Microsoft®

Windows® 7 Inside Out
Deluxe Edition

Ed Bott
Carl Siechert
Craig Stinson

D0862046

PUBLISHED BY
Microsoft Press
A Division of Microsoft Corporation
One Microsoft Way
Redmond, Washington 98052-6399

Copyright © 2011 by Ed Bott, Carl Siechert, Craig Stinson, and Ed Wilson

All rights reserved. No part of the contents of this book may be reproduced or transmitted in any form or by any means without the written permission of the publisher.

Library of Congress Control Number: 2011928844

ISBN: 978-0-7356-5692-5

Printed and bound in the United States of America.

Sixth Printing: March 2015

Microsoft Press books are available through booksellers and distributors worldwide. If you need support related to this book, email Microsoft Press Book Support at mspinput@microsoft.com. Please tell us what you think of this book at http://www.microsoft.com/learning/booksurvey.

Microsoft and the trademarks listed at http://www.microsoft.com/about/legal/en/us/IntellectualProperty/Trademarks/EN-US.aspx are trademarks of the Microsoft group of companies. All other marks are property of their respective owners.

The example companies, organizations, products, domain names, email addresses, logos, people, places, and events depicted herein are fictitious. No association with any real company, organization, product, domain name, email address, logo, person, place, or event is intended or should be inferred.

This book expresses the authors' views and opinions. The information contained in this book is provided without any express, statutory, or implied warranties. Neither the authors, Microsoft Corporation, nor its resellers or distributors will be held liable for any damages caused or alleged to be caused either directly or indirectly by this book.

Acquisitions Editor: Jeff Koch
Developmental and Project Editor: Valerie Woolley
Editorial Production: Curtis Philips
Technical Reviewer: Mitch Tulloch; Technical Review services provided by Content Master, a member of CM Group, Ltd.
Copyeditor: John Pierce
Indexer: Jan C. Wright
Cover: Twist Creative • Seattle

In memory of
Jean Varven Stinson
1952–2010

Contents at a Glance

Table of Contents

What do you think of this book? We want to hear from you!

Microsoft is interested in hearing your feedback so we can continually improve our books and learning
resources for you. To participate in a brief online survey, please visit:

www.microsoft.com/learning/booksurvey/

Part 2: File Management

Part 4: Security and Networking

Part 5: Tuning, Tweaking, and Troubleshooting

Part 6: Windows 7 and PC Hardware

What do you think of this book? We want to hear from you!

Microsoft is interested in hearing your feedback so we can continually improve our books and learning resources for you. To participate in a brief online survey, please visit:

www.microsoft.com/learning/booksurvey/

Foreword to *Windows 7 Inside Out*

Individually and collectively, the three authors who wrote *Windows 7 Inside Out* have been working with Windows for as long as many of the most senior developers at Microsoft. Ed, Carl, and Craig focus on Windows from a unique perspective—they are experts and enthusiasts who want to share their expertise and enthusiasm with you.

With Windows 7, our development team was dedicated to building a brand new release of the OS while also making sure your investments in hardware and software are effectively brought forward. We took a deliberate approach to building new features, refining existing features, and making sure at every step we were true to our goals of delivering an awesome release of Windows. Ed, Carl, and Craig do an awesome job of providing readers with the ins and outs of the full range of features of Windows 7, which will help you to get the most out of the product.

As we engineered Windows 7, we opened a dialog with a broad community of enthusiasts on our Engineering Windows 7 blog (*blogs.msdn.com/b/e7*). Through this blog, we discussed the engineering side of building Windows 7—from the bottom up, so to speak. We know that for many, these topics were interesting as Windows 7 was being developed. Through the blog and through all of our forms of learning as we developed Windows 7, we were asked many questions not just about the "how" but about the "why" of features. We offered our insights from the product development perspective. With their unique perspective, few are more qualified to offer further explanations of the ins and outs of Windows 7 than the authors of *Windows 7 Inside Out*.

With Windows 7 now in the hands of customers around the world, our collective interests turn to making the most of Windows 7. I know from 15 years of following the work of Ed, Carl, and Craig that they have the same commitment to delivering real-world advice from a perspective that is grounded in experience and knowledge of how Windows works. Over the years, they've met with many teams here in Redmond to talk about Windows and how they can help you, our shared customers and readers, be more productive. I hope you enjoy *Windows 7 Inside Out*.

Steven Sinofsky
President, Windows Division
Microsoft Corporation

Foreword

When we began designing Windows 7, we thought a lot about how you use your PC. Our goal was to make your experience simpler, so that you can concentrate on the tasks you're trying to accomplish. Since we released Windows 7 in 2009, we've been gratified by the positive response to our work from hundreds of millions of customers worldwide.

We didn't stop working on launch day, and neither did the authors of *Windows 7 Inside Out*. We've delivered a steady stream of updates to Windows in the past two years, including Service Pack 1, Internet Explorer 9, and Windows Live Essentials 2011.

In this Deluxe Edition, Ed, Carl, and Craig have once again done a thorough job of explaining not just *how* Windows works but *why* we designed it the way we did. They understand that Windows isn't just a collection of features—it's a series of end-to-end experiences. They've spent a tremendous amount of time in the Windows community over the past couple years learning from you, and they've incorporated that learning into this impressively expanded edition.

The authors of *Windows 7 Inside Out* have been doing what they do for a long time. They get Windows in a way that few others do. We hope this Deluxe Edition will help you make the most of Windows 7.

Julie Larson-Green
Corporate Vice President, Windows Experience
Microsoft Corporation
June 2011

Introduction

By some measures, Windows 7 sets a new standard for usability. It needs less out-of-the-box tweaking and troubleshooting than any Windows version we've ever used. The arrangement of folders and files in Windows Explorer, basic system security, User Account Control settings, and numerous other default configuration options are well thought out. Adding a new hardware device typically requires nothing more than just plugging it in, and setting up a network no longer entails invoking supernatural help.

Despite all that—or perhaps because of it—we have plenty of good stuff to share with you in this edition of *Windows 7 Inside Out*. The good news: we don't need to spend a lot of ink on Windows 7 features that work as expected. That allows us to concentrate on the many capabilities and features that are buried just beneath the surface. We cover the handful of essential tasks—backing up your computer, for example—that aren't configured automatically. We've also brought together countless shortcuts, tips, and tricks to help you perform tasks more quickly and with less aggravation.

This *Deluxe Edition* adds several chapters not included in the original edition, giving us the space to dive deeper into media applications, networking, scripting, and deployment of Windows throughout a small organization. Perhaps more important, spread throughout this edition are additional tips and explanations based on many, many hours of poking, probing, and studying Windows 7 in the two years since its release. This book also covers the latest changes to the operating system, notably Service Pack 1, as well as a new version of Internet Explorer and an impressively updated collection of programs in Windows Live Essentials 2011.

Who This Book Is For

This book offers a well-rounded look at the features most people use in Windows. It serves as an excellent reference for anyone who wants a better understanding of how Windows 7 works. If you're a Windows expert in training, or if your day job involves IT responsibilities, or if you're the designated computer specialist managing computers and networks in a home or small business, you'll discover many sections we wrote just for you. And if you consider yourself a Windows enthusiast, well, we hope you'll find enough fun and interesting tidbits to keep you interested—because, after all, we're unabashed enthusiasts ourselves.

Assumptions About You

This book, like others in the *Inside Out* series, is designed for readers who have some experience with the subject. It touches only briefly on some of the basic topics that you'll find covered in more detail elsewhere (for those, we recommend other Microsoft Press titles, such as *Windows 7 Step by Step* or *Windows 7 Plain & Simple*).

Whether your experience comes from Windows 7 or an earlier version, we expect that you are comfortable finding your way around the desktop, browsing folders with Windows Explorer, launching programs, using copy and paste operations, and finding information in a web browser. We don't assume that you're a hardware tinkerer, a hacker, a hardcore gamer, or a code jockey.

How This Book Is Organized

Part 1, "Getting Started," describes your initial Windows experiences: installing and configuring Windows, working with programs, adding Windows Live Essentials, personalizing Windows to your needs, and using Internet Explorer.

Part 2, "File Management," explains how to organize your folders and files, how to find those files when you need them, and how to back them up to ensure that they're always available. It also covers the ins and outs of Windows search technologies.

Part 3, "Digital Media," explores the rich media features of Windows 7, including playing, sharing, and syncing media. This edition includes expanded coverage of Windows Media Center and other Microsoft media products, such as the Xbox 360 and the elegant, powerful Zune software.

Part 4, "Security and Networking," explains how to set up a network so that you can share files, printers, Internet connections, and other resources among all your computers—and how to properly implement security measures so that you can do so safely.

Part 5, "Tuning, Tweaking, and Troubleshooting," covers routine maintenance tasks and explores tools and techniques for measuring and improving your computer's performance. Other topics include Windows PowerShell scripting, troubleshooting methods, and deployment of Windows to multiple computers.

Part 6, "Windows 7 and PC Hardware," looks at details of the devices on which Windows runs, including setup and configuration, management of hard disk drives, and use of input methods other than the keyboard and mouse (namely, pen, touch, and speech).

Part 7 comprises a handful of appendixes that provide reference information, including concise looks at the differences among Windows 7 editions, changes wrought by Service Pack 1, and accessory programs that are part of Windows.

Features and Conventions Used In This Book

This book uses special text and design conventions to make it easier for you to find the information you need.

Text Conventions

Convention	Meaning
Abbreviated commands for navigating the ribbon	For your convenience, this book uses abbreviated commands. For example, "Click Home, Insert, Insert Cells" means that you should click the Home tab on the ribbon, then click the Insert button, and finally click the Insert Cells command.
Boldface type	**Boldface** indicates text that you type.
Initial Capital Letters	The first letters of the names of tabs, dialog boxes, dialog box elements, and commands are capitalized. Example: the Save As dialog box.
Italicized type	*Italicized* type indicates new terms.
Plus sign (+) in text	Keyboard shortcuts are indicated by a plus sign (+) separating key names. For example, Ctrl+Alt+Delete means that you press the Ctrl, Alt, and Delete keys at the same time.

Design Conventions

INSIDE OUT   **This statement illustrates an example of an "Inside Out" heading**

These are the book's signature tips. In these tips, you get the straight scoop on what's going on with the software—inside information about why a feature works the way it does. You'll also find handy workarounds to deal with software problems.

Sidebar

Sidebars provide helpful hints, timesaving tricks, or alternative procedures related to the task being discussed.

TROUBLESHOOTING

This statement illustrates an example of a "Troubleshooting" problem statement

Look for these sidebars to find solutions to common problems you might encounter. Troubleshooting sidebars appear next to related information in the chapters. You can also use "Index to Troubleshooting Topics" at the back of the book to look up problems by topic.

Cross-references point you to locations in the book that offer additional information about the topic being discussed.

CAUTION!

Cautions identify potential problems that you should look out for when you're completing a task or that you must address before you can complete a task.

Note
Notes offer additional information related to the task being discussed.

 When an example has a related file that is included on the companion CD, this icon appears in the margin. You can use these files to follow along with the book's examples.

About the CD

The companion CD that ships with this book contains many resources to help you get the most out of your Inside Out book.

If you bought a digital edition of this book, you can enjoy select content from the print edition's companion CD. Visit *http://go.microsoft.com/FWLink/?Linkid=219280* to get your downloadable content. This content is always up-to-date and available to all readers.

What's on the CD

Your Inside Out CD includes the following:

- **Complete eBook**   Enjoy the entire electronic version of this title.

- **Resources**   Reference white papers, user assistance, and product support to help you use and troubleshoot the features of Windows 7.

- **Product Information** Explore the features and capabilities of Windows 7 and learn how other Microsoft products and technologies can help you at work and at home.

- **Tools** Link to tools for PowerShell, application compatibility, IEAK, WAIK, and Windows 7 Upgrade Advisor.

- **Sample Scripts** Discover more than 80 Windows PowerShell scripts you can customize and use to configure and manage computers running Windows 7. Here is a listing of the scripts arranged by the chapter in which each is introduced:

Chapter	PowerShell Scripts	Chapter	PowerShell Scripts

2	DisplayProcessor.ps1
	Get-OSVersion.ps1
	Get-ProcessorArchitecture.ps1
	Get-WindowsEdition.ps1
	ListOperatingSystem.ps1
		24	Get-MicrosoftUpdates.ps1
			Get-MissingSoftware-
			   Updates.ps1
			Get-PercentFreeSpace.ps1
			ListFreeSpace.ps1
			ScanForSpecificUpdate.ps1
			Start-Defrag.ps1
			TroubleshootWindows-
			   Update.ps1
			UninstallMicrosoftUpdate.ps1

7	Clean-IE.ps1		
9	Set-ExplorerCommandBar.ps1		

18	AddLocalUserToLocal-
	   Group.ps1
	BackupFolderToServer.ps1
	Change-LocalUser-
	   Password.ps1
	CreateLocalGroup.ps1
	CreateLocalUser.ps1
	EnableDisableUser.ps1
	FindAdmin.ps1
	Get-LocalGroupMembers.ps1
	Get-LocalGroups.ps1
	Get-LocalUsers.ps1
	Get-SystemRestore-
	   Settings.ps1
	ListUserLastLogon.ps1
	LocateDisabledUsers.ps1
	LocateLockedOutUsers.ps1
	Remove-LocalUserFrom-
	   LocalGroup.ps1
		24	ConfigureSoftwareUpdates-
			   Schedule.ps1
			DownloadAndInstallMicrosoft-
			   Update.ps1
			Get-DefragAnalysis.ps1
			Get-DiskDriveInventory.ps1
			Get-LogicalDiskInventory.ps1

		25	acceptPause.ps1 AutoServicesNotRunning.ps1 ChangeModeThenStart.ps1 ChangeServiceAccount- Logon.ps1 CheckServiceThenStart.ps1 CheckServiceThenStop.ps1 CountRunningServices.ps1 EvaluateServices.ps1 GetMultipleServices.ps1 getServiceStatus.ps1 MonitorService.ps1 ServiceDependencies.ps1 StartMultipleServices.ps1 StopMultipleServices.ps1
20	CreateShare.ps1 DeleteShare.ps1 Get-ShareInfo.ps1 GetShareAndPermission.ps1 ListAdminShares.ps1		
23	FindMaxPageFaults.ps1 Get-DiskUtilization.ps1 Get-ProcessorInformation.ps1 Get-ProcessorUtilization.ps1 GetTopMemory.ps1 TroubleshootPerformance.ps1	27	Test-64Bit.ps1
		28	CountErrors.ps1 FindUSBEvents.ps1 Get-DiagnosticEventLogs.ps1 GetErrorsFromAllLogFiles.ps1 GetEventLogErrors.ps1

Chapter	PowerShell Scripts	Chapter	PowerShell Scripts
29	FindPrinterDrivers.ps1	30	Get-DiskPerformance.ps1
	FindPrinterPorts.ps1		Get-PageFile.ps1
	Get-PrinterPorts.ps1		Get-VolumeDirty.ps1
	Get-PrintQueueStatistics.ps1		Get-VolumeInventory.ps1
	Get-SharedPrinter.ps1		Get-VolumeLabel.ps1
	InstallPrinterDriver.ps1		Set-VolumeAutoCheck.ps1
	InstallPrinterDriverFull.ps1		Set-VolumeLabel.ps1
	ListPrinterDrivers.ps1		
	ListPrinters.ps1		
	ListSharedPrintersAddPrint-Connection.ps1		
	TroubleshootPrinter.ps1		
	WorkWithPrinters.ps1		

System Requirements

Following are the minimum system requirements necessary to run the CD:

- A Pentium 500 megahertz (MHz) or faster processor (Pentium III is recommended as a minimum).

- Microsoft Windows XP with Service Pack (SP) 3 (32-bit), Windows Vista with SP1 (32-bit or 64-bit), Windows Server 2003 R2 (32-bit or 64-bit) with MSXML 6.0 installed, Windows Server 2008 R2, or Windows 7 (32-bit or 64-bit).

- At least 24 megabytes (MB) of random access memory (RAM); 512 MB is recommended.

- A hard drive with at least 527 MB of free space.

- A CD-ROM or DVD-ROM drive.

- A mouse or other pointing device.

- A 1024 x 768 or greater monitor display.

Other options required to use all features include the following:

- A multimedia computer for sound and other multimedia effects.

- Dial-up or broadband Internet access.

- Microsoft Internet Explorer 6 or later.

Acknowledgments

If we tried to list all the people who have helped us in one way or another on this project, we'd have to add another 50 pages. So we apologize in advance to those we don't thank by name.

We'd like to acknowledge the tremendous assistance offered for the original edition by Steve Ball, Mark Russinovich, Dan Plastina, Gabe Aul, Charlie Owen, Chris Flores, and Jerry Koh of Microsoft. They are among literally dozens of developers, product managers, and technical professionals at Microsoft who enthusiastically shared their time and their deep knowledge of Windows 7 with us.

Our thanks also to their bosses, Jon DeVaan and Steven Sinofsky, for their support in making those contacts possible.

For this edition, our coverage of Internet Explorer benefited greatly from many hours of meetings with Dean Hachamovich and his team. We also owe a big thanks to the countless bloggers, Microsoft MVPs, Windows enthusiasts, and readers who shared their questions and answers with us.

The signature feature of this edition is a collection of PowerShell scripts you'll find sprinkled throughout the book. Those would not exist without the assistance of Ed Wilson, who proved to us why they call him The Scripting Guy.

Our production team was led by our longtime collaborator Curt Philips, who somehow makes this grueling process look easier each time. Technical editor Mitch Tulloch brought his own considerable expertise to the task of making sure we got the details right; he also did a fine job putting together the companion CD. We owe a big debt to John Pierce, copyeditor, and Andrea Fox, proofreader, for helping us weed out typos and grammatical errors.

Our partners and collaborators at Microsoft Press have been a source of support for many terrific years: this edition would not have been possible without the support of Jeff Koch and the superb logistical talents of project editor Valerie Woolley.

Our literary agent and good friend Claudette Moore has provided much encouragement as we've all watched the book business transform, provided excellent guidance, talked us down a few times when it was necessary, and continued to make sure that this project came together to everyone's benefit.

Thanks to one and all.

Ed Bott, Carl Siechert, and Craig Stinson
June 2011

Support and Feedback

The following sections provide information on errata, book support, feedback, and contact information.

Errata & Support

We've made every effort to ensure the accuracy of this book and its companion content. Any errors that have been reported since this book was published are listed on our Microsoft Press site:

http://go.microsoft.com/FWLink/?Linkid=220284

If you find an error that is not already listed, you can report it to us through the same page.

If you need additional support, email Microsoft Press Book Support at *mspinput@microsoft.com*.

Please note that product support for Microsoft software is not offered through the addresses above.

We Want to Hear from You

At Microsoft Press, your satisfaction is our top priority, and your feedback our most valuable asset. Please tell us what you think of this book at

http://www.microsoft.com/learning/booksurvey

The survey is short, and we read *every one* of your comments and ideas. Thanks in advance for your input!

Stay in Touch

Let's keep the conversation going! We're on Twitter: *http://twitter.com/MicrosoftPress.*

What's New in Windows 7

W HAT has changed since we wrote the first edition of this book? For starters, PC manufacturers have sold hundreds of millions of new desktop and laptop systems running Windows 7. A few tens of millions of people have upgraded to Windows 7 from earlier versions. We've had nearly two years' worth of hands-on experience with Windows 7 ourselves—tweaking, testing, tuning, and occasionally troubleshooting, often in response to questions and comments from our readers.

Microsoft has been busy since then as well, releasing new security tools, new digital media software, and significant new releases of Internet Explorer and Windows Live Essentials— not to mention a steady stream of updates to improve the performance, reliability, and security of Windows 7. Oh, and many of those updates and hotfixes have been rolled into the first service pack, which was released in February 2011.

What's in Your Edition?

Microsoft offers Windows 7 in several editions, with a mix of features and capabilities intended for different hardware platforms, personal preferences, and business needs. In this book, we focus primarily on the three editions that you are most likely to encounter on new and upgraded PCs—Windows 7 Home Premium, Windows 7 Professional, and Windows 7 Ultimate (which is nearly identical to the Enterprise edition available for large corporate customers). A sidebar box like this one, typically placed at the beginning of each chapter, summarizes the differences in each edition as they relate to the content of that chapter. For a more detailed discussion of the differences between each edition, see Appendix A, "Windows 7 Editions at a Glance."

For recent upgraders, this is the question we hear most often: Is Windows 7 a major upgrade or just a collection of refinements? The answer depends on your starting point. If you've been using Windows Vista, the upgrade to Windows 7 should be relatively straightforward. Windows 7 is built on the same foundation as Windows Vista, so you've already sorted out compatibility hassles with programs and devices. After you learn the basics of the revamped Windows 7 desktop and adapt to changes in search and file management, you should feel right at home.

For those who are moving to Windows 7 from Windows XP, the learning curve will be steeper. You'll find fundamental changes in nearly every aspect of the operating system, and many of the expert techniques that you've learned through the years won't work any longer. Three feature sets that were introduced in Windows Vista will be of particular interest to anyone upgrading from Windows XP:

- Search capabilities are a key part of just about every Windows task. In Windows XP, this capability is available as an add-on that installs a search box on the taskbar. In Windows 7, you'll find a search box on the Start menu, in the upper right corner of any window or dialog box based on Windows Explorer, and in Control Panel.

- For anyone obsessed with performance and troubleshooting (we suspect most of our readers fall into this group), Windows 7 includes an impressive set of diagnostic and monitoring tools. Collectively, they offer a level of detail about system events that can be eye-opening and overwhelming.

- User Account Control was one of the most controversial and misunderstood additions to Windows Vista. This feature has been greatly modified in Windows 7, but anyone upgrading from Windows XP might be surprised by the extra layer of consent dialog boxes required for some common administrative tasks, especially when settling in with a new PC.

If you've upgraded from Windows Vista, you'll notice changes throughout Windows. In most cases, these refinements fall into the "fit and finish" category. Many of the changes are subtle enough that you might not even notice them at first. Some longstanding Windows annoyances are fixed, although others remain. You'll notice that some everyday tasks require fewer keystrokes and mouse clicks, and we predict you'll see fewer warnings and notifications as you go about your daily Windows routine.

Regardless of where you come from, our goal in this book is to help you navigate through this period of transition as quickly as possible, so that you can unlearn old habits, discover new features, and become comfortable and productive with Windows 7.

In this chapter, we take you on a quick tour of noteworthy features and capabilities in Windows 7, with appropriate pointers to chapters where you'll find more detailed information and advice.

The Missing Pieces

When you upgrade to Windows 7, you might be surprised to find some familiar programs have vanished. The most notable entry on the missing-programs list is an e-mail client or news reader. Likewise, Windows 7 includes only the bare-bones Photo Viewer program. To fill in the gaps, you need to seek out Windows Live Essentials 2011 (*w7io.com/20801*). This package includes Windows Live Mail, which replaces Outlook Express in Windows XP and Windows Mail from Windows Vista. It also includes Windows Live Photo Gallery, Windows Live Messenger, and Windows Live Movie Maker, among other programs. (For more details on Windows Live Essentials, see Chapter 8, "Adding Windows Live Programs and Services.")

The other piece of software you need to add as part of your initial installation of Windows 7 is a good antivirus program. You can download a free antivirus program called Microsoft Security Essentials that works well with any edition of Windows 7, or choose from a variety of third-party options. For information on what to look for, see "Using Security Software to Block Malware" on page 617.

If you purchase a new PC with Windows 7 already installed, don't be surprised to find that it already includes Windows Live Essentials 2011 and an antivirus program (often as a feature of an all-in-one security package). As always, if you prefer a different solution you are free to replace the included software with any Windows-compatible alternative.

Introducing the Windows 7 Family

When you begin to delve into details about how Windows 7 works, the discussion can quickly become complicated. The primary reason for confusion is that the operating system is actually distributed and sold in multiple editions. The lineup of available editions is less complicated than for Windows Vista, but you can still get tripped up if you read about an advanced feature and don't realize that it's missing from your edition.

How can you tell which Windows 7 edition is installed on your PC? The easiest way is to look at the top of the System window in Control Panel—click System in Control Panel; right-click the Computer icon on the Start menu and then click Properties; click Computer on the Start menu and then click System Properties on the command bar; or use the keyboard shortcut Windows logo key+Break. Under the Windows Edition heading, you will see the current installed edition, as shown in Figure 1-1.

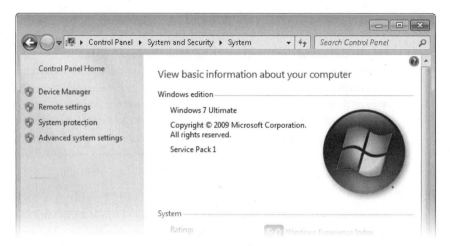

Figure 1-1 System in Control Panel shows which Windows 7 edition is installed. It also lets you see whether a service pack has been installed.

In this book, we concentrate on the three Windows 7 editions you are most likely to encounter on a mainstream home or business PC:

- **Windows 7 Home Premium**   This is the edition you are most likely to find installed on a new PC in the computer section at your local warehouse store or consumer electronics specialist. It includes roughly the same mix of features as its predecessor, Windows Vista Home Premium.

- **Windows 7 Professional**   This edition is the successor to Windows Vista Business and incorporates the same features as that operating system, notably advanced networking features that work with networks based on the Windows Server family. In a noteworthy change, however, Windows 7 Professional is a superset of Home Premium and thus includes all features (including Windows Media Center) found in the lesser edition.

- **Windows 7 Ultimate** and **Windows 7 Enterprise**   These editions are essentially identical, with the names reflecting the sales channel of each: Ultimate is available on retail and original equipment manufacturer (OEM) editions; Enterprise is available as an upgrade only to customers who buy volume licenses of Windows. This edition contains all features found in the Home Premium and Professional editions plus some advanced networking features, BitLocker encryption, and support for multiple languages. The Enterprise edition includes some additional usage rights available in the volume license agreement.

All of these editions are available in x86 (32-bit) and x64 (64-bit) options. When we wrote the previous edition of this book, 64-bit Windows was still a fairly exotic choice for most Windows users. Within just a few years, thanks in no small measure to the plummeting price of memory chips, that balance has shifted dramatically. Today, 64-bit Windows 7 is commonly installed on new computers, especially on systems with 4 GB or more of RAM.

> **Note**
>
> The default settings we describe in this book are those you will see if you perform a clean install of Windows 7 using a shrink-wrapped retail copy. If you purchase a new PC with Windows 7, your settings might be different. Computer manufacturers have the right to customize Windows when they install it on a new system; they can change default settings, customize desktop backgrounds and screen savers, tweak the home page and Favorites list in Internet Explorer, install third-party software, and configure the system so that it uses a different media player or browser than the Windows 7 default settings.

In this book, we offer only limited coverage of two specialized Windows 7 editions:

- **Windows 7 Starter**   This edition is available for sale only on low-powered hardware, such as lightweight "netbooks," and is limited in its feature set.

- **Windows 7 Home Basic**   Although its predecessor was available worldwide as the entry-level edition of Windows Vista, Windows 7 Home Basic is available only in emerging markets and is not authorized for sale in the United States, Western Europe, and the rest of the so-called developed world. It lacks support for the Aero interface and does not include Windows Media Center.

We also ignore the handful of variations of standard Windows 7 editions that have been modified to satisfy terms dictated by courts in various parts of the world. We never heard from a single reader who actually used the N or K versions of Windows Vista, which had Windows Media Player removed and were offered for sale in Europe and Korea, respectively. Windows 7 offers similar packages, and our experience suggests they have been equally unpopular, if not completely invisible.

Adjusting to the Windows 7 Interface

The basic building blocks of the Windows interface have remained unchanged for years, with only relatively minor tweaks to break the familiar routine. With Windows 7, those familiar pieces get the biggest makeover they've had since the turn of the century. In this section, we present a whirlwind tour of the Windows 7 desktop; you'll find more details (and our exclusive Inside Out advice on how to tweak things to match your preferences) in Chapter 4, "Personalizing Windows 7."

The basic layout of the Windows taskbar is the same as it has been for more than a decade: a Start button on the left side, a clock and some small icons on the opposite side, and room in between for buttons that represent programs.

By default, those taskbar buttons are noticeably bigger than the ones you're accustomed to from earlier Windows versions. They also serve a dual purpose: to start up programs and to switch between running application windows. You can pin program shortcuts to the taskbar so that they're always available (even when the program they represent isn't running) and drag buttons left or right to reorder them.

When you move your mouse over a taskbar button that represents a running program, the Aero interface shows you a live thumbnail preview of every window associated with that button. Hover the mouse over a preview, and a nifty new feature called Aero Peek hides other windows to show you only the one you've highlighted. Move the mouse away from the preview, and Windows restores your desktop.

For programs that support lists of recently opened files, you can right-click to display a Jump List, like the one shown in Figure 1-2. You can "pin" frequently used items to this list as well so that they're always available. If Internet Explorer 9 is installed, you can also create shortcuts to individual websites and pin them to the taskbar.

Every Windows user has, at some point in their computing lifetime, watched in horror as the number of icons in the notification area rose to double digits and threatened to overwhelm the rest of the taskbar. In Windows 7, notifications are hidden by default. You can customize individual notifications so that they're always visible, or click the arrow to the left of the visible icons to reveal and work with the collection of hidden icons. In the Notification Area Icons dialog box (shown in Figure 1-3), you can adjust each icon's behavior individually or use the links at the bottom of the dialog box to globally change the appearance and behavior of this area.

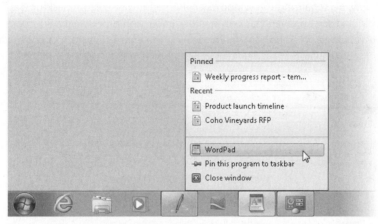

Figure 1-2 Jump Lists give you easier access to documents you've opened recently. With Internet Explorer 9 installed, you can also pin shortcuts for websites to the taskbar, like the shortcut to Hotmail, the third one from the right.

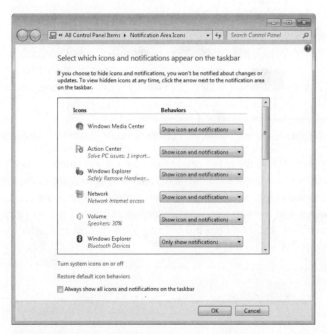

Figure 1-3 Use the Notification Area Icons dialog box to adjust the behavior of every icon in the notification area.

Arguably, personalizing the Windows environment with custom desktop backgrounds, sounds, and screen savers has only a minor impact on productivity. But those tweaks are still psychologically important. In Windows 7, the entire collection of personalization settings is consolidated in a single dialog box, shown in Figure 1-4.

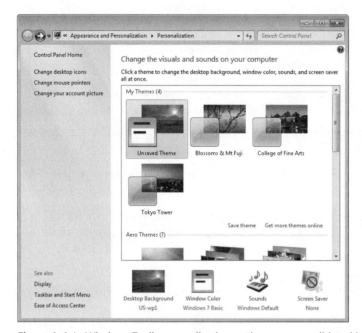

Figure 1-4 In Windows 7, all personalization options are consolidated in a single control panel.

If you dig deep enough into the many categories under the Personalization heading in Control Panel, you'll find a large and interesting selection of desktop backgrounds, which can be chained together into sets that refresh automatically at intervals you specify, plus new sound schemes and even an expanded collection of pictures that identify your user account, as shown next. You'll find our Inside Out advice on how to master the full range of personalization options in Chapter 4.

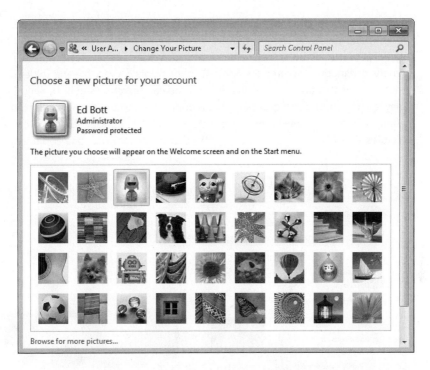

And finally, Windows 7 refines the concept of gadgets. These minimalist programs perform simple tasks such as displaying a clock or your favorite pictures in a small desktop window, retrieving RSS feeds, or monitoring CPU and network activity. In Windows Vista, gadgets reside by default in the sidebar and have to be dragged manually to the desktop. In Windows 7, gadgets float on the desktop at all times. Although the host process is still Sidebar.exe, the confining sidebar itself is gone, and a simple keyboard shortcut (Windows logo key+G) allows you to temporarily move all running gadgets to the top of the desktop, above any program windows, for easy reference.

Organizing and Finding Files

Over the years, Windows Explorer has evolved dramatically. In its earliest incarnation, it was a simple file browser to make it easier to traverse hierarchical directories on hard drives without having to use DOS commands. Today, Windows Explorer is a full-featured shell that helps you manage practically every aspect of the operating system. It still functions as a file manager, but old-timers might be surprised to note that drive letters and folder trees are de-emphasized in Windows 7, in favor of a navigation system that emphasizes a new file-organizing feature called *libraries*.

Chapter 1

The concept behind libraries can be confusing, especially if you're accustomed to navigating through the traditional Windows Explorer folder tree. A library is a virtual folder that contains links to actual folders located on your system or on a network. When you view a library in Windows Explorer, the contents pane displays every file and folder contained in the locations that are a part of that library. You can search this unified view, filter it, or display it using sorting and grouping that is appropriate to the type of data contained in that library. As part of a default installation, Windows 7 sets up four libraries: Documents, Music, Pictures, and Videos. Figure 1-5 shows the Pictures library with one additional local folder added to it.

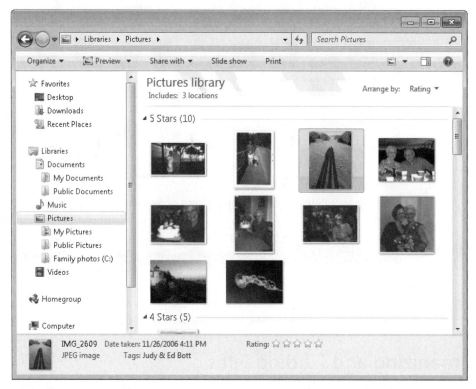

Figure 1-5 Libraries present a unified view of data files stored in multiple locations, allowing you to search, filter, sort, and group the entire collection.

The other major change in Windows Explorer is its excellent support for indexed searches, which can seem practically magical when you're looking for one particular document on a hard drive filled with thousands of files. Windows 7 removes many of the form-based, fill-in-the-blank, "select this check box" search tools that you might have learned to use in Windows XP or Windows Vista. Instead, context-sensitive options in the search box help you refine a search, as the example in Figure 1-6 shows.

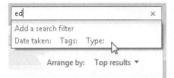

Figure 1-6 Enter free-form text in a search box to filter the contents of a library or folder, and then click to refine the search further using these filters.

Mastering Windows Explorer is a crucial stop on the way to becoming a Windows expert. That's why, in this edition, we devote two full chapters to the topic. Chapter 9, "Organizing Files and Information," introduces the building blocks of Windows Explorer, including a detailed discussion of libraries, metadata, and basic search techniques. In Chapter 10, "Using Windows Search," we document the powerful but sometimes arcane Windows Search syntax and provide examples of its effective use.

Saving, Sharing, and Playing Digital Media

These days, practically all of the media we consume is digital. Digital cameras have almost completely eliminated film, and more music is downloaded (legally or otherwise) than is sold on CDs. Even movies and TV are increasingly being delivered to your home as a stream of bits rather than on a shiny disc.

The natural hub for managing all these media files is a PC. In this book, we cover two full-featured tools included with Windows 7 that allow you to manage, play, and share digital music, movies, and photos: Windows Media Player and Windows Media Center. For this edition, we also add coverage of the Zune software, which provides a slick and modern alternative for managing and playing a music and video collection.

> **Note**
>
> As we noted earlier in this chapter, some digital media tools previously included as a part of earlier Windows versions are not included with Windows 7. On a clean installation of Windows 7, for example, you can import pictures from a digital camera and view them using Windows Explorer or Windows Photo Viewer. To edit those imported photos, however, you must use Windows Live Photo Gallery (part of Windows Live Essentials 2011) or third-party software.

Windows Media Player 12 is the latest incarnation of the core media manager/player program included in Windows. It's superficially similar to its predecessors in layout—with a navigation pane on the left side, a contents pane in the center, and tabs on the right for displaying lists of items to be played, synced, or burned to CD or DVD. Figure 1-7 shows Media Player in operation, with a selection of songs queued up and ready to play.

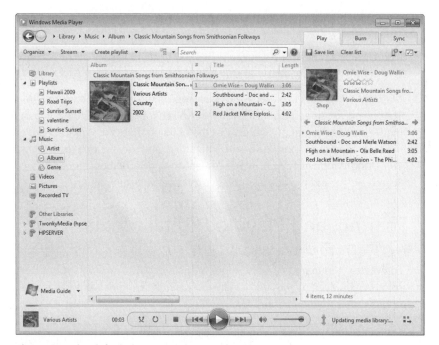

Figure 1-7 The default three-pane layout of Windows Media Player.

Most simple tasks in Windows Media Player work without any customization. If you double-click an album in the library, it begins playing through the default playback device (normally, your PC's speakers). When you insert a DVD, the player starts, switches to full-screen mode, and begins playing back the movie immediately.

What's new in Windows Media Player 12? The most significant change is one you might not notice immediately: the player now supports playback of additional file types, including standard and high-definition movies recorded on digital cameras and saved in H.264 and AVC formats. If you previously had to install a third-party package such as Apple's Quick-Time to play back those movies, you'll be pleasantly surprised to find that you can now play them using Windows Media Player.

The other significant new digital-media feature in Windows Media Player 12 is the ability to stream media between devices on a Windows network. After you enable this capability, you can select a remote device (such as the Xbox 360 shown in Figure 1-8) and use the Play To menu to send the contents of a playlist from your Windows 7 PC to that device over the network.

Figure 1-8 Use the media-streaming capabilities in Windows Media Player 12 to send digital music or movies from a PC to another device over your network.

We explain the fundamentals of building, maintaining, and enjoying a library of music and movies in Chapter 13, "Playing and Organizing Digital Media Files." For step-by-step instructions on how to set up and use media streaming, check out Chapter 14, "Sharing and Syncing Digital Media."

The other major media program in Windows 7 is Windows Media Center. For playing back media files, it shares much of the code from Windows Media Player. (One major capability that Media Center has that is not in Media Player is the ability to record TV from a TV tuner device.) Media Center uses what is known as a 10-foot interface, designed to be used in a living room with a remote control (although it's quite functional on a laptop or desktop PC as well). For more details about how to build your own media hub, see Chapter 15, "Using Windows Media Center."

For this edition, we've added an entirely new chapter for digital media fanatics. In Chapter 16, "Digital Media for Enthusiasts," we cover the nuts and bolts of using a PC in the living room, how to make best use of an Xbox 360 console on a PC network, how to master the Zune software, and how to manage tags and convert digital media file formats.

Networking in New Ways

In Windows Vista, Microsoft introduced the Network And Sharing Center as the one place to go for most network-related tasks. The concept annoyed some longtime Windows users, who discovered that common network tasks they had learned to accomplish with simple shortcuts in Windows XP now required extra clicks or keystrokes.

The Windows 7 Network And Sharing Center (shown in Figure 1-9) gets a usability overhaul designed to reduce clutter and make common tasks easier to find.

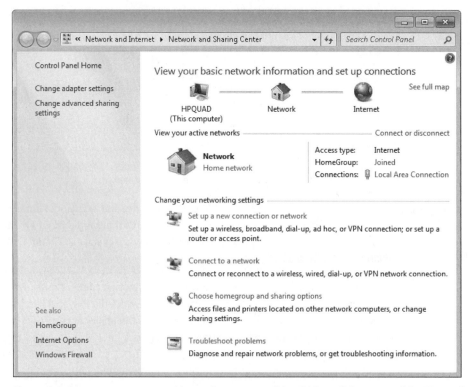

Figure 1-9 Most common networking tasks are accessible within a click or two of the Network And Sharing Center.

If you're accustomed to networking in Windows XP, you have a lot of catching up to do. In the networking section of this book, we explain how Internet Protocol version 6 (IPv6) and Internet Protocol version 4 (IPv4) work together, for example, and how the Link Layer Topology Discovery subsystem helps you build a visual map of your network. Networking changes that are new in Windows 7 include a much-improved interface for connecting to wireless access points.

The most significant addition to the networking capabilities in Windows 7 is the Home-Group feature, which allows two or more computers running Windows 7 to share files and printers and stream media without the hassle of managing individual user accounts and permissions. Figure 1-10 shows the interface for managing shared files in a homegroup.

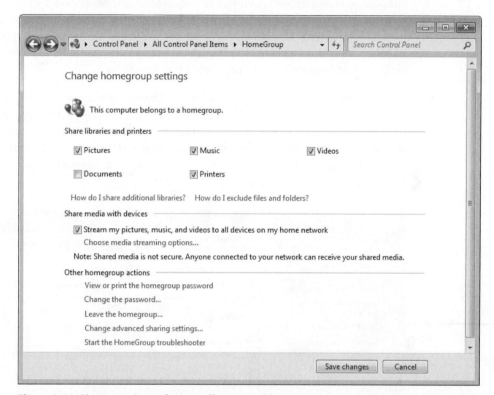

Figure 1-10 The HomeGroup feature offers a simplified interface for sharing files, printers, and digital media between computers running Windows 7.

If your network includes computers running earlier versions of Windows, you need to set up shared access by using more traditional techniques. The differences from Windows XP–based networks are profound. You can specify different levels of security for sharing, and on individual files and folders stored on NTFS volumes, you can specify which accounts and groups, if any, are allowed to access those files.

Our coverage of Windows 7 networking begins in Chapter 19, "Setting Up a Small Office or Home Network."

Keeping Your PC Speedy and Safe

The secret of remaining happy and productive with Windows, day in and day out, is to ensure that the system runs at peak performance, with no unexplained hangs or crashes to interrupt work or play. We know from talking to Microsoft developers that they made many kernel-level changes that collectively make Windows 7 feel faster than its predecessors. But that still leaves plenty of room for tweaking and, inevitably, troubleshooting. Fortunately, Windows 7 includes excellent tools for helping you monitor performance, diagnose balky programs and hardware, and fix problems when they occur.

The most noteworthy addition to the Windows 7 system-management toolkit is the Action Center. It consolidates messages, troubleshooting tools, and basic system-management functions in a single location. You can access it from its ever-present icon in the notification area or from the System And Security heading in Control Panel. Figure 1-11 shows a pair of security and maintenance messages, which are color-coded on your screen as red or yellow to indicate the level of importance.

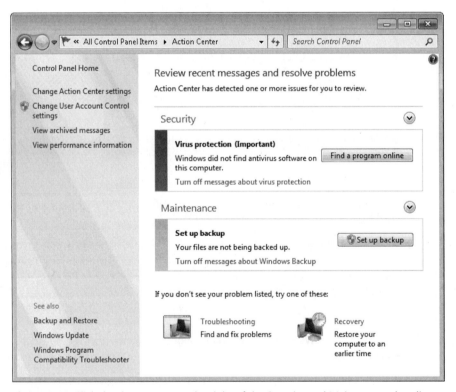

Figure 1-11 Click the down arrow to the right of the Security and Maintenance headings to see more messages.

We cover the ins and outs of Action Center and its companion tools in Chapter 24, "Performing Routine Maintenance."

When you're trying to troubleshoot problems such as application crashes or hardware failures, it's useful to have a log of important events. That's the function of the new Reliability Monitor, shown in Figure 1-12. It plots important system events, such as successful and unsuccessful installations of drivers and software as well as application crashes, on a timeline. By filtering the timeline to a specific day or week, you can identify individual events that might provide important clues to the cause of a problem.

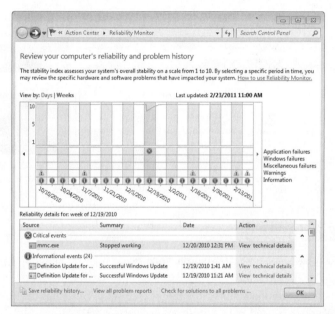

Figure 1-12 Reliability Monitor provides a convenient timeline of critical events and changes to your system configuration.

Finally, there's Resource Monitor, which debuted in Windows Vista but has been significantly enhanced for Windows 7. The amount of technical detail available here—covering CPU load, memory usage (shown in Figure 1-13), disk activity, and network performance—can be overwhelming, at least initially. We explain how to filter the useful information from the noise in "Monitoring Performance in Real Time" on page 841.

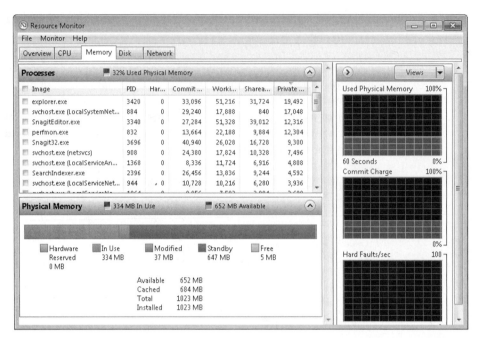

Figure 1-13 Resource Monitor displays in-depth information about every major aspect of system performance.

Using Internet Explorer 9

Windows 7 includes Internet Explorer 8 as its default program for browsing web pages and displaying HTML-formatted content. Even if you're new to Windows 7, you're probably already familiar with the features in Internet Explorer 8, which has been available as an upgrade for Windows XP and Windows Vista since early 2009.

In 2011, after a long public beta test, Microsoft released Internet Explorer 9, which is available as an upgrade for Windows Vista and Windows 7. Unless you have a compelling reason to continue using Internet Explorer 8, we strongly recommend upgrading. When you do, here's what you get:

- **Performance**   Internet Explorer 9 is able to tap into the graphics processing unit (GPU) on a modern PC and use its considerable horsepower to assist in displaying graphics. Other areas of the browser received extensive attention from developers to improve speed and responsiveness as well. If you thought previous versions of Internet Explorer were sluggish, you might be pleasantly surprised by this one.

- **Security**   In Windows Vista, Microsoft introduced the concept of Protected Mode browsing, which provides a significant layer of protection from potentially hostile

Chapter 1

web pages, scripts, and downloads. That architecture is present in Windows 7 as well, along with a host of new security features such as a SmartScreen filter that blocks known sources of dangerous code. Internet Explorer 9 includes a major new set of Tracking Protection tools that give you fine-grained control over your privacy, as shown in Figure 1-14.

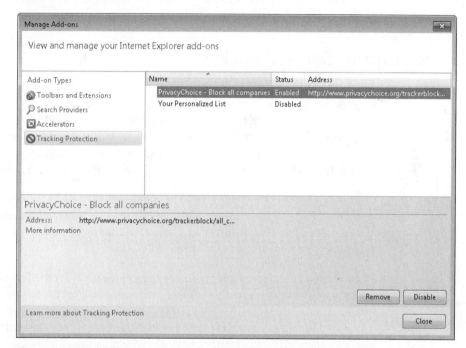

Figure 1-14 By adding a Tracking Protection list and enabling it, you can block websites that try to build a profile of you based on your online activities.

- **Usability**   What's most notable about the Internet Explorer 9 interface is what's missing. The address bar and search box have been combined. Toolbars, menus, and buttons are hidden. The window frame is thinner, and there's no text at all in the title bar. The overall effect is that the browser recedes into the background, allowing the website itself to take center stage. In addition, you can pin a website to the taskbar and return to that site (or a group of sites) with a single click.

- **Compatibility**   Over the years, Internet Explorer has earned its share of brickbats from web designers, who complained that it ignores web standards and requires cus-tom code to handle its many design and layout quirks. By contrast, Internet Explorer 9 was designed to conform to modern web standards. The changes in both Inter-net Explorer 8 and 9 are so sweeping, in fact, that you might experience problems properly displaying pages that were tweaked to display properly in earlier versions (especially Internet Explorer 6). We explain why formatting glitches occur and list the full range of solutions in "Dealing with Compatibility Issues" on page 248.

Internet Explorer is a large and complex program—so big, in fact, that it deserves two chapters in this edition. If you choose to use it as your default browser, you'll benefit greatly from a close reading of Chapter 6, "Using Internet Explorer," and Chapter 7, "Internet Explorer Compatibility, Security, and Privacy."

Updating to Service Pack 1

In February 2011, Microsoft officially released Windows 7 Service Pack 1. This package consolidates previously released updates for system reliability, program compatibility, and security into a single package. For a comprehensive listing of all included updates, see Appendix C, "Fixes Included in Windows 7 Service Pack 1." For more information about service packs in general, including links to the latest release for a specific Windows version, see Microsoft's official Service Pack information page at *support.microsoft.com/sp*.

You don't need to do anything special to update your system to Service Pack 1. For homes and small businesses, Windows Update handles this task automatically, downloading a relatively small update file and installing it as part of your regular update routine. No intervention is required on your part.

If you're an IT professional setting up one or more new PCs for the first time, check the installation media you're using. Packages manufactured after the release of Service Pack 1 should contain the necessary files already integrated into the setup DVD. If you're using an original Windows 7 disc, you can download the service pack files and "slipstream" them into an installation image for deployment in your organization. See Chapter 26, "Deployment and Migration," for details.

Installing and Configuring Windows 7

S OME Windows users never have to deal with the Windows setup program. If you buy a new computer with Windows 7 already installed and set up an effective backup routine, you might be able to use it forever without having to do anything more than minor maintenance or, in the worst case, a system recovery.

For upgraders, hobbyists, and inveterate tinkerers, however, the Windows 7 setup program is inescapable. Knowing the arcane secrets of upgrades, custom installations, and activation can spell the difference between a smooth-running system and a box of troubles. If you're upgrading from Windows Vista, many of the skills you've learned will transfer directly. If you're moving to Windows 7 from Windows XP, however, prepare to unlearn nearly everything you knew about setup. The image-based installation process in Windows 7 (fundamentally the same as its Windows Vista counterpart) is faster and much more reliable than its Windows XP equivalent, especially when it comes to upgrades.

In this chapter, we'll explain the subtleties and intricacies of the Windows setup program, explore the workings of the Windows Easy Transfer utility, and show you how to set up a computer with multiple versions of Windows.

Our coverage in this chapter focuses primarily on issues surrounding installation of Windows 7 on a single computer. For information about deploying Windows 7 throughout an organization, see Chapter 26, "Deployment and Migration."

What's in Your Edition?

All the tools and techniques we discuss in this chapter are available in all editions of Windows 7. Some features might be unavailable or have different default settings in Windows editions that have been customized by a computer maker for installation on a new PC.

Before You Start

Programs originally written for earlier versions of Windows (including Windows XP and Windows Vista) might not run properly under Windows 7. Likewise, some older hardware devices require drivers that have never been updated for use with Windows 7. The worst possible time to find out about either type of compatibility problem is right after you complete a fresh installation of Windows 7, when you try to use a favorite program or device.

To spare yourself unnecessary headaches, if the computer on which you plan to install Windows 7 is currently running Windows XP (with Service Pack 2 or later) or any edition of Windows Vista that you are planning to upgrade, download and run the free Windows 7 Upgrade Advisor first. This tool, available from *w7io.com/0201*, scans installed programs and devices and produces a report identifying any potential issues you're likely to confront as part of an upgrade.

The purpose of Upgrade Advisor is to identify hardware and software issues that might interfere with your ability to install Windows 7 or programs that might not run properly after the upgrade is complete. Figure 2-1 shows a typical Upgrade Advisor report. Scroll through the entire list to identify any urgent warnings or compatibility issues that require your immediate attention. If this tool identifies any potential problems with drivers or installed software, we recommend that you resolve those issues before continuing.

Note that Upgrade Advisor generates two reports: one that applies if you plan to upgrade to a 32-bit version of Windows 7, and one that applies to upgrades to 64-bit Windows 7. Click the tabs at the top of the window to switch between the two reports.

INSIDE OUT   Use dynamic updates

When you upgrade over an existing Windows version, the setup program offers to check for dynamic updates. If you have an active Internet connection, be sure to take advantage of this option. Dynamic updates can include any or all of the following: critical updates to the setup program itself; improved or new versions of boot-critical drivers for storage, display, and network hardware detected on your system; and compatibility updates (also known as *shims*) for programs you're currently running. Rolling these updates in at the beginning of the process increases the likelihood that the Windows 7 setup will run correctly. After completing installation, you'll still need to connect to Windows Update to download critical updates for Windows and the most recent drivers for detected hardware.

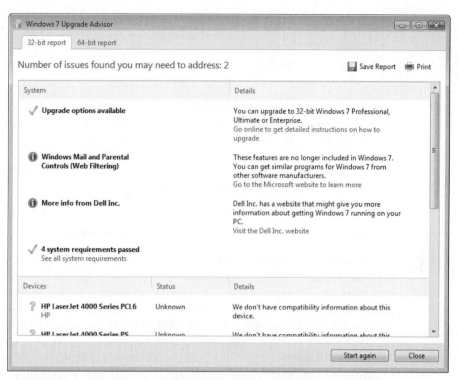

Figure 2-1 Read this upgrade report carefully before continuing with setup. In some cases, you might need to uninstall programs or find new drivers before going any further.

Understand the Licensing Issues

One important step before you install Windows 7 is ensuring that you purchase the right version. The choices are numerous, and making the wrong selection can mean paying more than you need to or ending up with a version that doesn't have the features you need or isn't properly licensed. Before you head to the mall, you need to consider the following:

- **Which edition has the features you need?**   Windows is available in six different editions, ranging from Windows 7 Starter through Windows 7 Ultimate. For a summary of the features in each edition, see Appendix A, "Windows 7 Editions at a Glance."

- **Should you use the 32-bit or 64-bit version of Windows?**   For help with this decision, see the following section, "Know Your Hardware."

- **Should you purchase a full version or an upgrade?**   This choice is dependent entirely on obtaining the appropriate Windows software license, a topic that is widely misunderstood. We try to clarify the choices in the following paragraphs.

Four different types of license are available for Windows 7:

- **OEM**   An OEM (original equipment manufacturer) license is one that's included with a new computer. This license is locked to the computer on which it's installed. That is, you can't transfer it to a new computer.

- **Full**   A full license is sold at retail and is intended for use on a computer that was not sold with Windows originally. A full license can be transferred to a different computer, as long the license is no longer being used on any other computers.

- **Upgrade**   An upgrade license is a discounted copy of Windows that can be installed only on a system that already has an OEM or full license.

- **Volume**   Volume licenses are sold in bulk to corporate customers in quantities of five or more at a time. A volume license is available as an upgrade only.

Who qualifies for an upgrade or volume license? All editions of Windows XP and Windows Vista qualify you to upgrade. Specifically:

- Any PC that was purchased with Windows XP or Vista preinstalled (look for the sticker on the side) is qualified. This is true whether the PC came from a large royalty OEM or a system builder. You can install a retail upgrade of Windows 7 on that PC. You cannot, however, use the OEM license from an old PC to upgrade a new PC without Windows installed.

- Any retail full copy of Windows XP or Windows Vista can serve as the qualifying license as well. If have a full retail copy (not an OEM edition) on an old PC, you can uninstall that copy from the old PC and use it as the baseline full license for the new PC.

Older copies of Windows, including Windows 95/98/Me or Windows 2000, do not qualify for upgrade pricing. You also need a full license for the following types of Windows installations:

- In a virtual machine (except for Windows XP Mode; for details, see "Running Legacy Applications in Windows XP Mode" on page 178)

- On a Mac or other computer that does not come with Windows preinstalled

- Dual boot (unless it's for a brief evaluation during the upgrade process, you need a full license for each installation after the first)

> **Note**
>
> It's important to understand that the legal restrictions imposed by license requirements are wholly independent of technical restrictions on installation. For example, the license permits upgrading from Windows XP to Windows 7, but it's not possible to perform an in-place upgrade; you must perform a custom install. Conversely, it is technically possible to install an upgrade version on an unlicensed computer, but doing so violates the license agreement.

Know Your Hardware

Microsoft has published minimum hardware requirements for the retail editions of Windows 7 (Home Premium, Professional, and Ultimate). The specifics are listed in Table 2-1. Note that RAM and disk space requirements are slightly higher for 64-bit versions of Windows 7.

Table 2-1 **Windows 7 Hardware Requirements**

Component	Minimum System Requirement
Processor (CPU)	1-GHz or faster, 32-bit (x86) or 64-bit (x64) processor
Memory	1 GB RAM (32-bit) 2 GB RAM (64-bit)
Graphics processor	Support for DirectX 9 graphics with WDDM 1.0 or higher driver
Hard disk	16 GB available disk space (32-bit) 20 GB available disk space (64-bit)

A DVD or other optical storage device is optional but useful for many tasks. For most everyday tasks, you also need a mouse or other pointing device, a keyboard, audio playback capabilities, and Internet access. In addition, certain Windows 7 features require additional hardware, such as a television tuner card (for viewing and recording television in Windows Media Center).

Chapter 2

INSIDE OUT   Find the hardware bottlenecks

Defining an acceptable level of performance is strictly a matter of personal preference. Some tasks, such as rendering 3D graphics or encoding video files, demand a lot from the CPU and the graphics processing unit and will benefit greatly from a more muscular processor and display adapter. For most everyday activities, including web browsing, sending and receiving e-mail, and creating standard business documents, the speed of the CPU is less critical. If you have a fast hard disk with ample free space and at least 1 GB of memory, you should have no trouble keeping multiple applications running smoothly. If you use large, memory-intensive programs such as Adobe Photoshop, 2 GB of RAM should be considered a bare minimum.

Deciding Between 32-Bit and 64-Bit Versions

As noted earlier, the hardware requirements for installing and running a 64-bit edition of Windows 7 are slightly steeper. So what's the benefit of 64-bit? Unlike a 32-bit version, a 64-bit version can efficiently handle more than 4 GB of RAM. This ability (along with copious amounts of RAM) results in better performance when you run several programs at once and when you're working with extremely large data files.

The downside of 64-bit versions is compatibility with older applications and hardware. In general, programs for 32-bit Windows work on a 64-bit system. However, some do not—particularly utilities that work at a low level, such as antivirus programs. In addition, you can't run 16-bit applications or 32-bit installers with 64-bit Windows. Support for hardware devices can be problematical because 64-bit driver support is nonexistent for many older devices.

Before you decide between a 32-bit and a 64-bit version, be sure to check the corresponding tabs in the Windows 7 Upgrade Advisor. Upgrade Advisor determines first whether your system is capable of running a 64-bit version of Windows, and it also identifies devices and programs that might be incompatible.

Another way to check for 64-bit capability is with a Windows PowerShell script on the companion CD, in the Scripts folder. Locate the script named Get-ProcessorArchitecture.ps1, which displays the value X64 when you run it on a computer with a 64-bit processor.

> **Note**
>
> If you intend to install a 64-bit version of Windows 7, you'll need to confirm that digi-tally signed drivers are available for all devices you intend to install. This compatibility bar is far more stringent than with 32-bit versions, where you can choose to install drivers that have not been digitally signed by the Windows Hardware Quality Labs. In 64-bit versions of Windows 7, unsigned boot drivers will not load.

Avoiding Software Compatibility Problems

When upgrading, be especially vigilant with utility software that works at the system level. If you use a system utility that was originally written for a previous Windows version, it's prudent to assume that it will require an upgrade to work properly with Windows 7. Most applications that are certified to be compatible with Windows Vista are also compatible with Windows 7, but that is not universally true. For essential programs, it's important that you verify compatibility first.

Which classes of software are most likely to cause problems with an upgrade or a clean installation of Windows 7? Here is a list of likely culprits:

- Antivirus and antispyware software

- Software firewalls and other security programs

- Programs whose feature set includes the capability to burn CDs and DVDs

- Disk-partitioning utilities and other low-level system maintenance programs

As a precaution when upgrading, you should consider disabling or uninstalling antivirus software and other system utilities that might interfere with setup. After setup is complete, reinstall or reenable the programs and then test to be sure that they're working properly.

If Upgrade Advisor identifies any programs as incompatible with Windows 7, we strongly recommend that you uninstall those programs before continuing with the upgrade.

Backing Up Data and Settings

If you're planning an upgrade, don't underestimate Murphy's Law (most often described as "Anything that can go wrong will go wrong"). Use a reliable backup program or Windows Easy Transfer (described in "Transferring Files and Settings from Another Computer" on page 66) to make a safe copy of important data files before continuing with the upgrade.

Chapter 2

> **Note**
>
> If you use the Windows XP Backup program on your old computer (or on your current computer if you plan to upgrade) to save data files to a network drive or another disk, be aware that the backup program in Windows 7 uses a different, incompatible format and cannot open or restore files backed up using that earlier format. Microsoft makes available a free program that restores (but cannot create) backups in the .bkf format used by Windows XP. For information about the Windows NT Backup Restore Utility for Windows 7 and links to download the appropriate version for your system, visit support article 974674 (*w7io.com/974674*).

If you own a software utility that can create an image copy of your existing system volume, this is an excellent strategy. Some hard-disk upgrade packages sold at retail outlets include this sort of tool; Norton Ghost (*w7io.com/0202*) and Acronis True Image (*w7io.com/0203*) are highly regarded examples of third-party imaging tools. A disk image stored on an external hard disk is excellent protection against data disasters.

Setting Up Windows 7

As we mentioned briefly at the beginning of this chapter, the setup program in Windows 7 is based on the architecture introduced with Windows Vista and is unlike its Windows XP predecessor. The reengineered process is specifically designed to run very quickly, with an absolute minimum of attention required from you. In this section, we'll explain the ins and outs of the most common scenarios you'll confront when installing or upgrading Windows 7 on a single PC. We assume that you have a bootable DVD containing a full copy of Windows 7, suitable for use in a clean installation or upgrade.

> **Note**
>
> Windows 7 is sold in a variety of packages, and not all are covered in the scenarios we discuss here. For a discussion of the different types of licenses and installation media available to you, see "Activating and Validating Windows 7" on page 59.

As part of the setup process, you need to make a series of relatively simple but important decisions:

- **Which Windows 7 edition do you want to install?** The edition you choose will normally be the version you purchased; however, retail copies of the Windows 7 DVD contain program code for all three Windows editions available through the retail channel—Home Premium, Professional, and Ultimate—as well as the Home Basic and Starter editions, which are not intended for installation by end users. As we explain later in this section, you can install and run any of these editions for up to 30 days without entering a product key or activating your copy of Windows 7.

- **Do you want to perform a custom installation or an upgrade?**   A custom installation starts from scratch; you need to reinstall your programs and re-create or transfer settings from another system. An upgrade retains installed programs and settings, at the risk of creating some compatibility issues.

- **Do you need to adjust the layout of the system disk?**   The Windows 7 installation program includes disk-management tools that you can use to create, delete, format, and extend (but not shrink) partitions on hard disks installed in your computer. Knowing how these tools work can save you a significant amount of time when setting up Windows.

- **Do you want to install Windows 7 alongside another operating system?**   If you want to set up a dual-boot (or multiboot) system, you'll need to understand how different startup files work so that you can manage your startup options effectively. Understanding these details is especially important if you plan to use Windows 7 and Windows XP in a dual-boot configuration.

If the system on which you plan to install Windows 7 is already running Windows XP, Windows Vista, or Windows 7, you can start the setup program from within Windows. As an alternative, you can start the system from the installation media. Depending on which option you choose, you'll notice some important differences.

If you run setup from within Windows

- You *can* upgrade Windows Vista (SP1 or later), provided that the new Windows 7 edition is the same as or higher than the Windows Vista edition. For details about supported upgrade paths, see "Upgrading a Previous Windows Version" on page 46.

- You *can* reinstall Windows 7. (You can also use this option to upgrade from one edition of Windows 7 to a more advanced edition; however, the Windows Anytime Upgrade option, described later in this chapter, is far preferable.)

- You *cannot* run the 64-bit setup program on a PC running a 32-bit version of Windows, or vice versa.

- You *can* run the Windows 7 Upgrade Advisor from an option on the startup screen.

- You *cannot* perform an in-place upgrade of Windows XP.

Chapter 2

- You *can* install Windows 7 on the same volume as an existing Windows version. (You'll find step-by-step instructions in the following section.)

- You *cannot* make any changes to the layout of a disk; you must use existing partitions, and the setup program will not recognize or use unallocated space on an attached hard drive.

If you boot from the Windows 7 DVD

- You *cannot* upgrade an existing Windows version. Your only option is a custom install.

- You *can* delete existing partitions, create new partitions, extend an existing disk partition to unallocated space, or designate a block of unallocated space as the setup location.

- You *can* install Windows 7 on the same volume as an existing Windows version.

Performing a Clean Installation

The simplest (and best, in most cases) setup scenario of all is installing Windows 7 in a newly created partition on a system that does not currently have any version of Windows installed. This is the case if you start with a brand-new hard disk, or if you wipe out a partition that contains an existing version of Windows. The safest way to embark on a clean installation is to boot from the Windows 7 DVD. Insert the Windows 7 DVD, and restart your computer. Watch for a boot prompt; typically, you need to press a key to boot from the DVD. After the setup process begins, you can follow the instructions as outlined in this section.

TROUBLESHOOTING

You get a Boot Manager error when you boot from the Windows 7 DVD

If you boot from a DVD for a 64-bit version of Windows on a computer that isn't capable of using a 64-bit operating system, you'll see a Windows Boot Manager error. Install Windows using the media for a 32-bit version instead.

TROUBLESHOOTING

You can't boot from the Windows 7 DVD

For a bootable CD or DVD to work properly, you must set the boot order in the BIOS so that the drive appears ahead of the hard disk drive and any other bootable media; we recommend setting the DVD drive as the first boot device, followed by the hard disk, floppy disk (if present), and any other bootable devices in whichever order you prefer. The boot options available for every computer are different, as is the technique for accessing the BIOS setup program. During boot, watch for a message that tells you which key to press for setup. If you're lucky, the BIOS setup program on your computer includes a Boot section where you can specify the order of boot devices; if this option isn't immediately apparent, look for a page or tab called Advanced CMOS Settings or something similar.

What if your computer lacks the capability to boot from a DVD drive? This problem is most likely to affect you if you're trying to install Windows 7 on a notebook computer that doesn't include an integrated DVD drive, or if the DVD drive in an existing system is damaged. Try one of the following alternatives to work around the problem (you'll need temporary access to a computer with a functioning DVD drive to complete any of these steps):

- Copy the DVD files to a folder on your hard disk, and run the setup program from that location.

- Copy the DVD files to a partition on an external hard disk, set that partition as active, and boot from the external drive. This option might require adjusting the order of boot devices in your system BIOS.

- Copy the DVD files to a USB flash drive, and run setup from that location. The drive must have enough space to accommodate all installation files (2.5 GB for 32-bit, 3.2 GB for 64-bit). The procedure for preparing the flash drive to be a bootable device is cumbersome but straightforward. Step-by-step instructions are in this blog post by Microsoft's Jeff Alexander: *w7io.com/0204*.

- On another computer, use a full-featured DVD-burning program such as Nero (*w7io.com/0205*) or Roxio Creator (*w7io.com/0206*) to copy the Windows 7 DVD to an ISO image file. Then install an ISO image-mounting program such as Virtual CloneDrive (*w7io.com/0207*) or Daemon Tools (*w7io.com/0208*), and point it at the ISO file you created. The mounted image file appears as a DVD drive in the Computer window, and you can run the setup program from that virtual drive.

Any of the preceding options allow you to upgrade the current Windows installation or to install a clean copy on a separate volume or on the same volume, alongside the current copy of Windows. You must boot from a removable storage device (an external hard drive or USB flash drive) if you want to delete the current partition on which Windows is installed and install a clean copy in that location.

Chapter 2

When you boot from the Windows 7 DVD, your first stop is a pair of screens that allow you to set up the installation language and choose your language preferences for Windows itself. These should normally be the same and typically match the Windows version you purchased. After you accept the license agreement, you'll reach the Which Type Of Installation Do You Want dialog box shown here:

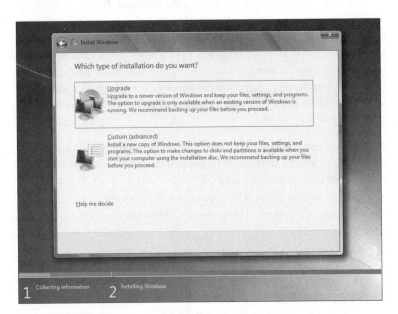

Because you booted from the DVD, the Upgrade option does not work, although it appears to be available (if you try to select it, you'll get an error message). Click the Custom (Advanced) option to continue with a clean installation. The Where Do You Want To Install Windows dialog box, shown in Figure 2-2, lists all physical disks, partitions, and unallocated space.

In this example, we assume that you're using a freshly formatted disk with no existing partitions and that you want to use all unallocated space as your system drive. For alternative scenarios involving multiple partitions or changes to existing partitions, see "Setup and Your Hard Disk" on page 42.

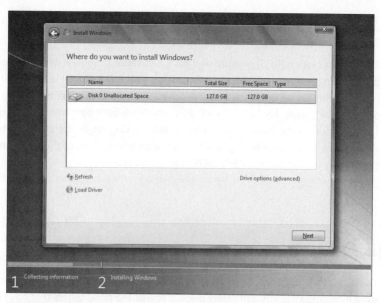

Figure 2-2 In this simple scenario, with a single physical disk that does not contain any partitions, you can click Next to create a partition and install Windows using the entire physical drive.

TROUBLESHOOTING

Setup doesn't detect your hard disk

The Windows 7 DVD includes drivers for most commonly used IDE and SATA disk controllers. If you have an older PC or an unusual disk configuration, the setup program might not recognize your disk controller. In that case, you'll be prompted to provide a driver when you reach the Where Do You Want To Install Windows dialog box. For 32-bit (x86) versions of Windows 7, you should be able to supply a driver that is compatible with Windows Vista or Windows 7 on a USB flash drive, on a floppy disk, or on a CD or DVD. For the last option mentioned, remove the Windows 7 DVD and insert the disc containing the storage driver; after the driver loads successfully, remove the disc and reinsert the Windows 7 DVD.

TROUBLESHOOTING

During setup, some peripherals don't work properly

Check your system BIOS. An outdated BIOS can cause problems with disk partitioning, power management, peripheral configuration, and other crucial low-level functions. To find out whether an update is available, check with the manufacturer of your computer or its motherboard. For "white label" PCs, which are built by small system builders from standard parts, identifying the BIOS and tracking down the appropriate source for updates isn't always easy; you'll find detailed information at the indispensable (and thoroughly independent) Wim's BIOS (*wimsbios.com*).

INSIDE OUT   It's OK to share a partition

Thanks to the radically revised setup architecture introduced in Windows Vista and also used in Windows 7, you can safely discard one of the basic tenets that have governed installation decisions since the beginning of the Windows era. You want to point Windows 7 setup to a partition on which another version of Windows is already installed? As long as you have sufficient free disk space and you don't plan to use the copy of Windows on that volume any more, go right ahead. When you choose to do a clean installation in this nondestructive configuration, Windows 7 setup moves the old Windows, Program Files, and user profile folders (Documents And Settings for Windows XP, Users for Windows Vista or Windows 7) to a folder named Windows.old.

Why would you want to do this? Let's say you currently have a system that has a single disk with a single partition and plenty of free disk space. You want to start fresh with a clean installation, but you have lots of valuable data and you don't want to lose any of it. Performing a nondestructive clean installation gives you the fresh start you're looking for, with your data files safely ensconced in the Windows.old folder. You can no longer start up your old Windows installation, but you can copy any of the saved files from that folder to your new user profile whenever you're ready. (In addition, all the device drivers from your previous installation are available for your use; you'll find them in Windows.old\Windows\System32\DriverStore\FileRepository.)

Why is this option acceptable now? In Windows XP and earlier versions, the operation of the setup program invariably involved some commingling of files in the old and new Windows installations. Those unwanted system files and leftovers from previously installed programs defeated the purpose of doing a clean installation. But the image-based Windows setup used by Windows Vista and Windows 7 quarantines your old files and allows you to do a truly clean installation of your new operating system.

After you select the disk location where you want to install Windows 7, setup proceeds automatically, copying files and configuring hardware devices with no further input required from you. The Installing Windows dialog box provides a progress bar to indicate how close to completion you are. After the technical portion of a clean installation is complete, you need to fill in some basic information and set some essential systemwide options:

1. **Choose a user name and a computer name.**   The user name you enter here becomes the first user account, which is a member of the Administrators group. Setup suggests a default computer name by removing any spaces and tacking the "-PC" suffix to the user name you enter. You're free to replace the autogenerated name with a more descriptive name if you prefer.

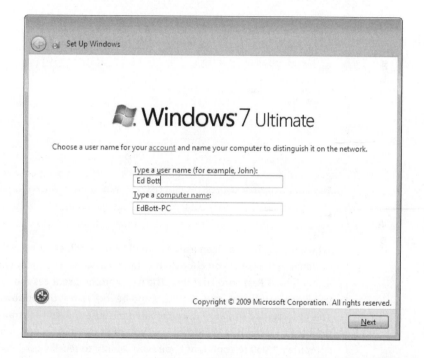

2. **Set a password for your user account.**   Although you're not required to assign a password to this account, we strongly recommend you do so.

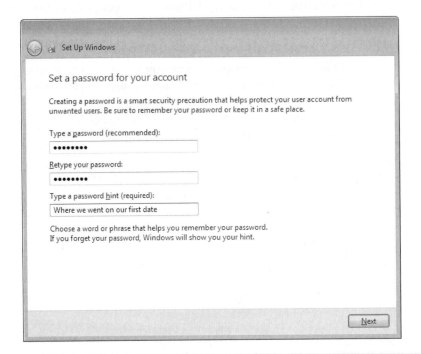

Note

When you perform a clean installation of Windows 7, entering a password is optional. However, if you choose to enter a password, you must enter something in the Type A Password Hint box. The password hint reduces the likelihood that you'll one day forget your password and be locked out of your own computer. This unfortunate situation is exacerbated because the Administrator account is disabled by default in Windows 7, so you can't use it as a back door into your computer. If you're confident about your ability to recall your password and you don't want to offer any clues to a would-be intruder, enter a nonsense word or phrase (or just a single punctuation mark) here. For more information, see "Setting a Logon Password" on page 663.

3. **Enter your Windows product key.**   You can enter the product key included with your purchased copy, or you can bypass this dialog box and install Windows without entering a product key. (For more details on these options, see "Activating and Validating Windows 7" on page 59.)

4. **Select Automatic Update settings.**   For most people, the first option, Use Recommended Settings, is the correct one.

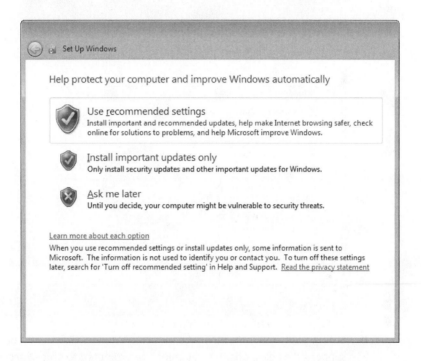

5. **Review your time and date settings.**   A clean installation of Windows 7 from U.S. English media sets the time zone to Pacific (U.S. and Canada), with Daylight Saving Time enabled. Changing the time zone does not change the time displayed. After selecting your time zone, check the date and time carefully. Incorrect values in any of the settings on this page can cause complications later.

6. **Set up your network.**   If you're installing Windows 7 on a notebook with a supported wireless adapter, you might be prompted to enter a security passphrase for your wireless access point before you reach the dialog box shown next. The network location setting determines basic network security, including firewall settings and sharing options. On most home or small business networks connected to the Internet through a router, you can safely select the Home Network or Work Network option. Click Public Network if your computer is directly connected to a cable or DSL modem (that is, with no router or gateway appliance separating your computer from the modem) or if you connect to the Internet by means of a dial-up modem. If you choose Home Network, the next dialog box allows you to create or join a homegroup.

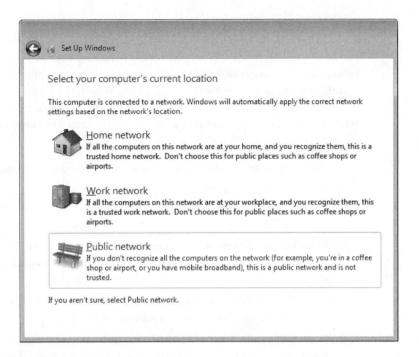

For more details about your network options, see Chapter 19, "Setting Up a Small Office or Home Network."

After completing the final step in this process, setup takes you to a logon screen.

INSIDE OUT   Perform a clean installation with upgrade media

A common misconception about installing Windows is that you must use a full version of Windows to perform a clean install; this is false. If you already have a qualifying version of Windows (in short, Windows XP or Windows Vista; for details, see "Understand the Licensing Issues" on page 25), you can use an upgrade version. In fact, many legitimate upgrade paths (for example, from any version of Windows XP) require a clean installation, but they do not require you to purchase a full version of Windows.

Before you begin the installation, we strongly encourage you to back up your data and settings by using Windows Easy Transfer. Although the installation process can retain your existing files in the Windows.old folder, Windows Easy Transfer provides a method that is much more convenient and comprehensive. For details, see "Transferring Files and Settings from Another Computer" on page 66. Then, after you complete the installation, use Windows Easy Transfer to restore your data.

Chapter 2

To install Windows 7, simply boot from the upgrade DVD (or other media, such as a bootable USB flash drive), and then follow the remaining steps as described on the preceding pages. If you get an Invalid Product Key error when you enter the product key (step 3), proceed without entering a product key. After setup finishes (including downloading updates and rebooting as required), open the Start menu and type **activate**. Select Activate Windows, enter your product key, and after a few moments you should see an Activation Was Successful message.

If activation fails for some reason, you can use the following workaround:

1. Open an elevated Command Prompt window. To do that, click the Start button and type **cmd**. Press Ctrl+Shift+Enter to run Cmd.exe as an administrator. Click Yes in the User Account Control dialog box that appears.

2. At the command prompt, type **slmgr /ipk** *productkey*, where *productkey* is your 25-character upgrade product key. Include the hyphens that separate each group of five characters. This command installs the product key.

3. Click OK in the dialog box that appears, and then enter **slmgr /ato** at the command prompt. This command activates Windows.

4. To check the activation and license status, at the command prompt type **slmgr /dli** (for a summary report) or **slmgr /dlv** (for a detailed report).

Setup and Your Hard Disk

In the previous section, we described the steps for a clean installation on the simplest of all PC configurations: a single hard disk, containing a single partition to be used as the system drive. Out in the real world, especially among Windows enthusiasts, we know that disk configurations are often much more complex.

On most desktop PCs and on some notebooks, you can connect multiple physical disk drives. You can choose to install Windows 7 to a volume on any IDE or SATA drive (including eSATA drives, which attach to the system via an external cable but appear to Windows as an ordinary internal drive). You cannot, however, install Windows to an external drive connected via USB or IEEE 1394 (FireWire).

INSIDE OUT   What's that mysterious 100-MB partition?

If you install Windows 7 on a clean disk with no existing partitions, it creates a System Reserved partition of 100 MB at the beginning of the disk and uses the remainder of the unallocated space to create your system drive. That small partition isn't assigned a drive letter, so you won't even know it exists unless you look in the Disk Management console (as shown here) or use DiskPart or a similar low-level utility to inspect the disk structure.

Disk 0	System Reserved	(C:)
Basic	100 MB NTFS	126.90 GB NTFS
127.00 GB	Healthy (System, Active)	Healthy (Boot, Page File, Crash Dump, Primary Partition)
Online		

This system partition, new in Windows 7, serves three functions. First, it holds the Boot Manager code and the Boot Configuration Database (which we explain in more detail in "Understanding and Managing the Windows 7 Startup Process" on page 50). Second, it provides a safe location for recovery tools. (For more information, see "Making Repairs with the Windows Recovery Environment" on page 1046.) And third, it reserves space for the startup files required by the BitLocker Drive Encryption feature (which we discuss in "Encrypting Information" on page 418).

Multiboot capabilities and Windows Recovery Environment can be implemented without this System Reserved partition, but BitLocker requires it. Because the clean-install process creates the partition, you won't have to repartition your system drive (a genuinely tedious process) if you ever decide to encrypt your system drive using BitLocker.

With a new hard disk or an existing one, you might have any of several good reasons to tinker with disk partitions. You might prefer to segregate your operating system files from your data files by placing them on separate volumes, for example, or you might be planning to set up a dual-boot or multiboot system. In any event, it's always easier to make partitioning decisions before setup than it is to resize and rearrange volumes after they're in use.

For a full inventory of all disk-management tools and techniques available in Windows 7, see Chapter 30, "Managing Disks and Drives."

To make adjustments to existing disk partitions, boot from the Windows 7 DVD (or a bootable hard drive or USB flash drive) and run through Windows setup until you reach the Where Do You Want To Install Windows dialog box, shown earlier in Figure 2-2. Click Drive

Options (Advanced) to expand the collection of tools below the list of disks and partitions, as shown in Figure 2-3.

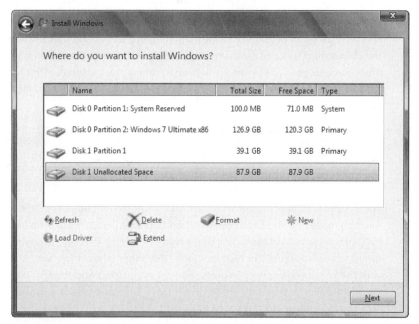

Figure 2-3 Use the disk-management tools in this phase of the Windows 7 setup process to manage disk partitions for more efficient data storage and multiboot configurations.

You can accomplish any of the following tasks here:

- **Select an existing partition or unallocated space on which to install Windows 7**   Setup is simple if you already created and formatted an empty partition in preparation for setting up Windows, or if you plan to install Windows 7 on an existing partition that currently contains data or programs but no operating system, or if you want to use unallocated space on an existing disk without disturbing the existing partition scheme. Select the partition or unallocated space, and click Next.

- **Delete an existing partition**   Select a partition, and then click Delete. This option is useful if you want to perform a clean installation on a drive that currently contains an earlier version of Windows. Because this operation deletes data irretrievably, you must respond to an "Are you sure?" confirmation request. After deleting the partition, you can select the unallocated space as the destination for your Windows 7 installation or create a new partition. Be sure to back up any data files before choosing this option.

- **Create a new partition from unallocated space**   Select a block of unallocated space on a new drive or on an existing drive after deleting partitions, and click New to set up a partition in that space.

By default, the setup program offers to use all unallocated space on the current disk. You can specify a smaller partition size if you want to subdivide the disk into multiple drives. If you have a 1,500-GB drive, for example, you might choose to create a small partition on which to install Windows and use the remaining space to create a second volume with its own drive letter on which to store data files such as music, pictures, documents, and recorded TV.

- **Extend an existing partition by using unallocated space**   If you want to upgrade an existing copy of Windows and you're not happy with your existing partition scheme, you can use the Extend option to add unallocated space to any partition. If you originally set up a 60-GB notebook hard drive with a 10-GB partition for Windows XP and set aside the remaining 50 GB for data files, you might be unable to upgrade to Windows 7 because your system drive doesn't meet the requirement of at least 15 GB of free space. The solution? First, back up your data files to an external drive. Then delete the data partition, select the partition you want to make larger, and click Extend. Choose the total size of the extended partition in the Size box (the default is to use all available unallocated space), and click Apply. You can now restore your backed-up data files and continue with Windows setup.

INSIDE OUT   ### Use labels to tell volumes apart

In both the Disk Management console and the disk-management tools available via Windows setup, it can be confusing to tell which partition is which. Confusion, in this case, can have drastic consequences if you inadvertently wipe out a drive full of data instead of writing over an unwanted installation of Windows. One good way to reduce the risk of this sort of accident is to label drives well. In Figure 2-3, for instance, you can see at a glance that the second partition on Disk 0 contains a current installation of Windows 7 Ultimate x86 and that the smaller partition on Disk 1 is empty.

Chapter 2

Alert observers will no doubt notice that one option is missing from that list. Unfortunately, the setup program does not allow you to shrink an existing disk partition to create unallocated space on which to install a fresh copy of Windows 7. The option to shrink a volume is available from the Disk Management console after Windows 7 is installed, but if you want to accomplish this task before or during setup, you'll need to use third-party disk-management tools.

Upgrading a Previous Windows Version

To perform an in-place upgrade of your existing copy of Windows, you must be running either Windows Vista with Service Pack 1 or later installed or Windows 7. The installed edition (32-bit or 64-bit) must match the upgrade edition; you can't install 32-bit Windows 7 over a 64-bit Windows installation or vice versa. Finally, you must have enough free disk space to accommodate the new installation of Windows 7—typically, 15 to 20 GB. The exact upgrade paths available are listed in Table 2-2.

Table 2-2 Supported Paths for In-Place Upgrades from Windows Vista

If Your Current Operating System Is	You Can Upgrade To
Windows Vista Home Basic	Windows 7 Home Basic, Home Premium, Ultimate
Windows Vista Home Premium	Windows 7 Home Premium, Ultimate
Windows Vista Business	Windows 7 Professional, Ultimate, Enterprise
Windows Vista Ultimate	Windows 7 Ultimate

If you want to upgrade your existing copy of Windows XP to Windows 7, you'll need to jump through a few hoops. Direct upgrades from Windows XP are not possible, so you'll have to perform a clean installation. You can use the Windows Easy Transfer utility to migrate your files and settings from the old computer to the new one, and then you'll need to reinstall applications that are compatible with Windows 7. For more details, see "Performing a Clean Installation" on page 32, paying particular attention to the Inside Out tip at the end of that section.

To begin an in-place upgrade, start your existing copy of Windows and run the Windows 7 setup program. If you're using the Windows 7 DVD, you can kick off setup from the Auto-Play dialog box, open the contents of the DVD in Windows Explorer and double-click Setup, or enter **d:\setup.exe** (substituting the letter of your DVD drive for *d*) at any command prompt, including the Run dialog box (Windows logo key+R). In the Install Windows dialog box, click Install Now to begin.

The upgrade process involves significantly fewer steps than a clean installation. After accepting the license agreement, you see the dialog box shown in Figure 2-4. If you have a working Internet connection, we strongly recommend that you accept the default option to download the latest updates for installation.

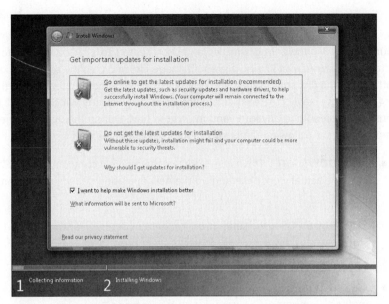

Figure 2-4 For an upgrade installation, you'll avoid headaches if you take advantage of the option to download security updates and new drivers as part of setup.

Next, you're prompted to choose the type of installation you want. Click Upgrade to begin setup.

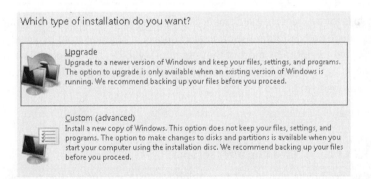

Before beginning the actual upgrade, the setup program runs a brief compatibility test analogous to the Windows 7 Upgrade Advisor. If this test detects any potential software or hardware compatibility issues, you'll see a Compatibility Report dialog box listing the issues and recommending steps to resolve them. You can (and should) interrupt setup at this point to uninstall a program or driver if setup recommends that you do so; or, if you're satisfied that the issue won't affect your upgrade, click Next to continue.

An upgrade from Windows Vista takes significantly more time than a clean installation. In fact, the upgrade actually gathers settings and drivers from your existing installation; moves your existing Windows, Program Files, and Users folders to a new folder; performs a clean installation of Windows 7 using a prebuilt image file; migrates the settings and drivers it gathered in the first step to the new copy of Windows 7; moves user data to the correct locations in the newly created user profiles; and finally restarts Windows 7. All of this happens without requiring any intervention on your part. During the upgrade, the setup program creates the following temporary hidden folders in the root of your system drive:

- **$WINDOWS.~BT**   This folder contains the minimal copy of Windows 7 that manages the actual work of setting up the new operating system and migrating files and settings.

- **$UPGRADE.~OS**   The setup program gathers settings for the operating system and stores them in this temporary folder to be applied to Windows 7 after installation is complete.

- **$WINDOWS.~LS**   This folder contains the large image file (in Windows Image format) and temporary files used during the upgrade.

- **$INPLACE.~TR**   User-specific and machine-specific settings are temporarily stored here after being gathered during the first stage of the upgrade.

- **$WINDOWS.~Q**   This folder contains the original Windows installation.

If setup fails for any reason, it automatically rolls back the installation, removing the newly installed image and restoring the original Windows installation from its saved location. After a successful upgrade, most of these temporary folders are deleted. The $INPLACE.~TR and $WINDOWS.~Q folders are preserved to allow you to recover files and settings that were not properly migrated.

INSIDE OUT   Clean up after setup

After you complete an upgrade from Windows Vista and are satisfied that all your data files are intact and all settings were properly migrated, you can clean up the bits and pieces the upgrade process leaves behind. The quickest and safest way to accomplish this goal is to use the Disk Cleanup utility. Select the Files Discarded By Windows Upgrade option, and click OK. If you performed a clean installation of Windows 7 on the same partition as an existing copy of Windows, use the Previous Installation(s) Of Windows option, which removes the Windows.old folder and its contents. For more details on how to use this option, see "Cleaning Up with Disk Cleanup" on page 892.

Creating and Configuring a Multiboot System

If your computer already has any version of Windows installed *and* you have a second disk partition available (or enough unallocated space to create a second partition), you can install a clean copy of Windows 7 without disturbing your existing Windows installation. At boot time, you choose your Windows version from a startup menu. Although this is typically called a dual-boot system, it's more accurate to call it a multiboot configuration, because you can install multiple copies of Windows or other PC-compatible operating systems.

Having the capability to choose your operating system at startup is handy if you have a program or device that simply won't work under Windows 7. When you need to use the legacy program or device, you can boot into your other Windows version without too much fuss. This capability is also useful for software developers and IT professionals who need to be able to test how programs work under different operating systems.

For experienced Windows users, installing a second copy of Windows 7 in its own partition can also be helpful as a way to experiment with a potentially problematic program or device driver without compromising a working system. After you finish setting up the second, clean version of Windows 7, you'll see an additional entry on the startup menu that corresponds to your new installation. (The newly installed version is the default menu choice; it runs automatically if 30 seconds pass and you don't make a choice.) Experiment with the program or driver and see how well it works. If, after testing thoroughly, you're satisfied that the program is safe to use, you can add it to the Windows 7 installation you use every day.

INSIDE OUT   The ins and outs of system drive letters

Which drive letter will your clean installation of Windows 7 use? As with previous versions of Windows, the assigned drive letter varies depending on how you start setup. If you currently have a working copy of any Windows version on drive C and you install a clean copy of Windows 7 on a different partition, drive letters are assigned using the following logic:

- If you begin the installation process by booting from the Windows 7 media and choose a partition other than the one containing your current copy of Windows, the new installation uses the drive letter C when you start up. The volume that contains the other Windows installation uses the next available drive letter when you start your new installation of Windows. When you choose the previous Windows installation from the startup menu, it uses the drive letter C, and your new Windows 7 installation is assigned the next available drive letter. In this configuration, you can be certain that your current operating system is always on the C drive, but drive letters assigned to volumes you use for data might shift in unexpected ways.

- If you begin the installation process by running the setup program from within your current version of Windows and use the Custom (Advanced) option to perform a clean installation on a partition that does not have a drive letter assigned to it, each installation will use the drive letter C as well, with the drive letter for other partitions shifting accordingly depending on which choice you made from the Windows boot menu.

- If you begin the installation process by running the setup program from within your current version of Windows and use the Custom (Advanced) option to perform a clean installation on a partition that currently has a drive letter assigned to it, the new installation uses that drive letter. Other volumes maintain their original drive letters when you start your newly installed copy of Windows 7. Thus, if you run setup from within Windows and choose to install a clean copy of Windows on drive E, the system drive for the new installation will be E as well.

There's no inherent reason to prefer one of these options over the other. If you find comfort in the consistency of knowing that system files and program files are always on the C drive and you don't want to have to worry about software that is hard-wired to locations on the C drive, you'll probably want to choose the first or second option. If you prefer the nonstandard but supported option to use drive letters to keep track of which Windows version is running at any given time, you'll prefer the third option. But any of these configurations should work reliably with any combination of properly written software, hardware, and settings.

Understanding and Managing the Windows 7 Startup Process

Windows 7, Windows Vista, and Windows Server 2008 share a common startup process. If you've learned the ins and outs of a multiboot system with Windows Vista or Windows Server 2008, your accumulated knowledge will serve you well with Windows 7. However, if your only experience with multiboot systems involves Windows XP, Windows Server 2003, and Windows 2000, you'll need to read this section carefully.

Fundamental changes in the boot loader change the way you manage multiple operating system installations that include Windows 7 or Windows Vista. The Ntldr and Boot.ini files from an installation of Windows XP, Windows 2000, or Windows Server 2003 are used only in a secondary role in a multiboot configuration with Windows 7, Windows Vista, or Windows Server 2008.

The startup process in Windows 7 begins when your computer performs its power-on self test (POST), which is followed by the POST for each adapter card that has a BIOS, such as advanced storage adapters and video cards. The system BIOS then reads the master boot record (MBR)—the first physical sector on the hard disk defined as the boot device—and transfers control to the code in the MBR, which is created during setup of Windows 7 or Windows Vista. This is where Windows takes over the startup process. Here's what happens next:

1. The MBR reads the boot sector—the first sector of the active partition—which contains code that starts the Windows Boot Manager program, Bootmgr.

2. The Windows Boot Manager reads the contents of the Boot Configuration Data (BCD) store, which contains configuration information about all operating systems installed on the computer. It uses this data to build and display the boot menu.

3. When you make a selection from the boot menu, you trigger one of the following actions:

   • If you select an instance of Windows 7 or Windows Vista, the Windows Boot Manager starts the OS loader, Winload.exe, from the %SystemRoot%\System32 folder for that installation.

   • If you choose the option to resume Windows 7 or Windows Vista from hibernation, the Boot Manager loads Winresume.exe and restores your previous environment.

   • If you choose the Earlier Version Of Windows option from the boot menu, the Boot Manager locates the volume containing that installation, loads its Windows NT–style Legacy OS loader (Ntldr.exe), and, if necessary, displays a new startup menu drawn from the Boot.ini file on that volume.

When you select an installation of Windows 7 from the boot menu, Windows starts by loading its core files, Ntoskrnl.exe and Hal.dll, reading settings from the registry, and loading drivers. That's followed by the Windows Session Manager (Smss.exe), which starts the Windows Start-Up Application (Wininit.exe), which in turn starts the Local Security Authority (Lsass.exe) and Services (Services.exe) processes. After that, you're ready to log on.

Understanding the boot process can help you to pinpoint problems that occur during startup. For more information, see "Using Advanced Boot Options" on page 1041.

INSIDE OUT
Use virtual machines instead of hassling with multiboot menus

You can create truly elaborate multiboot configurations using more than a decade's worth of Windows versions. But unless you're running a hardware testing lab, there's no good reason to do that. The much simpler, smoother alternative is to use virtualization software to run multiple versions of Windows on virtual hardware that faithfully re-creates the operating environment. During the course of researching and writing this book, we installed Windows 7 in virtual machines to capture details of several crucial tasks and processes that can't easily be documented on physical hardware, and we saved many hours compared to how long those tasks would have taken had we set up and restored physical hardware. Microsoft's Windows Virtual PC (*w7io.com/0209*) runs on Windows 7 Professional and Ultimate systems only. The Hyper-V virtualization software, which runs on Windows Server 2008, can be used over a local area network by clients running Windows 7. (For more information about Hyper-V, visit *w7io.com/0210*.) VMware (*vmware.com*) offers excellent virtualization software for use on desktop Windows machines and servers. The free VirtualBox package from Sun Microsystems (*virtualbox.org*) is compatible with all Windows 7 editions and can host an extensive selection of guest operating systems. Using any of these solutions, you can install even the most ancient Windows version. Backing up a machine's configuration and restoring it is as simple as copying a file. Legally, you'll need a license for every operating system you install in a virtual machine. If you have a license to use Windows for evaluation purposes, this option is a lifesaver.

To add Windows 7 to a system on which an existing version of Windows is already installed, first make sure that you have an available partition (or unformatted disk space) separate from the partition that contains the system files for your current Windows version.

The target partition can be a separate partition on the same physical disk, or it can be on a different hard disk. If your system contains a single disk with a single partition used as drive C, you cannot create a multiboot system unless you add a new disk or use software tools to shrink the existing partition and create a new partition from the free space. (The Windows 7 Disk Management console, Diskmgmt.msc, includes this capability; to shrink partitions on a system running an older Windows version, you'll need third-party software. For details, see "Shrinking a Volume" on page 1116.) The new partition does not need to be empty; however, it should not contain system files for another Windows installation. Run the setup program, choose the Custom (Advanced) option, and select the disk and partition you want to use for the new installation.

The setup program automatically handles details of adding the newly installed operating system to the Boot Configuration Data store.

And how do you edit and configure the Boot Configuration Data store? Surprisingly, the only official tool is a command-line utility called Bcdedit. Bcdedit isn't an interactive program; instead, you perform tasks by appending switches and parameters to the Bcdedit command line. To display the complete syntax for this tool, open an elevated Command Prompt window (using the Run As Administrator option) and type the command **bcdedit /?**.

For everyday use, most Bcdedit options are esoteric, unnecessary—and risky. In fact, the only option that we remember using more than once in the past four years is the command to change the text for each entry in the boot menu. By default, the setup program adds the generic entry "Windows 7" for each installation. If you set up a dual-boot system using two copies of Windows 7 (one for everyday use, one for testing), you'll be unable to tell which is which because the menu text will be the same for each. To make the menu more informative, follow these steps:

1. Start your computer, and choose either entry from the boot menu. After startup is complete, make a note of which installation is running.

2. Click Start, type **cmd** in the Search box, and press Ctrl+Shift+Enter. Click Yes in the User Account Control box to open an elevated Command Prompt window.

3. Type the following command: **bcdedit /set description "*Menu description goes here*"** (substitute your own description for the placeholder text, and be sure to include the quotation marks). Press Enter.

4. Restart your computer, and note that the menu description you just entered now appears on the menu. Select the other menu option.

5. Repeat steps 2 and 3, again adding a menu description to replace the generic text and distinguish this installation from the other one.

A few startup options are still available from the Startup And Recovery dialog box (open the System option in Control Panel, click the Advanced System Settings link in the left pane, and click Settings under the Startup And Recovery heading). As shown next, you can choose which installation is the default operating system (this is where descriptive menu choices come in handy) and how long you want to display the list of operating systems. The default is 30 seconds; we typically set this value to no more than 10 seconds (you can choose any number from 1 through 999). To set the boot menu so that the default operating system starts automatically, clear the Time To Display check box or enter **0** (zero) for its value in seconds. These options write data directly to the Boot Configuration Data store.

Chapter 2

The syntax of the Bcdedit command is daunting, to say the least. It's also something you're unlikely to use often enough to memorize. Those facts are enough for us to strongly recommend using a graphical editor for the BCD store instead. A slick utility called DualBootPRO (*dualbootpro.org*) has been in our toolkit for years. It includes the capability to repair the Windows boot loader or uninstall it and return to booting from the Legacy OS Boot Loader (Ntldr.exe). DualBootPRO also works in Windows XP, so you can boot to either operating system and then adjust boot settings. A free alternative, which is equally powerful if slightly more difficult to use, is EasyBCD, from NeoSmart Technologies (*w7io.com/0211*). Both utilities offer the ability to customize multiboot installations and to repair a damaged boot loader or switch on the fly to the old-style Windows XP boot loader.

How do you remove Windows 7 (or Windows Vista) from a dual-boot installation and restore the Windows XP boot loader? Insert the Windows 7 DVD and type the following command at a command prompt, substituting the letter of your DVD drive for *d*:

```
d:\boot\bootsect.exe /nt52 all
```

You can now delete all system files from the volume containing the Windows installation you no longer plan to use. For even more effective removal, use the Disk Management console in Windows XP to reformat the drive and start fresh.

TROUBLESHOOTING

You installed Windows XP, and Windows 7 is no longer on the boot menu

Each time you install a version of Windows, it rewrites the MBR to call its own boot loader. If you install Windows 7 (or Windows Vista) as a second operating system on a PC where Windows XP is already installed, the Windows boot menu incorporates the options from the older boot menu. But if you install a fresh copy of Windows XP (or Windows Server 2003) on a system that is already running Windows 7, you'll over-write the MBR with one that doesn't recognize the Windows 7 boot loader. To repair the damage, open a Command Prompt window in the older operating system and run the following command from the Windows 7 DVD, substituting the letter of your DVD drive for *d* here:

```
d:\boot\ bootsect.exe /nt60 all
```

When you restart, you should see the Windows 7 menu. To restore the menu entry for your earlier version of Windows, open an elevated Command Prompt window and type this command:

```
bcdedit /create {ntldr} –d "Menu description goes here"
```

Substitute your own description for the placeholder text, being sure to include the quotation marks. The next time you start your computer, the menus should appear as you intended.

An even easier solution is to use one of the boot-editing utilities we highlight in this section. Both DualBootPRO and EasyBCD run on Windows XP, Windows Vista, Windows 7, and Windows Server 2003 or 2008, and they can be used to switch quickly from a Windows XP–style boot loader to its Windows 7 counterpart and back again.

Installing Windows 7 and Linux in a Multiboot Configuration

It's possible to install Windows 7 and Linux in a multiboot configuration that works much like the Windows multiboot setup described on the preceding pages. You can set it up to use the Windows 7 boot menu, or you can use a Linux boot loader (most commonly, GRUB) if you prefer. The procedure is a bit more complex than the proce-dure for installing another version of Windows, and it varies somewhat depending on which Linux distribution you use and which Linux tools (such as partition editors, boot loaders, and the like) you prefer. It's generally easier to set up such a system if the Win-dows partition is set up first, but it can be done either way: Windows and then Linux, or Linux and then Windows.

An Internet search for *dual boot linux Windows 7* turns up plenty of detailed instructions, and if you add the name of your Linux distribution to the search input you're likely to find the specific steps needed to make it work with Windows 7. As an example, check out the fully illustrated and meticulously detailed steps prepared by *APC* magazine (*w7io.com/0212*) that cover most combinations of Windows and Linux.

Upgrading from Another Windows 7 Edition

The basic procedure for upgrading from one edition of Windows 7 to another is unlike anything Microsoft has ever created before. The Anytime Upgrade feature was first introduced in Windows Vista, but the name is about all that the Windows 7 version of this feature has in common with its immediate predecessor.

So what's changed? If you purchase a new PC with Windows 7 Starter, Home Basic, Home Premium, or Professional installed, you'll find an unpretentious link beneath the name of your edition in the System applet in Control Panel: Get more features with a new edition of Windows 7.

Click that link, and it opens the Windows Anytime Upgrade dialog box, shown in Figure 2-5.

If you're ready to upgrade, choose the top option to buy the upgrade online from Microsoft. (This option might not be available in some geographic locations.) After selecting the edition you want to upgrade to, you're taken straight to a dialog box that allows you to initiate the upgrade process. You also receive a product key in the same format as the Windows product key that comes with a new retail version of Windows 7. (This upgrade key is for your use in the event that you need to reinstall Windows later.)

If you purchase an Anytime Upgrade package from a brick-and-mortar retailer, the upgrade key will be included with the package and you can click the bottom option to continue. After you enter the Anytime Upgrade product key, the remainder of the process is automatic.

What's most startling about the Anytime Upgrade process in Windows 7 is how quick and unobtrusive it is. The upgrade typically takes 10 minutes or less, in sharp contrast to the identically named feature in Windows Vista, which required a complete reinstallation of Windows and several hours.

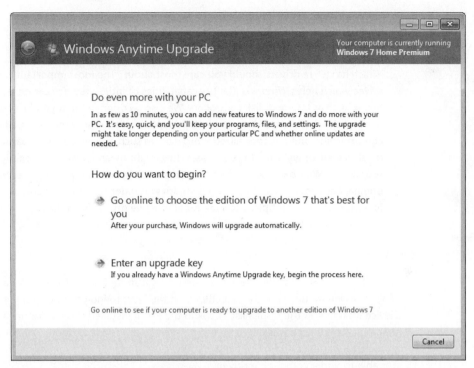

Figure 2-5 Upgrading from one edition of Windows 7 to another takes less than 10 minutes. You can buy an upgrade key online or from a local retailer.

It doesn't require you to insert the original installation media or download any code. It simply unlocks the features in the upgraded edition. The upgrade process restarts the computer on its own, once. You don't need to restart the computer at the end of the upgrade.

Installing and Updating Drivers

The Windows 7 installation DVD includes signed hardware drivers that support an enormous number of devices. Thousands of additional drivers are available from Windows Update, with hundreds of new devices added every month. (To give you an idea of the scale of the ongoing driver development effort, consider that Microsoft added roughly 1,600 new drivers per month in the first year after Windows Vista was released, and that pace has not slowed down.) Assuming that you're working with a relatively modern PC with no esoteric parts, the chances are good that virtually all of your hardware will work immediately after you finish Windows setup. (That's certain to be true if you purchase a new PC with Windows 7 already installed; in that case, the manufacturer is required to install drivers for all devices included with the system.)

INSIDE OUT   Pay special attention to these drivers

Which hardware drivers should you care most about? The most important is the chipset driver, which helps Windows identify capabilities of integrated devices on the mother-board, such as USB and disk controllers. We also recommend that you be sure you have the best driver available for your display adapter, network adapter, sound adapter, stor-age controller, and any specialized input devices such as a wireless keyboard, trackpad, touch screen, or webcam. In some cases, this might mean replacing a generic driver supplied by Windows 7 with one designed especially for your hardware, even if the original equipment manufacturer (OEM) driver is older than the Windows 7 alternative. In most cases, the best place to look for alternative drivers is on the support website for the manufacturer of your PC or the peripheral you're trying to use.

To verify that every installed device is working as it should, open Device Manager. (Begin typing **device manager** in the search box on the Start menu or in Control Panel, and click Device Manager in the results list.) Look in the list of installed devices for any warning icons that indicate a device was detected but no driver was installed. Figure 2-6, for example, shows a Multimedia Audio Controller (in this case, a sound card) for which Windows 7 was not able to find a compatible driver.

If you have any USB or IEEE 1394 (FireWire) devices—such as printers, external hard drives, cameras, or scanners—connect them now and confirm that they work correctly. If you downloaded any updated drivers before setting up Windows 7, this is the time to install them. In many cases, a visit to Windows Update will locate the correct driver for a device.

For a complete discussion of Device Manager and drivers, see Chapter 29, "Setting Up and Configuring Hardware."

Figure 2-6 The yellow exclamation point alongside the item under the Other Devices category indicates that it is missing a compatible device driver.

Activating and Validating Windows 7

Windows 7 includes a set of antipiracy and antitampering features that Microsoft refers to collectively as *Windows Activation Technologies* (in previous Windows versions, these were included under the Windows Genuine Advantage branding). The various checks and challenges in Windows 7 are, in essence, enforcement mechanisms for the Windows 7 license agreement, which is displayed during the process of installing the operating system (you must provide your consent to complete setup). We're not lawyers, so we won't attempt to interpret this license agreement. We do recommend that you read the license agreement, which is fairly straightforward and is written clearly enough that even a nonlawyer can understand it. In this section, we explain how the activation and validation mechanisms in Windows 7 affect your use of the operating system.

Entering a Product Key

When you perform a clean installation or upgrade an existing Windows installation by using a retail copy of Windows 7, you might be prompted to enter a 25-character alphanumeric product key that uniquely identifies your licensed copy of Windows.

Here are some key facts you should know about this procedure:

- **The product key is entered automatically on any copy of Windows that is pre-installed on a new PC by a large computer maker.**   If you use the Windows 7 media supplied by the PC manufacturer to reinstall this copy of Windows, you won't be required to enter a product key.

- **Your product key matches your edition of Windows.**   If you purchase a full or upgrade version of Windows 7 from a retail outlet, the installation media (typically a DVD) contains a configuration file that automatically installs the edition you purchased. The product key works only with that edition.

- **You are not required to enter a product key when installing Windows 7.**   If you leave the Product Key box blank and click Next, the setup program continues. You will be prompted to enter a valid product key later, when you activate Windows.

If you choose to install Windows 7 without entering a product key, you might be asked to select the edition you want to install (a file named Ei.cfg, in the Sources folder on the installation disc, can restrict these options to a specific edition; if that file exists, you will not see this list of options). You can then use the installed copy of Windows 7 without restriction for 30 days. Before the end of that 30-day grace period, you must enter a valid product key and activate your copy, as described in the next section. If you fail to complete these steps, Windows displays notifications at startup that urge you to activate your installation; additional reminders appear on the desktop and in the notification area. To make the notifications more visible, Windows replaces your personalized desktop background with a stark black background.

INSIDE OUT   Extend your activation grace period by 30 days

The 30-day period before activation is required is called the *grace period*. If, at the end of that 30 days, you are not ready to activate, you can extend the grace period by an additional 30 days and continue your evaluation. Open a Command Prompt window by using the Run As Administrator option and type the following command: **slmgr /rearm**. When the command completes, restart your computer. (You can verify that it worked by opening an elevated Command Prompt window and typing **slmgr /dli**.) You can run this command a total of three times, giving you up to 120 days of use before activation is required.

Activating a Retail Copy of Windows

Just as with Windows XP and Windows Vista, you must *activate* your installation of a retail copy of Windows 7 within 30 days, either by connecting to a Microsoft activation server over the Internet or by making a toll-free call to an interactive telephone activation system.

The activation mechanism is designed to enforce license restrictions by preventing the most common form of software piracy: casual copying. Typically, a Windows 7 license entitles you to install the operating system software on a single computer. If you use the same product key to install Windows 7 on a second (or third or fourth) system, you might be unable to activate the software automatically. One important exception to this rule is the Windows 7 Family Pack, which allows Windows 7 Home Premium edition to be installed and activated on up to three PCs in the same home.

In the Set Up Windows dialog box where you enter your product key, the Automatically Activate Windows When I'm Online check box is selected by default. If you leave this option selected, Windows will contact the activation servers three days after installation and complete the activation process for you. At any time, you can confirm your system's activation status by looking at the Windows Activation section at the bottom of the System dialog box. (Click Start, right-click Computer, and click Properties.) This dialog box displays the number of days left in the grace period and includes links where you can manually activate or change your product key.

If the 30-day grace period expires and you have not successfully activated your installation, you'll see the dialog box shown in Figure 2-7. Click Activate Windows Online Now to begin the Internet activation process. If you left the Product Key box blank when installing Windows 7, you'll be prompted to enter a valid product key before you can complete activation.

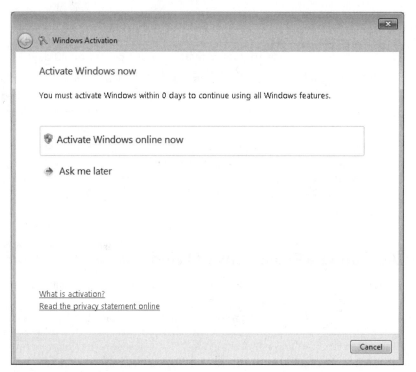

Figure 2-7 If you fail to activate Windows 7 within 30 days after installation, you're greeted with this dialog box when you log on.

Under most circumstances, activation over the Internet takes no more than a few seconds. If you need to use the telephone, the process takes longer because you have to enter a 50-digit identification key (either by using the phone's dial pad or by speaking to a customer service representative) and then input the 42-digit confirmation ID supplied in response.

INSIDE OUT   Don't rush to activate your installation

When you install a retail copy of Windows 7, the default settings delay automatic activation for three days. We recommend that you clear the Automatically Activate Windows When I'm Online check box when entering your product key. This option gives you a full 30 days to verify that Windows 7 works properly on your hardware and that you won't be required to replace any hardware or the entire computer. After you're confident that Windows 7 is completely compatible with your hardware, you can open the System dialog box and choose the manual activation option.

What if you skip past this setting during setup and forget to change it? Disabling automatic activation requires a registry edit. (As always, the standard disclaimers apply: Don't try this unless you understand the consequences, including the risk that editing the registry incorrectly can damage your system configuration.) Open Registry Editor and select the key HKLM\Software\Microsoft\Windows NT\CurrentVersion\SoftwareProtectionPlatform\Activation. In the right pane, double-click the Manual value and change it from 0 to 1.

The activation process is completely anonymous and does not require that you divulge any personal information. If you choose to register your copy of Windows 7, this is a completely separate (and optional) task.

You're allowed to reinstall Windows 7 an unlimited number of times on the same hardware. During the activation process, Windows transmits a hashed file that serves as a "fingerprint" of key components in your system. When you attempt to activate Windows using the same product key you used previously, the activation server calculates a new fingerprint and compares the value against the one stored in its database. If you're reinstalling Windows 7 on the original hardware, the fingerprints will match and activation will be automatic.

Just as with earlier Windows versions, the activation process is designed to prevent attempts to tamper with the activation files or to "clone" an activated copy of Windows and install it on another computer. What happens if you upgrade the hardware in your computer? When you activate your copy of Windows 7, a copy of the hardware fingerprint is stored on your hard disk and checked each time you start your computer. If you make substantial changes to your system hardware, you might be required to reactivate your copy of Windows. Because the activation mechanism assumes (mistakenly) that you've tried to install your copy of Windows on a second computer, Internet activation might not work. In this case, you're required to manually enter a new activation code, which can be obtained from the telephone activation–based support center. For Windows XP, Microsoft published a detailed description of the algorithm it used to determine whether hardware changes were significant enough to require reactivation. For Windows Vista and Windows 7, Micro-soft has chosen not to publish those details but has stated that if you replace a defective motherboard, you'll be required to reactivate your copy of Windows. (If you upgrade your PC with a new motherboard, that is considered a new PC and might require a new license.)

INSIDE OUT   Recover your product key

When you install a retail copy of Windows, the product key gets filed away, usually never to be seen again. But you might need to retrieve the product key at some point. If you have Windows 7 installed on multiple computers in your home or office, for example, you might lose track of which product key goes with which computer, result-ing in confusion and hassle if you need to reinstall Windows, or if you retire a computer and want to transfer its full (not OEM) Windows license to a new computer. To find out which product key is in use on a given computer, we recommend a utility called Recover Keys (*w7io.com/20201*). This application displays the product keys that were used to install any version of Windows or Microsoft Office on a computer. (Unfortu-nately, its popular, free predecessor, Magical Jelly Bean Keyfinder, finds product keys only for older versions of Windows and Office.)

Activation Requirements for OEM Installations

If you purchase a new computer with Windows 7 already installed on it, the licensing pro-cedures are different, as are the rules for activation. In the arcane parlance of Windows, system makers are known as *original equipment manufacturers*, or OEMs. To make matters more confusing, not all OEMs are created equal; instead, they're divided into two classes:

- Large system builders (Microsoft refers to these firms as *named* or *multinational* OEMs or, informally, as *royalty OEMs*) are allowed to install and preactivate Windows using a technology called System Locked Preinstallation (SLP). The preinstalled copy of Windows (including the recovery disc) contains configuration files that look for specific information in the system BIOS. As long as the BIOS matches, no activation is required. When you purchase a new computer from one of these large companies, a sticker containing a unique product key is affixed to the PC's case, but that key isn't used to activate Windows initially. Instead, the OEM uses a single master key to activate large numbers of computers. If you need to reinstall Windows, you can use the recovery disc provided by the manufacturer, and you won't be asked for a product key at all, nor is activation required—as long as you start your computer using the SLP disc on the same computer (or one with the same motherboard/BIOS combination).

- Smaller firms that build PCs can also preinstall Windows. These OEM copies are called *System Builder copies*, and they do require activation. The rules of the System Builder program require the PC manufacturer to use specific tools to preinstall Windows so that you accept a license agreement and activate the software when you first turn on the PC. In addition, the manufacturer is required to supply the purchaser with the Windows 7 media (typically a DVD) and affix a product key sticker to the PC's case. If you need to reinstall Windows on this computer, you must enter the product key and go through activation again.

The license agreement for a retail copy of Windows 7 allows you to transfer it to another computer, provided that you completely remove it from the computer on which it was previously installed. An OEM copy, by contrast, is tied to the computer on which it was originally installed. You can reinstall an OEM copy of Windows an unlimited number of times on the same computer. However, you are prohibited by the license agreement from transferring that copy of Windows to another computer.

Product Activation and Corporate Licensing

Businesses that purchase licenses in bulk through a Microsoft Volume Licensing (VL) program receive VL media and product keys that require activation under a different set of rules than those that apply to retail or OEM copies. Under the terms of a volume license agreement, each computer with a copy of Windows 7 must have a valid license and must be activated. Under new activation procedures that apply to Windows 7 and Windows Vista, businesses can purchase product keys that allow multiple activations, or they can use Key Management servers to activate computers within their organization.

For more details on Volume Licensing programs see Chapter 26, "Deployment and Migration."

Dealing with Product Validation

After you successfully activate your copy of Windows 7, you're still subject to periodic anti-piracy checks from Microsoft. This process, called *validation*, verifies that your copy of Windows has not been tampered with to bypass activation. It also allows Microsoft to undo the activation process for a computer when it determines after the fact that the product key was stolen or used in violation of a volume licensing agreement.

Validation takes two forms: an internal tool that regularly checks licensing and activation files to determine that they haven't been tampered with, and an online tool that restricts access to some downloads and updates.

If your system fails validation, your computer continues to work, but you'll see some differences: the desktop background changes to black (and if you change it to something else, Windows changes it back to black after one hour), an "activate now" reminder that also tells you your copy of Windows is "Not Genuine" appears on the desktop, and an Activate

Now dialog box appears periodically. In addition, your access to Windows Update is somewhat restricted; you won't be able to download optional updates, new drivers, or certain other programs from the Microsoft Download Center until your system passes the validation check.

> **Note**
>
> An unactivated copy of Windows (or one that has failed validation) can still be used. All Windows functions work normally, all your data files are accessible, and all your programs work as expected. The nagging reminders are intended to strongly encourage you to resolve the underlying issue. Some forms of malware can result in damage to system files that has the same effect as tampering with activation files. Another common cause of activation problems is a lazy or dishonest repair technician who installs a stolen or "cracked" copy of Windows 7 instead of using your original licensed copy. Links in the Windows Activation messages lead to online support tools, where you might be able to identify and repair the issue that's affecting your system. Microsoft offers free support for activation issues via online forums as well, with separate forums for enterprise customers (*w7io.com/0214*) and individuals (*w7io.com/0215*). Telephone support is also available at no charge.

Transferring Files and Settings from Another Computer

If you upgrade your computer from Windows Vista to Windows 7, all of your data and most of your programs should survive the journey intact. But what do you do with your data and settings if you purchase a new computer, or if you decide to do a clean installation on your existing system, or if your old computer was running Windows XP and can't be directly upgraded? With Windows 7, you can use a utility called Windows Easy Transfer to handle much of the grunt work.

This utility is a significant upgrade to the version that appeared in Windows Vista (which in turn was a greatly improved replacement for Windows XP's Files And Settings Transfer wizard). With its help, you can migrate settings and files from your old Windows installation (Windows XP, Windows Vista, or Windows 7) to the new one.

Although the utility has its limitations, it's highly flexible and offers an impressive number of customization options. New in Windows 7 is a post-migration report that shows you which files and settings were transferred and then lists all programs that the utility was able to detect on the old installation; you can use this report as a checklist to reinstall programs on the new computer.

INSIDE OUT   Use Windows Easy Transfer with a single PC

When you use Windows Easy Transfer, the "old PC" and "new PC" don't have to be different physical machines. This utility will get the job done if you want to completely replace your existing Windows installation with a clean install of Windows 7. Use Windows Easy Transfer to save settings and files from your current Windows installation (your "old PC") to an external hard disk or network location. After you complete the clean install of Windows 7 on the same hardware, restore the saved files and settings to your "new PC."

Note

You can transfer files and settings from a 32-bit version of Windows to a 64-bit version, but the transfer won't work in reverse. You can't use this utility to copy files or settings from a 64-bit Windows version to a 32-bit version.

Windows Easy Transfer is simple and straightforward in operation, but describing it is another story. It would take a whiteboard the size of a Jumbotron scoreboard to map out all the possible paths you can follow when using this utility. So rather than describe every step, we'll list the broad outlines and count on you to find your way through the process.

Note

Windows Easy Transfer works with files and settings, but it does not transfer the programs themselves. If you want to transfer programs as well as files from your old PC to a new one, you need to use third-party software, such as LapLink's PCmover (*w7io.com/0216*).

Making a Connection

To accomplish the transfer, you need to establish a data connection between the old and new computers. When you run the Windows Easy Transfer utility and click past the introductory screen, you're greeted with the list of options shown in Figure 2-8.

Chapter 2

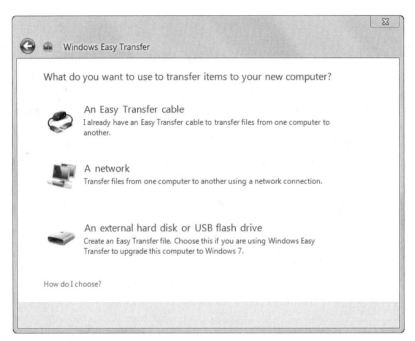

Figure 2-8 The first two Windows Easy Transfer options require a physical connection between two PCs. The third option is intended for upgraders.

Your three transfer options are as follows:

- **Easy Transfer cable**   This custom cable, available for purchase from many vendors (just search the web for "Easy Transfer cable"), allows high-speed transfers over a direct connection between USB 2.0 ports on both computers. You cannot use a standard USB cable for this task. If you connect the cable before running Windows Easy Transfer, the program assumes you plan to use it as the transfer mechanism and skips the other options.

- **Network**   You can connect two computers over a local area network and transfer settings directly from the old computer to the new one. A Fast Ethernet (100 Mbit/sec) or gigabit Ethernet connection is by far your best choice, especially if you want to transfer a large number of data files.

- **Removable media, including USB flash drives and external hard disks**   If a direct connection isn't practical or possible (if you're planning to wipe out an existing partition so that you can do a clean installation on the same computer, for example), you can save the Windows Easy Transfer output to a file and then restore it after you finish setup. You must have enough free space on the external storage device to accommodate all files to be transferred. The Windows Easy Transfer utility calculates the amount of data it expects to transfer and warns you if the destination you select has insufficient space.

INSIDE OUT   Use a shared network location for Windows Easy Transfer storage

Although you wouldn't know it from the Windows Easy Transfer interface, you can store files and settings from one computer on a shared network folder and retrieve them later. The trick? Don't choose the second option, A Network, which works in real time with two physical PCs connected over a wired or wireless network. Instead, choose the third option, An External Hard Disk Or USB Flash Drive. After specifying that this is your old computer, go through the process of calculating which files will be transferred, and then click Save. In the Save Your Easy Transfer File dialog box, select a shared network folder and enter a file name. When you're ready to restore the files and settings, connect to the same location over the network and begin the transfer.

If you're replacing your old computer with a new one running Windows 7, your best bet is to connect the two computers over a local area network (or using an Easy Transfer cable) and then run Windows Easy Transfer. This technique is not only the fastest way to get your new computer up and running, it's also the best way to avoid losing data. Because your existing data files remain intact on the old computer, you can recover easily if the process inadvertently leaves behind a crucial data file. If neither of these options is available, you can use an external hard drive to physically store the data and settings to be transferred.

If you have any other programs running, stop them now; then start the Windows Easy Transfer utility on both computers.

- On the old computer, you can use the Windows 7 DVD (browse to the \Support\ Migwiz folder on the DVD and double-click Migsetup.exe). If the installation disc isn't available, or you want to make sure you have the most recent version of the utility, run Windows Easy Transfer on the new computer first and follow the prompts to copy the program files to an external hard disk, a USB flash drive, or a shared network folder; then connect your old PC to the device or network location and run the Windows Easy Transfer shortcut there. If the old computer is running Windows 7, this step isn't necessary; you can run Windows Easy Transfer from the Start menu.

- On the new computer, click the Start button and then choose All Programs, Accessories, System Tools, Windows Easy Transfer. (You can also type **Windows Easy Transfer** in the search box on the Start menu or type **migwiz** at any command prompt, including the Start menu search box.) Click Next on the Welcome To Windows Easy Transfer page.

Chapter 2

If you're using an Easy Transfer cable, start by plugging the cable into the old PC, which will need to install a driver for the device. When the driver is successfully installed, follow the prompts to begin the transfer. After you specify that this is the old PC, you'll be prompted to plug in the cable on your new PC, where Windows Easy Transfer should make the connection automatically and begin cataloging files and settings that need to be transferred.

If you're transferring over a network, start with the old PC, and then run Windows Easy Transfer on the new PC. The connection should be made automatically. You'll need to enter a numeric key on the new PC (automatically generated on the old PC) to initiate the connection.

Choosing What to Transfer

When you reach the Choose What To Transfer From This Computer page, Windows Easy Transfer automatically catalogs all files and settings that are available for transfer, calculates their size, and displays the results in a dialog box like the one shown here:

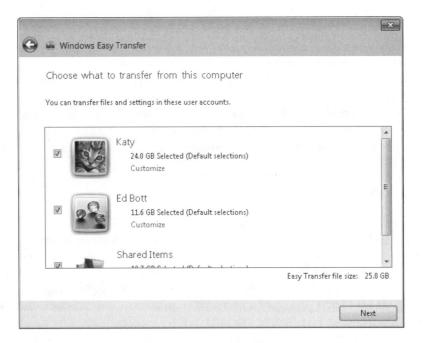

Each user account on the old PC gets its own top-level entry in this list, followed by a Shared Items entry that grabs files from the folder hierarchy for the Public user profile and settings for programs that are installed for all users.

The default settings for individual user profiles migrate files from your user profile, including documents, music, pictures, and videos, as well as per-user program settings and

Windows settings like your desktop background and screen saver. The utility also migrates Internet Explorer Favorites and preferences; folder and taskbar options; and account settings, messages, and address books from supported e-mail programs, including Microsoft Outlook Express, Windows Mail, and Outlook, among other programs.

If you want to replicate the setup of your old PC on your new one, click Next, and then find something else to do while the transfer takes place. (Transferring 100+ GB of data over a network can take hours.) If you simply want to transfer your personal files and settings to the new PC, clear the check boxes next to the Shared Items entry and any other accounts; then click Next.

For more granular control over exactly what gets transferred, click the Customize link beneath your user account entry or the Shared Items entry. That displays a list of folders and program settings like the one shown in Figure 2-9.

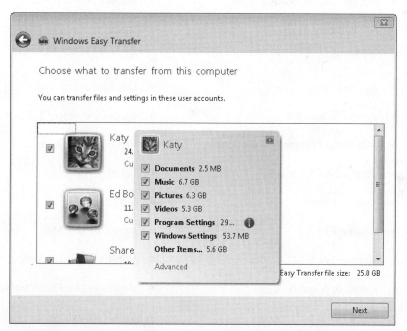

Figure 2-9 Clear any check box to skip the selected item type. Click Advanced to specify individual folders and drives that you want to include or exclude.

If you have an enormous collection of music and videos, you might prefer to copy those files to an external hard disk and import them later. In that case, clear the Music or Videos check box for your user profile (Public Music and Public Videos in the Shared Items category).

Allow the mouse pointer to hover over the blue Information icon to see a list of which programs will have their settings migrated.

Windows Easy Transfer does not migrate program files; instead, it copies the settings and preference files to the correct location on the new computer and uses those preferences when you install the program on the new computer. Registry settings and preference files for a long list of programs are copied automatically. (Click Customize and allow the mouse pointer to hover over the blue Information icon to see a list of which programs will have their settings migrated for the selected account.) Naturally, this list is heavy on Microsoft programs, but it also includes a lengthy list of third-party products. Here's the complete list of programs covered as of the initial release of Windows 7:

- Ad-Aware 6 Professional
- Adobe Creative Suite 2
- Adobe ImageReady CS
- Adobe Photoshop CS
- Adobe Photoshop 9
- Adobe Reader 9.0
- AOL Instant Messenger 5 and 6
- Corel Paintshop Pro 9
- Google Chrome
- Google Picasa 3
- Google Talk 1
- iTunes 6, 7, and 8
- Lotus Notes 6, 7, and 8
- Lotus SmartSuite
- Microsoft Money Plus Home & Business 2008
- Microsoft Office 2003 and 2007

- Microsoft Works 9.0
- Mozilla Firefox 3
- Opera 9
- Peachtree 2009
- Quicken Deluxe 2009
- QuickTime Player 5, 6, and 7
- RealPlayer Basic 11
- Safari 4
- Skype 3
- Windows Live Mail
- Windows Live Messenger
- Windows Live Photo Gallery
- Windows Live Writer
- WinZip (8, 9, or 10)
- WordPerfect Office 11, 12, and X3
- Yahoo! Messenger
- Zune Software 3

Restoring Files and Settings on Your New Computer

If you use a network or cable connection to transfer files between two computers with Windows Easy Transfer, you control both ends of the process. After you enter the correct security keys on each end, establish a connection, and specify which files and settings you want to copy to your new PC, click Transfer. When the operation is complete, you'll see a detailed status report on the new computer indicating which files and settings were transferred.

If you've saved the files and settings to a USB flash drive, an external hard disk, or a shared network drive, run Windows Easy Transfer on the new computer, specify that you're using an external hard disk or USB flash drive, and click This Is My New Computer. Choose the location, type a password (if you set one when saving the data), and click Next.

If the user names on the old and new computers are different, you have a choice to make. If you simply click Transfer, Windows will create a new account for each account that you saved that doesn't have a match on the new computer. If you want the settings from the old computer to go to a specific account on the new computer, click Advanced Options (at the bottom of the Choose What To Transfer From This Computer page). That opens a dialog box like the one shown here. You can choose to match existing accounts or click Create User and type in a new name to create an account on the fly.

If you copied files from a secondary drive on the old computer and want those files to go on a drive with a different letter on the new PC, click the Map Drives tab and match the old and new drive letters. After completing both match-ups, click Save, and then click Transfer to complete the operation.

After the Windows Easy Transfer utility completes its restoration, it automatically displays a report of what it did. (You can call up this report later by clicking the Windows Easy Transfer Reports shortcut, which is also in All Programs, Accessories, System Tools.) Check for any errors, and correct them if necessary.

Unfortunately, as we noted earlier, Windows Easy Transfer doesn't migrate installed programs. Instead, when the process is complete, the Easy Transfer Report displays a list of programs that were installed on your old computer that you might need to install on the new one. The example shown here displays a selection of third-party programs.

If you chose to install some programs before running this step, you'll notice that some programs in the list are marked with a green check mark as Already Installed. The links under each entry in the list take you to the program developer's website, which typically includes the download link. You can leave this report window open, and it will update each entry in the list automatically as you complete it.

Tweaking and Tuning Your Windows Installation

Technically, Windows 7 setup is complete when you reach the desktop and log on for the first time. In the real world, there's still a short checklist of system settings you'll want (or need) to go through soon. Most of the items in the following list are one-time tasks that you'll set and forget. The list doesn't include performance tweaks or maintenance tasks that you perform occasionally, nor does it include personalization settings you might want to change over time. What all of these settings have in common is that they are per-machine settings, not per-user settings.

To learn how to adjust personal settings for your user account, see Chapter 4, "Personalizing Windows 7."

Adjust Basic Display Settings

Your screen resolution determines how many pixels are available for Windows to use when displaying on-screen objects. Objects on the screen appear larger at lower resolutions and smaller when you switch to a higher resolution. If setup correctly detected the capabilities of your monitor and display adapter, your display should be set to the monitor's native resolution. To adjust the resolution, right-click any empty space on the desktop and click Screen Resolution on the shortcut menu (or open Control Panel and click Adjust Screen Resolution under Appearance And Personalization). The Screen Resolution dialog box that opens shows the full range of supported resolutions for your video adapter and display (as determined by Plug and Play). In Figure 2-10, for example, you can move the Resolution slider to any of eight settings, ranging from 800 by 600 at the low end of the scale to 1680 by 1050 at the high end.

On analog monitors, you can adjust the display to any resolution and get acceptable results. On flat-panel LCD displays, you'll get best results by setting this value to match the display's native resolution, which corresponds to the number of pixels on the display. If your video memory is extremely limited, you might need to choose a lower color depth to enable higher resolutions.

If you've connected multiple monitors, you can adjust display settings independently for each one. Click a monitor icon to select settings for that display.

For instructions on how to adjust other display-related settings, including the DPI Scaling option that improves readability at high resolutions, see "Making Text Easier to Read" on page 157.

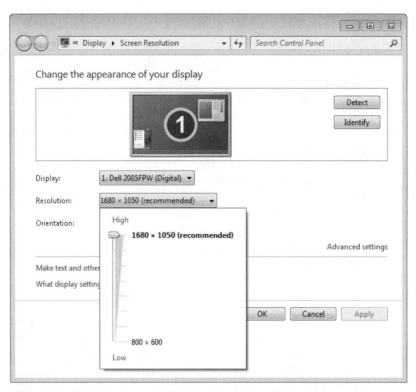

Figure 2-10 The (recommended) label appears alongside the setting for the native resolution of the current display.

Update the Windows Experience Index

The Windows Experience Index (WEI) measures the performance of key subsystems of your PC, including the display adapter, memory, CPU, and hard disk. In Windows Vista, the individual benchmark tests that make up the WEI ran automatically at the end of setup, adding several minutes to the total installation time; in Windows 7, setup defers this task until you choose to run it manually. To fill in these scores and determine whether each subsystem is performing as expected, open System Properties. In the place where the rating would normally appear, you should see a link reading "System rating is not available." Click that link to kick off the Windows System Assessment program and fill in the missing scores.

For a more detailed discussion of what the Windows Experience Index measures and how to interpret its findings, see "Using the Windows Experience Index" on page 835.

Check Your System's Security

A default installation of Windows 7 includes basic security safeguards that protect your PC from a variety of threats—with one important exception. Windows 7 does not include anti-virus software. If you purchased a new PC with Windows 7 already installed, the PC maker might have included a full or trial version of a third-party antivirus program. You can use this software or replace it with Microsoft Security Essentials or another package you prefer. To confirm whether you have antivirus software, open Action Center (it's at the top of the System And Security category in Control Panel) and look under the Security heading. The warning message shown in Figure 2-11 indicates that your system requires additional soft-ware for full protection.

If you choose to use a different program in place of any of the Windows default security features, you should check here after installing the other program to ensure that it's cor-rectly reporting its coverage to Windows.

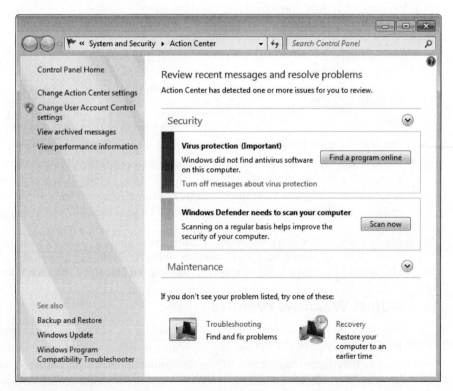

Figure 2-11 If you choose to use a third-party security program, make sure it reports its status accurately to Security Center.

For details on how to use Action Center, including instructions for disabling its notifications, see "Introducing Action Center" on page 872. For details and how to view and adjust security settings, see "Monitoring Your Computer's Security" on page 600.

Test Network and Internet Connections

Network And Sharing Center, available under the Network And Internet category in Control Panel, provides one-stop access to all networking settings. With most hardware, Windows 7 doesn't require any special setup to enable access to the Internet and to other computers on your network. To verify that your network is functioning properly, check the graphical display at the top of Network And Sharing Center. It should resemble the one shown here. If you see a red X between your Network icon and the Internet icon, click it to start the Network Troubleshooter.

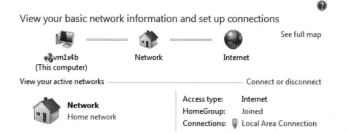

This is also a good time to perform some functional tests. Can you access favorite web pages in your preferred browser? Can you open, save, and change files in shared network folders? The options elsewhere in Network And Sharing Center allow you to create, join, or leave a homegroup; tweak adapter settings; fine-tune advanced file sharing; and perform other advanced tasks that might be appropriate for your network configuration.

For details about making network connections and working in Network And Sharing Center, see Chapter 19, "Setting Up a Small Office or Home Network." For information about sharing files across your network, see Chapter 20, "Sharing and Managing Network Resources."

Adjust Windows Features

The basic feature set of Windows 7 is determined by the edition you install, and a standard installation makes all the features in your edition available without asking you (or allowing you, for that matter) to pick and choose. In addition to these core features, a small set of advanced and specialized features is available as well. To review the full list and enable or disable any of the features on it, open Programs in Control Panel and click Turn Windows Features On Or Off (under Programs And Features).

What Happened to Windows Mail?

Unlike its predecessors, Windows 7 includes no default e-mail program, no instant-messaging program, no movie-editing software, and only rudimentary DVD-writing and photo-viewing applications. If you upgrade from a previous edition, your settings for Windows Mail, Windows Photo Gallery, and other programs that have been left out of Windows 7 will be preserved, but the programs themselves will be missing. You'll need to download and install the most recent versions of those programs separately from Windows Live (*download.live.com*). For details of what is included in the Windows Live family, see Chapter 8, "Adding Windows Live Programs and Services."

The Windows Features dialog box, shown in Figure 2-12, indicates which features are available for your edition. A check mark means the feature is currently enabled, and a blank box means the feature is disabled. If you see a filled box, the feature is partially enabled; click the plus sign to the left of the entry to see more details about it.

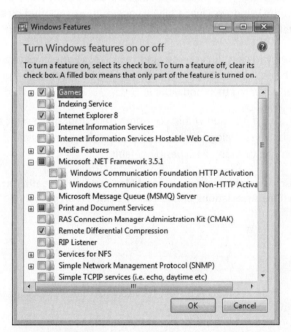

Figure 2-12 Some of the features in this list are familiar, but most involve esoteric networking options. Click any item in the list to see descriptive help text for that option.

Chapter 2

You might be surprised to see that Windows 7 offers the ability to remove some features that were untouchable in previous editions: Internet Explorer 8, for example, along with Windows Media Center and Windows Media Player. Removing one or more of those options (as well as the default selection of games) might be appropriate on a PC intended for use in a business environment where you want to lock down access to potential distractions.

The Windows Features list might change over time as you add Windows features to your system. For example, if you install Windows Virtual PC, it is added to the list, allowing you to subsequently disable that feature if you need to.

Choose Default Programs

One of the great strengths of the Windows platform is the staggering number of programs from which you can choose. Many of those options are designed to handle the same functions as programs included with Windows 7. For example, you might prefer Mozilla Firefox to Internet Explorer for daily web browsing, and fanatic iPod or iPhone owners will almost certainly prefer iTunes to Windows Media Player. If you prefer a third-party program (including programs in the Windows Live family) to one of those included by default with Windows 7, use the Default Programs dialog box to make your preference official.

To open Default Programs, click its link on the Start menu. As Figure 2-13 shows, you can adjust settings for each program that appears in this dialog box, setting the program to use all available defaults or adjusting them individually.

Even if you've already used a function within your preferred program to set it as the default, it's worth a visit to this dialog box to see if another program has managed to hang on to the right to open one or more file types by default.

For a more detailed discussion of how programs and file types work together, see "Setting Default Programs, File-Type Associations, and AutoPlay Options" on page 195.

Figure 2-13 Use the top option to make this program the default for all file types it can handle; the bottom option allows you to adjust defaults individually.

Personalize Power and Sleep Settings

If you install a retail version of Windows 7, the operating system sets default power-saving and sleep options based on the type of hardware you're using. On a PC that you purchase with Windows 7 already installed, the PC maker might set its own power and sleep defaults. In either case, you should check the current settings to ensure that they match your personal preferences. If necessary, you can adjust individual power settings or create a new power scheme. You'll find Power Options in Control Panel, under the Hardware And Sound category.

For more details about the ins and outs of power management, see "Setting Power and Sleep Options" on page 162.

Fine-Tune System Protection Options

The System Protection feature is one that you probably won't appreciate until you have to use it, at which point you'll be very, very grateful to the anonymous programmer who dreamed it up. System Protection takes periodic snapshots of system files and configuration details, allowing you to run the System Restore utility to undo changes and roll back a system configuration to a time when it was known to work correctly. In Windows 7, those volume snapshots also include real-time backups of individual data files, allowing you to recover from unwanted edits or unexpected deletions by restoring a previous version of a deleted or changed file.

Those backed-up files and settings come at a cost in disk space, however. On a system where available storage is in short supply, you might want to reduce the amount of disk space set aside for System Protection. To configure System Protection settings, on the Start menu, right-click Computer and choose Properties; then click System Protection, select a drive, and click Configure. Figure 2-14 shows the settings dialog box for a system volume approximately 140 GB in size. You can move the Max Usage slider to adjust disk space usage or use the options at the top to disable all or part of the System Protection feature on this drive.

For more details on how to choose the right settings for System Protection, see "Configuring System Protection Options" on page 461.

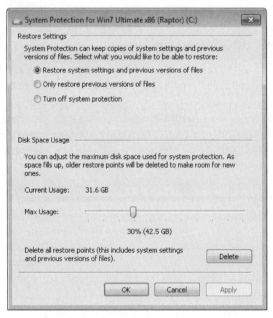

Figure 2-14 Use these settings to restrict the amount of space that Windows 7 uses for System Restore snapshots and previous versions of files.

Create Additional User Accounts

If you anticipate that your computer will be used by more than one person, set up an account for each additional user now. Creating standard accounts for users ensures that they won't be able to install malware or incompatible software in system folders and will be unable to install unsigned device drivers that can cause system instability. They'll also be blocked from deleting essential system files.

For details on how to create and manage user accounts in Windows 7, see "Working with User Accounts" on page 651.

Set Up a Regular Backup Schedule

When you've finished with setup and tweaked basic system settings to match your preferences, it's a perfect time to set up a regular backup schedule. The first step, of course, should be to back up your newly installed and properly tweaked and tuned system by creating a system image. This option is available as part of the built-in system-image feature, which is part of the program in all retail editions of Windows 7. (If you prefer, you can choose from a multitude of third-party products that offer similar backup features.) After the image is complete, be sure to create a system repair disk so that you can restore the backed-up image easily in the event of a disk failure or other problem.

For a full discussion of the many backup options available in Windows 7, see "Using the Windows Backup Program" on page 436.

Obtaining Help and Support

A s the Windows operating system becomes more complex—even while it's suppos-edly growing more intuitive with each successive version—some parts will remain unclear to some users, creating a need for help and support systems.

Creating a help system that meets the needs of all users has been the subject of much research, and the help system in Windows has evolved as dramatically as Windows itself. Most experienced Windows users quickly learned to skip right past the help files in Windows 95 and 98, which were aimed at novices and were hampered by a help engine that was extremely awkward to navigate. The reservoir of help content in Windows Me (Millennium Edition) and Windows 2000 was much deeper, and the HTML-based interfaces were slicker and easier to use than their predecessors. However, in both of those Windows versions, the online help file was still essentially a user manual that had been carved into small pieces, and it grew increasingly outdated with each Windows update. Windows XP added a Help And Support center, which served as an entry point to a tremendous collection of resources for Windows users at every level of experience. Windows Vista and Windows 7 have expanded that resource trove with narrated video demonstrations to explain key concepts, updated help topics (available whenever your computer is connected to the Internet), and handy links to other online help resources.

This chapter offers a brief survey of the Windows Help And Support application (the help application is simple and straightforward enough that little explanation is required), followed by a somewhat more detailed treatment of Windows Remote Assistance, a program that lets you connect your computer to that of another user so that you can offer assistance to or seek help from that other user. We'll conclude with a survey of technical resources aimed at IT professionals.

Note that if you're coming to Windows 7 from Windows XP and have used Remote Assistance there, you'll find significant improvements in Windows 7. Windows Remote Assistance now offers substantially better performance and security enhancements. But the biggest change is its far superior network connectivity, which makes it easier to connect to another person's computer even when both computers are behind routers that use Network Address Translation (NAT).

What's in Your Edition?

All features described in this chapter are available in all editions of Windows 7.

Using Windows Help And Support

Figure 3-1 shows the home page of Windows Help And Support. You can get there by choosing Help And Support on the right side of the Start menu, or, more simply, by holding down the Windows key and pressing F1. (If you have configured your Start menu *not* to include the Help And Support item and you forget the Windows key+F1 shortcut, open the Start menu, and type **help** in the search box. Help And Support will appear either at or near the top of the search results.)

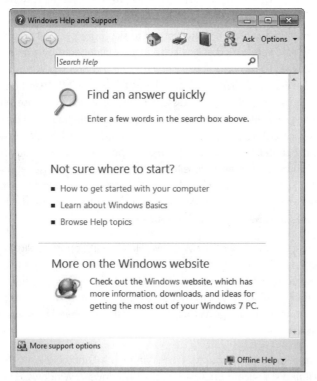

Figure 3-1 The Help And Support home page has austere navigation and search tools, along with links to a variety of resources. Many computer manufacturers add their own links and content to this page.

The toolbar at the top of each help window includes only a few buttons, as shown in Table 3-1.

Table 3-1 Help Toolbar Buttons

	The browser-style Forward and Back buttons enable you to retrace your steps through the help system.
	The Help And Support Home button returns you to the home page.
	The Print button prints the currently displayed topic.
	The Browse Help button displays your current location within the table of contents, from which you can navigate up or down the hierarchy to a topic of interest.
Ask	The Ask button leads to a page with links to other help resources, including places where you can ask for help (such as Windows communities or newsgroups) and places where you can look for more help on your own (such as the Windows website). The More Support Options link that appears at the bottom of each help window leads to this same topic.
Options ▾	The Options button opens a short menu of commands, two of which duplicate the function of toolbar buttons. Other commands let you adjust the size of text displayed in the help window and find a word or phrase within the currently displayed page.

Ensuring Access to Online Help Topics

Opening the Options menu and clicking Settings takes you to the Help Settings dialog box, shown in Figure 3-2. The first of the two check boxes here is your ticket to online help topics. This content on Microsoft web servers is continually updated. If you leave the option selected (its default state), whenever your computer is connected to the Internet you'll have access to the latest version of each help topic. Unless you have a dial-up Internet connection, there's seldom a good reason to clear the check box.

The second check box, Join The Help Experience Improvement Program, if selected, allows Microsoft to collect information about how you use help; such information can assist the company in its efforts to improve the system. If you're working with a slow Internet connection, you'll probably want to clear this check box. If you're curious about what kind of information Microsoft collects and how it uses that data, you can click the link to read the privacy statement online.

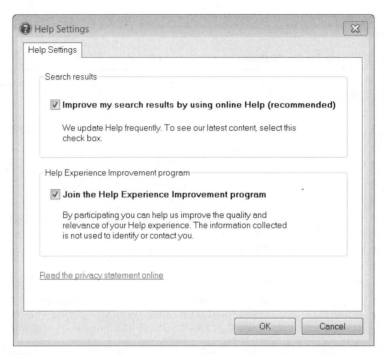

Figure 3-2 Unless you have a very slow Internet connection, it's best to ensure your access to online help topics by selecting the first check box in the Help Settings dialog box.

TROUBLESHOOTING

You can't display help from older programs

The original format for help files is the .hlp file format. This long-lived and widely used format has been used in help files for all versions of Windows from Windows 3.1 (in 1992) through Windows XP, along with all types of applications for Windows. If you use older applications, there's a good chance that you'll find some .hlp files on your computer's hard drive. Alas, the program needed to display those files, Winhlp32.exe, is not included in Windows 7. The Winhlp32.exe program has not been updated for many years and has officially been put out to pasture. Newer programs, as well as Windows itself, now use one of the newer help engines to display help files saved in one of the newer formats.

If you have some ancient .hlp files that you must use, you can download Winhlp32.exe from the Microsoft Download Center. For details, see Microsoft Knowledge Base (MSKB) article 917607 (*w7io.com/0301*).

Browsing Through Windows Help And Support

If you're reading this book from front to back, you might be the type who'd like to read through Windows Help And Support as well. Or you might find it easier to find a subject by drilling down through a table of contents–like hierarchy. Either way, the Browse Help button (or the Browse Help Topics link on the home page) is your entrée to the help topics that interest you.

To explore the available help, click a subject heading. You'll be rewarded with links to more narrowly focused subject headings as well as links to detailed help topics, as shown in Figure 3-3. Links near the top of the page trace your path to a topic; you can use these "bread crumbs" to quickly find your way back to an intermediate subject page.

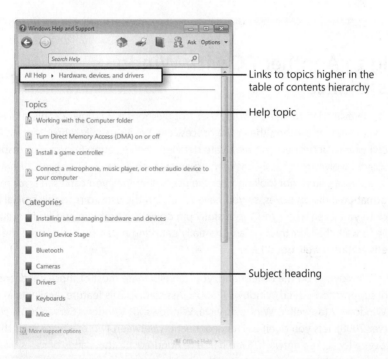

Figure 3-3 The Browse Help button lets you explore help topics organized by subject, similar to the table of contents in a printed book.

Searching for Help Topics

Finding a particular help topic is straightforward. Simply type your search word or phrase in the search box (in the toolbar at the top of the help window) and press Enter. Windows then displays links to up to 30 of the best results, with the ones most likely to be useful to you at the top of the list. If you're using online help, it searches the online topics; otherwise, it looks only at your local (offline) content.

INSIDE OUT Find articles in the Microsoft Knowledge Base

The Microsoft Knowledge Base (MSKB) is a repository of thousands of articles with detailed troubleshooting solutions and other useful information. The Windows 7 help system (unlike its predecessor in Windows XP) does not search MSKB articles, but you can use Help And Support as a launch pad for MSKB searches. Instead of using the search box, click the Ask button, and then click Microsoft Customer Support under the Contact Technical Support heading. To go directly to the advanced search page for MSKB, use this link: *w7io.com/0302*. For an MSKB article about how to search MSKB, see *w7io.com/0303*.

Connecting to Another PC with Windows Remote Assistance

If you've ever tried to help a novice user troubleshoot a Windows problem over the phone, you know how frustrating the entire process can be. It's usually difficult for an inexperienced user to accurately communicate detailed configuration information, especially if the problem involves technically challenging areas, such as hardware drivers or network protocols. Because you're not looking over the user's shoulder, you can't see error messages or informational dialog boxes, so you have to rely on the user to read this crucial information back to you. Even when you successfully pin down the problem and find a solution, you have to walk the user through a potentially daunting repair process. And if the registry needs editing—well, good luck.

With Windows 7, on the other hand, you can eliminate most of those headaches by using a cool support tool called Windows Remote Assistance. This feature, available in all versions of Windows 7 (as well as Windows Vista, Windows XP, Windows Server 2003, and Windows Server 2008), lets you open a direct connection between two machines over the Internet or over a local area network. Even if you're hundreds or thousands of miles away, you can watch as the user demonstrates the problem and take control of the screen to make repairs quickly and accurately. You can investigate Control Panel settings, run diagnostic tools, install updates, and even edit the registry of the problem-plagued PC. Repairs that might have taken hours the old-fashioned way can be accomplished in a few minutes using this tool.

Remote Assistance is designed for informal, peer-to-peer use by Windows users without an extensive technical background. Although the user interface hides most of its complexities, a basic understanding of how Remote Assistance connections work can help you make reliable connections without compromising the security of either computer.

How Remote Assistance Works

The two parties in a Remote Assistance session are called the *novice* and the *expert*. (On some screens and in some documentation, the expert is referred to as the *helper* and the novice is sometimes called the *user*.) To use Remote Assistance, both parties must be using a Windows version that includes Remote Assistance (Windows 7, Windows Vista, Windows XP, Windows Server 2003, or Windows Server 2008), both must have an active Internet connection or be on the same local area network, and neither can be blocked by a firewall.

The connection between novice and expert can be established in a variety of ways. If both parties are using Windows 7, a new Easy Connect feature is the simplest approach; a simple password exchange is all that's required. Alternatively, the novice can send a Remote Assistance invitation by using an instant messenger program or in e-mail. The expert then accepts the invitation and enters an agreed-upon password. Finally, the novice approves the expert's acceptance.

After the connection is established, a terminal window on the expert's computer displays the desktop of the novice's machine. The expert views the desktop in a read-only window and exchanges messages with the novice using text chat. If the expert wants to work with objects on the novice's computer, he or she can request control.

In a slight variation of this process, the expert can initiate the Remote Assistance session, perhaps in response to a telephone plea for help from the novice. We describe both connection processes in detail in the sections that follow.

At the heart of each Remote Assistance connection is a small text file called an *RA ticket*. (More formally, its type is Windows Remote Assistance Invitation and its extension is .msrcincident.) This file uses encrypted data in XML fields to define the parameters of a Remote Assistance connection. When you use Windows Live Messenger to manage the connection, the RA ticket is never visible. (In fact, Messenger uses a connection string that includes only part of the RA ticket information—just enough to establish connection.) When a novice sends a Remote Assistance request via e-mail, however, the RA ticket rides along as an attachment to the message. The expert has to double-click this file to launch the Remote Assistance session.

Chapter 3

Remote Assistance vs. Remote Desktop Connection

Remote Assistance in Windows 7 uses some of the same underlying technology as Remote Desktop Connection, a program that allows you to connect to your computer from a remote location and use it as though you were sitting right in front of it. Here are some of the key differences that set these programs apart:

- In a Remote Assistance session, both users must be present at their respective computers and must agree to establish the connection. Remote Desktop Connection can be initiated from one computer without the assent of someone at the remote target computer.

- With Remote Assistance, you can connect to a computer running any edition of Windows 7. The target (host) computer for a Remote Desktop Connection session must be running the Professional, Enterprise, or Ultimate edition. (You can initiate the connection from any Windows 7 edition. You can even initiate the connection from a web browser, which is not possible with Remote Assistance.)

- Remote Assistance provides a shared view of an existing session (that is, the users at each end see the same screen and can share control), whereas Remote Desktop Connection starts a new session on the remote computer. The remote session takes over completely, and the local user loses interactive access, seeing instead a logon screen with a label identifying the user account that is logged on from a remote location.

- In a Remote Assistance session, the remote user has the same rights and privileges as the local user. With Remote Desktop Connection, remote users can do whatever their account credentials allow them to do.

- Remote Assistance connections can be established over the Internet with most standard configurations. Microsoft offers an Internet Connectivity Evaluation tool, which you can find at *w7io.com/20304*, that can help you determine your system's support for Remote Assistance. In most cases, Remote Assistance will work unless both the expert and the novice are behind symmetric NATs. With Remote Desktop Connection, the target computer must be on the same network (including a virtual private network, or VPN), and it cannot be behind a NAT router.

These two programs, of course, are intended to serve very different needs. But their similarities sometimes make it possible to use one in place of the other.

Remote Assistance is able to reach computers behind nearly any NAT router by simultaneously attempting several types of connections until it finds one that works:

- **IPv4 address**   This type of connection is used when both computers can be directly addressed using IPv4, such as on a local area network or when both computers have public IP addresses.

- **IPv6 address**   This type of connection is used when both computers are on an IPv6 network.

- **UPnP NAT address**   This type of connection is used to connect through a UPnP router, which provides NAT traversal.

- **NAT traversal via Teredo**   And this type of connection is used when all the other methods fail. After using a public Teredo server to determine NAT port mapping and to initiate communication, this connection then encapsulates IPv6 data in IPv4 packets, enabling it to tunnel through an IPv4 network.

For more information about NAT, IPv4, IPv6, and Teredo, see Chapter 19, "Setting Up a Small Office or Home Network."

Chapter 3

TROUBLESHOOTING

Teredo can't make a connection

If you can't make a connection and you're certain that a firewall isn't blocking the connection, be sure that UPnP is enabled on your router. (See the instructions for your router for details. If you no longer have the manual, check the manufacturer's website.) Teredo doesn't work with routers that use symmetric NAT. To find out if you have an incompatible router, at a command prompt type **netsh interface teredo show state**. (This can be abbreviated as **netsh int ter sho st**.) If the Type line shows Symmetric or Port Restricted, your best bet is UPnP.

With the Windows XP version of Remote Assistance, connecting two systems behind NAT routers was difficult at best. Trying to explain to an inexperienced user who's already flustered because of computer problems all the complex configuration steps needed to bypass NAT made Remote Assistance impractical for most such setups. NAT is a great system for extending the limited number of available IP addresses and for securing computers on a small network, but it is the bane of users trying to make peer-to-peer connections, whether for voice, video, gaming—or Remote Assistance. Now, the only obstacle to end-to-end connections for Remote Assistance on computers running Windows Vista or Windows 7 is a firewall.

Windows Firewall has an exception defined for Remote Assistance. (An exception is a group of rules that enable an application to communicate through the firewall.) By default, the exception is enabled only for private networks, such as a workgroup in a home or small office. The exception is disabled for public networks (such as an Internet cafe or public Wi-Fi hotspot) and for domain networks. If you try to make a Remote Assistance connection when the exception is disabled, you'll see a message like the one shown in Figure 3-4.

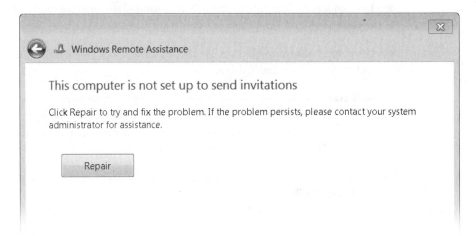

Figure 3-4 If you see this message, you need to enable the Remote Assistance exception in Windows Firewall.

To correct the problem, click Repair. The troubleshooter will figure out what's wrong and then present a Try These Repairs As An Administrator link. Click that link, give the troubleshooter a moment or two to carry out the necessary repair, and you should be good to go. If the troubleshooter for any reason doesn't perform as expected, open Windows Firewall. In the left pane, click Allow A Program Or Feature Through Windows Firewall. Then click Change Settings (which requires administrator privileges), select Remote Assistance, and click OK.

Asking for Assistance

To begin a Remote Assistance session, the novice must ask for help. If both parties are using Windows 7, the simplest way to do this is by means of a feature called Easy Connect. Alternatively, the novice can send the assistance request via instant messaging or by transferring an invitation file (for example, via e-mail).

INSIDE OUT   Know the rules

The specific rules that make up the Remote Assistance exception vary depending on the profile type. For example, UPnP connections are enabled only in the private and domain profiles—not in the profile for public networks. Teredo connections are enabled only in the private and public profiles to prevent its use on corporate domains. The domain profile contains additional rules that enable help-desk personnel to offer assistance using Distributed Component Object Model (DCOM). You might want to examine the rules that define the Remote Assistance exception, whether it's to satisfy your innate curiosity or to configure comparable rules for a third-party firewall. To do so, follow these steps:

1. Open Windows Firewall With Advanced Security.

2. In the console tree, select Inbound Rules or Outbound Rules.

3. In the actions pane, click Filter By Group, Filter By Remote Assistance.

4. In the details pane, double-click a rule to review its specifics.

Requesting Assistance with Easy Connect

To use Easy Connect to invite someone to help you, follow these steps:

1. Open Windows Remote Assistance, which can be done in any of the following ways:

   - On the Start menu, click All Programs, Maintenance, Windows Remote Assistance. More simply, type **remote** in the Start menu search box, and then click Windows Remote Assistance (not Remote Desktop Connection).

   - At a command prompt, type **msra**.

   - In Windows Help And Support, click the Ask button and then click the Windows Remote Assistance link.

2. In the Windows Remote Assistance window, click Invite Someone You Trust To Help You.

3. If you have previously used Easy Connect, the next dialog box shows you when and with whom that previous session took place, giving you the opportunity to reconnect with a single click. (See Figure 3-5.) If instead you want to establish a new connection, click Invite Someone To Help You.

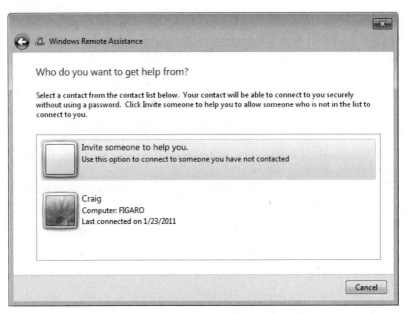

Figure 3-5 Easy Connect makes it simple to reconnect, as well as to establish a new connection.

4. If you're setting up a new connection, Windows Remote Assistance presents a 12-character alphanumeric password:

Convey this password to your helper by phone, e-mail, or instant messaging.

Accepting an Invitation to Help Using Easy Connect

After the novice has invited the expert by using Easy Connect, the expert does the following:

1. Open Windows Remote Assistance. (See step 1 in the preceding list.)

2. Click Help Someone Who Has Invited You.

3. Click Help Someone New (or, to reestablish a prior connection, select that connection from the list).

4. Click Use Easy Connect.

5. Enter the 12-character password. (The password is not case-sensitive.)

    Windows Remote Assistance uses the password to match the novice with the expert (or present an error message if the password has been entered incorrectly). Then the novice is asked to confirm the connection:

Connecting the Novice and the Expert with Windows Live Messenger

Another simple way to use Remote Assistance is through an instant messenger connection. The novice initiates the session by following these steps:

1. Sign in to Windows Live Messenger, and then open a chat window with your prospective helper if one is not already open.

2. In the chat window, click Activities, and then click Request Remote Assistance. Your request appears as part of the conversation.

3. After the expert accepts your request (by pressing Alt+C or clicking Accept in the chat window), a password appears on your screen. Convey that password to your helper. If you have any doubt at all that the person at the other end of the instant messaging connection is who he or she appears to be, call the expert and provide the password by phone or send it by e-mail.

4. After the expert has correctly entered the password, a confirmation prompt appears on your screen. Check the e-mail address in the prompt to be certain that you're chatting with who you think you are—after all, this person will be able to see and (with your additional consent) operate your computer—and then click Yes.

Chapter 3

After the Remote Assistance connection is established, you no longer need the instant messenger session; you can close that window if you want to. You can resume your online discussion in the Remote Assistance chat pane.

Using an Invitation File to Request Assistance

If the expert and novice don't use the same instant messaging system, the novice can create an invitation file. The invitation file can be transferred to the expert via e-mail, a shared folder on the network or Internet, or even on physical media, such as a USB flash drive. Follow these steps:

1. Open Windows Remote Assistance.

2. In the Windows Remote Assistance window, click Invite Someone You Trust To Help You.

3. Click Invite Someone To Help You.

4. Click Save This Invitation As A File, and then specify a file location.

5. Windows Remote Assistance presents a 12-character password. Convey the invitation file to your helper by whatever means you favor, and then give that person the password—preferably in person or by phone. (If you include the password along with the invitation file, anyone who intercepts the message can pose as the expert and connect to your computer.)

6. After the expert has launched the invitation file and entered the password, a confirmation prompt appears on your screen. Confirm.

CAUTION

Don't make your invitation lifespan longer than necessary. Although several protections are in place to prevent its misuse, a Remote Assistance file is an invitation to connect to your computer. It's best to keep the window of opportunity as small as possible. Note that when you close the Windows Remote Assistance window on the novice's computer, you effectively cancel the invitation, regardless of the time.

INSIDE OUT   Change the invitation duration

By default, a Remote Assistance invitation expires six hours after it's created. For the best security, reduce the expiration time if the expert can respond quickly to your request. Conversely, you might need to create a longer-lasting invitation if you don't expect your chosen expert to be available during that time. To modify the duration of invitation files you create, follow these steps:

1. Open Control Panel, click System And Security, and then click System.

2. In the Tasks list, click Remote Settings (requires administrator privileges).

3. On the Remote tab, click Advanced to display the dialog box shown in Figure 3-6. Specify the amount of time that you want invitation files to remain valid.

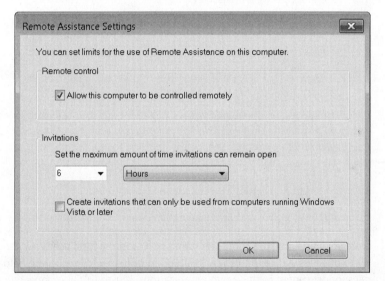

Figure 3-6 You can specify the time in minutes, hours, or days, up to a maximum of 99.

Offering Remote Assistance via DCOM

If you start Windows Remote Assistance by typing **msra /offerra** at a command prompt, you'll see a dialog box similar to the one following:

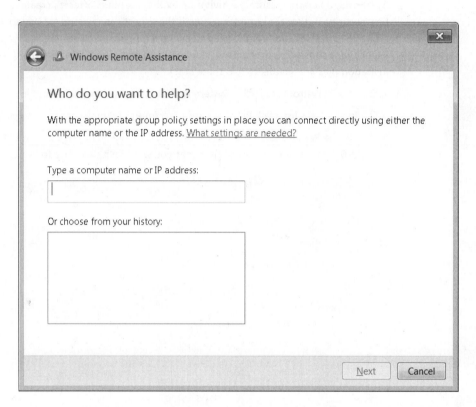

Here you can enter the computer name or IP address for a user you want to assist. The ability to offer assistance in this way is intended primarily for corporate help desks and technical support centers within large organizations. It uses DCOM connectivity and requires prior configuration of the novice's computer, including configuration of that computer's firewall and user accounts; this is most easily done through Group Policy on a domain-based network. If you're trying to assist someone on a small network in a home or business, this option isn't for you; your best bet is to establish the Windows Remote Assistance connection through the methods described earlier. (The reason DCOM connectivity is not readily available in workgroups is primarily security. Allowing anyone to offer assistance to someone else is rife with danger.)

INSIDE OUT

Make it easier for the novice to request assistance

The ability to offer assistance via DCOM is impractical except for experts in a domain environment. If you must rely on your novice friends to initiate a request by sending you an invitation, you can help them out by creating a shortcut on their desktop that creates an invitation and attaches it to an e-mail message; all they need to do is click Send. To do that, use the /Email option with Msra.exe. For details, at a command prompt type **msra /?**.

Working in a Remote Assistance Session

After a Remote Assistance connection is established, a Windows Remote Assistance window opens on the expert's machine, as shown in Figure 3-7.

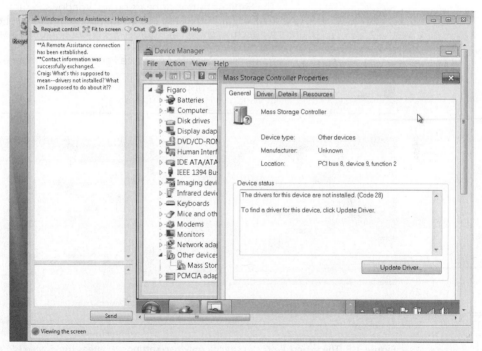

Figure 3-7 The novice's desktop appears on the expert's computer in a window topped with a toolbar containing Remote Assistance controls.

Chapter 3

As the expert, you use the toolbar at the top of the Windows Remote Assistance screen to take control of the remote desktop, open a chat window, send a file, or disconnect when the session is complete. The novice has similar options available. The toolbar provides the functions shown in Table 3-2.

Table 3-2 Toolbar Functions Available in a Windows Remote Assistance Session

Request control	Request Control allows (with the novice's consent) the expert to take control of the novice's computer. For details, see "Sharing Control of the Novice's Computer" on page 103. While the expert has control, each party's toolbar has a Stop Sharing button with which either user can return exclusive control to the novice.
Actual size	Clicking Actual Size toggles the expert's view of the novice's screen between the actual size and a scaled view that fits in the Windows Remote Assistance screen without the use of scroll bars.
Chat	Clicking Chat opens a chat pane that works much like an instant messaging program.
Settings	The Settings button appears on the Windows Remote Assistance toolbar for both users, but it summons a different set of options for each, as shown in Figure 3-8. For details about these settings, see "Sharing Control of the Novice's Computer" on page 103 and "Improving Remote Assistance Performance" on page 106.
Help	Clicking Help displays a list of Windows Remote Assistance topics in Windows Help And Support.

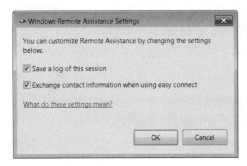 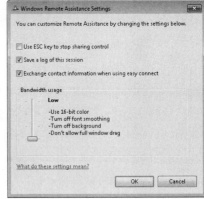

Figure 3-8 The expert (left) can specify only two settings, whereas the novice (right) can also control performance options.

The novice sees a slightly modified version of this toolbar:

On the novice's toolbar, the Stop Sharing button becomes active if the expert asserts control; as its name suggests, it lets the novice suspend control sharing. The Pause button makes the novice's screen temporarily invisible to the expert—until the novice clicks Continue.

Sharing Control of the Novice's Computer

For obvious security reasons, clicking Request Control sends a request to the novice, who must grant permission before the expert can actually begin working with the remote desktop. (See Figure 3-9.) While the expert has control, the novice's computer responds to input from the keyboard and mouse of *both* the expert and the novice. At any time, the novice can cut off the expert's ability to control the session by tapping the Esc key; alternatively, either party can return exclusive control to the novice by clicking Stop Sharing.

Figure 3-9 The novice must decide whether to allow the expert to share control.

Regardless of his or her expert credentials, the expert's actions in a Windows Remote Assistance session are governed by the privileges assigned to the novice user's account. When connecting to a machine belonging to a user with a standard user account, for instance, you might be unable to edit the registry or make necessary configuration changes unless you can supply the password for an administrator account on the novice's computer.

Terminating a Remote Assistance Session

Either party can terminate a Windows Remote Assistance connection at any time. The novice does this by clicking the Cancel button on his or her Windows Remote Assistance toolbar. The expert does it by clicking the Close button in the Windows Remote Assistance window.

Using Remote Assistance with Earlier Windows Versions

Windows 7 is not the first version of Windows to include Remote Assistance; it's also available in Windows Vista, Windows XP, Windows Server 2008, and Windows Server 2003. For the most part, experts and novices on any of these platforms can use Windows Remote Assistance to help each other. There are some limitations:

- If either computer is running an earlier version of Windows, Windows Remote Assistance in Windows 7 reverts to the capabilities of the earlier version. New connectivity features such as Easy Connect and NAT traversal using Teredo are unavailable.

- Windows Remote Assistance in Windows 7 does not support voice chat, which was supported in Windows XP.

- Pausing a session is a feature that was introduced in Windows Vista. (The expert can't see what occurs while a session is paused.) If a novice running Windows 7 pauses a session, an expert running Windows XP receives no indication that the session has been paused.

- You cannot offer assistance from a computer running Windows XP.

- Invitation files created on a computer with the "Windows Vista or later" option enabled (shown in Figure 3-6) are completely encrypted and cannot be used on computers running earlier versions.

Maintaining Security

Windows Remote Assistance is a powerful tool. In the wrong hands, it's also potentially dangerous because it allows a remote user to install software and tamper with a system configuration. In a worst-case scenario, someone could trick an unsuspecting novice into granting access to his or her machine and then plant a Trojan horse application or gain access to sensitive files.

Windows Remote Assistance was designed and built with security in mind, and several enhancements were introduced with the Windows Vista version. For example:

- A password is required for all connections, whether by Easy Connect, invitation file, or instant messenger.

- The novice must agree to accept each incoming connection and must approve each request to share control.

- Invitation files expire six hours after they're created or when the Windows Remote Assistance session is closed.

- Windows Remote Assistance uses a dynamic port assignment.

- By default, the Windows Firewall exception for Remote Assistance is enabled only on private networks.

For these reasons and more, Windows Remote Assistance is sufficiently secure out of the box. You can take the following additional precautions to completely slam the door on Windows Remote Assistance–related security breaches:

- Set a short expiration time on Windows Remote Assistance invitations sent via e-mail. An expiration time of one hour should be sufficient for most requests. (Note that the invitation must be accepted within the specified time; you don't need to specify the length of the Windows Remote Assistance session.) An expired RA ticket file is worthless to a potential hacker.

- Because e-mail is fundamentally insecure, do not send a password with an invitation. Instead, communicate the password by telephone or in a separate e-mail message.

- Manually expire an invitation when it's no longer needed. To do so, simply close the Windows Remote Assistance screen.

- If both the expert and novice use Windows Vista or Windows 7, use encrypted invitation files. Open System in Control Panel. In the Tasks list, click Remote Settings. On the Remote tab, click Advanced. Then select Create Invitations That Can Only Be Used From Computers Running Windows Vista Or Later. (See Figure 3-6.)

- Disable Remote Assistance on any machine for which the possible benefits of a Windows Remote Assistance session are outweighed by potential security risks. To completely disable Remote Assistance on a given machine, open System, click Remote Settings, click the Remote tab, and then clear Allow Remote Assistance Connections To This Computer. If that step seems too drastic, you can limit Remote Assistance capabilities so that an expert cannot take control of the remote machine. On the Remote tab, click Advanced, and then clear Allow This Computer To Be Controlled Remotely.

Chapter 3

Improving Remote Assistance Performance

You might shudder at the thought of accessing another desktop over a dial-up connection. Surprisingly, the performance can be quite usable. You wouldn't want to use this sort of connection for everyday work, but for troubleshooting, it's good enough.

You can maximize Remote Assistance performance over a slow link by observing these guidelines:

- If possible, use Windows Vista or Windows 7 for both the novice and expert. The version of Remote Assistance in these releases of Windows incorporates a number of performance enhancements compared to the version included in Windows XP, but most of these improvements are effective only when both computers are running Windows Vista or Windows 7.

- Close any unnecessary applications on the novice machine.

- Don't let the novice move the mouse on the novice machine, if possible, when the expert is in control of the screen.

- Reduce the visual complexity of the novice machine as much as possible. Reduce the display resolution to 800 by 600 and use only as many colors as is absolutely necessary. If the novice has a multimonitor setup, disable that for the duration of the Remote Assistance session.

- Turn off desktop animations and other sophisticated visual effects, and avoid opening windows that contain complex graphics unless absolutely necessary.

The last two suggestions can be implemented by using the Settings button on the novice machine. The Bandwidth Usage slider (see Figure 3-8) has four settings; for details about each setting, move the slider. The slower your connection, the lower you should set this slider.

Help and Support Resources for IT Professionals

If you're an IT pro, you might be looking for a deeper level of help than many of the articles in Windows Help And Support provide. Don't disregard the help application altogether, though. If you simply search Windows Help And Support for "IT Pros," you'll find a sizable list of topics aimed at the technically adept user—including networking information, migration strategies, registry management strategies, and a good deal more. These topics can serve as springboards for more detailed online investigations.

The most important online resources to know about are the Microsoft Knowledge Base and the Windows Client TechCenter. The Microsoft Knowledge Base, MSKB, is described earlier in this chapter, on page 90. The Windows Client TechCenter, accessible at *w7io.com/20310* and shown in Figure 3-10, is a portal to learning resources for Windows XP, Windows Vista, and Windows 7.

Figure 3-10 The Windows Client TechCenter is a portal to Windows 7, Windows Vista, and Windows XP support resources.

On the Windows Client TechCenter home page you'll find tools for troubleshooting errors and events and searching the Microsoft Knowledge Base, links to Windows client blogs and forums, information about webcasts, and quite a lot more. Click Windows 7 on the top menu to focus your work specifically on the latest Windows client. Click Library on the top menu to go to the Windows 7 node of the vast Microsoft TechNet Library. (See Figure 3-11.) A walk through the outline in the left pane of the Microsoft TechNet Library will give you a good idea of the range and depth of the available information.

Chapter 3

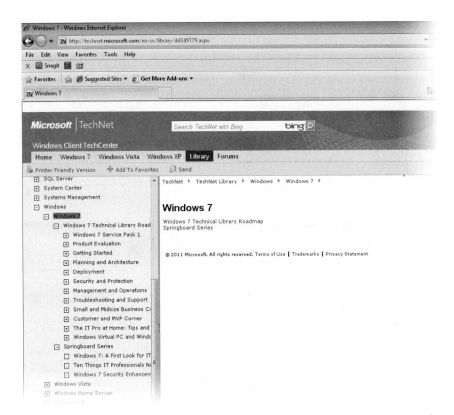

Figure 3-11 The Microsoft TechNet Library hosts a wealth of IT-oriented technical information about Windows 7 and other topics.

If you're interested in communicating with other members of the IT community about topics related to Windows 7, be sure to click Forums on the Windows Client TechCenter main menu. Figure 3-12 illustrates some of the available Windows 7 IT Pro forums.

Figure 3-12 The Forums item on the Windows Client TechCenter menu provides access to the IT community.

Personalizing Windows 7

O NE of the most obvious changes that Microsoft made in moving from Windows Vista to Windows 7 is the taskbar, which has a bold new look, lots of new functionality, and new ways to customize, all of which we explain in this chapter. We also cover the many new techniques that make it easier to perform various window tasks, such as maximizing, resizing, and so on.

A subtler change is the inclusion of the word *Personalize* prominently in the user interface of the new operating system. Certainly, earlier versions of Windows could be tailored, customized, and modified to suit a user's needs and preferences—in a word, personalized. But the *P* word itself was missing. Now, when you right-click your desktop, the shortcut menu that pops up features an icon-festooned Personalize command. Personalize Windows is also one of the items that appear in the new operating system's Getting Started task list.

So the message is clear: It's your operating system; make it reflect your tastes, your needs, your style. Make it work for you. More than any previous version of Windows, Windows 7 provides myriad tools for doing just that—tools that we survey in this chapter.

What's in Your Edition?

The ability to personalize your computing environment by changing desktop backgrounds, window colors, and sounds is not available in Windows 7 Starter edition. Lack of Aero support in Starter edition means you can't get transparent window frames, live taskbar previews, and other visual effects, and Aero Peek is unavailable. And Starter edition does not support the use of multiple monitors. All other features described in this chapter are available in all editions.

Working with the New Taskbar and Start Menu

The *taskbar* is that strip of real estate along one screen edge (bottom by default) that contains the Start menu button, program buttons, and status icons. The taskbar made its first appearance in Windows 95. In the years since, it has slowly evolved: installing Internet Explorer 4 in Windows 95 also added a Quick Launch toolbar and other toolbars; Windows XP reduced clutter by introducing taskbar grouping; and Windows Vista added taskbar previews, small window representations that increased your chances of clicking the correct taskbar button for the program you wanted to bring to the front.

The evolution continues in Windows 7, but at a generation-skipping pace. The Windows 7 taskbar (see Figure 4-1) continues to serve the same basic functions as its progenitors—launching programs, switching between programs, and providing notifications—but in a way that makes these basic tasks easier and more efficient.

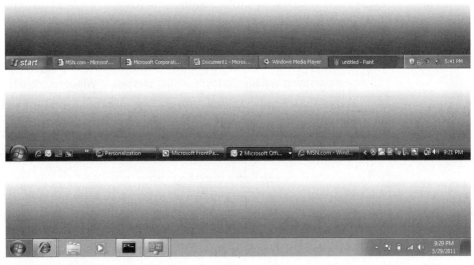

Figure 4-1 Although the taskbar designs in Windows XP (top), Windows Vista (center), and Windows 7 (bottom) contain the same basic elements, the appearance has evolved a bit—and the functionality has advanced by leaps and bounds.

Opening and Monitoring Programs from Taskbar Buttons

As in previous Windows versions, the taskbar houses the Start menu button, a button for each running program, and the notification area. You can use these task buttons to switch from one running program to another. You can also click a task button to minimize an open window or to restore a minimized window. But in a departure from earlier Windows versions, which had separate bands dedicated to a Quick Launch bar (from which you can open programs) and to taskbar buttons (which represent programs that are currently running), the Windows 7 taskbar combines these functions. That is, buttons between the Start button and the notification area can be used both for opening programs and for switching between programs.

Adding and Removing Pinned Programs, Documents, and Folders

Programs that you use often (the ones that you might've had on the Quick Launch toolbar in the past) can be easily pinned to the taskbar so that a single click launches them. To open a program that is pinned to the taskbar, you don't need to open the Start menu or dig down to find a desktop shortcut. To pin a program to the taskbar, simply drag its icon or a shortcut (from the desktop, from the Start menu, or from any other folder) to the taskbar. Alternatively, right-click a program icon wherever you find it and choose Pin To Taskbar.

To remove a pinned program from the taskbar, right-click the pinned icon and choose Unpin This Program From Taskbar. This command also appears on other shortcuts to the program, including those on the desktop and on the Start menu.

You can also pin frequently used documents and folders to the taskbar by using similar methods:

- To pin a document to the taskbar, drag its icon or a shortcut to the taskbar. If the taskbar already has a button for the program associated with the document, Windows adds the document to the Pinned section of the program's Jump List. (For more information about Jump Lists, see "Using Jump Lists on the Taskbar and Start Menu" on page 119.) If the document's program is not on the taskbar, Windows pins the program to the taskbar and adds the document to the program's Jump List.

- To pin a folder to the taskbar, drag its icon or a shortcut to the taskbar. Windows adds the folder to the Pinned section of the Jump List for Windows Explorer.

- To open a pinned document or folder, right-click the taskbar button and then click the name of the document or folder.

- To remove a pinned document or folder from the Jump List, right-click the taskbar button and point to the name of the document or folder to be removed. Click the pushpin icon that appears.

Chapter 4

INSIDE OUT Restore the Quick Launch toolbar

Some habits die hard. If you just can't bear to give up the Quick Launch toolbar, you can display it in Windows 7. To do so, add the hidden Quick Launch folder as you would any other folder. (For details, see "Using Additional Toolbars" on page 124.) In the New Toolbar dialog box, type **%AppData%\Microsoft\Internet Explorer\Quick Launch** in the Folder box.

To mimic the appearance of the Quick Launch toolbar in previous Windows versions, unlock the taskbar. (Right-click the taskbar and, if there's a check mark by Lock The Taskbar, choose that command.) Right-click the Quick Launch toolbar and clear the Show Title and Show Text commands. Then drag the handle (the dotted line) on the left side of the Quick Launch toolbar so that it's next to the Start button, and drag the handle on the right side of the toolbar to set the width you want. Then relock the taskbar.

If you later decide you don't need the Quick Launch toolbar after all, right-click the taskbar and select Toolbars, Quick Launch to remove the check mark and the toolbar.

Opening Programs

To open a program, click its taskbar button. A few simple (but not obvious) tricks let you do more:

- To open a new instance of a program, Shift+click its taskbar button. This is useful for programs that are already running, for which an ordinary click switches to the existing instance or, if you already have multiple open instances, displays the window thumbnails. (If you have a wheel mouse or other three-button mouse, middle-click serves the same purpose as Shift+click.)

- To open a new instance with administrative privileges, Ctrl+Shift+click a taskbar button.

Switching Tasks

When you open a pinned program, the appearance of its taskbar button changes to indicate that the program is running, as shown in Figure 4-2. The icon for a running program has a buttonlike border, and when you mouse over the button, the background color becomes similar to the program's window colors. A program that has more than one window or tab open appears as a stack of buttons. Opening other programs adds a button for each program to the taskbar.

Stacked buttons represent multiple windows

An outlined button represents a single window

Figure 4-2 Taskbar buttons for programs that are not running have an icon but no border and share the same background as the taskbar itself.

As in previous Windows versions, you can switch to a different program by clicking its task-bar button. Much of the guesswork required to pick the correct taskbar button in previous versions is gone in Windows 7, however. Now, when you hover the mouse pointer over a taskbar button, a thumbnail image of the window appears next to the taskbar button. If a taskbar button represents more than one window (because the program has multiple open windows), hovering the mouse pointer over the taskbar button displays a preview of each window.

Still not sure which is the correct window? Use another new Windows 7 feature, *Aero Peek*. Hover the mouse pointer over one of the preview images, and Windows brings that window to the fore and indicates the location of all other open windows with outlines, as shown in Figure 4-3.

Figure 4-3 Aero Peek makes it easy to see the contents of a window, even when it's buried among a stack of open windows.

> **Note**
>
> Taskbar preview images and Aero Peek are available only when you use an Aero theme. (For more information about Aero and themes, see "Understanding and Using Windows Aero" on page 139.) If you're not using an Aero theme, hovering the mouse pointer over a taskbar button displays each window's full title.

When the preview (or the title bar, if you're not using Aero) of the window you want is displayed, simply click that preview to switch to that window. You also have the option of closing a window by clicking the red *X* in the upper right corner of the preview or by middle-clicking anywhere in the preview image. Other basic window tasks are available on the context menu that appears when you right-click the preview image.

INSIDE OUT   Use shortcut keys for taskbar buttons

The first 10 taskbar buttons are accessible by keyboard as well as by mouse. Press Windows logo key+1 for the first, Windows logo key+2 for the second, and so on (using 0 for the tenth). Using one of these shortcuts is equivalent to clicking the corresponding taskbar button: if the button's program isn't running, it starts; if it has a single open window, you switch to that window; if it has multiple open windows, Windows displays previews of all windows and a "peek" view of the first window.

Note that you can move taskbar buttons, which therefore determines the key number that opens a particular icon. To move a taskbar button, simply drag it to the location you want.

Another useful shortcut key is Windows logo key+T, which brings focus to the first item on the taskbar, as indicated by a faint glow at the bottom of that taskbar button. At that point, you can repeatedly press Windows logo key+T, Shift+Windows logo key+T, or the arrow keys to select other taskbar buttons. When a taskbar button is selected, you can press Spacebar to "click" the button, press the Menu key to display its Jump List, or press Shift+F10 to display its context menu.

As you use Windows 7, you'll notice other enhancements to the taskbar. Some taskbar previews do more than simply show a thumbnail image of the window; for example, the preview for Windows Media Player includes basic player controls (Previous, Pause/Play, and Next). And with some taskbar buttons, you don't even need to display a preview to know what's going on with the program; windows or dialog boxes that show a progress bar, for example, indicate their progress with a colored background in the taskbar button itself.

INSIDE OUT   Use Ctrl+click to cycle through windows

If you're not using Aero, you don't get thumbnail previews and you can't use Aero Peek to view full-size windows or tabs before you switch to them. However, if you hold down the Ctrl key while you click a taskbar button that represents a group of windows, you'll see each window in turn. Release the Ctrl key when you see the one you want.

Opening Programs from the Start Menu

Although improvements to the taskbar in Windows 7 have reduced the number of necessary trips to the Start menu (shown here), the Start menu continues to provide access to nearly everything you need to do in Windows.

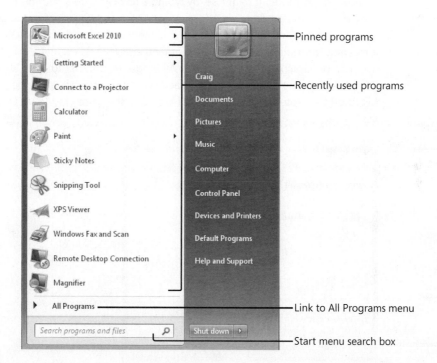

Like the default Start menu in Windows XP and Windows Vista, the Windows 7 Start menu is a two-column affair, the left side of which is reserved for the programs you use most often or that you have used most recently. Windows 7 devotes the right side of the menu to various important system folders, such as your Documents and Pictures folders, Control Panel, and Devices And Printers.

Four areas of the Start menu make it easy to run the programs and open the documents you need most. They are listed here in descending order of convenience and ease of use:

- **Pinned programs** The area in the upper left corner of the Start menu, above the horizontal line, is reserved for the programs you want to be accessible at all times. After you pin an item to this part of the Start menu, it stays there (unless you subsequently remove it).

- **Recently used programs** Windows populates the area directly below pinned programs with programs that you have used recently. You can change the number and types of programs that appear here; for details, see "Customizing the Left Side of the Start Menu" on page 130.

- **Start menu search box** The Start menu includes a search box (at the bottom on the left, directly below All Programs). You can get to anything on the menu, no matter how deeply nested it might be, by typing a few characters into this box. In the preceding illustration, for example, Microsoft OneNote 2010 does not appear on the left side of the menu because we haven't pinned it to the top of the menu or used it recently. Navigating to this program's menu entry would require a couple of clicks and a bit of scrolling (one click to open All Programs, another to open Microsoft Office). As Figure 4-4 shows, three characters in the search box are enough to bring Microsoft OneNote 2010 to the Programs area of the search results, at the top of the Start menu.

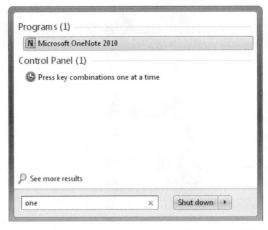

Figure 4-4 Typing **one** into the search box is sufficient to bring Microsoft OneNote 2010 to the top of the Start menu.

Provided you're not completely averse to typing, the search box pretty much eliminates the hassle of finding items that are buried several folders deep within the menu structure. The Start menu search box doesn't limit its searches to programs, however;

it's an entry point to the full-fledged search capabilities of Windows 7. For complete details, see Chapter 10, "Using Windows Search."

- **All Programs folder**   Clicking All Programs opens a hierarchically arranged list of program icons similar to that found in earlier Windows versions. The All Programs menu is generated by merging the contents of two folders:

  - A personal folder, located at %AppData%\Microsoft\Windows\Start Menu\ Programs

  - An "all users" folder, located at %ProgramData%\Microsoft\Windows\Start Menu\Programs

  As you might expect, items stored in the personal folder appear only on your own Start menu. Items stored in the "all users" folder appear on the Start menu of everyone who has an account on your computer.

Adding and Removing Pinned Programs

To add a program to the pinned programs area of the Start menu, right-click it wherever you see it (elsewhere on the Start menu, for example) and choose Pin To Start Menu. The item will take up residence at the bottom of the pinned programs area. If you'd like to give it a more prominent location, drag it upward.

> **Note**
> If no shortcut menu appears when you right-click an item, and you can't drag the item to the pinned programs area, open the Customize Start Menu dialog box. (For details, see "Personalizing the Start Menu" on page 128.) In the list of options, select Enable Context Menus And Dragging And Dropping.

To remove an item from the pinned programs area, right-click it and choose Unpin From Start Menu.

Using Jump Lists on the Taskbar and Start Menu

A powerful addition to the taskbar and Start menu is the *Jump List*, a menu of options closely related to the program associated with a taskbar button or an entry on the Start menu. Programs that are written to take advantage of Jump Lists in Windows 7 might include on the Jump List various common commands and tasks that can be performed with that program.

Jump Lists can be big timesavers even with older programs. For those programs, Windows adds to the Jump List a list of recently used documents, making it easy to reopen a recent document quickly.

In addition, each taskbar Jump List includes commands to open the program, to pin (or unpin) the program to the taskbar, and to close all open windows represented by the button.

Figure 4-5 shows Jump Lists for Internet Explorer.

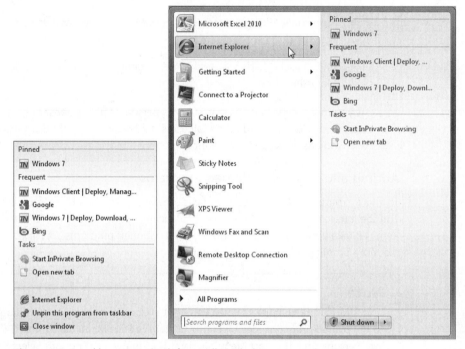

Figure 4-5 A taskbar Jump List (left) usually includes commands not on a Start menu Jump List (right).

To open a taskbar Jump List, use one of these techniques:

- Right-click the taskbar button.

- Using a stylus (or your finger, if you have a touch-capable computer), drag the task-bar button away from the edge of the screen in a flicking motion. When you release, the Jump List appears.

- The preceding technique was created for use with tablet and touch computers, but it also works with a mouse: point to the taskbar button, press the left mouse button, drag away from the taskbar, and release the mouse button.

On the Start menu, a Jump List is available only for programs that have been pinned and those in the recently used list. To display the Jump List associated with a Start menu item,

Chapter 4

click the arrow next to the program name or simply hover the mouse pointer over the menu item.

Most of the Jump List content is created by the program's author or, in the case of recent items, generated by Windows. To keep favorite documents always available on the Jump List, you can pin an item in the recent documents list: point to it and click the pushpin icon, or right-click it and choose Pin To This List.

To protect your privacy or simply to clean up a cluttered list, you can remove an item from the recent list or the pinned list: right-click and choose Remove From This List (or, for pinned items, Unpin From This List).

INSIDE OUT   Clear recent items from all Jump Lists

The recent items lists on Jump Lists, grouped by program, largely replace the need for a Recent Items menu on the Start menu, which is disabled by default in Windows 7. (If you want to restore the Recent Items menu, open the Customize Start Menu dialog box and select Recent Items.) Like the Recent Items menu in previous Windows versions, the recent items shown on Jump Lists are derived from the contents of the folder %UserProfile%\Recent. Note that you can't add items to recent lists by making direct additions to %UserProfile%\Recent. For the purposes of building these lists, Windows simply ignores anything in the Recent folder that it didn't put there itself.

To clear all recent items (but not pinned items) from Jump Lists and from the Recent Items menu, right-click the Start button and choose Properties. On the Start Menu tab of the Taskbar And Start Menu Properties dialog box, clear the Store And Display Recently Opened Items In The Start Menu And The Taskbar check box. Windows clears out the %UserProfile%\Recent folder when you do this.

Personalizing the Taskbar and Start Menu

The new look of the taskbar and the default selection of commands on the Start menu are not for everyone. In this section, we describe the tools and methods for customizing them to work the way you like.

Changing the Taskbar's Appearance and Behavior

As described in the following sections, you can modify the order, size, appearance, and grouping of taskbar buttons and change the overall taskbar size and location. Many of these changes are made most easily through the Taskbar And Start Menu Properties dialog box (see Figure 4-6), which you can open by right-clicking an unoccupied area of the taskbar and choosing Properties.

Figure 4-6 You can also display this dialog box by right-clicking the Start button, choosing Properties, and clicking the Taskbar tab.

Changing the Order of Taskbar Buttons

One of the most useful personalizations you can make doesn't require a visit to any dialog box. To change the order of buttons on the taskbar, simply drag them to the place you want. Pinned program icons retain their order between sessions, allowing you to quickly find your most used programs in their familiar (to you) location.

Changing the Size, Appearance, and Grouping of Taskbar Buttons

Two items on the Taskbar tab of Taskbar And Start Menu Properties control the size and appearance of taskbar buttons:

- **Use Small Icons**   Select Use Small Icons if you want to reduce the height of taskbar buttons, making them similar to the button size in earlier Windows versions.

- **Taskbar Buttons**   The default setting for Taskbar Buttons is Always Combine, Hide Labels. This setting suppresses the display of labels (window titles) and causes Windows to always group multiple windows from a single application into a single taskbar button.

With either of the other settings (Combine When Taskbar Is Full or Never Combine), Windows displays the window title (or as much as it can fit) on the taskbar button, much like it does in earlier versions of Windows. (See Figure 4-7.) The difference between these settings is that with Combine When Taskbar Is Full, each window gets its own separate taskbar button until the taskbar becomes too crowded, whereupon Windows groups windows from a program into a single taskbar button. With Never Combine, taskbar buttons continue to diminish in size as you open more windows.

Figure 4-7 Selecting Use Small Icons and Combine When Taskbar Is Full results in a taskbar similar to what you see in Windows XP or Windows Vista.

Changing the Taskbar's Size and Appearance

The default height of the taskbar is enough to display one taskbar button. (If you switch between large and small icons, the taskbar automatically adjusts its height to fit.) You can enlarge it—and given the typical size and resolution of computer displays these days, enlarging it is often a great idea. Before you can change the taskbar's dimensions, you need to unlock it. Right-click an unoccupied area of the taskbar, and if a check mark appears next to the Lock The Taskbar command, click the command to clear the check mark. Then position the mouse along the border of the taskbar farthest from the edge of the screen. When the mouse pointer becomes a two-headed arrow, drag toward the center of the screen to expand the taskbar. Drag the same border in the opposite direction to restore the original size.

Getting the Taskbar Out of Your Way

By default, the taskbar remains visible even when you're working in a maximized program. If that's inconvenient for any reason, you can tell it to get out of the way. In the Taskbar And Start Menu Properties dialog box, shown in Figure 4-6, select Auto-Hide The Taskbar. With this option selected, the taskbar retreats into the edge of the desktop whenever any window has the focus. To display the taskbar, move the mouse pointer to the edge of the desktop where the taskbar is "hidden."

> **Note**
>
> Regardless of how you set the auto-hide option in the Taskbar And Start Menu Properties dialog box, you can make the taskbar visible at any time by pressing the Windows logo key or Ctrl+Esc.

Moving the Taskbar

The taskbar docks by default at the bottom of the screen (the main screen, if you have more than one), but you can move it to any other edge, including any edge of a secondary screen. To move the taskbar, select a Taskbar Location On Screen option in Taskbar And Start Menu Properties.

As an alternative, you can manipulate the taskbar directly: Unlock it (right-click an unoccupied spot and choose Lock The Taskbar—unless no check mark appears beside that command, which means that the taskbar is already unlocked). Then drag any unoccupied part of the taskbar in the direction you want to go. (Don't drag the edge of the taskbar closest to the center of the screen; doing that changes the taskbar's size, not its position.)

Using Additional Toolbars

A seldom-used feature of the taskbar is its ability to host other toolbars. Optional toolbars might provide shortcuts to folders, documents, and applications, or they might be miniapplications that operate entirely within the confines of the taskbar. Toolbars you can choose to install include the following:

- **Address** The Address toolbar provides a place where you can type an Internet address or the name and path of a program, document, or folder. When you press Enter or click the Go button, Windows takes you to the Internet address, starts the program, opens the document, or displays the folder in a Windows Explorer window. The Address toolbar is functionally equivalent to the Start menu's Run command or the address bar in Windows Explorer or Internet Explorer.

- **Links** The Links toolbar provides shortcuts to Internet sites; it is equivalent to the Links toolbar in Internet Explorer.

- **Tablet PC Input Panel** The Tablet PC Input Panel toolbar provides a single tool—an icon you can click (or, more likely, tap with a stylus) to display or hide the panel that encompasses the writing pad and touch keyboard. (For details about using the Tablet PC Input Panel, see "Using the Writing Pad and Touch Keyboard" on page 1145.)

- **Desktop** The Desktop toolbar provides copies of all the icons currently displayed on your desktop. In addition, it includes links to your Libraries, Homegroup, Computer, Network, Control Panel, and other user profile folders. When you click the toolbar's double arrow, a cascading menu of all the folders and files on your system appears.

> **Note**
>
> Pinned icons on the taskbar obviate the Quick Launch toolbar, a regular taskbar feature since the days of Windows 95. But if you prefer to use it, we show you how: see the tip "Restore the Quick Launch toolbar" on page 114.

Installing and Removing Toolbars   To install a new toolbar or remove one you're currently using, right-click any unoccupied part of the taskbar or any existing toolbar. Choose Toolbars from the shortcut menu that appears, and then choose from the ensuing submenu. A check mark beside a toolbar's name means that it is already displayed on the taskbar. Clicking a selected toolbar name removes that toolbar.

> **Note**
>
> You can also display any of the predefined toolbars (listed earlier) or remove any currently displayed toolbar by using the Toolbars tab of the Taskbar And Start Menu Properties dialog box.

Sizing and Positioning Toolbars   Before you can change a toolbar's size or position on the taskbar, the taskbar itself must be unlocked. To do that, right-click an unoccupied area of the taskbar and, if a check mark appears next to the Lock The Taskbar command, click the command to clear the check mark.

When the taskbar is not locked, a dotted vertical bar appears at the left edge of every toolbar. (If the taskbar is displayed vertically against the left or right edge of the desktop, the bar is horizontal and appears at the top of the toolbar.) This is the toolbar's handle. To reposition a toolbar within the taskbar, drag the handle.

> **Note**
>
> Unlike Windows XP, Windows 7 insists that toolbars be docked to the taskbar.

Creating a New Toolbar   Any folder on your system can become a toolbar. To create a new toolbar, right-click an existing toolbar or a spot on the taskbar, choose Toolbars, and then choose New Toolbar. In the next dialog box, navigate to a folder and click Select Folder.

The folder's name becomes the name of the new toolbar, and each item within the folder becomes a tool.

Chapter 4

Controlling How Notifications Appear

In previous versions of Windows, the *notification area* (also sometimes called the system tray or the status area) often becomes crowded with tiny icons—many of which don't "notify" you of anything. To deal with notification-area congestion, Windows 7, by default, keeps a few icons visible at all times but hides the icons that you aren't actually using. And unlike in previous Windows versions, the notification area doesn't consume an increasingly large chunk of the taskbar; new icons are corralled in a box that appears only when you click the arrow at the left end of the notification area to display the hidden items.

You can personalize this behavior in the Notification Area Icons control panel. To get there, display the hidden notification area icons and click Customize. Alternatively, begin typing **notification** in the Start menu search box or the Control Panel search box, and then click Notification Area Icons.

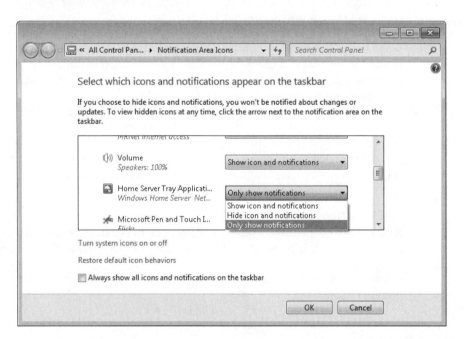

For each notification area icon, you can select one of three options:

- **Show Icon And Notifications**   Selecting this option displays the icon on the taskbar at all times.

- **Hide Icon And Notifications**   With this option, the icon appears only when you click the arrow at the left end of the notification area. Notifications from the program are squelched.

- **Only Show Notifications**   Like the previous option, this one hides the icon, but it allows its program to pop up notification messages.

The system icons (Clock, Volume, Network, Power, and Action Center) can be remanded to the box of hidden icons by selecting either of the last two options. But if you'd rather banish one or more of them altogether, click Turn System Icons On Or Off. The dialog box shown in Figure 4-8 appears.

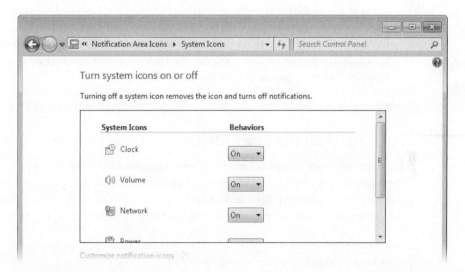

Figure 4-8 Windows displays four (or five, for battery-powered computers) notification area icons unless you modify the System Icons options here.

One final option can come in handy if you don't like having to click the arrow to display hidden icons (and you don't mind having a string of notification area icons as long as your arm). If you want to see all your notification area icons at all times, select Always Show All Icons And Notifications On The Taskbar. This is an all-or-nothing proposition, but remember that you can turn off any of the system icons you don't use. Also, some well-behaved programs have an option (usually accessible by clicking the notification area icon and choosing Options) to not display their icons.

INSIDE OUT
Drag notification area icons

Perhaps the easiest way to specify the appearance option for a notification area icon is to simply drag the icon—a technique you can apply to system icons (except Clock) as well as to other notification area icons. Dragging an icon to the hidden area sets it to Only Show Notifications, whereas dragging it to the taskbar is equivalent to selecting Show Icon And Notifications. Dragging also lets you specify the order of icons in each area.

INSIDE OUT
Use a keyboard shortcut for notification area tasks

If you're one of those users whose fingers never leave the keyboard, you can press Windows logo key+B to move the focus to the notification area. Use the arrow keys to highlight different icons on the taskbar, or, when the arrow is highlighted, press Spacebar to display the hidden icons. You can then use arrow keys to select an icon, and the Menu or Shift+F10 keys to display the icon's menu.

Personalizing the Start Menu

Although Windows 7 does not offer a "classic" Start menu as found in Windows XP and Windows Vista, it offers plenty of other personalization options. Begin your fine-tuning on the Start Menu tab of the Taskbar And Start Menu Properties dialog box (shown in Figure 4-9), which you reach by right-clicking the Start button and choosing Properties.

Many more options become available when you click Customize to display the Customize Start Menu dialog box, shown in Figure 4-10.

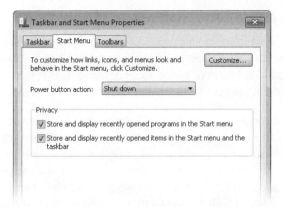

Figure 4-9 Options and check boxes on the Start Menu tab of the Taskbar And Start Menu Properties dialog box let you control the default action of the Power button and erase evidence of what you've been doing at your computer.

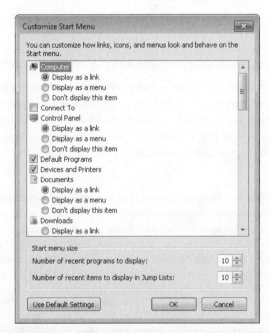

Figure 4-10 Don't fail to scroll down in this crowded dialog box to expose many more options.

Customizing the Left Side of the Start Menu

Quite apart from choosing which programs appear in the pinned programs section at the top of the left side of the Start menu (see "Adding and Removing Pinned Programs, Documents, and Folders" on page 113 for information about customizing that aspect of the menu), you have several choices that control the menu's left side.

For starters, your choices under Privacy on the Start Menu tab of Taskbar And Start Menu Properties (shown earlier in Figure 4-9) determine whether Windows keeps track of recently used programs and displays them below the pinned programs and whether Windows keeps track of recently opened documents and displays them as a Jump List associated with a pinned or recently used program. If you choose to keep these options enabled, you can proceed to the Customize Start Menu dialog box (shown in Figure 4-10) and use the settings under Start Menu Size to specify the maximum number of recent programs to include on the Start menu (the allowable range is 0 through 30) and the maximum number of recent items to include on each Jump List (0 through 60).

INSIDE OUT   Control which programs are included in the recent list

The list of recently used programs—the items that appear below the pinned programs on the left side of the Start menu—is controlled by Windows. The list includes only shortcuts to executable files you open, such as .exe files and .msc files. The following items are excluded by default (for more information, see Knowledge Base article 279767, "Frequently Used Programs Not Automatically Added to the Start Menu," at *w7io.com/0401*):

- Programs listed in the AddRemoveApps value of the registry key HKLM\Software\Microsoft\Windows\CurrentVersion\Explorer\FileAssociation. By default, the following items are excluded: Setup.exe, Install.exe, Isuninst.exe, Unwise.exe, Unwise32.exe, St5unst.exe, Msoobe.exe, Lnkstub.exe, Control.exe, Werfault.exe, Wlrmdr.exe, Guestmodemsg.exe, Msiexec.exe, Dfsvc.exe, and Wuapp.exe. By modifying this registry value, you can tailor the exclusion list to suit your needs.

- Items whose shortcut names include any of the following text: Documentation, Help, Install, More Info, Readme, Read Me, Read First, Setup, Support, What's New, or Remove. This list of exclusion strings is specified in the AddRemoveNames value of HKLM\Software\Microsoft\Windows\CurrentVersion\Explorer\FileAssociation.

- Items in the Games folder (Professional, Ultimate, and Enterprise editions only). Apparently to prevent workers who goof off from getting in trouble, business editions of Windows 7 exclude games from the list of recently used programs.

Other options scattered about the Customize Start Menu dialog box (all selected by default) determine the appearance and behavior of the left side of the Start menu:

- **Sort All Programs Menu By Name**   When this option is selected, Windows always sorts the All Programs menu alphabetically. Clear this option to display the menu in the order that items were added to it, or in the order you create by moving items around the menu.

- **Use Large Icons**   Clear this option if you want to fit more items on the left side.

- **Enable Context Menus And Dragging And Dropping**   When this option is selected, you can move items on the left side of the menu and on the All Programs menu by dragging. In addition, context menus (which appear when you right-click an item on the left side of the menu or on the All Programs menu) are enabled. Clearing this option disables both capabilities.

- **Highlight Newly Installed Programs**   When this option is selected, new programs are highlighted with a colored background so that they're easy to find; if you find that distracting, clear the option.

- **Open Submenus When I Pause On Them With The Mouse Pointer**   When this option is selected, Jump Lists and cascading menus appear on the right side of the Start menu when you hover the mouse; when this option is cleared, you must click the arrow to display these items.

Customizing the Right Side of the Start Menu

The right side of the Start menu has an assortment of buttons that open various data folders and system folders. Options in Customize Start Menu (shown in Figure 4-10) let you add to or subtract from this collection, and they let you control the behavior of certain items.

Chapter 4

INSIDE OUT   Change your Start menu picture

The picture that appears at the top of the right side of the Start menu is the one associated with your user account (the one that also appears on the Welcome screen). If you're not happy with it, click it. That takes you to the User Accounts section of Control Panel, where you can specify a different picture.

Choosing Link, Menu, or No Show   Several of the items in the Customize Start Menu list offer you the choice of Display As A Link, Display As A Menu, and Don't Display This Item. The first option displays a button that opens the folder in Windows Explorer, whereas the second option displays a button that opens the folder's contents as a submenu sprouting from the side of the Start menu. Following is a list of folders you can customize in this manner:

- Computer
- Control Panel
- Documents
- Downloads
- Games

- Music
- Personal Folder
- Pictures
- Recorded TV
- Videos

INSIDE OUT   Use links and submenus interchangeably

You can have it both ways. If you opt for submenus, you can still open items in Windows Explorer. Just right-click and choose Open.

Displaying Other Folders   Other folders don't offer the link vs. submenu option, but your Start menu customization is not complete until you decide whether to include any of these folders for single-click access:

- Favorites Menu (displays your Favorites menu as a cascading submenu)
- Homegroup (displays shared resources on your home network)
- Network (displays computers and devices on your network)
- Recent Items (displays your 15 most recently opened documents, from all applications)
- Default Programs (opens the Control Panel tool for specifying which program opens each document type)
- Devices And Printers (opens the Control Panel tool for managing your computer hardware)
- System Administrative Tools (displays a menu of advanced system-management programs)

- Connect To (displays a list of available network connections)

- Help (opens Help And Support)

Displaying the Run Command   The Run command, a perennial favorite of computer enthusiasts, is no longer a standard Start menu feature. You can make sure it's still part of your Start menu by selecting Run Command in the Customize Start Menu dialog box.

You might find you can live comfortably without the Run command. When you're tempted to type a program in the Run dialog box, try typing it in the Start menu search box instead. The Search feature won't always get you where you want to go (it's no good when you need a command-line switch, for example), but it's more versatile than you might expect. Typically, you can run an executable by simply typing its name in the search box and pressing Enter, just as you would in the Run dialog box. On the other hand, the Run dialog box remembers command strings that you have entered before, and the search box has nothing to replace that.

INSIDE OUT   Open the Run dialog box with a keypress

Whether or not your Start menu includes it, you can always get to the Run dialog box by pressing Windows logo key+R.

Controlling Where the Search Box Searches

Two options in the Customize Start Menu dialog box let you customize the behavior of the Start menu search box:

- **Search Other Files And Libraries**   The default setting, Search With Public Folders, includes in a Start menu search the same document files and folders that are included in other searches. (For details, see "Configuring Search and Indexing Options" on page 368.) With the other settings, you can limit the scope of a search to exclude public folders, or you can completely disable the search of documents and folders.

- **Search Programs And Control Panel**   With this option selected (the default setting), searches look for program names and Control Panel tools or tasks that match your search text.

For more information, see "Searching from the Start Menu" on page 379.

Chapter 4

Mastering Window Management with Windows 7 Tricks

Windows 7 includes a host of keyboard shortcuts and mouse gestures that greatly simplify the everyday tasks of managing windows: resizing, moving, minimizing, switching, and so on. These new methods are easily learned and remembered—but they're not easily discovered. In this section, we'll show you the way.

And don't worry: All the keyboard shortcuts and other tricks you've used in previous versions of Windows continue to work the same way in Windows 7.

Resizing and Moving Windows

New mouse gestures in Windows make it easy to work with certain windows without being distracted by the clutter of others:

- *Aero Snap* has three functions. The first one makes it easy to maximize a window or restore it to its previous size and position. Simply drag the title bar to the top of the screen to maximize it, or drag the title bar away from the top edge to restore it. (Although Windows has long offered comparable capability with the Maximize and Restore buttons in the title bar, this new gesture offers a much bigger target. This feature also makes it possible to move a maximized window from one screen to another on a multimonitor system.)

  The second Aero Snap function makes it easy to split the screen space between two windows for side-by-side editing or comparisons: drag a window title bar to the left edge of the screen, and it snaps to fill the left half of the screen. (Note that the window resizes when the mouse pointer hits the edge of the screen. To use this feature with minimal mouse movement, start your drag action by pointing at the title bar near the edge you're going to snap to.) Drag a title bar to the right edge to fill the right half of the screen. Begin dragging a window that has been resized this way away from the edge of the screen, and it returns to its previous size and position.

  The third function is useful if you want full-height, side-by-side windows but you don't want them to fill exactly half the screen width. It's also good for obtaining maximum window height without making text lines too long to read, especially on widescreen monitors. Drag the top window border (not the title bar) to the top edge of the screen, or drag the bottom border to the bottom edge of the screen. With either action, when you reach the edge the window snaps to full height, without changing its width. When you drag the border away from the window edge, the opposite border snaps to its previous position.

- *Aero Shake* minimizes all windows except the one you want to use. To do that, point to the window's title bar, hold down the mouse button, and quickly move it back and forth a few times. Suddenly, all windows except that one retreat to the taskbar.

This one takes a bit of practice, but once you get the hang of it, you'll probably use it often. It requires only three "shakes"—a smooth left, right, left motion is best—not maniacal shaking.

> **Note**
>
> Although the names of these features include the word *Aero*, you do not need to have Aero enabled to use these mouse gestures. Without Aero, you lose some of the associated visual effects, but the outcomes are the same.

Windows 7 includes keyboard shortcuts that correspond with the preceding mouse gestures. These are shown in Table 4-1.

Table 4-1 Keyboard Shortcuts and Mouse Gestures for Resizing and Moving Windows

Task	Keyboard Shortcut	Mouse Gesture
Maximize	Windows logo key+ Up Arrow	Drag title bar to top of screen
Resize window to full screen height without changing its width	Shift+Windows logo key+Up Arrow	Drag top or bottom border to edge of screen
Restore a maximized or full-height window	Windows logo key+ Down Arrow	Drag title bar or border away from screen edge
Minimize a restored window	Windows logo key+ Down Arrow	Click the Minimize button
Snap to the left half of the screen	Windows logo key+ Left Arrow*	Drag title bar to left edge
Snap to the right half of the screen	Windows logo key+ Right Arrow*	Drag title bar to right edge
Move to the next monitor to the left	Shift+Windows logo key+Left Arrow	Drag title bar
Move to the next monitor to the right	Shift+Windows logo key+ Right Arrow	Drag title bar
Minimize all windows except the active window (press again to restore windows previously minimized with this shortcut)	Windows logo key+ Home	"Shake" the title bar
Minimize all windows	Windows logo key+M	
Restore windows after minimizing	Shift+Windows logo key+M	

* Pressing this key repeatedly cycles through the left, right, and restored positions. If you have more than one monitor, it cycles these positions on each monitor in turn.

Chapter 4

The new taskbar in Windows 7 also uses a new trick to expose the traditional window menu: hold the Shift key as you right-click a taskbar button. For a button that represents a single window, the menu includes commands to Restore, Move, Size, Minimize, Maximize, and Close the window. Shift+right-clicking a grouped taskbar button displays commands to arrange, restore, minimize, or close all windows in the group.

INSIDE OUT   Disable Aero Snap and Aero Shake

If you find it disconcerting to have windows snap to a certain size and position when you drag their title bars, you can disable Aero Snap. Unfortunately, the setting for doing so is no more obvious than the mouse gestures themselves. In the Start menu search box or in Control Panel, type **mouse** and then click Change How Your Mouse Works. Near the bottom of the window that appears, select Prevent Windows From Being Automatically Arranged When Moved To The Edge Of The Screen. Selecting this option disables Aero Snap and Aero Shake altogether, including keyboard shortcuts.

Viewing the Desktop and Gadgets

Sometimes you need to get to the bottom of things, whether it's to use a desktop icon, view a desktop gadget, or simply enjoy your gorgeous desktop background. Windows 7 has some ways to simplify these tasks.

If you're using Aero, you can view the desktop with an overlay of outlines representing all open windows, as shown in Figure 4-11; simply point to the Show Desktop tool, the empty space at the right end of the taskbar. (If your taskbar is on the left or right side of the screen, Show Desktop is at the bottom.) When you move the mouse pointer away, the previous window arrangement returns. You can get the same effect by pressing Windows logo key+Spacebar.

For a more lasting effect, click Show Desktop, and all windows are hidden. (This works with or without Aero enabled.) To restore the previous arrangement, click Show Desktop again. If you prefer to use the keyboard, Windows logo key+D toggles between these two views.

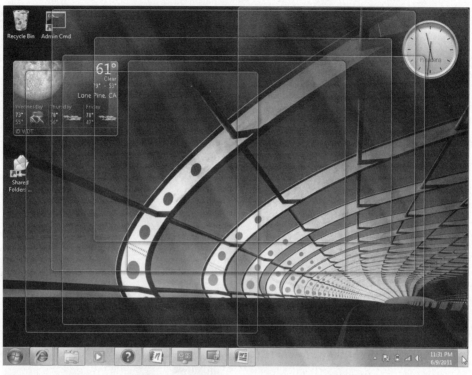

Figure 4-11 View the desktop, including gadgets, without a single mouse click.

You can bring your gadgets to the fore without minimizing or hiding your open windows; simply press Windows logo key+G. For more information about desktop gadgets, see "Using and Customizing Desktop Gadgets" on page 160.

Switching Between Windows

In addition to the taskbar-centric methods described in "Switching Tasks" on page 114, the time-honored task-switching keyboard shortcuts continue to work in Windows 7. Alt+Tab cycles between the open windows (and, with Aero enabled, invokes Aero Peek); Shift+Alt+Tab reverses the order. Windows logo key+Tab cycles through the open windows by using the visually flashy Flip 3D feature introduced in Windows Vista.

Personalizing Theme Elements: Visuals and Sounds

The most obvious way to personalize your Windows experience is to customize its visual appearance—the desktop background, the window colors, and so on—and to select the sounds that Windows uses to let you know what it's up to. These settings are made in the aptly named Personalization, a Control Panel tool that appears when you right-click the desktop and choose Personalize. You can also open Personalization, which is shown in Figure 4-12, by starting to type **personalization** in the Start menu search box or in the Control Panel search box, and then clicking the Personalization link that appears.

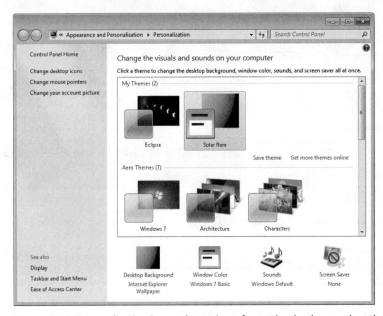

Figure 4-12 Personalization is your home base for setting backgrounds, colors, sounds, screen savers, desktop icons, and mouse pointers.

A *theme* in Windows 7 is an *über* configuration that combines and names the various personalization settings that you can make. Themes can incorporate the following:

- Desktop background

- Window color

- Settings that you make in the "advanced" Window Color And Appearance dialog box

- Sound scheme

- Screen saver

- Desktop icons

- Mouse pointer scheme

Note that these are all settings that pertain to your own profile; that is, they're specific to your user account. Settings that apply to all users at your computer, such as screen resolution, are not included in the current theme.

Windows 7 includes some terrific predefined themes, and you can select one simply by clicking it in Personalization. (Alternatively, type **theme** in the Start menu search box, and then click on Change The Theme when it appears in the search results.) The theme is applied right away, so if you don't like what you see and hear, you can select another before you close Personalization.

For information about saving your own settings as a theme and using themes that others have created, see "Saving, Sharing, and Finding Theme Settings" on page 152.

Understanding and Using Windows Aero

This chapter contains several references to *Windows Aero*, which is the default graphical user interface in most editions of Windows. The Aero interface uses *desktop composition* to achieve effects such as these:

- Transparent window frames

- Live previews of running programs via buttons on the taskbar

- Live previews of the windows that you can switch to by pressing Alt+Tab

- Flip 3D—a feature that shows all open windows (and the desktop) as a three-dimensional stack when you press the Windows logo key+Tab

- Smoother window dragging

- Interactive window controls (Close buttons that glow on hover, for example)

- Animated window closings and openings

With desktop composition on, applications write to video card memory buffers instead of directly to the screen, and the Desktop Window Manager feature of Windows 7 arranges the video surfaces in the appropriate order and presents the results to the screen.

In a nutshell, the requirements to use Aero are as follows:

- Windows 7 Home Premium, Professional, Ultimate, or Enterprise (Aero is not available with Windows Starter edition, and only a subset of Aero features is available in Windows 7 Home Basic)

- A DirectX 9–class graphics processing unit (GPU) with a Windows Display Driver Model (WDDM) 1.0 or higher display driver

- An Aero-based theme (one from the Aero Themes category in Personalization or one based on any of those themes)

Turning Aero Off

Even if you're not wild about transparency and animation, there's plenty to like about Aero. Smoother window dragging, the preview icons on the taskbar, and the improved task-switching features are well worth the price of admission—for most users. Nevertheless, admission is not entirely free; the Aero interface uses more graphics memory than the non-Aero interface—especially because achieving smoother window movement requires Aero to store the contents of all open windows in video memory, not just the windows that are currently visible.

If Aero slows you down or annoys you for any other reason, you can turn it off. In Personalization, choose any of the themes in the Basic And High Contrast Themes category. For a solid, if stolid, user interface that retains the new look and feel of Windows 7 without taxing your graphics subsystem, choose Windows 7 Basic.

What if you like transparency but don't care for the animated opening and closing of windows or certain other effects? In the Start menu search box, type **effects** and then click Adjust The Appearance And Performance Of Windows. Clearing the Animate Windows When Minimizing And Maximizing check box, on the Visual Effects tab in Performance Options, turns off these animated transitions. Other options let you squelch other unwanted Aero effects.

Customizing the Desktop Background

You can perk up any desktop with a background image. Your background can be supplied by a graphics file in any of several common formats (.bmp, .gif, .jpg, .png, and .tif). And you're not stuck with a static image, either. You can set up a slide show of images, and you can even use an RSS feed to supply new images.

To select a background, right-click the desktop, choose Personalize from the shortcut menu, and then click Desktop Background. The Picture Location box in Desktop Background (shown in Figure 4-13) provides a selection of useful categories. The Windows Desktop Backgrounds category itself is divided into several image categories. The Top Rated Photos category includes pictures from your own Pictures library to which you've assigned a four-star or five-star rating. You might want to maximize the dialog box to get a better look at the offerings.

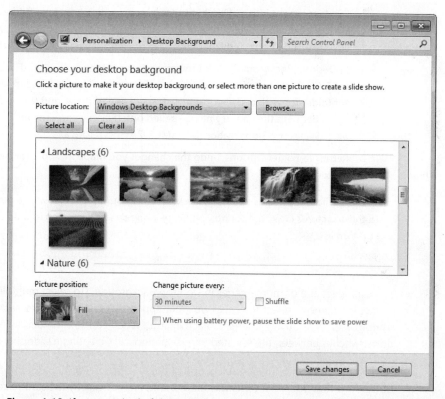

Figure 4-13 If you get tired of the wallpaper selections that come with Windows, you can always use your own pictures instead.

If you don't find what you need, click Browse. Folders to which you navigate via the Browse button will subsequently appear in the Location list, making it easy for you to go back and grab a different image from the same folder.

Chapter 4

INSIDE OUT
Find more great photographs hidden in your Windows installation

In the Windows Desktop Backgrounds picture location, you might've noticed a category with your country name or region as its name; the category includes a number of photographs taken in that place. With a little digging, you can find pictures of other places already installed on your hard drive. To do so, follow these steps:

1. Display "super-hidden" files. In the Start menu search box, type **folder options**. On the View tab of Folder Options, select Show Hidden Files, Folders, And Drives and clear Hide Protected Operating System Files (Recommended). Click Apply.

2. In Desktop Background, click Browse, and navigate to %Windir%\Globalization\MCT. (On most systems, %Windir% is C:\Windows.) The MCT folder has a subfolder for each installed country. Expand one of these, and then select the subfolder with the country name spelled out. (For example, the full path might be C:\Windows\Globalization\MCT\MCT-ZA\South Africa.)

3. Return to Folder Options, undo the changes you made in step 1 (or simply click Restore Defaults), and click OK.

The newly found pictures appear in Desktop Background. And it's easy to get back to these pictures later; the country name now appears as an option in the Picture Location list.

You can select one or more images in Desktop Background. (To select multiple images, click a category name or select the check box that appears when you point to each image you want to use. Alternatively, Ctrl+click each image.) When you select multiple images, Windows switches between the selected images periodically, creating a slide show effect.

After you choose your images, select one of the five Picture Position options to let Windows know how you want to handle images that are not exactly the same size as your screen resolution.

Then, if you've selected more than one image, specify how often you want Windows to change the background; the settings range from 10 seconds to 1 day. Selecting Shuffle causes the backgrounds to be chosen randomly from your selected images; otherwise, Windows cycles through the images in the order in which they appear in Desktop Background.

INSIDE OUT   Use pictures from an RSS feed

If you want an ever-changing collection of pictures to use as your desktop background, you can configure a theme to obtain images from an RSS feed. If you post your own photos to a photo-sharing site, for example, you could configure your computer to pick up those pictures and use them. (Not every photo feed works, however. You must use one that includes the photo as an enclosure. Flickr is one service that uses enclosures.) Because Windows 7 doesn't provide an interface for enabling RSS-fed images as desktop backgrounds, the easiest way to set one up is to edit an existing .theme file that includes a slide show. Open it in Notepad. Then, in the [Slideshow] section, remove the ImagesRootPath line and all Item*n*Path lines. Replace them with a line like this (using the URL to the RSS feed, of course):

```
RSSFeed=http://www.example.com/rssfeed
```

For complete details about .theme files, see the MSDN article "Creating and Installing Theme Files" at *w7io.com/0402*.

Here are some other ways to change the wallpaper:

- Right-click an image file in Windows Explorer, Windows Photo Viewer, or Windows Live Photo Gallery and choose Set As Desktop Background. This centers the selected image.

- Right-click an image in Internet Explorer and choose Set As Background. This displays the selected image using the current picture position setting.

- Open any image file in Paint, open the Paint menu (the icon to the left of the Home tab), and choose Set As Desktop Background. A submenu lets you choose among Fill, Tile, and Center picture positions.

Selecting Colors and Modifying Color Schemes

With a beautiful desktop background in place, your next personalization step might be to select a complementary color for the window borders, Start menu, and taskbar. To do that, right-click the desktop, choose Personalize, and then click Window Color.

If you're using an Aero theme, Window Color And Appearance appears, as shown next. If none of the 16 choices meets your needs exactly, you can click Show Color Mixer and dial in your own blend of Hue, Saturation, and Brightness.

Chapter 4

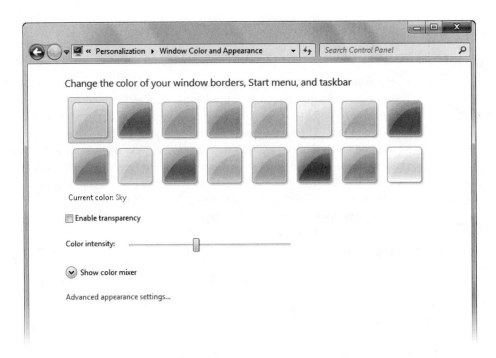

You can also adjust the transparency of your window frames. Dragging the Color Intensity slider to the right makes window frames darker and less transparent. If you want lighter colors but don't fancy transparency at all, clear the Enable Transparency check box. You might find this "Aero sans trans" approach convenient at times if you need to generate pictures of windows for presentation purposes and don't want the pictures to include distracting "behind the scenes" material.

If you're not using an Aero theme, clicking Window Color displays a different Window Color And Appearance dialog box, as shown next.

> **Note**
>
> This same dialog box appears when you click Advanced Appearance Settings in the Aero version of Window Color And Appearance. There's no particular reason to go there if you're using Aero, however, because most settings in this dialog box apply only to basic and high-contrast (that is, non-Aero) themes.

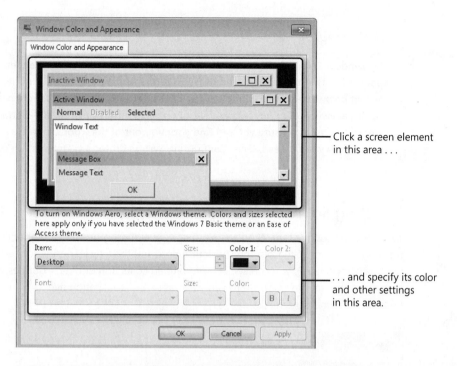

Click a screen element
in this area . . .

. . . and specify its color
and other settings
in this area.

Each basic and high-contrast theme comprises a group of settings that specifies fonts and sizes of certain interface elements, as well as colors. In the sample window of the Window Color And Appearance dialog box, click the screen element you want to change, and then use the lists and buttons at the bottom of the dialog box to make your color, font, and size selections. For title bars, you can specify two colors; Windows creates a gradient from Color 1 (at the left end of the title bar) to Color 2 (at the right end). The Item list includes some items that don't appear in the sample window, so you might want to review it in its entirety before you move on.

The Color button for each item opens a selection of standard colors. If you don't see the one you're looking for, click the Other button. Windows then displays a Color dialog box. Should you fail to find exactly the color you want in the Basic Colors palette, you can define your own custom colors. Change the color that appears in the Color box by adjusting the positions of the hue/saturation crosshair and the luminosity arrow or by specifying numeric values. When you have found the color you want, click Add To Custom Colors. If you want to replace an existing custom color, select it before you specify your new color.

Chapter 4

CAUTION

The Window Color And Appearance dialog box itself has a distinctly twentieth-century appearance. The squared-off windows in its sample area betray its ancient heritage, and the text below the sample window gives fair warning. You won't find Undo or Default buttons anywhere. Experiment carefully and keep your own mental cookie trail. If you want to be absolutely sure you can find your way out of the woods, create a restore point before you proceed. (See "Configuring System Protection Options" on page 461.)

Selecting Sounds for Events

To specify the sounds that Windows plays as it goes through its paces, right-click the desktop, choose Personalize from the shortcut menu, and then click Sounds. In the Sound dialog box (shown here), you can select a predefined collection of beeps, gurgles, and chirps that Windows plays in response to various system and application events. Simply choose an item in the Sound Scheme list.

In the same dialog box, you can customize the sound schemes. To see what sounds are currently mapped to events, scroll through the Program Events list. If an event has a sound associated with it, its name is preceded by a speaker icon, and you can click Test to hear it. To switch to a different sound, scroll through the Sounds list or click Browse. The list displays .wav files in %Windir%\Media, but any .wav file is eligible. To silence an event, select (None), the item at the top of the Sounds list.

If you rearrange the mapping of sounds to events, consider saving the new arrangement as a sound scheme. (Click Save As and supply a name.) That way, you can experiment further and still return to the saved configuration.

The Sound dialog box is also the place to silence the Windows Startup sound. Perhaps you've had this experience: You arrive a moment or two late for a meeting or class, discreetly turn on your computer at the end of the table or back of the room, and then cringe as your speakers trumpet your arrival. True, the Windows Startup sound is less raucous in Windows 7 than it was in Windows XP. But it's still a recognizable item, apt to cause annoyance in libraries, classrooms, concert halls, and other hushed venues. You can't substitute your own tune, but you can turn the startup sound off. In the Sound dialog box, clear the Play Windows Startup Sound check box.

INSIDE OUT   Mute your computer

If you like event sounds in general but occasionally need complete silence from your computer, choose No Sounds in the Sound Scheme list when you want the machine to shut up. (Be sure to clear the Play Windows Startup Sound check box as well.) When sound is welcome again, you can return to the Windows Default scheme—or to any other scheme you have set up. Switching to the No Sounds scheme won't render your system mute (you'll still be able to play music when you want to hear it), but it will turn off the announcement of incoming mail and other events.

If you want to control sound levels on a more granular level—perhaps muting some applications altogether and adjusting volume levels on others—right-click the volume icon in the notification area and choose Open Volume Mixer. (Alternatively, click the icon and then click Mixer.) Volume Mixer provides a volume slider (and a mute button) for each output device and each running program that emits sounds.

Choosing a Screen Saver

Screen savers don't save screens. (In long-gone days when screens were invariably CRTs and many offices displayed the same application at all hours of the working day, having an image move about during idle times probably did extend the service life of some displays.) And they certainly don't save energy. But they're fun to watch. To see the current offerings, right-click the desktop, choose Personalize from the shortcut menu, and then click Screen Saver.

> **Note**
>
> If you use a multimonitor setup, some of the screen savers supplied with Windows (specifically, 3D Text and Photos), unfortunately, "save" only the primary screen. The others go blank when the screen saver goes into action.

The Screen Saver Settings dialog box (shown here) includes a handy On Resume, Display Logon Screen check box. If you work in an environment where privacy is not a big concern, you can save yourself some hassle by clearing this check box. (Password entry might also be required when your computer wakes from sleep; for details, see "Customizing a Power Plan" on page 164.)

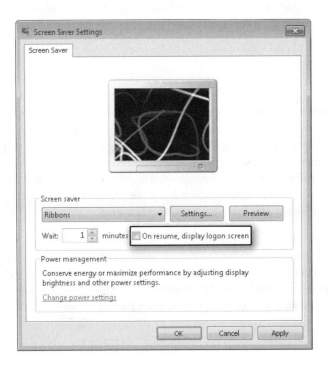

Customizing Mouse Pointers

As you have undoubtedly noticed, Windows has dispensed with the time-dishonored hour-glass mouse pointer. That might be a welcome development, particularly if you've logged a lot of hours with earlier versions of Windows. On the other hand, if you think an hourglass depicts the passage of time more unambiguously than a rolling doughnut, you can easily bring back the old shape. You can customize the entire array of pointer shapes your system uses by right-clicking the desktop, choosing Personalize, and then clicking Change Mouse Pointers (in the left pane of Personalization, shown in Figure 4-12). On the Pointers tab of the Mouse Properties dialog box, you can select a pointer type in the Customize box, and then click Browse to select an alternative pointer shape. (The Browse button takes you to %Windir%\Cursors and displays files with the extensions .cur and .ani. The latter are animated cursors.)

Just as Windows encapsulates a collection of sound choices as a sound scheme, it wraps up a gamut of pointer shapes as a mouse-pointer scheme. The system comes with a generous assortment of predefined schemes, making it easy for you to switch from one set of pointers to another as needs or whims suggest. Figure 4-14 shows the list.

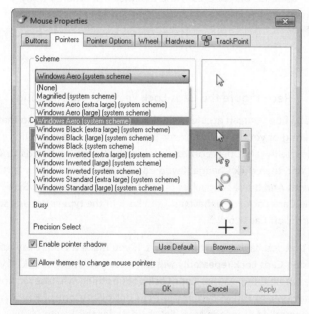

Figure 4-14 Some of the predefined mouse-pointer schemes are better suited for challenging light conditions than the default (Windows Aero) scheme.

If you sometimes use your portable computer in lighting conditions that make it hard for you to find the pointer, consider switching to one of the large or extra large schemes. If nothing else, those will give your eyeballs a larger target to pursue.

For something perhaps more novel than large or animated pointers, try one of the inverted schemes. These make your mouse pointer appear to pass behind the text on your screen rather than in front of it. (It's an acquired taste.)

Chapter 4

If you're inclined to roll your own mouse scheme (by using the Browse button to assign cursor files to pointer types), be sure to use the Save As command and give your work a name. That way you'll be able to switch away from it and back to it again at will.

It's worth taking a minute or two to explore the remaining tabs in the Mouse Properties dialog box. Some of the more useful options there are Button Configuration (on the Buttons tab), which lets you swap the roles of the left and right mouse buttons; Display Pointer Trails, in the Visibility section of the Pointer Options tab (this one makes the mouse cursor even easier to find in lousy lighting conditions); and Select A Pointer Speed, in the Motion section of the Pointer Options tab. This last option governs the rate at which the pointer travels in response to mouse movement. If you have switched to a high-DPI setting (see "Making Text Easier to Read" on page 157) and a higher-resolution display, you might also need to increase the pointer speed to accommodate the increased number of pixels on your screen.

INSIDE OUT   Reconfigure the Caps Lock key to avoid shouting

If you occasionally find yourself accidentally stuck in Caps Lock mode, so that your e-mails are shouting or your text documents look like a letter from the IRS, consider the following simple tweak. Open Control Panel, click Change Keyboards Or Other Input Methods, and then click Change Keyboards. On the Advanced Key Settings tab of the Text Services And Input Languages dialog box, choose Press The SHIFT Key. This action makes the Caps Lock key behave as it did back in the typewriter era, so that pressing Shift turns off Caps Lock.

Note, however, that you can't have it both ways. If you make the Shift key turn off Caps Lock, then pressing Caps Lock repeatedly will still leave you in Caps Lock. If you want to get rid of the whole thing, so that Caps Lock does nothing whatsoever, open Registry Editor and navigate to HKLM\System\CurrentControlSet\Control\Keyboard Layout. Add a Binary value called Scancode Map. Set the data for this key to

00000000 00000000 02000000 00003A00 00000000

Close Registry Editor, reboot, and you'll never be stuck in Caps Lock again.

Configuring Desktop Icons

A fresh, cleanly installed Windows 7 desktop (as opposed to one generated by an upgrade installation) includes a single lonely icon—Recycle Bin. If you want other system icons, right-click the desktop, choose Personalize, and click Change Desktop Icons (in the left pane). The Desktop Icon Settings dialog box, shown here, provides check boxes for five system folders—Computer, the root folder of your own profile (User's Files), Network, Recycle Bin, and Control Panel.

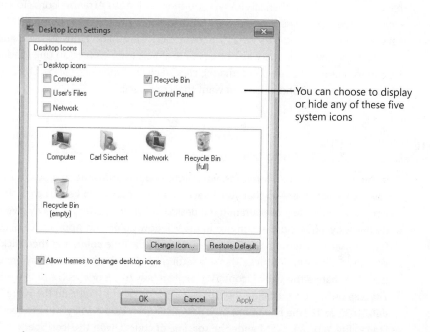

You can choose to display or hide any of these five system icons

If you're really into customization, you can change any of the five icons that appear in the large box in the center. Note that the Control Panel icon does not appear in this center box even if you select its check box; Windows doesn't provide a way to change it.

To change an icon, select it in the center box and click Change Icon. You'll find an interesting assortment of alternative icons in the file %Windir%\System32\Imageres.dll. (Be sure to use the horizontal scroll bar to see them all.) If none of these suit you, try browsing to %Windir%\System32\Shell32.dll.

Note

The icons you choose for system folders become part of a theme, if you save the configuration as described in the next section. However, other settings for desktop icons, including which ones you choose to display, their size, and their arrangement, are not saved in the theme file, allowing you to safely change themes without the risk of changing any of these customizations.

Chapter 4

After you've populated your desktop with icons, you might want to control their arrangement. If you right-click the desktop, you'll find two commands at the top of the shortcut menu that can help in this endeavor. To make your icons rearrange themselves when you delete one of their brethren, click View and then click Auto Arrange Icons. To ensure that each icon keeps a respectable distance from each of its neighbors (and that the whole gang stays together at the left side of your screen), click View, Align Icons To Grid. And if your icons occasionally get in the way (for example, if you want to take an unimpeded look at the current desktop background image), click View, and then click Show Desktop Icons. (Return to this command when you want the icons back.)

INSIDE OUT   Customize icon spacing and size

If you're really into desktop icons, you might find it worthwhile to move the ones you have closer together—so that you'll have room for more or to keep the current collection from completely overrunning the desktop. The most effective way we've found to do this is by adjusting the icon size in the Window Color And Appearance dialog box for non-Aero themes. (In the Start menu search box, type **color**, and then click Change Window Colors And Metrics.) The Size setting for the Icon item, curiously enough, does not change the size of icons. (We explain how to change icon size in a moment.) The Size setting does change the icons' spacing, however. Reducing the value from the default 32 to 16 (the minimum) produces a compact icon display without sacrificing readability. You can also change the spacing, of course, with the Icon Spacing (Horizontal) and Icon Spacing (Vertical) items, which have a default value of 43.

To adjust the icon size, click the desktop, hold the Ctrl key, and then turn the mouse scroll wheel forward or back. This method produces a continuous zoom effect; if you want to get back to a standard size, right-click the desktop, click View, and select a size.

To change the sort order of your desktop icons, right-click the desktop and click Sort By. You can sort on any of four attributes: Name, Size, Item Type, or Date Modified. Sorting a second time on any of these attributes changes the sort order from ascending to descending (or vice versa).

Saving, Sharing, and Finding Theme Settings

If you've got all the visual and aural aspects of your profile set up just the way you want them, and you want to be able to experiment further but still return to the current settings, it's time to revisit Personalization (right-click the desktop and choose Personalize), shown earlier in Figure 4-12 on page 138. At the top of the themes list, in the My Themes category, you'll see Unsaved Theme if you made changes to whatever theme was previously in effect. To make those changes reusable, click Save Theme and supply a name. (The name you furnish is the display name that appears in Personalization; you needn't follow restrictive file-naming rules that prohibit several common punctuation symbols.)

If you make additional changes, you'll once again generate an Unsaved Theme entry. There's no limit to the number of themes you can create. Windows saves each group of settings as a .theme file in your %LocalAppData%\Microsoft\Windows\Themes folder. (A .theme file is a standard text file that describes all the theme settings. For complete details about theme files, see "Creating and Installing Theme Files" at *w7io.com/0402*.) You can delete unwanted items from the My Themes list; simply right-click the item you no longer want and choose Delete Theme. Note that you can't delete the theme that's currently in use.

After you create a theme you like, you might want to use it on your other computers or share it with other users. Because a .theme file is just a text file, it doesn't contain the graphic images of your desktop, the sound files you use for various events, or other neces-sary files that make up the entire theme experience. For the purpose of sharing themes, Windows uses a .themepack file, which includes the .theme file as well as all other nonstan-dard theme elements. A .themepack file uses the standard compressed folder (.zip archive) format to envelop its component files. To create a .themepack file of an item in My Themes, first select it to make it the current theme. Then right-click it and choose Save Theme For Sharing. Unless you specify otherwise, Windows saves the .themepack file in the default save location of your Documents library.

To use a theme that was saved in .theme or .themepack format, simply double-click it. (Of course, a .theme file won't offer the full experience if the theme's components aren't avail-able on your computer in folders to which you have access.)

Because themes are so easily portable, you can find many compelling Windows 7 themes online. Start your quest by clicking Get More Themes Online (under My Themes in Person-alization), where Microsoft offers a nice selection.

Chapter 4

CAUTION !

If you search for themes elsewhere on the Internet, be sure to download theme files only from people or companies you know and trust. Some theme elements (most notably, screen savers, which include executable program code) have long been notori-ous vectors for viruses and spyware. (A study released in 2009 by the security software vendor McAfee found "screen savers" to be the web's most dangerous search term, because the results pages often lead to malware downloads. As Windows 7 gains in popularity, searches for "free themes" are likely to produce risky results too. The study is available as a PDF file at *w7io.com/0403*.) Also, other types of malware could be dis-guised as a theme pack. (That is, you think that by double-clicking a file you're install-ing a theme, but you could in fact be installing a nefarious program instead.)

INSIDE OUT   Change the Windows logon screen

You won't find an option in Control Panel's Personalization tool that allows you to change the image that appears when you log on to Windows. You can change this aspect of the Windows interface, however, by making a small registry edit. For details, see "Customizing the Logon Screen" on page 670.

Configuring Your Display

The previous sections about themes and desktop backgrounds describe how to put eye-pleasing elements on your screen. Another important personalization step is to properly configure your display hardware for your purposes and preferences, which is the subject of the following sections.

Configuring Screen Resolution

Changing the screen resolution changes the number of pixels that Windows displays on your screen. Increasing the resolution—say, from 1024 by 768 to 1600 by 1200—lets you see more action on your display: more windows, more text, larger graphics, and so on—with various tradeoffs. Text at a given point size appears smaller at higher resolutions. A mouse at a given pointer speed requires more arm and wrist motion to traverse a high-resolution screen than a low-resolution one. And higher resolutions use more video memory. In short, the right resolution for you depends on your hardware, your preferences, and visual acuity.

To change the screen resolution, right-click the desktop and choose Screen Resolution. To make a change, click Resolution and drag the slider up or down. (See Figure 4-15.)

> **Note**
> A change in screen resolution affects all accounts at a particular computer, not just the account that makes the change.

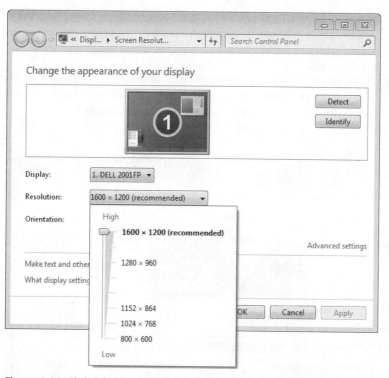

Figure 4-15 Click Advanced Settings to adjust the color depth or examine the drivers for the display adapter and monitor.

Configuring a Multimonitor Display

Extending your desktop across two or more monitors can be a great way to increase your productivity. You can do your main work on one screen and keep auxiliary information, e-mail, or even Windows Media Player open and visible on the second. Or if you work with large spreadsheets or database tables, you can spread them across multiple screens so that you can see more data without having to set your resolution to stratospheric levels.

If your display adapter supports two monitors (these days, most do), the Screen Resolution dialog box show two boxes, labeled 1 and 2, when you have a second monitor connected. (Of course, if you have more than two monitors attached, Windows displays a numbered box for each one.) You can click these boxes to configure the monitors independently. If adjusting the settings for monitor 1 appears to be affecting what you consider to be monitor 2, click Identify. Windows displays large white numerals on your screen temporarily

Chapter 4

to let you know which screen is which. If it happens that screen 2 is on the left of screen 1, drag the boxes in Screen Resolution so that they match the physical layout of your monitors.

Assuming you want to add screen space to your visual layout, be sure to select Extend These Displays in Multiple Displays. If you prefer to have your second monitor function as a duplicate display (for example, to make a presentation easier for a group of clients to see), select Duplicate These Displays.

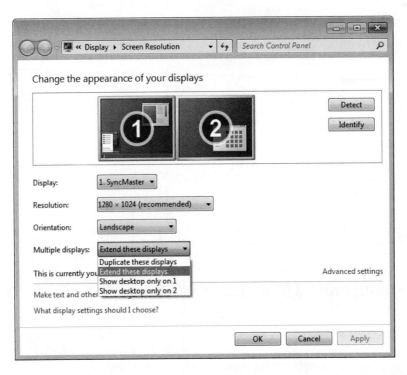

Some third-party programs exist to enhance your multimonitor experience. For example, with DisplayFusion from Binary Fortress Software *(w7io.com/0408)*, you can put a different desktop background on each monitor or have a single image span multiple monitors.

INSIDE OUT   Change multimonitor options with a keyboard shortcut

Windows logo key+P, the keyboard shortcut for switching to a network projector, also provides a quick and easy way to switch between multimonitor display arrangements.

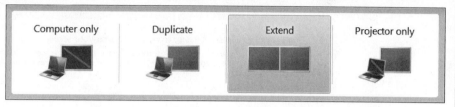

Making Text Easier to Read

In earlier versions of Windows, users who wanted larger text sometimes bumped up the point size for one or more screen elements. Scaling up this way was problematic, though, because not all elements of the Windows user interface could be scaled successfully. Dialog box text in particular was a problem, so users sometimes found themselves looking at large title bars and scroll bars and large menu text, but small dialog-box text. Windows 7 offers a better way.

If you like to work at high screen resolutions but you find yourself straining to read the text, you can try the following:

- Look for scaling ("zoom") commands in the text-centric programs you use. Many programs, including most modern word processors, include these scaling features. Scaling text up to a readable size this way is a good solution for particular programs but doesn't change the size of icon text, system menus (such as the Start menu), or system dialog boxes.

- To enlarge part of the screen, use the Magnifier tool. (For more information, see "Adjusting Ease of Access Options" on page 167.)

- Use the scaling options in the Display control panel—the "better way" offered by Windows 7. Adjusting the scaling to a higher level enables you to have readable text at higher screen resolutions.

Chapter 4

To adjust display scaling, right-click the desktop and choose Personalize. In Personalization, click Display, a link in the left pane. (Alternatively, type **display** in the Start menu search box and click Display.) Select one of the options shown here:

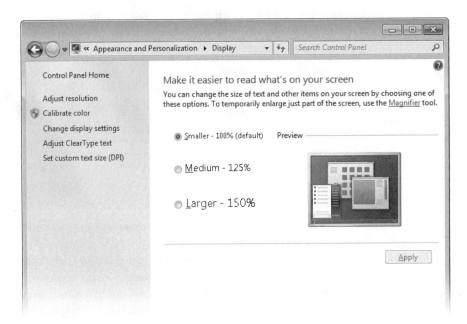

For a greater range of settings, as well as greater precision, click Set Custom Text Size (DPI). (DPI stands for *dots per inch*.) Figure 4-16 shows the Custom DPI Setting dialog box.

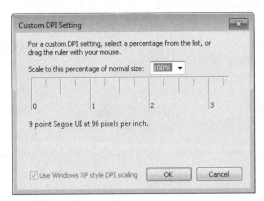

Figure 4-16 You can set the scaling from 100% to 500% of normal (96 DPI).

To change the scaling factor, drag any part of the ruler. Alternatively, you can select a value in the Scale To This Percentage Of Normal Size list or type directly in this box. What scaling factor is right? It depends on many things—the size and resolution of your screen, the programs you use, your eyes, and your preferences. You will likely need to try more than one combination of screen resolution and scaling factor to get your system exactly the way that works best for you.

The Use Windows XP Style DPI Scaling check box offers a measure of compatibility for (mostly older) applications that are not written to use high DPI settings. Some compromise is required: when selected, some elements (dialog box text or icons, for example) might not align or resize properly, whereas clearing this option causes blurry text in some applications. By default, for a DPI setting of 120 (125%) or lower, the option is selected; for larger sizes it is cleared.

When you change DPI scaling, you must log off before the change takes effect. After you log on again, test some text-centric applications to see if you like the result. If you don't, return to the Display dialog box and try another setting.

TROUBLESHOOTING

Some programs produce fuzzy text

If you're running Aero and have applied a nondefault font scaling factor, some of your older programs might produce fuzzy text. Newer DPI-aware programs get information about the current scaling factor from the operating system and adjust themselves accordingly. Older applications that were not designed with DPI scaling in mind assume they are running under the default scale of 96 DPI, and the operating system scales them. A side effect of this is that fonts and icons can sometimes appear fuzzy. If you find a particular program's display unsatisfactory, right-click its entry in the Start menu, choose Properties from the shortcut menu, and click the Compatibility tab. In the Settings section, select Disable Display Scaling On High DPI Settings.

Using Font Smoothing to Make Text Easier on the Eyes

ClearType is a font-smoothing technology that reduces jagged edges of characters, thus easing eye strain. Although it is optimized for LCD (flat panel) displays, ClearType is turned on by default on all systems, regardless of display type. Microsoft believes that ClearType improves readability on both cathode-ray tube (CRT) and LCD displays, but if you're a CRT user you should probably try turning ClearType off to see which works better for you. (You can also turn font-smoothing off altogether by clearing the Smooth Edges Of Screen Fonts check box on the Visual Effects tab of Performance Options, but it's hard to imagine any benefit from doing so.)

To check or change your font-smoothing settings, type **cleartype** in the Start menu search box, and then click Adjust ClearType Text. Doing so opens the ClearType Text Tuner, which, in its first screen, has a check box that turns ClearType on when it is selected. The ensuing screens that appear each time you click Next offer optometrist-style choices ("Which is better, number 1 or number 2?") to help you reach ClearType perfection.

Windows includes seven new fonts that are optimized for ClearType. The names of six of these—Constantia, Cambria, Corbel, Calibri, Candara, and Consolas—begin with the letter *c*—just to help cement the connection with ClearType. If you're particularly prone to eye fatigue, you might want to consider favoring these fonts in documents you create. (Constantia and Cambria are serif fonts, considered particularly suitable for longer documents and reports. The other four are sans serif fonts, good for headlines and advertising.) The seventh ClearType-optimized font, Segoe UI, is the typeface used for text elements throughout the Windows user interface. (Windows also includes a ClearType-optimized font called Meiryo that's designed to improve the readability of horizontally arrayed Asian languages.)

For information about how ClearType works, visit Microsoft's ClearType site, at *w7io.com/0404*.

Calibrating Your Display's Colors

To get the most accurate rendition of images and colors on your screen, you should calibrate it. You've probably noticed, but perhaps not fiddled with, the buttons on your monitor that control various display settings. A new tool included with Windows 7, Display Color Calibration, helps you to calibrate your screen using your monitor's display controls as well as various Windows settings. With Display Color Calibration, you set gamma, brightness, contrast, color balance, and other settings, all of which are explained in the on-screen descriptions.

To run Display Color Calibration, in the Start menu search box, type **display** and then click Calibrate Display Color. (Even easier, type **dccw**, the name of the executable file for Display Color Calibration, and press Enter.) Calibrate Color is also an option in the Display control panel. No matter how you start it, Display Color Calibration opens a full-screen application that leads you through the steps of adjusting your display by making settings and adjusting monitor controls until the images displayed at each step look their best.

Using and Customizing Desktop Gadgets

One of the most conspicuous new features in Windows Vista was Windows Sidebar, a repository for miniprograms (called *gadgets*) that can amuse, inform, and distract you all day long. Windows 7 continues to support gadgets, but they're no longer constrained to the sidebar along one edge of your screen; they can be scattered anywhere on your desktop.

You can easily add or remove gadgets whenever you feel the need for something new on your computer screen. The gadget gallery that comes with Windows includes about a dozen offerings, but it has a handy link to a much larger online gallery.

To add a gadget to your desktop, right-click the desktop and choose Gadgets to summon the gadget gallery.

For clues about what a gadget might do, select it and click Show Details. To install a gadget, you can either drag it to the desktop or right-click it and choose Add. After you have installed a gadget, you'll probably want to prod it with your mouse (try both buttons, and click on various parts) to see what tricks it knows and what options it offers. Each gadget is different, but they're all designed to make their features discoverable. Many gadgets sprout a wrench icon when you point to them; click it to make settings and customizations. Some gadgets (Weather, for example) include a Make Smaller or Make Larger icon, which changes the amount of information the gadget displays.

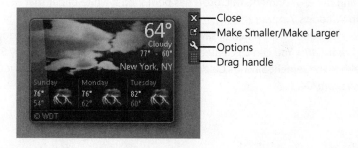

Chapter 4

Many gadgets rely on online updates (weather and stocks, for example). When you don't have an Internet connection, these gadgets show information from the last online update and include a time stamp at the bottom that shows how old the data is.

To remove a gadget, click the Close button. Gadgets that you close remain in the gallery for easy recovery; if you want to remove a gadget from your computer, open the gadget gallery, right-click the gadget, and choose Uninstall. If you'd rather hide your gadgets temporarily without removing them, right-click the desktop and choose View, Show Desktop Gadgets to remove the check mark and hide your gadgetry.

To get to the online gadget site, click Get More Gadgets Online in the bottom right corner of the gadget gallery. If you download a gadget from this site, it takes up residence in the gallery, so you can easily close it and reopen it whenever you want. The search box in the gadget gallery is also a list. By opening the list, you can filter the gallery to show recently installed gadgets or gadgets from particular publishers.

INSIDE OUT   Display desktop gadgets with a single keystroke

Bring all your gadgets to the foreground at any time by pressing Windows logo key+G. If you want to view just your gadgets without the clutter of other open windows, press Windows logo key+D. (Press it again to restore the windows.)

Setting Power and Sleep Options

Do power settings really make a difference? In a word, yes. You can not only achieve greater battery life on a portable computer with the appropriate settings, but you can save considerable amounts of energy on desktop computers. The green effect of reducing power consumption can be significant, whether you interpret "green" to mean saving dollars or saving the environment. Microsoft has published a white paper that describes the changes in Windows 7 power management and helps you to assess the energy savings, financial savings, and environmental savings of proper power management; download it from *w7io.com/0405*. You can calculate your own savings by using the Energy Star Computer Power Management Savings Calculator, a Microsoft Excel spreadsheet you can download at *w7io.com/0406*.

Selecting a Power Plan

Power management in Windows 7 is significantly different from power management in Windows XP, both in its user interface and in its under-the-hood operation. Windows provides three predefined power plans, and some computer manufacturers include additional predefined plans. To select a power plan, open Power Options (in the Start menu search box, type **power** and click Power Options), shown in Figure 4-17.

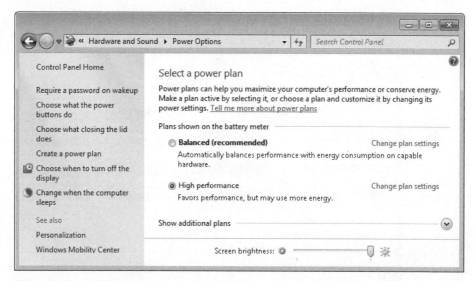

Figure 4-17 Use the Create A Power Plan link in the left pane to add to the list of ready-made power schemes. Click Change Plan Settings to adjust individual options for a plan.

On a portable computer, there's an easier way to switch plans: click the Power icon in the notification area and make your selection.

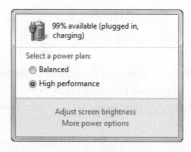

Customizing a Power Plan

To customize the current power plan, click one of the links in the left pane of Power Options or click Change Plan Settings next to the name of any plan. As you dig into Power Options, you'll discover a wealth of useful settings, especially on notebook computers, where you can make adjustments that are different based on whether a system is running on batteries or on AC power.

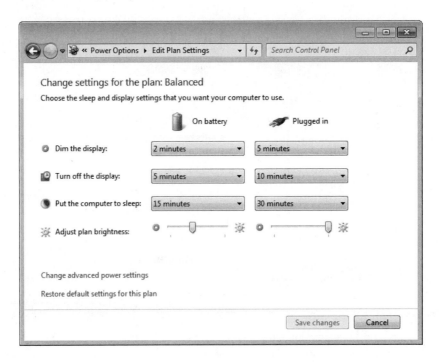

You can do additional fine-tuning by clicking Change Advanced Power Settings in the window shown.

> **Note**
>
> If you've made changes to a predefined power plan, you can restore its default settings by clicking Change Plan Settings and then clicking Restore Default Settings For This Plan. Not sure what those default settings are? The United States Environmental Protection Agency will tell you; visit *w7io.com/0407*.

Understanding Sleep States

When you click Choose What The Power Buttons Do (in the left pane of Power Options), you'll see that for each power switch, you can specify Do Nothing, Sleep, Hibernate, or Shut Down. What do these terms mean?

- Do Nothing disables the switch.

- Sleep switches to a low-power sleep state that allows quick resumption.

- Hibernate copies an image of memory to the hard disk and powers off the computer, enabling you to return to where you left off.

- Shut Down performs an orderly shutdown of Windows and switches off the power.

By default, when you choose Sleep, Windows 7 uses *hybrid sleep*, which combines the benefits of the low-power sleep state (the system uses just enough power to keep everything in volatile memory, ready to resume quickly) and hibernation (saves the contents of memory to a hard disk so that nothing is lost if power is shut off or the battery drains completely).

Setting Power Options with Powercfg

Windows 7 includes a command-line program called Powercfg that enables you to incorporate routine power-setting changes in scripts or batch files. This power user's power-management tool includes options that are not available in the graphical user interface. To see the full range of Powercfg's capabilities, open an elevated Command Prompt window (right-click Command Prompt and choose Run As Administrator). Then type **powercfg /?**. You might want to redirect output from this query to a text file (for example, by appending **>powercfg helptext.txt** to the command), because the list of options is long. Here are some you might find useful:

- To change the monitor timeout, disk timeout, standby timeout, or hibernate timeout value in the current power scheme, use **powercfg –x** *setting value*.

- To make a particular power scheme active on the system, use **powercfg –s** *Scheme_GUID*.

- To retrieve the name of the current power scheme, use **powercfg –getactivescheme**.

- To enable or disable hibernation, use **powercfg –h [on|off]**. Note that this is the only way to completely disable hibernation.

- To generate a report analyzing the system for common energy-efficiency and battery-life problems, close all applications, and then type **powercfg –energy.** After the program finishes running and the command prompt returns, type **energy-report.html**, and a diagnostic report opens in your web browser.

Chapter 4

Working with Fonts

The days when your choice of fonts ended just beyond Arial and Times New Roman are long gone; if you include all the language variants and style variants (bold, italic, and so on), Windows 7 comes with hundreds of fonts. Something else that is gone (and won't be missed): the Add Fonts dialog box, which has been in every version of Windows virtually unchanged since Windows 3.1.

The headquarters for font management is Fonts in Control Panel, which is shown next. From this list of fonts, you can select a font (or a font family, which appears as a stack) and then click Preview to open a window that shows the font's characters in sizes ranging from 12 point to 72 point. (A *point* is a printer's measurement that is still used in modern digital typography. There are 72 points to an inch.)

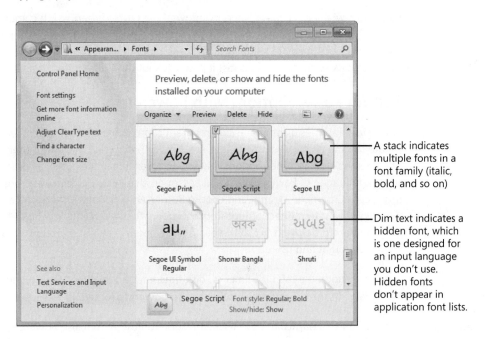

A stack indicates multiple fonts in a font family (italic, bold, and so on)

Dim text indicates a hidden font, which is one designed for an input language you don't use. Hidden fonts don't appear in application font lists.

The primary font format used by Windows is OpenType, which is a format jointly developed by Microsoft and Adobe as an extension of Apple's TrueType format. Windows also supports TrueType fonts and PostScript Type 1 fonts. To install a new font, you can drag its file from a folder or compressed .zip archive to Fonts in Control Panel. But it's not necessary to open Fonts; the simplest way to install a font is to right-click its file in Windows Explorer and choose Install. Because font file names are often somewhat cryptic, you might want to double-click the file, which opens the font preview window, to see what you're getting. If it's a font you want, click the Install button.

CAUTION

Download and install fonts only from people or companies you know and trust.

Note

PostScript Type 1 fonts normally consist of two or three files. The one you use to install the font—regardless of which method you use—is the .pfm file, whose file type is shown in Windows Explorer as Type 1 Font File.

Adjusting Ease of Access Options

The Windows family has a longstanding commitment to making computing accessible and easier to use for persons with vision, hearing, or mobility impairments. Windows 7 groups these options into the Ease Of Access Center, which you can find in Control Panel or by using its keyboard shortcut, Windows logo key+U.

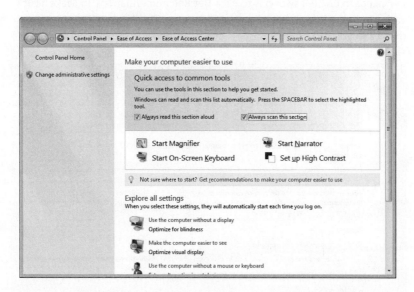

The Ease Of Access Center provides a prominent link to each of the following tools, which can be used alone or in combination:

- **Magnifier**   This tool enlarges part of the screen, making it easier for persons with vision impairments to see objects and read text. (You can also launch Magnifier with a keyboard shortcut: Press Windows logo key+plus sign to launch it and zoom in. Press again to zoom in more, or press Windows logo key+minus sign to zoom out.)

- **Narrator** This tool converts on-screen text to speech and sends it to your computer's speakers. This option allows people who are blind or have severe vision impairments to use Windows.

- **On-Screen Keyboard** This tool provides an alternate means for Windows users with impaired mobility to enter text using a pointing device. Options that appear when you click Options let you control how On-Screen Keyboard works—you can choose whether to select a letter by clicking, for example, or by allowing the pointer to pause over a key for a specific amount of time.

- **High Contrast** This tool uses a high-contrast color scheme (by default, white text on a black background) that makes it easier for visually impaired users to read the screen.

Many more tools—including Windows stalwarts Mouse Keys (uses the numeric keypad to control the mouse pointer), Sticky Keys (lets you press key combinations one key at a time), and Filter Keys (ignores repeated keystrokes)—are available through links at the bottom of the Ease Of Access Center. However, the easiest way to configure your computer for adaptive needs in one fell swoop is to click Get Recommendations To Make Your Computer Easier To Use, a link near the center of the page. The link launches a wizard, shown here, that walks you through the process of configuring accessibility options.

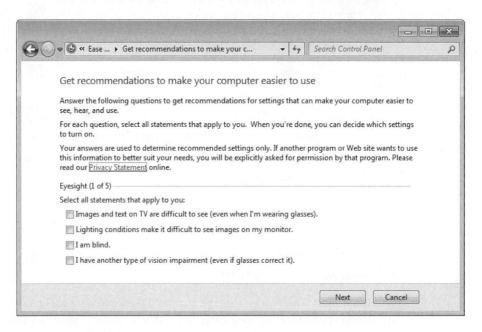

If you want accessibility options to be available at all times, even before logging on to the computer, click the Change Administrative Settings link in the left pane of the Ease Of Access Center. This option (shown next) applies any changes you make to the logon desktop. If you choose not to enable this option, you can still turn accessibility features on or off at the logon screen; click the small blue Ease Of Access icon in the lower left corner of the logon screen to display a list of available settings, and then press the Spacebar to enable each one.

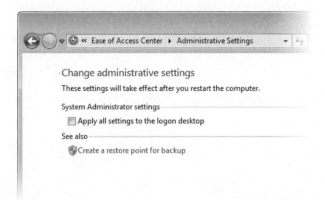

Windows 7 offers another useful accessibility tool in speech input. For details, see "Using Speech Recognition and Voice Commands" on page 1148.

Adding, Removing, and Managing Programs

You don't need a wizard or a Control Panel applet to install an application in Windows 7. Setting up a new program from a CD or DVD is typically a straightforward matter of inserting the disc and following the instructions that appear courtesy of your AutoRun settings. Setting up a program that you download is usually a matter of clicking Run or Open after the download has finished. In neither scenario do you need a wizard to hold your hand.

That's the theory, at any rate. In practice, there might be hurdles to surmount or hoops to jump through when it comes to installing programs. Potential complications come in two flavors:

- User Account Control (UAC)

- Compatibility issues

The first of these is usually no more than a minor annoyance. The second can be vexatious, but it usually arises only with programs designed for an earlier generation of operating system.

In this chapter, we'll survey the hoops and hurdles and everything else having to do with the addition, removal, updating, and management of applications in Windows 7. We'll also look at Windows XP Mode, a free download for Windows 7 (Professional, Enterprise, and Ultimate) that can let you run legacy applications that can't run directly in Windows 7.

What's in Your Edition?

With the exception of Windows XP Mode, all of the tools and techniques described in this chapter are available in all editions of Windows 7. Windows XP Mode requires Windows 7 Professional, Windows 7 Ultimate, or Windows 7 Enterprise.

Dealing with User Account Control

Rare exceptions aside, the rule in Windows 7 is this: To install a program, you need administrative credentials. Software installers—the programs that install programs—typically create files in system folders (subfolders of %ProgramFiles%) and keys in protected registry locations, and these are actions that require elevated privileges.

Installing the program files and registry keys in protected locations protects your programs (hence, you) from tampering by malicious parties, but unless you have disabled User Account Control altogether, you need to deal with UAC prompts to complete the process. If you install a program while running under an administrative account, a UAC prompt will request your consent for the actions the installer is about to undertake. If you install while running under a standard account, you will be asked to supply the name and password of an administrative user.

For more information about User Account Control, see "Preventing Unsafe Actions with User Account Control" on page 629.

Windows 7 employs installer-detection technology to determine when you have launched an installation process. This technology enables the operating system to request credentials at the time the process is launched rather than wait until the installer actually attempts to write to a protected location.

The system presumes that any process with a file name containing particular keywords (such as *install*, *setup*, or *update*) or whose data includes particular keywords or byte sequences is going to need elevated privileges to complete its work, so the UAC prompt appears as soon as the installer process begins. After you have satisfied the UAC mechanism, the process runs in the security context of TrustedInstaller, a system-generated account that has access to the appropriate secure locations.

The same technology that detects an installation process also recognizes when you're about to update or remove a program. So you can expect to see UAC prompts for these activities as well.

INSIDE OUT   Turn off Start menu notifications

After you install a program, Windows announces additions to the Start menu by high-lighting the changes on the menu itself. It's reasonably intelligent about this; it doesn't highlight additions that aren't programs (shortcuts to documents, for example), it removes the highlight for items that you ignore for at least a week, and it doesn't high-light anything that you install within an hour of installing Windows itself. Nevertheless, some users would rather it didn't highlight any Start menu changes. If you're in that camp, right-click the Start button and choose Properties. On the Start Menu tab of the Taskbar And Start Menu Properties dialog box, click Customize. Then, in the Customize Start Menu dialog box, clear Highlight Newly Installed Programs.

TROUBLESHOOTING

No UAC prompt appears, and the install fails

If installer-detection technology fails to detect your installer, and if your installer tries to write to a protected area (in file storage or the registry), your setup will fail—typi-cally with an error message like this:

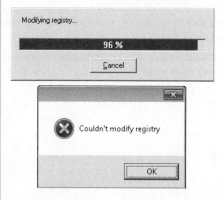

To solve this problem, first do whatever is necessary to back out of the failed instal-lation (click OK, Exit, Cancel, or whatever else seems appropriate). Then try to find the executable file for the installer. It will *not* be named Setup or Install (because if it were, it would not have evaded the detector), but it will be an .exe file. When you find it, right-click it in Windows Explorer and choose Run As Administrator. Supply your administrative credentials, and let the installer run.

Chapter 5

TROUBLESHOOTING

The setup process hangs on reboot

If you launch a setup program as a standard user and supply the name and password of an administrative account, and if the setup program requires a system reboot to complete installation, you might not be able to finish the installation unless you log back on (after the reboot) as that administrative user, rather than under your own standard-user account. Installer routines that include a reboot typically record post-reboot instructions in the registry key HKLM\Software\Microsoft\Windows\Current-Version\RunOnce. The value of the RunOnce key is, as the key name suggests, run one time—and then discarded. The hitch is that RunOnce values are executed only when an administrator logs on. If you log on as a standard user, the RunOnce instructions are ignored, and your setup process might appear to hang. The solution is to log off and log back on as an administrator. To forestall problems of this kind, you might want to adopt the practice of elevating your own account to administrative status, using the User Accounts section of Control Panel, before you begin installing applications. Afterward, if you're more comfortable running as a standard user, you can return to Control Panel and demote yourself.

Dealing with Compatibility Issues

Most recent application programs should install and run without problems in Windows 7. Certain older ones might not. Windows 7 attempts to recognize potential compatibility problems *before* you install. Immediately after running a program's installer, you might, for example, see a message like the one shown in Figure 5-1.

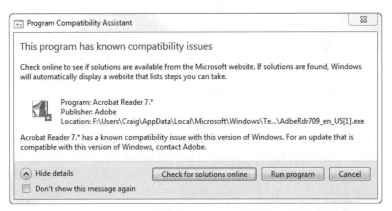

Figure 5-1 Windows flags some potential compatibility problems and recommends solutions before you install.

Problems of this kind commonly arise if you try to install an outdated version of an application. In such cases (as in this example), clicking Check For Solutions Online takes you to the application vendor's website, where you can download a later version that will run with no problem in Windows 7. If you're sure that no help is available online, however, and you want to try installing the software despite the potential compatibility problem, click Run Program.

If an installation routine runs but fails for any reason to complete successfully (in some cases, even if you simply cancel out of the setup process), you will likely see a Program Compatibility Assistant message, comparable to the one shown in Figure 5-2. If the Assistant is mistaken and you really have successfully installed your program, click This Program Installed Correctly. Otherwise, click Reinstall Using Recommended Settings. The Program Compatibility Assistant will then apply one or more compatibility tweaks (unfortunately, without telling you what it's doing) and try again to run your installer.

Figure 5-2 The Program Compatibility Assistant appears when an installation program does not reach a successful conclusion.

In some cases, a program written for an earlier version of Windows might install successfully but still not run well. In such situations, the Program Compatibility troubleshooter is your friend. This wizard lets you take measures designed to convince your program that it's running in the environment for which it was designed.

To run the Program Compatibility troubleshooter, open Programs in Control Panel. Then, under Programs And Features, click Run Programs Made For Previous Versions Of Windows. The wizard will try to detect which program or programs are giving you problems, but if it doesn't find them, you can choose from a list of running programs. Then follow the step-by-step instructions.

INSIDE OUT Set a restore point

The setup routines for most recent programs automatically create a restore point before making any changes to your system. A restore point is a snapshot of your current system state. If an installation destabilizes your system, you can use System Restore to return to the snapshot state. (For more information about using System Restore, see "Configuring System Protection Options" on page 461 and "Making Repairs with the Windows Recovery Environment" on page 1046.) The installers for some older programs do not create restore points, unfortunately, and it is precisely these older programs that present the most potential hazard. If you're about to install a program that's not of recent vintage (say, one written for Windows 9x), it's not a bad idea to create a restore point manually before you begin. (Open System And Security in Control Panel, click System, click System Protection in the left pane, and then click Create. Bring along your administrative credentials.)

With some programs, you can go straight to the Program Compatibility troubleshooter by right-clicking the program's shortcut on the Start menu (or the desktop) and choosing Troubleshoot Compatibility:

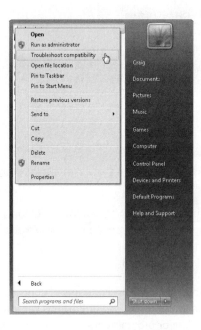

As an alternative to using the Program Compatibility wizard, you can modify the properties of the program's shortcut. Open the Start menu, find the program you want to adjust, right-click its Start menu entry, and choose Properties from the shortcut menu. Then click the Compatibility tab. Figure 5-3 shows an example of what you'll see.

Figure 5-3 Options on the Compatibility tab of a program shortcut's properties dialog box might enable some older programs to run in Windows 7.

Select the Run This Program In Compatibility Mode For check box, and then choose one of the available operating system options. Use the Settings options to deal with programs that experience video problems when run at higher resolutions and color depths.

Some programs work properly only when run with administrative privileges. Although Microsoft has been advising developers for years to avoid this requirement except for applications that perform administrative functions, this advice was routinely ignored in an era when nearly all user accounts were administrator accounts—the usual situation on computers running Windows XP. You can get these programs to run properly by selecting Run This Program As An Administrator. Although the program runs, it's not without some inconvenience: you'll need to respond to a UAC elevation prompt every time you run the program.

Chapter 5

Running Legacy Applications in Windows XP Mode

Windows XP Mode is an optional download for the Professional, Enterprise, and Ultimate editions of Windows 7 that consists of a licensed copy of Windows XP with Service Pack 3, saved in Microsoft Virtual Hard Disk Image (.vhd) format. When run in Windows Virtual PC or another compatible software program, this virtualized installation of Windows XP allows you to run mission-critical applications that might not run satisfactorily in Windows 7. Windows XP Mode is also suitable for developers who need to test applications in older environments without devoting physical hardware to the task. You can, for example, run an older version of Internet Explorer on the same desktop with Internet Explorer 9, or Microsoft Office 2003 alongside Office 2010—feats that would be impossible without the virtualized earlier operating system. Windows XP Mode also comes in handy if you happen to have an older device with a proprietary driver that hasn't been updated for Windows Vista or Windows 7. If it worked great in Windows XP but doesn't work in Windows 7, don't throw it out; install it in Windows XP Mode.

> **Note**
>
> When Windows Virtual PC was first released, it required a computer with hardware-assisted virtualization (HAV), which means the microprocessor has to support either Intel Virtualization Technology (Intel VT) or AMD Virtualization (AMD-V). With the release of an updated version of Windows Virtual PC in 2010, that is no longer the case. Nonetheless, you'll see better Windows XP Mode performance on a system with HAV. To determine if your computer supports HAV and see if it's enabled, download and run the hardware-assisted virtualization detection tool from *w7io.com/20501*. Note that HAV must be enabled in the BIOS; it's often disabled by default. Instructions for enabling HAV on several popular computer brands can be found at *w7io.com/20502*.

Downloading and Installing Windows XP Mode

Setting up Windows XP Mode requires two free downloads—first is a small download that enables the Windows Virtual PC host program, followed by a separate download that installs, configures, and activates the licensed copy of Windows XP SP3. Follow these steps:

1. Go to *w7io.com/0502* and click Download Windows XP Mode And Windows Virtual PC.

2. Select your Windows 7 system type (32 bit or 64 bit) and language.

3. Follow the website's instructions to download and install Windows Virtual PC and then Windows XP Mode.

4. Restart your system.

5. Launch Windows XP Mode by opening the Start menu, choosing All Programs, clicking Windows Virtual PC, and then clicking Windows XP Mode.

6. Accept the license agreement, and then enter a password for the default administrative account:

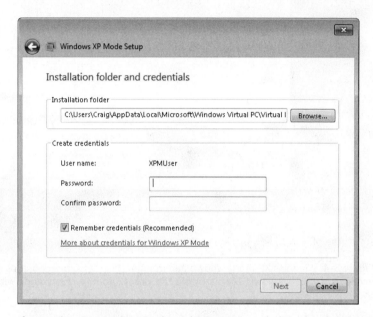

If you select Remember Credentials (Recommended) in this dialog box, whenever you launch Windows XP Mode from your Windows 7 desktop or Start menu, you'll be logged on automatically with the saved credentials.

7. Allow the setup process to complete, and then customize and secure your new Windows XP installation to suit your needs and preferences. If you create additional user accounts, be aware that the system will let you create accounts without passwords but won't let you log on to those accounts.

Running Windows XP Mode

To launch the virtualized Windows XP environment, open the Start menu, click All Programs, and then click the Windows Virtual PC folder. There you'll find a shortcut for Windows XP Mode. This action launches Windows Virtual PC, which in turn hosts Windows XP Mode. As Figure 5-4 shows, the Windows XP environment appears initially as a window on your Windows 7 desktop.

Chapter 5

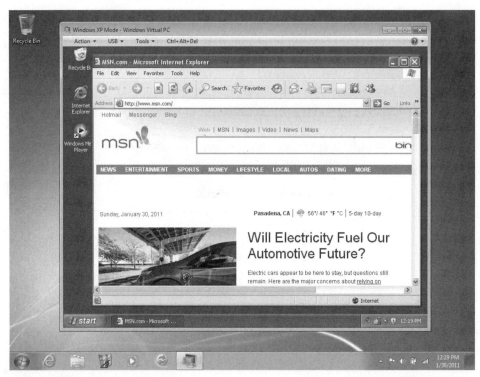

Figure 5-4 Windows XP Mode, shown here running Internet Explorer 6, runs initially as a window on your Windows 7 desktop. You can kick it into full-screen mode with a command on the Action menu.

To turn the full screen over to the virtual environment and remove its own window frame, either maximize it or open the Action menu and choose View Full Screen. In full-screen mode, the menu bar at the top of the Windows XP Mode window appears, in slightly modified form, as a toolbar on the desktop. Click the Restore button on this toolbar to return to windowed display.

To end a Windows XP Mode session, click the Close button on the Windows XP Mode window or its counterpart on the full-screen toolbar. Initially, the virtual environment is configured to hibernate when closed. If that doesn't suit you, choose Settings on the Tools menu, and then click Close in the Windows XP Mode—Windows Virtual PC Settings dialog box. Options here include Hibernate, Shut Down, Turn Off, and Prompt For Action. (See Figure 5-5.)

The advantage of hibernating, of course, is that it enables you to restart the XP environment quickly. If you switch to Shut Down, a click of the Close button generates an orderly shutdown sequence, with prompts to save unsaved work. Turn Off, in contrast, simply pulls the plug on the virtual machine—no questions asked. Turn Off might be a little drastic as a default close option, but if you configure the environment to prompt on close, Turn Off is handy for those times when you want an immediate shutdown and have nothing important to save.

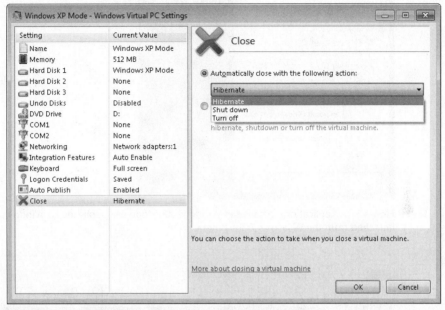

Figure 5-5 For the sake of speedy restarts, the virtual environment, by default, hibernates when you close it.

Installing Applications

Windows Virtual PC is configured by default to share your computer's optical drives with Windows 7. While the virtual environment is running, AutoRun is disabled. To install an application from a CD or DVD in Windows XP Mode, therefore, run the virtual environment, pop in the disc, open My Computer in Windows XP, and run the application's setup program.

After you have installed a program in this manner, Windows Virtual PC (in its default configuration) publishes that program to Windows 7. Thereafter, you can run it "seamlessly" by launching it from the Windows 7 Start menu. As Figure 5-6 shows, applications installed in Windows XP Mode are given Start menu shortcuts in the folder Windows XP Mode Applications.

Applications installed in Windows XP Mode and launched from the Windows 7 Start menu run on the Windows 7 desktop, without visible Windows XP Mode paraphernalia. This is done by running the applications in a Terminal Services session in the virtualized Windows XP machine; the Windows 7 host accesses the session by using Remote Desktop Protocol (RDP). Applications installed in Windows XP Mode might take longer to launch because the virtual environment must be initialized. Once launched, however, they cohabit agreeably with your Windows 7 programs. (See Figure 5-7.)

Chapter 5

Figure 5-6 Applications installed in Windows XP Mode are published to Windows 7 and can be launched from the Windows 7 Start menu.

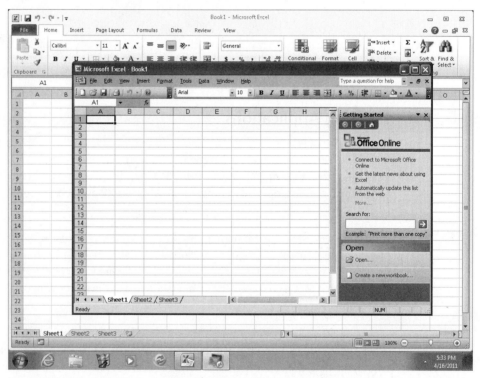

Figure 5-7 Microsoft Office Excel 2003, installed in Windows XP Mode and launched from the Windows 7 Start menu, can share the Windows 7 desktop with Excel 2010, as shown here.

Messages generated by an application running seamlessly also appear on the Windows 7 desktop, identified by the word Remote:

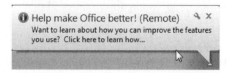

Sharing Data with Windows 7

Whether running seamlessly or housed within a Windows XP Mode frame, applications running in the virtual Windows XP environment share the Clipboard with Windows 7. You can't drag and drop between the two environments, but you can use ordinary cut and paste procedures to transfer data.

Windows Virtual PC, by default, creates a single virtual hard disk, which appears in the Windows XP My Computer folder as drive C. Your host computer's own disk resources are identified and are accessible in My Computer as drive *d* on *computername*:

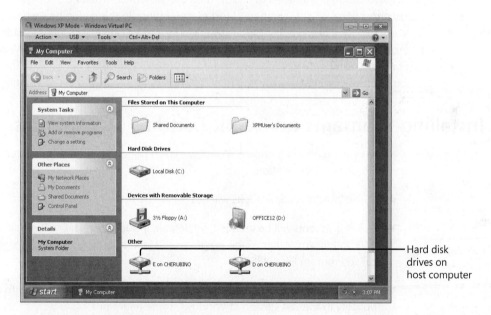

Hard disk drives on host computer

Sharing Devices with Windows 7

Provided that the Virtual Windows PC integration features are enabled (as they are by default), storage devices, including flash drives and other external media, are automatically shared between the virtual environment and Windows 7. Other kinds of USB 2 devices can be used in both environments, but you have to attach them in Windows XP Mode to use them there and then release them to make them available to Windows 7.

To use an unshared USB device in Windows XP Mode, follow these steps:

1. Attach and turn on the device.

2. On the Windows Virtual PC USB menu, choose Attach *devicename*. Windows XP will install a driver if one hasn't already been installed.

3. Use the device.

To release the device, making it available to Windows 7, open the USB menu again and choose Release *devicename*. When a Windows XP Mode program is running in seamless mode, you'll find the Manage USB Devices option on the Jump List for the program button on the taskbar.

Configuring Windows Virtual PC

Figure 5-5, earlier in this section, illustrated the Windows Virtual PC Settings dialog box, in connection with Close options. Most of the settings in this dialog box, when the dialog box is accessed from within Windows XP Mode, are read-only. To configure other settings, including integration features, close the virtual environment. Then open the Windows 7 Start menu and click All Programs, Windows Virtual PC, Virtual Machines. In the Windows Explorer window that appears, right-click Windows XP Mode and choose Settings.

Installing Programs on 64-Bit Editions of Windows

If you're running an x64 edition of Windows, you'll notice the following differences when it comes to program installation:

- 16-bit Windows applications will not install.

- 64-bit programs will be installed, by default, in subfolders of the Program Files folder (%ProgramFiles%), but 32-bit programs will land in subfolders of a separate folder, called Program Files (x86).

- Although most programs designed for a 32-bit environment will run with full functionality in the x64 version of Windows, some might not.

In its x64 editions, Windows 7 provides both 32-bit and 64-bit versions of some programs, including Internet Explorer. The 32-bit version runs by default; to run the 64-bit version, click Start, All Programs, Internet Explorer (64-Bit). Why include both? In an ideal world, you'd use the native 64-bit version to take advantage of its better resource handling and speed. However, many popular add-ins for Internet Explorer are available only in 32-bit form; to use them, you must run the 32-bit version of Internet Explorer.

In general, it's not essential to know whether a program you're running is a 32-bit or 64-bit program. You can easily find out, however, by opening Windows Task Manager. (Press Ctrl+Shift+Esc.) On the Processes tab, 32-bit processes are identified with "*32" next to the process name:

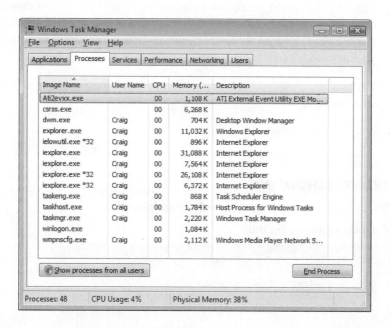

INSIDE OUT   Use a virtual machine to run 32-bit applications

Although most 32-bit applications work fine in x64 editions of Windows 7, some do not. Hardware-dependent programs—such as the software that comes with a scanner or the control panel for a graphics card—are likely to be among the recalcitrant ones. (You'll also need a 64-bit device driver to use these devices; for more information, see "A Crash Course in Device Drivers" on page 1076.) If you have a hardware device and accompanying software that won't work in your 64-bit Windows edition, one work-around is to install virtual machine software (such as Windows Virtual PC or VMware Workstation) and set up a 32-bit (x86) Windows edition in a virtual machine. (You'll need a separate license for each copy of Windows.) Then install the hardware and its software in the virtual machine. This way, you can enjoy the benefits of 64-bit comput-ing while continuing to use legacy products until their developer provides 64-bit sup-port or you replace the product.

Chapter 5

Managing Startup Programs

Setting up a program to run automatically when you start Windows is easy. If the program's installer doesn't offer to do this for you (many do) and you want the program to run every time you begin a Windows session, create a shortcut for the program in the Startup folder of your Start menu. Here's one good way to do it:

1. Open the Start menu, choose All Programs, right-click Startup, and then choose either Open (to create a shortcut for your user account only) or Open All Users (to create a shortcut for all accounts at your computer). This will open the appropriate Startup folder in Windows Explorer.

2. On the Start menu, find the item that you want to launch automatically when you start Windows.

3. Drag the item to the Startup folder.

TROUBLESHOOTING

You can't create a shortcut in the Startup folder

If you see a message like this:

you're in the All Users Startup folder (%ProgramData%\Microsoft\Windows\Start Menu\Programs\Startup) instead of your own Startup folder (%AppData%\Microsoft\Windows\Start Menu\Programs\Startup). The All Users folder holds shortcuts for everyone with an account at your computer. Program installers (running under the TrustedInstaller account) can create shortcuts there, but you cannot unless you provide administrative credentials. To do that, go ahead and create a shortcut on your desktop, and then drag the shortcut to the All Users Startup folder in Windows Explorer. A Destination Folder Access Denied message appears; click Continue, and then, if prompted, enter the name and password of an administrator account to complete the process.

To get to your own Startup folder, be sure that you choose Open, not Open All Users, when you right-click the Startup folder shortcut on the Start menu.

Controlling Startup Programs with the System Configuration Utility

The problem that many users have with startup programs is not with creating them (that's easy, and in many cases it happens more or less automatically), but getting rid of them. Having too many startup programs not only makes your system take a longer time to start, it also has the potential to waste memory. If you don't require a program at startup, it's a good idea to get it out of your startup path.

Unfortunately, tracking down programs that start automatically isn't as easy as you might think. A program can be configured to run at startup in many ways, not just by having a shortcut in a Startup folder. To wit:

- **Run key (machine)**   Programs listed in the registry's HKLM\Software\Microsoft\ Windows\CurrentVersion\Run key are available at startup to all users.

- **Run key (user)**   Programs listed in the HKCU\Software\Microsoft\Windows\Current- Version\Run key run when the current user logs on. A similar subkey, HKCU\Software\ Microsoft\Windows NT\CurrentVersion\Windows\Run, can also be used.

- **Load value**   Programs listed in the Load value of the registry key HKCU\Software\ Microsoft\Windows NT\CurrentVersion\Windows run when any user logs on.

- **Scheduled tasks**   The Windows Task Scheduler (see "Using Task Scheduler" on page 966) can specify tasks that run at startup. In addition, an administrator can set up tasks for your computer to run at startup that are not available for you to change or delete.

- **Win.ini**   Programs written for 16-bit Windows versions can add commands to the Load= and Run= lines in the [Windows] section of this startup file, which is located in %SystemRoot%. The Win.ini file is a legacy of the Windows 3.1 era.

- **RunOnce and RunOnceEx keys**   This group of registry keys identifies programs that run only once, at startup. These keys can be assigned to a specific user account or to the machine:

  - HKLM\Software\Microsoft\Windows\CurrentVersion\RunOnce

  - HKLM\Software\Microsoft\Windows\CurrentVersion\RunOnceEx

  - HKCU\Software\Microsoft\Windows\CurrentVersion\RunOnce

  - HKCU\Software\Microsoft\Windows\CurrentVersion\RunOnceEx

Chapter 5

- **RunServices and RunServicesOnce keys**   As the names suggest, these rarely used keys can control automatic startup of services. They can be assigned to a specific user account or to a computer.

- **Winlogon key**   The Winlogon key controls actions that occur when you log on to a computer running Windows 7. Most of these actions are under the control of the operating system, but you can also add custom actions here. The HKLM\Software\Microsoft\Windows NT\CurrentVersion\Winlogon\Userinit and HKLM\Software\Microsoft\Windows NT\CurrentVersion\Winlogon\Shell subkeys can automatically launch programs.

- **Group Policy**   The Group Policy console includes two policies (one in Computer Configuration\Administrative Templates\System\Logon, and one in the comparable User Configuration folder) called Run These Programs At User Logon that specify a list of programs to be run whenever any user logs on.

- **Policies\Explorer\Run keys**   Using policy settings to specify startup programs, as described in the previous paragraph, creates corresponding values in either of two registry keys: HKLM\Software\Microsoft\Windows\CurrentVersion\Policies\Explorer\Run or HKCU\Software\Microsoft\Windows\CurrentVersion\Policies\Explorer\Run.

- **BootExecute value**   By default, the multistring BootExecute value of the registry key HKLM\System\CurrentControlSet\Control\Session Manager is set to *autocheck autochk **. This value causes Windows, at startup, to check the file-system integrity of your hard disks if your system has been shut down abnormally. It is possible for other programs or processes to add themselves to this registry value. (Note: Microsoft warns against deleting the default BootExecute value. For information about what to do if your system hangs while Autocheck is running, see Microsoft Knowledge Base article 151376, "How to Disable Autochk If It Stops Responding During Reboot," at *w7io.com/0503*.)

- **Shell service objects**   Windows loads a number of helper dynamic-link libraries (DLLs) to add capabilities to the Windows shell.

- **Logon scripts**   Logon scripts, which run automatically at startup, can open other programs. Logon scripts are specified in Group Policy in Computer Configuration\Windows Settings\Scripts (Startup/Shutdown) and User Configuration\Windows Settings\Scripts (Logon/Logoff).

In Windows Vista, Windows Defender, the antispyware utility included with the operating system, offered a list of your startup programs as part of its Software Explorer. That feature of Windows Defender has been removed. However, the System Configuration utility, still included with Windows 7, can help you see what's running at startup and disable particular startup items if you choose to. Figure 5-8 shows the Startup tab of the System Configuration utility.

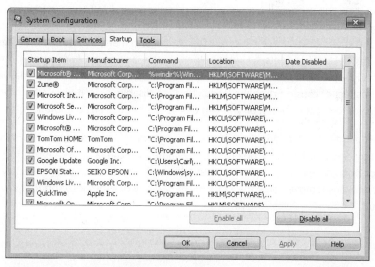

Figure 5-8 To disable a startup item in System Configuration, clear its check box.

To run System Configuration, type **msconfig** in the Start menu's search box, and then press Enter. Click the Startup tab to see what your system is busy doing at startup, and clear the check boxes for any items you want to disable. After you disable one or more items, those items will appear at the bottom of the list (in the default sort order) the next time you run System Configuration, and the date and time of their disabling will appear in the column at the right.

System Configuration is dandy for temporarily lightening your system's startup overhead, and for those who don't relish registry edits, it's a fine way to disable startup behavior established by registry keys. Note, however, that the utility's startup list does not include items established via Group Policy or the Windows 7 Task Scheduler, nor in many of the other dark recesses in which startup programs can hide.

For an alternative, less cramped, and more readable listing of your system's startup programs, open the Start menu, choose All Programs, Accessories, and then System Tools, and run System Information. In the left pane of the System Information window, open Software Environment, and then click Startup Programs. Because the System Information window can be maximized, it's handier for reading long registry paths than is the fixed-size System Configuration window. Like System Configuration, however, it omits policy and scheduled startup tasks.

Chapter 5

Using Autoruns

For the most comprehensive listing of items that run at startup, as well as a handy tool to prevent certain programs from starting, we recommend Autoruns, a free utility from Windows Sysinternals. Autoruns, which you can download from *w7io.com/2001*, shows all the registry keys and startup locations listed earlier, and it also shows Explorer shell extensions, services, desktop gadgets, browser helper objects, and more. Autoruns is particularly useful for finding processes that don't belong (such as a Trojan horse or other malware) or that you suspect of causing problems. You can then disable these items without removing them while you test your theory, or you can delete their auto-start command altogether.

Select an item, and its details appear at the bottom of the screen, as shown here. Disable an item by clearing the check box next to its name; you can later reenable it by selecting the check box. To clear an item from the auto-start list, select it and choose Entry, Delete. (Note that deleting removes only the entry in the registry or other location that causes the item to run; it does not delete the program.)

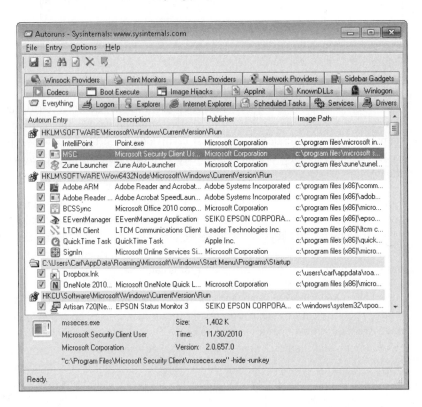

Although the tabs at the top of the Autoruns window filter the list of auto-start items into various categories, the number of items can still be daunting. One nice feature of Autoruns is its ability to filter out components that are part of Windows or are digitally signed by Microsoft, as these are presumably safe to run. Commands on the Options menu control the appearance of these items.

You can also use the Compare feature in Autoruns to compare before and after snapshots of the data the program finds. Run Autoruns before you install a new program, save the data, run Autoruns again after you install the program, and compare the results to see what changes to auto-start behavior were made by the program installation.

Managing Running Programs and Processes with Windows Task Manager

Windows Task Manager is a tool that serves two essential purposes. You can use it to track aspects of your system's performance, and you can use it to see what programs and processes are running and terminate items when the normal shutdown methods aren't working.

For information about using Task Manager to monitor system performance, see "Monitoring Performance in Real Time" on page 841.

The easiest way to run Task Manager is by means of its keyboard shortcut, Ctrl+Shift+Esc. Figure 5-9 shows the Applications tab and Processes tab of Task Manager.

Figure 5-9   Task Manager is useful for terminating recalcitrant applications and processes, as well as for monitoring system performance.

In Task Manager, the Applications tab lists all running programs that have corresponding taskbar buttons. Each entry in the Task column consists of descriptive text identical to the text displayed in the program's title bar.

Chapter 5

The Applications tab also includes a Status column. Most of the time, the entries in this list will read *Running*. If an application hangs or freezes for any reason, you will see the words *Not Responding* in this column instead. In that case, you can attempt to shut down the misbehaving program by selecting its entry and clicking End Task. Don't be too quick on the trigger, however; Not Responding doesn't necessarily mean that an application is irredeemably lost. If the program is using every bit of resources to handle a different task, it might simply be too busy to communicate with Task Manager. Before you decide to end the program, give it a chance to finish whatever it's doing. How long should you wait? That depends on the task. If the operation involves a large data file (performing a global search and replace in a large Microsoft Access database, for instance), it's appropriate to wait several minutes, especially if you can hear the hard disk chattering or see the disk activity light flickering. But if the task in question normally completes in a few seconds, you needn't wait more than a minute.

The items listed on the Applications tab represent only a portion of the total number of programs and services running on a Windows computer at any given time. To see the entire list of running processes and gain access to a broader selection of tools for managing them, click the Processes tab.

Note

To find out what process is associated with a given application, right-click the application on the Applications tab and choose Go To Process from the shortcut menu.

INSIDE OUT   Be smart about shutdowns

When you shut down an application by clicking the End Task button on the Applications tab, the effect is the same as if you had chosen to shut down the program using its menus or by right-clicking its taskbar button and choosing Close. If the program can respond to the shutdown request, it should prompt you for confirmation or give you a chance to save open files, if necessary. By contrast, the End Process button on the Processes tab zaps a process immediately and irrevocably, closing any open files without giving you a chance to save them. Whenever possible, you should try the End Task option first and reserve the drastic End Process option for situations in which you have no alternative.

Initially, the Processes tab lists programs and services that are directly accessible to the current user. To see everything, including processes running under system accounts and the accounts of other logged-on users (if you use Fast User Switching), click Show Processes From All Users.

For each process, Task Manager includes the following information by default: Image Name (the name of the process), User Name (which user started the process), CPU (the percentage of the CPU's capacity that the process is currently using), Memory (Private Working Set) (the amount of memory the process requires to perform its regular functions), and Description (a text field identifying the process). To display additional information for each process, open the View menu and choose Select Columns.

If you need to shut down a process, select it and click End Process.

INSIDE OUT   Assign a program to a specific processor

If you have a dual-core or multiprocessor system, you can assign a process to a specific processor—but only after the process is already running. To do this, right-click the process on the Processes tab and choose Set Affinity. In the dialog box that appears (shown here), select the processor you want to use. (If all CPUs are selected, Windows sets the process affinity as it sees fit.)

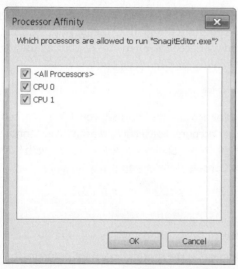

If an "access denied" message appears when you try to set processor affinity, return to the Processes tab, select Show Processes From All Users, and provide your administrator credentials at the UAC prompt. Task Manager then runs as an elevated process, enabling you to set affinity for any process.

Running a Program as an Administrator or Another User

As mentioned earlier in this chapter, you can run a program as an administrator by right-clicking any shortcut for the program (in the Start menu or elsewhere), choosing Run As Administrator, and satisfying the UAC prompt with either consent or credentials. Here are two additional ways to do it:

- Start a Command Prompt session as Administrator (by right-clicking a shortcut for Cmd.exe and choosing Run As Administrator). Then, in the Command Prompt window, type the name of the executable file for whatever program you want to run as an administrator. To run Registry Editor, for example, type **regedit**. Because you've already passed UAC inspection for the Command Prompt session, and because whatever you run from Command Prompt is a child process of Command Prompt, you don't have to deal with any further UAC prompts. This method is excellent for situations where you need to run a sequence of programs as an administrator. Keep one administrative-level Command Prompt window open, and run your programs from the command line.

- Type the name of the program you want to run in the Start menu search box, and then press Ctrl+Shift+Enter.

To run a program under a different user account, you can right-click the program shortcut and choose Run As Different User from the shortcut menu. You will be prompted to enter the password for the specified user account. Alternatively, you can use the runas command from the Command Prompt window or a shortcut. The syntax is

```
runas /user:username programname
```

After you issue the command or activate the shortcut, you'll be prompted to enter the password for the specified user account. For security reasons, you cannot save the password with the shortcut. Note that the Runas command does not work with Windows Explorer or with Microsoft Management Console (MMC) snap-ins.

INSIDE OUT Add Runas to shortcut menus

Although Runas doesn't appear on the shortcut menu for programs in Windows 7, you can restore this capability by running ShellRunas, a program you can download from Windows Sysinternals at *w7io.com/20504*.

Uninstalling Programs

To remove an installed Windows program, open Control Panel and click Uninstall A Program. (You'll find that under the Programs heading.) The list of programs you can uninstall does not include usage information, but it does list the size of each program. Click the program you want to remove, or select it and click Uninstall/Change.

Here are some basic facts you should know about uninstalling programs:

- Windows 7 warns you if you attempt to remove a program while other users are logged on. For safety's sake, you should always completely log off any other user accounts before attempting to remove a program.

- Many uninstall programs leave a few traces of the programs behind, either inadvertently or by design. For instance, programs that create data files typically do not remove custom user settings and data files as part of the uninstall process.

- You can remove programs using Control Panel only if they were originally installed with a Windows-compatible setup program. Some older programs and simple utilities work by copying their files to a folder. In this case, you uninstall the program by manually removing its files and shortcuts.

- In some cases, a poorly written uninstall routine might leave a phantom entry behind in the list of installed programs, even after it has successfully removed all traces of the program itself. When you click such an entry in Control Panel, Windows offers to remove the orphaned entry from the list. If that doesn't work for some reason, you can remove entries manually by using Registry Editor. Detailed instructions are available in Knowledge Base article 314481, "How to Manually Remove Programs from the Add or Remove Programs Tool" (*w7io.com/0504*). Although written for Windows XP, the procedure also applies to Windows 7.

Setting Default Programs, File-Type Associations, and AutoPlay Options

Most of the programs you use in Windows are associated with particular file types and protocols. These associations are what enable you, for example, to double-click a Windows Media Audio (.wma) file in Windows Explorer and have your favorite audio program play the file, or click an Internet hyperlink in a document or e-mail message and have your favorite web browser take you to the appropriate website. The Windows setup program establishes many of these associations for you when the operating system is installed. The setup programs for various applications also create associations with the file types those programs can use. (Sometimes such programs, when installed, change existing file-type associations; generally, but not invariably, they ask for your permission before doing this.)

But regardless of how the associations between programs and file types and protocols are currently set, Windows makes it easy for you to see and modify the settings. You can inspect and alter current defaults by clicking Default Programs, on the right side of the Start menu, or opening Control Panel, clicking Programs, and then clicking Default Programs. Either way, you arrive at the section of Control Panel shown in Figure 5-10.

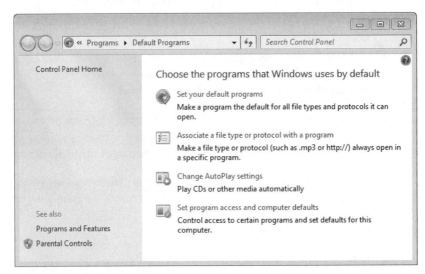

Figure 5-10 The designers of Windows 7 considered this aspect of Control Panel to be so important that they gave it its own Start menu entry.

Setting Default Programs

The first item on this menu, Set Your Default Programs, approaches the issue of associations from the standpoint of particular vital applications. You undoubtedly have a good many other applications in addition to these (and you might not have all of these), but the programs listed here are all capable of handling multiple file types and protocols. This list gives you a way to assign programs to *all* the items they can handle—should you choose to do that. (You can also assign programs to a subset of their possible associations.)

To illustrate how this works, we'll select Windows Live Mail in the dialog box shown in Figure 5-11.

As Figure 5-12 shows, the dialog box responds by indicating that Windows Live Mail currently is the default program for one of the file types or protocols it is capable of handling.

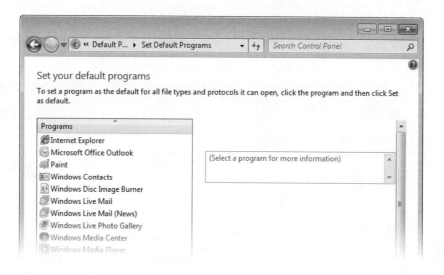

Figure 5-11 The Set Your Default Programs dialog box lets you approach associations from the standpoint of certain vital applications—such as your web browser(s) and e-mail client(s).

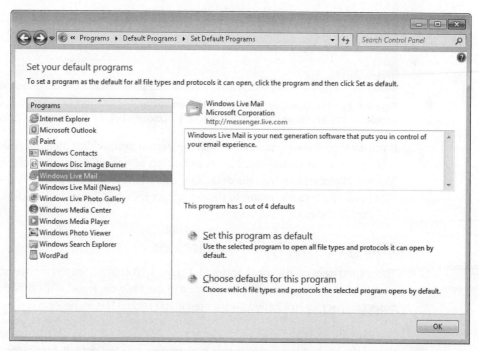

Figure 5-12 In this example, Windows Live Mail is set as the default handler for one of the four protocols it is capable of handling.

To see which defaults Windows Live Mail currently "owns" (and modify particular ones if you want), click Choose Defaults For This Program. The dialog box then lists file extensions and protocols that are possibilities for Windows Live Mail. (See Figure 5-13.)

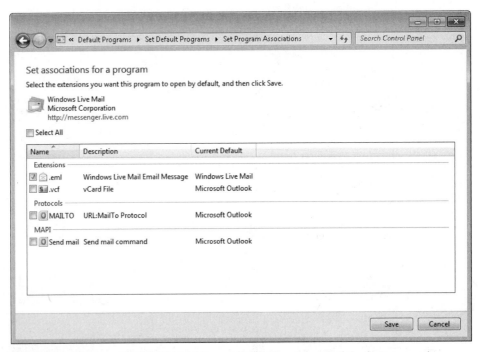

Figure 5-13 Windows Live Mail "owns" the .eml extension; the rest of the file types and protocols that Windows Live Mail is capable of handling belong to Microsoft Outlook.

If you want to make Windows Live Mail the default program for other extensions or protocols, you could select the check boxes associated with these protocols and then click Save. To make Windows Live Mail the default for everything, select the Select All check box and click Save. Alternatively, return to the dialog box shown in Figure 5-12 and click Set This Program As Default.

Changing File-Type Associations

The second item on the menu shown in Figure 5-10 approaches the matter of file-to-program associations from the perspective of the file type. Figure 5-14 shows a list of file types comparable to what you would see if you clicked this menu item.

The file-type list is alphabetized by extension. For each extension, the list shows a description of the file and the program that is currently set as the default application for that file type. So, for example, in Figure 5-14, you can see that the extension .bmp represents bitmap image files, and that Windows Photo Viewer is the program currently associated with such files. In other words, double-clicking a .bmp file in Windows Explorer, as things now stand, will open that file in Windows Photo Viewer.

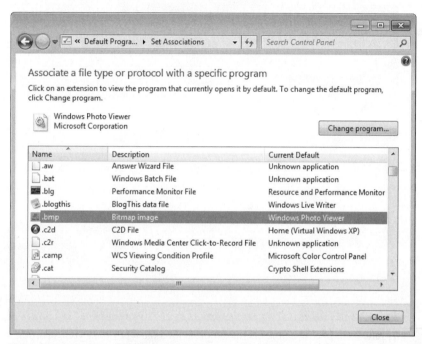

Figure 5-14 The list of file extensions shown in this dialog box lets you change the program or programs associated with individual file types.

To change the default, click Change Program. As Figure 5-15 shows, the Open With dialog box that appears has a section called Recommended Programs and a section called Other Programs. The Recommended Programs section includes the current default (Windows Photo Viewer) and other programs that are registered as being capable of opening files of the current type (bitmap images, in this case). The dialog box also includes an Always Use The Selected Program To Open This Kind Of File check box, which appears dimmed and is unavailable. The reason the check box is unavailable is that Windows assumes that because you have arrived in the Open With dialog box by way of the Default Programs command (on the Start menu or in Control Panel), the only business you have here is to change the program that's always used to open the selected file type. (As you'll see in a moment, there's another way to get to this dialog box.)

The Other Programs section of this dialog box will at first appear unpopulated. To make its contents visible, click the little arrow at the end of the dividing line between the Recommended Programs section and the Other Programs section. (We've already done that in Figure 5-15.)

Chapter 5

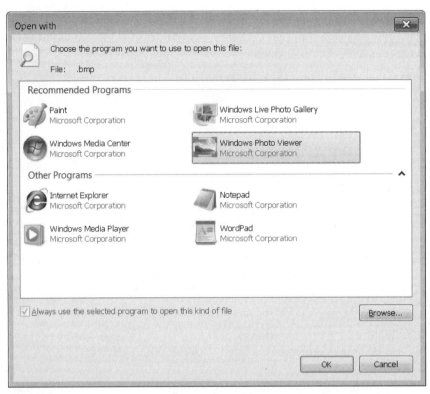

Figure 5-15 To change the default program for a file type, make your selection in the Recommended Programs section of this dialog box, and then click OK.

Be careful. The programs listed in Other Programs are simply commonplace applications installed on your system. They are almost guaranteed to be bad choices for the selected file type. If you select one of these and click OK, it will become the default program for the current file type, no matter how unsuitable it might be. You can fix that easily enough by returning to the Open With dialog box. But the spurned program will make a nuisance of itself by remaining in the Recommended Programs section. If, for example, you're curious about how a bitmap image might look when rendered by Notepad, you might be tempted to make Notepad, temporarily, the default application for that file type. If you do this, Notepad will become one of the recommended programs for opening bitmap files—even though you'll probably never want to use it again for that purpose. (See Figure 5-16.)

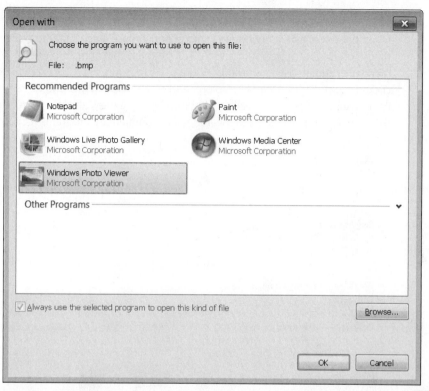

Figure 5-16 If you make a program the default application for a file type and then change your mind, that program will remain in the Recommended Programs section of the dialog box.

TROUBLESHOOTING

You want to remove a program from the Recommended Programs section of the Open With dialog box

The contents of the Recommended Programs list are determined in part by the registry key HKCU\Software\Microsoft\Windows\CurrentVersion\Explorer\FileExts*filetype*\ OpenWithList (where *filetype* is the extension of the file type in question). So, for example, in the case shown in Figure 5-16, the ...\.bmp\OpenWithList key includes several values, one of which is Notepad.exe. Deleting the unwanted item in the OpenWithList key removes it from the Recommended Programs list. (Some items in the Recommended Programs and Open With lists appear as the result of values within the HCR\ *filetype* key and its subkeys. However, accidental additions to the lists, as described in the preceding section, are always made in the HKCU hive.)

Chapter 5

Changing the Default Application from Windows Explorer

If you right-click a file in Windows Explorer and choose Open With from the shortcut menu, the programs that appear in the submenu are those that appear in the file type's Recommended Programs list, as shown in Figure 5-15. In Figure 5-17, for example, we've right-clicked a .bmp file in Windows Explorer and chosen Open With, and we're presented with Paint, Windows Live Photo Gallery, Windows Media Center, and Windows Photo Viewer—the same four programs that appear in the Recommended Programs section of Figure 5-15.

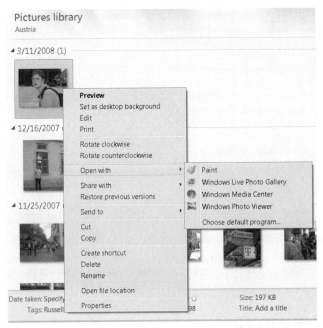

Figure 5-17 The options that appear when you right-click a file in Windows Explorer and choose Open With are those that appear in the file type's Recommended Programs list in Control Panel.

Notice that the programs are listed alphabetically, and the menu does not indicate which one is the current default. The assumption is that if you've gone to the trouble of choosing Open With, it's because you want, this time, to open the file in a nondefault program.

You can use this Open With menu either to open the selected file one time in a nondefault application or to change the default. To do the latter, click Choose Default Program on the menu shown in Figure 5-17. The Open With dialog box that appears will be just like the one shown in Figure 5-15, with one major exception: the Always Use The Selected Program To Open This Kind Of File check box will be available. Note that it will be available *and selected*. If you don't want to make a change to the default (if you're just looking around or curious about what might show up in the Other Programs section of the dialog box), be

sure to clear the check box before you select a program and click OK. (If you do uninten-
tionally reset the default, you can always return to this Open With dialog box and fix the
problem.)

INSIDE OUT   Use a third-party tool to manage file-type associations

The built-in tools described in the preceding sections are perfectly adequate for specifying the default program for a particular file type. But if you want to change other
attributes of a file type, such as its description or icon and whether it appears as an
option when you choose New in Windows Explorer, you'll need to use a third-party
utility. One we like is File Type Doctor, which is a component of Creative Element Power
Tools (*w7io.com/20503*), shown here. In addition to viewing and modifying these file-
type properties, you can use File Type Doctor to easily add context menu items—commands that appear on the menu when you right-click a file of the specified type.

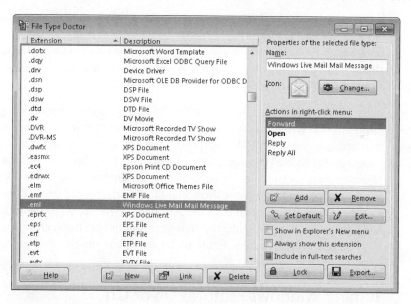

Setting Program Access and Computer Defaults

The dialog box that appears when you choose Default Programs on the Start menu and
click Set Program Access And Computer Defaults (shown in Figure 5-18) is designed to give
Windows users the option to remove access to a number of Microsoft programs that were
tightly integrated into the original version of Windows XP.

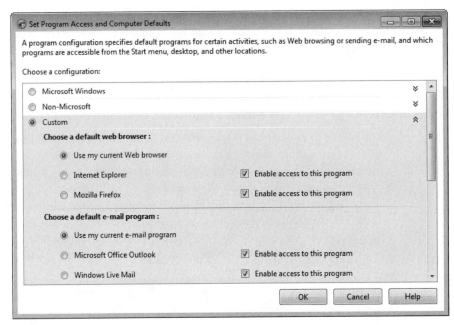

Figure 5-18 You can use this dialog box to remove certain Microsoft programs from menus in Windows.

In the Set Program Access And Computer Defaults dialog box, the default selection on all newly installed systems is Custom. This essentially means that you are willing to make your own decisions about what Microsoft middleware programs are visible and accessible on your system. This works for most users. If you want to remove the evidence of a particular Microsoft item, such as Internet Explorer, clear the Enable Access To This Program check box beside the program's name. Note that this action does not uninstall the program; it merely removes the program from the Start menu, desktop, and other locations. To abjure all Microsoft middleware, select the Non-Microsoft option. If you change your mind and want the Microsoft tools back, return to the dialog box and click Microsoft Windows or Custom.

Turning Windows Features On or Off

If you want to disable certain default Windows features, you can use the Set Program Access And Computer Defaults dialog box just shown. A simpler, more direct, and more versatile way to get the job done is to open Control Panel, choose Programs, and then, under Programs And Features, choose Turn Windows Features On Or Off. As Figure 5-19 shows, you can disable or reenable many different Windows features in the Windows Features dialog box that appears. Some of the entries in this list (those with outline controls beside them) contain subentries. You can disable subentries without lopping off the whole category by opening the outline heading. To banish Spider Solitaire, for example, while leaving the other games in place, open the Games entry and clear the Spider Solitaire check box.

Figure 5-19 The Windows Features dialog box provides a simple way to disable or reenable selected programs.

Note that the Windows Features dialog box lists features that are not enabled by default. The Indexing Service entry, for example, refers to a service that was used in earlier versions of Windows, not the service that builds and maintains the Windows 7 search index. Unless you are sure you need a feature that is not enabled by default, it's better to leave its setting alone.

Setting AutoPlay Options

AutoPlay is the feature that enables Windows to take appropriate action when you insert a CD or DVD into a drive. The operating system detects the kind of disc you have inserted—an audio disc, a program, or a DVD movie, for example—and takes the action that you have requested for that type of media. If you have not already made a decision about what the operating system should do, an AutoPlay dialog box appears when the disc is detected, and Windows presents a list of possible actions (including in some cases an option to do nothing at all). A check box in this dialog box lets you specify that the action you're currently choosing should be the default for all discs of the current type. Figure 5-20 shows an example of the AutoPlay dialog box.

If you have used the AutoPlay dialog box shown in Figure 5-20 to set a default action for a particular media type, and you subsequently change your mind and want a different default, open the Start menu, click Default Programs, and then click Change AutoPlay Settings. The dialog box that appears, shown in Figure 5-21, provides a drop-down list of possible actions for each media type. You can make your selection from this list and then click Save.

Chapter 5

Figure 5-20 The AutoPlay dialog box that appears when you first insert an optical disc of a given type lets you tell Windows how to process the disc—either this time or every time.

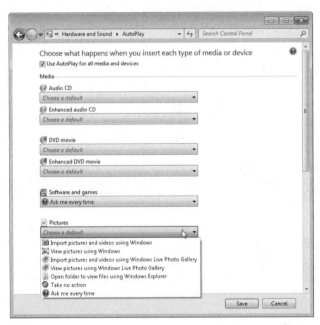

Figure 5-21 For each optical media type, Windows lets you choose from a list of appropriate default possibilities.

INSIDE OUT   You don't want a default action?

To have *no* default action for a given optical media type, choose Ask Me Every Time. To suppress the AutoPlay dialog box completely, choose Take No Action.

INSIDE OUT   AutoRun has been disabled on some USB media

AutoRun is the mechanism that proposes a default action when you insert an optical disc in the drive. In Figure 5-20, for example, the contents of a file called AutoRun on the inserted CD is responsible for suggesting the action *Run index.html*. Because of the rising incidence of malware that uses AutoRun to induce unwary users into running Trojan horses (the Conficker worm, about which you can read at *w7io.com/0505*, is a conspicuous example), the designers of Windows 7 decided to disable AutoRun capability on USB devices other than removable optical media.

Because of this security change, some devices that executed programs automatically when plugged into a Windows Vista computer might appear not to work in Windows 7. If your device seems inert when attached to your Windows 7 system, don't assume it's broken. Open Computer in Windows Explorer, and then open the entry for your device. You will probably find a file there called AutoRun. Opening that file in Notepad will reveal the name of the program that would run automatically had AutoRun not been disabled for your device. Run that program from Windows Explorer.

Using Internet Explorer

T is no exaggeration to call Internet Explorer 9 Microsoft's most ambitious browser release ever. Microsoft officially released this important upgrade on March 14, 2011, after a full year of public testing. The improvements over Internet Explorer 8 are profound: a streamlined user interface, dramatically faster performance (especially on PCs with modern graphical processing units), major enhancements to security and privacy, and a new type of shortcut that allows you to pin a website to the taskbar or Start menu and treat it as if it were a Windows program.

If you recently moved to Windows 7 from Windows XP, Internet Explorer 9 will be completely new to you, because the new browser does not run on that old platform. If you're upgrading from Windows Vista, you might have already become familiar with Internet Explorer 9. If you gave up on Internet Explorer in the past, we think you should give this version a second look.

We've divided our coverage of Internet Explorer 9 into two chapters. In this chapter, we cover the essentials of browsing and searching, including details about changes to the way Internet Explorer handles multiple tabs. We also explain how to manage and troubleshoot add-ons. You'll find details about security, privacy, and the new Internet Explorer 9 Download Manager in Chapter 7, "Internet Explorer Compatibility, Security, and Privacy."

What's in Your Edition?

All of the tools and techniques we describe in this chapter are available in all editions of Windows 7. Our discussion is based on the features and user interface available in Internet Explorer 9, which is available as a free upgrade for all Windows 7 editions.

What's New in Internet Explorer 9

If you've used a previous version of Internet Explorer, the first thing you're likely to notice in Internet Explorer 9 is what you *don't* see on the screen. There's no branding beyond the familiar blue E logo on the taskbar button. There's no text or program icon in the title bar. By design, the browser's primary role is as a frame that hosts web pages while calling as little attention as possible to itself. Figure 6-1 displays what you see when you open a new tab:

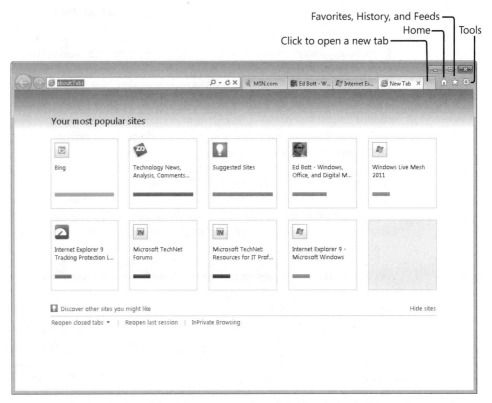

Figure 6-1 Internet Explorer 9 banishes menus and toolbars, leaving a single row that contains the address bar (also known as the One Box), tabs, and three command buttons.

All but the most essential interface elements in the browser have been removed or hidden in the default view of Internet Explorer 9. There's no search box in the upper right corner, no status bar along the bottom. The Command bar and Favorites bar are hidden, with virtually all of their functions taken over by the three gray command buttons in the upper right corner. The Refresh and Stop buttons are also gray. (All of these buttons change to color if you pass a mouse pointer over them.) The only element that's bigger and brighter than its predecessor is the Back button in the top left corner, which turns from gray to bright blue if you have any previously visited pages available to return to.

Tabs for open pages are smaller, crisper in design, and located in a band to the right of the address bar. (You can position the browser tabs on their own row if you prefer.) Internet Explorer 9 adds a few new fillips to the tabbed browsing experience, including the ability to tear off tabs and drag them into a new window or dock them to the side of the display by using Aero Snap. If you drag a tab to the taskbar, you can pin it there and use the website as if it were an application. (We explain how to use these features effectively in "Using Tabs and Tab Groups" on page 217 and "Working with Pinned Sites" on page 231.)

For notifications (of blocked pop-up windows, for example), Internet Explorer 8 uses an Information bar above the page you're viewing. For actions that require your input (whether to save or run a download, enable an ActiveX control, and so on), dialog boxes pop up and demand your attention. In Internet Explorer 9, by contrast, all of those messages and action buttons appear in the Notification bar along the bottom of the window, where you can address them at your convenience—or ignore them completely while you continue using the browser. The Save button shown in Figure 6-2 is tied to another new feature—the simple but effective Download Manager, which we discuss in more detail in "Managing Downloads" on page 274.

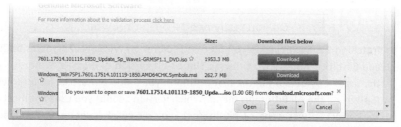

Figure 6-2 Notifications and requests for input no longer appear in dialog boxes that demand attention but instead show up discreetly in the Notification bar at the bottom of the browser window.

Internet Explorer 9 combines the address bar and the now-defunct search box into what Microsoft informally calls the One Box. (In Help files and options dialog boxes, Internet Explorer 9 still uses the term *Address bar*. We do the same throughout this chapter.) As you type, it sifts through your history and favorites and adds search results from the current search provider (if you've enabled this option). The result is a list of possible destinations that is uncannily accurate in predicting where you're likely to want to go.

Internet Explorer 9 is noticeably faster than its predecessors, in our experience, and it introduces some significant security improvements—see "Controlling ActiveX" on page 254 for one especially important example. Its greatly enhanced privacy controls include a collection of Tracking Protection features that allow you to block sites that try to profile you based on your online behavior. We describe these features in detail in "Protecting Your Privacy" on page 263.

All these changes combined make a compelling case for Internet Explorer 9. As a result, we strongly recommend this update, and we have written this chapter with that assumption in mind.

Installing and Uninstalling Internet Explorer 9

A clean installation of Windows 7, with or without Service Pack 1, includes Internet Explorer 8 as the default web browser. You can update the browser to Internet Explorer 9 by using Windows Update or download a standalone installer from *w7io.com/20601*.

The installation process is fairly quick and straightforward. Choose the update that matches your operating system: use the 32-bit installer if you're running a 32-bit version of Windows 7; choose the 64-bit update if you are running 64-bit Windows. If you're not sure which version of Windows 7 is installed on your PC, click Start, click Computer, then click System Properties. The System Type field, under the System heading, answers the 32-bit/64-bit question.

INSIDE OUT   Do you really need a 64-bit browser?

Installing the 64-bit version of Internet Explorer on Windows 7 updates both the 32-bit and 64-bit versions of the browser. The 32-bit version of Internet Explorer is pinned to the taskbar by default (in the first position); you'll find a shortcut for Internet Explorer (64-bit) on the All Programs menu. Which version should you use? For most situations, the correct answer is the 32-bit Internet Explorer, which is set up as the default browser during installation. The web isn't picky about how many bits your OS uses.

If you're curious, we recommend that you try using the 64-bit Internet Explorer 9 for a while. You probably won't notice any difference until you run into a site that requires an add-on that isn't available in a 64-bit version. At that point you'll have to make a choice: forgo the functionality offered by the add-on or switch back to the 32-bit browser to see all content on the page. Someday, all add-ons will be written with a 64-bit browser in mind. That day is probably still a few years (and at least one more browser version) away.

For an excellent explanation of the issues involved with 64-bit Internet Explorer, see the Q&A by Eric Lawrence, a programmer on the Internet Explorer team, at *w7io.com/20604*.

If you change your mind, you can uninstall Internet Explorer 9 and roll back to your previously installed copy of Internet Explorer 8. To begin the process, close all Internet Explorer windows, open Control Panel, and type **update** in the search box. In the results list, click View Installed Updates. You can scroll through the list of updates to find the entry for Windows Internet Explorer 9 (it's filed under the Microsoft Windows heading) or type **Internet** in the search box to filter the Installed Updates list. Select the entry for the update and click Uninstall. You'll need to restart to complete the process of restoring Internet Explorer 8.

Internet Explorer 9 is a complete replacement for Internet Explorer 8. The two versions of Internet Explorer cannot coexist in the same Windows installation. If you need to keep the older version around for compatibility testing, you should do so on a separate PC or in a virtual machine. Because Internet Explorer 8 is supported on Windows XP (albeit without the extra security of Protected Mode), one relatively simple option that avoids many licensing and setup hassles is to use it in a virtual machine in Windows XP Mode. For details, see "Running Legacy Applications in Windows XP Mode" on page 178.

INSIDE OUT   Working with multiple web browsers

If you have installed one or more third-party web browsers in addition to Internet Explorer, you can specify which program you prefer to use as your default browser. Doing so associates that program with Internet shortcuts, HTML files, and other files normally viewed in a browser.

In general, most web browsers offer to set themselves up as the default browser during installation. If you've set a different web browser as your default, you'll see a notification at the bottom of the Internet Explorer window each time you begin a new session. Click Yes to make Internet Explorer the default, or click No to dismiss the notification. (If you prefer to use a browser other than Internet Explorer as your default, you can banish these reminders by clicking the down arrow to the right of the No button and clicking Don't Ask Again.)

To manually set Internet Explorer as the default browser, click Tools, choose Internet Options, click the Programs tab, and click the Make Default button in the Default Web Browser section. As we discuss in Chapter 5, "Adding, Removing, and Managing Programs" (see "Setting Default Programs" on page 196), the Start menu's Default Programs command gives you more granular control over web-related settings. There, for example, you can associate particular file types and protocols with Internet Explorer and others with a different browser.

To deploy a custom version of Internet Explorer in an organization, use the Internet Explorer Administration Kit (*w7io.com/20602*). Using the IEAK, you can manage the browser upgrade process and customize most parts of the installation. In addition to customizing home and search pages, you can add search providers, populate the Favorites folder, tweak compatibility settings, and tighten security to match your company's policy.

Microsoft recognizes that some organizations might have valid compatibility reasons to delay an upgrade to Internet Explorer 9. To prevent users from being tempted to upgrade on their own, administrators can use the Internet Explorer 9 Blocker Toolkit (*w7io.com/20603*), which tweaks a registry key that tells Windows Update to omit Internet Explorer from the list of updates offered to that computer. It does not prevent users from downloading the Internet Explorer 9 update package and trying to install it manually.

Browsing with Internet Explorer

The Internet Explorer 9 interface is simple and clean—maybe even too clean. In the default view, all controls are lined up in a single row, as shown here. Although the address bar is in its customary place, it's capable of performing a few new tricks to justify its new alias, the One Box. It also can include up to six additional controls at the end, each of which is identified here.

ActiveX Filtering/
Tracking Protection — Refresh — Stop

Search — Click and drag to resize address bar — Compatibility view — Show address bar AutoComplete

INSIDE OUT Using the Clipboard with Internet Explorer 9

You can also use the Clipboard to jump to a specific page or to search for keywords without having to use the address bar. This capability is especially useful if you're reading a document or an e-mail message that contains links in text format. Start by copying the address to the Clipboard. Next, right-click on the contents of any open tab in Internet Explorer (but not on the tab itself) and click Go To Copied Address. If the Clipboard contains a word or phrase, the menu option that appears is slightly different. Click Search Using Copied Text to send the contents of the Clipboard to the default search provider. Note that these right-click menu options are not available with the New Tab page (about:Tabs). The keyboard shortcut, Ctrl+Shift+L, works on any page.

You can still visit a web page by double-clicking a saved Internet shortcut or by typing a web address (with or without the *http://* prefix) and pressing Enter. In that case, the address bar shows the full web address, which is technically known as a Uniform Resource Identifier (URI) or Uniform Resource Locator (URL).

Using the Address Bar for Faster Navigation

Over time, Internet Explorer captures a history of the sites you visit. You can return to any of those sites, or visit a page you previously saved as a favorite, by typing one or more keywords into the address bar. Internet Explorer uses Windows Search to compare the text you type with your history and the contents of the Favorites folder. As soon as you type a couple of characters, a categorized list of results appears; it changes dynamically as you continue typing. If you've enabled search suggestions, the list also contains matching pages from the current search provider. Figure 6-3 displays one such set of results, using suggestions from Wikipedia.

Figure 6-3 The neatly categorized list of results refreshes in real time as you type in the address bar. Click the down arrow to the right of the History or Favorites heading to see an expanded list of results.

The results list includes your browsing history and favorites by default. The list of results as initially displayed shows only the two or three most likely contenders for each of these categories. (The order is based on a relevancy algorithm whose exact contents are not publicly shared.) You can see a greatly expanded set of results from either category by clicking the down arrow to the right of the History or Favorites heading, which shows up to 20 results.

If you subscribe to any RSS feeds, you can include those in your search results as well. For details, see "Using (or Refusing) AutoComplete" on page 225. For more on how to use feeds, see "Working with RSS Feeds and Web Slices" on page 242.

Two separate configuration options control how the address bar works with external search providers, including Microsoft's Bing (the default search provider) and alternatives such as Google and Wikipedia. The first is a check box that allows you to enable or disable all search features in the address bar. To view this setting, click Tools, then click Manage Add-Ons. Click Search Providers in the Add-On Types list. (You can also get to this setting from the Internet Options dialog box. On the General tab, click the Settings button under the Search heading.)

If the Search In The Address Bar check box is selected, the following features are available to you:

- Type one or more search terms and press Enter. Internet Explorer opens your default search provider and sends the text you entered for use as search parameters. If you use Bing or Google, the search terms can include advanced operators (such as site:microsoft.com) to refine your search. Tip: When searching for a single word, enter a space before you press Enter to avoid having Internet Explorer use the first match-ing address in the AutoComplete list.

- If the current search provider supports search suggestions, those entries appear at the bottom of the results list as you type. If you find these suggestions distracting or are concerned about the privacy implications of sending your keystrokes to a search provider, you can disable this feature. Look for the Turn Off Suggestions link at the bottom of the results list. Click Turn On Suggestions to reenable this feature.

- Not happy with the results? To modify your search, or to repeat the search with a different provider, click the Search icon at the end of the address bar (it looks like a magnifying glass). Doing so replaces the current contents of the address bar with a question mark, followed by the terms you entered. You can then edit the search terms or click the icon for a different search provider at the bottom of the results list.

For more on how to integrate search engines into Internet Explorer, see "Adding, Removing, and Managing Search Providers" on page 237.

As you pass the mouse pointer over items in the History, Favorites, and Feeds groups, you'll notice a small X to the right of each one. (Allow the mouse pointer to hover over the X and it turns red.) Click this X to permanently delete an entry from the list. This option is espe-cially useful for any page in your browsing history that you know leads to a dead end—if you misspell a domain name or follow a misleading search result, for example. Note that clicking the red X for a saved favorite permanently deletes that shortcut from your Favorites folder.

Using Tabs and Tab Groups

Like all modern browsers, Internet Explorer on Windows 7 allows you to keep multiple pages open on separate tabs in the same application window and switch between them quickly via mouse click or key press. This feature is a tremendous timesaver for anyone doing research or trying to juggle multiple tasks.

In addition, tab grouping allows you to visually identify groups of related tabs. When you open a new tab by clicking a link in the current tab, Internet Explorer displays the original tab and the newcomer in the same color, showing you at a glance that the two tabs hold related content. Any additional tabs you generate from pages in the current tab group also acquire the same color. Right-clicking a tab within the tab group reveals commands to close all tabs in the current group, close all tabs *not* in the current group, and remove the current tab from the group.

You can open a new browser tab in any of several ways:

- To open a new, blank tab, press Ctrl+T, or click the New Tab button, just to the right of the current tabs.

- To open a link in a new tab without shifting focus from the current tab, right-click the link and choose Open In New Tab, or hold down Ctrl while clicking the link, or use the middle mouse button to click the link.

- To open a link in a new tab and shift focus to the newly opened tab, hold down Ctrl and Shift and click using the left or middle mouse button.

- To duplicate a tab, press Ctrl+K, or right-click the tab and choose Duplicate Tab from the shortcut menu.

To close any open tab, click the small X at the right side of its tab, or press Ctrl+W, or click the middle mouse button. You don't need to select a tab first to close it—just hover the mouse pointer over the tab to make the X visible.

You must have at least one tab open in a browser window. If you close the last remaining tab, the entire browser window closes.

INSIDE OUT Customizing the New Tab window

If you poke around in Internet Explorer's advanced settings, you'll find references to a couple of pages with unusual URIs: about:blank and about:Tabs. The former is a convenient way to open a new blank tab with absolutely no clutter. The latter produces the New Tab window, which consists of two rows of five icons that reflect the most popular pages based on your browsing history. (There are other about: addresses, but they're mostly used for error pages, like about:navigationfailure and about:securityrisk.)

You can click any of the thumbnails on the New Tab page to go straight to that page. If you find yourself visiting a page regularly but don't want or need to see it here, click the X in the top right corner of the thumbnail to banish it from the list, or right-click and use the shortcut menu. That same shortcut menu also offers the option to open the site in a new tab.

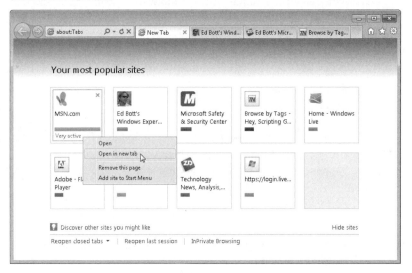

As you make the browser window smaller, the thumbnails on the New Tab page get smaller. Eventually, Internet Explorer throws out the last two thumbnails on the second row, leaving two rows of four shortcuts. If you make the browser window bigger, however, the number of thumbnails doesn't expand. You're stuck with two rows unless you tweak the registry.

All the standard disclaimers about the dangers of Regedit.exe apply, of course. (For more details, see "Avoiding Registry Mishaps" on page 928. If you understand the risks, go to HKCU\Software\Microsoft\Internet Explorer\TabbedBrowsing\NewTabPage, add a DWORD value called NumRows, and set it to a value between 2 and 5, corresponding to the number of rows you want to see on about:Tabs.

Alas, that's about the limit when it comes to customization options. There's no easy way to manually add a new site or change the order of sites on the New Tab page. And beware: Internet Explorer uses your browsing history to determine the order of sites on the New Tab page. If you use the Delete Browsing History option, Internet Explorer starts with a clean slate, and you'll need to wait a while for the page to rebuild itself.

The division of space between the address bar and the tabs is initially determined by the width of your display. At screen widths of 1280 pixels or more, two-thirds of the window width is given over to tabs. If your screen width is less than 1280 pixels, tabs get half of the window width. At any time, of course, you can drag the divider to the right of the Stop button to change the width of the address bar. If you need still more room, right-click any open tab and click Show Tabs On A Separate Row. That gives the address bar full use of the space between the Back and Forward buttons on the left and the command buttons on the right. With this option selected, tabs appear below the address bar. (There's no option to place tabs above the address bar.)

Reopening Closed Tabs

Did you accidentally close a tab before you were quite finished with it? No problem; open the New Tab page and use the Reopen Closed Tabs menu at the bottom. You can also right-click any open tab and choose Reopen Closed Tab. This menu shows every page you've closed using the current Internet Explorer window. (Use the keyboard shortcut Ctrl+Shift+T to quickly reopen the most recently closed page.)

The New Tab page also includes a Reopen Last Session link that reloads every page that was open the last time you closed Internet Explorer. This can spare you some anguish if you accidentally close the browser when you meant to close only the current tab. It can really rescue you if you sit down at your machine and find that your system has been restarted in your absence.

There's one big gotcha lurking in the Reopen Last Session link, however. What happens if you have two or more Internet Explorer sessions open, each in a separate window, and you close them all? In that case, Reopen Last Session brings back only the tabs that were open in the session that was closed last. (To recover closed tabs in that case, open the Favorites Center, click the History tab, and choose View By Order Visited Today from the drop-down menu above the list.)

Managing Multiple Tabs

Switching between browser tabs is literally as simple as pointing to a tab and clicking. If more tabs are open than will fit in the browser window, a scrolling arrow appears to the left of the first tab or to the right of the last tab (or both). Click to scroll in the indicated direction and see tabs that are open but not currently visible. You can also use keyboard

Chapter 6

shortcuts to quickly cycle between tabs: press Ctrl+Tab to move from left to right or Ctrl+Shift+Tab to go from right to left.

When you have a lot of tabs open, particularly if you are working with more than one browser window, you might find that the easiest way to navigate is to hover your mouse over the Internet Explorer icon on the taskbar. Windows displays either thumbnails or names of all open tabs, and you can point to the one you want. If you point to a tab in a browser window, a ScreenTip shows the page title and web address.

To change the order of tabs, drag any tab to a new position in the same window. (If you drag a tab between members of a tab group, the moved tab joins the group.) If you find you have too many tabs in a single window and you want to move a group of related pages to their own window, grab one of the tabs and drag it up or down, away from the other tabs. (Drag it to either side of the display to snap it into position using Aero Snap.) When you release the mouse button, the tab appears in its own browser window. You can now drag each related tab from the old browser window to the new one, dropping it into its rightful place alongside the tabs in the new window.

Setting Tabbed Browsing Options

If you regularly open large numbers of tabs, you will probably want to tweak the way Internet Explorer handles tabs. To see your available options, click Tools, then click Internet Options, and then click the Settings button in the Tabs section on the General tab. That opens the dialog box shown in Figure 6-4, which shows options in Internet Explorer 9. (The options for Internet Explorer 8 are nearly identical.)

Most of the options shown here are self-explanatory. The most radical option is the one at the top of the dialog box, which allows you to completely disable tabbed browsing. The following options deserve special mention:

- **Open Only The First Home Page When Internet Explorer Starts**   This option allows you to define multiple pages as your home page without slowing you down when you first open Internet Explorer. By selecting this option, you load only the top item in the home page list at startup but can open all the pages in that list later by pressing Alt+Home or clicking the Home button.

- **When A New Tab Is Opened, Open**   This drop-down list lets you substitute a blank page or your first home page for Internet Explorer's default New Tab page.

- **Enable Quick Tabs**   If you like to open lots and lots of browser tabs, you will no doubt mourn the loss of the Quick Tabs button, which appeared at the left side of the tabs row in Internet Explorer 8 but is gone in Internet Explorer 9. As it turns out, the feature is merely disabled. Select this check box, click OK, and restart Internet Explorer. With this setting enabled, you can press Ctrl+Q to see a visual display of all open tabs in the current browser session, like the one shown in Figure 6-5.

Figure 6-4 Use any of the options shown here to change the behavior of tabbed browsing—or disable it completely.

Figure 6-5 The Quick Tabs window displays thumbnails of all tabs open in the current browser window. Click to switch to a tab, or click the X in the tab's upper right corner to close that tab.

Chapter 6

INSIDE OUT   Select and scroll with the caret

If you look carefully at Internet Explorer's menus, you might notice an option called Caret Browsing. To toggle this setting, click Tools, then File, or tap the Alt key and look for this option on the View menu. Or just click its keyboard shortcut, F7. Turning this feature on plants a blinking vertical bar, much like a word processor's insertion point, wherever you click the mouse. The caret makes it easier to select text. Hold down Shift, with or without Ctrl, and use the arrow keys to extend the selection from the current caret position. If you've ever tried to select text with the mouse alone and wound up grabbing more than you intended, you'll welcome this feature.

You might also find caret browsing handy for scrolling text on web pages. Put the caret on the bottom line of the display, for example, and the Down Arrow key moves through blocks of text one line at a time instead of by larger chunks.

Setting the Home Page(s)

As a tabbed browser, Internet Explorer allows you to define one or more home pages, each of which loads in its own tab when you open a new browser session or click the Home button. You can create a multitab home page manually by entering the addresses for all pages (each on its own line) in the box at the top of the General tab of the Internet Options dialog box. But there's an easier way.

Right-click the Home button and then click Add Or Change Home Page. The resulting dialog box contains three options, as shown here.

Use the top two options to set the current tab as your only home page or to add it to the current set of home page tabs. Choose the third option if you want all current browser tabs to open when you click Home. Be careful, though; if you add too many tabs to your home page list, you can make Internet Explorer slower to start.

To remove a tab from your current home page list, clear its entry from the Home Page box at the top of the General tab in the Internet Options dialog box.

Note that a pinned site has its own home page settings, separate from the default settings we discuss here. For details, see "Working with Pinned Sites" on page 231.

Unhiding the Command Bar and Other Missing Interface Elements

Over the years, bits of the Internet Explorer interface have been whittled away, version by version. The menu bar was hidden away beginning with Internet Explorer 7, for example. The Command bar, Favorites bar, and status bar have been shoved into a closet for Internet Explorer 9. To make any of these elements visible, right-click anywhere to the immediate right of the New Tab button—or right-click the title bar at the top of the browser window. That action reveals a menu like the one shown here.

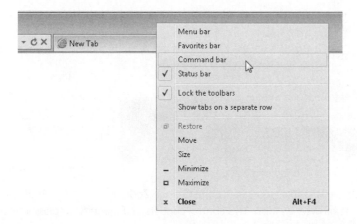

The menu bar and the Command bar represent old interfaces that have been kept around for compatibility purposes. You'll find most of the same menu options via the new command buttons for Internet Explorer 9. A few options (mostly obscure) are found only on the older menus. You'll search in vain for the handy New Session command, for example, which is available when you click File on the menu bar. Likewise, many third-party add-ons place custom options on the Tools menu. If you need items from the menu bar only now and then, you can simply press the Alt key; that displays the menu bar temporarily and then hides it again after you choose a command or click somewhere else.

Zooming In or Out to Make Text Readable

Internet Explorer provides several methods for making text and graphics on a web page larger or smaller. The fastest way is to use Internet Explorer's keyboard shortcuts: hold down

the Ctrl key and press the Plus key to increase the page magnification in 25-percent increments, up to a maximum of 1,000 percent. Hold Ctrl and press Minus to decrease the page
magnification in 25-percent increments. (The final step below 25 percent is 10 percent.)
Press Ctrl+0 to return to normal (100 percent) magnification.

Do you prefer to pick from a menu? No problem. Click Tools, and then click Zoom to display the menu shown here. Note that the Custom option at the bottom of the menu allows
you to set the zoom level to any whole number between 10 and 1,000—233 percent, for
example.

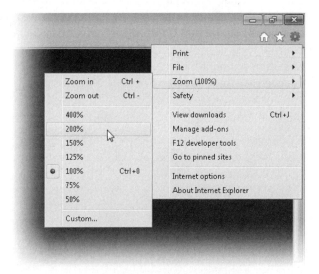

If the status bar is visible, you can use the Change Zoom Level control in the lower right
corner of the browser window. This control consists of a magnifying glass icon alongside
the current magnification level (expressed as a percentage).

Click the arrow to display the same Zoom menu available from Settings. Click the zoom
level to change the page magnification. If the current zoom level is 100 percent, that click
bumps the magnification up to 125 percent. Clicking a second time increases it to 150 percent. For any value other than 100 percent or 125 percent, clicking the Change Zoom Level
control returns the page to 100 percent.

An even simpler method, provided you have a wheel mouse, is to hold down Ctrl and wheel forward (to zoom in) or backward (to zoom out). Each turn of the wheel changes the magnification by five percent. Zooming with the mouse wheel has one other important characteristic: Internet Explorer maintains the position of whatever object you're pointing to when you begin zooming. Suppose, for example, that you're zooming in to get a better look at a graphic element lying near the right edge of the screen. If you use the keyboard or the Zoom Level control at the bottom of the screen, the element you care about will eventually waltz out of the window. But if you zoom in by pointing to it and rolling the wheel, the element retains its position relative to your mouse pointer as it gets larger.

If you're using a computer with a touch screen, such as a Tablet PC, you can also use touch gestures to zoom in on particular elements of a web page. For details, see "Using Gestures in Windows 7" on page 1142.

Zoom levels in Internet Explorer 8 and Internet Explorer 9 are persistent by default. That means the program retains your settings and applies them to new tabs and new sessions. This represents a change from Internet Explorer 7. If you prefer the old approach, click Tools and then click Internet Options. Click the Advanced tab in the Internet Options dialog box, and then, under the heading Accessibility, select Reset Zoom Level For New Windows And Tabs.

INSIDE OUT   Press F11 for full-screen display

To make the most efficient use of the browser window, press F11 to switch Internet Explorer into full-screen mode. This mode hides the title bar and moves the address bar, tabs, and command buttons to the top of the window. As soon as you move the mouse pointer away or click in the page itself, they slide away again. In full-screen mode, Internet Explorer is maximized, even if it was previously in a window, and the Windows taskbar is covered. You can still display the taskbar by pressing the Windows logo key, and you can return Internet Explorer to its normal display style by pressing F11 a second time.

Using (or Refusing) AutoComplete

Internet Explorer's AutoComplete features can help reduce keystrokes by remembering URLs you type, data you enter into web forms, and logon names and passwords you use. As you begin entering data in a field on a web form, AutoComplete consults its list of previous entries and proposes possible matches—thereby reducing the amount of typing you have to do. Likewise, when Internet Explorer detects matching user name and password fields on a web page, it asks if you want to save the data as a matched pair. If you click Yes, the values you enter are encrypted and saved in the registry.

Not everyone welcomes this kind of assistance, though. Depending on your preferences and your level of caution, you might want to use all, none, or only some of the browser's AutoComplete services.

To enable or disable AutoComplete options, click Tools, Internet Options, click the Content tab, and then click Settings in the AutoComplete section of the dialog box. In the ensuing dialog box (shown in Figure 6-6), you can select any or all of the following check boxes:

- **Address Bar**   This option, with its subordinate options, controls which categories are displayed below the address bar when you begin typing (see "Using the Address Bar for Faster Navigation" on page 215). Browsing History and Favorites are selected by default, as is the option to use the Windows Search index for faster performance.

- **Forms**   This option enables autocompletion of data that you type into web pages, such as the names and shipping addresses that you supply on e-commerce sites.

- **User Names And Passwords On Forms**   When this option is selected, Internet Explorer remembers logon credentials for various sites that you visit.

Figure 6-6 You can turn various AutoComplete options on or off individually.

CAUTION

> If you select User Names And Passwords On Forms, Internet Explorer always prompts you before collecting a new password. The password itself appears on screen as a string of asterisks and is encrypted for storage on your disk. A person reading over your shoulder or prowling your hard disk will therefore not be able to pick up your password when AutoComplete supplies it. However, anyone who has physical access to your computer when you are logged on to your user account could interact with websites for which you have saved AutoComplete user name and password data, effectively impersonating you. Unless you are sure that no one else will ever use your account, you might want to decline the browser's offer to remember logon credentials.

If you want Internet Explorer to prompt you before it saves logon credentials for new sites that you visit, be sure to select Ask Me Before Saving Passwords. If you clear the User Names And Passwords On Forms option, the AutoComplete feature will retain entries that it already has recorded but will not record new ones.

Managing Favorite Sites and Recent History

Internet Explorer maintains a repository of shortcuts to your favorite websites in the Favorites folder within your user profile. Any time you discover a site that you know (or suspect) you'll want to return to, you can add a shortcut to that site to the Favorites folder. To return to a favorite site, select it from the Favorites menu or the Favorites Center in Internet Explorer or from the Favorites folder in Windows Explorer. Or enter a word or two in the search box on the Start menu to display any saved favorites that match your search term.

Most of the techniques we describe in this section work the same in Internet Explorer 8 as they do in Internet Explorer 9. The biggest difference is that the Favorites button (a star that glows gold when you move the mouse pointer over it) has moved. It's on the left side of the browser tabs in Internet Explorer 8 but has relocated (and shed the text label) in Internet Explorer 9. You'll now find it in the middle of the group of three buttons to the right of the browser tabs. Click it to open the Favorites Center.

Don't be misled by the name; the Favorites Center has three tabs and also allows you to view and search your browsing history and the contents of any subscribed RSS feeds. To display the Favorites Center, click the Favorites button or press Alt+C. Figure 6-7 shows the Favorites Center in its default position in Internet Explorer 9.

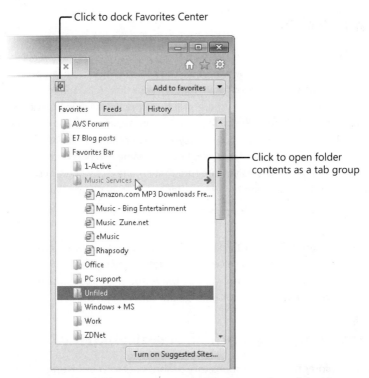

Click to dock Favorites Center

Click to open folder contents as a tab group

Figure 6-7 Click a folder name to expand its contents, then click a shortcut to open it in the current window. Click the blue arrow to the right of a folder to open all its shortcuts as a tab group.

The Favorites Center normally opens in a free-floating window just below the Favorites button. While it's open, you can drag the left edge to make it wider or narrower. Internet Explorer saves this preferred width and uses it the next time you open the Favorites Center. After you click to open a shortcut or a tab group (or click anywhere else in the browser window), the Favorites Center closes immediately. If you need to spend extra time exploring your browsing history or sifting through your favorites, click the button in the top left corner to pin the Favorites Center along the left side of the browser window.

To jump directly to any of the three available panes, learn their keyboard shortcuts: Ctrl+I for Favorites, Ctrl+G for Feeds, Ctrl+H for History. Add the Shift key to any of these shortcuts to open the respective tab in its pinned position: Ctrl+Shift+H, for example, pins the Favorites Center and switches to the History tab.

Windows Live Mesh includes an option to sync the contents of your Favorites folder on multiple PCs. For details, see "Synchronizing Files and Favorites with Windows Live Mesh" on page 295.

Both versions of the browser include a toolbar called the Favorites bar. (In earlier versions of Internet Explorer, this was called the Links bar.) Its purpose is to make particular favorites particularly easy to open—if you're willing to surrender some space in the browser window for one-click access. In Internet Explorer 9 the Favorites bar is normally hidden. To make it visible, right-click the title bar and select Favorites Bar from the list of available toolbars.

Adding, Editing, and Organizing Favorites

Internet Explorer makes it easy to add the currently displayed page (or all tabs in the current browser window) as a favorite. Any of the following methods will work:

- Press Ctrl+D.

- Click Favorites (or press Alt+C or Ctrl+I) to open the Favorites Center, and then click Add To Favorites.

- Pin the Favorites Center, and then drag the icon to the left of the web page address in the address bar into the Favorites list. If you want the item to go inside an existing subfolder that isn't open, point to the folder icon and wait. After a brief pause the folder opens, and you can drop the shortcut in its proper place within the subfolder.

- Right-click anywhere within the current page and choose Add To Favorites from the shortcut menu. This action adds the current page to the Favorites folder. If you point to a link on the page and choose this menu option, the newly created shortcut picks up the title and address of the link.

All of these methods, except the drag-and-drop procedure, produce the Add A Favorite dialog box, shown in Figure 6-8.

Figure 6-8 Internet Explorer proposes to use the page title as the name for the favorite. Replace the default page title with a shorter, simpler name to make the favorite easier to find.

The contents of the Name box are drawn from the page title, as defined by the owner of the site you're visiting. You can (and usually should) replace the page name with one that is descriptive and relevant to the reasons you chose to save the favorite in the first place.

Chapter 6

INSIDE OUT   Always rename favorites

Get in the habit of assigning a descriptive name when you save a favorite. Make sure the name you choose contains the words your future self is likely to use as search terms in the One Box. And steer clear of extra-long file names. Web designers often create outrageously long page titles, packing descriptions and keywords together, with the goal of ranking higher on search engines. Shorter, more meaningful names are easier to spot when you're scrolling through a folder full of shortcuts.

The Create In drop-down box allows you to save the new favorite within the top level of the Favorites folder, or you can choose an existing subfolder or create a new subfolder. Each favorite is saved as an Internet shortcut (a file with the extension .url) in the Favorites folder in your user profile.

You can edit these shortcuts the same way you edit any other kind of shortcut. Right-click any shortcut or folder in the Favorites Center to rename, copy, or delete the shortcut. You can also use Windows Explorer to rename your favorites and organize them into folders. You'll find the Favorites folder in your user profile (just type Favorites in the Start menu's search box). Right-click a shortcut in either location and choose Properties; that dialog box allows you to see and edit the address for the shortcut.

To save all open tabs in the current window as a folder of new favorites, open the Favorites Center, click the down arrow next to Add To Favorites, and choose Add Current Tabs To Favorites. After you specify a folder name and location, Internet Explorer saves all open tabs in that folder. If the folder name you enter already exists, the current tabs are added to that folder.

INSIDE OUT   Support your alter ego with the New Session command

Do you have multiple identities? The New Session command opens a new browser window without carrying over session cookies. That means, for example, that you can log on to one Hotmail account, start a new session, and log on to a second Hotmail account without logging off the first. New Session is on the File menu, on the traditional menu bar. If you aren't displaying the menu bar, press Alt+F to open the File menu.

Working with Pinned Sites

One of the most useful innovations in Internet Explorer 9 is the introduction of *pinned sites*. The idea behind this feature is straightforward: you open a website in a tab and then drag its icon from the address bar (or drag the tab itself) onto the taskbar, where it's pinned just like a program. If the site has a custom icon (also known as a *favicon*), the shortcut for the pinned site uses it instead of the generic Internet Explorer icon.

Here, for example, we've created four pinned sites and lined them up side by side on the right side of the taskbar. Notice the custom Jump List for the Hotmail shortcut. Any web developer can insert a snippet of code onto a site to create a similar custom list.

On the Windows 7 taskbar, pinned website shortcuts look exactly like locally installed apps, especially if the site developer has uploaded a full-size icon for Windows to use on the taskbar.

When you open a pinned site, its appearance is subtly different from a normal website. It maintains its privileged position on the taskbar, complete with personalized icon, which makes it easy for you to quickly get back to a site you use regularly. The personalized icon appears in the upper left corner of the browser window as well, and the Back and Forward buttons take on the same color as the icon.

Philosophically, these special shortcuts represent a way to divide web content into two distinct types. For basic browsing, you can save a site as a favorite, which is an ordinary shortcut that opens in an ordinary Internet Explorer window, with its tab identified by the big blue E icon on the associated taskbar button. With pinned sites, the shortcut you create uses the favicon supplied by the website owner, and when you open the site two visual differences are immediately obvious. First, the Back and Forward buttons shift slightly to the right, and the favicon for the site appears in the newly vacated space. And second, those navigation buttons pick up the predominant color of the favicon, just as program buttons in the Windows 7 taskbar pick up the icon's color when a mouse pointer passes over them.

This pair of screenshots shows the difference between a page opened in a standard Internet Explorer window (top) and the same page launched from a pinned site shortcut.

There's no Home button in the group of commands in the top right of the window. Instead, right-click the icon to the left of the Back button to add extra home pages to the pinned site. In a pinned site window, you can open new tabs just as you can in a standard Internet Explorer session.

INSIDE OUT   Pinned site shortcuts aren't just for the taskbar

It makes sense to pin your most favorite favorites, the websites you visit every day and leave open all day, to the taskbar. For other sites, avoid cluttering up the taskbar and pin a site to the Start menu instead. Click Tools, then click File, Add Site To Start Menu. You can also drag a tab from the browser window and drop it on Start. For sites on the New Tab page, right-click and then click Add Site To Start Menu. The advantage of saving pinned site shortcuts here is that Windows categorizes them as programs for search purposes, and it returns results from the Start menu instantly, before it even begins to search the rest of the index. Thus, when you start typing a search term, you see a list at the top of the Start menu that includes both installed programs and websites you've saved as pinned shortcuts.

When you pin a site to the taskbar or Start menu, the saved shortcut uses a new registered file type for Windows, officially known as a Pinned Site Shortcut. It is almost exactly like a regular Internet shortcut except that it has a .website file name extension instead of a .url extension. In fact, you can turn a regular web shortcut into a pinned site shortcut, or vice versa, by changing the extension.

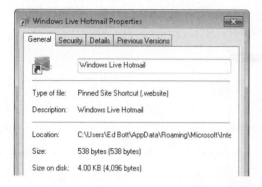

There is nothing magical about a pinned site shortcut. The .website extension tells Windows to call Internet Explorer with a set of special startup switches:

"C:\Program Files (x86)\Internet Explorer\iexplore.exe" -w "%l" %*

The **–w** switch is what causes Internet Explorer 9 to treat this process as a pinned website rather than a standard web page. The remaining parameters tell Internet Explorer to use the saved location and any other switches from the saved shortcut.

Using Your Browser History to Revisit Familiar Sites

Internet Explorer hides your browsing history on the third tab in the Favorites Center. You can get there by clicking Favorites and then clicking the History tab, or use the keyboard shortcut Ctrl+H (to open the Favorites Center in its regular location) or Ctrl+Shift+H (to pin the Favorites Center to the left side of the browser window).

As Figure 6-9 shows, you can sort the History list in various ways. Click the drop-down list to view by date ("I know I visited that site last Tuesday") or by order visited today ("I saw that page this morning").

More important, perhaps, the list includes a Search History option. The search tool won't find content buried on a page, but it will find words that appear in page titles. For example, suppose you visited the website of an airport shuttle service and looked at the home page, a page called Rates, and another called Reservations. You don't remember the name of the company or which day you were pondering a limo ride, but you do remember you went to the Reservations page. Search your history for Reservations, and you'll find what you need.

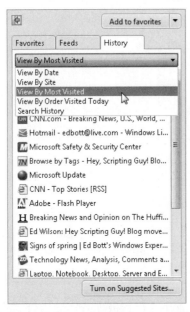

Figure 6-9 You can sort the History list in a variety of memory-jogging ways. For best results, try the Search History option.

Managing and Troubleshooting Add-Ons

Browser add-ons can be a mixed blessing. On the plus side, they allow you to greatly extend the capabilities of Internet Explorer. It's hard to imagine accomplishing anything online without the help of Adobe's Flash Player and Microsoft's Silverlight, for example. Both are ActiveX add-ons. Microsoft Office and Windows Live Essentials include useful add-ons for Internet Explorer, as do many third-party programs.

The downside is that a poorly written (or deliberately hostile) add-on can be a drag on performance and can introduce security risks. In extreme examples, an ill-behaved add-on can cause the browser to crash or become unstable. Too many add-ons (even harmless ones) can cause clutter and noise that you might prefer not to deal with.

Internet Explorer 9 supports a variety of add-on types. ActiveX controls, extensions, browser helper objects, and toolbars typically use a standard Windows installer package. Markup-based add-ons such as accelerators and search providers are typically installed from the browser itself. Use the Manage Add-Ons dialog box to see information about any installed add-on, regardless of its type. You can inspect version numbers, see how many times an add-on has been used or blocked, and view details of the performance impact of any add-on. More importantly, you can disable an add-on completely, either as a troubleshooting step or as a way to improve the performance and reliability of Internet Explorer.

Managing Toolbars and Extensions

The most powerful (and potentially invasive) group of add-ons is available at the top of the Manage Add-Ons dialog box. Click Tools, Manage Add-Ons, and then click Toolbars And Extensions in the Add-On Types list. That opens the dialog box shown in Figure 6-10.

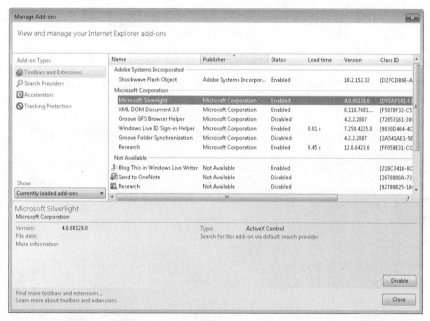

Figure 6-10 Select an item from the list of installed add-ons to enable or disable it. You can view a summary of details about the item in the pane below the list.

When you select an item in the list of add-ons, you can see more details about it in the pane below, including the publisher's name, the version number and file date (if available), and the add-on type. In the lower right corner of the dialog box is a button that allows you to enable or disable the add-on.

INSIDE OUT

Get more information from the Manage Add-Ons dialog box

By default, the Toolbars And Extensions list contains five columns and is grouped by publisher. You can add columns to this listing by right-clicking any column heading and clicking Columns on the shortcut menu. Available columns include File, Folder, and one obscure but extremely useful entry: Class ID. That option shows you the long GUID that identifies the selected add-on in the registry. Knowing that information can be tremendously helpful when troubleshooting. The same right-click menu allows you to choose a different grouping or sort order for the list. Group by Status, for example, and you can see at a glance which add-ons are enabled and which are disabled.

If you're ready to be completely overloaded with information about an add-on, double-click its name in the list, or click the More Information link in the information pane below the list. If the selected add-on is an ActiveX control, you see an information-rich dialog box like the one shown here.

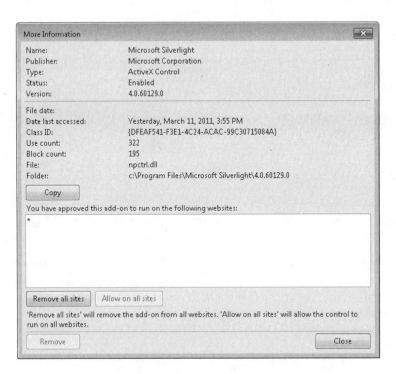

When you install a well-known ActiveX control, such as the Adobe Flash player or Microsoft's Silverlight, it is approved to run automatically on all websites you visit. That setting is reflected in the More Information dialog box for the add-on, where an asterisk—the wild-card character for "all"—appears in the You Have Approved This Add-on To Run On The Following Websites box.

If you're more cautious than the average Windows user, you might want the option to approve websites on a site-by-site basis for a particular ActiveX control. In that case, click the Remove All Sites button. From that point forward, you'll see a polite request in the Notification bar at the bottom of the Internet Explorer window when you visit a site that uses that control. If you make this change to the Shockwave Flash Object add-on, for example, you'll see this notification when you visit a page that uses Flash:

If you trust the website and want to allow it to use the installed add-on, click Allow. The arrow to the right of the Allow button lets you automatically allow the add-on for all websites. You can safely ignore the notification and continue browsing if you don't want to use the add-on with that site.

Internet Explorer 9 also offers a global feature called ActiveX Filtering, which allows you to disable all ActiveX controls and then reenable them on a per-site basis. For details, see "Controlling ActiveX" on page 254.

Adding, Removing, and Managing Search Providers

As we explained earlier in this chapter, Internet Explorer allows you to search for information without actually visiting a website. All you have to do is enter search terms in the address bar. If your current search provider supports search suggestions, you see them in the results list below the address bar. If you press Enter or click Go, Internet Explorer opens the default search provider and passes your search terms to it.

On a clean installation of Windows 7, the default search provider is set to Microsoft's Bing, but you can add other search providers to the list of available search engines. If you have more than one search provider installed, you can change the default search provider. Each installed search provider appears in a neat row at the bottom of the results list when you type in the One Box; use those icons to choose an alternative search provider.

To manage the list of available search providers, click the search button (the magnifying glass icon) at the end of the address bar and then click Add at the bottom of the results list. Alternatively, click Tools, Manage Add-Ons, and then click Search Providers in the Add-On Types list. Either route leads to the dialog box shown in Figure 6-11, which lists all installed providers.

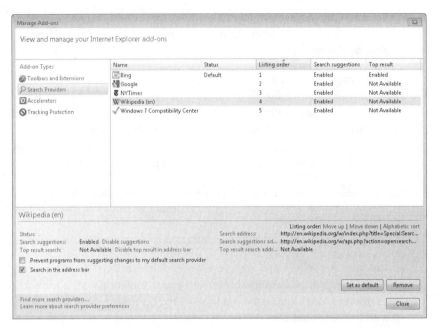

Figure 6-11 This page lists all installed search providers. The pane below the list allows you to disable or remove a provider and to change the order in which providers appear.

In this dialog box, click Find More Search Providers (the tiny link is in the lower left corner), which takes you to the Internet Explorer Add-Ons Gallery. There, you can sift through an extensive selection of search providers that you can add to your installation. When you click Add To Internet Explorer to add a search provider, a dialog box like this one appears.

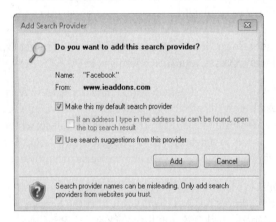

If you're adding a search provider because you want to use it for occasional specialized searches, clear the top check box, which offers to set the provider as the default. If you select Use Search Suggestions From This Provider, the search box provides AutoComplete functionality, potentially helping you to define your search more clearly before you get to the actual search page—and, at any rate, saving you keystrokes.

Certain search providers are identified on the Search Providers page as offering Visual Search. These providers add graphic thumbnails to their search suggestions when those thumbnails are available.

Configuring Accelerators

Accelerators debuted in Internet Explorer 8 and are essentially unchanged in Internet Explorer 9. These innovative, markup-based add-ons are designed to save you keystrokes, mouse clicks, and context switching. When you select text (or a document or link) on a web page, the browser assumes you want to do something with that selection and displays a blue button with an arrow pointing northeast:

If you click the blue arrow, Internet Explorer displays a list of default accelerators for each of several categories. You might, for example, see an accelerator that will transfer your selection directly to an e-mail program, another that offers to translate the text into a different language, another that shares a link with your Facebook account, and so on. (If the blue arrow is distracting or too small, you can right-click instead; all installed accelerators are available at the bottom of the shortcut menu.)

As Figure 6-12 shows, some accelerators perform their duties in a pop-out window that doesn't require you to leave the current page.

The menu that pops up when you click the Accelerators button lists only those accelerators that are registered as default for a given category. Click All Accelerators to choose from the entire list of installed accelerators.

By default, Internet Explorer 9 includes a handful of accelerators. You can supplement this group with additional options from the Internet Explorer Add-Ons Gallery. To manage installed accelerators, click Manage Accelerators at the bottom of the All Accelerators menu, or click Tools, Manage Add-Ons, and then select Accelerators from the Add-On Type list. The resulting dialog box, shown in Figure 6-13, allows you to change category defaults or to remove or disable accelerators.

Chapter 6

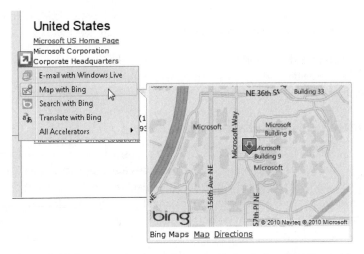

Figure 6-12 Some accelerators let you see their results without requiring you to leave the current page.

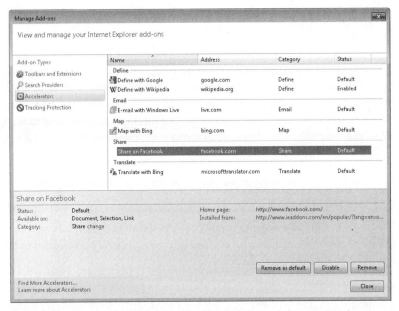

Figure 6-13 Use the Find More Accelerators link (lower left corner) to browse and install additional add-ons, and then manage categories here.

Troubleshooting Problems Caused by Add-Ons

As we noted at the start of this section, add-ons can be a mixed blessing. Every add-on requires its own (usually small) allotment of system resources and can add incrementally to the time required to start Internet Explorer and load a web page. In the Manage Add-Ons dialog box, Internet Explorer lists the load time and navigation time for all entries in the Toolbars And Extensions group. A delay of as little as 0.2 seconds can be noticeable, and if multiple add-ons are competing for resources each time you open a web page, the delay can be especially annoying.

Some programs include add-ons for Internet Explorer that were designed for use with an earlier version of Internet Explorer and are incompatible (or problematic) with the current version. If Internet Explorer detects a potential compatibility issue, you might see an error message offering to check for an update or to disable the add-on.

If Internet Explorer does not detect a troublesome add-on at startup but you suspect that an add-on is causing problems—sluggish performance, for example, or unwanted behavior of some kind—you might be able to verify your suspicion by starting Internet Explorer with all add-ons disabled. To do this, click Start and choose All Programs; then click Accessories, System Tools, Internet Explorer (No Add-Ons). It might be quicker to type **iexplore –extoff** in the Start menu search box.

If that step resolves the issue you're seeing, it's a strong indication that the problem is a balky add-on. The next step in the troubleshooting process is to use the Manage Add-Ons dialog box to disable all available add-ons. Click Toolbars And Extensions in the Add-On Types list, click to select any add-on, and then begin reenabling them one by one until you find the one that's causing the problem.

If you're unable to identify the source of a problem, you can try the extreme approach of resetting Internet Explorer to its default settings. That step disables all add-ons and restores default privacy and security settings. To begin, click Tools, Internet Options, and then click the Reset button at the bottom of the Advanced tab. Doing so displays the dialog box shown here.

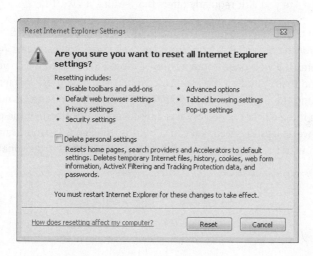

Note that a reset does not affect your personal settings, nor does it remove or disable markup-based add-ons such as search providers and accelerators. If you want to remove all of these settings as well and give Internet Explorer a fresh start, select the Delete Personal Settings check box before you click Reset.

Working with RSS Feeds and Web Slices

When is a web page not exactly a web page? When it's a web *feed*. Feeds are delivered using the HTTP protocol, but they're put together programmatically by using Extensible Markup Language (XML) and the Really Simple Syndication (RSS) standard. A web feed is basically a well-structured list of items, each with a headline, a body, date and time stamps, and other standard details. The page is designed to be regenerated after new items are posted; the latest feed is downloaded at a regular interval and reconstituted at the receiver's end by an RSS reading tool.

Web feeds allow you to avoid having to constantly check a news site or blog to find out if anything new has been posted. When you use Internet Explorer as a feed reader, you can subscribe to an RSS feed and allow the browser to download the feed on a schedule you set up. When a new post appears, the link for that site turns bold, and clicking it shows the unread material in your browser window.

Web feeds work in browsers and in RSS client software, and they work on any computing platform, even on phones. Web *slices*, on the other hand, are available only in Internet Explorer 8 or later. Think of them as miniature feeds that are drawn from part of a page and that don't require you to shift context to get some dollop of information—the current weather forecast, for example. Web slices, once installed, live on your Favorites bar. Like RSS feeds, their headings turn bold when their content has been refreshed. Web slices are not widely used, but if a site you visit regularly offers this feature, it's worth checking out.

In Internet Explorer 9, you need to jump through a few hoops to discover RSS feeds. Look on the page itself for the orange RSS icon. From any web page, you can press Alt+T to open the Tools menu. If a web page contains one or more RSS feeds to which you can subscribe, you'll find them listed on the Feed Discovery menu. If you use this feature regularly, consider making the Command bar visible. The Feeds button on the Command bar changes to orange if the current page contains a discoverable RSS feed. (If the page contains one or more web slices to which you can subscribe, the Feeds button turns green.) Click the down arrow to the right of the Feeds button or press Alt+J to see what's available.

Then click the item to which you want to subscribe.

When you open a feed in Internet Explorer, the browser applies a uniform style sheet to the page, and you see the feed's contents in the browser window, as shown in Figure 6-14. The box at the top of the page shows the feed's title as set by the site developer. The box on the right allows you to filter the list of items by typing a term in the search box; if items in the feed include categories, you can use those tags to filter the list.

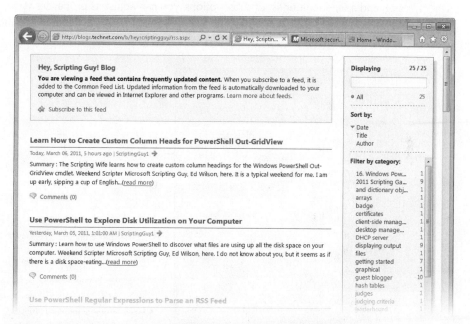

Figure 6-14 Some RSS feeds contain only brief summaries of longer posts or media files. Click the Read More link to open the associated item.

To add a new feed to the list in the Favorites Center, click the Subscribe To This Feed link. That action opens the dialog box shown here. These settings, which are similar to those you enter when you create a web favorite, allow you to give the feed a descriptive name and, optionally, add it to your Favorites bar.

To view all feeds on your subscribed list, open the Feeds list in the Favorites Center. After you add a feed to your list of subscriptions, you can adjust its properties by right-clicking the feed name in the Favorites Center and choosing Properties. Figure 6-15 shows the properties available for you to change.

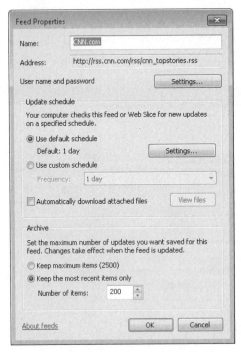

Figure 6-15 For a news-related web feed, you might prefer more frequent updates rather than sticking with the default daily schedule.

When you view an RSS feed directly in Internet Explorer, you might notice a mention of the Common Feed List. This feature allows other programs to share the list of subscribed feeds available from Internet Explorer. If you use Microsoft Outlook, for example, you'll find an RSS Feeds tab in the Account Settings dialog box. Any feeds you add or change using Internet Explorer show up here, and vice versa. Using Outlook to retrieve the contents of an RSS feed allows you to see each item in its own Outlook message window, with feeds organized into folders by name and Outlook's full search capabilities available. If you live in Outlook from sunrise to sunset, this option offers an easy way to bring the news into an environment where you're likely to see it.

CHAPTER 7

Internet Explorer Compatibility, Security, and Privacy

IN the previous chapter, we focused on the essentials of browsing in Internet Explorer. In this chapter, we look at a handful of features that allow you to exert control over what appears in the browser window.

Our discussion starts with an in-depth explanation of the compatibility features included in Internet Explorer 9. If a page isn't rendering correctly, you might be able to fix it by clicking a button.

To help you cope with potential online threats, Internet Explorer 9 includes a broad assortment of security features, the most important of which is Protected Mode. In this chapter, we explain how Protected Mode works, and we dive into details about other important security features. We also explain how the new Download Manager helps safeguard you from potentially dangerous files.

In recent years, online advertising has grown into an enormous industry, with advertisers and specialized web analytics firms vying for ways to capture data about your online habits so that they can serve more targeted ads to you. To tilt the balance of privacy back in your favor, Internet Explorer 9 includes a group of interesting new Tracking Protection features, which we describe in detail in "Protecting Your Privacy" on page 263.

What's in Your Edition?

All of the tools and techniques we describe in this chapter are available in all editions of Windows 7. Our discussion is based on the features and user interface available in Internet Explorer 9, which is available as a free upgrade for all Windows 7 editions.

Dealing with Compatibility Issues

With Internet Explorer 8, Microsoft inched closer to the goal of being fully compliant with World Wide Web Consortium (W3C) and Internet Engineering Task Force (IETF) standards. Internet Explorer 9 dives emphatically over the line, offering greatly improved support for modern layout standards, including support for version 3 of the cascading style sheets standard and version 5 of the W3C's Hypertext Markup Language standard. These changes are often loosely grouped under the HTML5 and CSS3 headings.

Because earlier versions of Internet Explorer are so entrenched in the market, however, many web developers have designed their sites in conformance with older, proprietary layout rules rather than with established web standards. As a result, a site designed to look good using the nonstandard markup required by Internet Explorer 7 might produce layout errors in Internet Explorer 8 or Internet Explorer 9.

Internet Explorer 9 includes a complicated set of options designed to deal with some common compatibility issues. The most obvious feature is the Compatibility View button in the address bar, which instructs the browser to display all pages from the current domain as if they were being viewed in Internet Explorer 7. But the full range of compatibility options is far more complex than that, and knowing at least the broad outlines can help you understand why a given page fails to render correctly in Internet Explorer.

> **Note**
>
> If you're a web developer, these details are tremendously important, and you should study them carefully to ensure that you deliver a good experience to anyone who visits your site using Internet Explorer. For a general overview, see the blog post "IE's Compatibility Features for Site Developers" (*w7io.com/20702*). You'll find two comprehensive articles at the Microsoft Developer Network (MSDN): "Defining Document Compatibility" (*w7io.com/20701*) explains how this feature works, with details on how to specify document compatibility mode for a web page you create and how to determine the document mode of a page you access in Internet Explorer. "Understanding the Compatibility View List" (*w7io.com/20703*) provides an in-depth discussion on how Microsoft's compatibility list is created.

Internet Explorer's rendering engine (officially known as Trident) uses two settings to determine how to render a page. The first is the browser mode, which includes the User-Agent (UA) string that Internet Explorer sends as part of a request to a web server and that controls how it responds to conditional comments on a web page. The second important setting is the document mode, which determines how Trident displays the page. A website designer who wants to ensure that pages are displayed using a predictable set of layout rules can add HTML markup in the header of a page to force Internet Explorer 9 to use a specific document mode.

Internet Explorer 9 includes four possible values for browser mode:

- **IE9**   This is the default mode for Internet Explorer 9 and represents the most standards-compliant rendering.

- **IE9 Compatibility View**   This is the browser-mode setting that Internet Explorer 9 uses if you click the Compatibility View button. The browser behaves as if it is Internet Explorer 7; the User-Agent string identifies the browser as Internet Explorer 7 but includes a token (Trident/5.0) to signal that the browser is really Internet Explorer 9.

- **IE8**   Internet Explorer reports a User-Agent string, version vector, and document mode as if it were Internet Explorer 8.

- **IE7**   Internet Explorer reports a User-Agent string, version vector, and document mode as if it were Internet Explorer 7.

Document mode can be specified by the site owner in the page markup itself. Internet Explorer 9 looks first to the <!DOCTYPE> directive on a page to decide how to lay it out. Web developers can override the default behavior by adding an X-UA-Compatible tag to the HTML markup for a page. That tag instructs Internet Explorer to display the page as if it were being viewed by an older version of the browser. There are four possible document-mode settings. The first three items on the following list apply when <!DOCTYPE> is set to strict or is unknown:

- **IE9 Standards**   This is the default mode used by Internet Explorer 9 to render a page using its most standards-compliant behavior.

- **IE8 Standards**   This behavior matches that of Internet Explorer 8.

- **IE7 Standards**   This behavior matches that of Internet Explorer 7.

- **Quirks**   Quirks mode is the most primitive document mode of all. If the <!DOCTYPE> directive is missing or is set to Quirks mode, Internet Explorer uses a behavior that is similar to that of Internet Explorer 5.

To see at a glance which browser mode and document mode are in use for a given page, press F12, or click Tools and then click F12 Developer Tools. This opens an information-packed dialog box that is normally docked at the bottom of the browser window but can also be allowed to float. The current settings are shown to the right of the menu; you can click either one to change its value. Figure 7-1 shows the settings for a page that does not include an X-UA-Compatible tag and for which we clicked the Compatibility View button.

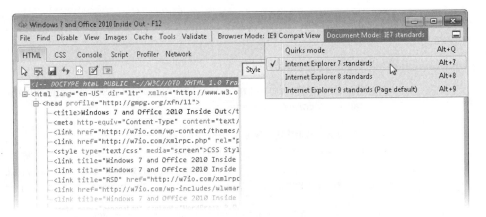

Figure 7-1 The browser-mode and document-mode settings shown here were applied when we clicked the Compatibility View button.

A handful of Compatibility View settings are well hidden in Internet Explorer 9. To get to them, you must tap Alt to display the menu bar, then click Tools, Compatibility View Settings to open the dialog box shown in Figure 7-2.

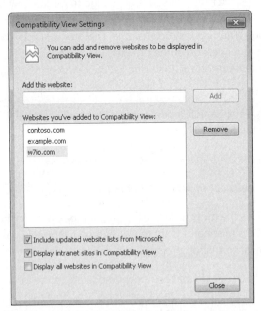

Figure 7-2 The first check box at the bottom of this dialog box allows you to enable or disable Microsoft's Compatibility View list.

Microsoft's Compatibility View list can also manipulate the document-mode setting for a page, as we explain in the next section.

Using the Compatibility View List

When you run Internet Explorer for the first time in Windows 7, you must decide whether to use Microsoft's Compatibility View list to control the display of certain websites. Most Internet Explorer 9 users opt in to this list. You can use the Compatibility View Settings dialog box to enable or disable this feature at any time.

This list is designed to customize how a website appears to Internet Explorer 9. In general, the entries on this list are from high-traffic sites that were designed for use in an earlier version of Internet Explorer and don't display properly using Internet Explorer 9's standards-compliant mode. For example, if a domain is on the list with a value of docMode="EmulateIE8", the effect is the same as if all pages in that domain had been set to use IE8 Standards mode.

In Internet Explorer 8, changes to the Compatibility View list are delivered via Windows Update. In Internet Explorer 9, this list is maintained on an XML page hosted on Microsoft.com and can thus be updated immediately. To view the most current local version of this list in Internet Explorer 9, enter the following in the address bar:

file:\\%LOCALAPPDATA%\Microsoft\Internet Explorer\IECompatData\iecompatdata.xml

Note that a website developer can override the settings on Microsoft's Compatibility View list by including an X-UA-Compatible tag in the header.

Using the Compatibility View Button

When you click the Compatibility View button, Internet Explorer 9 displays pages as if they were created using the IE7 Standards document mode. In its request for the page, the browser identifies itself with the Internet Explorer 7 User-Agent string, which means conditional comments in the page markup are interpreted for that older browser. The gray broken-page icon turns blue when it's been clicked.

Compatibility View

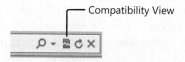

Here are some other noteworthy details about Compatibility View:

- Intranet sites (sites in your Local Intranet security zone) are displayed in Compatibility View by default. To change this behavior, clear the Display Intranet Sites In Compatibility View check box in the Compatibility View Settings dialog box.

- When you visit a domain included in Microsoft's Compatibility View list, the Compatibility View button is not available in the address bar.

- For domains that are in the Internet zone and are not included on Microsoft's Compatibility View list, the Compatibility View button is available. Clicking that button saves the current domain in the Compatibility View Settings dialog box, which allows Internet Explorer to remember the setting when it returns to any page in that domain. Click Compatibility View again to remove the domain from your personalized list.

- If the markup on a page includes an X-UA-Compatible tag, the Compatibility View button is not available.

Monitoring and Maintaining Security

The bedrock of security in Internet Explorer is its consistent use of Windows permissions to limit what web pages and add-ons can do with files, registry keys, and other objects. This security fence around the browser window is called Protected Mode. It was introduced in Internet Explorer 7, and it requires security features found only in Windows Vista and Windows 7. If you've recently upgraded from Windows XP, Protected Mode is a welcome new addition.

In the following sections, among other things, we explain how Protected Mode defangs potentially dangerous add-ons by restricting their access to system files and redirecting files they save or create to locked-down virtualized locations. We show how to use a new feature in Internet Explorer 9 that offers significant protection from vulnerabilities in ActiveX controls, a frequent source of security headaches through the years. We also explain how Internet Explorer's use of security zones lets you apply different levels of security to different categories of sites.

Working with Protected Mode

Using a web browser exposes you to special security risks; by clicking a link in an e-mail message or mistyping a web address, you can find yourself on a site that contains hostile script or downloadable code intended to take over your system. To mitigate these threats, Internet Explorer runs in Protected Mode. This special mode, which is active in all external Internet Explorer security zones except the Trusted Sites zone, takes advantage of a wide range of security-related features, notably User Account Control (UAC). When Protected Mode is enabled (the default setting), Internet Explorer runs with severely limited privileges. The purpose of these restrictions is to prevent a website from installing programs without your permission or changing system settings.

In Windows 7, every running application process and object (such as a file created by an application) has an integrity level (IL) defined by the Mandatory Integrity Control feature. The three most common options—Low, Medium, and High—represent the trustworthiness of that process or object. By default, processes that are started by a standard user have an

IL of Medium, and elevated processes have an IL of High. Windows uses policies to block processes of lower integrity (and thus lower trustworthiness) from reading or modifying objects of higher integrity. These integrity levels allow Windows to control access in a way that cannot be defined by user or group permissions in access control lists (ACLs).

In Protected Mode, all processes and files associated with Internet Explorer run with a Low integrity level. As a result, Internet Explorer is prevented from writing to areas of the file system or the registry that require a higher privilege, and web sites running in the browser are prevented from interacting with processes of higher integrity levels without your explicit permission. Add-ons such as ActiveX controls and toolbars use the same Low IL, preventing them from gaining access to any parts of the file system except those specifically created for storing potentially unsafe data and programs.

How Do You Check a File's Integrity?

To see the integrity level for a file or folder, open a Command Prompt window and use the icacls command followed by the name of the file or folder. If the integrity level is something other than the default Medium, the last line will look like this:

```
C:\>icacls "C:\Users\Ed Bott\AppData\Local\Temp\Low"

NT AUTHORITY\SYSTEM:(I)(OI)(CI)(F)
BUILTIN\Administrators:(I)(OI)(CI)(F)
XPS435\Ed Bott:(I)(OI)(CI)(F)
Mandatory Label\Low Mandatory Level:(OI)(CI)(NW)
```

To see the integrity level of a running process, use the Sysinternals tool Process Explorer. We describe the ins and outs of this amazingly powerful diagnostic tool in "Advanced Performance Analysis Tools and Techniques" on page 868.

Folders and files created by Internet Explorer in Protected Mode inherit its Low integrity level. When Internet Explorer needs to work with files or folders in a higher integrity level, a broker process intercepts the operation and asks for your consent before continuing. This represents an important concept of Protected Mode: whenever any action requires a higher privilege level, such as an ActiveX installation or an attempt to save a file, a broker process must be invoked.

On a default installation of Internet Explorer 8 or Internet Explorer 9, with User Account Control on, Protected Mode is enabled for the Internet and Restricted Sites zones and is off in the Intranet and Trusted Sites zones. (We discuss security zones in more detail in the following section.) If you disable User Account Control, Protected Mode is also disabled in all zones. It is never advisable to disable Protected Mode in the Restricted Sites zone. It is possible to disable Protected Mode in the Internet zone. We recommend doing so only if you are fully cognizant of the risks inherent in doing so. The following steps include the strong recommendation that you reenable Protected Mode immediately after you finish the activity that conflicts with it.

To disable Protected Mode for the Internet zone, follow these steps:

1. In Internet Explorer, click Tools, and then click Internet Options.

2. Click the Security tab, select Internet from the list of zones at the top of the dialog box, and clear the Enable Protected Mode check box.

3. Click OK to continue, and close the Internet Options dialog box. Close all instances of Internet Explorer. After you restart Internet Explorer, Windows displays a warning that the current security settings will put your computer at risk. Click OK to continue.

When Protected Mode is off, navigating to any web page displays a warning message at the bottom of the browser window:

To reenable this important security feature, click Turn On Protected Mode. If you choose to hide this warning, you need to return to the Internet Options dialog box, click the Security tab, and select the Enable Protected Mode check box.

Another method for working around Protected Mode restrictions for a specific website is to add the site to the Trusted Sites zone, where Protected Mode is not in effect. We recommend that you exercise caution before using this technique, however; adding a site to the Trusted Sites zone enables a wide range of potentially risky behaviors, and it's easy to forget to remove the site from the Trusted Sites zone after you finish working with it.

Controlling ActiveX

ActiveX controls are small programs that run inside the browser window to enhance the functionality of a website. They're used for such things as enabling you to play games with other Internet users, displaying stock tickers, and displaying animation. The best known of all ActiveX controls, of course, is Adobe's Flash Player. Outside the U.S., ActiveX is widely used, especially in banking applications. Microsoft's various update sites use ActiveX controls to compare installed patches and updates on your system with those available on Microsoft's servers. ActiveX controls contain binary code and, like executables that you run from the Start menu or a command line, they have full access to your computer's resources, although they are subject to some security restrictions.

> **Note**
>
> You cannot download an ActiveX control, scan it for viruses, and install it separately. ActiveX controls must be installed on the fly. Although the inability to scan for viruses in advance might sound like a security risk, you're protected from known viruses if you've configured your antivirus software to perform real-time scanning for hostile code. If the ActiveX control contains the signature of a known virus or worm or engages in suspicious behavior, the antivirus software will intercept it and refuse to allow the installation to proceed. As with any program you download and install, of course, you need to exercise caution and be confident that the download is safe before allowing it on your computer.

Even a seemingly safe ActiveX control from a trusted source can lead to trouble, however. Over the years, ActiveX controls have been associated with a frightening number of security vulnerabilities that resulted from an attacker's ability to exploit a flaw in an apparently benign control.

To tip the balance back in your favor, Windows 7 and Internet Explorer collectively offer two features aimed at blocking ActiveX-related problems. The first feature, ActiveX opt-in, kicks in whenever you visit a website that tries to run an ActiveX control that isn't on a small list of widely used controls. In that case you're prompted to approve the use of the control—on the current site or on all sites. If you're not certain of the site's safety, resist the urge to click Yes. This feature is available in Internet Explorer 8 as well.

The second feature, available only in Internet Explorer 9, is a potentially much bigger addition to your online security. Clicking ActiveX Filtering on the Safety menu acts like a master switch that universally disables all ActiveX controls on all sites. When you enable this option, the only immediate change is the check mark that appears next to it.

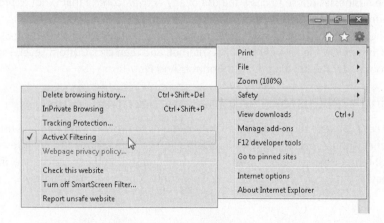

With ActiveX Filtering on, content that requires any ActiveX control is silently disabled when you visit a new website, with no prompts to install or reenable the plugin. (That effect can be disconcerting and difficult to troubleshoot if you are expecting a Flash video to play or a bank balance to appear on the screen.) The only indication that content has been blocked is a vivid blue icon that immediately follows the web page address in the address bar. Click that icon and you'll see a message that refers to ActiveX Filtering, like the one shown in Figure 7-3.

Figure 7-3 Click the blue icon in the address bar to turn off ActiveX Filtering for the current site. Doing so disables filtering for all pages on that domain.

When you enable ActiveX Filtering, you set yourself up for a minor succession of annoyances. On sites that use ActiveX controls, some features might not work, and you might be prompted to install controls that are, in fact, already installed. To restore such a site to working order, you have to click the blue icon and then click Turn Off ActiveX Filtering. Internet Explorer saves your preference. The domain name is added as a DWORD value to the registry, in the HKCU\Software\Microsoft\Internet Explorer\Safety\ActiveXFilterExceptions key, so that any future visits to that domain work as expected.

Some businesses refuse to allow the use of any ActiveX control that is not approved by an administrator. Others disallow all ActiveX controls. If you need to tighten the security settings imposed on ActiveX controls in the Internet zone, click Tools and choose Internet Options. On the Security tab, click Internet, and then click Custom Level. Then adjust options under the heading ActiveX Controls And Plug-Ins.

Using and Customizing Internet Security Zones

Internet Explorer's security zones are key elements to browsing the web and using the Internet without fear. By default, all websites you visit are assigned to the Internet zone, and Internet Explorer severely restricts the action of sites in the Internet zone. If you're concerned about security, you can lock down security zones even more tightly.

By default, Internet Explorer allows you to work with four security zones:

- The Internet zone includes all sites that are not included in any other category.

- The Local Intranet zone is for sites on your local network—typically behind a firewall. Protected Mode is turned off by default in this zone.

- The Trusted Sites zone allows you to specify sites on which you allow certain actions—such as running ActiveX controls or scripts—that you might not permit on other sites in which you have a lower degree of trust. Protected Mode is off by default in this zone.

- The Restricted Sites zone allows you to specify sites where you want to specifically disallow actions that might otherwise be permitted.

How Security Zones Affect the Way You Browse

When you open a web page using Internet Explorer, Windows checks to see which security zone that page is assigned to and then applies restrictions to that page based on the settings for that zone. Initially, any sites you connect to internally (that is, sites on your home or business network) are automatically assigned to the Local Intranet zone. Internet Explorer includes a group of predefined settings—High, Medium-High, and Medium are available in any zone; Medium-Low and Low are unavailable in the Internet zone. You can assign one of these preset security levels to a zone by using the slider control on the Security tab of the Internet Options dialog box, as shown in Figure 7-4.

If you choose to enable intranet settings, the Local Intranet zone is accorded a Medium-Low level of security settings. All other sites on the Internet are lumped into the Internet zone, which is given a Medium-High security level. As you roam the Internet, if you come upon a site that you trust completely, you can move that site into the Trusted Sites zone. Internet Explorer, by default, applies a Medium level of security settings to the Trusted Sites zone. When you discover a site that warrants a high degree of wariness, you can move that site into the Restricted Sites zone. The security settings that apply there are, by default, described as High.

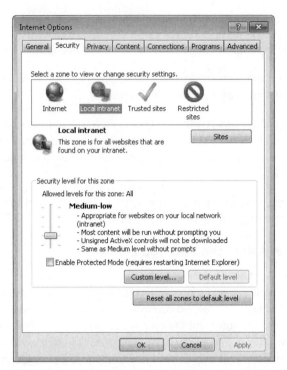

Figure 7-4 Use this dialog box to add sites to specific zones or to modify the security settings associated with a zone.

To manually add a site to your Trusted Sites or Restricted Sites zone, follow these steps:

1. On the Security tab of the Internet Options dialog box, select Trusted Sites or Restricted Sites.

2. Click Sites. You'll see the following dialog box (or one similar if you selected Restricted Sites):

3. The URL for the current site appears in the Add This Website To The Zone box. Edit or replace this value if necessary, and then click Add.

By design, the Trusted Sites zone is most appropriate for use with secure sites, where you already have a high degree of confidence that the site you're interacting with is legitimate. Thus, the default settings for this zone require that Internet Explorer verify that the site's server is secure (in other words, that its URL begins with *https:*) before establishing a connection. To add a non–Secure Sockets Layer (SSL) site to the list, clear the check box at the bottom of the Trusted Sites dialog box. (After adding the site, you can select the check box again.) When you add a domain (such as *http://example.com*) to either of these zones, all URLs located within that domain are assigned to the zone you select.

By default, Internet Explorer populates the Local Intranet zone with the following:

- All intranet sites that you haven't moved into either the Trusted Sites zone or the Restricted Sites zone

- All sites that bypass your proxy server, if one exists on your network

- All network servers accessed via UNC paths (*server_name*)

To remove one or more of these categories (so that the affected category joins the Internet zone), select Local Intranet in the Internet Options dialog box and then click Sites. You'll see the following dialog box. Clear the appropriate check boxes.

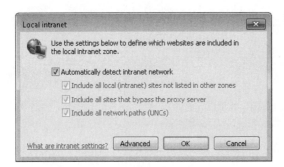

If you want to add a site to the Local Intranet zone, click the Advanced button. Then type the site's URL and click Add.

Changing a Zone's Security Settings

Any site placed in a security zone is subject to the same privileges and restrictions as all other sites in that zone. Thus, if you change the overall security settings associated with the zone, you change the security settings for all of its member sites. You can change the security settings for a zone to one of the predefined groups by following these steps:

1. On the Security tab of the Internet Options dialog box (shown earlier in Figure 7-4), click the icon for the zone you want to adjust.

CAUTION

If you previously made any customizations to security settings for a particular zone, those settings are wiped out as soon as you click Default Level. If you make specific changes to allow a program or site to work correctly, be sure you document those settings so that you can reapply them after changing other security settings.

2. If you previously customized the security settings for the selected zone, click the Default Level button in the Security Level For This Zone section to reveal a slider control. If the zone is using default settings already, you can skip this step.

3. Move the slider up to apply more stringent security measures or down to be more lenient. As you move the slider from level to level, the description to the right of the slider summarizes the current level's settings.

To fine-tune the settings for a zone or to read all the particulars about the current level of settings, click Custom Level. In the Security Settings dialog box that appears, you can use the option buttons to adjust individual settings.

If you customized a security zone's settings and you want to start over from a clean slate, open the Security Settings dialog box, choose a predefined level from the Reset To drop-down list, and then click Reset.

Using Scripts Wisely

Scripts are snippets of code, written in a scripting language such as JavaScript or VBScript, that run on the client computer (that is, *your* computer, not the web provider's) to enhance the functionality of a web page. Scripts should be distinguished from Active Server Pages (web pages with the extension .asp or .aspx), which employ a server-side scripting technology and don't, by themselves, represent a security hazard.

Scripts are generally harmless and are widely used in modern web design. However, security experts sometimes advise users to disable active scripting as a security measure. If you decide to take this extreme step, be prepared for many of your favorite websites to stop working properly.

If you're still determined to disable scripting, follow these steps:

1. Choose Internet Options from the Tools menu.

2. On the Security tab, click the Internet icon and then click Custom Level.

3. In the Settings list, locate Active Scripting (under the Scripting heading) and click Disable.

4. Click OK to save your settings, and then click OK to close the Internet Options dialog box.

To permit scripts to run on specific sites after disabling them globally, you have to add the sites—manually, one at a time—to the Trusted Sites zone. If globally disabling scripts and enabling them site by site is too extreme, but you're still concerned about security risks from scripts, consider choosing Prompt instead of Disable in the Settings list.

Identifying Deceptive (Phishing) Websites

A signature feature of Internet Explorer is its capability to inspect websites and block access to or provide a warning about those that appear suspicious. These so-called phishing sites are designed by scammers to closely resemble online commerce and banking sites. The scammer's goal is to fool you into visiting the site (usually by enticing you to click a link in an e-mail message) and have you fill in sensitive information such as your logon credentials, account numbers, and details about your identity.

SmartScreen Filter, an updated version of the Phishing Filter introduced with Internet Explorer 7, detects known and suspected phishing sites and does its best to deter you from falling prey to such sites. The feature does its detective work with the help of an allow list, a set of rules, and a server-based block list that is continually updated. The initial check is heuristic, looking at the content of the page itself; if all the images are from a bank's website, for example, but the submit button goes to a URL containing an IP address, red flags go up.

If SmartScreen Filter thinks you're headed to a dodgy page, it displays a bold, bright red warning before you ever get there, as shown here. An icon in the address bar identifies the address as an Unsafe Website, and a banner-sized link on the warning page itself provides one-click egress to the safety of your home page; the smaller More Information link leads to a menu option where you can disregard the warning and load the page. If you do proceed to a site that SmartScreen Filter has flagged, your address bar remains blood red as a warning.

You can enable or disable this feature at any time: click the Tools button, and then click Safety, Turn On SmartScreen Filter; if the feature is already enabled, you'll see Turn Off SmartScreen Filter on the menu. Other options on the Safety menu let you perform an ad-hoc check of a site (which is useful if you do not have the filter turned on, but available even if you do) and report a site that appears unsafe to you but has not been flagged by the filter.

You can disable the SmartScreen Filter for particular security zones. To turn it off for sites in your Trusted Sites zone, for example, choose Tools, Internet Options and click the Security tab. Select Trusted Sites, click Custom Level, and then, under Use SmartScreen Filter, select Disable.

For more information about phishing and other hazards of the online world, see Microsoft's Online Privacy & Safety page at *w7io.com/0603*.

Protecting Your Privacy

The web is a complicated place. When you click a shortcut or type an address to open a web page, the content that appears in your browser window might be drawn from several websites, some of them unrelated to the domain that appears in the browser's address bar. So when you think you're visiting just one website, you might actually be exchanging information with many sites.

In some cases, this sharing is benign, a by-product of how the web works. A site might keep its HTML pages in one domain and image files on another, for example, resulting in finished pages drawn from both sites. But the online advertising business has learned how to turn third-party content into amazingly effective tracking devices. The tools they use include the following:

- **Cookies**   These are tiny text files, associated with a specific domain, that can store information about you and your computer. The contents of the cookies can be retrieved by the website when you return to that domain. We discuss cookies in more detail in "Managing Cookies" on page 270.

- **Tracking pixels**   Also known as "web beacons" or "web bugs," these are tiny image files, often made up of a single clear pixel. A third-party analytics firm can create a tracking pixel with a unique file name associated with its client's domain. When you visit the client's page, you also load the invisible image from the analytics firm, which chalks up another visit to that page in its database.

- **Scripts**   Snippets of script from a third-party site can be extraordinarily useful for advertisers and analytics firms who gather information about you: your location, your operating system, and your preferred browser, for example.

- **Ads**   The majority of online advertisements are served from third-party networks, allowing advertisers to upload an ad to a single server and have it appear on any number of websites.

To see just how many different locations can contribute to a single web page, visit a popular site like Microsoft.com using Internet Explorer 9, click Tools, click Safety, and then click Webpage Privacy Policy. That opens a dialog box like the one shown here:

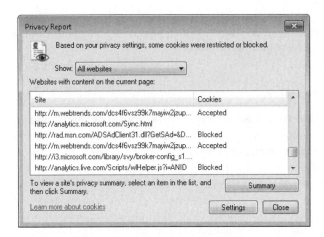

In this example, what appears to be a single web page is actually made up of more than 52 individual elements from five different domains.

By cleverly combining these elements, advertisers and analytics firms can build up an impressively accurate picture of you. A single third-party site might have its tracking tools on hundreds or thousands of popular sites. As you visit those sites and read pages, perform searches, follow links, and fill in forms, all of those details are being stored on the third-party server, with a serial number from a cookie attached to each item so that they can all be correlated with you and your PC. It's easy (and very profitable) for someone to correlate that data into a profile of you. The resulting profile allows a third-party ad network to display targeted advertisements that are more likely to be relevant to your interests. Unfortunately, that mass of data also allows these companies to infer conclusions about your health, your income, your employment status, and other aspects of your personal life. And therein lies the problem.

Protecting Yourself from Online Tracking

Internet Explorer 9 includes a Tracking Protection feature that is specifically designed to throw roadblocks in the path of websites that want to collect and use information about you without your consent. This feature is available in two variations. Both are disabled by default, but they can be enabled with relative ease.

- **Personalized Tracking Protection list**   This is a *heuristic* form of protection. With this feature enabled, Internet Explorer watches your browsing activity and automatically creates and maintains a list of sites that make third-party connections to Internet Explorer. You can manually block or allow individual sites or automatically block all connections to all sites on the list. This capability is available in Internet Explorer 8 (under the name InPrivate Filtering), but it requires a registry edit to persist across sessions. In Internet Explorer 9, you can enable a personalized list that remains active even after you restart your browser or your PC.

- **Third-Party Tracking Protection lists**   This is a *curated* form of protection, in which an individual or group creates a Tracking Protection list that you download and install in Internet Explorer. The list identifies sites, scripts, and pages that, in the opinion of the list's curator, represent an unwanted intrusion on privacy. After you enable that list, any sites or pages on the list are blocked from making third-party connections.

In the remainder of this section, we discuss how to enable and use these features. In either case, start by clicking Tools, then click Safety, and then click Tracking Protection. That opens the Manage Add-Ons dialog box, with the Tracking Protection category selected from the Add-On Types list.

Using a Personalized Tracking Protection List

In a default installation of Internet Explorer 9, the Tracking Protection section of the Manage Add-Ons dialog box contains a single entry—Your Personalized List—which is disabled by default. To begin using this feature, select the Your Personalized List entry and then click the Enable button. When you do, the entry under the Status column changes to Enabled, as shown here.

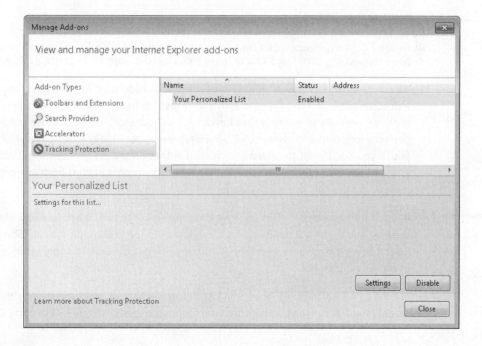

Although the feature is technically enabled, it's not actually doing anything to protect your privacy yet. Before that can happen, you need to click the Settings button. That opens the Personalized Tracking Protection List dialog box, shown in Figure 7-5, where you must make some choices.

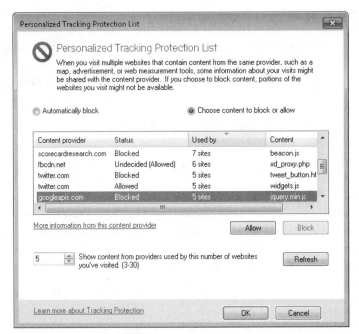

Figure 7-5 With a Personalized Tracking Protection list, you can automatically block all third-party connections from listed sites or make individual decisions for each site, as shown here.

It's crucial to understand what the list of content providers shown here really represents. Individual entries on this list represent addresses that have been identified as making third-party connections to multiple sites in your browsing history. Some of those connections are perfectly innocent and even useful; others represent potentially intrusive ways of tracking you. If you don't want to evaluate individual entries on the list, you can select Automatically Block, which tells Internet Explorer to block third-party connections from any entry on this list and any that are added to it later.

If you want to be more selective, leave the Choose Content To Block Or Allow setting selected and then click the Block or Allow button for each entry on the list. (Sort by the Content Provider column, and then use Shift+click or Ctrl+click to apply settings to groups of entries simultaneously.)

The Personalized Tracking Protection List dialog box lists all content providers that have made a third-party connection from a minimum number of different first-party sites. The default threshold is 10, but you can reduce that to as low as three. (If you change this number, you must click Refresh to update the list's contents.) Sites are sorted initially in order of increasing activity. To see which third-party sites have been the most active in your browsing history, you need to scroll to the bottom of the list or reverse the sort order.

The Content Provider column lists the domain, and the Content column lists the file (if any) that is common to all those third-party interactions. The Used By column shows how many first-party sites in your browsing history contain that specific third-party content. If, for example, a web analytics firm uses a tracking pixel called pixel.gif on multiple sites, you will see it show up on this list after you visit enough of that company's first-party partners.

TROUBLESHOOTING

Your Personalized Tracking Protection list is empty

The Personalized Tracking Protection list is built from your browsing history and only shows sites that have made a minimum number of third-party connections based on your browsing history. If you clear the browsing history or reset Internet Explorer without specifying that you want this information saved, you'll need to wait until you've visited enough sites to rebuild the list.

INSIDE OUT   Clear your Personalized Tracking Protection list

When you first enable your Personalized Tracking Protection list, all sites are set to Undecided (Allowed). After you choose Block or Allow for an individual entry in the Content Providers list, you can switch between those two states, but there is no way to return that site to its previous Undecided state. You can, however, delete all your Block/Allow choices and return the entire list to its original state, with all sites listed as Undecided. To do so, open Registry Editor, navigate to HKCU\Software\Microsoft\ Internet Explorer\Safety\PrivacIE, and delete the UserFilterData key. Internet Explorer will re-create this key as soon as you make the first Block/Allow decision for the personalized list.

Using a Third-Party Tracking Protection List

Personalized Tracking Protection lists are potentially problematic for two reasons. First, you have to allow a certain amount of tracking before you can identify sites to block. Second, deciding which sites to block or allow is a time-consuming task. The alternative is to turn the work over to a Tracking Protection list (TPL) created by an independent person or organization, such as a consumer protection group. Here's how the feature works in Internet Explorer 9.

Someone—anyone—creates a list of domains and substrings (such as file names used with scripts). The list is formatted using Microsoft's Tracking Protection List specification, with each entry marked for Internet Explorer 9 to block (or allow) when a matching domain or substring tries to make a third-party connection. The list creator then publishes that list on a web page, using a simple JavaScript command.

When you click a link to that list, you see a dialog box like this one:

Click Add List to download the formatted file to your computer, where it is copied to %LocalAppData%\Microsoft\Internet Explorer\Tracking Protection. The file is saved using a GUID as the file name and .tpl as the file name extension. The newly installed list appears in the Manage Add-Ons dialog box and is set to Enabled.

From that point on, Internet Explorer uses the rules contained on that TPL before it sends an HTTP request to a third-party site. The same rules apply to requests that originate with an ActiveX control.

If a domain is on the Block list, no request is sent to its server. If a site is on an Allow list, the request goes through. If a domain is set to be blocked, any tracking activity (such as that generated by tracking pixels and scripts) is blocked. And although ad blocking is not the primary purpose of this feature, it is an unintended side effect.

Here are a few other facts worth knowing about Tracking Protection:

- TPLs affect third-party content only and are ignored for direct requests. If example.com is on a Block list, Internet Explorer will reject any third-party requests to that domain but will serve up the page normally if the address shown in the address bar is on the example.com domain.

- You can install multiple Tracking Protection lists and enable or disable any list at any time. You can also remove a list.

- From the Manage Add-Ons dialog box, you can select Tracking Protection and double-click any installed TPL to inspect its contents and copy it to a text file. (See Figure 7-6.)

Figure 7-6 If you see –d in front of a domain, third-party requests are blocked. Click Copy, and then paste the list's contents into a text editor for easier inspection.

- TPLs include an auto-update mechanism. The default update period is 7 days, but a list publisher can set this value to any interval between 1 and 30 days.

- If you have multiple lists, Internet Explorer uses a hierarchy to resolve conflicts. Allow rules always trump Block rules. Thus, if the same domain or substring is on one list with a Block entry and another with an Allow entry, third-party content from that domain will be allowed.

- If you enable the Personalized Tracking Protection list and manually specify which sites to block or allow, those settings override any entry on a third-party TPL.

Managing Cookies

A *cookie* is a small text file that enables a website to store persistent information on your hard disk. The website creates the cookie on your first visit to that page, updates it in response to your actions, and then reads the cookie on your subsequent visits to the site. Cookies can be used for a variety of purposes, such as storing logon information, shopping preferences, pages that you have visited, searches that you have performed, and so on. In general, cookies provide benefits to users as well as to web content providers. They make the websites you visit more responsive to your needs and preferences.

Cookies are divided into two broad categories:

- **First-party cookie**   A cookie used by the site that you are currently viewing. First-party cookies are generally used to personalize your experience with a website.

- **Third-party cookie**   A cookie used by a site other than the one you're currently viewing—such as an advertiser on the site you're currently viewing.

In addition, a cookie can be *persistent*, with a fixed expiration date—we've seen cookies that are programmed to expire more than 20 years in the future. By contrast, *session cookies* are designed to store information for the current session only (or for a set period of time, so that your session automatically times out if you don't interact with the server in a specific amount of time). Session cookies are deleted when you leave a site or close the browser window.

In and of themselves, cookies are mostly harmless. They don't contain executable code, and they can't be used to spread viruses or malware. A cookie can provide a website only with information that you supply while visiting the site (a cookie can't scurry around your hard disk reading your address book and financial records, for example), and this information can be read only by pages in the same domain as the one that created the cookie. Privacy concerns arise when advertisers and web-analytics companies begin to correlate the information from third-party cookies to build a profile of your activities. Because it's not always obvious who's sending you a cookie and what purposes that cookie serves, some people are understandably wary about allowing cookies on their systems.

All versions of Internet Explorer that are supported on Windows 7 allow you to block or accept cookies on the basis of the cookies' content and purposes, in accordance with your preferences. Sites that support the Platform for Privacy Preferences (P3P) supply information about their use of cookies in the form of a *compact privacy statement*—special HTML tags embedded in the site's HTTP header that indicate the source, purpose, and lifetime of cookies used on that site. When you access a site, Internet Explorer compares the site's compact privacy statement with your current privacy preferences and then accepts, blocks, or restricts the cookies.

To see the current settings for cookies, click Tools, open the Internet Options dialog box, and click the Privacy tab (shown in Figure 7-7). The default setting is Medium.

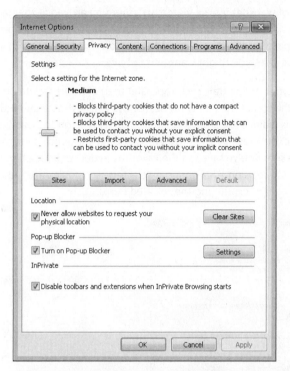

Figure 7-7 Use the slider in this dialog box to select a policy for accepting, rejecting, and restricting cookies based on their source and purpose.

> **Note**
>
> Your privacy settings apply only to sites in the Internet zone. By default, all cookies are accepted in the Trusted Sites and Local Intranet zones.

INSIDE OUT   Don't waste time obsessing over cookies

Managing cookies manually is a tedious and error-prone process. If you are using Internet Explorer 9, the new Tracking Protection options are much more effective at safeguarding your privacy.

Clearing Personal Information

Internet Explorer keeps a copy of HTML pages, images, and media you've viewed recently. It also maintains a list of websites you've visited, whether you arrived at the page by clicking a link or typing an address. This cached information—combined with cookies, saved form data, and saved passwords—can give another person who has access to your computer more information than you might want him to have.

To wipe away most of your online trail, click Tools and then click the Delete Browsing History option at the top of the Safety menu. (Or use the keyboard shortcut Ctrl+Shift+Delete.) This dialog box, shown in Figure 7-8, allows you to clear some or all categories of information. The Preserve Favorites Website Data check box allows you to keep information related to sites you've saved in the Favorites folder while deleting elements collected from more casual browsing. This option is selected by default. After you adjust any options, click Delete to begin expunging the selected items.

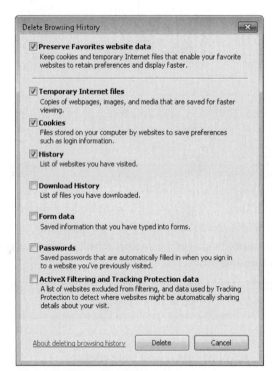

Figure 7-8 The options in the Delete Browsing History dialog box let you specify which elements of your history you want to erase.

INSIDE OUT   Use a PowerShell script to keep Internet Explorer clean

If you're fanatical about clearing your tracks with Internet Explorer, you'll want to check out a PowerShell script we've included in the Scripts folder on the companion CD. The Clean-IE script allows you to clear the browser cache more thoroughly than Internet Explorer can. Use Clean-IE.ps1 with the **–action history** parameter to perform a complete cleanup. For detailed instructions on how to work with PowerShell scripts, see "Running PowerShell Scripts" on page 999.

Browsing Privately

You can clear your personal information at any time (see the preceding section), but if you want to cover your tracks only for particular websites, a simpler solution is to visit those sites in private browsing sessions. You can open a private session by clicking Tools and choosing Safety, InPrivate Browsing; by pressing Ctrl+Shift+P; or by choosing InPrivate Browsing from the bottom of the New Tab page. Internet Explorer opens a new window when you do this, without modifying your current session; thus, you can keep private and nonprivate sessions open at the same time. As Figure 7-9 shows, the distinctive blue label to the left of the address bar makes it easy to tell that a session is private.

Figure 7-9 Internet Explorer changes the address bar to let you know that a browsing session is private.

While you browse privately, neither your browsing history nor any data that you enter in web forms is recorded. Session cookies are retained in memory but are deleted at close. Temporary Internet files are stored on disk and are deleted when you close the session.

Be aware that browsing privately is not the same as browsing anonymously. Sites you visit can record your IP address, and your network administrator or Internet service provider can see which sites you connect to and can capture any unencrypted information that you transmit or receive.

InPrivate Browsing disables toolbars and extensions by default. If you want them enabled, click Tools, open the Internet Options dialog box, and then clear the Disable Toolbars And Extensions When InPrivate Browsing Starts check box.

Managing Downloads

Among the most welcome additions to Internet Explorer 9 are several features designed to make it easier to download programs, media files, documents, and other files that aren't intended to be viewed directly in a web browser.

When you click a link that begins a download, Internet Explorer displays a notification bar at the bottom of the browser window. If the download is a program, the notification looks like this:

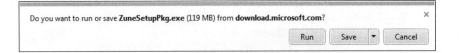

You can click Run to download a temporary copy of the program and begin installing it as soon as the download finishes. The temporary copy is deleted after installation is complete. If you prefer to save the file so that you can run it later, you have three options:

- Click Save to download a copy of the program and save it to your default download location.

- Click the arrow to the right of the Save button and then click Save As if you want to specify a folder other than the current default location.

- Click the arrow to the right of the Save button and then click Save And Run if you want to download a copy to the default location and begin installation as soon as the download is complete.

As part of the download process, Internet Explorer checks the file using its SmartScreen Filter, another feature that is new in Internet Explorer 9. Files that are known to be safe are waved through, while those that are dangerous are flagged and blocked. If the program you're attempting to download is from a small developer that the SmartScreen Filter doesn't recognize, you'll see a notification like this one:

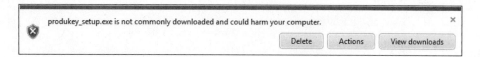

If you're certain the file is safe, click Actions to open a separate dialog box in which you can approve the download.

> **Note**
>
> Although that red shield is designed to get your attention, it doesn't mean that the file you're downloading is unsafe. SmartScreen Filter is a reputation-based system that derives its input from information that Windows users supply to Microsoft. The "not commonly downloaded" message means that not enough information is available for SmartScreen Filter to make a recommendation about the download. You should exercise caution, but if you're satisfied that the download is from a trusted source, go ahead.

For downloads that are not executables, such as Zip archives and Word documents, the Run and Save And Run options change to Open and Save And Open, respectively.

If you choose to save a file, the notification bar at the bottom of the window changes when the download is complete. Here's what it looks like for a nonexecutable file:

The arrow to the right of the Open button leads to an Open With option, with which you can specify that you want to open the downloaded file using a program other than the one that is set as the default for that file type.

The two buttons on the right of the notification bar are available for any completed download. Click Open Folder to open Windows Explorer and display the contents of the folder where you downloaded the file. Click View Downloads to open the Download Manager. This feature, which is new in Internet Explorer 9, keeps track of every file you've downloaded. Figure 7-10 shows the Download Manager in action.

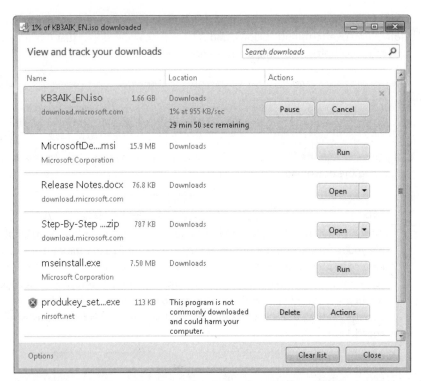

Figure 7-10 Every file you've downloaded appears in this list. Click the X in the top right corner of any item to remove its entry (but keep the downloaded file). Click Clear List to remove all entries from the list.

While a download is in progress, you can view its status (complete with an estimate of the time remaining) in the notification bar and in the Download Manager. In either location, you can pause a download temporarily and then resume it later.

From the Download Manager window, you can open or run any previously downloaded file. To see a file in the folder where you downloaded it, click the folder link in the Location column. To open Download Manager, click View Downloads in the notification bar. If no download is in progress, you can open the Download Manager and view its entire history by clicking Tools, View Downloads, or by using the keyboard shortcut Ctrl+J.

By default, Internet Explorer saves all files in the Downloads folder in your user profile. You can use the Save As option to specify a different location for a single download. To change the default location for all files you download in the future, click Options and use the Browse button to select your preferred location.

To Trust or Not to Trust?

Microsoft offers a digital signing technology, called Authenticode, that can be used to guarantee that an executable item comes from the publisher it says it comes from and that it has not been changed, deliberately or otherwise, since it left the publisher's hands. The digital signature verifies each bit of the signed file by comparing it to a hash value; if even a single bit of the file has changed, the comparison fails and the signature is invalid. Windows 7 blocks installation of any code that has an invalid signature—by definition, this indicates that the program file is corrupt (possibly because it was damaged during downloading) or has been tampered with.

When an executable file isn't digitally signed, it's impossible to make a definitive determination of whether it's safe. In those circumstances, you can't be too cautious. You can tip the odds in your favor by using common sense. Make sure the download is from a verifiable source. Use your favorite search engine to look for complaints about the program or its publisher; be sure to search the web and popular newsgroups (see, for example, Microsoft's extensive selection of forums—*w7io.com/0602*), and don't install anything until you're comfortable that you can resolve any reported problems if they crop up on your PC. Be sure to scan any downloaded files for viruses and spyware before installation. Finally, set a System Restore point or, even better, create an image backup before installing any software so that you can undo the configuration changes if you're unhappy with the results.

A digital signature doesn't promise that the signed item is healthy and benevolent. It confirms only that the bits you're about to download are the authentic work of a particular party and haven't been tampered with on their way to you. However, it is prudent to regard an unsigned item, or an item without a valid signature, as a potential threat.

Assuming the signature is valid, you can use the information contained within that signature to make an additional determination—do you trust the person or organization that attached the signature to the file? If the publisher is reputable and the Security Warning message reports that the item has been digitally signed, you must then decide how much confidence you have in the publisher.

Normally, you make choices about whether to install a signed item on an individual basis. But you can choose to trust a particular publisher and allow its software to be installed automatically without any prompting. Or you can decide that the publisher of a particular program is not trustworthy and you do not want any products from that publisher to be installed on your computer, under any circumstances.

Adding Windows Live Programs and Services

WE don't blame you if you're a little confused about Windows Live. Over the years, Microsoft has applied the Windows Live branding to a wide variety of software and services. Some are replacements for programs that were part of a default installation in earlier Windows versions. Others are replacements for services that were once lumped under the MSN brand. Still others—programs and services—are new, with no antecedents.

In this chapter, we cover both sides of the Windows Live family:

- **Windows Live Essentials** is a collection of programs, utilities, and browser add-ons that serve as valuable extensions of Windows 7. The current Windows Live Essentials lineup includes separate mail and messaging clients; a comprehensive program that allows you to import, edit, and share digital photos; and a utility for synchronizing the contents of folders across multiple PCs (even if they're not running Windows). Many PC manufacturers install Windows Live Essentials on new computers; it's also available, in whole or in part, as a free download.

- **Windows Live services** allow you to communicate with other people, share documents and photos, send messages using e-mail and social networks, chat using text or video, and synchronize files and favorites among multiple PCs and mobile devices. These services can be used on their own in a web browser, but they're most effective when used in conjunction with Windows Live Essentials programs.

What's in Your Edition?

Every Windows Live program and service we discuss in this chapter is available in any edition of Windows 7.

The content in this chapter is based on Windows Live Essentials 2011 and its companion services. Because these programs and services are designed to be upgraded regularly, it is possible that the versions you encounter will differ, perhaps significantly, from those we describe here.

Getting Started with Windows Live Programs and Services

In this chapter, we assume that you have set up a Windows Live ID and that you have linked online services from that Windows Live account to the corresponding programs from the Windows Live Essentials collection. That's the way to get the most out of these programs and services, as we explain later in this section.

Those connections aren't mandatory, however. You can use many Windows Live programs and services independently, if you insist. The Windows Live Mail program, for example, works just fine even without a Hotmail account. And although it might seem incongruous given the name, several of the core Windows Live web services don't require Windows at all. You can use the Hotmail and SkyDrive features from any modern browser (not just Internet Explorer) on a computer or a device running any operating system (not just Windows).

Installing and Configuring Windows Live Essentials

If the programs in the Windows Live Essentials collection seem familiar, it's not your imagination. The core members of the suite replace programs that were previously included in a full Windows installation.

Microsoft divides the full list into two groups. Four programs get shortcuts on the All Programs menu:

- **Windows Live Mail** is a replacement for the Windows Mail program that was part of Windows Vista. (That program was, in turn, a replacement for Outlook Express in Windows XP.) It supports connections to Internet-standard mail accounts and many popular web-based mail services.

- **Windows Live Photo Gallery** is a vastly improved version of the Windows Vista Photo Gallery program. It allows you to import photos from a digital camera or memory card, organize and tag those photos, and share them with social media networks. Choosing this option also installs SQL Server 2005 Compact Edition.

- **Windows Live Movie Maker** allows you to edit and share video files, especially those you capture with a camcorder or phone. The program is part of a tandem with Photo Gallery; neither program can be installed or removed individually.

- **Windows Live Messenger** is a descendant of MSN Messenger and Windows Messenger, which were once part of Windows. It offers a full range of instant-messaging and chat options. The same service also allows you to connect to social media networks such as Facebook and LinkedIn, where you can watch what your friends are doing and share your own photos, links, and status updates.

You'll find shortcuts for three additional programs in a Windows Live subfolder on the All Programs menu:

- **Windows Live Family Safety** allows parents to exercise tighter control over when and how children use Internet Explorer and filters out potentially offensive or dangerous content.

- **Windows Live Mesh** provides a synchronization framework that you can use to effortlessly share the contents of folders, Internet Explorer favorites, and Microsoft Office settings between PCs. It also allows you to access your PCs from a remote location (to copy a file from your work PC to your notebook when traveling, for example). Installing Windows Live Mesh also installs the Windows Live Remote Client, an ActiveX control that enables remote functions in Internet Explorer, and several other support files for remote connections.

- **Windows Live Writer** is a specialized program that allows you to create, edit, and manage blog posts using just about any modern blogging service.

A full installation of Windows Live Essentials also includes a handful of Internet Explorer add-ons: the Bing Bar, the Microsoft Search Enhancement Pack, and Messenger Companion. If the Windows Live ID Sign-In Assistant is not already installed, it's added to your system. If Microsoft Office is installed, you get the Microsoft Office Outlook Connector, which enables support for Hotmail accounts in Microsoft Outlook 2003 or later. If Microsoft Silverlight is not already available on your PC, it is installed as well.

To add any or all of the Windows Live Essentials programs to your installation of Windows 7, visit *w7io.com/20801*. After you click the Download Now button and then click Run, the setup program allows you to install all Windows Live Essentials programs or choose which programs you want to install. If you select the latter option, you see the dialog box shown in Figure 8-1. By default all programs are selected; clear the check box for any program you don't want and then click Install.

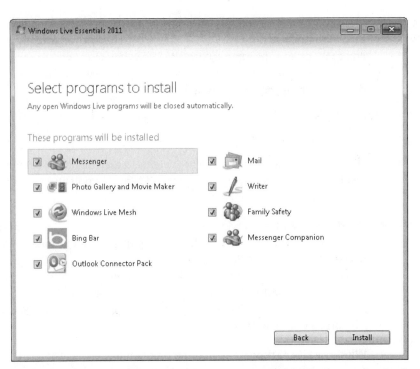

Figure 8-1 You can exclude any of the Windows Live Essentials programs by clearing the corresponding check box here.

If you want to remove individual Windows Live Essentials programs that you previously installed, open Programs And Features in Control Panel. Bing Bar, Microsoft Office Outlook Connector, and Windows Live Mesh ActiveX Control for Remote Connections have their own entries in the list. Select any of those entries and click Uninstall to begin the removal process.

For all other programs, click Windows Live Essentials 2011 and then click Uninstall/Change. That opens a dialog box that gives you the option to repair all programs or uninstall selected programs. Choose the latter option and you'll see a dialog box similar to the one shown in Figure 8-1. Click to select the programs you want to remove, and then click Uninstall.

Using Windows Live Web Services

To begin using Windows Live services, visit *home.live.com* in your web browser. If you're not already signed in, you're taken to a login page where you must enter the e-mail address and password for your Windows Live ID and click Sign In. After signing in, you see the Windows Live home page, which should resemble the one shown in Figure 8-2.

Figure 8-2 The Windows Live home page displays the most recent information from your Hotmail inbox and calendar and from any social networks connected to your Windows Live account.

At the top of every Windows Live page is a toolbar that gives you quick access to the most popular services, starting with Hotmail and Messenger. Click the Windows Live button at the left edge of the toolbar to return to the home page. Hover your mouse pointer over

Chapter 8

Chapter 8

the Windows Live button to display the menu shown here. To see all available Windows Live services, click All Services at the bottom of the menu, or manually enter *home.live.com/allservices* in the browser's address bar.

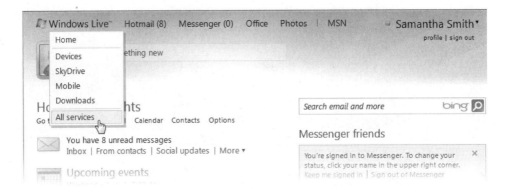

Similar menus appear when you allow the mouse pointer to rest over the other top-level toolbar items. The Hotmail button, for example, shows the number of unread messages (8, in this example), and its corresponding menu allows you to jump to the inbox, manage events on your Hotmail calendar, view and edit your saved contacts, or begin composing a new e-mail message.

In the upper right corner of the home page is the name of the logged-on user—presumably you—with links that allow you to view or edit your Windows Live account profile or to sign out from Windows Live.

TROUBLESHOOTING

A Windows Live service isn't working properly

Is your Hotmail or Messenger account refusing to allow you to sign in? Are you having problems accessing stored SkyDrive files or synchronizing files using Windows Live Mesh? Before you dive into extensive troubleshooting, it's a good idea to check the official Windows Live Service Status page at *status.live.com*. That page shows the current status for all Windows Live services, with details of any recent issues. (Click the View History link to see details for the previous two weeks.) If the status page doesn't list any issues for the service in question, click Report An Issue to access additional troubleshooting resources and submit a report or ask a question using the Windows Live Solution Center.

In the remainder of this section, we introduce the various Windows Live services, grouped by function, with notes about how they work with Windows Live Essentials programs. Where possible, we've provided a simple, easy-to-remember web address that you can use to go directly to that service. (In most cases, that address expands to a longer, more formal URI when you enter it in a browser.)

Messaging Services

The Messenger and Social Updates services are available from your Windows Live home page. All of your Messenger contacts are listed in the right column, just below the search box, with color-coded squares indicating their current status: green for Available, yellow for Away, red for Busy. You can set your own status by clicking the down arrow to the right of your user name in the top right corner of the page, as shown here.

Chapter 8

INSIDE OUT   Make yourself temporarily invisible

If you're trying to concentrate on a task and don't want to be disturbed by instant messages (IMs) from friends, you have two options. You can set your status to Busy and hope that your friends understand that you prefer not to be interrupted until further notice. Or you can choose the Appear Offline option. While this status is active, you are effectively offline to all of your friends. They are blocked from sending an unsolicited IM to you. When your status is set to Appear Offline, you can initiate a chat session with any of your available contacts and they can reply.

Chapter 8

To begin an IM session, you can click the name of a contact on the Messenger menu or under Your Friends (if you have a large contacts list, use the search box to filter the list). If the Messenger program from Windows Live Essentials is installed and running, your conversation takes place there; if that program is unavailable, your chat takes place in a small embedded window at the bottom of the browser, like the one shown here. This window remains visible on all Windows Live pages; click the Pop Out button to move the conversation to its own window.

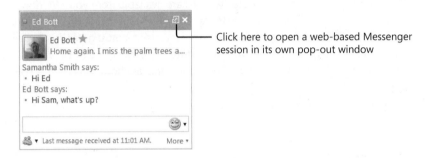

Click here to open a web-based Messenger session in its own pop-out window

For details on how to set up and use the Messenger program for instant messages and video chats, see "Using Windows Live Messenger" on page 321.

Mail and Related Services

In addition to storing messages you send and receive, your Hotmail account also contains a list of contacts and a personal calendar. Details about your contacts and calendar events are available for viewing and editing on separate pages. You'll find shortcuts for all three pages on the Hotmail menu on the Windows Live toolbar and at the bottom of the sidebar. Here's what's in each one

- Inbox (*mail.live.com* or *hotmail.com*) displays the contents of your Hotmail inbox. The view in the online inbox is similar to what you'll find in the Windows Live Mail program, with a sidebar on the left, a message list on the right, and an optional preview pane to show the contents of the currently selected message. Use the sidebar to switch to a different folder or apply one of several ready-made filters under the Quick Views heading. Figure 8-3, for example, shows the Photos view, which lists all messages that contain photos, including picture files sent as attachments and those that are part of an online photo album.

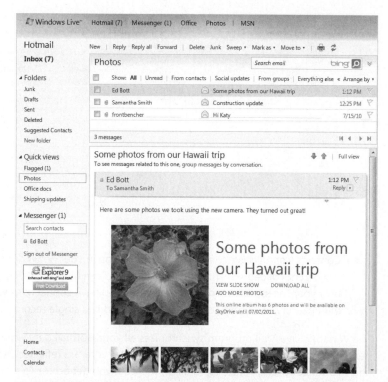

Figure 8-3 The web view of Hotmail includes a preview pane like the one found in the Windows Live Mail program. Here, it's positioned on the bottom, below the message list.

- Calendar (*calendar.live.com*) includes Day, Week, Month, and Agenda views of events you've scheduled. It also includes a to-do list. You can create additional calendars—private or shared. You can also make a calendar public, a useful option if you work with a community group or run a theater. Click Options (just below your user name in the top right corner) to open a settings page where you can set your time zone, the hours you want to see in Day and Week views, and whether you want to include an updated weather forecast in your calendar, as shown next.

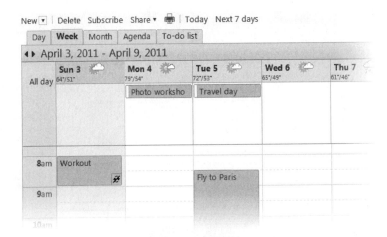

- Contacts (*contacts.live.com*) shows every person in your network of friends, family, coworkers, colleagues, and acquaintances. You can filter the list by source—showing only your Facebook friends, for example. If you have connections with contacts from multiple services, those contacts are combined in a single record.

The Windows Live Mail program synchronizes all your Hotmail data—messages, calendar items, and contacts. Any change you make in the program is reflected in the web view, and vice versa. When you use Hotmail on the web, you get access to a single inbox and its related folders. You can link up to five Hotmail accounts to a single Windows Live ID, but you can only view the inbox for one account at a time.

By contrast, in Windows Live Mail you can add other e-mail accounts, including secondary Hotmail addresses, Google Mail (Gmail) accounts, and POP3/SMTP accounts at an Internet Service provider. Each account gets its own node in the Windows Live Mail sidebar.

For more details, including how to set up and use multiple mail accounts, see "Using Windows Live Mail" on page 300.

Online Storage Services

Microsoft's cloud-based storage service, Windows Live SkyDrive, is available worldwide, offering 25 GB of free online storage to anyone with a Windows Live ID. (One significant limitation: individual files are limited to a maximum size of 50 MB.) When you sign in to Windows Live and visit your SkyDrive page (*skydrive.live.com* or *skydrive.com*), you can upload files (one at a time or in groups) and view, share, and manage your stored files. Figure 8-4 shows a well-stocked SkyDrive collection.

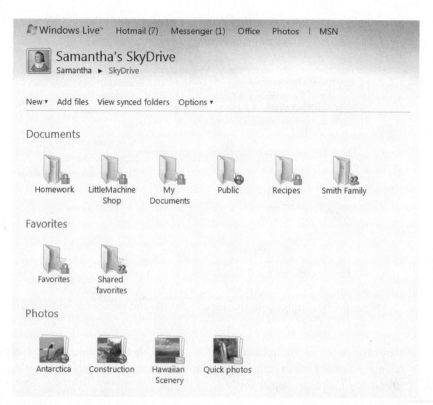

Figure 8-4 The icons beside each folder indicate whether it's private, public, or shared. Open any folder to add, edit, rename, or delete files within that folder.

SkyDrive categorizes your online files based on three available folder types—Documents, Favorites, and Photos—each of which can contain folders and subfolders. SkyDrive offers quick access to the contents of the Documents and Photos groups via shortcuts on the Windows Live toolbar:

- Office (*office.live.com*) displays all of the folders in the Documents group. By default, SkyDrive contains a private My Documents folder and a Public folder whose contents are available to any visitor, with no login required. You can apply custom permissions to folders and subfolders you create, allowing read-only access or assigning full rights to individuals or groups (categories) from your contacts list. Using the free Office Web Apps, you can view and edit existing documents or create new ones. Aim the mouse pointer at the Office button on the Windows Live toolbar to see a menu that lists the four supported document types.

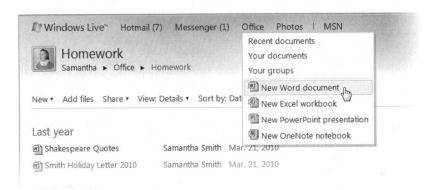

- Photos (*photos.live.com*) shows you all the digital files you've uploaded, arranged into albums that are the functional equivalent of folders. You can share folders with other people by assigning permissions to people and groups, or you can share an album via e-mail.

Both Windows Live Photo Gallery and Windows Live Mail offer excellent tools to help you create online albums in your SkyDrive, upload photos, and share them with other people through e-mail or social networks.

Using SkyDrive, you can also create storage spaces that are shared by groups of people using a Windows Live account. To begin working with Groups, visit *groups.live.com*.

For more details on how to store and share photos online, see "Using Windows Live Photo Gallery" on page 310.

An in-depth discussion of how to use SkyDrive with Office Web Apps is outside the scope of this book. For more details, pick up a copy of *Microsoft Office 2010 Inside Out*, by Ed Bott and Carl Siechert (Microsoft Press, 2010).

Synchronization Services

The last group of services is most interesting if your digital life includes two or more Windows PCs or a mobile phone. The Windows Live Mesh service allows you to synchronize the contents of folders across multiple PCs running Windows 7, Windows Vista, Windows Server 2008, and Mac OS X 10.5 or later. The service works in conjunction with the Windows Live Mesh client software, and you can manage individual PCs from the Devices page (*devices.live.com*). Using default settings, each device you connect to Windows Live Mesh is identified with its computer name (which might or not be descriptive) and a generic icon. After you sign in to Windows Live Mesh, click Personalize to change the name that you see on the Devices page and to choose from an assortment of computer icons, as we have done here.

In addition to syncing files between PCs, you can automatically sync as much as 5 GB of files in the Windows Live cloud by using SkyDrive synced storage. This feature gives you an effective online backup for truly important files, as well as access to those files from any computer.

For a full discussion of how to use Windows Live Mesh to keep multiple PCs in sync, see "Synchronizing Files and Favorites with Windows Live Mesh" on page 295.

If you have a Windows Phone (*windowsphone.live.com*), you can access many Windows Live services from the device. If you add the phone to your Devices page, you can manage settings, add contacts and calendar events, and view or share photos directly from that page. This feature works only with Windows Phone 7 or later. Earlier Windows Mobile devices can use a much more limited set of services.

Chapter 8

Managing Your Windows Live ID and Profile

A Windows Live ID consists of two elements: an e-mail address that uniquely identifies you, and a password that helps ensure that only you can access your associated e-mail and other services. (It's up to you to make that password strong and to keep it away from data thieves.) If you have a Windows Live Hotmail account (with an e-mail address in the *hotmail.com* or *live.com* domain) or a Windows Messenger account or an Xbox Live account, you already have a Windows Live ID. (Longtime Windows users might recall setting up a Microsoft Password years ago—it's the same thing as a Windows Live ID.) If you don't have any of these, you can create a Windows Live ID by going to *live.com* and clicking Sign Up.

INSIDE OUT   Use multiple Windows Live IDs

You're not limited to a single Windows Live ID. You can have multiple accounts, using any combination of e-mail addresses from Hotmail and other domains. You might want to use one ID to chat with your friends and another to share work-related files on SkyDrive. If you use a valid e-mail address that is not in the *hotmail.com* or *live.com* domain as your Windows Live ID, you can connect to any Windows Live service (or sign in on any site that uses Windows Live ID as an authentication method), with the noteworthy exception of Hotmail.

You can sign in to different services at the same time using different IDs. For example, you can use Windows Live Photo Gallery to upload photos to a SkyDrive account using one ID while you carry on a video chat using a different ID. To help manage multiple IDs, the Sign In dialog box allows you to select Remember My ID And Password, after which you can switch IDs by using a drop-down list. You can also link multiple IDs, allowing you to quickly switch between Hotmail accounts by using your web browser. To link IDs, click the down arrow to the right of your name on any Windows Live web page, and then click Account. Under the Other Options heading, choose Linked IDs, and then enter the credentials for your second (or subsequent) account. Click that same arrow to switch between linked IDs using choices at the bottom of the menu.

To sign in to a Windows Live service using a web browser, enter your ID and password on the Sign In page. Use the corresponding Sign In dialog box with a Windows Live Essentials program. If you open Windows Live Messenger, for example, and you're not already signed in, the dialog box appears automatically. Figure 8-5 shows what you see with Windows Live Messenger.

Figure 8-5 Select the top check box to save your ID and password in the drop-down list; click the box below it to sign in using the current ID automatically each time you start Messenger.

A similar dialog box (minus the status options) appears when you open Windows Live Mesh. For Mail, Photo Gallery, and Movie Maker—all of which can be used without connecting to a Windows Live account—you'll find a Sign In button at the far right of the Home tab. After you sign in, your profile picture appears in that space, and clicking the arrow beneath it displays this menu.

The relationship between Windows Live Mail and your Windows Live ID is worth looking at a little more closely. As you'll see later in this chapter, you can set up multiple e-mail accounts, any of which can be associated with a Windows Live ID. You can send and receive mail from all of those accounts regardless of whether you're signed in to Windows Live. So why bother signing in at all? Contacts and Calendar items for a given account are visible only when you are signed in. To designate an account that you want to keep signed in whenever you use Windows Live Mail, click the blue button at the left of the ribbon, click Options, and then click Mail. On the Connections tab, you can specify a Windows Live ID (with saved password) that you want to automatically sign in with each time you open Mail.

INSIDE OUT   Link a Windows Live ID to your user account

If you have a primary Windows Live ID and use it regularly, consider linking your Windows 7 user account and that ID. Doing so allows you to access shared files on your network using the Windows Live ID instead of a local user ID. It also allows you to connect to a remote computer and play media files using Windows Media Player.

Be sure you first install Windows Live Essentials, which adds the Windows Live ID Sign-In Assistant. To link the two IDs, open Control Panel and use the search box to find and open Link Online IDs. Here is what you'll see if your Windows user account is currently unlinked; click Link Online ID, enter your ID and password, and then click Sign In.

After you finish, this dialog box shows the e-mail address of the linked ID and contains options to update your credentials (if you change your password, for example) or to unlink the ID.

In Windows Live Messenger, you can sign in on multiple PCs and with multiple programs. From a single PC, you can sign in to Messenger using the Messenger program, the Mail program, and a web browser. When you're signed in at multiple places, messages appear in all those places. To sign out from one or all of those places, click your name in Window Live Messenger and use any of the Sign Out options on the menu.

To change options associated with your Windows Live account, click the arrow to the right of your user name and then click Options. (Or enter *home.live.com/options* in your browser's address bar.) Here, you can customize what appears on your Windows Live home page, change your profile picture, change Messenger Social options, and much more.

To manage your Windows Live account itself—including changing your name, managing linked IDs, and supplying an alternate e-mail address that you can use to reset a lost password—visit *account.live.com*. Note that you cannot change the e-mail address associated with a specific ID; if you want to use a new address, you must create a new ID.

Synchronizing Files and Favorites with Windows Live Mesh

Windows Live Mesh is an ambitious synchronization and remote access service that Microsoft officially launched in September 2010, roughly a year after the release of Windows 7. It replaces and unifies a hodgepodge of related sync services that Microsoft offered over the years; discontinued services in this category include Windows Live Sync (previously known as FolderShare), the favorites synchronization capabilities of the Windows Live Toolbar, and Live Mesh beta, which was a completely different product despite the similar name.

To get started, install the Windows Live Mesh application from Windows Live Essentials 2011, open it from the Start menu shortcut, and sign in using your Windows Live ID. That takes you to the Windows Live Mesh Status page for your computer. Figure 8-6 shows this page after we set up one folder to sync. We also personalized the name and icon for this computer, as described in "Synchronization Services" on page 290.

With the help of Windows Live Mesh, you can accomplish any of the following tasks:

- **Synchronize the contents of folders**   You can designate any folder to be synced with a matching folder on another connected device. Any additions or changes you make to the contents of your synced folders on one PC are replicated on other PCs, provided you've selected that device for syncing and you've signed in to Windows Live Mesh with the same user ID. For each folder you designate, you can, optionally, choose to synchronize files to SkyDrive synced storage so that any files you add or change in your local folder are also available from the web. If you're synchronizing files between two PCs on the same local network, the transfer takes place locally, at network speeds—no round trip to SkyDrive is required. SkyDrive synced storage is

Chapter 8

limited to 5 GB. For peer-to-peer syncing, the limits are far more generous: up to 200 folders, with each synced folder limited to 100,000 files and a total size of 50 GB.

- **Synchronize Internet Explorer and Microsoft Office settings**   These settings have no additional options. Click the links beneath the Program Settings heading to enable or disable either one. With Internet Explorer sync enabled, the entire contents of your Favorites folder is synchronized with other PCs on which this option is enabled and Windows Live Mesh is running under the same Windows Live ID.

- **Connect to computers remotely**   If Windows Live Mesh is running and your computer is online, you can connect to it over a network or over the Internet. This feature is similar to Remote Desktop, but it works on all editions of Windows 7, Windows Vista, and Windows Server 2008 or later. You cannot connect to a Mac running OS X, nor can you connect to a computer running Windows XP or Windows Server 2003.

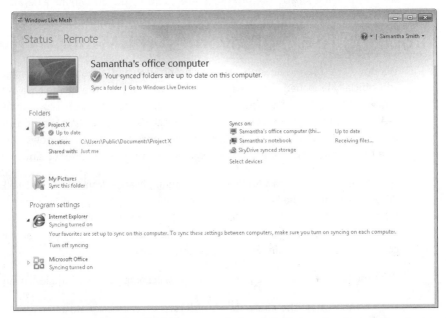

Figure 8-6 From this central point, you can designate folders and system settings to sync. Click the arrow to the left of any synced folder or setting to see more details about the folder.

For more on how to set up and use Remote Desktop connections, see "Connecting to Another Computer with Remote Desktop" on page 762.

To begin synchronizing a folder on your PC with other computers or with SkyDrive synced storage, start by opening Windows Live Mesh. Click Sync A Folder, select the local folder, and then click Sync. That opens the Select Devices dialog box, shown next, which lists all other computers that you've added to this account as well as SkyDrive Synced Storage.

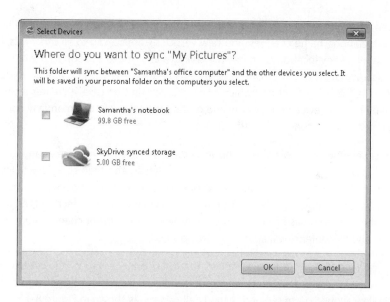

Select the SkyDrive Synced Storage check box if you want the contents of the folder to be available when your local PC is offline. Be selective: Remember that this dedicated storage space has a 5-GB limit (separate from the 25 GB available in your main SkyDrive folders).

TROUBLESHOOTING

A synced folder ends up in the wrong location on a secondary PC

Think carefully before you select the check box for another computer when you initially set up a synced folder. When you do this, Windows Live Mesh syncs the selected folder to a top-level folder within the user profile of the other computer. That works fine if you want to sync any of the default folders in your profile, such as My Documents or My Pictures. But what happens if you select a subfolder on your desktop PC to sync, like C:\Users\Ed\Documents\Work? When you click the other computer's check box in the Select Devices dialog box, Windows Live Mesh creates a Work folder in the user profile of the other PC. Instead of being located in the Documents folder as you expect, the new Work folder is in your user profile—C:\Users\Ed\Work—right alongside My Documents and My Pictures. If you want control over the location, leave the check box cleared, go to the other PC, and open Windows Live Mesh. You'll see a new entry under the Folders heading for the folder you just began syncing on the other PC (in this case, Work). Click Sync This Folder, select the folder you want to use (create the new folder, if necessary), and then click Sync.

Chapter 8

When a folder is synced to two or more locations, any changes made on one PC—additions, deletions, name changes, and new versions—are copied to all other PCs, immediately if possible. If any location is offline, the changes are synced as soon as the device reconnects to Windows Live Mesh. In some cases, Windows Live Mesh is unable to determine which file should be kept and which one discarded. In that case, it creates a copy of the file, appending the device name to the end of the file name. You can manually compare the documents and reconcile the differences.

You can enable or disable synchronization for a folder on any device at any time. Click the arrow to the left of the synced folder to see its details, and then click Select Devices from the bottom of the Syncs On list. Clear the check box next to the device you no longer want to sync with. Removing a device from the Syncs On list has no effect on the content in the folder where it has been synced previously, but any further changes you make to that folder and its contents will affect only the local copy.

To access your folders from a computer that isn't connected to Windows Live Mesh, navigate to *devices.live.com*, sign in with your Windows Live ID, and click View Synced Folders. That view allows you to see and manage all folders, as shown in Figure 8-7.

Figure 8-7 You can see and manage all available synced folders from the Devices page, even if they're not synced to SkyDrive.

For any folder whose contents are available in SkyDrive synced storage, clicking the folder name takes you to the SkyDrive copy of that folder, where you can download files and share their contents with up to nine other persons, using their e-mail addresses.

If a remote computer is online and signed in to Windows Live Mesh using the same Windows Live ID as yours, you can access it remotely, running programs and using Windows Explorer on the remote computer to manage files as if you were connected locally. As a security precaution, remote access via Windows Live Mesh is disabled by default. To enable access for your local PC, open Windows Live Mesh and click the Remote tab. That opens the dialog box shown in Figure 8-8.

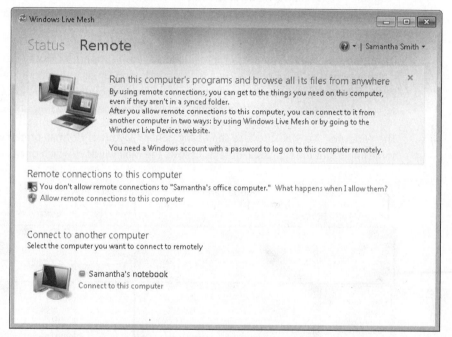

Figure 8-8 If you want to connect to this computer from another computer where you're signed in with Windows Live Mesh, you have to first allow remote connections.

Click Allow Remote Connections To This Computer. (You must supply the credentials of an administrator account to make this change.) That starts the Windows Live Mesh Remote Connections service. With that service running, you see a green light next to the computer name at the bottom of the Windows Live Mesh Remote tab, and you can click Connect To This Computer to launch the remote connection. As with Remote Desktop, only one user at a time—remote or local—can log on to the same Windows session. While you're accessing the computer remotely, the computer itself is locked to local users. They need to enter appropriate credentials—and kick you offline—to gain access.

Using Windows Live Mail

If you look carefully at Windows Live Mail, you can see traces of its many predecessors. Although the name is new, the program itself is the successor to the Windows Vista mail client, Windows Mail, which in turn replaced Outlook Express, the e-mail client and news-group reader that was included with Windows XP. Windows Live Mail is a full-featured, rich program. In this section, we assume you don't need help with the basics of composing, sending, and receiving e-mail, and we focus instead on the most important (and interesting) features that you're not likely to discover on your own.

It's not surprising that Windows Live Mail offers superb support for Hotmail accounts, but it also supports other popular e-mail services, including Gmail and Yahoo! Mail, as well as POP3 and IMAP e-mail accounts. (It does not support accounts on Microsoft Exchange servers, unless those accounts are configured to run in IMAP mode.)

The Windows Live Mail interface shares the general layout of Hotmail on the web, with some important differences. Figure 8-9 shows the Mail window, which opens by default.

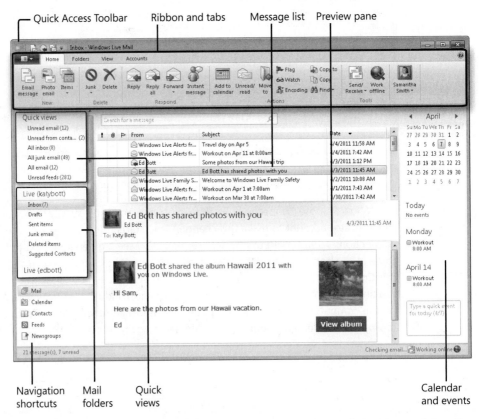

Figure 8-9 Options on the Home tab let you create new messages and manage your inbox. You can customize the appearance of every one of these elements by switching to the View tab.

The shortcuts in the lower left corner of the window are a crucial navigation element. The opening view shows the contents of your e-mail account. Click the Calendar or Contacts shortcut to switch to either of those views, both of which we discuss in more detail later in this section.

INSIDE OUT   Tame the ribbon

If you've used any recent version of Microsoft Office, you probably recognize the ribbon interface, which replaced pull-down menus with tabs. In our experience, people either love the ribbon or despise it, with little to no middle ground. If you fall into the "I hate it" group, the reason is probably your longtime familiarity with menus as a navigation tool. We've found that it helps tremendously to think of each tab as a menu turned sideways, with the row of tab headings playing the role of top-level menus.

The set of tabs varies depending on the type of item you're working with. Commands on each tab are organized into groups. If you make the overall window narrower, items in the groups compress, hiding first the text and then consolidating all commands under a single button with an arrow below it. Commands never change location, however. The blue button just to the left of the Home heading offers access to commands that were once on the File menu: New, Import, Export, Options, and so on.

You can click any heading to switch to a different tab. For example, the options on the View tab, shown here, allow you to customize the arrangement of any item in the main program window. You can show a two-line message list, for example, or move the reading pane to the right or hide it altogether.

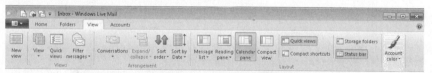

Still mourning for menus? Double-click the current heading to minimize the ribbon so that only its headings show. In that configuration, the headings look like top-level menus. When you click a heading, the contents of its tab appear; the tab disappears as soon as you choose a command or click elsewhere in the window.

To further reduce your frustration with the ribbon, consider moving the Quick Access Toolbar below the ribbon and then customizing it by adding your most frequently used commands. Click the down arrow to the right of the Quick Access Toolbar to move it below the ribbon. Right-click any command on any tab and then choose Add To Quick Access Toolbar to make that command available at any time, regardless of which tab is currently selected.

Chapter 8

In the New group on the Home tab, a few choices cover the basic data types. Click Email Message to begin addressing and composing a new message, or click Items and then choose a menu option to add a calendar event or a new contact. When you right-click the Windows Live Mail taskbar icon (or click and swipe upward), the resulting shortcut menu contains these three obvious choices as well. But there's another choice available in all these locations: Photo Email.

This specialized type of e-mail message allows you to upload your high-resolution photos to SkyDrive and then send thumbnails to e-mail recipients, with a link to the online album. That approach avoids overloading the recipients' inboxes or taxing a slow Internet connection.

Windows Live Mail embeds photo thumbnails in the message by using one of six available album styles (click the arrow to the right of the gallery in the Album Styles group to see the full selection). For some styles, like the one shown in Figure 8-10, you can add an album title. You can also specify the size of the uploaded photos and adjust privacy settings by using commands on the custom Photo Album Tools tab.

Figure 8-10 The tools shown here are available only when you create a new message using the Photo Email option.

If you intend to use this feature for more than casual photo sharing, be warned: There is no limit on the number of pictures you can send via photo e-mails. However, Microsoft specifically says it may "limit the number of files that each user can upload to a SkyDrive album each month."

When you begin creating a photo e-mail with Windows Live Mail, you use Windows Explorer to add pictures. You can also create a photo e-mail by starting with Windows Live Photo Gallery. Select photos you want to include, and then click Photo Email on the Create tab in that program.

Windows Live Mail and Windows Live ID Accounts

A Windows Live ID isn't required for using Windows Live Mail. However, certain features are available only with a Windows Live ID:

- You must be signed in to Windows Live to send photo e-mail messages—messages that simultaneously send to your recipient thumbnail images and a link to full-size images stored in a SkyDrive album. (If you're not signed in, you're prompted to do so before you can continue.)

- Various instant messaging functions—including the capability to send text messages to mobile phones—are available only when you're signed in to Windows Live.

- You must be signed in to Windows Live to view your online contacts list—the same one that you see if you use a web browser to view your Hotmail account. If you're not signed in to Windows Live, your local contacts list, which is completely independent of the online list, appears.

Managing Mail Accounts and Messages

When you start Windows Live Mail for the first time, the program guides you through the steps necessary to create your first account. (This process is particularly easy if you are signed in to Windows Live with a Hotmail account.) If you need to create an additional account, or if you declined to set one up at your first opportunity and are now ready to create your first account, open Mail (click the Mail shortcut in the lower left corner if necessary), and then click Email, the first command on the Accounts tab.

That opens a dialog box in which you enter account details—e-mail address, password, and the display name you want to use. The setup process is nearly foolproof when it comes to

Hotmail and Gmail accounts, and it can automatically discover settings for many other mail providers. For some external domains that the program recognizes (including addresses at *gmail.com* and *yahoo.com*), you'll see a yellow box alerting you to specific requirements and containing a link to more detailed help.

It's worth trying the automatic setup first. If it fails, you know immediately and can start over, this time selecting the Manually Configure Server Settings check box. Then enter credentials, server names, ports, and other details.

> **Note**
>
> When you enter the password for a new account, the Remember This Password option is selected by default. This is convenient if you have a strong Windows user password, you lock your computer when you step away from your desk, and no one has easy access to your computer. If someone else might have physical access to your computer and could access your e-mail account, clear the Remember This Password check box. You'll then be prompted for the password the first time you send or retrieve mail in each Windows Live Mail session.

Do you have more than one e-mail account? If you want to use multiple accounts in Windows Live Mail, you have to decide how to organize your messages. You have three choices, which we'll cover in the following sections.

Keep Your Accounts Separate

Each account is represented by a separate set of folders in the sidebar on the left, with each having its own Inbox, Sent Items, and other default folders. Click the arrow to the left of each account name to expand or collapse its folders, as shown next.

INSIDE OUT   See the contents of multiple inboxes in a single folder

There's no need to jump from inbox to inbox to check on multiple accounts. Instead, click Quick View on the View tab (or right-click the Quick Views heading in the navigation pane and click Select Quick View). Select the All Inbox check box and click OK. The Quick Views list, above your e-mail folders, now has an All Inbox shortcut that consolidates the contents of all your inboxes in a single virtual folder. The search box above this unified message list allows you to find messages from any inbox in any account.

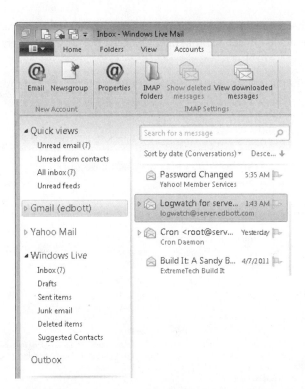

Right-click any account name and click Properties to change the settings for that account, including the name displayed here. If you use the search box above the message list, it searches only the contents of the currently displayed folder.

If you set up multiple accounts, a new option appears in the top right corner of any message you compose. Use the contents of the From list to choose which account you want to use to send the current message.

Fetch Mail from Other Accounts into a Single Inbox

In this configuration, use your Windows Live account to retrieve mail from other services and bring those messages into your inbox or into a separate folder. In general, this configuration works only with accounts that are enabled for POP3 access. Gmail can be configured to use POP3 by using instructions available from a Help link in this dialog box. Yahoo Mail reportedly offers this option only to Yahoo Mail Plus customers. Other Hotmail and Windows Live accounts are not supported using this option.

To begin, use a web browser to open Hotmail and sign in using the Windows Live ID you plan to use as the destination for all incoming messages. Switch to the inbox if necessary, click Options, and then click More Options. Under Managing Your Account, click Sending/ Receiving Email From Other Accounts. That opens a dialog box like the one shown here.

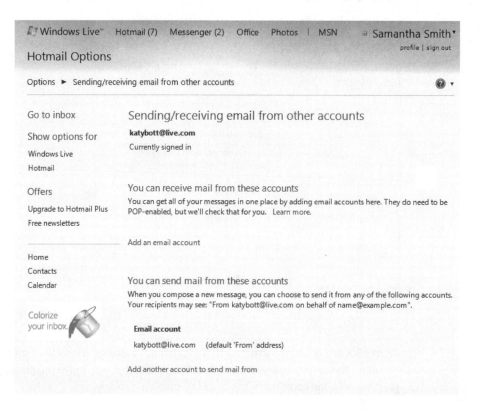

Click Add An E-Mail Account to enter the credentials for the external account (use the advanced options if you have unusual server or port settings). After you respond to a confirmation message in the other account, you're done. From now on, Windows Live connects to the other server several times an hour and downloads its new messages to your Hotmail inbox. When you check in with the primary account, you see the messages from the other accounts intermixed with those addressed to your Windows Live address.

This feature has one unavoidable side effect: you might see a significant lag between the time messages arrive in your secondary account and when they reach your primary inbox. That's because you can't control how often Windows Live checks that other account. In our experience, the delay can be 20 to 30 minutes. If that's not acceptable, the next option might be for you.

Forward Other Accounts to a Single Address

The last alternative is to go to those other, secondary e-mail accounts and configure them to forward all incoming messages to your primary account—presumably a Windows Live account. Each mail service uses a slightly different technique for accomplishing this, often adding X-Forwarded-To and X-Forwarded-For headers to the message. If you choose this route, you should get your forwarded mail with almost no delay.

You might, however, experience one gotcha: many mailing lists and other similar services require that you send replies from the same account at which you receive a message. If the secondary account is set up to forward new messages to a different account and Windows Live Mail isn't configured to send using the original account, your replies and administrative requests might be rejected.

How Secure Is Windows Live Mail?

By default, Windows Live Mail shares security settings with the Restricted Sites zone in Internet Explorer. You can confirm this setting by opening the Windows Live Mail menu (click the Windows Live Mail button, directly to the left of Home, click Safety Options, and then click the Security tab). It's worth noting that ActiveX controls and scripts are always disabled in Windows Live Mail, even if you've enabled them in the corresponding security zone for Internet Explorer.

Working with Contacts

To manage your contacts in Windows Live Mail, click the Contacts shortcut in the lower left corner of the window. If prompted, sign in to your Windows Live account. The initial view shows your Windows Live contacts as well as those from any social network that you've attached to Windows Live. Use the search box to filter the list and find details about any contact, as shown here.

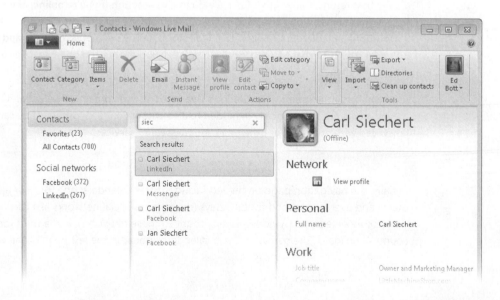

Adding new contacts is straightforward: on the Home tab, click Contact (the first command in the New group), or press Ctrl+Shift+C. The contact form divides information into seven tabs, with the Quick Add tab containing the bare minimum of information you're likely to need for a new contact. Click the Contact tab to manage multiple phone numbers and e-mail addresses for a contact. Use the Primary E-Mail Address drop-down list on this tab to specify which address Windows Live Mail should use by default when you begin composing a new e-mail message.

You can use the Contacts list as a jumping-off point for a new e-mail message. Select one or more contacts, and then click Email (on the Home tab) or right-click and choose Send Email from the shortcut menu. In either case, you get a new mail message window with the preferred e-mail address for each contact already included in the To field.

To add a recipient to an e-mail message that you've already begun to compose, click Add in the Contacts group on the Message tab. Use the search box to filter the list and find the name you're looking for. Select one or more names, and then click To, Cc, or Bcc to add the preferred e-mail addresses for the selected contacts to the respective fields.

Using the Calendar

Windows Calendar, a separate application in Windows Vista, has become a feature of Windows Live Mail in Windows 7. To see all events, sign in to your Windows Live account and click the Calendar shortcut in the lower left corner of Windows Live Mail.

> ### Why Should You Use a Windows Live Account?
>
> If you want to use the Contacts and Calendar features of Windows Live Mail, you'll have the best results if you sign in to a Windows Live account. If you're online, any changes you make in Windows Live Mail or in your web browser are synchronized to the other location immediately. Windows Live Mail stores a local copy of all contacts and calendar events so that you can view and edit existing events and add new ones even if you're offline.
>
> If you forgo the option of a Windows Live account, any contacts or calendar items you create are stored locally in hidden folders within your user profile. They cannot be synced with other PCs or other mail and messaging services.

Initially, the navigation page on the left includes three calendars: one for your appointments and events, a second for birthdays (drawn from social networks like Facebook, if you've connected your Windows Live account to those networks), and a third for your country's holidays. The names of these calendars appear in the left pane of the window, with check boxes that allow you to show or hide each calendar's contents in the display pane.

You can also include additional calendars from your Windows Live account—those you create and those that other Windows Live users share with you. Figure 8-11, for example, shows a Windows Live account that includes a group calendar and a shared calendar from another person.

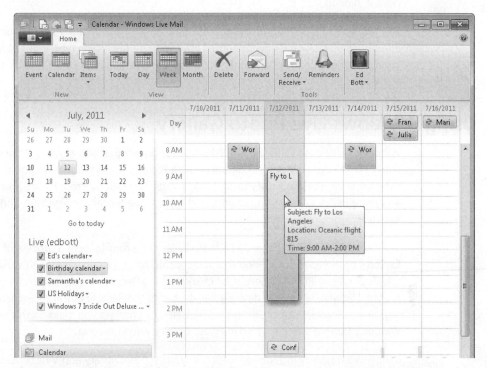

Figure 8-11 Calendars you add to your Windows Live account using the web interface are available in Windows Live Mail as well.

If you and your spouse both have Windows Live accounts, you can share calendars with ease and access details of each other's schedule in Windows Live Mail. (If you view the shared calendars in a web browser, you can see to-do list and agenda functions that are absent in the Windows Live Mail calendar.)

To share a calendar with another person, sign in to your Windows Live account at *mail.live.com* and click Calendar. Click Share and choose your personal calendar from the list. On the Sharing Settings page, click Share This Calendar and then click Add People to select contacts and assign permissions for each one. Click Save to send an invitation. When the people you invite accept, your calendar is added to their list of Hotmail calendars; they can see free/busy time, view details of events, or create events on your calendar, depending on the permissions you've assigned.

You can change the name and color assigned to a calendar by clicking its name in the navigation pane and choosing Properties. To hide a calendar, clear its check box. To add a calendar, click Calendar in the New group on the Home tab. To delete a calendar, click its name and choose Delete (note that the birthday calendar cannot be deleted; if you don't want it, hide it).

Entering an event is straightforward: select a date and time in any view in your calendar and double-click (or click Event in the New group on the Home tab). In the New Event form you'll find the necessary date and time fields and a versatile set of recurrence and reminder options.

Using Windows Live Photo Gallery

Windows Live Photo Gallery is a full-featured program that allows you to take complete control over your collection of digital photos. You can import digital photos and video clips; organize a photo library using folders, tags, and ratings; crop, adjust, and edit photos; and share individual pictures, albums, and videos—via e-mail, on SkyDrive, and on social networks.

The Photo Gallery executable (WLXPhotoGallery.exe) runs as a child process of Windows Explorer (Explorer.exe). Knowing that relationship helps explain why, when you add or edit a folder or file in Photo Gallery, your changes are reflected immediately in the Windows file system. Likewise, when you delete a file, it goes to the Recycle Bin. For supported formats, tags and ratings are saved within the file itself; any changes you make to this metadata in Windows Explorer are displayed in Photo Gallery, and vice versa.

Initially, your gallery includes all folders in your Pictures library and Videos library, displayed in thumbnails view. The arrangement of the default Photo Gallery window should be familiar: folders on the left, contents in the middle, an optional tag and caption pane on the right.

For a refresher course on how libraries work, see "Working with Libraries" on page 343. For more on how to get around without menus, see "Tame the ribbon" on page 301. For a discussion of how Windows Explorer handles metadata, see "Managing File Properties and Metadata" on page 360.

Figure 8-12 shows the default Windows Live Photo Gallery configuration without any adornments.

Navigation pane   Contents pane   Connections to web services   Tag and caption pane

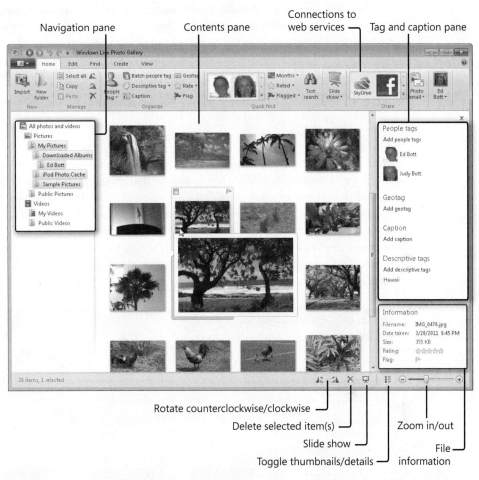

Rotate counterclockwise/clockwise

Delete selected item(s)

Slide show

Toggle thumbnails/details

Zoom in/out

File information

Figure 8-12 Rest the mouse pointer over any picture in the contents pane and, after a brief delay, a larger thumbnail pops up to give you a closer look. Move the mouse to close it.

Any folders you add to the Pictures or Videos library are automatically added to the respective views in Photo Gallery. To specify which folders are included in either library, click File (the blue button to the left of Home) and then click Include Folder. The New Folder button on the Home tab creates a subfolder in the currently selected folder or in the default Save folder if a library is selected.

Other commands on the Home tab include tools you can use to perform a variety of important tasks that we cover in more detail later in this section.

Chapter 8

The View tab, shown here, includes several options that help you arrange items displayed in the contents pane and see more details about some or all of them. The command on the far right, for example, toggles the display of the tag and caption pane.

Normally, the contents of the gallery are grouped automatically. On the View tab, click any of the commands in Arrange List to change that grouping. The Show Detail option lets you display and edit one piece of data—rating, caption, date taken, file size, and so on—beneath each thumbnail. Here, for example, we clicked Tag to group the gallery using descriptive tags and File Name to display a name under each picture. Because multiple tags can be applied to a single photo, the same picture can appear two or more times in the gallery. If you change a piece of metadata on one image (renaming a file, for example), the label beneath other copies of that image also changes.

Click All Details to see a dense block of information to the right of every thumbnail. This view is most useful if you're scanning a folder full of files and want to see all the metadata and images at the same time.

When you double-click a thumbnail, it opens in the same window, replacing the contents of the gallery and giving you access to an extended set of editing tools that we'll look at in more detail later in this section.

TROUBLESHOOTING

Your can't get back to the gallery

If you use Windows Live Photo Gallery long enough, you'll run into this puzzle. You double-click a picture from the gallery to open it in its own editing window and click a command on the Create or View tab to do something with it. When you're ready to close the picture and return to the gallery, there's no obvious way to get back.

The fix? Press the Backspace key, or switch to the Edit tab and then click the Close File command at the far right of the tab.

On the View tab, use the Zoom In and Zoom Out commands to increase or decrease the size of thumbnails in the contents pane. You can also use the Zoom slider at the bottom right, or the Zoom In and Zoom Out buttons on either side of it. For smooth zooms, point to the contents pane, hold down the Ctrl key, and move the mouse wheel. If you're a keyboard aficionado, press Ctrl+Plus key or Ctrl+Minus key to zoom, and use Ctrl+0 to toggle between thumbnails and details.

Importing Pictures into the Gallery

Windows Live Photo Gallery monitors your Pictures library and any additional folders that you have assigned to the gallery; any image added to one of those folders is automatically added to the gallery. That makes importing files into the gallery a simple, straightforward process: just copy them into a folder that's in the library.

If the image files are freshly captured in a digital camera or saved on a portable storage device, you have other options. Virtually all recent-vintage cameras support the Windows Image Acquisition (WIA) driver standard introduced in Windows XP or the newer Windows Portable Devices (WPD) standard introduced in Windows Vista. Plug in the camera, connect it to a USB port, and turn the camera on. In the AutoPlay window that appears, choose Import Pictures And Videos Using Windows Live Photo Gallery. (Avoid the similar-sounding Import Pictures And Videos Using Windows; this option offers fewer organizing features.)

TROUBLESHOOTING

Your pictures don't import as you expect

Open AutoPlay in Control Panel (under Hardware And Sound) and make sure the default action for Pictures is Import Pictures And Videos Using Windows Live Photo Gallery. If your camera has its own entry, you might need to connect it to your computer and adjust this setting from Device Stage. (See "Managing Devices with Device Stage" on page 1067 for more details.)

The Windows Live Photo Gallery Import Photos And Videos wizard is lean and straightforward. In fact, you can complete the import with two or three clicks if you're in a hurry. Figure 8-13 shows the initial window.

Figure 8-13 To get pictures into the gallery as quickly as possible, with a minimum number of options, choose the second option in this dialog box.

From start to finish, the import wizard is designed to help you accomplish three goals, either automatically or manually, using preferences you can reset on the fly:

- **Sort photos and videos into groups** You can dump all photos from a given import session into a single folder, or you can group photos into separate folders. Windows Live Photo Gallery does the grouping based on the date and time stamps for each photo. You can adjust the grouping manually and also mark individual photos or videos to be skipped during this import.

- **Specify a folder name (or names) for the imported photos** Give a folder name to the entire batch or to individual groups. If you skip this step, Photo Gallery uses the default settings.

- **Add tags** Here, too, you can add tags to the entire import or assign separate sets of tags to each group.

How you choose to accomplish each import operation depends on how diligent you want to be about folder naming and tagging; if consistent and complete folder naming and tagging is important to you, you'll probably want to spend a little time filling these details in each time you connect your digital camera to your computer. If you prefer the "shoebox" approach, you can accept all the defaults and go back later to review images, creating new folders and adding tags as needed.

The fastest way to get a group of pictures into the gallery is to select Import All New Items Now and not click the Add Tags link or type a folder name. Click Import, and all new pictures on the connected device are imported into the gallery using the default settings. Any photos or videos that you previously imported but left on the camera are ignored during this process.

If your camera contains a large number of photos taken at different times and places, you might prefer to allow Photo Gallery to sort the imported photos into separate folders. To do so, use the default option (Review, Organize, And Group Items To Import) and then click Next. That opens a dialog box showing the camera's contents divided into groups, as in Figure 8-14.

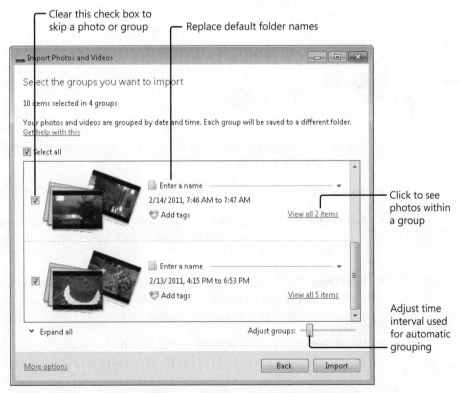

Figure labels:
- Clear this check box to skip a photo or group
- Replace default folder names
- Click to see photos within a group
- Adjust time interval used for automatic grouping

Dialog box text:
Import Photos and Videos

Select the groups you want to import

10 items selected in 4 groups

Your photos and videos are grouped by date and time. Each group will be saved to a different folder. Get help with this

☑ Select all

Enter a name
2/14/ 2011, 7:46 AM to 7:47 AM
Add tags   View all 2 items

Enter a name
2/13/ 2011, 4:15 PM to 6:53 PM
Add tags   View all 5 items

Expand all   Adjust groups:

More options   Back   Import

Figure 8-14 From this window, you can refine automatic grouping of imported photos, assign folder names, and look at individual pictures before deciding whether to keep or toss them.

Click to the right of any folder icon to give that group's folder its own descriptive name. Click Add Tags to apply tags to all photos in that group. If the grouping doesn't make sense, use the Adjust Groups slider to change the time interval from its default 4 hours to a value that's higher or lower.

The More Options link allows you to adjust any or all of the default settings. It leads to the dialog box shown here. (If you'd prefer to set these options before connecting a camera, open Windows Live Photo Gallery; click the blue button to the left of the Home tab to open the File menu, click Options, and then click the Import tab.)

Using this dialog box, you can adjust any or all of the following settings; refer to the Example text to see the effect of your changes:

- **Import To**   Designate which folder your imported pictures should be stored in.

- **Folder Name**   The drop-down list lets you choose a variety of combinations of the date imported, the date or date range when the pictures were taken, and the text you enter in the Add Tags box.

- **File Name**   The default setting here uses the file names originally created by your camera. You can choose instead to use the folder name, with or without the Date Taken information, plus a sequence number.

- **Other Options**   The check boxes in this section allow you to specify whether to immediately open the imported pictures in Windows Live Photo Gallery, erase pictures from the camera after the import is successful, and rotate pictures automatically when importing.

CAUTION

The option to erase pictures on import is potentially dangerous, especially for irre-placeable photos of once-in-a-lifetime events. If you leave this check box clear, you can decide on a case-by-case basis whether to erase pictures on the fly. Just select the Delete Files From Device After Importing option in the status dialog box that appears after you click Import.

Adding Tags to Image Files

Tags are an extraordinarily flexible way to organize files, especially digital photos. A tag can consist of a single word (*Hawaii*, *sunset*, *Judy*) or a phrase of up to 255 characters, and if there's a theoretical limit to the number of tags you can add to an image file, we haven't found it. Windows Live Photo Gallery distinguishes three types of tags—people tags, geo-tags, and descriptive tags—all with essentially the same purpose and effect: to categorize pictures so that you can find groups of related photos later by using the Find tab or the search boxes on the Start menu and in Windows Explorer.

To add a people tag to an image, make sure the tag and caption pane is visible, then select the image and click Add People Tags in the info pane. You can select names from the Con-tacts list that descends, or you can type in someone new.

To add a descriptive tag, click Add Descriptive Tags. Windows Live Photo Gallery tries to save you keystrokes as you type by presenting candidate tags that you've already used. This autocomplete feature also helps you maintain consistency in your tagging.

Geotags can be automatically saved to a photo if your camera has built-in GPS capabilities. For pictures that aren't automatically tagged with a location, you can click Add Geotag and start typing a place name. If Windows Live recognizes the place name, it might suggest a name in a standard format.

Tags assigned to images saved in the JPEG format are stored with the file itself and are thus preserved if the file is e-mailed or moved to a new computer.

Uploading and Sharing Photos

Windows Live Photo Gallery lets you create and share photos, videos, and photo albums using a variety of external services. By default, you can connect directly to Windows Live SkyDrive, Facebook, YouTube, Flickr, and Windows Live Groups. To connect to other services, including Picasa and SmugMug, visit the Windows Live Plug-ins site at *plugins.live.com* and search through the collection available for Photo Gallery.

Chapter 8

To upload and share a photo album, start by selecting a group of photos, and then click the icon for a connected service on the Create tab. Each service requires you to provide credentials first (this is automatic for SkyDrive if you're already signed in to Windows Live) and then offers options that allow you to change the album name or use an existing album, add captions, adjust permissions, and choose whether to resize images when uploading them. Here, for example, are the options available when you create an album on SkyDrive.

Photos in an online SkyDrive album are displayed initially as thumbnails. You can use the View menu to switch to either Details view or icons. The Sort menu includes a handy option to rearrange the contents of an album in a manner that pleases you, and the Slide Show command offers a tasteful presentation, with background colors tailored to the content of each slide. Those with whom you share your albums can download particular pictures by clicking More and then clicking Download.

Cropping and Editing Image Files

Windows Live Photo Gallery includes an easy-to-use and surprisingly powerful set of editing tools to help you crop out unnecessary parts of a picture, fix flawed images, and erase small flaws in otherwise perfect photos. To touch up or crop an image, you can select it in the gallery and click the Edit tab. To see a more expansive range of editing options, click View File or double-click the picture to open it in its own window.

To crop an image, start by clicking the arrow beneath the Crop command to display the list of available proportions, as shown in Figure 8-15.

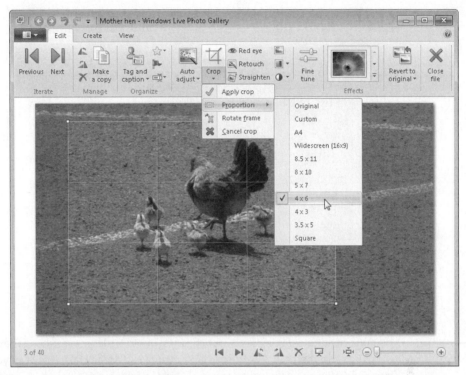

Figure 8-15 Choosing one of the preset proportions from this list is wise if you plan to print out a photo using a standard photo size.

Pick the proportion you want, move and resize the box so that it includes the portion of the image you want to keep, and then click Apply Crop (or just click the Crop button) to finish. If you want to use a standard photo size but in a different orientation, click Rotate Frame on the Crop menu.

Each of the entries in the Adjustments group, with the exception of Auto Adjust, allows you to make a single type of change to the image. Click Red Eye or Retouch, and then use the mouse to mark the section where you need a quick fix. Color and Exposure have drop-down lists of changes that apply changes ranging from subtle to extreme. Click Straighten to allow Photo Gallery to take its best guess at lining up the image.

Auto Adjust, as its name implies, automatically performs whatever editing the program thinks the image needs. Click the arrow below the command and choose Settings to specify which tweaks you want to make using this option. Fine Tune opens a pane on the right where you can exercise fine-grained control, as shown here.

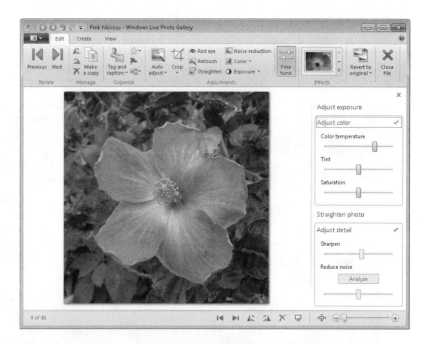

You don't need to explicitly save your changes; Photo Gallery saves changes automatically when you close the program or return to Gallery view. Meanwhile, a copy of your original, unedited picture is safely tucked away in a hidden folder within your local profile. If you change your mind *after* you return to the gallery, even days or weeks later, select the picture and click Revert To Original on the Edit tab.

To see all your saved original images, click the arrow beneath Revert To Original on the Edit tab and click Settings. That opens the Settings dialog box and displays the Originals tab, which provides a link that takes you straight to the folder itself and another option that allows you to specify a period of time after which you want Photo Gallery to move saved original images to the Recycle Bin.

Using Windows Live Messenger

With Windows Live Messenger, you can send and receive instant messages, transmit SMS text messages to mobile devices, transfer files, play games, and request remote assistance. If you have a webcam, you can participate in real-time video chats or transmit video clips to anyone on your list of Messenger contacts.

Windows Live Messenger contains some quirky and unconventional menu options. Like Internet Explorer, it hides its menu bar by default. If you need to access a feature available only from a menu, tap the Alt key to make the menus temporarily visible.

A tiny icon at the top of the Messenger window allows you to switch between Compact view (the narrow window that older versions used as a default) and Full view, which shows updates from people in your social network.

Before you can send messages, you have to have contacts. To add a Messenger contact, click Add and then choose Add A Friend. In the ensuing dialog box, you can enter the contact's instant messaging address (if the person has one) or their e-mail address. You can also enter a mobile phone number that you can use for text messaging, if the recipient's service permits it:

Every new contact receives an invitation via e-mail and has the opportunity to accept or decline. You are not notified if the intended recipient declines your invitation.

To begin an instant messaging conversation with a contact who is online, double-click the contact's name in your Friends list. In the instant message window, type your part of the conversation in the bottom line of the window:

Note that this chat window includes a menu of options along the bottom. Clicking Share allows you to send pictures or files to your contact. Click Voice Call to begin an audio-only conversation using the default communications device. If both parties have a webcam, you can start a video chat. If you have a webcam but the other party doesn't, you can record a video message and send it via e-mail. For any audio or video chat or file transfer, the party at the other end has the opportunity to accept or decline. Click Invite to bring other parties in and turn a conversation into a conference call.

If your contact is not online or not available when you want to communicate, you can send an oxymoronically named offline instant message. Your recipient will see your message when he or she logs back in. Alternatively, you can right-click the person's name and choose Send E-Mail. Or you can right-click the name, choose Enter A Mobile Number, supply the number, and transmit a text message.

PART 2

File Management

Organizing Files and Information

N the beginning, there was the command prompt, which begat drive letters and path names. In those dark days, when floppy disks ruled the PC world and file names were a mere eight characters long with three-letter extensions, finding your stuff wasn't a particularly difficult task.

Today, thanks to long file names, rich file properties, and customizable metadata—not to mention multiterabyte data drives—the challenges of organizing data are considerably tougher. The robust search capabilities built in to Windows 7 (which we discuss in more detail in Chapter 10, "Using Windows Search") offer a tremendous amount of help. In this chapter, we focus on more prosaic organizational tools that help you combine multiple locations into virtual folders and then filter, sort, and group as needed.

Unless you use your computer exclusively as a game machine or a media center, learning to manage your "stuff"—your documents, programs, and communications—is probably the single most critical computing skill you need to acquire. Because the continual growth in storage capacity encourages a corresponding increase in digital retentiveness, keeping track of stuff is more crucial than ever.

The redesigned Windows Explorer is rich with organizational power tools, including live-icon previews of file contents (for applications and document types that support that capability), a preview pane that allows you to peek inside a file's contents without actually opening it, and a details pane that displays file properties and lets you add descriptive tags to files. In this chapter, we dive deeply into this rich feature set and explain how Windows 7 organizes your data files, a crucial bit of inside knowledge that will serve you well.

What's in Your Edition?

All of the features we describe in this chapter are available in all editions of Windows 7.

Mastering Windows Explorer

You can't become a Windows expert without mastering Windows Explorer. This general-purpose tool is used throughout Windows, for general file-management tasks, for opening and saving files in Windows programs, and even in parts of the Windows shell such as Control Panel. The more you understand about how Windows Explorer works, the more effective you'll be at speeding through tasks without unnecessary delays.

The design of Windows Explorer in Windows 7 is significantly refined from its Windows Vista predecessor, and it's practically unrecognizable compared to its ancestor in Windows XP. To give you the lay of the land, we'll start by introducing the individual elements that allow you to navigate through Windows and display and arrange data.

As we explain in detail later in this chapter, Windows Explorer is extremely customizable. You can show or hide some navigation and display elements and choose from a dizzying array of views and column layouts. Figure 9-1 shows Windows Explorer with all of its basic elements visible. The contents of a single folder within the Pictures library are shown in Medium Icons view.

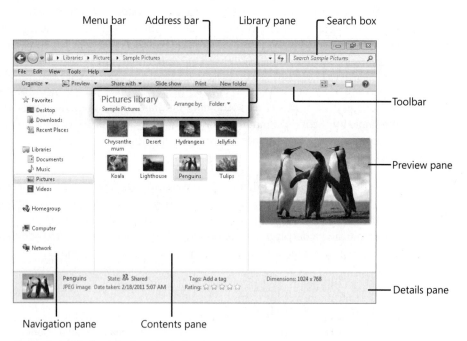

Figure 9-1 Windows Explorer includes the navigation and display elements shown here, some of which can be hidden.

The important landmarks, optional and otherwise, are as follows.

Navigation pane   The default view of the navigation pane, which appears at the left side of Windows Explorer, shows four or five nodes: Favorites, Libraries, Homegroup (visible only if the network location is set to Home), Computer, and Network. You can hide the navigation pane, adjust its width, or change its content to include only the Favorites node and a hierarchical folders list. We discuss the navigation pane and its customization options later in this section.

Details pane   Running across the bottom of the window, the details pane displays properties for the current selection. You can adjust its height by dragging the top border up or down. The details pane is shown by default but can be hidden.

For more details about how to view and edit the properties of files, see "Managing File Properties and Metadata" on page 360.

Preview pane   A button on the toolbar allows you to show or hide the preview pane with a single click. If the currently selected file has a preview handler, the file's contents are displayed in the preview pane. Default preview handlers allow you to view the contents of most graphics file formats, plain text files, and those saved in Rich Text Format (RTF). Select a media file, such as an MP3 music track or a video clip, and a compact media player appears in the preview pane. Programs that you install after setting up Windows, such as Microsoft Office and Adobe Reader, can add custom preview handlers as part of their program setup, allowing you to preview files created in the formats supported by those programs. Figure 9-2 shows the preview pane displaying the contents of a PDF file on a computer where Adobe Reader 9 has been installed.

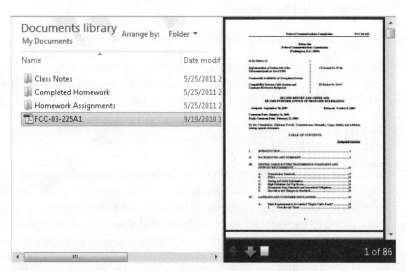

Figure 9-2 With the help of custom preview handlers like the one provided by Adobe Reader, you can preview the contents of documents that are not supported by default in Windows Explorer.

Chapter 9

Toolbar The toolbar (known as the command bar in Windows Vista) is not optional and cannot be customized via Control Panel. (For information about how to customize it by editing the registry, see "Customizing the Toolbar in Windows Explorer" on page 340.) A few elements on the toolbar are always available, including the Organize menu on the left and the three buttons on the far right, which (going from left to right) change views, show or hide the preview pane, and open a help window. Other buttons on the toolbar vary depending on the current selection; available commands are relevant to the selected file type or folder location.

Menu bar Sitting directly above the toolbar shown in Figure 9-1 on page 326 is the menu bar, which is normally hidden. You shouldn't need this relic from Windows XP in everyday use, as most of its offerings are now available on the Organize menu and through the Change Your View button (or, in some cases, on the shortcut menu that appears when you right-click in Windows Explorer). Nevertheless, some Windows XP veterans prefer to keep the menu bar visible because it takes up little space and leaves frequently needed function- ality (such as a command to open the Folder Options dialog box) in familiar places. (Expert network users might be accustomed to using an option on the Tools menu to map a shared network folder to a local drive letter; in Windows 7, this option appears on the toolbar, but it is visible only when you click Computer in the navigation pane.)

INSIDE OUT Get faster access to Folder Options

The fastest way to get to the Folder Options dialog box is to type **folder** in the Start menu's search box. Folder Options should pop to the top of the search results list, under the Control Panel heading.

If the menu bar isn't displayed, you can make it appear temporarily by pressing Alt or F10; the menu bar disappears after you open a menu and execute a command, if you click any- where else in Windows Explorer, or if you tap Alt again.

Library pane This navigation aid appears by default above the file list when a library is selected. It can be hidden.

Address bar Like its counterpart in a web browser, the address bar shows you where you are and helps you get where you want to go. (You can even type a URL here and launch your web browser, although that's hardly its principal function.) Back and Forward but- tons allow you to navigate between destinations you've visited in the current session, and the drop-down history list lets you revisit addresses you entered in previous sessions. Like its Windows Vista predecessor, this version of Windows Explorer uses a breadcrumb trail feature to help you navigate in the address bar. Figure 9-3 shows this feature in action. The

Class Notes folder is open, and each parent folder is represented with a name separated by a small arrow. Click any folder name to move straight to that location; click the down arrow, as shown, to display other subfolders at the same level.

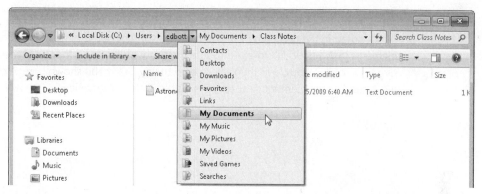

Figure 9-3 The breadcrumb trail allows you to jump to parent folders or subfolders in the path of the current folder.

We regularly hear from experienced Windows XP users who are perplexed by the absence of the familiar Up button. A design change in the Windows 7 address bar should help ease the transition; the address bar is designed to always show the link for the parent folder (sliding the name of the current folder to the right if necessary), allowing you to go up a level by clicking that link.

INSIDE OUT   Get the full path for a folder or a file

If you're moving from Windows XP to Windows 7, you'll notice that the address bar no longer shows you the full path of the current folder in the traditional manner, with backslash characters separating folder names. If you need to see the full path displayed that way, click anywhere to the right of the path in the address bar or right-click any part of the address bar and choose Edit Address. This shortcut menu also includes two additional options that allow you to copy the current address to the Clipboard. Click Copy Address to save the location in a format that is optimized for copying and pasting folders in Windows Explorer; use Copy Address As Text if you plan to paste the folder path into a document.

To copy the full path for an individual file, hold down the Shift key as you right-click the file, and then choose Copy As Path. This option is especially useful if you've found a file in Windows Explorer and you want to upload it to a website or open it in another program without browsing to the same location in an Open dialog box. Copy the full path for the file, and then paste it into the File Name box in the target program.

Chapter 9

Search box Typing in the search box begins a search whose scope is restricted to the current location and displays the search results immediately in the contents pane. The width of the search box can be adjusted by dragging its left edge in either direction.

For more details on how to search in Windows Explorer, see Chapter 10.

As we noted in the preceding list, you can show or hide some of the navigation and display elements in Windows Explorer. To toggle the show/hide setting for any of these items, click Organize, click Layout, and then select from the fly-out menu shown here. A check mark indicates that the element in question is visible in the current view.

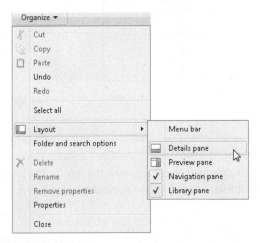

Navigating in Windows Explorer

In its default arrangement, Windows Explorer offers four or five starting points for navigating through files on your computer and on your network. The most prominent jumping-off point is the new Libraries feature, which we discuss in more detail later in this chapter (see "Working with Libraries" on page 343), but older, more traditional organizational structures are still there in the background. If you're a Windows veteran and you prefer working directly with the subfolders in your user profile folders or navigating through the hierarchy of drives and folders, you can do that.

In fact, if you prefer the Windows XP–style folder tree, you can replace the default navigation pane layout with a single flat tree. On the General tab of the Folder Options dialog box, under the Navigation Pane heading, select Show All Folders. If you want the folders tree in the navigation pane to automatically open to show the contents of the current folder, select Automatically Expand To Current Folder. (Both options are available on a shortcut menu when you right-click any empty space in the navigation pane.)

Figure 9-4 shows these two views of the navigation pane side by side. On the left is the default, Windows 7–style view; on the right is the Show All Folders view.

Figure 9-4 If you prefer navigating with a folder tree, customize the default navigation pane (left) by using the Show All Folders option (right).

Interestingly, *how* you start Windows Explorer also dictates *where* you start. Here's a quick cheat sheet of what each option does:

- Press Windows logo key+E to open Windows Explorer with Computer selected in the navigation pane. This has the same effect as clicking Computer on the Start menu.

- Click the Windows Explorer button on the taskbar to open Windows Explorer with Libraries selected in the navigation pane. This displays all available libraries (default and custom) for the logged-on user.

- Click the user name at the top of the Start menu's right column to open the user profile folder for the currently logged-on user. This option does not correspond to a top-level entry in the default navigation pane.

The Favorites list that appears at the top of the navigation pane provides direct transport to folders that might or might not be located somewhere along the current path. Windows Explorer populates this list with three links by default: the Desktop and Downloads folders from your user profile, and Recent Places. The third one is a shortcut that displays a filtered view of the Recent Items list, showing only folders and hiding files.

Chapter 9

You can add as many shortcuts as you want to the Favorites list. If you continually need to return to the same folder (say, for a project that you'll be working with for the next few weeks or months), you can add a link to that folder. To do this, display the folder's parent in Windows Explorer, drag the folder to the navigation pane, and then drop it on the Favorites heading. Initially, your new link will have the same name as the folder you dragged, but you can right-click and rename it.

INSIDE OUT   Use Windows Explorer techniques with dialog boxes

If you're opening or saving files in a Windows program that uses the Windows 7 *common dialog boxes* (a set of dialog boxes provided by the Windows application programming interface to give applications a consistent appearance and behavior), you will find essentially the same navigation tools provided by Windows Explorer. In fact, these dialog boxes use the same program code as Windows Explorer, with minor modifications to make them useful for opening and saving files.

Every trick you can use in a standalone Windows Explorer window will work in an Open or Save As dialog box. You can filter the contents of a window by using the search box. The dialog boxes are resizable as well, unlike their predecessors in Windows XP. That option is especially useful in combination with the preview pane. Click the toolbar button to make the preview pane visible, and then double-click the dialog box title bar so that it expands to use the full screen. In that fully expanded view, you should be able to find the file you're looking for with relative ease.

What's What and Where in a User Profile

A *user profile* contains all the settings and files for a user's desktop environment. In addition to personal documents and media files, this profile includes the user's own registry settings, cookies, Internet Explorer favorites, and user data and settings for installed programs.

By default, each user who logs on to a computer has a local user profile, which is created when the user logs on for the first time. Local user profiles are stored in %SystemDrive%\ Users. Each user's profile is stored in a subfolder where the user account name is the folder name (for example, C:\Users\Katy). The entire path for the current user's profile is accessible via another commonly used environment variable, %UserProfile%.

To open your user profile, click Start and then click your user name at the top of the right column. Using the default Windows Explorer view settings, what you see will look much like Figure 9-5. For a new user profile, Windows creates 11 subfolders, each intended to hold a different category of personal information. Programs that you install might create additional folders inside your profile folder.

Figure 9-5 The unhidden portion of your profile consists of 11 subfolders within a folder named for your user account.

INSIDE OUT   Why is it called My Documents again?

In Windows XP, the default data location for each user profile was the My Documents folder, with My Pictures and My Music created as subfolders in that location. Windows Vista introduced the concept of a user profile with separate subfolders for different data types and removed the "My" prefix from these locations. With Windows 7, the personal pronoun is back. Or is it? If you open a Command Prompt window and look at a raw directory listing of your user profile, you'll see that the actual name of the folder displayed as My Documents is simply Documents. The same is true for the Music, Pictures, and Videos folders. So where does the "My" come from? The display text comes from a custom Desktop.ini file that appears in each of these four folders. An entry at the top of the file points to a location within the system file Shell32.dll, which contains a localized name for this folder that varies according to your language. If you want to get rid of the pronoun, open your user profile folder, right-click the folder (My Documents, My Music, and so forth), and click Rename. Whatever text you enter here becomes the new value in the LocalizedResourceName value line in Desktop.ini.

In addition to these visible document folders, a user profile includes a number of hidden registry files, a hidden AppData folder, and several junctions provided for compatibility with

Windows XP. In the remainder of this section, we break out some of the more interesting folders and subfolders within this location.

Default User Data Folders

The 11 visible data folders are as follows:

- **Contacts**   This folder first appeared in Windows Vista and was designed to store contact information used by Windows Mail. It is not used by any programs included in Windows 7 and is maintained for compatibility purposes with third-party personal information management programs.

- **Desktop**   This folder contains items that appear on the user's desktop, including files and shortcuts. (A Public counterpart also contributes items to the desktop.) A link to this location appears by default in the Favorites section of the navigation pane.

- **Downloads**   This folder, which was introduced in Windows Vista and has no predecessor in Windows XP, is the default location for storing items downloaded from websites. A link to this location appears by default in the Favorites section of the navigation pane.

- **Favorites**   This folder contains Internet Explorer favorites. To open it quickly in Windows Explorer, use the shortcut **shell:favorites**.

- **Links**   This folder contains shortcuts that appear under the Favorites heading in the navigation pane. You can create shortcuts here directly, but it's easier to drag items from a file list or the address bar directly into the navigation pane.

- **My Documents**   This folder is the default location for storing user documents in most applications.

- **My Music**   This folder is the default location for ripped CD tracks. Most third-party music programs store downloaded tracks in a subfolder here.

- **My Pictures**   This folder is the default storage location for programs that transfer images from external devices (such as digital cameras).

- **My Videos**   This folder is the default location for programs that transfer video data from external devices.

- **Saved Games**   This folder is the default storage location for game programs that can save a game in progress. All games included in the Windows 7 Games Explorer use this folder.

- **Searches**   This folder stores saved search specifications, allowing you to reuse previous searches.

Application Data

The hidden AppData folder, introduced in Windows Vista, is used extensively by programs as a way to store user data and settings in a place where they'll be protected from accidental change or deletion. This folder (which performs the same function as the Application Data folder in Windows XP) contains application-specific data—customized dictionaries and templates for a word processor, junk sender lists for an e-mail client, custom toolbar settings, and so on. It's organized into three subfolders, named Local, LocalLow, and Roaming. The Roaming folder (which is also accessible via the environment variable %AppData%) is for data that is made available to a roaming profile (a profile stored on a network server; the server makes the profile available to any network computer where the user logs on). The Local folder (which is also accessible via the system variable %LocalAppData%) is for data that should not roam. The LocalLow folder is used only for Internet Explorer Protected Mode data.

Subfolders under AppData\Local include the following:

- **Microsoft\Windows\History**   This hidden folder contains the user's Internet Explorer browsing history. You can open it directly using the shortcut **shell:history**.

- **Temp**   This folder contains temporary files created by applications. The %Temp% variable points to AppData\Local\Temp.

- **Microsoft\Windows\Temporary Internet Files**   This hidden folder contains the offline cache for Internet Explorer as well as attachments saved from Microsoft Outlook messages. Use **shell:cache** to open it in Windows Explorer.

Subfolders under AppData\Roaming\Microsoft\Windows include the following:

- **Cookies**   This hidden folder contains Internet Explorer cookies and can be accessed directly using the shortcut **shell:cookies**.

- **Libraries**   You'll find files that define the contents of default and custom libraries here.

- **Network Shortcuts**   This folder contains shortcuts to network shares that appear in the Computer folder. The folder is not hidden; you can add your own shortcuts here, although it is easier to right-click in Computer and choose Add A Network Location.

- **Recent Items**   Shortcuts to recently used documents are automatically saved here; if you customize the Start menu to include a Recent Items link, the 15 most recent shortcuts appear on that list.

- **SendTo**   This folder contains shortcuts to the folders and applications that appear on the Send To submenu. Send To is a command that appears on the shortcut menu when you right-click a file or folder in Windows Explorer (or on the desktop). The SendTo folder is not hidden. You can add your own items to the Send To menu by creating shortcuts here. Use **shell:sendto** to open this folder and add or delete shortcuts.

- **Start Menu**   This folder contains items that appear on the Start menu. (The Start menu also includes items stored in a Public counterpart to this folder, %ProgramData%\Microsoft\Windows\Start Menu\Programs\Startup.)

- **Templates**   This folder contains shortcuts to document templates. These templates are typically used by the New command in Windows Explorer (on the shortcut menu) and are referenced by the FileName value in the HKCR*class*\ShellNew key, where *class* refers to the extension and file type.

INSIDE OUT   Expand the Send To menu

Normally, the Send To menu displays a limited selection of items, including the Desktop and your Documents library as well as any removable storage devices and mapped network drives. To see an expanded Send To menu that includes all folders in your user profile, hold down Shift and then choose Send To from the right-click shortcut menu.

Junctions Used for Compatibility with Windows XP

Most applications that write to locations within the user profile query the operating system as needed rather than write to absolute addresses. (As a side benefit, this technique allows applications to handle folders that have been relocated, as we describe in "Relocating Personal Data Folders" on page 416.) A well-behaved program that was originally written for Windows XP will thus have no trouble accommodating the changed names and locations of profile folders in Windows Vista and Windows 7. On the other hand, a program that looks for Documents And Settings (the root of profile folders in Windows XP) as an absolute address could encounter problems when it tries to open or save files.

The solution? Beginning with Windows Vista, each user profile contains junctions (reparse points) that redirect Windows XP folder names to the appropriate names as used in Windows Vista and Windows 7.

You can see how these junctions are set up by running a Command Prompt session and typing **cd %userprofile%** and then **dir /ads** (the /ads switch restricts output to directories that also have the system attribute). The output from this command will look something like Figure 9-6.

Chapter 9

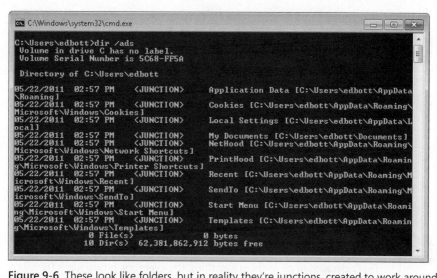

Figure 9-6 These look like folders, but in reality they're junctions, created to work around compatibility issues with programs written for the Windows XP folder structure.

The reparse points in this directory list are identified by the label <JUNCTION>. The fourth column in the display lists the Windows XP folder name (SendTo, for example) followed, in brackets, by the redirect address (C:\Users\edbott\AppData\Roaming\Microsoft\Windows\SendTo). If you display the same folder (%UserProfile%) in Windows Explorer, with hidden and system files visible, the junctions will look like shortcuts and won't include any information about their targets.

Table 9-1 lists the junction points created by default in the Users folder.

Table 9-1 Junction Points in the Windows 7 Users Folder

Junction Name	Target in Windows 7 File System
Application Data	%UserProfile%\AppData\Roaming
Cookies	%UserProfile%\AppData\Roaming\Microsoft\Windows\Cookies
Local Settings	%UserProfile%\AppData\Local
My Documents	%UserProfile%\Documents
NetHood	%UserProfile%\AppData\Roaming\Microsoft\Windows\Network Shortcuts
PrintHood	%UserProfile%\AppData\Roaming\Microsoft\Windows\Printer Shortcuts
Recent	%UserProfile%\AppData\Roaming\Microsoft\Windows\Recent
SendTo	%UserProfile%\AppData\Roaming\Microsoft\Windows\SendTo
Start Menu	%UserProfile%\AppData\Roaming\Microsoft\Windows\Start Menu
Templates	%UserProfile%\AppData\Roaming\Microsoft\Windows\Templates

Chapter 9

INSIDE OUT Why can't you open some folders in your user profile?

If you set Windows Explorer to show hidden files and folders and then double-click any of the junctions that map to locations in the Users folder (or the Documents And Settings junction that maps to the Users folder itself), you'll be rebuffed with an error message like this one:

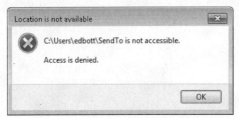

That's because in all of these junctions, the Everyone group has a Deny access control entry (ACE) preventing users from listing folder contents. This Deny ACE might seem drastic, but it's Windows' way of telling you to keep your hands off the compatibility infrastructure.

In every case, there's a proper path to the folder you're really looking for; you just need to unlearn the Windows XP structure.

The Deny ACE does not prevent you from deleting a junction, but you should never perform such a deletion unless you absolutely know what you are doing. Although a junction looks like an ordinary shortcut in Windows Explorer, it's not what it appears to be. Deleting a shortcut deletes a pointer, leaving the pointee unchanged. Deleting a junction has the same effect as deleting the location to which it points. Trust us: you don't want to discover this the hard way.

The VirtualStore Folder

Many legacy applications write data (such as configuration information) to areas that are ordinarily inaccessible to standard accounts. This behavior presented few problems in Windows XP because most users ran with administrative privileges. In Windows 7 (as in Windows Vista), the User Account Control (UAC) feature means that all users, even those with administrator accounts, run with a standard user token in ordinary operation. To prevent compatibility problems, UAC redirects problematic file and registry writes (and subsequent reads) to per-user virtualized locations. (For more details about UAC, see "Preventing Unsafe Actions with User Account Control" on page 629.)

> **Note**
> If you disable UAC, file and registry virtualization are disabled as well. If you log on using an account in the Administrators group with UAC disabled, any program you run can write directly to locations in the file system and the registry that would otherwise be protected by UAC.

So, for example, if an application, running in your security context, attempts to write to a location within %ProgramFiles%, the write will be redirected to a comparable location within %LocalAppData%\VirtualStore. When the application subsequently reads what it has written, the read request is redirected to the same virtualized location. As far as the application is concerned, everything is perfectly normal, and the operating system has prevented standard-user access to the %ProgramFiles% folder.

If you open a folder in which a virtualized write has occurred, a Compatibility Files link will appear on the Windows Explorer toolbar, as in this example from a program that insisted on writing a configuration file to the Windows folder:

Clicking Compatibility Files will take you to the VirtualStore location where the data is actually written.

A similar form of virtualization protects sensitive areas of the registry. Programmatic access to HKLM\Software is redirected to HKLM\Software\Classes\VirtualStore.

Note the following about virtualization:

- Virtualization does not affect administrative access to files or registry keys.
- Virtualization does not affect 64-bit processes.
- Virtualized data does not move with roaming profiles.
- Virtualization is provided for the sake of compatibility with current legacy programs; Microsoft does not promise to include it with future versions of Windows.

Common Profiles

Windows creates a local user profile for each user account, storing the profiles in subfolders of %SystemDrive%\Users with folder names that match the account names. In addition to these user profiles, the operating system creates two others:

- **Public**   The Public profile contains a group of folders that mirror those in your user profile. You can see the Public Documents, Public Music, Public Pictures, and Public Videos folders in their matching libraries. The advantage of these folders is that other users can save files to these locations from different user accounts on the same computer or from across the network. The Windows XP equivalent of the Public profile is called All Users, and this profile also serves to store application data designed to be available to all users. In Windows 7 and Windows Vista, this "all users" application data is stored in %SystemDrive%\ProgramData (which has its own system variable, %ProgramData%).

- **Default**   When a user logs on to a computer for the first time (and her account is not set up to use a roaming profile or mandatory profile), Windows creates a new local profile by copying the contents of the Default profile to a new folder and giving it the user's name. Note that the Default folder is hidden, and you must approve a UAC consent dialog box to add files to it. You can configure the Default profile the way you want new users' initial view of Windows to appear. Note, however, that some of the customizations that you might make to the Default profile might not be copied to profiles for new users. For more information about this topic, see the series of articles by Windows MVP Mitch Tulloch at *w7io.com/21101*.

If you enable the Guest account, it gets its own profile in the Users folder as well.

CAUTION!

In the unlikely event that Windows is unable to access your user profile when you log on, the system might create a temporary user profile in %SystemDrive%\Users\Temp, warning you at logon that it has done so. Any changes you make to this temporary profile (including any files you save in its data folders) will be deleted when you log off.

Customizing the Toolbar in Windows Explorer

The toolbar in Windows Explorer includes both invariant and context-sensitive items. The invariant items include the Organize menu, on the left, a New Folder button farther to the right, and the Help button all the way at the right, among others. Context-sensitive items include the Open button, which appears when a file or folder is selected in the Documents library; the Play button, which appears when a track is selected in the Music library; and many others. The Open button itself is context-sensitive; select a Microsoft Excel file, for example, and an Excel icon appears to the left of the word *Open*.

The Windows 7 user interface does not provide you with tools for customizing the toolbar. But, like just about everything else in Windows, the toolbar's settings are prescribed by the registry. You can perform some useful toolbar customizations by editing the appropriate registry values.

For information about working with the registry, see "Editing the Registry" on page 923.

In each of the four default libraries—Documents, Music, Pictures, and Videos—toolbar content is controlled by values in subkeys of HKLM\Software\Microsoft\Windows\CurrentVersion\Explorer\FolderTypes. The four keys associated with these default libraries and a fifth key for generic folders are listed in Table 9-2.

Table 9-2 **Library Folders and Associated Registry Keys**

Folder Type	Registry Key
Documents	{fbb3477e-c9e4-4b3b-a2ba-d3f5d3cd46f9}
Music	{3f2a72a7-99fa-4ddb-a5a8-c604edf61d6b}
Pictures	{0b2baaeb-0042-4dca-aa4d-3ee8648d03e5}
Videos	{631958a6-ad0f-4035-a745-28ac066dc6ed}
Generic	{5c4f28b5-f869-4e84-8e60-f11db97c5cc7}

Subordinate to each of these keys are subkeys named TasksItemsSelected and TasksNoItemsSelected. The string values of these keys govern the toolbar commands that appear when an item within the folder is selected and when no item is selected, respectively. Each value lists a set of commands separated by semicolons. So, for HKLM\Software\Microsoft\Windows\CurrentVersion\Explorer\FolderTypes\{fbb3477e-c9e4-4b3b-a2ba-d3f5d3cd46f9}\TasksItemsSelected, for example, you might see a string beginning with Windows.print;Windows.email;Windows.burn. To add a new toolbar command to the existing set, you would simply append the appropriate verb to the current string value.

What verbs might be appropriate? To see the possibilities, navigate in Registry Editor to HKLM\Software\Microsoft\Windows\CurrentVersion\Explorer\CommandStore\shell. The available verbs appear as subkeys of this key. Some useful candidates for inclusion (or exclusion, if you want to remove existing items) are listed in Table 9-3.

Changes to the toolbar for a folder type take effect the next time you display that folder type in Windows Explorer.

Chapter 9

Table 9-3 **Some Useful Registry Values and Their Toolbar Effects**

Registry Value	Effect of Toolbar Command
Windows.burn	Burns selected item to an optical disc
Windows.delete	Deletes selected item
Windows.email	Attaches selected item to an e-mail message
Windows.folderoptions	Displays the Folder Options dialog box
Windows.menubar	Toggles display of the menu bar
Windows.navpane	Toggles display of the navigation pane
Windows.newfolder	Creates a new folder in the current folder
Windows.properties	Displays the Properties dialog box for the selected item
Windows.readingpane	Toggles display of the preview pane

You can use the Windows PowerShell script called Set-ExplorerCommandBar.ps1, included on the companion CD in the Scripts folder, to simplify the task of adding commands to toolbars. The script, which must be run with administrative privileges, displays the graphical form shown in Figure 9-7.

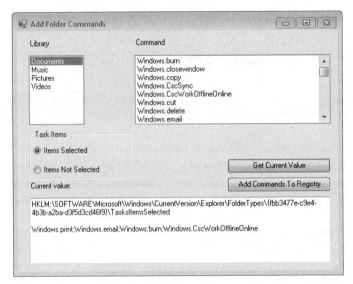

Figure 9-7 You can use the Set-ExplorerCommandBar PowerShell script to view or modify the current registry settings for a folder type's toolbar.

To use this form, select a folder type in the Library list, and then select either Items Selected or Items Not Selected. Use the Get Current Value button to see which commands are currently assigned to the toolbar. To add one or more items, select it or them in the Command list and click Add Commands To Registry.

Note that the script offers no Undo button, nor any way to subtract items from registry keys. Those tasks require that you either edit the registry manually or restore a registry backup. If you plan to experiment, consider creating a restore point before you start. If you're not pleased with the outcome, you might find it easier to perform a system restore than to roll back your changes via Registry Editor.

For information about using this and other scripts, see "Running PowerShell Scripts" on page 999. For more details about the design of this script, see the "Hey, Scripting Guy" blog post at *w7io.com/20902.*

Working with Libraries

As we noted earlier in this chapter, Windows 7 introduces a new organizational element called *libraries*, which make it easier to view, sort, search, and filter similar items, even when those items are stored in multiple physical locations. A library is, in essence, a virtual folder that aggregates the contents of multiple folders stored on your computer or on your network. You can sort, filter, group, search, arrange, and share the data in a library as if it were in a single location.

If you look only at the four default libraries included in a user profile, you might have trouble seeing the point of libraries, especially if you have a single user account and your computer isn't connected to a network. The true advantages of libraries don't become obvious until you customize the default libraries or create new, custom libraries. Consider the following scenarios:

- **Large digital media collections**   You keep your favorite music in the My Music folder on your notebook so that you have it available when you leave home. The bulk of your collection, including large high-definition movie files and albums you don't listen to regularly, are stored on an external hard drive. By arranging content on the external drive into Music, Pictures, and Videos folders and then adding those folders to the corresponding libraries in Windows Explorer, you have full access to your entire collection when you're home and connected to the external drive.

- **Workgroup projects**   You and some coworkers are collaborating on a project. Your drafts are stored in a subfolder of the Documents folder on your local hard disk. You also need access to shared graphics on a network file server, and final drafts from you and your coworkers will be saved in another shared network folder. By adding the local Drafts folder and the two network folders to a custom library, you can search and browse through all those files from one virtual location.

- **Homegroup projects**   At the end of every year, you create a holiday newsletter to send to friends and family. You create a custom library that includes one local folder where you copy photos that will go in the newsletter. You also save the draft of the newsletter here. With two clicks, you can share the custom library with your homegroup so that other family members can add their own files and photos to the project.

- **School-related or work-related projects**   You keep documents, notes, spreadsheets, and other files organized in subfolders, one for each client or project you're working on. Adding those subfolders to a custom library allows you to quickly browse a single subfolder or search through all folders at once. Searching for proposals, contracts, or homework assignments can help you find a document you did for a previous project, adapt it for a new project, and save it quickly in the correct subfolder.

Figure 9-8 illustrates two of these scenarios in use. The computer is a notebook with limited storage on the main drive (C) and a large external USB drive (D) with a large collection of MP3 and WMA tracks in a Music folder. We've added the Music folder from the external drive to the Music library and created a custom School library with three folders for class notes and homework. The search results show files from multiple locations within the search folder, all containing the search term *tulip*.

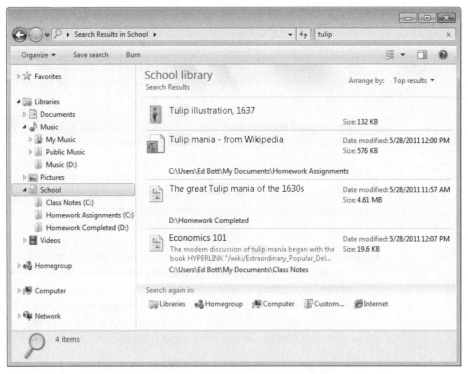

Figure 9-8 The custom library shown here includes three folders on two local drives. Search results cover all three locations.

To create a new library, click the Libraries heading in the navigation pane and then click the New Library button on the toolbar (or right-click Libraries and click New, Library). Give the new library a descriptive name and then press Enter. Your newly created library appears in the navigation pane. Click the Include A Folder button to populate the library.

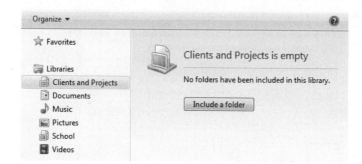

Using the Include Folder dialog box, select the folder you want to use as the default location for saving files in this library and then click Include Folder. That opens the library and lists the contents of the folder you just selected. At the top of the contents pane is the Library pane; the link below the library name lists the number of locations it includes—in this case, only one:

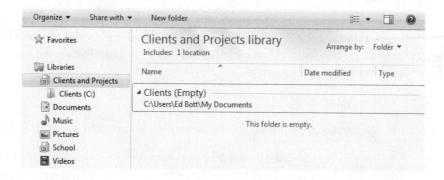

Clicking that link leads to the dialog box shown here, with Add and Remove buttons that you can use to change the lineup of locations that contribute to the library's content:

What locations can you add to a library? The most important consideration is that the folder must be indexed so that it can be included in searches. Folders and network shares in any of the following locations are eligible for inclusion:

- The system drive.

- An additional volume on an internal local drive formatted using NTFS or FAT32.

- An external USB or IEEE 1394 (FireWire) hard drive, formatted using NTFS or FAT32.

- A USB flash drive, but only if the device appears in the navigation pane, under the Computer heading, in the Hard Disk Drives section. If it appears under Devices With Removable Storage, it is not eligible.

- A shared network folder that is indexed using Windows Search; this includes any shared folder from another computer in your homegroup.

- A shared network folder that has been made available offline and is therefore available in your local index.

Chapter 9

For more details on how to manage the search index, see "Configuring Search and Indexing Options" on page 368.

You can also add a folder to a library by opening the folder location in Windows Explorer and choosing a library from the Include In Library menu on the toolbar. When you add a folder from a local drive to a library, Windows checks to see whether that location is in the search index already and adds it to the index if necessary. For additional customization options, right-click the library name in the navigation pane and then click Properties. Figure 9-9 shows a typical properties dialog box.

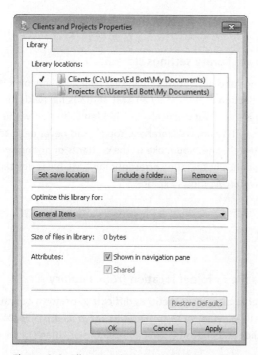

Figure 9-9 All customization options for a library are available in this dialog box.

This dialog box offers yet another way to include a folder in a library (or remove a folder). It also allows you to change the save location, which is the specific folder where files and folders are copied or moved when you drop them on the library icon in the navigation pane. The check mark indicates the current save location. Choose a different folder from the Library Locations list and click Set Save Location to make a change. The Shown In Navigation Pane check box indicates whether a library is visible in the navigation pane. If you've created a library specifically for sharing or for use with backups, you might want to hide it from the navigation pane to reduce clutter.

The Arrange By list at the right of the library pane allows you to change the way the contents of the library are displayed. By default, each library shows its contents arranged by folder, with each folder listed in alphabetical order, with a subheading and a separate file list for each one. From the Arrange By list, you can choose a different option, which applies the selected sorting or grouping to the aggregated folder contents. The exact choices available for each library are determined by its properties; to see what's available, look at the selection in the Optimize This Library For box in the properties dialog box. For the default Music library, for example, you can choose Album or Artist to combine all tracks from all locations into a single list grouped by the field you choose.

INSIDE OUT   Where are library settings stored?

Libraries are per-user settings and are not shared among user accounts on a Windows 7 PC. Each library in your collection is defined by an XML settings file (with the file name extension .library-ms) and is saved automatically in a hidden subfolder within your user profile (%AppData%\Microsoft\Windows\Libraries). You should never need to edit the files stored here directly. Any changes you make to the contents or arrangement of a folder are saved here automatically, and the corresponding XML file is deleted when you delete a library from within Windows Explorer.

INSIDE OUT   Open a file or folder location from a library

Because libraries are virtual folders, it's sometimes difficult to perform operations directly on their contents. If you want to see a file or folder in its actual location in Windows Explorer, right-click and choose Open File Location or Open Folder Location from the shortcut menu.

Using Compressed (Zipped) Folders

Depending on the file type, you can dramatically reduce the amount of disk space used by one or more files by compressing those files into a *zipped folder*. Don't be fooled by the name: a zipped folder (also known as a Zip file or archive) is actually a single file, compressed using the industry-standard Zip format and saved with the .zip file name extension. Any version of Windows can open a file saved in this format, as can other modern operating systems. The format is also accessible with the help of many third-party utilities. Thus, zipped folders are an ideal way to compress large files for e-mailing or transferring across a network, including the Internet.

> ## Note
>
> Windows Explorer compresses and decompresses files in zipped folders on the fly, displaying the contents of an archive in a window that closely resembles a folder. But most applications do not support this format. Thus, to view a WordPad document stored in a zipped folder, you need to double-click the zipped folder in Windows Explorer to display its contents and then double-click the file. If you try the same task using Word-Pad's Open command, you'll open the binary Zip file itself and display its unreadable contents. (If you want to edit a file stored in a Zip file, be sure to extract it to a local or network folder first.)

To create a new archive using zipped folders, follow these steps:

1. In Windows Explorer, display the folder in which you want the new archive to reside.

2. Right-click any empty space in the folder.

3. From the shortcut menu, choose New, Compressed (Zipped) Folder.

4. Name the folder.

To add files and folders to your archive, drag and drop them onto the zipped folder icon in Windows Explorer (or double-click to open the zipped folder in its own window and then drag items into it). You can also use the Clipboard to copy and paste items. To remove an item from the zipped folder, double-click to display the folder's contents and then right-click and choose Delete from the shortcut menu

Using the Send To menu, you can create an archive and copy one or more files or folders to it in one step. After selecting the files or folders you want to include in the new zipped folder, right-click and choose Send To, Compressed (Zipped) Folder. Windows creates an archive file with the same name as the current selected object. Use the Rename command (or press F2) to replace the default name with a more descriptive one.

To extract individual files or folders from a zipped folder, open it in Windows Explorer and then drag the items you want to extract to a new location, or use the Clipboard to copy and paste. To extract all items from a zipped folder to a specific location, right-click the zipped folder icon and choose Extract All, or open the zipped folder in Windows Explorer and click the Extract All Files button on the toolbar.

INSIDE OUT Add password protection to zipped folders

One feature that was available with zipped folders in Windows XP is gone from Windows 7. When creating a new archive, you no longer have the option to add a password to protect the file from casual snoops. The alternative is to use a third-party program. You have many choices, including the venerable WinZip (*winzip.com*), which costs $30 per copy. We prefer two freeware alternatives. The simple SecureZIP Express (*securezip.com*) was developed by PKWare, whose founder originally created the Zip format. A full-featured alternative is IZArc (*izarc.org*), which supports a huge number of compression formats, including ISO disk images, and also allows you to secure compressed files using 256-bit Advanced Encryption Standard (AES) encryption. It integrates neatly into Windows Explorer.

Arranging Data in Windows Explorer

The basic techniques for arranging data in folders have changed in subtle but significant ways in Windows 7. This version of Windows is far more reliable than its predecessors at recognizing the settings you've applied to a folder and retaining those settings so that they remain in place the next time you visit that folder.

You can adjust the display of any individual folder's contents by using the Change Your View menu, which appears on the right side of the toolbar throughout Windows Explorer. As Figure 9-10 shows, this menu is significantly changed from its Windows XP predecessor and also offers one noteworthy change over its equivalent in Windows Vista.

Figure 9-10 Use this menu to change the view of any folder, library, or search results list.

The choice at the bottom of the list, Content, is new in Windows 7. It's intended primarily for use with search results, and in the case of documents, it shows a fairly lengthy snippet of text with the matching search terms highlighted. (For an example, see Figure 9-7 on page 342.)

The three view options above Content—Tiles, Details, and List—offer icons and text listings of a fixed size and layout. The choices at the top of the menu allow you to display the folder's contents as icons of varying sizes. In Windows 7, as in Windows Vista, this menu includes a slider that allows you to move smoothly between icon sizes instead of being restricted to the predefined sizes. At medium sizes and above, the operating system displays thumbnails—previews of file or folder contents—if it finds something to display. This effect is most noticeable in folders dedicated to digital media, where you'll find cover art for albums and small but recognizable images of digital photos.

The range of options for the various icon views is not infinite. Although there are four discrete choices available on the Change Your View menu, ranging from Small to Extra Large, the actual number of sizes is 76. You can cycle smoothly through all 76 sizes by choosing Small Icons from the View menu and then holding down the Ctrl key as you use the wheel on your mouse (or the Up Arrow key) to step upward through the list. With each step, you'll see the icons shift to a new, larger size (although at some of the smaller sizes the change is barely perceptible).

Your other option to customize the display of objects in a file folder is to adjust the headings that are visible for that folder. In Windows 7, these headings are visible only in Details view, although you can access them using a right-click shortcut menu in other views. As you'll see in the next section, these headings are key to sorting and grouping a folder's contents and to arranging those contents.

Initially, all folders intended for the storage of user data (including those you create) are assigned one of five folder templates. These templates define the default headings that Windows Explorer considers appropriate for the content type. These headings are used atop columns in the Details view and are available on the Sort By menu in all other views. The logic is straightforward: you'll probably want to sort a folder full of MP3 tracks by track number, but that column would be superfluous in a folder full of Microsoft Word documents. And the Date Taken column is extremely useful for filtering digital photos, but it isn't much use with any other kinds of data.

Table 9-4 lists the default column headings available in each of these five templates. It also lists additional headings that you can add easily by right-clicking any heading in the Details view.

Chapter 9

Table 9-4 **Standard Folder Templates in Windows 7**

Template	Default Headings	Additional Headings
General Items	Name, Date Modified, Type, Size	Date Created, Authors, Tags, Title
Documents	Name, Date Modified, Type, Size	Date Created, Authors, Categories, Tags, Title
Pictures	Name, Date, Tags, Size, Rating (in libraries), and Name, Date, Type, Size, Tags (in folders)	Date Created, Date Taken, Dimensions, Rating
Music	Name, [Track] #, Contributing Artists, Album	Type, Size, Date Created, Date Modified, Album Artist, Bit Rate, Genre, Length, Protected, Rating, Year
Videos	Name, Date, Type, Size, Length	Date Created, Date Modified, Media Created, Dimensions

If the set of default headings and additional headings isn't enough, you can choose headings for other properties from an enormously long list in the Choose Details dialog box. To display this dialog box, switch to Details view, right-click the currently visible column headings and choose More from the bottom of the menu. If column headings aren't visible, tap the Alt key, choose View from the menu bar, and then click Choose Details. Using this dialog box, shown in Figure 9-11, you can show or hide headings by selecting or clearing check boxes; you can also use the Move Up and Move Down buttons to change the order in which headings appear.

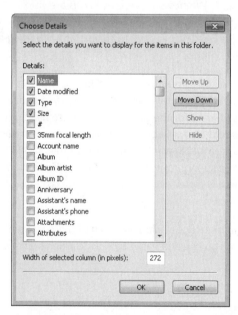

Figure 9-11 Use this dialog box to select which headings are available for sorting data in folders.

Although the Choose Details dialog box includes a Width Of Selected Column field, you'll probably find it easier to make size adjustments directly with the mouse. Drag the divider between columns to adjust a column's width.

INSIDE OUT   Customize folder templates

Not sure what folder "type" you're in? Right-click a blank space in the folder and choose Customize This Folder from the shortcut menu, or tap the Alt key to reveal the menu bar, and then choose View, Customize This Folder. (If this option isn't available, you're viewing a system folder whose template can't be changed.) On the Customize tab of the properties dialog box for the selected folder, look at the selection in the Optimize This Folder For drop-down list, which shows the folder type that's currently in effect.

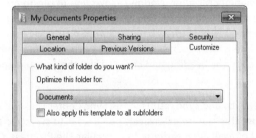

You can choose a different value from this list to change the template for the current folder. By default, your choice here applies only to the current folder; select Also Apply This Template To All Subfolders if you want your changes to ripple through to all child folders. You cannot, however, create a new template or rename an existing one.

INSIDE OUT Use Explorer tricks in Control Panel

The view controls found in Windows Explorer are used in some parts of Control Panel and Action Center as well. Many of the techniques for sorting, filtering, and grouping information that work in Windows Explorer work just as well in these Control Panel windows. Here are some examples:

- The list of installed programs under the Programs And Features headings is sorted alphabetically by default. This list is much easier to manage if you right-click in any empty space and group by the Publisher heading. You can also right-click the headings and click More to add headings, including the version number.

- The full Problem Reports list (in Action Center, click View Reliability History under the Maintenance heading, and then click View All Problem Reports at the bottom of the Reliability Monitor window) allows you to group problem reports by source, summary, date, or status. Grouping by source allows you to zero in on a particular issue and see how often it has occurred over time; grouping by status allows you to see which reports might require sending more information to Microsoft. Right-click any heading and choose from the Group menu to change the display.

- The list of partnerships and sync results in the Sync Center is useful in its default view, but if you use this feature extensively you'll want to switch to Details view and check the list of available headings. In particular, the Progress, Conflicts And Errors, and Last Sync headings can provide valuable information at a glance.

Sorting, Filtering, and Grouping

Regardless of the view settings you've chosen for a folder, you can adjust the way its contents are displayed at any time by changing the sort order, filtering the contents by one or more properties to include only selected items, and grouping and arranging the contents by a particular heading. These arrangements are not saved as part of the view for a folder, but the result can be dragged to the Favorites group in the navigation pane and saved for recall.

In any view, these options are available by right-clicking anywhere in the contents pane and choosing a Sort By or Group By option. In most cases, however, these actions are easier to accomplish by switching to Details view and using the column headings, which is also the preferred way to filter.

Sorting a Folder's Contents   To sort a folder in Details view, click the heading that you want to use as a sort key. For example, to sort by Date Modified, click the Date Modified heading. Click again on the same heading to reverse the sort order. The current sort order is indicated by a faint blue highlight on the column heading, with an up or down arrow above the heading name to indicate whether the sort is in ascending or descending order.

In all other views, right-click any empty space in the contents pane and select a value from the Sort By menu. A bullet next to Ascending or Descending indicates the current sort order; choose the other option to reverse the sort order.

Filtering Folder Contents   In Details view only, you can use headings to filter the contents of a folder. If you rest your mouse pointer on a heading, a drop-down arrow appears at the right. Clicking the arrow reveals a set of filter check boxes appropriate for that heading; in some cases (the Type heading, for example, as shown in Figure 9-12), the filter list is built on the fly from the contents of the current file list.

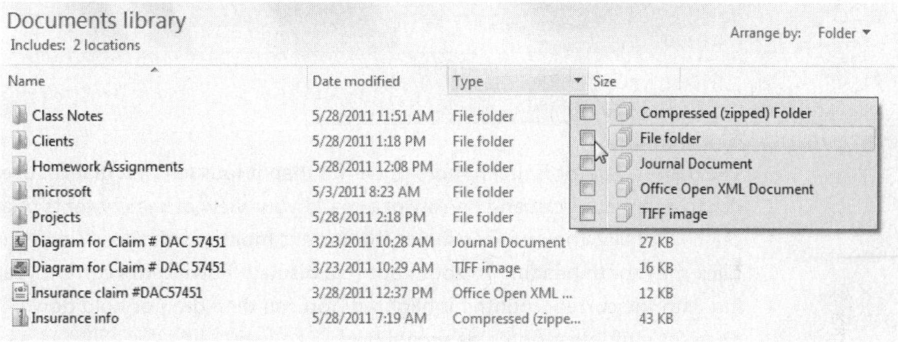

Figure 9-12 When you click the drop-down arrow next to a field heading, a set of filtering options, appropriate for the heading type, appears.

Select any check box to add that item to the filter list; clear the check box for an item to remove it from the filter. After you filter the list in Details view, you can switch to any other view and the filter will persist. (Look in the address bar to see the specific filter applied, and click the previous breadcrumb to remove all filtering without switching back to Details view.)

INSIDE OUT   Use the date navigator to zoom through time

If you click a date heading, the filter options display a date navigator like the one shown below, with common date groupings available at the bottom of the list. You can also click Select A Date Or Date Range and use the calendar to filter the file list that way.

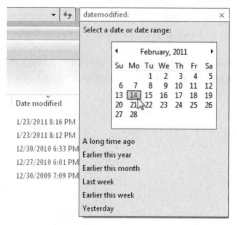

The date navigator is much more powerful than it looks at first glance. Use the calendar to zoom in or out and narrow or expand your view of the contents of a folder or a search. Initially, the calendar shows the current month, with today's date highlighted. Click the month heading to zoom out to a display showing the current year as a heading with the current month highlighted. You can then drag or hold down Ctrl and click to select multiple months, as shown here:

Click the year to zoom out again to show the current decade. Click once more to show the current century. In any calendar view, you can use the arrows to the left and right of the column heading to move through the calendar a month, year, decade, or century at a time. To zoom back in, click any month, year, decade, or century on the calendar control. This technique is especially valuable with folders or search results containing hundreds or thousands of files and folders.

If you filter by Size, you get a set of choices based on the file sizes that Windows deems appropriate, given the current folder contents, as shown here:

A filter can use multiple check boxes and multiple headings. So, for example, you could fil-ter a picture folder based on ratings as well as a "date taken" value, resulting in a file list like this one:

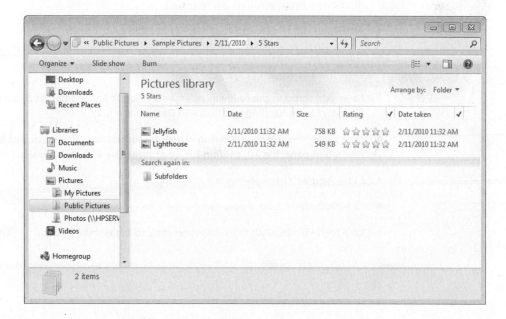

Chapter 9

When a folder is filtered, check marks appear to the right of headings used for filtering (see the Rating and Date Taken headings in the preceding illustration). The values on which you have filtered (for example, the specific tags) appear in the address bar.

When you select multiple check boxes in the same heading, Windows Explorer displays items that match any of the selected check boxes. When you select filtering check boxes from two or more separate headings, however, Windows Explorer displays only items that satisfy the criteria applied to each heading (in Boolean terms, it uses the conjunction AND between the headings).

INSIDE OUT   Zip through Windows Explorer with keyboard shortcuts

Pressing Ctrl+N in Windows Explorer opens a new window on the same folder. Ctrl+W closes the current window. (These keyboard shortcuts function the same way in Internet Explorer.) The following additional keyboard shortcuts work in Windows Explorer:

- Alt+Up Arrow—Go up one level.

- Alt+Right Arrow—Go forward.

- Alt+Left Arrow—Go back.

- Alt+D—Move the focus to the address bar, and select the current path.

- F4—Move the insertion point to the address bar, and display the contents of the drop-down list of previous addresses.

- Alt+Enter—Show properties of the selected file.

- Shift+F10—Open the shortcut menu for the current selection (which is the same as a right-click).

- F6—Cycle through the following elements: address bar, toolbar, navigation pane, file list, column headings (available in Details view only).

- Tab—Cycle through the following elements: address bar, search box, toolbar, navigation pane, file list, column headings (available in Details view only).

- F11—Toggle full-screen mode.

- Ctrl+Shift+N—Create a new subfolder in the current folder.

- Ctrl+Shift+E—Expands the navigation pane to the current folder.

Filtering a folder actually kicks off a specialized search, with the current folder designated as the search scope. If the filtered folder contains subfolders, you will see at the bottom of the list of results an invitation to Search Again In Subfolders, which reruns the search in those locations (and discards any results from the current folder).

Grouping Folder Contents   If sorting and filtering don't give you enough ways to organize or locate files, try grouping. Grouping generates a display comparable to the one shown in Figure 9-13.

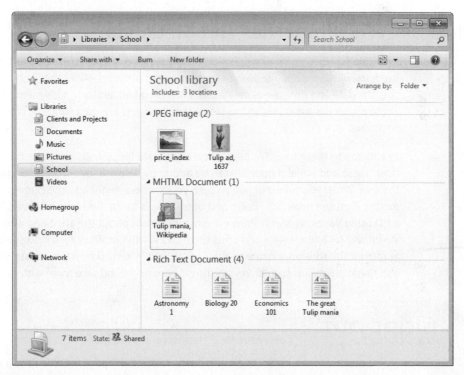

Figure 9-13 Use the expand/collapse controls to the left of a group heading to focus attention on particular items.

When you group, Windows Explorer collects all the items that have some common property (in Figure 9-13, type is the property), displaying each group under a heading that can be expanded or collapsed in most views. List view offers a particularly interesting perspective, with each group of results appearing under a column heading. The grouped arrangement is saved as part of the custom view settings for that folder; the next time you open the folder, it will still be grouped.

INSIDE OUT **Remove grouping from a folder**

To return a grouped folder to its ungrouped state, right-click in the contents pane (or tap Alt and then choose View from the menu bar). Then choose (None) from the Group By menu.

Managing File Properties and Metadata

Every file you view in Windows Explorer has a handful of properties that describe the file itself: the file name and file name extension (which in turn defines the file type), the file's size, the date and time it was created and last modified, and any file system attributes. These properties are stored in the file system itself and are used for basic browsing and searching.

In addition to these basic file properties, many data file formats can store custom *metadata*. These additional properties can be added by a device, by software, or directly by the user. When you take a digital picture, your camera might add the camera make and model, exposure time, ISO speed, and other details to the file when it's saved. When you rip a CD using Windows Media Player, it retrieves details about the artist and album from the Windows Metadata service and adds them to the MP3 or WMA files. Microsoft Word 2010 automatically adds your name to the Author field in a document you create; you can fill in additional properties such as keywords and comments and save them with the file.

INSIDE OUT **Rate your favorite digital media files**

For digital photos, music, and other media files, you'll notice that the Rating field is available in the details pane. Instead of providing a box to enter free-form text or a number, this field shows five stars, all of which are shown in gray initially. You can rate any file on a scale of one to five stars by clicking the appropriate star in the details pane or in a program that also supports ratings, such as Windows Media Player or Windows Live Photo Gallery. Adding ratings is a great way to filter large media collections so that they show only the entries you've previously rated highly. Ratings are also useful in playlists and screen savers and in the Favorites features in Windows Media Center.

The details pane, which runs along the bottom of Windows Explorer by default, displays a thumbnail of the selected file (if a thumbnail is available), plus a few properties. The number of properties shown depends on the height and width of the details pane. In the following illustration from a subfolder in the Pictures library, you can see only three properties—the file name, the type, and the date the photo was taken.

You can make more properties appear by enlarging the details pane. Widening the Windows Explorer window and dragging the details pane divider upward, for example, changes the property display dramatically. It also increases the thumbnail size, as shown here:

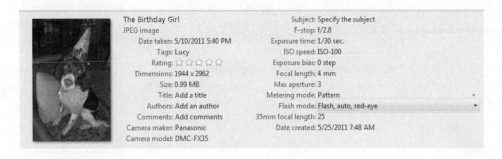

Even when enlarged to its maximum size, the details pane doesn't necessarily show all properties for a given file. For that, you need to right-click the file, click Properties, and then click the Details tab of the file's properties dialog box. Figure 9-14 shows the dialog box for the digital photo in the preceding example, with the first portion of the list of properties visible.

Figure 9-14 This dialog box shows the full set of properties for a file, organized by category.

Some properties of a file, such as its file size, are calculated by the file system or are otherwise fixed and cannot be directly modified. But you can enter or edit custom metadata if the format of the underlying file allows you to do so. Metadata is saved within the file itself, using industry-standard data storage formats. Software developers who need to create a custom file format can make its metadata available to Windows by using an add-in called a *property handler*, which opens the file format to read and write its properties. Because metadata is saved within the file itself, the properties you edit in Windows Explorer or a Windows program are fully portable. This means

- You can move files to other computers, even those running other operating systems, without losing their tags and other metadata.

- You can edit a file in an application other than the one in which it was created without losing any of the file's properties (assuming the other application properly adheres to the file format's standard for reading and writing metadata).

- A file's properties are visible to anyone who has read access to the file.

TROUBLESHOOTING

You cannot save metadata for some file types

You can edit custom properties (including tags) only in files saved using a format that accommodates embedded metadata. For digital image files, Windows supports the JPEG, GIF, and TIFF formats, but you cannot save metadata in bitmap images and graphics files saved in PNG format because these formats were not developed with metadata in mind. Among music file formats, MP3 and WMA fully support a wide range of properties designed to make it easy to manage a music collection; files saved in the uncompressed Wave Sound (.wav) format do not support any custom tags. Plain text and Rich Text Format (.rtf) files do not support custom metadata; files saved in Word formats expose a rich set of additional properties, as do all other native file formats from Microsoft Office programs.

In some cases, you'll find that you're unable to view or edit metadata in a file even though the underlying format supports metadata. In that case, the culprit is a missing property handler. In some cases, you can lose data in this situation if you're not careful. This might happen, for example, if you create a file using WordPad and save it in the Office Open XML Document format. If you then open that file using Word, you can add properties, such as author name, title, and comments. When you save the file, the file name extension (.docx) remains unchanged. However, if you reopen the document in WordPad you'll see an information bar at the top of the document warning you that the program does not support all the features of the file format:

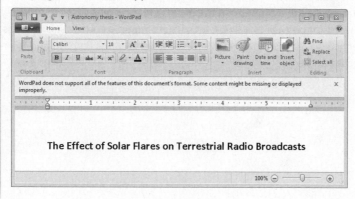

Chapter 9

If you make some changes and attempt to save the document under the same name or a different name, you'll see the following stern warning:

Believe that warning. If you choose the Save option, any custom properties you saved in an earlier version of the file will be stripped out permanently.

You can use the details pane to edit metadata as well. In the Music library, for example, you can fix errors or omissions in an individual track by selecting the track and then clicking an individual property in the details pane. Windows Explorer provides clues to help you spot properties that are currently blank but can be edited. In Figure 9-15, for example, the Album Artist field showed the text "Specify an album artist" until we clicked that text to reveal the editing box. The Save and Cancel buttons are visible only after you've clicked to begin editing.

To enter or change a property in the details pane, simply click and type. If you add two or more words or phrases to a field that accepts multiple entries (such as Tags or Authors), use semicolons to separate them. Click Save or just press Enter to add the new or changed properties to the file.

To edit properties that are not visible in the details pane, you need to right-click the file, choose Properties, and then select and edit values on the Details tab.

You can edit properties for multiple files at one time. This is especially useful when you're correcting an error in an album or artist name; just select all the songs in the album's folder. When more than one file is selected, you'll note that some properties in the details pane (such as track numbers and song titles) change to indicate that the specified field contains multiple values. Any change you make to any field will be written to all of the files in your selection.

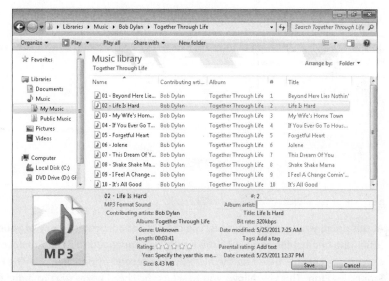

Figure 9-15 Click in any field in the details pane to make its contents visible. Click Save to write the edited properties to the file or files.

INSIDE OUT   Remove personal metadata for privacy's sake

Metadata within a file can tell a lot about you. Cameras record data about when a picture was taken and what camera was used. Microsoft Office automatically adds author and company information to documents and spreadsheets. With user-created tags, you can add personal and business details that might be useful on a local copy but are unwise to disclose to the wider world.

To scrub a file of unwanted metadata in Windows 7, select one or more files in Windows Explorer, right-click, and then click Properties. On the Details tab, click Remove

Properties And Personal Information. This opens the Remove Properties dialog box, an example of which is shown here:

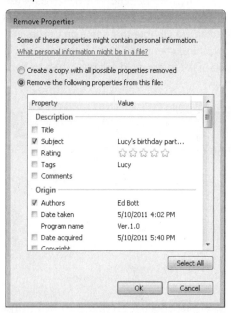

At this point, you have two choices. The default option creates a copy of your file (using the original file name with the word *Copy* appended to it) and removes all properties it can change, based on the file type. The second option, Remove The Following Properties From This File, allows you to select the check boxes next to individual properties and permanently remove those properties from the file when you click OK. (If no check box is visible, that property is not editable.)

Of course, common sense should prevail when it comes to issues of privacy. This option zeroes out metadata, but it does nothing with the contents of the file itself. You'll need to be vigilant to ensure that a digital photo doesn't contain potentially revealing information in the image itself or that sensitive personal or business details aren't saved within a document's contents.

Using Windows Search

ARTHUR C. Clarke once famously said, "Any sufficiently advanced technology is indistinguishable from magic." By that standard, Windows Search is sufficiently advanced. In our experience, we've found it uncanny, and often downright magical, at helping us quickly and efficiently find the exact file, e-mail message, or link we're looking for, even on an overstuffed hard drive or in an overflowing inbox.

If you're moving to Windows 7 from Windows Vista, the basics of search should already be familiar to you, although specific techniques have been significantly polished in the interests of usability. On the other hand, anyone accustomed to the search tools in Windows XP should prepare for some very welcome changes. Although the Windows 7 search infrastructure is a direct successor to a series of add-ins first developed for Windows XP, its implementation is dramatically different. The biggest change, of course, is that you no longer have to begin every search from a task pane (with or without the help of a cartoon dog) or a bolted-on toolbar.

Perhaps more than any other feature in Windows, these search tools have the potential to change the way you work. If your filing philosophy involves the digital equivalent of throwing everything into a giant shoebox, you'll be startled at how easy it is to find what you're looking for. Even if you consider yourself an extremely well-organized Windows user, we predict that you'll find ways to integrate these new search tools into your everyday routine.

What's in Your Edition?

All of the features we describe in this chapter are available in all editions of Windows 7.

Although the underlying architecture of Windows Search is similar to what you might have used in Windows Vista, specific techniques have changed significantly in Windows 7. The user interface is much simpler (the fill-in-the-blanks Advanced Search box is gone), but subtle differences in search behavior can trip up advanced users who try to apply techniques from earlier Windows versions. In this chapter, we explain how the search index works and how you can configure it to match your preferred searching style. We introduce the entry points for search (including the search box on the Start menu and in the upper right corner of every Windows Explorer window), with advice for squeezing more relevant results out of searches that originate in those little boxes. And for those who aspire to become search ninjas, we offer details about advanced query tools and techniques.

Configuring Search and Indexing Options

Windows Search is the collective name for a set of features that affect practically every aspect of Windows 7. At its heart, Windows Search relies on a speedy, powerful, and well-behaved indexing service that does a fine job of keeping track of files and folders by name, by properties, and (in supported formats) by contents.

All of those details are kept in the search index, a database that keeps track of indexed file names, properties, and the contents of files and e-mail messages. As a rule, when you do most common types of searches, Windows checks the index first and returns whatever results it finds there.

> **Note**
>
> The search index is stored by default in %ProgramData%\Microsoft\Search\Data. Default permissions for this folder are set to allow access only to the System account and to members of the Administrators group. This folder contains no user-editable files, and we recommend that you leave its contents undisturbed.

INSIDE OUT   When do searches skip the index?

Although we focus mostly on indexed searches in this section, Windows 7 actually includes two search engines. The second engine is informally known as *grep* search (the name comes from an old UNIX command derived from the full name *global | regular expression | print*). Windows Search uses the index whenever you use the search box on the Start menu, in the Search Home folder, in libraries, and in locations that are part of a homegroup. In those circumstances, search looks only in the index and ignores any subfolders that are excluded from the index.

Windows uses the grep search engine if you begin your search from the Computer window, from the root of any local drive (including the system drive), or from a local file folder. Grep searches include the contents of all subfolders within the search scope, regardless of whether they're included in the search index. For a more detailed examination of nonindexed searches, see "Advanced Search Tools and Techniques" on page 386.

To build the index that makes its magic possible, Windows Search uses several separate processes. The index is constructed dynamically by the Windows Search service, Search-Indexer.exe. The indexer crawls through all locations that are prescribed to be indexed, converting the content of documents (in supported formats) into plain text and then storing the text and metadata for quick retrieval.

The Windows Search service begins running shortly after you start a new Windows session. From that point on, it runs in the background at all times, creating the initial index and updating it as new files are added and existing ones are changed or deleted. *Protocol handlers* do the work of cracking open different data stores to add items to the index; Windows 7 includes protocol handlers for Microsoft Outlook and Windows Live Mail, for example, to enable indexing of your e-mail messages as well as your files. *Property handlers* allow Windows Search to extract the values of properties from items and store them properly in the index. *Filters* extract the contents of supported file types so that you can do full-text searches for those items.

Which Files and Folders Are in the Index?

Indexing every 0 and 1 on your hard disk would be an exhausting task—and ultimately pointless. When you search for a snippet of text, you're almost always looking for something you wrote, copied, or saved, and you don't want the results to include random program files that happen to have the same snippet embedded in the midst of a blob of code. So the default settings for the indexer make some reasonable inclusions and exclusions.

Certain locations are specifically included. These include your user profile (but not the AppData folder), the contents of the Start menu, and your Internet Explorer history. If your mail program includes a protocol handler, the files that contain your saved messages are indexed when you are logged on and the mail program is running. Offline files stored in the client-side cache (CSC) are automatically included in your local index. You can explicitly add other folders to the index, but Windows 7 eliminates the need to do that. Instead, just add the folder to a library; when you do so, Windows automatically adds that folder to the list of indexed locations and begins indexing its contents without requiring any additional steps on your part.

For more details on the workings of the Offline Files feature, see "Staying in Sync with Offline Files" on page 403.

To see which folders are currently being indexed, open the Indexing Options dialog box. You can find this in Control Panel, but it's usually quicker to type **index** in the Start menu search box. Indexing Options should appear at the top of the results list, under the heading Control Panel.

Chapter 10

> **CAUTION !**
>
> If you poke through the Windows Features list under Control Panel's Programs And Features category, you might notice an entry for Indexing Service (Cisvc.exe), which is missing from a default installation of Windows 7. You might be tempted to install and enable it. Don't. This service is a holdover from previous Windows versions and deserves its reputation as slow and difficult to use. It was supplanted by Windows Search beginning with Windows Vista, and the only reason this feature is still available (albeit buried deeply) is to support corporate applications that rely on this legacy service.

Figure 10-1 shows the list of indexed locations on a system where we've already added one custom folder to the index. The Archives folder at the top of the list is a new folder we created in the root of the system (C) drive and then added to the Documents library.

Figure 10-1 When you add a local folder to a library, it's automatically added to the list of locations included in the search index.

To add locations manually or to remove existing locations, click Modify. That displays the dialog box shown in Figure 10-2, where you can browse through a list of local drives, folders, and subfolders; select a check box to add a location to the index; or clear the check box to remove the corresponding location.

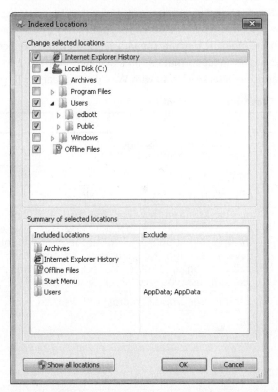

Figure 10-2 The best way to add locations to the local index is to add them to a library; doing so automatically selects the corresponding check box here.

CAUTION

> We strongly recommend that you *not* try to manage locations manually using the Indexed Locations dialog box. If you add a folder to a library and then remove it from the list of indexed locations, the folder will remain in the navigation pane under the associated library, but none of its contents will be visible in the library itself.

In its default view, the Indexed Locations list shows only locations that are accessible to your user account. To see (and manage) locations from other user profiles, click Show All

Locations. As the User Account Control (UAC) shield icon makes clear, you'll need to be logged on as an administrator (or provide an administrator's credentials) to continue.

Within that list of indexed locations, the Windows Search service records the file name and properties (size, date modified, and so on) of any file or folder. Files marked as System and Hidden are indexed but are displayed in search results only when you change Windows Explorer settings to show those file types. Metadata for common music, image, and video file formats is included in the index by default. The indexer also includes the contents of a file and its custom properties if the file format has an associated property handler and filter. The list of formats supported by filters included with Windows appears in Table 10-1.

Table 10-1 File Formats That Support Content Indexing

File Format	Extension
HTML	.ascx, .asp, .aspx, .css, .hhc, .hta, .htm, .html, .htt, .htw, .htx, .odc, .shtm, .shtml, .sor, .srf, .stm, .wdp, .vcproj
MIME	.mht, .mhtml
Office	.doc, .dot, .pot, .pps, .ppt, .xlb, .xlc, .xls, .xlt
Plain Text	.a, .ans, .asc, .asm, .asx, .bas, .bat, .bcp, .c, .cc, .cls, .cmd, .cpp, .cs, .csa, .csv, .cxx, .dbs, .def, .dic, .dos, .dsp, .dsw, .ext, .faq, .fky, .h, .hpp, .hxx, .i, .ibq, .ics, .idl, .idq, .inc, .inf, .ini, .inl, .inx, .jav, .java, .js, .kci, .lgn, .lst, .m3u, .mak, .mk, .odh, .odl, .pl, .prc, .rc, .rc2, .rct, .reg, .rgs, .rul, .s, .scc, .sol, .sql, .tab, .tdl, .tlh, .tli, .trg, .txt, .udf, .usr, .vbs, .viw, .vspcc, .vsscc, .vssscc, .wri, .wtx
XML (xmlfilt.dll)	.csproj, .user, .vbproj, .vcproj, .xml, .xsd, .xsl, .xslt
Favorites	.url
Journal File	.jnt
Rich Text	.rtf
WordPad	.docx, .odt
XML Paper Specification	.dwfx, .easmx, .edrwx, .eprtx, .jtx, .xmlps

To see which file formats support full-text indexing, open the Indexing Options dialog box and click the Advanced button (you'll need to supply an administrator's credentials to do so, although elevation is silent if your logon account is a member of the Administrators group). On the File Types tab of the Advanced Options dialog box (see Figure 10-3), you will find a long list of file name extensions. By default, the check box next to every item in this list is selected.

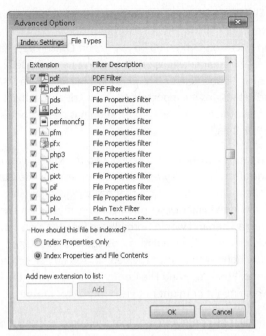

Figure 10-3 The File Types list shows whether and how each file type is included in the index.

INSIDE OUT   Add text from received faxes to the search index

Eagle-eyed readers might notice that no pictures are included in the list of formats in Table 10-1. That's perfectly normal, because images by definition consist of colored pixels rather than words, and they thus contain no content to index. But one image format is a noteworthy exception to that rule. If you use your PC's fax modem to receive pages sent from a remote fax machine, the received faxes are saved using Tagged Image File Format (TIFF), but the original document usually consists of at least some text. Windows 7 Home Premium and higher editions contain code that can perform optical character recognition on received faxes saved as TIFF files and include the recognized text in the search index. To enable this feature, open Control Panel and click Turn Windows Features On Or Off (under the Programs And Features heading). In the Windows Features dialog box, select Windows TIFF IFilter and then click OK.

Chapter 10

The list of formats on the File Types tab on your computer might include more file types if you've installed Windows programs that include custom property handlers and filters, such as those installed with Microsoft Office 2007 or Microsoft Office 2010. The list shown in Figure 10-3 includes several file name extensions that aren't part of a default Windows 7 installation. When we installed Adobe Reader 9 on this machine, it installed a PDF filter and assigned it to the file name extensions it supports, including .pdf and .pdfxml. Any file with one of these extensions that is stored in an indexed location has its full contents added to the index, courtesy of the PDF filter.

Each of the file types in this list can be indexed in one of two manners by using the option buttons below the list—Index Properties Only or Index Properties And File Contents. The latter option is selected by default for any file type that has a registered filter, and the name of the associated filter is listed in the Filter Description column. If you don't need to search content in a file type that has a filter and would normally be indexed, you can save some processing overhead by selecting the file type and choosing Index Properties Only. If you need content indexing where none is currently provided, you can try switching a file from Index Properties Only to Index Properties And File Contents. In that case, the indexer will use the Plain Text filter—which might or might not yield satisfactory results.

Windows Search does not index the content of files that are saved without a file name extension, nor does it index contents of files that are protected by Information Rights Management (IRM) or digital rights management (DRM).

A handful of locations are specifically excluded from indexing. Even if you manually specify that you want your system drive (normally C) to be included in the index, the following files and folders will be excluded:

- The entire contents of the \Windows folder and all its subfolders (Windows.000 and Windows.old folders are also excluded)

- \$Recycle.Bin (the hidden folder that contains deleted files for all user accounts)

- \Users\Default and all of its subfolders (this is the user profile template used to create a profile for a new user)

- The entire contents of the \Program Files and \Program Files (x86) folders and all of their subfolders

- The \ProgramData folder (except the subfolder that contains shortcuts for the shared Start menu)

Monitoring the Index, and Tuning Indexer Performance

The status message at the top of the Indexing Options dialog box offers real-time updates on what the indexer is doing at the moment. "Indexing complete" means there are no pending tasks. The text lists the number of items (files, folders, e-mail messages, and so on) that are currently in the index.

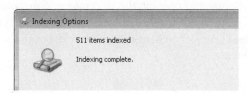

"Indexing paused" means the service has temporarily stopped all indexing tasks; you'll see this message if you check the indexer status shortly after you start the computer because the default setting for the Windows Search service is Automatic (Delayed Start).

If indexing tasks are currently under way, the status message will display an increase or decrease in the number of items indexed as new, changed, and deleted files are processed. The indexer is designed to throttle itself whenever it detects that the system is working on other, presumably more important tasks. As a result, you'll most likely be told that "Indexing speed is reduced due to user activity" when you first check.

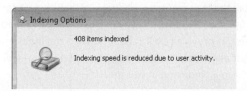

That message indicates that the indexing service has backed off in response to your activity and is operating at a fraction of its normal speed. If the number of files to be indexed is big enough (if you copied a folder full of several thousand documents, for instance), you'll see the indexing speed pick up dramatically after you keep your hands off the keyboard and mouse for a minute or so.

The exact speed of indexing depends on a variety of factors, starting with the speed of your CPU and hard disk or disk subsystem and including as well the number, size, and complexity of documents and whether their full contents are being indexed. Unfortunately, the status message in the Indexing Options dialog box doesn't include a progress bar and doesn't indicate how many files are yet to be indexed, so there's no easy way to tell whether the current task is barely under way or nearly complete. If you haven't recently added any new folders to the index but have simply been changing a few files in the course of normal work, the index should stay close to complete (assuming you've ever had a complete index).

Some websites for performance-obsessed Windows users complain about the performance hit that Windows Search causes; some even recommend disabling the Windows Search service to improve overall system performance. We recommend that you leave it running. In our experience, the Windows Search service uses only a small percentage of available CPU resources even at its busiest. The indexing service is specifically designed to back off when you use your computer for other activities, switching to low-priority input/output (I/O) and allowing foreground I/O tasks, such as opening the Start menu, to execute first. When Windows 7 first builds its index, or if you copy a large number of files to the system at once, indexing can take a long time and cause some hard-disk chattering, but you shouldn't notice any impact on performance.

INSIDE OUT   Kick the indexer into overdrive

If you're impatient, you might want the search indexer to work at full speed after you copy or move a large number of files to an indexed location. You could just step away from the mouse and keyboard to give the indexer unfettered access to system resources for as long as it takes to get the job done. Or, if you're using Windows 7 Professional or Ultimate, you can use the Local Group Policy Editor to configure the Disable Indexer Backoff policy and then manually stop and restart the Windows Search service.

A much better way is to install the Indexer Status gadget. This desktop gadget, created by Microsoft engineer Brandon Paddock, is available as a free download from *w7io.com/0902*. As shown here, it provides clear feedback when the indexer is working and also provides buttons that allow you to pause the indexer temporarily or disable the "back off" logic and perform all indexing at full speed.

The small, lightweight gadget shows how many files are currently being indexed. If no indexing is in process, the message displays the text "Index up-to-date." The group of three buttons on the left require administrative credentials. The first, Pause Indexer, suspends indexing activity. The second, Index At Normal Speed, returns to default behavior. The third button, Index Now, disables the back-off logic and allows indexing to proceed as a foreground task, allowing you to quickly rebuild the index or add a large number of new files. The button at the right side opens the Indexing Options Control Panel.

Windows Explorer accesses the index directly, so even if the indexer is busy processing new and changed files it shouldn't affect the speed of a search operation. In normal operation, retrieving search results from even a very large index should take no more than a few seconds. If you see hang-ups in either Windows Explorer or Microsoft Outlook when you perform a search, you need to look at the operation of the program itself to find the problem. (Outlook add-ins, for example, can dramatically slow down the program, and because Outlook runs as a child process of Explorer.exe, they can also affect Windows Explorer.)

Other Index Maintenance Tasks

The Indexing Options dialog box is also your gateway to buttons and check boxes that let you rebuild a corrupted index, change the location where the index stores its data, add folders to the index, change how the index deals with particular file types, and so on. To perform any of these maintenance tasks, display the Index Settings tab of the Advanced Options dialog box (shown in Figure 10-4).

Figure 10-4 You can use this dialog box to rebuild an index that has stopped functioning properly.

It's not supposed to happen, but if your index stops working properly (or if you just performed major file maintenance and you want to give the index a fresh start), click Rebuild, under the Troubleshooting heading. Then give your system time to re-create the index. Be aware that rebuilding the index might take a considerable amount of time.

Chapter 10

For security reasons, the contents of encrypted files are not included in the index by default. (Properties such as the name, date, and size of such files are indexed.) If you use Encrypting File System and you need those files indexed, select Index Encrypted Files under the File Settings head.

By default, the index files live in subfolders of %ProgramData%\Microsoft\Search. If you install a faster hard disk on your computer, you might be able to improve search performance by moving the index files to the new disk. (Note that the index must reside on a fixed disk.) Simply type or paste the full path of the folder you want to use in the Current Location box. (The path must not be greater than 128 characters in length.) Be prepared to restart your computer and wait while the index is rebuilt.

Although this option sounds like an appealing performance tweak, we recommend you think twice before trying it. The actual difference in performance is likely to be minor, and you can expect to encounter problems reestablishing the index if you have to restore your system drive from a backup and you don't also restore the volume containing the index.

Basic Search Techniques

You can search wherever you see a search box. Specifically, that means the following:

- From the search box at the bottom of the Start menu

- From the search box in the upper right corner of any Windows Explorer window

- From Control Panel

- From a common file dialog box

INSIDE OUT   What happened to the Search menu?

If you moved to Windows 7 from Windows XP, you'll no doubt notice that the Search option previously found on the right side of the Start menu is no longer available. That change was part of a voluntary settlement of a legal complaint brought by one of Microsoft's archrivals in the search business, Google. If you've grown to depend on a dedicated Search dialog box, press Windows logo key+F (F as in Find). This opens the Search Home window—essentially an instance of Windows Explorer with an empty search box highlighted. A search you begin from here will include the entire search index and exclude all nonindexed locations. You can achieve the same result by entering a term in the search box on the Start menu and then clicking the See More Results link just above the search box.

When you type in the search box on the Start menu, in a library, or in a homegroup location, the list of results is drawn from the search index. The list includes files whose names or properties contain the selected text; for files in formats that include appropriate property handlers and filters, the results will include items whose contents contain the text you entered. The *scope* of the search depends on your starting point. From the Start menu search box, you'll search the entire index, or you can restrict the scope to a specific location by selecting that location in Windows Explorer and using its search box.

The following rules govern how searches work:

- Whatever text you type must appear at the beginning of a word, not in the middle. Thus, entering **des** returns items containing the words *des*ire, *des*tination, and *des*troy, but not un*des*irable or sad*des*t. (You can override this behavior by using wildcard characters, as we explain in "Advanced Search Tools and Techniques" on page 386.)

- Search terms are not case-sensitive. Thus, entering **Bott** returns items with Ed Bott as a tag or property, but the results also include files and e-mail messages containing the words *bott*om and *bott*le.

- By default, searches ignore accents, umlauts, and other diacritical marks. If you routinely need to be able to distinguish, say, Händel from Handel, open the Indexing Options dialog box, click Advanced (you'll need administrative credentials), and then select Treat Similar Words With Diacritics As Different Words.

- To search for an exact phrase, enclose the phrase within quotation marks. Otherwise, you search for each word individually.

Searching from the Start Menu

The search box on the Start menu has a dual personality. Its primary role is to help you find shortcuts to applications on the Programs menu and tasks in Control Panel. When you type a search term that matches any item in either of those locations, the results appear almost instantaneously. But this box also offers complete access to everything else in the search index: websites in your history folder; saved favorites; messages in your e-mail store; appointments and contacts from Microsoft Outlook; any shared network folders that are included in any of your libraries; and, of course, files and folders in your file system.

INSIDE OUT   **Use the search box to find a website**

If you start an entry in the Start menu search box with *http:* or *www*, Windows assumes, quite logically, that you're trying to find a web page. In that case, the first result at the top of the search results list appears under the Internet heading. Searches from the local index appear beneath that result.

Chapter 10

The search box (here and elsewhere) is a "word wheel"—which means that the search begins as soon as you start typing, and each new character you type refines the results. If you type the letters *m* and *e* into the Start menu search box, you'll see results for Windows *Me*dia Center and Windows *Me*dia Player, as well as the Windows *Me*mory Diagnostic. You'll also see 42 Control Panel tasks (topped by Taskbar And Start *Me*nu), e-mail messages to and from friends whose names begin with those letters (like *Me*lissa and *Me*rle), and any document that has the word *me* (or a word that begins with those two letters). The list gets considerably shorter if you continue typing.

Because the word wheel action is snappy and the Start menu search is optimized to find items on the Start menu, typing a few characters here can be a great alternative to hunting up a program shortcut from the All Programs section of the Start menu. Typing the word **media** into the search box, for example, produces a list like the one shown in Figure 10-5.

Figure 10-5 Start menu searches return categorized shortcuts to programs, Control Panel tasks, documents, and other items included in the search index.

The scope of a search from the Start menu box covers the entire index, including document files, folders, Internet shortcuts, e-mail messages, objects on a Microsoft OneNote page, and more. Results are ranked and categorized, with the number of results in each category appearing in parentheses alongside the category heading. The initial display of results is limited to the space available on the left side of the Start menu, with each category limited, if necessary, to the top three results. If you're not sure what an item returned by the search is, you can hover your mouse over it and read a tip with more details about the item.

TROUBLESHOOTING

Your keyboard is stuck in the wrong language

On some hardware configurations used in the development of this book, we noticed the following anomaly: When we used Control Panel to install a new keyboard layout (Russian, for example), then used the new layout for some work, and subsequently returned to English, the Start menu search box retained the non-English layout. The problem appeared consistently on some systems and not at all on others. Should you find yourself confronted with this misbehavior, the solution is simple. Make sure the language you actually want to use is selected in the Notification Area. Open Windows Task Manager (for example, by pressing Ctrl+Shift+Esc). On the Processes tab, select explorer.exe, and then click End Process. Click End Process again to answer the confirmation prompt. Then choose File, New Task (Run), and type **explorer.exe** on the Open line. These steps will restore a well-mannered shell.

To see all results for a specific category, click the category heading. To see the complete set of results for all categories except Programs and Control Panel, click the See More Results link just above the search box. In either case, Windows Explorer opens and displays your search results in Contents view. Figure 10-6 shows the See More Results view for the Start menu search in the previous figure.

From this window, you can turn on the preview pane to view a document's contents without having to open it. You can also refine the search in a variety of ways. The most obvious of these refinements is the Search Again In list along the bottom of the file list. Start menu searches encompass the entire search index. You can rerun the search to look only in libraries or across other computers in your homegroup or on your computer only. Use the Custom link to hand-pick folders or libraries where you want to search, or click Internet to send the search terms to your default Internet search page.

If you're unhappy with the results of Start menu searches, you have two customization options available. To control the reach of Start menu searches, right-click the Start button and choose Properties. On the Start Menu tab, click Customize. Finally, scroll down the Customize Start Menu dialog box until you reach the two settings that begin with *Search*. The Search Programs And Control Panel option is selected by default. To see only programs and Control Panel tasks, leave this setting unchanged and select Don't Search under the Search Other Files And Folders heading.

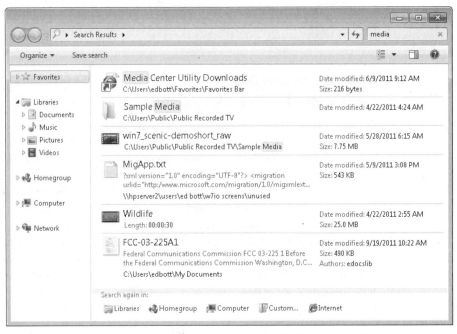

Figure 10-6 The Search Results window shows more details than the brief list of item names on the Start menu results list.

INSIDE OUT You can search for programs that aren't on the Start menu

Searching from the Start menu search box can be a good way to run a program that isn't on the Start menu—such as Registry Editor or an .msc console. (To run an .msc console, type the full name, including the .msc extension.) The Start menu's search looks for executables in system folders that are not ordinarily indexed. Because the search engine's word-wheel feature works only with indexed locations, however, you need to type the full name before it appears in the search results. You also need to identify the program by the full name of its executable file, rather than its friendly title. Typing **Registry Editor** in the search box gets you nothing (unless you happen to have created a shortcut and saved it under that name). Typing **regedit** summons the program.

Refining a Search in Windows Explorer

Searching from a Windows Explorer folder yields an uncategorized list of items from the current location—typically a folder or a library. It's a great way to find something when you have a general idea of where it is saved and you want to filter out extraneous hits from inappropriate locations. For example, if you're looking for songs by a particular artist, just click the Music library in the navigation pane and then start typing the artist's name in the search box.

INSIDE OUT   See all files in a folder and its subfolders

If you have opened Windows Explorer to a particular folder and you want to avoid the tedium of opening subfolders to view their contents, try using the wildcard character that's been around as long as Microsoft has been making operating systems. Entering an asterisk (*) in the search box immediately returns all files in the current folder and all its subfolders. Assuming the list is of manageable size, you can then group, filter, sort, or otherwise rearrange the items within it to find exactly what you're looking for.

Here again, the word wheel is your friend. Unless your fingers are as fleet as Rachmaninoff's, the odds are that any of his music you have will appear in the search results long before you get to the last syllable of his name (see Figure 10-7). (What's more, if you try to type the whole thing and make a mistake somewhere along the line, you're likely to wind up with nothing.)

Unlike in Windows Vista, there is no limit on the number of results that Windows 7 returns when you perform a search in a Windows Explorer folder (in one test of a well-used system, we searched for the word *the* and ended up with more than 75,000 items; a similar search for the even more common word *a* returned 145,000 items). Of course, scrolling through a results list containing thousands of items isn't likely to be all that helpful; instead, you probably want to refine your search.

Chapter 10

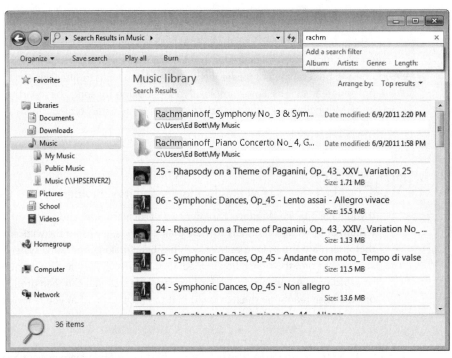

Figure 10-7 Select a folder or library to narrow the search scope, and use search filters (below the box in the upper right corner) to refine your results further.

The easiest way to narrow the results list is to use the Search Builder, a new feature in Windows 7. The Search Builder allows you to add search filters (which conveniently appear below the search box after you've typed a few characters) by pointing and clicking. In Figure 10-7, for example, four available search filters appear directly below the search box. Clicking any of the highlighted blue keywords here adds it to the search box and, where appropriate, calculates a list of options from which you can choose. Thus, if you click Artists you see a list of all artists available in the current location and can choose one. If your music collection includes dozens of renditions of "Somewhere over the Rainbow," click Title and then enter the text **rainbow**. Then click Artists and use the drop-down list to see a filtered list containing only the names of artists who are associated with songs in your collection that contain that word.

There's nothing magical about search filters. You could accomplish the same thing by mastering the advanced query syntax and then typing keywords and values manually into the search box; this option allows you to achieve the same results by simply pointing and clicking.

INSIDE OUT   Go wide to see more search filters

The number of search filter options that appears below the search box is constrained by the width of the search box. Thus, in Figure 10-7 it appears that only four search filters are available for the Music library. In reality, Windows Search offers up to eight filters for music folders. To see the entire selection, drag the handle between the address bar and the search box to the left. When you click in the newly widened search box, you'll see the full set, as shown here:

If you find search filters interesting and useful, we strongly recommend that you learn at least the fundamentals of advanced query syntax; see "Advanced Search Tools and Techniques" on page 386.

The exact selection of point-and-click search filters available in a particular library (or a folder within a library) depends on the template assigned to that folder. (For a refresher course on the five standard folder templates, see "Arranging Data in Windows Explorer" on page 350.) Table 10-2 lists the search filters for each folder type, in order from left to right; if you don't see all available search filters, widen the search box.

Table 10-2 Available Search Filters by Folder Type

Folder Type	Search Filters Available from the Search Box
Documents	Authors, Type, Date Modified, Size, Name, Folder Path, Tags, Title
Music	Album, Artists, Genre, Length, Folder Path, Year, Rating, Title
Pictures	Date Taken, Tags, Type, Date Modified, Name, Size, Folder Path, Rating
Videos	Length, Date Created, Type, Date Modified, Name, Folder Path, Tags, Rating
General Items	Kind, Date Modified, Type, Size, Name, Folder Path, Tags

Note that the search filters shown in Table 10-2 are available only for indexed searches. If you begin your search by opening a folder directly, rather than by accessing that folder from a library, Windows will perform a grep search, and the only available search filters will be Date Modified and Size.

Chapter 10

INSIDE OUT Reuse a search filter

If you've added a value to a search filter by using its drop-down list, how do you choose a different value? The tedious way is to delete the text from the search box and then start over. The much faster way is to click the value that appears after the property name. Doing so displays the drop-down list again, allowing you to make a different selection.

If you use multiple search filters, the search engine assumes you want to apply all filters to the result set, effectively using the AND operator. Each filter you add thus has the effect of further narrowing the current results set. You can change this behavior by manually grouping properties with parentheses and using the AND, OR, and NOT operators explicitly. For more information on how to accomplish this technique, see "Using Multiple Criteria for Complex Searches" on page 392.

INSIDE OUT Search from a common dialog box

Like the search box in Windows Explorer, the search box in a common Open or Save As dialog box takes as its default scope the current folder and its subfolders. Searching from a dialog box might not sound all that nifty at first. After all, if you're trying to open a file and you don't know exactly where it is, you can always hunt for it from a Windows Explorer folder, and then double-click it when the Windows Search engine ferrets it out. But searching from a dialog box can be quite useful if you're already in the dialog box and find yourself confronted with a superfluity of files. If you start from a library or a location within your homegroup, you can use the full array of search tricks, including search filters, to locate the exact file you're looking for.

Advanced Search Tools and Techniques

You might not consider yourself a search ninja, but if you've typed a keyword or two in the search box and built a point-and-click search filter, you've taken the first steps on that path. To become a search ninja, you must master Advanced Query Syntax (AQS), which is the official name for the set of rules that Windows Search follows when interpreting what you type in the search box. (You'll find detailed documentation of AQS at *w7io.com/0903*.)

In addition to keywords, AQS supports the following types of *search parameters*, which can be combined using search operators:

- **Kinds of items**   Folders, documents, pictures, music, e-mail messages, and so on

- **Data stores**   Specific databases and locations containing indexed items

- **File properties**   Size, date, tags, and so on

The most basic query typically begins with a keyword (or a portion of a word) typed in the search box. Assuming that you begin typing in a location that supports indexed searches (the Start menu search box or your Documents library, for example), the list of search results will include any item in that location containing any indexed word (in its name or properties or content) that begins with the letters you type.

You can then narrow the search by using additional parameters. In every case, these consist of a word that AQS recognizes as a property or other index operator, followed by a colon and the value for that operator. If you've used the Search Builder to construct search filters like **type:="Text Document"** and **size:small**, you've already seen this syntax at work. You can customize parameters you create by using the Search Builder or enter your own by typing them directly into a search box.

INSIDE OUT   Use search filters anywhere you find a search box

It's tempting (and wrong) to assume that the properties available as optional search filters under the search box are the only ones permitted for that folder. In reality, you can use any of the examples we list in this chapter in any search box, including the one on the Start menu. In some contexts, a particular property might not make sense, but you can still try. The Windows Explorer search box offers a slight aid to help you learn the correct syntax; when you enter a recognized property or operator followed by a colon, the text turns blue. If the property in question supports entry from a list, the search engine begins building that list immediately.

The value that immediately follows the colon can take several forms. If you want a loose (partial) match, just type a word or the beginning of a word. Thus, **type:Word** will turn up files of the type Microsoft Word Document, Microsoft Word 97 – 2003 Document, Microsoft Word 97 – 2003 Template, Microsoft Word Macro-Enabled Document, and so on. To specify a strict (exact) match, use an equals sign and, if necessary, quotation marks, as in this example: **type:="Microsoft Word Document"**.

Also in this section, we explain how you can use logical operators (AND, OR, and NOT) and parentheses to combine criteria. If you have fond memories of MS-DOS, you'll welcome using * and ? as wildcards, and we also show how an innocuous-looking tilde (~) dramatically changes the behavior of a search.

Of course, all of these techniques become much more useful when you're able to reuse your carefully crafted search criteria, as we explain in "Saving Searches and Clearing Search History" on page 395.

Searching by Item Type or Kind

To search for files with a particular file name extension, you can simply enter the extension in the search box, like this:

```
*.ext
```

(Note that this method of searching does not work for .exe or .msc files.) The results will include files that incorporate the extension in their contents as well as in their file names—which might or might not be what you want. You will get a more focused search by using the **ext:** operator, including an asterisk wildcard and a period like this:

```
ext:*.txt
```

> **Note**
>
> As with many properties, you have more than one way to specify an exact file name extension. In addition to **ext:**, you can use **fileext:**, **extension:**, or **fileextension:**.

File name extensions are useful for some searches, but you'll get even better results using two different search properties: Type and Kind. The Type property limits your search based on the value found in the Type field for a given object. Thus, to look for files saved in any Microsoft Excel format, type this term in the search box:

```
type:excel
```

To find any music file saved in MP3 format, type this text in the search box:

```
type:mp3
```

To constrain your search to groups of related file types, use the Kind property. Table 10-3 lists many (but not all) of the options available with this search term.

Table 10-3 **Limiting Items in Search Results by Kind**

Kind Syntax	Returns as Search Results
kind:=calendar kind:=appointment kind:=meeting	Appointments and meetings stored in Microsoft Outlook, iCalendar, and vCalendar files
kind:=communication	E-mail messages and attachments
kind:=contact kind:=person	vCard files, Windows Contact files, Outlook Contacts
kind:=doc kind:=document	Text files, Microsoft Office documents, Adobe Acrobat documents, HTML and XML files, and other document formats
kind:=email kind:=e-mail	Microsoft Outlook and Windows Live Mail messages, including messages saved as files
kind:=folder	File folders, search folders, compressed (Zip) files, and cabinet files
kind:=link	Shortcuts to programs and files, Internet shortcuts
kind:=music kind:=song	Windows Media playlists and audio files in MP3, WMA, or WAV format
kind:=pic kind:=picture	Picture files in any indexed format, including JPEG, GIF, bitmap, PNG, as well as icons and shortcuts to image files
kind:=program	Windows and MS-DOS applications, batch and VBScript files, saved registration entries, Windows Installer packages, and program shortcuts
kind:=tv	TV programs recorded by Windows Media Center
kind:=video	Movie files and clips in any indexed format

Changing the Scope of a Search

Several operators allow you to restrict a search to a particular folder or a database containing certain types of items. For example, to search only for items in your Microsoft Outlook profile, type this parameter in the Start menu search box:

```
store:mapi
```

You can also specify a folder or library location by using **folder:**, **under:**, **in:**, or **path:**. Thus, **folder:documents** restricts the scope of the search to your Documents library, and **in:videos mackie** finds all files in the Videos library that contain *Mackie* in the file name or any property.

INSIDE OUT Extending Windows 7's search capabilities

Although it's not easy to do so, you can add some Internet-based locations to Windows Explorer. Search results from these locations aren't integrated into local search results. Instead, you create a search connector and save it as an OpenSearch file, with the .osdx file name extension, and double-click to add it to the Favorites list in the navigation pane. When you click the search connector, the focus moves to the search box. Windows Explorer sends the query to the provider defined by the Search Connector Description file, using the search terms you entered. The results are returned as RSS or Atom feed items and displayed in Windows Explorer in the familiar Contents view. For technical details about the OpenSearch format, see the MSDN overview at *w7io.com/0904*. For a friendlier description, including links to some ready-made Open-Search files that you can download and install for searching popular websites, see "How to Install and Use Search Connectors in Windows 7," by Sarah Perez of Microsoft's Channel 10 blog at *w7io.com/0905*.

Searching for Item Properties

You can search on the basis of any property recognized by the file system. (The list of available properties for files is identical to the ones we discuss in "Arranging Data in Windows Explorer" on page 350.) To see the whole list of available properties, right-click any column heading in Windows Explorer and choose More from the shortcut menu. The Choose Details list that appears enumerates the available properties.

When you enter text in the search box, Windows searches file names, all properties, and indexed content, returning items where it finds a match with that value. That often generates more search results than you want. To find all documents of which Jean is the author, omitting documents that include the word *Jean* in their file names or content, you would type **author:jean** in the search box. (To eliminate documents authored by Jeanne, Jeannette, or Jeanelle, add an equals sign and enclose *jean* in quotation marks: **author:="jean"**.)

When searching on the basis of dates, you can use long or short forms, as you please. For example, the search values

```
modified:6/15/11
```

and

```
modified:06/15/2011
```

are equivalent.

To search for dates before or after a particular date, use the less-than (<) and greater-than (>) operators. For example:

`modified:>11/16/09`

would search for dates later than November 16, 2009. Use the same two operators to specify file sizes below and above some value.

Use two periods to search for items within a range of dates. To find all e-mail messages you received in September or October 2010, type this search term in the Start menu search box:

`received:9/1/2010 .. 10/31/2010`

You can also search for dates by using text in long or short forms. For example:

`received:Feb 2010`

lists all e-mail messages that landed in your indexed message store (Windows Live Mail or Microsoft Outlook) during the month of February 2010. The same technique works for days of the week.

INSIDE OUT   Make your searches flexible

You don't need to enter a precise date as part of a search term. Instead, Windows Search recognizes "fuzzy" date qualifiers like *today*, *tomorrow*, *this week*, and *last month*. This technique lets you create saved searches that you can use to quickly open a window showing only the files you've worked on this week or last week. A search that uses dates picked from the calendar wouldn't be nearly as useful next month for identifying current projects, but one built using these relative dates will continue to be useful indefinitely.

You can also use ranges to search by file size. The search filters suggest some common ranges and even group them into neat little buckets like the ones shown here, so you can type **size:** and then click **Gigantic** to find files greater than 128 MB in size.

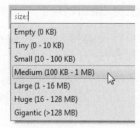

Again, don't be fooled into thinking that this list represents the full selection of available sizes. You can specify an exact size range, using operators such as >, >=, <, and <=, or you can use the ".." operator. For example, **size:0 MB..1 MB** is the same as **size:<=1 MB**. You can specify values using bytes, KB, MB, or GB.

Using Multiple Criteria for Complex Searches

You can use the Boolean operators AND, OR, and NOT to combine or negate criteria in the search box. These operators need to be spelled in capital letters (or they will be treated as ordinary text). In place of the AND operator, you can use a plus sign (+), and in place of the NOT operator, you can use a minus sign (–). You can also use parentheses to group criteria; items in parentheses separated by a space use an implicit AND operator. Table 10-4 provides some examples of combined criteria.

Table 10-4 Some Examples of Complex Search Values

This Search Value	Returns
Siechert AND Bott	Items in which at least one indexed element (property, file name, or an entire word within its contents) begins with or equals *Siechert* and another element in the same item begins with or equals *Bott*
title:("report" NOT draft)	Items in which the Title property contains the word *report* and does not contain a word that begins with *draft*
tag:tax AND author:Doug	Items authored by Doug that include *Tax* in the Tags field
tag:tax AND author:(Doug OR Craig) AND modified:<1/1/10	Items authored by Doug or Craig, last modified before January 1, 2010, with *Tax* in the Tags field

> **Note**
> When you use multiple criteria based on different properties, an AND conjunction is assumed unless you specify otherwise. The search value *tag:Ed Author:Carl* is equivalent to the search value *tag:Ed AND Author:Carl*.

Using Wildcards and Character-Mode Searches

File-search wildcards can be traced back to the dawn of Microsoft operating systems, well before the Windows era. In Windows 7, two of these venerable operators are alive and well:

- ***** The asterisk (also known as a star) operator can be placed anywhere in the search string and will match zero, one, or any other number of characters. In indexed searches, which treat your keyword as a prefix, this operator is always implied at the end; thus, a search for **voice** will turn up *voice, voices,* and *voice-over.* Add an asterisk at the beginning of the search term (***voice**), and your search will also turn up any item containing *invoice* or *invoices.* You can put an asterisk in the middle of a search term as well, which is useful for searching through folders full of data files that use a standard naming convention. If your invoices all start with INV, followed by an invoice number, followed by the date (INV-0038-20110227, for example), you can produce a quick list of all 2011 invoices by searching for **INV*2011***.

- **?**   The question mark is a more focused wildcard. In index searches, it matches exactly one character in the exact position where it's placed. Using the naming scheme defined in the previous bullet, you could use the search term **filename:INV-????-2011*** to locate any file in the current location that has a 2011 date stamp and an invoice number (between hyphens) that is exactly four characters long.

In both the previous examples, we described the behavior of searches in indexed locations, such as a library or a folder within a library. In other locations, the grep search engine kicks in. By default, anything you enter here is treated as a character search that can match all or any part of a word. Thus, if you open a data folder that is not in a library and enter the search term **voice**, you'll get back *voices* and *voice-over* and *invoice*. The behavior of wildcards varies slightly as well. In a grep search, **??voice** matches *invoice* but not *voice*. In an indexed search, the wildcards at the beginning of the term are ignored in favor of loose matches. (Extra question marks at the end of a search term are ignored completely.)

To force Windows Search to use strict character matches in an indexed location, type a tilde (~) as the first character in the search box, followed immediately by your term. If you open your Documents library and type **~??v** in the search box, you'll find any document whose file name contains any word that has a *v* in the third position, such as *saved* and *level* and, of course, *invoice.* This technique does not match on file contents.

Searching with Natural Language

If you don't fancy Boolean formulations, try the natural-language approach to searching. With natural language enabled, the search engine promises to accept queries in plain English. So, instead of typing **kind:email from:(Carl OR Ed) received:this week**, you can enter **email from Carl or Ed received this week**. The system looks for key words (like "email"), filters out prepositions (such as "from"), handles conjunctions without making you capitalize them, and assumes the rest of what you type consists of property values that it should try to match.

Chapter 10

To turn natural-language searching on, choose Organize, Folder And Search Options in Windows Explorer. In the Folder Options dialog box, click the Search tab. On the Search tab, select Use Natural Language Search.

Searching Nonindexed Locations

As we mentioned previously, when you search a folder that isn't included in the search index, Windows does a (relatively) slow grep search of the folder's contents. An information bar, similar to the one shown in Figure 10-8, appears to warn you that the search is likely to be slow. You can click the information bar to add your current search target to the index manually. (But don't do this until you've read "Which Files and Folders Are in the Index?" on page 369.) Be aware that just adding the folder to the index won't make the search any quicker until the system has had time to update the index.

Figure 10-8 This dialog box provides an unequivocal warning that searching the full contents will be slower than usual.

The search engine's initial pass in a nonindexed location goes blazingly fast because it looks only at file names and basic properties (Date Modified and Size). Look carefully at the Search Again In box along the bottom of the window and you'll see a File Contents option asking if you would like to search properties (such as tags) and the contents of files that include a property handler and filter. Click this option and watch the green progress bar move slowly across the address bar (depending on the number of files that need to be cracked open and inspected, this can take a very long time).

If you're willing to put up with occasionally slow searches, you can change this default. To do so, open the Folder Options dialog box, click the Search tab, and click Always Search File Names And Contents under the What To Search heading.

INSIDE OUT   Searching for files in system folders

Windows 7, by default, includes system folders when it searches nonindexed locations. This is a change from Windows Vista, where system folders were excluded by default. If you prefer the Windows Vista behavior—that is, if you really don't want stray files from system folders ever to appear in search results, open the Folder Options dialog box, click the Search tab, and clear the first option, Include System Directories, under When Searching Non-Indexed Locations.

When you connect to a shared folder on a networked computer, the search engine can detect whether Windows Search is running and whether the location you've accessed is already part of the remote index. If it is, great! Your query gets handed off to the remote search engine, which runs it on the other machine and returns its results to your computer. Note that for an indexed search of a shared folder, that folder must be included in the list of indexed locations on the remote computer, and the remote computer must be running version 4.0 or later of Windows Search.

Chapter 10

Saving Searches and Clearing Search History

After you have completed a search and displayed its results in Windows Explorer, you can save the search parameters for later reuse. Click the Save Search button that appears on the toolbar in a Search Results window (or drag the search icon from the address bar into the Favorites node in the navigation pane). The saved search is added to the Favorites list in the navigation pane and is also stored in %UserProfile%\Searches. If you use this location regularly, consider adding it to a library or to the Favorites list in the navigation pane.

When you save a search, you are saving its specification (technically, a *persistedQuery*), not its current results. The next time you double-click the Saved Search icon, Windows reexecutes the search against the current contents of the search index. (If you're interested in the XML data that defines the search, right-click the saved search in your Searches folder, choose Open With, and choose Notepad or WordPad.)

Each of your previous searches are also included in a history list. When you click in the search box, you'll see a drop-down list of searches that are available for reuse. In some cases, this is a tremendous convenience. But it's a nuisance if you mistyped a search term or created a set of search parameters that didn't produce useful results. To clear a single item from the list, click in the search box and then use the Up Arrow and Down Arrow keys to move through the list. Press Delete to remove the highlighted entry.

TROUBLESHOOTING

Your search returns unexpected results

If Windows Search does not perform as expected, try typing **fix search** in the Start menu search box. Then click Find And Fix Problems With Windows Search. The trouble-shooter that appears automatically finds and fixes any problems that it can detect. If it finds none, it leads you through a series of steps to identify and resolve your problem.

Advanced File Management

PERHAPS you have noticed that in the language of Windows dialog boxes, the word *advanced* does not invariably mean technically complex, obscure, esoteric, or arcane. Sometimes its meaning is closer to miscellaneous. In the spirit of this long-established usage, we offer in this chapter a file-management miscellany. We explore the very un-esoteric Recycle Bin and the less visible but more powerful recovery tool known as Previous Versions. We also explore various methods of managing files when you need to use them on more than one computer, techniques for separating your personal data files from your system files (should you desire to separate them), some ways to encrypt data, and a powerful and somewhat obscure file-management program called Robocopy. We'll also explore some relatively unknown keyboard methods for opening shell folders and Control Panel items.

What's in Your Edition?

The Offline Files and Encrypting File System features described in this chapter are available only in the Professional and Ultimate/Enterprise editions of Windows 7. BitLocker To Go volumes can be locked and unlocked in any edition of Windows 7, but those volumes can be created and their encryption settings managed only in the Ultimate/Enterprise editions. Likewise, BitLocker Drive Encryption is supported only in the Ultimate/Enterprise editions.

Recovering Lost, Damaged, and Deleted Files and Folders

It takes only a fraction of a second to wipe out a week's worth of work. You might accidentally delete a folder full of files or, worse, overwrite an entire group of files with changes that can't be undone. Whatever the cause of your misfortune is, Windows 7 includes tools that offer hope of recovery. If a file is simply lost, try searching for it using the tools described in Chapter 10, "Using Windows Search." For accidental deletions, your first stop should be the Recycle Bin, a Windows institution since 1995. If you don't find what you're looking for in the Recycle Bin, your next recourse is a considerably more powerful recovery tool called Previous Versions. We explain how to use both features in this section.

> **Note**
> Your very best hedge against losing important files is a recent backup. For detailed information about the Windows 7 Backup program, see Chapter 12, "Backup, Restore, and Recovery."

Recovering Files and Folders with the Recycle Bin

The Recycle Bin provides protection against accidental erasure of files. In most cases, when you delete one or more files or folders, the deleted items go to the Recycle Bin, not into the ether. If you change your mind, you can go to the bin and recover the thrown-out items. Eventually, when the bin fills up, Windows begins emptying it, permanently deleting the files that have been there the longest.

The following kinds of deletions do not go to the Recycle Bin:

- Files stored on removable disks

- Files stored on network drives, even when that volume is on a computer that has its own Recycle Bin

- Files deleted from a command prompt

- Files deleted from compressed (zipped) folders

You can bypass the Recycle Bin yourself, permanently deleting an item, by holding down the Shift key while you press the Delete key. You might want to do this if you need to get rid of some very large files and you're sure you'll never want those files back. Skipping the Recycle Bin in this case will reclaim some disk space.

You can also turn off the Recycle Bin's services permanently, as we explain in the following section.

Changing Recycle Bin Settings

To see and adjust the amount of space currently used by the Recycle Bin for each drive that it protects, right-click the Recycle Bin icon on your desktop and choose Properties from the shortcut menu. In the Recycle Bin Properties dialog box (shown in Figure 11-1), you can select a drive and enter a different value in the Custom Size box. Windows ordinarily allocates up to 10 percent of a disk's space for recycling. (When the bin is full, the oldest items give way to the newest.) If you think that amount of space is excessive, enter a lower value.

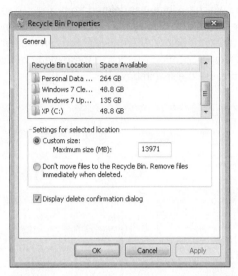

Figure 11-1 You can use the Recycle Bin Properties dialog box to alter the amount of space devoted to the bin—or to turn the feature off for selected drives.

> ### Note
>
> If you don't see a Recycle Bin icon on your desktop, it's probably hidden. To make it visible, right-click the desktop, choose Personalize, and then click Change Desktop Icons. In the Desktop Icon Settings dialog box, select Recycle Bin and click OK. If you use the Show All Folders option in Windows Explorer (see "Navigating in Windows Explorer" on page 330), you'll have access to the Recycle Bin from the bottom of the Folders pane.

If you'd rather do without the Recycle Bin for a particular drive, select the drive in the Recycle Bin Properties dialog box and then click Do Not Move Files To The Recycle Bin. Remove Files Immediately When Deleted. This action is equivalent to setting the maximum capacity to 0.

Whether the Recycle Bin is enabled or disabled, Windows normally displays a confirmation prompt when you delete something. If that prompt annoys you, clear the Display Delete Confirmation Dialog check box.

Chapter 11

Restoring Files and Folders

When you open the Recycle Bin, Windows displays the names of recently deleted items in an ordinary Windows Explorer window. In Details view (see Figure 11-2), you can see when each item was deleted and which folder it was deleted from. You can use the column headings to sort the folder—for example, to display the items that have been deleted most recently at the top, with earlier deletions below. Alternatively, you can organize the bin by disk and folder by clicking the Original Location heading. If these methods don't help you find what you're hoping to restore, use the search box.

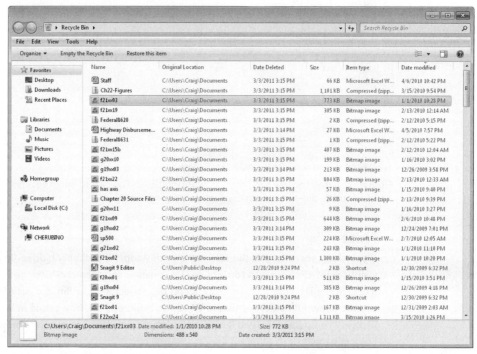

Figure 11-2 Sorting the Recycle Bin in Details view can help you find what you need to restore; so can the search box.

Note that deleted folders are shown only as folders; you don't see the names of items contained within the folders. If you restore a deleted folder, however, Windows re-creates the folder and its contents.

The Restore This Item command (on the toolbar) puts the item back in the folder from which it was deleted. If that folder doesn't currently exist, Windows asks your permission to re-create it. If no object is selected, a Restore All Items option is available on the toolbar. If your Recycle Bin contains hundreds or thousands of deleted files dating back weeks or months, this option can create chaos. It's most useful if you recently emptied the Recycle Bin and all of its current contents are visible.

If you want, you can restore a file or folder to a different location. Select the item, choose Edit, Move To Folder, and then specify the new location. (If the menu bar isn't currently visible, you can right-click the item, choose Cut, and then paste it in the new location.) Or, simplest of all, you can drag the item out of the Recycle Bin and put it where you want it.

Purging the Recycle Bin

A deleted file sitting in your Recycle Bin takes up as much space as it did before it was deleted. If you're deleting files to free up space for new programs and documents, transferring them to the Recycle Bin won't help. You need to remove them permanently. The safest way to do this is to move the items to another storage medium—a different hard disk or a removable disk, for example.

If you're sure you'll never need a particular file again, however, you can delete it in the normal way, and then purge it from the Recycle Bin. Display the Recycle Bin, select the item, and then press Delete.

To empty the Recycle Bin entirely, right-click the Recycle Bin icon on your desktop and choose Empty Recycle Bin from the shortcut menu. Or display the Recycle Bin and click Empty The Recycle Bin on the toolbar.

Restoring Previous Versions of Files and Folders

Need a time machine? With Previous Versions, you have it. This invaluable feature is a side benefit of the way the operating system now creates backup copies and restore points. With System Protection turned on (its default state), Windows creates a daily *restore point* that lets you roll your system back to an earlier state in the event that a new installation or some other event creates instability. (For more information, see "Fine-Tune System Protection Options" on page 82.) Restore points are built from *shadow copies*, which are essentially change logs for files and folders. Shadow copies are also created by the Windows Backup program (for more details, see Chapter 12). If you perform regular periodic backups, you have the Backup program's shadow copies as well as those created by System Protection.

You can't open or manipulate shadow copies directly. However, you can access their contents indirectly via the Previous Versions tab of the properties dialog box for any file, folder, or drive icon, or you can use the Restore Previous Versions command on the File menu in Windows Explorer. Using Previous Versions, you can open, copy, or restore a document or folder as it existed at an earlier point in time. This feature is a lifesaver if you accidentally delete files from a folder or want to "roll back" to an earlier version of a document you've been working on for days or weeks; if you have a shadow copy from a time before you made the deletions or changes, you can recover the earlier version by restoring individual files or replacing the folder's contents with the earlier version. (As an alternative to restoring the earlier version, you can create a copy of the earlier version of the file or folder and then compare its contents to the current version.)

The Previous Versions feature is independent of the Recycle Bin. Purging the Recycle Bin (or declining to use it) has no bearing on the availability of shadow copies.

To see what previous versions are available for a file or folder, right-click the item in Windows Explorer and choose Restore Previous Versions. The Previous Versions tab of the object's properties dialog box (see Figure 11-3) will list the available shadow copies. Select the one you want, and then click Open (to view the file or folder), Copy (to create a copy of it without changing the original), or Restore (to overwrite the object in its current state with the selected copy).

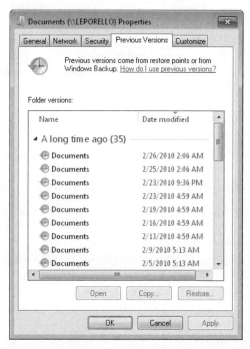

Figure 11-3 The Previous Versions feature enables you to recover a file or folder from a shadow copy saved days or weeks earlier.

> **Note**
> Previous versions are not available for system files or files in an offline cache. You can use the feature to restore earlier versions of uncached files on network shares, however. For more about offline caches, see the following section.

Staying in Sync with Offline Files

The trouble with shared network files and folders is that they're not always there when you need them. The situation is especially awkward with portable computers, which are designed to be disconnected from wired networks and carried out of range of wireless access points. If you're working with a group of files on a server at the office, how do you keep working on them when you no longer have access to the network?

If you are using the Professional or Ultimate/Enterprise edition of Windows 7, you can keep files in sync by using the offline files feature. With offline files, you can mark folders or files on any network share as Always Available Offline. Those files will then be available for use whether or not you are connected to the network, and Windows 7 will transparently keep everything in sync.

If your edition of Windows 7 does not support offline files, you can keep your work life synchronized by using Windows Live Mesh. This free web-based tool is particularly useful for collaborative projects in which multiple, perhaps widely dispersed, users contribute input to common shared folders. For information about using Windows Live Mesh, see Chapter 8, "Adding Windows Live Programs and Services."

The offline files feature lets users of Windows 7 Professional, Ultimate, or Enterprise "pin" files stored on network shares, making those files available on their own computers, whether or not the network is online. When you mark a folder or file as always available offline, Windows copies that item to a cache on your own computer. When you take your computer offline, you can go on working with the cached items as though you were still connected to the network. When you reconnect, Windows automatically synchronizes the cached items with their network counterparts.

The offline files feature is useful even if you never intentionally disconnect from the network. If the network goes down (or simply slows down significantly), Windows begins using cached items instead of their server-based counterparts; when the connection is restored or the logjam breaks, your files are synchronized. You can also simply opt to work with cached files instead of network-based files even when the network is online.

Synchronization of offline files normally occurs whenever you reconnect to the network—or, if you choose to work offline while you're connected to the network, whenever you return to online status. Background synchronization, by default, occurs approximately every six hours while you are connected. You can also perform ad hoc synchronization, synchronize on a schedule of your choosing, or set up an event-driven synchronization

Chapter 11

schedule—for example, stipulate that Windows should synchronize whenever you lock or unlock your Windows account. The option to synchronize on demand is particularly important; to ensure that your offline cache holds the latest versions of any files you intend to use when you go offsite, you should perform an ad hoc synchronization right before you disconnect.

Files cached for offline access are indexed by default, so you can search for them the same way you would any other indexed file.

Making Folders and Files Available Offline

To make a folder or file available offline, navigate to its network location, right-click, and choose Always Available Offline:

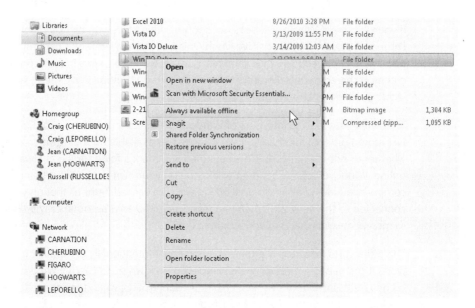

As soon as you choose this command, Windows begins copying the selected item to your local cache. You will see a progress report while this is occurring. On completion, you will see a report of success or failure. In the following example, two errors have occurred:

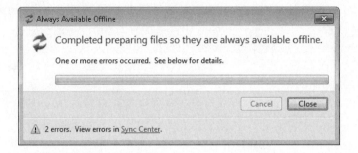

Clicking the Sync Center link reveals the problem:

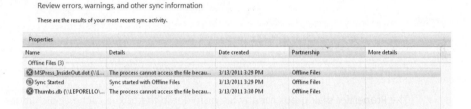

Two of the files on the server were in use and therefore couldn't be synchronized. In this circumstance, you could close the server copies (if you're the one using them) and perform a manual sync. Or if you don't need the offline copies right away, you could let the next scheduled background synchronization take care of the problem.

After you have made files available offline, certain changes in Windows Explorer allow you to confirm their new status (see Figure 11-4):

- Folders available offline are marked with a green icon, similar to the Sync Center icon in the notification area.

- The same green icon appears in the Windows Explorer details pane, along with the words *Always Available*.

- On the right-click context menu, a check mark appears beside the Always Available Offline command and a new Sync command appears below it.

- A Sync command appears on the toolbar.

Chapter 11

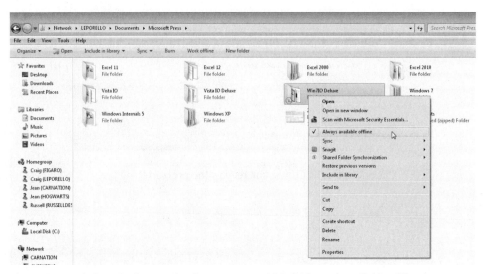

Figure 11-4   Windows Explorer makes it easy to see which folders are available offline.

The Properties dialog box for any file or folder in the offline cache also changes, acquiring a new Offline Files tab, complete with a Sync Now button:

TROUBLESHOOTING

The Always Available Offline command is not available

The offline files feature is enabled by default, but it can be disabled. If you're using the Professional or Ultimate/Enterprise edition of Windows 7 and you don't see the Always Available Offline command on the shortcut menu for a shared network item, open Control Panel on the server computer. Type **offline files** in the search box, and then choose Manage Offline Files. On the General tab of the Offline Files dialog box, click Enable Offline Files.

Working Offline

As mentioned, before disconnecting from the network (or clicking Work Offline on the Windows Explorer toolbar), you should always synchronize any folders or files you intend to use offline. Windows will not do this for you, and if a file is not up to date when you try to use it offline, Windows will deny you access. You can perform this synchronization in a variety of ways. The simplest is to right-click any folders containing files you want to work with, choose Sync from the shortcut menu, and then choose Sync Selected Offline Files. Alternatively, you can open Sync Center in Control Panel, select View Sync Partnerships, right-click Offline Files, and then choose Sync Offline Files. (On a portable computer, you can get to Sync Center by pressing Windows logo key+X to open the Windows Mobility Center; click the green icon to open Sync Center, or click the Sync button to sync all.)

There are several ways to get to your cached files while you're working offline. If you create a shortcut to any network folders you intend to use offline, you can open the cached folder offline by clicking its shortcut. If you map the network share to a drive letter, your offline files will be accessible via that drive letter. Alternatively, you can open Sync Center, click View Sync Partnerships, click Offline Files, click the share you want to use, and then click Browse on the toolbar:

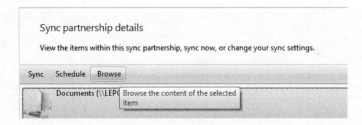

Understanding Synchronization and Resolving Sync Conflicts

When you synchronize your offline files with their server-based copies, Windows performs the following operations for each offline file:

- If you have changed the file while offline and the server-based copy has not been changed, Windows updates the server copy with your changes.

- If you have not made changes to your offline copy but the server copy has been changed, Windows updates the copy in your cache.

- If either the offline copy or the server copy of a file is deleted, the file on the other computer is deleted as well, unless the file on the remote computer was changed while you were offline.

- If one copy has been deleted and the other copy has been changed, Sync Center displays a dialog box that allows you to delete the versions in both locations or copy the changed version to both locations.

- If a new file has been added on the server to a folder that you have marked for offline availability, that new file is copied to your cache.

If both the server copy and your offline copy have changed, Sync Center records a sync conflict. You will have the opportunity to resolve the conflict, but typically the only way you know a conflict exists is by observing a change to the Sync Center icon in the notification area. A yellow caution marker adorns the conflicted icon:

Click this icon to open Sync Center, and then click View Sync Conflicts. Sync Center will display the names of any files that have changed in both the server and cache locations:

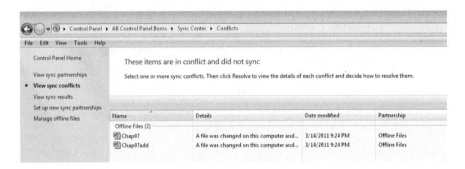

INSIDE OUT   ## Make the Sync Center icon visible in the notification area

If you don't see the Sync Center icon when you know you have a sync conflict, it's probably because your notification area isn't configured to display Sync Center notifications. It's a good idea to personalize the notification area so that these messages always appear. Otherwise, you might not know that conflicts exist. To do this, click the arrow at the left edge of the notification area, and then choose Customize. (Alternatively, right-click a blank spot in the notification area and choose Customize Notification Icons.) In the Notification Area Icons dialog box that appears, choose Show Icons And Notifications in the Behaviors column, beside Microsoft Sync Center. (For more about personalizing the notification area, see "Controlling How Notifications Appear" on page 126.)

Click the name of a file to resolve the conflict. As Figure 11-5 shows, you can keep either version or both, and the dialog box gives you some information about which file is newer and which is larger. If you know which one you want to keep, click it. If you want to inspect a version before deciding, right-click it and choose Open.

Figure 11-5 When synchronization reveals file conflicts between the server and the cache, you can choose which version to keep—or save both versions and sort out the differences later.

Setting Up a Synchronization Schedule

Windows synchronizes offline files by default about once every six hours. To set up additional regular synchronization points, open Sync Center, click View Sync Partnerships, click Offline Files, and then click Schedule on the toolbar. You'll see a list of items that you can schedule, shown here.

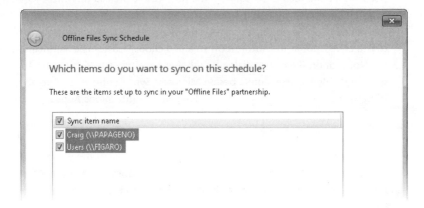

Make your selections and click Next. On the screens that follow, you can choose to sync at a scheduled time or on particular events.

Click At A Scheduled Time to set up a recurring schedule. In the Repeat Every setting, choose minutes, hours, days, weeks, or months; for folders where frequent updates are essential, you can specify that sync operations should occur every *n* minutes or hours.

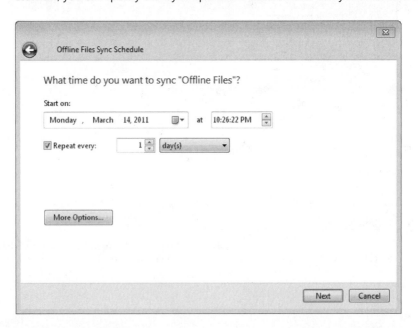

Chapter 11

Click When An Event Occurs to display the options shown here, where you can strike your own personal balance between keeping files up to date and avoiding interruptions to your work:

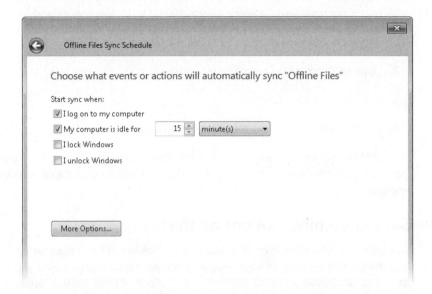

Regardless of which scheduling route you take, the More Options button leads to the dialog box shown in Figure 11-6, which allows you to favor power management by allowing sync cycles only when you're running on external power and pausing the schedule if the PC is asleep or hibernating.

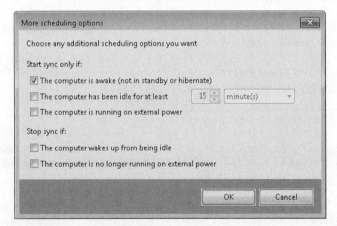

Figure 11-6 The default settings for a sync schedule prevent the Offline Files service from waking up a sleeping computer to sync files.

Encrypting Offline Files

If the files you take offline include private information and you share your computer with other users, you might want to encrypt them. The cached copies will then be hidden from all accounts but your own. To encrypt your offline files, follow these steps:

1. Open Control Panel.

2. Type **offline files** in Control Panel's search box.

3. Click Encrypt Your Offline Files.

4. On the Encryption tab of the Offline Files dialog box, click Encrypt.

Note that encrypting offline files affects the cached copies only, and that once you have exercised the encryption option, all subsequent additions to the cache will also be encrypted.

Setting Caching Options on the Server

Our discussion of the behavior of offline files and folders so far in this chapter has assumed that the caching property of each network share accessed for offline work is set at its default value. This value, called Offline Settings, is one of three possible settings. To adjust the caching property, do the following on the server computer:

1. Type **fsmgmt.msc** at a command prompt. This runs the Shared Folders management console.

2. In the console tree (the left pane), select Shares.

3. In the details pane (the right pane), double-click the share whose property you want to set (or right-click and then choose Properties).

4. On the General tab of the properties dialog box, click Offline Settings. The Offline Settings dialog box opens, as shown in Figure 11-7.

> **Note**
>
> If you prefer, you can access the Offline Settings dialog box directly from a shared folder. Right-click the folder icon and choose Properties. On the Sharing tab, click Advanced Sharing, and then click Caching in the Advanced Sharing dialog box.

Figure 11-7 Use this dialog box to control caching behavior for a shared folder.

5. Choose the behavior you prefer for files in the shared folder:

- The default setting, Only The Files And Programs That Users Specify Are Available Offline, stipulates that a computer connecting to the shared folder from across the network will cache only those files and folders that the user has explicitly marked as Always Available Offline.

- The second option, No Files Or Programs From The Shared Folder Are Available Offline, completely disables caching of files from that share.

- If you choose the third option, All Files And Programs That Users Open From The Share Are Automatically Available Offline, any file opened from a remote computer will be automatically cached for offline use. When you open a cached document from a client computer, the cached copy is used, but the original document on the server is also opened to prevent other people from changing the file while you have it open. This setting is more convenient and easier to use than the default manual caching. On the other hand, with automatic caching, Windows doesn't guarantee that your server resources remain in the cache. How long they stay there, in fact, depends on usage. As the amount of disk space you've allocated to the cache is consumed, Windows discards any documents that have not been used recently to make room for newer ones.

Chapter 11

Managing Disk Space

Because careless caching of large network shares could overwhelm the storage capacities of a mobile computer, Windows by default limits the size of the offline cache to something under 25 percent of the client computer's disk space. (The cache is stored by default in hidden system folders under %SystemRoot%\CSC. For information about relocating the cache, see Microsoft Knowledge Base article 937475, at *w7io.com/1002*.)

To see how much cache space you're using and how much is still available, open Control Panel, type **offline files** in the search box, and click Manage Offline Files. The Disk Usage tab of the Offline Files dialog box provides the statistics:

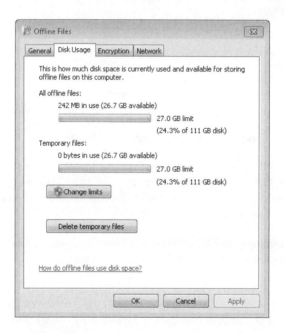

Note that the Temporary Files portion of this report is relevant only if you are using the All Files And Programs That Users Open From The Share Are Automatically Available Offline option, described in the previous section (see Figure 11-7). Windows will delete files from the temporary cache when necessary, but you can do the job yourself by clicking Delete Temporary Files. To increase or decrease the amount of space available for offline files, click Change Limits. The Offline Files Disk Usage Limits dialog box will appear:

Note that the second slider in this dialog box cannot be moved to the right of the first slider.

Removing Offline Access to Files and Folders

When you no longer need offline access to a network resource, open the sync item in Windows Explorer, right-click, and clear Always Available Offline. If the share involved is set for manual caching (the Only The Files And Programs That Users Specify Are Available Offline option; see Figure 11-7, on page 413), Windows purges the items from your cache in addition to removing the offline access attribute. If the share is set for automatic caching, items that are currently in the temporary cache remain there. To delete those files, open the Offline Files option in Control Panel, and on the Disk Usage tab, click Delete Temporary Files. Note, however, that this option does not affect files you have marked to be Always Available Offline.

To eliminate all items from the offline files cache so that you can start over, you need to make a small edit to the registry. Before taking this drastic step, make sure you synchronize all sync items that contain changes you made that haven't yet been copied to the server location. The following steps completely erase all files from your offline files cache:

1. Using an administrator's account, open Registry Editor (Regedit.exe) and navigate to HKLM\System\CurrentControlSet\Services\CSC\Parameters. (This key is not created until you use Offline Files for the first time.)

2. Right-click the Parameters key and click New, DWORD (32-Bit) Value.

3. For the name of the new value, type **FormatDatabase**. (Note that there's no space in that name.)

4. Double-click the new DWORD value and assign it a value of 1.

5. Restart your computer.

After you restart and log on to your account again, you'll notice that there are no longer any sync items in the Offline Files section of Sync Center.

Chapter 11

Relocating Personal Data Folders

Although the organizational scheme that Windows has adopted for personal data folders—the 11 visible subfolders of %UserProfile% (see Figure 9-5 on page 333)—is suitable for many users, the scheme has one potential defect: it combines data and system files on the same physical volume. For a variety of reasons, some users prefer to separate their documents and other profile data. These reasons might include the following:

- Large collections of data, particular digital media files, have a way of overwhelming the available space on system volumes, eventually necessitating their removal and relocation to a separate, larger volume.

- Separating data from system files makes restoration easier in the event of system corruption (for example, by malware).

- Separation reduces the size and time devoted to image backups, encouraging their regular use.

- Separation can make it easier, when the time comes, to upgrade the operating system.

On a large system volume, it might not be a problem to keep data files and system files together on the same disk. But if you have installed Windows on a solid-state drive—an excellent strategy for performance—your system-drive space is likely to be at a premium. It's a good idea to keep at least 20 percent of your system drive free. If you find your space shrinking below that threshold, you should probably consider relocating some of your personal data folders.

In earlier versions of the operating system, we routinely recommended that users accomplish this separation by redirecting their user profile subfolders to new locations. In Windows 7, an alternative makes equally good sense: store personal data in folders on a separate volume, and then include those folders in your libraries. (For information about using libraries, see "Working with Libraries" on page 343.) This approach leaves you with a default set of profile folders, which you can still use when it's convenient to do so, but it keeps the bulk of your personal information in a separate place.

Not everyone loves libraries, however, and there's no requirement to love them. You can still move some or all of your profile subfolders in Windows 7, just as you could in Windows XP and Windows Vista. To relocate a user profile folder by editing its properties, follow these steps:

1. Click your account name at the top of the Start menu's right column to open the root folder of your profile, right-click a folder that you want to relocate, and choose Properties from the shortcut menu.

2. On the Location tab of the properties dialog box, enter the address that you want to relocate to. For example, to move the Downloads folder from C:\Users\Craig\ Downloads to F:\Users\Craig\Downloads, you could simply replace the C with an F at the beginning of the path.

3. Click OK. Windows asks permission to create the target folder if it doesn't already exist. Click Yes. A Move Folder dialog box similar to this one appears:

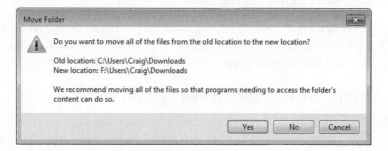

4. Unless you have some good reason not to move the existing files from the original location to the new one, click Yes.

It's really not a good idea *not* to click Yes in this dialog box. First, it's difficult to imagine why you would want some of your personal documents in a given category on one disk and the rest on another. (If you want to keep your existing files separate from those you save in the future, move the old files to a subfolder in the new location instead of leaving them in the old location.) Second, because %UserProfile% is a system-generated folder, not an ordinary data folder that corresponds to a fixed disk location, leaving some files behind will give you two identically named subfolders in %UserProfile%.

Encrypting Information

Windows 7 provides the following encryption tools for preventing the loss of confidential data:

- Encrypting File System (EFS) encodes your files so that even if someone is able to obtain the files, he or she won't be able to read them. The files are readable only when you log on to the computer using your user account (which, presumably, you have protected with a strong password). In fact, even someone else logging on to your computer won't have access to your encrypted files, a feature that provides protection on systems that are shared by more than one user.

- BitLocker Drive Encryption, introduced with Windows Vista, provides another layer of protection by encrypting entire hard-disk volumes. By linking this encryption to a key stored in a Trusted Platform Module (TPM) or USB flash drive, BitLocker reduces the risk of data being lost when a computer is stolen or when a hard disk is stolen and placed in another computer. A thief's standard approach in these situations is to boot into an alternate operating system and then try to retrieve data from the stolen computer or drive. With BitLocker Drive Encryption, that type of offline attack is effectively neutered.

- BitLocker To Go, new in Windows 7, extends BitLocker encryption to removable media, such as USB flash drives.

EFS is available on systems running Windows 7 Professional or Ultimate/Enterprise. Encrypting a drive using BitLocker or BitLocker To Go requires the Ultimate/Enterprise edition. You can use a flash drive encrypted with BitLocker To Go in any edition of Windows 7.

Using the Encrypting File System

The Encrypting File System (EFS) provides a secure way to store your sensitive data. Windows creates a randomly generated file encryption key (FEK) and then transparently encrypts the data, using this FEK, as it is being written to disk. Windows then encrypts the FEK using your public key. (Windows creates a personal encryption certificate with a public/private key pair for you the first time you use EFS.) The FEK, and therefore the data it encrypts, can be decrypted only with your certificate and its associated private key, which are available only when you log on with your user name and password. (Designated data recovery agents can also decrypt your data.) Other users who attempt to use your encrypted files receive an "access denied" message. Even administrators and others who have permission to take ownership of files are unable to open your encrypted files. EFS, which uses Advanced Encryption Standard (AES) with a 256-bit key as its default encryption algorithm, provides extremely strong protection against attackers.

You can encrypt individual files, folders, or entire drives. (You cannot encrypt the boot volume—the one with the Windows operating system files—using EFS, however. For that, you must use BitLocker Drive Encryption.) We recommend that you encrypt folders or drives instead of individual files. When you encrypt a folder or drive, the files it contains are encrypted, and new files that you create in that folder or drive are encrypted automatically. This includes temporary files that your applications create in the folder or drive. (For example, Microsoft Word creates a copy of a document when you open it for editing. If the document's folder isn't encrypted, the temporary copy isn't encrypted—giving prying eyes a potential opportunity to view your data.) For this reason, you should consider encrypting your %Temp% and %Tmp% folders, which many applications use to store temporary copies of documents that are open for editing, in addition to encrypting the folders where your sensitive documents are stored.

To encrypt a folder, follow these steps:

1. In Windows Explorer, right-click the folder, choose Properties, click the General tab, and then click Advanced, which displays the dialog box shown next. (If the properties dialog box doesn't have an Advanced button, the folder is not on an NTFS-formatted volume and you can't use EFS.)

2. Select Encrypt Contents To Secure Data. (Note that you can't encrypt compressed files. If the files are already compressed, Windows clears the compressed attribute.)

3. Click OK twice. If the folder contains any files or subfolders, Windows then displays a confirmation message.

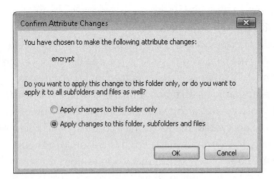

> ### Note
> If you select Apply Changes To This Folder Only, Windows doesn't encrypt any of the files currently in the folder. Any new files that you create in the folder, however, including files that you copy or move to the folder, will be encrypted.

After a file or folder has been encrypted, Windows Explorer displays its name in green. This minor cosmetic detail is the only change you are likely to notice. Windows will decrypt your files on the fly as you use them and re-encrypt them when you save.

CAUTION

> Before you encrypt anything important, you should back up your file recovery certificate and your personal encryption certificate (with their associated private keys), as well as the data recovery agent certificate, to a USB flash drive (UFD). Store the UFD in a secure location. If you ever lose the certificate stored on your hard drive (because of a disk failure, for example), you can restore the backup copy and regain access to your files. If you lose all copies of your certificate (and no data recovery agent certificates exist), you won't be able to use your encrypted files. No back door exists (none that we know of, at any rate), nor is there any practical way to hack these files. (If there were, it wouldn't be very good encryption.)

To encrypt one or more files, follow the same procedure as for folders. You'll see a different confirmation message to remind you that the file's folder is not encrypted and to give you an opportunity to encrypt it. You generally don't want to encrypt individual files because the information you intend to protect can too easily become decrypted without your knowledge. For example, with some applications, when you open a document for editing, the application creates a copy of the original document. When you save the document after editing, the application saves the copy—which is not encrypted—and deletes the original encrypted document. Static files that you use for reference only—but never for editing—can safely be encrypted without encrypting the parent folder. Even in that situation, however, you'll probably find it simpler to encrypt the whole folder.

Encrypting with BitLocker and BitLocker To Go

BitLocker Drive Encryption can be used to encrypt entire NTFS volumes, which provides excellent protection against data theft. BitLocker can secure a drive against attacks that involve circumventing the operating system or removing the drive to another computer. BitLocker is a powerful tool that can more than ruin your day if you don't know what you are doing. Because under some circumstances it can lock you out of your own computer or data, we recommend that before you apply BitLocker to your own systems you carefully read two white papers from Microsoft: "BitLocker Drive Encryption Deployment Guide for Windows 7" (*w7io.com/1004*) and "BitLocker Drive Encryption Step-by-Step Guide for Windows 7" (*w7io.com/1005*).

BitLocker To Go, a new feature in Windows 7, allows you to encrypt the entire contents of a USB flash drive or other removable device. If it's lost or stolen, the thief will be unable to access the data without the password.

> **Note**
> After you encrypt a removable drive by using BitLocker To Go on a PC running Windows 7 Ultimate or Enterprise, you can add, delete, and change files on that volume using any edition of Windows 7. Systems running Windows XP and Windows Vista can, with proper authentication, open (but not change) files on encrypted media using a reader program that is included on the volume itself. This reader program does not work with volumes formatted using NTFS; if you intend to use a removable drive on systems running older Windows versions, be sure to format it using FAT, FAT32, or exFAT before turning on BitLocker To Go encryption.

To apply BitLocker To Go, right-click the removable device in Windows Explorer and choose Turn On BitLocker from the shortcut menu:

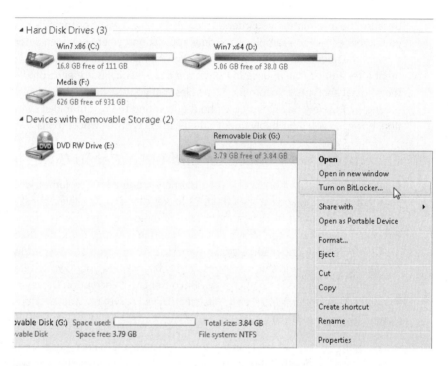

BitLocker To Go will ask how you want to unlock the encrypted drive—with a password, a smart card, or both. After you have made your selections and confirmed your intentions, the software will give you the opportunity to save and print your recovery key:

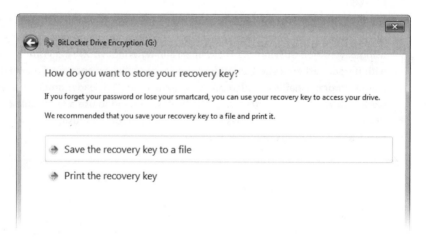

Your recovery key is a system-generated, 48-character, numeric backup password. If you lose the password you assign to the encrypted disk, you can recover your data with the recovery key. BitLocker To Go offers to save that key in a plain text file; you should accept the offer and store the file in a secure location.

With all preliminaries out of the way, BitLocker To Go begins encrypting your media. This takes a few minutes, even if the disk is freshly formatted. Any files currently on the disk are encrypted, as are any files subsequently added.

To read an encrypted disk, you will need to unlock it, using whatever method you have stipulated. You will also see an Automatically Unlock On This Computer From Now On check box. If your computer is secure and you're only concerned about having your data locked when the drive it's on is not plugged into this computer, you can safely exercise this option.

If you're prompted for a password that you have lost or forgotten, click I Forgot My Password. You will then have the opportunity to enter your recovery key. In case you have several recovery-key text files, BitLocker To Go gives you the key's identification code:

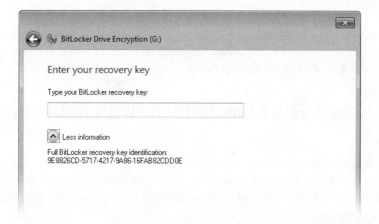

Find the text file whose name matches the identification code, copy the recovery key from this text file to the BitLocker dialog box, and you'll be granted temporary access to the files (and the access is good until you remove the disk or restart the computer). If you are using Windows 7 Ultimate or Enterprise, the dialog box that announces your temporary access includes a Manage BitLocker button. Clicking this button gives you an opportunity to reset the password that unlocks the drive:

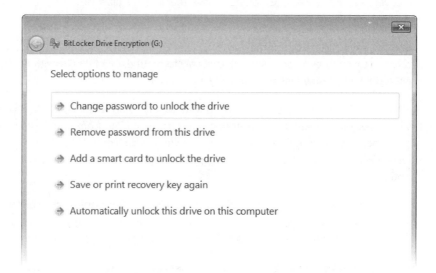

To remove BitLocker To Go encryption from a disk, open BitLocker Drive Encryption in the System And Security section of Control Panel and click Turn Off BitLocker. The software will decrypt the disk; allow some time for this process.

Industrial-Strength File Management with Robocopy and Robocopy GUI

Dragging files between folders with Windows Explorer is fine for some tasks, but when it comes to heavy-duty file management you need a better tool. If you're willing to do a little typing in exchange for power and flexibility that you can't get with Windows Explorer, get to know Robocopy.

Robocopy (the name is short for Robust File Copy) was introduced with the Windows Server 2003 Resource Kit and is included in all editions of Windows 7. Its many strengths include the ability to copy all NTFS file attributes and to mirror the contents of an entire folder hierarchy across local volumes or over a network. If you use the right combination of options, you can recover from interruptions such as network outages by resuming a copy operation from the point of failure after the connection is restored.

The Robocopy syntax takes some getting used to. If you're familiar with the standard Copy and Xcopy commands, you'll have to unlearn their syntax and get used to Robocopy's unconventional ways. The key difference is that Robocopy is designed to work with two directories (folders) at a time, and the file specification is a secondary parameter. In addition, there are dozens of options that can be specified as command-line switches. The basic syntax is as follows:

```
robocopy source destination [file [file]...] [options]
```

The *source* and *destination* parameters are specified as *drive:\path* or *\\server\share\path*. The *file* parameter can contain one or more literal file names, or it can use the familiar ? and * wildcards. Available options include dozens of switches that control copying, file selection, retry options, and the ability to create log files. For instance, this command copies the contents of one folder and all its subfolders from a local drive E to a shared folder on a Windows Home Server:

```
robocopy "E:\test" \\server\public\test\ /MIR /W:20 /R:15 /LOG: \\server\public\logs
```

The /MIR switch tells Robocopy you want to mirror the two folders, copying all folders (even empty ones) from the source directory and purging folders from the destination if they no longer exist on the source. The /W and /R switches set the wait and retry options; in this case, Robocopy will retry each copy up to 15 times, waiting 20 seconds between attempts. (The defaults allow 1 million retries at 30-second intervals, which allows copy operations to complete when an open file is closed even if hours or days have passed since the command was first launched.)

To see the full syntax, type **robocopy /?** at a command prompt.

Robocopy is a powerful tool, capable of moving, copying, and deleting files and folders faster than you can say "Whoops." We recommend experimenting with commands on non-essential files and folders first; when you're comfortable that you understand the effects of the syntax you're using, you can run the command against real data files.

And if you aren't keen on the idea of using a command-line tool, take heart. Microsoft engineer Derk Benisch has written a graphical front end, shown in Figure 11-8, that allows you to build a command by selecting check boxes instead of entering switches.

Robocopy GUI adds more than usability to Robocopy; it also lets you create a library of commonly used copy scripts. To read an article about Robocopy GUI and download the bits, visit *w7io.com/1001*.

Chapter 11

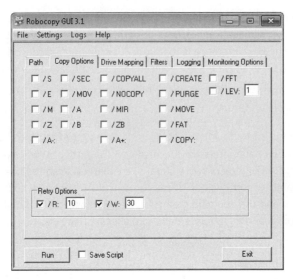

Figure 11-8 Download this utility to turn Robocopy's cryptic command lines into a friendlier set of check boxes.

Opening Shell Folders with the Shell Command

If you're a speedy typist or a user who likes working with undocumented Windows commands, you might want to acquaint yourself with the *shell* command. Enter this command in the Start menu search box, followed by a colon and the appropriate argument, press Enter, and Windows takes you straight to a shell folder—without passing Go. For example, if you type **shell:personal** in the search box and press Enter, Windows displays the Documents folder in your user profile. Granted, in this case it's probably quicker to user the mouse (unless, of course, you've removed the Documents item from your Start menu), but some of the *shell* command's arguments do take you places that aren't so easily accessible. The following list presents some of the more interesting and potentially useful variants of this command. Note that in each case you must leave no spaces between the word *shell* and the first word of the argument, but that some of the multiword arguments include spaces and others do not. (Don't look for consistency here; just follow directions!) Spaces that appear are required. Capitalization, on the other hand, is optional.

- **Shell:Profile**   Opens your user profile folder.

- **Shell:Personal**   Opens the Documents folder in your user profile.

- **Shell:SendTo**   Opens the SendTo folder, which is normally hidden at %UserProfile%\AppData\Roaming\Microsoft\Windows\SendTo.

- **Shell:Public**   Opens the default collection of shared folders on your machine.

- **Shell:Startup**   Opens a folder containing shortcuts that are automatically loaded when you start Windows with your account.

- **Shell:Common Startup**   Opens a folder containing shortcuts that are automatically loaded when any user starts Windows on your computer.

- **Shell:ConnectionsFolder**   Opens Network Connections in Control Panel.

- **Shell:Programs and shell:Common Programs**   These two folders combine to create the All Programs list on your Start menu. The first folder contains programs specific to your account; the second contains programs available to all accounts at your computer.

- **Shell:AppData**   Opens the folder %UserProfile%\AppData\Roaming.

- **Shell:Local AppData**   Opens the folder %UserProfile%\AppData\Local.

- **Shell:Cookies**   Opens a folder of cookies saved by Internet Explorer.

- **Shell:Cache**   Opens Internet Explorer's Temporary Internet Files folder.

Tables 11-1 through 11-9 list other arguments for the Shell command.

Table 11-1 **Folders from Current User Profile**

Command	Folder Opened
Shell:Profile	User profile of logged-on user
Shell:UsersFilesFolder	Same as shell:profile
Shell:Personal	Documents folder from profile of logged-on user
Shell:My Music	Music folder from profile of logged-on user
Shell:My Video	Videos folder from profile of logged-on user
Shell:Contacts	Contacts folder from profile of logged-on user (deprecated)
Shell:Desktop	Desktop folder from profile of logged-on user
Shell:Downloads	Downloads folder from profile of logged-on user
Shell:Favorites	Internet Explorer Favorites folder from profile of logged-on user
Shell:Searches	Searches folder from profile of logged-on user; contains saved searches
Shell:Links	Links folder from profile of logged-on user; contains shortcuts from Favorites node in Windows Explorer navigation pane

Table 11-2 **Folders from Public User Profile**

Command	Folder Opened
Shell:Public	Public User Profile folder
Shell:Common Desktop	Public Desktop folder
Shell:Common Documents	Public Documents folder
Shell:CommonDownloads	Public Downloads folder
Shell:CommonMusic	Public Music folder
Shell:CommonPictures	Public Pictures folder
Shell:CommonVideo	Public Videos folder
Shell:SampleMusic	Sample Music folder (by default in public Music folder)
Shell:SamplePictures	Sample Pictures folder (by default in public Pictures folder)
Shell:SampleVideos	Sample Videos folder (by default in public Videos folder)

Table 11-3 **Other Per-User Folders**

Command	Folder Opened
Shell:Start Menu	Start Menu folder from profile of logged-on user
Shell:Startup	Startup folder from profile of logged-on user
Shell:Programs	Start menu Programs folder from profile of logged-on user
Shell:Quick Launch	Quick Launch folder from profile of logged-on user
Shell:Recent	Recent folder from profile of logged-on user
Shell:SendTo	Send To folder from profile of logged-on user
Shell:User Pinned	All shortcuts that have been pinned to the taskbar and Start menu by the currently logged-on user
Shell:ImplicitAppShortcuts	In User Pinned folder, contains shortcuts to system-managed Start menu items, including Control Panel, Help And Support, and auto-published applications from Windows Virtual PC
Shell:GameTasks	Custom Games Explorer shortcuts for logged-on user
Shell:Administrative Tools	Administrative Tools subfolder from All Programs section of Start menu
Shell:Ringtones	Ringtones folder, which stores custom files created by Windows ringtone editor using a compatible phone in Device Stage
Shell:Templates	Templates folder from profile of logged-on user (rarely used)
Shell:Gadgets	User-installed Windows gadgets, including those that have been removed from the desktop but are still available
Shell:Playlists	Playlists subfolder in Music folder from profile of logged-on user

Command	Folder Opened
Shell:PrintHood	User-created printer shortcuts
Shell:CD Burning	Burn folder, used to store temp files before they are burned to disc

Table 11-4 Internet Explorer and Security Folders

Command	Folder Opened
Shell:Cache	Internet Explorer Temporary Internet Files
Shell:Cookies	Internet Explorer cookies (open Low subfolder to see cookies for sites with low integrity level)
Shell:History	Internet Explorer history
Shell:SystemCertificates	Signed copies of digital certificates for system; use Certificate Manager to view details and add or remove certificates
Shell:CryptoKeys	Crypto folder; stores machine keys
Shell:DpapiKeys	Protect folder; holds user keys for data encryption, including Encrypting File System
Shell:CredentialManager	Credentials folder

Table 11-5 Virtual Folders

Command	Folder Opened
Shell:MyComputerFolder	Computer folder
Shell:RecycleBinFolder	Recycle Bin
Shell:Fonts	Settings for installed fonts and font families
Shell:Games	Games Explorer
Shell:Libraries	Libraries node in Windows Explorer
Shell:UsersLibrariesFolder	Same as Shell:Libraries
Shell:DocumentsLibrary	Default Documents library
Shell:MusicLibrary	Default Music library
Shell:PicturesLibrary	Default Pictures library
Shell:VideosLibrary	Default Videos library
Shell:HomeGroupFolder	Homegroup node in Windows Explorer
Shell:NetworkPlacesFolder	Network node in Windows Explorer
Shell:NetHood	User-created network shortcuts
Shell:ConnectionsFolder	Network Connections
Shell:PrintersFolder	Printers And Faxes
Shell:AppUpdatesFolder	Installed updates, including those delivered by Windows Update and Microsoft Update
Shell:CSCFolder	Offline Files folder
Shell:SearchHomeFinder	Search Results window, with focus in search box (equivalent to pressing Windows logo key+F)

Chapter 11

Table 11-6 **Control Panel Folders**

Command	Folder Opened
ShellControlPanelFolder	Control Panel, displaying All Control Panel Items in icon view
Shell:AddNewProgramsFolder	Get Programs item in Control Panel
Shell:ChangeRemoveProgramsFolder	Programs And Features folder
Shell:SyncSetupFolder	Sync Setup in Sync Center
Shell:SyncResultsFolder	Sync Results in Sync Center
Shell:ConflictFolder	Conflicts in Sync Center
Shell:InternetFolder	Internet Explorer (32-bit)

Table 11-7 **System Folders**

Command	Folder Opened
Shell:Windows	Windows installation folder
Shell:System	System32 folder
Shell:SystemX86	Windows\SysWOW64 on 64-bit systems
Shell:UserProfiles	Users folder, which contains profiles for all local users and a Public profile
Shell:ProgramFiles	Program Files folder
Shell:ProgramFilesX86	Program Files (x86) folder on 64-bit Windows systems
Shell:ProgramFilesX64	Program Files folder on 64-bit Windows systems
Shell:ProgramFilesCommon	Common Files subfolder of Program Files folder
Shell:ProgramFilesCommonX86	Program Files (x86) subfolder of Program Files on 64-bit Windows systems
ShellProgramFilesCommonX64	Common Files subfolder of Program Files folder on 64-bit Windows systems

Table 11-8 **Application Data**

Command	Folder Opened
Shell:AppData	Roaming AppData folder from profile of logged-on user
Shell:Local AppData	Local AppData folder from profile of logged-on user
Shell:LocalAppDataLow	User Local AppData (low integrity level) folder from profile of logged-on user

Table 11-9 Per-Machine Folders

Command	Folder Opened
Shell:Common AppData	ProgramData folder, which holds global settings saved by applications
Shell:Common Start Menu	Start Menu folder, containing shortcuts and subfolders for all users
Shell:Common Programs	Start menu programs for all users
Shell:Common Startup	Startup folder for all users
Shell:Default Gadgets	Default Windows gadgets
Shell:ResourceDir	Resources folder, which contains Windows themes, including Aero and ease-of-access themes
Shell:CommonRingtones	Stores default ringtones for use with Windows ringtone editor using a compatible phone in Device Stage
Shell:PublicGameTasks	Custom Games Explorer shortcuts for all users
Shell:Common Templates	Templates folder for all users; rarely used
Shell:Device Metadata Store	DeviceMetadataStore folder, which contains digitally signed files, downloaded from Microsoft, with icons and custom settings for Device Stage items

Using GUIDs to Open Control Panel Items and System Folders

A GUID (globally unique identifier) is a string of 32 hexadecimal digits enclosed within braces, with hyphens separating the digits into groups of eight, four, four, four, and twelve characters. Windows uses GUIDs to identify all kinds of objects, including Control Panel items and certain system folders. If you create a new folder and give it any name followed by a period and a GUID, the folder becomes a shortcut to the object associated with that GUID. So, for example, if you create a new folder and name it

CP Tasks. {ED7BA470-8E54-465E-825C-99712043E01C}

that folder becomes a shortcut to a categorized list of Control Panel tasks. Table 11-10 lists 39 GUIDs that can be used in this way in Windows 7. Note that capitalization in the GUID is unimportant.

Chapter 11

Table 11-10 **GUIDs and Associated Folders**

GUID	Associated Folder
{BB64F8A7-BEE7-4E1A-AB8D-7D8273F7FDB6}	Action Center
{D20EA4E1-3957-11D2-A40B-0C5020524153}	Administrative Tools
{1D2680C9-0E2A-469D-B787-065558BC7D43}	All .NET Frameworks and COM Libraries
{ED7BA470-8E54-465E-825C-99712043E01C}	All Tasks (Control Panel)
{9C60DE1E-E5FC-40F4-A487-460851A8D915}	AutoPlay
{B98A2BEA-7D42-4558-8BD1-832F41BAC6FD}	Backup and Restore
{0142E4D0-FB7A-11DC-BA4A-000FFE7AB428}	Biometric Devices
{D9EF8727-CAC2-4E60-809E-86F80A666C91}	BitLocker Drive Encryption (Ultimate Edition only)
{20D04FE0-3AEA-1069-A2D8-08002B30309D}	Computer Folder
{1206F5F1-0569-412C-8FEC-3204630DFB70}	Credential Manager
{00C6D95F-329C-409A-81D7-C46C66EA7F33}	Default Location
{17CD9488-1228-4B2F-88CE-4298E93E0966}	Default Programs
{A8A91A66-3A7D-4424-8D24-04E180695C7A}	Devices and Printers
{C555438B-3C23-4769-A71F-B6D3D9B6053A}	Display
{D555645E-D4F8-4C29-A827-D93C859C4F2A}	Ease of Access Center
{93412589-74D4-4E4E-AD0E-E0CB621440FD}	Font Settings
{15EAE92E-F17A-4431-9F28-805E482DAFD4}	Get Programs
{67CA7650-96E6-4FDD-BB43-A8E774F73A57}	HomeGroup
{E9950154-C418-419E-A90A-20C5287AE24B}	Location and Other Sensors
{1FA9085F-25A2-489B-85D4-86326EEDCD87}	Manage Wireless Networks
{8E908FC9-BECC-40F6-915B-F4CA0E70D03D}	Network and Sharing Center
{7007ACC7-3202-11D1-AAD2-00805FC1270E}	Network Connections
{208D2C60-3AEA-1069-A2D7-08002B30309D}	Network Folder
{05D7B0F4-2121-4EFF-BF6B-ED3F69B894D9}	Notification Area Icons
{96AE8D84-A250-4520-95A5-A47A7E3C548B}	Parental Controls
{78F3955E-3B90-4184-BD14-5397C15F1EFC}	Performance Information and Tools
{ED834ED6-4B5A-4BFE-8F11-A626DCB6A921}	Personalization
{025A5937-A6BE-4686-A844-36FE4BEC8B6D}	Power Options
{7B81BE6A-CE2B-4676-A29E-EB907A5126C5}	Programs and Features
{9FE63AFD-59CF-4419-9775-ABCC3849F861}	Recovery
{241D7C96-F8BF-4F85-B01F-E2B043341A4B}	RemoteApp and Desktop Connections
{58E3C745-D971-4081-9034-86E34B30836A}	Speech Recognition

GUID	Associated Folder
{9C73F5E5-7AE7-4E32-A8E8-8D23B85255BF}	Sync Center
{BB06C0E4-D293-4F75-8A90-CB05B6477EEE}	System
{C58C4893-3BE0-4B45-ABB5-A63E4B8C8651}	Troubleshooting
{60632754-C523-4B62-B45C-4172DA012619}	User Accounts
{4026492F-2F69-46B8-B9BF-5654FC07E423}	Windows Firewall
{E95A4861-D57A-4BE1-AD0F-35267E261739}	Windows SideShow
{36EEF7DB-88AD-4E81-AD49-0E313F0C35F8}	Windows Update

One way you might consider using some of these GUIDs is to give yourself single-click access to Control Panel items that would otherwise take multiple clicks. For example, you might create a folder in your Documents folder, call it Custom Control Panel Shortcuts, and then populate it with GUID shortcuts to the Control Panel items you use most frequently. You could also drag such a containing folder to the taskbar or the Start menu for even quicker access.

Chapter 11

Backup, Restore, and Recovery

I N the Unabridged Edition of Murphy's Law, you'll find an entire chapter of corollaries that apply to computers in general and your important data files in particular. Murphy says, "Anything that can go wrong will go wrong." That's certainly true of hard disks, where it's not a matter of whether they'll fail but when. When a disk crashes, it's usually impossible to recover your data without spending a small fortune at a data recovery service.

Even if your hardware never lets you down, human error can wreak havoc with data. You can press the wrong key and inadvertently delete a group of files you meant to move. If you're not paying attention, you might absent-mindedly click the wrong button in a dialog box, saving a new file using the same name as an old one, wiping out weeks' worth of work in the process.

In any of these circumstances, you're almost certainly going to lose data. When a hard disk crashes, for instance, all files you've created or saved since your last backup are gone for good. But you can avoid the worst data losses if you get into the habit of backing up regularly.

In this chapter, we cover the backup tools included with Windows 7, which contain everything you need to undo the damage from data disasters and human errors. We also explain how to configure and use the powerful but nearly invisible backup and recovery features known collectively as System Protection.

What's in Your Edition?

All editions of Windows 7 include the Windows Backup program and have the capability to perform file backups and create and restore system images. The capability to specify a network location as a backup destination is restricted to the business editions: Professional, Ultimate, and Enterprise. All System Protection features discussed in this chapter, including the capability to create restore points and recover previous versions of files and folders, are available in all editions.

If you're looking for assistance on how to fix problems that affect your computer's ability to start, see "Making Repairs with the Windows Recovery Environment" on page 1046.

Using the Windows Backup Program

The Windows Backup program (Sdclt.exe) is installed by default in all editions of Windows 7. Its feature set is dramatically improved over its predecessor in Windows Vista, which was roundly (and deservedly) criticized for its inflexibility and for Microsoft's decision to remove important features from the program in home editions. And it's light-years beyond the NT Backup program included with Windows XP, which was designed before the turn of the millennium.

Before you create a backup, you are strongly encouraged to run through a brief setup routine. The purpose of this one-time operation is twofold: to help you choose a backup type (system image, data files, or both), and then to help you build a schedule that will automate future backups. You can save one and only one collection of backup settings.

For your first backup, you can start from either of the following two locations:

- Under the Maintenance heading in Action Center, click the Set Up Backup button.

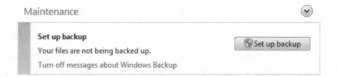

- In Control Panel, click Back Up Your Computer under the System And Security heading (if you use icons view in Control Panel, click Backup And Restore), and then click Set Up Backup, as shown in Figure 12-1.

> **Note**
> You can skip the initial setup if you simply want to create a one-time backup of your system volume (an excellent idea if you just finished performing a clean installation with all your drivers and programs installed and ready to use). Click the Create A System Image link in the left pane.

The basic steps for performing a backup are simple and straightforward. You have to make some decisions first, which in turn dictate which tools you use and what actions you need to take.

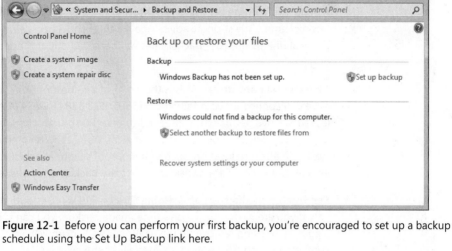

Figure 12-1 Before you can perform your first backup, you're encouraged to set up a backup schedule using the Set Up Backup link here.

1. Select a destination where your backup will be saved. The Set Up Backup dialog box, shown in Figure 12-2, lists all available destinations. Note that the system volume is not included in this list.

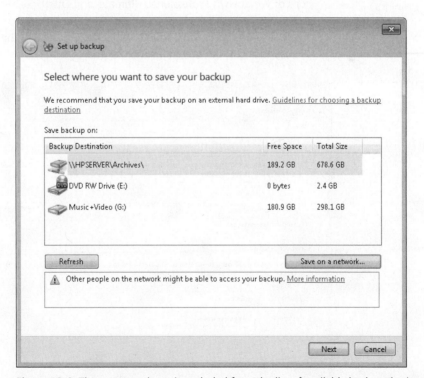

Figure 12-2 The system volume is excluded from the list of available backup destinations, and network locations are available only on business editions of Windows 7.

Your choices include the following:

- **A separate volume on the same internal hard drive that holds your system volume**   We strongly advise against this option because in the event of a physical disk failure your backup files will be wiped out at the same time as the originals.

- **An external hard drive**   This is the simplest and best option. The external drive can connect to your PC via a USB 2.0, IEEE 1394, or eSATA cable. You can leave the drive permanently attached to your PC so that scheduled backups happen regularly, or you can unplug it after the backup is complete and then store it in a secure location, such as a fireproof safe or a locked cabinet. For extremely valuable data, consider storing the backup drive offsite.

- **Removable media such as writable CDs or DVDs**   This option is available only if you are performing a one-time image backup; you can't define a scheduled backup using removable media. Windows Backup will prompt you to swap media as needed. This option is especially useful after you perform a clean installation and before you add any data files.

- **A shared network folder**   This option is available only on the business editions of Windows 7: Professional, Ultimate, and Enterprise. It's an excellent choice for file-based backups if another PC or server on your network has ample storage space. You'll need to enter credentials that the scheduled task can use to access the shared location, as shown here:

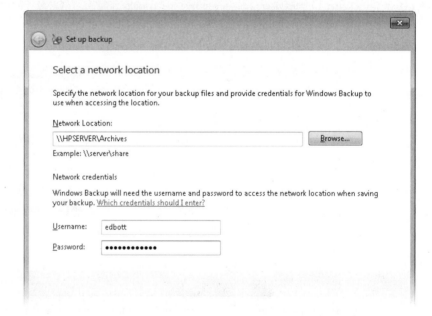

INSIDE OUT   Use Windows Home Server or Windows Small Business Server

Two network operating systems that are widely used in home networks and in small businesses overcome these limitations of Windows Backup. With Windows Home Server or Windows Small Business Server Essentials, you don't need a business edition of Windows 7 to save backups on a network drive; the backup software included in these operating systems works with any Windows 7 edition to store backups on a network drive. And you're not limited to a single system image backup. For more information, see "Implementing a Backup Strategy in a Server-Based Environment" on page 453.

As we note later in this chapter, using a network location to store system image backups has one major downside: you can store only the most recent image file per computer. For more details, see "Creating a System Image Backup" on page 444.

2. Choose a backup type. The easy option is the first one shown here: Let Windows Choose (Recommended). This option is selected by default, and if you click Next without changing the selection, Windows will do the following: create a system image and save it in the location you specified earlier; back up all local files that are stored in libraries, on the desktop, and in default folders within all user profiles; and create a scheduled task to repeat the backup weekly.

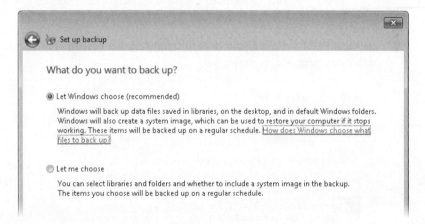

If you prefer to exercise fine-grained control over what gets backed up and when, select the second option, Let Me Choose, and then click Next. We'll describe these options in more detail in the following section.

3. Create a backup schedule. By default, the Windows Backup program runs automatically, using the same settings you just saved, at 7:00 P.M. every Sunday night. If you prefer to back up more or less frequently or at a different time, click Change

Schedule on the Review Your Backup Settings page to open the How Often Do You Want To Back Up window shown here:

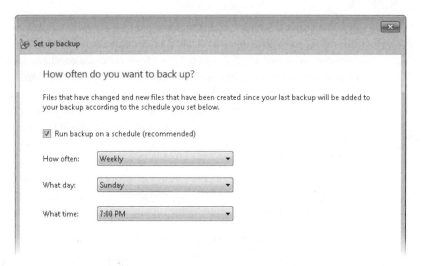

Your scheduling options are extremely limited (although you can manually edit the scheduled task if you want an option that isn't listed here). You can choose Daily, Weekly, or Monthly backups, picking a day of the week or a date each month and a time when automatic backups will take place. After the original full backup, updates to your backup set include only files that have changed since the last backup.

After the initial setup is complete, click Save Settings And Run Backup to perform the backup operation. While your backup is running, the Backup And Restore Control Panel displays its progress, as shown here:

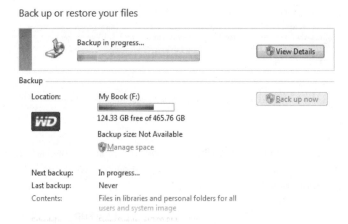

While a backup is in progress, you can click View Details to see more information and to stop the backup.

Customizing a Backup

If you choose the default settings, you can be assured that all data files in all user profiles on your PC will be backed up, along with the contents of any local folder included in a library in any user profile. (Shared network folders in a library are never backed up.) If the backup destination has sufficient room, the backup will also include an image of the system drive.

If you want more granular control of exactly which files and folders are backed up, begin setting up a new backup and click Let Me Choose when you reach the What Do You Want To Back Up window. That opens a dialog box like the one shown in Figure 12-3.

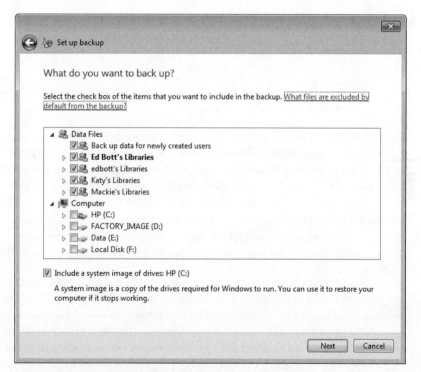

Figure 12-3 Windows Backup normally backs up only libraries and user profiles, but you can choose specific locations for backup instead.

The customization options here are divided into two hierarchies. At the top of the list is the Data Files heading, which includes an entry for each existing user account. Clear the check box to the left of any entry to remove all files from that user profile from the current backup settings. (You might want to do this if you've created an account that you use exclusively for testing and you're certain that none of the files it contains are worth preserving. If you've enabled the Guest account, you'll probably want to exclude it from backups as well.)

Although the entry for each account under the Data Files heading suggests that it includes only libraries, that description isn't entirely accurate. When you fully expand the list of available options for an entry in the Data Files list, you see a selection similar to the one shown here:

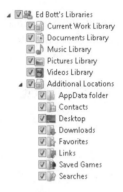

Every one of the libraries for the selected account, including the standard libraries created by Windows and any custom libraries you've created, is selected by default. You can skip one or more libraries by clearing the associated check box, but it's an all-or-nothing proposition: you can't choose to include some locations within a library and exclude others. You might want to skip backups for a specific library, especially if it's full of large files for which you have a separate backup strategy. If you're already synchronizing hundreds of gigabytes of files in the Music and Videos folders with another computer on your network, for example, you might leave those space-gobbling files out of your regular backup settings.

The entry just after the final library for each account in this list is Additional Locations. Click the arrow to its left to expand it, and you'll see that it includes the AppData folder for the selected account, which contains data files and settings that are typically created and managed by programs. Microsoft Outlook and Windows Live Mail, for example, store user data here; if this location isn't backed up, you risk losing all your e-mail messages and contacts in the event of a disk failure. Countless other programs from Microsoft and third-party software developers store user data here as well; one popular example is Mozilla Firefox, which stores user profiles and settings in a subfolder of AppData.

The other options under the Additional Locations heading represent the default folders from your user profile other than those already included in the standard libraries; Desktop, Downloads, and Favorites are included in Additional Locations, but not Documents, Music,

Pictures, and Videos, which are part of other libraries. Note that additional subfolders within your user profile folder (whether created by you or by a program) are not added to this list and thus will not be included by default in your backup settings.

For a full explanation of what's in a user profile, see "What's What and Where in a User Profile" on page 332.

INSIDE OUT Use custom libraries for foolproof backups

Do you store important data files outside your user profile? Custom libraries can help you ensure that those files are always backed up. Create a new library, call it Backup, and make sure it's selected in your current backup settings. Add locations to the new library that you want to be sure are backed up. The files themselves remain in their original location, but as long as they're on a local drive they'll be backed up. If you remove a folder from the Backup library, it will no longer be backed up. Any new folder you add here, even if it's outside your user profile, will automatically be included in your next backup.

There is one important exception: Folders and files stored on a network drive are not backed up, even if you include the folder in a library that gets backed up.

The Computer tree at the bottom of this dialog box exists for those who prefer old-school backup programs that back up everything in designated locations. The list includes every local volume on an internal hard disk (removable drives are not included). You can select an entire drive or drill into each one to include and exclude specific folders and subfolders in your backup settings.

INSIDE OUT Future-proof your backup settings

When you're setting up a new general-purpose backup routine, we recommend that you leave the first option, Back Up Data For Newly Created Users, intact. Its purpose is to make sure that your backups will include libraries and data files for any new user accounts you create in the future. If you clear this check box, only the data files and locations you specify when you create your backup settings will be backed up. When should you clear this box? If you've set up a regular backup routine specifically intended to back up only a single user's data files and some custom locations, you might want to avoid the prospect of having unwanted locations added to your backup sets later.

Chapter 12

The final option in the What Do You Want To Back Up dialog box is an option to include a system image with your backup. You can save a system image automatically with each backup or use the techniques we describe later in this chapter to create a system image on demand.

INSIDE OUT What's not backed up?

Every file on your computer that matches the criteria you select is backed up, regardless of which user account it belongs to. But not every file is included in a file backup. Even if you select every box under the Data Files and Computer headings, Windows excludes some files. For starters, files stored on any disk formatted with the FAT or FAT32 file system are ignored; drives to be backed up must be formatted with NTFS. System files are excluded, as are program files and any files in the Recycle Bin. Temporary files are backed up only on drives that are larger than 1 GB in size.

Creating a System Image Backup

With a system image backup (previously known as a Complete PC Backup in Windows Vista), you can rebuild your computer from bare metal in the event of a catastrophic failure—or if you just want to start fresh. You don't need to install, update, and activate Windows, reinstall all your applications, and then configure your applications to work the way you like; instead, you boot into the Windows Recovery Environment, choose an image file to restore, and then complete the process by restoring from your latest file backup, which is likely to be more recent than the image. The image files that Windows Backup creates are largely hardware independent, which means that—with some limitations—you can restore your backup image to a new computer of a different brand and type without missing a beat.

As we noted earlier in this chapter, you can create a system image backup as part of your regularly scheduled backup routine. However, if your goal is to quickly create a complete copy of the contents of all drives that contain Windows system files, you can do so here without having to mess with backup settings. In the Backup And Restore Control Panel, click Create A System Image in the left pane and follow the prompts to select a backup destination. The disk space requirements for an image-based backup can be substantial. Windows will warn you if the destination you choose doesn't have sufficient free disk space.

When you create a system image backup, it stores the complete contents of all selected drives during its first backup. If the backup target is a local (internal or external) hard drive, subsequent backup operations store only new and changed data. Therefore, the subsequent, incremental backup operation typically runs much faster, depending on how much data has been changed or added since the previous image backup operation. If you choose a shared network folder as the backup destination (using Windows 7 Professional, Ultimate, or Enterprise), you can save only one image backup. Any subsequent image backup wipes out the previous image backup.

INSIDE OUT   Save multiple image backups on a network

If you specify a shared network folder as the destination for an image backup, beware of the consequences if you try to reuse that location for a subsequent backup of the same computer. If the backup operation fails for any reason, the older backup will be overwritten, but the newer backup will not be usable. In other words, you'll have no backup.

You can avoid this risk by creating a new subfolder in the shared network folder to hold each new image backup. The disadvantage, of course, is that each image file will occupy as much space as the original disk, unlike an incremental image backup on an external hard drive, which stores only the changed data.

If you have multiple hard drives, Windows displays a dialog box like the one shown in Figure 12-4, in which you choose the volumes you want to include in the backup. By default, any volume that contains Windows system files is selected. You can optionally choose to include other drives in the backup image as well.

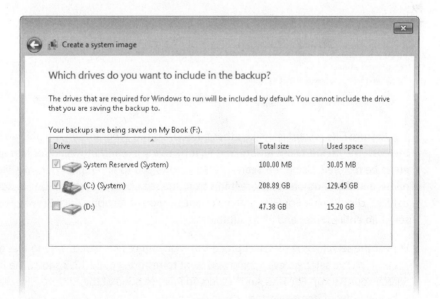

Figure 12-4 The Windows boot volume (indicated by the logo on the drive icon) and system volumes must be included in a system image. Other volumes are optional.

After you confirm your settings, click Next and then click Start Backup to begin the process of building and saving your image.

System images are stored in virtual hard disk (.vhd) format. Although the data is not compressed, it is compact because the image file does not include the hard drive's unused space and some other unnecessary files, such as hibernation files, page files, and restore points. Incremental system image backups on a local drive are not written to a separate folder. Instead, new and updated files (actually, the changed blocks in those files) are written to the same .vhd file. The older blocks are stored as shadow copies in the .vhd file, allowing you to restore any previous version.

The final step of the image backup process offers to help you create a system repair disc on a writable CD or DVD. We highly recommend that you take advantage of this option; if you don't have a blank disc or don't want to take the minute or so to create the repair disc at this point, you can do so later using the link in the left pane of the Backup And Restore Control Panel.

Restoring Files from a Backup Set

Backing up is pointless if you never need to restore a file. You should be so lucky.

To restore one or more files, open the Backup And Restore Control Panel. If the file was backed up from a location within your user profile or one of your libraries, click Restore My Files. To restore files from another user's account or to select a different backup, you need to click one of the other links here and supply an administrator's credentials.

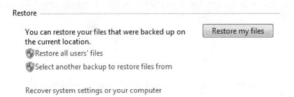

The Restore Files wizard is unlike other backup/restore programs you might have used in the past. The list starts out empty. You fill it by searching and browsing for files and folders to be restored. Using the Search button allows you to enter all or part of a file or folder name, and then add one or more items from the search results to your list. To add individual files, click Browse For Files and make one or more selections. Click Browse For Folders to select an entire folder and all its subfolders.

Repeat the search-browse-select process as many times as needed, adding files and folders until you've selected everything you want to restore. Figure 12-5 shows the Browse Or Search Your Backup For Files And Folders To Restore page of the Restore Files dialog box with a handful of items selected.

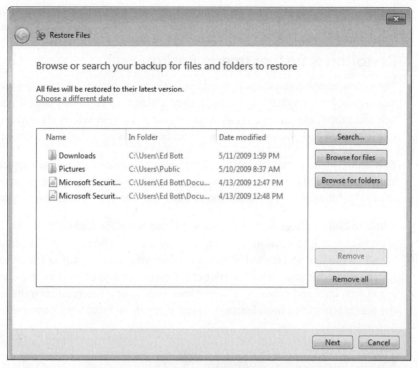

Figure 12-5 Use the three buttons to the right of this list to search or browse for files and folders you want to restore from the most recent backup.

Click Next to specify the location where you want to restore the selected files. If you're simply recovering an accidentally deleted file, you'll want to restore it to its original location; if you want to sift through a group of recovered files before deciding which ones to keep, restore them to a new folder, as shown here.

You might find it easier to restore a file by using the Previous Versions feature in Windows Explorer, as described in "Restoring Previous Versions of Files and Folders" on page 401.

Restoring a System Image Backup

The system image capabilities in Windows Backup are intended for creating an emergency recovery kit for a single PC. In that role, they function exceptionally well. If your hard drive fails catastrophically, or if you want to wipe your existing Windows installation and start with a clean image you created a few weeks or months ago, you've come to the right place.

Your options (and potential gotchas) become more complex if you want to use these basic image backup and restore tools to work with a complex set of physical disks and partitions, especially if the disk layout has changed from the time you created the original image.

In this chapter, we assume that you have created an image backup of your system disk and want to restore it to a system that is essentially the same (in terms of hardware and disk layout) as the one you started with. In that case, you can restart your computer using the system repair disc you created as part of the system image backup (or use the Windows 7 installation DVD and choose the Repair Your Computer option). Either route leads you to the dialog box shown here. Select the second option to restore your computer using a system image.

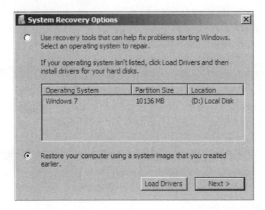

Click Next to select the image backup to restore from. If you're restoring the most recent image backup to the same system on which it was originally created *and* the backup is stored on an external hard drive attached to the computer, your job is easy. The latest system image should be available for your selection. Verify that the date and time and other details of the image match the one you want to restore, and then click Next to continue.

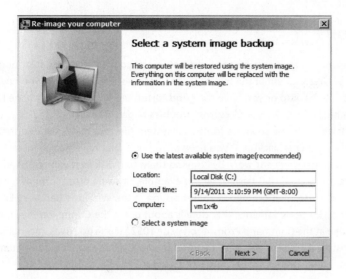

If the image file you're planning to restore from is on a network share or if you want to use a different image, choose Select A System Image and then click Next. You'll see a dialog box that lists additional image files available on local drives. Select the correct file, and click Next to select an image created on a specific date if more than one is available. If the image file you're looking for is on a shared network folder, click the Advanced button and then enter the network location and a user name and password that have authorized access to that account.

Restoring an image backup completely replaces the current contents of each volume in the image file. The restore program offers to format the disk or disks to which it is restoring files before it begins the restore process; if you have multiple drives or volumes and you're nervous about wiping out valuable data files, it offers an option to exclude certain disks from formatting.

The important point to recognize about restoring a system image is that it replaces the current contents of system volumes with the exact contents that existed at the time of the image backup you select. That means your Windows system files and registry will be returned to health (provided the system was in good shape when you performed your most recent backup and that no hardware-related issues have cropped up since then). Whatever programs were installed when you backed up your system will be restored entirely. All other files on the restored disk, including your documents, will also be returned to their prior states, and any changes made subsequent to your most recent backup will be lost.

Chapter 12

CAUTION!

If you keep your documents on the same volume as your system files, restoring a system image is likely to entail the loss of recent work—unless, of course, you have an up-to-date file backup or you have the good fortune to have made an image backup almost immediately before your current troubles began. The same is true if you save documents on a volume separate from your system files but have included that data volume in your image backup. If you have documents that have not been backed up, you can avoid losing recent work by copying them to a disk that will not be affected by the restore process—a USB flash drive, for example, or some other form of removable media. You can use the Command Prompt option in the Windows Recovery Environment to copy these documents. (For details about using the Command Prompt option, see "Working at the Command Prompt" on page 1052.) If you do have a recent file backup, you can restore files after you have restored the image backup and your system is running again.

Note

The main hardware limitation for restoring a system image backup is that the target computer must have at least as many hard drives as the source system, and each drive must be at least as big as its corresponding drive in the source system. This means, for example, that you can't restore a system image from a system that has a 500-GB hard drive to a system with a 320-GB hard drive, even if the original system had less than 100 GB of data on its drive. Keep in mind also that on a system with multiple hard drives, the BIOS determines which one is the bootable drive, and this is the one on which Windows will restore the image of your system volume. (You have no choice in the matter, aside from reconnecting the drives or, if your BIOS permits it, selecting a different bootable drive.)

If your new computer meets the space requirements, restoring a system image should work. This is true even when the source and target computers use different disk controllers, such as SCSI, PATA (IDE), or SATA. Similarly, other differences—such as different graphics cards, audio cards, processors, and so on—shouldn't prevent you from restoring a system image to a different computer because hardware drivers are isolated from the rest of the image information and are rebuilt as part of the restore process.

TROUBLESHOOTING

You can't find the backup image file

When you try to restore from a backup image stored on an external hard drive, you might discover to your horror that the image can't be found. Connect the hard drive to another computer and be sure the image files are, in fact, in the \WindowsImage-Backup folder, as expected. Then run Chkdsk on the USB drive. (Run it from a Command Prompt window or from the Tools tabs of the disk's properties dialog box in Windows Explorer.) Although rare, we've encountered situations where a (slightly) corrupted drive would not work, but the problem was resolved with Chkdsk.

Managing Saved Backups

The first time you back up files, Windows performs a complete backup of the files you specify. Subsequent scheduled backups are incremental backups, which include only new files and files that have changed. The incremental backups are stored separately from the original, complete backup, which means that—in the case of files that change—the backup set includes each file as it existed at the time of each backup. (A *backup set* comprises the original backup and all incremental backups.)

A file backup—like a system image backup—relies upon the Volume Shadow Copy Service to create a volume snapshot when a backup operation runs. This "point-in-time" image enables the backup program to reliably back up files that are open or in use and constantly changing, such as a .pst file for Microsoft Outlook data. The Volume Shadow Copy Service also keeps track of changes made between shadow copies. For more information, see "Volume Shadow Copy Service" on the Microsoft TechNet site at *w7io.com/21201*.

Backups are saved to the location you specify in a folder that has the same name as your computer. That folder contains a subfolder for each backup set; the set folder contains a subfolder for the original backup and each subsequent incremental backup, using a naming convention that includes the date and time when the backup was created. Within the backup folders, the archived files are saved in ordinary .zip files, each with a maximum size of 200 MB. This makes the data accessible even from a computer that's not running Windows 7; simply use the tool of your choice to browse the content of the .zip files. This storage method has another benefit: if you back up to removable media such as CDs and your backup spans several discs, even if one disc is damaged you can retrieve your data from all undamaged discs, thereby limiting the amount of lost data.

To see a summary of disk space in use by your current collection of backups, click Manage Space in the Backup And Restore Control Panel. The resulting display, like the one shown next, shows how much disk space is in use on the current backup destination.

Chapter 12

To see a full list of backed-up files by set, click View Backups. This dialog box allows you to delete a full set of backups from a specific period, including the initial backup and all incremental changes. Under the System Image heading, click Change Settings to remove all backed-up images or save the most recent image and delete all previous ones.

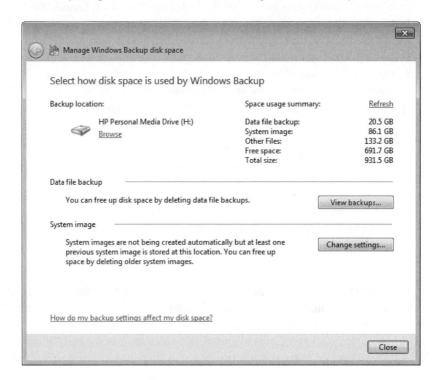

TROUBLESHOOTING

Your backup folders are "empty"

If you use Windows Explorer to browse to your backup folders, when you rest the mouse pointer over a folder name, the pop-up tip might identify it as an "Empty folder." Alarmed, you right-click the folder and choose Properties, only to find that the folder apparently contains 0 bytes, 0 files, and 0 folders. Don't worry. This is the normal condition when your backups are stored on an NTFS volume because, by default, only the System user account has permission to view the files. (That's a reasonable security and reliability precaution, which prevents you or another user from inadvertently delet-ing a key backup file.) If you're confident of your ability to work safely with backup files in their native format, the solution is simple: Double-click the folder name. Follow the prompts, including a User Account Control (UAC) consent dialog box, to permanently add your user account to the folder's permissions list, giving you Full Control access to the folder.

INSIDE OUT   Monitor backup operations with Event Viewer

You can view the results of backup operations in Event Viewer. Doing so allows you to send alerts or take other actions depending on the outcome of the backup process. In Event Viewer, you'll find these events in the Applications and Services\Microsoft\ Windows\Backup folder. For more information about Event Viewer, see "Digging Deeper with Event Viewer" on page 1023.

Implementing a Backup Strategy in a Server-Based Environment

Windows Backup, the program described in the first part of this chapter, is ideal for backing up (and restoring, when necessary) the content of a standalone computer. And in a workgroup environment (such as a small home network), it does an effective job of backing up individual workstations, either to external drives or—with one of the business editions of Windows 7—to a shared network drive.

But ensuring that all computers on your network are reliably backed up requires constant vigilance. You must periodically check the Action Center or Windows Backup on each computer to be sure that the backup process ran as scheduled and without errors. If you need to check more than a handful of computers, this oversight can become burdensome.

A server-based network provides numerous advantages over a workgroup environment, and one of the greatest advantages is the ability to let you configure server-based backups. You can configure and manage such backups from a central location, and you can configure backups to save archives on a network drive that's physically separate from the computers being backed up.

In the small office/home office space, Microsoft offers two network operating systems that include excellent client backup tools:

- **Windows Home Server 2011**   Windows Home Server (WHS) is designed for use in a home with up to 10 computers. Besides improved backup, its other benefits include the ability to easily store, organize, and share photos, videos, music, and documents; to stream media throughout your home and over the Internet; and to provide remote access over an Internet connection to computers in your home.

- **Windows Small Business Server 2011 Essentials**   Essentials is one of two editions of Windows Small Business Server 2011 (SBS), and it's promoted as an ideal first

Chapter 12

server for small businesses. It supports up to 25 users and is designed to work with online services such as hosted e-mail and Office 365.

> **Note**
>
> The other SBS edition, Windows Small Business Server 2011 Standard, includes a robust version of Windows Server Backup for backing up servers, but it does not include software for backing up other networked computers. You can use Windows Backup, as described earlier in this chapter, to store backups on a shared network drive, but this doesn't provide a centrally managed solution. You'll be better off with a third-party backup solution. Another alternative is to set up an additional server running Windows Storage Server 2008 R2, which provides client backup that is nearly identical to that in Windows Home Server 2011 and Windows Small Business Server 2011 Essentials, as described in the following sections.

In the following sections, we describe and illustrate the backup capabilities of Windows Home Server 2011. Performing backups in Windows Small Business Server 2011 Essentials works the same. Both operating systems perform a daily automatic backup of every computer on the network, and also back up the server itself.

Configuring Computers for Backup

Because backup is an integral feature of Windows Home Server and Windows Small Business Server 2011 Essentials, configuring computers to be backed up is a no-brainer. When you add a computer to the network, a process you initiate by using your web browser to open *http://server/connect* (where *server* is the computer name of your WHS or SBS server), a wizard leads you through the brief procedure.

You need to make only one choice regarding backup (see Figure 12-6); default settings take care of the rest. The server backs up all local drives (except for those formatted as FAT or FAT32), including a complete system image that allows a bare-metal restore.

To review or change the backup settings for a computer, after you've added it to the network, open the Windows Home Server 2011 Dashboard (or the SBS equivalent), click the Computers And Backup tab, and select the computer name. See Figure 12-7.

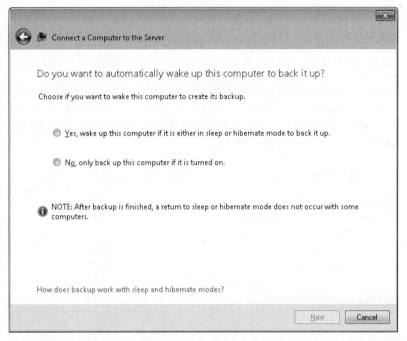

Figure 12-6 You decide whether you want the server to wake sleeping computers to be backed up.

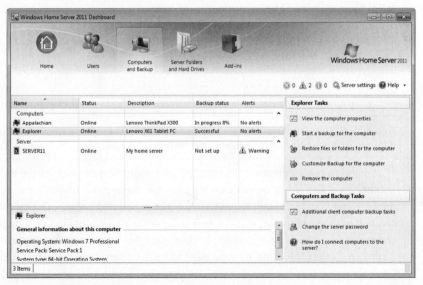

Figure 12-7 You manage backup features for all networked computers from the Computers And Backups tab in the Dashboard.

Chapter 12

Then, in the tasks pane, click Customize Backup For The Computer. In the wizard that appears, you can select which drives and folders you want backed up in a process similar to that used by Windows Backup (see "Customizing a Backup" on page 441), except it uses only the folder hierarchy and not libraries for making selections.

To modify the backup schedule, under Computers And Backup Tasks click Additional Client Computer Backup Tasks. In the dialog box that appears (see Figure 12-8), you can specify the time at which backups occur, and you can specify the number of daily, weekly, and monthly backups to be retained.

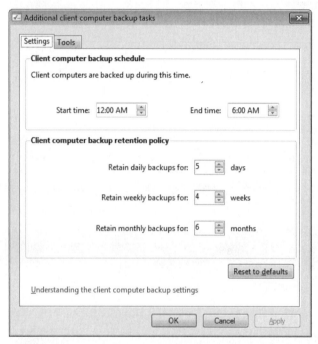

Figure 12-8 The server stores the last backup of the week and last backup of the month for the number of weeks and months you indicate here.

In addition to the automatic daily backups, you might find occasion to create a backup at another time. This might be the case if a portable computer is often disconnected from the network and you don't want to wait for the next scheduled backup. Or you might want to create a backup before you install a new program or make other major changes to your computer. To perform an immediate backup, click the Computers And Backup tab in the Dashboard, select the computer you want to back up, and then click Start A Backup For The Computer.

Alternatively, you can initiate a backup from the computer you want to back up. Open the Windows Home Server 2011 Launchpad, click Backup, and then click Start Backup.

Backing Up the Server

Backing up all the client computers is important, of course, but keep in mind that those backups are stored on the server. You'll want to back up the server not only to provide additional protection for the computer backups, but also to provide a means to restore the server itself should it suffer a hard drive failure or other data loss.

You can use an external hard drive for backup. We recommend that you cycle between two or three drives, swapping among them weekly. Store the unattached drives in a safe place away from the server. This could be an off-site location, or you might want to use a fire-proof media safe.

> **Note**
>
> Through the use of an add-in for WHS or SBS, you can back up the server to cloud-based storage, such as Amazon Simple Storage Service (Amazon S3).

To configure server backup, first connect all the external drives that you plan to use for backup. In the Dashboard, click the Computers And Backup tab, select the server, and in the tasks pane click Set Up Backup For The Server. You'll soon arrive at a dialog box that shows all connected drives, as shown in Figure 12-9. Unlike in the comparable dialog box in Windows Backup (shown earlier in Figure 12-2), you can select multiple drives here, making it easy to rotate among them when performing backups. In the next dialog box (Figure 12-10), you assign a label to each drive in the rotation. You should place a corresponding physical label on the drive case.

> **CAUTION**
>
> The wizard warns you, but we'll add our own warning: The server configuration process removes all data from the drives you will use for server backup.

In the remaining dialog boxes, you specify a schedule for server backups (the default is twice daily) and specify which folders to back up.

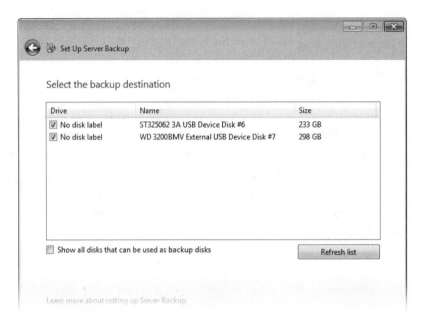

Figure 12-9 Select Show All Disks to include internal drives—but keep in mind that using an internal disk for backup doesn't provide the same measure of disaster protection as using disks that can be physically removed.

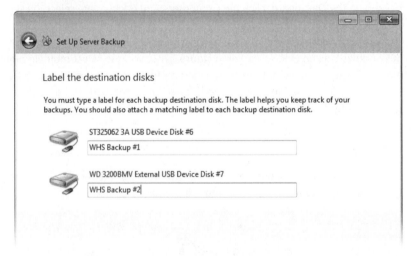

Figure 12-10 The label comes in handy when you need to restore one or more files because Windows tells you which disk to attach.

INSIDE OUT   Recover from a server failure

With a good set of server backups, you can restore a server in short order. You can restore to the same hardware or, in the case of hardware catastrophe, to a new server. You'll find step-by-step directions in "How to Perform a Bare Metal Restore on Small Business Server 2008" (which also applies to SBS 2011) at *w7io.com/21202*. If you don't have good backups, don't give up hope. A troubleshooting discussion at *w7io.com/21203* describes other data recovery techniques.

Restoring Files from a Backup

To restore one or more files, open the Dashboard, click the Computers And Backup tab, select the computer, and click Restore Files Or Folders For The Computer. In the wizard that appears, you select which backup set you want to restore from, select the folders or files you want to restore (see Figure 12-11), and then specify a restore location.

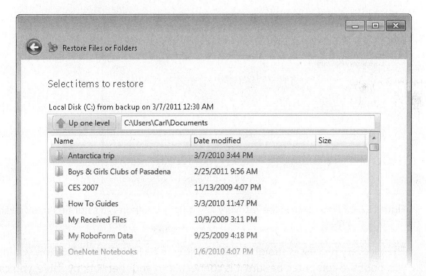

Figure 12-11 Hold down Ctrl to select multiple folders or files within a folder. Note, however, that if you go up a level or open a subfolder, your selections are lost. Therefore, to restore files from different folders, you need to run separate restore operations.

Restoring a System Image

If you need to restore a computer completely (to the same hardware or to a new computer) you create a bootable USB flash drive to initiate the process. You'll need a flash drive with a capacity of at least 512 MB.

CAUTION!

All data on the USB flash drive is deleted when you create a recovery key.

Begin at the server and run the Dashboard. On the Computers And Backup tab, click Additional Client Computer Backup Tasks. In the dialog box that appears, click the Tools tab and then click Create Key, as shown in Figure 12-12, Follow the on-screen instructions to create a bootable recovery key, and then use it to boot the computer you plan to restore. Note that you might need to make settings in the computer's BIOS to enable booting from a USB device.

Figure 12-12 You can use the recovery key on any computer; it's not tied to a specific computer or backup set.

The recovery process is straightforward, with only a few obstacles to slow you down. Before you boot the computer, be sure it is connected to your network by cable; you cannot use a Wi-Fi connection for the recovery process. When you boot, you need to know whether you're restoring a 64-bit operating system or a 32-bit version.

Configuring System Protection Options

System Restore made its first shaky appearance in the late, unlamented Windows Me. With each successive version of Windows, this important feature has taken on whole new responsibilities. System Restore is now part of a larger feature known as System Protection, whose primary job is to take periodic snapshots of designated local storage volumes. These snapshots make note of differences in the details of your system configuration (registry settings, driver files, third-party applications, and so on), allowing you to undo changes and roll back a system configuration to a time when it was known to work correctly. In Windows 7 (as in Windows Vista), the volume snapshots also include data files on designated drives. The effect of this expansion is to create real-time backups of individual data files, allowing you to recover from unwanted edits or unexpected deletions by restoring a previous version of a file or folder from Windows Explorer.

For a full description of how the Previous Versions feature works and how to use it, see "Restoring Previous Versions of Files and Folders" on page 401.

Periodically checking the status of System Protection is an essential part of a comprehensive backup strategy: Is the feature enabled and working properly on the drives where you need its protection? Is the proper amount of space set aside for it, not too much or too little?

The mechanics of System Protection in Windows 7 are substantially changed from those of its predecessors in Windows Vista and Windows XP. It uses disk space more intelligently and offers significantly more customization options. In this section, we explain how this feature works and what it backs up, how to turn it on or off for a given disk, and how to create a manual restore point.

If you're looking for step-by-step instructions on how to use System Restore to recover from a crash, see "Rolling Back to a Stable State with System Restore" on page 466. For information about recovering files that have been inadvertently edited or deleted, see "Recovering Lost, Damaged, and Deleted Files and Folders" on page 397. For technical details about the implementation of System Restore in Windows 7, see the associated MSDN reference pages "Volume Shadow Copy Service" (*w7io.com/1102*) and "System Restore" (*w7io.com/1103*).

Normally, automatic restore points are created at least once every seven days. (This is a significant change from Windows Vista, which created snapshots daily.) Restore points are also created automatically before the following major system events:

- **Installation of any application that uses an installer that complies with System Restore requirements**   In practice, any program that qualifies for the Windows Vista or Windows 7 logo will create a new restore point before performing any installation tasks (including removal).

- **Installation of any updates provided through Windows Update or Microsoft Update** System Restore creates a restore point before the installation of the update begins, whether the update is installed automatically or manually.

- **System Restore** If you choose to use System Restore to roll back to an earlier configuration, the system creates a fresh restore point first. If necessary, you can undo the restore operation by choosing the freshly created restore point.

- **Any backup operation performed by Windows Backup** Restore points are created by Windows Backup as part of both file backups and system images.

INSIDE OUT What's in a restore point?

Restore points created by Windows Vista and Windows 7 include information about changes made to any files on that volume since the previous snapshot was created. If you have enabled the option to monitor system settings, snapshots contain two additional data points: a full copy of the registry at the time of the snapshot, and a list of files that include any of 250+ file name extensions specifically designated for monitoring. This list (which cannot be modified) contains many file types that are clearly programs and system files, with extensions such as .exe, .dll, and .vbs. But it also includes other files that you might not think of as system files, including .inf and .ini, and some that are truly head-scratchers, such as .d01 through .d05 and .d32. (Apparently .d06 through .d31 are unmonitored.) The entire list is available at *w7io.com/1104*. It's most useful for programmers and system administrators, but you might want to take a look at it if you're curious why using System Restore deleted a file that you thought was perfectly safe.

To access the full set of System Restore options, open System in Control Panel and click the System Protection link in the left pane. (To go directly to the System Properties dialog box, click Start, type **systempropertiesprotection**, and press Enter.) The resulting dialog box, shown in Figure 12-13, lists all available NTFS-formatted drives (internal and external). The value under Protection Settings indicates whether restore points are being created automatically for each drive.

Using the System Properties dialog box, you can enable or disable automatic monitoring for any local drive. In addition, you can specify whether you want restore points for a given drive to include system configuration settings and previous versions of files or to save previous versions only. By design, system protection is fully enabled for the system drive and is disabled for all other local drives.

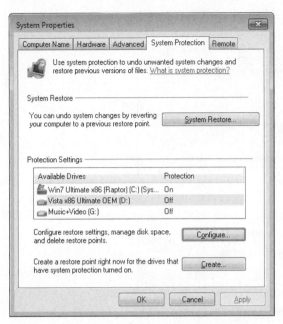

Figure 12-13 By default, System Restore monitors changes to the system drive. Select another drive and click Configure to enable System Protection for that drive.

CAUTION

System Restore is a powerful and useful tool, and you shouldn't disable it on your system drive without a good reason. If you're extremely low on disk space and a hard disk upgrade is impractical or impossible (as on some notebook computers), you might choose to do so, although you should try limiting its use of disk space, as we explain later in this section, before shutting it down completely.

If you've set aside one or more drives exclusively for data, you might want to enable the creation of automatic restore points on those drives, which has the effect of creating shadow copies of files you change or delete on that drive. This step is especially important if you've relocated one or more profile folders to drives other than the one on which Windows is installed. To enable or disable the creation of automatic restore points for a drive, open the System Properties dialog box, select the drive letter from the list under Protection Settings, and click Configure. Figure 12-14 shows the recommended settings for a secondary drive that contains data files and system image backups only. We chose the second option, Only Restore Previous Versions Of Files, rather than the default, which also tracks system settings.

Figure 12-14 For this drive, which is used to store data files only, we enabled System Protection but configured it to ignore system settings and only save previous versions of files.

The information under the Disk Space Usage heading shows both the current usage and the maximum amount of space that will be used for snapshots before System Protection begins deleting old restore points to make room for new ones. By default, a clean installation of Windows 7 sets aside space for system protection based on the size of the hard drive. On a volume larger than 64 GB, the default amount of reserved space is 5 percent of the disk or 10 GB, whichever is less. On a volume that is smaller than 64 GB, the default disk space usage is limited to a maximum of 3 percent of the drive's total space. (The minimum space required is 300 MB.)

> **Note**
>
> The disk space usage rules for system protection in Windows 7 represent a significant change over those in place for Windows Vista and Windows XP. If you upgrade a PC from Windows Vista to Windows 7, Windows does not adjust the maximum disk space settings previously in place. Thus, for an upgrade, you might discover that a given drive has reserved as much as 30 percent of your free disk space for volume snapshots. In that case, you might want to manually lower the reserved space, using the steps in this section.

To adjust the maximum amount of disk space available for volume snapshots, click the System Protection tab in the System Properties dialog box, select a drive letter from the list of available drives, click Configure, and move the Max Usage slider to the value you prefer. For drives greater than 64 GB in size, you can choose any value between 1 percent and 100 percent; for drives that are smaller than 64 GB, the minimum reserved space is 300 MB.

INSIDE OUT   Don't follow old System Restore advice

In Windows Vista, the tools for configuring system protection were relatively inflexible. By default, the system set aside 15 percent of each drive for System Restore snapshots. This value could be adjusted using the DiskPercent value in the registry key HKLM\ Software\Microsoft\WindowsNT\CurrentVersion\SystemRestore\Cfg. Although this key is created on a clean installation of Windows 7, it does not appear to have any effect. In addition, the only way to adjust the size of reserved space for System Protection files in Windows Vista was by opening an elevated command prompt and using the Vssadmin Resize Shadowstorage command. Although the Vssadmin command is still available in Windows 7, you can accomplish the same goal in much simpler fashion with the Max Usage slider in the System Protection dialog box.

You can also manually create a restore point at any time for all drives that have system protection enabled by clicking the Create button at the bottom of the System Protection tab. If you're concerned about disk space usage and you're confident that you won't need to use any of your currently saved restore points in the near future, you can click the Delete button under the Disk Space Usage heading to remove all existing restore points without changing other System Protection settings.

Note

The default location for System Restore data is *d*:\System Volume Information, where *d* is the letter of each drive. Each restore point is stored in its own subfolder, under a name that includes a unique 32-character alphanumeric identifier called a GUID. This location cannot be changed. On an NTFS drive, these files are not accessible to users, even those in the Administrators group; the default NTFS permissions grant access only to the System account, and there is no easy way to view these files or to take owner-ship of them (nor should you even consider doing so, as these data structures are not intended for use by anything other than a program working through tightly controlled application programming interfaces).

Chapter 12

If you've set up a dual-boot system with Windows XP and Windows 7 (or Windows Vista) on the same system, you should be aware of one unfortunate side effect caused by this configuration. When you boot into Windows XP, the system wipes out all restore points created by the later Windows version. New restore points are created at the usual times when you return to Windows 7, but all previous restore points are gone. This unfortunate state of affairs is caused because Windows XP doesn't recognize the format of the newer restore points; assuming they're corrupt, it deletes them and creates new ones.

INSIDE OUT   Customize System Restore intervals

As we noted earlier, Windows 7 creates restore points in response to specific system events, including the installation of a program, a device driver, or an update delivered via Automatic Updates. Using a scheduled task, the system checks at every startup and at midnight every day to see when the last restore point was created. If more than seven days have passed, the system automatically creates a new restore point. If you prefer to have regular checkpoints created more often, you can do so in either of two ways. The easiest way is to schedule a daily backup; Windows also creates a restore point with each backup. The more complicated solution involves a script and a custom scheduled task.

Create a text file using the following code:

```
Set oRP = getobject("winmgmts:\\.\root\default:Systemrestore")
newRestore = oRP.createrestorepoint ("Created by my scheduled task", 0, 100)
```

Running this script will create a restore point using the generic description "Created by my scheduled task." Save the file using a name such as Instant_RP and the file name extension .vbs. Then, using the techniques we describe in "Using Task Scheduler" on page 966, create a scheduled task to run the script at the interval you prefer.

Rolling Back to a Stable State with System Restore

In the previous section, we described how to set up the System Protection feature so that it creates regular snapshots of your system configuration. In this section, we explain how to make use of those snapshots.

The System Restore utility provides controlled access to snapshots created by the System Protection feature. It can't perform miracles—it won't bring a dead hard drive back to life, unfortunately—but it can be a lifesaver in any of the following situations:

- **You install a program that conflicts with other software or drivers on your system.**   If uninstalling the program doesn't cure the problem, you can restore your system configuration to a point before you installed the program. That should remove any problematic files or registry settings added by the program.

- **You install one or more updated drivers that cause performance or stability problems.**   Rather than using the Roll Back Driver command in Device Manager, use System Restore to replace the new, troublesome driver (or drivers) with those that were installed the last time you saved a restore point.

- **Your system develops performance or stability problems for no apparent reason.**   This scenario is especially likely if you share a computer with other family members or coworkers who have administrator accounts and are in the habit of casually installing untested, incompatible software and drivers. If you know the system was working properly on a certain date, you can use a restore point from that date, undoing any changes made since then and, if all goes well, returning your system to proper operation.

CAUTION!

Don't count on System Restore to protect you from viruses, worms, Trojan horses, and other malware. Use a reliable and up-to-date antivirus program.

Using System Restore

The quickest way to get to System Restore is to type **rstrui** at a command prompt. Here are a few alternatives:

- Open the Start menu, click All Programs, click Accessories, click System Tools, and then click System Restore.

- On the System Protection tab of the System Properties dialog box, click System Restore.

- In the Start menu search box, type **restore** and then, in the list of search results, click the System Restore shortcut under the Programs heading.

- Open Control Panel, type **system restore** in the Search box, and click Restore System Files And Settings From A Restore Point.

Chapter 12

If you're running under a standard user account, you'll need to enter an administrator's credentials in a UAC dialog box to continue.

When the System Restore wizard appears, it might recommend the most recent restore point. To see a complete list of available restore points, select Choose A Different Restore Point and click Next. If the restore point you're looking for is older than the oldest entry in the list, click Show More Restore Points to see the complete, unfiltered list, as shown in Figure 12-15.

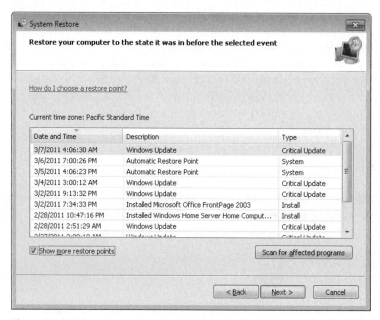

Figure 12-15 You must select the check box at the bottom of this dialog box to see more than the five most recent restore points.

What impact will your choice of restore points have? To see a full list of programs and drivers that will be deleted or restored, select the restore point you're planning to use, and then click Scan For Affected Programs. That displays a dialog box like the one shown in Figure 12-16, highlighting every change you've made since that restore point was created. This capability is new in Windows 7.

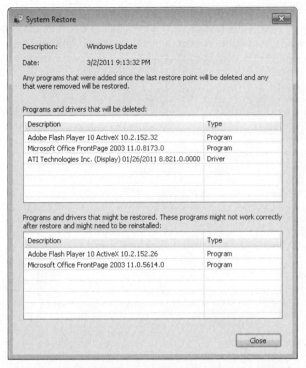

Figure 12-16 Check this report before using System Restore to roll back to an earlier configuration so that you know what changes the operation will make.

After selecting a restore point, click Next to display a confirmation dialog box like the one shown in Figure 12-17. The summary shown here lets you know which drives will be affected and gives you a chance to create a password reset disk—an important precaution if you've recently added or changed a password for your user account.

When you're satisfied, click Finish. That takes you to *one more* confirmation prompt, advising you that the restore process must not be interrupted. Answer Yes, and the system creates a new restore point and then begins replacing system files and registry settings with those in the previous restore point you selected. As part of the restore process, your computer will restart and various messages will appear, all counseling you to be patient and not to interfere with the goings-on.

When System Restore reinstates a previously saved configuration using a restore point, your data files—documents, pictures, music files, and the like—are not tampered with in any way. (The only exception is if you or a program created or saved a file using file name extensions from the list of monitored extensions, as described in the previous section.) Before System Restore begins the process of returning your system to a previous restore point, it creates a new restore point—making it easy for you to return to the present if this time machine doesn't meet your expectations.

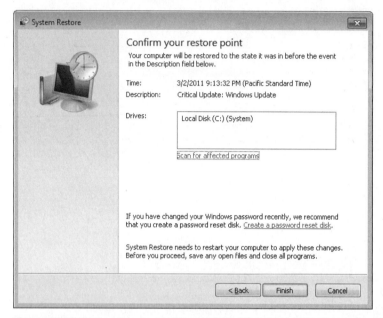

Figure 12-17 Review this description carefully. After you begin the system restore operation, it cannot be interrupted.

When the process is complete and you have logged back on to Windows 7, do some testing to see if the restoration has improved the stability of your system. If it has not and you want to return the system to the state it was in before you restored it, retrace your steps to System Restore. At or near the top of the list of available restore points, you will find one labeled Undo: Restore Operation. Choose that one and you're back where you started.

System Restore Dos and Don'ts

You don't have to be a science fiction aficionado to appreciate the hazards of time travel. Here are some to be aware of:

- If you create a new user account and then use System Restore to roll back your system configuration to a point before the new account was created, the new user will no longer be able to log on, and you will receive no warning. (The good news is that the new user's documents will be intact.)

- System Restore does not uninstall programs, although it does remove executable files, dynamic-link libraries (DLLs), and registry entries created by the installer. To avoid having orphaned program shortcuts and files, view the list of programs and drivers that will be affected when you return to the restore point you're about to roll back to. If you don't want the program anymore, uninstall it in the normal way before running the restore operation. If you want to continue using the program, reinstall it after the restore is complete.

- Any changes made to your system configuration using the Windows Recovery Environment are not monitored by System Protection. This can produce unintended consequences if you make major changes to system files and then roll back your system configuration with System Restore.

- Although you can restore your system to a previous configuration from Safe Mode, you cannot create a new restore point in Safe Mode or in the Windows Recovery Environment. As a result, you cannot undo a restore operation that you perform in either of these ways. You should use System Restore from Safe Mode or the Windows Recovery Environment only if you are unable to start Windows normally to perform a restore operation.

For information about the Windows Recovery Environment, see "Making Repairs with the Windows Recovery Environment" on page 1046.

TROUBLESHOOTING

All restore points are gone

You encounter a problem so you decide to perform a system restore. You open System Restore and, to your horror, no restore points are listed.

As noted earlier in this chapter, system restore points are deleted whenever you boot into Windows XP on a system configured for dual-boot.

But a nasty bug can also cause Windows to delete all restore points each time the system boots—even if your only operating system is Windows 7. This can occur if the page file is badly fragmented. There's no way to get those deleted restore points back, but you can prevent the problem from recurring by deleting the page file, defragmenting your hard drive, and creating a new page file. For details, see Microsoft Support article 2533911 (*w7io.com/21204*).

PART 3
Digital Media

Playing and Organizing Digital Media Files

WINDOWS 7 includes version 12 of Windows Media Player, a full-featured program that allows you to play, rip, copy, tag, rate, find, organize, synchronize, burn, and share digital media files. Windows Media Player 12 works with all sorts of media, but it's especially well suited for the task of managing digital music files.

In this chapter, we start with a list of digital media formats that can be played back directly in Windows 7 without requiring third-party software. We explain how to play music, videos, and DVDs and how to customize the Windows Media Player interface. We discuss organizational strategies and explain how to edit tags for digital downloads. We also provide instructions on the best ways to copy music from CDs to your media library, maintaining a balance between audio quality and disk space.

Throughout all four chapters in this section, we assume you've correctly installed and configured all the hardware necessary to use the features under discussion, including sound cards, speakers, CD/DVD burners, and TV tuners. We also assume that you've installed the most recent edition of Windows Live Essentials, which contains programs for managing digital photos and movies. (For details on this free collection of Windows software, see Chapter 8, "Adding Windows Live Programs and Services.")

What's in Your Edition?

Windows Media Player 12 works identically in all editions of Windows 7, with one exception: although you can watch DVDs using any edition, the required DVD decoder is not included with the Starter or Home Basic editions; you need to install a third-party decoder or upgrade to a DVD-ready Windows 7 edition before you can watch a DVD in Windows Media Player. In this chapter, we touch briefly on the basic picture importing and viewing capabilities in Windows Photo Viewer, which are identical in all editions.

TROUBLESHOOTING

You can't hear any sound from your speakers

Modern PCs often have multiple playback channels, in both digital and analog formats. Audio playback hardware can be found in a variety of locations: on your motherboard; as an optional feature on an add-in video card, with multichannel sound typically delivered over an HDMI cable; on an add-in sound card; or through headphones connected physically to a USB port or wirelessly using a Bluetooth connection. It's not unusual to find multiple audio playback options in a single PC, especially one that has been upgraded extensively.

If your hardware and drivers appear to be installed correctly but you're unable to hear any sound, right-click the speaker icon in the notification area at the right side of the taskbar and choose Playback Devices from the shortcut menu. This opens the Sound dialog box from Control Panel, with the Playback tab selected. Look for a green check mark next to the device currently designated as the default playback device. In the following example, digital audio is being delivered over the same HDMI connection that carries the video signal, and a set of USB headphones is used only for communications programs. To use headphones as the default playback device, click the Headset Earphone option (the exact wording varies depending on how the driver developer chose to implement it) and then click Set Default.

For details on how to configure hardware and install drivers to unlock the functionality of those devices, see Chapter 29, "Setting Up and Configuring Hardware."

Which File Formats and Codecs Does Windows 7 Support?

To understand digital media formats, you have to understand the difference between *container formats* and *codecs*. Container formats define the way data is stored within a media file or streamed over a network. A codec is a piece of software used to compress and decompress digital media (in fact, the word *codec* is formed by combining the first few letters from the words *compress* and *decompress)*. For Windows to play back a sound or video clip, it must be able to open the format and process its compressed contents. As a result, you might find that some files in supported container formats can't be played back in Windows Media Player because the required codec is not available.

Windows Media Player 12 can play back a long list of media file formats and supports many widely used codecs. The list of supported formats includes every one that was available in Windows Media Player 11 with Windows Vista and Windows XP. Windows 7 adds support for some popular formats that required third-party playback programs in previous Windows versions. Table 13-1 lists the newly supported file types.

Table 13-1 File Formats Newly Supported in Windows Media Player 12

File Type	File Name Extension(s)	Description
3GPP/3GPP2 Audio/Video	.3gp, .3gpp, .3g2, .3gp2	Allows delivery and playback of multimedia over 3G wireless networks.
ADTS Audio	.aac	Used for streaming audio content from media players or websites in Advanced Audio Coding (AAC) or MPEG-4 Audio formats.
AVCHD Video	.m2t, .m2ts, .mts	High-definition video container format used by many portable video recorders. It typically uses the H.264 video compression codec (also known as MPEG-4 AVC).
MP4 Video	.m4v, .mp4, .mp4v	This widely used high-definition video container format typically uses H.264 video compression.
MPEG-2 TS Video	.ts, .tts	A streaming format used to deliver synchronized digital audio and video; commonly used in European digital TV systems.
MPEG-4 Audio	.m4a	Also known as Advanced Audio Coding (AAC), this is the default format used by Apple's iTunes software and online music store; files in this format that use Apple's FairPlay copy protection are not supported, nor are those that use Apple Lossless Format.
QuickTime Movie	.mov	A container format used by many portable video cameras.

As you can see from this list, the changes in Windows Media Player 12 will be especially welcome to anyone who has purchased unprotected music from Apple's iTunes Store. Files in this format can now be included in a Windows Media Player Music library and played back alongside those in the MP3 and Windows Media Audio (WMA) formats. In addition, Windows Media Player 12 now directly supports the most common high-definition video formats, especially those that use the H.264 video compression codec. Finally, if you have a digital camera that records video to a flash memory card in the QuickTime Movie (file extension .mov) or AVCHD formats, you can now play those files directly in Windows without installing third-party software.

These improvements, while welcome, do not begin to cover every available audio and video format. Digital media enthusiasts in particular are likely to need additional software to play back formats that aren't supported directly.

Adding and Updating Codecs

A default installation of Windows Media Player includes codecs that can handle most widely used formats and is capable of downloading updated codecs automatically. You can also download and install third-party codecs that are designed to work with Windows Media Player but are not endorsed or supported by Microsoft. You do so at your own risk—a buggy codec can cause the Player to crash, freeze, or suffer reduced performance, even when working with clips in a format completely different from the one supported by the rogue codec.

Enthusiasts who rip and share digital video files are the most common source of codec-related issues with Windows Media Player. Some enthusiast sites offer so-called codec packs, which install a collection of third-party codecs that have the potential to cause at least as many problems as they solve. Before you install one of these packages, we recommend that you research it extensively—and, of course, have a backup image ready. In some cases, especially when playing content that was encoded using an older media-authoring program, you might decide to take the risk and install an untested codec. If you do, be sure to set a restore point first. (For more details on how to use System Restore, see "Configuring System Protection Options" on page 461.)

The two most commonly used video codecs, both of which are frequently used in AVI files, are DivX and Xvid. Windows Media Player 12 includes support for these codecs as part of its H.264 package. In some cases, however, files produced using these codecs are saved in container formats that are incompatible with Windows 7; this is the case with the Matroska Video file type (.mkv), which requires additional software to play back using Windows Media Player. For more information about these codecs, along with download and installation instructions, visit the DivX website at *divx.com* and the Xvid home page at *xvid.org*. If you're curious about Matroska, you'll find specifications, FAQs, and downloads at *matroska.org*.

When you first run Windows Media Player, one of the custom setup options allows you to pick and choose which file formats to associate with it; you can review and change these options any time by opening the Default Programs option from Control Panel or the Start menu, clicking Set Your Default Programs, and choosing Windows Media Player from the list of programs.

On a clean installation of Windows 7, the listing for Windows Media Player should read This Program Has All Its Defaults. If you've used any third-party media software since installing Windows, it's possible that another program might have taken control of some media file formats. In that case, the description in the right half of the Set Default Programs dialog box will look like the one shown in Figure 13-1. As the dialog box indicates, this installation of Windows Media Player has 46 of its 53 defaults. The remaining seven file types normally handled by Windows Media Player are now controlled by the Zune software on this computer.

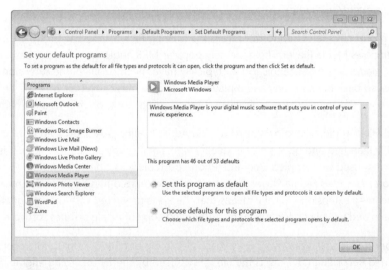

Figure 13-1 If you install other media software, such as Microsoft's Zune program, it might take control of formats normally owned by Windows Media Player.

To restore all default file associations for Windows Media Player, click Set This Program As Default. To inspect (and if necessary adjust) settings individually, click Choose Defaults For This Program.

Popular container formats supported in Windows 7 include Advanced Systems Format files, which can contain audio, video, or both. Windows Media Audio (file name extension .wma) and Windows Media Video (.wmv) are ASF files that have been compressed using Windows Media Audio and Windows Media Video codecs, respectively. Files in either format can be packaged using digital rights management (DRM) and can be encoded at various levels of quality (which in turn affects the disk space used per file). The generic .asf file name extension indicates that the file was compressed with a different codec and that ASF is simply a "wrapper" around the actual codec.

Windows Media metafiles are XML files that can be created and viewed in a plain text editor. They're typically designed to be redirectors, which allow Windows Media Player to open and play streaming media sources on web servers. The file name extensions typically end in *x*: .asx, .wax, .wvx, .wmx.

Audio Video Interleave (.avi) and QuickTime Movie (.mov) are widely used container formats used to play back video clips (with or without audio tracks) on Windows-based computers. AVI is a Microsoft-developed format, whereas QuickTime was developed by Apple. Support for QuickTime Movie files in Windows Media Player 12 is primarily designed for compatibility with portable cameras that use this format for recording. For files in this format that you encounter on the web, you might still need Apple's QuickTime Player (*apple.com/quicktime*).

A group of widely used formats from the Moving Pictures Experts Group are supported in Windows Media Player. The extremely popular MP3 audio format is the best known. Digital media files that use this format typically have the .mp3 file name extension and can be played back in nearly any audio player or portable music jukebox. MPEG-2 encoded video files are DVD quality and typically use .mpeg, .mpg, .mpv, or .m2v as a file name extension.

MPEG-4 Audio, also known as Advanced Audio Coding (AAC), evolved from the popular MP3 standard and boasts higher quality with significantly smaller file sizes. It is the default format used with Apple's iPod and iPhone portable music devices and the iTunes online store. Windows Media Player plays back AAC-formatted files that use the .m4a extension; the .m4p extension typically means that the file is protected with digital rights management and will play back only in an authorized copy of Apple's iTunes software.

For recorded TV, Windows 7 plays back files in either of two formats. Microsoft Digital Video Recording (.dvr-ms) is the file format used by the TV recording engine in older versions of Windows Media Center. Windows TV (.wtv) is the file format used by the TV recording engine included with Windows Media Center in Windows 7.

TV recording is enabled only in Windows Media Center and requires a TV tuner. For more details, see "Recording and Watching TV" on page 556.

And finally: When is a media file format not a file format at all? When it's a CD audio track. If you open an audio CD in Windows Explorer, you'll see each track listed as a CD Audio file, with the file name extension .cda. These files are representations of audio tracks, and they cannot be copied to the Windows file system in their native format or played back except from an audio CD.

Using Windows Media Player

Windows Media Player has been a part of Microsoft Windows for nearly two decades. Through the years, Microsoft has steadily improved its capabilities, polished its design, and tightened its links to other parts of Windows. All editions of Windows 7 include Windows Media Player 12.

You can use Windows Media Player to play sound and video files stored on a local disk (including removable media such as flash drives, CDs, and DVDs) or stream the output across a network (or over an Internet connection) to and from other computers, servers, or devices. You can *rip* tracks from audio CDs (that is, copy them to your hard disk) in a broad range of quality levels, create custom CDs using a CD or DVD drive that has recording capabilities, and download songs to a portable audio player, as long as it isn't an iPod or a Zune. You can use the player as a jukebox to listen to all your favorite songs, in custom sequences that you devise (called playlists) or in random order. If you have a DVD drive, you can use the Player to screen your favorite movies and concert videos on a desktop or portable PC.

Windows Media Player also serves as the engine for other media-related features in Windows 7. For example, when you use Windows Media Center to play music, view pictures, or watch a video, Windows Media Player is actually doing the work in the background.

The arrangement of the basic building blocks in Windows Media Player hasn't changed much over the past decade, although its visual design is greatly streamlined and much more sophisticated in Windows 7. For the most part, you'll switch between two primary views of Windows Media Player. The Player Library view, shown in Figure 13-2, is used to browse, search, and arrange your media library. It consists of five main elements, some of which might be hidden:

- **Address bar**   Contains a breadcrumb trail that helps you find your current place in the library. The Back and Forward buttons to the left of the address bar work just as they do in Internet Explorer. Below the address bar is a toolbar whose contents change depending on the current selection. At the right of the toolbar is a search box.

- **Navigation pane**   This customizable, resizable pane serves the same basic function as its counterpart in Windows Explorer. You can choose any major node in the media library, select removable media such as CDs and DVDs, work with portable devices, and view any libraries that are available over the network.

- **Details pane**   The contents of this pane change depending on the type of content you select from the library and which view is applied. In Windows Media Player 12, the Now Playing option is no longer available for this pane.

- **List pane**   This resizable pane displays the contents of the current playlist when the Play tab is selected. The Burn and Sync tabs allow you to create or edit a list of tracks to be burned to a CD (or DVD) or transferred to a compatible portable device, respectively. An info box above the list shows album art for the current track. Click any tab to show or hide its associated list.

- **Playback controls**   Manage playback of audio and video files, using DVD-style controls to play, pause, fast-forward, and rewind files; this area also includes a variety of special-purpose buttons that control volume and the appearance of the Player. If a file is playing, details appear to the left of the controls. The button to the right of the playback controls allows you to quickly switch from Library view to Now Playing view.

Figure 13-2 Five basic elements of the Windows Media Player interface.

INSIDE OUT
For the list pane, wider is better

Making the list pane wider also makes it more informative. As you expand the pane's width, it displays additional fields. When you are playing music, for example, the default list shows the song title and playing time for each track on the list; for most tracks, all or part of the artist's name is also visible (in gray). When you drag the left border of the pane to its maximum width, the graphical one-to-five-star ratings appear on the list. Because the rating field is "live," you can click to adjust each track's star rating as you listen to an album or a playlist.

The toolbar beneath the address bar offers access to Windows Media Player features and options specific to the part of the library you're currently working with. General options (including the ability to change the layout and choose which columns are visible) can be found on the Organize menu. The same options are also available via more conventional menus, which are normally hidden. To make these menu choices visible temporarily in the form of a cascading menu, tap the Alt key. To show or hide the menu bar with its traditional pull-down menus, press Ctrl+M or press Alt and click Show Menu Bar.

After you begin playing an album or a playlist, you can click the Switch To Now Playing button in the lower right corner of the Player Library view. That immediately changes the view to the minimal one shown here, with a 240-by-240 pixel album cover, basic playback controls, a display of the track/album name above the cover, and a Switch To Library button in the top right corner that takes you back to the full Player Library view.

The search box allows you to search the library for any item in the currently selected category. If you begin your search with a particular view already selected, the text you enter in the search box filters that view only. So, if you select the Artist view under the Music heading in the navigation pane and type **Dylan** in the search box, you'll see all items where that name appears in the Artist field. If you start from the main heading for the Music library, however, the search results show matches for song titles and albums as well.

INSIDE OUT Find hidden information in the playback controls

The playback controls at the bottom of the Player window illustrate the universal advice for Windows tinkerers: when in doubt, click and right-click. If you follow that advice, you'll be amply rewarded. Clicking the icon in the lower left corner while a music track is playing, for instance, cycles through a tiny thumbnail of the album cover art, an icon that indicates whether the track is playing from a local file or streaming from a network server, and a miniature frequency spectrum. Hover the mouse pointer over this region to see the bit rate of the current track. Click the time indicator to cycle through different views of elapsed and remaining time. Right-click the Play/Pause button to choose slow, normal, and fast playback modes. If you're ripping a CD, a progress indicator to the right of the playback controls tells you how many tracks remain to be ripped; click the message to jump directly to the track list from the CD.

The keyboard shortcuts Ctrl+1 and Ctrl+3 also allow you to switch between the Player Library and Now Playing views. Ctrl+2 takes you to the decidedly retro Skin view, a feature that never quite caught on; it continues to exist only for backward compatibility, and we don't cover it in this book.

Playing Music

When you play back a music file or an audio CD in Windows Media Player, the playback controls look and function like those on common consumer devices, such as CD and DVD players.

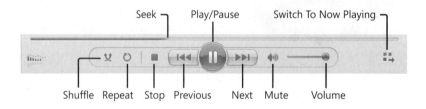

The oversized Play button becomes a Pause button (as shown here) while a track is playing. The Mute button is a toggle; click one time for silence, a second time for sound. The Next and Previous buttons move ahead and back one item within the current playlist. Click and hold the Next button to fast-forward through the current track. You can drag the Seek slider in the blue progress bar just above the playback controls to move to a different place within the item that's currently playing. For example, to start the current track over again, drag the Seek slider all the way to the left.

The Player plays the current playlist—which might be an album from your library, a CD, or a selection of tracks you've picked individually—in order, once, unless you turn on Shuffle or Repeat (or both):

- If you turn on Shuffle by clicking the Shuffle button on the playback bar, by pressing Ctrl+H, or by choosing Play, Shuffle, the Player moves through the playlist in random order.

- If you turn on Repeat by clicking the Repeat button on the playback bar, by pressing Ctrl+T, or by choosing Play, Repeat, the Player plays the current playlist continuously—that is, it repeats the playlist each time it finishes the final track. As we explain later in this chapter (see "Working with Playlists" on page 490), you can configure playlist options so that any tracks you skip on the initial pass are also skipped on repeat passes.

Playing an audio CD in Windows Media Player is almost as easy as playing it on any conventional CD player: insert disc, close drive, enjoy music. The *almost* has to do with your CD (or DVD) drive's AutoPlay settings. If you have set up your system so that the default AutoPlay action for audio CDs is Play Audio CD Using Windows Media Player, your disc starts playing within a few moments after you insert it (provided that the Player is not busy doing something else). If you haven't chosen a default AutoPlay action for audio CDs, Windows displays the AutoPlay dialog box. To set the AutoPlay default and begin playing the CD in one action, leave the Always Do This For Audio CDs check box selected and click Play Audio CD Using Windows Media Player.

For more details on how to change default AutoPlay settings for specific media types, see "Setting Default Programs, File-Type Associations, and AutoPlay Options" on page 195.

Windows 7 and Digital Photography

In this chapter, we talk mostly about digital music and videos, and in Chapter 15, "Using Windows Media Center," we dig deeper into recorded TV. That covers all but one of the nodes in the Windows Media Player navigation pane. So why is there a Pictures heading? No one expects you to browse or view digital photos using Windows Media Player, but you can create and edit playlists made from photos, which can then be played back in Windows Media Center.

Windows 7 by default includes only the most basic tools for working with digital photos. Windows Photo Viewer allows you to import pictures from a digital camera, view them in a resizable window, play a basic slide show, attach a picture to an e-mail message, and burn pictures to a data CD or DVD. For more advanced tasks, such as editing and cropping a photo or removing red-eye from flash photos of people, you need to install a more advanced program. If you don't have a preferred third-party alternative, we strongly encourage you to download and install Windows Live Photo Gallery, which we describe in more detail in "Using Windows Live Photo Gallery" on page 310.

If you're a digital photo enthusiast, we also encourage you to take a look at Windows Media Center. It offers some rudimentary editing tools, but its real hidden gem is the capability, new in Windows 7, to create and play custom slide shows or just play favorites based on your ratings. We discuss all of these scenarios in Chapter 15.

Watching Videos and DVDs

Windows 7 Home Premium and higher editions contain everything you need to watch standard DVDs in Windows Media Player. For Starter and Home Basic editions, you need to add a small but crucial software decoder before DVDs will play back properly. (This same software is required to play back videos recorded in MPEG-2 format.) Typically, this decoder is included with DVD playback software, which is often provided by the PC manufacturer. For this chapter, we assume you have a suitable decoder already installed.

After all the requisite hardware and software is in place, playing a DVD movie in Windows Media Player is as transparently simple as playing an audio CD. If Windows Media Player is the AutoPlay application for DVD movies, it starts automatically and begins playing your movie. If it isn't, start Windows Media Player yourself. Then click Library, click the icon for the DVD in the navigation pane, and click Play. You can also click the Videos library in the navigation pane and choose a file saved in your Videos library.

Note

In this chapter, we *don't* discuss playback of high-definition content on Blu-ray discs. Windows 7 includes some support for data storage on Blu-ray media, but it does not include the software needed to play movies distributed in this format. For that, you need a compatible drive, a display adapter and video driver that explicitly support Blu-ray playback, a display that supports High-Bandwidth Digital Content Protection (HDCP), and a third-party player program. For Windows 7, we're aware of three software publishers that offer programs designed to add Blu-ray playback to Windows: CyberLink Software makes PowerDVD (*w7io.com/1203*), ArcSoft offers Total Media Theater (*w7io.com/1201*), and Corel offers a program formerly developed by Inter-Video, WinDVD (*w7io.com/1202*). Blu-ray playback is an option typically available only in the most advanced (and expensive) of these products. We recommend that you spend some time reading reviews and user forums before settling on one.

For information on using Windows Media Center to play DVDs, see "CDs, DVDs, and Devices" on page 555.

While your movie is playing in Windows Media Player, playback controls appear at the bottom of the Player, with title information and a Switch To Library button in a black bar across the top, as shown in Figure 13-3. Right-click anywhere in the Player window and use the shortcut menu to show or hide the DVD title and chapter list. This list provides one means of navigation within the movie—you can jump to a particular chapter by double-clicking it on the Play tab of the list pane. You can also get to the movie's own menu screens by clicking the DVD button (to the left of the playback controls) or by clicking the arrow to the right of the DVD button and choosing Root Menu or Title Menu.

Use the playback controls to play or pause your movie, to fast-forward or rewind, or to adjust the volume. To jump to the DVD menu (which typically includes options for choosing the language of the soundtrack, adjusting audio settings, and showing subtitles), click the DVD icon at the bottom of the Now Playing screen, to the left of the playback controls, or choose View, DVD Features. (Remember, the traditional menus are normally hidden; to make them visible tap the Alt key.) You can also adjust the soundtrack and subtitles from the Play menu by choosing Audio And Language Tracks or Lyrics, Captions, And Subtitles.

Figure 13-3 DVD playback and navigation controls are readily accessible within the Player window, but they distract from the playback experience.

To fully appreciate the DVD playback experience, you probably don't want to see any part of the Player except the portion that shows the movie itself. Click the View Full Screen button to switch from the Player window to a full-screen display. You can toggle between these views by double-clicking the movie or by pressing Alt+Enter.

In full-screen mode, the playback controls along the bottom of your screen normally fade from view after a few seconds and reappear whenever you move the mouse. The controls remain visible when you cause them to reappear while playback is paused. To switch back to a window, double-click the playback window or press Alt+Enter again.

Customizing the Navigation Pane

If you used Windows Media Player 11 in Windows XP or Windows Vista, you'll find the navigation pane in Windows Media Player 12 more consistent in its organization and certainly easier to use. The top of the list contains your existing playlists, followed by media libraries arranged by category. Any currently connected portable devices appear at the bottom of the navigation pane. Shared libraries from other PCs or devices appear in a separate group below your local libraries, with the list of available online stores at the bottom of the pane.

If you find this lengthy list overly cluttered (or, conversely, if you find that one or more of your favorite options are missing), you can customize it. To see all available options for changing which items are visible here, click Organize and then click Customize Navigation Pane. This opens the dialog box shown in Figure 13-4.

Chapter 13

Figure 13-4 Use this dialog box to change which libraries and views are visible in the navigation pane.

Each bold-faced entry in the list represents a top-level node in the navigation pane. Underneath each heading is a list of available views. By default, every top-level node is visible, but most views are hidden—only three views under the Music heading are shown by default. If you don't want to see a particular node (Other Media or Pictures, for example), clear the check box to its left. If you want to see a particular view for a given heading, including the ability to browse your Music library by folder, select the check box for that view.

To remove all shared network libraries from the navigation pane, right-click the Other Libraries heading and choose Hide Other Libraries. To hide the entry for an individual user's library, right-click its name beneath the Other Libraries heading and choose Remove From List. To restore the Other Libraries hierarchy, open the Customize Navigation Pane dialog box, choose Other Libraries from the drop-down list at the top of the dialog box, and click Show Other Libraries.

The View Options menu above the details pane, to the left of the search box, allows you to customize the display of information in a given view, in much the same way that Windows Explorer works with files. In the default views of the Music library, you can switch between Icon, Tile, and Details arrangements (or Expanded Tiles if you select the main Music heading). The Details option provides a plain list of albums, artists, or genres, with no album art or thumbnails. You can also customize the list of columns visible in the details pane: right-click the visible column headings and then click Choose Columns, or click Organize, Layout, and then click Choose Columns. As Figure 13-5 shows, you can use this option to display a Yes/No field in the Protected column (identifying tracks that are copy-protected with Windows Media DRM) and to show the file path. Clicking a column heading to sort on one of these fields allows you to quickly locate groups of media files that meet a common criterion.

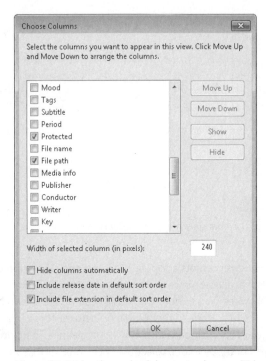

Figure 13-5 Use these check boxes to show or hide columns in Details view.

Working with Playlists

A *playlist* is a customized list of digital media files that Windows Media Player can play back as a unit, in either linear or random order. If you want to combine tracks from multiple albums or rearrange the order of tracks on a CD, you use a playlist. Windows Media Player 12 also supports (indeed, requires) using playlists for creating custom CDs and for synchronizing files with a portable device.

For a more detailed discussion of burn lists, see "Burning Music and Other Media to CDs and DVDs" on page 529. For more on how to use playlists as sync lists, see "Synchronizing Digital Media with Portable Devices" on page 520.

You can build a playlist on the fly for a specific purpose—to cue up music for a party, for example, or to burn a custom CD to play in the car. After the task is done, you can clear the list or save it for reuse. Saved lists are stored by default in the Playlists subfolder of the current user profile's My Music folder. You can also create and save Auto Playlists, which are essentially saved searches whose results are updated automatically each time you open them.

INSIDE OUT ### Separate duplicate albums in different formats

Your library might contain multiple copies of the same album (or of different tracks from a single album). If you rip a CD to your collection using WMA format or buy an album from the iTunes Store in AAC format, you might decide to make an MP3 copy for ease of use with devices that don't support the original format. By default, Windows Media Player sorts these duplicates for you, as shown here. If you don't like this behavior, you can disable it by opening the Choose Columns dialog box (shown in Figure 13-5) and clearing Include File Extension In Default Sort Order.

Creating and Editing Custom Playlists

The current playlist appears in the list pane at the right of the Player window. (If the list pane isn't visible, click the Play tab; click the Play tab again to hide the list pane if it's currently showing.) Use the navigation pane, the search box, or another playlist to choose which tracks you want to include, and then use any of the following techniques to create a custom playlist:

- Drag individual songs, albums, playlists, or artists from anywhere in the details pane and drop them in the list pane.

- Select one or more tracks, albums, or artists; right-click and then click Add To, Play List. The shortcut menu also includes options to send the current selection to the burn list or sync list or to add the selected items to any existing playlist.

- Double-click any album. It begins playing, and its contents appear in the Now Playing list in the list pane, where you can add or remove tracks or rearrange the order of tracks on the album.

- Select one or more supported media files in Windows Explorer, and then drag them into the list pane; or right-click and then click Add To, Windows Media Player List on the shortcut menu. Click the Play or Burn buttons in the Windows Explorer toolbar to add the selected tracks to the current playlist or burn list, respectively.

- To remove tracks you've added to the playlist, select one or more items, right-click, and click Remove From List.

You can drag items up and down in the list to change their order. When you're satisfied with the arrangement, click Save List at the top of the list pane, enter a descriptive name, and press Enter.

Use the drop-down List Options menu at the top of the list pane (shown in Figure 13-6) to sort list items, randomly shuffle the list, or save the playlist as a file in a location of your choosing. Use the Clear List button to start fresh, removing the list contents immediately, with no confirmation required.

Figure 13-6 Use this drop-down menu to sort, shuffle, or save the current playlist. Clear the list to start over.

Windows Media Player 12 introduces a nifty option for handling items you skip while playing back an unsaved playlist. This option might be useful if you created a large playlist from a diverse selection of albums and randomly shuffled its contents. As you play it back, you skip individual tracks that don't fit with the flow of the playlist. When you eventually click Save List, Windows Media Player displays the dialog box shown here.

Note that skipped items within the list appear in gray. You can save the playlist exactly as it appears in the list pane or remove the skipped items before saving. The Skip During Playback option doesn't affect the saved list; instead, it tells Windows Media Player to remember which items you skipped during the current playback session and skip them if you replay the list. If you close or clear the list, all indications of skipped tracks are discarded.

Saved playlists appear at the top of the navigation pane. By default, the Playlists section of the navigation pane shows only the five most recently used playlists. You can customize the navigation pane to show all playlists or none. (See "Customizing the Navigation Pane" on page 488 for instructions.) When you select a playlist from the navigation pane, the items that make up the list appear in the details pane, where you can edit the properties of individual items or assign star ratings. In this view, you can right-click and use the Remove From List option on the shortcut menu to winnow the list down; you can also sort by any heading and manually change the order of items in the playlist. Any additions, deletions, or changes in track order that you make to the list in the details pane are saved immediately.

Using Auto Playlists

Playlists you create using Windows Media Player can retrieve results dynamically on the basis of criteria you define. Unlike regular playlists, which are static and define a list of specific tracks in a specific order, Auto Playlists are saved searches that return different results depending on the current contents of your library. You can use Auto Playlists to find tracks that you added recently but have not yet rated, for instance, or to create a playlist of tracks from a specific genre or by a specific artist that you've also rated highly. Details of each Auto Playlist you create are stored in an XML file in the default Playlists subfolder. Copy that file to another computer, and the Auto Playlist becomes available on that computer as well.

To create a new Auto Playlist from any library view, click the down arrow to the right of Create Playlist on the toolbar, and then click Create Auto Playlist. Enter a name in the box at the top of the New Auto Playlist dialog box, and then begin clicking to add criteria to your search. By default, every new Auto Playlist includes Music In My Library as the first criterion. Start with the first green plus sign, and use drop-down lists to define criteria. After you click OK to save the list, you can right-click and choose Edit to adjust the criteria. In the example shown in Figure 13-7, we created an Auto Playlist that includes songs that are performed by a trio of our favorite female artists and are all rated four stars or better.

> ### Note
> If you used Windows Easy Transfer to migrate your Windows settings from Windows XP, your collection includes a group of preset Auto Playlists, all of which are stored in the My Playlists folder. Windows Media Player seamlessly combines the contents of these two lists in the library. In fact, selecting Playlists from the navigation pane shows all saved playlists from any folder in any monitored location.

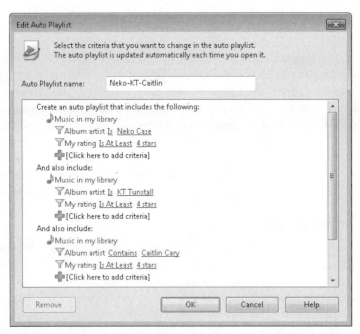

Figure 13-7 Build an Auto Playlist one criterion at a time. Enter each criterion in its own branch, and then click OK to save.

When you create an Auto Playlist, all criteria within a single group must be satisfied for the Player to add matching items to the playlist results. When you create different groups of criteria, the Player combines them with a logical OR. Thus, any track that matches all the criteria within any one group gets added to the list. The group of criteria at the bottom of the Auto Playlist window allows you to restrict the playlist itself to a maximum size, number of items, or playing time.

TROUBLESHOOTING

The file name for a playlist doesn't match its display name

When you create a playlist (regular or Auto), the text you enter before you first save the list is used in two places. The playlist title appears between the <title> and </title> tags in the XML file that contains the playlist definition. The player also uses that text as the file name that gets saved into the Playlists folder. You can rename the saved playlist within Windows Media Player (for an Auto Playlist, you can also change its name in the Edit Auto Playlist dialog box). In either case, however, your change is written only to the XML file; the file name remains the same. To rename the file itself, right-click the playlist name, click Open File Location, and then rename the file in Windows Explorer.

Importing and Exporting Playlists

When you click the Save List button, your playlist is saved as an XML file in Windows Media Playlist format, with a .wpl extension. You'll find the file itself in the Playlists subfolder of whatever folder is set as the save location in your Music library. If you use the Save List As choice on the List Options menu, you can choose M3U Playlist (.m3u) as an alternative format. This is a wise choice if you suspect that you'll play your playlists on a different device or in a program that doesn't support the Windows Media Playlist format.

Windows Media Playlist files use XML tags to specify the file name of each track in the list. Each track also includes the globally unique IDs—the two long alphanumeric strings—that define the track and its associated album. By contrast, M3U files are plain text. In either format, the saved playlist uses relative path references for each track that is saved on the same drive as the Playlists folder. Any track stored on a different drive (including shared network folders) is represented by its fixed file path. When you move a playlist to a new computer, Windows Media Player might have trouble locating the files you're trying to play if they're in a different location than they were on the other machine.

If you use the Zune software, it automatically creates its own versions of playlists that you create in Windows Media Player; for details, see "Mastering the Zune Software" on page 570.

Ripping CDs

Windows Media Player can copy, or *rip*, tracks from audio CDs and store them as files on your hard disk. The copies you make are completely unrestricted: you can listen to the saved tracks on your PC, burn a collection of tracks to a custom CD, or copy those tracks to another PC or to a portable device. Before you use Windows Media Player to rip your first CD, however, it's smart to answer the following questions:

- What format do you want to use?

- At what bit rate should you copy?

- Where should you store your files?

- What naming convention do you want to use?

Your answers to the questions in the preceding list dictate specific settings in Windows Media Player. We discuss each of these settings in more detail in this section. You can adjust settings any time—changing to a different, higher-quality format before ripping a CD you're especially fond of, for instance.

Before you can rip an audio CD, you have to insert the disc in your CD or DVD drive. When Windows Media Player recognizes the presence of an audio CD, it adds the CD's icon to the navigation pane. Click that icon, and you'll see a list of tracks on the CD. To copy the tracks on the CD to matching files on your hard disk using the currently selected file format, bit rate, naming scheme, and location, click Rip CD on Windows Media Player's toolbar. (Note that you can play a CD and rip it at the same time.)

When you're connected to the Internet, Windows Media Player consults its online data sources to determine the name of your disc, as well as the names of the artist(s) and tracks and the genre of music the disc contains. This information is used to automatically tag and name tracks you rip to your collection from CD.

We discuss the ins and outs of metadata and how to edit tags in more detail later in this chapter; see "Managing Metadata and Album Art" on page 504.

By default, Windows Media Player selects the check boxes to the left of all track names when you choose to copy a CD to disk. To copy particular tracks only, clear the check boxes beside tracks that you don't want to copy. To clear or select all the check boxes at once, click the check box in the column heading.

To begin ripping, click Rip CD. Copying begins immediately. Entries in the Rip Status column tell you which tracks are pending, which are being copied, and which have been ripped to the library. You can do other things in Windows Media Player while this is going on, including listening to an album or a playlist from your library.

Windows Media Player copies each CD track to a separate file and stores it, by default, in the Music folder of the currently logged-on user (%UserProfile%\Music). The Player uses the information about each track—the name of the artist, album, and song, for instance—as downloaded via the Internet from the Windows Metadata service and inserts that information into the saved file as metadata. It then uses these details to organize your collection of saved files into a hierarchy, with a folder for each artist and a subfolder for each album by that artist.

INSIDE OUT   Find a classical music database

The Windows Metadata service uses information from a variety of suppliers, including Allmusic (previously known as AMG) and Muze (for U.K. titles). As of the beginning of 2011, the ever-growing allmusic.com database included more than 2.2 million albums and more than 20 million tracks. (You can find the latest statistics at *w7io.com/1204*.) The service is heavily skewed in favor of pop and rock titles and has much less information about classical music CDs. If you want to copy a classical collection to your hard disk, your best bet is to find a third-party CD player that uses an alternative Internet service called the Gracenote Media Recognition Service, also known as CDDB (Gracenote is owned by Sony Corporation of America). The Gracenote Media Database of classical discs is extensive, and after you rip your discs using the other product, you can save the resulting files in a folder monitored by Windows Media Player to add them to your library. For more information, visit *gracenote.com* and search in the Solutions section.

Choosing an Audio Format and Bit Rate

For practical purposes, files copied from audio CDs to your hard disk must be compressed; if you rip tracks to your hard disk using the uncompressed WAV format, a typical 60-minute CD will consume more than half a gigabyte of disk space. Compressing the files means you can store more music on your hard disk, and it makes the process of backing up and streaming music files easier and more efficient.

When it comes to compression, your first choice is simple: lossy or lossless? Most popular algorithms used to compress audio (and video) files are *lossy*, which means that they achieve compression by eliminating data. In the case of audio files, the data that's tossed out during the compression process consists mostly of frequencies that are outside the normal range of human hearing. However, the more you compress a file, the more likely you are to degrade its audio quality to the point where you'll notice it. Windows Media Player allows you to rip tracks using the Windows Media Audio Lossless format, which stores music files more efficiently than uncompressed WAV files without sacrificing any informa-tion. In theory, at least, a track ripped in this format should be indistinguishable from the original.

Deciding on the type and amount of compression involves a tradeoff between disk space and audio quality. The level of compression is determined by the bit rate you select for your copied files. Higher bit rates preserve more of the original sound quality of your audio tracks but result in larger files on your hard disk or portable player. Lower bit rates allow you to pack more music into limited space at a cost in fidelity.

INSIDE OUT Use different bit rates for different devices

Even a truly massive music collection can fit comfortably in a fraction of the free space on today's terabyte-and-up hard drives. Saving disk space is more of a concern on por-table devices with limited storage. For those occasions, why not get the best of both worlds? Save the original copy on your local hard drive or server, at the highest bit rate you're comfortable with. When syncing music with your portable device, use the sync software settings to transcode each track to a lower bit rate for more efficiency in stor-age. We explain how to accomplish this task in Windows Media Player in "Synchroniz-ing Digital Media with Portable Devices" on page 520.

To set your preferences, click the Rip Settings button on the Player toolbar. Click Format, and then choose one of the six available formats, as shown here. If you choose a format that allows lossy compression, click the Audio Quality option to select from choices avail-able for that format.

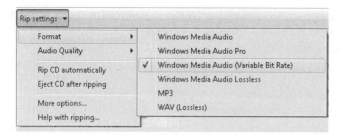

The following options are available, listed in order of compatibility with other hardware and software:

- **MP3** is the longtime standard for digital music files and has nearly universal sup-port. If you want the widest freedom to share, play, and reuse files, this is your safest choice. The MP3 format supports variable bit-rate encoding, but Microsoft's MP3 codec allows you to rip tracks at fixed bit rates only, in four steps, ranging from the default setting of 128 Kbps up to 320 Kbps. (If you want to rip MP3 tracks at variable bit rates, you need to use a different program.) Most commercial music services (with the noteworthy exception of Apple's iTunes Store) offer files in MP3 format at 192 Kbps or higher.

- **Windows Media Audio**, which uses fixed bit rates, is the default choice. You can keep the default bit rate of 128 Kbps or choose one of five other settings, ranging from 48 Kbps to 192 Kbps. In previous versions of Windows Media Player, it was possible to increase this bit rate by tweaking a registry setting. That trick no longer works in Windows Media Player 12. If you want higher-quality encoding in WMA format, choose the Variable Bit Rate option.

- **Windows Media Audio (Variable Bit Rate)** allows the encoder to vary the compression applied to portions of a file, depending on the amount of information in it. Using a variable bit rate (VBR) can result in files of much higher quality compared to files of similar size created using fixed bit rates. Options on the Bit Rate menu are expressed in ranges, starting with 40 to 75 Kbps and topping out at 240 to 355 Kbps. The VBR format might cause problems with some portable players and home audio devices, especially older ones; before you choose this option, make sure that files in this format play back properly on devices you plan to use regularly.

- Choose **Windows Media Audio Lossless** if you plan to use Windows Media Player to burn custom CDs that are essentially equal in quality to the music source. This is also your best choice if you want to play tracks on a high-end audio system (including a home theater system connected to Windows Media Center) without compromising quality. Because this format is lossless, no options are available on the Audio Quality menu.

- **WAV (Lossless)** is the correct choice if you want nearly perfect copies of the tracks on a CD and you want those copies to be usable with any burning program. WAV files use nearly twice as much space as Windows Media Audio Lossless files and cannot be streamed as easily as compressed formats, making them unsuitable for all but temporary storage.

- **Windows Media Audio Pro** is primarily intended for high-fidelity output on phones and other devices with limited storage capacity. Its default bit rate is 64 Kbps, although you can choose options ranging from 32 Kbps to 192 Kbps. This format is not supported by all devices (in fact, we've never seen it used out here in the real world), so check compatibility carefully before choosing it.

Chapter 13

INSIDE OUT   Make a perfect copy of a CD track

If you right-click the icon for an audio CD in Windows Explorer and choose Explore from the shortcut menu, you'll see that each track is listed as a small file with the file type CD Audio Track, the .cda extension, and a date and time stamp of December 31, 1994, at 5:00 P.M. Most of that information is completely wrong and represents a confused attempt by Windows Explorer to make sense of a format it wasn't designed to read.

CD Audio is not a file format; instead, these pointers serve as shortcuts to the actual files, which are stored in a format that is essentially identical to a WAV file. You can't copy a CD track directly to your hard drive from Windows Explorer, and the default ripping options compress the resulting file so that it loses some quality. Using Windows Media Player 12, you can rip a track using the WAV (Lossless) format or specify the Windows Media Audio Lossless format, which produces a file that is smaller than a WAV file but still quite large. Either format will work if your goal is to create a nearly identical copy of a CD using burning software. The WAV format is certain to work with all third-party CD-burning programs, unlike Windows Media Audio Lossless.

Notice we said "a *nearly* identical copy." The process of ripping a track from a CD is not perfect, especially if the media is scratched. Tiny errors caused by the mechanical operation of the drive components—a single bit here and a couple of bits there—will inevitably creep in when you rip a file, even if you use a lossless format. Similar errors can result when you use the "copy CD" option available in most commercial CD-burning software. These errors are mostly imperceptible to the human ear, but if you repeat the rip/mix/burn cycle several times, the errors can add up and create a click, pop, or other noticeable glitch during playback.

Perfectionists who want to make a perfect copy of a single music track or an entire CD need to take special precautions to prevent these errors from occurring. For these tasks, we recommend Exact Audio Copy, written by Andre Wiethoff and available for download from *exactaudiocopy.de*; this highly regarded program can reliably extract every bit of digital information from the disc, without allowing any data to be lost. As of November 2010, the program includes full support for Windows 7.

Most of the options available on the Rip menu are also available in a slightly different arrangement on the Rip Music tab of the Options dialog box. Instead of choosing the bit rate from a menu, you use the Audio Quality slider, shown in Figure 13-8, to select a bit rate. Moving the slider to the left produces smaller files with lower quality; moving it to the right produces larger files with better audio quality.

Figure 13-8 The Rip Settings section of this dialog box duplicates choices available on the Rip menu on the Player toolbar.

Deciding How to Name Your Files and Where to Store Them

Unless you specify otherwise, Windows Media Player saves ripped CD tracks in the Music folder in your user profile (which is also the default save location in the Music library). If you want ripped tracks to go to a different location, click the Rip Music tab in the Options dialog box, and then click Change under the Rip Music To This Location heading. This capability is especially useful if you store your music library in a shared folder or on a network device such as a Windows Home Server.

If you are online when you copy a CD, Windows Media Player connects to the Windows Metadata service and gets whatever information is available about that CD. Typically, this information includes the name of the album and the songs it contains, the names of performers and composers, information about musical genres, and album art. Windows Media Player uses some of this information to create file names for your copied CD tracks. (All of the information Media Player gets from this online repository of information can be used in one way or another, even if it doesn't become part of your file names. The album art, for example, appears on the Library tab, in the Now Playing list, when you play tunes from that album, and in Windows Explorer when you use Thumbnails view.)

By default, the file names for your tracks are made up of the track number, followed by a space character, followed by the song title (which probably includes spaces). Such a file name might look like this: 09 Tell Me All The Things You Do.wma. This naming scheme works fine in Windows Media Player, which uses metadata to sort, group, and display items in your collection. However, if you copy a group of songs to a portable player that doesn't use subfolders, that device might display and sort only by the file name. Therefore, when you choose a file-naming convention in Windows Media Player, give some thought to how your files will work on your portable device. In that context, if you want to keep all songs from a given artist or album together, the most important information is probably the artist or album name (or both), followed by the track number.

In any event, you can tell Media Player how you want your files named as follows:

1. Click Options on the Organize menu, and then click the Rip Music tab.

2. Click File Name to open the File Name Options dialog box.

3. Select the check boxes for the information categories that you want to include in your file names, and clear the other check boxes. As you adjust your choices here and in the following two steps, the example in the Preview area of the dialog box shows the effect on file names.

4. If you want to, use the Move Up and Move Down buttons to change the order in which name elements appear.

Chapter 13

5. Use the Separator drop-down list to choose the character that appears between elements of a track name (if you don't want to use spaces). You can choose dashes, dots, underlines, or no separator character at all.

6. Click OK.

Managing Your Media Library

The contents of the Windows Media Player library are drawn directly from the corresponding libraries that are part of your user profile. Thus, adding an item to the library is as simple as copying it to a folder within the corresponding library. If you click the Organize menu, you'll find a Manage Libraries menu with four choices on it: Music, Videos, Pictures, and Recorded TV. Choosing any of these options takes you to the same dialog box you use to manage libraries in Windows Explorer.

For more details about how to select which folders are part of a library, see "Working with Libraries" on page 343.

Windows Media Player includes the option to assign ratings to every item in your media library. For music and picture files, this capability unlocks several features in Windows Media Center, specifically the capability to "play favorites." Giving four or five stars to your favorite tunes and photos makes it easy to create playlists and slide shows guaranteed to contain only items you're certain to enjoy.

Using Ratings

Every music track in your library has a star rating, assigned on a scale of one star (lowest) to five stars (highest). Auto ratings are assigned by default and appear in the Rating column with a soft blue tint over the stars. Ratings you assign explicitly appear in gold. By default, all new tracks are auto-rated at three stars; tracks in WMA format that are listed in the Windows Media database are auto-rated using values from that source. When you first play a track, its auto rating increases to four stars. (The rating goes up only if you play all the way through a track; if you click the Next button while a track is playing, Windows Media Player assumes you did so because you didn't like the selection.)

If you choose to do so, you can assign ratings to tracks, one at a time or in groups. You can adjust a rating for one or more tracks by opening an album or a playlist and clicking the values under the Rating head. If the playlist is visible, you can drag it to its full width to make ratings visible for all selected tracks. In any view except Now Playing, you can select one or more tracks, right-click and choose Rate, and then pick a rating from the menu. As soon as you assign a rating, Windows Media Player stops using auto rating for that track. (To completely remove a rating you've assigned, choose Unrated. In this case, the track will once again pick up a default auto rating.)

INSIDE OUT   Preview a music track

You don't have to add a track to a playlist to hear it. Windows Media Player 12 includes
a new feature that allows you to preview any track from the Player Library view. When
you allow the mouse pointer to hover over the track name for a second or two, a small
blue window pops up, displaying the track name, album name, and album cover. Click
the Preview link and leave the mouse pointer over the preview box to begin listening.
While the track is playing, the elapsed time of the track is displayed; click the Skip link,
as shown here, to jump forward 15 seconds at a time. When you've heard enough,
move your mouse away from the preview box to stop playback immediately.

Managing Metadata and Album Art

If you're connected to the Internet and you've accepted the default settings, Windows
Media Player automatically downloads information about any disc or media file you play
for the first time, including the track name(s), album name, album cover, and information
about artists and composers for each track. This information is stored as part of the library
when you rip a CD or when you add one or more MP3 or WMA files to your Music folder. If
you downloaded the tracks from a music service, some of this metadata (composer names,
contributing artists, and so on) might be missing. To retrieve all details for the selected
album, right-click the album cover and click Find Album Info; if Windows Media Player
believes it has a perfect match for a complete album, it displays a dialog box like the one
shown in Figure 13-9. If you're satisfied that all the information is correct, click Finish to
update any missing information for the selected tracks.

In some cases, the update check is unable to find a match for all the tracks on an album.
In that case, you're given the opportunity to manually match up the tracks from your collection with the downloaded track lineup. The cause of such a mixup might be as simple as
a discrepancy between the song name in your saved file and the name listed in the database. If you find a typo in a song listing from the metadata service, or if a detail it provides
clashes with your preferences, you can change the listings on the fly. Click the Edit button
beneath the album name to manually edit album and track information.

Figure 13-9 If the Windows Metadata service finds a perfect match for your album, you can click Finish to update all tracks with full details.

The algorithm that identifies tracks is truly sophisticated. It actually plays back the track, creates a "fingerprint" for it, and then searches the online database based on that identifier. The result is that Windows Media Player is uncannily accurate at finding the correct track. In fact, the fewer the details available in metadata, the more accurate the Player is likely to be.

Album art, once retrieved from the Internet, is cached on your computer. Thereafter, even if you're no longer online, you can display the album art in Now Playing view, in the Player Library view, and in any Windows Explorer view that includes thumbnails.

INSIDE OUT   Add your own album art

What do you do if the Windows Media database doesn't have an album cover for your album? If you can find the correct album art anywhere online, you can add it to the library with just a couple of clicks. Start by locating the album art (ideally, at a size that is at least 200 pixels square) at your favorite online music store or fan site. In the browser window, right-click the cover image and copy it to the Clipboard. Now return to the Player, open the album, right-click the generic album cover image in the details pane, and click Paste Album Art. (This menu choice is available only if a suitable image is on the Clipboard.) This saves the copied image as a pair of hidden JPEG files in the folder for that album and also caches copies of the JPEG file for individual tracks.

Regardless of the source of your music files, errors and inconsistencies are bound to creep in to your library. Simple misspellings of track names are probably the most common error, but other problems can occur, too. Variations in the spelling or styling of an artist's name can result in that artist's work being filed in two different places.

You can edit any of the incorrect information directly. You can do this on the Audio CD page (if you're tackling this task before ripping a CD) or from the Player Library view (if you've already added the tracks). Right-click the Album, Album Artist, Genre, or Release Date fields under the Album heading and click Edit to change these details for all tracks. Right-click the Title, Contributing Artist, or Composer fields in the track list and choose Edit (or select the track name and press F2) to edit these details for individual tracks.

> **Note**
>
> Previous versions of Windows Media Player included a feature called Advanced Tag Editor, which provided a rich editor for viewing and changing all metadata associated with a music track. This feature is not included in Windows Media Player 12. To edit metadata that isn't visible in Windows Media Player, use Windows Explorer or a third-party program.

While you're editing, you can move from column to column by pressing Tab or Shift+Tab, and move from row to row by pressing the Up Arrow or Down Arrow.

If you want to change the information in the Contributing Artist or Composer field for a group of tracks or an entire album, select all the rows first. (Click the first entry and then Shift+click the last entry, or press Ctrl+A to select all items in the currently visible list.) Then right-click and choose Edit. Move to the column you want to edit by pressing Tab or Shift+Tab, make the edit in one row, and then press Enter to duplicate the edit to the entire column.

> **Note**
>
> The Rating and Track Number fields cannot be edited until you have actually added the tracks to your library. The Length field is always determined by the file itself and can never be manually edited.

How and Where Is Metadata Stored?

All editable data that appears in your library is stored as metadata within your media files. In addition, some information that is specific to your collection is stored in the library index—details about the play count for a specific track, for instance, or when the track was added to the library. When you edit details about a track in the library, such as the name of a song or an artist, Windows Media Player rewrites the information in the underlying file. (To change file names, you need to work in Windows Explorer.) For music files, Windows Media Player can read and write these details by way of tags stored directly in the file, using one of the following three formats:

- **ID3v1**   This relatively old format is still in wide use for MP3 files. It consists of six fields, each of fixed size, stored in 128 bytes at the end of the file. Windows Media Player can read ID3v1 tags but does not write them.

- **ID3v2**   Modern media players that use the MP3 format typically store metadata using these tags, which can contain dozens of fields, each holding an unlimited number of characters. Because these tags are often used to help identify streaming media, they are stored at the beginning of the media file. If you edit the details associated with an MP3 file in Windows Media Player, it writes the data to the file using this type of tag.

- **WMA**   These tags are the native format used for Windows Media Audio files. The metadata is stored at the beginning of the file, and the format is functionally equivalent to ID3v2 tags.

When you import files into Windows Media Player, the data stored in these tags is used to populate the fields in the library. When you edit details of a track in your library, Windows Media Player writes the information back to the file containing that track, using either an ID3v2 or a WMA tag. This change is permanent. The Player continually scans for changes to metadata within files. If you use an external tag editor or Windows Explorer to change information stored in a WMA or an MP3 file, the changes are reflected in your library the next time you open it, usually within a few minutes.

Working with (and Around) Digital Rights Management

In Windows 7, you're likely to encounter media files that use Microsoft's Windows Media Digital Rights Management (DRM) technology—that is, digital content that has been encrypted by using digital signatures and whose use is governed by a licensing agreement with the content provider—whenever you acquire music or movies from an online subscription service or when you use Windows Media Center to record TV shows from premium cable or satellite channels. The media usage rights (previously called a license) that are associated with DRM-protected files specify how you can use the file and for what period of time; these rights are designed to prevent unauthorized copying or distribution of the media item. The media usage rights are determined by the content vendor and should be disclosed when you agree to purchase or download the item; Windows Media Player enforces the terms of that agreement.

Living Without DRM

We recognize that copy protection and digital rights management schemes that restrict your right to use media files are controversial. If you're philosophically opposed to the idea of restricted usage rights, you have plenty of options to download music in DRM-free formats. These days, every major music store, including the 800-pound gorilla of the industry, the iTunes Store, sells its wares in unrestricted MP3 or AAC files. DRM in the music industry lives on in subscription services like the Zune Marketplace, where you can download music files whose playback rights have to be renewed each month.

In the United States, over-the-air television broadcasts are all digital and unencumbered by DRM. They offer a rich source of programming, including huge amounts of HDTV. Finding movies to watch on a PC is a much more difficult task if you're determined to avoid DRM. DVDs use a weak form of copy protection, while Blu-ray discs use exceptionally strong encryption. We're not aware of any mainstream movie services that allow unrestricted downloads, although you have many options for streaming TV shows and movies over the Internet to your Windows PC. If you want to completely avoid acquiring media files that include restrictions on your digital rights, choose Options from the Organize menu. On the Privacy tab in the Options dialog box, clear Download Usage Rights Automatically When I Play Or Sync A File.

We don't recommend the extreme option of downloading bootleg tools and utilities to decrypt digitally protected files. Under the Digital Millennium Copyright Act of 1998, distributing and using those tools to circumvent access protection on copyrighted material is a criminal offense. As a result, most such tools are hard to find and can lead to some very dark corners of the Internet, where you might download more than you bargained for.

When you download a song, movie clip, or other protected media file from an online store, the content provider might encrypt the file with a wrapper that defines your media usage rights. Windows Media DRM agreements can be for an indefinite period of time or can be set to expire after some period of time. In some cases, the media usage rights agreement will allow you to play the media item only on the computer on which the item was originally downloaded. In other cases, the agreement allows you to copy or move the item to other computers and personal music players (but not necessarily to CDs or DVDs). For some protected files, you can read the terms of an item's license by examining the item's Properties dialog box. Find the file in the player's media library, right-click it, choose Properties, and then click the Media Usage Rights tab. You'll see a list like the one shown here.

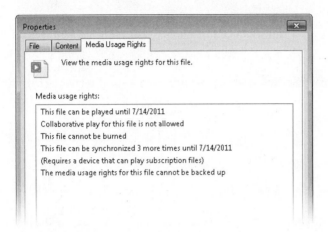

If you have bought licenses that allow you to play the items for an indefinite period of time on a single computer, how do you move the media item to another computer? In Windows Media Player 10 and earlier versions, you could back up licenses on one machine and restore them on another (giving up your privileges on the original computer, of course). In Windows Media Player 11 and later, this feature no longer exists. To move protected files from one computer to another, you must use whatever procedure the original content provider specifies. (For music files that include burn rights, this can be as simple as burning the tracks to a CD, then ripping the newly created CD in an unprotected format such as MP3.) In extreme cases, you might be unable to play back the original file.

CHAPTER 14

Sharing and Syncing Digital Media

WHEN you think of Windows Media Player, you probably think of it as a program that allows you to enjoy your own music or video collection on a single PC. But that's only one of the roles this multifaceted program can play in our connected world. On a home network (especially one joined to a Windows 7 homegroup), Windows Media Player allows you to fetch media from one location and play it locally or sling it to another PC or networked device. It also offers some basic features that allow you to transfer all or part of your media collection to a disc or device so that you can take it on the road or to the office.

In Windows 7, you can access music and videos from a library on another PC, with or without the help of a homegroup; you can even access your personal music library over the Internet. You can use a variety of techniques to stream content stored on other PCs and network-connected digital media devices. In addition, with a new feature called Play To, you can "push" content from one PC or device to another. In this chapter, we explain how each of these network options works and walk you through the steps you need to complete before you can begin using them.

Synchronizing with portable devices has been a signature feature of Windows Media Player for as long as we've been writing about it. Those features still work with older MP3 players and with generic flash drives. If your portable device has an Apple, Zune, or Windows Phone logo on it, however, you need to use separate software for synchronization, as we explain in this chapter.

And finally, we explain a classic form of sharing: how to use Windows 7 to burn CDs and DVDs filled with music, videos, and slide shows. For some DVD-related tasks, you might need to use a separate software tool, Windows DVD Maker, which is included with Windows 7.

What's in Your Edition?

Windows Media Player is included in all editions of Windows 7. However, some of the features we describe in this section require the use of a homegroup, which can be created only by a computer running Windows 7 Home Premium or higher. Computers running the Starter or Home Basic edition can join a homegroup that has already been created. Windows DVD Maker is available only in Home Premium and higher editions.

Sharing Digital Media over a Network

Sometimes it's hard to contain a large music collection on a single PC, especially if multiple family members have different tastes. So, what do you do when the new album you want to listen to is on a computer in the other room? Physically copying the tracks from one machine to another is one option, but if the PCs in question are part of the same network, you also have these three alternatives:

- **Play media directly from another computer in your homegroup**   This option is particularly convenient when your digital media is stored on another computer running Windows 7. If both computers have joined a homegroup, you can browse the other computer's libraries (Music, Pictures, and Videos, in particular) and add anything you find there to a Windows Media Player playlist.

  For more details on how to create, manage, and use shared libraries in a homegroup, see "Working with Libraries" on page 343 and "Sharing Files, Digital Media, and Printers in a Homegroup" on page 720.

- **Play tunes from a shared media library**   Shared libraries appear at the bottom of the navigation pane in Windows Media Player; you can access the contents of a shared library if the owner of that library has granted you permission to do so. This option doesn't require Windows 7; in fact, the shared library can be on a computer running any operating system. When you browse and play media this way, you do so using streaming protocols.

- **Use Windows Media Player as a remote control to play music or videos on another PC or device**   This scenario requires that you use the Play To menu in Windows Media Player 12 in Windows 7. The music tracks, video clips, pictures, or recorded TV programs can be "played to" another Windows 7 PC or a compatible digital media device.

Of course, all of this network magic happens only with your permission, which means that some configuration steps are required. As we explain later in this section, you must specifically authorize other computers on your network to access your shared library (a process that happens automatically when you join a homegroup). You must also specifically enable the option for other computers to play content on your PC.

In the Player Library view of Windows Media Player, a Stream menu is available on the toolbar at all times, just to the right of the Organize menu. From this menu, you determine which computers and devices on your network are allowed to access your media library.

By default, when you join a homegroup, streaming is enabled for all devices and PCs. You'll find this option on the Change Homegroup Settings page, under the Share Media With Devices heading. You can also enable universal access by clicking the Stream menu in

Windows Media Player and adding a check mark to the left of Automatically Allow Devices To Play My Media. (If this command doesn't appear, you must first choose Turn On Media Streaming and then click Turn On Media Streaming. If you are not currently joined to a homegroup, this option is displayed as Turn On Media Streaming With Homegroup, and selecting the option enables the Homegroup feature.)

Learn More About Digital Media and Networks

The specifications for sharing media over a network aren't proprietary to Windows. Instead, they represent published standards from a group called the Digital Living Network Alliance (DLNA), which was founded in 2003. DLNA standards define the capabilities of PCs and consumer electronics devices. In theory, you should be able to purchase a DLNA-certified media player for your living room and have confidence that you'll be able to stream media files to it from your Windows 7 PC. For more on the DLNA standards and compatible devices, check out the organization's website at *dlna.org*.

For more precise control over which devices are allowed access to your media library and which are blocked, click Stream and then click More Streaming Options. That opens the dialog box shown in Figure 14-1.

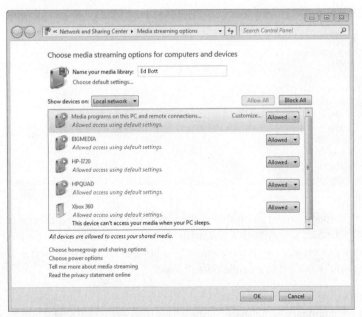

Figure 14-1 This list of devices capable of accessing a shared media library includes other PCs on the network as well as digital media devices such as the Xbox 360.

Chapter 14

This dialog box is busy and filled with options, so it's worth taking a closer look. At the top of the dialog box, you have the option to give your library a descriptive name that will appear on network devices in the navigation pane under Other Libraries; the default is your user account name. The list in Figure 14-1 includes several other PCs on the local network as well as an Xbox 360. Using this dialog box, you can instantly block access to all listed devices by clicking Block All. To allow or block an individual PC or device, use the drop-down menu to its right.

In the next section, we explain how to play media files once these configuration chores are complete.

Sharing Media Libraries

After you enable media sharing on one PC, you can access its library from another PC by looking under the Other Libraries heading in Windows Media Player. By default, this list shows all libraries on all networked computers where the Windows Media Player Network Sharing Service is running, even those where your access to the shared library is blocked. The format for each listing is the library name followed by the computer name in parentheses.

Assuming you've been allowed access to a shared library, you can see its full contents by expanding the list of headings beneath its entry in the Other Libraries group. The choices closely resemble those available on your computer, as shown in this example:

Browsing through one of these shared libraries is similar to the experience of browsing through your own library, with a few twists. For starters, you can't customize the available views shown here; you can browse music by album, artist, or genre, and in the case of other libraries, you're limited to a single default view.

In addition, the owner of the shared library can use both star ratings and parental ratings to limit what appears in the shared library. This is an extremely useful feature when you are working with very large shared libraries, where performance can suffer in streaming situations. You can set these restrictions for a shared library as a default setting and then adjust them on a case-by-case basis. To filter the contents of your library in this fashion, follow these steps:

1. In Windows Media Player, click Stream, More Streaming Options.

2. To adjust settings for all connected PCs and devices, click Choose Default Settings under the name of your media library. To adjust settings for an individual PC or device, move your mouse pointer over the entry for that device, and then click the Customize link.

3. In the Customize Media Streaming Settings dialog box (see Figure 14-2), adjust the options in either list. If you're working with an individual device or PC, you must clear the Use Default Settings check box before these options are available.

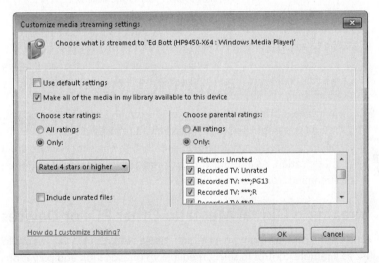

Figure 14-2 With these customized settings, only tracks, pictures, and video clips that you've rated highly are visible when other PCs browse your shared media library.

4. Click OK to apply your changes. If you begin playing one or more music tracks or video clips from a shared library on another computer, the selected items appear in your playlist. To confirm that you're streaming the file rather than playing it directly, right-click its entry in the playlist and view its properties. When you do, you'll see a noteworthy difference from the file name and path you see on a file being played directly from a disk or a shared folder. The complicated URI shown next is typical.

In this case, the streaming engine is using IPv6; depending on your network configuration, you might see an IPv4 address here instead. Because items in the playlist are being accessed via a streaming protocol, the files themselves are not available for modification. As a result, you can't rate tracks, rename them, or edit metadata when streaming from a shared library.

Streaming Digital Media to Other PCs or Devices

One of the most intriguing new digital media features in Windows 7 allows you to use your PC as a remote control to select media from one location and play it on another PC or device. The target device can be any DLNA-compatible renderer, including Windows Media Player 12 on another PC running Windows 7.

So, if you have a Windows 7 PC connected to your high-end audio system in the living room, you can put together a playlist on your notebook PC and "push" it to the living room. The tracks (or video clips or recorded TV shows) can be anywhere on your network, and getting things started is as simple as right-clicking the album, playlist, or video clip and choosing the target device from the Play To menu.

The Play To menu is visible only if a compatible device is on the network and available for playback duties. In the case of Windows Media Player 12, that requires some advance prep-

aration. First, you have to allow your computer to be controlled remotely. From the Stream
menu, click Allow Remote Control Of My Player, as shown in Figure 14-3.

Figure 14-3 The check mark to the left of the second option means any network computer can
play music or video on your PC using Windows Media Player.

That step opens the dialog box shown in Figure 14-4, where you must click one of the
options to enable or disable remote control on the current network. (This option requires
that your network location be set to Home or Work, and it is disabled if the network location is Public.)

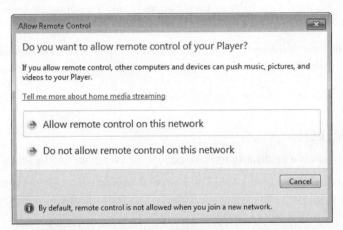

Figure 14-4 You must specifically authorize other devices to play content to your PC, and you
can revoke that decision any time by choosing the second option here.

Finally, open Windows Media Player on the target device and leave it running. (You can
minimize it if you prefer.) From the PC you want to use as a controller, select the media you
want to play and choose the target device from the Play To menu. If everything is configured correctly, you'll see a Play To controller like the one shown in Figure 14-5.

Figure 14-5 This remote control program allows you to stop, skip, or repeat items being played to a remote device or PC.

Note that the time to the right of the current track is displayed as a countdown showing how much time remains. On the target computer, music tracks appear in the playlist one at a time.

TROUBLESHOOTING

You can't enable or disable remote control of Windows Media Player

In some circumstances, you might find yourself unable to enable remote control of your player. Clicking Allow Remote Control On This Network doesn't have any effect, and your PC doesn't appear in the Play To menu of another networked device.

Microsoft engineers we talked to about this issue can't identify the reason why it occurs, but they were able to provide us with the fix. Open Registry Editor and navigate to HKCU\Software\Microsoft\MediaPlayer\Preferences. Right-click the DMR key beneath that branch of the registry and delete it. Now try enabling remote control again. Windows Media Player will create a new group of settings for this key, and this time the setting should stick.

Remote Streaming over the Internet

Your massive media collection is on your PC at home. You're on the road, using your note-book PC to access the Internet. If both PCs are running Windows 7, you can connect your notebook to your home PC and play back any files stored in the Windows Media Player library.

The secret ingredient for making this connection work is linking your online ID with your user account on both PCs. In theory, any secure online credential can be used with this feature; at the time we wrote this section, more than a year after the commercial release of Windows 7, the only supported credentials are those provided with your Windows Live ID. Assuming you have already set up a Windows Live ID (*live.com*), click the Stream menu in Windows Media Player and then click Allow Internet Access To Home Media. (If this is the first time you're using this Live ID with Windows 7, you might need to install the Windows Live ID Sign-in Assistant first.) In the Internet Home Media Access dialog box, shown in Fig-ure 14-6, click Link An Online ID to begin the process of associating your Windows Live ID with your user account. Once this is done, click the Allow Internet Access To Home Media option.

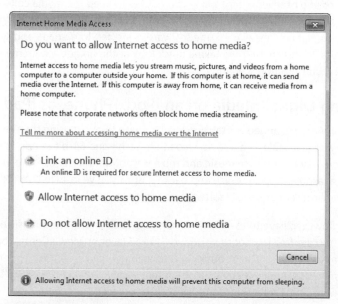

Figure 14-6 Before you can enable Internet access to your media library, you have to link an online ID to your user account.

Link the same online ID to your user account on the PC you plan to use for remote access to your home media library. As long as your home PC is turned on and the Windows Media Network Sharing Service is running, you can connect to the remote library from the Other Libraries node in Windows Media Player.

Synchronizing Digital Media with Portable Devices

Do you own a portable music player or a smartphone that also plays music and movies? If so, we might be able to help you synchronize the contents of that device with all or part of the digital media collection on your PC. We say "might" because the tools and techniques you need to use for that synchronization process vary depending on who made your device.

The synchronization tools built into Windows Media Player 12 are the direct descendants of features designed years ago for a category of portable devices that collectively fell under Microsoft's PlaysForSure certification. (Microsoft officially discontinued the PlaysForSure logo and associated branding in 2008.) You can still use Windows Media Player as the synchronization hub with generic media players and older PlaysForSure devices. And, as we explain in this chapter, you can also use the sync tools in Windows Media Player to transfer tracks and albums between PCs by using portable storage media such as flash drives.

But Windows Media Player is of no help if you have an iPod, iPhone, or iPad. For these devices, which dominate their respective markets, you need to use Apple's iTunes software (*itunes.com*) or one of several third-party alternatives to keep the media collections on your device and your PC in sync. Likewise, Microsoft's Zune players and Windows Phone 7 devices require that you install the Zune software (*zune.net*) to manage and sync music and media files. In this chapter, we take a quick look at the unique requirements of each of these three synchronization scenarios.

Managing Digital Media on an iPod, iPhone, or iPad

If you own an Apple-branded portable device, it's hard to avoid using the iTunes program. Apple's software (available as a free download for 32-bit and 64-bit Windows versions) offers the only way to purchase music and movies through the iTunes Store. It's also the only option available to synchronize and back up apps you've installed on the device and to update the firmware or system software on the device.

You do not, however, have to use iTunes for playing back unprotected music or video files on your PC. You are free to choose Windows Media Player or Media Center (or an alternative program) to handle playback duties and to manage the contents of your media library. If you choose to use iTunes strictly to sync content with your iPod, iPhone, or iPad, you should be aware of the following potential sticking points:

- **Supported music formats**   Windows Media Player and Media Center can play tracks saved or downloaded in the default iTunes format, AAC (with a .m4a file-name extension), as can Microsoft's Zune software. However, any tracks you save or download in WMA format cannot be synced to or played on a device running Apple's iOS operating system. For the sake of interoperability, you should be sure that all tracks in your music library are in MP3 or AAC format.

- **Copy protection**   Any music, movies, or TV shows that use Apple's FairPlay digital rights management (DRM) must be played using iTunes on a PC or a portable device. Likewise, any music or video files that use Windows Media DRM are unplayable in iTunes.

- **Files and folders**   By default, iTunes creates a subfolder in the Music folder within your user profile and stores its library files in that location. This allows any tracks or albums that are part of the iTunes library to be included automatically in your Windows Media Player library. If you want the Windows and iTunes libraries to be independent, you need to move the iTunes folder to a location outside the Windows Music library and adjust your iTunes configuration accordingly.

- **Library details**   iTunes builds and maintains its own library. Any information that is stored within a music file using standard tag formats is added to the iTunes library automatically. Play counts and ratings are stored in iTunes only and are not available to other Windows programs.

- **Album art**   iTunes maintains an album art cache that is completely independent of the one used in Windows Media Player. If you use both programs, you need to manage two different sets of cover art for your collection.

If your library includes music files that are in formats that iTunes does not support, consider using a third-party program to sync your collection with the device.

Synchronizing with a Zune Player or Windows Phone

The Zune brand name covers a wide swath of technological ground, including portable music players, Windows Phone 7 devices, an online music and video store (Zune Marketplace), and a subscription music service (Zune Pass). For our purposes, the most important piece is the Zune software, which helps you synchronize your Windows PC with Zune services and compatible devices.

The Zune software displays the contents of your Music, Pictures, and Videos libraries in separate windows under the Collection heading; it also adds a Podcasts library to your user account. Click any heading to display that library's contents, and then sort, group, search, tag, and play those items. When you connect a device to the PC, you see the summary view shown in Figure 14-7. Click any of the links above the device name to browse the current contents of the Music, Videos, Pictures, or Podcasts libraries on that device.

For a more detailed look at how the Zune software works, see "Mastering the Zune Software" on page 570.

Chapter 14

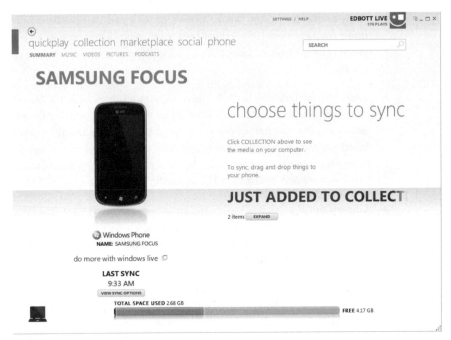

Figure 14-7 Use this Summary tab to check how much space is available on a portable Zune device.

When you first connect a Zune-compatible portable device to your PC, the Zune software offers the sync options shown here.

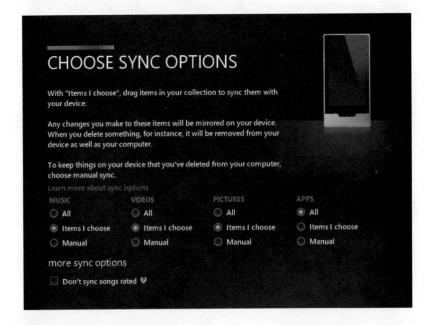

By default, the Music, Videos, and Pictures sync options are set to Items I Choose. With this setting, you can right-click an item in that library—a song, an album, a playlist, or an artist in the Music library; a picture or folder (album) in the Pictures library; a series in the Videos library—and then choose Sync With <Device_name>. Syncing an artist name is a particularly effective way to ensure that your device automatically receives a sync copy when you add a new song or album from that artist to the Music library on your PC.

If part of the media library on your PC is small enough to fit comfortably within the storage capacity of your device, choose All to keep the full contents of that library in sync. If the capacity of the portable device forces you to be selective about what goes on the portable device, choose one of the other two options for that library.

Use the Manual option if you want to copy items to the Zune device by dragging them from the Zune collection. To remove them, you need to browse the contents of the device in the Zune software and manually select items to delete. Any items you delete from the PC library remain in the corresponding device library (and vice versa).

Chapter 14

INSIDE OUT   Keep Windows libraries separate from Zune

In our experience, Zune devices work exceptionally well with Windows libraries. In the Zune software, if you click Settings and then click Software, the Collection tab shows four categories under the Windows 7 Libraries heading. A Manage button next to each one opens the Windows Explorer Library Locations dialog box, where you can add or remove folders. What if you want to maintain the two locations independently? If you're in that camp, you can break the connection between the Zune collection and Windows libraries. At the bottom of the Collection tab, click Manage Separately. That changes the heading on the Collection tab to Monitored Folders and changes the user interface so that you can add or remove folders individually for each category. To restore the link between the Zune collection and your Windows libraries, click Align Folders at the bottom of the Collection pane.

Syncing with Portable MP3 Players and Removable Storage Media

For most other devices designed for use with Windows, including phones based on the Windows Mobile operating system, you can use Windows Media Player to establish a working relationship between your device and your music collection (videos, too, if your portable device supports video playback). You can also use these techniques with generic removable drives based on flash memory. After you complete the initial configuration, you can connect the device to your PC (typically via a USB port) and synchronize the contents of the device automatically or manually.

> **Note**
>
> Don't let the term "synchronization" fool you. In this case, synchronization is not a two-way street. If you add songs to your portable device from another source, they are not automatically copied to your computer the next time you synchronize. You have to perform that operation yourself, as we explain at the end of this section.

The sync capabilities in Windows Media Player rely on Media Transfer Protocol (MTP). Storage can be on flash memory—Compact Flash (CF) or Secure Digital (SD) cards, for instance—or on a hard disk. For compatible devices, Windows supplies drivers automatically—just connect the device to your computer. After driver installation is complete, you see an icon for the device at the bottom of the Library section of Windows Media Player's navigation pane. Figure 14-8 shows Windows Media Player with two devices available for synchronization, an SD card and a portable Sansa e260 MP3 player.

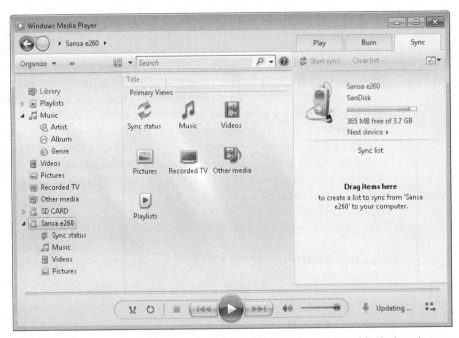

Figure 14-8 You can sync all or part of a digital media library to removable devices that appear at the bottom of the navigation pane.

Chapter 14

Windows Media Player allows you to set up synchronization partnerships with up to 16 devices on a single computer, each with its own settings. For portable music players, the benefits are obvious—plug in headphones or speakers and listen to the synchronized tunes (or watch videos) directly. For removable flash drives, sync features in Windows Media Player give you the ability to transfer media libraries from one PC to another or to carry a subset of your music library from your home PC to the office. Depending on the capabilities of your device, you might be able to sync only music files, or you might be able to include photos, video clips, and recorded TV shows.

Manual or Automatic Sync?

Before you can sync media files with a portable device, you have to set up the device. During initial setup, Windows Media Player makes some default choices based on your device configuration and the size of your media collection. If the storage capacity on the device is more than 4 GB *and* your entire Player library occupies less space than the total capacity of the device, Windows Media Player sets up an *automatic sync* relationship. Your entire library is automatically synchronized to the device each time you connect. If the device has a capacity of less than 4 GB, or if your library is larger than the total capacity of the device, Windows Media Player configures the device for a *manual sync*.

In the case of a manual sync, the option that gives you the most control over the contents of your device is to drag items (including existing playlists, individual tracks, entire albums, or artist names) into the sync list pane, create a list on the fly, and then click Start Sync to begin transferring items to the device.

If you prefer, you can define custom sync settings using existing or new playlists. To customize sync settings, first insert the device and verify that it appears in the navigation pane. Then click the Sync tab to display the sync list, use the Next Device link if necessary to select the correct device, and then click Set Up Sync from the Sync Options menu, which you open by clicking the unlabeled button in the upper right corner of the Sync tab. (Alternatively, you can right-click the device name in the navigation pane and choose Set Up Sync). If this is the first time you're setting up the device in question, you're given an opportunity to give it a friendly name in place of the generic device name or drive letter it receives by default. After that, you see the Device Setup window. Figure 14-9 shows this window after we created an automatic sync routine.

Chapter 14

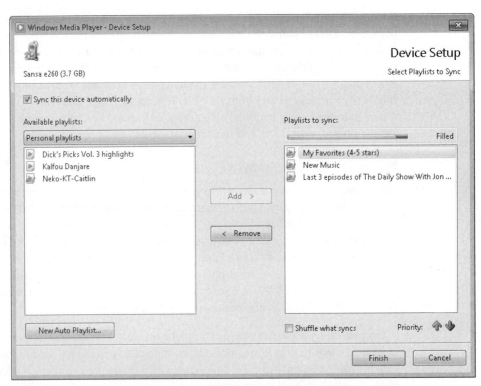

Figure 14-9 Use auto playlists to fill a portable device with favorite tracks and fresh content.

Note that in this example, Sync This Device Automatically is selected. As a result, any time you connect the device to the computer while Windows Media Player is running, it compares the current contents of the device with the contents of the Playlists To Sync list. All available playlists show in the pane on the left; select anything from that list and click Add to move it to the list of content that will be synchronized. Use the up and down arrows beneath the right pane to adjust the priority of items. This order is crucial if the playlists you select contain more content than will fit on the device. In that case, Windows Media Player moves through each list in order, from top to bottom, stopping when the device is full. (To randomize this selection instead, select the Shuffle What Syncs check box beneath the Playlists To Sync list.)

INSIDE OUT   Speed up file syncs

Each time you sync audio or video files with a portable player whose quality settings are lower than those of your music library, Windows Media Player transcodes those files—converting them to the lower bit rate in a temporary folder before copying them to the device itself. If you have ample space on your primary hard disk, you can speed up this process by allowing more room for the Transcoded Files Cache and configuring Windows Media Player to perform this operation in the background. You can also move this temporary folder to a different drive depending on your system configuration.

By default, Windows Media Player uses the Transcoded Files Cache folder on the system drive (in %LocalAppData%\Microsoft\Media Player) for temporary files. If you don't have enough room on your system drive or prefer to store these temporary files elsewhere, change this setting. Click Organize, and then click Options. Click the Devices tab in the Options dialog box, and then click the Advanced button. That opens the File Conversion Options dialog box, shown here. Select a different location and, if necessary, adjust the space set aside for transcoded files.

You might be tempted to lower the size of the Transcoded Files Cache from its default setting. That strategy is probably safe if all you ever plan to do is sync music files to a portable player. But this location is also used when you transfer movie clips or recorded TV shows to a portable device or burn them to a DVD, and if you change this setting now you could run into problems later. Our advice? Don't change this value unless you're desperately short of disk space and an upgraded hard disk is not an option.

Chapter 14

Customizing Sync Settings

For you to adjust device-specific settings after the initial setup, the device must be connected. Right-click the device in the navigation pane, and then click Properties. This opens a dialog box like the one shown in Figure 14-10, where you can change the device's name without having to go through initial setup again. For generic flash-memory devices and portable players that support this feature, you can also limit the amount of space that Windows Media Player uses; this option allows you to reserve space on the device if you also use it to store programs or data files that you carry on the road.

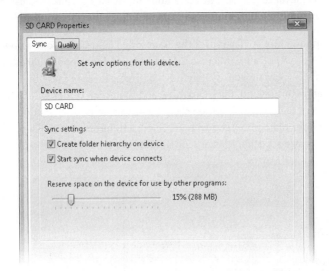

Figure 14-10 Some of these synchronization options are unavailable when the hardware doesn't support changes to those features.

When transferring music, videos, and recorded TV shows to a portable device that has limited storage space, you might want to adjust options on the Quality tab of its Properties dialog box. Under the Music and Videos And TV Shows headings, choose Select Maximum Quality Level and then use the slider to adjust the bit rate you want to use for all items in that category. With these settings enabled, files stored in your library are converted before being copied from the PC to the device.

Transferring Media Files from a Portable Device to a PC

When a device is connected to Windows Media Player, you can expand its entry in the navigation pane to see its sync status and to view its contents. The Sync Status entry shows all items that have been synced to the device and, more importantly, alerts you if any items were skipped, either for lack of space or because digital media rights were not available for those tracks.

If you're using a portable flash drive to copy items from a Player library on one PC to another, first make sure you've successfully synced all items from the original PC to the device. Then connect the device to the second PC and open Windows Media Player. In the navigation pane, click a heading under that device to view its contents, and then drag any or all items from the library pane to the sync list. When you do so, a Copy From Device button appears at the top of the sync list, as shown here:

Click this button to begin transferring the items from the removable storage media to your Player library.

Burning Music and Other Media to CDs and DVDs

If you have a CD or DVD burner, Windows Media Player can use it to burn a custom selection of songs to a recordable disc. You don't need to use Windows Explorer or a third-party CD-burning or DVD-burning program to do this (although you might choose to use another program if you find that Windows Media Player lacks a feature you find essential).

With a compatible drive, Windows Media Player can burn any of the following three types of discs:

- **Audio CD**   This type of disc plays back in any CD player, including the one in your car. One major caveat: the burning engine in Windows Media Player does not support the CD-Text standard, so any disc you burn here will not display album and track information on a car CD player that can read this information.

- **Data CD**   Typically, these discs consist of MP3 and WMA files. You can play back a data CD on another computer or on a player that recognizes MP3 and WMA tracks (as most recent-vintage car players do). Unless you change the default burn settings, Windows Media Player uses metadata from selected tracks to organize your list by folder and adds a playlist in Windows Playlist (WPL) format.

- **Data DVD**   This type of disc is similar to a data CD, with the major advantage that it holds significantly more data. Note that a data DVD is not the same as a video DVD and might not play back in some consumer DVD players.

To start, insert a blank CD or DVD in the drive and click the Burn tab to display the burn list. Drag songs, albums, playlists, or artists to the list pane to build the list; if you're planning to burn a data CD or DVD, you can add pictures and video clips (in WMV format) as well.

For more details on how to create, edit, and save lists, see "Working with Playlists" on page 490.

The box above the burn list displays the current disc setting. For audio CDs, the display shows how much time is available and how much will be used by the current burn list; the running time of the current selection is shown at the top of the burn list itself. Figure 14-11 shows an audio CD that still has room for a few more tracks.

Figure 14-11 As you fill the burn list, the display above the list tells you how much time you'll use on an audio CD.

For a data disc, the display shows available and used disc space. The example shown here uses the same list of tracks as in Figure 14-11, but this data disc is nowhere near being full, thanks to compressed audio files.

If the total time or disc space in your burn list is greater than the capacity of the blank disc, Windows Media Player adds Next Disc markers at the break points and changes the display at the top of the list to indicate how much time (or space) remains on the last disc. You can accept the disc breaks as defined or edit the playlist by adding and removing tracks. Drag individual tracks up or down to change their order. Click and drag a disc heading to rearrange the order of discs. A blue icon to the left of any track indicates that the track contains restricted media usage rights that don't allow burning.

To switch between audio and data disc formats, use the List Options menu, which sits unobtrusively at the top of the list pane, as shown here.

Other options on this menu allow you to shuffle or sort the burn list, give the disc a name that will be visible in the Computer window within Windows Explorer, and specify whether you want the disc to be ejected automatically after burning. Click More Burn Options to open the dialog box shown in Figure 14-12.

Figure 14-12 By default, all settings in this dialog box are enabled.

These settings apply to all CDs you burn using Windows Media Player. Two particularly interesting settings are under the Audio CDs heading. By default, volume levels are automatically adjusted for tracks on audio CDs. This option is useful for mix CDs, where the content is drawn from a variety of sources and volume levels can vary widely. You might want to disable this option if you're burning tracks from a single source and you want to maintain their fidelity. To change this setting, select or clear the Apply Volume Leveling Across Tracks option. The second option in this category, Burn CD Without Gaps, turns on cross-fading for audio CDs to avoid the two-second gap that would otherwise be present. This setting is especially important for live recordings and classical pieces where the audio should play continuously across track breaks.

When you're ready to begin creating your disc, click the Start Burn button at the top of the list pane. The burning process takes a little while. Windows Media Player first checks each track to make sure that its media usage rights (if any) permit copying. For an audio CD, it converts MP3, WMA, and MPEG-4 Audio (AAC) files to a temporary WAV audio file. (Because WAV files are uncompressed, you might need as much as 700 MB of temporary storage to accommodate this process.) Finally, it begins burning the selected tracks or files to your blank disc.

You can follow the progress of all these operations by watching the Status column on the Burn tab, or you can return to another part of Windows Media Player and perform other tasks.

By default, Windows Media Player ejects your disc when the copy is complete. If you've prepared a multidisc burn list, this option makes it easy to replace the completed disc with a fresh blank one and click Start Burn to continue. The Eject operation can be dangerous, however, if your computer is a tower model stored on the floor next to your knee. If you're unaware that a disc has popped out, you could inadvertently bump the drive and injure your knee, snap the drive tray, or both. If you don't want burned discs to eject automatically, clear the Eject Disc After Burning option on the List Options menu.

Using DVDs to Share Pictures and Videos

Every edition of Windows 7 can burn data DVDs for backup and for playback on other computers. The premium editions of Windows 7 (Home Premium and higher) include Windows DVD Maker, which you can use to create custom discs in DVD format that can be played back in the living room on a consumer DVD player connected to your TV (or on another computer, using its DVD playback software).

DVD Maker includes no pull-down menus. Instead, you use a two-step wizard: First, you put together the pictures or videos (or both) that will go on your DVD. Next, you add a title and create a DVD menu that can be navigated with a remote control. When both of these steps are complete, you burn the project. Windows DVD Maker supports digital video files in WMV or AVI container formats but not those saved in MPEG-4 formats; you can use photos in any format that Windows 7 recognizes.

You'll find the Windows DVD Maker shortcut on the Start menu, near the top of the All Programs menu. After you bypass the opening screen, you can begin building the list of items that will go on your new DVD. Figure 14-13 shows a DVD project after we added a handful of video files to it.

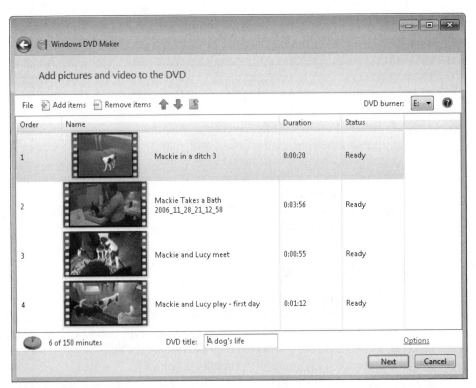

Figure 14-13 Be sure to enter a disc title in the box at the bottom of this dialog box before going on to the next step.

To add content, click the Add Items button above the contents pane and choose video or picture files from Windows Explorer. Use the Remove Items button to delete the current selection (with no warning or confirmation!) from the current list. Enter a disc title in the box at the bottom of the dialog box, and click Next to continue.

The Ready To Burn DVD step, shown in Figure 14-14, allows you to choose from a variety of menu styles and then customize the menu to suit your preferences.

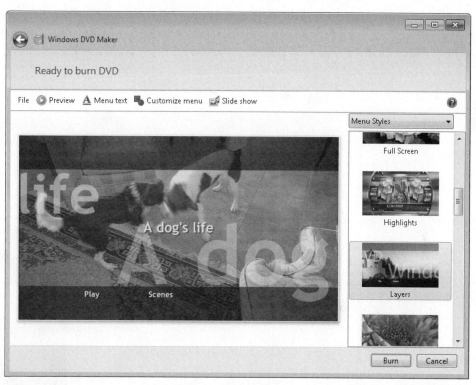

Figure 14-14 You can accept one of the canned menu styles, such as the Layers option shown here, or use the row of buttons along the top to customize the menu.

The four buttons along the top of this dialog box allow you to preview the DVD based on its current content and settings, customize the menu, and synchronize a slide show with music. The following choices are available:

- **Preview**   Takes you to a page that allows you to test-drive the DVD using on-screen controls that mimic those on a DVD player's remote control. You can see not only what menus look like but how they work. Preview buttons are available from other customization screens as well.

- **Menu Text**   Includes edit controls where you can change the DVD title; customize the text that identifies the Play and Scenes buttons; choose fonts, font colors, and font styles; and add notes.

- **Customize Menu**   Includes the same font choices as in the Menu Text option, as well as options to customize the video clips and sounds that play while the menu is visible. By default, DVD Maker picks snippets from the items in your project and uses them to add zing to the menu. If the snippets it chooses are inappropriate, you can

create your own short custom video files, save them in WMV format, and use them
here. You can also choose a different background audio track to play along with the
menu. Click Change Style to accept the changes you just made. Note the Save As
New Style button, which allows you to add your custom options to the menu list so
that you can reuse the changes you make here.

- **Slide Show**   Includes options suitable for DVDs that include only photos. This page
  allows you to include audio files as the sound track, change the length of time each
  picture is visible on the screen, and select transition effects. The most interesting
  option is the Change Slide Show Length To Match Music Length box, which automatically adjusts the intervals between photos so that the show begins and ends with
  the music.

When you've finished customizing the menus, insert a blank disc in the DVD drive, click the
Burn button, and be prepared to wait. When the burn is complete, be sure to label the disc
(if you haven't done so already). It's also worth previewing the resulting disc in a compatible player to be sure that everything went as expected. If you notice any glitches, it's easier
to fix them now than it is to try to re-create the entire project later.

Using Windows Media Center

W HEN you picture a media center, you probably imagine it in the living room, hooked up to a widescreen high-definition TV and a surround-sound system. But the Windows Media Center interface is also at home in dorm rooms, hotel rooms, offices, bedrooms, and other relatively small places where a computer display is big enough to stand in for a TV and where you can use a remote control or a mouse to operate a jukebox filled with music, movies, slide shows, and videos.

Windows Media Center is included with all the premium editions of Windows 7, and its feature set is identical in each one. Its most basic function is to serve as a simpler alternative interface to Windows Media Player. Media Center uses the same media libraries you manage in Windows Explorer and Windows Media Player, so when you add or tag content in one place, it appears in Media Center as well. And it does much more when you add the right hardware.

With a TV tuner and a signal source—an antenna or a cable TV or satellite connection—you can configure Media Center to act as a digital video recorder whose capacity is limited only by the amount of disk space you give it. Add an Xbox 360 in its role as a hardware extender, and a single Media Center PC is also capable of feeding music, pictures, movies, and live or recorded TV to multiple rooms over a wired or wireless network.

What's in Your Edition?

Windows Media Center is included in Home Premium, Professional, and Ultimate editions. All the features we describe in this chapter are available in those editions. Some features require additional hardware. In addition, we assume that your computer, if it's part of a network, is joined to a homegroup and is not joined to a Windows domain.

Our immediate goal is to help you get Media Center up and running, regardless of where you live or what room your PC is located in.

Setting Up and Customizing Media Center

Media Center does not run by default when you start Windows. You have to start the program by using the Media Center shortcut on the Start menu or by pressing the green button on a remote control that's been set up for use with the PC you want to start. The main executable file for the Media Center program is Ehshell.exe. You'll find it and its fellow program and settings files in %SystemRoot%\Ehome; as its name suggests, the main program serves as a shell that in turn calls other functions, such as Windows Media Player.

INSIDE OUT   Get answers to complex questions online

Even if we were to devote every one of the 1,000-plus pages in this book to Media Center–related topics, we'd have to leave out some details. If you're having issues with getting specific hardware to work properly or you're looking for the latest Media Center add-ins, we suggest you stop by *thegreenbutton.com*. (The site name comes from the green button at the center of every Media Center–compatible remote control, which takes you to the Start menu.) This online community was founded by Media Center enthusiasts, and although it's now owned by Microsoft, it has retained its independent character. Ian Dixon's *thedigitallifestyle.com* is also a valuable resource for questions about Media Center and related technologies.

If your system configuration is simple—especially if it doesn't include a TV tuner or connect to a fancy surround-sound system—setting up Media Center can take literally one click (or one tap on a remote control). The first time you run Media Center, you see the Welcome carousel and then the Get Started screen, shown next. The oversized Express link is highlighted by default; if you click Express (as most people will), you launch immediately into the Windows Media Center experience, ready to play music, movies, or videos or browse through your library of digital photos.

In general, the Express configuration is perfectly adequate for most purposes and allows you to begin using Media Center immediately. (If you have a TV tuner, you can set it up now using the Custom option or defer that task till later, as we describe in "Recording and Watching TV" on page 556.)

If you want to fine-tune your Media Center experience, choose the Custom setup option and run through the options we explain in this section. You start with a required setup section that checks your network and Internet connection and offers you several opportunities to read the Media Center privacy statement. Assuming your network is set up already, the only substantive option is on the Enhanced Playback page, where you get to decide whether to download information from the Internet, including cover art for albums and DVDs, information about movies, and TV listings. Most people will click Yes here.

After you finish the required setup, you can go through any of the four choices on the Optional Setup page:

- If you have one or more TV tuners installed, the first option on the Optional Setup page allows you to configure the tuner and the downloadable program guide to work with your channel lineup; we cover this task in more detail in "Recording and Watching TV" on page 556.

- The next option (at the top of the menu if you're lacking a TV tuner) is a wizard that allows you to configure your monitor or TV. The wizard includes a video clip that helps you identify and fix problems with aspect ratios, color settings, and so on.

- Next on the menu is a speaker setup wizard that lets you specify how many speakers you have and test them for correct connections and performance.

- The final option allows you to specify which folders Media Center should use to build its library. By default, your library contains all folders that are currently included in the default Music, Pictures, and Videos libraries for the logged-on user account. Media Center also creates a Recorded TV library during setup and adds the contents of the local Recorded TV folder from C:\Users\Public. (The Movies folder is unique to Media Center and can be managed only there.) You can add or remove folders from any of these libraries by using this option in Media Center, or you can use the corresponding interface in Windows Explorer, Windows Media Player, or the Zune software; the results are reflected in all locations. You can populate the Media Center library with folders from a local volume or from shared folders on the network, as shown in Figure 15-1, where shared media folders on a Windows Home Server and other networked computers are available.

For details on how to change the list of folders monitored in your default media libraries, see "Working with Libraries" on page 343.

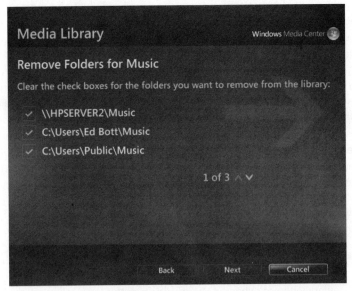

Figure 15-1 Media Center libraries reflect the contents of your Music, Pictures, and Videos libraries. You can manage them in Media Center or in Windows Explorer.

At any time after you complete this initial setup, you can customize your Media Center configuration by using a list of additional options on the Settings menu. To display this menu, use either of the following techniques:

- Using the Media Center remote control, press the green button to go to the Start menu, and then select Settings from the Tasks strip. (If you are currently viewing music, pictures, or other content, press More Info on the remote control and choose Settings from the shortcut menu.)

- Using the mouse and keyboard, click the green button in the upper left corner of the Media Center window to go to the Start menu. (If the green button isn't visible, click anywhere within the Media Center window and move the mouse to make it appear.) Then use the Up Arrow and Down Arrow keys to move through the main menu options; press Left Arrow when you reach Tasks to select Settings, and then press Spacebar or Enter.

You'll find an assortment of useful options on the General menu, where you can adjust the Media Center settings shown in Table 15-1.

Table 15-1 **Media Center General Options**

Menu Choice	Available Options
Startup And Windows Behavior	Tweak the behavior of the Media Center window, including whether it starts automatically with Windows.
Visual And Sound Effects	Choose a color scheme, set a background color to fill the screen when the video signal uses less than the full screen (black, white, or a shade of gray), and enable or disable transition effects and sounds for menu actions.
Windows Media Center Setup	Configure your Internet connection, speakers, TV signal, and TV or monitor. The Run Setup Again choice resets all Media Center options and allows you to start fresh.
Parental Controls	Lock out access to programs based on TV or movie ratings; access is controlled by a four-digit PIN you select.
Automatic Download Options	Control whether and when Media Center retrieves album art and other information from the Internet. The Download Now option forces the program guide to refresh immediately.
Optimization	Select the single check box here to specify a time, once per day, when Windows will restart the Ehshell.exe process (the Media Center shell). This restart doesn't happen if you're watching or listening to content or if the recorder is busy.
About Windows Media Center	Display the Media Center version number and the terms of service for the online program guide.
Privacy	Read the privacy statement, and adjust some privacy settings that affect Internet connections and the TV program guide.

Chapter 15

INSIDE OUT   Let Media Center start itself

If you have set up a Windows-based PC whose primary function is to run Media Center, why stop at the Windows desktop every time you start? From the Tasks strip, choose Settings, then General, and then Startup And Window Behavior. Select the Start Windows Media Center When Windows Starts option, as we have done here. The Always Keep Windows Media Center On Top option makes certain that the taskbar doesn't block access to Media Center functions, as it can.

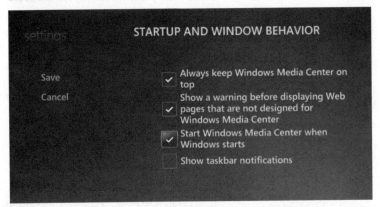

To force Media Center to use full-screen mode and suppress the Minimize, Restore, and Close buttons in the top right corner, go to the Media Center Start menu and select the Media Only option at the far right of the Tasks strip.

If your user account is the only one on the system and has no password, you'll go straight to the Media Center Start menu each time you power up your PC. Running with a password-free account creates problems when you need to access password-protected resources on a server, however, and it prevents you from logging on remotely using Remote Desktop tools. To start automatically with a password-protected account, open the Run dialog box (press Windows logo key+R), type **netplwiz**, and then press Enter. On the Users tab of the User Accounts dialog box, clear the Users Must Enter A User Name And Password To Use This Computer check box. Click OK or Apply, and enter the user name and password when prompted. This option bypasses the Log On screen and automatically logs on using the specified account each time you start the computer. For security's sake, we recommend that you create a dedicated account for Media Center use and control which shared resources are available for access by that account.

Mastering the Media Center Interface

Some brilliant (but anonymous) observer of technology once pointed out that we work with computers from 2 feet away but typically sit 10 feet from a TV. And thus was born the concept of the 10-foot interface, which dictates the design of Windows Media Center. Every menu and option in Media Center was created so that you can see it from across the room and navigate through menus, lists, and libraries with a remote control using four arrows and a big OK button.

The Start menu, shown in Figure 15-2, is the jumping-off point for all Media Center activities. You can return to the Start menu from anywhere within Media Center by pressing the green button on the remote control (or, if you're navigating with a mouse, by clicking the green Media Center logo in the upper left corner, a target that is visible only after you move the mouse).

Figure 15-2 The Media Center Start menu is organized into strips. Use the up and down arrow buttons on a remote control to move through the main menu; the left and right arrows choose options for the selected strip.

With its oversized text and a clean design, the Start menu is easy to see and use from a distance. Clicking the up or down arrows on the remote control moves through the options on the main menu—Music, Pictures + Videos, and so on—each of which is called a *strip*. (If you go the wrong direction, just keep going. Most Media Center menus are circular, so if you press the up arrow from the top of the menu you'll begin again at the bottom of the menu.) Use the left and right arrow buttons on the remote control to select an option on the current strip, and then press OK to select it.

Chapter 15

INSIDE OUT Pick your favorite remote control

All Media Center–compatible remote controls are not created equal. Different designs are available from PC makers and from third-party hardware designers. Every design has some common features (the green button, for example, and basic navigation controls), but different designers add their own touches to differentiate their designs. One element worth looking for if you plan to use a Media Center PC connected directly to a PC without a separate sound system is an extra power button to turn a TV on or off. For complex home theater installations, you'll probably want a universal remote control that can handle every component. Our personal preference in this category is just about anything from Logitech's extensive Harmony line (*logitech.com/harmony*). The setup software runs on Windows 7 and can assign functions to match your Media Center remote control without requiring any programming skills. From personal testing, we can confirm that these units consistently score highly on the crucial Spousal Acceptance Factor rating.

Most of the Start menu options are self-explanatory; the Music, Pictures + Videos, and Movies strips all lead to galleries of the associated content that can be sorted and grouped in a wide variety of ways, along with options to set up custom playlists of your favorite items, tune in radio stations, and so on. The Extras strip is where you'll find games and online services, and the Tasks strip is where you go to customize Media Center settings and hardware. Third-party software developers can add custom strips to the Start menu as well. For a good example of this capability, Media Center users in the United States can check out the Sports strip, which is linked with several online sports information sources and ties into the program guide when a TV tuner is installed and configured.

The Now Playing strip is visible only when you're playing music, watching a video or recorded TV program, or playing a slide show. This strip includes a live thumbnail representation of whatever is currently playing, with a title beneath it. Select this thumbnail to play that content in a full screen.

For some items, you can display a Details window that provides information about the selected item as well as commands and other actions you can take. (For a picture, the View and Resume Slide Show commands are at the top of the list, with another group of options under the Additional Commands heading.) For some items, the Details window is split into multiple panes, as is the case with the recorded TV program shown in Figure 15-3. The headings at the top of the Details window allow you to move from pane to pane. In this example, press the right arrow to move to the Other Showings pane, where you can see a list of upcoming episodes in the same series as the current selection.

Figure 15-3 Use the left and right arrows to switch to a different details pane.

Chapter 15

INSIDE OUT   More Info = right-click

Years of experience have probably taught you to right-click whenever you need additional options throughout Windows. In Media Center, the remote control equivalent of a right-click is a press of the More Info button, which inevitably leads to a useful context menu. Select a song in the Now Playing queue and the choices allow you to change its rating, burn the track to a CD, or see additional albums or tracks by that artist. Click More Info when a picture is selected and the top choice is Picture Details, which leads to a Details window where you can rotate the picture, crop it, or remove red eye, among other actions.

In this case, you have four details panes to choose from. In the Actions pane, shown in Figure 15-3, Play is selected by default, but you can use the up and down arrows to choose a different option, such as burning a copy of the program to a CD or DVD. Use the left and right arrows to switch between panes. In this example, the Other Showings pane is to the right. You need to scroll in either direction to ascertain that the other panes are Synopsis and Cast + Crew.

Pressing the More Info button when a video or recorded TV program is playing brings up a multipane menu along the bottom of the screen. Use the left and right arrow buttons to move from pane to pane and see which options are available.

Navigating and Entering Text with a Remote Control

In addition to the green button, which takes you to the Media Center Start menu (or returns you to your previous location if you're currently at the Start menu), the following special navigation keys are available on the remote control:

- **Back**   This button functions just like the Back button in a web browser, taking you to the previous page or menu. Its memory, alas, is not unlimited; it remembers only the eight most recent pages.

- **Channel/Page Up/Down**   These keys move one screen at a time through music and picture galleries and through the TV program guide. When you're watching live TV, they allow you to "channel surf" by switching the tuner to the next higher or lower channel as filtered by the guide.

- **Replay/Skip**   While you are playing back a TV show, these buttons jump 7 seconds back or 30 seconds forward, respectively. Within the TV program guide, they move 12 hours forward or backward. In the Music Library, they skip to the previous or next song in the current queue, respectively.

- **Live TV**   Use this button to immediately begin playing whatever program is on the currently selected TV channel.

- **Recorded TV**   This button serves as a shortcut that opens the Recorded TV library and displays its contents.

- **Guide**   Press this button to open the TV program guide. If a program is already playing, pressing Recorded TV or Guide allows the current program to continue to play in the background as you browse the library or guide in the foreground.

In some cases, the remote control doesn't have all the keys you need to enter the information required for the task at hand. If you select Search from the Music strip on the Start menu, for example, you need to enter a search term such as the name of an artist or album. The keyboard works just fine for this task, but coaxing text out of the numeric keypad at the bottom of the remote control is slightly more problematic. The solution is the On Screen Keyboard that appears when you navigate to a text box and press OK. Use the arrow buttons to move around the keyboard layout and press OK to tap the virtual key, as shown here:

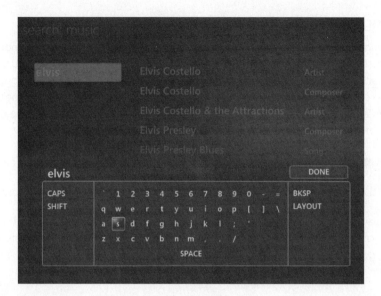

Older versions of Windows Media Center required you to enter text by using the numeric keypad (a technique many people have mastered on a mobile phone). That old-school option is still available in Windows 7. Instead of pressing OK in a text box, press any numeric key. That opens the layout shown here:

Continue to press keys on the numeric keypad to cycle through the letters and numbers available for that key, or use the OK button and the virtual keypad instead. Continue pressing the key until you reach the character you want. If the next character you want to enter is assigned to a different key, you can press that key immediately. You can switch between three different alphanumeric keypad mappings by pressing the Channel Up and Channel

Down buttons on the remote control or by using the Mode button on the virtual keypad. Use the Layout option to toggle between the virtual keyboard and the virtual keypad.

Using Media Center with a Mouse or Keyboard

Although the Media Center interface was designed for ease of use with a remote control, it also responds well to more conventional forms of input. If you move the mouse (or touch the trackpad on a notebook PC) while Media Center is running, navigation controls appear in two of the four corners. Use the back arrow and the green Media Center logo in the upper left corner to emulate pressing the corresponding buttons on a remote control. Playback and volume controls appear in the lower right corner, as shown here:

The playback controls in the center are familiar to anyone who's ever used a DVD player. The four controls on the left allow you to record the current TV program, switch to the program guide, and use the Channel/Page Up and Channel/Page Down buttons, respectively. The three buttons on the right allow you to mute, lower, or raise the volume.

All of these elements go away after five seconds of inactivity on the mouse's part.

You can also use a keyboard to gain full access to Media Center functions. The techniques we describe here work with a wired keyboard or one built into a notebook PC; if you have a wireless keyboard with sufficient range, you can control your Media Center PC from the comfort of your couch, using the keyboard as a replacement for or supplement to the remote control.

Some keyboard commands are obvious: the Up Arrow, Down Arrow, Left Arrow, and Right Arrow keys work just like the navigation controls on the remote, and pressing Enter or Spacebar is the same as pushing OK. Page Up and Page Down map to the Channel Up/ Down buttons. In search boxes, you can type search terms directly and use the Backspace key to clear the most recently typed character.

Table 15-2 lists some other combinations that might be less obvious but are still useful. In particular, the numeric keypad on a full-size keyboard can fill in for a lot of tasks that you would otherwise handle with a remote control while watching live TV and while viewing the guide.

Chapter 15

Table 15-2 **Media Center Keyboard Shortcuts**

Menu Choice	Keyboard Shortcut
Media Center Start menu (start Media Center, if necessary)	Windows logo key+Alt+Enter
Recorded TV	Ctrl+O or Ctrl+Shift+T
Guide	Ctrl+G
Music Library	Ctrl+M
Video Library	Ctrl+E
Picture Library	Ctrl+I
Movie Library	Ctrl+Shift+M
Radio	Ctrl+A
Go back to previous screen	Backspace
Toggle full screen/window	Alt+Enter
Go to channel number (Live TV or Guide)	Enter number using the 0–9 keys
Up one channel (while playing TV)	Plus (+) or Equal (=)
Down one channel (while playing TV)	Minus (–)
Record	Ctrl+R
More Info/Display shortcut menu	Ctrl+D
Play	Ctrl+Shift+P
Pause/Play (toggle)	Ctrl+P
Stop	Ctrl+Shift+S
Replay (Back)	Ctrl+B
Skip (Forward)	Ctrl+F
Rewind	Ctrl+Shift+B
Fast Forward	Ctrl+Shift+F
Mute	F8
Volume up	F9
Volume down	F10
Audio language options (TV or DVD)	Ctrl+Shift+A
Subtitles/Closed Captions	Ctrl+U

Chapter 15

Playing Music, Pictures, Videos, and Movies

From the Media Center Start menu, you can jump directly to any of four libraries: Music, Pictures, Videos, and Movies. The basic layout of each library is simple, with minor variations to account for the different ways you're likely to browse or play different types of content. Figure 15-4 shows the Music library, which is probably the most complex of the bunch.

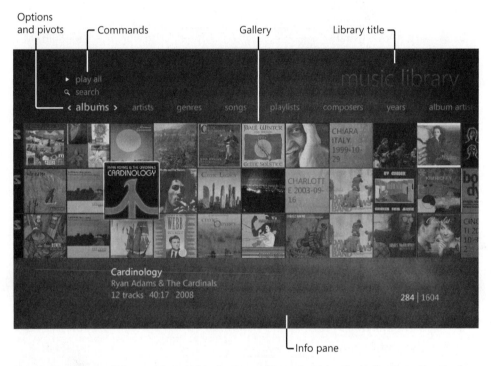

Figure 15-4 The basic layout of every Media Center library includes these elements. Use the bar above the gallery to filter or sort.

Here's a quick guided tour of these basic navigation elements:

- The library title appears in the upper right corner. If you're browsing through the Pictures or Videos library, the current folder name appears here.

- In the center of the display is the gallery, which lists the content you're currently browsing. Use the right and left arrow buttons to scroll through the gallery. Depending on how you've filtered and sorted the current contents, you might be able to view large or small thumbnails or switch to a list view that packs more information (albeit with less graphic pizzazz) into the visible portion of the gallery. Press More Info to change views using the menu shown next.

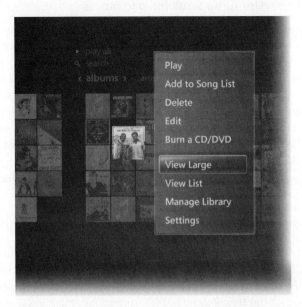

- Immediately above the gallery is a single row of options that you can select to display a different set of data or to sort the current set. (Among Media Center aficionados, each such view is called a *pivot*.) In the Music library, for example, you can scroll through all songs or playlists, or you can choose categories such as genres or years to filter the library to show only albums tagged with the item you choose. In the Pictures library, you can filter by tag, date taken, and ratings or browse by folder.

- In the upper left corner of the Music and Pictures libraries you'll find commands: Play All and Search in the Music library, and Play Slide Show in the Pictures library.

- Information about the selected item appears below the gallery. In thumbnail views like the album view shown in Figure 15-4, the selected item appears larger than its neighbors. In the lower right corner is a count of the current view, which reveals that the selected album is number 284 in an alphabetically sorted list of 1,604 albums.

In any view in any library, you can jump through the list by entering characters from the keyboard or the remote's keypad; Media Center immediately takes you to the first entry in the list that matches the characters you enter. In Artists view, for example, if you press the 7 key three times in succession, you get the letter R. Press the 6 key three times to show the letter O, and then press 5 three times quickly to get the letter L. If you have any albums by The Rolling Stones in your collection, you'll go straight to their entry in the list.

INSIDE OUT   Use Turbo Scroll for long moves

In any gallery view, you can press and hold the left or right arrow button to move through the gallery in either direction. If you keep either button held down for approximately two seconds, navigation shifts into Turbo Scroll mode. In lists of albums, covers appear as milestones as you whiz through the list; alphabetical hints beneath the gallery tell you where you are. In folders filled with photos, the display tells you where you are numerically speaking. Turbo Scroll also works in TV listings. To adjust the settings, you have to roll up your sleeves and edit a setting in the registry, specifically HKLM\SOFTWARE\Microsoft\Windows\CurrentVersion\Media Center\Settings\Turbo-Scroll. Find the DWORD value GuideDelay (if it doesn't exist, create it), and set it to the interval you want, in milliseconds. Entering a value of 3,000 would initiate TurboScroll approximately three seconds after you begin scrolling.

In the Music library, you can add search results, individual songs, or entire albums to the current queue. If you choose Play All, the current album replaces the contents of the current Now Playing list. Choose Add To Now Playing if you want the current album to be added to the end of the Now Playing list. Similar options are also available from the Details window for an album or song.

In the Pictures library, the most interesting feature is the ability to build slide shows quickly using only the remote control. Start by opening the Pictures library, choose Slide Shows from the options above the gallery, and then choose Create Slide Show. Follow the steps to browse by folder, tag, or date, and use the OK button to fill in the check box on pictures you want to add to the slide show list, as shown in Figure 15-5.

Repeat this process as many times as necessary, going to different folders or selecting different tags to find all the pictures you want in your slide show. When you finish, choose the Next button, rearrange the order of pictures if necessary, and save the results. The playlist appears in the Pictures library, available when you select the Slide Shows pivot.

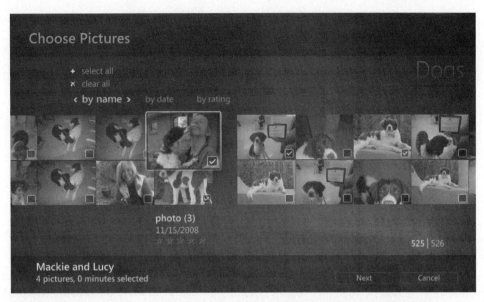

Figure 15-5 Use the OK button to add photos in the current view to a custom slide show.

The Movie library contains cover art and details for DVDs and for recorded TV programs that are categorized as movies. If you have a collection of movies that you have ripped into digital file formats using widely available DVD backup tools, you can add them to the library as well. Just use the Media Library tools on the Settings menu to specify at least one folder where your ripped DVDs are located.

Using Ratings and Playing Favorites

The larger your collection of digital pictures and music, the more likely you are to have some items you love and some that are there only because you can't force yourself to delete them. A major improvement in Windows 7 Media Center allows you to quickly go through a folder (or an entire hard drive) full of pictures and rate them on the standard scale of one to five stars using only the remote control. You can also rate songs while they're playing, using the 1 to 5 buttons on the numeric keypad (or 0 to remove any previously applied rating).

Begin by opening a folder full of pictures or switching to the Date Taken pivot, select the first picture in the gallery, and press OK. That opens the picture in full-screen view, with no menus or other options visible. To rate the current picture, press the number that matches the rating you want to give it. If this is the first time you've tried this, you'll be asked whether you want to enable shortcuts, as shown next.

Chapter 15

Choose the default, Enable Shortcuts, and the rating you just applied will appear in the upper left corner. Use the left and right arrows to move through the entire selection of pictures, using the number buttons to rate each one. (To remove a rating, press 0.)

All the work you put into rating your music and pictures pays off when you use new features in Windows 7 Media Center to create slide shows or playlists based on what you define as favorites. You can define separate criteria for music and pictures. To see your current settings, choose Settings from the Tasks strip, choose Pictures (or Music), and then choose Favorite Pictures (or Favorite Music). The resulting set of options allows you to define what constitutes your favorites.

For instructions on how to create a custom playlist (or auto playlist) that can be used to define your favorites, see "Working with Playlists" on page 490.

Both the Music strip and the Pictures + Videos strip on the Start menu offer a Play Favorites option that immediately begins playing tunes or a slide show based on the criteria you previously defined. (If you use both Play Favorites options, you get a slide show with a musical background.) The favorites-based slide show (known internally among Microsoft developers as Ambient) will also launch as a screen saver when you invoke the new Play Favorites option on the Start menu. The slide show features some impressive visual effects, zooming in and out, fading your photos from black and white to color as they come into focus. It's a dazzling effect, guaranteed to be a crowd pleaser if you put in the time to rate pictures first.

CDs, DVDs, and Devices

If you want music CDs and DVDs to begin playing in Media Center as soon as you insert them into a drive, you need to adjust AutoPlay settings. In the absence of custom settings, Media Center expects you to manually cue up and play these forms of media.

When you insert a music CD into the drive of a PC running Windows Media Center, the new CD appears in the top left slot in the Music library. When you select the CD, you see information about the CD, and a menu gives you the option to play the CD or rip its tracks using the format and bit rate currently set on the Rip Music tab in the Windows Media Player Options dialog box.

For more details on how to adjust settings for CDs you copy to your PC, see "Ripping CDs" on page 496.

To play a DVD in Media Center, choose Movies from the Start menu, and then choose Play DVD. Use the More Info button to display a shortcut menu with additional options, including a Zoom menu, which adjusts letter-boxed pictures so that they display to best advantage with your screen dimensions, and a Title Menu option, which jumps to the DVD's menu.

If you've already set up a portable music player for synchronization with Windows Media Player, you can perform the same tasks from the Media Center interface. You'll find the Sync option on the Start menu in the Tasks menu. Prepare to be a little disappointed by the options available here, however. Unlike the rich interface in Windows Media Player, your only option in Media Center is to sync with one or more playlists. And it won't work with an Apple-branded device (such as an iPod or iPhone) or a Windows Phone or Zune player.

Chapter 15

Accessing Shared Libraries

If your PC is joined to a homegroup, you have access to every shared media library from within Media Center. To browse through the contents of a library on another PC on the network, look for the Shared option, on the far right of the menu above the gallery in the Music, Pictures, Videos, and Recorded TV libraries. Click that to see a list of all other PCs in your homegroup that have matching content to share with you.

From a navigation point of view, there's almost no difference between using a shared library and a local one. The name of the computer doing the sharing appears in the title section in the top right corner of the library, and you'll see an occasional warning that some options are unavailable. When accessing a shared library, be aware of possible performance issues, especially when accessing large shared libraries. Also be aware that copy-protected content will play back only on the device on which it was originally recorded and can't be shared with other PCs.

Recording and Watching TV

For playing music, videos, and DVDs and viewing pictures, Media Center provides an alternative interface to Windows Media Player, but its feature set is essentially the same. What makes Media Center really shine is its unique ability to play back live TV, record individual TV shows or series, and allow you to manage a collection of recorded TV programs from a comfy chair with nothing more than a remote control.

Before you can begin recording TV, you need to have the right hardware. The most important ingredient, of course, is a TV tuner. Tuners can be internal cards or external devices (typically connected through a USB port). After installing a tuner, you next have to provide a television signal (from an over-the-air antenna, a cable TV connection, or a satellite converter box). You need a Media Center remote control and its infrared receiver (which can be built into the computer or attached to a USB port on the PC). And you need disk space, lots of it.

We apologize in advance to our readers outside the United States for our inability to cover the hardware and content providers found in those markets. Broadcast and satellite technologies vary depending on geographic location, and many of the changes in Windows 7 are specifically designed to improve the TV experience in locations such as Japan and Western Europe. Because the authors of this book live in the United States, and thus have hands-on experience only with U.S. broadcast technologies, this chapter covers only the standards commonly used in the United States.

Setting Up One or More TV Tuners

Windows Media Center can recognize and use analog and digital TV tuners, as well as a special class of tuners that work with CableCARD devices supplied by a cable TV provider. In the United States, all over-the-air (OTA) broadcasts are in digital format and use the Advanced Television Systems Committee (ATSC) standard; connecting an antenna to one or more digital tuners allows you to record OTA high-definition TV (HDTV) signals. You can connect an analog tuner directly to a cable input if your cable provider supports this configuration. To record digital output from a cable or satellite connection, you must connect the output of a converter box to the tuner or use a CableCARD device that performs the functions of a set-top box. In Windows 7, you can install up to four tuners of each type.

Setting up one or more TV tuners requires that you install drivers for the tuner hardware. If you've selected a popular, well-supported device, the drivers should be installed automatically and updated by Windows Update. If Windows Update doesn't recognize the device, visit the manufacturer's website and download the latest drivers. If no Windows 7 drivers are available, try drivers listed as compatible with Windows Vista.

After you connect a video source (antenna, cable box, CableCARD, or satellite converter), you need to configure the TV signal. If you haven't yet set up your hardware, you can do so by choosing Live TV Setup from the TV strip on the Start menu. Or choose Settings from the Tasks strip, choose TV, and then select Set Up TV Signal. In this procedure, you need to identify your signal provider, enter a ZIP Code so that you can receive the correct program guide listings, and specify which physical connections your tuner is using. We recommend that you allow Media Center to perform an automatic setup first; if the results aren't satisfactory, you can repeat the setup and choose manual options instead.

For ATSC tuners, Media Center scans all OTA channels as part of its setup process and displays the signal strength of each one. The scan loops through all channels continuously, allowing you to adjust the orientation of the antenna for best reception. You can also hide any channel whose signal is too weak for proper reception. After setup is complete, you can repeat this scan at any time by choosing Settings, TV, TV Signal, and then selecting Digital TV Antenna Signal Strength, as shown next.

Chapter 15

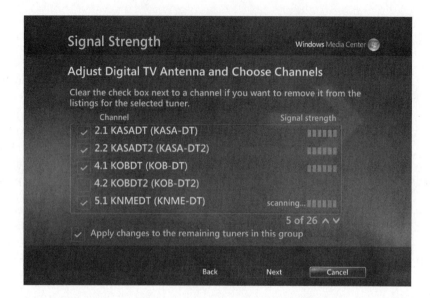

Finally, you need to configure the program guide. For large digital cable and satellite networks, the most important step in this process is removing access to channels you never watch. To customize the guide, open Settings, choose TV, and then choose Guide. If you choose Edit Channels, you're taken to a screen where you can select or clear the check box next to a channel listing to add it to or remove it from the guide. You can also change the order of channels and sort them by name instead of number.

Windows 7 also offers the capability to edit settings for individual channels. You can do this from the overall Edit Channels screen (just select a single channel's entry and press OK) or by selecting a channel in the program guide and then pressing More Info. Either option takes you to a settings page like the one shown in Figure 15-6.

You can change the channel name or number, but the real payoff comes for Media Center users with multiple TV tuners who want to specify which sources get preference when recording from a channel. Let's say you have a digital cable tuner and an over-the-air tuner both capable of receiving the same channel. In the guide, the channel appears as 13.1 for the OTA tuner and 213 for the cable tuner. Using the Edit Listings option, you can combine the two channels under a single number. Then, using the Edit Sources option, you can specify that you want the non-copy-protected OTA tuner to have first shot at recording anything on that channel, with the digital cable tuner kicking in only if the other tuner is occupied.

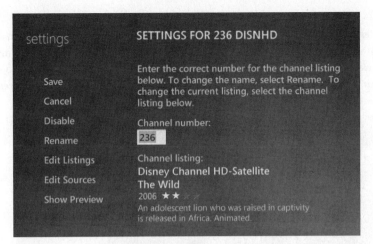

Figure 15-6 Use the settings here to fine-tune the display of a channel and define priority for tuners.

Finally, you can create Favorite Lineups, which are subsets of the program guide that you create based on your interests and preferences. You might want to create a Favorite Lineup called Movies, for example, containing only channels that specialize in movies. To create a Favorite Lineup, right-click anywhere on the guide, choose Edit Favorites, and then choose Add New.

Setting Up a Digital Cable Tuner

To watch or record high-definition content from premium channels that are available only through a cable subscription, you must have a digital tuner that is capable of decrypting the protected content being delivered by your TV provider. Windows Media Center supports a standard called the Open Cable Unidirectional Receiver (OCUR), also known as a digital cable tuner (DCT).

When Windows 7 was originally released, the use of these devices was limited to new PCs that were specifically built for this purpose, and successfully configuring a DCT required a second product key for the tuner itself. In 2009, these requirements were greatly relaxed. If you have a PC that satisfies the hardware requirements (most modern consumer PCs do) and is running Windows 7 Home Premium, Professional, or Ultimate, you can purchase a CableCARD-ready tuner and do the upgrade yourself. We highly recommend Ceton Corporation's InfiniTV 4 (*cetoncorp.com*), which is available as a PCI Express card that requires only a single CableCARD for four tuners.

Chapter 15

After connecting the hardware device, open the Media Center Start menu, choose Extras Library from the Extras strip, and choose Digital Cable Advisor. (You might have to wait a few minutes for this add-in to appear in the library.) The advisor confirms that your system meets the hardware requirements, takes care of the activation requirements, and downloads the necessary support files.

Your cable company provides the CableCARD, which uses the PC Card form factor and is designed to slide into a slot on the DCT. Many cable companies require that this component be delivered and activated by their installer. If you set up a DCT and attach the incoming cable feed without inserting a CableCARD, it functions as a "clear QAM" digital tuner and allows you to receive any unprotected channels (both standard and high definition) that are available over your digital cable connection.

After your CableCARD device is successfully "paired" with a tuner and then activated on your account, it cannot be moved. If you try to swap CableCARD devices between tuners, you'll end up losing all access to the programming you've paid for, and fixing the mess will probably require another visit from a cable installer. (You can, however, move the tuner and CableCARD as a unit to a new PC without having to reactivate the CableCARD device.)

DCTs can be tricky to install, at least initially. If you have trouble getting digital cable to work, start the troubleshooting with your cable company. (You might need to escalate your request a level or two before you find someone who understands the nuances of CableCARD support in Windows.)

Recording TV Programs and Series

The biggest advantage of using Media Center for TV recording is that program listings are free and updated regularly. To see what's on TV right now or at any time until approximately two weeks into the future, choose Guide from the Start menu or press the Guide button on the remote control. In the guide, a red dot next to a listing means it's set to record. A red dot with a shadow denotes a series recording.

Use the Channel Up and Channel Down buttons on the remote control (or the Page Up and Page Down keys on the keyboard) to move up or down a screen at a time. To jump to a particular channel, enter its number on the numeric keypad. Virtually everything in the guide can be selected for interaction. If you press OK after selecting the thin Categories bar on the left side, for instance, it expands to show a list of available categories, which you can use to filter the guide's contents.

INSIDE OUT   Use the search box

Search capabilities aren't available directly from the TV program guide, but you can search current listings by going to the Media Center Start menu and choosing Search from the TV strip. You can search by title, keyword, categories, movie actor, or movie director. The same search box is available from the Add Recording menu.

To record an individual upcoming program, highlight its entry in the program guide and press the Record button on the remote control, or press OK to display more details and then choose Record from the menu on the Details page. TV programs that are part of a series offer a text description, with options to record individual episodes or an entire series. Movies offer a richer details page that includes art and an option to read reviews and see additional cast information, as shown in Figure 15-7.

The Record button on the remote cycles through three settings. Press Record a second time to add the current selection as a series recording using default settings. Press Record a third time to cancel the recording.

> **Note**
> The Other Showings option is useful when you want to record an upcoming program that's on at the same time as one you've already chosen to record. Rather than cancel the original recording, choose Other Showings to see a list of alternate times and dates. If you're lucky enough to find an additional showing at a more convenient time, you can choose one of those dates and avoid the conflict.

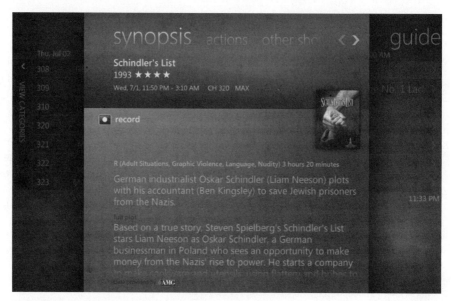

Figure 15-7 Movies, unlike programs and series, include ratings, reviews, and cast details drawn from an online database.

To record a series, start with any listing in that series. Press OK to see the details for that show, and then choose one of the following options:

- **Record Series**   Use this option if you want to add the recording to your series list using all the current default settings. (To view and adjust these settings, choose TV, choose Recorder, and finally select Recording Defaults.)

- **Advanced Record**   Select this option from the Actions pane if you want the series recordings to always start a minute (or two or three) early or end a little later. You can also choose how many copies of the series to keep on hand at any given time. For a series recording of a nightly news show, for example, you might want to keep only one show, discarding yesterday's news as soon as today's news begins recording.

To see all upcoming recordings, go to the Start menu, select Recorded TV, and choose View Scheduled. On this list, you can choose Series to see all series recordings you've set up. This list allows you to rank series to determine which one should be recorded in the event that programs from different series are on at the same time and you don't have enough available tuners to service the series requests. (If you have two tuners, this sort of conflict is less likely to be a problem, but the rules still come into play if you have *three* shows on at the same time. With four available tuners, you're unlikely to ever encounter a series conflict.)

About File Formats and Copy Protection

Media Center saves recorded TV programs in the Windows Recorded TV Show format, which uses the file name extension WTV. This file format replaces the Microsoft Recorded TV Show format (DVR-MS), which was used in previous Windows versions. Both are container formats that use the MPEG-2 standard for video encoding and MPEG-1 Layer II or Dolby Digital AC-3 for audio. WTV files include metadata about the content and any digital rights management (DRM) applied to it.

Like its predecessor, the WTV format consumes a large amount of space. An hour-long, standard-definition TV program can consume well over 3 GB of disk space at the highest quality supported by Media Center. High-definition content uses even more space: we've seen two-hour programs use as much as 16 GB of disk space. That makes it difficult to record a movie and then burn it to a standard DVD, which has a maximum capacity of roughly 4.5 GB. (If you select the Burn DVD option for one of these large files, Media Center offers to burn it at a "lower quality" but gives you no way to know just how much lower the quality will be, nor can you adjust the quality level manually.)

Over the years, a number of third-party tools have appeared that support converting DVR-MS files to formats that gobble less disk space; many have been updated to include support for WTV files. The version of Windows Movie Maker included with Windows Live Essentials Version 2011 supports both formats. If your preferred video editing tool supports only the older format, you can manually convert a WTV file for editing. Open the Recorded TV folder in Windows Explorer, right-click the file you want to convert, and click Convert To Dvr-ms Format from the shortcut menu. If disk space is scarce, beware: this process creates a copy of the file and leaves the original intact.

The Windows Recorded TV format, like its predecessor, also honors copy protection applied to recordings by the content provider. You can copy a protected program—such as a movie from a premium channel such as Home Box Office—and play it back on the same system on which it was recorded or on a Media Center Extender connected to that PC. But you can't play it back on another PC using Windows Media Player or Media Center (if you try, you'll see an error message). Unprotected files can be freely moved from one PC to another.

You can identify a copy-protected recording fairly easily from within Media Center. Select the program from the Recorded TV library and choose More Info. At the bottom of the Synopsis pane in the Details window, you'll see a Copy Protected label.

Windows 7 incorporates a new DRM technology called PlayReady. If you run into a DRM-protected program you might be prompted to install or upgrade PlayReady. The theoretical benefits of the PlayReady technology are that it allows sharing of content by multiple connected devices (such as those on a home network) and makes it possible to synchronize protected content between devices. Only time will tell whether these theoretical advantages become real.

Chapter 15

The clean, mostly uncluttered Media Center interface sometimes leads to options appearing in unlikely places. A good example is the History option, which shows you all the programs you've recorded, which ones failed to record because of a conflict or a hardware or signal problem, and those that were deleted either automatically or manually. This option is found, in unintuitive fashion, on the View Scheduled page. Options here allow you to sort by date or by status (if you start seeing Bad Tuner messages, it's time to do some troubleshooting). You can also clear the history.

Watching and Managing Recorded TV

To watch programs you've previously recorded, go to the Start menu and choose Recorded TV from the TV strip (or use the shortcut button on the remote control). Every recorded item in the list has a name and a thumbnail image (the thumbnail is generated using an algorithm that is uncanny in its ability to find an image that fits, usually a face). Figure 15-8 shows a large collection of all current recordings in List format. Click More Info and choose View Large from the shortcut menu to see much larger thumbnails for each program in a list that scrolls horizontally.

Figure 15-8 The List view of all recorded programs is more efficient than the default Large view—but it's somewhat harder to read.

Select any program from the list and press OK to see the Details window for that program. Options in the Actions pane allow you to change when the program is automatically deleted or burn it to a CD or DVD for archival purposes (if the program isn't copy protected, of course).

INSIDE OUT   The fastest way to delete a recording

From Recorded TV, you can delete any program—with no intermediate steps and only a single confirmation. Select the entry in the list, and then push the Clear button (usually found below the numeric keypad, in the lower left corner of the remote control). This brings up an "Are you sure?" dialog box with Yes conveniently selected. Press OK, and the program is gone. And when we say "gone," we mean it. Recordings you delete from Media Center do not go to the Recycle Bin and cannot be recovered using any supported tools in Windows or Media Center.

Sooner or later—usually sooner—you'll run out of disk space, at which point Media Center begins throwing out old recordings to make way for new ones. You can check on available disk space at any time: start by choosing Settings from the Tasks strip on the Start menu, then choose TV, then Recorder, and finally Recorder Storage. If you want to make sure that you reserve some space on your primary disk for documents and other data files, adjust Maximum TV Limit.

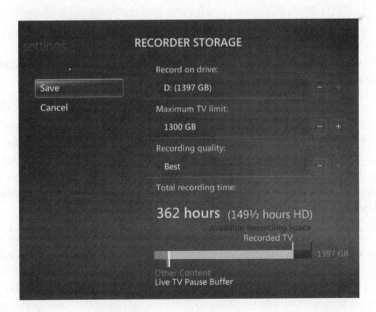

Chapter 15

Using an Xbox 360 as a Media Center Extender

Your PC is in the den, hooked up to an antenna or a cable connection (or both) and is dutifully recording your favorite TV programs to a large hard disk. That same PC also contains your libraries of music, movies, and digital pictures. Your most comfortable chair is in the living room, opposite a large-screen TV connected to a high-end audio system guaranteed to impress your friends and annoy your neighbors. How do you get those sounds and images off the PC in the den and into your living room? One excellent option is to set up an Xbox 360 console in the living room and use it as a Media Center Extender.

What Happened to Those Other Media Center Extenders?

Beginning in early 2008, a handful of manufacturers of consumer electronics and networking gear introduced stand-alone Media Center Extenders. These devices, which were originally intended for use with Windows Vista, were designed to be small and quiet so that they would fit comfortably in a living room. Unfortunately, the marketplace rejected them roundly, and by the time Windows 7 was released, all of them had been discontinued. If you have one of these orphaned devices (or if you find a secondhand unit for sale from a reputable seller), we have some good news for you: it will work just fine with Windows 7. These devices don't have the graphics capabilities of an Xbox 360, so some features are implemented differently, but the setup process is the same as we describe here.

When you use an Xbox 360 in its Media Center Extender mode, it communicates over a network with a Media Center PC. The system is capable of streaming high-definition video and surround sound over a network connection to the Xbox 360, which in turn routes it to the TV and audio equipment connected to it.

When you are working in Extender mode, you use a variant of the Media Center interface that is almost identical to the one on the PC itself. You don't need a keyboard or any internal storage; instead, the Xbox 360 acts as a remote console, accepting the input from your remote control in the living room and sending those requests over the network to the PC in the den, office, or basement, which in turn delivers high-definition TV, movies, music, or digital pictures back over the network to your big screen and sound system.

To use an Xbox 360 as a Media Center Extender, you have to connect it to your network and associate it with a Media Center–capable PC on the same network. If this is the first time you are connecting this device, Windows should detect its presence and display a message offering to set up a connection between the PC and the extender. You can also kick off this process manually by selecting Add Extender from the Tasks strip on the Start menu. Or you can right-click the icon for the extender device in the Network folder in Windows Explorer, and then click Configure.

The setup process is relatively simple: From the Xbox 360 console, choose System Settings, Computers, Windows Media Center, and then Setup. Make a note of the eight-digit setup key displayed on the Setup screen. Now go to the Media Center PC, choose Add Extender from the Tasks strip on the Media Center Start menu, and enter that eight-digit setup key on the Extender Setup screen, as shown here:

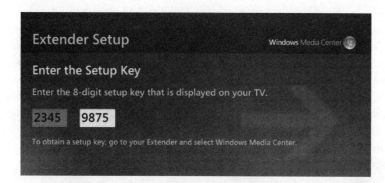

After you enter the correct value, the setup process enables the Media Center Extender service (Mcx2svc), configures the Windows Firewall to allow the extender to work on your network, and sets up your media libraries.

Media Center's extender feature operates by setting up a Remote Desktop session with the Media Center PC. You can connect as many as five extenders to a single Windows 7 PC. Each extender uses resources on the host PC. If you intend to use multiple extenders simultaneously, be sure you have a muscular hardware platform with a fast CPU and plenty of memory.

Behind the scenes, the way that extenders use media libraries on the associated Media Center PC can be confusing, at least initially. When you watch content directly on a PC, Media Center uses the libraries that belong to the logged-on user account. But each device configured as an extender on that PC uses its own unique account to log on: MCX1 for the first extender, MCX2 for the next, and so on. Each such account is restricted for use only by the associated extender. The first time you use the extender, you are prompted to set up a library, which includes all folders from the user account you're using when you perform the setup. If you later customize the folders where you store music, pictures, and other media files, you'll need to repeat those customizations on the extender.

Extenders do not automatically work with all types of content that you can play on the Media Center PC to which they're connected. All Windows Media codecs are supported, of course, as are MP3 and AAC. So you can play any TV programs you record with Media

Center and any music in standard formats. But you can't play a DVD or Blu-ray disc on your Media Center PC and stream the output to an extender. File formats that are supported on the PC but are not natively supported on the extender are normally transcoded to a supported format, such as MPEG-2 or H.264.

INSIDE OUT   Tuning an extender's performance

Streaming high-definition videos and recorded TV between a PC and an extender is a demanding task. A wired connection can usually provide sufficient bandwidth, but wireless connections can be problematic, especially if multiple computers are competing for the same bandwidth. To test (and, if necessary, tune) your network performance, open the Settings page and select Extender. This option shows a list of all extenders that have been configured to work with your device. With the extender turned on and connected to the network, you should see a menu like the one shown here when you select the extender from the list. (You can also run this test from the extender itself; from the Start menu, choose Tasks, and look for the Tune Network option.)

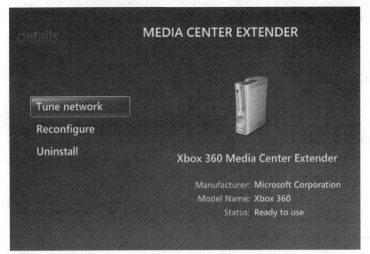

Be sure that nothing is playing on the extender, and then choose Tune Network to begin a brief performance test. At the end of the test, you receive a summary that tells you whether your network performance is acceptable or you need to perform some tuning.

Chapter 15

Digital Media for Enthusiasts

Is your digital music collection big enough to deserve a dedicated hard drive? Do you break into a cold sweat at the thought that your Media Center might not record the latest episode of your favorite TV series? Have you thought of setting up a PC in the living room so you can connect it directly to your big-screen HDTV and surround-sound system?

If the answer to any of those questions is yes, then you're a digital media enthusiast, and this chapter is for you. Casual music listeners and light TV watchers can move along.

In this chapter, we focus on a pair of Microsoft products that aren't officially part of Windows 7 but make exceptional additions to the platform. We start with the Zune software, which offers an attractive, easy-to-use alternative to Windows Media Player. We also explain how to unlock the digital media features of an Xbox 360 console so that it can share media libraries and a Zune collection on your Windows 7 PC.

Finally, we look at some of the unique challenges that digital media enthusiasts face. When you move a PC out of the office and into the living room, you face some potential logistical hurdles. We can help you anticipate and head off these hassles.

What's in Your Edition?

The Zune software, a free download, runs on all editions of Windows 7. Some Xbox 360 media-sharing features require a homegroup, which can only be set up by a PC running Windows 7 Home Premium or higher. Our advice for setting up a PC in the living room assumes you're using Windows Media Center, which is also available only in Home Premium and higher editions.

Mastering the Zune Software

You don't need a dedicated Zune device to use the Zune software. All you need is a free download from *zune.net*. A Windows Live ID is optional, but it's highly recommended.

Installing the Zune software doesn't replace Windows Media Player, although you can use Zune for just about any media playback and organizational task that you would otherwise use Windows Media Player for. Because the two programs share your Windows libraries, you can freely shift between them for different tasks. Any changes you make to tags and metadata in one program are reflected immediately in the other.

What makes the Zune software different from Windows Media Player?

For starters, it's much richer graphically, and it uses a more modern set of interface conventions called Metro. Using Windows Media Player often feels like you're browsing with good ol' Windows Explorer, with tabs and toolbars and buttons. The Zune software is more like an artfully designed web page; it's been thoroughly decluttered—it even lacks the border you normally see around a more conventional Windows program.

In general, the Zune software offers a simpler interface than Windows Media Player. If you look closely enough, you'll find several Media Player tasks that Zune can't do. Most are advanced or esoteric, such as the option to synchronize playlists with flash drives. A few, though, are basic, such as the option to rip a CD to WAV (Lossless format) or play back tracks in WAV format: Zune can't do that.

For more details on how to split default tasks between the Zune software and Windows Media Player, see "Synchronizing with a Zune Player or Windows Phone" on page 521.

The Zune software is well connected to the Zune Marketplace, where you can buy or rent movies and TV shows and purchase an album or a song. You can play back that content on your PC, on a Zune-compatible device, or on an Xbox 360. It also offers a subscription-based option called the Zune Pass (not available in all countries). For a monthly fee, you can listen to any song or album in the Zune Marketplace on up to three PCs, on an Xbox 360, or on a Windows Phone or Zune player.

Zune does have a few capabilities you won't find in Windows Media Player, such as the ability to subscribe to podcasts from the Zune Marketplace. The Smart DJ feature lets you command Zune to build a playlist of compatible tracks by starting with a song, an album, or an artist of your choosing. Use Mixview to discover new music that's compatible with tunes you already like.

Figure 16-1 shows how content from your collection and from the Zune Marketplace come together on the screen when you search for something—in this case, a band with an extensive catalog of albums available in the Zune Marketplace.

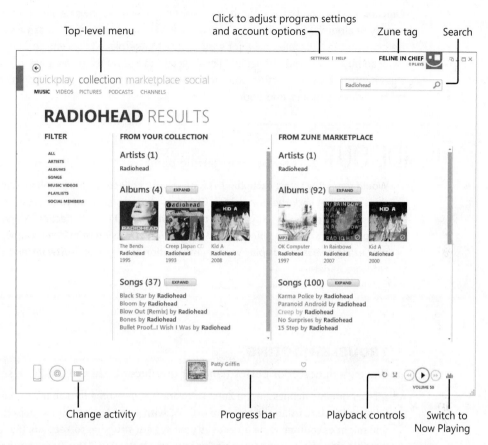

Figure 16-1 The contents displayed in the Zune program window are drawn from your collection and from the Zune Marketplace.

The row of options in the top left corner is a menu, although it certainly doesn't look much like the menus you're accustomed to in other Windows programs. The first four options—Quickplay, Collection, Marketplace, and Social—are always available. A fifth option, Phone or Device (but not both), appears on the menu only if a Windows Phone or other Zune-compatible device is attached to your computer. If the Zune software detects the presence of a CD in a local drive, a Disc menu appears as well.

For more on the details of how to sync content from your Windows library to a Zune-compatible device, see "Synchronizing with a Zune Player or Windows Phone" on page 521.

The cluster of options in the top right corner include a Settings menu, a search box, and an option to sign in using your Windows Live ID. The latter option unlocks your Zune tag—an online profile where you can share your listening and viewing history with friends. (Click the top-level Social menu to see what old friends are up to and add new ones.)

Chapter 16

Quickplay takes you to the default Zune start page, which shows newly added items and a history of albums, video clips, and playlists you've played recently. You can also "pin" favorite items to the Quickplay page for easy access. Marketplace takes you to a page where you can buy or rent digital media. Click Collection to jump to the area we focus on most in this chapter—it's your starting point for managing and playing your personal collection of music, videos, pictures, and podcasts.

INSIDE OUT   Choose your starting point

Would you rather start each Zune session in your collection? No problem. Click Settings and then click the General tab. There you'll find an option to select which page you want to see each time you start the software: Quickplay, Collection, Marketplace, or Social. The same tab allows you to turn sound effects on or off, control the display of warning messages, display version information for the Zune software, and check for software updates.

TROUBLESHOOTING

You experience poor performance or graphics glitches in the Zune software

All that graphic richness in the Zune software requires some muscle from your graphics adapter. If you're using the software on a PC with good-but-not-great graphics support, you might encounter some glitches as your system struggles to keep up. (For a list of possible side effects, see Microsoft Support article 945030, "The Zune software is not displayed correctly on the computer," at *w7io.com/21601*).

Fortunately, there's an easy fix. On the Zune Settings page, click Software and then click the Display tab, where you'll find a variety of settings that allow you to adjust the graphical richness of the Zune software. Background themes are purely a matter of personal preference and have little or no impact on performance. Click the check box to disable the Now Playing screen, which is beautiful but demanding, and use the Screen Graphics slider to select from four settings that affect GPU usage. Explanatory text beneath the slider tells you what effect each setting has. (Hardware acceleration is enabled in all settings except Basic, where it's turned off completely.) Note that you must close and restart the Zune software to make this change effective.

Screen graphics

Basic ——————— Premium

Shows album grid in now playing; hardware acceleration is turned on

---

Two icons—one representing a phone or other device, the other a disc—are always visible in the lower left corner of the Zune screen. If a device is connected or a disc is available, the corresponding icon turns black. The third icon allows you to create, edit, and manage playlists without having to visit the Playlists section of your music collection.

All three icons serve dual roles:

- Drag content from your collection and drop it on an icon. Drag an album or a selection of songs onto the playlist icon to create a new custom playlist or add them to an existing playlist. Drag a similar selection or a custom playlist onto the disc icon to add those items to the burn list.

- Click an icon to switch to activities that are appropriate for that device. If an audio CD is available for playback or ripping, for example, or if you've created a burn list, you can click the disc icon to jump straight to the appropriate page.

The center space along the bottom of the main Zune window displays the progress of whatever activity you're involved in at the time. If you're playing a music track or a video clip, for example, the dot on the progress bar shows your current position; drag that dot left or right to go forward or back in the track or clip.

Finally, in the lower right corner you'll find a cluster of playback controls. Figure 16-2 shows the full array of controls available when you're playing a track or an album from your music collection. (Some of these controls are hidden if you've selected content from the Videos or Pictures area of your collection.)

Figure 16-2 Aim the mouse pointer at the volume controls below the playback buttons to display this volume slider and Mute button.

The playback controls should be familiar: Repeat and Shuffle on the left, then a large Play/Pause button surrounded by Previous and Next buttons, and a Mute button and Volume slider below. (The volume controls are hidden by default and appear as shown here only when you point to the word *Volume* beneath the Play/Pause button.)

When music is playing and you're doing something else—entertaining friends, reading a book, or just relaxing—you might want to switch the display to Now Playing view. This view strips away just about everything from the top of the screen and adds a colorful background drawn from a collage of your album art. The playback controls remain, and the main Zune display shows information about the current track. A list appears when needed to show you what you just listened to and what's playing next; it goes away after a period of inactivity. Click the Switch To Now Playing button (just to the right of the Next button) and your Now Playing screen should look like the one shown in Figure 16-3, only personalized using your collection.

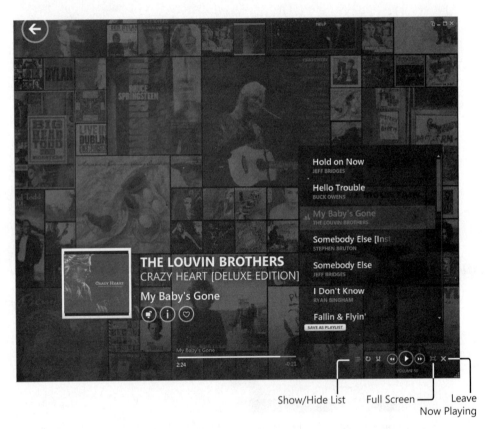

Show/Hide List   Full Screen   Leave
Now Playing

Figure 16-3 The Now Playing list disappears after a few seconds of inactivity. Move the mouse to bring it back.

Click Full Screen to expand Now Playing so that it completely covers the display, including the Windows taskbar. This mode is particularly striking if your PC is connected to a high-definition TV screen.

In Now Playing, you have two places where you can rate the current track. Click the large heart icon under the track title to indicate that you like the track. Click again to change that icon to a "don't like," which looks like a broken heart. Click again to remove the rating completely. (You can also rate a track by right-clicking its entry in the Music area of your collection.) Note that Zune's like/don't like ratings correspond to five stars and one star on the Windows Media Player scale.

To leave Now Playing, press Esc, or click the Back button in the top left corner, or click Leave Now Playing (the small X in the lower right corner).

Using Zune to Manage a Digital Media Collection

The easiest way to add content to your Zune collection is to copy files directly to the corresponding Windows library. As we noted earlier, any changes you make there are reflected immediately (or very soon thereafter) in the corresponding Zune collection. If you purchase an album from your favorite online music store, just make sure to download its files into a folder that's included with the matching library.

For more details on how Windows 7 libraries work, see "Working with Libraries" on page 343.

You can also add to your collection by using the Zune software to rip a CD or by making a purchase or subscribing to a podcast in the Marketplace.

INSIDE OUT   Reset your Zune collection

In some cases, a Zune collection can become corrupted. One symptom is album art that doesn't match the underlying track. In this case, the best option is to give Zune a completely fresh start with your local media collection by using one of the following three options. The first is a manual fix: after shutting down the Zune software, open %LocalAppData%\Microsoft\Zune\ in Windows Explorer and delete ZuneStore.sdf. That single file contains all the details about your collection, and Zune will rebuild it using metadata from the media files themselves. You can also accomplish the same goal by using the Zune media collection reset tool (*w7io.com/21602*) or the Microsoft Fix it page at *w7io.com/21603*. If you have a large collection, you'll need to set aside time the next time you start the Zune software so that the program can rebuild this index file.

To make your way through a media collection, start by clicking Collection, and then choose one of the five available media types—Music, Videos, Pictures, Podcasts, or Channels. A search box is available to help you narrow the selection. You can also group, sort, and filter the contents; your options vary depending on the type of media. Figure 16-4 shows the choices available when you click Music.

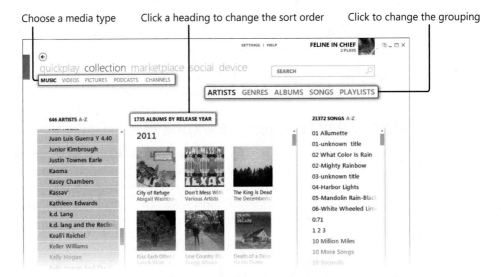

Choose a media type   Click a heading to change the sort order   Click to change the grouping

Figure 16-4 Click any heading to change the sort order for the list below it. You can resize columns, but you can't change the size of album art in the center.

By default, this large music library is grouped by artist, with the library's contents available in the center section and a list of songs on the right. Click the headings over the Artists or Songs column to reverse the sort order (Z to A instead of A to Z). Click the headings above the list of albums to cycle through all available sort orders: in this case, Artist, Date Added, A-Z, or Release Year.

You can click any album to see just its songs. Click any artist name to filter the selection to albums and songs by that artist. The heading displays the number of items in the filtered list. In any column, you can Ctrl+click or Shift+click to select multiple entries.

If you've filtered the list by artist or genre, click the heading over the first column to select the entire list and remove the filter.

Five options on the right allow you to change the grouping of the current view. Click Albums, for example, to remove the first column completely and display albums in a grid with larger cover art than the Artists view. Songs and Playlists display as multicolumn lists. The size of album art and the arrangement of columns are fixed and can't be customized.

The default display under Videos is simple, with all your videos on the left, and details about the current video in a pane on the right. Click the headings over the list of video clips to cycle through four sort orders: Title, Date Added, Content Type, Category. Use the headings above the details pane to filter the list. We clicked Personal here to filter the list so that it shows only video clips taken with a digital camera:

When you select a video and click Play, it replaces the contents of the Zune program window with the videos version of the Now Playing screen. This view has a black background, a progress bar, and playback controls on the bottom that appear when you move the mouse and disappear after a few seconds of inactivity. If you click Leave Now Playing, the clip continues to play in the background and is visible in the tiny thumbnail to the left of the progress bar.

The Pictures area in Zune is simple, almost rudimentary. The Albums column on the left displays the folders and subfolders in your Pictures library. The contents of the selected folder appear to the right. From this area, you can sync pictures to a Zune-compatible phone or device or play a slide show. If you need to do anything else with one or more photos, use Windows Live Photo Gallery. From the Zune software, you can right-click any selection and choose Edit And Share, or use the link at the bottom of the Albums column: Edit And Share With Windows Live Photo Gallery.

For more details on how to edit and share photos, see "Using Windows Live Photo Gallery" on page 310.

Chapter 16

The Zune software does a tremendous job of keeping you up with your favorite podcasts. Click Marketplace, Podcasts to search through the large, categorized collection (don't worry—almost all podcasts are free). Then click Collection, Podcasts to see which shows are in your subscription list. Use the Series Settings button to adjust options for an individual podcast, as we did in Figure 16-5.

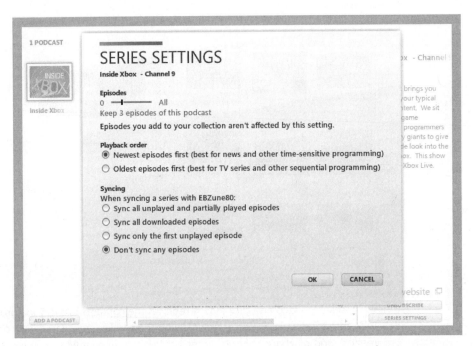

Figure 16-5 When you subscribe to a podcast, you can specify how many shows you want to keep and which order to play them in.

The Channels tab is only useful if you are a Zune Pass subscriber.

Ripping CDs

If you've ripped a CD using Windows Media Player, you'll have no trouble adapting to the equivalent procedure in the Zune software. The first step is to click Settings, Software; on the Rip tab, choose a format (WMA or MP3) and a bit rate. (For an overview of your options, see the discussion in "Ripping CDs" on page 496. Note that the WAV and Windows Media Audio Pro formats are not available when using Zune to rip a CD.)

With that bit of housekeeping out of the way, insert the audio CD and click Disc (this menu is available only if a suitable CD is inserted). If you have an active Internet connection, the Zune software looks up the album and fills in its title and track information. Right-click the album cover art and choose Edit if you want to change the album artist, title, or genre, and then click Start Rip to begin copying the CD to the default folder in the Music library.

Editing Album Details, Tags, and Other Metadata

When you rip a CD, the Zune software automatically adds album and track details from Microsoft's Windows Metadata service and stores them as tags in the resulting music files. Tracks or albums from a music service or other source are typically tagged by the individual or service that created the original file.

If your inner perfectionist is unhappy with the details stored with an album or a track, you can change them at any time. Right-click a track name or an album cover and then choose Edit to open a tag editor like the one shown in Figure 16-6.

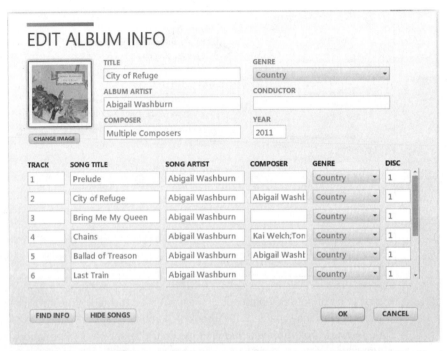

Figure 16-6 Enter a number in the Disc field to separate tracks from multidisc collections in the Zune collection. Disc numbers aren't recognized in Windows Media Player.

You can edit any field here. Items in the top portion of the box apply to all tracks on an album; those in the bottom half are specific to individual tracks. Click Change Image to paste a saved image file in place of the current cover art.

Other options on the same right-click menu allow you to rename an album or a track (Rename), update information about the album by using the Windows Metadata service (Find Album Info), or replace the cover image for an album (Update Album Art).

You can right-click and choose Edit for videos as well. The dialog box shown next allows you to save metadata that is used for grouping and categorizing a video in the Videos collection.

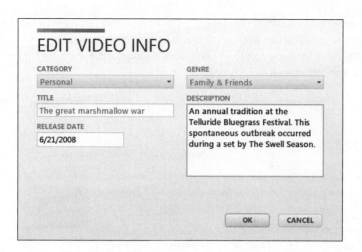

Metadata for pictures cannot be edited in the Zune software. Instead, right-click and choose Edit And Share to open the selected item or items in Windows Live Photo Gallery.

Any changes you make here are saved as metadata within the original file. If you want to see or edit the file itself, right-click an item and choose Properties. That opens a dialog box that shows the file name and extension, as well as details about the file. The value in the Location field is a hyperlink; click it to open Windows Explorer with the selected file high-lighted in its current location.

Creating and Managing Playlists

Most of the general principles that apply to playlists in Windows Media Player apply in the Zune software as well. (For a refresher, see "Working with Playlists" on page 490.) There are, however, some differences in details. The Zune Playlist format (with a file name extension of .zpl) is an XML variation that consists of plain text, but it's not compatible with the Windows Media Player format. If you have any playlists saved in the older format, the Zune software creates copies in Zune Playlist format when if finds them in your Music library.

Click Collection, Music, Playlists to view playlists you've already created. To modify the order of tracks in a playlist, drag tracks up or down. Right-click any track and choose Remove From Playlist to remove a track. Any changes you make are saved immediately; you don't need to explicitly save them.

The Zune program supports three distinct types of lists. You can create a list manually, using content you supply. You can also create lists automatically, using criteria you specify or by allowing the Zune software to use its own musical judgment. Figure 16-7 shows a collection of playlists that includes all three types.

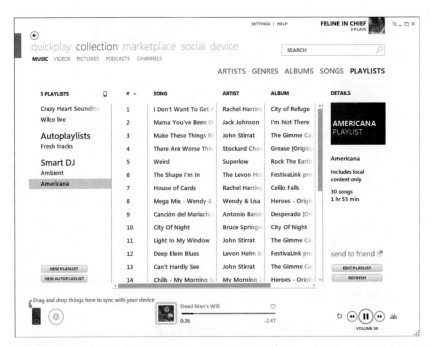

Figure 16-7 Smart DJ playlists are based on a track, an album, or an artist. Click Refresh to build a new version of the list on the fly.

Use the New Playlist button to create a new conventional playlist. After you supply a title, you can click Artists and begin dragging songs to the list to fill it. Click New Autoplaylist to create a list based on a single set of criteria—limited to a specific artist or genre, including a specific range of release dates, and so on. You can also use ratings and the Added On date; if you've added a large number of new albums to your collection lately, you might choose to specify that you want the list to include only tracks added in the past 14 days, arranged by album, excluding tracks that you've marked as Don't Like. Like their Windows Media Player counterparts, these autoplaylists dynamically refresh their contents each time you open them.

Finally, Zune offers the Smart DJ feature, which puts together a list of tracks automatically, using artists and songs that are compatible (at least in the opinion of the Zune database) with a starting point you specify. Pick a track, an album, or an artist, right-click, and choose either Play Smart DJ Mix or Create Smart DJ Playlist. Both options begin playing a mix of tracks immediately, but the latter option also saves the results so you can return to it later.

You can't edit a Smart DJ list, but you can change its properties. Click Playlists, select a list from under the Smart DJ heading, and click Edit Playlist to open the dialog box shown here. Note that the option to add songs from the Zune Marketplace is available only if you are a Zune Pass subscriber.

EDIT SMART DJ PLAYLIST

Americana

PLAYLIST SOURCE

◉ My local collection only

○ Draw from songs in my collection and songs at Zune Marketplace

○ Marketplace music only

Zune Marketplace songs are available only when you have a Zune Pass.
Try a Zune Pass with a free 14-day trial. ⬈

PLAYLIST DURATION

◉ Songs ○ Minutes

30

Number of songs depends on availability.

REFRESH RATE

☐ Auto refresh every 5 days

So how do you edit the contents of an autoplaylist or a Smart DJ list? If you want to keep the arrangement of tracks on this type of list, double-click the list name to begin playing it, switch to Now Playing, and click the Save As Playlist button below the track list. Give the new playlist a name to save it as a standard playlist whose contents you can reorder or change as needed. Note that the saved list is not linked to the autoplaylist or Smart DJ list you started with.

Connecting a PC to a Home Entertainment System

Moving a PC to the living room and pressing it into full-time service as a media hub poses some unique challenges. In your office or den, you can normally make any necessary adjustments using an attached keyboard and mouse. In a living room, where the PC is tucked away in a corner or inside a cabinet, making those changes is a bit trickier.

In this section, we share some secrets we've learned over the years about how to reduce the hassles of using a PC in the living room.

Chapter 16

Make Sure Your PC Is Properly Ventilated

The greatest unseen enemy for PCs in any living room is heat. Any PC that has enough CPU power and graphics muscle to deliver a high-definition picture is going to generate heat. Under normal circumstances, fans inside the PC's case vent this heat away from sensitive components and out through openings in the PC's case, drawing in cooler outside air to replace it. This ventilation process can fail, with potentially catastrophic results, if you hide your media PC in a cabinet that doesn't allow sufficient airflow. When heat builds up past a critical point, you might see glitches in the display. Under extreme circumstances, the system will shut down and can suffer permanent damage. If you plan to enclose your PC in a cabinet, make sure the space around it has adequate ventilation, and monitor temperatures inside and outside the PC to ensure that they're within an acceptable range. A wide variety of software utilities are available to help you keep track of internal temperatures, including Core Temp (*w7io.com/21604*) and HWMonitor (*w7io.com/21607*). You can also use a standard room thermometer in the enclosed space to keep tabs on the ambient temperature.

Connecting Your PC to a TV and External Amplifier

For best results, your living-room PC needs to make digital connections to both a big-screen TV (or a widescreen monitor dedicated for use as a TV) and to an amplifier capable of producing multichannel surround sound. Most modern PCs have digital audio and video capabilities built in to the motherboard.

For video, you'll get the best results with an HDMI connection, which uses a single physical connection to deliver digital video and audio. Some newer PCs use an alternative to HDMI called DisplayPort, which offers a wide variety of digital audio and video outputs; few TVs support direct DisplayPort input, so you'll likely need a converter to pair this type of output with an HDMI input on a TV. If your PC's primary video output uses a Digital Video Interconnect (DVI) connector, you can use an adapter to connect the DVI port to an HDMI input on the TV.

Depending on your setup, you might not be able to transfer audio over the same cable you use for video and will need another source for audio. The most important issue is how you plan to play back audio:

- **Will you play back audio through your TV's speakers?** For a relatively recent TV, a single HDMI connection should handle video and audio. This option is simple, but sound quality might be limited, and surround sound probably isn't available.

- **Will you play back audio using a stereo amplifier/receiver and speakers?**   If so, the ideal configuration allows you to connect your PC to the receiver and then use a second HDMI cable to pass the video on to the TV. If your receiver doesn't have HDMI inputs or doesn't support HDMI pass-through, you'll need a separate digital audio connection from the PC to the receiver.

INSIDE OUT   Don't overpay for cables

How much do you need to spend for quality HDMI cables? We've seen some stagger-ing price tags on name-brand cables sold at consumer-electronics stores. But you don't need to spend a fortune on cables. A well-built generic cable that meets the HDMI standard should deliver the same number of bits at the same rate as its more expen-sive brand-name cousins. Shop around, especially at reputable online dealers, and you might save enough to buy another terabyte or two of storage.

If you can't use HDMI or DisplayPort for audio, you'll need to make a connection using the standard for consumer electronics equipment, the Sony/Philips Digital Interconnect Format, better known as S/PDIF. Your PC should have a digital audio output using one of three types:

- Optical connections (also known as Toshiba Link, or TOSLINK) typically use square connectors on either end and transmit the digital audio signal in a beam of light over a fiber optic cable. Their effective maximum range is about 20 feet.

- Coaxial connections use RCA connectors on either end and carry the digital audio over a wire. Their effective maximum range is around 30 feet.

- Mini-jacks that carry an S/PDIF signal are sometimes found on notebooks, often shar-ing the same connector used for headphones. You need an adaptor to connect this output to an RCA-style S/PDIF input on a receiver.

Compensating for Overscan

When you connect a Windows 7 PC to a TV, you're likely to run head-on into a fundamen-tal difference between computer monitors and TVs. Monitors have a default resolution, defined in pixels. TV broadcasting evolved during the era of cathode-ray tubes, which used scan lines to create the on-screen image. To avoid the chance that a picture would be distorted at the edges, TV makers cut off 3 percent or so (sometimes more) from the available image and then centered it on the display. (For an excellent overview of the

Chapter 16

whole issue, see Ben Drawbaugh's explainer: "HD 101: Overscan and why all TVs do it," at *w7io.com/21605*.)

The odd thing is that today's all-digital TVs still do this, centering the image to fill your display, with part of all four edges extending outside the available area. That's fine if you're watching a TV show or a DVD—this type of programming is specifically designed so that nothing important is in the overscan area. But you might be startled the first time you open the Windows desktop on a big-screen TV and discover that the taskbar and Start button are invisible (or at least partly hidden) because overscan has pushed them below the bottom edge of the display.

To deal with overscan, you might need to make two separate sets of adjustments. Start with the TV itself and look for an option that affects overscan—ideally, a way to replace it with 1:1 pixel mapping. If that hardware option isn't available, or if it doesn't solve the problem, you'll need to dig into the configuration utility provided by your display driver.

If you've installed the most recent drivers for an Nvidia adapter, open the Nvidia Control Panel and click Adjust Desktop Size And Position, as shown in Figure 16-8. Click Resize Desktop and then move the two slider controls so that the four arrows are in the four visible corners of the screen.

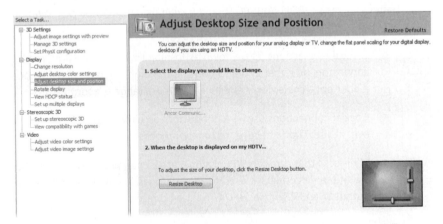

Figure 16-8 In the Nvidia Control Panel, click Resize Desktop to correct overscan on a TV connected to a PC.

For AMD/ATI adapters, you'll find a similar option in the Catalyst Control Center. Click Desktops And Displays, and then click Scaling Options. The slider shown here allows you to correct for overscan in the hardware by enabling underscan in the video output. (Note that the Catalyst Control Center was redesigned in early 2011 and now includes the AMD logo and an updated interface. The overscan/underscan options still work the same way.)

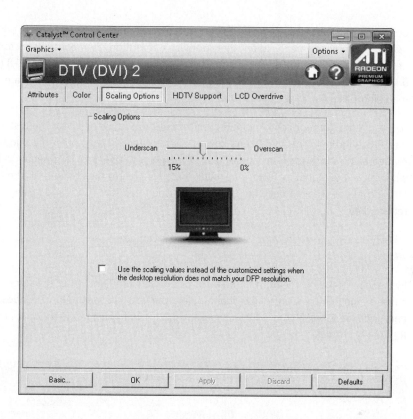

Managing Remote Controls and Wireless Input Devices

If your living-room PC is tucked away out of sight, in a corner or in a cabinet, any task that requires a keyboard and a mouse is, by definition, going to be awkward. You can reduce some of that awkwardness by equipping the PC with a wireless keyboard (ideally one that also includes some sort of trackpad option for handling mouse duties). Both Bluetooth and RF-powered devices work well for this sort of task. Make sure the device you choose can control your computer when it starts up and before Windows is loaded—that's an essential feature for troubleshooting.

Remote controls are simpler to set up. Windows Media Center is designed to work with remote controls that use Philips RC6 infrared technology. As long as you have fresh batteries and a clear line of sight between your remote control's emitter and the infrared receiver attached to your PC, you should be able to begin controlling Media Center with no need to install custom drivers or perform any extra setup.

One complication arises if you have two PCs in the same room, each equipped with an infrared receiver. Unless you take great pains to position them perfectly, you'll probably

Chapter 16

be frustrated to find that pressing the buttons on one remote control causes both PCs to respond. If moving one PC to another room isn't an option, then consider customizing the Remote Control ID. You can set unique Remote Control IDs in a range from 1-8 (an ID of 0 allows a PC to respond to any remote). If each PC and its assigned remote are set to a matching pair, your problem is solved.

To begin configuration, pick the number you want to use as the ID for the first PC/remote pair. Press and hold the DVD Menu key on the remote, and then press the number button that corresponds to the Remote Control ID you want to use (1-8) for 5 seconds. Remotes with visible LED signal indicators will blink twice to confirm the change. On the Media Center PC that you want to pair with that remote, open Registry Editor and locate the following registry key:

HKLM\SYSTEM\CurrentControlSet\Services\HidIr\Remotes
745a17a0-74d3-11d0-b6fe-00a0c90f57da

In the value pane on the right, double-click CodeSetNum0 and enter the same number you chose as the Remote Control ID. Finally, delete the values CodeSetNum1, CodeSetNum2, and CodeSetNum3. Figure 16-9 shows what you'll see if you change the value for the Remote Control ID to 5.

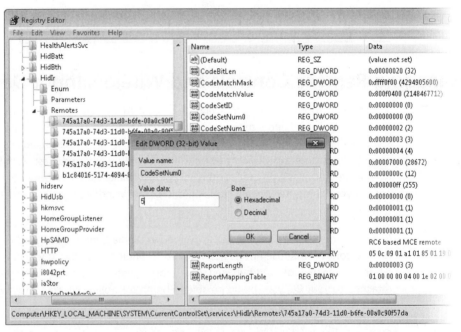

Figure 16-9 Change this value in the registry and then assign a matching ID to your remote control to pair the remotes and prevent interference with other PCs.

If you're interested in learning more about Media Center remote controls and the codes that drive them, you'll want to read Shane Kent's "All About Media Center Remotes (Advanced)" at *w7io.com/21606*.

Integrating an Xbox 360 into a Home Network

Earlier, we discussed how to make an Xbox 360 function as a Media Center extender (see "Using an Xbox 360 as a Media Center Extender" on page 566. But if you have an Xbox 360 console on the same network as a Windows 7 PC, you can do much more.

For starters, if you set up a homegroup you can share your Windows media libraries with an Xbox 360. To browse their contents, go to the Xbox 360 Dashboard, open Music Library, Video Library, or Picture Library, and select the PC name and user account for your library.

If you installed the Zune software on a PC, you can share its collection on an Xbox 360 as well. Click Settings, Software, and open the Xbox 360 tab. By default, none of the options shown here are selected. Click the check box for each type of media you want to share, give the collection a name, and click OK. Your shared collection appears in the same place as shared libraries—look for the Zune icon to the right of the library name.

Chapter 16

Although it seems like a logical thing to do, you can't copy content from a PC to an Xbox 360. You can, however, rip audio CDs directly onto the memory card or hard disk in an Xbox 360 console so that they're stored locally. This option can be especially useful if you want access to your music collection even when your PC is sleeping or turned off.

I
N the early days of personal computing, security was a mere afterthought—when it was considered at all. But as personal computers have become more powerful, more complex, and more connected, they've also become more vulnerable. Because Microsoft Windows is so widely used, computers running any version of Windows make an especially juicy target for those who would like to steal your valuable personal data, appropriate your computing resources and bandwidth, or simply create havoc.

So, does this mean you need to treat security as an all-consuming obsession and worry about the security implications of every keystroke and mouse click? Fortunately, no. In part, that's because security has been engineered into the design and development process of Windows 7. Several key architectural underpinnings of Windows have been reworked to make them simpler and more secure by design. Thanks to new development tools designed to detect common programming flaws, code that allows buffer overflows and other security holes that have to be patched later is less common than in previous releases. Countless new features (some are visible, such as User Account Control and Windows Firewall, but there are also many under-the-hood improvements) have significantly raised the bar for malcontents who try to attack your computer. The bad guys don't give up easily, however.

What's in Your Edition?

All security features of Windows 7 described in this chapter work identically in all editions of Windows 7, with the exception of a handful of features, such as Network Access Protection, which are available only with business editions on Windows-based enterprise networks. A tip near the end of this chapter describes some additional settings you can make in Local Security Policy, a console that is available only in the Professional, Ultimate, and Enterprise editions.

In this chapter, we examine in detail the kind of threats you're likely to face at home and at work, and we detail how you can build an effective, multilayered security regimen. We would also like to point out, with no small measure of pride, that when Microsoft introduced its own antimalware program, it used the same name as the title of this chapter—a title we've used for a decade in at least five consecutive editions of this book. We cover Microsoft Security Essentials (and much more) in depth.

Understanding Security Threats

A decade ago, the threat landscape for Windows users was dominated by viruses and worms. That era hit its low point in 2003–2004, when a series of fast-spreading viruses and worms with colorful names like Blaster and Sasser incapacitated millions of PCs and shut down entire networks.

The modern threat landscape is much more complex and, unfortunately, more insidious. Today, an attacker is likely to be part of an organized crime ring, not an attention-seeking vandal, and attacks are typically designed to go unnoticed for as long as possible.

This is the dark side of software. A rogue program, installed without your knowledge and running without your awareness, can perform malicious tasks and transfer data without your consent. This category of software is often referred to as *malware*. The most pernicious form of malware allows intruders to take control of the computer without the owner's knowledge.

The goal of the bad guys is to get you, by hook or by crook, to run their software. They might, for example, convince you to install a *Trojan*—a program that appears legitimate but actually performs malicious actions when it's installed. This category of malware doesn't spread on its own but instead uses social engineering (often using popular social networking sites such as Facebook and Twitter) to convince its victims to cooperate in the installation process. As part of its payload, a Trojan can include a downloader that installs additional malicious and unwanted programs. Some Trojans install a "backdoor" that allows an outside attacker to remotely control the infected computer.

What's in it for the bad guys? Money, mostly, gathered in a variety of ways, depending on how the attackers got through your defenses.

A *password stealer* runs in the background, gathers user names and passwords, and forwards them to an outside attacker. Keyboard monitoring programs called *keyloggers* can monitor users' activities and capture account numbers and passwords. The stolen credentials can then be used to make purchases, clean out bank accounts, or commit identity theft.

Bad guys prey on fear with *rogue security software* (also known as *scareware*), which mimics the actions and appearance of legitimate antivirus software. If you install one of these programs, it inevitably reports the presence of a (nonexistent) virus and offers to remove it—for a fee, of course. The worst offenders in this category engage in a form of digital blackmail, encrypting data and unlocking it only upon payment of a ransom. (Microsoft Security provides examples of rogue security software and advice on how to avoid it at *w7io.com/21701*.)

Viruses, Spyware, and Unwanted Software: What's the Difference?

Throughout this chapter, we refer to different types of malicious and unwanted software. Use this scorecard to sort out the players:

- A *virus* is a program that can copy itself, usually by attaching itself to another object. Viruses can infect program files, documents (in the form of macro viruses), or low-level disk and file-system structures such as the boot sector and partition table. Viruses can run when an infected program file runs; they can also reside in memory and infect files as the user opens, saves, or creates the files. Infections spread when an infected file is transferred to another computer over a network, over the Internet, or on removable media, and is then executed on the target computer. In addition to their all-important reproductive capability, viruses are typically written to destroy or corrupt data files, wipe out installed programs, or damage the operating system itself.

- *Rootkits* are among the most worrying forms of malware, specifically designed to burrow into the most sensitive areas of the operating system, where they can evade detection and removal. The rootkit's job is to cloak the actions of another program—such as a backdoor or keylogger—and prevent it from being detected even by an administrator.

- A *worm* is a program that replicates by copying itself from one computer to another on a network. Many modern worms also contain virus code, backdoors, and downloaders.

- *Spyware* and *adware* are terms that have been applied to a variety of unwanted programs, including advertiser-sponsored software that tracks a user's web surfing habits; programs that display pop-up ads or install unexpected toolbars, favorites, and links in your web browser; programs that redirect Internet Explorer to a search engine or home page that's different from the one you specify; and more. Note that spyware doesn't necessarily "spy" on you. A common characteristic of anything dubbed "spyware" is that it does its deeds—malicious or otherwise—without your informed consent. For the purposes of this chapter, our definition of spyware is "any program that is installed without the user's full and informed consent, often through deceptive means, and that displays advertising, records personal information, or changes a computer's configuration without the user's explicit permission."

You can review "top ten" lists of current malware threats and detections, along with links to details about each one, at the Microsoft Malware Protection Center, *w7io.com/1518*.

Computers that have been taken over by other forms of malware are sometimes referred to as *zombies* or *bots* (short for robots). Armies of these zombies, called *botnets*, can be used to launch crippling attacks against websites, to send spam without revealing the true sender's address, and to propagate themselves.

The most sophisticated attacks are targeted against individuals and organizations. The goal in these cases might be financial, aimed at business bank accounts, or the intruders might be interested in industrial or political espionage. These attacks typically exploit previously unreported vulnerabilities.

And how does an innocent PC become a victim? These are the most common vectors for security breaches:

- Attackers can exploit a vulnerability in Windows or one of its components, including Internet Explorer. This type of attack is often carried out by convincing the target to click a link in an e-mail message; that link leads to a website that contains the exploit code, which executes silently without tipping off the victim (this type of attack is often called a *drive-by download*). An attack that is unleashed on the same day that an unpatched vulnerability becomes widely known among security researchers is called a *zero-day exploit*.

- In some cases, attackers target third-party software. This category has constituted the majority of reported vulnerabilities in recent years. Successful attack vectors have come through the distribution of "poisoned" data files in widely used formats, such as digital image files and PDF documents.

- Some attacks exploit flaws in networking software that allow malware to spread to vulnerable computers using network shares.

- There's the direct route, in which an attacker convinces his target to install unwanted or malicious software by disguising its true actions. So-called *Trojan horse* programs can be malicious or merely misleading.

- Finally, don't overlook the risk of intrusions and theft from people with access to your PC, either physically or over a network. Physical security, including a lock screen protected by a strong password, is the first line of defense. That's especially important in a business setting where your computer might be accessible to an untrusted person.

Phishing attacks, which use social engineering to convince visitors to give away their login credentials, are a separate but potentially devastating avenue to identity theft that can strike in any browser using any operating system. We cover this and other browser-based security issues in "Monitoring and Maintaining Security" on page 252.

The Microsoft Malware Protection Center issues a twice-yearly report on the changing threat landscape, using data from hundreds of millions of Windows users and other sources. You can read the latest Microsoft Security Intelligence Report at *w7io.com/1501*.

Securing Your Computer: A Defense-in-Depth Strategy

A multidimensional threat landscape requires an appropriately diverse approach to protecting your PC and your network. Microsoft security experts often describe this strategy as "defense in depth." The idea is to ensure that you take advantage of a broad range of appropriate security features rather than rely on a single piece of technology (such as a suite of security software) to stymie a would-be intruder. On a home or small business network, those layers of security include the following:

Use a hardware router to protect your broadband connection   This is an essential part of physical security, even if your network consists of a single PC. We provide an overview of the technology in "Configuring Your Network Hardware" on page 689.

Enable a software firewall and keep it turned on   You can use Windows Firewall, which is included with Windows 7, or a firewall that you obtain elsewhere. To learn more, see "Blocking Intruders with Windows Firewall" on page 604.

Set up standard user accounts and keep User Account Control enabled   Standard accounts help to prevent (or at least minimize) the damage that an untrained user can do by installing untrusted programs. User Account Control (UAC) helps in this regard by restricting access to administrative tasks and virtualizing registry and file-system changes. For details, see "Introducing Access Control in Windows" on page 642, and "Preventing Unsafe Actions with User Account Control" on page 629.

Keep Windows and vulnerable programs up to date   Windows Update (and its opt-in sister service, Microsoft Update) can handle this chore for Windows, Office, and other Microsoft programs. You're on your own for third-party programs. We cover your options in "Keeping Your System Secure with Windows Update" on page 875.

Install protection against viruses and malware and keep it up to date   Windows Defender, which is included with Windows 7, provides basic antispyware protection. To block more dangerous forms of malware, however, you need to use a separate program. PC makers often include third-party security software with new PCs; you can get effective protection by using Microsoft Security Essentials, which is free. For details, see "Setting Up and Using Microsoft Security Essentials" on page 621.

Protect yourself from threats in e-mail messages   At a minimum, your e-mail solution should block or quarantine executable files and other potentially dangerous attachments. In addition, effective anti-spam features can block scripts and prevent phishing attempts. You can get all of this protection by way of Windows Live Essentials, as we explain in "Using Windows Live Mail" on page 300.

Chapter 17

Use parental controls to keep kids safe   If you have children who use your computer, Parental Controls in Windows can help you keep them away from security threats. It also includes options you can use to restrict their computer activities in other ways. For details, see "Controlling Your Children's Computer Access" on page 675.

Action Center monitors many of these areas to be sure you're protected, and it displays an alert if something needs attention. For details, see "Monitoring Your Computer's Security" on page 600.

What's New in Windows 7

Although Windows 7 doesn't have the number of new, highly visible security features that were added to the Windows arsenal with Windows Vista, it has improved upon several of those features. Some—such as User Account Control, Windows Defender, and Windows Firewall—sport new, simpler interfaces and new capabilities. In addition, Windows 7 also has numerous under-the-hood improvements and security features for computers on large networks that are of interest primarily to software developers and information technology professionals—and hackers, who now have many additional challenges and obstacles to face. Among the key security improvements are these:

- **Windows Firewall**   Windows Firewall is substantially changed from the version in Windows XP. As in Windows Vista, it is a two-way firewall, monitoring outbound traffic as well as inbound, and it fully supports Internet Protocol version 6 (IPv6). In Windows 7, Windows Firewall adds multiple access firewall profiles, a feature that provides appropriate protection for each connected network when you're connected to more than one at a time—an increasingly common situation. With an advanced configuration console for Windows Firewall, administrators have granular control over firewall rules and other settings.

- **User Account Control (UAC)**   UAC reduces the inherent danger of using an administrator account for everyday tasks by requesting your consent when an application needs to do something with systemwide effect. Furthermore, architectural changes wrought by UAC make it practical for most people to use a standard account for daily computing. In Windows 7, UAC is far less intrusive than in Windows Vista because fewer tasks trigger UAC prompts and new configuration options make it easier to control UAC so that it doesn't control you.

- **Windows Defender**   Windows Defender, an antispyware program, continuously monitors system settings to prevent the installation of known spyware and to alert you to the presence of spyware-like activity. The new interface in the Windows 7 version has fewer confusing options than its Windows Vista predecessor—which is appropriate for a program that normally runs silently in the background. Its protection is rudimentary, and we strongly recommend replacing it with Microsoft Security Essentials or another more comprehensive security program.

- **Internet Explorer**   Internet Explorer runs in Protected Mode, which lessens the likelihood of installing malicious code. Effectively, it runs isolated in a "sandbox" with reduced privileges, able to write data only in locked-down temporary folders unless you grant permission to act outside the protected area. Internet Explorer 9 raises the security bar even higher with fine-grained restrictions on ActiveX controls, an improved SmartScreen phishing filter, and a built-in framework to give you complete control over websites that want to track your browsing habits. (For more information, see "Monitoring and Maintaining Security" on page 252.)

- **Windows Biometric Service**   The Windows Biometric Service provides support for fingerprint biometric devices so that you can use a fingerprint reader to log on to your computer and to enter administrative credentials in response to UAC elevation prompts.

- **Data encryption**   BitLocker Drive Encryption (available only in Enterprise and Ultimate editions) encrypts entire hard drives—making the data they contain completely inaccessible to a thief who makes off with a computer. In Windows 7, BitLocker To Go can also be used to protect removable storage drives, such as portable hard drives and USB flash drives.

If you're coming to Windows 7 from Windows XP, you might be unaware of the following additional security features and enhancements that are part of Windows Vista and now Windows 7:

- **Parental Controls**   Parental Controls provide tools to help parents guide their kids' use of the Internet, games, and other programs.

- **Data redirection**   When User Account Control is enabled, an application that attempts to write to a protected system folder (such as %ProgramFiles% or %SystemRoot%) gets transparently redirected to a virtual file store within the user's profile. Similarly, if an application attempts to write to systemwide areas of the registry (such as the HKEY_LOCAL_MACHINE hive), it is redirected to virtual keys within the user's section of the registry. Applications that attempt to read from these protected file and registry locations look first to the virtual stores. File and registry virtualization allows standard users to run older applications—including many of those that required administrator access under Windows XP—while at the same time preventing malicious applications from writing to areas that could bring down the entire system.

Chapter 17

- **Buffer overrun protection**   Address Space Layout Randomization (ASLR) is one of several underlying technologies that defend against buffer overrun exploits. With ASLR, each time you boot Windows, system code is loaded into different locations in memory. This seemingly simple change stymies a class of well-known attacks in which exploit code attempts to call a system function from a known memory address. ASLR and numerous other esoteric programming changes are one result of Microsoft's adoption of the Security Development Life Cycle, a process that minimizes security bugs in program code.

- **Additional security on 64-bit computers**   With the 64-bit versions of Windows, only digitally signed device drivers can be installed. This feature, called PatchGuard, ensures that kernel-level code is from a known source and has not been altered, as a means to prevent the installation of rootkits and any other code that tries to alter the underlying operating system.

- **Restrictions on removable drives**   Through the use of Group Policy, administrators can control the use of removable storage devices, such as USB flash drives and external hard drives. These restrictions can help prevent the theft of sensitive or proprietary data. In addition, they can be used to seal an entry point for viruses and other malware brought in from home. In addition, AutoRun is disabled for removable storage devices such as USB flash drives, lessening the chance that an attacker can fool you into running a hostile program simply by clicking an entry in the AutoPlay list.

Monitoring Your Computer's Security

In Windows 7, security-related options have been gathered in Action Center, an application that replaces Security Center found in Windows XP and Windows Vista. Ordinarily, the only indication of this program's presence is its flag icon in the notification area, which serves as a reminder that Action Center is on the job, monitoring your computer's essential security settings as well as maintenance and troubleshooting tasks. You can open Action Center by clicking its notification area icon (see Figure 17-1) or by clicking the message that emanates from that icon when your computer's security settings need attention. You can also open Action Center from Control Panel.

The Security section in Action Center provides at-a-glance information about your security settings. Items that need your attention have a red or yellow bar, as shown in Figure 17-2. A red bar identifies important items that need immediate attention, such as detection of a virus or spyware or that no firewall is enabled. A yellow bar denotes informational messages about suboptimal, but less critical, settings or status, such as when Windows Update is not set to automatically download and install critical updates. Next to the bar appear explanatory text and buttons that let you correct the problem (or configure Action Center so that it won't bother you).

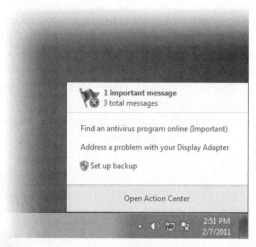

Figure 17-1 Clicking the notification area icon displays a menu that includes links that let you directly address current problems, as well as a link to open Action Center itself.

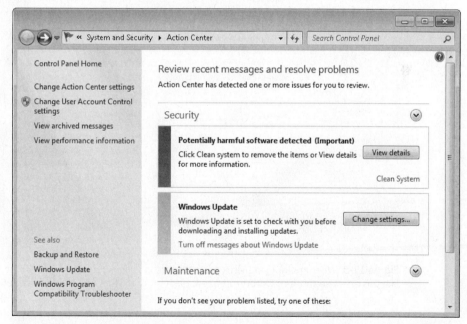

Figure 17-2 Action Center collects security, maintenance, and troubleshooting information and settings in a single window.

If all is well, the Security category is collapsed and you see nothing in that category when you open Action Center. Click the arrow to expand the category, and you'll see all the security-related items that Action Center monitors, as shown in Figure 17-3.

Action Center is designed to work with third-party firewall, antivirus, and antispyware programs, as well as with the programs built in to Windows 7 (Windows Firewall and Windows Defender) and those available separately from Microsoft, such as Microsoft Security Essentials. Systems with more than one program installed in any of these categories include a link to show a list of such programs. For example, Figure 17-3 shows a system on which Sunbelt's VIPRE antivirus and antispyware software is installed and temporarily disabled. The dialog box that appears when you click the link to view installed programs allows you to turn on any installed program that is currently turned off.

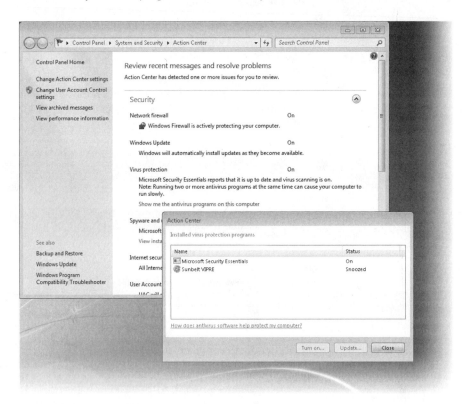

Figure 17-3 When multiple antivirus programs are installed, you can click a link to show a list like this one. Use the Turn On button to enable a program that is currently disabled.

Note

Running more than one antivirus program can cause problems because the programs compete with each other to process each bit of information that passes through the computer. For this reason, Action Center doesn't allow you to turn on an antivirus program until all others have been turned off. Antispyware programs, on the other hand, generally don't have such conflicts, so you can safely run multiple programs if you really feel the need to do so.

In Windows 7 (unlike earlier versions of Windows), Windows Firewall can coexist with third-party firewall programs. Windows now defines firewall categories (such as port filtering and IPsec filtering); different firewalls can handle different categories, letting you use the best tool for each task. A properly written third-party firewall can take ownership of a category, and Windows Firewall no longer protects that category, even when Windows Firewall is turned on. If the third-party firewall is stopped or removed, however, and no other firewall is registered for the category, Windows Firewall takes over. Using multiple firewalls can cause system performance to degrade, so use this option only if you are certain you understand the interactions between the two security software packages.

If you don't want to be bothered with alerts from Action Center about one or more security features, click Change Action Center Settings. After clearing items you don't want monitored in the dialog box shown in Figure 17-4, you won't receive any further alerts, and thereafter Action Center passively indicates the status as Currently Not Monitored.

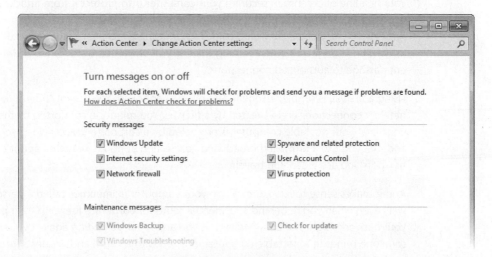

Figure 17-4 You can selectively disable and enable Action Center monitoring here, or you can manage monitored items individually by clicking links in the main Action Center window.

For more information about Action Center, see "Introducing Action Center" on page 872.

INSIDE OUT Hardening older programs against new attacks

The definitive fix for a vulnerability in Windows or in a third-party program is for the program's developer to supply a patch. But what do you do while you're waiting for the patch? And how do you deal with vulnerabilities in legacy applications that can't be easily repaired?

That's the goal of Microsoft's Enhanced Mitigation Experience Toolkit (EMET), a simple but powerful configuration utility that allows you to harden applications that weren't originally designed to take advantage of Windows security features. (You'll find it at *w7io.com/21704*.)

Using EMET allows you to configure some important Windows security features for older programs that weren't written with those features in mind. Microsoft describes it as "a living tool, designed to be updated as new mitigation technologies become available." For more details and a walkthrough, see "The one security tool every Windows user should know about" at *w7io.com/21705*.

Blocking Intruders with Windows Firewall

Your first line of defense in securing your computer is to protect it from attacks by outsiders. Once your computer is connected to the Internet, it becomes just another node on a huge global network. A *firewall* provides a barrier between your computer and the network to which it's connected by preventing the entry of unwanted traffic while allowing transparent passage to authorized connections.

Using a firewall is simple, essential, and often overlooked. You'll want to be sure that all network connections are protected by a firewall. You might be comforted by the knowledge that your portable computer is protected by a corporate firewall when you're at work and that you use a firewalled broadband connection at home. But what about the public hotspots you use when you travel?

And it makes sense to run a firewall on your computer (sometimes called a personal firewall) even when you're behind a residential router or corporate firewall. Other people on your network might not be as vigilant as you are about defending against viruses, so if someone brings in a portable computer infected with a worm and connects it to the network, you're toast—unless your network connection has its own firewall protection.

CAUTION❗

This bears repeating. In today's environment, you should run firewall software on each networked computer; don't rely on corporate gateway firewalls and gateway antivirus solutions to protect your computer from another infected computer inside the perimeter. Although it's not a good idea to run more than one third-party software firewall on a computer, you should run a software firewall as an extra layer of protection behind your hardware firewall.

Windows includes a two-way stateful-inspection packet filtering firewall called, cleverly enough, Windows Firewall. Windows Firewall is enabled by default for all connections, and it begins protecting your computer as it boots. The following actions take place by default:

- The firewall blocks all inbound traffic, with the exception of traffic sent in response to a request sent by your computer and unsolicited traffic that has been explicitly allowed by creating a rule.

- All outgoing traffic is allowed unless it matches a configured rule.

You notice nothing if a packet is dropped, but you can (at your option) create a log of all such events.

Note

Some people wonder why Windows Firewall, unlike some third-party firewalls, doesn't block outbound traffic by default. You'll find security experts on both sides of this argument, but the reason is that Windows Firewall is designed to protect and maintain a secure computer. If malware is making outbound connections, your computer has *already been compromised.* (The misbehaving program should be caught by your antivirus or antispyware defenses.) Blocking outbound traffic by default would generate a blizzard of pop-up warning messages (because so many programs legitimately connect to the Internet or other network computers), which some experts feel would greatly dilute their significance, causing many users to simply ignore them.

Chapter 17

Stateful-Inspection Packet Filtering Explained

Most firewalls work, at least in part, by *packet filtering*—that is, they block or allow transmissions depending on the content of each packet that reaches the firewall. A packet filter examines several attributes of each packet and can either route it (that is, forward it to the intended destination computer) or block it on the basis of any of these attributes:

- **Source address**   The IP address of the computer that generated the packet

- **Destination address**   The IP address of the packet's intended target computer

- **Network protocol**   The type of traffic, such as Internet Protocol (IP)

- **Transport protocol**   The higher-level protocol, such as Transmission Control Protocol (TCP) or User Datagram Protocol (UDP)

- **Source and destination ports**   The number that communicating computers use to identify a communications channel

Packet filtering alone is an inadequate solution; incoming traffic that meets all the packet filter criteria could still be something you didn't ask for or want. *Stateful-inspection packet filtering* goes a step further by restricting incoming traffic to responses to requests from your computer. Here's a simplified example of how stateful-inspection filtering works to allow "good" incoming traffic:

1. You enter a URL in your browser's address bar.

2. The browser sends one or more packets of data addressed to the web server. The destination port is 80, the standard port for HTTP web servers; the source port is an arbitrary number from 1,024 through 65,535.

3. The firewall saves information about the connection in its state table, which it uses to validate returning inbound traffic.

4. After the web server and your computer complete the handshake needed to open a TCP connection, the web server sends a reply (the contents of the web page you requested) addressed to your computer's IP address and source port.

5. The firewall receives the incoming traffic and compares its source and destination addresses and ports with the information in its state table. If the information matches, the firewall permits the reply to pass through to the browser. If the data doesn't match in all respects, the firewall silently discards the packet.

6. Your browser displays the received information.

Compared with the firewall included in Windows XP, Windows Firewall has been enhanced in several ways:

- Windows Firewall supports monitoring and control of both incoming and outgoing network traffic.

- Through its Windows Firewall With Advanced Security console, Windows Firewall provides far more configuration options, and it can be configured remotely. A new wizard makes it easier to create and configure rules. Configuration of Internet Protocol security (IPsec)—a mechanism that provides for authentication, encryption, and filtering of network traffic—is also done in the Windows Firewall With Advanced Security console.

- In addition to the usual criteria (addresses, protocols, and ports), firewall rules can be configured for services, Active Directory accounts and groups, source and destination IP addresses for incoming and outgoing traffic, transport protocols other than TCP and UDP, network connection types, and more.

- Windows Firewall maintains three separate profiles, with the appropriate one selected depending on whether the computer is connected to a domain, a private nondomain network, or a public network.

Note that if you use Windows XP Mode, the virtual machine should have its own firewall enabled. Because the virtual machine runs Windows XP Service Pack 3 (SP3), it uses the Windows XP firewall. For more information about Windows XP Mode, see "Running Legacy Applications in Windows XP Mode" on page 178.

Using a Third-Party Firewall

As noted earlier in this chapter, Windows Firewall is designed to be compatible with firewall programs from third-party providers. When you install a third-party firewall, it can register itself to take ownership of and manage certain firewall categories, such as port blocking, IPsec policy, and boot-time policy. The third-party program reports its status in Action Center, just as Windows Firewall does.

Even if you have a third-party firewall, you should leave Windows Firewall turned on and leave the Windows Firewall service set to run automatically. This is needed to enforce IPsec policies, and it also ensures that Windows Firewall continues to manage any categories that are not protected by the third-party program.

Chapter 17

Using Windows Firewall in Different Network Locations

Windows Firewall maintains a separate profile (that is, a complete collection of settings, including rules for various programs, services, and ports) for each of three network location types:

- **Domain** Used when your computer is joined to an Active Directory domain. In this environment, firewall settings are typically (but not necessarily) controlled by a network administrator.

- **Private** Used when your computer is connected to a home or work network in a workgroup configuration.

- **Public** Used when your computer is connected to a network in a public location, such as an airport or library. It's common—indeed, recommended—to have fewer allowed programs and more restrictions when you use a public network.

If you're simultaneously connected to more than one network (for example, if you have a Wi-Fi connection to your home network while you're connected to your work domain through a virtual private network, or VPN, connection), Windows uses the appropriate profile for each connection with a feature called *multiple active firewall profiles* (MAFP). (This is not the case in Windows Vista. That operating system uses the most restrictive applicable profile whenever you connect to multiple networks at the same time.)

You make settings in Windows Firewall independently for each network profile. The settings in a profile apply to all networks of the particular location type to which you connect. (For example, if you allow a program through the firewall while connected to a public network, that program rule is then enabled whenever you connect to any other public network. It is not enabled when you're connected to a domain or private network, unless you allow the program in those profiles.)

For more information about network locations, see "Understanding Network Locations" on page 687.

Managing Windows Firewall

Windows Firewall is a Control Panel application that provides a simple interface for monitoring firewall status and performing routine tasks, such as allowing a program through the firewall or blocking all incoming connections. To open Windows Firewall, type **firewall** in the Start menu search box or in Control Panel. Click Windows Firewall to display a window similar to the one shown in Figure 17-5.

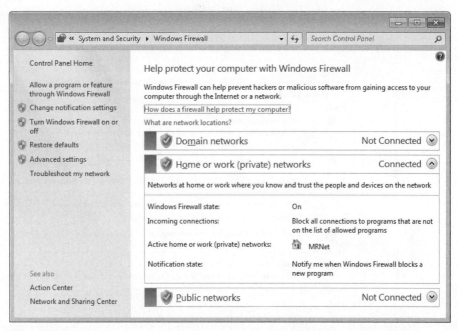

Figure 17-5 Windows Firewall shows status and settings for each currently connected network. The Domain Networks profile appears only on computers that have been joined to a domain.

Enabling or Disabling Windows Firewall

The main Windows Firewall application, shown in Figure 17-5, is little more than a status window and launchpad for making various firewall settings. The first setting of interest is to enable or disable Windows Firewall. To do that, click Turn Windows Firewall On Or Off to open the screen shown next. From here you can enable (turn on) or disable (turn off) Windows Firewall for each network type. In general, the only reason to turn off Windows Firewall is if you have installed a third-party firewall that you plan to use instead of Windows Firewall. Most of those, however, perform this task as part of their installation.

As you'll discover throughout Windows Firewall, domain network location settings are available only on computers that are joined to a domain. You can make settings for all network location types—even those to which you're not currently connected. Settings for the domain profile, however, are often locked down by the network administrator by using Group Policy.

Chapter 17

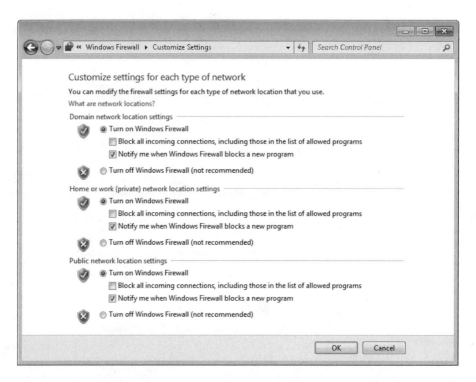

The Block All Incoming Connections check box in Customize Settings provides additional safety. When it's selected, Windows Firewall rejects *all* unsolicited incoming traffic—even traffic from allowed programs or that would ordinarily be permitted by a rule. (For information about firewall rules, see the next section, "Allowing Connections Through the Firewall.") Invoke this mode when extra security against outside attack is needed. For example, you might block all connections when you're using a public wireless hotspot or when you know that your computer is actively under attack by others.

> **Note**
>
> Selecting Block All Incoming Connections does not disconnect your computer from the Internet. Even in this mode, you can still use your browser to connect to the Internet. Similarly, other outbound connections—whether they're legitimate services or some sort of spyware—continue unabated. If you really want to sever your ties to the outside world, open Network And Sharing Center and disable each network connection. (Alternatively, use brute force: physically disconnect wired network connections and turn off wireless adapters or access points.)

Allowing Connections Through the Firewall

In some situations, you want to allow other computers to initiate a connection to your computer. For example, you might use Remote Desktop, play multiplayer games, or chat via an instant messaging program; these types of programs typically require inbound connections so that others can contact you.

The simplest way to enable a connection is to click Allow A Program Or Feature Through Windows Firewall, a link in the left pane of the main Windows Firewall window. The list of programs and features that initially appears in Allowed Programs, shown in Figure 17-6, depends on which programs and services are installed on your computer; you can add others, as described in the following sections. In addition, program rules are created (but not enabled) when a program tries to set up an incoming connection. To allow connections for a program or service that's already been defined, simply select its check box for each network location type on which you want to allow the program. (You'll need to click Change Settings before you can make changes. Note that the Domain column is only available on a computer that has been joined to a Windows domain.)

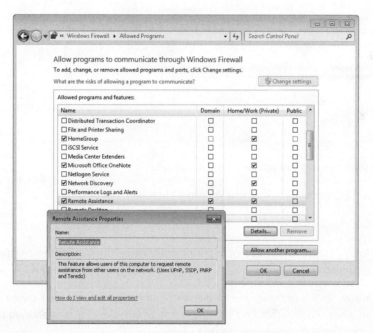

Figure 17-6 Selecting an item and clicking Details displays a description of the program or service.

In each of these cases, you enable a rule in Windows Firewall that pokes a small hole in the firewall and allows a certain type of traffic to pass through it. Each rule of this type increases your security risk to some degree, so you should clear the check box for all programs you don't need. If you're confident you won't ever need a particular program, you can select it and then click Remove. (Many of the list items included with Windows don't allow deletion, but as long as their check boxes are not selected, there's no danger.)

The first time you run a program that tries to set up an incoming connection, Windows Firewall asks for your permission by displaying a dialog box similar to the one shown here. You can add the program to the allowed programs list by clicking Allow Access. (If the computer is joined to a Windows domain, a third option, Domain Networks, will be available.)

When such a dialog box appears, read it carefully:

- Is the program one that you knowingly installed and ran?

- Is it reasonable for the program to require acceptance of incoming connections?

- Are you currently using a network location where it's okay for this program to accept incoming connections?

If the answer to any of these questions is no—or if you're unsure—click Cancel. If you later find that a needed program isn't working properly, you can open the allowed programs list in Windows Firewall and enable the rule.

Alternatively, you can set up the program from the Allowed Programs window shown in Figure 17-6 without waiting for a Windows Security Alert dialog box to appear. Follow these steps:

1. Click Allow Another Program. The Add A Program dialog box appears.

2. In Add A Program, select the program for which you want to allow incoming connections. Or click Browse and navigate to the program's executable file if it isn't shown in the Programs list.

3. Click Network Location Types.

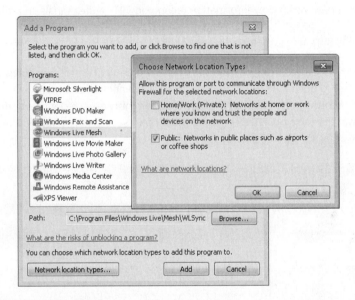

4. Select the network location types on which you want to allow the program, click OK, and then click Add. (You can also select network locations in Allowed Programs after you add the program.)

Restoring Default Settings

If you've played around a bit with Windows Firewall and perhaps allowed connections that you should not have, you can get back to a known, secure state by clicking Restore Defaults in Windows Firewall. Be aware that doing so removes all rules that you've added for all programs. Although this gives you a secure setup, you might find that some of your network-connected programs no longer work properly. As that occurs, you can add again each legitimate program that needs to be allowed, as described on the previous pages.

Advanced Tools for Managing Windows Firewall

If you have any experience at all with configuring firewalls, you'll quickly realize that the Windows Firewall application in Control Panel covers only the most basic tasks. Don't take that as an indication that Windows Firewall is underpowered. To the contrary, you can configure all manner of firewall rules, allowing or blocking traffic based on program, port, protocol, IP address, and so on. In addition, you can enable, disable, and monitor rules; configure logging; and much more. With advanced tools, you can also configure Windows Firewall on remote workstations. Because the interface to these advanced features is rather daunting, Windows Firewall provides the simplified interface described on the preceding pages. It's adequate not only for less experienced users, but also for performing the routine firewall tasks needed by information technology (IT) professionals and others.

Nonetheless, our tour of security essentials would not be complete without a visit to Windows Firewall With Advanced Security, a snap-in and predefined console for Microsoft Management Console (MMC) that offers granular control over rules, exceptions, and profiles. To open it, in Windows Firewall click Advanced Settings. (If you're using a standard account and you haven't yet entered administrative credentials during this Windows Firewall session, you'll need to enter them now.) Windows Firewall With Advanced Security appears, as shown in Figure 17-7.

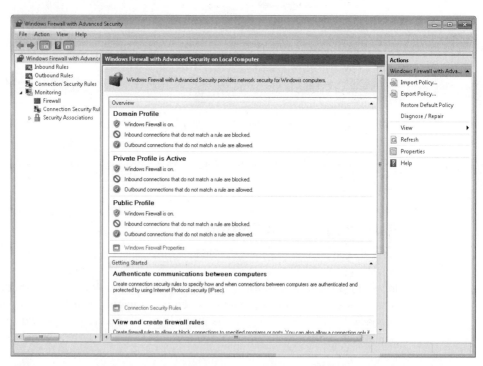

Figure 17-7 In the left pane, click Inbound Rules or Outbound Rules to view, configure, create, and delete firewall rules. The Domain Profile appears even on a computer that is not part of a Windows domain.

Chapter 17

The initial view presents information similar to that shown in Windows Firewall. Go just a few steps farther into the cave, however, and you could be lost in no time. The "Windows Firewall with Advanced Security Getting Started Guide" can brighten your path; view it at *w7io.com/1502*.

INSIDE OUT   Open Windows Firewall With Advanced Security directly

You don't need to open Windows Firewall to get to Windows Firewall With Advanced Security. In the Start menu search box, type **wf.msc** and press Ctrl+Shift+Enter to run it as an administrator.

If you're not intimidated by the Windows Firewall With Advanced Security console, you might want to try the command-line interface for managing Windows Firewall. Because it can be scripted, it can be useful if you need to make firewall settings repeatedly, whether on a single computer as conditions change or on a fleet of computers. To use the command-line interface, you use the Netsh command with the Advfirewall context. You can get some terse help by typing **netsh advfirewall** in a Command Prompt window. For additional information about Netsh commands for Windows Firewall, see the Microsoft TechNet reference at *w7io.com/1503*.

Staying Secure with Windows Update

One essential step in keeping your system secure is to be sure that you stay current with updates to Windows 7. Microsoft issues frequent updates that provide replacements for installed device drivers as well as fixes to code that has been found to be faulty. Some updates provide enhanced performance or reliability, while others patch security holes.

Windows 7 includes Windows Update (shown next), a program that can perform updates for you automatically or, if you prefer, at your direction. Windows Update is often considered to be a routine maintenance procedure, and we describe it in detail in "Keeping Your System Secure with Windows Update" on page 875.

Chapter 17

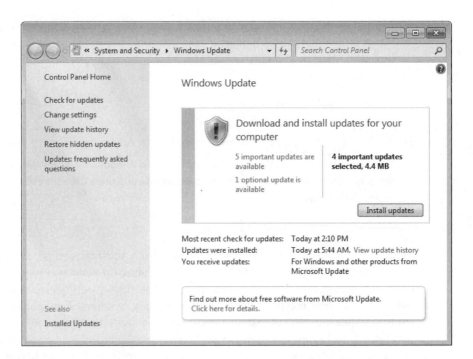

As we point out there, in recent years most widely exploited vulnerabilities in Windows have been patched quickly—usually *before* they became widespread problems. In fact, many of the worst outbreaks were based on vulnerabilities that had been patched months or years earlier. Windows users who installed the updates promptly were able to avoid infection, whereas those who failed to keep their systems updated fell victim.

Security need not become an obsession (and Windows Update makes keeping your system secure quite painless), but you might want to stay a bit ahead of the security game by making periodic visits to security-related websites or subscribing to security-related newsletters or RSS feeds. The following list describes some resources you might want to check out:

- Microsoft's security home page at *w7io.com/1504* offers links to information about the latest security updates (which you already have installed if you use Windows Update), current security threats, security training sessions, guidance centers, and other information. In addition you'll find links to security information written specifically for home users, educators, small businesses, midsize businesses, software developers, IT professionals, and other targeted groups of computer users.

- Microsoft TechNet Security TechCenter (*w7io.com/1505*) provides more technical details, aimed primarily at IT professionals.

- You can review the latest security bulletins a few days *before* the update is released via Windows Update. Learn about the Microsoft Security Bulletin Advance Notification Service at *w7io.com/1506*.

- You can view the latest issue of the Microsoft Security Newsletter at *w7io.com/1507*; to subscribe, visit *w7io.com/1508*. The newsletter includes webcast schedules and links to numerous security-related blogs and newsgroups, in addition to timely articles.

- You can sign up for alerts (sent via e-mail, RSS, or instant messenger) of security information from Microsoft at *w7io.com/1509*.

Using Security Software to Block Malware

The best way to fight unwanted and malicious software is to keep it from being installed on any PC that is part of your network.

Historically, the most common source of widespread computer virus outbreaks is the class of hostile software that replicates by sending itself to other potential victims as an attachment to an e-mail message. The accompanying message often uses social-engineering techniques designed to lure inattentive or gullible users into opening the infected attachment. For example, some viruses arrive as attachments that mimic delivery failure reports from an e-mail server administrator. The attachment, in .zip format, ostensibly includes details of the failed message but actually contains the virus payload.

INSIDE OUT   Beware of .zip files attached to e-mail messages

These days, most mail servers reject all incoming messages with executable files attached; even if the server doesn't stop such messages, modern e-mail clients make it difficult or impossible to run executable attachments. That simple measure completely stops most viruses written before 2003.

To work around the blockade, attachment-based viruses now typically send their payloads using the standard .zip format for compressed files. If the user opens the attachment, the contents of the compressed file appear—in Windows Explorer or in the third-party utility assigned to handle .zip files. Double-clicking the executable file within the compressed archive sets the virus in motion. Virus writers use a variety of tricks with .zip files. In some cases, they include a bogus extension in the file name and then append a large number of spaces before the real file name extension so that the actual file type doesn't appear in the window that displays archived files. Some viruses even encrypt the .zip attachment and include the password as part of the message. That allows the infected attachment to slip past some virus scanners. Most real-time scanners will detect a virus in a .zip file, either when it arrives or when the user tries to extract the file. The moral? Be wary of all attachments, even when they appear to be innocent.

Chapter 17

Although viruses that spread through e-mail attachments were responsible for the majority of attacks in the last decade, other modes of transmission now represent a greater threat. By their nature, attachments (as well as files transferred with an instant messaging program, a more recent attack vector) require some cooperation from an unwitting or distracted user; that requirement dramatically limits their potential to spread unchecked. As a result, authors of hostile software are always on the lookout for techniques they can use to spread infections automatically.

The Conficker worm, which made headlines in 2009, provides an example: one of its propagation methods relies on AutoPlay, the feature that displays a menu of options when you insert a removable drive, such as a USB flash drive. On unprotected computers it displays an option to "open folder to view files" when a victim inserts an infected USB flash drive in the computer and AutoPlay runs. When clicked, that option actually executes the worm, which then attempts to spread to other computers. Windows 7 doesn't have the vulnerability that Conficker exploits in earlier (unpatched) Windows versions, but it also closes the AutoPlay vulnerability, as AutoRun (the feature that placed the bogus option in the AutoPlay dialog box) is disabled on removable drives.

Another popular mechanism is the use of scripts—written in languages such as Java-Script, JScript, or Microsoft Visual Basic Scripting Edition (often abbreviated as VBScript or VBS)—that automatically take actions on the intended victim's computer when he or she visits a web page or views an HTML-formatted e-mail message. Protected Mode in Internet Explorer is one defense against this type of intrusion.

For details about Protected Mode and other defensive measures in Internet Explorer, see "Monitoring and Maintaining Security" on page 252.

Yet another increasingly common mode of transmission uses e-mail to send a link to a compromised website. If the intended victim clicks the link, she's taken to a page that attempts to install hostile code automatically, using an exploit that attacks the browser or a helper program. In other scenarios, the visitor is prompted to download a seemingly harmless file. The file, which might be disguised as a codec or system update required to view a salacious file, usually turns out to be a Trojan.

Spyware typically gets installed by deceitfully asking permission to do something other than what it actually does or, in some cases, by exploiting browser vulnerabilities. In this regard, most spyware is fundamentally different from earlier types of malware; it typically relies on social engineering to install instead of exploiting vulnerabilities.

In our opinion, any program that tries to sneak onto your PC without your full knowledge and consent should be blocked. An important layer in a basic PC protection strategy, therefore, is to use up-to-date antivirus software. Windows 7 itself does not include any antivirus software, but it's readily available from Microsoft and many other vendors.

Choosing an Antivirus Program

Antivirus programs run as a system service and typically use a scanning engine to compare files against a database of virus definitions (sometimes called the signature file). Most also use *heuristic analysis* of the behavior of program files to flag suspicious activity from a file that isn't included in the list of known threats. The most effective programs scan each file that you access in any way, including downloads from the Internet and e-mail attachments you receive. (This feature is typically called real-time scanning, virus monitoring, or something similar and shouldn't be confused with scheduled scans, which periodically inspect all files stored on your computer to root out malware.)

If you buy a new PC from a retail outlet, it's likely that the PC maker included an antivirus program as part of its standard installation. For commercial programs, this sort of installation is often a trial version that must be converted to a paid subscription after the trial expires. (The PC maker typically gets a share of the revenue you pay.) If you don't want the trial software, we recommend that you uninstall it immediately and install an antivirus program of your own choosing.

Plenty of good antivirus programs are available at a wide range of prices, including some very well respected free programs. You can start your search at the Windows 7 Consumer Security Software Providers page, *w7io.com/1510*, which provides links to publishers of Windows 7–compatible security software, including antivirus programs. (If you haven't yet installed antivirus software, you'll find a link to this page in Action Center. Next to Virus Protection, click Find A Program Online.)

The Windows 7 Consumer Security Software Providers page provides no independent evaluation. So how do you choose? Besides the usual review sites managed by computer magazines, you should look to ICSA Labs, which tests antivirus programs and certifies those that meet its criteria for effectiveness. You can find lists of certified programs at *w7io.com/1511*. Another independent tester is Austria-based AV-Comparatives.org (see *w7io.com/1512*).

The most important thing to understand about security software is this: it is not perfect. Malware authors and security software companies are engaged in a constant, endless game of cat and mouse. That's why antivirus definitions are updated so frequently. The best security companies detect new threats quickly and have false positives—legitimate programs flagged as malicious—rarely or never.

Microsoft's entry in the consumer antivirus arena is Microsoft Security Essentials (see *w7io.com/1513*). The program is available free of charge to individuals and for small businesses with up to 10 Windows PCs. Microsoft Security Essentials is based on the antivirus feature of Microsoft Forefront Endpoint Protection (formerly Forefront Client Security), a business-oriented program for protection against viruses and spyware; for more information, see *w7io.com/21703*.

Chapter 17

Do You Even Need an Antivirus Program?

Some computer experts—computer *security* experts, even—proudly point out that they don't use antivirus software. Why not? Some question its efficacy, particularly at blocking zero-day exploits for which virus definitions have not been created. Others point to the fact that, like every additional running program, an antivirus program adds another level of complexity and another potential attack surface for malicious software. Indeed, at one time or another, virtually every major antivirus program has been found to have some vulnerability to remote exploits. Finally, what puts some folks over the edge is the performance hit imposed by antivirus programs that constantly work in the background to examine each file as it's read from disk; the slowdown is usually small but measurable.

How is it possible to maintain a virus-free computer without the assistance of an anti-virus program? Remember that antivirus protection is just one of many security lay-ers in a well-protected computer network. To have any hope of surviving unscathed without that layer, several other forms of protection must be in place. The network's Internet gateway should provide filtering that prevents viruses from entering through a web browser or instant messenger connection; this capability is typically available only in commercial-grade firewall appliances or in a separate gateway computer that's con-figured for this purpose.

The e-mail server should also have virus-blocking capability. (Many ISPs and web-based mail services block all mail that contains a known virus.) In theory, those network-level layers should prevent any malware from reaching your computer, but the computer itself must be properly secured in other ways: all patches up to date, firewall enabled, User Account Control enabled, and a standard account set up for each user.

The most important protective layer—and the one that is most easily overlooked—is user education and self control. Everyone who uses the computer must have the disci-pline to read and evaluate security warnings when they're presented and to allow the installation only of software that is known to be safe. (Although a user with a standard account is incapable of installing or running a program that wipes out the entire com-puter, he can still inflict enough damage on his own user profile to cause considerable inconvenience.) Countless successful virus attacks worldwide have proven that most users do not have adequate awareness of safe computing methods. Indeed, our stan-dard advice for most users is don't even think of connecting to the Internet without antivirus software! Only people who really know what they're doing, and who remain vigilant, should consider joining those anti-antivirus experts.

Based on several years of experience, we unhesitatingly recommend Microsoft Security Essentials. It's lightweight, unobtrusive, and consistently effective based on independent tests. In the following section, we describe how to install, configure, and use Microsoft Security Essentials.

Scanning for Viruses Without an Antivirus Program

On the second Tuesday of each month, as part of its normal security releases, Microsoft releases an updated version of a utility called the Malicious Software Removal Tool (MSRT). This utility is not designed to block new viruses from entering a computer; rather, its function is to clean up systems that have been infected with well-known and widespread viruses and other forms of malware. The MSRT is delivered by Windows Update, and on most computers, this tool runs silently and then deletes itself; it alerts you if it finds any infections, and lets you know if they were successfully removed.

If you prefer to scan one or more systems manually, you can download the current executable version of the MSRT from *w7io.com/1514*. Because this utility is updated at least monthly, we do not recommend that you save this file. For details about this tool, read Microsoft Knowledge Base article 890830 (*w7io.com/1515*).

If you suspect that a Windows-based PC has been compromised by malware, you can use one of many web-based detection tools to scan your system. Most major third-party security software companies offer a service of this type. You'll find Microsoft's free Microsoft Safety Scanner, for example, at *w7io.com/1516*. If you're suspicious of a file that you've downloaded or received as an attachment, you can upload it directly to Microsoft by using the online form at *w7io.com/21702*. VirusTotal (*virustotal.com*) offers a similar service that uses multiple scanning engines to check a suspect file.

Periodic scanning by the MSRT or an online tool does not provide continuous protection against virus infections. For that, you need to install and run an antivirus program.

Setting Up and Using Microsoft Security Essentials

Microsoft Security Essentials is a drop-in replacement for Windows Defender, with a similar user interface but a much deeper approach to malware protection. To download and install the latest version, visit *w7io.com/1513*. The download is small, and the installation process (which requires administrative credentials, of course) is quick. After setup completes, you're prompted to update your virus and spyware definitions to the latest version and perform a quick initial scan for any existing malware. We strongly recommend completing these tasks as soon as possible.

Chapter 17

To open the Microsoft Security Essentials console, click Start, type **security** in the search box, and click the program's shortcut. Or click the program's icon in the notification area, which is normally green but changes color if the program requires any attention—to yellow if a scan turns up a threat rated Low or if your definitions are out of date, and to red if a Serious threat is detected.

In the console, click Home to see the results of the most recent scan. The color changes to yellow or red if any detected threats have not yet been dealt with.

This page also tells you whether real-time protection is enabled; for a closer look, click Settings, click Real-Time Protection, and examine the four categories shown in Figure 17-8.

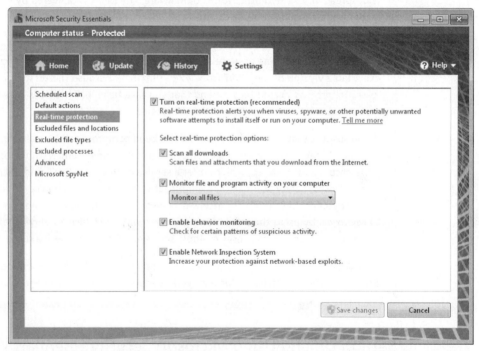

Figure 17-8 In the unlikely event that real-time protection causes performance problems, you can adjust its behavior here.

To temporarily disable real-time protection (if it is interfering with the installation of a legitimate program, for example), clear the Turn On Real-Time Protection (Recommended) check box. Doing so causes the Computer Status banner at the top of the program window to glow red and change from Protected to At Risk. The icon in the notification area also turns red, and you will receive multiple warnings from Action Center.

You can dial back the effect of real-time protection in a less dramatic way by using the four check boxes beneath that big red switch. In particular, if you are confident of your ability to keep your system from being compromised, you can change the Monitor All Files setting to Monitor Only Incoming Files.

Microsoft Security Essentials uses Windows Update to retrieve definition files and periodic updates to the detection engine. As part of the setup process, it might enable automatic updating. You cannot disable or reschedule updating for Microsoft Security Essentials except by changing the global Windows Update settings.

Also as part of the default setup, Microsoft Security Essentials schedules a scan of your system to run every Sunday morning at 2:00 A.M. You can change the type of scan or adjust the schedule from the Scheduled Scan section, shown in Figure 17-9.

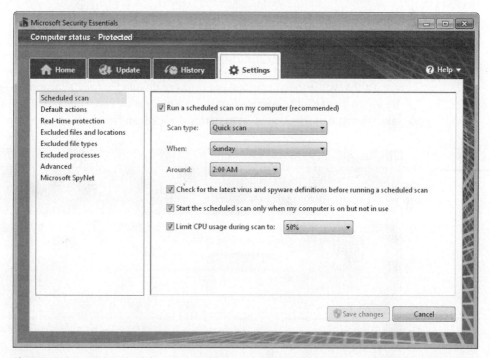

Figure 17-9 You can schedule scans weekly or choose Daily from the top of the When list to run a scan every night.

The default scheduled scan runs weekly on the day you specify. Want to scan more often? The top choice on the When menu is Daily.

INSIDE OUT   Set your PC to scan using the proper amount of system resources

A complete scan can take a long time. Automatic scans run at low priority and use algorithms to determine when your computer is idle; this enables scans to run efficiently when you're not using your computer and to stay out of the way when you are. For a well-equipped desktop PC, you might prefer to get this housekeeping over as soon as possible. If you're working on a slower notebook, on the other hand, you might want to throttle the scanning engine even further. In the Scheduled Scan section, adjust the Limit CPU Usage During Scan option from its default of 50 percent to a higher or lower level.

Manually Scanning for Malware

The combination of real-time protection and periodic scheduled scanning is normally sufficient for identifying and resolving problems with malware and spyware. However, if you suspect that you've been infected—or if you've disabled automatic scanning—you can initiate a scan on demand. To immediately run a quick scan, click Home. Under Scan Options, select the type of scan you want to perform; click Scan Now to begin the scan.

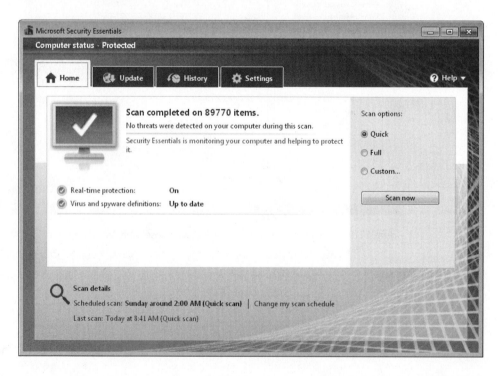

INSIDE OUT   **Run a scan from a script or a scheduled task**

Microsoft Security Essentials includes a command-line utility that you can use to auto-mate scans with a script or a scheduled task. You'll find MpCmdRun.exe in %Program-Files%\Microsoft Security Client\Antimalware. For details about using the utility, open an elevated Command Prompt window and run the program with no parameters.

The Quick option kicks off a scan that checks only the places on your computer that mal-ware and spyware are most likely to infect, and it is the recommended setting for frequent regular scans. Choose Full if you suspect infection (or you just want reassurance that your system is clean) and want to inspect all running programs and the complete contents of all local volumes. Click Custom if you want to restrict the scan to any combination of drives, folders, and files.

A full scan can be burdensome, especially if you have hundreds or thousands of files scat-tered around local disks. To minimize the time and system resources, you can specify that Microsoft Security Essentials skip over locations and file types that you know are safe and haven't been tampered with.

On the Settings page, you'll find four options that affect scanning:

- **Excluded Files And Location**   In this box, you can specify files or folders that you know to be safe. This is an appropriate option if you have a folder full of previously downloaded system utilities that routinely trigger alerts. Do not use this option with folders where you routinely download new files.

- **Excluded File Types**   Similarly, you can exclude from scans all files with the file name extensions (such as common scripts) that you specify.

- **Excluded Processes**   If you find that a program is routinely detected as a potential threat despite your telling Microsoft Security Essentials to allow it, consider add-ing the program to this list. Be sure to specify the process name (Myprogram.exe) and not the program name. This strategy is less risky than excluding the containing folder; if you grant blanket approval for files in the containing folder, and later some real spyware ends up in the folder, you risk allowing malware to sneak onto your sys-tem with no warning.

- **Advanced**   The options shown next control the scope of Microsoft Security Essen-tials scans when selected. Note that archive files—the subject of the first option and enabled by default—are the storage mechanism for compressed folders as well as .zip and .cab files. The Scan Removable Drives option is off by default. Enable it if you are preparing to transport files to a new computer and you want to verify that they're harmless.

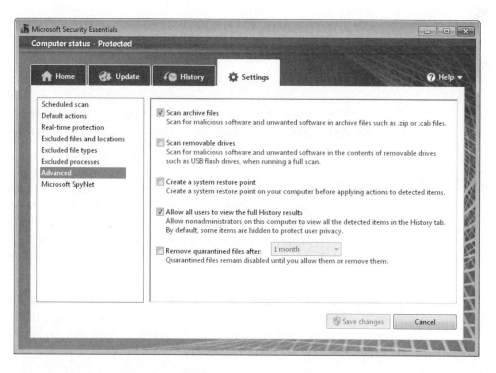

Dealing with Detected Threats

If Microsoft Security Essentials detects the presence of malware or spyware as part of its real-time protection, it slides up a warning above the notification area, similar to the one shown here.

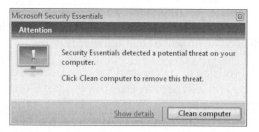

Click the Clean Computer button to immediately remove the threat. Click Show Details to display a dialog box that offers more information and more options. As Figure 17-10 shows, the list at the top of the window shows the name, alert level, and current status of the detected item or items; if you're certain of the consequences, you can click to select an alternative action from the one shown on the drop-down Recommended Action list.

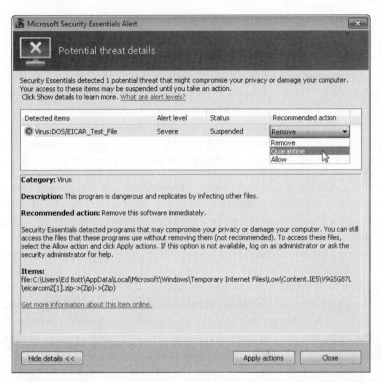

Figure 17-10 If you're not certain what a detected item is, click the Get More Information link at the bottom of this dialog box.

The default action for each alert level can be customized by clicking Settings and then clicking Default Actions. For each detected item, you can specify one of three actions:

- **Remove**   Microsoft Security Essentials permanently removes the files from your computer.

- **Quarantine**   The detected item is moved to a restricted folder (%ProgramData%\ Microsoft\Microsoft Antimalware\Quarantine) whose permissions include a Deny access control entry that locks out the built-in Users and Everyone groups. Executable files in this folder cannot be run, nor can the folder's contents be accessed from Windows Explorer. Items moved here can only be managed from the Microsoft Security Essentials console (preferred) or an elevated Command Prompt window.

- **Allow**   Microsoft Security Essentials allows the program to be installed or to run and adds the program to the allowed list. Further contact with the file no longer produces an alert. You should allow only software that you know to be safe.

After you make your choice, click Apply Actions.

INSIDE OUT
Take action—but which action?

How do you decide what to do based on the rather cryptic information that's presented? Begin with the Potential Threat Details screen. If that information isn't useful, click Show Details and then click Get More Information About This Item Online. That takes you to the Microsoft Malware Protection Center, where you can read a full report on the detected item. Examine each of the details and consider whether the recommended action is reasonable for the type of program you *think* you're installing.

If you're still unsure, search the web for the names of any programs or files shown; you're likely to find many sites that better describe the source and potential risks with a particular file or program. (You're also likely to find a number of sites packed with misinformation, and it's sometimes hard to tell the difference. Until you find a site that gives you confidence, check several sites to find a consensus. And when you do find one of those good sites, bookmark it for the next time you have to deal with an uncategorized risk.) Dealing with potentially risky software is not clear-cut. Not everyone agrees on what constitutes a risky program; some people are willing to accept the risk in return for benefits derived from the program. Furthermore, some perfectly safe, perfectly legitimate programs work in ways similar to some spyware, and they could be flagged as spyware. Ultimately, you have to decide.

TROUBLESHOOTING
You can't get rid of a detected threat

Some types of malware and spyware are pernicious and use every trick in the book to avoid being removed, coming back to life like the monster in a horror film and reinstalling themselves after you thought you had driven a stake through the program's heart. After you take action to disable a malware or spyware infestation (either remove or quarantine), be even more vigilant in case it rears its ugly self again. In the aftermath of a cleanup, be sure that all real-time protection options are enabled. Consider running an occasional manual scan. And watch out for the sequel.

If an infestation does return, you're dealing with a tough one, and you're going to need some up-to-date expert advice to help you through the process of manually removing it. Because every threat is different, we can't provide useful generic instructions here—but we can point you to an excellent resource: the aptly named BleepingComputer.com forums (*w7io.com/21706*), where you'll find links to diagnostic and removal tools and volunteer experts to help solve problems.

Preventing Unsafe Actions with User Account Control

Windows Vista introduced one of the most controversial—and potentially most effective—security changes in User Account Control (UAC). In short, UAC intercedes whenever a user or program attempts to perform a system administrative task and asks for the consent of a computer administrator before commencing what could be risky business. As implemented in Windows Vista, UAC took a lot of heat because some users saw it as intrusive, annoying, or both. Even after modifications in Service Pack 1, many Windows Vista users ended up turning off UAC altogether.

Microsoft has made considerable changes to UAC in Windows 7. Users, whether logged on with an administrator account or a standard account, see far fewer prompts than in Windows Vista. In Windows 7, standard users can view Windows settings (in Device Manager, for example) without requiring elevation. (They still need administrative credentials to make changes, however.) Standard users can install updates and drivers from Windows Update, pair Bluetooth devices, and reset the network adapter—all tasks that require elevation in Windows Vista—without a peep from UAC in Windows 7. In other cases, such as with certain file operations and installing programs from Internet Explorer, several prompts are merged. In addition, Windows 7 provides more flexibility in configuring UAC to work the way you want; in Windows Vista, unless you dig into Local Security Policy, UAC is either on or off. For more information about changes to UAC in Windows 7, read the TechNet article "What's New in User Account Control" at *w7io.com/1522*.

To understand why UAC is effective, you need to look at security as it existed before the release of Windows Vista. Computer security experts have long espoused *least privilege*, a rule that states that you give only enough access for a person to perform his or her job. (This basic security tenet is sometimes referred to as LUA, an acronym that, depending upon whom you ask, stands for "limited user account," "least user access," "least-privileged user account," or something similar.) In earlier versions of Windows, by default all accounts are set up as administrator accounts, with full privileges to do anything on the computer—including the ability to easily and inadvertently install viruses and perform other harmful tasks. This is a clear violation of LUA, and security experts recommended setting up users with limited accounts (comparable to standard accounts in Windows 7). Because these accounts have fewer rights and more restrictive permissions, users and programs running with limited accounts can do less damage. As it turns out, however, using a limited account in Windows XP is practically impossible, primarily because most applications of the day were written with the assumption that users would have full administrative privileges, and those programs don't run properly (or at all) when you start them from a limited account.

By contrast, in Windows 7, accounts you set up after the first one are nonadministrator standard accounts by default; although they can carry out all the usual daily computing tasks, they're prevented from performing potentially harmful operations. These restrictions apply not just to the user; more importantly, they also apply to any programs launched by the user. Even administrator accounts run as so-called "protected administrator" accounts, in which they have standard-user privileges except when they need to perform administrative tasks. (This is sometimes called Admin Approval Mode.)

For information about user accounts, see Chapter 18, "Managing User Accounts, Passwords, and Logons."

Newer, security-aware programs are written so that they don't require administrator privileges for performing everyday tasks. Programs that truly need administrative access (such as utility programs that change computer settings) request elevation. And what about those older programs—many still in use—that require administrator privileges? Windows 7 has several ways of making most of them work properly. In one way or another, the program is made to act as if it's being run by an administrator. One method, for example, is file and registry virtualization (also known as data redirection). When a program attempts to write to (and subsequently read from) a file or registry key on which only administrators have write access, Windows instead uses a file or key within the current user's profile. In some cases, a program must be marked as requiring elevation, in which case it triggers a UAC prompt each time it runs—and then actually runs using an administrator's credentials.

For more information about program compatibility, see "Dealing with Compatibility Issues" on page 174.

What Triggers UAC Prompts

The types of actions that require elevation to administrator status (and therefore display a UAC elevation prompt) include those that make changes to systemwide settings or to files in %SystemRoot% or %ProgramFiles%. Among the actions that require elevation are the following:

- Installing and uninstalling applications

- Installing device drivers that are not included in Windows or provided through Windows Update

- Installing ActiveX controls

- Changing settings for Windows Firewall

- Changing UAC settings

- Configuring Windows Update

- Adding or removing user accounts

- Changing a user's account type

- Configuring Parental Controls

- Running Task Scheduler

- Restoring backed-up system files

- Viewing or changing another user's folders and files

Within Windows, you can identify in advance many actions that require elevation. A shield icon next to a button or link indicates that a UAC prompt will appear if you're using a standard account.

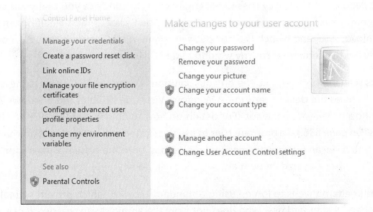

If you used Windows Vista, you'll notice that if you log on with an administrator account (and if you leave the default UAC settings unchanged), you'll see fewer consent prompts. That's because the default setting prompts only when a program tries to install software or make other changes to the computer, but not when you make changes to Windows settings (even those that would trigger a prompt for a standard user with default UAC settings). Windows uses *auto-elevation* to elevate without prompting certain programs that are part of Windows. Programs that auto-elevate are from a predefined list, they must be digitally signed by the Windows publisher, and they must be stored in certain secure folders.

Chapter 17

Is Auto-Elevation a Security Vulnerability?

The changes Microsoft made to User Account Control in Windows 7 represent a trade-off between convenience and security. (For details of these changes, see this post from the Engineering Windows 7 blog: *w7io.com/21707*.) Some researchers have argued that the decision to automatically elevate certain tasks is a security hole. As they demonstrated with sample code, a program can inject itself into one of these tasks, allowing it to execute with no warning if you are logged on using a Protected Administrator account.

Is this a fundamental weakening of Windows security? In our opinion, no. Instead, it's a sobering illustration of a simple fact: User Account Control isn't a security silver bullet. It's one layer of a defense-in-depth strategy.

Some Windows users assume that UAC consent dialog boxes represent a security boundary. They don't. They simply represent a place for an administrator to make a trust decision. If a bad guy uses social engineering to convince you that you need his program, you've already made a trust decision. You'll click at least a half-dozen times to download, save, and launch the bad guy's program. A UAC consent request is perfectly normal in this sequence, so why wouldn't you click one more time?

If this scenario bothers you, the obvious solution is to adjust UAC to its highest level. This matches the default settings of Windows Vista and disables the Windows 7–specific auto-elevate behavior. (For details on how to do this, see "Modifying UAC Settings" on page 636.) If a program tries to use this subterfuge to sneak system changes past you, you'll see an unexpected consent dialog box from the system. But as soon as you provide those elevated credentials, the code can do anything it wants.

A better alternative is to log on using a standard account, which provides a real security boundary. A standard user who does not have the administrator password can make changes only in her own user profile, protecting the system from unintended tampering. (For more information, see "Working Around UAC Without Disabling It" on page 638 and "Effectively Implementing User Accounts on a Shared Computer" on page 659.)

Even running as a standard user doesn't provide complete protection. Malware can be installed in your user profile without triggering any system alarms. It can log your keystrokes, steal your passwords, and send out e-mail using your identity. Even if you reset UAC to its highest level you could fall victim to malware that lies in wait for you to elevate and then does its own dirty work alongside you.

As we said, enabling UAC is only one part of a multilayered security strategy. It works best when supplemented by a healthy skepticism and up-to-date antivirus software.

Dealing with UAC Prompts

At logon, Windows creates a token that is used to identify the privilege levels of your account. Standard users get a standard token, but administrators actually get two: a standard token and an administrator token. The standard token is used to open Explorer.exe (the Windows shell), from which all subsequent programs are launched. Child processes inherit the token of the process that launches them, so by default all applications run as a standard user—even when you're logged on with an administrator account. Certain programs request elevation to administrator privileges; that's when the UAC prompt is displayed. If you provide administrator credentials, Windows then uses the administrator token to open the program. Note that any processes that the successfully elevated program opens also run as administrator.

As an elevation-requesting application attempts to open, UAC evaluates the application and the request and then displays an appropriate prompt. As an administrator, the most common prompt you're likely to see is the *consent prompt*, which is shown in Figure 17-11. Read it, check the name of the program, click Yes, and carry on.

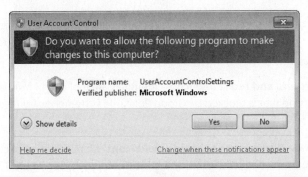

Figure 17-11 Clicking Show Details displays a link to the program's certificate.

If you use a standard account, when a program requires elevation you'll see the *credentials prompt*, which is shown in Figure 17-12. If the user is able to provide the credentials (that is, user name and password, smart card, or fingerprint, depending on how logon authentication is configured on the computer) of an administrator, the application opens using the administrator's access token.

Chapter 17

Figure 17-12 To perform an administrative task, a standard user must enter the password for an administrator account.

You'll encounter other UAC prompts as well. A colored background near the top of the prompt dialog box provides a quick visual clue to the type of program that's requesting elevation:

- **Red background and red shield icon**   Identifies an application from a blocked publisher or one that is blocked by Group Policy. Be extremely wary if you see one of these.

- **Yellow-orange background and red shield icon**   Identifies an application (signed or unsigned) that is not yet trusted by the local computer. (See Figure 17-13.)

- **Blue-green background**   Identifies an administrative application that is part of Windows. (See Figures 17-11 and 17-12.)

- **Gray background**   Identifies an application that is Authenticode signed and trusted by the local computer.

By default, the UAC dialog box sits atop the *secure desktop*, a separate process that no other application can interfere with. (If the secure desktop wasn't secure, a malicious program could put another dialog box in front of the UAC dialog box, perhaps with a message encouraging you to let the program proceed. Or a malicious program could grab your keystrokes, thereby learning your administrator logon password.) When the secure desktop is displayed, you can't switch tasks or click the windows on the desktop. (In fact, they're not really windows. When UAC invokes the secure desktop, it snaps a picture of the desktop, darkens it, and then displays that image behind the dialog box.)

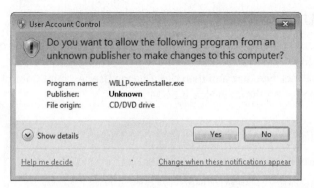

Figure 17-13 When you install a new program, you'll see a UAC prompt.

TROUBLESHOOTING

There's a delay before the secure desktop appears

On some systems, you have to wait a few seconds before the screen darkens and the UAC prompt appears on the secure desktop. There's no easy way to solve the slow-down, but you can easily work around it. In User Account Control Settings (described in the next section, "Modifying UAC Settings"), you can take it down a notch. The setting below the default provides the same level of UAC protection (albeit with a slight risk that malware could hijack the desktop), except that it does not dim the desktop.

Note

If an application other than the foreground application requests elevation, instead of interrupting your work (the foreground task) with a prompt, UAC signals its request with a flashing orange taskbar button. Click the taskbar button to see the prompt.

It becomes natural to click through dialog boxes without reading them or giving them a second thought. But it's important to recognize that security risks to your computer are real, and that actions that trigger a UAC prompt are *potentially* dangerous. Clearly, if you know what you're doing and you click a button to, say, set the Windows Update settings, you can blow past that security dialog box with no more than a quick glance to be sure it was raised by the expected application. But if a UAC prompt appears when you're not expecting it—stop, read it carefully, and think before you click.

Chapter 17

Modifying UAC Settings

User Account Control is not for everybody, but in Windows 7 you can tone it down without disabling it altogether. To review your options and make changes, in the Start menu search box or in Control Panel, type **uac** and then click Change User Account Control Settings. A window similar to the one shown in Figure 17-14 appears.

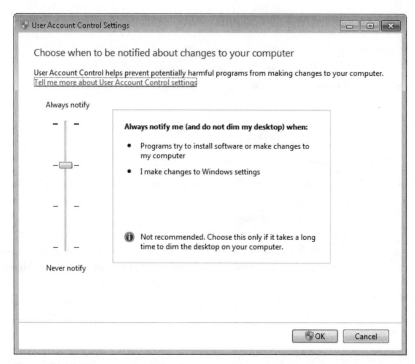

Figure 17-14 The topmost setting is comparable to UAC in Windows Vista; the bottom setting turns off UAC.

Your choices in this window vary slightly depending on whether you use an administrator account or a standard account. (Specifically, the second option from the top is different.) For standard accounts, the top setting is the default; for administrator accounts, the second setting from the top is the default. Table 17-1 summarizes the available options.

To make changes, move the slider to the position you want. Be sure to take note of the advisory message in the bottom of the box as you move the slider. Click OK when you're done—and then respond to the UAC prompt that appears! Note that when you're logged on with a standard account, you can't select one of the bottom two options, even if you have the password for an administrator account. To select one of those options, you must log on as an administrator and then make the change.

Table 17-1 **User Account Control Settings**

Slider Position	Prompts when a program tries to install software or make changes to the computer	Prompts when you make changes to Windows settings	Displays prompts on a secure desktop
Standard user account			
Top (Default)	✔	✔	✔
Second	✔	✔	
Third	✔		
Bottom (Off)			
Administrator account			
Top	✔	✔	✔
Second (Default)	✔		✔
Third	✔		
Bottom (Off)			

TROUBLESHOOTING

User Account Control settings don't stick

If you find that nothing happens when you make a change to User Account Control settings, be sure that you're the only one logged on to your computer. Simultaneous logons that use Fast User Switching can cause this problem.

INSIDE OUT   Use Local Security Policy to customize UAC behavior

Users of the Professional, Enterprise, and Ultimate editions of Windows 7 can use the Local Security Policy console to modify the behavior of UAC. Start Local Security Policy (Secpol.msc), and open Security Settings\Local Policies\Security Options. In the details pane, scroll down to the policies whose names begin with "User Account Control." For each policy, double-click it and click the Explain tab for information before you decide on a setting. With these 10 policies, you can make several refinements in the way UAC works—including some that are not possible in the User Account Control Settings window. (Administrators on Windows-based enterprise networks can also configure these options using Group Policy management tools.) For details about each of these policies, see "UAC Group Policy Settings" at *w7io.com/1523*.

Chapter 17

Regardless of your UAC setting, the shield icons still appear throughout Control Panel, but you won't see UAC prompts if you've lowered the UAC protection level. Clicking a button or link identified with a shield immediately begins the action. Administrators run with full administrator privileges; standard users, of course, still have only standard privileges.

> **CAUTION !**
>
> Don't forget that UAC is more than annoying prompts. Only when UAC is enabled does an administrator run with a standard token. Only when UAC is enabled does Internet Explorer run in a low-privilege Protected Mode. Only when UAC is enabled does it warn you when a rogue application attempts to perform a task with systemwide impact. And, of course, disabling UAC also disables file and registry virtualization, which can cause compatibility problems with applications that use fixes provided by the UAC feature. For these reasons, we urge you not to select the bottom option in User Account Control Settings, which turns off UAC completely.

Working Around UAC Without Disabling It

Although the UAC prompts are sometimes intrusive, that's the point. First, they provide a not-so-subtle reminder that what you're about to do has a systemwide effect. But more importantly, UAC prevents a malicious application from silently installing in a system-controlled location without your knowledge. Most spyware, viruses, and other malware get installed as a direct, albeit unintended, result of a user action, such as clicking a link. When you click a link that you think is going to display some pretty pictures, wouldn't you be pleased to have UAC tell you that it's attempting to install a program?

One misperception about UAC is that it doesn't let you do certain things, or that it "locks you out" of your own computer. In fact, UAC doesn't prevent anything—all it does is inform you when an application requires administrator access. Remember that even when you're logged on with an administrator account, you ordinarily run as a standard user. Need to run something that requires full administrator privileges? Simply respond to the prompt. (If you find that you can't access certain folders and files, it's likely that the restriction is imposed by NTFS permissions—which are only tangentially related to UAC.)

Most people encounter lots of UAC prompts while setting up a new computer, configuring it, and installing programs. After that, they seldom see a prompt from UAC and forget that it's even there. But if you frequently tweak your computer's settings or install new programs, consider these tricks for running into fewer prompts:

- **Use an administrator Command Prompt window** Because child processes inherit the access token of the process that opens them, programs that you run from an administrator command prompt run as an administrator without further prompting. You'll need to respond to just a single prompt when you open the Command Prompt window. Then you can enter commands, open Microsoft Management Console (MMC) consoles, start programs, and edit the registry without further prompting.

To open an administrator Command Prompt window, use one of these methods:

- Click the Start menu, click All Programs, and find the Command Prompt shortcut in the Accessories subfolder. Right-click the shortcut, and click Run As Administrator (or press Ctrl+Shift+Enter, which is the little-known but extremely useful keyboard shortcut that has the same effect as clicking the Run As Administrator option).

- In the Start menu search box, type **cmd**. Then press Ctrl+Shift+Enter or right-click the cmd entry in the results list and click Run As Administrator.)

- Create a shortcut to Cmd.exe. Open the shortcut's properties dialog box and, on the Shortcut tab, click Advanced. Select Run As Administrator.

Naturally, you can run only programs for which you know the name and location of the executable file, as well as any required command-line parameters. (You can often glean this information by examining an application's shortcut.) Also note that you cannot run Windows Explorer, Internet Explorer, or Control Panel as administrator, even when you start from an administrator command prompt. (You can run Control Panel applications if you know the command line; it's just the main Control Panel window that does not run with elevated privileges.)

- **Run as a standard user**   As a standard user, you'll probably encounter *fewer* elevation prompts than you do as an administrator. In this situation, many applications refuse to run or they run with limitations. (For example, they might not display all settings, or they might not save settings you make.) On occasions when you do need to use such an application with full capabilities, right-click and choose Run As Administrator. Or, in the Start menu search box, type the program name and press Ctrl+Shift+Enter.

- **Use a hardware biometric device**   If you ordinarily use a standard user account—always a good practice—and you're required to type the password for your administrator password when UAC presents a credential prompt (see Figure 17-15), you'll find it easier to use biometric authentication, such as a fingerprint reader or a webcam equipped with facial-recognition software. Fingerprint readers are often included as a standard feature on many business-class notebook PCs. After the device and any required software is set up properly, you can simply swipe your finger instead of typing a lengthy password.

Chapter 17

Figure 17-15 You can set up your user accounts so that one finger logs on to your standard account, and a different finger can log on to an administrator account or provide administrator credentials for a UAC elevation prompt.

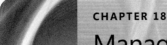
Managing User Accounts, Passwords, and Logons

T HE user account, which uniquely identifies each person who uses the computer, is an essential component in security and in providing a personalized user experience in Windows. Windows 7 allows you to restrict access to your computer so that only people you authorize can use the computer or view its files. User accounts in Windows 7 provide the means by which you can

- Require each user to identify himself or herself when logging on.

- Control access to files and other resources that you own.

- Audit system events, such as logons and the use of files and other resources.

Of course, if your computer is in a secure location where only people you trust have physical access to it, you might not have such concerns. But you should still create a user account for each person who uses the computer because associated with each account is a user profile that stores all manner of information unique to that user: favorite websites, desktop background, document folders, and so on. With features such as the Welcome screen and Fast User Switching, described in this chapter, you can log on or switch between user accounts with only a few clicks.

What's in Your Edition?

For the most part, the tools for managing user accounts work the same in all Windows 7 editions. The core Control Panel application for managing user accounts works slightly differently on computers that are joined to a domain than on those in a workgroup; only the Professional, Ultimate, and Enterprise editions can join a domain. A few account-management tasks are most easily performed with a console called Local Users And Groups; it's not available in the Starter and Home Premium editions. All these tasks can be performed with one or more other tools, however, and we describe each one in this chapter.

Fast User Switching, the feature that allows you to log on with another account without logging off the first account, is not available in Starter edition.

The last topic in this chapter, Parental Controls, describes a feature that is not available on computers that are joined to a domain.

Introducing Access Control in Windows

The Windows approach to security is discretionary: each securable system resource—each file or printer, for example—has an owner who has discretion over who can and cannot access the resource. Usually, a resource is owned by the user who creates it. If you create a file, for example, you are the file's owner under ordinary circumstances. (Computer administrators, however, can take ownership of resources they didn't create.)

> ## Note
> To exercise full discretionary control over individual files, you must store those files on an NTFS volume. For the sake of compatibility, Windows 7 supports the FAT and FAT32 file systems used by early Windows versions and many USB flash drives, as well as the exFAT file system used on some removable drives. However, none of the FAT-based file systems support file permissions. To enjoy the full benefits of Windows security, you must use NTFS. For more information about file systems, see "Choosing a File System" on page 1111.

To determine which users have access to a resource, Windows assigns a *security identifier* (SID) to each user account. Your SID (a gigantic number guaranteed to be unique) follows you around wherever you go in Windows. When you log on, the operating system first validates your user name and password. Then it creates a *security access token*. You can think of this as the electronic equivalent of an ID badge. It includes your user name and SID, plus information about any security groups to which your account belongs. (Security groups are described later in this chapter.) Any program you start gets a copy of your security access token.

With User Account Control (UAC) turned on, administrators who log on get two security access tokens—one that has the privileges of a standard user and one that has the full privileges of an administrator.

Whenever you attempt to walk through a controlled "door" in Windows (for example, when you connect to a shared printer), or any time a program attempts to do so on your behalf, the operating system examines your security access token and decides whether to let you pass. If access is permitted, you notice nothing. If access is denied, you get to hear a beep and read a refusal message.

What Are Security Identifiers?

Windows security relies on the use of a security identifier (SID) to identify a user. When you create a user account, Windows assigns a unique SID to that account. The SID remains uniquely associated with that user account until the account is deleted, whereupon the SID is never used again—for that user or any other user. Even if you re-create an account with identical information, a new SID is created.

A SID is a variable-length value that contains a revision level, a 48-bit identifier authority value, and a number of 32-bit subauthority values. The SID takes the form S-1-*x*-*y1*-*y2*-.... S-1 identifies it as a revision 1 SID; *x* is the value for the identifier authority; and *y1*, *y2*, and so on are values for subauthorities.

You'll sometimes see a SID in a security dialog box (for example, on the Security tab of a file's properties dialog box) before Windows has had time to look up the user account name. If a SID on a Security tab doesn't change to a name, it's because it's a SID for an account that has been deleted; you can safely delete it from the permissions list because it'll never be used again. (If you have a multiboot system, it could be the SID for an account in another installed operating system. If that's the case, you should not delete it.) You'll also spot SIDs in the hidden and protected $Recycle.Bin folder (each SID you see in this folder represents the Recycle Bin for a particular user) and in the registry (the HKEY_USERS hive contains a key, identified by *SID*, for each user account on the computer), among other places. The easiest way to determine your own SID is with the Whoami command-line utility. For details, see "Learning About Your Own Account with Whoami" on page 650.

Not all SIDs are unique (although the SID assigned to your user account is always unique). A number of commonly used SIDs are constant among all Windows installations. For example, S-1-5-18 is the SID for the built-in Local System account, a hidden member of the Administrators group that is used by the operating system and by services that log on using the Local System account. You can find a complete list of such SIDs, called *well-known SIDs*, in Microsoft Knowledge Base article 243330 (*w7io.com/1601*).

In determining whom to let pass and whom to block, Windows consults the resource's *access control list* (ACL). This is simply a list of SIDs and the access privileges associated with each one. Every resource subject to access control has an ACL.

What Are ACLs?

Each folder and each file on an NTFS-formatted volume has an ACL (also known as DACL, for *discretionary access control list*, and commonly called *NTFS permissions*). An ACL comprises an access control entry (ACE) for each user who is allowed access to the folder or file. With NTFS permissions, you can control access to any file or folder, allowing different types of access for different users or groups of users.

To view and edit NTFS permissions for a file or folder, right-click its icon and choose Properties. The Security tab lists all the groups and users with permissions set for the selected object, as shown below. Different permissions can be set for each user, as you can see by selecting each one.

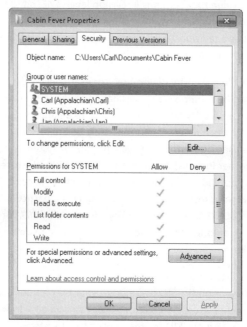

To make changes to the settings for any user or group in the list, or to add or remove a user or group in the list, click Edit. (Use caution. Setting NTFS permissions without understanding the full consequences can lead to unexpected and unwelcome results, including a complete loss of access to files and folders. The permission-setting capabilities of the Sharing wizard provide far greater flexibility and power than were possible in the basic Windows XP interface. Before you delve into the inner workings of NTFS permissions on the Security tab, be sure to try the Share With command or the Sharing tab, both of which invoke the Sharing wizard unless it has been disabled.)

The access granted by each permission type is as follows:

- **Full Control**   Users with Full Control can list contents of a folder, read and open files, create new files, delete files and subfolders, change permissions on files and subfolders, and take ownership of files.

- **Modify**   Allows the user to read, change, create, and delete files but not to change permissions or take ownership of files.

- **Read & Execute**   Allows the user to view files and execute programs.

- **List Folder Contents (folders only)**   Provides the same permissions as Read & Execute but can be applied only to folders.

- **Read**   Allows the user to list the contents of a folder, read file attributes, read permissions, and synchronize files.

- **Write**   Allows the user to create files, write data, read attributes and permissions, and synchronize files.

- **Special Permissions**   The assigned permissions don't match any of the preceding permission descriptions. To see precisely which permissions are granted, click Advanced.

This manner of allowing and blocking access to resources such as files and printers is essentially unchanged since Windows NT. UAC, which was introduced in Windows Vista, adds another layer of restrictions based on user accounts. Although UAC is sometimes confused with (blamed for?) the restrictions imposed by discretionary access control lists (described in the preceding paragraphs), it's actually unrelated. UAC is a method of implementing the rule of least-privilege user access—a fancy way of saying that a user account should have only the minimum privileges required to perform a task; this practice is intended to prevent malicious programs from using the power of an account to do bad things.

With UAC turned on, applications are normally launched using an administrator's standard user token. (Standard users, of course, have only a standard user token.) If an application requires administrator privileges, UAC asks for your consent (if you're logged on as an administrator) or the credentials of an administrator (if you're logged on as a standard user) before letting the application run. With UAC turned off, Windows works in the same (rather dangerous) manner as previous versions: administrator accounts can do just about anything (sometimes getting those users in trouble), and standard accounts don't have the privileges needed to run many older programs.

For more information about UAC, see "Preventing Unsafe Actions with User Account Control" on page 629.

Chapter 18

Another feature that first appeared in Windows Vista places one more doorway on the way to object access. Somewhat like the discretionary ACLs used to secure file objects, registry keys, and the like, each securable object in Windows 7 has an integrity level (IL) access control entry, which can be low, medium, or high. (Objects that don't have an IL specified have an implicit value of medium.) Each process (program) is also marked with an IL: Protected Mode ("low rights") in Internet Explorer is low, standard processes are medium, and processes that require elevation to administrator are high. A process can open an object for write access only if its IL is equal to or higher than that of the object.

Permissions and Rights

Windows distinguishes two types of access privileges: permissions and rights. A *permission* is the ability to access a particular object in some defined manner—for example, to write to an NTFS file or to modify a printer queue. A *right* is the ability to perform a particular systemwide action, such as logging on or resetting the clock.

The owner of a resource (or an administrator) assigns permissions to the resource via its properties dialog box. For example, if you are the printer owner or have administrative privileges, you can restrict someone from using a particular printer by visiting the properties dialog box for that printer. Administrators set rights via the Local Security Policy console. (This console is available only in the Professional, Enterprise, and Ultimate editions of Windows 7. In the other editions, rights for various security groups are predefined and unchangeable.) For example, an administrator could grant someone the right to install a device driver.

> **Note**
>
> In this book, as in many of the Windows messages and dialog boxes, *privileges* serves as an informal term encompassing both permissions and rights.

User Accounts and Security Groups

The backbone of Windows security is the ability to uniquely identify each user. While setting up a computer—or at any later time—an administrator creates a user account for each user. The *user account* is identified by a user name and is (optionally) secured by a password, which the user provides when logging on to the system. Windows then controls, monitors, and restricts access to system resources on the basis of the permissions and rights associated with each user account by the resource owners and the system administrator.

Account type is a simplified way of describing membership in a security group, a collection of user accounts. Windows classifies each user account as one of three account types:

- **Administrator**   Members of the Administrators group are classified as administrator accounts. By default, the Administrators group includes the first account you create when you set up the computer and an account named Administrator that is disabled and hidden by default. Unlike other account types, administrators have full control over the system. Among the tasks that only administrators can perform are the following:

  - Create, change, and delete user accounts and groups

  - Install and uninstall programs

  - Configure automatic updating with Windows Update

  - Install an ActiveX control

  - Install or remove hardware device drivers

  - Share folders

  - Set permissions

  - Access all files, including those in another user's folder

  - Take ownership of files

  - Copy or move files into the %ProgramFiles% or %SystemRoot% folders

  - Restore backed-up system files

  - Grant rights to other user accounts and to themselves

  - Configure Parental Controls

  - Configure Windows Firewall

- **Standard user**   Members of the Users group are classified as standard user accounts. (In Windows XP, Users group members are called limited accounts.) Many tasks that were available only to administrators in previous Windows versions can be performed in Windows 7 by standard users. These additional tasks do not affect overall system security, and their prohibition in Windows XP and Windows 2000 made it impractical for most people to run without full administrative privileges; in Windows 7—as in Windows Vista—it makes sense to use a standard account. A partial list of tasks available to standard user accounts includes

  - Change the password and picture for their own user account

  - Use programs that have been installed on the computer

- Install system and driver updates using Windows Update

- Install approved ActiveX controls

- Configure a secure Wi-Fi connection

- Refresh a network adapter and the system's IP address

- View permissions

- Create, change, and delete files in their document folders and in shared document folders

- Restore their own backed-up files

- View the system clock and calendar, and change the time zone

- Set personalization options, such as themes, desktop background, and so on

- Select a display dots-per-inch (DPI) setting to adjust text size

- Configure power options

- Log on in Safe Mode

- View Windows Firewall settings

- **Guest** Members of the Guests group are shown as guest accounts. Guest accounts have privileges similar to standard accounts, with some limitations. A user logged on with the Guest account (but not any other account that is a member of the Guests group) cannot create a password for the account.

> **Note**
>
> User accounts that are not a member of the Administrators, Users, or Guests group do not appear in User Accounts in Control Panel. There's seldom reason to set up an account that doesn't belong to one of these groups, but if you do need to work with such accounts, you must use one of the other user account management tools. For details, see "Using Other Account Management Tools" on page 661.

Assigning an appropriate account type to the people who use your computer is straightforward. At least one user must be an administrator; naturally, that should be the person who administers the computer. All other regular users should each have a standard user account. Use a guest account if you have guests or occasional users; that way, they can use your computer without gaining access to your files. For more detailed recommendations, see "Effectively Implementing User Accounts on a Shared Computer" on page 659.

What Happened to the Administrator Account?

Every computer running Windows has a special account named Administrator. Traditionally in Windows, Administrator has been the primary account for managing the computer. Like other administrator accounts, the Administrator account has full rights over the entire computer. There's one key difference in Windows 7: the Administrator account is disabled by default.

In Windows 7, there's seldom a need to use the Administrator account instead of another administrator account. With default settings in Windows, the Administrator account does have one unique capability: it's not subject to UAC, even when UAC is turned on for all other users. All other administrator accounts (which are sometimes called *Protected Administrator* accounts) run with standard-user privileges unless the user consents to elevation. The Administrator account runs with full administrative privileges at all times and never needs your consent for elevation. (For this reason, of course, it's rather risky. Any application that runs as Administrator has full control of the computer—which means applications written by malicious or incompetent programmers can do significant damage to your system.)

For other ways to live with UAC, see "Working Around UAC Without Disabling It" on page 638.

Security groups allow a system administrator to create classes of users who share common privileges. For example, if everyone in the accounting department needs access to the Payables folder, the administrator can create a group called Accounting and grant the entire group access to that folder. If the administrator then adds all user accounts belonging to employees in the accounting department to the Accounting group, these users will automatically have access to the Payables folder. A user account can belong to one group, more than one group, or no group at all.

In large networks based on Active Directory domains, groups can be a valuable administrative tool. They simplify the job of ensuring that all members with common access needs have an identical set of privileges. We don't recommend creating or using groups other than the built-in Administrators, Users, and Guests groups on standalone and workgroup-based computers, however.

Permissions and rights for group members are cumulative. That means that if a user account belongs to more than one group, the user enjoys all of the privileges accorded to all groups of which the user account is a member.

Local Accounts and Groups vs. Domain Accounts and Groups

Windows stores information about user accounts and security groups in a security database. Where the security database resides depends on whether your computer is part of a workgroup or a domain.

A *workgroup* setup (or a standalone computer) uses only local user accounts and local groups—the type described in this chapter. The security database on each computer stores the local user accounts and local groups that are specific to that computer. Local user accounts allow users to log on only to the computer on which you create the local account. Likewise, a local account allows users to access resources only on that same computer. (This doesn't mean that you can't share your resources with other network users, even if you're not part of a domain. For details, see Chapter 20, "Sharing and Managing Network Resources.")

The alternative is to set up the network as a domain. A Windows *domain* is a network that has at least one machine running Windows Server as a domain controller. A *domain controller* is a computer that maintains the security database, including user accounts and groups, for the domain. With a *domain user account,* you can log on to any computer in the domain (subject to your privileges set at the domain level and on individual computers), and you can gain access to permitted resources anywhere on the network.

In general, if your computer is part of a Windows domain, you shouldn't need to concern yourself with local user accounts. Instead, all user accounts should be managed at the domain controller. But you might want to add certain domain user accounts or groups to your local groups. By default, the Domain Admins group is a member of the local Administrators group, and Domain Users is a member of the local Users group; members of those domain groups thereby assume the rights and permissions afforded to the local groups to which they belong.

Learning About Your Own Account with Whoami

Windows includes a command-line utility called Whoami (Who Am I?). You can use Whoami to find out the name of the account that's currently logged on, its SID, the names of the security groups of which it's a member, and its privileges. To use Whoami, open a Command Prompt window. (You don't need elevated privileges.)

Then, to learn the name of the logged-on user, type **whoami**. (This is particularly useful if you're logged on as a standard user but running an elevated Command Prompt window—when it might not be obvious which account is currently "you.") If you're curious about your

SID, type **whoami /user**. To see a list of your account's group memberships, type **whoami /groups /fo list**. To learn which privileges are enabled for the logged-on account, type **whoami /priv /fo list**. For a complete list of Whoami parameters, type **whoami /?**.

Working with User Accounts

When you install Windows 7 on a new computer, you create one user account, which is an administrator account. If you upgrade to Windows 7 from Windows Vista and you had local accounts set up in your previous operating system, Windows migrates those accounts to your Windows 7 installation. Accounts that you migrate from Windows Vista maintain their group memberships and passwords.

Through User Accounts in Control Panel, Windows provides a simple post-setup method for creating new accounts, making routine changes to existing accounts, and deleting accounts. When you launch User Accounts in Control Panel, you'll see a window similar to the one shown in Figure 18-1.

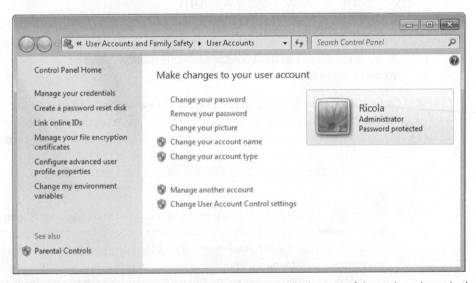

Figure 18-1 User Accounts on a domain-based computer lacks most of the options shown in the center of this workgroup version of User Accounts.

INSIDE OUT   Access User Accounts quickly

You can jump straight into User Accounts without going through Control Panel. Simply open the Start menu and click the account picture in the upper right corner of the Start menu.

If your computer is a member of a domain, User Accounts has far fewer options; you can change your picture and change your password. In a domain environment, all management of user accounts beyond these basic tasks and those shown in the left pane of User Accounts is normally handled at the domain level. You can manage local accounts on a domain-joined computer by using the Advanced User Accounts Control Panel. For more information, see "Using Other Account Management Tools" on page 661.

Creating a New User Account

To create a new user account, in the User Accounts window shown in Figure 18-1, click Manage Another Account. The Manage Accounts window appears, as shown in Figure 18-2. (To get there directly, in the main Control Panel window click Add Or Remove User Accounts, under User Accounts And Family Safety.)

Click Create A New Account, which takes you to the window shown in Figure 18-3, where you can create a new account with a minimum of fuss. You need to supply only a name for the account and decide whether you want to set up the account type as standard user or administrator.

Note

The name you provide when you create a new account with Windows is used for both the user name and the full name. The *user name* is the primary name used internally by Windows. You use it when you log on without the benefit of the Welcome screen (such as in certain networking situations) and when you specify the account name in various commands and dialog boxes for setting permissions. The *full name* is the name that appears on the Welcome screen, at the top of the Start menu, and in User Accounts. You can change either name at any time after the account is created.

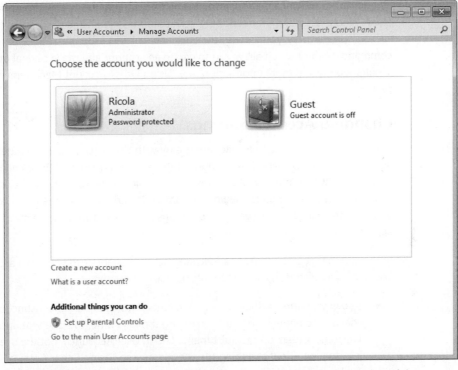

Figure 18-2 Manage Accounts shows all local user accounts that are a member of the Administrators, Users, or Guests groups.

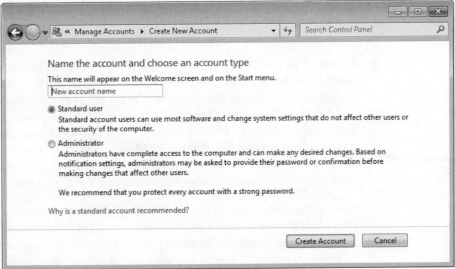

Figure 18-3 Creating an account couldn't be much easier; just specify a name and account type.

Chapter 18

If you want to specify any other information about the account—including setting a password—you must make changes after you create the account, as described in the following section. Alternatively, you can use the Local Users And Groups snap-in or the Net User /Add command, both of which allow you to create an account and make several other settings simultaneously. For more information, see "Using Other Account Management Tools" on page 661.

Changing Account Settings

Making routine changes to an account is easy with User Accounts. To change your own account, start at the main User Accounts page, shown in Figure 18-1. To change another user's account (you must have administrative privileges to do so), click Manage Another Account to display the page shown in Figure 18-2, and then click the name of the account you want to change. You'll see links to options similar to those you can make to your own account.

In this window, you can make the following account changes to your own account or (if you're an administrator) other accounts on your computer:

- **Account name**   Although User Accounts doesn't explain the distinction, when you change the name here you're changing the full name (the one that appears on the Welcome screen, on the Start menu, and in User Accounts), not the user name. (For information about changing the user name, see "Using Other Account Management Tools" on page 661.)

- **Password**   You can create a password and store a hint that provides a reminder for a forgotten password. If the account is already password protected, User Accounts allows you to change the password or remove the password. For more information about passwords, see "Setting a Logon Password" on page 663.

- **Picture**   If you don't want a user to be identified as a flower (or whatever icon Windows selects for the account), you can change the picture associated with the account name on the Welcome screen, at the top of the Start menu, and in User Accounts. Clicking the change-picture link shows all the pictures stored in %AllUsersProfile%\Microsoft\User Account Pictures\Default Pictures, but you're not limited to those choices. Click Browse For More Pictures, and you can select any picture in bitmap, GIF, JPEG, or PNG format, such as a picture of yourself or a favorite scene. Windows reduces and crops the picture to fit the picture box.

- **Parental Controls**   Clicking this link takes you to Parental Controls, where you can place restrictions on the user by limiting the hours of use, filtering web content, and specifying which games and other programs can be run. You must have administrator privileges to view or change Parental Controls settings, and you can't configure

Parental Controls settings for administrator accounts. For details about Parental Controls, see "Controlling Your Children's Computer Access" on page 675.

- **Account type**   With User Accounts, you can change the account type to Administrator (which adds the account to the Administrators group) or Standard User (which adds the account to the Users group). If you want to add the account to other groups, you must use Advanced User Accounts, Local Users And Groups, or the Net Localgroup command. For more information about those alternatives, see "Using Other Account Management Tools" on page 661. (You must have administrator privileges to change the account type.)

For your own account (that is, the one with which you're currently logged on), you can make the following additional changes by clicking links in the left pane:

- **Manage Your Credentials**   This link opens Credential Manager (known as Stored User Names And Passwords in earlier Windows versions), which lets you manage stored credentials that you use to access network resources and websites.

- **Create A Password Reset Disk**   This link launches the Forgotten Password wizard, from which you can create a password reset disk. For more information, see "Recovering from a Lost Password" on page 666.

- **Link Online IDs**   With Link Online IDs, you can associate an online ID (a Windows Live ID, for example) with your user account in Windows. Depending on the online ID provider, linking an account in this way might enable you to share resources in a homegroup in new ways or to access your data from any computer signed in to the online ID. For more information, see "Deciding What to Share—And What Not to Share" on page 721.

- **Manage Your File Encryption Certificates**   This link opens a wizard that you can use to create and manage certificates that enable the use of Encrypting File System (EFS). EFS, which is available only in Windows 7 Professional and above, is a method of encrypting folders and files so that they can be used only by someone who has the appropriate credentials.

- **Configure Advanced User Profile Properties**   This link is used to switch your profile between a local profile (one that is stored on the local computer) and a roaming profile (one that is stored on a network server in a domain environment). With a local profile, you end up with a different profile on each computer you use, whereas a roaming profile is the same regardless of which computer you use to log on to the network. Roaming profiles require a domain network based on Windows Server. To work with user profiles other than your own, in Control Panel open System and click Advanced System Settings; on the Advanced tab, click Settings under User Profiles.

Chapter 18

- **Change My Environment Variables**   Of interest primarily to programmers, this link opens a dialog box in which you can create and edit environment variables that are available only to your user account; in addition, you can view system environment variables, which are available to all accounts. For more information, see "Using Environment Variables" on page 1178.

- **Manage Your Fingerprint Data**   This link, which appears only on computers with an installed fingerprint reader or similar biometric device, provides a path to the program (usually provided by the manufacturer of the biometric device) in which you register and manage fingerprints to be used for logging on.

TROUBLESHOOTING

A server continually prompts for logon credentials

For reasons too various to enumerate, you might find that a server you log on to regularly—an e-mail server, for example—prompts for credentials at each logon, even though you have selected a check box that promises to store your user name and password. To address this annoyance, open Credential Manager (click the picture at the top of the right side of the Start menu, and then click Manage Your Credentials in the left pane of the User Accounts dialog box). Click Add A Generic Credential (to the right of the Generic Credentials heading). The following dialog box appears:

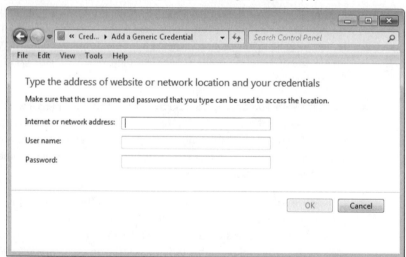

Enter the address of your server, your user name, and your password. Windows will cooperate by storing the credentials locally and using them at subsequent logons.

Using the Guest Account for Visitors

The Guest account is designed to allow an infrequent or temporary user such as a visitor to log on to the system without providing a password and use the system in a restricted manner. By default, the Guest account is disabled; no one can use an account that's disabled.

To enable the Guest account, open User Accounts, click Manage Another Account, and click the Guest account icon. In the window that appears, click Turn On. The Guest account thereafter shows up on the Welcome screen, and anyone can use it. Users of the Guest account have access to items in the Public folder as well as those in the Guest profile.

Deleting an Account

You can delete any account except one that is currently logged on. To delete an account, open User Accounts, click Manage Another Account, and click the name of the account you want to delete. Then click Delete The Account. User Accounts gives you a choice, shown in Figure 18-4, about what to do with the account's files:

- **Delete Files**   After you select Delete Files and confirm your intention in the next window, Windows deletes the account, its user profile, and all files associated with the account, including those in its Contacts, Desktop, Documents, Downloads, Favorites, Links, Music, Pictures, Saved Games, Searches, and Videos folders.

- **Keep Files**   Windows copies certain parts of the user's profile—specifically, files and folders stored on the desktop and in the Documents, Favorites, Music, Pictures, and Videos folders—to a folder on your desktop, where they become part of your profile and remain under your control. The rest of the user profile, such as e-mail messages and other data stored in the AppData folder; files stored in the Contacts, Downloads, Saved Games, and Searches folders; and settings stored in the registry are deleted after you confirm your intention in the next window that appears.

Figure 18-4 Select Keep Files to avoid losing files in the account's Documents and other folders.

Chapter 18

> **Note**
>
> User Accounts won't let you delete the last local account on the computer, even if you're logged on using the account named Administrator. This limitation helps to enforce the sound security practice of using an account other than Administrator for your everyday computing.

After you delete an account, of course, that user can no longer log on. Deleting an account also has other effects you should be aware of. You cannot restore access to resources that currently list the user in their access control lists simply by re-creating the account. This includes files to which the user has permission and the user's encrypted files, personal certificates, and stored passwords for websites and network resources. That's because those permissions are linked to the user's original SID—not the user name. Even if you create a new account with the same name, password, and so on, it will have a new SID, which will not gain access to anything that was restricted to the original user account.

You might encounter another predicament if you delete an account. If you use a tool other than User Accounts to delete the account, the user's original profile remains in the Users folder. If you later create a new account with the same name, Windows creates a new profile folder, but because a folder already exists with that user's name (for example, C:\Users\Jan), it appends the computer name to the user name to create a convoluted folder name (for example, C:\Users\Jan.Sequoia). The extra folder not only consumes disk space but leads to confusion about which is the correct profile folder. (In general, the one with the longest name is the most recent. But you can be certain only by examining files in the profile folder.) To avoid this problem, use User Accounts to delete accounts because it properly deletes the old profile along with the account.

INSIDE OUT   Delete an unused profile when you delete an account

If you delete an account with a tool other than User Accounts, the account's profile continues to occupy space in the Users folder and in the registry. You don't want to delete the files or registry entries directly because a simple mistake could affect other accounts. Instead, in Control Panel open System and click Advanced System Settings. Click the Advanced tab, and then click Settings under User Profiles. Select the account named Account Unknown (the deleted account), and click Delete.

Effectively Implementing User Accounts on a Shared Computer

Whether you're setting up a computer for your family to use at home or to be used in a business, it's prudent to set it up securely. Doing so helps to protect each user's data from inadvertent deletions and changes as well as malicious damage and theft. When you set up your computer, consider these suggestions:

- **Control who can log on**   Create accounts only for users who need to use your computer's resources, either by logging on locally or over a network. Delete or disable other accounts (except the built-in accounts created by Windows).

- **Change all user accounts except one to standard accounts**   You'll need one administrative account for installing programs, creating and managing accounts, and so on. All other accounts—including your own everyday account—can run with standard privileges. If you are the de facto administrator for a computer, we recommend that you create two accounts for yourself: a standard account that you normally use for logging on, and an administrator account that you can use for elevation when needed. (You might have noticed that some of this chapter's illustrations show an account named Ricola and another named RicolaAdmin; they are set up as an implementation of this suggestion.)

  It's easy to set up accounts this way. If you're working with a freshly installed version of Windows 7 on which you haven't yet installed applications or made personalizations to the single account created during setup, use that account as your administrator account. (If you've already given it your name during setup, you might want to modify the name to indicate that it's your administrative account. See "Changing Account Settings" on page 654 for details.) Create a new standard account to use as your everyday account. (See "Creating a New User Account" on page 652.) Log off, and then log on with your standard account. Whenever Windows requires elevation, it displays the name of your administrator account; enter its password to gain administrator privileges.

  If you've been using Windows for a while and have already customized the administrator account created during setup as your own, you're better off keeping it as your everyday account. But you can still easily implement this suggested practice. While logged on with your administrator account, create a new administrator account, which will be the account you use when Windows requires elevation. Then change your current account to a standard account. (You must create the new administrator account before you demote your account, because Windows requires the existence of at least one administrator account.) Note that you don't lose your administrator privileges until you log off; the next time you log on with your (now standard) account, all your programs and personalizations remain exactly as before, but you now run with standard privileges.

Chapter 18

INSIDE OUT Log on with your standard account all the time. Really.

Note that you'll rarely, if ever, need to log on using your administrator account. Instead, when Windows requires elevation while you're logged on with your standard account, you simply enter the password for your administrator account.

Certain programs won't run (or are not fully functional) if you launch them while logged on with a standard account. To get around obstacles like this, don't log off and then log on with your administrator account. In most cases, a better solution is to use the "run as administrator" feature. To do that, right-click the program's shortcut (on the Start menu or in Windows Explorer) and choose Run As Administrator. Alternatively, select the shortcut and press Ctrl+Shift+Enter. Windows then prompts for your administrator password.

A handful of programs won't work, even with this trick. (Device Manager is an example. If you start it from a shortcut in Control Panel while logged on as a standard user, it displays settings but doesn't let you change any settings. And its right-click menu doesn't include a Run As Administrator command.) You can usually run such recalcitrant programs by launching them from an elevated Command Prompt window. That is, run Command Prompt as an administrator (in the Start menu search box, type **cmd**, press Ctrl+Shift+Enter, and then enter your administrator password) and then enter the program's executable name at the command prompt. (For example, to run Device Manager as an administrator, in an elevated Command Prompt window type **devmgmt.msc**. Device Manager then runs with full functionality, exactly as if you had logged off and then logged on with your administrator account.)

- **Be sure that all accounts are password protected**   This is especially important for administrator accounts and for other accounts whose profiles contain important or sensitive documents. You might not want to set a password on your toddler's account, but all other accounts should be protected from the possibility that the tyke (or your cat) will accidentally click the wrong name on the Welcome screen.

- **Restrict logon times**   You might want to limit the computing hours for some users. The easiest way for home users to do this is with Parental Controls; for details, see "Restricting Logon Hours" on page 677.

- **Restrict access to certain files**   You'll want to be sure that some files are available to all users, whereas other files are available only to the person who created them. The Public folder and a user's personal folders provide a general framework for this protection. You can further refine your file protection scheme by selectively applying permissions to varying combinations of files, folders, and users.

- **Turn on the Guest account only when necessary**   You might occasionally have a visitor who needs to use your computer. Rather than logging on with your own account and exposing all your own files and settings to the visitor, turn on the Guest account in such situations.

Using Other Account Management Tools

Windows 7 includes no fewer than four different interfaces for managing users and groups:

- **User Accounts**   Located in Control Panel, User Accounts provides the simplest method to perform common tasks. It is the one we describe throughout most of this chapter.

- **Advanced User Accounts**   If your computer is joined to a domain, clicking the Manage User Accounts link in User Accounts opens Advanced User Accounts. (The title bar of the dialog box doesn't include the word Advanced, however.) If your computer is not joined to a domain, you can open this version by typing **netplwiz** at a command prompt.

    The capabilities of Advanced User Accounts are few (you can remove local user accounts, set passwords, and place a user account in a single security group), but it has a handful of unique features that you might find compelling. With Advanced User Accounts, you can

    - Change an account's user name. (For information about the difference between the user name and the full name, see "Creating a New User Account" on page 652.)

    - Configure automatic logon. (For more information, see "Bypassing the Logon Screen" on page 671.)

    - Eliminate the Ctrl+Alt+Delete requirement on domain-joined computers. (For details, see "Managing the Logon Process" on page 668.)

- **Local Users And Groups**   This Microsoft Management Console (MMC) snap-in—which is available only in Windows 7 Professional, Ultimate, and Enterprise editions—provides access to more account-management features than User Accounts and is friendlier than command-line utilities. You can start Local Users And Groups, shown in Figure 18-5, in any of the following ways:

    - In Computer Management, open System Tools, Local Users And Groups.

    - At a command prompt, type **lusrmgr.msc**.

Chapter 18

- In Advanced User Accounts, click the Advanced tab, and then click the Advanced button.

Figure 18-5 Through its austere interface, Local Users And Groups offers more capabilities than User Accounts.

- **Command-line utilities** The Net User and Net Localgroup commands provide the most complete and direct access to various account tasks.

If you are an administrator who spends a lot of time managing user accounts on your network, you might want to acquaint yourself with the Net User and Net Localgroup commands. These provide a complete set of tools for creating, modifying, and deleting user accounts (Net User) and security groups (Net Localgroup). Here is a sampling of tasks you can perform with Net User:

- To see detailed information about a user named *username*, including information about when the user's password was set, when it is due to expire, and whether the user is allowed to change the password, type **net user *username***.

- To add a user named *username* to the user accounts database, type **net user /add *username***. To delete this account, type **net user /delete *username***.

- To remove *username*'s ability to change his or her password, type **net user *username* /passwordchg:no**. To reenable it, type the same command with **/passwordchg:yes**. (The default is yes.)

- To disable the password requirement for *username*, type **net user *username* /passwordreq:no**.

For a full list of Net User commands, type **net help user**. For a full list of Net Localgroup options, type **net help localgroup**.

Several PowerShell scripts included in the Scripts folder on the companion CD provide additional ways of working with users and groups, either on your own computer or a remote computer. Get-LocalUsers.ps1 lists local users and their descriptions; Get-LocalGroups.ps1 lists local groups and their descriptions. Use the –computer switch to specify a remote computer, or run the script without this switch to get information from your own machine. To create a local user or local group, use CreateLocalUser.ps1 or CreateLocalGroup.ps1. To set a local user password on one or more computers, use Change-LocalUserPassword.ps1. To add a user, use AddLocalUserToLocalGroup.ps1. For details about the use of any of these scripts, open the script in a text editor and read the .Synopsis section at the beginning of the script. For general information about running PowerShell scripts, see "Running PowerShell Scripts" on page 999.

Setting a Logon Password

Associating a password with your user account is your first line of defense against those who would like to snoop around in your files. Because the Welcome screen shows every user account, if you don't set passwords, anyone who has physical access to your computer can log on by simply clicking a name on the Welcome screen. If the chosen name belongs to an administrator account, the person who clicks it has full, unfettered access to every file and setting on the computer. Requiring a password for each account (particularly administrator accounts) goes a long way toward securing your computer.

> ## Note
>
> You needn't worry about someone who's not in your homegroup logging on to your computer remotely (over the network, the Internet, or with Remote Desktop Connection, for example) if your account doesn't have a password. Security features in Windows prevent remote logon by any account with a blank password. When you don't have a password in Windows, the risk comes only from people who have physical access to your computer.
>
> This feature is enforced by a policy setting, which is enabled by default. If you have the Professional, Enterprise, or Ultimate edition, you can confirm that the policy setting is enabled, as follows. At a command prompt, type **secpol.msc** to open Local Security Policy. Open Local Policies\Security Options and be sure that the Accounts: Limit Local Account Use Of Blank Passwords To Console Logon Only policy setting is enabled. (If you use the Starter or Home Premium edition, you needn't worry; the policy setting can't be disabled.)

Chapter 18

Creating a Secure Password

A password is of little value if it's easily guessed by an intruder. Obviously, you shouldn't use your name or something equally transparent. However, even a random word provides little security against a determined intruder—some hackers use tools that try every word in the dictionary. By observing the following guidelines, you can create a password that's difficult to crack in a reasonable amount of time:

- Use at least eight characters. Longer is better, which is why some security experts suggest using a *pass phrase*. A password or phrase can (and should) include spaces and punctuation; the maximum length is 127 characters.

- Use a mixture of uppercase letters, lowercase letters, numbers, and punctuation.

- Avoid including your name or user name in the password.

- Use random sequences instead of words, or intersperse numbers and punctuation within words—W!nd()wS 7 1ns!dE ()uT for example.

With a little thought, it's pretty easy to come up with a password that is memorable and secure. For example, start with a phrase about yourself or your hobbies—one that you can easily remember, such as *I'm addicted to Solitaire.* Make a few letter substitutions, misspell a word or two, and you come up with *I'm +lcted 2 $ol!ta!re.* It's long, uses all four types of characters, contains no dictionary words, and is easy to remember—so you won't be tempted to write it on a sticky note attached to your monitor.

TROUBLESHOOTING

You can't log on

Even when you're *certain* you know the password, you might have trouble logging on. First, be aware that passwords are case sensitive: You must type capital letters and lowercase letters exactly as you did when you created the password. If you still can't get on, be sure the Caps Lock key is not on.

Setting a Password

The simplest way to set a password for yourself or for another user (if you have administrator privileges) is with User Accounts in Control Panel. Click the name of the user for whom you want to set a password and then click Create A Password. A window like the one shown in Figure 18-6 appears.

Figure 18-6 User Accounts allows you to provide a password reminder hint that becomes available on the Welcome screen.

To change your password, you must provide your old password as well as a new one.

INSIDE OUT   Use Ctrl+Alt+Delete to access password options

The fastest path to a password-setting screen for your own account is to press Ctrl+Alt+Delete and then click Change Password. There you can set a password along with an updated hint.

You can use other account management tools to set a password, but User Accounts is the only tool (along with Ctrl+Alt+Delete, described above) that lets you specify a password hint. The password hint appears after you click your name on the Welcome screen and type your password incorrectly. Be sure your hint is only a subtle reminder—not the password itself—because any user can click your name and then view the hint.

CAUTION !

If another user has files encrypted with EFS, do not create a password for that user; instead, show the user how to create a password for his or her own account. Similarly, do not remove or change another user's password unless the user has forgotten the password and has absolutely no other way to access the account. (For more information, see the following section, "Recovering from a Lost Password.") If you create, change, or remove another user's password, that user loses all personal certificates and stored passwords for websites and network resources. Without the personal certificates, the user loses access to all of his or her encrypted files and all e-mail messages encrypted with the user's private key. Windows deletes the certificates and passwords to prevent the administrator who makes a password change from gaining access to them—but this security comes at a cost!

TROUBLESHOOTING

You can't access encrypted files because an administrator changed your password

When an administrator removes or changes the password for your local account, you no longer have access to your encrypted files and e-mail messages. That's because your master key, which is needed to unlock your personal encryption certificate (which, in turn, is needed to unlock your encrypted files), is encrypted with a hash that includes your password. When the password changes, the master key is no longer accessible. To regain access to the master key (and, by extension, your encrypted files and e-mail messages), change your password back to your old password. Alternatively, use your password reset disk to change your password.

When you change your own password (through User Accounts or with your password reset disk), Windows uses your old password to decrypt the master key and then re-encrypts it with the new password, so your encrypted files and e-mail messages remain accessible.

Recovering from a Lost Password

It's bound to happen: someday when you try to log on to your computer and are faced with the password prompt, you will draw a blank.

Windows offers two tools that help you to deal with this dilemma:

- **Password hint**   Your hint (if you created one) appears below the password entry box after you make an incorrect entry and then click OK. You can create a hint when you set a password with User Accounts.

- **Password reset disk**   A password reset disk allows you (or anyone with your password reset disk) to change your password—without needing to know your old password. As standard practice, each user should create a password reset disk and keep it in a secure location. Then, if a user forgets the password, he or she can reset it using the password reset disk.

> ### Note
> You can make a password reset disk only for your local user account. If your computer is joined to a domain, you can't create a password reset disk as a back door to your domain logon password. However, in a domain environment, a domain administrator can safely reset your password, and you'll still have access to your encrypted files. Also, on a computer joined to a domain, password hints are never shown, even for local user accounts.

Both solutions require a little forethought on your part. You must create the hint when you set your password, and you must create the password reset disk before you actually need it.

To create a password reset disk, you need to know your current password and have removable media available. (You can use a floppy disk, USB flash drive, external hard drive, or memory card.) Follow these steps:

1. Log on using the account for which you want to create a password reset disk.

2. If you need to use a USB flash drive as a password reset disk, insert it in your computer's USB slot.

3. In Control Panel, open User Accounts.

4. In the left pane, click Create A Password Reset Disk to launch the Forgotten Password wizard.

5. Follow the wizard's instructions.

You can have only one password reset disk for each user account. If you make a new one, the old one is no longer usable.

To use the password reset disk when password amnesia sets in:

1. On the logon screen, make an entry in the password box. If you guess right, you're in! If you're wrong, Windows informs you that the password is incorrect.

2. Click OK. The logon screen reappears, but with additional text below the password box.

3. If the first bit of additional text, your password hint, jogs your memory, enter your password. If not, click Reset Password to open the Password Reset wizard.

   The Password Reset wizard asks for the location of the password reset disk, reads the encrypted key, and then asks you to set a new password, which it then uses to log you on. Your password reset disk remains usable for the next attack of forgetfulness; you don't need to make a new one.

If you can't remember the password, the hint doesn't refresh your memory, and you don't have a password reset disk, you're out of luck. An administrator can log on and change or remove your password for you, but you'll lose access to your encrypted files and e-mail messages and your stored credentials.

Managing the Logon Process

Unlike in Windows XP, which provides a radically different logon experience for computers joined to a domain than for those in a workgroup or not connected to a network, the process is similar for all users of Windows 7. The key differences:

- By default, on a computer joined to a domain, users must press Ctrl+Alt+Delete before the logon screen appears. This requirement can be removed from domain computers or added to others, as described in the following tip.

- The Welcome screen for a workgroup or standalone computer shows an icon for each account on the computer, as shown in Figure 18-7. By contrast, after pressing Ctrl+Alt+Delete, a domain user sees only one user account, along with a Switch User button that enables you to log on using an account other than the one shown. (This is the same screen that a workgroup user with a password-protected account sees after clicking his or her account name.)

Figure 18-7 At startup, a workgroup computer—but not a computer joined to a domain—shows all user accounts on the Welcome screen.

INSIDE OUT   Skip the Ctrl+Alt+Delete requirement

On a domain-based computer, if you don't want to bother pressing Ctrl+Alt+Delete to reach the logon screen, make the following change:

1. Open User Accounts in Control Panel, and then click Manage User Accounts to open Advanced User Accounts.

2. In the User Accounts dialog box that appears, click the Advanced tab.

3. Under Secure Logon, clear Require Users To Press Ctrl+Alt+Delete.

Be aware that doing so removes a security feature. Because the design of the Windows security system prevents any other application from capturing this particular key combination, pressing Ctrl+Alt+Delete ensures that the next screen that appears, the logon screen, is displayed by the operating system and not by a rogue application that's trying to capture your password, for example.

INSIDE OUT   Hide the name of the last user to log on

On a computer joined to a domain, by default the name and picture of the last user who logged on appears on the logon screen. On a system that's used primarily by a single user, this is a convenient feature that allows the user to log on again without typing his or her name each time. For a computer that's shared by many users, you might prefer not to show the last user. You can prevent the last-used name from appearing by typing **secpol.msc** at an elevated command prompt to open Local Security Policy. In Local Security Policy, open Local Policies\Security Options. Then enable the policy setting named Interactive Logon: Do Not Display Last User Name.

Customizing the Logon Screen

You probably don't spend much time looking at the logon screen; after all, whenever you're using your computer you're already logged on. Nonetheless, you might prefer a different image for the desktop background. Or, if you have difficulty reading the text on the logon screen, you can use a higher dots per inch (DPI) setting.

Setting a Custom Desktop Background

To use a desktop background other than the default image shown in Figure 18-7 (or one provided by the manufacturer of your computer), follow these steps:

1. In the Start menu search box, type **regedit** and press Enter to open Registry Editor.

2. In Registry Editor, navigate to the HKLM\Software\Microsoft\Windows\CurrentVersion\Authentication\LogonUI\Background key.

3. If a DWORD value named OEMBackground does not exist, create one. Set this value's data to 1.

4. In Windows Explorer, navigate to %Windir%\System32\Oobe\Info\Backgrounds. (If the subfolders of Oobe do not exist, create them.)

5. Copy the image you want to this folder, using these guidelines:

   - The image must be in .jpg format, and the file size cannot exceed 256 KB.

   - Scale the image to the pixel dimensions of your primary monitor's native (or default) resolution, and name the file Background*www*x*hhh*.jpg, where *www* and *hhh* represent the width and height, in pixels (for example, Background1600x1200.jpg).

- Because this feature doesn't support all screen resolutions, create a copy of the image file and name it BackgroundDefault.jpg. If Windows is unable to use the resolution-specific image, it uses this one and stretches it to fit.

If that procedure sounds too daunting, download the Tweaks.com Logon Changer, a utility that compresses your image file (to stay under the file-size limit) as well as safely diving into the registry and deeply nested folders for you. Get it from *w7io.com/1603*.

Making the Logon Text Bigger

If you use a high-DPI setting to enlarge text while you're logged on, you might be disappointed to see that your setting doesn't apply to the logon screen. To remedy that situation, follow these steps:

1. In the Start menu search box, type **regedit** and press Enter to open Registry Editor.

2. In Registry Editor, navigate to the HKU\.Default\Control Panel\Desktop key.

3. If a DWORD value named LogPixels does not exist, create one.

4. Double-click the LogPixels value. Be sure that Base is set to Decimal, and then set the value to the desired resolution in dots per inch. The default setting is 96 DPI; larger values increase the text size. For example, setting the value to 120 increases the size by 25 percent. (96 times 1.25 is 120.)

Log off to see the changes. The first time each user logs on after making this change, Windows applies the new DPI setting to the user's desktop as well as the logon screen. Users who want to change to a different text size can do so by visiting Display in Control Panel. For details, see "Making Text Easier to Read" on page 157.

TROUBLESHOOTING

Context menus are unreadable after setting the logon screen text size

After you set the logon screen text to a comfortably legible size, you might discover that the text for context menus (right-click menus) and other items has become microscopic. The fix is easy: open Personalization and select a different theme.

Bypassing the Logon Screen

If your computer has only one user account (aside from built-in accounts, such as Administrator and Guest), and if that user account doesn't have a password, Windows automatically logs on that user during startup. You won't see the Welcome screen or any other logon screens; Windows launches straight to your desktop.

Chapter 18

You might want to set up your computer to log on automatically even if it has more than one user account and even if your preferred user account is password-protected. This kind of logon can be convenient in several situations: if you're the primary user of the computer, but other people occasionally need to use it; if you occasionally need to log on as a different user to install software or perform other tasks; or if you have set up a password for your account (so that you can use scheduled tasks or connect remotely, operations that are available only to accounts with passwords) but still want to log on automatically at startup.

CAUTION!

Automatically logging on means that the system effectively enters your user name and password when you turn on the power. Anyone who has physical access to your computer can then log on as you and have access to all computer resources (including websites for which you've saved passwords) that you normally have.

If your computer is not joined to a domain, you can set it up to log on automatically by following these steps:

1. At a command prompt, type **netplwiz** to open Advanced User Accounts.

2. On the Users tab, clear the Users Must Enter A User Name And Password To Use This Computer check box and then click OK. Note that the Users Must Enter A User Name And Password To Use This Computer check box doesn't appear if your computer is a member of a domain. Only computers that aren't part of a network or are part of a workgroup can bypass the logon screen. Domain users must enter a user name and password, even to log on locally.

The Automatically Log On dialog box appears.

3. Type the user name and password for the account that you want to log on with each time you start your computer.

After you make this change, you can use other accounts on the computer by logging off and then logging on to another account or by using Fast User Switching.

Users of any computer—those joined to a domain as well as workgroup and standalone computers—can configure automatic logon by downloading and using a free utility named Autologon, which was created by Mark Russinovich at Sysinternals (now part of Microsoft). You can download Autologon from *w7io.com/1602*.

INSIDE OUT   Bypass automatic logon or prevent others from bypassing it

If you've configured your system to log on automatically, you can suppress the automatic logon by holding down the Shift key as the system boots. If you want to prevent users from bypassing the automatic logon (thereby ensuring that your system always starts with a particular account), you can use a registry setting to make the system ignore the Shift key. Use Registry Editor to navigate to HKLM\Software\Microsoft\WindowsNT\CurrentVersion\Winlogon. If the string value IgnoreShiftOverride doesn't exist, create it. Set this value to 1 to ensure that your system always starts with its auto-logon account.

Logging Off, Switching Users, or Locking Your Computer

When you're finished using your computer, you want to be sure that you don't leave it in a condition in which others can use your credentials to access your files. To do that, you need to log off, switch users, or lock your computer:

- **Log Off**   With this option, all your programs close and dial-up connections are ended. To log off, click the arrow in the lower right corner of the Start menu and click Log Off. (See Figure 18-8.)

- **Switch User**   With this option (sometimes called Fast User Switching), your programs continue to run. Your account is still logged on, but (if it's protected by a password) only you can return to your session. To switch users, click the arrow in the lower right corner of the Start menu and click Switch User. This takes you to the Welcome screen, where you can click the name of the account you want to switch to.

    Fast User Switching, a feature that made its first appearance in Windows XP, allows multiple users to be logged on to a computer at the same time. As the feature name suggests, you can quickly switch between users. This might be convenient, for example, if one user logs on, opens several documents, and begins downloading a huge file from the Internet. Meanwhile, another user comes along and wants to quickly check e-mail. No problem: the second user can log on, log off, and return control to the first user. While the second user is logged on, the first user's applications (such as the download process) continue to run.

- **Lock**   With this option, your programs continue to run, but the logon screen appears so that no one can see your desktop or use the computer. Only you can unlock the computer to return to your session; however, other users can log on in their own sessions without disturbing yours. To lock a computer, click the arrow in the lower right corner of the Start menu and click Lock.

Figure 18-8 To change the default action of the power button to something other than Shut Down, right-click the Start menu, choose Properties, and select a Power Button Action option.

In any case, if you want to prevent others from using your account, you must protect your account with a password. When you choose any of these options, Windows hides whatever you were working on. Your computer continues to run (subject to power management settings), and any resources shared by your computer remain available to other users on the network.

INSIDE OUT   Use keyboard shortcuts

To lock your computer, you can press Windows logo key+L. (You might also find it more convenient to use this shortcut for switching users; the only difference is that it takes you to the logon screen—which has a Switch User button—instead of to the Welcome screen.)

For any of these actions—log off, switch users, or lock—you can start by pressing Ctrl+Alt+Delete, which displays a menu that includes all three options.

Controlling Your Children's Computer Access

Parental Controls is a feature that enables parents to help manage how their children use the computer. As a parent, you can set restrictions (different for each child, if you like) on which programs your children can run and which games they can play, and you can set hours of use for the computer. With the addition of controls from Microsoft and other providers, you can specify which websites your children can visit and view activity logs that detail each child's computer activity.

Note

In addition to technological measures in Windows 7 and other products, Microsoft also offers plenty of educational information for parents and kids to assist them in staying safe online. Visit the "Family Safety" page at *w7io.com/1604* to view parent's guides, safety tips, and more.

The requirements for using Parental Controls are simple:

- You must have at least two user accounts set up on your computer—an administrator account for the parent and a standard account for the child. (More adults? More kids? Create a separate account for each person. Be sure that each child to whom you want to apply Parental Controls has a standard account because parental controls can't be applied to administrator accounts.)

- All administrator accounts on the computer should be protected by a password. (This isn't an absolute requirement, but without password protection, anyone can bypass or turn off Parental Controls. Note also that you need only one password-protected administrator account to manage Parental Controls. Other parents with standard accounts can use the administrator parent's credentials to run Parental Controls.)

- Your computer cannot be joined to a domain. On domain-joined computers, the Parental Controls feature is disabled, even when you're connected to your home network (or no network).

For information about creating and managing user accounts, see "Working with User Accounts" on page 651. For information about password protection for user accounts, see "Setting a Logon Password" on page 663.

Configuring Parental Controls

To begin using Parental Controls, open it in Control Panel. (It's in the User Accounts And Family Safety category.) After consenting to the User Account Control prompt (or entering an administrator password if you're logged on as a standard user), you'll see a window like the one shown in Figure 18-9.

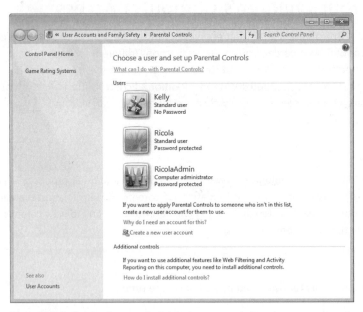

Figure 18-9 If any of your administrator accounts is not password-protected, Windows displays a prominent warning—and a link to correct the problem—in this window.

To set restrictions for a child, click the child's account name and then click On, Enforce Current Settings, as shown in Figure 18-10.

Settings from other providers can supplement (or replace) the controls included with Windows

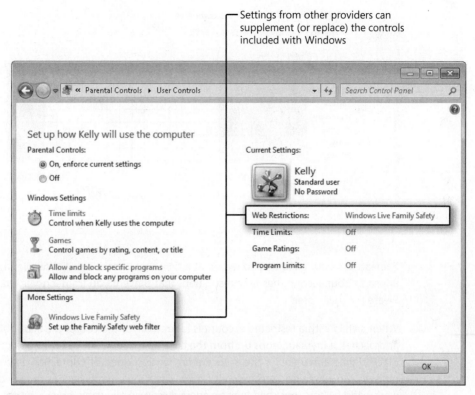

Figure 18-10 Using a window like this one, you can set different restrictions for each child.

Restricting Logon Hours

To control the times at which your child can use the computer, in the User Controls window (shown in Figure 18-10), click Time Limits. You can then specify, for each day of the week, which hours are allowed and which are blocked.

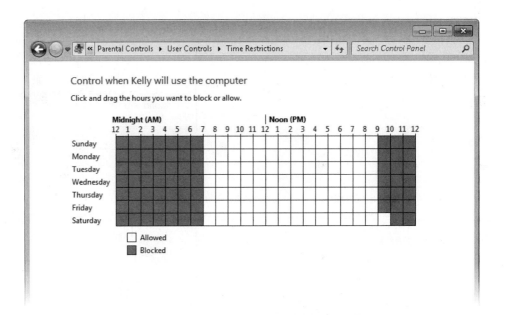

Thereafter, if your child tries to log on at a time that's not allowed, a simple message appears: "Your account has time restrictions that prevent you from logging on at this time. Please try again later."

When a child with a restricted account is logged on, as the end of the allowable time approaches, a message pops up from the taskbar. If your child is still logged on when the blocked time arrives, he or she is unceremoniously logged off. Note, however, that this log-off is akin to switching users; open windows and running applications remain open, and no work is lost. When your child logs on again during an allowable time, everything is just as it was before the child was logged off.

INSIDE OUT Find out how much time is left

When Parental Controls is in effect, it displays an icon in the notification area. (By default, the icon is hidden, meaning it's visible only when you click the arrow at the left end of the notification area.) Hovering the mouse pointer over the icon displays the current status of Parental Controls, including how much time remains until the user will be logged off.

> Parental Controls are turned on. Time left: 0hrs, 11mins

By double-clicking the icon, your child can view (but not modify) all of the Parental Controls settings imposed on his or her account.

Controlling Access to Games

To control which computer games your child is allowed to play, in the User Controls window (shown in Figure 18-10), click Games. In the window shown in Figure 18-11, click Set Game Ratings to specify the ratings codes for allowable games. You can also block games that contain specific types of objectionable content, even if the game's rating falls into the acceptable range. (Scroll down on the game ratings page to see these types of content, many of which you probably never imagined could appear in something called a "game.") In addition, you can review a list of installed games and explicitly block or allow certain titles.

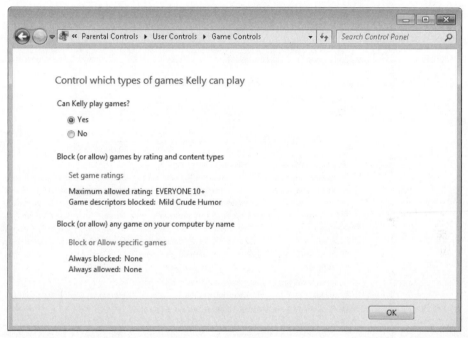

Figure 18-11 Time for a timeout? You can block access to all games simply by selecting No near the top of this window.

> ### Note
>
> Some games are not recognized by Windows as games. Therefore, they're not affected by settings you make in the game controls section of Parental Controls, nor do they appear in the list of games that you can explicitly block or allow. To control use of these games, use the general program-blocking capabilities of Parental Controls, as described in the following section.

By default, Parental Controls uses the game rating system established by the Entertainment Software Rating Board (ESRB), which has been widely adopted by publishers of games sold in the United States. To use a different rating system, return to the main Parental Controls page. (See Figure 18-9 earlier in this chapter.) In the left pane, click Game Rating Systems.

Blocking Programs

To control which programs your child is allowed to run, in the User Controls window (shown in Figure 18-10), click Allow And Block Specific Programs. The Application Restrictions window, shown in Figure 18-12, lists the executable files for programs installed on your computer, grouped by storage location (folder).

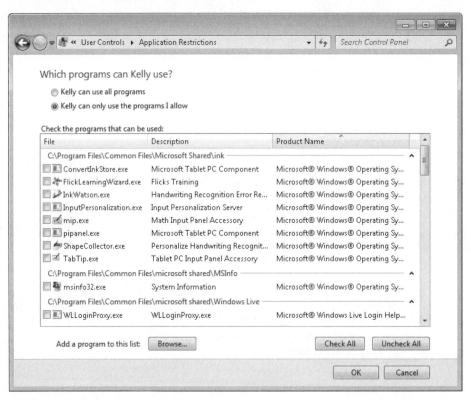

Figure 18-12 Blocking programs through Parental Controls does not remove them from the child's Start menu; it just prevents their use.

If you want to restrict your child's use to just a handful of programs, you can easily do so here. Conversely, if you want to give free rein *except* for a handful of programs (for example, you might want to prevent the use of your personal finance program so that your financial records aren't inadvertently compromised), click Check All—and then clear the check box by the programs you want to block.

> **Note**
>
> Most of the basic accessory programs included with Windows—such as Notepad, Calculator, and Help And Support—are not included in the list of blockable programs, nor can you add them to the list. These programs are always allowed.

When your child attempts to run a blocked program, a dialog box appears.

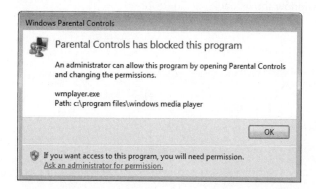

Clicking OK dismisses the dialog box, whereas clicking the Ask An Administrator For Permission link requests the password of an administrator, and then gives you a chance to ignore the request by clicking Keep Blocking. If you click Always Allow, the program is added to the list of allowed programs, and your child won't be prompted again.

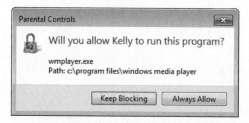

Using Other Controls to Keep Your Children Safe

Parental Controls in Windows Vista includes two controls that are not in Windows 7:

- Web filtering lets you specify lists of sites to allow and sites to block.

- Activity reporting monitors and reports computer activity, including when each child logged on and off, which programs she ran, which websites she visited, whom she has corresponded with via e-mail and instant messaging, and so on.

Chapter 18

Although those controls are no longer part of Windows, Parental Controls is designed to incorporate additional controls that provide comparable functionality as well as other features. One such add-in is Windows Live Family Safety, which performs web filtering and creates activity reports that you can view from anywhere you have access to a web browser and an Internet connection. You can learn more about Windows Live Family Safety and download it from *w7io.com/1605*.

These additional controls can be provided by Microsoft or others. To install or use an add-in control, follow the instructions under Additional Controls, near the bottom of the main Parental Controls window shown earlier in Figure 18-9.

CHAPTER 19

Setting Up a Small Office or Home Network

S ETTING up a network is no longer the complex and sometimes frustrating process it used to be. With Microsoft Windows XP, the Network Setup wizard performs many of the tasks necessary to configure network computers. Because of advances in hardware technology as well as in Windows itself, the wizard isn't necessary for configuring wired networks in Windows 7. On a network where every computer is running Windows (any version), in fact, you might find that your wired network requires no configuration at all—after you finish setting up Windows, your network is available for immediate access. Modern hardware and Windows 7 combine to bring similar ease of configuration to wireless networks. (For advice on what to do when the pieces of your network don't fit together so neatly, see Chapter 22, "Fixing and Tweaking Your Network.")

You can maximize your chances of a trouble-free network setup by selecting the right hardware and installing it properly. When you start Windows after connecting your network, a quick visit to Network And Sharing Center is usually all that's necessary to confirm that IP addresses, workgroup names, Windows Firewall settings, registry settings, and system policies are properly configured to facilitate a working network. Although Windows does all this with nary a nudge from you, you can always fine-tune network settings to suit your networking needs.

What's in Your Edition?

This chapter explains how to configure a peer-to-peer network for a small workgroup (typically consisting of 10 or fewer computers)—a network of computers that are not part of a domain run by a member of the Windows Server family. The steps we describe in this chapter for setting up and configuring a network work identically in all Windows 7 editions, with one exception: a computer running Starter edition can join a homegroup but cannot create one.

Introducing Windows 7 Networking

With a minimal investment in hardware, you can connect two or more computers and form a simple peer-to-peer network. Because these networks aren't built around a server, they don't allow you to manage users and shared resources centrally; instead, each computer contains its own database of authorized user accounts and shared folders, drives, and printers. Setting up a workgroup-based network offers the following advantages:

- **Shared storage**   By designating certain folders as shared resources, you avoid the need to swap files on removable media or to maintain duplicate copies of files; instead, everyone on the network can open a shared document.

- **Shared printers**   Sharing a printer allows any authorized network user to print to that device.

- **Shared media**   You can open shared media files (music, pictures, and video) stored on another computer or device or stream media from one computer to other computers and devices on the network.

- **Shared Internet connection**   With a router to which all your networked computers are connected, every computer can use the router's connection to the Internet. An alternative is to use Internet Connection Sharing (ICS), with which you can set up Internet access on a single computer and then allow every computer on the network to share that connection. ICS is an acceptable sharing method if you have a dial-up connection to the Internet; ICS lets you control it from any computer on the network. However, using a hardware router offers significant security and performance advantages over ICS and is clearly the way to go if you have high-speed, always-on Internet service, such as that provided by cable or DSL.

What's New in Windows 7

Networking in Windows 7 improves on earlier versions primarily with ease-of-use enhancements. Among the most useful improvements:

- HomeGroup makes child's play of the previously daunting tasks of connecting the computers in your home and sharing the information they contain. When you join a home network, Windows automatically invites you to join a homegroup. Documents, pictures, music, and other files you choose to share are then accessible from all your home network's computers. For information about setting up HomeGroup, see "Using HomeGroup to Connect Your Computers at Home" on page 710; for details about using homegroups, see "Sharing Files, Digital Media, and Printers in a Homegroup" on page 720.

- Wi-Fi Protected Setup (WPS), a standard promulgated by the Wi-Fi Alliance (*wi-fi.org*) and embraced by many hardware manufacturers, enables simple and secure configuration of the gamut of wireless network devices, including routers, wireless access points, computers, printers, cameras, game consoles, media extenders, and personal digital assistants (PDAs). WPS is fully integrated in Windows 7. For details, see "Setting Up a Wireless Network" on page 695.

- Mobile broadband support provides a driver-based system for working with connections to mobile broadband services such as 3G. Instead of having to install and learn proprietary connection software, you can now connect a mobile broadband adapter and begin using it in essentially the same way as any other network adapter.

In addition, Windows 7, when connected to a server running Windows Server 2008 R2, enables new networking features such as DirectAccess, which enables connections to an enterprise server without creating a virtual private network (VPN) connection; VPN Reconnect, which automatically reestablishes a VPN connection when Internet connectivity is restored; and BranchCache, which improves response time and reduces wide area network (WAN) traffic by caching server content in a local office. These enterprise-scale features are beyond the scope of this book.

These usability improvements come atop a major networking makeover implemented in Windows Vista, which is based on a protocol stack that was completely rewritten for Windows Vista. Dubbed the Next Generation TCP/IP stack, this redesign of the network underpinnings provides improvements in security, performance, and convenience that are largely invisible to ordinary users.

For example, additional security comes in the ability of the Windows Filtering Platform to implement packet filtering at all levels of the Transmission Control Protocol/Internet Protocol (TCP/IP) stack. Performance is enhanced by Receive Window Auto-Tuning, which dynamically determines the optimal receive window size based on changing network conditions; in previous Windows versions, you were required to tweak the registry to set a fixed-size receive window for your type of Internet connection. The Next Generation TCP/IP stack implements Internet Protocol version 6 (IPv6) in a dual-stack architecture; instead of having to install a separate protocol (with its own transport and link layers) as in previous versions, IPv4 and IPv6 are incorporated in a single Windows driver, with a shared transport layer and link layer. Enabling IPv4 and IPv6 by default is more convenient for the user who needs both—because there's nothing extra to install—but also easier for developers. Native support for wireless devices is built in to the Next Generation TCP/IP stack, which also reduces demands on developers and users who must deal with add-in support in earlier versions of Windows.

And if all of the preceding jargon means nothing to you—well, that's the point. Improvements like these (and dozens of others) have made networking almost transparent to users, so you don't need to spend time understanding how the layers in a protocol stack communicate and, worse, how to configure them to do so.

Using Network And Sharing Center

Many of the tasks related to configuring the hardware and software for a network, viewing network resources, setting up shared resources on your own computer, and diagnosing network problems can be managed from Network And Sharing Center, which is shown in Figure 19-1.

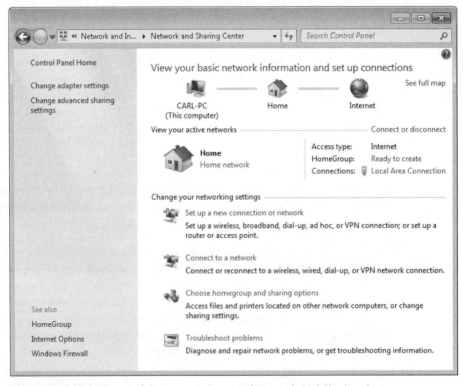

Figure 19-1 Clicking one of the icons at the top of Network And Sharing Center opens your Computer folder, Network folder, or default web browser's home page.

You can open Network And Sharing Center in any of the following ways:

- In the notification area, click the Network icon and then click Open Network And Sharing Center.

- In the Start menu search box, begin typing **network** until Network And Sharing Center appears; click it.

- If your Start menu includes a Network command on the right side, right-click it and then click Properties.

- In Control Panel, click Network And Internet, and then click Network And Sharing Center.

- In Windows Explorer, with the Network folder displayed, click the Network And Sharing Center button on the toolbar.

> **Note**
>
> **Many of the tasks related to configuring networks require elevation to administrator privileges, as indicated by the shield icon next to commands and on command buttons.**

Understanding Network Locations

With computers that connect to different types of networks—such as a corporate domain, an Internet café, and a private home network—often within the same day and sometimes even simultaneously, using the same network security settings for all networks would lead to security breaches, severe inconvenience, or both. Windows uses network locations to categorize each network and then applies appropriate security settings. When you initially connect to a network, Windows asks you to select a network location, as shown in Figure 19-2. Select one of the three options:

- **Home Network**   Select this option when you're connecting to a trusted network, such as your own network at home. You should select Home Network only for a network that is protected by a residential gateway (a term we'll explain shortly) or comparable Internet defense, and one where you're confident that malicious users aren't connected. When you make this choice, Windows enables the HomeGroup feature for sharing with other users on the network.

- **Work Network**   Select this option when you're connecting to a trusted network, such as your company network at work. When you choose Work Network, Windows turns on network discovery, which lets you see other computers on the network and lets other users see your computer.

- **Public Network**   Use this option for networks in public places, such as wireless hotspots in coffee shops, hotels, airports, and libraries. This type of network typically has a direct connection to the Internet. Network discovery is turned off for public locations.

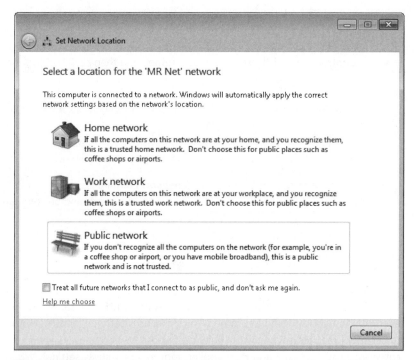

Figure 19-2 Windows asks you to choose a network location the first time you connect to a new network.

> **Note**
>
> In Windows Vista, the Home and Work options are functionally identical; the only difference is the default icon that Windows assigns to represent the network. In Windows 7, however, there is a key difference: only Home networks can use the Home-Group feature.

If you have a mobile computer that connects to multiple networks, keep in mind that Windows keeps three groups of network security settings: one for private (home or work) networks, one for public-location networks, and one for use when your computer is joined to a domain-based network. A visit to Windows Firewall shows that it maintains three profiles: Home Or Work (Private) Networks, Public Networks, and Domain Networks; each is associated with a network location type.

For more information about Windows Firewall, see "Blocking Intruders with Windows Firewall" on page 604.

This is important because, for example, when you are connected to a public network and Windows Firewall is turned on, some programs and services ask you to let them communicate through the firewall. Consider carefully whether you want to unblock such programs; if you do, that program is unblocked for all networks identified as "public location" networks.

The location of the current network is shown in Network And Sharing Center, below the name of the network.

To change the network location, in Network And Sharing Center, click the link that identifies the network location. In the dialog box that appears (same as in Figure 19-2), click the appropriate location.

Workgroups vs. Domains

Computers on a network can be part of a workgroup or a domain.

In a *workgroup*, the security database (including, most significantly, the list of user accounts and the privileges granted to each one) for each computer resides on that computer. When you log on to a computer in a workgroup, Windows checks its local security database to see if you've provided a user name and password that matches one in the database. Similarly, when network users attempt to connect to your computer, Windows again consults the local security database. All computers in a workgroup must be on the same subnet. A workgroup is sometimes called a *peer-to-peer network*.

By contrast, a *domain* consists of computers that share a security database stored on one or more domain controllers running Windows Server. When you log on using a domain account, Windows authenticates your credentials against the security database on a domain controller.

In this chapter (and throughout this book), we focus primarily on workgroup networks.

Configuring Your Network Hardware

Before you can set up the networking features in Windows, you need to assemble and configure the proper hardware. In addition to two or more computers, you'll need the following components to set up a home or small office network:

- **Network adapters**   Each computer needs an adapter to communicate with the other computers on the network. (An adapter is sometimes called a *network interface card*, or NIC.) Network adapters can be internal or external. Internal adapters are often incorporated directly onto the motherboard of a desktop or notebook PC, or they can be installed in a PCI slot on a desktop PC or a mini-PCI slot hidden within the guts of a notebook computer. External adapters are typically connected to a USB port. Most wired network adapters conform to the Ethernet standard. Wireless adapters conform to one of several 802.11 (Wi-Fi) standards.

- **A central connection point**   Use a *hub* or *switch* to connect the computers in an Ethernet network. This function is sometimes integrated in a *router* or *residential gateway*. On a wireless network, a *wireless access point* handles these duties.

  In this chapter, we sometimes use the term *hub* in its generic sense to refer to a central connection point for networks that use a star-bus topology, such as Ethernet. However, a *hub* (using its more precise definition) is just one of several types of connection points commonly used in home and small office networks:

  - **Hub**   A hub is the simplest and slowest of these devices, all of which have several jacks (called *ports*) into which you can plug cables attached to computers and other network devices. In a hub (which is sometimes called a *repeater*), data that is received on one port is broadcast to all its ports, which produces a lot of unnecessary network traffic.

  - **Switch**   By keeping track of the unique Media Access Control (MAC) address for each connected device, a switch is able to receive data and in turn send it only to the port to which the destination device is attached. A switch is faster and more secure than a hub.

  - **Router**   Unlike hubs and switches, which are used to connect computers on a single network, a router is typically used to connect two or more networks. In a small network, a router typically is used to connect the local area network to the network at an Internet service provider (which, in turn, uses routers to connect to the Internet backbone).

    A *residential gateway* is a router that typically adds Network Address Translation (NAT) and Dynamic Host Configuration Protocol (DHCP) capabilities. (NAT enables multiple computers on a network to share a single public IP address. DHCP is a system for assigning an IP address to each computer on a network.) In addition, many residential gateways include a stateful packet inspection firewall and other security features.

    A *wireless gateway* adds wireless capability to a residential gateway, thereby enabling connections to computers with Wi-Fi adapters as well as computers with wired adapters. To add wireless capability to a network centered around a nonwireless residential gateway, use a *wireless access point*.

- **Cables**   On an Ethernet network, you connect each network adapter to the hub using an eight-wire Category 5, Category 5e, or Category 6 patch cable with an RJ-45 connector on each end. (Cat 5 is designed for Fast Ethernet, with speeds up to

100 Mbps, whereas Cat 5e and Cat 6 cables are designed for Gigabit Ethernet, with speeds up to 1 Gbps.) HomePNA networks use standard balanced pair telephone wire to connect to an existing telephone jack with a standard telephone connector (RJ-11), or television-style coaxial cable using a standard F connector. Power-line networks typically use Cat 5 cables to connect computers to adapters that plug into a power outlet. By definition, wireless networks require no cables, except typically between the wireless access point and the Internet.

Although it's not required, most networks also include one additional hardware component: a modem or other device to connect your network to the Internet.

Wired or Wireless?

When setting up a network in a home or office for use with Windows 7, you can choose from several technologies, including

- **Ethernet**   This popular networking standard, developed in the mid-1970s, has stood the test of time. The original Ethernet standard (also known as 10Base-T) is capable of transferring data at maximum speeds of 10 megabits per second. The Fast Ethernet standard (also known as 100Base-T) can transfer data at 100 megabits per second and is currently the mainstream system used in most homes and small office networks. A newer standard called Gigabit Ethernet allows data transfers at 1 gigabit (1,000 megabits) per second. In an office or home that is wired for Ethernet, you can plug your network adapter into a wall jack and install a hub at a central location called a *patch panel*. In a home or office without structured wiring, you need to plug directly into a hub.

- **Wireless**   In recent years, wireless networking technology has enjoyed an explosion in popularity, thanks to its convenience, steadily decreasing prices, and ubiquity. Wireless connections are now available in many hotels, trains, buses, ferries, and airplanes in addition to the more traditional hotspot locations such as cafés and libraries.

   Although wireless local area networks (WLANs) were originally developed for use with notebook computers, they are increasingly popular with desktop computer users, especially in homes and offices where it is impractical or physically impossible to run network cables. The most popular wireless networks use one of several variants of the IEEE (Institute of Electrical and Electronics Engineers) 802.11 standard, also known as Wi-Fi. Using base stations and network adapters with small antennas, Wi-Fi networks using the 802.11g standard transfer data at a maximum rate of 54 megabits per second using radio frequencies in the 2.4 GHz range. (Some manufacturers of wireless networking equipment have pushed the standard with proprietary variations that approximately double the speed.) 802.11g-based networks have largely supplanted those based on an earlier standard, 802.11b, which offers a maximum speed of 11 megabits per second. The newest standard, 802.11n, offers approximately a tenfold improvement in speed (600 megabits per second) as well as significantly greater range. Unlike the earlier standards, the 802.11n standard allows use of the 5 GHz frequency range as well as 2.4 GHz. However, not all 802.11n hardware supports both bands.

Most 802.11g hardware works with 802.11b networks as well. Likewise, most 802.11n hardware is backward compatible with 802.11g and 802.11b devices. For a summary of the current state of 802.11n development, see the Wikipedia page at *w7io.com/1701*.

INSIDE OUT   Maximize the speed of your Wi-Fi network

Although the newer Wi-Fi standards are backward compatible with hardware that uses the older, slower standards, be aware that all traffic on your network runs at the speed of the slowest wireless standard in use; if you've just bought an 802.11n router, you might want to pony up a few dollars more to replace your old 802.11b and 802.11g network adapters.

For the maximum throughput, use 5 GHz 802.11n devices throughout your network. The 5 GHz band is subject to less radio interference than 2.4 GHz and is capable of a higher maximum theoretical data rate. If you must maintain compatibility with older 2.4 GHz devices, the ideal solution is to use a dual-band wireless access point, putting the 802.11n traffic on the 5 GHz channels and the 802.11b/g traffic on the 2.4 GHz radio. The procedure for configuring a wireless network in this fashion depends on the access point you use; check its documentation for details.

Another Wi-Fi standard you might encounter is 802.11a, which can reach maximum speeds of 54 Gbps. It broadcasts in the 5 GHz frequency range and is therefore incompatible with 802.11b, 802.11g, and some 802.11n equipment, except for specialized dual-band and multiband gear.

A number of other wireless network standards promulgated by the IEEE's 802.11 Working Group promise benefits such as better security. Be aware that, despite the confusingly similar names, network equipment using one of the wireless standards is generally compatible only with other equipment using the same standard. For the latest technical details, you can read the sometimes dense and dry commentary at the official site of the 802.11 Working Group, *ieee802.org/11*. For a more readable summary, try the website run by the Wi-Fi Alliance at *wi-fi.org*.

- **Phone line**   Networks that comply with early versions of the HomePNA standard operate at speeds of roughly 10 megabits per second; the latest HomePNA 3 standard works at speeds of up to 320 megabits per second. HomePNA networks don't require a central connection point such as a router or hub; instead, they employ a daisy-chain topology in which all network adapters communicate directly by plugging into existing telephone jacks and transmitting data on the same wires that carry telephone, fax, and television signals, without interfering with those communications. For more information, visit the HomePNA Alliance at *homepna.org*.

- **Power line**   Another technology that uses existing wiring communicates over power lines. Two trade associations—HomePlug Powerline Alliance and Universal Powerline Association—have developed standards (which are not compatible with each other) for power-line communications, and each one can be found on devices from a small number of manufacturers. Speeds up to 200 megabits per second are claimed. You can find more information at the HomePlug Powerline Alliance (*homeplug.org*) and Universal Powerline Association (*upaplc.org*) websites.

Ethernet and wireless are the dominant networking technologies in homes and offices. The availability of inexpensive wireless network gear has relegated phone-line and power-line technologies to niche status; they are most attractive in older homes where adding network cable is impossible and wireless signals are impractical because of distance, building materials, or interference.

In many homes and offices, it's impractical to rely exclusively on one type of network. For example, it might not be feasible to run cables to every location where you want a computer. Yet, a wireless network might not be adequate because the signal can't reach all locations given the number and type of walls and floors that separate computers. In such a case, you can install two or more networks of different types and use a router or a bridge to connect the disparate networks.

For details about bridges, see "Bridging Two Networks" on page 790.

Installing and Configuring a Network Adapter

On most systems, you don't need to take any special configuration steps to set up a network adapter, regardless of whether it's for an Ethernet, wireless, HomePNA, or power-line adapter. The Plug and Play code in Windows handles all the work of installing drivers. If you install an internal adapter and Windows includes a signed driver for that adapter, the driver should be installed automatically when Windows detects the adapter. (If Windows cannot find a built-in driver, you'll be prompted to supply the location of the driver files.) For an external adapter connected to a USB or IEEE 1394 port, the driver installs in the same way as one for an internal adapter, and thereafter it loads and unloads dynamically when you attach or remove the adapter.

For more details about installing hardware, see "Installing a New Plug and Play Device" on page 1056.

As with all hardware devices, you can inspect the properties of a network adapter from Devices And Printers or from the Device Manager console. (See "Changing Settings for an Installed Device" on page 1082 for details.) Alternatively, you can view an adapter's properties from Network And Sharing Center, but it takes a few more clicks to get there. Most network adapters include an Advanced tab in the properties dialog box, from which you can configure specialized hardware settings. These settings are invariably hardware-specific, and they can vary dramatically. In general, you should accept the default settings on the Advanced tab of the network adapter's properties dialog box except when you're certain a change is required.

Making Connections

On a standard Ethernet network, all computers must be connected via one or more routers, switches, or hubs.

If you're going to connect your network to a broadband Internet service, you should use a router or residential gateway as the primary hub. Most such products designed for use in homes and small offices combine a router and hub; in this type of device, you connect your external DSL or cable modem to the Internet connector (often labeled as wide area network, or WAN) on the router and then connect each computer on the network to a port on the local area network (LAN) side.

If you use a dial-up connection for Internet service, you can use any type of hub to connect your computers.

On wireless networks, a wireless access point typically serves as a hub.

You must be able to run a cable from the hub to each computer on your network. It's not always feasible to make a direct connection from each computer or other networked device to the central hub. (Furthermore, the central hub might not have enough ports to connect all devices.) To make additional connections in an Ethernet network, use another hub or switch.

Figure 19-3 shows a schematic diagram of a typical network in a home or small business. This network includes both wired and wireless segments.

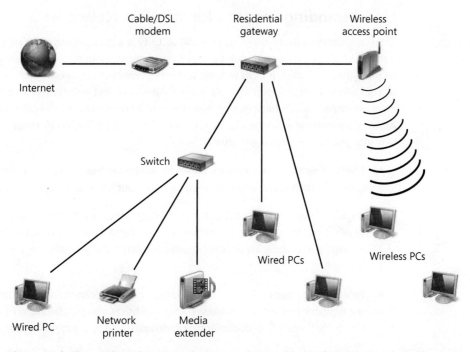

Figure 19-3 The residential gateway device can also provide the functionality of a cable modem, wireless access point, or both, eliminating the need to have separate devices.

Setting Up a Wireless Network

Configuring each device on a wireless network so that they all communicate with each other (and not with nearby networks that share the same airwaves) has traditionally been a tricky task. Understanding the alphabet soup of abbreviations—SSID, WEP, WPA, PSK, and MAC, to name a few—and providing appropriate values for each is a task for a true wizard. Fortunately, Windows 7 includes a wizard for each configuration task in wireless networking. These wizards, combined with configuration support such as Wi-Fi Protected Setup (which encompasses an earlier technology called Windows Connect Now) in modern wireless networking equipment, truly make setup simple.

Before we get into the details of setup and configuration, however, we discuss security. Because wireless signals potentially expose your network to anybody who comes near, it's important to understand and consider security implications before you make your first wireless connection.

Understanding Security for Wireless Networks

On a conventional wired network, physical security is a given: if someone plugs a computer into your hub, you'll know about it immediately, and you can trace the physical wire back to the intruder's computer. On wireless networks, however, anyone who comes into range of your wireless access point can tap into your network and intercept signals from it. Finding open access points has become something of a sport; participants call it *war driving*. Although some war drivers seek open access points just for fun, other users who find their way into your network present several risks:

- **Theft of service** An intruder might be able to access the Internet using your connection, which could degrade the quality of your Internet service.

- **Denial of service** An intruder who is unable to connect to your network can still cause some degree of havoc by flooding the network with connection requests. With enough persistence, an attacker could completely deny legitimate users access to the network.

- **Privacy violations** An intruder with the right tools can monitor all data sent over the network and can therefore see which websites you visit (along with your passwords for those sites), documents you download from a shared network folder, and so on.

- **Theft or destruction of data** Outsiders who successfully connect to your network can browse shared folders and printers. Depending on the permissions assigned to these resources, they can change, rename, or delete existing files or add new ones.

- **Network takeover** An intruder who manages to log on to the network and exploit an unpatched vulnerability can install a Trojan horse program or tamper with permissions, potentially exposing computers on the LAN to attacks from over the Internet.

To prevent any of these dire possibilities, you can and should configure the best available security for your access point and all wireless devices on your network. Depending on your hardware, you should have a choice of one or more of the following options:

- **Wired Equivalent Privacy (WEP)** WEP is a first-generation scheme for protecting authorized users of a wireless network from eavesdroppers by encrypting the data flow between the networked computer and the access point. WEP suffers from some known security flaws that make it extremely easy for an attacker to "crack" the key using off-the-shelf hardware. As a result, WEP is inappropriate for use on any network that contains sensitive data. Most modern Wi-Fi equipment supports WEP for backward compatibility with older hardware, but we strongly advise against using it unless no other options are available. To enter a WEP key, you supply a string of ASCII or hex characters (5 ASCII or 10 hex characters for a 64-bit key; 13 ASCII or 26 hex characters for a 128-bit key). The key you provide when setting up your wireless adapter must match the key on your access point, and all devices on the network must use the same encryption strength—either 64 or 128 bits.

- **Wi-Fi Protected Access (WPA)**   WPA is a newer, stronger encryption scheme that was specifically designed to overcome weaknesses of WEP. On a small network that uses WPA, clients and access points use a shared network password (called a *pre-shared key*, or *PSK*) that consists of a 256-bit number or a passphrase that is from 8 to 63 bytes long. (A longer passphrase produces a stronger key.) With a sufficiently strong key based on a truly random sequence, the likelihood of a successful outside attack is slim. Most network hardware that supports the 802.11g standard also supports WPA. With older hardware, you might be able to add WPA compatibility via a firmware upgrade.

- **Wi-Fi Protected Access 2 (WPA2)**   Based on the 802.11i standard, WPA2 provides the strongest protection yet for consumer-grade wireless networks. It uses 802.1x-based authentication and Advanced Encryption Standard (AES) encryption; combined, these technologies ensure that only authorized users can access the network and that any intercepted data cannot be deciphered. WPA2 comes in two flavors: WPA2-Personal and WPA2-Enterprise. WPA2-Personal uses a passphrase to create its encryption keys and is currently the best available security for wireless networks in homes and small offices. WPA2-Enterprise requires a server to verify network users. WPA2 can work with all flavors of Wi-Fi, including 802.11b, 802.11g, 802.11n, and 802.11a. All wireless products sold since early 2006 must support WPA2 to bear the Wi-Fi CERTIFIED label.

You must use the same encryption option on all wireless devices on your network—access points, routers, network adapters, print servers, cameras, and so on—so choose the best option that is supported by all your devices. If you have an older device that supports only WEP (and it can't be upgraded with a firmware update) consider retiring or replacing that device.

The alternative to these encryption methods is to use no security at all, an option that produces an "open" network. If you own a coffee shop or bookstore and your goal is to provide free Internet access for your customers, this option is acceptable as long as you make sure to protect other computers on your network from unauthorized access. (The primary tools for doing so are a firewall, sharing permissions, and folder permissions.) But for most people, the risks of running an open network are unacceptable.

Configuring a Router or Wireless Access Point

You begin setting up your wireless network by configuring the wireless access point (or a router that includes a wireless access point), which is the hub of your Wi-Fi network. The process is simple if you use a device that supports Wi-Fi Protected Setup (WPS); most routers sold since 2008 do, although it's not always clear from the product literature. Older routers and other noncompliant devices offer a variety of third-party solutions or ask you to perform configuration manually. (If you're not sure whether your router supports WPS, try the following steps. If this method doesn't work, check the instructions that came with your router.)

You can set up a Wi-Fi Protected Setup–compliant router or access point by using either a wired or wireless connection. To configure a wireless access point or router that supports Wi-Fi Protected Setup, follow these steps:

1. Open Network And Sharing Center. (Click the Network icon in the notification area, and then click Open Network And Sharing Center.) Click Set Up A New Connection Or Network.

2. In the Set Up A Connection Or Network wizard, select Set Up A New Network and click Next. Wait for the wizard to find the unconfigured router or access point. When it appears, as shown here, select it and click Next.

TROUBLESHOOTING

The router doesn't appear in the Set Up A Network wizard

If, after waiting for a minute or two, the router you want to set up does not appear in the wizard, either it is already configured or it does not support Wi-Fi Protected Setup.

You can reset a configured router by following the manufacturer's instructions (in many cases, you use a paper clip to press a recessed reset button). Be aware that doing so removes all configuration data from the router. If it's already configured, you might be better off skipping this procedure altogether and connecting your devices to the router, as explained in the next section, "Connecting to a Wireless Network" on page 702.

For routers that do not support WPS, check the instructions that came with the router for information about configuring wireless settings.

INSIDE OUT   Bypass Network And Sharing Center

With a computer that has a Wi-Fi adapter, you can go directly to the Set Up A Network wizard without going through Network And Sharing Center. If Windows detects a wireless network and you're not currently connected to one, the Network icon in the notification area shows an orange glow. Click the icon, and you'll see a connection for your new router—usually with the name of the router's manufacturer. Click the connection, click the Connect button, and Windows displays the message shown here.

Click OK, and then follow the procedure beginning with step 3.

3. Enter the eight-digit PIN (sometimes identified as "WPS PIN") on the router's label, and then click Next.

4. Enter a name for your wireless network. This name, also known as the SSID (for service set identifier), can contain only letters, numbers, and underscores. Windows suggests using the name of your computer with "_Network" appended; because it's the name by which all devices on a WLAN identify the network, you might want to come up with something more meaningful.

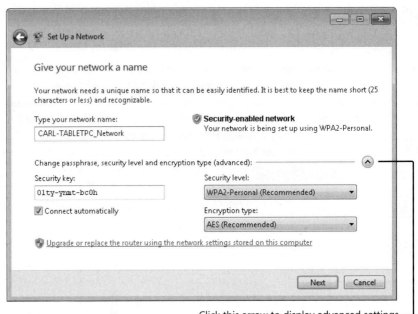

Click this arrow to display advanced settings

INSIDE OUT Use your existing wireless settings

If the router you're setting up replaces an existing router, you can apply wireless networking settings from your old router to your new one. By doing this, you won't need
to reconfigure any other wireless devices on your network because their existing configuration will work with the new router. (However, be aware that your old—and possibly unsecure—security method remains intact.) To use your existing settings, click the
Upgrade Or Replace The Router Using The Network Settings Stored On This Computer
link, which is near the bottom of the dialog box shown above.

5. Click the arrow to display advanced settings. Then select the best security method
   supported by all your wireless devices—WPA2-Personal (best), WPA-Personal, WEP, or
   No Security.

6. Enter a passphrase, which Windows uses to generate a security key. Windows
   suggests a security key, but you can replace it with one of your own choosing. (You
   might prefer to use a memorable phrase instead of random characters. If you do,
   choose a phrase that's not easily guessed, make it long, and consider incorporating
   letter substitution or misspellings to thwart attackers. Because you seldom have to

type the passphrase—it's ordinarily needed only during setup, and even then it's usually transferred automatically from a USB flash drive [UFD] or, at worst, by cut and paste—using a memorable phrase for WPA is less appealing than it is for, say, a login password.) A passphrase for WPA or WPA2 can be up to 63 characters long and can contain letters (case-sensitive), numbers, and spaces (no spaces at the beginning or end, however). A WEP security key must be exactly 26 hexadecimal characters (numbers 0–9 and letters A–F) or 10 letters (case-sensitive), numbers, and symbols. Click Next, and Windows transmits the configuration information to the router or access point.

7. You can click Close to complete the wizard. But before you do, we recommend that you click the Copy The Network Profile To A USB Drive link, plug a USB flash drive into your computer, select it from the list, and click Next. You don't need to use a UFD dedicated to the purpose; all the files (Autorun.inf and Setupsnk.exe in the root folder, plus a handful of files in the Smrtntky folder) take only a few kilobytes of space and don't interfere with other files on the UFD.

    You can use the UFD to quickly set up other wireless devices—including game consoles, printers, and computers running Windows XP, Windows Vista, or Windows 7— so they can connect to your wireless network. It also comes in handy when a visiting friend wants access to your wireless network to use its Internet connection, or when you upgrade the firmware in your router and it loses all its settings.

INSIDE OUT   Print configuration details

The final page of the Set Up A Network wizard offers an opportunity to print configuration details. The document includes the network name (SSID) for your wireless network and the passphrase or security key that you created along with other details, so it's handy to have for future reference.

If you click Close before you print the document, you have another option: open the \Smrtntky\Wsetting.txt file on the UFD. This plain-text document also includes other details of your WLAN configuration.

Many routers that don't support WPS have comparable, proprietary systems—usually provided on a setup CD—for configuring the router's SSID, encryption, and other settings. Check the instructions that came with your router for more information.

INSIDE OUT Beef up security at the access point

If your data is sensitive and your network is in an apartment building or an office complex where you can reasonably expect other people to wander into range with wireless adapters, you should take extra security precautions in addition to enabling WPA. Consider any or all of the following measures to protect your wireless access point from intruders:

- Change the network name (SSID) of your access point to one that doesn't match the hardware defaults and doesn't give away any information about you or your business.

- Disable remote administration of the access point; if you need to change settings, you can do so directly, using a wired connection.

- If you decide to allow remote administration of the access point, set a strong password.

- Upgrade the firmware of your wireless hardware (access point and adapter) to the most recent versions, which might incorporate security fixes.

- Consider using virtual private networks for wireless connections.

On larger networks with one or more domain servers available, you can set up a Remote Authentication Dial-In User Service (RADIUS) server to allow the most secure option of all, 802.1x authentication. In addition, consider enabling Internet Protocol security (IPsec).

Connecting to a Wireless Network

In this section, we assume that you have already connected a wireless access point to your network and set it up using the instructions in the previous section or the instructions provided by the manufacturer. Here we explain how to connect a computer that has a wireless network adapter to your wireless network.

Whenever your computer's wireless network adapter is installed and turned on, Windows scans for available wireless access points. If it finds at least one (and you're not already connected to a wireless network), the Network icon in the notification area glows orange to let you know that connections are available.

Network

Connecting to a Network by Using the WPS Button

An optional component of the Wi-Fi Protected Setup standard is a push button setup method. When present, this method provides the simplest way to connect a computer running Windows 7 to a wireless network.

To make a network connection, click the Network icon in the notification area. Alternatively, in Network And Sharing Center, click Connect To A Network. Doing so opens a panel that shows all currently available network connections, as shown in Figure 19-4. This panel, sometimes called View Available Networks (VAN), shows wireless networks and, if your computer has appropriate adapters, available mobile broadband (such as 3G), virtual private network (VPN), and dial-up networks.

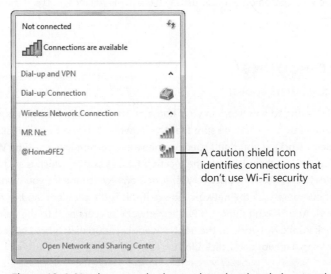

Figure 19-4 Nearby networks that are broadcasting their network names (SSIDs) are visible here. Hover the mouse pointer over a name to show details of the connection's signal strength, speed, and security.

Click the network you want to join, and then click the Connect button that appears. If you haven't connected to that particular network before, you'll see a dialog box similar to the one shown in Figure 19-5. You can enter the security key that was created when configuring the router. (See step 6 in the preceding section, "Configuring a Router or Wireless Access Point.") But if your router has a WPS button, press it; the router broadcasts some configuration information and in a few moments you have a secure, encrypted connection to the network with no additional typing or clicking required.

To confirm that your computer is part of the network, open the Network folder in Windows Explorer, and you should be able to see other computers and devices on your network.

Figure 19-5 The WPS button on a router usually has a Wi-Fi Alliance logo similar to that shown in the dialog box.

TROUBLESHOOTING

No other computers appear

If you're connecting to a network in your home or office (as opposed to a public hot-spot, such as an Internet café), be sure that the network is defined as a private network (either home or work). If you don't specify a network location the first time Windows detects a network, by default it sets the location type as public, which is safer. However, on a public network, network discovery is turned off—which means you won't be able to see other computers on the network. To see if this is the problem (and to resolve it), open Network And Sharing Center. If Public Network appears next to the name of your network, click Public Network. In the Set Network Location dialog box, select Home Network or Work Network and click Close.

Using a USB Flash Drive

If you created a USB flash drive with configuration settings for your wireless network, you can use it to connect a computer running Windows 7, Windows Vista, or Windows XP to the network. Plug the UFD into the computer that you want to add to the wireless network. When the AutoPlay dialog box appears, click Connect To A Wireless Network. Click OK a couple of times, and you're done. (If Connect To A Wireless Network does not appear in the AutoPlay dialog box, click Open Folder To View Files—or, if the AutoPlay dialog box doesn't appear at all, open Windows Explorer and browse to the USB flash drive—and double-click SetupSNK, a program in the UFD's root folder.)

Chapter 19

INSIDE OUT   Create a wireless connection UFD

If you didn't create a UFD with wireless network configuration information when you set up the wireless access point or router (or you lost it), it's easy (but not obvious how) to create one. On any computer already connected wirelessly, open Network And Sharing Center. Under Connect Or Disconnect, click Wireless Network Connection (shown here). In the dialog box that appears, click Wireless Properties, and then click Copy This Network Profile To A USB Flash Drive.

You can also create a connection UFD for a wireless network to which you're not currently connected. In Network And Sharing Center, click Manage Wireless Networks. Double-click the name of the network for which you want to create a UFD, and then click Copy This Network Profile To A USB Flash Drive.

Note

These instructions describe the process in Windows 7 specifically, although the process is nearly identical on computers running Windows Vista or Windows XP. For computers running other operating systems, the process of configuring a wireless network connection varies; see the operating system documentation or the documentation for the wireless network adapter for more information.

Connecting to a Network Without WPS or a USB Flash Drive

Using a router's WPS button or having configuration settings on a UFD (as described in the previous sections) makes it dead simple to add a computer to a wireless network. However, these options aren't always available. This might be the case if you're visiting someone else's WLAN, if you didn't create a UFD when you configured your wireless network, or if the UFD is simply not available.

Click the notification area's Network icon, click a network, and click Connect to display a dialog box like the one shown earlier in Figure 19-5. Enter the security key that was created when configuring the router to join the network.

INSIDE OUT   View the security key

If you've forgotten the security key, you can find it on a computer that's already connected to the wireless network. On that computer, click the Network icon in the notification area, right-click the network name, and choose Properties. On the Security tab, select Show Characters to display the network security key.

Connecting to a Hidden Network

Some wireless networks are set up so that they don't broadcast their SSID. (Configuring a router to not advertise its name has been incorrectly promoted by some as a security measure. Although it does make the network invisible to casual snoops, lack of a broadcast SSID is no deterrent to a knowledgeable attacker. Furthermore, attackers can learn the SSID even when they're not near your wireless access point because it's periodically broadcast from your computer, wherever it happens to be.) Connecting to such hidden networks is a bit more challenging because its name doesn't appear in View Available Networks (shown earlier in Figure 19-4). Instead, it's shown in the list as Other Network. Click that item to connect, just as you would for any other wireless network, and Windows asks you to provide the SSID.

You can also set up your computer so that it connects to a particular nonbroadcasting wireless network whenever you're in range, as follows:

1. Open Network And Sharing Center, and click Set Up A New Connection Or Network.

2. In the Set Up A Connection Or Network wizard, select Manually Connect To A Wireless Network and click Next.

3. Specify the network name (SSID), the type of security used by the network, the encryption type if the network uses WPA or WPA2 security, and the security key or passphrase. Select Connect Even If The Network Is Not Broadcasting. (What is the privacy risk mentioned in the dialog box? When this option is turned on, your computer sends out probe requests to locate the wireless network; an attacker can detect these probe requests and use them to determine the network's SSID. Your computer continues to send these requests even when you're away from your network's access point.) Click Next.

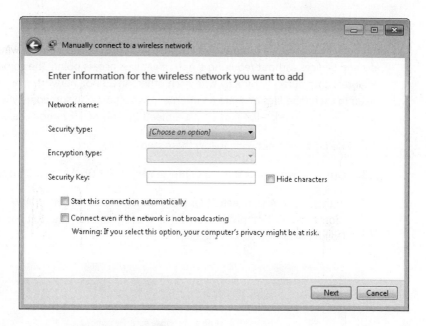

Chapter 19

4. Click Next, and then click Close.

Setting Up Per-User Wireless Network Connections

By default, when you set up a wireless connection on your computer, it's available to all users of your computer. You can optionally make a connection available only to the user who's currently logged on. To make that option available, you must make a setting before you set up the wireless network connection, as follows:

1. In Network And Sharing Center, click Manage Wireless Networks.

2. On the toolbar of the Manage Wireless Networks window, click Profile Types.

3. In the Wireless Network Profile Type dialog box, select Use All-User And Per-User Profiles.

Thereafter, when you set up a new wireless network, Windows asks whether you want the network to be available to all users or only to yourself. You can't apply this setting to an existing network; to do that, you must delete the network (in Manage Wireless Networks, select the network and click Remove) and then re-create it (in Manage Wireless Networks, click Add).

Setting Up an Ad Hoc Network

An *ad hoc network* is a temporary network that connects two or more wireless computers and devices without requiring a hub or wireless access point. The computers' network adapters communicate directly with each other. An ad hoc network is handy when you need to exchange files or share an Internet connection with someone who isn't normally part of your network—for example, in a meeting. Another common use: multiplayer games.

To set up an ad hoc network, follow these steps:

1. Open Network And Sharing Center, and click Set Up A New Connection Or Network.

2. In the Set Up A Connection Or Network wizard, select Set Up A Wireless Ad Hoc (Computer-To-Computer) Network and click Next. On the next page, click Next. Doing this brings you to the page shown here:

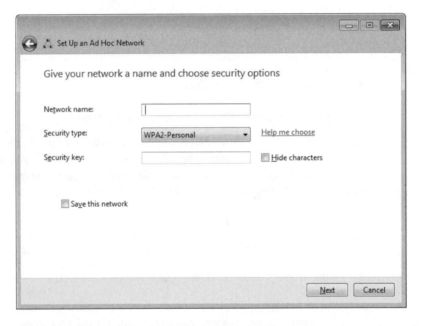

3. Specify a network name. The name can be up to 32 characters long; can contain letters, numbers, and underscores; and is case-sensitive.

4. Specify a security type. Ad hoc networks support WEP and WPA2-Personal encryption; the only other option is an open, unsecured network. An open network is the easiest for others to join—whether that's an advantage or disadvantage depends on

whether potential interlopers might be nearby and whether you expect to transmit sensitive information.

5. If you choose to encrypt the ad hoc network, enter a security key or passphrase in one of these forms:

   - For WPA encryption, up to 63 characters (letters, numbers, and spaces)

   - For WEP encryption, 5 or 10 case-sensitive characters (letters, numbers, and punctuation) *or* a 13-digit or 26-digit hexadecimal number (numbers and letters A–F)

6. If you plan to use the ad hoc network again, select Save This Network. If you do not, Windows automatically deletes the network after the user who set up the network or all other users on the network disconnect.

7. Click Next. If your computer is connected directly to the Internet (through a network adapter other than the wireless adapter you're using for the ad hoc network) and you want to share the Internet connection, click Turn On Internet Connection Sharing.

8. Click Close.

The network is now set up and ready to use. Others can join the network just as they join any other wireless network: Click the network icon in the taskbar's notification area, select the ad hoc network, and click Connect. If the ad hoc network is secured with WEP or WPA encryption, another dialog box asks for the security key; enter it and click Connect.

To share files, file sharing must be enabled. For more information, see Chapter 20, "Sharing and Managing Network Resources."

Connecting Wireless Devices to Your Network

A simple, standard method for connecting other devices with wireless capabilities—such as printers, cameras, PDAs, media players, and mobile phones—hasn't yet been widely adopted. At the time of this book's printing, Wi-Fi Protected Setup is just beginning to make inroads with device manufacturers. Until the devices are made to support connection by using the router's WPS button or entering the router's PIN, you'll need to enter the security key or use other methods, as described in the instructions that came with the device.

Using HomeGroup to Connect Your Computers at Home

HomeGroup is a new feature of Windows 7 that makes it easy to share resources among your computers at home. These "resources" can include printers as well as files from your documents, pictures, music, and video libraries. Gone are the days when, to print a document, you copied it to a USB flash drive and then carried it to the computer to which your printer is attached. And you no longer need to remember on which computer you stored a batch of pictures; with HomeGroup you can search a particular library or machine, or you can search across all computers in a homegroup. Files on other computers are as easily accessible as if they were on your own computer.

(Oh, and if you're confused by the capitalization of the term, you're not alone. According to Microsoft, the correct spelling is HomeGroup when describing the feature and the associated Control Panel option where you configure it; the collection of Windows 7 computers joined together this way is called a *homegroup*, with no capitalization. In Windows Explorer, in dialog boxes and menus, and in this book, the term might be capitalized to indicate that it is part of the name of an option.)

> **Note**
>
> The HomeGroup feature works only with computers running Windows 7. To share files with computers running earlier versions of Windows, or for users of those computers to access files on your Windows 7 computer, you must use network sharing methods compatible with those older versions. For details, see "Sharing Resources with Older Windows Versions" on page 732.

In this chapter, we describe the basics of setting up a homegroup. For details about using and customizing HomeGroup, see "Sharing Files, Digital Media, and Printers in a Homegroup" on page 720.

Creating a Homegroup

Windows 7 offers to create a homegroup when you install Windows and when you connect to a network that you identify as a home network. (That is, you select Home Network as the network location.) If you decided to forego those opportunities, you can set up Home-Group at any later time; in the Start menu or Control Panel search box, type **homegroup** and click HomeGroup.

If no homegroup exists on your network, a dialog box opens to inform you of that fact. Click Create A Homegroup to open the wizard shown in Figure 19-6.

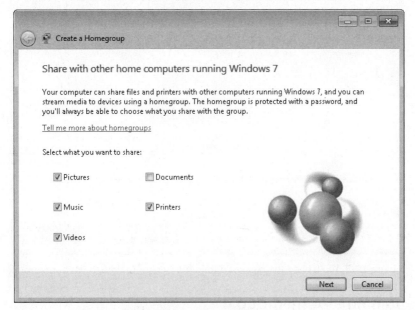

Figure 19-6 You can safely leave the default selections in place; you can change them at any time.

Click Next, and the wizard generates a password for your homegroup, as shown in Figure 19-7. (Behind the scenes, the wizard also sets up the requisite user accounts and security groups, services, firewall rules, and shares.) Click Finish, and you're done.

> **Note**
>
> A computer running Windows 7 Starter edition cannot create a homegroup. It can, however, join a homegroup created by a computer running Windows Home Premium or above.

Figure 19-7 You'll need the password to join other computers to the homegroup.

Joining a Homegroup

After a homegroup has been created, other computers on the network can join it by using a similarly brief process. When you connect your computer to the home network, the wizard opens automatically, displaying a screen similar to the one shown earlier in Figure 19-6. (The text at the top is slightly different, informing you that a homegroup already exists.) If you missed that chance to join the homegroup, open HomeGroup in Control Panel and click Join Now to reach this same wizard screen.

Click Next, and the wizard asks you to enter the homegroup password. (If you don't have the password, return to a computer that has already joined the homegroup. On that computer, open HomeGroup and click View Or Print The Homegroup Password. Alternatively, on that computer, open Windows Explorer, right-click Homegroup, and choose View The HomeGroup Password.)

Chapter 19

Join a Homegroup

Type the homegroup password

A password helps prevent unauthorized access to homegroup files and printers. You can get the password from Carl on CARL-PC or another member of the homegroup.

Where can I find the homegroup password?

Type the password:

Enter the password and click Next, and you're ready to view resources from other computers in the homegroup. To do that, open Windows Explorer. In the left pane, expand Homegroup to see a subfolder for each user account on each computer in the homegroup, as shown in Figure 19-8.

Figure 19-8 Joining a homegroup enables access to libraries on other computers.

By default, you have read access to the personal folders in each library (for example, My Pictures) and read/write access to the public folders in each library (for example, Public Pictures.) In the next chapter, we explain how to customize the settings so that each user has the necessary access privileges, but no more. In addition, we take a peek under the hood to get a better idea of how HomeGroup works.

Connecting to Windows Home Server

Although the built-in networking features of Windows 7, particularly HomeGroup, are adequate for sharing files and printers on a small home network, you might want to consider using a server-based network. A good option is Windows Home Server, which runs on a dedicated server computer. Windows Home Server 2011, which uses the industrial-strength Windows Server 2008 R2 at its core, offers several advantages over a simple workgroup network, including:

- **Automatic daily backups of all networked computers** Without any user configuration or intervention, each computer is backed up to a drive on the server—that is, a drive that's physically separate from the computer being backed up. The backups are full-image backups that allow restoration of files from any time in the preceding days and weeks. You can also use these backups to fully restore a computer to working condition after replacing a failed hard drive or other component. Although easy access to previous versions and bare-metal restore capability are features of the Windows Backup program in Windows 7, you must configure the program on each computer. And Windows Home Server supports Apple Mac computers as well as computers running earlier versions of Windows, which have inferior backup solutions.

  For details about Windows Backup, see "Using the Windows Backup Program" on page 436. For more information about backup in Windows Home Server, see "Implementing a Backup Strategy in a Server-Based Environment" on page 453.

- **Remote access** You can configure Windows Home Server to allow secure access over the Internet to all files on each computer. In addition, Windows Home Server can act as a web server to share photos and videos over the Internet.

- **Media streaming** Music, video, and photos stored on Windows Home Server can be streamed to media devices throughout the home and over the Internet.

  For details about media streaming, see "Sharing Digital Media over a Network" on page 512.

- **Document storage and management** Documents stored on the server can easily be shared and accessed throughout the home and remotely.

- **Centralized computer management**   Through the use of the Dashboard and Launchpad programs available on each computer, you can control all aspects of Windows Home Server.

For more information about Windows Home Server, visit *w7io.com/21901*.

The process of setting up a Windows Home Server network is much like that of setting up any other, as discussed earlier in this chapter. The hardware setup is the same, and the server can be located anywhere on the network using standard connections, just like any other computer.

> **Note**
>
> In this book, we don't describe setup and configuration of the server itself; our focus is on the workstations running Windows 7. You can buy a server with Windows Home Server preinstalled, or you can purchase the server software separately and install it on a server device. For information about installing and configuring Windows Home Server 2011, go to *w7io.com/21902*.

The main difference is that you must perform a one-time installation of the Windows Home Server Connector software on each computer on the network.

To set up the connector for Windows Home Server 2011, on each networked computer use your web browser to go to *http://server/connect*, where *server* is the server name of the Windows Home Server device. This opens a web page from which you can download the software for connecting a Windows computer. Download and run the software, affirm User Access Control when prompted, and follow the on-screen instructions to complete the setup. (You'll need to know the administrative password for your Windows Home Server.) Upon completion, your computer is part of the Windows Home Server network.

> **Note**
>
> If you're using Windows Home Server V1 (the original version, which is commonly known simply as Windows Home Server), you'll need the software CD that came with Windows Home Server. If you can't locate the CD, use Windows Explorer on each computer to browse to the Software folder on the home server, and run the Setup program you find there.

You'll also want to set up an account for each user. Doing so controls that user's access to shared folders on the Windows Home Server and to remote access capabilities. To add a user account, open the Windows Home Server 2011 Dashboard. You can do so at the Windows Home Server device or from any computer that has the Windows Home Server Connector software installed. (The ability to manage the server from another computer is not only a convenience, but in many cases a necessity; oftentimes Windows Home Server devices do not have a monitor, keyboard, or mouse attached.) On the Home tab of the Dashboard, shown in Figure 19-9, click Common Tasks, and then click Add A User Account.

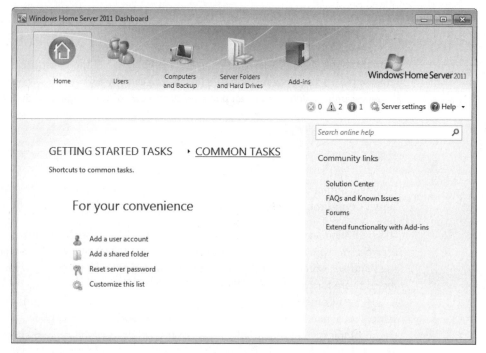

Figure 19-9 The Dashboard in Windows Home Server 2011 is the place for all server management tasks.

In the wizard that appears, you'll be asked for the user's name and password; you should use the same user name and password set up for the user on his or her computer.

The wizard then asks you to specify access permissions for each shared library on the server. Your options are Read/Write, Read Only (the default), and No Access.

In the final step, the wizard asks you to configure remote web access capabilities for the user, as shown next. These options control access to server resources and to computers on your network only via the Internet. Note, too, that you must configure remote web access for Windows Home Server. For more information, see "Configuring Your Server and Computers" on page 783.

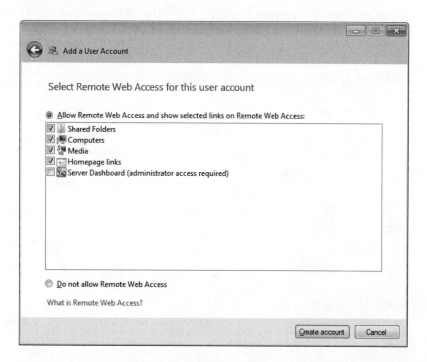

Windows Home Server 2011 includes support for HomeGroup, a Windows 7 feature described earlier in this chapter. Using HomeGroup, you can provide access to shared folders without creating a user account for each user on the network.

> ## Note
>
> When a person logs on to a computer that's part of the homegroup *and* that person also has a user account on Windows Home Server, the most restrictive permission set for each folder applies. For example, if you set the Pictures library to Read Only in the HomeGroup settings and you set it to Read/Write for a particular user account, that person gets Read Only access when logged on to a computer in the homegroup. However, if the same person logs on to a computer that is not joined to the homegroup, he or she has Read/Write access to the Pictures library. Because of the confusion this can create, we recommend that you choose only one method for sharing—per user or HomeGroup. The first option provides greater customization (you can easily set different permissions for each user), whereas the latter method offers simplicity.

To join the Windows Home Server device to the homegroup, in the Dashboard click Server Settings and then click HomeGroup. If you haven't yet set up a homegroup on your network, you can do so here, using a process similar to that described in "Creating a Homegroup" on page 710. On networks with an existing homegroup, the Server Settings dialog box provides a path to join the homegroup, as shown here. Click Join Now, and then enter the homegroup password.

After joining the server to the homegroup, you can find shared files stored on the server under the Homegroup heading in Windows Explorer.

Sharing and Managing Network Resources

B y sharing your computer's resources—such as its folders, printers, and media library—you let other people who use your computer and other people on your network use these resources. With Windows 7, using shared resources and sharing your own resources with other users—either locally or across the network—is simple and straightforward. Browsing a network folder is just like browsing a folder on your own hard disk. Sending a document to a network printer is just like printing at your own computer. Playing music and viewing photos from a shared media library lets you benefit from the hours somebody else spent ripping CDs and tagging photos.

For home users, Windows 7 introduces an entirely new sharing paradigm with the Home-Group feature, which provides easy sharing of libraries (and other folders and files that you specify) in Windows Explorer, Windows Media Player, and Windows Media Center.

HomeGroup is not the right solution in all cases, however. Windows 7 also puts a new face on the sophisticated security settings for resource sharing that have been an integral—and often confusing—part of earlier versions of Windows. This face, in the form of the Sharing wizard, makes it easy to implement security appropriate for computers shared by multiple users and for many small network workgroups. With the Sharing wizard, settings for local sharing (via NTFS permissions) and network sharing can be set in one place—and with greater flexibility and improved security compared with the Windows XP solution, Simple File Sharing.

What's in Your Edition?

Sharing with other users of your computer and other users on your network works identically in all editions of Windows 7, with one minor exception: users of Starter edition can join a homegroup but cannot create one. One feature mentioned in this chapter, the Print Management console, is not available in Starter and Home Premium, but all its functionality is available in other tools.

> **Note**
>
> In this chapter, we describe resource sharing as it applies in a workgroup environment. We do not cover sharing in a domain-based environment.

Sharing Files, Digital Media, and Printers in a Homegroup

HomeGroup is a networking feature, new in Windows 7, that is designed to provide easy sharing in a home environment without needing technical expertise. With HomeGroup, Microsoft has striven to strike a balance between security and convenience—a balance that has been somewhat elusive through the evolution of Windows. Although Simple File Sharing in Windows XP is convenient and relatively easy to set up, it's inflexible and its security is weak. Sharing in Windows Vista is considerably more secure and more flexible, but it's not easy to configure properly, and it requires sacrifices that some home users are reluctant to make, such as requiring the use of a logon password for all accounts.

Microsoft usability researchers found that many home users choose not to use logon passwords. Because everyone in the home is fully trusted and because the computer is in a physically secure location (a locked home) that precludes computer use by unknown or untrusted users, these users find the logon password to be nothing more than an unnecessary obstacle to computer use. This can be a real annoyance to family users who simply want to share media throughout the house, share a printer, and share documents. For this reason, HomeGroup is designed to work equally well with computers and users that do not use logon passwords and those that do. Even without password protection, it keeps your files safe from users outside the homegroup. (It does so through the use of a special password-protected user account—HomeGroupUser$—and a HomeUsers security group that have network access privileges. For more information about the inner workings of HomeGroup, see "HomeGroup: How It Works" on page 731.)

HomeGroup offers the following benefits:

- Easy sharing of libraries and other files throughout the homegroup in Windows Explorer

- Easy access to shared media libraries in Windows Media Player and Windows Media Center

- Ability to stream media to devices (other computers, media extenders and players, digital picture frames, and so on) by using Play To

- Easy sharing of USB-connected printers among all homegroup members

The requirements to implement and use HomeGroup are few:

- At least one computer running Windows 7 Home Premium or above to create the homegroup

- All computers in the homegroup running Windows 7

- The network location for all computers set to Home Network

> **Note**
>
> HomeGroup can be useful even in networks that include computers running a mix of operating systems: Windows 7, earlier versions of Windows, Mac OS X, and Linux. Although only the Windows 7 computers can use HomeGroup features, HomeGroup coexists nicely with the traditional sharing methods that you'll need to use to share with users of other operating systems. (For details about those methods, see "Sharing Resources with Older Windows Versions" on page 732.)
>
> If you have only a single computer with Windows 7 but you also have networked media devices (for example, an Xbox 360 or a digital picture frame), HomeGroup can also be useful. On that computer, after you create a homegroup, you can discover these devices and play media to them more easily than you can with earlier Windows versions.

For users, setting up HomeGroup is a straightforward process. On one computer—it doesn't matter which one because HomeGroup is a true peer-to-peer networking system without a designated server/controller—you create a homegroup. Then, on other computers, you join the homegroup.

For details about setting up HomeGroup, see "Creating a Homegroup" on page 710 and "Joining a Homegroup" on page 712.

Deciding What to Share—And What Not to Share

When you first create or join a homegroup, Windows asks which libraries you want to share, as shown in Figure 20-1. Not surprisingly, the libraries shown here correspond to the libraries you see in Windows Explorer. (For more information about libraries, see "Working with Libraries" on page 343.)

> **Note**
>
> If your computer is joined to a domain, these sharing options are not available when you join a homegroup. For details, see "Using HomeGroup with a Domain-Based Computer" on page 730.

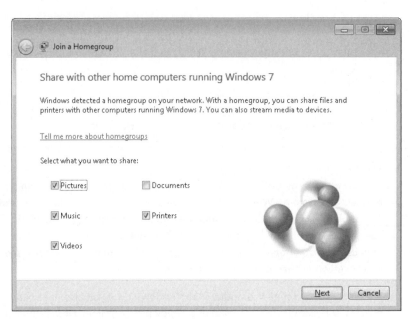

Figure 20-1 The sharing options refer to libraries, not to content types.

You can change your library selections at any time by visiting HomeGroup, which you can open by typing **homegroup** in the Start menu search box or Control Panel, or by right-clicking Homegroup in Windows Explorer and choosing Change HomeGroup Settings. All those routes lead to HomeGroup, as shown in Figure 20-2.

Fortunately, you're not limited to sharing only the content of the Documents, Music, Pictures, or Videos libraries. If you would like to share other folders or files with users of other computers in your homegroup, you can use any of these methods:

- Add the folder (or folders) to an existing library. (You can do that by opening the library and clicking the Locations link, or by right-clicking the item you want to add and choosing Include In Library.) Folders and files that you add to a shared library are automatically shared, with no additional steps required.

- Create a new, custom library. (In Windows Explorer, right-click Libraries and choose New, Library, or right-click the folder and choose Include In Library, Create New Library.) Then share the library as explained next.

- Share a folder that's not in a library.

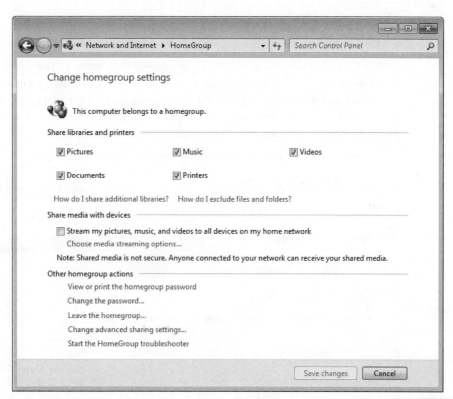

Figure 20-2 With HomeGroup in Control Panel, you specify whether to share each of the standard libraries: Documents, Music, Pictures, and Videos.

To share a single folder and its contents, open Windows Explorer and select the folder (or items) you want to share. On the toolbar (shown next) or on the right-click menu, click Share With and then choose Homegroup (Read) or Homegroup (Read/Write). Which command you select, of course, determines whether a homegroup user on another computer can create, modify, and delete folders and files within the shared folder. Both options share the selected item with your entire homegroup.

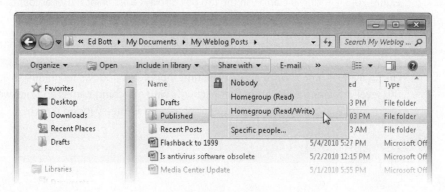

Chapter 20

> ## CAUTION !
>
> Don't share the root folder of a drive (for example, D:\). Although sharing the root folder has long been common practice, we recommend against doing so. Because of the way permissions are inherited, changing permissions on the root folder can cause a variety of access problems. A better solution is to create a subfolder of the root folder, put everything you want to share into it, and share the subfolder.

To share with only certain individuals, choose Share With, Specific People. Doing so opens the File Sharing dialog box shown in Figure 20-3.

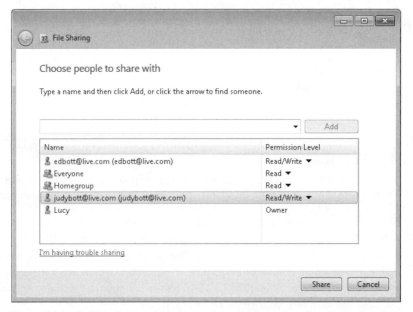

Figure 20-3 Clicking the arrow in the top box displays a list of local user accounts as well as homegroup users who have linked their Windows Live IDs to user accounts.

Using this feature with homegroups allows you to set per-user permissions that override homegroup permissions. So, if you allow homegroup users Read access, you can allow specific individuals Read/Write access. The time-honored Windows technique to implement this level of sharing is to set up user accounts with matching names and passwords on different PCs. That can lead to management hassles and messy logon screens.

Figure 20-3 shows off a useful, little-known feature in Windows 7 that lets you bypass those hassles by linking a Windows Live ID to your local user account. When you choose the Specific People option, any such linked IDs on any PC in the homegroup are available from the drop-down list, with no requirement for matching local user accounts. For more details on linking Windows Live IDs and user accounts, see "Link a Windows Live ID to your user account" on page 294.

TROUBLESHOOTING

When you try to share a file, it's unavailable on other network PCs

A quirk in the user interface for file sharing can cause confusion if you don't understand what's really happening. The Share With menu is available for files as well as folders. If you try to share a file with the homegroup or with specific people, Windows accepts the settings and shows the file as shared in Windows Explorer. But it's unavailable on other PCs.

The reason? To access a share over the network, you need to supply a share name, which by definition can apply only to a folder, a library, or a volume. You can indeed assign permissions to individual files, but if the folder they reside in isn't shared (either directly or as part of a parent folder), those files are inaccessible over the network.

You also use the Share With command on the toolbar or the right-click menu to *prevent* sharing of a particular folder or file within a shared library or folder. Simply choose Share With, Nobody to stop sharing the selected items.

Similarly, you can override the default sharing settings for private folder profiles within a library—normally these are shared with read access—by selecting a folder or file within the shared library or folder and clicking Share With. (Public folders play by a different set of rules, as we explain in "Sharing Files with Public Folders" on page 737.)

Note

A *computer* joins a homegroup and, therefore, all users on that computer have access to the homegroup's shared resources. However, sharing options are maintained on a per-user basis; on a computer with more than one user account, each user decides which of his or her libraries to share. The first time a user goes to HomeGroup in Control Panel after the computer has been joined to a homegroup, a screen like the one shown here appears.

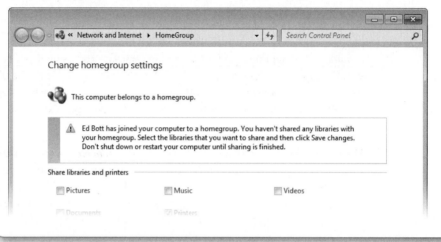

Browsing Shared Folders and Files

If your network profile is set to Home, you've probably noticed the Homegroup node in the navigation pane of Windows Explorer. Figure 20-4 shows an example.

You can use folders and files in the Homegroup node just as you use folders and files in your own libraries. Tasks you can perform include

- Preview and open files

- Play music, pictures, or video (in a folder filled with music files, look for the Play All button on the toolbar)

- Search through all files within a folder, a library, a user node, or the entire homegroup

- Add a shared folder to one of your local libraries

- Add, modify, and delete files (only in libraries or folders shared with read/write access)

Figure 20-4 Each subfolder under Homegroup represents the folders shared by a user. Note that the computer named Appalachian has two users who are sharing files: Carl and Jan.

When you add a file to a shared library on another computer (for example, by dragging a song file to a shared Music library), the file goes into the library's public folder (in our example, it would go to the %Public%\Music folder on the remote computer).

INSIDE OUT   Add Homegroup to the Start menu

You can add a link to the Homegroup folder to the right side of the Start menu, making it easy to browse homegroup resources. To add the link, right-click the Start button and choose Properties. On the Start Menu tab, click Customize. In the Customize Start Menu dialog box, select Homegroup.

You can also browse shared media libraries using Windows Media Player. Shared libraries appear in the navigation pane under Other Libraries. For more information about Windows Media Player, see "Sharing Media Libraries" on page 514.

If you use Windows Media Center, you'll discover that shared media files appear there too. In Media Center, choose the Shared option above a gallery (music, pictures, videos, or recorded TV) to see a list of shared libraries, as shown here. For more information about Windows Media Center, see Chapter 15, "Using Windows Media Center."

INSIDE OUT   Use HomeGroup in multiple homes

With HomeGroup in Windows 7, you cannot join multiple homegroups; you must leave one homegroup before you can join another. Those who frequently visit another home, such as a vacation home or the home of a trusted friend, might find this limitation to be disappointing. However, there is a way to have an "extended homegroup" that spans multiple physical locations. Suppose you have two homes, each with a desktop computer, and a laptop computer that travels between the homes. In the first home, have the desktop and the laptop join a homegroup. Then take the laptop to the second home, start it up and connect it to the network, and then join the second desktop to the laptop's homegroup. Additional computers in each home can also join the homegroup. If the traveling laptop stores all your music, for example, you'll be able to play it in whichever home the laptop currently resides (or you can use the laptop to "play to" other computers and devices). The laptop will also have seamless access to shared resources in the home, including libraries and printers.

Streaming Media in a Homegroup

Media streaming is the process of delivering media (pictures, music, video, and recorded TV) over a network in a continuous flow of data. With streaming, you can play to network devices such as digital media receivers and digital picture frames, as well as to computers. HomeGroup enables and simplifies the streaming process. To enable streaming of media on your computer to other devices, in HomeGroup (shown earlier in Figure 20-2), select Stream My Pictures, Music, And Videos To All Devices On My Home Network.

For more information about configuring streaming options and playing to other devices, see "Sharing Digital Media over a Network" on page 512.

Sharing a Printer

In the bad old days of home networking, many users found that the easiest way to print a document was to send it via e-mail or carry it on a USB flash drive to the computer with an attached printer. HomeGroup greatly simplifies the process. If a homegroup member computer has a printer connected to one of its USB ports, and if the computer's user has chosen to share its printers (by selecting the Printers check box in HomeGroup, shown in Figure 20-2), all homegroup users have access to that printer.

If the printer has been certified by the Windows Logo Program, it shows up automatically in the Devices And Printers folder of all homegroup users. HomeGroup obtains the driver files from the host computer whenever possible or downloads them from the Internet if necessary (for example, if the host computer runs 32-bit Windows and your computer has 64-bit Windows installed), and then installs the driver without requiring any user intervention. (Note that it might take a few minutes after joining or connecting to a homegroup for HomeGroup to discover the shared printer and install the driver.)

When you share a printer that is not Windows Logo–certified, HomeGroup displays a pop-up message to notify other homegroup members that a printer is available. If you miss the pop-up, you can view the notification in HomeGroup, as shown here. Click Install Printer to set it up on your computer. (The reason for this extra step is security: HomeGroup won't install an unsigned third-party driver without your consent.)

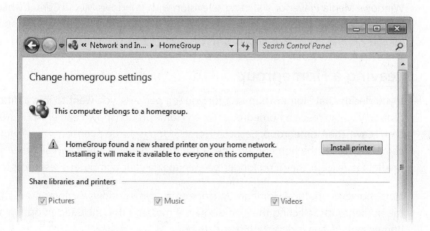

If the shared printer is connected to a desktop computer (but not a laptop) that is in sleep mode, sending a print request to the printer uses Wake On LAN to awaken the computer so that it can perform the print job. After completing the print job, the computer returns to sleep.

Windows sets the most recently shared printer to be the default printer unless you have manually selected a default printer. Note that it's the default printer only for your home network, however. With a feature called Location Aware Printing, if you have a mobile domain-joined computer that travels between work and home, it retains its default printer on each network and automatically changes the default to the home printer when you connect to the home network.

Using HomeGroup with a Domain-Based Computer

A computer that is joined to an Active Directory domain (typically, a business network based on Windows Server) can join a homegroup, making it easy and productive to bring home a work computer and have access to home resources such as media, documents, and printers. It's also secure, due to differences in the way HomeGroup works on a domain-joined computer.

The principal difference is that a domain-joined computer can see and use all shared resources in the homegroup, but other homegroup members cannot see anything on the domain-joined computer. (This is done to protect your business documents and files from inadvertent access by others in your home.) When you create or join a homegroup using a domain member computer, the dialog box does not include any of the sharing options (Pictures, Music, Videos, and so on) that appear for other homegroup users.

Some corporate administrators might not relish the idea of you listening to music with Windows Media Player or watching television with Windows Media Center while you're working at home; those taskmasters can use Group Policy to prevent the computer from joining a homegroup. (For details, see "Disabling HomeGroup," following.)

Leaving a Homegroup

If you decide that HomeGroup isn't for you (or, perhaps, you want to join a different home-group), you can leave a homegroup. Open HomeGroup (shown earlier in Figure 20-2) and click Leave The Homegroup. Because HomeGroup is a true peer-to-peer network, when any computer leaves the homegroup, the homegroup remains intact and all other members are unaffected (except they'll no longer be able to see your computer's resources, of course).

Note, however, that the Homegroup icon remains in Windows Explorer even after you leave the homegroup. Selecting the icon displays a message that includes an option to join a homegroup (if one is detected) or create one.

Disabling HomeGroup

If you see no need for HomeGroup and are annoyed by the presence of the empty Homegroup node in the navigation pane of Windows Explorer, it's easy to banish the feature altogether. Simply change your network location to Work Network.

To do that, open Network And Sharing Center and, under View Your Active Networks, click Home Network. In the dialog box that appears, click Work Network. The next time you start Windows Explorer, the Homegroup icon is gone.

HomeGroup: How It Works

The simplicity of setting up and using HomeGroup belies its complexity. The basic sharing mechanism uses standard sharing protocols that have been part of Windows for many years. Here's the short version: HomeGroup grants share permissions and applies an access control entry (ACE) to each shared object, allowing access to a group called HomeUsers. A password-protected account (which is required for accessing shared objects over a network connection) named HomeGroupUser$ is a member of HomeUsers and acts as your proxy in accessing shared network resources. (In fact, even if your user account is password protected, HomeGroup still uses the HomeGroupUser$ account instead of your account to connect to a remote computer, unless you select the Use User Accounts And Passwords To Connect To Other Computers option in Advanced Sharing Settings. For more information about this setting, see "Configuring Your Network for Sharing" on page 734.)

CAUTION!

Do not change the password for the HomeGroupUser$ account; doing so is a recipe for disaster. (Note that the account password is not the same as the homegroup password.)

But there's much more going on with HomeGroup. Creating or joining a workgroup creates the HomeGroupUser$ account and the HomeUsers group, and adds all local accounts to the group. HomeGroup setup also configures Windows Firewall. (Specifically, it enables certain rules in the Core Networking, Network Discovery, and HomeGroup groups. And for computers that are not joined to a domain, it enables rules in the File And Printer Sharing, Windows Media Player, and Windows Media Player Network Sharing Service groups.) In addition, it configures the HomeGroup Provider and HomeGroup Listener services. (HomeGroup also relies on Function Discovery and several other networking services.)

An administrator can also disable HomeGroup by using Group Policy. Open Local Group Policy Editor (Gpedit.msc), and navigate to Computer Configuration\Administrative Templates\Windows Components\HomeGroup. Double-click the Prevent The Computer From Joining A Homegroup policy and select Enabled. After rebooting, the computer can't join a homegroup. Furthermore, the Homegroup node does not appear in Windows Explorer, even if the network location is Home Network.

Sharing Resources with Older Windows Versions

Convenient as it is, HomeGroup isn't appropriate for all networks. First, it's designed for use in a home, where you fully trust everybody. Hence, it has limited abilities for applying different access requirements to various objects and for various users. Second, HomeGroup works only on computers running Windows 7. Computers running earlier versions of Windows or other operating systems must use different methods for sharing and accessing network resources.

These methods are fully supported in Windows 7 and can be used alongside HomeGroup if you want to. The underlying system of share permissions and NTFS permissions for controlling access to objects remains in Windows 7.

Understanding Sharing and Security Models in Windows

Much like Windows Vista, Windows 7 offers two ways (aside from HomeGroup) to share file resources, whether locally or over the network:

- **Public folder sharing**   When you place files and folders in your Public folder or its subfolders, those files are available to anyone who has a user account on your computer. (The Public folder replaces the functionality of the Shared Documents folder in Windows XP.) Each person who logs on has access to his or her own profile folders (Documents, Music, and so on), and *everyone* who logs on (including members of the Guests group) has access to the Public folder.

   Settings in Advanced Sharing Settings (accessible from Network And Sharing Center), determine whether the contents of your Public folder are made available on your network and whether a user name and password is required for access. If you turn on password-protected sharing, only people who have a user account on your computer (or those who know the user name and password for an account on your computer) can access files in the Public folder. Without password-protected sharing, everyone on your network has access to your Public folder files if you enable network sharing of the Public folder.

- **"Any folder" sharing**   By choosing to share folders or files outside the Public folder, you can specify precisely which user accounts are able to access your shared data, and you can specify the types of privileges those accounts enjoy. You can grant different access privileges to different users. For example, you might enable some users to modify shared files and create new ones, enable other users to read files without changing them, and lock out still other users altogether.

You don't need to decide between sharing the Public folder and sharing specific folders because you can use them both simultaneously. You might find that a mix of sharing styles works best for you; each has its benefits:

- Sharing specific folders is best for files that you want to share with some users but not others—or if you want to grant different levels of access to different users.

- Public folder sharing provides a convenient, logical way to segregate your personal documents, pictures, music, and so on from those that you want to share with everyone who uses your computer or your network.

- Public folder sharing is the easiest to set up, although with the benefit of the Sharing wizard, sharing a specific folder certainly isn't complex.

What Happened to the Windows XP Sharing Models?

Windows veterans know that in a workgroup environment, Windows XP has two sharing models, dubbed *Simple File Sharing* and *classic sharing*.

Simple File Sharing is the default sharing model on all editions of Windows XP, except on computers that are joined to a domain. In fact, with Windows XP Home Edition, Simple File Sharing is the *only* way to share files over a network. As it turns out, Simple File Sharing is a little too simple, because it is notoriously inflexible and not very secure. With Simple File Sharing, you can share only folders, and you can't adjust permissions for files or subfolders in a shared location. Those shared folders are available to all network users; you can't specify different access permissions for different users. And your choice of permissions for a shared folder is limited: full control or read only.

On the other hand, classic sharing (which is largely unchanged from the sharing model used in Windows NT and Windows 2000) can be quite complex. Although classic sharing has tremendous flexibility, it also causes lots of confusion. This confusion often leads to configuration errors that end up with files being inaccessible to legitimate users or wide open to anybody who stumbles onto your computer. Further complicating matters is the poorly understood relationship between share permissions (which control network access to shared objects) and discretionary access control lists (DACLs) or NTFS permissions (which control all access to a secured object, from network and local users alike).

The same technologies that underlie Simple File Sharing and classic file sharing in Windows XP—namely, DACLs, share permissions, and user rights—also power sharing in Windows 7. Yet the implementation—primarily through HomeGroup, the Sharing wizard, and Network And Sharing Center—is radically different.

Configuring Your Network for Sharing

If you plan to share folders and files with other users on your network using options other than those available in the HomeGroup feature, you need to take a few preparatory steps. (If you plan to share only with others who use your computer by logging on locally, you can skip these steps.)

1. **Be sure that all computers use the same workgroup name**   If all computers on your network run Windows 7 or Windows Vista, this step isn't absolutely necessary, although it does improve network discovery performance. However, if you have a mixed network that includes some computers running Windows XP or other earlier versions of Windows, it's essential for enabling computers on the network to see each other. For details, see "Renaming Your Workgroup" on page 817.

2. **Be sure that your network's location is set to Home Network or Work Network**   This setting provides appropriate security for a network in a home or office. For details, see "Understanding Network Locations" on page 687.

3. **Be sure that Network Discovery is turned on**   This should happen automatically when you set the location to Home Network or Work Network, but you can confirm the setting—and change it if necessary—in Advanced Sharing Settings, which is shown in Figure 20-5. To open Advanced Sharing Settings, in Network And Sharing Center, click Change Advanced Sharing Settings. Alternatively, in the Start menu search box, type **sharing** and then click Manage Advanced Sharing Settings.

4. **Select your sharing options**   In Advanced Sharing Settings, select from these network options:

   - **File And Printer Sharing**   Turn on this option if you want to share specific files or folders, the Public folder, or printers; it must be turned on if you plan to share any files (other than media streaming) over your network.

     The mere act of turning on file and printer sharing does not expose any of your computer's files or printers to other network users; that occurs only after you make additional sharing settings.

   - **Public Folder Sharing**   If you want to share items in your Public folder with all network users (or, if you enable password-protected sharing, all users who have a user account and password on your computer), turn on Public folder sharing. If you do so, network users will have read/write access to Public folders. With Public folder sharing turned off, anyone who logs on to your computer locally has access to Public folders, but network users do not.

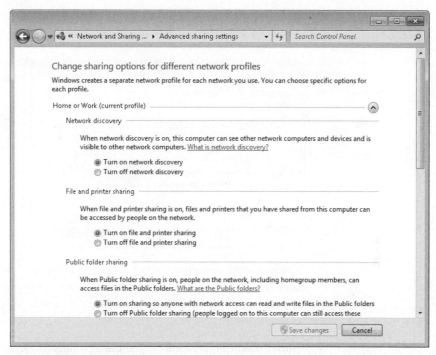

Figure 20-5 Be sure to set options in the Home Or Work profile, not the Public profile. Settings for each profile are in an expandable group in Advanced Sharing Settings.

- **Media Streaming**   Turning on media streaming provides access to pictures, music, and video through streaming protocols that can send media to computers or to other media playback devices. For more information, see "Sharing Digital Media over a Network" on page 512.

- **File Sharing Connections**   Unless you have very old computers on your network, leave this option set to 128-bit encryption, which has been the standard for most of this century.

- **Password Protected Sharing**   When password-protected sharing is turned on, network users cannot access your shared folders (including Public folders, if shared) or printers unless they can provide the user name and password of a user account on your computer. With this setting enabled, when another user attempts to access a shared resource, Windows sends the user name and password that the person used to log on to his or her own computer. If that matches the credentials for a local user account on your computer, the user gets immediate access to the shared resource (assuming permissions to use the particular resource have been granted to that user account). If either the user name or the password does not match, the user is asked to provide credentials in a dialog box like the one shown here:

With password-protected sharing turned off, Windows does not require a user name and password from network visitors. Instead, network access is provided using the Guest account. This is essentially the same as Simple File Sharing in Windows XP.

- **HomeGroup Connections**   If you use a homegroup for sharing, it's generally best to use the default setting, Allow Windows To Manage Homegroup Connections (Recommended). With this setting, when a user at a computer that is also a homegroup member attempts to use a shared resource on your computer, Windows connects using the HomeGroupUser$ account.

  When a user connects from a computer that is not a homegroup member, Windows first tries to authenticate using that person's logon credentials; if that fails, Windows uses Guest (if password-protected sharing is off) or prompts for credentials (if password-protected sharing is on). If you select Use User Accounts And Passwords To Connect To Other Computers, homegroup computers work like nonhomegroup computers, instead of using the HomeGroup-User$ account. Linking a Windows Live ID to each user account can simplify this process.

5. **Configure user accounts**   If you use password-protected sharing, each person who accesses a shared resource on your computer must have a user account on your computer. They could, of course, use the user name and password from another account, but they'll be required to enter that information each time they access the shared resource or save those credentials in mapped drives or the Credential Manager. (For more on this utility, see "Changing Account Settings" on page 654.)

Although it requires some extra preparation time up front, in the long run you'll find it much easier to share resources over the network if, on each computer that will have shared resources, you create a user account for each user who will access those resources. Use the same user name as that person uses on his or her own computer and the same password as well. If you do that, network users will be able to access shared resources without having to enter their credentials after they've logged on to their own computer.

Chapter 20

INSIDE OUT   Use the best and easiest method for sharing on a small network

If you're in a group of trusted users who have similar needs for access to shared resources on your computer, you can forego the considerable hassle of setting up identical accounts for each user on each computer. Instead, on the computer with shared resources, create a standard user account for accessing shared resources. (Call it Share, for example.) You must assign a password to this account.

If the sharing computer is in a homegroup, use HomeGroup in Control Panel to share the libraries you want to share. These folders are automatically available to the user named Share because that account is a member of the HomeUsers group. If the computer is not in a homegroup (or if you want to share folders or files that are not in a library), you must share each object with the Share account; for details, see "Sharing Files and Folders from Any Folder" on page 738. In Advanced Sharing Settings, be sure that File And Printer Sharing and Password Protected Sharing are turned on.

You can then access the shared items from another computer on your network. (For details, see "Finding and Using Shared Resources on a Windows Network" on page 750.) When prompted, a user must enter the user name (Share, in our example) and its password. This method works well for any type of client that needs access to your computer's shares, including computers running OS X, Linux, and earlier versions of Windows.

Sharing Files with Public Folders

To share items in your Public folder and its subfolders with other users of your computer, you don't need to do a thing. By default, all users with an account on your computer (including Guest) can log on and create, view, modify, and delete files in the Public folders. The person who creates a file in a Public folder (or copies an item to a Public folder) is the file's owner and has Full Control access. All others who log on locally have Modify access.

To share items in your Public folder with network users, in Advanced Sharing Settings, turn on Public folder sharing, as described in the preceding section. You can't select which network users get access, nor can you specify different access levels for different users. Sharing via the Public folder is quick and easy—but it's inflexible.

INSIDE OUT   Use an easier (but less secure) method for sharing on a small network

As an alternative to setting up an account for sharing, you can use anonymous sharing (using the Guest account), which works much like Simple File Sharing in Windows XP. Use this method only if you trust everyone on your network—such as in a home network shared by your family.

To use this method, on each computer with resources to share, turn off Password Protected Sharing. For each folder you want to share, use the Share With command to share with Guest or Everybody; for this type of open sharing, it doesn't really matter which you use. (Note that shared homegroup libraries also need to be shared in this way.)

Users from any computer can then gain access to any shared resource on your computer, and they won't be prompted for a user name or password.

Sharing Files and Folders from Any Folder

Whether you plan to share files and folders with other people who share your computer or those who connect to your computer over the network (or both), the process for setting up shared resources is the same as long as the Sharing wizard is enabled. We recommend that you use the Sharing wizard even if you normally disdain wizards. It's quick, easy, and certain to make all the correct settings for network shares and NTFS permissions—a sometimes daunting task if undertaken manually. Once you've configured shares with the wizard, you can always dive in and make changes manually if you need to.

To be sure the Sharing wizard is enabled, open Folder Options. (Type **folder** in the Start menu search box or, in Windows Explorer, click Organize, Folder And Search Options.) Click the View tab, and near the bottom of the Advanced Settings list, see that Use Sharing Wizard (Recommended) is selected.

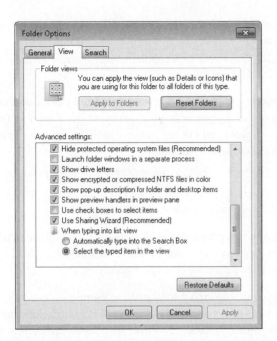

With the Sharing wizard at the ready, follow these steps to share a folder or files:

1. In Windows Explorer, select the folders or files you want to share. (You can select multiple objects.)

2. On the toolbar, click Share With, Specific People. (Alternatively, right-click and choose Share With, Specific People.) The File Sharing dialog box, shown in Figure 20-3 on page 724, appears.

3. In the entry box, enter the names or Windows Live IDs of the users with whom you want to share. You can type a name in the box or click the arrow to display a list of available names; then click Add. Repeat this step for each person you want to add.

   The list includes all users who have an account on your computer, plus Everyone. If you've joined a homegroup, the list also includes any Windows Live IDs that have been linked to user accounts on any PC that is part of the homegroup. Guest is included if password-protected sharing is turned off. If you want to grant access to someone who doesn't appear in the list, click Create A New User, which takes you to User Accounts in Control Panel. (This option appears only if your computer is not joined to a homegroup.)

> **Note**
>
> If you select Everyone and you have password-protected sharing enabled, the user must still have a valid account on your computer. However, if you have turned off password-protected sharing, network users can gain access *only* if you grant permission to Everyone or to Guest.

4. For each user, select a permission level. Your choices are

   - **Read** Users with this permission level can view shared files and run shared programs, but they cannot change or delete files. Selecting Read in the Sharing wizard is equivalent to setting NTFS permissions to Read & Execute.

   - **Read/Write** Users assigned the Read/Write permission have the same privileges you do as owner: they can view, change, add, and delete files in a shared folder. Selecting Read/Write sets NTFS permissions to Full Control for this user.

> **Note**
>
> You might see other permission levels if you return to the Sharing wizard after you set up sharing. Contribute indicates Modify permission. Custom indicates NTFS permissions other than Read & Execute, Modify, or Full Control. Mixed appears if you select multiple items and they have different sharing settings. Owner, of course, identifies the owner of the item.

5. Click Share. After a few moments, the wizard displays a page like the one shown in Figure 20-6.

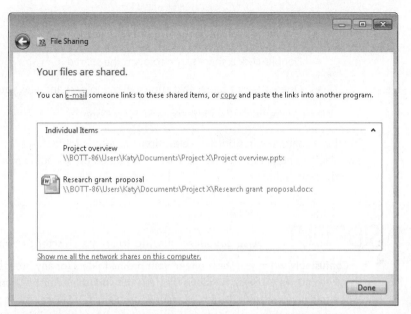

Figure 20-6 The Sharing wizard displays the network path for each item you've shared.

6. In the final step of the wizard, you can do any of the following:

- Send an e-mail message to the people with whom you're sharing. The message includes a link to the shared folder or file.

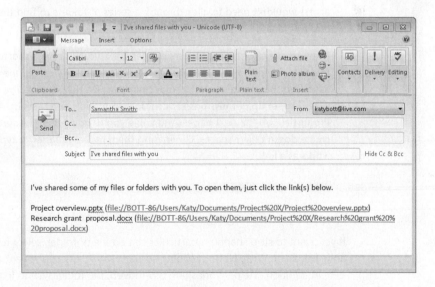

- Copy the network path to the Clipboard. This is handy if you want to send a link via instant messenger or other application.

- Double-click a share name to open the shared item.

- Open a search folder that shows all the folders and files you're sharing.

When you're finished with these tasks, click Done.

Creating a share requires privilege elevation, but after a folder has been shared, the share is available to network users no matter who is logged on to your computer—or even when nobody is logged on.

INSIDE OUT   Use advanced sharing to create shorter network paths

Confusingly, when you share one of your profile folders (or any other subfolder of %SystemDrive%\Users), Windows creates a network share for the Users folder—not for the folder you shared. This isn't a security problem; NTFS permissions prevent network users from seeing any folders or files except the ones you explicitly share. But it does lead to some long Universal Naming Convention (UNC) paths to network shares. For example, if you share the Travel subfolder of Documents (as shown in Figure 20-6), the network path is \\CARL-PC\Users\Carl\Documents\Travel. If this same folder had been anywhere on your computer outside the Users folder, no matter how deeply nested, the network path would instead be \\CARL-PC\Travel. Other people to whom you granted access wouldn't need to click through a series of folders to find the files in the intended target folder.

Network users, of course, can map a network drive or save a shortcut to your target folder to avoid this problem. But you can work around it from the sharing side too: use advanced sharing to share the folder directly. (Do this after you've used the Sharing wizard to set up permissions.) For more information, see "Setting Advanced Sharing Properties" on the next page. (And while you're doing that, be sure the share name you create doesn't have spaces. Eliminating them makes it easier to type a share path that works as a link.)

Stopping or Changing Sharing of a File or Folder

If you want to stop sharing a particular shared file or folder, select it in Windows Explorer and click Share With, Nobody. Doing so removes access control entries that are not inherited. In addition, the network share is removed; the folder will no longer be visible in another user's Network folder.

To change share permissions, choose Share With, Specific People. In the File Sharing dialog box (shown earlier in Figure 20-3), you can add users, change permissions, or remove users. (To stop sharing with a particular user, click the arrow by the user's name and choose Remove.)

Setting Advanced Sharing Properties

With Advanced Sharing, you configure network shares independently of NTFS permissions. (For more information about this distinction, see "How Shared Resource Permissions and NTFS Permissions Work Together" on page 746.) To open Advanced Sharing, right-click a folder, choose Properties, and click the Sharing tab. Or, if the Sharing wizard is disabled, select a folder and on the toolbar (or right-click menu) choose Advanced Sharing. Both methods display the Sharing tab, which is shown in Figure 20-7.

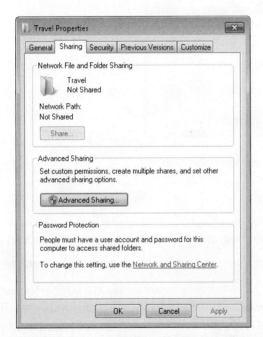

Figure 20-7 The Share button under Network File And Folder Sharing summons the Sharing wizard, but it's available only when the Sharing wizard is enabled.

> **Note**
> The Sharing tab is part of the properties dialog box for a folder, but not for files. Also, when the Sharing wizard is disabled, the Share button appears on the toolbar only when you select a single folder. Only the Sharing wizard is capable of making share settings for files and for multiple objects simultaneously.

Chapter 20

To create or modify a network share using advanced settings, follow these steps:

1. On the Sharing tab, click Advanced Sharing to display the Advanced Sharing dialog box.

2. Select Share This Folder, as shown here:

3. Accept or change the proposed share name.

> **Note**
>
> **If the folder is already shared and you want to add another share name (perhaps with different permissions), click Add and then type the name for the new share.**

The share name is the name that other users will see in their own Network folders. Windows initially proposes to use the folder's name as the share name. That's usually a good choice, but you're not obligated to accept it. If you already have a shared folder with that name, you'll need to pick a different name.

4. Type a description of the folder's contents in the Comments box.

Other users will see this description when they inspect the folder's properties dialog box in their Network folder (or use Details view).

5. To limit the number of users who can connect to the shared folder concurrently, specify a number in the box. Windows 7 permits up to 20 concurrent network connections, which means that up to 10 users can access a share at one time. (If you need to share a resource with more than 10 users at once, you must use Windows Server.)

6. Click Permissions.

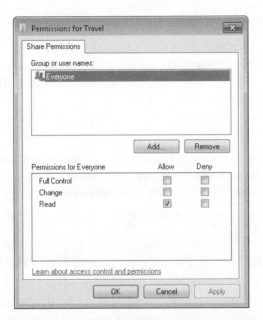

The default shared resource permission associated with a new share is Read access to Everyone.

CAUTION

When you share a folder, you also make that folder's subfolders available on the network. If the access permissions you set for the folder aren't appropriate for any of its subfolders, either reconsider your choice of access permissions or restructure your folders to avoid the problem.

7. In the Group Or User Names list, select the name of the user or group you want to manage.

The shared resource permissions for the selected user or group appear below in the permissions list.

8. Select Allow, Deny, or neither for each access control entry:

- **Full Control**   Allows users to create, read, write, rename, and delete files in the folder and its subfolders. In addition, users can change permissions and take ownership of files on NTFS volumes.

- **Change**   Allows users to read, write, rename, and delete files in the folder and its subfolders but not create new files.

- **Read**   Allows users to read files but not write to them or delete them.

If you select neither Allow nor Deny, it is still possible that the user or group can inherit the permission through membership in another group that has the permission. If the user or group doesn't belong to another such group, the user or group is implicitly denied permission.

Note

To remove a name from the Group Or User Names list, select it and click Remove. To add a name to the list, click Add to open the Select Users Or Groups dialog box, where you can enter the names of the users and groups you want to add.

How Shared Resource Permissions and NTFS Permissions Work Together

The implementation of shared resource permissions and NTFS permissions is confusingly similar, but it's important to recognize that these are two separate levels of access control. Only connections that successfully pass through both gates are granted access.

Shared resource permissions control *network* access to a particular resource. Shared resource permissions do not affect users who log on locally. You set shared resource permissions in the Advanced Sharing dialog box, which you access from the Sharing tab of a folder's properties dialog box.

NTFS permissions (also known as discretionary access control lists, DACLs) apply to folders and files on an NTFS-formatted drive. For each user to whom you want to grant access, you can specify exactly what that user is allowed to do: run programs, view folder contents, create new files, change existing files, and so on. You set NTFS permissions on the Security tab of the properties dialog box for a folder or file.

It's important to recognize that the two types of permissions are combined in the most restrictive way. If, for example, a user is granted Read permission on the network share, even if the account has Full Control NTFS permissions on the same folder, the user gets only read access when connecting over the network. In effect, the two sets of permissions act in tandem as "gatekeepers" that winnow out incoming network connections. An account that attempts to connect over the network is examined first by the shared resource permissions gatekeeper. The account is either bounced out on its caboodle or allowed to enter with certain permissions. It's then confronted by the NTFS permissions gatekeeper, which might strip away (but not add to) some or all of the permissions granted at the first doorway. In many advanced sharing scenarios, it's common practice to simply configure the shared folder with Full Control permissions for Everyone and then configure NTFS permissions to control access as desired.

In determining the effective permission for a particular account, you must also consider the effect of group membership. Permissions are cumulative; an account that is a member of one or more groups is granted all the permissions granted explicitly to the account as well as all permissions granted to each group of which it's a member. The only exception to this rule is Deny permissions, which take precedence over any conflicting Allow permissions.

Using PowerShell Scripts to Manage Shared Folders

The Scripts folder of the companion CD contains a handful of PowerShell scripts that you can use to enumerate and manage shared folders. You can find much of this information in the Computer Management console (Compmgmt.msc), but the scripts allow a way to programmatically gather the information, which can be useful if you're administering an unfamiliar PC.

- **Get-ShareInfo.ps1** lists all available shares on the local computer.

- **GetShareAndPermission.ps1** accomplishes a similar goal but also lists permissions assigned to each folder. (To view the latter information, you'll need to run the script using an administrator's credentials.)

- **ListAdminShares.ps1** enumerates the normally hidden administrative shares on a local or remote computer.

Two additional simple scripts might be useful when incorporated into scripts that tackle larger jobs:

- **CreateShare.ps1** allows you to create a share on the local machine using default permissions. Use the –folderpath and –sharename parameters to identify the folder you want to share; if the specified folder doesn't exist, the script creates it.

- **DeleteShare.ps1** is a cleanup tool that allows you to remove a share on a local computer. Use the –computername parameter to delete a share from a remote computer.

For information about the use of a particular script, open the script in Notepad and read the .Synopsis section. For general information about running Windows PowerShell scripts, see "Running PowerShell Scripts" on page 999.

Sharing a Printer

Although Windows doesn't have a Sharing wizard for sharing a printer over the network, the process is pretty simple. You configure all options for a printer—whether you plan to share it or not—by using the printer's properties dialog box, which you access from the Devices And Printers folder in Control Panel.

To make a printer available to other network users, right-click a printer and click Printer Properties. On the Sharing tab, select Share This Printer and provide a share name, as shown in Figure 20-8.

Figure 20-8 The share name can include spaces.

Unlike shared folders, which maintain separate share permissions and NTFS permissions, a single set of permissions controls access to printers, whether by local users or by network users. (Of course, only printers that have been shared are accessible to network users.)

When you set up a printer, initially all users in the Everyone group have Print permission for documents they create, which provides users access to the printer and the ability to manage their own documents in the print queue. By default, members of the Administrators group also have Manage Printers permission, which allows them to share a printer, change its properties, remove a printer, and change its permissions; and Manage Documents permission, which lets them pause, restart, move, and remove all queued documents. As an administrator, you can view or modify permissions on the Security tab of the printer properties dialog box.

Setting Server Properties

In addition to setting properties for individual printers by using their properties dialog boxes, you can set other properties by visiting the Print Server Properties dialog box. To get there, select a printer in the Devices And Printers folder, and then click Print Server Properties on the toolbar.

The first three tabs control the list of items you see in the properties dialog box for a printer:

- The Forms tab controls the list of forms that you can assign to trays using the Device Settings tab in a printer's properties dialog box. You can create new form definitions and delete any that you create, but you can't delete any of the predefined forms.

- The Ports tab offers the same capabilities as the Ports tab in a printer's properties dialog box.

- The Drivers tab offers a list of all the installed printer drivers and provides a centralized location where you can add, remove, or update drivers.

The Advanced tab offers a potpourri of options:

- You can specify the location of spool files (but only after you click Change Advanced Settings and supply an administrator's credentials). You might want to change to a folder on a different drive if, for example, you frequently run out of space on the current drive when you attempt to print large documents.

- The Beep On Errors Of Remote Documents check box causes the print server to notify you audibly of problems with a remote printer.

- The two Show Informational Notifications... check boxes control pop-up status messages near the notification area.

INSIDE OUT Use the Print Management console

Users of Windows 7 Professional, Enterprise, or Ultimate edition have a tool that places all print management tasks in one convenient console. Print Management (Printmanagement.msc), shown here, provides a place for managing printers, drivers, queues, and shares. If your edition includes Print Management, you can start it by typing print in the Start menu search box and then clicking Print Management.

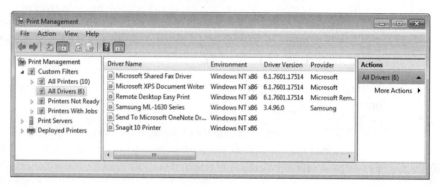

Finding and Using Shared Resources on a Windows Network

The Network folder is your gateway to all available network resources, just as Computer is the gateway to resources stored on your own system. The Network folder (shown in Figure 20-9) contains an icon for each computer on your network; double-click a computer icon to see that computer's shared resources, if any.

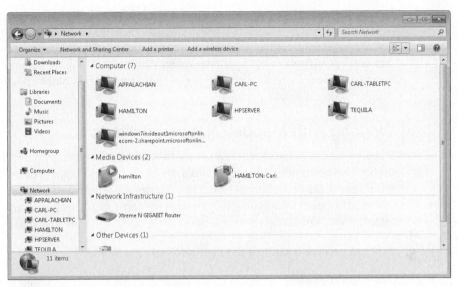

Figure 20-9 Unlike in Windows XP, the Network folder in Windows 7 shows all computers on your network, not just those in your workgroup.

To open a shared folder on another computer, double-click its icon in the Network folder. If you have the proper permissions, this action displays the folder's contents in Windows Explorer. It's not always that easy, however. If the user account with which you logged on doesn't have permission to view a network computer or resource you select, a dialog box asks you to provide the name of an account (and its password, of course) that has permission. Don't be fooled by the Domain reference below the User Name and Password boxes; on a workgroup, that value refers to the local computer.

Chapter 20

Perhaps the trickiest part of using shared folders is fully understanding what permissions have been applied to a folder and which credentials are in use by each network user. The first rule to recognize is that *all network access is controlled by the computer with the shared resources*; regardless of what operating system runs on the computer attempting to connect to a network share, it must meet the security requirements of the computer where the shared resource is actually located.

Working with Mapped Network Folders

Mapping a network folder makes it appear to applications as though the folder is part of your own computer. Windows assigns a drive letter to the mapped folder, making the folder appear like an additional hard drive. You can still access a mapped folder in the conventional manner by navigating to it through the Network folder. But mapping gives the folder an alias—the assigned drive letter—that provides an alternative means of access.

To map a network folder to a drive letter, follow these steps:

1. Open Computer in Windows Explorer, and on the toolbar, click Map Network Drive. (Alternatively, after you open a computer in the Network folder, right-click a network share and choose Map Network Drive.)

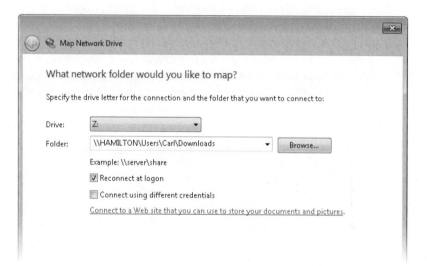

2. Select a drive letter in the Drive box. You can choose any letter that's not already in use.

3. In the Folder box, type the path to the folder you want or, more easily, click Browse and navigate to the folder.

4. Select Reconnect At Logon if you want Windows to connect to this shared folder automatically at the start of each session.

5. If your regular logon account doesn't have permission to connect to the resource, select Connect Using Different Credentials. (After you click Finish, Windows will ask for the user name and password you want to use for this connection.)

6. Click Finish.

In the Computer folder, the "drive" appears in the Network Location group. As a top-level item in Computer, it also appears in the breadcrumb bar when you click the arrow to the right of Computer, as shown here:

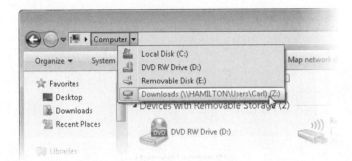

If you change your mind about mapping a network folder, simply right-click the folder's icon in your Computer folder. Choose Disconnect on the resulting shortcut menu, and the connection will be severed.

Connecting to a Network Printer

To use a printer that has been shared, open the Network folder and double-click the name of the server to which the printer is attached. If the shared printers on that server are not visible, on the toolbar, click View Remote Printers. Right-click the printer and choose Connect. Alternatively, from the Devices And Printers folder, click Add A Printer and use the Add Printer wizard to add a network printer.

CHAPTER 21
Advanced Windows Networking

F OR most users of Windows at home or in a small office, HomeGroup and the other networking methods and procedures described in the preceding chapters provide all the needed connectivity. In these environments, accessing shared files, media, and printers throughout a local area network is easily achieved.

But there's much more to networking, various facets of which are the subject of many volumes larger than this tome. In this chapter, we touch upon a few of these more complex features.

What's in Your Edition?

Most—but not all—of the information in this chapter applies to computers running one of the business editions of Windows 7—Professional, Enterprise, or Ultimate. The main exception is the section on Windows Live Mesh, which works with all Windows editions.

Only computers running Windows 7 Professional, Enterprise, or Ultimate can join a domain.

This chapter also covers Remote Desktop. If you want to set up your computer to allow inbound access using Remote Desktop, you must be running the Professional, Enterprise, or Ultimate edition. However, you can use the Remote Desktop Connection client software under any Windows 7 edition to *connect to* a computer that has enabled incoming connections via Remote Desktop. Because Windows Home Server 2011 relies on Remote Desktop, computers that allow inbound access must be running Professional, Enterprise, or Ultimate. All other features of Remote Web Access in Windows Home Server work with all Windows editions.

Similarly, you need Professional, Enterprise, or Ultimate to set up your Windows 7 computer as a VPN server, but you can use any edition to connect to it.

Many Windows 7 users, of course, work with computers attached to large corporate networks. Administration of a corporate domain is beyond the scope of this book, but here we offer a glimpse into what life in a domain is like from the user's perspective. This information also provides a starting point for further learning by de facto administrators of small domain-based networks.

In this chapter we also look beyond the desktop, to situations in which accessing shared files and printers is not enough; you want access to an *entire computer*. With tools available in Windows, you can do exactly that, and much of this chapter is devoted to showing you how. We look into several different remote access tools, each with slightly different capabilities and complexities:

- Remote Desktop provides "the closest thing to being there," with the ability to display desktop background images, play videos, and so on. It's ideal for connecting to another computer on your internal network. It also works well for connections over the Internet—but only after you properly configure your network router and firewall, which is not always easy to do.

- For connecting to a computer at your home from elsewhere on the Internet, Windows Home Server 2011 greatly simplifies the configuration process and provides the full-fidelity experience of Remote Desktop.

- The easiest end-to-end connections over the Internet are made with Windows Live Mesh, which requires virtually no configuration. However, it has its limitations: You can connect only between a pair of your own computers (that is, you can't use a computer in an Internet café—or even a friend's computer—without joining it to your own collection of Windows Live devices). Furthermore, its video and audio capabilities are limited.

In this chapter we also discuss using a virtual private network (VPN) connection, which enables secure, encrypted communication with a remote server, even when you're working in an open Wi-Fi hotspot. (An even better solution, if the server you're connecting to is running Windows Server 2008 R2, is DirectAccess, which we briefly touch upon.)

Working in a Domain-Based Network

Elsewhere in this book, we describe setup, configuration, and usage of peer-to-peer (or *workgroup*) networks. This is the type of network most commonly found in homes and small businesses, and it does not require a server; each computer on the network is an equally empowered peer.

In contrast, an Active Directory domain-based network requires at least one computer running a version of Windows Server. The most significant difference is that all computers and user accounts on the network can be centrally managed through the server. User accounts can be added and removed; permissions can be set for different users and groups on various objects, including folders, files, and printers; applications and updates can be installed throughout the network—all from a single location.

When you have more than a handful of computers in a network, they become much easier to manage when configured as a domain. For example, instead of re-creating a database of user accounts on each computer, a domain administrator creates each account only once—using the server's Active Directory Domain Services. A domain environment also enables features such as roaming user profiles (these allow users to log on at any network computer and have their usual profile—including files, settings, and preferences—in place); a fully searchable directory service that allows network users to easily find shared resources, contacts, users, and other objects; centralized user data management and backup; and much more. Administration of an Active Directory domain-based network is (well) beyond the scope of this book. Our focus here is on the user experience: What do users need to know to become, for lack of a better term, masters of their domain?

Chapter 21

INSIDE OUT   Use Remote Server Administration Tools

Although this book isn't about server administration, we can't help offering one tip: If your responsibilities include managing servers in a domain running Windows Server 2008 R2, Windows Server 2008, or Windows Server 2003, take a look at Remote Server Administration Tools (RSAT), a free suite of tools for server management that runs on Windows 7. You can learn more about RSAT by viewing two articles on TechNet: "Remote Server Administration Tools for Windows 7" (*w7io.com/22105*) and "What Are the Remote Server Administration Tools?" (*w7io.com/22106*). You can download RSAT from *w7io.com/22107*.

How can you tell if a computer is joined to a domain? Click the Start button, right-click Computer, and choose Properties to display System in Control Panel, as shown in

Figure 21-1. Under Computer Name, Domain, And Workgroup Settings, a domain-joined computer will show the word *Domain*.

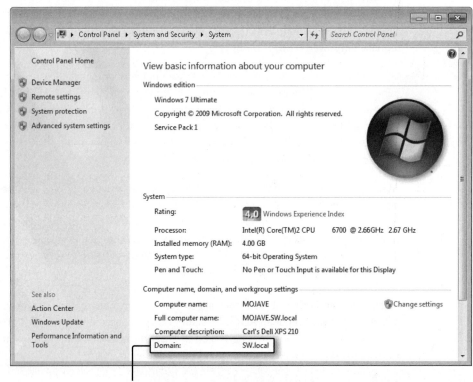

This computer is a member of the domain named SW.local

Figure 21-1 To join (or leave) a domain, click Change Settings, and then click Change in the dialog box that appears. Either action requires the credentials of a domain administrator.

Differences in the Logon Process

Users of a domain computer see one difference right off the bat: By default, on a computer joined to a domain, users must press Ctrl+Alt+Delete to display the logon screen. (If you don't want to burden users with this requirement, you can change the default. For details about this change and other ways to customize the logon experience, see "Managing the Logon Process" on page 668.)

Thereafter, the visible differences between using a computer joined to a domain and one that's part of a workgroup are few and subtle. In the Windows XP era, using a domain-joined computer was almost like using a different operating system. (In one of our earlier books, *Microsoft Windows XP Inside Out Deluxe*, it took eight pages just to list the differences an ordinary user would encounter—without even mentioning any of the administrative and under-the-hood differences.)

One of the more significant differences in earlier Windows versions is gone in Windows 7: domain users can now use Fast User Switching. (For information about Fast User Switching, see "Logging Off, Switching Users, or Locking Your Computer" on page 674.) A related change allows workgroup users to lock their computer by pressing Windows logo key+L, a feature that was formerly available only on domain-joined computers.

If you forget your password for logging on to the domain, you won't get any help from a displayed password hint, nor can you use a password reset disk—two features of non-domain computers. (For more information, see "Recovering from a Lost Password" on page 666.) Your only recourse is for a domain administrator to reset your password. Fortunately, after the reset you regain full use of any encrypted files on your computer—which is not the case when a local administrator changes the password on a workgroup computer.

Security Groups and Policy Restrictions in a Domain

User groups—collections of user accounts—are typically used to much greater effect in a domain-based network. In a workgroup, you typically have only two user groups in active use: Administrators and Users. In a domain, it's not uncommon for administrators to create user groups for departments, job functions, locations, and other logical divisions. User accounts can be assigned to one or more groups, as appropriate. Permissions and user rights at an extremely granular level can be applied to computers and to folders, files, printers, and other shared network resources. On a properly configured network, a complex interaction of group memberships and permissions allows individual users access to all the network resources they need to perform their job—and nothing more.

For more information about permissions and user rights, see "Introducing Access Control in Windows" on page 642. For more information about user groups, see "Local Accounts and Groups vs. Domain Accounts and Groups" on page 650.

Group Policy comprises thousands of policy settings that let an administrator control nearly every aspect of a computer running Windows—its appearance, which programs can be run or installed, what settings can be made through Control Panel, whether it can be turned off, and much, much more. Although the Group Policy feature is built in to all editions of Windows, in a workgroup it's rarely used because it takes so much time (and expertise) to administer—and any settings must be made separately on each computer. In a domain-based network, however, policies can be applied based on group membership and other criteria, and all management tasks can be performed at the server and applied throughout the network. In a domain environment, applying Group Policy settings becomes practical.

For details about Group Policy, see "Using Group Policy" on page 935.

Chapter 21

The key takeaway here is that, through proper application of user groups, permissions, user rights, and Group Policy, computers and network resources in a domain can be made to work quite differently from the behavior you'll experience in a workgroup—and it can all be controlled by a domain administrator.

Network Profiles in a Domain

As explained earlier in this book, Windows Firewall uses a network profile associated with each network location. Windows Firewall maintains three different profiles: Home or Work (which are functionally identical for Windows Firewall purposes), Public, and Domain. Windows Firewall automatically uses the appropriate profile for the network to which your computer is currently connected. When your domain-joined computer connects to the domain network, Windows Firewall automatically invokes the Domain profile. You can see which type of network you're connected to by opening Network And Sharing Center, as shown in Figure 21-2.

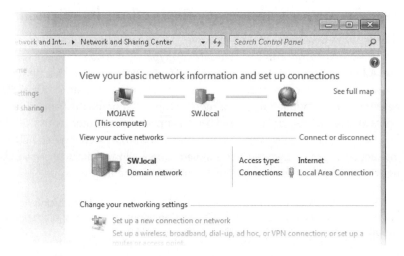

Figure 21-2 The Domain network profile is used whenever a domain member computer is connected to the domain network.

Note that only a computer that is joined to the domain uses the domain profile, which is typically configured and managed by a domain administrator. If you attach a computer that is not joined to the domain to a domain-based network so that you can use its Internet connection or other network resources, Windows asks you to select one of the other network location types (Home, Work, or Public).

Note also that you can click the network location type in Network And Sharing Center to change the current network to a different location type—unless the location shown is Domain Network. The only way to enable the domain profile is to connect a domain-joined computer to the domain network. And the only way to switch to another location type is to disconnect the computer from the network.

For more information about network profiles, see "Understanding Network Locations" on page 687. For details about Windows Firewall, see "Blocking Intruders with Windows Firewall" on page 604.

Using a Domain-Joined Computer Away from the Domain

When you disconnect a domain member computer from the domain network and reconnect to a different network, it uses the appropriate network location type for the new location. (If you're connecting to a new network for the first time, Windows asks which network location to use.) In other words, a domain-joined computer is perfectly happy to hit the road.

Your computer is particularly content when you take it home and join a homegroup in your home network; HomeGroup is fully compatible with and introduces some unique features to work-at-home scenarios. While you're connected to the home network, you have access to all documents, media, and printers that are shared in the homegroup. However, you can't share libraries or printers on your domain-joined computer, ensuring that other homegroup members don't have access to your business documents and files. In short, you get all the benefits of HomeGroup while preventing exposure of your work files.

> **Note**
>
> A computer that is a domain member can join an existing homegroup on a home network, but it cannot create a homegroup.

For more information, see "Using HomeGroup with a Domain-Based Computer" on page 730. For a list of settings a domain administrator can make to ensure smooth, secure transitions from your workplace network to your home network, see the TechNet article "Settings to Allow Computers That Are Members of a Domain to Join a Homegroup" at *w7io.com/22104*.

Chapter 21

Connecting to Another Computer with Remote Desktop

Sharing computer resources over a network, when properly configured, gives you access to all the files you might need, wherever they're stored. But sometimes even that is not enough. You might need to run a program that is installed only on another computer, or you might need to configure and manage another computer's files and settings in ways that can be done only by sitting down in front of that computer. As it turns out, there is an alternative to direct physical access: Remote Desktop. By using a Remote Desktop session, you can operate a computer by remote control over a local network or over the Internet.

When you use a Remote Desktop connection, you're able to operate that computer as if you were sitting right in front of it. You have access to all of the other computer's files, applications, and network resources. You can connect to your work PC from your home office and run a query on a corporate database using an application that isn't available at home. If you work all night to finish an important presentation and forget to bring it to the office, you can connect to your home computer from your office network and use Remote Desktop to retrieve the file and meet your deadline. And unlike earlier versions of Remote Desktop, the version in Windows 7 can play videos and other media, and its bidirectional audio support makes it possible to use the remote computer for Voice over Internet Protocol (VoIP) telephony applications and speech recognition.

On a home or small business network, you can use Remote Desktop as a remote management console. From your main desktop, you can connect to any computer on your network and install updates, change system settings, or perform other routine maintenance tasks without having to leave the comfort of your couch or cubicle.

What can't you do? Any task that requires direct access to video hardware will fail to work using the virtualized hardware in a Remote Desktop session. So you can't watch a recorded TV show using Windows Media Center running on a remote PC, nor can you use Windows Live Movie Maker. Ironically, you also can't make any changes to Remote Desktop settings over a Remote Desktop session.

With Remote Desktop, applications run on the remote computer; your computer is effectively used as a dumb terminal. You can use a low-powered computer—an inexpensive netbook or even an old clunker—and enjoy the speed and power of the remote computer. Remote Desktop connections are encrypted, so your information is secure, even if you're making a connection over the Internet.

The basic requirements for using Remote Desktop are pretty simple: you need two computers that are connected via a local area network, the Internet, or a dial-up connection.

> **Note**
>
> The computer that you want to control—the one at the remote location—is called the *remote computer*. The computer you want to use to control the remote computer is called the *client computer*.

These are the requirements for the two computers:

- **Remote computer**   You need a computer running Windows 7 Professional, Enterprise, or Ultimate. (Windows 7 Starter, Home Basic, and Home Premium editions do not include the software required for hosting Remote Desktop sessions.) The remote computer can also use Windows Vista (Business, Enterprise, or Ultimate editions), Windows XP Professional (or Windows XP Media Center or Tablet PC editions), Windows Home Server, Windows Server 2008, or Windows Server 2003. This computer must have a connection to a local area network or to the Internet. If you're going to connect to this computer over the Internet, its Internet connection must have a known, public IP address. (For ways around this last requirement, see "Configuring Your Network for Remote Desktop Connections" on page 765.)

  > **Note**
  >
  > It is possible to set up an incoming Remote Desktop connection to use a dial-up modem that's configured to answer incoming calls automatically. For reasons of practicality, we don't recommend this configuration, nor do we cover it in this book.

- **Client computer**   You can access Remote Desktop from a computer running any version of Windows. Windows 7 Service Pack 1 includes version 7.1 of the Remote Desktop Connection program (Mstsc.exe), which is included in all editions. If you plan to connect to or from other operating systems, download the most recent version from one of these sources:

  - For Windows Vista or Windows XP Service Pack 3 (SP3), download Remote Desktop Connection version 7.0 from *w7io.com/22101*.

  - For Windows XP SP2, download Remote Desktop Connection version 6.1 from *w7io.com/1801*.

- For older versions of Windows, including Windows 2003 Server and Windows 2000, version 5.1 of the Remote Desktop client software can be downloaded from *w7io.com/1803*.

- Mac clients can download a compatible version of the client software from Microsoft's Office:Mac site, at *w7io.com/1802*.

- An open-source Linux client, FreeRDP, is available from *w7io.com/22102*.

Alternatives to Remote Desktop

Remote Desktop is an elegant and well-engineered solution to a common problem, but it's not your only option when you need to connect to another PC. If you're looking for alternatives, especially for a system running Windows 7 Starter or Home Premium edition, Microsoft has one excellent option in its Windows Live family. You can also consider a third-party program that offers similar features, or use one of several browser-based services.

Windows Live Mesh, which is included with Windows Live Essentials 2011, includes remote capabilities that are strikingly similar to those of Remote Desktop, with a noteworthy difference: you can host a Windows Live Mesh session on any edition of Windows 7. For more information, see "Connecting Remotely with Windows Live Mesh" on page 779.

Among commercial third-party programs, Laplink Gold has a stellar reputation and a long history. Remote access is only one of its many features, which also include PC-to-PC file transfer and synchronization. For more information, visit *w7io.com/1805*.

An excellent free alternative is UltraVNC (*uvnc.com*), which is one of many variants of the Virtual Network Computing (VNC) software first developed by Olivetti and Oracle Research Labs and released as open source in 2002. RealVNC (*realvnc.com*) uses the same code base and offers a version that is free for personal use.

Browser-based alternatives typically work on a subscription model. You create an account with an online service (paid or free) and run a service on the PC to which you want to enable remote access. You can then connect to that PC over the Internet by opening a web browser, going to the service's home page, and logging in. To see if this option is right for you, look at GoToMyPC (*gotomypc.com*), LogMeIn (*logmein.com*), or Laplink Everywhere (*w7io.com/1806*).

Configuring Your Network for Remote Desktop Connections

When you enable Remote Desktop on Windows 7 Professional, Enterprise, or Ultimate, the remote computer listens for incoming connections on port 3389. Enabling Remote Desktop also creates an exception in Windows Firewall that allows authenticated traffic on this port.

That makes Remote Desktop easy to use over a local network where no third-party security software is installed. But it doesn't solve the many problems you face when trying to connect to Remote Desktop over the Internet. To connect through the Internet, you must be able to reach the remote computer using a known public IP address, and you have to get through a router and past any security software in between the two computers. If you're sitting in a hotel room or an airport, connecting to Remote Desktop poses several challenges imposed by firewalls, routers, and IP addresses. The solutions to these issues depend on your specific hardware configuration, but we can offer the following general advice.

Configuring a Router for Remote Desktop

If the remote computer is connected to the Internet through a router, you need to accomplish two tasks. First, you have to ascertain the router's public IP address. Then you have to configure the router to forward Remote Desktop Protocol traffic it receives on port 3389 to the remote computer.

To find the router's IP address, open its browser-based administration interface and find the status screen. The public IP address is typically labeled as the WAN (wide area network) address; don't use the local area network (LAN) address, which is the private IP address used to forward traffic to computers on your local network.

To make sure Remote Desktop Protocol (RDP) traffic reaches your remote PC, look for a "port forwarding" page in the same router administration interface (it's often buried within an advanced configuration section). You'll need to specify the local (private) IP address of the remote computer and tell the router that you want all traffic on port 3389 to be forwarded to that PC instead of being discarded. Figure 21-3 shows this configuration on a NETGEAR router, allowing incoming Remote Desktop requests to be forwarded to a computer with a local (private) IP address of 192.168.1.107.

Chapter 21

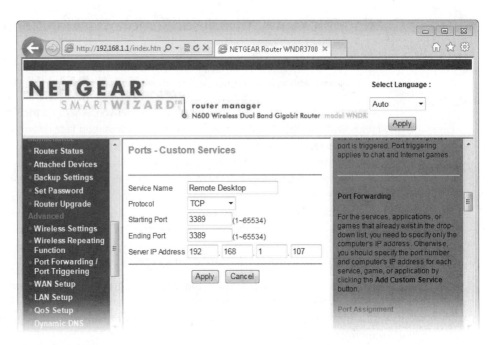

Figure 21-3 Every router has a different configuration interface, but the basic concepts of port forwarding are similar to the one shown here, which will forward traffic on port 3389 to a local PC with the specified private IP address.

INSIDE OUT   Use dynamic DNS to avoid IP address confusion

Using a bare IP address for Remote Desktop connections is easy but potentially risky. If you forget the public IP address assigned to your computer, you'll be unable to make a connection. Worse, if your ISP decides to change your IP address, you'll be stymied until you discover the new address, which is a challenge if you're away from home. The solution is to use a dynamic DNS service, such as those offered by Dynamic Network Services (*dyndns.com*) and TZO (*tzo.com*). (A web search for "dynamic DNS service" will turn up many more options.) Such services map the public IP address on your router to a domain name that doesn't change. Dynamic DNS services typically rely on software installed on your remote computer, which notifies the service provider's domain name servers if your IP address changes. Because the domain name server correlates your domain name with its current IP address, you (or anyone you designate) can always find your computer by using your registered domain name instead of a numeric IP address.

Using a Windows Server as a Remote Desktop Gateway

The mechanics of configuring a home or small office network for remote access can be daunting, and port forwarding suffers from the limitation that it allows remote access to one and only one PC on your local network. For a simpler (but certainly not free) solution to these problems, consider adding a Windows server to your network. For information about using Windows Home Server 2011 for remote access, see "Connecting Remotely to a Windows Home Server Network" on page 782.

For larger or more sophisticated networks, you can use the Remote Desktop Gateway feature of Windows Server 2008 R2. When users connect to a server that has been configured to use this service, they can use a web-based interface to connect to any computer on the network that has Remote Desktop enabled. A network administrator can also designate individual programs that can be run in Remote Desktop sessions. When you connect to one of these RemoteApp programs, it runs in a window on your desktop that looks just like any other program being run from a local source; the only clue that it's running from another computer is the word *remote* in parentheses after the program's name in Windows Task Manager.

For more information about Remote Desktop Gateway, see *w7io.com/22108*.

Chapter 21

Enabling Inbound Remote Desktop Connections

If you intend to connect to a remote computer while you're away from home or out of the office, you must first enable Remote Desktop on that computer. To set up a computer running Windows 7 Professional, Enterprise, or Ultimate to accept Remote Desktop connections, follow these steps:

1. Open the System Properties dialog box. (Press the Windows logo key+Break or, in Control Panel, open System And Security, System.) In the left pane, click Remote Settings. (Or use the undocumented command **systempropertiesremote**.)

2. Under Remote Desktop, change the default setting (Don't Allow Connections To This Computer) to either of the options that begin with Allow Connections, as shown next.

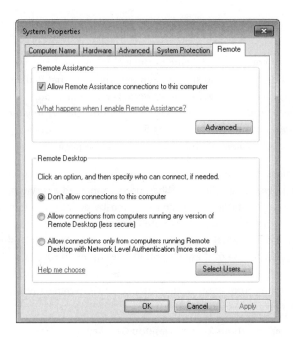

- If you anticipate that you will need to access your computer from a computer running Remote Desktop Connection software version 6.0 or earlier, select Allow Connections From Computers Running Any Version Of Remote Desktop (Less Secure). You must also choose this option if you plan to connect through Windows Home Server version 1 (but not Windows Home Server 2011).

- If you are certain that you will access your computer only by using Remote Desktop software version 6.1 or higher (included with Windows 7, Windows Vista, Windows XP SP3, Windows Server 2008, and Windows Server 2008 R2), select Allow Connections Only From Computers Running Remote Desktop With Network Level Authentication (More Secure).

At this point, the current user account and any user account that is a member of the local Administrators group can be used to connect remotely to the computer, provided that the account has a logon password.

> **Note**
> As a security precaution, accounts that use a blank password cannot be enabled for remote connections.

3. If you want to change which users can connect remotely, click Select Users. The Remote Desktop Users dialog box appears.

- To add a user to the Remote Desktop Users group, click Add. Then type the user's name in the Select Users dialog box that appears (or click Advanced, Find Now to select names from a list). You can type the name of any local user account or, if your computer is in a domain, any domain user account. You can add multiple users by separating each user name with a semicolon.

- To delete a user from the Remote Desktop Users group, select the user's name in the Remote Desktop Users dialog box and click Remove.

INSIDE OUT   Change the Remote Desktop port number

You can use a different port for Remote Desktop connections. Although there's seldom reason to do so, changing to a different port can provide increased security because you don't expose a listening port where intruders might expect to find Remote Desktop. You can also use this capability to provide access to multiple remote PCs through a single router. For details about changing the port, see Microsoft Support article 306759 (*w7io.com/1807*). For example, you might use the default port of 3389 on a computer named Rock, and assign port 3390 to Remote Desktop on a PC named Paper. Then, using your router's administrative interface, you would map incoming traffic on port 3389 to Rock and traffic on port 3390 to Paper. To connect to Rock from the Internet, use the Remote Desktop Connection software normally. To connect to Paper, append a colon followed by the port number after the computer name (paper:3390) in the Remote Desktop Connection dialog box.

That's all you need to do to set up the remote computer. Windows configures rules for Remote Desktop in Windows Firewall when Remote Desktop is enabled, allowing connection requests on port 3389 to be received from any IP address.

If your connection has to pass through a router to get to your computer, be sure you take the additional steps outlined earlier in "Configuring a Router for Remote Desktop" on page 765. If you have replaced Windows Firewall with a third-party software firewall, you need to configure it to allow incoming access to TCP port 3389.

Using a Remote Desktop Connection

If you've enabled incoming remote connections on your PC at home or in the office and verified that your network and firewall have the welcome mat out (for visitors with suitable credentials only, of course), you're ready to begin using Remote Desktop Connection. In the Start menu search box, type **remote** and then click Remote Desktop Connection. A dialog box like the one shown in Figure 21-4 appears. In the Computer box, type the name of the remote computer or its IP address.

Figure 21-4 You can specify the remote computer by name or IP address.

> **Note**
>
> After a successful connection to a remote desktop, the name of the remote computer is added to the drop-down list in the Computer box. Thereafter, you can simply select it from the list (if it isn't already selected) instead of typing the name each time.
>
> In addition, if Remote Desktop Connection is pinned to your taskbar or Start menu (or if it's in the Start menu's recently used list), the name of each computer to which you've successfully connected appears on the Jump List. By using the Jump List and saved logon credentials, you can bypass this dialog box completely.

TROUBLESHOOTING

Your firewall blocks outbound access

If you use a third-party firewall that blocks unknown outbound traffic to the Internet, it prevents your initial attempt to connect to your remote desktop. Configure the firewall to enable Mstsc.exe (the file name of the Remote Desktop Connection program) to make outbound TCP connections on port 3389.

If you're willing to accept the default settings (about which we'll go into great detail later in this section), you can click Connect at this point. Here's what happens next.

Are both your client computer and the remote computer running Windows 7, Windows Vista, Windows Server 2008, Windows Server 2008 R2, or Windows Home Server 2011? In that case, your connection uses Network Level Authentication and displays the Windows Security dialog box shown here. After you enter your credentials and they're approved, Windows initiates the Remote Desktop Connection.

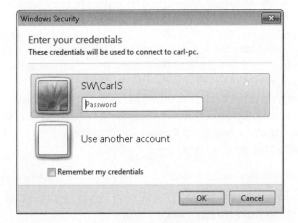

When you connect to a computer running Remote Desktop on an older version of Windows (such as Windows XP, Windows Home Server version 1, or Windows Server 2003), the procedure is different. Windows opens a Remote Desktop window (or switches to full screen) and initiates a session to the remote computer, changes the background of the Remote Desktop Connection window to match the settings on the remote machine, and then displays a logon dialog box. When you enter approved credentials, you're given access to your desktop.

If the account you used for the remote connection is already logged on to the remote computer—or if no one is logged on to the remote computer—the remote computer's desktop appears on your computer, either in a window or a full-screen display.

If a different user account is logged on to the remote computer, Windows lets you know that you'll be forcing that person to log off and gives you a chance to cancel the connection. On the other end, the logged-on user sees a similar notification that offers a short time to reject the remote connection before it takes over. It's important to note that only one user at a time can control the desktop of a computer running Windows. Whoever is currently logged on has the final say on whether someone else can log on.

While you're connected to the remote computer, the local display (if it's turned on) does not show what you see on the client computer but instead shows the Welcome screen. A person who has physical access to the remote computer can't see what you're doing (other than the fact that you are logged on remotely).

Changing Screen Resolutions and Display Settings

When you connect to a remote computer using Remote Desktop Connection, the remote computer takes over your entire screen. It uses the resolution of the client computer, regardless of the resolution set on the remote computer. Along the top of the screen, in the center, a small title bar appears. This title bar lets you switch between your own desktop and the remote desktop. The Minimize, Maximize, and Restore buttons work as they do in other programs.

The Pushpin button locks the title bar in place. If you click the pushpin, the title bar disappears completely, retracting into the top of the screen. To make the title bar reappear, "bump" the mouse pointer to the top edge of the screen. To keep the title bar visible at all times, click the pushpin again. The Close button disconnects the remote computer (but does not log you off the remote computer) and closes Remote Desktop Connection. You can pick up where you left off by reopening Remote Desktop Connection and reconnecting or by logging on locally at the remote computer.

INSIDE OUT   Move the title bar

If the title bar covers a part of the screen that you need to see, you can move it instead of hiding it altogether with the pushpin button. Simply slide it left or right.

You might prefer to use less than your full screen resolution for the remote desktop. (This option is especially useful if you have a large monitor and the work you want to do with Remote Desktop is just another task among several.) You must set the resolution—along with a number of other options—before you connect to the remote computer. After you start Remote Desktop Connection, click the Options button (shown in Figure 21-4) to expand the dialog box. Then click the Display tab, which is shown in Figure 21-5. You can set the screen resolution to any size that is supported on the client hardware, from 640 by 480 up to the current resolution of the client computer (not the remote computer). Set it to full screen by moving the slider all the way to the right.

Figure 21-5 Screen resolution is determined by the client computer.

If you have a multimonitor setup at your local computer, you might be excited to learn that Remote Desktop allows the use of multiple monitors. Temper that excitement with the knowledge that this feature works only with Windows 7 Ultimate and Enterprise editions, and the resulting remote display is "spanned" to spread across your multiple monitors as if they were a single display. To configure the connection for use with more than one monitor, select Use All My Monitors For The Remote Session.

Accessing Local Resources

While you use Remote Desktop Connection, it's immediately apparent that you have control of the remote computer. You see its desktop, Start menu, and so on. That's terrific if the remote computer has everything you need. But you'll often want to use local resources and information from the client computer as well as from the remote computer. In addition, you might want to move information between the two computers. With Remote Desktop Connection, you can do so easily by clicking the Options button to expand the Remote Desktop Connection dialog box to its full size and then adjusting any of the options on the Local Resources tab, shown in Figure 21-6.

Figure 21-6 Configure these Remote Desktop Connection settings before you make the connection—you can't change settings while the connection is active.

The following options are available:

- **Remote Audio** If your music collection is on the remote PC and you want some tunes at your current location, click Settings and select Play On This Computer. If you want both computers to be silent, choose Do Not Play. After clicking Settings, you can also tell Remote Desktop Connection whether to pay attention to the microphone (or other audio input) on the client computer.

- **Keyboard** When you press a Windows keyboard shortcut such as Alt+Tab, do you want to treat the Remote Desktop session as a window on the client computer, or do you want the remote session to handle your keyboard shortcuts?

- **Printers** When this option is selected, your local printers appear in the remote computer's Printers folder. Their entries have "(from *clientcomputername*)" appended to each printer name. To print to a local printer, select its name in the Print dialog box from any application.

- **Clipboard** When you copy or cut text or graphics on either the remote computer or the local computer, it's saved on the Clipboard in both locations. The Clipboard contents are then available for pasting in documents on either computer. Similarly, you can cut or copy files or folders from a Windows Explorer window on either computer and paste them into a folder on the other computer. Clear this option if you want to keep the contents of the two Clipboards separate.

The More button leads to additional devices in the Local Devices And Resources category. Smart cards are automatically enabled, and serial ports are disabled by default. Local drives and Plug and Play devices are also disabled by default. They can be enabled individually in this dialog box, as shown in Figure 21-7. These options are most useful if you're expecting to do most or all of your work with the Remote Desktop session in full-screen view and you don't want to continually flip back to your local desktop for file management tasks.

Figure 21-7 You control which (if any) client computer resources are available in the Remote Desktop Connection window.

TROUBLESHOOTING

You receive a security warning when you try to log on remotely

Remote Desktop Connection considers any connections to local hard drives to be a potential security risk. As a result, you'll see an extra security dialog box ("Do you trust this remote connection?") if you choose to make any local drives or Plug and Play devices available on the remote desktop. If you're comfortable with the configuration you've chosen, click Connect. If you want to adjust the connect settings, click the Details button to expand the dialog box. Then clear the check box for any category of resources.

Chapter 21

Using the Keyboard with Remote Desktop Connection

When the Remote Desktop Connection window is active, almost every key you press is passed to the remote computer. Certain key combinations, however, can be processed by the client computer, depending on the setting you make in the Keyboard section of the Local Resources tab of the Remote Desktop Connection dialog box (shown in Figure 21-6). You can specify that the key combinations shown in the first column of Table 21-1 are sent to the remote computer all the time, only when the remote desktop is displayed in full-screen mode, or never.

Table 21-1 **Special Keys in Remote Desktop Connection**

Key Combination for Local Session	Equivalent Key Combination for Remote Desktop Session	Description
Alt+Tab	Alt+Page Up	Switches between programs
Alt+Shift+Tab	Alt+Page Down	Switches between programs in reverse order
Alt+Esc	Alt+Insert	Cycles through programs in the order they were started
N/A	Ctrl+Alt+Break	Switches the remote desktop between a window and full screen
Ctrl+Alt+Delete	Ctrl+Alt+End	Displays the Windows Security screen
Ctrl+Esc	Alt+Home	Displays the Start menu
Alt+Spacebar	Alt+Del	Displays the Control menu of the active window (does not work when using Remote Desktop in full-screen mode)
Shift+Print Screen	Ctrl+Alt+Plus Sign (on numeric keypad)	Captures a bitmap image of the remote desktop and places it on the remote computer's Clipboard
Alt+Print Screen	Ctrl+Alt+Minus Sign (on numeric keypad)	Captures a bitmap image of the active window and places it on the remote computer's Clipboard

If you select On This Computer, key combinations from the first column of Table 21-1 are always applied to the client computer. To get the equivalent function on the remote computer, press the key combination shown in the second column. The same is true if you select Only When Using The Full Screen and the remote session is displayed in a window.

If you select On The Remote Computer, key combinations from the first column are applied to the remote computer. Key combinations in the second column are ignored (unless they have some function in the active application on the remote desktop). The same is true if you select Only When Using The Full Screen and the remote session is displayed in full-screen mode. One exception is the Ctrl+Alt+Delete combination, which is always applied to the client computer. Regardless of your Local Resources tab setting, you must press Ctrl+Alt+End to obtain the same result on the remote computer. As an alternative, in the remote session, open the Start menu and choose Windows Security.

Configuring Performance Options

When you first use Remote Desktop Connection, you might notice that the remote desktop doesn't display a background. Disabling the background is one of several settings you can make that affect the perceived performance of your remote session. How you set these options depends in large measure on the speed of the connection between the two computers. If you're using a dial-up connection, you should disable as many features as possible to reduce the amount of information that must be transmitted across the wire and keep the mouse and windows movements responsive. On the other hand, if you're connecting to another desktop over a fast local area network, you might as well enable all features to enjoy the full experience of working at the remote computer.

The performance-related options are on the Experience tab of the Remote Desktop Connection dialog box, shown in Figure 21-8. To quickly select an appropriate set of prepackaged options, select the speed of your connection from the list box.

Figure 21-8 Remote Desktop Connection has a default collection of settings for each connection speed.

Use those settings or select your own options. Three options on the Experience tab deserve further explanation:

- **Visual Styles**   Clearing the Visual Styles check box disables the Aero themes and Windows 7 Basic theme, causing everything to be displayed using the Windows Classic theme—the one used in earlier versions of Windows. For more information about themes, see "Personalizing Theme Elements: Visuals and Sounds" on page 138.

- **Persistent Bitmap Caching**   Unlike with the other options on the Experience tab, you get the fastest performance if you *select* (not clear) Persistent Bitmap Caching. Bitmap caching can speed up your connection by storing frequently used images on a local drive.

- **Desktop Composition**   This option must be selected if you plan to use Windows Aero visual effects. Aero support is available only if both the remote computer and the client are running Windows 7 Ultimate or Enterprise edition. If you use multiple monitors for a remote desktop connection, desktop composition cannot be used. For information about Aero, see "Understanding and Using Windows Aero" on page 139.

Saving a Remote Desktop Configuration

Changes you make in the expanded Remote Desktop Connection dialog box are automatically saved in a hidden file named Default.rdp (stored in your default save location for documents), and they're automatically used the next time you open Remote Desktop Connection. But you might want to have several different Remote Desktop Connection configurations for connections to different computers. If you have a portable computer, you might want different settings for use with different connections to the same computer (for example, a slow Wi-Fi connection from a hotel versus a fast LAN at your branch office).

You can also save your credentials (user name and password) along with the other settings. To do so, enter your user name in the Logon Settings section of the General tab and select Allow Me To Save Credentials. You'll be prompted to save the password (in encrypted form, of course) when you log on.

To save a configuration, simply make all your settings, click the General tab, and click Save As.

To reuse a stored configuration at a later time, start Remote Desktop Connection, click Options, click Open, and then double-click the stored file. More simply, select it from the Jump List for Remote Desktop Connection (on the taskbar or Start menu), or double-click the stored file in Windows Explorer.

Ending a Remote Session

When you're through with a Remote Desktop Connection session, you can lock, disconnect, or log off. These options appear in the lower right corner of the remote session's Start menu, in place of the shutdown and power options that appear on a local session's Start menu. (You must click the arrow to see all the options.)

Locking the computer keeps the remote session connected and all programs running, but it hides everything behind a logon screen that requests a password; this is comparable to pressing Windows logo key+L to lock your computer.

If you disconnect, your programs continue to run on the remote computer, but the remote connection is ended. The Welcome screen is visible on the remote computer, and it's available for another user. If you log on later—either locally or through a remote connection—you can pick up right where you left off. As an alternative to the Start menu command, you can disconnect by simply clicking the Close button on the title bar of the remote session.

Logging off closes all your programs and exits your user session before disconnecting.

You cannot turn off or restart the remote computer using options on the Start menu. To perform either task in a remote session, open the Start menu and choose Windows Security. In the lower right corner of the Windows Security screen, click the arrow next to the red power button to select an option. Choosing any of these options, of course, disconnects your remote session; if you want to use the remote computer after a restart, you'll need to reconnect.

Connecting Remotely with Windows Live Mesh

Windows Live Mesh is a component of Windows Live Essentials, a bundle of free add-ins for Windows from Microsoft. As we explain in "Synchronizing Files and Favorites with Windows Live Mesh" on page 295, Windows Live Mesh provides an easy way to synchronize files, favorites, and other settings between your computers. But Windows Live Mesh also offers perhaps the absolute easiest way to remotely access the desktop of one of your computers. It works with all editions of Windows 7 (as well as Windows Vista with Service Pack 2, Windows Server 2008 R2, and Windows Server 2008 with Service Pack 2) and, beyond its initial installation and making a single setting, requires no configuration on either computer or any network router.

It does have some limitations compared to Remote Desktop, including:

- Windows Live Mesh must be installed on both computers, and both must be in the collection of devices associated with your Windows Live ID. This makes it impractical for use on a public computer, or even on a friend's computer.

- Windows Live Mesh uses some assumptions about the speed of your Internet connection and is configured accordingly. Therefore, desktop background images don't appear during a remote connection; the desktop is black. (You can use Personalization in Control Panel to select a different solid color for the background if you prefer.) Sounds are not transmitted, and video playback is painful, at best. Unlike with Remote Desktop, these settings are not configurable.

- You can connect to only a single computer at a time.

To enable remote access to a computer, open Windows Live Mesh and click Remote. Initially, you'll see a screen similar to the one shown earlier in Figure 8-8 on page 299. Simply click Allow Remote Connections To This Computer and respond to the User Access Control prompt—the computer is now ready to receive connection requests.

To connect to one of your computers, open Windows Live Mesh and click Remote. An icon for each of the other computers associated with your Windows Live ID appears, as shown in Figure 21-9. Some computers (such as the one named Explorer in the figure) are shown as unavailable—a status that occurs unless all the following conditions are true:

- The remote computer must be powered on and running (that is, not in a sleep state), and it must be connected to the Internet.

- Remote connections via Windows Live Mesh must be enabled on the remote computer, as described in the preceding paragraph.

- The remote computer can't have any other open remote connections to it.

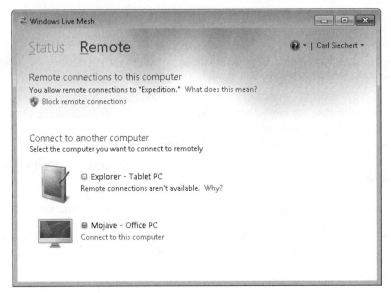

Figure 21-9 A green light appears next to the name of each computer that is available for connection.

To complete the connection, click Connect To This Computer. A connection status window appears on your computer while a dialog box appears on the remote computer, informing the user there (if any) that you're trying to make a remote connection. The user on that computer can deny your request (which he or she might choose to do because the computer is unavailable for anyone else's use while you have a remote connection open), allow your request immediately, or do nothing—in which case access is allowed after 30 seconds.

INSIDE OUT   Change the icons and names for your computers

By default, the Windows Live Mesh shows each computer using a standard computer image as an icon and the computer's name. If you have more than a couple of computers in your Windows Live Mesh network, you might want to make them easier to differentiate and identify. To do that, in Windows Live Mesh, click the Status tab and then click Go To Windows Live Devices. That leads to a page that shows all the computers and other devices, such as mobile phones, associated with your Windows Live ID. Simply click Personalize next to a device name, and you can specify a descriptive name and select an icon that more resembles your computer.

When the connection is made, the remote computer's desktop appears in a window on your local computer, ready for you to log on. You can then interact with the remote computer as if you're sitting right in front of it. As with Remote Desktop, to direct certain keystrokes to the remote computer instead of your client computer, you'll need to use the keystrokes shown earlier in Table 21-1.

If the resolution of the remote computer's screen is greater than that of your client computer, the remote session is reduced in size to fit your screen. This becomes most apparent when the remote computer has more than one monitor, as shown in Figure 21-10. When the Windows Live Mesh window for the remote computer can't show the entire screen at full size, a View window becomes available. Using the View window, you can zoom in or out and click to show different parts of the display.

Figure 21-10 also shows the only menu available in a Windows Live Mesh remote session, which appears when you click the computer name. As you can see, the menu is short and your options are few.

Chapter 21

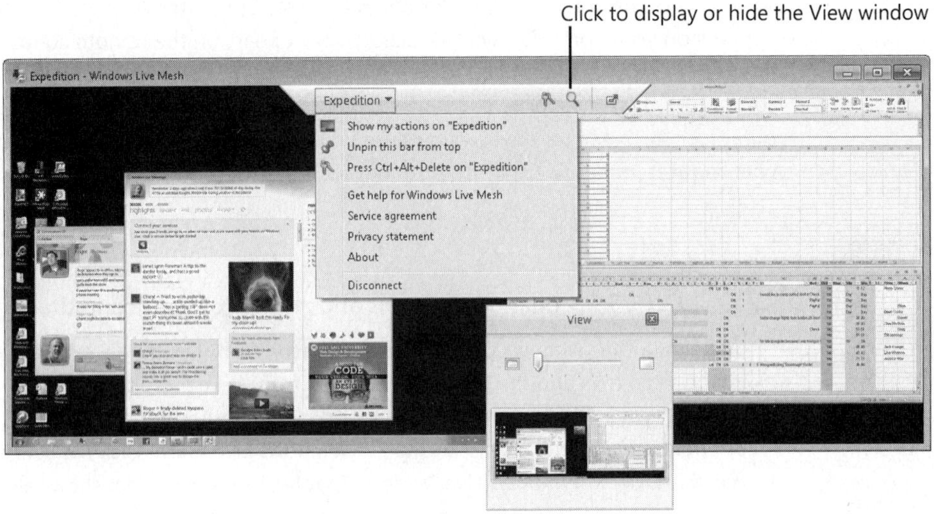

Click to display or hide the View window

Figure 21-10 If the remote computer has two monitors, as shown here, you might need the View window to maneuver around the screen.

Connecting Remotely to a Windows Home Server Network

As noted earlier in this chapter, configuring a home or small office network for remote access using Remote Desktop can be a formidable task. Furthermore, such a configuration has a major limitation: using a router for port forwarding allows remote access to only one PC on your local network. Windows Home Server 2011 (WHS) solves both these problems.

Windows Home Server 2011 is designed for use on home and very small office networks. One of its key features is an easy remote access interface. When you enable remote access on the server, you can connect to that server over the Internet and browse shared folders. If you've enabled Remote Desktop on any computers that are connected to the Windows Home Server, you can connect to those computers through the server's Remote Access interface. (The target computers must be running a supported Windows edition; you cannot make a Remote Desktop connection to a computer running Windows 7 Home Premium through Windows Home Server.)

The Windows Home Server option has other advantages as well, including a configuration tool that automates port forwarding for most UPnP-capable routers and sets up dynamic DNS.

Configuring Your Server and Computers

Before you can connect remotely to your WHS network, you need to set up Remote Web Access on the server. To do that, open the Windows Home Server 2011 Dashboard and then, under Getting Started Tasks on the Home tab, click Set Up Remote Web Access. (Alternatively, click Server Settings and then click the Remote Web Access tab.)

If Remote Web Access is properly configured, the status message at the top of the window reads "Available," your network's external IP address appears under Router, and the URL for accessing your server remotely appears under Domain Name. On a fresh installation of Windows Home Server, however, the window is more likely to look similar to the one shown in Figure 21-11.

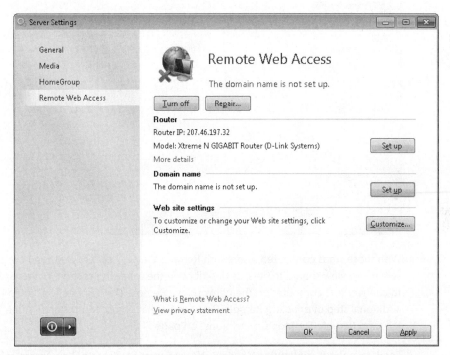

Figure 21-11 You must set up a domain name for remote access.

Under Router, click Set Up to run a wizard that configures your router. Then, under Domain Name, click Set Up to run a wizard that assists in obtaining a domain name if you need one and then directing your network's IP address to that domain name.

Next you need to visit the Users tab in the Dashboard and enable remote access for each user who plans to connect from outside the network. Double-click a user's name and, in the dialog box that appears, click the Remote Web Access tab, shown next. Select the first option and then select which WHS features and resources you want to make available to the selected user when he or she connects via the Internet.

With those steps completed, users with Remote Web Access allowed can connect to the server and view shared folders, as described in the following section. However, if you want to connect to a computer on the network in a Remote Desktop session, you must take the additional step of enabling Remote Desktop on that computer; for details, see "Enabling Inbound Remote Desktop Connections" on page 767.

For details about configuring Windows Home Server for Remote Web Access, refer to the online help in Windows Home Server.

Making a Remote Connection

With your Windows Home Server network ready to accept connections via Remote Web Access, the next step is simple: Enter your network's URL (which you can find in the Server Settings dialog box under Domain Name) in your web browser. The built-in web server in WHS asks for your user name and password; use the normal credentials assigned to your user account. (In the WHS Dashboard, you can specify the user name, password, and other settings by double-clicking a user name on the Users tab.)

You'll soon be greeted by your Remote Web Access home page, as shown in Figure 21-12. From here, you can navigate among your shared folders and your media library. You can also connect to any computer on which Remote Desktop has been enabled for your user account. When you click Connect, a Remote Desktop session opens. Although it's running in a web browser, it performs nearly identically to Remote Desktop on a local area network, as described under "Using a Remote Desktop Connection" on page 770.

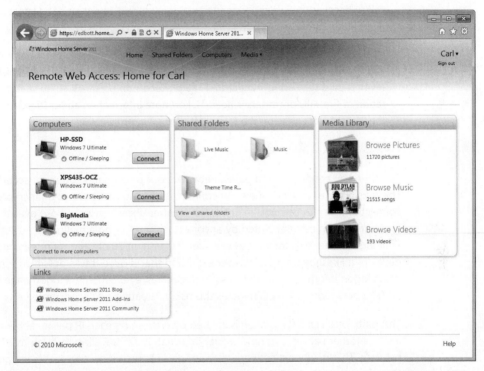

Figure 21-12 The links that appear on the home page depend on settings on the Remote Web Access tab of the properties dialog box for a user.

Using a Virtual Private Network for Remote Access

A *virtual private network (VPN)* is a secure means of connecting to a private network (such as your office intranet) via the public Internet. Unlike Remote Desktop, which we described earlier in this chapter, with a VPN your remote computer becomes another node on the network, rather than displaying the desktop of a computer already on the network.

INSIDE OUT   Use DirectAccess

If you have the Ultimate or Enterprise edition of Windows 7 and if the server you want to connect to is running Windows Server 2008 R2, you might be able to use Direct-Access, a new feature of Windows, instead of a VPN. (DirectAccess capability must be configured on the Windows Server 2008 R2 network.) Like a VPN, DirectAccess provides intranet access to a server over an Internet connection. But instead of you having to manually initiate a VPN connection, DirectAccess connects to the intranet automatically whenever the computer connects to the Internet, and it uses the latest encryption and security protocols.

Like a VPN, DirectAccess incorporates IPsec tunneling technologies to encrypt all data and encapsulate IPv6 traffic over IPv4 (for routing over the Internet, which relies on IPv4). Data is sent using standard HTTPS protocols on port 443, so no special configuration of firewalls or routers is needed. For more information about DirectAccess, visit the DirectAccess page on the Microsoft site: *w7io.com/22103*.

Any time you connect over a public network, your privacy and computer security is at risk. The risks are exacerbated when you connect to the Internet over an unencrypted Wi-Fi connection, such as one you might use in a coffee shop or hotel. Those over-the-air communications can be intercepted by anyone nearby, allowing a malicious hacker to grab your login credentials for various websites you visit. In 2010, security researcher Eric Butler developed Firesheep, a web browser extension that proved it was possible in some cases to glean logon information from transmitted cookies, even when the logon page itself uses HTTPS encryption. A VPN eliminates this risk by creating a fully encrypted end-to-end path.

This path (often called a *tunnel*) is created by encrypting each IP packet and wrapping it inside another packet with new header information for traveling through the intervening network. That is, when a network frame or packet created on one of the computers is destined for a computer on the other side of the tunnel, the entire frame is encrypted and a new header that routes the encrypted frame through the intervening network is attached. When the new frame gets to the other side, the new header is stripped off, and the original frame is decrypted and routed forward just as though it had never left the original local network.

Tunneling protocols are the core of VPNs. VPN communications in which both the server and client are running Windows 7 or Windows Server 2008 use the newest tunneling protocol, Secure Socket Tunneling Protocol (SSTP). It provides encryption over a Secure Sockets Layer (SSL) connection using TCP port 443—the same connection types you use when connecting to a secure website (https://). By using a widely used standard port, SSTP works with most firewalls without creating special rules.

Configuring a VPN Server

VPNs are most often used at the gateway to corporate networks, allowing employees to connect to the network and use resources (including Remote Desktop connections) as if they were back in the office. For the most part, these setups use third-party VPN solutions specifically designed for high-volume usage. For a standalone computer or a small network, where you need only a single incoming connection at any time, Windows 7 includes everything you need.

You can make any computer on your network a remote access server so that you (and others, if you choose to share access) can connect to it via a VPN and then access shared folders on your local drives. If your computer is connected to a local area network, incoming VPN connections can also browse the network and access shared resources elsewhere on the network.

To enable others to connect to your computer, follow these steps:

1. Open Network And Sharing Center and, in the tasks pane, click Change Adapter Settings.

2. Press Alt+F to open the File menu, which is hidden by default. Press N or click New Incoming Connection. A wizard appears.

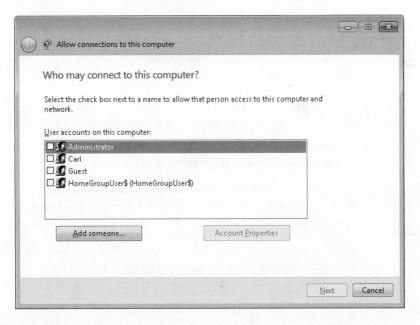

3. Select one or more names from the list of user accounts defined for this machine. You can use the Add Someone button to create a new user account on the fly. Click Next to continue.

4. On the How Will People Connect? page, select Through The Internet and click Next.

5. On the next wizard page, select the networking software you want to use with your incoming connection. By default, IPv4 is selected and IPv6 is not. Adjust these settings if you plan to use IPv6 connections. (Most people won't need this option.) Click Allow Access.

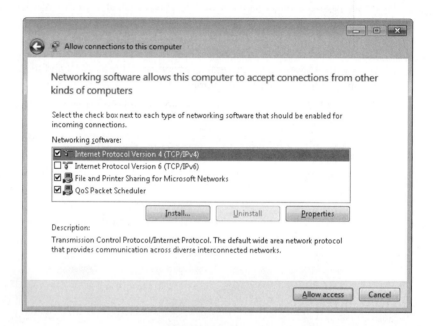

INSIDE OUT Be sure your VPN connection uses encryption

A secure VPN connection must use encrypted communications. You can enforce encryption requirements at the server or in the client.

On the server side (if you're using Windows 7 as a VPN server), open Network Connections, right-click Incoming Connections, and choose Properties. On the Users tab, be sure that Require All Users To Secure Their Passwords And Data is selected.

On the client computer, open Network Connections, right-click the VPN connection, and choose Properties. On the Security tab, select Require Encryption (Disconnect If Server Declines) or Maximum Strength Encryption (Disconnect If Server Declines).

To accept an incoming VPN connection from the Internet, your computer must be reachable with a public IP address. This IP address is assigned to you by your Internet service provider. If your computer is on a private network behind a router, you'll need to forward TCP port 1723 to the computer you want to accept incoming connections. You'll also need to allow the Generic Routing Encapsulation (GRE) protocol through the router. Most routers can do this in one step if you enable the incoming VPN option in their advanced setup pages. (For information about port forwarding and dynamic IP addresses, see "Configuring a Router for Remote Desktop" on page 765. The ports and protocols might be different, but the configuration procedures are similar for both access types.)

Connecting to a Virtual Private Network

To connect to your corporate VPN or to a computer where you've already configured an incoming VPN connection, follow these steps. (Note that you can connect to your Windows 7 VPN server with any version of Windows. The steps are similar for all Windows versions.)

1. Open Network And Sharing Center and, under Change Your Network Settings, click Set Up A New Connection Or Network.

2. In the Choose A Connection Option dialog box, click Connect To A Workplace and click Next.

3. On the How Do You Want To Connect? page, click Use My Internet Connection (VPN).

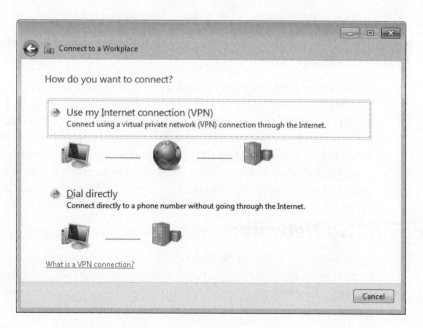

4. On the following page, click in the Internet Address box and enter the IP address or qualified domain name of the computer you want to connect to. In the Destination Name box, enter the name you want to use for this connection. Adjust other options in this dialog box as needed and click Next.

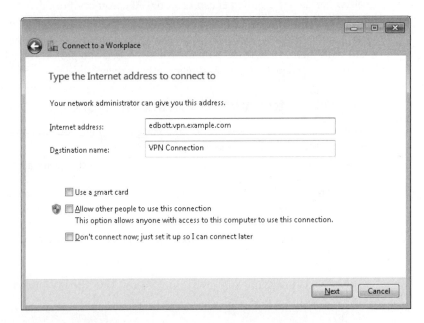

5. On the following page, enter the user name and password required to connect to the VPN connection.

To connect to a VPN, click the Network icon in the notification area, click the VPN connection you want to use, and then click Connect. If you don't already have a connection to the Internet open, Windows offers to connect to the Internet. Once that connection is made, the VPN server asks for your user name and password (if you chose not to save the credentials with the other connection settings). After entering the proper credentials, click Connect, and the network resources should be available to you in the same way they are when you connect directly to the network.

Bridging Two Networks

As we noted in Chapter 19, "Setting Up a Small Office or Home Network," Windows supports a variety of network media types, including Ethernet, Home Phoneline Networking, and wireless connections. In some cases, your home or small business network might consist of two or more different types of physical networks. For instance, you might have two desktop computers in your upstairs den connected to an Ethernet router and residential gateway, which serves as your connection to the Internet. In the basement, you have another computer that you want to add to the network. Running network cable to that distant location is impractical, and it's too far away for a reliable wireless connection. You do have a phone jack in that location, however, so you've installed a phone-line network adapter and plugged it into that jack. Upstairs, you've installed a phone-line adapter in one of the desktop computers.

You now have two networks. The upstairs computers can communicate easily, and one of them communicates with the basement computer as well. But the basement computer can't reach the other upstairs computer, and it's cut off from the Internet as well. How do you bring all three computers into the same network? You create a network bridge, which brings the two networks together seamlessly and creates a virtual connection between the separate network segments. In this example, you would bridge the two network connections on the computer with the two adapters.

Bridging also can be useful if you have a mix of different vintage Wi-Fi equipment on your network. You can keep each technology (for example, 802.11b and 802.11n) on a separate network to maintain maximum security and speed on each network. Then, on a computer with multiple Wi-Fi adapters, bridge the separate networks.

Although the steps to create a bridge are simple, the concepts behind it are potentially confusing. Here's what you need to know:

- You can create a bridge using any two (or more) Ethernet, IEEE-1394, or Ethernet-compatible wireless adapters. You cannot add a virtual private network (VPN) connection, a dial-up Internet connection, or a direct cable connection to a network bridge.

- Although it's technically possible, you should never bridge a connection that has a public Internet address with one that connects to a private network. In that configuration, you should use Internet Connection Sharing instead.

- When you use a network bridge, the machine that has the bridge enabled must be turned on to allow other computers to communicate across the virtual network. If you shut down that computer, you also shut down the bridge.

To create a bridge, in Network Connections select the first connection, hold down Ctrl, and then select each additional connection. Right-click and choose Bridge Connections from the shortcut menu.

Chapter 21

After you create the bridge, a new device, Network Bridge, appears in the Network Connections folder, as shown here:

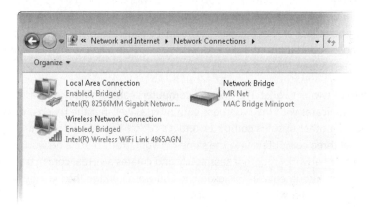

After you create the bridge, the settings for individual connections are no longer available. To view details of your network configuration, double-click the Network Bridge icon. To change details of the bridged connection, right-click the Network Bridge icon and click Properties. The resulting dialog box, shown in Figure 21-13, lets you adjust configuration details for individual adapters or configure IP settings for the bridged connection.

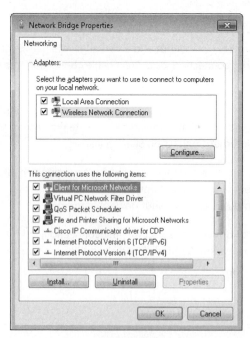

Figure 21-13 To remove adapters from the network bridge, clear the appropriate check boxes in the Adapters section of this dialog box.

You can have only one network bridge on a single computer, although you can, in theory, have as many as 68 network adapters joined in a bridge. To add or remove network adapters from the bridge, right-click the connection icon in the Network Connections window and choose Add To Bridge or Remove From Bridge. If you decide you no longer want to use the network bridge, you can remove it by right-clicking the Network Bridge icon and clicking Delete.

Chapter 21

Fixing and Tweaking Your Network

W HEN you encounter network problems, the troubleshooting process can be tricky because it's difficult to determine where the fault lies. In some cases, network problems are directly related to hardware, either on the local computer, elsewhere on your network, or at another stop on the connection between your computer and an Internet destination. But the problem can also be caused by a faulty configuration on your computer.

Windows 7 has tools for automatically detecting and, in many cases, resolving network problems. In this chapter, we introduce these tools and explain how to identify and repair common configuration problems on home and small business networks, including TCP/IP address errors, improper subnet settings, and Domain Name System (DNS) problems. We also explain how to identify situations in which a network is performing at less than its optimum speed, and we show you how to modify various network-related settings.

> ### What's in Your Edition?
>
> The networking features described in this chapter work identically in all Windows 7 editions.

Viewing Status in Network And Sharing Center

Network And Sharing Center is the place to go for a quick overview of your network connections and the condition of your network. And, if you're experiencing problems with your network, it serves as a launchpad to various diagnostic tools.

For details about opening Network And Sharing Center, see "Using Network And Sharing Center" on page 686.

When connectivity is broken between your computer and the rest of your network, or if your Internet connection is broken, Network And Sharing Center displays a red X or a yellow caution sign in the line that symbolizes the connection, as shown in Figure 22-1. (A symbol also appears in the network·icon in the taskbar notification area to alert you to a problem even if Network And Sharing Center isn't open.)

Figure 22-1 An X indicates trouble.

Click the X or caution sign to launch Windows Network Diagnostics, which tries to determine the cause and fix the problem or suggest a solution. Sometimes, the problem is as simple as a loose connection.

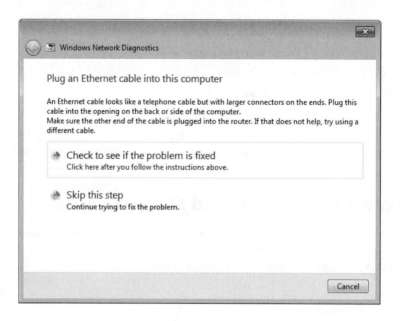

Other situations might point to problems outside your network.

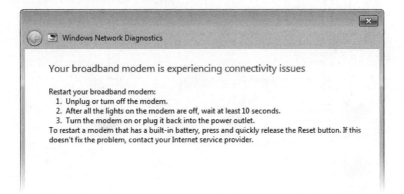

This feature of Network And Sharing Center—the X that indicates a broken connection—is suggestive of the basic troubleshooting process for many connectivity problems: namely, isolate the problem. If the diagnostic capabilities leave you at a dead end, you'll find that restarting the affected network hardware often resolves the problem, because the hardware is forced to rediscover the network. Here is a good general procedure:

1. Isolate the problem. Does it affect all computers on your network, a subset of your network, or only one computer?

2. If it affects all computers, try restarting the Internet device (that is, the cable or DSL modem). If it doesn't have a power switch, unplug it for a few moments and plug it back in.

3. If the problem affects a group of computers, try restarting the router to which those computers are connected.

4. If it affects only a single computer, try repairing the network connection for that computer. In Network And Sharing Center, click Change Adapter Settings. Then, in Network Connections, select the connection and click Diagnose This Connection. For more details, see "Repairing Your TCP/IP Configuration" on page 811.

Diagnosing Problems Using Network Map

Network mapping, a feature that was new in Windows Vista, uses the Link Layer Topology Discovery (LLTD) protocol to find the other computers and devices on your network, and then it displays them in a schematic representation. To display the map, in Network And Sharing Center click See Full Map. Figure 22-2 shows an example.

Chapter 22

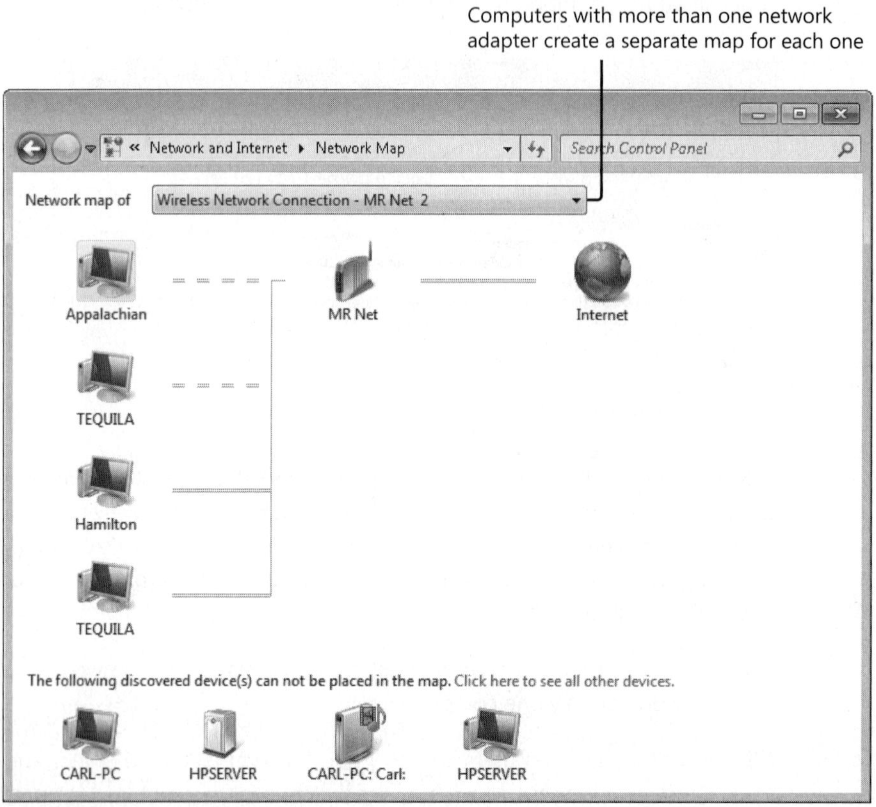

Computers with more than one network
adapter create a separate map for each one

Figure 22-2 The computer you're using is always shown in the upper left corner of Network Map. Notice that the computer named Tequila has a wireless connection (represented by a dotted line) and a wired connection (represented by a solid line) to the router.

Network mapping works with wired and wireless networks, but only on private (home or work) network locations; by default, you can't view a map of a domain-based network or a public network. LLTD maps only the computers in a single subnet—the typical setup in a home or small office.

You might notice that some computers and devices are shown separately at the bottom of the window, or they might be missing altogether. In addition, you will probably see multiple entries for some PCs that offer services beyond file sharing. For example, the two Hpserver devices at the bottom of the display shown in Figure 22-2 represent different services on a server running Windows Home Server. It supports UPnP but not LLTD, and thus it can't be placed on the map correctly. This occurs because not all operating systems and devices include LLTD support, or because the devices might not be configured properly.

INSIDE OUT   Use Network Map on a domain computer

By making changes through Group Policy, you can enable network mapping on domains, public networks, or both. (This option will be unavailable if a Group Policy object disables these policy settings.) To make this change, follow these steps:

1. At a command prompt or in the Start menu search box, type **gpedit.msc** to open the Local Group Policy Editor. (The Local Group Policy Editor is available on computers running the Professional, Enterprise, or Ultimate edition of Windows 7. These are also the only editions that can join a domain.)

2. Navigate to Computer Configuration\Administrative Templates\Network\Link-Layer Topology Discovery.

3. Double-click the Turn On Mapper I/O (LLTDIO) Driver policy.

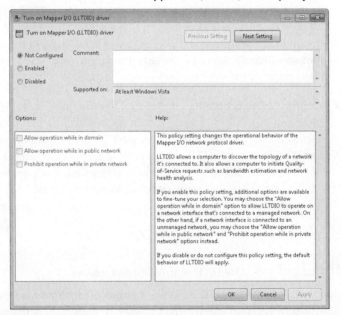

4. Select Enabled, and then select Allow Operation While In Domain.

5. Click Next Setting.

6. Repeat the selections for the Turn On Responder (RSPNDR) Driver policy setting, and then click OK.

Note that, depending on the size of the network, creating a network map on a domain-based network can be inordinately slow, which is why it is disabled by default. Note also that you can use these same policy settings to enable network mapping on a public network and, if you want, disable network mapping on a private network. For security and convenience, we don't recommend either of these options.

Chapter 22

Devices shown at the bottom generally fall into one of the following categories:

- **Computers running Windows XP**   LLTD is installed by default in Windows 7 and Windows Vista, but it is not included in earlier Windows versions. An LLTD client is available for Windows XP, and it should be available through Windows Update. (To find out if it's installed, look at the properties for the network connection and see if LLTD appears in the list of installed protocols.) You can download and install the protocol without Windows Update; for details, see Knowledge Base article 922120 (*w7io.com/1902*). Note that if you have already installed Service Pack 3 for Windows XP, you'll need the hotfix available from *w7io.com/1905*. LLTD is not currently available for other versions of Windows.

- **Other network devices**   LLTD (along with another network discovery–related technology, Plug and Play Extensions, or PnP-X) is part of the Windows Rally technologies, an initiative for network hardware devices that gained steam in 2006. Devices that include LLTD support became widely available in 2007 and later, but earlier devices are not fully recognized by Network Map. Most devices sold in recent years support UPnP, which should get the device somewhere in the map window; however, Network Map displays only limited information about the device and offers only limited control of the device.

- **Configuration problems**   In Network And Sharing Center, be sure that your network is not identified as a public network, and be sure that network discovery is turned on. In Network Connections, view the properties of your network connection and be sure that two LLTD-related protocols, Link Layer Topology Discovery Mapper I/O Driver and Link Layer Topology Discovery Responder, are installed and enabled (that is, their check boxes are selected). Whether you use Windows Firewall or another firewall, be sure it has an exception enabled for file and printer sharing.

INSIDE OUT   Use LLTD with Windows Server

It's possible to use the LLTD client for Windows XP on Windows Server 2003, as described in *Windows IT Pro* magazine (*w7io.com/1903*, subscription required), and on the first version of Windows Home Server (which is based on Windows Server 2003), as described by Microsoft MVP Donavon West (*w7io.com/1904*). These workarounds are not supported by Microsoft, so apply them with caution. (Be sure you have a current backup and set a restore point.)

Network Map is more than a pretty picture. If you hover the mouse pointer over a computer or other device, you get more information about the device, including information such as its IPv4 and IPv6 addresses and its Media Access Control (MAC) address.

Network infrastructure devices (such as routers) that include Wi-Fi Protected Setup support offer a menu of choices when you right-click them, usually including one that leads to the device's configuration page. Right-clicking a computer icon displays relevant options for that computer, such as connecting to it using Remote Desktop Connection. For computers and other devices with shared resources, you can double-click them in Network Map to open them, just as you can in the Network folder.

Network Map, like the "mini-map" in Network And Sharing Center, indicates broken network connections with an X. Click Diagnose And Repair to attempt a solution.

Troubleshooting Network Problems

Windows 7 has built-in network diagnostic capabilities, so in many cases, if there is a problem with your network connection, Windows knows about it before you do, displays a message, and often solves the problem.

To discover and resolve problems, Windows uses the Network Diagnostics Framework (NDF). When a network-dependent activity (for example, browsing to a website) fails, NDF automatically springs into action. NDF is designed to address the most common network-related issues, such as problems with file-sharing, website access, newly installed network hardware, connecting to a wireless network, and using a third-party firewall.

Chapter 22

For more information about NDF, see "New Network Diagnostic Framework and Network Tracing Features in Windows 7" at *w7io.com/1901*.

If you encounter network problems that don't trigger an automatic response from Windows, you should first try to detect and resolve the problem with one of the built-in troubleshooters. In Network And Sharing Center, click Troubleshoot Problems to display the choices shown in Figure 22-3. (Alternatively, in the Troubleshooting control panel, click Network And Internet.)

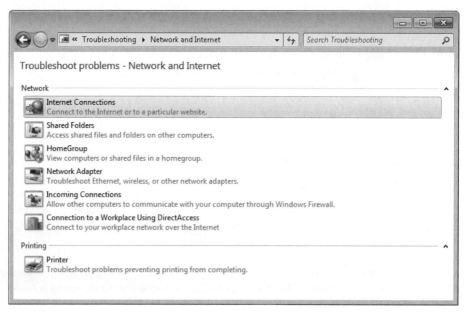

Figure 22-3 Click any of these options to launch a troubleshooter that performs numerous diagnostic and corrective steps.

Each of the troubleshooting wizards performs several diagnostic tests, corrects some conditions, suggests actions you can take, and ultimately displays a report that explains the wizard's findings. For more information about troubleshooting wizards and interpreting their reports, see "Using Troubleshooters to Solve Problems" on page 1016.

Troubleshooting HomeGroup Problems

The HomeGroup troubleshooting wizard provides a good example of how these troubleshooters work. If you're having problems seeing shared resources in a homegroup and you didn't have the benefit of the troubleshooter's assistance, you'd need to check the following settings, among others:

- The network location profile must be set to Home Network.

- In Windows Firewall With Advanced Security, you need to ensure that the following groups of rules are enabled on private networks:

    - Core Networking

    - Network Discovery

    - HomeGroup

    - File/Printer Sharing (not on domain-joined machines)

    - Windows Media Player (not on domain-joined machines)

    - Windows Media Player Network Sharing Service (not on domain-joined machines)

- The following services must be configured so that they can run:

    - HomeGroup Listener

    - HomeGroup Provider

    - Function Discovery Provider Host

    - Function Discovery Resource Publication

    - Peer Name Resolution Protocol

    - Peer Networking Grouping

    - Peer Networking Identity Manager

Running the HomeGroup troubleshooter—which you can launch from HomeGroup or by right-clicking HomeGroup in Windows Explorer as well as from the list of troubleshooters shown in Figure 22-3—checks each of these items and more. When you get to the wizard's

Chapter 22

last window, click View Detailed Information to see a troubleshooting report that lists the potential problems that the wizard attempted to identify and fix, as shown here:

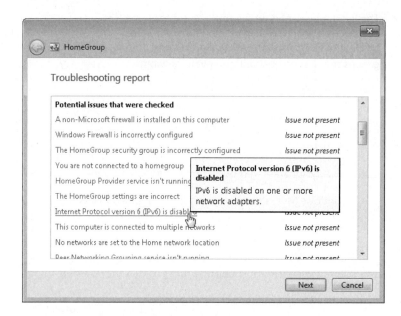

Network Troubleshooting Tools

When the troubleshooters don't solve the problem, it might be time to dig deeper into the Windows toolbox. Windows 7 contains an assortment of utilities you can use to diagnose, monitor, and repair network connections. Table 22-1 lists some of the more useful networking-related command-line utilities and summarizes how you can use them. To learn more about each utility, including its proper syntax, open a Command Prompt window and type the executable name followed by **/?**.

A more powerful tool is available as a free download from Microsoft. Network Monitor is a protocol analyzer that lets you capture network traffic, view it, and analyze it. Download it at *w7io.com/1906*, and learn more about it on the Network Monitor blog at *w7io.com/1907*.

Chapter 22

Table 22-1 **Windows Network Utilities**

Utility Name	What It's Used For
Get MAC Address (Getmac.exe)	Discovers the Media Access Control (MAC) address and lists associated network protocols for all network cards in a computer, either locally or across a network.
Hostname (Hostname.exe)	Displays the host name of the current computer.
IP Configuration Utility (Ipconfig.exe)	Displays all current Transmission Control Protocol/Internet Protocol (TCP/IP) network configuration values, and refreshes Dynamic Host Configuration Protocol (DHCP) and DNS settings.
Name Server Lookup (Nslookup.exe)	Displays information about Domain Name System records for specific IP addresses and/or host names so that you can troubleshoot DNS problems.
Net services commands (Net.exe)	Performs a broad range of network tasks. Type **net** with no parameters to see a full list of available command-line options.
Netstat (Netstat.exe)	Displays active TCP connections, ports on which the computer is listening, Ethernet statistics, the IP routing table, and IPv4/IPv6 statistics.
Network Command Shell (Netsh.exe)	Displays or modifies the network configuration of a local or remote computer that is currently running. This command-line scripting utility has a huge number of options, which are fully detailed in Help.
PathPing (Pathping.exe)	Combines the functions of Traceroute and Ping to identify problems at a router or network link.
TCP/IP NetBIOS Information (Nbtstat.exe)	Displays statistics for the NetBIOS over TCP/IP (NetBT) protocol, NetBIOS name tables for both the local computer and remote computers, and the NetBIOS name cache.
TCP/IP Ping (Ping.exe)	Verifies IP-level connectivity to another Internet address by sending Internet Control Message Protocol (ICMP) packets and measuring response time in milliseconds.
TCP/IP Route (Route.exe)	Displays and modifies entries in the local IP routing table.
TCP/IP Traceroute (Tracert.exe)	Determines the path to an Internet address, and lists the time required to reach each hop. It's useful for troubleshooting connectivity problems on specific network segments.

Chapter 22

Troubleshooting TCP/IP Problems

Transmission Control Protocol/Internet Protocol (TCP/IP) is the default communications protocol of the Internet; in Windows 7, it's installed and configured automatically and cannot be removed. Most of the time, your TCP/IP connection should just work, without requiring any manual configuration. When you encounter problems with TCP/IP-based networks, such as an inability to connect with other computers on the same network or difficulty connecting to external websites, the problems might be TCP/IP related. You'll need at least a basic understanding of how this protocol works before you can figure out which tool to use to uncover the root of the problem.

Checking for Connection Problems

Anytime your network refuses to send and receive data properly, your first troubleshooting step should be to check for problems with the physical connection between the local computer and the rest of the network. Assuming your network connection uses the TCP/IP protocol, your most potent weapon is the Ping utility. When you use the Ping command with no parameters, Windows sends four echo datagrams—small Internet Control Message Protocol (ICMP) packets—to the address you specify. If the machine at the other end of the connection replies, you know that the network connection between the two points is alive.

> ## Note
>
> Where does the name *Ping* come from? Some claim that it's short for Packet Internet Groper. However, the author of this utility, which was written for BSD UNIX in 1983, says it was originally named after the sound a submarine's sonar system makes when it sends out pulses looking for objects in the sea.

To use the Ping command, open a Command Prompt window (Cmd.exe) and type the command **ping *target_name*** (where *target_name* is an IP address or the name of another host machine). The return output looks something like this:

```
C:\>ping www.example.com

Pinging www.example.com [192.0.34.166] with 32 bytes of data:

Reply from 192.0.34.166: bytes=32 time=31ms TTL=48
Reply from 192.0.34.166: bytes=32 time=30ms TTL=48
Reply from 192.0.34.166: bytes=32 time=30ms TTL=48
Reply from 192.0.34.166: bytes=32 time=33ms TTL=48

Ping statistics for 192.0.34.166:
    Packets: Sent = 4, Received = 4, Lost = 0 (0% loss),
Approximate round trip times in milli-seconds:
    Minimum = 30ms, Maximum = 33ms, Average = 31ms
```

If all the packets you send come back properly in roughly the same time, your TCP/IP connection is fine and you can focus your troubleshooting efforts elsewhere. If some packets time out, a "Request timed out" message appears, indicating that your network connection is working but one or more hops between your computer and the target machine are experiencing problems. In that case, repeat the Ping test using the –n switch to send a larger number of packets; **ping –n 30 192.168.1.1**, for example, sends 30 packets to the computer or router at 192.168.1.1.

> **Note**
>
> **The –n switch is case-sensitive; don't capitalize it.**

A high rate of timeouts, also known as *packet loss*, usually means the problems are elsewhere on the network and not on the local machine. (To see the full assortment of switches available for the Ping command, type **ping** with no target specified.)

If every one of your packets returns with the message "Request timed out," the problem might be the TCP/IP connection on your computer or a glitch with another computer on that network. To narrow down the problem, follow these steps, in order, stopping at any point where you encounter an error:

1. Ping your own machine by using any of the following commands:

   ```
   ping ::1
   ping 127.0.0.1
   ping localhost
   ```

   The standard IP addresses are shown on the first two lines, and the standard hostname is shown on the third line. (The first line is the IPv6 address for your own computer; the second line is the IPv4 address.) If your local network components are configured correctly, each of these three commands should allow the PC on which the command is run to talk to itself. If you receive an error, TCP/IP is not configured properly on your system. For fix-it details, see "Repairing Your TCP/IP Configuration" on page 811.

2. Ping your computer's IP address.

3. Ping the IP address of another computer on your network.

4. Ping the IP address of your router or the default gateway on your network.

5. Ping the address of each DNS server on your network. (If you don't know these addresses, see the next section for details on how to discover them.)

Chapter 22

6. Ping a known host outside your network. Well-known, high-traffic websites are ideal for this step, assuming that they respond to ICMP packets.

7. Use the PathPing command to contact the same host you specified in step 6. This command combines the functionality of the Ping command with the Traceroute utility to identify intermediate destinations on the Internet between your computer and the specified host or server.

INSIDE OUT Choose your test site carefully

In some cases, pinging an external website results in a string of "Request timed out" messages, even when you have no trouble reaching those sites. Don't be misled. Some popular sites, including Microsoft's home page, *www.microsoft.com*, block all ICMP traffic, including Ping packets, as a routine security measure. Some routers and residential gateways are also configured to block certain types of ICMP traffic. Try pinging several sites before concluding that your Internet connection is broken.

If either of the two final steps in this process fails, your problem might be caused by DNS problems, as described later in this chapter. (For details, see "Resolving DNS Issues" on page 812.) To eliminate this possibility, ping the numeric IP address of a computer outside your network instead. (Of course, if you're having DNS problems, you might have a hard time finding an IP address to ping!) If you can reach a website by using its IP address but not by using its name, DNS problems are indicated.

If you suspect that there's a problem on the Internet between your computer and a distant host or server, use the Traceroute utility (Tracert.exe) to pinpoint the problem. Like the Ping command, this utility works from a command line. You specify the target (a host name or IP address) by using the syntax **tracert *target_name***, and the utility sends out a series of packets, measuring the time it takes to reach each hop along the route. Timeouts or unusually slow performance indicate a connectivity problem. If the response time from your network to the first hop is much higher than the other hops, you might have a problem with the connection to your Internet service provider (ISP); in that case, a call to your ISP's support line is in order. Problems farther along in the traceroute might indicate congestion or hardware problems in distant parts of the Internet that are out of your ISP's hands. These symptoms might disappear when you check another URI that follows a different path through the Internet.

If your testing produces inconsistent results, rule out the possibility that a firewall program or Network Address Translation (NAT) device (such as a router or residential gateway) is to blame. If you're using a third-party firewall program, disable it temporarily. Try bypassing your router and connecting directly to a broadband connection such as a DSL or cable modem. (Use this configuration only for testing and only very briefly because it exposes your computer to various attacks.)

If the Ping test works with the firewall or NAT device out of the picture, you can rule out network problems and conclude that the firewall software or router is misconfigured. After you complete your testing, be sure to enable the firewall and router again!

Diagnosing IP Address Problems

On most networks, IP addresses are assigned automatically by Dynamic Host Configuration Protocol (DHCP) servers; in some cases, you may need (or prefer) to use static IP addresses, which are fixed numeric addresses. Problems with DHCP servers or clients can cause network connections to stop working, as can incorrectly assigned static IP addresses.

To see details of your current IP configuration, follow these steps:

1. In Network And Sharing Center, click Change Adapter Settings.

2. Double-click the icon for the connection about which you want more information. (Alternatively, you can select the icon and click View Status Of This Connection on the toolbar.)

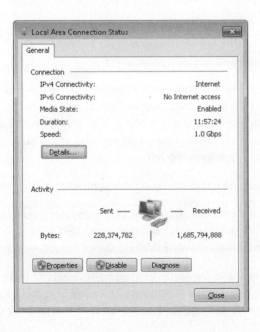

3. Click Details to see the currently assigned IP address, subnet mask, and default gateway for this connection. (If you have IPv4 and IPv6 connectivity, the Network Connection Details dialog box shows information for both.) In the following example, you can tell that the IP address was automatically assigned by the DHCP server in a router; details indicate that DHCP is enabled and the DHCP server address matches that of the router.

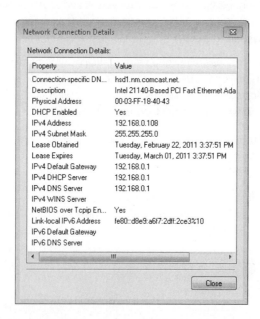

You can also get details of your IP configuration by using the IP Configuration utility, Ipconfig.exe, in a Command Prompt window. Used without any parameters, typing **ipconfig** at a command prompt displays the DNS suffix, IPv6 and/or IPv4 address, subnet mask, and default gateway for each network connection. To see exhaustive details about every available network connection, type **ipconfig /all**.

The actual IP address you see might help you solve connection problems:

- If the address is in the format 169.254.*x*.*y*, your computer is using Automatic Private IP Addressing (APIPA). This means your computer's DHCP client was unable to reach a DHCP server to be assigned an IP address. Check the connection to your network.

- If the address is in one of the blocks of IP addresses reserved for use on private networks (for details, see "Setting IP Addresses" on page 824), make sure that a router or residential gateway is routing your Internet requests to a properly configured public IP address.

- If the address of your computer appears as 0.0.0.0, the network is either disconnected or the static IP address for the connection duplicates an address that already exists on the network.

- Make sure you're using the correct subnet mask for computers on your local network. Compare IP settings on the machine that's having problems with those on other computers on the network. The default gateway and subnet mask should be identical for all network computers. The first one, two, or three sets of numbers in the IP address for each machine should also be identical, depending on the subnet mask. A subnet mask of 255.255.255.0 means the first three IP address numbers of computers on your network must be identical—192.168.0.83 and 192.168.0.223, for instance, can communicate on a network using this subnet mask, but 192.168.1.101 will not be recognized as belonging to the network. Likewise, with a subnet mask of 255.255.0.0, the first two numbers in each address must match—172.16.2.34, 172.16.4.56, and 172.16.83.201 are all valid addresses on a subnet with this mask. In every case, the gateway machine must also be a member of the same subnet. (If you use a router, switch, or residential gateway for Internet access, the local address on that device must be part of the same subnet as the machines on your network.)

> **Note**
>
> Are you baffled by subnets and other related technical terms? For an excellent over-view of these sometimes confusing topics, read Knowledge Base article 164015, "Understanding TCP/IP Addressing and Subnetting Basics" (*w7io.com/1908*), which offers information about IPv4. For comparable details about IPv6, see the "Introduction to IPv6" white paper at TechNet (*w7io.com/1909*).

Repairing Your TCP/IP Configuration

If you suspect a problem with your TCP/IP configuration, try either of the following repair options:

- **Use the automated repair option**   Right-click the connection icon in Network Connections and click Diagnose.

- **Renew your IP address**   Use the **ipconfig /renew** command to renew your IPv4 address from the DHCP server; use **ipconfig /renew6** to renew the IPv6 address.

> **Note**
>
> If these methods don't work, you can use the Netsh utility to restore the TCP/IP stack to its original configuration when Windows was first installed. The utility restores all registry settings relating to the TCP/IP stack to their original settings, which is effectively the same as removing and reinstalling the protocol. The utility records a log of the changes it makes. For details about this drastic, but effective, solution, see Microsoft Knowledge Base article 299357 (*w7io.com/299357*). Although the article was written for Windows Vista, its advice applies to Windows 7 as well. Another option is to uninstall and reinstall the network adapter, as described in "Enabling and Disabling Individual Devices" on page 1094.

Resolving DNS Issues

The Domain Name System (DNS) is a crucial part of the Internet. DNS servers translate host names (*www.microsoft.com*, for instance) into numeric IP addresses so that packets can be routed properly over the Internet. If you can use the Ping command to reach a numeric address outside your network but are unable to browse websites by name, the problem is almost certainly related to your DNS configuration.

Here are some questions to ask when you suspect DNS problems:

- **Do your TCP/IP settings point to the right DNS servers?** Inspect the details of your IP configuration, and compare the DNS servers listed there with those recommended by your Internet service provider. (You might need to call your ISP to get these details.)

- **Is your ISP experiencing DNS problems?** A misconfigured DNS server (or one that's offline) can wreak havoc with your attempts to use the Internet. Try pinging each DNS server to see whether it's available. If your ISP has multiple DNS servers and you encounter problems accessing one server, remove that server from your TCP/IP configuration temporarily and use another one instead.

- **Have you installed any "Internet accelerator" utilities?** Many such programs work by editing the Hosts file on your computer to match IP addresses and host (server) names. When Windows finds a host name in the Hosts file, it uses the IP address listed there and doesn't send the request to a DNS server. If the owner of the server changes its DNS records to point to a new IP address, your Hosts file will lead you to the wrong location.

Temporary DNS problems can also be caused by the DNS cache, which Windows maintains for performance reasons. If you suddenly have trouble reaching a specific site on the Internet and you're convinced there's nothing wrong with the site, type this command to clear the DNS cache: **ipconfig /flushdns**.

INSIDE OUT   Translate names to IP addresses and vice versa

The Nslookup command is a buried treasure in Windows. Use this command-line utility to quickly convert a fully qualified domain name to its IP address. You can tack on a host name to the end of the command line to identify a single address; type **nslookup ftp.microsoft.com**, for instance, to look up the IP address of Microsoft's File Transfer Protocol (FTP) server. Or type **nslookup** to switch into interactive mode. From this prompt, you can enter any domain name to find its IP address. If you need more sophisticated lookup tools, you can find them with the help of any search engine. A good starting point is DNSstuff (*w7io.com/22201*), which offers an impressive collection of online tools for looking up domains, IP addresses, and host names. The site also offers form-based utilities that can translate obfuscated URLs and dotted IP addresses, both of which are widely used by spammers to cover their online tracks.

Maximizing Network Performance

Is your network running more slowly than it should? A fast, easy way to measure the performance of all active network connections is to use Windows Task Manager. To view current networking statistics, open Windows Task Manager by pressing Ctrl+Shift+Esc and then click the Networking tab.

For more information about how to use Windows Task Manager, see "Using Windows Task Manager" on page 841.

In the example shown next, two network connections are active, so two graphs appear, one for each connection. Note that neither connection is close to saturating available network bandwidth.

On most networks, the speed of the connection to the Internet is the limiting factor for network performance. Fast Ethernet connections, with a theoretical maximum transfer speed of 100 megabits per second, run 10 to 30 times faster than even the fastest cable or DSL connections, and Gigabit Ethernet dials that up by another factor of 10. Wireless connections that are having difficulty reaching an access point might display performance problems as they automatically throttle down to lower connection speeds. This slowdown will be most obvious when you are trying to transfer large files between two computers on the network.

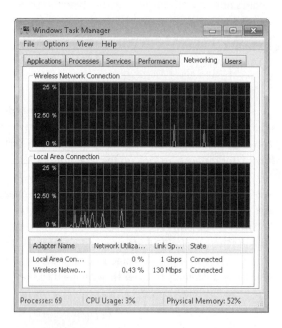

CAUTION

The Internet is awash with sites that claim to offer helpful advice and utilities that you can use to tweak settings such as the TCP Receive Window (RWIN) and Maximum Transmission Unit (MTU) values, with the goal of improving the performance of a TCP/IP-based network. Beware! Most of these articles are based on TCP/IP settings from previous Windows versions and do not apply to Windows 7, which generally does a good job of configuring connections properly. (The Cable Guy at TechNet explained TCP/IP performance enhancements in Windows Vista, which also apply to Windows 7; see *w7io.com/1910*.) In fact, tweaking settings without understanding their consequences is a near-certain route to slower performance, and it might result in connection problems when your tweaked packets hit routers and other connection points on the Internet that can't handle them. If you feel compelled to experiment, set a System Restore checkpoint first, and read the definitive and exhaustive Tweaking FAQ at the Broadband DSLreports.com site, *w7io.com/1911*, before you fire up Registry Editor.

Changing Network Settings

The default network settings in most cases produce a working network environment with minimal fuss and bother. However, you might want to modify some of the settings for your network.

Specifying the Order and Connection Properties of Preferred Wi-Fi Networks

The first time you connect to a wireless network, Windows adds that network to the top of the list of networks that use your wireless connection. If you take your computer to a different location and connect to a new network, that location is added to the list of wireless networks.

Each time you turn on your computer or enable your wireless adapter, Windows attempts to make a connection. The WLAN AutoConfig service tries to connect to each network in the list in the order that those networks appear. Unlike Windows XP, which included in its preferred networks list only networks that broadcast their SSID, Windows 7 includes non-broadcast networks also. This makes it possible to set a nonbroadcast network to a higher priority than an available broadcast network; Windows XP exhausts the list of broadcast networks before attempting to connect to an available nonbroadcast network.

You can alter the order of networks in the list and configure any entry for manual rather than automatic connection. To manage the settings of entries on the list of preferred networks, in Network And Sharing Center, click Manage Wireless Networks to open the window shown in Figure 22-4.

To change the order of entries in the list, select the entry you want to move and then click Move Up or Move Down. Alternatively, you can drag a network to the position you want it.

TROUBLESHOOTING

Windows switches between preferred networks

If you're within range of more than one preferred network, Windows might switch repeatedly between the networks as signal strengths vary. This causes delays as your computer negotiates each new connection and sometimes drops the connection altogether. To prevent this from happening, in Manage Wireless Networks, double-click one of the interfering networks. On the Connection tab, clear Connect To A More Preferred Network If Available and then click OK.

Chapter 22

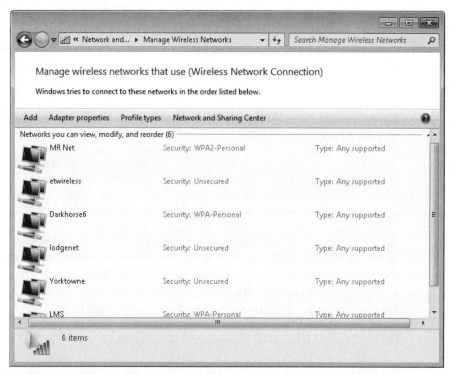

Figure 22-4 The list includes all wireless networks associated with a particular network adapter. If you have more than one wireless adapter installed, the toolbar includes a Change Adapter button.

Manage Wireless Networks is also the place to review and, optionally, change connection settings for a network. To do that, double-click a network, which opens the network's properties dialog box, shown in Figure 22-5.

To change an entry in the networks list from automatic to manual, or vice versa, select or clear Connect Automatically When This Network Is In Range. Settings on the Security tab let you specify the type of security and encryption and enter the security key or passphrase; if that information has changed since you set up the connection initially, you can change it here instead of creating a new network.

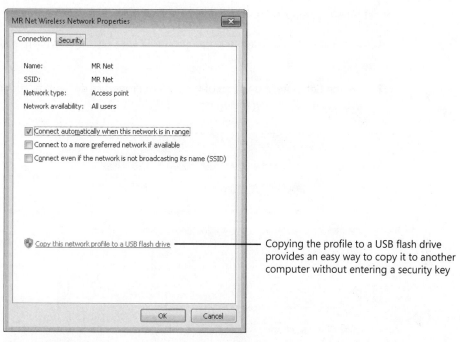

Copying the profile to a USB flash drive provides an easy way to copy it to another computer without entering a security key

Figure 22-5 Settings on the Connection tab determine whether Windows should attempt to connect automatically.

Renaming Your Workgroup

A workgroup is identified by a name; all computers in a workgroup must be in the same local area network and subnet, and all must share the same workgroup name. In Windows 7, the workgroup name is largely invisible and irrelevant; when you open the Network folder or look at a network map, Windows displays all computers in the network, regardless of which workgroup they're in. (However, network discovery is faster when all computers are in the same workgroup.)

That was not the case in Windows XP and earlier versions of Windows, which display in their network folders only computers in the same workgroup as your computer. Therefore, if your network includes computers running earlier versions of Windows, you should use the same workgroup name for all computers so that they can see each other. The default name for a new workgroup in Windows 7, Windows Vista, and Windows XP Professional is WORKGROUP; in Windows XP Home, it is MSHOME.

Chapter 22

To set the workgroup name in Windows 7, follow these steps:

1. In the Start menu search box or in Control Panel, type **workgroup**, and then click Change Workgroup Name.

2. On the Computer Name tab of the System Properties dialog box, click Change, which displays the following dialog box:

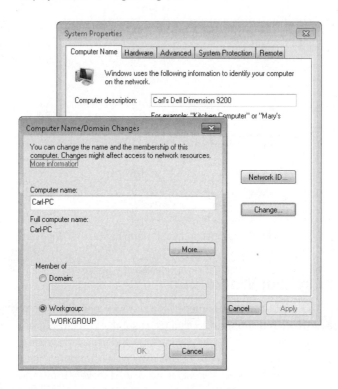

3. In the Computer Name/Domain Changes dialog box, select Workgroup and type the name of the workgroup (15-character maximum; the name can't include any of these characters: ; : < > * + = \ | / ? ,). Then click OK in each dialog box.

4. Restart your computer.

Except for the first step, the process for changing the workgroup name in Windows XP is nearly identical: Right-click My Computer and choose Properties. Then follow steps 2 through 4 in the procedure just shown.

Renaming Your Network

You can change the name and the icon for your network. This information appears in Network And Sharing Center and in the information that pops up when you click the network icon in the taskbar notification area. The network initially takes on the name of the wireless SSID or, if you join a domain, the domain name. (The default name of a wired network is Home or Network.)

To make the change, in Network And Sharing Center, under View Your Active Networks, click the icon for your network. Type the name you want in the Network Name box. If you want to select a different icon, click Change, where you'll find icons suggestive of a library, office building, park bench, airport, coffee shop, and more.

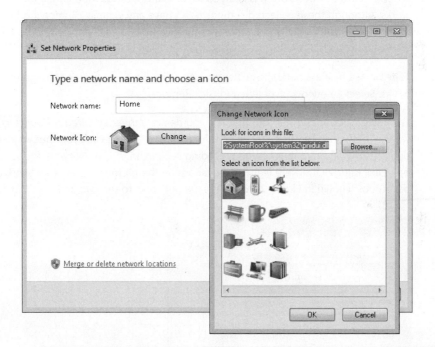

Chapter 22

Note

Changing the network name does not affect the workgroup name, wireless SSID, or domain name. And the name you choose is visible only on your computer; other computers can assign different names to the same network with no ill effects.

INSIDE OUT   Rename from Manage Wireless Networks

The Manage Wireless Networks window (shown earlier in Figure 22-4) can be a more convenient place to change the network name because it lets you rename networks to which you're not currently connected. Simply right-click a network and choose Rename.

Removing a Network

A computer that travels often is likely to accumulate settings for a large number of networks. Although these collected settings don't have any significant impact on performance or disk space, you might find it helpful to remove from the list entries that you don't plan to use again, such as one for a network at a hotel you don't expect to revisit.

To remove a wireless network, in Network And Sharing Center, click Manage Wireless Networks. Select a network to delete and click Remove.

Windows includes another tool that lets you delete unneeded wired networks as well as wireless networks. To use it, in Network And Sharing Center, click your network's icon to open the dialog box shown in the preceding section. In the Set Network Properties dialog box, click Merge Or Delete Network Locations. In the Merge Or Delete Network Locations dialog box (shown in Figure 22-6), select the networks to remove and click Delete.

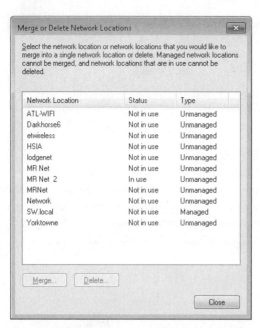

Figure 22-6 Connections to a domain are identified as Managed network locations.

Managing Network Connections

After you've installed your networking hardware (wired or wireless) and configured drivers and other supporting software, Windows creates a local connection that includes the following networking features:

- **Client For Microsoft Networks**   A network client provides access to computers and resources on a network; this client allows you to connect to computers running any 32-bit or 64-bit Windows version.

- **QoS Packet Scheduler**   This feature enables Quality of Service features provided on corporate networks and by Internet service providers. For the most part, these advanced features will not be widely used until Internet Protocol version 6 (IPv6) is also widely used.

- **File And Printer Sharing For Microsoft Networks**   This service allows other computers on your Windows-based network to access shared resources on your computer.

- **Internet Protocol Version 6 (TCP/IPv6)**   TCP/IP is the default network protocol in Windows 7, and IPv6 is the latest incarnation. For more information about IPv6, see "Understanding IPv6" on page 823.

- **Internet Protocol Version 4 (TCP/IPv4)**   The ubiquitous TCP/IPv4 provides easy connectivity across a wide variety of networks, including the Internet. Although TCP/IP has plenty of options you can configure, most users can safely accept the default settings without having to make any configuration changes.

- **Link Layer Topology Discovery Mapper I/O Driver**   The Link Layer Topology Discovery (LLTD) protocol is used to create the network map, which provides a graphical view of the devices on your network and shows how they are connected. The LLTD mapper is one of two items required for creating a network map.

- **Link Layer Topology Discovery Responder**   Besides the mapper, LLTD also relies on a responder, which answers requests from the mapper.

For more details about TCP/IP configuration, see "Setting IP Addresses" on page 824 and "Troubleshooting TCP/IP Problems" on page 806. For information about network mapping, see "Diagnosing Problems Using Network Map" on page 797.

This default collection of clients, services, and protocols is generally all you need to work with a Microsoft network (that is, one where all computers are running 32-bit or 64-bit versions of Windows).

Chapter 22

To see information about currently defined network connections, in Network And Sharing Center, click Change Adapter Settings. Figure 22-7 shows the information and configuration options available from this window.

Figure 22-7 Try using Details view to see more information about each connection.

INSIDE OUT   Rename your connections

Windows tags your main network connection with the Local Area Connection or Wireless Network Connection label. When you add connections, they get equally generic titles, such as Local Area Connection 2. Get in the habit of renaming all connections in this folder with descriptive names. The names you assign appear in Windows Task Manager graphs, Network And Sharing Center, notification area icons, status dialog boxes, and any other place where you can expect to see information about connections. Descriptive names make it much easier to troubleshoot, especially when you have multiple connections active. For instance, on a computer that's serving as an Internet Connection Sharing host, you might give your two network adapters distinctive names like "Comcast Cable Modem" and "Home Network Connection." To edit a connection label, right-click the connection icon, choose Rename from the shortcut menu, and then type the descriptive name.

Understanding IPv6

Internet Protocol version 6 (IPv6) is a network layer that is designed to overcome shortcomings of the original Internet Protocol, IPv4. (That's right; the first version was dubbed IPv4, and the second version is IPv6.) The most significant difference is the much larger address space. The 32-bit IPv4 addressing scheme provides for a theoretical maximum of approximately 4 billion unique addresses, which seemed like a lot when the Internet and Internet Protocol were conceived nearly three decades ago. (Because of the way IP addresses are allocated, the actual number in use is far less.) As a stopgap measure to overcome the limited number of IP addresses, private IP addresses and Network Address Translation were implemented, because this system allows a large number of computers to share a single public IP address.

Alas, on February 3, 2011, the Internet Assigned Numbers Authority (IANA) announced that it had allocated the last remaining addresses in the IPv4 pool. There will be no shortage of addresses with IPv6, which uses 128-bit addresses—providing a pool of 3.4×10^{38} addresses. (That's over 50 octillion addresses for every person on earth. Not many people have that many computers and other electronic devices, each of which will ultimately be reachable by its IPv6 address.)

Although NAT has been promoted as a security measure that shields networked computers behind a NAT firewall from external attack—which it does reasonably well—the security benefit was largely an afterthought; its real *raison d'être* is to ease the address shortage. IPv6 brings true security improvements, achieving the long-sought goal of security implemented at the network layer level; standards-based Internet Protocol security (IPsec) support is part of every IPv6 protocol suite.

Other improvements in IPv6 include easier configuration and more efficient routing.

Unfortunately, although IPv6 is being rapidly rolled out in many Asian countries, its adoption in the West is likely to take many years. Full implementation requires not only support at the host operating system—which we now have in Windows 7, Windows Server 2008 R2, and other recent versions of Windows—but application and hardware support as well, including the routers that tie together the various nodes of the Internet and the firewalls that keep them apart. Replacing the existing hardware (not just routers, but also printers and other network-connected devices) and other infrastructure will require huge investment and much time.

Until the transition to IPv6 is complete many years hence, you can gain several of its benefits with Windows 7. Today, computers running Windows 7 can communicate over IPv4 and IPv6 networks at the same time. This means that if your local area network (or your ISP) supports IPv6, Windows will use it because IPv6 is the primary protocol in

Chapter 22

Windows 7. Several crucial Windows 7 features depend on IPv6, so we strongly advise against disabling it unless you understand the consequences. At the time we wrote this chapter, many Internet service providers were still conducting tests before officially implementing their IPv6 infrastructure. Check with your ISP to see if you need to make any changes to your network.

You can also access IPv6 websites and other resources even if the intervening network infrastructure doesn't support IPv6, because Windows will automatically fall back to a tunneling system such as Teredo. (Teredo is an IPv6 transition technology that allows end-to-end communication using IPv6 addresses; NAT translation tables on Teredo client computers allow it to communicate through routers that use NAT. Other tunneling systems effectively embed IPv6 data in IPv4 packets.)

While you wait for the transition to IPv6 to be complete, you can find plenty of detailed information (business-related and technical) about IPv6 at the Microsoft IPv6 website, *microsoft.com/ipv6*. And if you *really* want the details, we recommend *Understanding IPv6, Second Edition*, by Joseph Davies (Microsoft Press, 2008).

Setting IP Addresses

Networks that use the TCP/IP protocol rely on *IP addresses* to route packets of data from point to point. On a TCP/IP network, every computer has a unique IP address for each protocol (that is, TCP/IPv4 and TCP/IPv6) in use on each network adapter. An IPv4 address—the type that will continue to be used on most networks for many years to come—consists of four 8-bit numbers (each one represented in decimal format by a number from 0 through 255) separated by periods. An IPv6 address consists of eight 16-bit numbers (each one represented in hexadecimal format) separated by colons. In addition to the IP address, each computer's TCP/IP configuration has the following additional settings:

- A *subnet mask*, which tells the network how to distinguish between IP addresses that are part of the same network and those that belong to other networks

- A *default gateway*, which is a computer that routes packets intended for addresses outside the local network

- One or more *Domain Name System (DNS) servers*, which are computers that translate domain names (such as *www.microsoft.com*) into IP addresses

Windows 7 provides several methods for assigning IP addresses to networked computers:

- **Dynamic Host Configuration Protocol (DHCP)**   This is the default configuration for Windows 7. Most ISPs start with a pool of IP addresses that are available for use by their customers. ISPs use DHCP servers to assign IP addresses from this pool and to set subnet masks and other configuration details as each customer makes a new connection. When the customer disconnects, the address is held for a period of time and eventually released back to the pool so that it can be reused. Many corporate networks use DHCP as well to avoid the hassle of managing fixed addresses for constantly changing resources; all versions of Windows Server include this capability. The Internet Connection Sharing feature in Windows 7 includes a full-fledged DHCP server that automatically configures all TCP/IP settings for other computers on the network. Most routers and residential gateways also incorporate DHCP servers that automatically configure computers connected to those devices.

- **Automatic Private IP Addressing (APIPA)**   When no DHCP server is available, Windows automatically assigns an IP address in a specific private IP range. (For an explanation of how private IP addresses work, see the sidebar "Public and Private IP Addresses" on page 829.) If all computers on a subnet are using APIPA addresses, they can communicate with one another without requiring any additional configuration. APIPA was introduced with Windows 98 and works the same in all versions of Windows released since that time.

  For detailed technical information about APIPA, including instructions on how to disable it, read Knowledge Base article 220874, "How to Use Automatic TCP/IP Addressing Without a DHCP Server" (*w7io.com/220874*).

- **Static IP Addressing**   By entering an IP address, subnet mask, and other TCP/IP details in a dialog box, you can manually configure a Windows workstation so that its address is always the same. This method takes more time and can cause some configuration headaches, but it allows a high degree of control over network addresses.

  Static IP addresses are useful if you plan to set up a web server, a mail server, a virtual private network (VPN) gateway, or any other computer that needs to be accessible from across the Internet. (New features in Windows, such as Teredo and Windows Internet Computer Name, make it possible to access a computer over the Internet even without a static IP address, however.) Even inside a local network, behind a router or firewall, static IP addresses can be useful. For instance, you might want to configure the router so that packets entering your network on a specific port get forwarded to a specific computer. If you use DHCP to assign addresses within the local network, you can't predict what the address of that computer will be on any given day. But by assigning that computer a static IP address that is within the range of addresses assigned by the DHCP server, you can ensure that the computer always has the same address and is thus always reachable.

- **Alternate IP Configuration**   This feature allows you to specify multiple IPv4 addresses for a single network connection (although only one address can be used

Chapter 22

at a time). This feature is most useful with portable computers that regularly connect to different networks. You can configure the connection to automatically acquire an IP address from an available DHCP server, and you can then assign a static backup address for use if the first configuration isn't successful.

To set a static IP address, follow these steps:

1. In the Network Connections folder, select the connection whose settings you want to change. On the toolbar, click Change Settings Of This Connection. (Alternatively, right-click the icon and choose Properties.)

2. In the list of installed network items, select Internet Protocol Version 4 (TCP/IPv4) or Internet Protocol Version 6 (TCP/IPv6), and then click Properties.

3. In the Internet Protocol (TCP/IP) Properties dialog box, select Use The Following IP Address and fill in the blanks. You must supply an IP address, a subnet mask (for IPv6, the length of the subnet prefix, which is usually 64 bits), and a default gateway.

4. Select Use The Following DNS Server Addresses, and then fill in the numeric IP addresses for one or more DNS servers as well. Figure 22-8 shows the dialog box with all fields filled in.

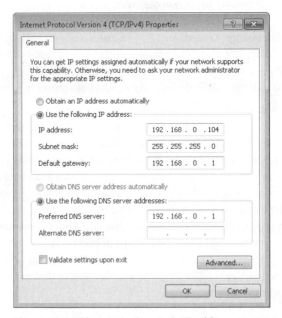

Figure 22-8 When assigning static IP addresses, you must fill in all fields correctly. To avoid making a mistake that could cause you to lose your network connectivity, select Validate Settings Upon Exit.

5. Click OK to save your changes. You do not need to reboot after changing your IP configuration.

When you configure an alternate IP configuration for a network connection, Windows looks first for a DHCP server to assign an IP address automatically. If no DHCP server is available, the system falls back to the static IP address defined on the Alternate Configuration tab. To set up an alternate IP configuration, follow these steps:

1. In the Internet Protocol Version 4 (TCP/IPv4) Properties dialog box shown in Figure 22-8, select Obtain An IP Address Automatically.

2. Click the Alternate Configuration tab (it appears after you select Obtain An IP Address Automatically), and then select User Configured.

3. Enter the IP address, subnet mask, default gateway, and DNS servers for the alternate connection. (You can safely ignore the fields that ask you to enter a preferred and alternate WINS server. WINS stands for Windows Internet Naming Service, a name resolution system that maps a computer's NetBIOS name to an IP address. WINS servers are used on large corporate networks to allow domain servers to communicate with computers running older Microsoft operating systems, including Windows NT, Windows 95, Windows 98, and Windows Me. For virtually all home and small business networks, the WINS server details are unnecessary and irrelevant.)

4. Click OK to save your changes. You do not need to restart after setting up an alternate configuration.

Configuring Power Management

Most network connections support Wake On LAN—the ability to wake a sleeping computer by sending a message over the network. This feature lets you take advantage of power-saving features, yet still have access to your computer, perhaps to perform a scheduled backup during the night or to play media files from a shared folder.

To check on the power management settings for a network connection:

1. In Network Connections, select the connection and click Change Settings Of This Connection. (Alternatively, right-click the connection and choose Properties.)

2. In the connection properties dialog box, click Configure to display the properties dialog box for the network adapter hardware.

Chapter 22

3. On the Power Management tab, shown here, select Allow This Device To Wake The Computer.

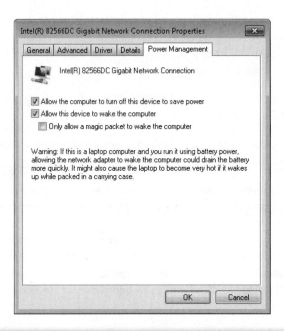

Note

You might find that your computer is a light sleeper, and that it wakes up at times you don't want it to. If that's the case, select Only Allow A Magic Packet To Wake The Computer. For more details, see Knowledge Base article 941145 at *w7io.com/941145*.

Public and Private IP Addresses

Any computer that is directly connected to the Internet needs a public IP address—one that can be reached by other computers on the Internet—so that information you request (web pages and e-mail, for instance) can be routed back to your computer properly. When you connect to an Internet service provider, you're assigned a public IP address from a block of addresses registered to that ISP. If you use a dial-up connection, your ISP probably assigns a different IP address to your computer (drawn from its pool of available addresses) each time you connect. If you have a persistent connection to your ISP via a DSL or cable modem, your IP address might be permanent—or semi-permanent if you turn off your computer when you leave your home or office to travel and your assigned IP address is changed when you reconnect on your return.

On a home or small office network, it's not necessary to have a public IP address for each computer on the network. In fact, configuring a network with multiple public addresses can increase security risks and often requires an extra fee from your ISP. A safer, less costly solution is to assign a single public IP address to a router or residential gateway (or a computer that performs that function). All other computers on the network connect to the Internet through that single address. Each of the computers on the local network has a private IP address that is not directly reachable from the outside world. To communicate with the Internet, the router on the edge of the network uses a technology called Network Address Translation (NAT) to pass packets back and forth between the single public IP address and the multiple private IP addresses on the network.

The Internet Assigned Numbers Authority (IANA) has reserved the following three blocks of the IP address space for use on private networks that are not directly connected to the Internet:

- 10.0.0.0–10.255.255.255

- 172.16.0.0–172.31.255.255

- 192.168.0.0–192.168.255.255

In addition, the Automatic Private IP Addressing feature in all post-1998 Windows versions uses private IP addresses in the range 169.254.0.0 through 169.254.255.255.

Routers and residential gateways that use NAT almost always assign addresses from these private ranges. Linksys routers, for instance, typically assign addresses starting with 192.168.1.x. The Internet Connection Sharing feature in Windows 7 (as in previous versions of Windows) assigns private IP addresses in the 192.168.0.x range. If you're setting up a small business or a home network that will not be connected to the Internet, or that will be connected through a single proxy server, you can freely use these addresses without concern for conflicts. Just make sure that all the addresses on the network are in the same subnet.

Tuning Up and Monitoring Performance

U LTIMATELY, the performance of your PC is a matter of personal preference. For some, waiting a few seconds as the system starts is no big deal. For others, it's worth spending hours of tweaking and tuning to shave a few milliseconds off the time it takes for an application to launch.

The software engineers who designed and built Windows 7 paid close attention to making sure that it takes full advantage of the hardware on which it's installed. We know from personal experience and extensive hands-on testing that they've succeeded admirably, but we also know that it's possible for performance problems to crop up unexpectedly. Our goal in this chapter is to help you measure performance accurately and fix problems when they occur, with a minimum of fuss and effort. And no, we don't believe you need an engineering degree, an oscilloscope, or expensive third-party software to determine the cause of and solution to performance problems.

Let's make it clear, right from the start, that we don't believe there is a secret formula, magic bullet, or special MakeRocketShipGoFast registry hack that will suddenly send your system zooming into warp speed. Our formula for getting great performance out of a Windows PC is much more prosaic: start with quality parts, make sure everything has the right drivers and is up to date, and then look at ways to speed you through your workday and make games go faster.

Windows 7 includes a number of tools that you can use to pinpoint performance bottlenecks. In this chapter, we help you identify all those tools plus a handful of extras that are not included with the operating system but should be a part of your toolkit as well. These tools include those that provide a snapshot of available system resources and how they're being used, as well as others that allow you to monitor performance over time and zero in on problems and solutions.

What's in Your Edition?

The information in this chapter applies equally to all editions of Windows 7.

Establishing a Performance Baseline

Before you begin trying to improve performance, it's crucial to make sure that all the major subsystems that affect performance are working properly and that you have a proper baseline for comparing the results of any changes you make. Only after you're certain that nothing is broken or improperly configured can you begin trying to make those subsystems work more efficiently.

What causes a PC to perform poorly? In our experience, the most common causes (listed in no particular order) are these:

- **Defective hardware**   Memory and disk errors are most obvious when they cause system crashes, but hardware-related problems can also cause performance to drag. Before you do any serious benchmarking or performance investigation, we recommend that you run a memory test (such as the one available as part of the Windows Recovery Environment) and a thorough disk diagnostic program. The latter is often available as a free download from disk drive makers. Seagate's SeaTools utility (*w7io.com/2002*), for example, was designed for use with Seagate and Maxtor drives. Western Digital offers several utilities under the Data Lifeguard label for its drives (*w7io.com/2003)*. Check with the manufacturer of your hard drive to see what options are available for your hardware.

   For more details on using the built-in repair tools in Windows 7, see "Making Repairs with the Windows Recovery Environment" on page 1046.

- **Outdated or flawed device drivers**   Writing device drivers is an art, not just a science. If one or more crucial system components are using drivers that were originally written for Windows Vista, you might benefit from an upgrade. (The same holds true if a component such as a storage controller is using a generic, Windows-supplied driver instead of one written specifically for that device.) We have seen performance problems vanish immediately after a simple driver upgrade. Always be certain you're using the best possible drivers for all system devices. (Don't assume that a newer driver is automatically better than an older one, however; any driver update has the potential to cause new problems.)

- **Inadequate hardware resources**   Are the individual hardware components of your system up to the work you're trying to do? Windows 7 should perform basic tasks well on even low-end hardware that was designed and built in 2008 or later. But more demanding tasks, such as high-definition media playback or media encoding, can push some systems to the breaking point. If your system is older (or if it's a budget model that incorporates older technology), make sure your hardware is within the specifications of the software you're trying to run.

- **Active background tasks**   Every system includes some programs designed to run as a background task, including antivirus software and some Windows maintenance tasks. If your system is configured to run some programs automatically, you might need to adjust their schedules or operating parameters to make certain they don't steal resources you need for work (or play). Later in this chapter, we discuss how to pinpoint processes and services that are temporarily using resources and having an impact on system performance.

  For instructions on how to identify programs that run automatically at startup or when you log on, see "Managing Startup Programs" on page 186.

- **Out-of-control processes or services**   Sometimes, a program or background task that normally runs just fine will spin out of control, consuming up to 100 percent of CPU time or grabbing increasing amounts of memory or other system resources. In the process, of course, performance of all other tasks slows down or grinds to a halt. Knowing how to identify and kill this sort of process or service and prevent it from recurring is a valuable troubleshooting skill.

- **Malware**   Viruses, Trojan horse programs, spyware, and other forms of unwanted software can wreak havoc on system performance. Be sure to check for the possibility that malware is lurking on a system that is exhibiting other unexplained performance problems.

After you've confirmed that none of the issues in the preceding list are affecting your system's performance, you're ready to take some initial measurements so that you have a valid baseline with which to compare the results from any changes you make later. Windows 7 includes several tools that you can use to get a here-and-now picture of your system's health and performance. These tools (which will be familiar to anyone who has upgraded from Windows Vista) include the following:

- The Windows Experience Index and its command-line companion, the Windows System Assessment Tool (Winsat.exe)

- The System Health report (also known as System Diagnostics)

- Resource Monitor

Using the Windows Experience Index

How well does your PC run Windows? You can attach a numerical rating called the Windows Experience Index (WEI) to it and get at least a crude measurement. If you're willing to look at several screens' worth of raw data, you can get a much better idea.

To see your PC's rating, open System in Control Panel. In the center of the dialog box, you'll see a single numeric rating like the one shown here:

Click Windows Experience Index to see all five categories that go into the overall rating, as shown in Figure 23-1.

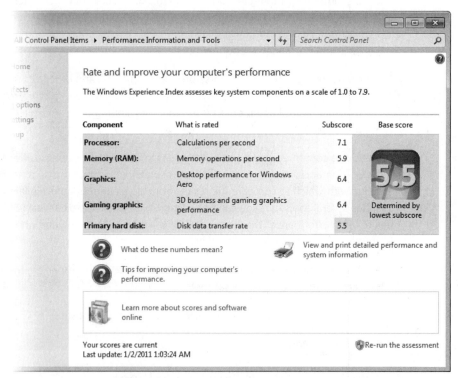

Figure 23-1 The Windows Experience Index measures five elements of your system's performance and returns a score based on the weakest element.

If you're familiar with the WEI from Windows Vista, you'll notice at least one significant difference immediately. The scale now goes from a minimum of 1.0 to a maximum of 7.9 (up from 5.9) in each category.

INSIDE OUT   Why do the ratings stop at 7.9?

When Windows Vista debuted in 2007, the individual WEI ratings stopped at 5.9. Using hardware designed in 2007 and later, we saw test scores hit this ceiling in every category. We expect the same will be true of Windows 7, where steady progress in hardware design should cause new systems to bump up against the higher ceiling of 7.9 sooner rather than later. As a result, you might see systems with CPUs of very different specifications that show identical ratings in the Processor category of the WEI. You might be able to feel the difference in raw speed and see the difference in detailed tests using WinSAT, but the numeric results for both CPUs will be 7.9. Microsoft has already demonstrated its capability and willingness to change the WEI scale by adjusting the top end of the scale so that it goes to higher numbers (perhaps even all the way to 11, in honor of the classic film comedy *This Is Spinal Tap*).

The extension of the scale accommodates newer hardware and allows for more accurate comparisons. For example, in the disk category, only a speedy solid-state drive (SSD) will post scores in the 6.0–7.9 range; current-generation SATA drives never exceed 5.9. Similarly, to get a score over 6.0, a graphics adapter must achieve high performance scores, it must support DX10, and it must have a WDDM 1.1 driver. Older adapters that support only DX9 (or rely on a WDDM 1.0 driver) won't make the cut. Testing of multithreaded operations ensures that only multicore processors suitable for demanding multitasking loads achieve CPU scores in the 6s or 7s.

For a more detailed look at how Microsoft developed the Windows Experience Index, with specific information about increasing the upper limit from 5.9 in Windows Vista to 7.9 in Windows 7, see Microsoft Support article 2461905 (*w7io.com/22301*). You can find additional details about how ratings relate to a computer's ability to perform specific tasks and how ratings show whether a computer has the appropriate muscle for various purposes at *w7io.com/22302*; scroll to the bottom, and click Show All.

So where do those numbers come from? The Windows Experience Index is drawn from the results of a series of tests performed by the Windows System Assessment Tool. The tool runs in the background to exercise different system components, calculates a score for each performance metric, and then displays a composite score based on the lowest of the five subscores. You can see details about these tests by clicking View And Print Detailed Performance And System Information.

Chapter 23

The test categories that make up the WEI are as follows:

- **Processor**   Gauges processor speed by running a series of tests that perform two different types of encryption and decryption, and compression and decompression using two different algorithms.

- **Memory (RAM)**   Assesses memory bandwidth by performing large copies between memory buffers, which simulates a heavy load such as that used in media applications.

- **Graphics**   Simulates desktop composition processes performed by Desktop Window Manager. If the score is too low to provide reasonable performance with the Aero interface, Windows disables Aero.

- **Gaming Graphics**   Assesses the system's ability to run Direct3D applications (such as games) and to perform video playback and encoding.

- **Primary Hard Disk**   Measures disk performance by testing sequential and random read and write operations.

A scheduled task runs WinSAT automatically (by default, once a week), so it remains updated even as you change components and drivers. You can do this manually as well: return to the Performance Information And Tools page shown in Figure 23-1 and click Re-Run The Assessment (you'll need administrative credentials to do this).

INSIDE OUT   Be sure to check the details

In the previous edition of this book, we expressed some cynicism about the WEI and its value. In Windows 7, we're happy to report, there's considerably more substance beneath these numbers. The WinSAT tests performed by Windows 7 are much more thorough and more granular than those performed by Windows Vista. In fact, we highly recommend that you check the detailed results carefully. Pay special attention to the Notes section at the end, where you might discover that your hard disk is falling short on some workloads. If you see this note, it's an indication that your drive is exhibiting problems related to write caching. Depending on the software you use, you might not notice a performance problem, but for some tasks the difference is noticeable. In that specific case, you might need to replace your hard drive to ratchet performance back up to acceptable levels.

Drivers have a profound influence on WEI scores. If you use a Windows Display Driver Model (WDDM) 1.0 graphics driver originally written for Windows Vista, you'll find that the score for graphics tests is capped at 5.9. Updating to a Windows 7–compatible WDDM 1.1 driver will enable WinSAT to run an expanded series of tests and return a score that could be significantly higher.

To see the full set of WinSAT test results, use the command-line Windows System Assessment Tool (Winsat.exe). Using WinSAT, you can rerun the entire suite (type **winsat formal** at an elevated command prompt) or retest individual parts of the Windows Experience Index (type **winsat –?** for the full syntax or visit *w7io.com/22304* for additional details). You can also save the output as an XML file or redirect the verbal output of the tests to a text file for subsequent review. To see the most recent set of detailed results, type **winsat query** in a Command Prompt window. This report shows the raw test results instead of the WEI scores, which provides a more detailed look at your system's performance.

Windows 7 keeps a history of WinSAT performance results that you can use for comparisons. You'll find them in %SystemRoot%\Performance\WinSAT\DataStore, each one stamped with the date and time it was run. Minor variations in results between WinSAT runs are normal, usually as a result of other processes and services interfering with resource usage. Keeping even an informal record of detailed results over time can help you determine whether a significant change in test scores is normal or a sign of a problem to be found and fixed.

Generating a System Health Report

To obtain a more detailed, action-oriented report of your system's current state of well-being, open Performance Information And Tools (from System in Control Panel, click Windows Experience Index), and then click Advanced Tools in the left pane. On the Advanced Tools page, click Generate A System Health Report. (This task requires administrative credentials.) When you initiate the test, Resource And Performance Monitor opens and begins collecting data for at least 60 seconds; when it ends, it displays its results in the predefined System Diagnostics Report format comparable to the one shown in Figure 23-2.

The System Diagnostics Report starts out with the worst news right at the top. Below this Warnings section, you'll find a section summarizing basic system checks, in which each of five test sets gets a green "Passed" or a red "Failed."

Click the plus-sign outline control next to any item in this list to see a wealth of detail.

Scrolling down into the report, you'll come to a Resource Overview section, with more green (and possibly red) balloons. If you see a small note or flag icon to the right of an entry, rest your mouse pointer there to read a "tip" window containing interesting details about the item in question.

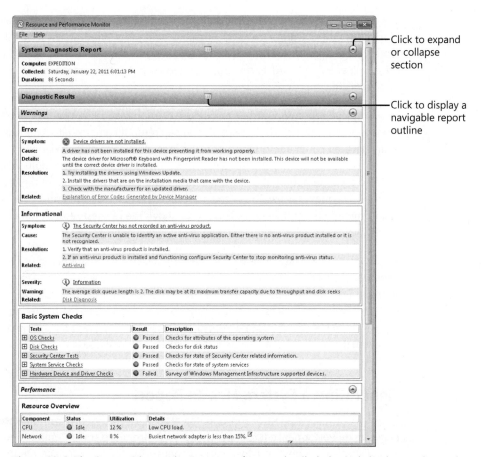

Click to expand or collapse section

Click to display a navigable report outline

Figure 23-2 The System Diagnostics Report performs a detailed physical checkup and puts the bad news (if any) right up front.

Farther still into the report, you'll see a set of expandable headings: Software Configuration, Hardware Configuration, CPU, Network, Disk, Memory, and Report Statistics. Use the outline controls at the right side of these headings to expand and collapse each section. To jump quickly between headings without scrolling, click the icon in the center of each main section heading to display an outline; click an outline entry to go directly to a section. It's all worth reading, particularly if you run across an item with a red flag next to it, indicating that it contains important details and recommendations.

Monitoring Performance in Real Time

Windows 7 offers two valuable tools for monitoring the performance of your system in real time. The first of these, Windows Task Manager, has been around through many versions of Windows and will therefore probably be familiar to many readers of this book. In addition to showing you what applications, processes, and services are running (and giving you a way to terminate recalcitrant items), it offers performance graphs that show a minute's worth of CPU usage, memory usage, and network capacity usage. By adding nondefault columns to the Processes tab of Task Manager, you can examine per-process details in depth.

For zeroing in on performance issues with extraordinary levels of detail, Windows 7 offers an advanced tool called Resource Monitor. This utility debuted in Windows Vista but has received a top-to-bottom makeover in this release, addressing several of the usability flaws we identified in the previous edition of this book. Resource Monitor allows you to keep an eye on different aspects of your system simultaneously, and it also allows you to isolate processes and look at exactly how and where they're using CPU, memory, disk, and network resources.

We take a brief look at the venerable Performance Monitor, which is largely rendered unnecessary by Resource Monitor, in "Advanced Performance Analysis Tools and Techniques" on page 868.

Using Windows Task Manager

Windows Task Manager pops up in response to the keyboard shortcut Ctrl+Shift+Esc. (You can also press Ctrl+Alt+Delete and then choose Start Task Manager.) Task Manager's instant accessibility is one of its more endearing traits, especially when something appears to have gone awry. Its executable file, Taskmgr.exe, runs at a Base Priority of High, allowing it to kick into action even when another program running at Normal priority is refusing to surrender control. If you need to stop an application (or process) that doesn't respond to the usual measures, or if your system suddenly slows down and you want to know who's eating your processor cycles, Task Manager is your best friend.

The Performance tab of Task Manager, shown in Figure 23-3, gives you a quick overview of CPU and memory usage. The bar graphs at the left report current data—the percentage of your CPU's capacity and the amount of physical memory (in gigabytes) in use—while the line graphs to the right show (by default) one minute's worth of data, with updates at one-second intervals. In Figure 23-3, for example, the Memory bar graph shows that 1.20 GB are currently in use, while the Physical Memory item in the status bar at the bottom of the window reports that 60 percent of the system's available RAM is in use. The CPU Usage History and Physical Memory Usage History line graphs, meanwhile, make it clear that we have opened several large applications in rapid succession within the last minute.

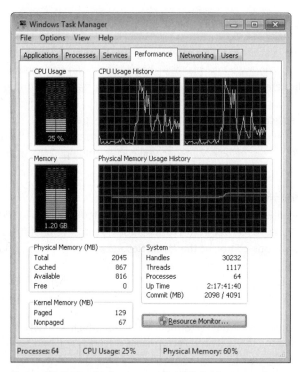

Figure 23-3 The Performance tab of Task Manager gives you a big-picture view of CPU and memory usage.

Numbers below the graphs amplify the graphical presentation. (For a detailed explanation of what these numbers mean, see "Basic Strategies for Improving Performance" on page 852.)

To change the update speed (and therefore the duration of the line graphs), choose View, Update Speed. The Normal option on this menu updates the display once per second; High switches to double that pace, and Low changes the display to update every 4 seconds. Use this command's Paused option to freeze all the Performance graphs. If the Task Manager display is paused, you can force an update at any time (without resuming continuous updating) by choosing View, Refresh Now or by pressing F5.

If you have a multiprocessor system (one using a dual-core or quad-core CPU, for example), you can choose between seeing a single line graph that represents all processors or separate graphs for each. Use commands on the View, CPU History submenu to switch between these alternatives.

By default, Task Manager stays on top of other open windows even when another window has the focus. Choose Options, Always On Top to toggle that behavior on or off. Regardless of what settings you choose on the View menu, Task Manager displays, in the notification area, a miniature version of the CPU Usage bar graph. You can minimize Task Manager and still keep an eye on CPU usage by glancing over at the notification area as you work. (Be aware, though, that continuous monitoring of your system performance by means of Task Manager—or any other real-time tracking tool—will itself consume some of your processor time.)

In its default view, the Processes tab lists programs and services that are directly accessible to the user. Note that in the example shown here, 64 processes are currently running (as evidenced by the value in the lower left corner of the status bar at the bottom of the dialog box). So why does the list display only 20 entries?

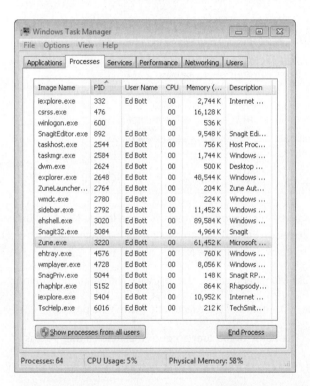

The short list shows only processes that were started by and can be directly controlled by the current user account. If you click Show Processes From All Users (and if necessary provide the required administrative credentials), the list expands to include all currently running processes. In the example shown next, the entries in the User Name column now include the currently logged-on user (running Internet Explorer) as well as a Media Center Extender account (its automatically generated account name begins with Mcx) and the built-in System, Network Service, and Local Service accounts.

Chapter 23

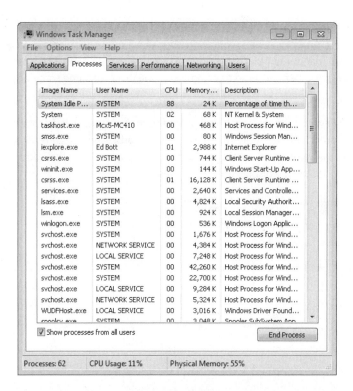

On a system running a 64-bit version of Windows 7, the Image Name column includes 32-bit and 64-bit processes. Each 32-bit process on such a system is identified by the *32 label at the end of its entry in the Image Name column.

For each process, Task Manager includes the following information by default:

- **Image Name**   The name of the executable file for the process

- **User Name**   The name of the user account that started the process

- **CPU**   The percentage of total CPU capacity that the process is currently using

- **Memory (Private Working Set)**   The amount of memory that is currently dedicated to the process and is not available for other applications to use

  For more details about how to analyze memory usage, see "Ensuring That You Have Adequate RAM" on page 852.

- **Description**   A descriptive name for the process, taken from the value stored in the File Description field of the executable file

INSIDE OUT   Get more details about a process

Task Manager separates its display of what's running on your computer into two tabs. The Applications tab lists each running program by name; the Processes tab is a much longer list that shows every executable file that's running, including child processes, services, and processes that run in the background.

In Windows XP, you can right-click on any item in the Applications list and choose Go To Process from the shortcut menu. But once you reach the Processes tab, you're at a dead end. If a process is sucking the life out of your CPU, or if you find a mysterious process that you can't identify and that you think might be associated with malware, you're on your own. You have to use search tools to find the file responsible for that process and then figure out what it is.

Windows 7 (like Windows Vista) simplifies this process. When you right-click any item in the Processes list, you'll see several new choices on its shortcut menu:

- Click Open File Location to open Windows Explorer and see the file responsible for the running process. Often, just knowing which folder it appears in is enough to help ease your mind about a process with a mysterious name.

- The Properties menu choice, also new in Windows Vista and Windows 7, leads directly to the properties dialog box for the associated file, where a greatly expanded Details tab includes copyright information and other relevant text drawn from the file itself. That information can help you decide whether a file is legitimate or needs further investigation.

- Finally, for processes that are running as Windows services, you can click the Go To Service(s) option, which takes you to the Services tab and highlights all of the individual services associated with that process. For an instance of Svchost.exe, the list might number a dozen individual services.

Processes are sorted initially by the order in which they were started, with the most recent entries at the top. You can sort by any column by clicking the column heading (click a second time to reverse the sort order). Clicking the Memory or CPU heading to sort in descending order is a good way to identify processes that are using more than their fair share of memory or CPU time.

With a modest amount of work, you can customize the Processes tab so that it shows far more information about each running process than the lean default view. To change the columns displayed on this tab, choose View, Select Columns, and then add or remove entries from the dialog box shown here:

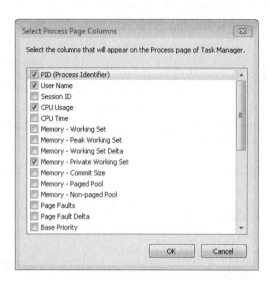

Most of these columns correspond to entries available in Resource Monitor (which we cover in detail in the next section). After selecting the columns you want to see, click OK. You can then rearrange the display by dragging column headings to the left or right and dragging the border of any column heading to change its width. If necessary, resize the Task Manager window to see more data.

INSIDE OUT   Add the Process ID column

The default arrangement of columns on the Processes tab does not include the Process Identifier (PID) column. This column is shown on the Services tab, where it's extremely useful in enabling you to see which processes are running as part of the same Svchost.exe instance. For detailed troubleshooting or performance analysis, we recommend that you display this column on the Processes tab. To find out what's inside a particularly busy Svchost process, make a note of its PID and then switch to the Services tab and sort by the PID column. The associated services will appear in a block using that PID.

Using Resource Monitor

Like the Performance tab in Task Manager, Resource Monitor gives you both instantaneous and recent-history readouts of key performance metrics. Also like Task Manager, Resource Monitor can show you, in excruciating detail, what each process is doing. An early version of this utility debuted in Windows Vista, and in the previous edition of this book we criticized several aspects of its design and operation. Someone at Microsoft must have read that chapter, because every one of those concerns has been addressed in this upgrade. The version of Resource Monitor in Windows 7 is extremely usable and packed with enough information to keep you busy for hours or days.

To open Resource Monitor, click its shortcut on the All Programs menu (under Accessories, System Tools). Or just type **resource** in the Start menu search box and click the shortcut that appears at the top of the list. (In either case, you need administrative credentials.) Or take the direct route: type **perfmon /res** in the Start menu search box or at a command prompt.

> **Note**
>
> You can open Resource Monitor by clicking the button at the bottom of the Performance tab in Task Manager (shown earlier in Figure 23-3). This is, in our opinion, the preferred way to use this utility. Start with a quick overview from Task Manager, and if you need more information call on Resource Monitor.

When you first open Resource Monitor, you see the Overview tab shown in Figure 23-4, which provides both detailed tables and charts that summarize performance in four areas.

Tabs along the top of the Resource Monitor window allow you to switch to a different context and focus on a specific type of resource usage. The basic layout of each tab is similar and consists of a handful of common elements.

One or more tables contain details about the resource featured on that tab. The first table on each tab is called the *key table*; it contains a list of all processes currently using the selected resource, with a check mark to the left of each process that allows you to filter the data displayed in additional tables on the tab. The key table at the top of the Overview tab lists all running processes, in a display that is similar to the Processes tab of Task Manager.

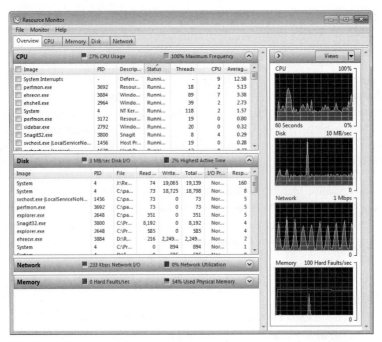

Figure 23-4 The Overview tab of Resource Monitor shows instantaneous and recent-history data for four vital system resources: CPU, disk, network, and memory.

Within each table, you can add or hide columns, change the order of columns, and resize columns. To see the full list of available columns for an individual table, right-click the column headings for that table and choose Select Columns. On the CPU tab, for example, you can add the following normally hidden columns to the Processes table: User Name, to help identify the owner of a process; Operating System Context, to identify the Windows version a program was originally written for; Platform, to distinguish 32-bit and 64-bit processes on a 64-bit Windows installation; and Elevated, which identifies processes running with full administrative privileges. You can sort any column by clicking the heading; click again to reverse the sort order.

The heading atop each table serves several purposes. At its most basic, it contains a label that identifies the table's contents. You can also click the arrow at the right side of the heading to expand or collapse its contents. To the right of the label is one or more elements that summarize the information in that table. In Figure 23-5, for instance, the header above the Processes table shows the percentage of physical memory in use, while the informational graphics in the Physical Memory header show the amount of RAM in use and available.

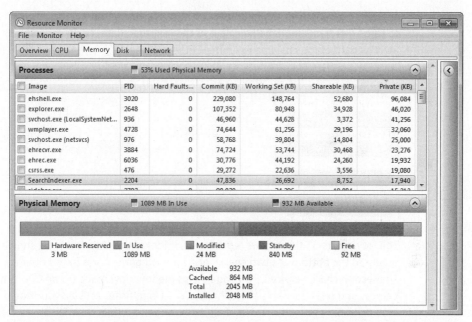

Figure 23-5 Informational graphics in each table's header summarize the contents of the table itself.

For each of four resources—CPU, disk, network, and memory—the Overview tab presents instantaneous and recent-history graphs of two metrics. The recent-history data appears in the chart pane on the right. The instantaneous readouts are in the small squares to the right of the label in the header above each table. Each graph uses colors—green and blue—to distinguish its two data sets. The performance metrics are shown in Table 23-1.

Table 23-1 **Performance Metrics Displayed on the Overview Tab**

Resource	Green Display	Blue Display
CPU	Percent of CPU capacity in use	Percent of full clock speed at which CPU is running
Disk	I/O activity for all disks (scale changes depending on workload)	Percentage of disks' available throughput in use
Network	Network activity (scale changes depending on workload)	Percent of network capacity in use
Memory	Hard faults per second	Percent of physical RAM in use

For most (but not all) of the graphs in the chart pane, you'll see two lines—one blue and one green. The color keys correspond to the information on the header for the associated table. Thus, on the Overview tab, the green line on the CPU graph shows total CPU usage in real time, while the blue line shows the maximum frequency at which the CPU is operating. If you find the graphs distracting, you can hide them by clicking the right-facing arrow in the header above the graphs; you can also use the choices on the Views menu to switch to Large, Medium, and Small displays of the real-time data. The display shown here is the Small variant of the chart pane on the CPU tab.

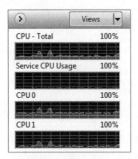

The four charts on this tab are worth a closer look. At the top is a chart showing total CPU usage. At the bottom are two charts, one for each of the cores in this dual-core processor. The second chart, Service CPU Usage, helps identify how much of the CPU is being used by background services. If this chart shows steady, significant activity, you should take a closer look at running processes to see if any are using more than their fair share of the CPU.

INSIDE OUT Save a favorite layout

One of our criticisms of Resource Monitor's predecessor in Windows Vista was its inability to remember layout changes you made. In Windows 7, that's fixed, and then some. When you reopen Resource Monitor, it remembers the settings you had selected when you closed it previously and restores those settings. Not only that, but you can save the display state—active tab, window size, column widths and additional columns within tables, and whether tables are expanded or collapsed. (The only setting not saved is the set of filters you've applied to the current view.) To save your current display settings, click Save Settings As from the File menu, enter a descriptive name, and then click Save. To load a saved configuration, choose Load Settings from the File menu, select your saved configuration file, and then click Open. Alternatively, double-click the saved configuration file in Windows Explorer to open Resource Monitor with your configuration settings loaded.

For each graph, the line on the horizontal axis (the time scale) represents 5 seconds; with 11 lines, that means the display encompasses 55 seconds, not 60 seconds, as the legend incorrectly notes. The vertical axis contains 10 lines and always depicts a percentage of the current scale.

In Figure 23-6, you can see the four graphs from the Overview tab on a desktop PC that is using the Balanced power scheme. The CPU is currently running at 75 percent of its clock speed but has spent the last 45 seconds or so running at 80–95 percent of its full rated speed. The hard disks have seen brief spikes of activity in this time slice, loading code as new programs launched and then quieting down. Very little is happening on the network at the current time; about 30 seconds earlier, there was a brief burst of activity from the network that used only a small fraction of the gigabit speeds available. At this instant, the system is experiencing virtually no hard faults, at the rate of 1 per second (having peaked at roughly 100 a short time ago), and is using 43 percent of its physical memory.

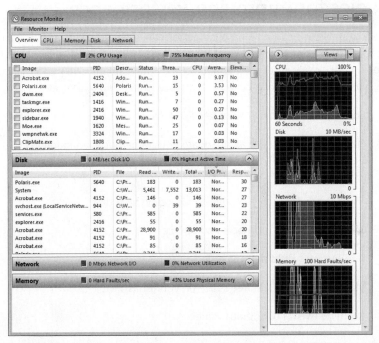

Figure 23-6 Click the heading above any table to expand the table and reveal details about individual processes using that category of system resource.

You can stop data collection at any time and freeze the display of information completely, a useful feature if you've just observed a spike in activity and then watched it calm down, and you now want to examine the details. Click Monitor, and then click Stop Monitoring to pause the display. Click Start Monitoring on the same menu to resume the data collection and display.

Filtering the display of data in Resource Monitor is an especially valuable technique when you're trying to track down the cause of a particular burst of activity (and possibly an

Chapter 23

associated slowdown). You can also use this technique to identify services, handles, and modules associated with a particular process. On the CPU tab, for instance, you might notice that an instance of Svchost.exe is using a disproportionate amount of the CPU and doesn't seem to be showing signs of stopping. To find out why, select the check box to the left of its entry in the Processes table. The entry immediately moves to the top of the list, and the tables below pick up an orange header, indicating they're filtered by the selected item. A similar orange line appears on the graph to the right to help you isolate resource usage for the filtered items.

Basic Strategies for Improving Performance

Now that we've established a baseline performance level for the hardware components and software that make up a Windows 7 PC and introduced the major diagnostic tools, it's time to look more closely at techniques and settings that can improve performance. In this section, we cover the following basic performance-enhancing strategies:

- Ensuring that you have adequate RAM

- Ensuring that you have an adequate virtual-memory configuration

- Tuning and troubleshooting SuperFetch

- Using ReadyBoost to compensate for a slow hard disk

- Managing startup programs and services

- Keeping your disks defragmented

- Maintaining adequate free space on your disks

- Avoiding tweaks of dubious value

Ensuring That You Have Adequate RAM

Random access memory (RAM) is the vital stuff that keeps Windows running smoothly. Having enough physical (main) memory helps reduce the operating system's dependence on virtual memory, thereby maximizing the number of times Windows is able to fetch information from fast memory chips and minimizing the number of times it has to get data from your (relatively slow) hard disk. How much memory do you need?

Microsoft's official hardware requirements for Windows 7 specify that a system must have at least 1 GB of RAM to run 32-bit Windows, and 2 GB if you plan to install 64-bit Windows. In our experience, doubling these minimums will provide a better ride for most installations.

INSIDE OUT

Use a PowerShell script to fix common performance problems

A PowerShell script called TroubleshootPerformance.ps1 can be found in the Scripts folder on the companion CD. This script in turn calls several troubleshooting scripts included with Windows and provides an interactive way to fix some performance problems. When you run the script, it runs each troubleshooter and displays available repair options. For example, in the run shown here, the script found that several startup programs are installed—which prolongs the startup process and can unnecessarily use resources as those programs continue to run—and then lets you choose which, if any, you want to prevent from running at startup. For more information about using this script, see "Running PowerShell Scripts" on page 999.

```
C:\Windows\system32\cmd.exe - powershell

PS C:\Users\Carl\Documents\scripts> .\troubleshootperformance
Checking power mode...
Checking for logged-on users...
Checking the disk programmed input/output mode...
Checking to see if multiple antivirus programs are installed...
Checking startup programs list...
Checking SuperFetch...
Checking visual effects settings...


Please select the resolutions to apply
The following resolutions are available to address the problems that were found.
 Additional resolutions will become available if the pack is rerun as an adminis
trator.

Several programs are running at startup
[1] Prevent unnecessary startup programs from running at startup (my programs on
ly)

[?] Help
[x] Exit
:1

Running resolution 'Prevent unnecessary startup programs from running at startup
 (my programs only)'...
Preventing programs from running at startup...

Which programs do you want to prevent from running at startup?
Select the programs that you do not want to run when Windows starts.

[1] Windows Live Messenger
[2] Windows Desktop Gadgets
[3] TomTom HOME
[4] Microsoft Office 2010
[5] Google Update
[6] EPSON Status Monitor 3
[7] Windows Live Mesh
[8] Dropbox
[9] Microsoft OneNote
[10] None of the above

[?] Help
[x] Exit
```

But don't assume that more memory is always better. As it turns out, there is such a thing as too much memory, especially if you're running a 32-bit Windows version. First, there's the question of how much RAM (how many memory modules and in what sizes) your computer can physically accommodate. And then there's a hard mathematical limitation: because of the nature of address spaces, 32-bit versions of Windows can use no more than 3.5 GB of RAM, and often considerably less. The exact amount varies depending on the hardware in question; for more details, see Microsoft Support article 978610, "The usable memory may be less than the installed memory on Windows 7–based computers," at *w7io.com/978610*.

With a 64-bit version of Windows 7, this limitation on physical memory vanishes and is replaced by limits that are defined differently for each edition of Windows. Table 23-2 has the details for all editions.

Table 23-2 **Physical Memory Limitations in Windows 7**

Windows 7 Edition	Limit in 32-Bit Windows	Limit in 64-Bit Windows
Starter	4 GB	8 GB
Home Basic	4 GB	8 GB
Home Premium	4 GB	16 GB
Professional	4 GB	192 GB
Enterprise/Ultimate	4 GB	192 GB

INSIDE OUT   How the System Properties dialog box reports RAM

As we note in this chapter, a computer running a 32-bit (x86) version of Windows can address a maximum of 3.5 GB of physical memory. In Windows 7, the System Properties dialog box displays two values when it encounters a discrepancy between the amount of addressable memory and the amount of physical RAM installed. Thus, on a system with 4 GB of physical RAM, the value reported under the System heading for Installed Memory (RAM) will show 4.00 GB (3.50 GB Usable); the second value might be less, depending on your hardware configuration.

Memory management is confusing, perhaps more so than any other aspect of PC performance. If you scour the web for information on this topic, you will surely run into misguided advice and technical errors. Knowing the meaning of the following specialized memory-measurement terms helps you make sense of it all:

- *Physical memory* refers to actual RAM chips or modules, typically installed on a computer's motherboard. The amount of physical RAM available to Windows might be less than the total physical amount if another system component is using that memory for its own purposes, as is the case with "shared memory" video subsystems on portable computers. Physical memory measurements (total and in use) are reported on the Performance tab of Task Manager and on the Memory tab of Resource Monitor.

- *Virtual memory* consists of physical memory plus the amount of space in the page file, which is stored on the hard disk. We discuss virtual memory in more detail in the next section, "Ensuring That You Have an Adequate Virtual-Memory Configuration" on page 856.

- *Kernel memory* is owned by Windows and is used to provide system services to applications. Paged memory can be backed up to the page file and replaced by application memory if necessary; nonpaged memory must remain in physical RAM at all times.

- *Cached memory* holds data or program code that has been fetched into memory during the current session but is no longer in use now. If necessary, the Windows memory manager will flush the contents of cached memory to make room for newly summoned data.

- *Free memory* represents RAM that does not contain any data or program code and is free for use immediately.

- *Working Set* is the term that defines the amount of memory currently in use for a process. Private Working Set is the amount of memory that is dedicated to that process and will not be given up for other programs to use; Shareable Working Set can be surrendered if physical RAM begins to run scarce. Peak Working Set is the highest value recorded for the current instance of this process.

- *Commit Charge* (also called *commit size*) is the total amount of virtual memory that a program has touched (committed) in the current session, including memory that has been paged out of physical memory to the disk-backed page file. The Memory and Physical Memory counters on Task Manager's Performance tab represent the sum of this value for all processes and the kernel. The Commit Charge Limit is the total amount of physical RAM and page file available—in other words, the maximum virtual memory.

- *Hard faults* are also known as *page faults*. Despite the negative connotation of the name, this is not an error condition. Rather, it represents an instance where a block of memory needed by the operating system or an application has to be fetched from the page file on the hard disk instead of from physical memory. A consistently high number of hard faults per second indicates a large—perhaps excessive—reliance on virtual memory, with consequent adverse performance effects.

Chapter 23

The best way to gauge the adequacy of your currently installed RAM is to keep an eye on the Memory graph in Resource Monitor (see Figure 23-5 and the accompanying text in "Using Resource Monitor" on page 847). The green portion of the bar indicates the percentage of your physical memory that's currently in use; shades of blue indicate cached memory that is available on demand (Standby). It's also important to watch the green line on the graphs to the right, which indicates the number of hard faults per second your system is generating; if you see it spike off the top of the graph for extended periods of time, you'll want to take a closer look at how memory is being used.

A PowerShell script included on the companion CD provides another way to determine which applications are generating the most hard faults. The script called FindMaxPage-Faults.ps1, which you can find in the Scripts folder, lists the top hard fault producers among currently running programs. (Note that it shows the total number of faults generated, not hard faults per second, as shown in Resource Monitor.)

For more information about using these scripts, see "Running PowerShell Scripts" on page 999.

Pay special attention to these numbers when you're asking the most of your computer; you might even consider performing a stress test by successively opening the applications you use most often. Switch between programs, open and edit some data files, browse a couple dozen web pages, and generally try to use more system resources than you can imagine using at one time under normal circumstances. If you find yourself bumping up against the ceiling regularly, you might get a noticeable performance boost from additional RAM.

Don't get hung up on mere percentages, though. If you routinely hit a maximum of 85 percent memory usage on a machine running 64-bit Windows 7 with 6 GB of physical RAM, you have 900 MB of free RAM, which is plenty of headroom.

Many users attempt to fix a computer that's perceived to be slow by adding more memory. As noted earlier, in some cases that "solution" can be wasteful and ineffective, but for a single computer at least you're not out much money. However, if you're charged with specifying requirements for a fleet of computers, buying too much (or too little) memory can be costly indeed. Microsoft has a white paper, titled "Memory Sizing Guidance for Windows 7," that can help you to develop a test plan for determining the optimum memory configuration for your needs. You can download the white paper at *w7io.com/22303*.

Ensuring That You Have an Adequate Virtual-Memory Configuration

Physical memory might be the vital lubricant of a happily humming Windows machine, but Windows is not designed to run on RAM chips alone, no matter how many of them you have. In addition to using physical RAM to store programs and data, Windows creates a hidden file on your primary hard disk and uses that file to manage pages of data pulled from scattered sections of the hard disk and used in physical memory when necessary. The *page file* acts as an extension of main memory—or, in other words, as virtual memory.

In olden days (especially in the early to mid 1990s), the memory manager's disk-backed storage was commonly called the "swap file," because its primary use was to overcome physical memory shortages. Today, the page file is an integral part of memory management, used by SuperFetch and the boot prefetcher to optimize your system for performance.

In Windows 7, Microsoft has chosen to deemphasize visible measurements of page file usage in common performance-monitoring tools. The Commit fraction in the lower right corner of Task Manager's Performance tab is useful for helping you gauge the adequacy of your virtual memory setup. Note, however, that while the numerator of the fraction indicates how much virtual memory your system is currently using, the denominator reports the sum of physical memory and current page file size.

In a default installation, Windows creates the page file in the root folder on the same drive that holds the Windows system files. The size of the page file is determined by the amount of RAM in your system. By default, the minimum size on a 32-bit (x86) system is 1.5 times the amount of physical RAM if physical RAM is less than 1 GB, and equal to the amount of physical RAM plus 300 MB if 1 GB or more is installed. The default maximum size is three times the amount of RAM, regardless of how much physical RAM is installed. On a PC with a processor that supports Physical Address Extension (PAE)—which is to say, on any PC that is capable of running Windows 7—the maximum size of the page file is 16 TB. That amount of disk space will no doubt seem horribly confining someday, perhaps even in our lifetimes, but for now it's more than enough. You can see the page file in a Windows Explorer window if you configure Windows to show hidden and system files; look for Pagefile.sys in the root of your system drive.

To see the current configuration of your system's virtual memory, open the System dialog box in Control Panel and click the Advanced tab. (For an excellent, undocumented shortcut to this dialog box, click Start, type **systempropertiesadvanced** with no spaces, and press Enter.) Under the Performance heading, click Settings. In the Performance Options dialog box, click the Advanced tab, and (finally!) under the Virtual Memory heading, click Change. Figure 23-7 shows the Virtual Memory dialog box, with default settings for a machine with 2 GB of RAM (default, that is, except that we cleared the Automatically Manage Paging File Size For All Drives check box to make the rest of the dialog box easier to read).

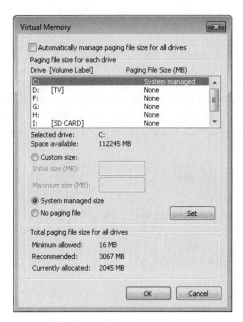

Figure 23-7 By default, Windows manages the page file size for you; clear the check box at the top of this dialog box to manage the page file manually.

By default, Windows creates a single page file in the root folder on the same volume that holds the Windows system files and manages its size for you. The Currently Allocated number near the bottom of the dialog box shows you how large the file is now. If conditions on your system change (you run an unusually large assortment of memory-intensive applications, for example), Windows might expand the page file. It might then return the file to its original size (or a smaller size) if the demand subsides. All this happens without intervention or notification if you leave the Automatically Manage Paging File Size For All Drives check box selected.

If you don't want Windows to do this for you, you have the following options:

- You can move the page file to a different volume if you have more than one.

- If you have more than one volume, you can establish more than one page file.

- For any page file, you can choose between System Managed Size and Custom Size.

- If you choose Custom Size, you can specify an initial size and a maximum size.

- You can remove a paging file from a volume by selecting the volume and choosing No Paging File. (You can even get rid of all paging files this way, although doing so is not recommended, even on systems with a lot of RAM.)

Should you get involved in page file management, and, if so, how?

If you have more than one physical disk, moving the page file to a fast drive that doesn't contain your Windows system files is a good idea. Using multiple page files split over two or more physical disks is an even better idea, because your disk controller can process multiple requests to read or write data concurrently. Don't make the mistake of creating two or more page files using multiple volumes on a single physical disk, however. If you have a single hard disk that contains C, D, and E volumes, for example, and you split the page file over two or more of these, you might actually make your computer run more slowly than before. In that configuration, the heads on the physical disk have to do more work, loading pages from different portions of the same disk sequentially, rather than loading data from a single contiguous region of the hard disk.

If you are short of hard disk space, you might consider setting a smaller initial page file size. Monitor peak usage levels over time; if the peak is well below the current page file size, you can consider reducing the initial size to save disk space. On the other hand, if you're not short of disk space, there's nothing to be gained from doing this and you might occasionally overload your custom settings, thereby degrading the performance of your system.

Should you enlarge your page file? Most users won't need to do this. But you might want to keep an eye on the green line in the Memory chart on the Overview tab of Resource Monitor (see the full discussion under "Using Resource Monitor" on page 847). If that line is spiking off the top of the graph a great deal of the time during your normal work, you might consider increasing the maximum size of your page file. (Disregard page file spikes and disk activity in general that takes place while you're not actually working. This is likely to be the result of search indexing, defragmentation, or other background processes and does not indicate a problem with your actual work performance.)

> **Note**
> For an extremely detailed discussion of virtual memory page file management in Windows, we recommend the blog post "Pushing the Limits of Windows: Virtual Memory?" by Microsoft Technical Fellow Mark Russinovich, at *w7io.com/2004*.

Tuning and Troubleshooting SuperFetch

Windows 7 incorporates an active performance-enhancing technology called SuperFetch. This intelligent caching routine, which debuted in Windows Vista, is designed to overcome performance problems caused by the biggest bottleneck on most PCs today, the disk I/O subsystem. SuperFetch observes your computer usage patterns over extended stretches of time (noting the programs you run and the days and times you typically run them) and adjusts caching behavior to optimize performance of the programs and data files you use most frequently.

SuperFetch runs as a service and actively fills unused memory with program and data files it believes you are likely to run in the current session, based on prior observations of your working habits. The irony of SuperFetch is that its performance-analyzing, cache-creating ways can actually impair performance, at least temporarily.

You can see SuperFetch in operation by using the details pane for disk activity in Resource Monitor. Look for an instance of Svchost.exe running under the System account and hosting more than a dozen services. Its impact on CPU performance should be negligible, and in normal operation it runs at Very Low priority, fetching code and data at a rate of a few pages per second. SuperFetch can have a noticeable if temporary impact on disk performance when it is in learning mode. You're most likely to see temporary slowdowns caused by SuperFetch under these specific circumstances:

- After you first install and run Windows 7, the system begins a series of tuning actions in which it tunes the boot prefetcher and SuperFetch caching. These runs normally begin at least 40 seconds after all boot operations have stopped. Assuming that you use your normal assortment of applications during the first three or four boot cycles, you should see a profound improvement in times to start Windows and to load programs.

- When you add new software, especially large, complex programs, the system shifts into a learning mode to improve boot prefetching. This can have an impact on your next several boot cycles as the system identifies the new files and loads them into the SuperFetch cache.

- Adding or changing hardware devices and drivers can also throw SuperFetch into learning mode, potentially causing minor impacts on performance and slowing down system starts.

Beyond knowing of its existence and allowing it to perform properly, you can do little to fine-tune or optimize the performance of SuperFetch.

Using ReadyBoost to Compensate for a Slow Hard Disk

ReadyBoost uses external memory devices (such as USB 2.0 flash drives and Secure Digital cards) to cache disk content of all kinds, reducing the need for time-consuming hard disk access. When a supported external memory device is available, ReadyBoost caches data and program code in flash memory and is able to retrieve small chunks of that memory, when needed, more quickly than Windows could if it relied only on the hard disk.

INSIDE OUT   Do you really need ReadyBoost?

Although ReadyBoost got a lot of favorable press when it debuted with Windows Vista a few years ago, it never quite lived up to its promise. And with steady improvements in hardware design since that time, it's become even more of a specialized tool. On a modern, full-size notebook or desktop PC that is designed to run Windows 7, chances are you'll see little or no improvement by using ReadyBoost. The scenarios in which this technology is most likely to be helpful involve a combination of bottlenecks: limited RAM and a slow hard disk, possibly combined with a low-power CPU. That combination is most likely to be found on small, portable devices popularly known as netbooks. Adding a flash drive of 2 GB or more and dedicating it to ReadyBoost might show noticeable performance improvements in that scenario.

There is at least one scenario in which even a computer with ample RAM and a speedy hard disk can benefit: if you use many programs simultaneously. In this case, Super-Fetch is likely to be less effective because the needed data might be forced out of memory by another request. ReadyBoost provides a dedicated area for SuperFetch data, mitigating this problem.

Generally, however, with a fast hard drive and sufficient RAM for caching, you're unlikely to notice any benefit from ReadyBoost. In fact, if you have Windows 7 installed on a fast solid-state disk (SSD), ReadyBoost, SuperFetch, and boot prefetching are all disabled. None of those tools offer a performance boost in that configuration.

All data cached via ReadyBoost is encrypted and backed up on the hard disk. Encryption ensures that the data can't be read on another system if the removable device is stolen, and backup enables Windows to revert to the hard disk cache in the event that the ReadyBoost drive is removed.

Windows supports the following form factors for ReadyBoost:

- USB 2.0 flash drives

- Secure Digital (SD) cards

- CompactFlash cards

- Memory Stick devices on Peripheral Component Interconnect (PCI), PCI Express (PCIe), and Serial Storage Architecture (SSA) buses; most internal card readers in portable computers use one of these bus types

When you connect a device of one of these types to your system, Windows runs a quick performance test to see if the device meets minimum standards required for ReadyBoost. It must have at least 2.5 MB/second throughput for 4-KB random reads and 1.75 MB/second throughput for 1-MB random writes. Devices that perform at twice this minimum level can be designated as "enhanced for ReadyBoost," a claim you might find on product packaging.

In addition, the device must have at least 230 MB available for the ReadyBoost cache.

> **Note**
> ReadyBoost does not support external card readers. If Windows Explorer shows a volume letter for a drive without media (as it does, for example, for card-reader drives or floppy drives), inserting flash media for that volume letter will not give you a ReadyBoost drive. Similarly, ReadyBoost does not support the use of external USB hubs; to use a USB flash drive, it must be connected to a built-in USB port.

Windows 7, unlike Windows Vista, supports multiple ReadyBoost drives. If you add two 4-GB USB flash drives to a system, you can combine them to create a single 8-GB ReadyBoost cache.

To use ReadyBoost, first plug a suitable external memory device into your computer. If an AutoPlay window offers the Speed Up My System Using Windows ReadyBoost option, click it. If no AutoPlay dialog box appears, right-click the device icon in the Computer window and click the ReadyBoost tab.

When you initially insert the device, Windows runs several brief performance tests to determine whether the device is ready for ReadyBoost. If any of these tests fail, the drive is rejected and you see a red X and a message telling you that the device "does not have the required performance characteristics." If you think the result is in error, click Test Again to rerun the performance benchmark. A device that passes the test will show a dialog box like the one in Figure 23-8.

At this point, you have two choices:

- If you want all available storage on the flash device to be used for a ReadyBoost cache, select Dedicate This Device To ReadyBoost. This option is appropriate if the USB drive is meant to be a long-term fixture on a desktop computer.

- If you want to reserve some space on the drive for data files, select Use This Device, adjust the slider to specify the amount of space you want to use for ReadyBoost, and then click OK. This option is most useful for scenarios in which you're traveling with a large (4 GB or more) flash drive and you need only 2 GB or so to get the most from ReadyBoost.

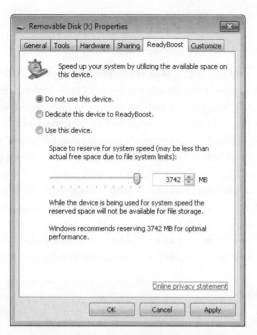

Figure 23-8 If you see this dialog box, your device passed the ReadyBoost performance test and is available for use as a supplemental cache.

For the greatest benefit, Microsoft recommends a ReadyBoost cache equal to at least twice the size of your system RAM. For example, a ReadyBoost cache of 4 GB or more is appropriate on a 2-GB system. The maximum cache size supported by Windows 7 is 32 GB.

> **Note**
>
> For cache sizes greater than 4 GB, the device must be formatted using exFAT or NTFS. Microsoft recommends exFAT for the best performance.

Managing Startup Programs and Services

A common performance problem occurs when Windows automatically loads an excessive number of programs at startup. The result, especially on systems with minimal memory, can be unpleasant: startup takes an unnecessarily long time, applications that you never use steal memory from programs you use frequently, and the page file gets more of a workout than it should. Some programs, such as antivirus utilities, need to start up automatically. But in many cases, you're better served by running programs when you need them and closing them when they're not needed.

INSIDE OUT   Take charge of startup with Autoruns

Windows 7 has a few tools you can use to peek at programs and services that run automatically at startup or logon, most notably the System Configuration utility, Msconfig.exe. But that built-in tool pales in comparison to the undisputed heavyweight champion of the category. We refer, of course, to Autoruns, which is available for free from Windows Sysinternals. It monitors programs in your Startup folder and in registry keys, showing you the exact order in which those programs will run. You can also configure Autoruns to show Explorer shell extensions, toolbars, browser helper objects, Winlogon notifications, and auto-start services, among other categories. Shortcut menus allow you to search for more information about a process or service whose name is unfamiliar, and clearing a check box to the left of each entry disables that item. The Everything tab shown here gives you an unfiltered look at everything your system starts automatically. You'll find the latest version of Autoruns at *w7io.com/2001*.

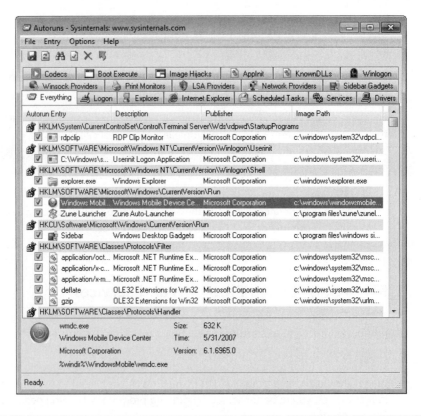

Overcrowded startups are most common on computer systems sold in retail outlets, where Windows is preinstalled along with a heaping helping of applications. In some cases, the bundled programs are welcome, but a free software program is no bargain if it takes up memory and you never use it.

A program can be configured to run at startup in a variety of ways. For a survey of these many ways—and how to take appropriate defensive action—see "Managing Startup Programs" on page 186.

Keeping Your Disks Defragmented

A "fragmented" hard disk, in which large files are stored in discontiguous sectors, makes read and write heads work overtime and puts a drag on performance. In the early days of personal computing, fragmentation was a common cause of severe performance degradation; that's much less true with Windows 7, which performs disk defragmentation as a weekly scheduled task. The Disk Defragmenter utility (Defrag.exe) runs as a background task, silently shifting the furniture while your system is idle. (The default schedule has defrag running at 1 A.M. every Wednesday. If your machine is turned off at that hour, the task runs as soon as possible after you come back online. It always runs as a low-priority background task, however, so you shouldn't find it obtrusive.)

For more information about using the defragmentation utility, see "Defragmenting Disks for Better Performance" on page 886.

Maintaining Adequate Free Space on Your Disks

A hard disk cluttered with stuff you no longer need might or might not be an impediment to performance (it certainly can be if the disk is home to a page file), but it's a nuisance at best. If a volume is running short of space, you can tidy up a bit with the Disk Cleanup wizard. Open Computer in Windows Explorer, right-click the disk in question, and choose Properties. Then, on the General tab of the Properties dialog box, click Disk Cleanup. Initially, you're given the opportunity to clean up your own files only; click Clean Up System Files to identify and, optionally, delete potentially unnecessary files created by the operating system. You'll need administrative credentials to go for the latter option.

For a more detailed discussion of this utility's features and capabilities, see "Cleaning Up with Disk Cleanup" on page 892.

Chapter 23

INSIDE OUT   Recover space used by service pack backup files

When you install a service pack for Windows, the files replaced by the service pack are stored on your hard disk in case you have problems with the service pack and need to uninstall it. These files can occupy a couple of gigabytes or more. After you're certain that you won't need to uninstall the service pack (we recommend waiting a month or longer to be sure no problems arise), you can recover that space by using the Deployment Image Servicing and Management tool (Dism.exe) to remove the backup files. Open an elevated Command Prompt window (click the Start button, type **cmd**, and press Ctrl+Shift+Enter) and enter the following command at the prompt:

```
dism /online /cleanup-image /spsuperseded
```

This geeky alternative to Disk Cleanup is functionally equivalent to selecting Service Pack Backup Files in that program (visible only after clicking Clean Up System Files), but it's considerably faster.

Avoiding Tweaks of Dubious Value

Among diehard tweakers, the urge to squeeze out every last bit of performance from a computer is irresistible. As a result, even a casual web search turns up dozens of tips intended to help you improve performance in Windows. Many of these tips repeat information that we cover in this chapter, including the truism that the best way to tune up Windows is to throw hardware at it. Nothing speeds up a sluggish system like a healthy dose of extra RAM.

Unfortunately, many of the Windows-tuning tips we've seen are of dubious value, and a few can actually hurt performance when indiscriminately applied. Some of these spurious tips are derived from techniques that worked with older Windows versions but are irrelevant or counterproductive now. Others are based on seemingly logical but erroneous extrapolations of how would-be experts think Windows works.

Page File Confusion

By far the most common instances of performance-related misinformation revolve around the subject of page files, sometimes incorrectly called swap files. We routinely run across two widely published myths about the proper configuration of virtual memory in Windows:

- **Myth #1: If your computer has a large amount of memory installed, you should eliminate your page file completely.** This is bad advice. Although you can configure Windows so that it does not set aside any virtual memory, no reputable source has ever published benchmarks establishing any performance gains from doing so, and Windows simply wasn't designed to run without a page file. If the goal is to conserve disk space, a more sensible strategy is to configure Windows to create a page file with a relatively small minimum size and monitor its usage over time to see how much virtual memory the operating system actually uses in daily operation.

- **Myth #2: Creating a page file of a fixed size improves performance.** This is also potentially bad advice. The logic behind this tip dates back to the earliest days of Windows. On 1990s-vintage hardware, dynamically resizing the swap file caused noticeable delays in system response and also resulted in excessive fragmentation. The memory management subsystems in modern Windows versions have been tuned to minimize the likelihood of performance problems.

Prefetch Pros and Cons

To improve the speed of starting applications, Windows continually monitors files that are used when the computer starts and when you start applications. For known programs, it creates an index (in the %SystemRoot%\Prefetch folder) that lists segments of frequently used programs and the order in which they're loaded. This prefetching process improves performance by allowing the operating system to quickly and efficiently grab all the files required by a program when you start it up.

A widely circulated tip of dubious value recommends that Windows users clean out the Prefetch folder and consider disabling the Prefetch function. Some sites even provide links to utilities that automate these functions.

Clearing out the Prefetch folder forces Windows to run programs inefficiently—but only once, because Windows rebuilds the Prefetch layout for a program the next time you run that program. Disabling the Prefetch function eliminates Windows' ability to optimize program loading. In either case, it's hard to find a logical reason why the tweak should result in a performance improvement.

Is it necessary to clear out the Prefetch cache occasionally to eliminate obsolete files and to minimize wasted disk space, as some websites claim? Hardly. A typical Prefetch folder uses well under 100 MB of disk space, and Windows automatically flushes unused entries that are older than a few weeks. Our take? The developers responsible for the memory management subsystem of Windows did a remarkable job when they devised this feature. To discourage tinkering, the default permissions on the Prefetch folder do not allow access to Standard users and to administrator accounts when UAC is turned on. Although you can change these permissions with a click, we see no reason to bother doing so. Let Prefetch work as designed.

Shutting Down Services

We've also seen sites focusing on Windows services. One sensible piece of advice is to mini-mize the use of unnecessary background applications and system services. If you install a third-party program that runs as a service and is constantly performing some sort of back-ground task, you should know about it and decide for yourself whether the steady drain on system resources is acceptable. However, a few sites take this advice to an extreme, urging Windows users to go through the list of system services that come with Windows and shut down many of them, including Windows Search, System Restore, and Automatic Updates.

This is, to put it bluntly, really terrible advice.

For starters, the potential payoff is minuscule at best. Most system services run as part of a larger instance of Svchost.exe. Disabling that service leaves the host and its other services running. Disabling most services saves a few kilobytes (with a K) of RAM, which isn't enough to make even a mild dent in performance except under the most extreme circumstances. And there's typically no impact on CPU usage either, because these "unnecessary" services work only when called upon; if you don't use them, they don't impact your CPU load.

We don't agree that the average Windows user should perform this sort of radical surgery on Windows. In less-than-expert hands, the Services console is a minefield; some Windows services can be safely disabled, but indiscriminately shutting down services is a prescription for trouble. That advice is doubly true for features designed to protect system reliability and security.

Advanced Performance Analysis Tools and Techniques

For virtually every performance tuning and tweaking task you're likely to accomplish, the tools built into Windows are more than adequate. That's especially true with the vastly improved Resource Monitor in Windows 7. But if you crave more information, we can rec-ommend two specialized tools.

Performance Monitor (Perfmon.exe)   This tool should be familiar to grizzled Windows veterans, having been around since well before the turn of the millennium. The underlying code is still in Windows, powering both Resource Monitor and the System Health report (which we covered earlier in this chapter). Its old-style interface still offers some capabili-ties that can't easily be achieved any other way. It allows you to track a much longer list of performance metrics than is available in either of its simpler cousins, Task Manager and Resource Monitor. You can also use it to log performance data to disk files or export to pro-grams such as Microsoft Excel for detailed analysis.

The fastest way to open Performance Monitor is the direct route: type **perfmon** in the Start menu search box or at a command prompt. The Performance Monitor console, shown in

Figure 23-9, provides several views of performance, including a System Summary and the graphical display shown here, which we've customized to track the performance of the ReadyBoost cache. Full coverage of this complex utility is beyond the scope of this book. For more details about its operation, see *Windows 7 Resource Kit,* by Mitch Tulloch, Tony Northrup, and Jerry Honeycutt (Microsoft Press, 2009).

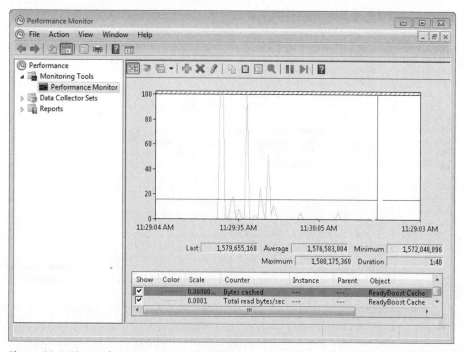

Figure 23-9 The Performance Monitor interface is a throwback to older Windows versions, but its data-mining capabilities are unmatched.

Process Explorer   This tool is another old-timer, originally developed by Mark Russinovich as a third-party utility for Winternals, the software company he and partner Bryce Cogswell founded in 1996. When Microsoft bought Winternals and its Sysinternals software library in 2006, some feared that development would stop cold. Thankfully, that fear turned out to be misplaced. Cogswell and Russinovich are now Microsoft employees; the Sysinternals website is still alive and well (although the *sysinternals.com* URL now redirects to a page at Microsoft's TechNet); and its flagship program, Process Explorer, is updated regularly and is fully compatible with Windows 7. To download Process Explorer, visit *w7io.com/2005.*

Process Explorer combines the best of Task Manager, Resource Monitor, and Performance Monitor in a single, highly customizable display. Its two-pane display, shown in Figure 23-10, provides system information, a hierarchical view of all running processes (including services), and an overwhelming number of technical details about how each process uses

CPU and memory. It all runs in real time, making it an ideal troubleshooting tool. For serious performance tuning and troubleshooting, it has no peer.

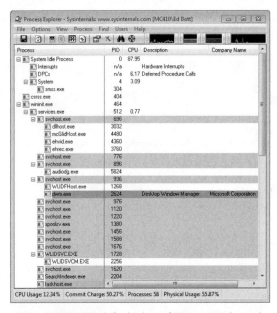

Figure 23-10 This default view of Process Explorer shows all running processes and services in a color-coded, hierarchical tree view. Right-click any process for more options.

When you right-click any entry in the Process list, you get a dialog box with an amazing amount of information about the process. You can kill, suspend, or restart a process any time. Double-click any process to see what that process is really up to.

The thing we love most about Process Explorer is its no-hassle installation and operation. The standalone executable requires no installation, only the acceptance of a license agreement. Copy the program to a convenient location and double-click to run it. When you close the program, it leaves no traces in memory and only a single registry key to store your preferences.

Performing Routine Maintenance

Y OUR personal computer is a curious combination of digital data and temperamental machinery. To keep your system running smoothly, it pays to perform some regular maintenance tasks. In particular, it's important to do the following on a regular basis:

- Download and install the latest updates from Microsoft. These updates ensure that your hardware and software will remain stable and secure.

- Download and install the latest versions of drivers used by your system's devices.

- Check your disks for file system and media errors.

- Defragment your hard disks to optimize file access.

- Perform regular backups of data and system files.

In Windows 7, many of the essential maintenance tools run automatically—or will do so after you perform some essential setup steps. We describe most of those setup chores, and the options associated with them, in this chapter. Backup, because it is particularly vital and because it presents a more extensive set of configuration choices, is discussed separately in Chapter 12, "Backup, Restore, and Recovery."

What's in Your Edition?

The features described in this chapter are available in all editions of Windows 7.

Introducing Action Center

By default, Windows monitors your system and notifies you if any security or maintenance issues merit your attention. Immediately after the system has detected a noteworthy event, you might see a balloon message in the notification area—near the lower right corner of your screen in the default screen layout. For example, if a backup fails because of lack of space on the target disk, you might see a balloon notification to that effect:

Clicking the balloon gives you a chance to take immediate action, typically by means of a troubleshooting dialog box like this:

Balloon messages alerting you to important security and maintenance issues are generated by Action Center, a new feature in the Windows 7 landscape. If you overlook or ignore the balloon, you can deal with the problem later by means of the Action Center icon, which is also in the notification area. When it's happy, the Action Center icon looks like this:

When it's not, it changes to look like this:

Clicking the icon in its troubled state reveals the nature of the problem (or problems, if more than one has accumulated) and tells you what you can do:

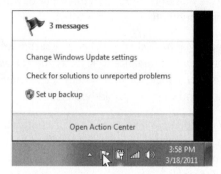

You can take corrective action by clicking an imperative statement in the middle of this message (for example, Change Windows Update Settings), or you can learn more about the condition of your system by clicking Open Action Center. Figure 24-1 illustrates what you might see if you open Action Center.

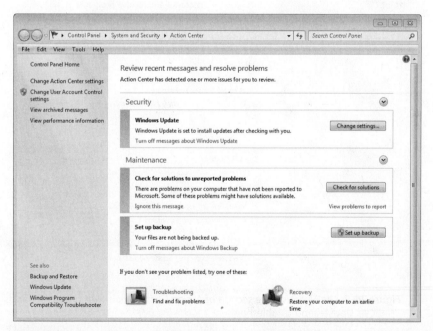

Figure 24-1 Action Center identifies potential security and maintenance problems and suggests corrective steps.

If Action Center has an important message to deliver, that message is flagged with a prominent red bar, and a button or link provides you with the means to address the problem.

Chapter 24

Less important messages are flagged with a yellow bar. Below the alert text in all cases, you'll also find a link that allows you to suppress subsequent messages on the same topic. So, for example, if you prefer not to see messages relating to the status of your virus protection, you can turn that form of monitoring off.

Action Center, which you can also reach via the System And Security section of Control Panel, is both a troubleshooting tool and a maintenance tool. It lets you review and address any current issues affecting the security or stability of your system. It also provides links to Backup And Restore, Windows Update, and various troubleshooters.

Messages served by Action Center fall under two broad headings: Security and Maintenance. You can expand and collapse each of these headings by means of controls at the right. Figure 24-2 shows the Maintenance section expanded. (For information about security issues, see Chapter 17, "Security Essentials.")

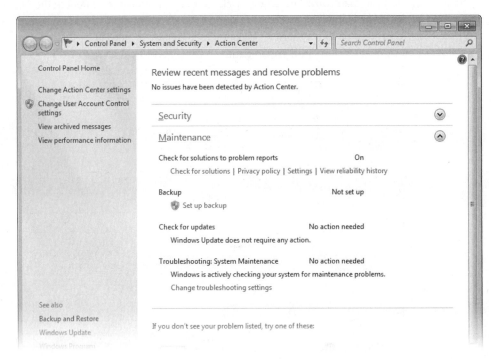

Figure 24-2 The Maintenance section of Action Center deals with problem reports, backup, Windows Update, and troubleshooting.

For information about the problem reports, system history, and configuring Action Center's troubleshooting behavior, see Chapter 28, "Troubleshooting Windows Errors and Crashes." For information about Windows Backup, see Chapter 12, "Backup, Restore, and Recovery." In the following section, we discuss Windows Update.

Keeping Your System Secure with Windows Update

Windows Update is a service that provides online updates for Windows 7. With it, you can obtain updates to Windows that include security updates, performance improvements, and support for new devices. If you're coming to Windows 7 from Windows XP, you'll find Windows Update completely overhauled. It's now a Control Panel application (in the System And Security section of Control Panel) and no longer uses a web-based interface. (Of course, it still requires an active Internet connection.) As before, it can be opened from the All Programs section of the Start menu or the Tools menu (on the menu bar, not the Tools button on the toolbar) in Internet Explorer, as well as from Control Panel. You'll also find a Windows Update link in the left pane of Action Center.

> **Note**
>
> Keeping Windows up to date is an absolutely essential step in maintaining a secure computer and avoiding malware. In recent years, the most widely exploited vulnerabilities in Windows have been patched quickly—usually *before* these issues became widespread problems. Windows users who installed the updates promptly were able to avoid infection, whereas legions of others (who failed to keep their systems updated) fell victim.

Depending on how you have Windows Update configured, you might not need to visit the Windows Update window at all because it does its work quietly in the background, keeping your computer up to date with the latest fixes and improvements. (It's still a good idea to check the list of available updates at least once a month to find optional updates such as hardware drivers and nonessential fixes to Windows features you use regularly.) You can view its current settings, see what it has been up to, and find out what else it has in store for you by starting at its main window, shown in Figure 24-3. The top part of the window displays the current status and alerts you to any actions you should take.

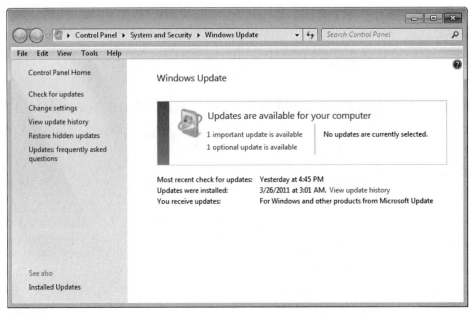

Figure 24-3 Windows Update lets you know if important or optional updates are available to download and install.

INSIDE OUT   Get updates for other Microsoft products

By default, Windows Update can download and install updates for Windows 7 and features, such as Internet Explorer, that are part of the operating system. You can also merge the functionality of Microsoft Update, a service for managing updates to Microsoft Office and several other Microsoft products, into Windows Update so that you no longer need to visit Office Online to get updates. If you do not already have Windows Update integrated with Microsoft Update, you will see the message "Find out more about free software from Microsoft Update" on the Windows Update home page. To enable checking of other products, click Click Here For Details beside this message. This action takes you to the Microsoft Update website for some quick installation steps. (You need to do this only once. Thereafter, the Windows Update home page indicates that you receive updates "For Windows and other products from Microsoft Update.")

Windows Update classifies updates into three categories: important (which includes security and critical performance updates), recommended (among other things, updates to signed drivers that affect performance or reliability and fixes to noncritical bugs), and optional (updated drivers that don't affect reliability or performance, interesting but unnecessary enhancements, and so on). Security updates—the most important items of the important category—are routinely released on the second Tuesday of each month (informally known as "patch Tuesday"). Other updates are not distributed on a regular basis; instead, they're published when the need arises, such as when a fix is developed for a newly discovered problem. You can make a habit of regularly visiting Windows Update to see what's new, but there's an easier way: install updates automatically. To review in greater detail (and modify, if you wish) your current Windows Update settings, click Change Settings. The page that appears (shown in Figure 24-4) lets you specify the degree of automation you want.

Figure 24-4 The Change Settings dialog box lets you specify how much automation you want from Windows Update.

The drop-down controls under Important Updates let you specify how and when you want those vital updates downloaded and installed. Under the recommended setting, Windows Update downloads and installs important updates for you, at the time you specify (for example, every day at 3 A.M.). With this option selected, Windows Update will also reboot your system if an update requires it. If you don't want this level of automation, you can choose to have updates downloaded but not installed until you give the go-ahead. Or you can opt simply to be notified when updates are available, allowing you to both download and install them on demand. The Important Updates drop-down list also gives you the not-recommended option of calling the whole thing off.

If you select the check box below Recommended Updates, Windows Update applies the same level of automation to recommended updates that it applies to important updates. Regardless of your setting for important updates, Windows Update refrains from downloading optional updates.

If you use the Install Updates Automatically (Recommended) option and your computer is in a low-power "sleep" state at the specified update time *and* if your computer is connected to AC power, Windows Update wakes the computer to perform the installation. If your computer is off or asleep but not plugged in, Windows Update waits until the next scheduled installation time.

If you have either the Download Updates But Let Me Choose Whether To Install Them or Check For Updates But Let Me Choose Whether To Download And Install Them option selected, Windows Update notifies you with a pop-up message when new updates are available for your review. You can click the message to open Windows Update. If you miss the pop-up message, the information awaits you the next time you open Windows Update. When you arrive there, click Install Updates to finish installing all updates or, if you want to review them first, click View Available Updates. Windows Updates presents a list of the updates that are ready to install. You can read about each update in the panel to the right of the list.

INSIDE OUT   Hide updates that you don't ever want to install

If you choose not to download and install an update, it's available for you the next time you visit Windows Update...and the next time, and the time after that as well. You might have a good reason for not accepting a particular update—perhaps it makes improvements to a Windows feature you never use—and there's no reason it should clutter your list of available updates. To remove an item from the list without installing it, you hide it. But the trick for hiding updates in the list is itself somewhat hidden.

In the list of available updates, right-click any update that you don't want to see again and choose Hide Update. If you later change your mind—or if you just want to see a list of the updates you've chosen to hide—on the main Windows Update page, click Restore Hidden Updates.

TROUBLESHOOTING

Windows Update fails to download and install updates

When Windows Update fails, it displays an error code on its home page, along with a link you can click to get help about the problem. The first place to start solving the problem is, of course, with the Get Help link. Sometimes that doesn't work either.

In that case, check your Internet connection. If it's not working, that accounts not only for the failure of Windows Update, but also for the failure of the link to additional help.

Updating Device Drivers

Windows Update can deliver updated drivers for many commonly used devices, either as recommended updates (if the drivers are considered to affect system stability) or optional updates (if they are not). If your devices meet the standards imposed by Microsoft's Windows Logo certification program, you can generally rely on Windows Update to keep their drivers current. Some device drivers are not ordinarily supplied by Windows Update, however; to get updates for such devices, you need to visit either the device vendor's website or, in some cases, your computer vendor's website. In certain cases, when hardware vendors make particularly large update downloads available, Windows Update might choose to alert you with a message and a link to the vendor's website, rather than offer the download directly.

Using Windows Update Manually

Whether you choose one of the automatic update options or choose the Never Check For Updates (Not Recommended) option, you can always manually check for updates to Microsoft products. To check for updates to Windows 7, open Windows Update and click Check For Updates (in the left pane).

Removing an Update

If you find that a particular update creates a problem, you can try removing it. Not all updates can be removed, however. (In particular, security-related updates usually cannot be removed. In addition, updates upon which other updates or other Windows features are dependent cannot be removed.) To find out if an update can be removed—and to go ahead and do the deed, if you choose—in Windows Update, click Installed Updates (in the left pane). Doing so takes you to a page within the Programs section of Control Panel that lists all uninstallable updates.

Chapter 24

> **Note**
>
> The installed updates page might lead you to believe that no updates have been installed. (For some reason, the "No updates are installed on this computer" message gives people that impression.) In fact, this page lists only the updates that can be uninstalled. To see a list of all updates that have been installed, return to Windows Update and click View Update History.

Updating More Than One Computer

The simplest way to keep all the computers on your network up to date is to enable automatic updating on each computer. If you have a small network in a home environment, go to each computer, open Windows Update, click Change Settings, and be sure it's set to download and install automatically.

But that's not always practical or efficient. If you have a dial-up connection to the Internet, for example, you'll spend a lot of time connected as each computer independently downloads large updates. And in larger networks, even those with lightning-fast Internet connections, administrators might want to control which updates get installed (and when) rather than leave it up to individual users.

Microsoft provides the following ways to manage updates in situations where setting Windows Update to automatic on all computers is impractical:

- Microsoft Update Catalog (*w7io.com/2101*) is a website that offers standalone installable versions of each update for Windows. Microsoft Update Catalog offers updates for all currently supported versions of Windows, which means you can also use this service to find updates for computers on your network that are not running Windows 7. You can search for updates based on keywords and then sort by the product, date of most recent update, classification, and size. After you find the updates of interest, download them once and store them in a shared network folder, where they can be installed from any computer.

- Administrators of large networks can use Windows Server Update Services (WSUS) to manage and deploy updates throughout an organization. The WSUS server, which runs on a computer running Windows Server 2003 or Windows Server 2008, manages downloading updates from Microsoft. Computers on the network then obtain updates from the WSUS server instead of directly from Microsoft's update servers. For details about WSUS, visit *w7io.com/2102*.

Using PowerShell Scripts to Manage Updates

Several Windows PowerShell scripts included in the Scripts folder of the companion CD provide additional ways of working with Windows Update on your local computer or remote computers. For example, Get-MicrosoftUpdates.ps1 returns detailed information about a specified number of the most recent updates installed on your own or a remote computer. Get-MissingSoftwareUpdates.ps1, illustrated in Figure 24-5, lists updates that have not been installed. You can supply a missing update's GUID as a parameter to the DownloadAndInstallMicrosoftUpdate.ps1 script to do what that script's name implies.

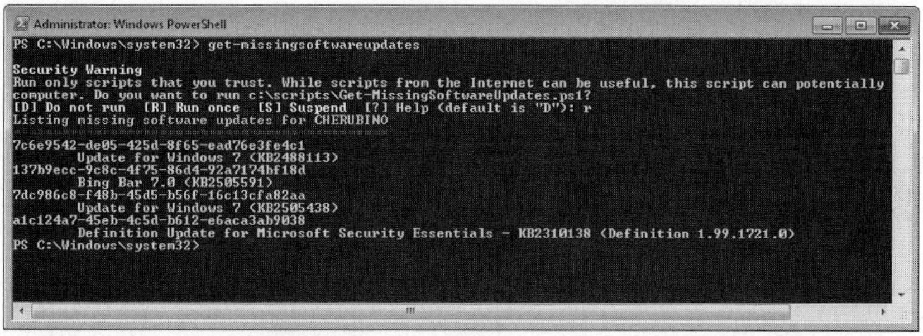

![screenshot of Administrator: Windows PowerShell window showing get-missingsoftwareupdates output]

Figure 24-5 The Get-MissingSoftwareUpdates.ps1 script reports the names and GUIDs of any updates that have not been installed.

Other update-related scripts on the companion CD include ConfigureSoftwareUpdates-Schedule.ps1 and TroubleshootWindowsUpdate.ps1. For information about the use of a particular script, open the script in Notepad and read the .Synopsis section. For general information about running Windows PowerShell Scripts, see "Running PowerShell Scripts" on page 999.

Checking Disks for Errors

Errors in disk media and in the file system can cause a wide range of Windows problems, ranging from an inability to open or save files to blue-screen errors and widespread data corruption. Windows is capable of recovering automatically from many disk errors, especially on drives formatted with NTFS.

To perform a thorough inspection for errors, you can manually run the Windows Check Disk utility, Chkdsk.exe. Two versions of this utility are available—a graphical version that performs basic disk-checking functions, and a command-line version that provides a much more extensive set of customization options.

To check for errors on a local disk, follow these steps:

1. Open Computer, right-click the icon belonging to the drive you want to check, and then choose Properties from the shortcut menu.

2. On the Tools tab, click Check Now. (If you're using a standard account, you'll need to supply credentials for an account in the Administrators group to execute this utility.)

3. In the Check Disk dialog box, shown next, select from the following options:

   - **Automatically Fix File System Errors**   This option, which is enabled by default, configures Windows to automatically repair any errors it detects in the file system. If this option is not selected, Check Disk reports any errors it finds but does not correct them. This option is the equivalent of running the Chkdsk command with the /F switch, as described later in this section.

   - **Scan For And Attempt Recovery Of Bad Sectors**   Select this option to perform an exhaustive check of the entire disk, locate bad sectors, and recover readable information stored in defective locations. Note that selecting this option automatically repairs file system errors as well, even if the previous option is cleared. This option is the equivalent of running the Chkdsk command with the /R switch.

If you simply want to see a report of file system errors without making any changes to disk structures, leave both boxes clear.

4. Click Start to begin the disk-checking process. The green progress bar provides feedback as the error-checking tool goes through several phases.

If you select the Automatically Fix File System Errors option on a drive that currently has open files, Windows is unable to run the utility immediately. In that case, you see the message shown here:

Click Schedule Disk Check to configure Windows startup so that the disk check utility runs the next time the computer is started. The disk check occurs early in the startup sequence, before Windows shifts into graphical mode; during this period, your computer is not available for you to perform any other tasks. When your computer starts, Windows notifies you that it's about to perform a scheduled disk check; by default, you have 10 seconds to cancel the operation and boot normally instead.

After Check Disk completes its operation, it reports its results. If the disk check turns up no errors, you see a Disk Check Complete dialog box. If Check Disk uncovers any errors, it writes a message to the System event log and displays a dialog box listing the errors it found and the repairs it made.

CAUTION

Although Check Disk is a useful tool and sometimes a lifesaver, it can cause you headaches if used without some planning. After it has started, the Check Disk operation cannot be stopped except by pressing your computer's power switch. On large drives (hundreds of gigabytes or more), the full disk check can take hours or even days to complete.

Check Disk runs automatically after an abnormal shutdown only if a specific bit in the registry is set, indicating that the file system is "dirty"—that is, that some pieces of data were not properly written to the disk when the system was shut down. If the file system wasn't doing anything when the system shut down, the dirty bit will not be set. Because NTFS volumes keep a journal of all disk activities, they are able to recover and remain clean even if you shut down in the middle of a disk write. Check Disk is most likely to run automatically at startup only on FAT32 volumes, after an unexpected shutdown.

INSIDE OUT   Cancel checks with Chkntfs

Two additional and well-hidden Windows commands are crucial to the operation of the Check Disk utility. The first of these, Autochk.exe, runs automatically any time you specify that you want to schedule a disk check to run at startup; it cannot be run interactively. The second, Chkntfs.exe, is especially useful if you change your mind and decide you want to cancel a scheduled check. At a command prompt, type **chkntfs /x d:** (where *d* is replaced by a drive letter) to exclude the drive specified. Chkntfs has another nifty trick: it can tell you whether a disk is dirty. At a command prompt, simply type **chkntfs d:**. For more details about these commands, see Knowledge Base article 248461, "Description of Enhanced Chkdsk, Autochk, and Chkntfs Tools in Windows 2000" (*w7io.com/2103*) and Knowledge Base article 160963, "CHKNTFS.EXE: What You Can Use It For" (*w7io.com/2104*). These Knowledge Base articles were originally written for earlier versions of the operating system, but the information is still valid for Windows 7.

The command-line version of Check Disk gives you considerably more options. It also allows you to set up regular disk-checking operations using the Task Scheduler (as described in "Using Task Scheduler" on page 966). To run this command in its simplest form, open a Command Prompt window using the Run As Administrator option, and then type **chkdsk** at the prompt. This command runs Chkdsk in read-only mode, displaying the status of the current drive but not making any changes. If you add a drive letter after the command (**chkdsk d:**, for instance), the report applies to that drive.

You can use any combination of the following switches at the end of the command line to modify its operation:

- **/F**   Instructs Chkdsk to fix any errors it detects. This is the most commonly used switch. The disk must be locked. If Chkdsk cannot lock the drive, it offers to check the drive the next time you restart the computer or to dismount the volume you want to check before proceeding. Dismounting is a drastic step; it invalidates all current file handles on the affected volume and can result in loss of data. You should decline the offer. When you do, Chkdsk will make you a second offer—to check the disk the next time you restart your system. You should accept this option. (If you're trying to check the system drive, the only option you're given is to schedule a check at the next startup.)

- **/V**   On FAT32 volumes, /V displays verbose output, listing the name of every file in every directory as the disk check proceeds. On NTFS volumes, this switch displays cleanup messages (if any).

- **/R**   Identifies bad sectors and recovers information from those sectors if possible. The disk must be locked. Be aware that this is a time-consuming and uninterruptible process.

The following switches are valid only on NTFS volumes:

- **/I**   Performs a simpler check of index entries (stage 2 in the Chkdsk process), reducing the amount of time required.

- **/C**   Skips the checking of cycles within the folder structure, reducing the amount of time required.

- **/X**   Forces the volume to dismount, if necessary, and invalidates all open file handles. This option is intended for server administrators. Because of the potential for data loss, it should be avoided.

- **/L[:*size*]**   Changes the size of the file that logs NTFS transactions. If you omit the *size* parameter, this switch displays the current size. This option is intended for server administrators. Because of the potential for data loss, it also should be avoided in normal use.

- **/B**   Reevaluates bad clusters.

Chapter 24

TROUBLESHOOTING

When you run Chkdsk in the Windows Recovery Environment, some options are not available

The Chkdsk command used when you boot to the Windows Recovery Environment is not the same as the one used within a full Windows session. Only two switches are available for this version:

- **/P**   Performs an exhaustive check of the current disk

- **/R**   Repairs damage on the current disk

If your system is able to boot to Windows either normally or in Safe Mode and you suspect that you have disk errors, you should use the full Chkdsk command.

For more details, see "Making Repairs with the Windows Recovery Environment" on page 1046.

Defragmenting Disks for Better Performance

On a relatively new system with a speedy processor and plenty of physical memory, hard disk performance is the single biggest bottleneck in everyday operation. Even with a zippy hard disk, it takes time to load large data files into memory so that you can work with them. The problem is especially noticeable with movies, video clips, DVD-burning projects, databases, ISO image files, and virtual hard disks, which can easily take up multiple gigabytes, sometimes in a single file.

On a freshly formatted disk, files load fairly quickly, but over time, performance can degrade because of disk fragmentation. To understand how fragmentation works, it helps to understand the basic structure of a hard disk. The process of formatting a disk divides it into *sectors*, each of which contains space for 512 bytes of data. The file system combines groups of sectors into *clusters*, which are the smallest units of space available for holding a single file or part of a file.

On any NTFS volume greater than 2 GB in size, the cluster size is 4 KB. Thus, when you save a 200-MB video clip, Windows divides the file into roughly 50,000 pieces. When you save this file for the first time on a freshly formatted, completely empty hard disk, Windows writes it in contiguous clusters. Because all the clusters that hold individual pieces of the file are physically adjacent to one another, the mechanical components of the hard disk can work very efficiently, scooping up data in one smooth operation. As a bonus, the hard disk's onboard cache and the Windows disk cache are able to anticipate the need for data and fetch nearby clusters that are likely to contain other parts of the file, which can then be retrieved from fast cached memory rather than from the relatively slow disk.

Unfortunately, hard disks don't stay neatly organized for long. When you add data to an existing file, the file system has to allocate more clusters for storage, typically in a different physical location on the disk. As you delete files, you create gaps in the once-tidy arrangement of contiguously stored files. As you save new files, especially large ones, the file system uses all these bits of free space, scattering the new files over the hard disk in many noncontiguous pieces. The resulting inefficiency in storage is called *fragmentation*; each time you open or save a file on a badly fragmented disk, disk performance suffers, sometimes dramatically, because the disk heads have to spend extra time moving from cluster to cluster before they can begin reading or writing data.

The Disk Defragmenter in Windows 7 improves on earlier versions in many ways, not the least of which is you shouldn't need to do anything to benefit from it. Disk Defragmenter runs as a low-priority background task that kicks off once a week, in the middle of the night, without requiring any attention from you.

Using Disk Defragmenter

The Disk Defragmenter utility improves performance by physically rearranging files so that they're stored in contiguous clusters. In addition to consolidating files and folders, the utility also consolidates free space, making it less likely that new files will be fragmented when you save them. The Disk Defragmenter process starts according to a schedule that you can adjust. To view the current settings, click the Disk Defragmenter shortcut (in the System Tools subfolder of the Accessories folder on the All Programs menu), or right-click any drive icon in the Computer window and click Defragment Now on the Tools tab.

Figure 24-6 shows the simple Disk Defragmenter interface. The Schedule section of the dialog box shows whether scheduled defragmentation is on or off and when the next run is to occur. The Current Status section shows the date and time of each disk's most recent defragmentation. Buttons let you reconfigure the schedule, analyze a selected disk to see how fragmented it might be, and perform an immediate defragmentation.

Click Configure Schedule to change when Disk Defragmenter runs automatically. By default, the utility runs weekly at about 1:00 A.M. each Wednesday. You can schedule operation to be daily, weekly (you pick the day of the week), or monthly (you pick the date), and you can choose the time of day (round numbers only), as shown in Figure 24-7.

Chapter 24

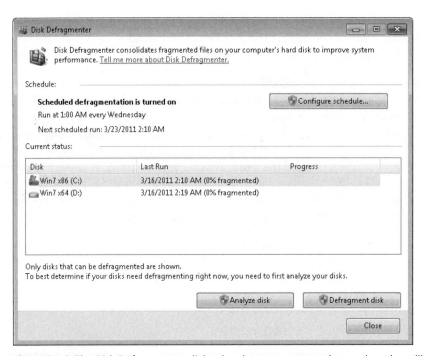

Figure 24-6 The Disk Defragmenter dialog box lets you see at a glance when the utility is set to run and when it last performed.

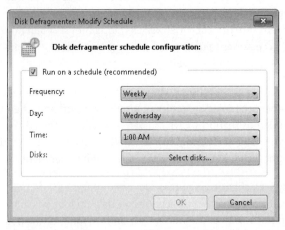

Figure 24-7 Pick a daily, weekly, or monthly schedule for Disk Defragmenter to begin running as a background task.

For details about managing scheduled tasks, see "Using Task Scheduler" on page 966.

If your computer is off at the appointed time, Disk Defragmenter will run at the first idle time after it's back up again. If your computer is nearly always either off or in use at 1 A.M., you might want to reconfigure the schedule. Choose a time when the machine is usually on but not in use—a regular lunch break, for example.

If your computer has more than one hard disk (more precisely, more than one *volume*, because each hard disk can be partitioned into multiple volumes), you can specify which ones you want Disk Defragmenter to act upon. Click Select Disks to display the dialog box shown in Figure 24-8, in which you can remove the check mark from any volumes you don't want to defragment.

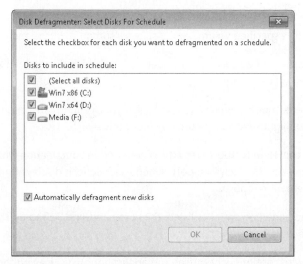

Figure 24-8 Selecting Automatically Defragment New Disks causes Disk Defragmenter to include any hard disks you add to your system in its routine.

INSIDE OUT   Dedicate a partition for CD or DVD burning

The best way to avoid disk fragmentation is to start with a completely clean slate. If you routinely work with CD images, for instance, consider creating a separate partition that's big enough to temporarily hold the files you're working with. A 2-GB partition, for instance, is big enough to hold a CD image and all temporary files associated with it. (You'll need roughly 10 GB for a DVD-burning partition.) Keep that drive empty except when you plan to create a CD, at which time you can copy files to it for burning. Using this strategy, you can be certain that fragmentation won't have a deleterious impact on your CD-burning performance.

Chapter 24

Running Disk Defragmenter from a Command Line

The command-line version of Disk Defragmenter allows you to exercise fine-grained control over the defragmentation process, and it uses the same program code as the scheduled version. To use this command for a specific drive, type **defrag** *d:* in an elevated Command Prompt window, where *d* is the drive letter or mount point of an existing volume. (For an explanation of mount points, see "Mapping a Volume to an NTFS Folder" on page 1119.) To see the full range of the Defrag utility's capabilities, type **defrag /?**. Among the more useful switches are the following:

- **/c** Defragments all volumes on the computer. Use this switch without specifying a specific drive letter or mount point.

- **/a** Analyzes the specified volume and displays a summary of the analysis report.

- **/f** Consolidates the free space on the specified volume, reducing the likelihood that large new files will be fragmented.

- **/r** Defragments multiple volumes in parallel. If your volumes are on physically separate disks, you might save a bit of time by using this switch.

- **/v** Displays complete (verbose) reports. When used in combination with /a, this switch displays only the analysis report. When used alone, it displays both the analysis and defragmentation reports.

In addition to the documented switches listed, the command-line Defrag utility includes this useful but undocumented switch:

- **/b** The /b switch optimizes boot files and applications while leaving the rest of the drive undisturbed.

The command-line Disk Defragmenter does not provide any progress indicator except for a blinking cursor. To interrupt the defragmentation process, click in the Command Prompt window and press Ctrl+C.

INSIDE OUT   Defragmenting particular files

Do you still want to defragment files larger than 64 MB, despite Microsoft's assurance that those files don't need defragmenting? Mark Russinovich's Contig utility, a free download from Microsoft's Sysinternals website (*w7io.com/2105*) will do the job. Contig is a file-specific defragmenter. You can use it to analyze and defragment individual files or groups of files meeting wildcard specifications.

TROUBLESHOOTING

The Disk Defragmenter utility does not fully defragment the drive

A volume must have at least 15 percent free space before Disk Defragmenter can completely defragment the volume. If you have less free space available, the operation will run, but only partial defragmentation will result. From a Command Prompt window, run Defrag with the /a switch to see statistics (including free space) regarding the specified volume.

You cannot defragment a volume that Windows has marked as possibly containing errors. To troubleshoot this possibility, type **chkdsk** *d:* **/f** at any command prompt, substituting the letter of the drive in question. Chkdsk will report and repair any file system errors it finds (after restarting, in the case of a system or boot volume).

Disk Defragmenter does not defragment files in the Recycle Bin. Empty the Recycle Bin before defragmenting.

Additionally, Disk Defragmenter does not defragment the following files: Bootsect.dos, Safeboot.fs, Safeboot.csv, Safeboot.rsv, Hiberfil.sys, and Memory.dmp. In addition, the Windows page file is never defragmented. (See "Defragmenting Particular Files" on the previous page to learn how to work around this issue.)

Disk Defragmenter ignores fragments that are more than 64 MB in size, both in its analytical reports and in operation. According to Microsoft's benchmarks, fragments of this size (which already consist of at least 16,000 contiguous clusters) have a negligible impact on performance. Thanks to disk latency, a large file divided into 10 fragments of 64 MB or greater in size will not load measurably slower than the same file in a single unfragmented location; under those circumstances, it's best to leave the fragments alone.

Disk Defragmenter will pass over any files that are currently in use. For best results, shut down all running programs before running the utility. For even better results, log off and log back on (using an account in the Administrators group) before continuing.

Defragmenting Solid-State Media

Because flash disks and other solid-state media don't employ moving parts to save and retrieve data, file fragmentation on these drives is likely to impose a smaller performance penalty than it does on rotating media. For this reason, as well as to avoid decreasing performance lifespan, Disk Defragmenter does not perform scheduled defragmentation of solid-state drives. You can still defragment a solid-state drive if you choose, but only on an ad hoc basis. To do this, run Disk Defragmenter, select the disk you want to defragment, and then click either Analyze Disk or Defragment Disk.

Chapter 24

Managing Disk Space

In the digital era, Parkinson's Law has an inescapable corollary: data expands to fill the space allotted to it. Gargantuan hard disks encourage consumption, and digital media files (not to mention Windows itself) supply plenty of bits to be consumed. It's surprisingly easy to run low on disk space, and the consequences can be deleterious to your system. If you run low on storage, Windows might not have enough room to expand its page file in response to system needs, or it might be unable to create temporary files. In addition, essential features such as Windows Search and System Restore might stop working properly. At that point, you start seeing ominous error messages and (possibly) degraded performance.

To pare down on disk space consumption, you can do any or all of the following:

- Clear out temporary files that you no longer need.

- Uninstall programs you don't need.

- Uninstall Windows features you don't need.

- Delete documents you don't need.

Cleaning Up with Disk Cleanup

The simplest way to make room on any drive is with the help of the Disk Cleanup utility, Cleanmgr.exe. If you click a "low disk space" warning, this tool opens automatically. To begin working directly with a single local drive, right-click the drive icon in the Computer window, choose Properties from the shortcut menu, and then click Disk Cleanup on the General tab of the properties dialog box. Alternatively, you can click All Programs on the Start menu, then Accessories, then System Tools, and then Disk Cleanup.

Disk Cleanup begins by calculating the amount of space it can recover. Then it presents its findings, categorized, in a dialog box similar to the one shown in Figure 24-9.

You can see at a glance how much space you can recover by deleting a category of files. If you're not sure what's included in a file category, select it in the list and read the descriptive text. For some file categories, a View Files button is available; click it to open a folder containing the file category.

With the assistance provided by the Description box, Disk Cleanup options are fairly self-explanatory. For the most part, these options merely consolidate functions already scattered throughout the Windows interface. For instance, you can empty the Recycle Bin, clear out the Temporary Internet Files folder, and purge files from the Temp folder. (Avoid cleaning out the Downloaded Program Files folder, which contains generally useful ActiveX and

Java add-ins.) Removing the Hibernation file can save a large amount of disk space—an amount equal to the amount of RAM installed on your computer; choose this option only if you never hibernate your system.

Figure 24-9 Disk Cleanup displays the categories of files it can delete and the amount of space per category that it can reclaim.

CAUTION

Disk Cleanup includes one confusing option that can leave an inordinate amount of wasted space on your hard disk if you don't understand how it works. When you run Disk Cleanup, one of the available options offers to delete Temporary Files; the accompanying Help text explains that these are unneeded files in the Temp folder. Unfortunately, this option might display a value of 0, even if your Temp folder contains hundreds of megabytes of useless files. The reason? Although the Help text hints at the answer, it doesn't clearly explain that this value lists only files in your Temp folder that are more than one week old. If you want to completely clean out this folder, you'll need to do so manually. Close all running programs and type **%temp%** in the Start menu search box; from the resulting Windows Explorer window, delete everything you find. You might discover that some files are not available for deletion until you restart your computer.

Cleaning Up System Files

Provided you have administrative credentials, you can add a few potentially large file categories to the initial list of deletable items by clicking Clean Up System Files. For example, if you performed a clean install of Windows 7 on a partition that you previously used for an earlier version of Windows, you might be able to reclaim gigabytes of disk space by eliminating the Windows.old folder. These files appear under the heading Previous Windows Installation(s). If you upgraded Windows Vista to Windows 7 (as opposed to performing a clean install), you might be able to recover a sizable chunk of disk space by deleting files under the heading Files Discarded By Windows Upgrade.

Clicking Clean Up System Files also adds a More Options tab to the Disk Cleanup dialog box, as shown in Figure 24-10.

The Clean Up button under Programs And Features takes you to the Uninstall Or Change A Program dialog box in Control Panel, where you can remove Windows features and programs. (For details, see "Tweaking and Tuning Your Windows Installation" on page 75 and "Uninstalling Programs" on page 195.) The Clean Up button under System Restore And Shadow Copies lets you remove all but the most recent System Restore checkpoints, shadow copies (previous file versions), and Complete PC Backup images. This option can recover a significant amount of space, but you should choose it only if you're certain you won't need to restore a backup or roll back your configuration to one of the saved versions you're about to delete.

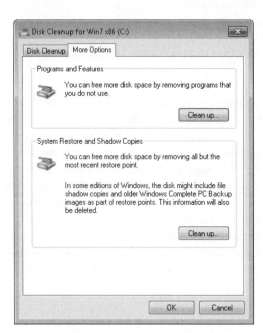

Figure 24-10 The More Options tab appears only if you click Clean Up System Files.

While getting rid of programs you no longer use is always a good idea, the option to eliminate all but the most recent restore point should be considered a desperate measure. Restore points can sometimes provide a way to restore stability to a system that has become unruly. Keep them if you can.

For information about using restore points, see "Rolling Back to a Stable State with System Restore" on page 466. For information about shadow copies, see "Restoring Previous Versions of Files and Folders" on page 401.

Cleaning Up at the Command Line

Disk Cleanup offers some cool command-line switches that are documented only in a pair of obscure Knowledge Base articles. Through the use of these switches, you can save your preferences and rerun the cleanup process automatically using those settings. To do so, you need to use the following switches with Cleanmgr.exe:

- **/Sageset:*n***   Opens a dialog box that allows you to select Disk Cleanup options, creates a registry key that corresponds to the number you enter, and then saves your settings in that key. Enter a number from 0 through 65535 in place of *n*.

- **/Sagerun:*n***   Retrieves the saved settings for the number you enter in place of *n* and then runs Disk Cleanup without requiring any interaction on your part.

To use these switches, follow these steps:

1. Open a Command Prompt window and type the command **cleanmgr /sageset:200**. (The number after the colon is completely arbitrary; you can choose any other number from 0 through 65535 if you prefer.) You must supply credentials from a member of the Administrators group to begin this task.

2. In the Disk Cleanup Settings dialog box, choose the options you want to apply whenever you use these settings.

3. Click OK to save your changes in the registry.

4. Open Task Scheduler from Control Panel, and start the Create Basic Task wizard. Follow the wizard's prompts to name the task, and schedule it to run at regular intervals. When prompted to select the program you want Windows to run, type **cleanmgr.exe** in the Program/Script box and type **/sagerun:200** in the Add Arguments box.

5. Repeat steps 1 through 4 for other Disk Cleanup options you want to automate.

INSIDE OUT   Make the most of Disk Cleanup shortcuts and tasks

Disk Cleanup shortcuts can be tremendously useful for routine maintenance. For instance, you might want to create a shortcut for Cleanmgr.exe with a saved group of settings that automatically empties the Temporary Internet Files folder and Recycle Bin and another that purges installation files and system dump files. If you create a short-cut that empties the Recycle Bin, it's best not to add it to your list of Scheduled Tasks, where it can inadvertently toss files you later discover you wanted to recover; instead, save this shortcut and run it as needed.

Strategies for Preserving Space on System Drives

The issue of space conservation on a system drive becomes crucial if you have Windows installed on a small-capacity disk—for example, if you have adopted the strategy of install-ing the operating system on an ultra-fast, expensive, and relatively small solid-state drive (SSD). Because it's important to keep an adequate amount of free space on the system drive—we recommend a minimum of 20 percent of the disk's capacity—you'll want to think about relocating certain folders and files that would ordinarily inhabit the system drive.

You'll get the most space savings by moving large data folders, such as Documents, Down-loads, Music, and Videos. For information about how to do this, see "Relocating Personal Data Folders" on page 416.

The next item to consider moving is your page file, Pagefil.sys. For details about the page file and information about how to move it (should you choose to do so), see "Ensuring That You Have an Adequate Virtual-Memory Configuration" on page 856.

Finally, you can consider removing the hibernation file. Windows supports two types of low-power states. One is sleep, and the other is hibernation. Hibernation is essential for notebooks, but less so for desktops, especially those that have a reliable uninterruptible power supply. Hibernation works by reserving space in a hidden file called hiberfil.sys, which is stored in the root of the system drive. By default, this file uses 75% of your total installed memory. You can reclaim this space on a desktop PC with a small system drive by disabling hibernation. To do so, you need to open an elevated Command Prompt. In the command window, type **powercfg –h off** and press Enter. (To reenable hibernation, use the same command, but change **off** to **on**.) From that same command prompt, you can verify the size of both your paging file and your hibernation file: use the command **dir c:\ /as**.

Conserving Space with NTFS File Compression

One of the many advantages the NTFS file system offers over older systems, such as FAT32, is slick and essentially seamless on-the-fly file compression. To compress a file (or an entire folder) stored on an NTFS-formatted volume, all you have to do is set an attribute for that object; Windows decompresses the file or folder automatically when you access it.

To compress a file or folder, right-click its icon in Windows Explorer, choose Properties from the shortcut menu, and click the Advanced button on the General tab. In the Advanced Attributes dialog box, shown in Figure 24-11, select Compress Contents To Save Disk Space. Note that an NTFS file can be compressed or encrypted but not both; the options are mutually exclusive.

Figure 24-11 You can compress a single file, a folder full or files, or an entire drive—but only on a drive formatted with NTFS.

INSIDE OUT   Use compression sparingly

A little compression goes a long way. In general, NTFS compression is most effective when used on files that are not already compressed. Bitmap images, Microsoft Word documents, and database files are highly compressible. Because music files (in MP# and WMA formats) and JPEG and GIF images are already compressed, NTFS compression provides little benefit and incurs a noticeable performance hit. By all means, avoid compressing the folders that contain Windows system files and log files that the operating system uses regularly. The negative effect on performance is especially severe here.

To compress an entire volume at once, right-click the drive icon in Windows Explorer and follow the same procedure. You'll be asked to confirm that you really want to do this for every file in the volume. When you say yes, the system begins compressing files, one at a time. The process can take hours to complete; fortunately, it needs to be done only once. You can continue working while Windows is busy compressing files. If the system needs to compress an open file, you'll be notified with a dialog box. At that point, you can close the file in question and click Retry, or click Ignore or Ignore All.

When you compress a folder, that attribute affects files that you move or copy later, according to the following rules:

- If you create a new file in a compressed folder, the new file is compressed.

- If you copy a file into a compressed folder, the file is compressed.

- If you move a file from a different NTFS volume into a compressed folder, the file is compressed.

- If you move a file into a compressed folder on the same NTFS volume, the file retains whatever compression setting it had originally; in other words, its compression attribute remains unchanged.

- If you move a compressed file into an uncompressed folder on the same NTFS volume, the file retains the compressed attribute. However, if you move a compressed file to an uncompressed folder on a different NTFS partition, the file loses the compression attribute.

INSIDE OUT   Highlight compressed files

If you use on-the-fly compression, take advantage of an option in Windows Explorer that displays compressed files and folders in an alternative color. That way you can see at a glance which files and folders are compressed. To verify that this feature is enabled, open Windows Explorer and choose Organize, Folder And Search Options. On the View tab, make sure that Show Encrypted Or Compressed NTFS Files In Color is selected. By default, the names and other details of compressed files appear in blue within Windows Explorer.

Using Advanced System Management Tools

N this chapter, we look at a handful of programs and management consoles that can help you attain greater mastery over Windows. We'll start with tools for unearthing details about your system—its hardware, software environment, running programs and services, and so on. Because the Services utility described later in the chapter (as well as a good many other management tools not covered here) is hosted by Microsoft Management Console, we'll precede our discussion with a consideration of MMC. We'll follow with a guide to editing the registry and a discussion of Group Policy.

What's in Your Edition?

The Local Group Policy Editor is available only in the Professional, Ultimate, and Enterprise editions of Windows 7. The other programs described in this chapter work the same way in all editions.

Viewing System Information

For answers to basic questions about your operating system and computer, there's no better place to start than the System application in Control Panel, shown in Figure 25-1. No matter where you are in Windows or what your preferred input method is, this display is only a few clicks or keystrokes away. The simplest way to get there is to right-click Computer and choose Properties. This works just about any place that the Computer shortcut appears, including on the Start menu, on the desktop, and in a Windows Explorer window.

The System application displays the Windows edition currently running, system details (including processor type, installed memory, and whether the current operating system is a 32-bit or 64-bit version), details about the computer name and domain or workgroup, and the current activation status.

Chapter 25

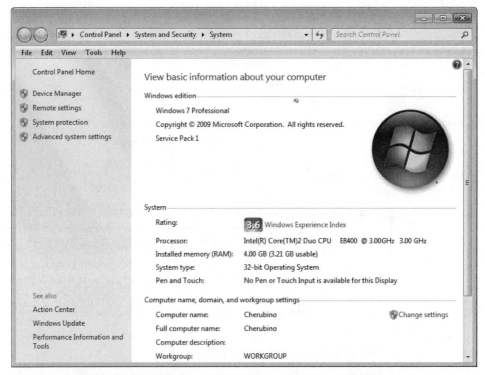

Figure 25-1 The System application in Control Panel provides basic details about your computer's configuration.

Links scattered around the dialog box lead to additional sources of information. Two in particular are worth noting here:

- Click Device Manager in the left pane to view detailed information about your installed hardware, including information about drivers. You can also open Device Manager directly, without first passing through System, by typing **devmgmt.msc** at a command prompt.

  For details about how to use the information displayed in Device Manager, see Chapter 29, "Setting Up and Configuring Hardware."

- Click Windows Experience Index to show a numeric breakdown of the five elements that make up the base score shown in the System window. Click View And Print Details to display a more detailed (but still not exhaustive) inventory of system components—motherboard and processor, storage, graphics, and network hardware. Knowing the numeric Experience Index rating for each subsystem is an important first step in improving system performance, as we explain in "Using the Windows Experience Index" on page 835.

Digging Deeper with Dedicated System Information Tools

For the most exhaustive inventory of system configuration details in a no-frills text format, Windows offers three tools that provide varying levels of technical information:

- **Systeminfo**   Systeminfo.exe is a command-line utility that displays information about your Windows version, BIOS, processor, memory, network configuration, and a few more esoteric items. Figure 25-2 shows sample output.

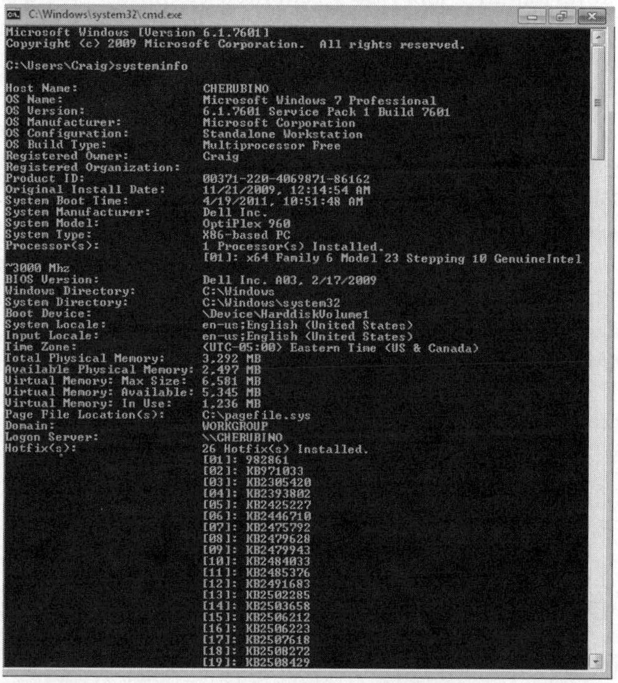

Figure 25-2 The command-line utility Systeminfo.exe provides an easy way to gather information on all your network computers in a single database.

To run Systeminfo, open a Command Prompt window, type **systeminfo**, and then press Enter. In addition to the list format shown in the figure, Systeminfo offers two formats that are useful if you want to work with the information in another program: Table (fixed-width columns) and CSV (comma-separated values). To use one of these formats, append the /FO switch to the command, along with the Table or Csv parameter. You'll also need to redirect the output to a file. For example, to store comma-delimited information in a file named Info.csv, enter the following command:

```
systeminfo /fo csv > info.csv
```

The /S switch allows you to get system information about another computer on your network. (If your user name and password don't match that of an account on the target computer, you'll also need to use the /U and /P switches to provide the user name and password of an authorized account.) When you've gathered information about all the computers on your network, you can import the file you created into a spreadsheet or database program for tracking and analysis. The following command appends information about a computer named Badlands to the original file you created:

```
systeminfo /s badlands /fo csv >> info.csv
```

- **Windows Management Instrumentation Command-Line Utility**   This tool is better known by the name of its executable, Wmic.exe, which is located in the Windows\ System32\Wbem folder. Wmic provides an overwhelming amount of information about hardware, system configuration details, and user accounts. It can be used in either of two ways. Enter **wmic** from a command prompt and the utility runs in console mode, allowing you to enter commands and view output interactively. If you add global switches or *aliases*, which constrain the type of output you're looking for, you can see the output in a Command Prompt window or redirect it to a file. For example, the command **wmic qfe list brief /format:htable > %temp%\hotfix.html** produces a neatly formatted HTML file; open that file in Internet Explorer to see a list of all installed updates on the current system. To see the full syntax for Wmic, open a Command Prompt window and type **wmic –?**.

- **System Information**   System Information—often called by the name of its executable, Msinfo32.exe—is a techie's paradise. It provides all manner of information about your system's hardware and software in a no-frills window that includes search capabilities. The following sections discuss System Information in greater detail.

Finding and Decoding Information in System Information

System Information displays a wealth of configuration information in a clear display, as shown in Figure 25-3. You can search for specific information, save information, view information about other computers, and even view a list of changes to your system.

To start System Information, type **msinfo32** at a command prompt, or click Start and choose All Programs, Accessories, System Tools, System Information.

You navigate through System Information much as you would through Windows Explorer or an MMC console: click a category in the left pane to view its contents in the right pane. To search for specific information, use the Find What box at the bottom of the System Information window. (If the Find bar is not visible, choose Edit, Hide Find.) The Find feature is basic but effective. Here are a couple of things you should know:

- Whenever you type in the Find What box to start a new search, Find begins its search at the top of the search range (the entire namespace unless you select Search Selected Category Only)—not at the current highlight.

- Selecting Search Category Names Only causes the Find feature to look only in the left pane. When this check box is cleared, the text in both panes is searched.

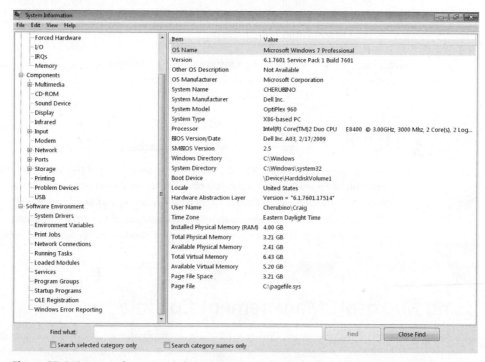

Figure 25-3 System Information is for viewing configuration information only; you can't use it to actually configure settings.

Exporting System Information

Using System Information, you can preserve your configuration information—which is always helpful when reconstructing a system—in several ways:

- Save the information as an .nfo file. You can subsequently open the file (on the same computer or on a different computer with System Information) to view your saved information. To save information in this format, choose File, Save. Saving this way always saves the entire collection of information.

- Save all or part of the information as a plain text file. To save information as a text file, select the category of interest and choose File, Export. To save all the information as a text file, select System Summary before you export.

- You can print all or part of the information. Select the category of interest; choose File, Print; and be sure that Selection is selected under Page Range. To print everything, select All under Page Range—and be sure to have lots of paper on hand. Depending on your system configuration and the number of installed applications, your report could top 100 pages.

Regardless of how you save your information, System Information refreshes (updates) the information immediately before processing the command.

INSIDE OUT   Save your system information periodically

Saving system configuration information when your computer is working properly can turn out to be very useful when you have problems. Comparing your computer's current configuration with a known good baseline configuration can help you spot possible problem areas. You can open multiple instances of System Information to display the current configuration in one window and a baseline configuration in another.

Using Microsoft Management Console

Microsoft Management Console (MMC) is an application that hosts tools for administering computers, networks, and other system components. By itself, MMC performs no administrative services. Rather, it acts as the host for one or more modules called *snap-ins*, which do the useful work. MMC simply provides user-interface consistency so that you or the users you support see more or less the same style of application each time you need to carry out some kind of computer management task. A combination of one or more snap-ins can be saved in a file called a Microsoft Common Console Document or, more commonly, an MMC *console*.

Creating snap-ins requires expertise in programming. You don't have to be a programmer, however, to make your own custom MMC consoles. All you need to do is run MMC, start with a blank console, and add one or more of the snap-ins available on your system. Alternatively, you can customize some of the MMC consoles supplied by Microsoft or other vendors simply by adding or removing snap-ins.

Why might you want to customize your MMC consoles? Because neither Microsoft nor any other vendor can anticipate your every need. Perhaps you would like to take some of the functionality from two or more existing MMC consoles and combine the functionality into a single console. (You might, for example, want to combine the Services console with the Event Viewer console, the latter filtered to show only events generated by services. You might also want to include a link to a website that offers details about services and service-related errors.) Or perhaps you would like to simplify some of the existing consoles by removing snap-ins that you seldom use.

Running MMC Consoles

MMC consoles have, by default, the extension .msc, and .msc files are associated by default with MMC. Thus, you can run any MMC console by double-clicking its file name in a Windows Explorer window or by entering the file name at a command prompt. Windows 7 includes several predefined consoles; the most commonly used ones, described in Table 25-1, can be easily found by typing their name in the Start menu search box.

Table 25-1 **Useful Predefined Consoles**

Console Name (File Name)	Description
Computer Management (Compmgmt.msc)	Includes the functionality of the Task Scheduler, Event Viewer, Shared Folders, Local Users And Groups, Reliability And Performance Monitor, Device Manager, Disk Management, Services, and WMI Control snap-ins, providing control over a wide range of computer tasks.
Device Manager (Devmgmt.msc)	Uses the Device Manager snap-in to enable administration of all attached hardware devices and their drivers. See Chapter 29 for more information.
Event Viewer (Eventvwr.msc)	Uses the Event Viewer snap-in to display all types of logged information. See "Digging Deeper with Event Viewer" on page 1023 for details.
Performance Monitor (Perfmon.msc)	Uses the Performance Monitor snap-in to provide a set of monitoring tools far superior to Performance Monitor in earlier Windows versions. See Chapter 23, "Tuning Up and Monitoring Performance," for details.
Services (Services.msc)	Uses the Services snap-in to manage services in Windows. For details, see "Managing Startup Programs and Services" on page 863.
Task Scheduler (Taskschd.msc)	Uses the Task Scheduler snap-in for managing tasks that run automatically. For details, see "Using Task Scheduler" on page 966.
Windows Firewall With Advanced Security (Wf.msc)	Uses the Windows Firewall With Advanced Security snap-in to configure rules and make other firewall settings. For details, see "Advanced Tools for Managing Windows Firewall" on page 614.

Chapter 25

MMC Consoles and User Account Control

Consoles can be used to manage all sorts of computer hardware and Windows features: with a console you can modify hard-drive partitions, start and stop services, and install device drivers, for example. In other words, MMC consoles perform the types of tasks that User Account Control (UAC) is designed to restrict. In the hands of someone malicious (or simply careless), consoles have the power to wreak havoc on your computer.

Therefore, when using an MMC console you're likely to encounter a User Account Control request for permission to continue. If UAC is enabled on your computer, the type of request you get and the restrictions that are imposed depend on your account type and the console you're using. Some consoles, such as Device Manager (Devmgmt.msc), display a message box informing you that the console will run with limitations. (In effect, it works in a read-only mode that allows you to view device information but not make changes.) Others block all use by nonadministrative users. To ensure that you don't run into an "access denied" roadblock when performing administrative tasks while logged on with a standard account, always right-click and choose Run As Administrator.

Running a Console in Author Mode

MMC consoles can be run in Author mode or in three varieties of User mode. Author mode gives you full access to MMC's menus and options. In User modes, elements of MMC's functionality are removed. To run a console in Author mode, right-click its file in a Windows Explorer window and choose Author from the shortcut menu. Alternatively, you can run a console in Author mode by using the following command-line syntax:

```
name.msc /a
```

where *name* is the file name of the console file.

> **Note**
> If the console mode was set to Author mode when the console was last saved, the console opens in Author mode without the use of the Author command or the /A command-line option.

Using MMC Consoles

Notwithstanding the fact that MMC is intended to provide user-interface consistency across administrative applications, actual MMC consoles can take on quite a variety of appearances. Compare the Event Viewer console (Eventvwr.msc) shown in Figure 28-9 on page 1023 with the Disk Management console (Diskmgmt.msc) shown in Figure 30-1 on page 1101, for example.

MMC is designed to be extremely flexible. Snap-ins can add elements to the MMC user interface, and console designers can hide or display UI elements as needs dictate. Nevertheless, *most* of the consoles that come with your operating system look somewhat like the one shown in Figure 25-4, so we can make a few generalizations about their use:

- **Console tree, details pane, and action pane**   The console can be divided vertically into panes. The leftmost pane, whose display is optional, contains the *console tree*, which shows the organization of the console and allows for easy navigation between snap-ins. Outline controls in the console tree function as in Windows Explorer. The center pane, called the *details pane*, shows information related to the item currently selected in the console tree. The *action pane*, which (optionally) appears on the right side of the window, lists links to actions that are appropriate for the items selected in the other two panes. Up arrows and down arrows let you expand or contract a section of the action pane; clicking a right arrow displays a submenu.

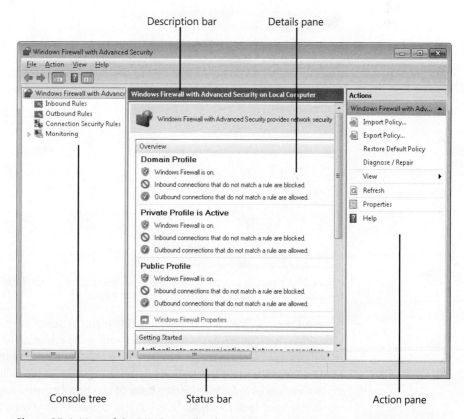

Figure 25-4 Most of the MMC consoles that come with Windows 7 include a console tree, a details pane, and an action pane.

The vertical split bar between the panes can be dragged to the left or right, like its counterpart in Windows Explorer. To display or hide the console tree or the action pane, use the toolbar buttons (one controls each pane) or the Customize command on the View menu.

- **Action and View menus**   The Action menu, if present, provides commands specific to the current selection, providing an alternative to the action pane. In other words, this is the menu you use to carry out administrative tasks. The View menu, if present, allows you to choose among alternative ways of presenting information. In many MMC consoles, for example, the View menu offers Large Icons, Small Icons, List, and Details commands, similar to the view options in Windows Explorer. The View menu might also include a Customize command. This command presents the Customize View dialog box shown in Figure 25-5, which allows you, among other things, to hide or display the console tree.

Figure 25-5 You can use the Customize View dialog box to control various elements of the MMC console, which are identified in Figure 25-4.

- **Shortcut menus**   Whether or not an Action menu or action pane is present, you'll sometimes find that the easiest way to carry out an administrative task is to right-click the relevant item in the console tree or the details pane and choose an action from the item's shortcut menu. That's because the shortcut menu always includes all the actions available for the selected item. (If you don't immediately find the command you need, look for an All Tasks command; the action you want is probably on the All Tasks submenu.) The shortcut menu also always includes a Help command.

- **Working with content in the details pane**   If the details pane provides a tabular presentation, you can manipulate content by using the same techniques you use in Windows Explorer. You can sort by clicking column headings, control column width by dragging the borders between column headings (double-click a border to make a column just wide enough for the widest entry), and rearrange columns by dragging headings.

  To hide or display particular columns, look for an Add/Remove Columns command on the View menu. Here you can specify which columns you want to see in the details pane, as well as the order in which you want to see them.

- **Exporting details pane data to text or .csv files**   Many MMC consoles include commands on the Action menu for saving data in binary formats. In most consoles that produce tabular displays, however, you can also use the Export List command to generate a tab-delimited or comma-delimited text file, suitable for viewing in a word-processing, spreadsheet, or database program. If this command is available, you'll find it on the Action menu or any shortcut menu.

Creating Your Own MMC Consoles

Creating your own MMC console or modifying an existing one involves the following steps (not necessarily in this order):

- Run MMC with no snap-in, or open an existing MMC console in Author mode.

- Display the console tree if it's not already visible.

- Add or remove snap-ins, folders, and, if appropriate, extensions (modules that extend the functionality of snap-ins).

- Manipulate windows and other display elements to taste.

- Add items to the Favorites menu if appropriate.

- Name the console and choose an icon for it.

- Choose Author mode or one of the three User modes, and further restrict user options if appropriate.

- Use the File menu to save your .msc file.

Running MMC with No Snap-in

To run MMC with no snap-in, simply type **mmc** on a command line. An empty, Author-mode MMC console appears. MMC is a multiple-document-interface (MDI) application (the Console Root window is a child window), although most of the consoles supplied with

Windows do their best to disguise this fact. You can create consoles with multiple child windows, and those windows can be maximized, minimized, restored, resized, moved, cascaded, and tiled, all within the confines of the main MMC window.

Displaying the Console Tree

If the console tree is not visible in the application you're creating or modifying, choose Customize View from the View menu. In the Customize View dialog box (shown earlier in Figure 25-5), select the Console Tree check box. Alternatively, if the standard toolbar is displayed, click the Show/Hide Console Tree button.

Adding Snap-ins and Extensions

The contents of a console can consist of a single snap-in, or you can craft a hierarchically organized, completely personalized, everything-but-the-kitchen-sink management tool. To add a snap-in to your application, follow these steps:

1. Choose File, Add/Remove Snap-In (or press Ctrl+M) to display the dialog box shown in Figure 25-6.

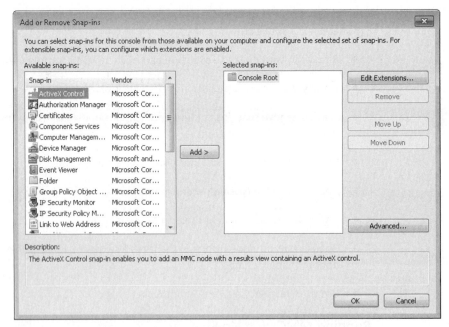

Figure 25-6 By default, MMC snap-ins are arranged in a single-level list.

2. If you want a multilevel console tree, click Advanced, select Allow Changing The Parent Snap-In, and then click OK.

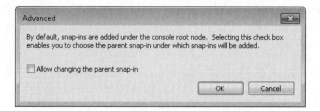

3.   In the Parent Snap-In list, select the parent of the new snap-in. The parent can be Console Root or a folder or snap-in that you've already added. (In a brand new MMC application, your only choice is Console Root.)

4.   In the Available Snap-Ins list, select the snap-in you want, and then click Add.

     If the selected snap-in supports remote management, a dialog box similar to the one shown in Figure 25-7 appears.

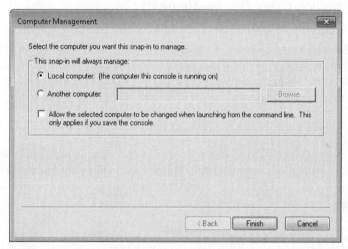

Figure 25-7 Some snap-ins can be configured to manage another computer on your network. In this dialog box, specify which computer you want to manage.

5.   Select Local Computer to manage the computer on which the console runs, or supply the name of the computer you want to manage. Some snap-ins that allow remote management let you specify the target computer at run time by means of a command-line switch; select the check box to enable this option.

     Some snap-ins come with optional extensions. You can think of these as snap-ins for snap-ins—modules that provide additional functionality to the selected snap-in. Some snap-ins comprise many extensions, and you can optionally select which ones you want to enable or disable.

6. To modify the extensions to a snap-in, select the snap-in in the Selected Snap-Ins list in the Add Or Remove Snap-Ins dialog box shown earlier in Figure 25-6, and then click Edit Extensions. Select which extensions you want to use. Click OK.

7. Repeat steps 3 through 6 to add more snap-ins. Click OK when you're finished.

8. If you added one or more folders as containers for other snap-ins, in the console tree right-click the new folder, choose Rename, and supply a meaningful name.

Managing Windows

With the New Window From Here command on the Action menu, you can create a new child window rooted in the current console-tree selection. You might want to use this command to create multiple-window applications. After you've created your windows, you can use Window menu commands to tile or cascade them.

Controlling Other Display Elements

The Customize View command on the View menu allows you to hide or display various elements of the MMC visual scene, including taskbars and menus. Note that selections in the Customize View dialog box (shown in Figure 25-5) take effect immediately—you don't need to click an Apply button or leave the dialog box. Therefore, you can easily try each option and see whether you like it.

Using the Favorites Menu

The Favorites menu allows you to store pointers to places within your console tree. If you create a particularly complex MMC console, you might want to consider using favorites to simplify navigation. To add a console-tree item to your list of favorites, select that item and then choose Add To Favorites from the Favorites menu.

Naming Your Console

To assign a name to your console, choose File, Options. Your entry in the field at the top of the Console tab in the Options dialog box will appear on the title bar of your console, regardless of the file name you apply to its .msc file. If you do not make an entry here, MMC replaces Console1 with the console's eventual file name. Click Change Icon to select an icon for the console. You can select an icon from any dynamic-link library (DLL) or executable file.

> **Note**
> You can rename Console Root (or any other folder in the console tree) by right-clicking it and choosing Rename.

Restricting User Control of Your Console

In the Console Mode list on the Console tab of the Options dialog box (choose File, Options), you can select among MMC's three User modes. In any of these modes, users can't add or remove snap-ins or make other changes to the console. The different modes control how much of the console tree users are able to see and whether they can open new windows.

- **User Mode—Full Access**   Users have full access to the console tree and can open new windows by using either the New Window From Here or Window, New Window command. (Changes to the window arrangement can't be saved in User mode, however.)

- **User Mode—Limited Access, Multiple Window**   Users have access only to parts of the console tree that are visible. (For example, if you create a hierarchically organized console, open a new window from a node below the console root, and then close the console root window before saving, users will be unable to reach the console root and other nodes at or above the level at which the new window was opened.) Users can open new windows with the New Window From Here command, but the New Window command (which would provide access to the console root) does not appear on the Window menu.

- **User Mode—Limited Access, Single Window**   In this most restrictive mode, users have access only to parts of the console tree that are visible. MMC operates in single-window mode, essentially losing its MDI character; users can't open new document windows, nor can they resize the single document window.

If you choose one of the three User modes, the two check boxes at the bottom of the Options dialog box become available. Your choices are as follows:

- **Do Not Save Changes To This Console**   With this check box cleared (its default), MMC saves the state of your application automatically when a user closes it. The user's selection in the console tree, for example, is preserved from one use to the next. If you always want your users to see the same thing each time they run the console, select this check box.

- **Allow The User To Customize Views**   This check box, selected by default, keeps the Customize View command available, allowing your users, for example, to hide or display the console tree. Clear the check box if you want to deny users access to this option.

Chapter 25

Saving a Console

The final step in the process of creating an MMC console is, of course, to save the file. Choose File, Save As; enter a file name in the Save As dialog box; and choose a location (the default location is the Administrative Tools folder in the Start Menu\Programs folder for your profile). Click Save. The resulting console file is saved with the .msc extension.

Managing Services

A service is a specialized program that performs a function to support other programs. Many services operate at a very low level (by interacting directly with hardware, for example) and need to run even when no user is logged on. For this reason, they are often run by the System account (which has elevated privileges) rather than by ordinary user accounts. In this section, you'll learn how to view the installed services; start, stop, and configure them; and install or remove them. We'll also take a closer look at some of the services used in Windows 7 and show you how to configure them to your advantage. A new (and great, we might add) method for viewing services on your computer is through the Services tab of Task Manager. This chapter also looks at this new feature.

Using the Services Console

You manage services with the Services snap-in for Microsoft Management Console, shown in Figure 25-8. To view this snap-in, type **services.msc** at a command prompt. (You must have administrator privileges to gain full functionality in the Services console. Running as a standard user, you can view service settings, but you can't start or stop most services, change the startup type, or make any other configuration changes.)

The Extended and Standard views in the Services console (selectable by clicking a tab near the bottom of the window) have a single difference: the Extended view provides descriptive information of the selected service in the space at the left edge of the details pane. This space also sometimes includes links for starting, stopping, or pausing the selected service. Unless you need to constrain the console display to a small area of your screen, you'll probably find the Extended view preferable to the Standard view.

The Services console offers plenty of information in its clean display. You can sort the contents of any column by clicking the column title, as you can do with other similar lists. To sort in reverse order, click the column title again. In addition, you can do the following:

- Start, stop, pause, resume, or restart the selected service, as described in the following section

- Display the properties dialog box for the selected service, in which you can configure the service and learn more about it

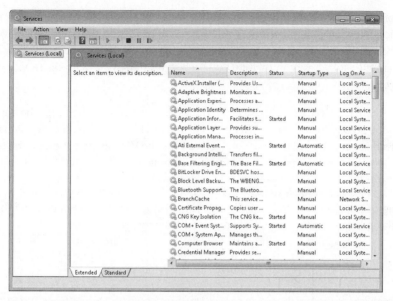

Figure 25-8 Use the Services console to start, stop, and configure services.

Most of the essential services are set to start automatically when your computer starts, and the operating system stops them as part of its shutdown process. But sometimes you might need to manually start or stop a service. For example, you might want to start a seldom-used service on the rare occasion when you need it. (Because running services requires system resources such as memory, running them only when necessary can improve performance.) On the other hand, you might want to stop a service because you're no longer using it. A more common reason, however, for stopping a service is because it isn't working properly. For example, if print jobs get stuck in the print queue, sometimes the best remedy is to stop and then restart the Print Spooler service.

INSIDE OUT   Pause instead of stopping

If a service allows pausing, try pausing and then continuing the service as your first step instead of stopping the service. Pausing can solve certain problems without canceling jobs in process or resetting connections.

Starting and Stopping Services

Not all services allow you to change their status. Some prevent stopping and starting altogether, whereas others permit stopping and starting but not pausing and resuming. Some services allow these permissions to only certain users or groups. For example, most services allow only members of the Administrators group to start or stop them. Which status changes are allowed and who has permission to make them are controlled by each service's discretionary access control list (DACL), which is established when the service is created on a computer.

To change a service's status, select it in the Services console. Then click the appropriate link in the area to the left of the service list (if you're using the Extended view and the link you need appears there). Alternatively, you can use the VCR-style controls on the toolbar, or right-click and choose the corresponding command.

You can also change a service's status by opening its properties dialog box and then clicking one of the buttons on the General tab. Taking the extra step of opening the properties dialog box to set the status has only one advantage: you can specify start parameters when you start a service using this method. This is a rare requirement.

Configuring Services

To review or modify the way a service starts up or what happens when it doesn't start properly, view its properties dialog box. To do that, simply double-click the service in the Services console. Figure 25-9 shows an example.

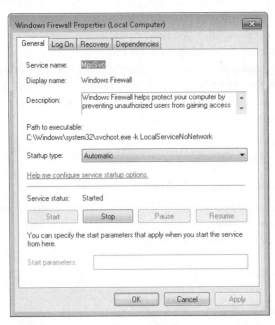

Figure 25-9 You specify a service's startup type on the General tab, where you can also find the actual name of the service above its display name.

Setting Startup Options

On the General tab of the properties dialog box (shown in Figure 25-9), you specify the startup type:

- **Automatic (Delayed Start)**   The service starts shortly after the computer starts in order to improve startup performance and user experience.

- **Automatic**   The service starts when the computer starts.

- **Manual**   The service doesn't start automatically at startup, but it can be started by a user, program, or dependent service.

- **Disabled**   The service can't be started.

You'll find other startup options on the Log On tab of the properties dialog box, as shown in Figure 25-10.

Figure 25-10 On the Log On tab, you specify which user account runs the service.

> **Note**
>
> If you specify a logon account other than the Local System account, be sure that account has the requisite rights. Go to the Local Security Policy console (at a command prompt, type **secpol.msc**), and then go to Security Settings\Local Policies\User Rights Assignment and assign the Log On As A Service right to the account.

Specifying Recovery Actions

For a variety of reasons—hardware not operating properly or a network connection being down, for example—a service that's running smoothly might suddenly stop. Settings on the Recovery tab of the properties dialog box, shown in Figure 25-11, allow you to specify what should happen if a service fails.

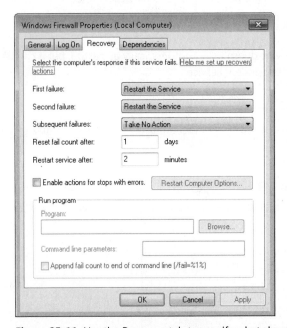

Figure 25-11 Use the Recovery tab to specify what should happen if the service fails.

You might want to perform a different action the first time a service fails than on the second or subsequent failures. The Recovery tab enables you to assign a particular response to the first failure, the second failure, and all subsequent failures, from among these options:

- **Take No Action**   The service gives up trying. In most cases, the service places a message in the event log. (Use of the event log depends on how the service was programmed by its developers.)

- **Restart The Service**   The computer waits for the time specified in the Restart Service After box to elapse and then tries to start the service.

- **Run A Program**   The computer runs the program that you specify in the Run Program box. For example, you could specify a program that attempts to resolve the problem or one that alerts you to the situation.

- **Restart The Computer**   Drastic but effective, this option restarts the computer after the time specified in the Restart Computer Options dialog box elapses. In that dialog box, you can also specify a message to be broadcast to other users on your network, warning them of the impending shutdown.

Viewing Dependencies

Many services rely on the functions of another service. If you attempt to start a service that depends on other services, Windows first starts the others. If you stop a service upon which others are dependent, Windows also stops those services. Before you either start or stop a service, therefore, it's helpful to know what other services your action might affect. To obtain that information, go to the Dependencies tab of a service's properties dialog box, shown in Figure 25-12.

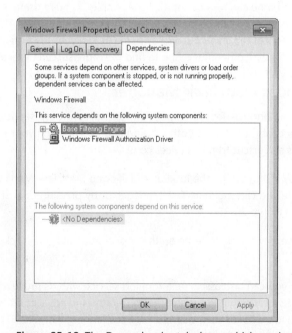

Figure 25-12 The Dependencies tab shows which services depend on other services.

Determining the Name of a Service

As you view the properties dialog box for different services, you might notice that the service name (shown at the top of the General tab) is often different from the name that appears in the Services console (the display name) and that neither name matches the name of the service's executable file. (In fact, the executable for many services is either Services.exe or Svchost.exe.) The General tab (shown in Figure 25-9) shows all three names.

So how does this affect you? When you work in the Services console, you don't need to know anything other than a service's display name to find it and work with it. But if you use the Net command to start and stop services, you might find using the actual service name more convenient; it is often much shorter than the display name. You'll also need the service name if you're ever forced to work with a service's registry entries, which can be found in the HKLM\System\CurrentControlSet\Services*service* subkey (where *service* is the service name).

And what about the executable name? You might need it if certain users have problems running a service; in such a case, you need to find the executable and check its permissions. Knowing the executable name can also be useful, for example, if you're using Windows Task Manager to determine why your computer seems to be running slowly. Although the Processes tab and the Services tab show the display name (under the Description heading), because of the window size it's sometimes easier to find the more succinct executable name.

Managing Services from Task Manager

Using the Services tab in Windows Task Manager, you can start and stop services and view several important aspects of the services, both running and available, on your computer. You can also use this as a shortcut to the Services console.

Access Task Manager by right-clicking the taskbar and clicking Start Task Manager, by pressing Ctr+Alt+Delete and clicking Start Task Manager, or by pressing Ctrl+Shift+Esc. The Services tab is shown in Figure 25-13.

To start or stop a service, right-click its name on the Services tab and then click Start Service or Stop Service.

Using the Services tab, you can also associate a running service with its process identifier (PID) and then further associate that PID with other programs and services being run under that PID. For example, Figure 25-13 shows several services running with PID 512. Right-clicking one of the services with PID 512 gives two options, one to stop the service and one called Go To Process. By clicking Go To Process, the Processes tab is opened with the particular process highlighted.

> **Note**
> Most service-related processes run under an account other than your own and therefore aren't available when you attempt to use the Go To Process option. To view these processes, click the Show Processes From All Users option on the Processes tab in Task Manager.

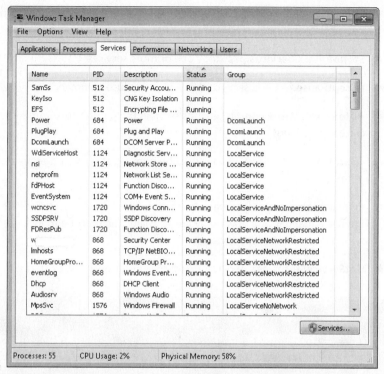

Figure 25-13 By sorting on the Status column, you can see which services are running and which are stopped.

Managing Services with Windows PowerShell Scripts

The Scripts folder on the companion CD includes a number of Windows PowerShell scripts that can be used for managing services on your own or a remote computer. Figure 25-14 illustrates output from one of these scripts, ServiceDependencies.ps1. This script generates a report of all services on a local or remote computer, including information for each about its current state, its start mode, and the names of any services on which it depends.

Other scripts on the CD that you might find useful include the following:

- **ChangeModeThenStart.ps1** changes the start mode of a service, then attempts to start that service.

- **CheckServiceThenStart.ps1** starts a service if it isn't already running; if it is running, the script reports that.

- **StartMultipleServices.ps1** starts one or more services.

- **CheckServiceThenStop.ps1** checks to see if a service will accept a stop command prior to attempting to stop it.

- **StopMultipleServices.ps1** stops one or more services.

- **AcceptPause.ps1** lists services that accept a pause command.

- **AutoServicesNotRunning.ps1** lists services that are set to automatic but are not currently running.

- **CountRunningServices.ps1** reports the number of services that are currently running.

- **EvaluateServices.ps1** generates a report telling how many services are auto, how many are manual, and how many are disabled. The report also includes detailed information about each service.

- **GetServiceStatus.ps1** generates a list of services grouped by status.

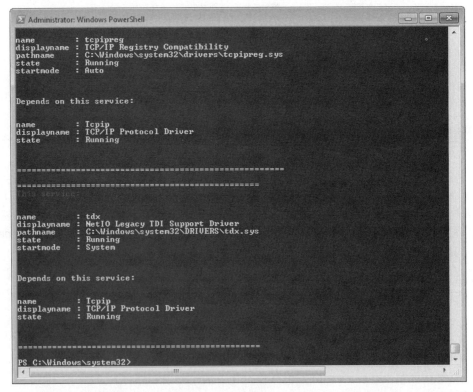

Figure 25-14 Output from the ServiceDependencies.ps1 script includes information about each script's name, path, state, start mode, and dependent services.

> For information about using any of these scripts, display the script in a text editor and read the .Synopsis section. For general information about running Windows PowerShell scripts, see "Running PowerShell Scripts" on page 999.

Editing the Registry

Windows 7 is designed in such a way that direct registry edits by end users are generally unnecessary. When you change some detail about your system's configuration using Control Panel, Control Panel writes the necessary updates to the registry for you, and you needn't be concerned with how it happens. When you install a new piece of hardware or a new program, a myriad of registry modifications take place; again, you don't need to know the details. On the other hand, because the designers of Windows couldn't provide a user interface for every conceivable customization you might want to make, sometimes working directly with the registry is the only way to get a job done. And sometimes, even when it's not the only way, it might be the fastest way. Windows includes a registry editor that you should know how to use—safely. This section tells you how.

Understanding the Structure of the Registry

Before you begin browsing or editing the registry, it's good to know a bit about how this database is built. Figure 25-15 shows a portion of a system's registry, as seen through Registry Editor, the registry editor supplied with Windows 7. As shown in the figure, the registry consists of the following five *root keys*: HKEY_CLASSES_ROOT, HKEY_CURRENT_USER, HKEY_LOCAL_MACHINE, HKEY_USERS, and HKEY_CURRENT_CONFIG. For simplicity's sake and typographical convenience, this book, like many others, abbreviates the root key names as HKCR, HKCU, HKLM, HKU, and HKCC, respectively.

Root keys, sometimes called *predefined keys*, contain subkeys. Registry Editor displays this structure as an outline. In Figure 25-15, for example, HKCU has been opened to show the top-level subkeys: AppEvents, Console, Control Panel, Environment, EUDC, Identities, Keyboard Layout, Network, Printers, Software, System, and Volatile Environment. A root key and its subkeys can be described as a path, like this: HKCU\Console. Root keys and their subkeys appear in the left pane in Registry Editor.

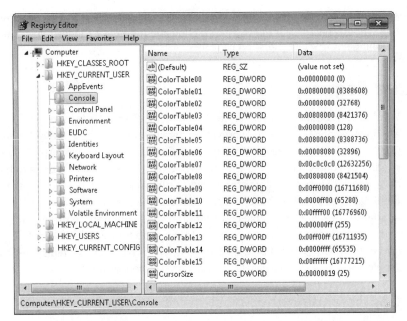

Figure 25-15 The registry consists of five root keys, each of which contains many subkeys.

> ## Note
>
> The registry is the work of many hands, and capitalization and word spacing are not consistent. With readability as our goal, we have made our own capitalization decisions for this book, and our treatment of names frequently differs from what you see in Registry Editor. No matter. Capitalization is irrelevant. Spelling and spacing must be correct, however.

Subkeys, which we call *keys* for short, can contain subkeys of their own. Whether they do or not, they always contain at least one *value*. In Registry Editor, that obligatory value is known as the *default value*. Many keys have additional values. The names, data types, and data associated with values appear in the right pane. As Figure 25-15 shows, the HKCU\ Console key has many values—ColorTable00, ColorTable01, and so on.

The default value for many keys—including HKCU\Console—is not defined. You can therefore think of an empty default value as a placeholder—a slot that could hold data but currently does not.

All values other than the default always include the following three components: name, data type, and data. As Figure 25-15 shows, the ColorTable00 value of HKCU\Console is of data type REG_DWORD. The data associated with this value (on the system used for this figure) is 0x00000000. (The prefix *0x* denotes a hexadecimal value. Registry Editor displays the decimal equivalent of hexadecimal values in parentheses after the value.)

A key with all its subkeys and values is commonly called a *hive*. The registry is stored on disk as several separate hive files. The appropriate hive files are read into memory when the operating system starts (or when a new user logs on) and assembled into the registry. You can see where the hives of your system physically live by examining the values associated with HKLM\System\CurrentControlSet\Control\HiveList. Figure 25-16 shows the HiveList key for one of the systems used for this book.

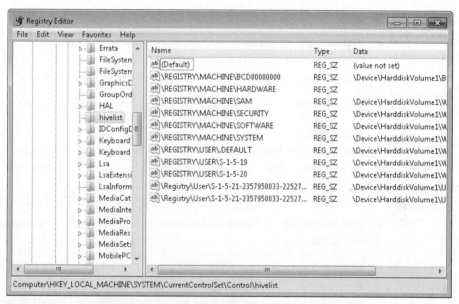

Figure 25-16 You can find the names and locations of the files that make up your registry in HKLM\System\CurrentControlSet\Control\HiveList.

Notice that one hive, \Registry\Machine\Hardware, has no associated disk file. This hive, which records your hardware configuration, is completely volatile; that is, Windows 7 creates it anew each time you turn your system on. Notice also the path specifications for the remaining hive files. Windows assigns drive letters after assembling the registry, so these paths do not specify drive letters.

Two predefined keys—HKCR and HKCU—are not shown in the HiveList key at all. Like the file system in Windows—which uses junctions, symlinks, and other trickery to display a virtual namespace—the registry uses a bit of misdirection (implemented with the REG_LINK data type) to create these keys. Both are representations of keys actually stored within HKLM and HKU:

- HKCR is merged from keys within HKLM\Software\Classes and HKU*sid*_Classes (where *sid* is the security identifier of the currently logged-on user).

- HKCU is a view into HKU*sid*.

You can view or edit the registry's actual locations or its virtual keys; the results are identical. The HKCR and HKCU keys are generally more convenient to use.

Registry Data Types

The registry uses the following data types:

- **REG_SZ**   The *SZ* indicates a zero-terminated string. This is a variable-length string that can contain Unicode as well as ANSI characters. When you enter or edit a REG_SZ value, Registry Editor terminates the value with a 00 byte for you.

- **REG_BINARY**   The REG_BINARY type contains binary data—0s and 1s.

- **REG_DWORD**   This data type is a "double word"—that is, a 32-bit numeric value. Although it can hold any integer from 0 to 2^{32}, the registry often uses it for simple Boolean values (0 or 1) because the registry lacks a Boolean data type.

- **REG_QWORD**   This data type is a "quadruple word"—a 64-bit numeric value.

- **REG_MULTI_SZ**   This data type contains a group of zero-terminated strings assigned to a single value.

- **REG_EXPAND_SZ**   This data type is a zero-terminated string containing an unexpanded reference to an environment variable, such as %SystemRoot%. (For information about environment variables, see "Using Environment Variables" on page 1178.) If you need to create a key containing a variable name, use this data type, not REG_SZ.

Internally, the registry also uses REG_LINK, REG_FULL_RESOURCE_DESCRIPTOR, REG_RESOURCE_LIST, REG_RESOURCE_REQUIREMENTS_LIST, and REG_NONE data types. Although you might occasionally see references in technical documentation to these data types, they're not visible or accessible in Registry Editor.

Registry Virtualization

One of the key elements of security in Windows 7 is that it prevents applications running under a standard user's token from writing to system folders in the file system and to machinewide keys in the registry, while at the same time enabling users with a standard account to run applications without running into "access denied" roadblocks. Many applications that require administrator-level access are still in use in Windows 7, but standard users can run them without hassle. That's because in Windows 7, UAC uses *registry virtualization* to redirect attempts to write to subkeys of HKLM\Software. (Settings in HKLM apply to all users of the computer, and therefore only administrators have write permission.) When an application attempts to write to this hive, Windows writes instead to a per-user location, HKCR\VirtualStore\Machine\Software. Like file virtualization, this is done transparently; the application (and all but the most curious users) never know this is going on behind the scenes.

> **Note**
>
> When an application requests information from HKLM\Software, Windows looks first in the virtualized key if it exists. Therefore, if a value exists in both the VirtualStore hive and in HKLM, the application sees only the one in VirtualStore.

Note that because the virtualized data is stored in a per-user section of the registry, settings made by one user do not affect other users. Running the same application in Windows XP, which doesn't use virtualization and therefore looks only at the actual HKLM hive, presents all users with the same settings. This can lead to confusion by users who are accustomed to sharing an application in Windows XP and find that it works differently in Windows 7.

INSIDE OUT   Copy virtualized registry entries to other user accounts

The hive that stores virtualized registry data, HKCR\VirtualStore\Machine\Software, can also be found in HKU*sid*_Classes\VirtualStore\Machine\Software, where *sid* is the security identifier of the user who is currently logged on. If you want to make sure that a certain application works identically for a different user, you can copy that application's subkey to the corresponding HKU subkey for the other user.

For more information about UAC and virtualization, see "Preventing Unsafe Actions with User Account Control" on page 629.

> **Note**
>
> Registry virtualization is an interim solution to application compatibility problems. It was introduced with Windows Vista, and Microsoft intends to remove it from future versions of the operating system. For more information about registry virtualization, see *w7io.com/22502*.

Avoiding Registry Mishaps

The primary tool in Windows 7 for working directly with the registry is Registry Editor. You won't find it anywhere on the Start menu, however, and it doesn't show up in the Start menu search box when you type its name; you must use the name of its executable file, Regedit.exe. To start Registry Editor at a command prompt, type **regedit**.

The two most important things to know about Registry Editor are that it copies your changes immediately into the registry and that it has no Undo command. Registry Editor doesn't wait for you to issue a File, Save command (it has no such command) before making changes in the registry files. And after you have altered some bit of registry data, the original data is gone forever—unless you remember it and restore it yourself or unless you have some form of backup that you can restore. Registry Editor is therefore a tool to be used sparingly and soberly; it should not be left open when not in use.

So that you can recover from ill-advised edits to the registry, before you make any changes you should back up the registry using one or both of these methods:

- Use the Export command in Registry Editor to back up the branch of the registry where you plan to work.

- Use System Restore to set a restore point.

Backing Up Before You Edit

One relatively safe way to edit your registry is to back up the section you're interested in before you make any changes to it. If something goes wrong, you can usually use your backup file to restore the registry to the state it was in when you backed up.

Registry Editor can save all or portions of your registry in any of the four different formats described here:

- **Registration Files** The Registration Files option creates a .reg file, a text file that can be read and edited in Notepad or a similar program. A .reg file can be merged into the registry of a system running Windows 7, Windows Vista, Windows XP, or

Windows 2000. When you merge a .reg file, its keys and values replace the corresponding keys and values in the registry. Using .reg files allows you to edit your registry "off line" and add your changes to the registry without even opening Registry Editor. You can also use .reg files as an easy way to share registry settings and copy them to other computers.

- **Registry Hive Files**   The registry hive format saves a binary image of a selected portion of the registry. You won't be able to read the resulting file (choose one of the text-file options if that's what you need to do), but if you need to restore the keys you've worked on, you can be confident that this format will do the job correctly.

  Registry hive file is the format of choice if you want to create a backup before working in Registry Editor. That's because when you *import* a registry hive file, it restores the entire hive to exactly the way it was when you saved it. (The .reg file types, when merged, restore all the saved keys and values to their original locations, which repairs all deletions and edits. But the process does not remove any keys or values that you added.) Note, however, that a registry hive file has the potential to do the greatest damage if you import it to the wrong key; see the caution in the following section.

- **Win9x/NT4 Registration Files**   The Win9x/NT4 Registration Files option also generates a .reg file, but one in an older format used by earlier versions of Windows. The principal difference between the two formats is that the current format uses Unicode and the older format does not. Use the Win9x/NT4 Registration Files option only if you need to replicate a section of your registry in the registry of an older system.

- **Text Files**   The Text Files option, like the Registration Files option, creates a file that can be read in Notepad or another text editor. The principal advantage of this format is that it cannot accidentally (or intentionally) be merged into the registry. Thus, it's a good way to create a record of your registry's state at a particular time. Its disadvantage, relative to the .reg file format, is its size. Text files are considerably larger than corresponding .reg files, and they take longer to create.

To export a registry hive, select a key in the left pane, and then on the File menu, click Export. (Easier yet: right-click a key and click Export.) In the Save As Type list in the Export Registry File dialog box, select one of the four file types. Under Export Range, select Selected Branch. The resulting file includes the selected key and all its subkeys and values.

Restoring the Registry from an Exported Hive

If you need to restore the exported hive from a registry hive file, select the same key in the left pane of the Registry Editor window, click Import on the File menu, and specify the file. You'll see a confirmation prompt letting you know that your action will overwrite (replace) the current key and all its subkeys. This is your last chance to make sure you're importing the hive into the right location, so take a moment to make sure you've selected the correct key before you click Yes.

CAUTION !

Importing a registry hive file replaces the entire content of the selected key with the contents of the file—regardless of its original source. That is, it wipes out everything in the selected key and then adds the keys and values from the file. When you import, be absolutely certain that you've selected the correct key.

If you saved your backup as a .reg file, you use the same process to import it. (As an alternative, you can double-click the .reg file in Windows Explorer without opening Registry Editor.) Unlike with a the registry hive file, however, the complete path to each key and value is stored as part of the file and it always restores to the same location. This approach for recovering from registry editing mishaps is fine if you did not add new values or subkeys to the section of the registry you're working with; it returns existing data to its former state but doesn't alter the data you've added.

TROUBLESHOOTING

You mistakenly deleted data from the HKLM\System\CurrentControlSet hive

As those dire warnings pointed out, improper changes to the registry can prevent your computer from operating properly or even booting. This is particularly true for changes to the HKLM\System\CurrentControlSet hive. Because keys in that hive are so essential, Windows maintains a backup, which you can restore when necessary. To do that, begin by shutting down your computer. Start your computer and, during the boot process, press F8. Use the arrow keys to select Last Known Good Configuration and then press Enter.

Using System Protection to Save the Registry's State

The System Protection utility takes snapshots of your system's state, at prescribed time intervals or on demand, and allows you to roll your system back to an earlier state (called a *restore point*) if you experience problems. Most of the registry is included in the restore point. Creating a restore point before you begin working in the registry is an excellent way to protect yourself against mishaps.

For information about using System Restore, see "Rolling Back to a Stable State with System Restore" on page 466.

Browsing and Editing with Registry Editor

Because of the registry's size, looking for a particular key, value, or data item can be daunting. In Registry Editor, the Find command (on the Edit menu; also available by pressing Ctrl+F) works in the forward direction only and does not wrap around when it gets to the end of the registry. If you're not sure where the item you need is located, select the highest level in the left pane before issuing the command. If you have an approximate idea where the item you want is located, you can save time by starting at a node closer to (but still above) the target.

After you have located an item of interest, you can put it on the Favorites list to simplify a return visit. Open the Favorites menu, click Add To Favorites, and supply a friendly name (or accept the default). If you're about to close Registry Editor and know you'll be returning to the same key the next time you open the editor, you can skip the Favorites step because Registry Editor always remembers your last position and returns to that position in the next session.

Registry Editor includes a number of time-saving keyboard shortcuts for navigating the registry. To move to the next subkey that starts with a particular letter, simply type that letter when the focus is in the left pane; in the right pane, use the same trick to jump to the next value that begins with that letter. To open a key (revealing its subkeys), press Right Arrow. To move up one level in the subkey hierarchy, press Left Arrow; a second press collapses the subkeys of the current key. To move to the top of the hierarchy, press Home. To quickly move between the left and right panes, use the Tab key. In the right pane, press F2 to rename a value, and press Enter to open that value and edit its data. Once you get the hang of using these keyboard shortcuts, you'll find it's usually easier to zip through the subkey hierarchy with a combination of arrow keys and letter keys than it is to open outline controls with the mouse.

Changing Data

You can change the data associated with a value by selecting a value in the right pane and pressing Enter or by double-clicking the value. Registry Editor pops up an edit window appropriate for the value's data type.

Adding or Deleting Keys

To add a key, select the new key's parent in the left pane, open the Edit menu, point to New, and click Key. The new key arrives as a generically named outline entry, exactly the way a new folder does in Windows Explorer. Type a new name. To delete a key, select it and then press Delete.

Adding or Deleting Values

To add a value, select the parent key, open the Edit menu, and point to New. On the submenu that appears, click the type of value you want to add. A value of the type you select appears in the right pane with a generic name. Type over the generic name, press Enter twice, enter your data, and press Enter once more. To delete a value, select it and press Delete.

Using .Reg Files to Automate Registry Changes

The .reg files created by the Export command in Registry Editor are plain text, suitable for reading and editing in Notepad or any similar editor. Therefore, they provide an alternative method for editing your registry. You can export a section of the registry, change it offline, and then merge it back into the registry. Or you can add new keys, values, and data to the registry by creating a .reg file from scratch and merging it. A .reg file is particularly useful if you need to make the same changes to the registry of several different computers. You can make and test your changes on one machine, save the relevant part of the registry as a .reg file, and then transport the file to the other machines that require it.

Figure 25-17 shows a .reg file. In this case, the file was exported from the HKCU\Software\Microsoft\Windows\CurrentVersion\Explorer\Advanced key, shown in Figure 25-18.

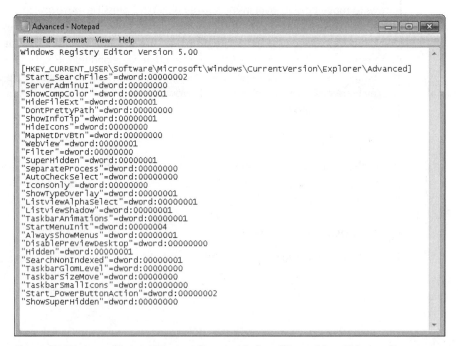

Figure 25-17 A .reg file is a plain-text file suitable for offline editing. This .reg file was exported from the key shown in Figure 25-18.

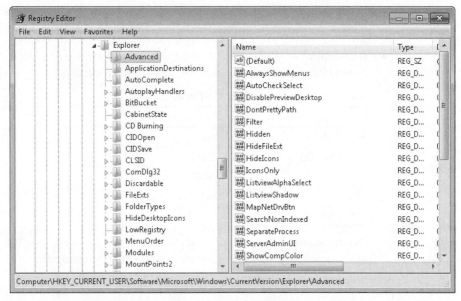

Figure 25-18 This key's name, values, and data are recorded in the .reg file shown in Figure 25-17.

Identifying the Elements of a .Reg File

As you review the examples shown in the two figures, note the following characteristics of .reg files:

- **Header line**   The file begins with the line *Windows Registry Editor Version 5.00*. When you merge a .reg file into the registry, Registry Editor uses this line to verify that the file contains registry data. Version 5 (the version shipped with Windows 7) generates Unicode text files, which can be used in Windows XP, Windows 2000, and Windows Vista, as well as Windows 7. If you want to share registry data with a system running Windows 95/98/Me or Windows NT, select the Win9x/NT4 Registration Files option when you export the file in Registry Editor. To create from scratch a .reg file that's suitable for import into Windows 95/98/Me or Windows NT, use the header *REGEDIT4* instead of *Windows Registry Editor Version 5.00*.

- **Key names**   Key names are delimited by brackets and must include the full path from the root key to the current subkey. The root key name must not be abbreviated. (Don't use HKCU, for example.) Figure 25-17 shows only one key name, but you can have as many as you please.

- **The default value**   Undefined default values do not appear in .reg files. Defined default values are identified by the special character @. Thus, a key whose default REG_SZ value was defined as MyApp would appear in a .reg file this way:

  ```
  "@"="MyApp"
  ```

- **Value names**   Value names must be enclosed in quotation marks, whether or not they include space characters. Follow the value name with an equal sign.

- **Data types**   REG_SZ values don't get a data type identifier or a colon. The data directly follows the equal sign. Other data types are identified as shown in Table 25-2:

Table 25-2 **Data Types Identified in .Reg Files**

Data Type	Identifier
REG_BINARY	hex
REG_DWORD	dword
REG_QWORD	hex(b)
REG_MULTI_SZ	hex(7)
REG_EXPAND_SZ	hex(2)

A colon separates the identifier from the data. Thus, for example, a REG_DWORD value named Keyname with value data of 00000000 looks like this:

```
"Keyname"=dword:00000000
```

- **REG_SZ values**   Ordinary string values must be enclosed in quotation marks. A backslash character within a string must be written as two backslashes. Thus, for example, the path C:\Program Files\Microsoft Office\ is written like this:

```
"C:\\Program Files\\Microsoft Office\\"
```

- **REG_DWORD values**   DWORD values are written as eight hexadecimal digits, without spaces or commas. Do not use the 0x prefix.

- **All other data types**   All other data types—including REG_EXPAND_SZ, REG_MULTI_SZ, and REG_QWORD—appear as comma-delimited lists of hexadecimal bytes (two hex digits, a comma, two more hex digits, and so on). The following is an example of a REG_MULTI_SZ value:

```
"Addins"=hex(7):64,00,3a,00,5c,00,6c,00,6f,00,74,00,00,75,00,73,00,5c,00,\
31,00,32,00,33,00,5c,00,61,00,64,00,64,00,64,00,69,00,6e,00,73,00,5c,00,\
64,00,71,00,61,00,75,00,69,00,2e,00,31,00,32,00,61,00,00,00,00,00,00,00
```

- **Line-continuation characters**   You can use the backslash as a line-continuation character. The REG_MULTI_SZ value just shown, for example, is all one stream of bytes. We've added backslashes and broken the lines for readability, and you can do the same in your .reg files.

- **Line spacing**   You can add blank lines for readability. Registry Editor ignores them.

- **Comments**   To add a comment line to a .reg file, begin the line with a semicolon.

Using a .Reg File to Delete Registry Data

.Reg files are most commonly used to modify existing registry data or add new data. But you can also use them to delete existing values and keys.

To delete an existing value, specify a hyphen character as the value's data. For example, to use a .reg file to remove the value ThumbnailSize from the key HKCU\Software\Microsoft\ Windows\CurrentVersion\Explorer, add the following lines to the .reg file:

```
[HKEY_CURRENT_USER\Software\Microsoft\Windows\CurrentVersion\Explorer]
"ThumbnailSize"=-
```

To delete an existing key with all its values and data, insert a hyphen in front of the key name (inside the left bracket). For example, to use a .reg file to remove the key HKCR\.xyz\ shell and all its values, add the following to the .reg file:

```
[-HKEY_CLASSES_ROOT\.xyz\shell]
```

Merging a .Reg File into the Registry

To merge a .reg file into the registry from within Registry Editor, open the File menu and click Import. Registry Editor adds the imported data under the appropriate key names, overwriting existing values where necessary.

The default action for a .reg file is Merge—meaning merge with the registry. Therefore, you can merge a file into the registry by simply double-clicking it in Windows Explorer and answering the confirmation prompt.

Using Group Policy

Group Policy is a highly touted feature of Active Directory, which is part of Microsoft Windows Server. In that environment, Group Policy is indeed an enormously powerful feature that lets administrators configure computers throughout sites, domains, or organizational units. In addition to setting standard desktop configurations and restricting what settings users are allowed to change, administrators can use Group Policy to centrally manage software installation, configuration, updates, and removal; specify scripts to run at startup, shutdown, logon, and logoff; and redirect users' profile folders (such as Documents) to network server drives. Administrators can customize all these settings for different computers, users, or groups.

In a domain environment, Group Policy enables an administrator to apply policy settings and restrictions to users and computers (and groups of each) in one fell swoop. With a workgroup, you must make similar Group Policy settings on each computer where you want such restrictions imposed.

Nonetheless, Group Policy can be a useful tool for managing computers on a small network or even for managing a single computer. Using only local Group Policy settings on a computer running Windows 7, you can manage registry-based policy settings—everything from configuring the desktop to hiding certain drives to preventing the creation of scheduled tasks. You can restrict the use of Control Panel applications on a granular level (for example, disable the appearance of individual tabs within tabbed dialog boxes, such as Internet Options). These settings—and thousands more—are stored in the HKLM and HKCU branches of the registry, which you can edit directly. But Group Policy provides two distinct advantages: it's much easier—and safer—to use than a registry editor, and it periodically updates the registry automatically (thereby keeping your policies in force even if the registry is somehow modified by other means).

In Windows XP, using local Group Policy settings on a standalone computer or one that's part of a workgroup isn't practical in most situations because all policy settings made by the computer's administrator affect everyone who uses the computer, including the administrator. An administrator who tries to make a machine safe for inexperienced users (say, by removing access to certain potentially dangerous parts of Control Panel) also finds himself or herself subject to the same restrictions. All that changed with Windows Vista, which introduced *Multiple Local Group Policy objects* (MLGPO). With MLGPO in Windows Vista or Windows 7, you can make Group Policy settings that affect all users, settings that affect only administrators, settings that affect only nonadministrators, and settings that affect individual named users.

Using the Local Group Policy Editor, you can also assign scripts for computer startup, computer shutdown, user logon, and user logoff, and you can specify security options. You'll find these settings in the Windows Settings folders.

Understanding Multiple Local Group Policy Objects

A *Group Policy object* (often abbreviated as GPO) is simply a collection of Group Policy settings. In a domain based on Windows Server, Group Policy objects are stored at the domain level and affect users and computers on the basis of their membership in sites, domains, and organizational units. Each computer running Windows 7 also has three levels of *local Group Policy objects*. Because local Group Policy doesn't rely on a server version of Windows, that's our focus in this book.

The levels of local Group Policy objects—collectively known as MLGPO—are

- **Local Computer Policy**   Local Computer Policy is the most widely applicable level of policy settings. Policy settings applied in Local Computer Policy affect all users on the computer, exactly the same as the Local Group Policy object in Windows XP. Local Computer Policy is the only level that includes computer settings as well as user settings.

- **Administrators Policy and Non-Administrators Policy**   The second level comprises a collection of settings that apply to members of the Administrators security group and a second collection of settings that apply to all other users. That is, while an administrator is logged on to the computer, he or she receives policy settings from the Administrators local Group Policy object; anyone else who logs on receives policy settings from the Non-Administrators local Group Policy object. This level, which was introduced with Windows Vista, includes only user settings.

- **User-Specific Policy**   The last level of local Group Policy objects, also introduced with Windows Vista, is a GPO that applies settings whenever a specific user account is logged on. You can create a separate user-specific local Group Policy object for any or all local user accounts on the computer. User-specific local GPOs include only user settings.

How Group Policy Works

The majority of the Group Policy settings are in the Administrative Templates extension of the Group Policy Object Editor snap-in. When you configure a policy in the Administrative Templates folder (that is, you select either Enabled or Disabled and, optionally, set a value) for Local Computer Policy, Group Policy stores that information as a custom registry setting in one of the two Registry.pol files. Group Policy uses the copy of Registry.pol in %SystemRoot%\System32\GroupPolicy\Machine for settings you make in the Computer Configuration\Administrative Templates folder in Group Policy, and it uses the copy in the %SystemRoot%\System32\GroupPolicy\User folder for settings you make in User Configuration\Administrative Templates. (User settings for Administrators Policy, Non-Administrators Policy, and user-specific local GPO work in the same way, but they are stored in Registry.pol files in subfolders of %SystemRoot%\System32\GroupPolicyUsers.)

Computer-related Group Policy settings—those stored in Machine\Registry.pol—are copied to the appropriate registry keys in the HKLM hive when the operating system initializes (that is, during startup, when resuming from sleep or hibernation, and when connecting to a docking station) and during the periodic refresh. User-related settings (in User\Registry.pol) are copied to the appropriate keys in HKCU when a user logs on, resumes, or docks and during the periodic refresh.

> **Note**
>
> Group Policy settings—either local or Active Directory–based—take precedence over user preferences (that is, settings that you make through Control Panel and other methods available to ordinary users). This is because Group Policy settings are not written to the "normal" registry key for a particular setting; instead, they're written to a value in a "policies" key. For example, if you use the Taskbar And Start Menu Properties dialog box to remove the Music item from the Start menu, the data in the Start_Show-MyMusic value in the HKCU\Software\Microsoft\Windows\CurrentVersion\Explorer\Advanced key changes. But if you use Group Policy, the NoStartMenuMyMusic value in the HKCU\Software\Microsoft\Windows\CurrentVersion\Policies\Explorer key changes instead. In cases of conflicts, the value in the Policies key overrules the other.

The *periodic refresh* occurs at intervals that you define as a Group Policy setting. By default, the Registry.pol files are copied to the registry every 90 minutes plus a random offset of 0 to 30 minutes. (The random offset is intended for Active Directory–based policies; on a large network, you wouldn't want all the refresh activity occurring simultaneously. For local Group Policy, the offset serves no useful purpose but is added anyway.) By enabling and modifying the Group Policy Refresh Interval For Computers setting in Computer Configuration\Administrative Templates\System\Group Policy and the Group Policy Refresh Interval For Users setting in User Configuration\Administrative Templates\System\Group Policy, you can change the interval and the random offset. You can set the interval to any value from 0 minutes (in which case settings are refreshed every 7 seconds) through 64,800 minutes (45 days).

> **Note**
>
> The Gpupdate command replaces the functionality of the Secedit /Refreshpolicy command, which was introduced in Windows 2000.

Resolving Conflicts Among Multiple Local Group Policy Object Settings

As you can imagine, it's possible—likely even—that a computer with policy settings in three levels of local GPOs will not only have different settings applied at each level, but in some cases contradictory settings for particular policy settings. After all, the whole point of MLGPO is to be able to apply different settings to different users. But in the case of conflicts, how does Windows know which GPO takes precedence? And, as a computer administrator, how can you reliably predict which GPO overrules another?

As it turns out, it's easy to know. Windows applies the local Group Policy settings in this order:

1. Settings from Local Computer Policy, which includes computer settings and user settings

2. Settings from Administrators Policy or Non-Administrators Policy, depending on group membership of the current user

3. Settings from the user-specific local Group Policy object

Windows uses a "most specific wins" process for determining precedence. Therefore, any policy settings in the Administrators or Non-Administrators local GPOs overrule settings in the Local Computer Policy GPO. And settings in the user-specific GPO trump all.

Note, however, that a policy setting of Not Configured does not overwrite a policy setting from another level. For example, if you set a policy setting in Local Computer Policy to Enabled (or Disabled), and the same policy setting is set to Not Configured in Administrators Policy, the setting is not overwritten; it remains enabled (or disabled).

How Local Group Policy Settings Interact with Active Directory–Based Group Policy Settings

If your computer is joined to a domain, it might be affected by Group Policy settings other than those you set in the local Group Policy objects. Group Policy settings are applied in this order:

1. Settings from the local Group Policy objects (as detailed in the previous section)

2. Settings from site Group Policy objects, in administratively specified order

3. Settings from domain Group Policy objects, in administratively specified order

4. Settings from organizational unit Group Policy objects, from largest to smallest organizational unit (parent to child organizational unit), and in administratively specified order at the level of each organizational unit

As with the levels of local MLGPO, policies applied later overwrite previously applied policies, which means that in a case of conflicting settings, the highest-level Active Directory–based policy settings take precedence. The policy settings are cumulative, so all settings contribute to the effective policy. The effective policy is called the *Resultant Set of Policy (RSoP)*.

To see which settings are in effect for a particular user, you can use a command-line tool, Gpresult.exe. To display your RSoP, simply type **gpresult /r** in a Command Prompt window. Type **gpresult** with no parameters for information about other options.

Using the Local Group Policy Editor

You make Group Policy settings using the Group Policy Object Editor snap-in for Microsoft Management Console (MMC). To open this snap-in, which is shown in Figure 25-19, type **gpedit.msc** in the Start menu search box. Using the Local Group Policy Editor console requires administrative privileges.

Types of Policy Settings

The Computer Configuration branch of Group Policy includes a variety of computer-related settings, and the User Configuration branch includes a variety of user-related settings. The line between computer settings and user settings is often blurred, however. Your best bet for discovering the policies you need is to scan them all. You'll find a treasure trove of useful settings, including many that can't be made any other way short of hacking the registry. In the Administrative Templates folders, you'll find several hundred computer settings and even more user settings, which makes this sound like a daunting task—but you'll find that you can quickly skim the folder names in the Local Group Policy Editor, ignoring most of them, and then scan the policies in each folder of interest.

To learn more about each policy, simply select it in the Local Group Policy Editor, as shown in Figure 25-19. If you have selected the Extended tab at the bottom of the window, a description of the selected policy appears in the center pane.

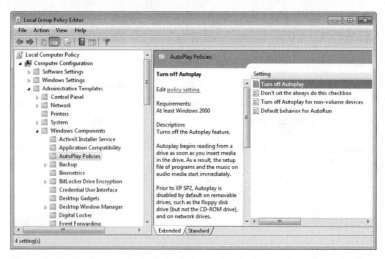

Figure 25-19 The Extended tab includes a description of the selected policy.

You can download a comprehensive list of all policy settings from the Administrative Templates folder, in Microsoft Excel (XLS) format, by visiting *w7io.com/22501*. The list is huge—more than 3,100 entries—but you can use Excel to sort, filter, or search the list to find policy settings of interest. The list also provides other details about each setting, such as the scope of the setting (machine or user), the registry value it controls, and whether a setting change requires a logoff or reboot to take effect.

> **Note**
>
> Some settings appear in both User Configuration and Computer Configuration. In a case of conflicting settings, the Computer Configuration setting always takes precedence.

Creating a Custom Console for MLGPO

The predefined Gpedit.msc console includes a snap-in only for Local Computer Policy. Remember that settings in Local Computer Policy apply to all users, including yourself and any other administrators. If you want to take advantage of MLGPO to apply different Group Policy settings to different users, you'll need to add snap-ins for Administrators Policy, Non-Administrators Policy, and any user-specific GPOs you want to manage. You can do so by opening Gpedit.msc in Author mode, but you'll probably find it easier to start with a fresh MMC console. Follow these steps to create your own Local Group Policy Editor console.

1. In the Start menu search box, type **mmc**, and then press Enter to open Microsoft Management Console.

2. Choose File, Add/Remove Snap-In (or press Ctrl+M).

3. In the Available Snap-Ins list in the Add Or Remove Snap-Ins dialog box, select Group Policy Object Editor, and then click Add.

4. In the Select Group Policy Object dialog box, click Finish. This adds Local Computer Policy to the Selected Snap-Ins list.

5. With Group Policy Object Editor still selected in the Available Snap-Ins list, click Add again.

6. This time, in the Select Group Policy Object dialog box, click Browse.

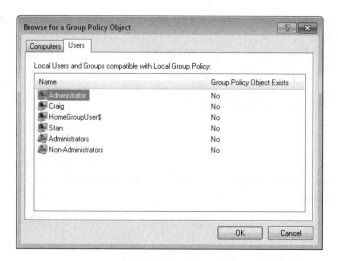

7. On the Users tab, select Administrators (not Administrator, which represents the user account named Administrator). Click OK, and then click Finish.

8. Repeats steps 5 through 7 to add snap-ins for Non-Administrators Policy and for any users for whom you want to apply user-specific policy settings.

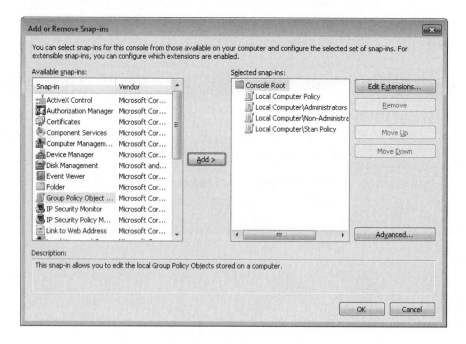

9. In the Add Or Remove Snap-Ins dialog box, click OK.

As shown in Figure 25-20, your console is now complete and fully functional for editing policy settings at any level of local Group Policy.

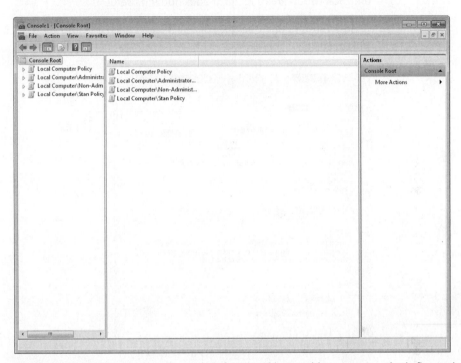

Figure 25-20 At this point, your console is functional but could use some aesthetic fine tuning.

This is a console document that you'll probably want to save and use often, so you might want to invest a little bit of time cleaning it up, as follows:

1. Click the Show/Hide Action Pane button on the toolbar to hide the action pane. In the Local Group Policy Editor, it adds nothing useful.

2. Choose File, Options. Give the console a name, such as **Multiple Local Group Policy Object Editor**.

3. In the console tree, right-click Console Root and choose Rename. Give it a name such as **Local Group Policy objects**.

4. Figure 25-21 shows the finished console. There's one last step, and it's an important one: save your console! Choose File, Save, and give it a name; we suggest MLGPO.msc.

Figure 25-21 With your new MLGPO console, you can edit policy settings at any level. Here we examine Control Panel settings for nonadministrative users.

Changing Policy Settings

Each policy setting in the Administrative Templates folders of the Local Group Policy Editor (or your custom MLGPO console) has one of three settings: Not Configured, Enabled, or Disabled. By default, all policy settings in the local Group Policy objects are initially set to Not Configured. (The policy settings in the Windows Settings folders do not have a Not Configured option and therefore have other default policy settings.)

To change a policy setting, in the Local Group Policy Editor, simply double-click the name of the policy setting you want to change or click the Properties link that appears in the center pane of the Extended tab. The properties dialog box then appears. The dialog box for each policy setting under Administrative Templates looks much like the one shown in Figure 25-22.

Beside the settings option buttons is a large area where you can write a comment. The Help pane below this Comment area includes detailed information about the policy setting (the same information that appears in the center pane of the Extended tab). The pane to the left of the Help pane offers options relevant to the current policy. The Previous Setting and

Next Setting buttons make it convenient to go through an entire folder without opening and closing individual dialog boxes.

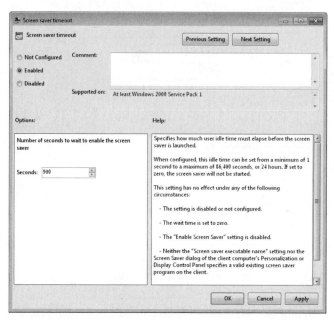

Figure 25-22 The properties dialog boxes for all Administrative Templates policy settings are similar to the one shown here.

> ## Note
>
> Pay close attention to the name of each policy setting because the settings can be counterintuitive. A number of policy settings begin with the word *Disable* (for example, Disable The Security Page in User Configuration\Administrative Templates\Windows Components\Internet Explorer\Internet Control Panel). For those policy settings, if you want to *allow* the specified option (in this example, display of the Security tab in the Internet Options dialog box), you must select the Disable setting (in other words, you must disable the disabling policy.) Conversely, if you want to prohibit the option (that is, hide the Security tab), you must select Enable.

Controlling Which Policy Settings Are Displayed

The Group Policy Object Editor snap-in, which forms the core of the Local Group Policy Editor and your custom MLGPO consoles, provides some easily overlooked options that you won't find in other MMC snap-ins: you can remove administrative templates, and you can restrict the view to show only the policies that have been configured.

Hiding Unwanted Snap-in Components   Without you adding any custom templates, Windows itself includes over 100 .admx files. Many undoubtedly include policy settings that hold no interest for you. You can remove some of the clutter from your console by hiding the templates that you don't plan to use. To inhibit the display of certain templates, follow these steps:

1. In your console, choose File, Add/Remove Snap-In (or press Ctrl+M).

2. In the Selected Snap-Ins list in the Add Or Remove Snap-Ins dialog box, select one of the local GPO snap-ins. (It doesn't matter which one because settings you make here apply to all local GPO snap-ins in this console.) Then click Edit Extensions.

3. Select Enable Only Selected Extensions, and then clear the check box next to the extensions you want to hide.

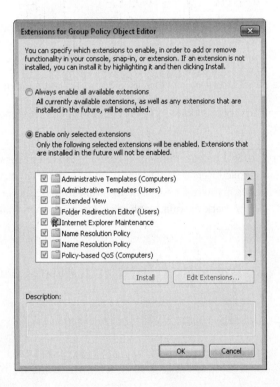

Note that most of the extensions control the display of folders other than the lengthy list within the Administrative Templates folder; many relate to subfolders of Windows Settings. Nonetheless, clutter is clutter. It's also sometimes difficult to divine exactly which folders will be hidden by disabling certain extensions. Aside from relying on trial and error, your best bet is to check the Group Policy Settings Reference spreadsheet (*w7io.com/22501*) for assistance.

Deleting Group Policy Settings

After you configure local GPO policy settings, you can, of course, go back and make changes to your settings at any time. But you can also remove a local GPO altogether, removing its settings *en masse*.

If you find occasion to undo all your settings for a particular local GPO (that is, one of the levels of MLGPO), it's easy to do, as follows:

1. Open your Multiple Local Group Policy Object Editor console.

2. Choose File, Add/Remove Snap-Ins (or press Ctrl+M).

3. In the Available Snap-Ins list, select Group Policy Object Editor, and then click Add.

4. In the select Group Policy Object dialog box, click Browse.

5. In the Browse For A Group Policy Object dialog box, click the Users tab.

6. Right-click the name of the local GPO that you want to remove and choose Remove Group Policy Object.

This action is irreversible, as it deletes the Registry.pol file and the folder within %System-Root%\System32\GroupPolicyUsers that contains it. Be sure this is what you want to do before you pull the trigger. If you're certain that you want to undo all your changes for that particular local GPO and go back to square one, click Yes in the confirmation dialog box.

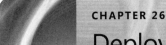

CHAPTER 26

Deployment and Migration

Most of the information in this book applies to your work on a single computer running Windows 7. (Of course, you might apply that information to many other computers—but you do so one computer at a time.) In this chapter, we address topics of interest to those who are responsible for setting up and maintaining Windows on a small fleet of computers.

What's in Your Edition?

For the most part, the tools described in this chapter are not included with any Windows 7 edition; rather, they are tools that you can download from Microsoft. (The handful of Windows 7 tools we mention are included in all editions.) These deployment tools work with all editions of Windows 7.

In this chapter we also discuss volume license programs available from Microsoft. This type of license agreement is generally available only for the business-oriented Windows 7 editions: Professional, Enterprise, and Ultimate.

Deployment of Windows and setup of new computers generally occur at one of three broad levels:

- Install Windows on a single computer. For details, see Chapter 2, "Installing and Configuring Windows 7."

- Install Windows and certain Microsoft applications on several computers in a home or small business using tools and techniques that facilitate multiple installations. Tools such as the Windows Automated Installation Kit for Windows 7, the Express Deployment Tool, and the Microsoft Deployment Toolkit allow you to preconfigure Windows and applications.

- Deploy Windows 7 and other applications throughout a large organization using advanced deployment tools from Microsoft. Tools such as Windows Deployment

Services and System Center Configuration Manager, along with the Microsoft Deployment Toolkit and Windows Automated Installation Kit for Windows 7, allow an administrator to create customized images and deploy them to remote computers from a central location.

Although you'll find bits of information in this chapter that apply to each of these scenarios, our focus is on the middle group. If you manage the computers in a small business, are a computer consultant, or even a serious hobbyist, the information in this chapter can help you to save time when you set up new computers.

Expediting Multiple Windows Installations by Installing from a USB Flash Drive

In Chapter 2, we explain in great detail various procedures for installing Windows 7 (upgrade, clean installation, multiboot configuration, and so on; see "Setting Up Windows 7" on page 30 for details). These procedures all have one thing in common: The setup procedure runs from a Windows 7 DVD. This can present a problem on computers that do not include a DVD drive, an increasingly common configuration on portable computers, which can use the space previously allocated for a DVD drive to increase battery capacity or to reduce the overall size and weight. And as DVDs continue their evolutionary decline, following in the footsteps of floppy disks and CD-ROMs before them, even many desktop computers now arrive sans DVD drive.

One solution, of course, is to use a portable DVD drive that attaches to a USB port. But there's a much better solution available: Create a bootable USB flash drive (UFD) from which you can install Windows 7. This low-cost solution offers another great benefit: It dramatically reduces the time needed to install Windows 7 compared to installing from a DVD. On some systems, we've performed a complete installation in just over 15 minutes. This makes a Windows 7 setup UFD an ideal method for installing Windows repeatedly (in a test environment, for example) or on several systems in relatively short order. (Note that the computer's BIOS must support booting from a UFD; many older systems do not.)

Because you can boot from the UFD, you can use it to install Windows onto a machine that doesn't already have an operating system in place (assuming, of course, that you comply with the terms of the licenses you have for Windows 7).

In the sections that follow, we describe two different methods for creating a bootable Windows 7 setup UFD. Use the first method, which uses a downloadable tool available from Microsoft, if you have an ISO image of the Windows 7 setup DVD. Use the second method if you have a Windows 7 installation DVD. (With the appropriate utility programs, you can mount an ISO image and extract its files—the same as you'd find on a DVD. Conversely, you can create an ISO image from a DVD. Either way, it's an extra step—which is why we recommend using the method that's suited to the file type you already have.)

For either method, you'll need a USB flash drive with a capacity of 4 GB or more.

> **CAUTION!**
>
> Regardless of which method you use for creating the UFD, be aware that all existing files on the UFD are permanently deleted during this procedure.

After you create the Windows 7 setup UFD, you use it in much the same way as you use a Windows 7 setup DVD: You can run Setup.exe from the root folder of the UFD, or you can boot from the UFD. (To boot from the UFD, your computer's BIOS must be configured to allow booting from USB devices.)

INSIDE OUT   Be sure you start with the right media

Before you go to the trouble of creating a UFD, be sure you have the right Windows 7 setup files. Aside from the usual concerns (Windows 7 edition and bitness), for successful installations you need an image that's appropriate for your license key (that is, OEM, retail, or volume license).

If you purchase Windows from the online Microsoft Store, you have the option of downloading a collection of compressed setup files or a single, uncompressed ISO image. Choose the ISO image. Instead of burning the ISO image to a writable DVD, you use it to create the UFD.

If you have a subscription to Microsoft Developer Network (MSDN), TechNet, or Microsoft Action Pack Subscription (MAPS), you might also be eligible to download an ISO image that you can use to create an installation UFD. (For more information about these programs, see "Evaluation Programs" on page 963.)

Creating a Bootable UFD with the Windows 7 USB/DVD Download Tool

The Windows 7 USB/DVD Download Tool lets you create a bootable UFD from an ISO image you download from the Microsoft Store. (You can also use it to create a DVD from the downloaded image.) Follow these steps to create the UFD:

1. Download the Windows 7 USB/DVD Download Tool setup program from *w7io.com/22613* and run it.

2. Run the newly installed Windows 7 USB/DVD Download Tool. (You'll find a shortcut on the Start menu.)

3. Click Browse, navigate to your ISO image file, and click Open. Then click Next.

4. On the Step 2 page, click USB Device.

5. On the Step 3 page, select your USB flash drive and then click Begin Copying.

In the fourth and final step, you don't need to do anything except wait a few minutes while the tool formats your UFD and copies files to it.

TROUBLESHOOTING

The Windows 7 USB/DVD Download Tool doesn't work

The tool is somewhat finicky and for various reasons might be unable to successfully create a bootable UFD. You can find some troubleshooting tips and workarounds at the Microsoft Store site (*w7io.com/22605*). If you still have problems, we recommend using the second method, as described in the following section. Although the second method is intended for use with a Windows 7 setup DVD, you can use an ISO image—the same file you would use in the preceding procedure. To make it work, you'll need a program that mounts an ISO image as a virtual drive. For that purpose, we recommend Virtual Clone Drive. The How-To Geek provides a description and a link to the download site at *w7io.com/22606*.

Creating a Bootable UFD from a Windows 7 Setup DVD

If you have a Windows 7 setup DVD and you want to create a bootable UFD for installations, this is the easiest method. Follow these steps:

1. Insert the USB flash drive into one of your computer's USB ports.

2. In the Start menu search box (or other command prompt), type **diskpart** and press Enter. After granting your approval at the UAC prompt, DiskPart (a disk partition–management program with a command-line interface) opens.

3. At the DISKPART prompt, type **list disk**. DiskPart displays a list of the computer's disk drives.

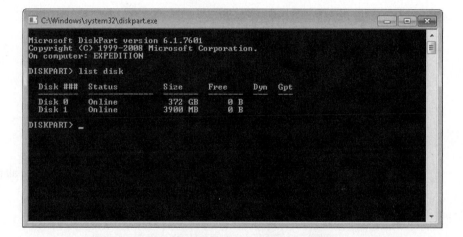

4. Use the disk size to determine which disk number represents the UFD you plan to use. In our example, 3,900 MB is close to the nominal size of our UFD (4 GB), so disk 1 is our target drive.

CAUTION!

Be absolutely certain you pick the correct drive. Remove all other removable drives if you have any doubt and enter **list disk** again. The drive you select will be formatted and all its existing data lost in the steps to follow.

5. At the DISKPART prompt, enter the commands on the next page, substituting the number of your UFD in place of *1* in this example's first command (Select Disk). Enter only the text shown in bold; DiskPart displays the other text.

```
DISKPART> select disk 1

Disk 1 is now the selected disk.

DISKPART> clean

DiskPart succeeded in cleaning the disk.

DISKPART> create partition primary

DiskPart succeeded in creating the specified partition.

DISKPART> active

DiskPart marked the current partition as active.

DISKPART> format fs=fat32 quick

100 percent completed

DiskPart successfully formatted the volume.

DISKPART> assign

DiskPart successfully assigned the drive letter or mount point.

DISKPART> exit
```

6. Insert the Windows 7 setup DVD. Using Windows Explorer, select all the files and folders in the root folder of the DVD, and copy them to the root folder of the UFD, thus preserving the folder structure.

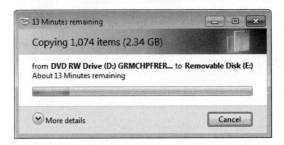

Using Your Bootable UFD

If you plan to run setup from a running copy of Windows, simply use Windows Explorer to navigate to the root folder of the UFD and then double-click Setup.exe. If you plan to boot from the UFD, you might have to jump through a few hoops. (For details about the implications of running setup from Windows vs. booting from media, see "Setting Up Windows 7" on page 30.)

By default, most computers do not look for boot files on USB devices. If you insert the UFD and reboot your computer, only to see it booting into its previously installed operating system, you'll need to boot again—this time interrupting the boot process. The key you press to stop booting and open the boot or BIOS menu varies depending on the computer manufacturer; it might be F2, F12, Tab, Del, or a dedicated button. (For example, Lenovo computers use a blue ThinkVantage button for this purpose.) As your computer boots, watch the computer manufacturer's splash screen for clues.

When you interrupt the boot process, some computers offer an option that lets you select a one-time boot device. If given that opportunity, take it, and select the USB flash drive. Otherwise, you'll need to dig around in the computer's BIOS settings to find the boot device settings; be sure that USB devices are enabled for booting ahead of your normal hard disk drive.

Slipstreaming the Service Pack Files

Our goal in this section is to expedite the installation of Windows 7, particularly when you're doing it repeatedly. If you're working from an original (pre–Service Pack 1) Windows 7 DVD, the first thing you need to do after installation is install the service pack. This extra step eats up a lot of time, thereby missing the goal.

In the Windows XP era, it was practical to "slipstream" the latest service pack by combining the files from the original setup CD with those from a service pack onto a new CD, which could then be used to install Windows and the service pack in one fell swoop. Unfortunately, this is no longer feasible. Whereas Windows XP used a file copy method for installation, Windows 7 (like Windows Vista) uses an image file. To incorporate the service pack files, you'd need an editor to open the image file; add, replace, and edit parts of it appropriately; and resave it. Microsoft offers a combination of tools that make it feasible to create a custom install image for Windows with SP1 already applied—in short, you'd install Windows 7 on a computer or virtual machine, apply SP1, and then use Sysprep, ImageX, and Windows PE to capture and apply the image—but this doesn't easily produce a standalone bootable Windows 7 SP1 setup DVD. A search of the web turns up some third-party tools and techniques for creating a slipstreamed image file, but we haven't found one that we can recommend.

Therefore, your best option when making a Windows 7 setup UFD is to start with a version of Windows that already includes Service Pack 1. If your only Windows 7 DVD predates the Service Pack, we strongly recommend that you get an updated DVD or ISO image. In addition to the sources mentioned earlier, you might be able to obtain an updated DVD from the manufacturer of your computer. For other solutions, see the following section, "Deploying Windows and Microsoft Office on Several Computers."

Deploying Windows and Microsoft Office on Several Computers

Microsoft makes available a wealth of tools for administrators of large-scale networks to use in rolling out Windows and other applications to a vast number of computers in an automated fashion. They let an administrator create customized images that work with the assorted hardware scattered about the organization and that meet the specific needs of different types of users. The tools can then manage automated delivery and installation of the images to desktops and servers throughout the organization. Through the use of the P2V Migration for Software Assurance tool, administrators can even maintain the current systems as virtual machines while backing up and converting systems, providing a safety net for legacy applications. The tools needed to perform these tasks are components of the Microsoft Deployment Toolkit (MDT).

For details about these enterprise-scale tools, visit the MDT website (*w7io.com/22601*) or see *Windows 7 Resource Kit*, by Mitch Tulloch, Tony Northrup, and Jerry Honeycutt (Microsoft Press, 2009). Mitch Tulloch has also written a series of articles about these tools, which you can find at *w7io.com/22602*. In addition, Microsoft Press makes available a free e-book, "Deploying Windows 7: Essential Guidance from the *Windows 7 Resource Kit* and *TechNet Magazine*"; you can download it at *w7io.com/22607*.

Tools for creating images that can be installed on new computers (which don't have the complications of migrating existing user accounts, applications, data, and settings) are also available for computer manufacturers (known in the industry as original equipment manufacturers, or OEMs) in the form of the Windows 7 OEM Preinstallation Kit (OPK). Tools in the OPK allow OEMs to meet Microsoft licensing requirements (Windows must be preinstalled on the hard drive), customize the installation by adding the OEM's branding, preinstall applications, create an out-of-box experience (OOBE) for customers' initial setup, and create master images for easy duplication.

For details about the Windows OPK, visit *w7io.com/22609*. On that web page, you'll find links to download the OPK as well as links to full documentation.

The MDT and OPK tools are not intended for hobbyists or for use on small networks, however. Although they offer seemingly endless options and capabilities, the tools can be inordinately complex to master and use. Unless you're responsible for managing hundreds of computers in an organization, you can spend far more time learning and implementing MDT than you could ever hope to save by using it. Similarly, the full OPK is best suited to full-scale computer manufacturers. Some of the tools are available only to customers with Software Assurance agreements or to computer manufacturers.

Fortunately, Microsoft makes available other tools that are more appropriate for smaller deployments, as described in the following sections.

> **Note**
>
> It might occur to you to customize Windows and other applications the way you like, create a system image with Windows Backup, and then restore the image to a new computer as a means of installing Windows on multiple computers. Unfortunately, this won't work. Among the problems you'll encounter: you'll have duplicate security identifiers (SIDs) on each computer, and the cloned computers will fail Windows activation. (For more information about activation, see "Activating and Validating Windows 7" on page 59.)

Introducing the Windows Automated Installation Kit

The Windows Automated Installation Kit (Windows AIK) provides many capabilities of the full MDT. Designed for IT professionals as well as OEMs and system builders, the Windows AIK is a set of tools and documentation for installing customized versions of Windows and other applications on new computers. The major components of Windows AIK are:

- **Windows System Image Manager**   Also known as Windows SIM, this tool opens Windows images, creates answer files for unattended installation, and manages stored images.

- **ImageX**   This tool captures and modifies Windows images and applies the images to disk volumes.

- **Deployment Image Servicing and Management**   Better known as DISM (rhymes with "prism"), this tool is used to apply updates, drivers, and language packs to a Windows image.

- **Windows Preinstallation Environment**   Windows PE is a bare-essentials operating system that's used to install a Windows image onto a new computer.

- **User State Migration Tool**   The USMT migrates users' data and settings from their old computer to a new computer running Windows 7. For more information about USMT, see "Migrating User Data" on page 960.

The Windows AIK for Windows 7 can be downloaded from *w7io.com/22611*, and you can download the documentation from *w7io.com/22612*. In addition, you might want to get the Windows Automated Installation Kit Supplement for Windows 7 SP1; for more information about its content, as well as a link to download it, visit *w7io.com/22614*. The process of creating and deploying a Windows image with Windows AIK generally involves these steps:

1. **Create an answer file.**   Using a file from the Windows 7 DVD and Windows SIM, you create a new answer file, to which you can add and configure Windows settings. You then save the settings in the form of an answer file.

2. **Build a reference installation.** You install Windows onto a reference computer using the answer file you created in step 1. You then use Sysprep, a tool included with Windows 7, to configure the system image for general use by cleaning up hardware- and user-specific settings and to make additional settings.

3. **Create bootable Windows PE media.** Using a script furnished with Windows AIK, you create a bootable CD-ROM that runs Windows PE entirely in RAM and includes the ImageX tool, which you'll need for capturing disk images.

4. **Capture the installation onto a network share.** Use the disc you created in step 3 to boot the reference computer and capture the image with ImageX. Then copy the image to a shared network location.

5. **Deploy from the network share.** Using the Windows PE disc, boot a new computer and then use DiskPart to partition and format its hard disk drive. Use ImageX to copy the image from the network location to the hard drive.

This brief summary glosses over the fact that the customization options and capabilities are numerous. Taken to extremes, preparation of the image can take many hours of fiddling around and testing. The end product is a computer ready to boot and finalize setup. This abbreviated setup process takes only a few minutes.

Introducing the Express Deployment Tool for System Builders

Early in 2011, Microsoft released a new tool that is ideal for smaller deployments onto new computers that you build. (You must be a "system builder"—a manufacturer or assembler of computer hardware that includes at least a hard disk drive, a central processing unit, a motherboard, a power supply, and a case—to use this tool in conformance with its license agreement.) Designed for system builders, the Express Deployment Tool (EDT) provides a subset of the capabilities in the full OPK, but it streamlines the process dramatically. Using the EDT, you can set up a reference PC (the master image) in 2 hours or less. After you've done that, you can install the image onto new PCs in about 10 minutes.

Images created with the EDT can include:

- Windows 7

- Microsoft Office 2010

- Windows Live

- Microsoft Security Essentials

- Bing Bar

To use the Express Deployment Tool, you need to download and run its setup program. (You can find a link on the Express Deployment Tool page at *w7io.com/22608*.) In addition, you need to download and install the full Windows 7 OEM Preinstallation Kit (*w7io.com/22609*) and image files or OPKs for Office and other applications you want to include.

The Express Deployment Tool is organized in a series of steps, culminating in the creation of an image in ISO format that you can then use with Windows PE (a component of the OPK) to deploy an image onto a new machine. Figure 26-1 shows the EDT midway through the process of adding applications to the image.

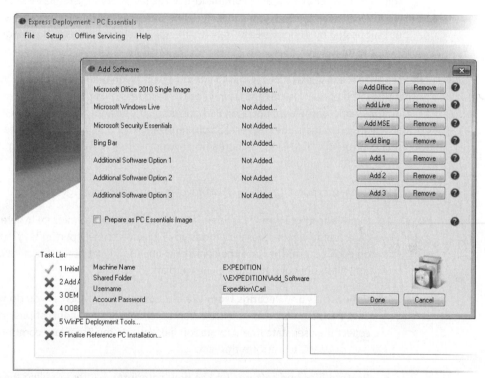

Figure 26-1 The list of tasks for preparing a deployment image is shown in the lower left corner of the EDT. You select the task to work on from the Setup menu.

Although the steps are clearly delineated, the online help is minimal. (In fact, as good as this tool is, it's clearly intended for a small audience of technically capable system builders. At least in its early releases, the EDT installer and the program itself are not digitally signed, and the error-handling is less than robust.) You'll find additional assistance in "Express Deployment—Step by Step Guide for System Builders," which you can download at *w7io.com/22610*. The guide is also included when you download the EDT setup program.

Migrating User Data

In Chapter 2, we describe Windows Easy Transfer, a program included with Windows 7 that assists in moving user account information, documents, and user settings (known collectively as *user state*) from your old computer to a new computer running Windows 7. (For details, see "Transferring Files and Settings from Another Computer" on page 66.) Windows Easy Transfer is an interactive program that's ideal for transferring the user state of a few computers.

For medium- or large-scale deployments, User State Migration Tool (USMT) offers a better solution. It's a set of scriptable command-line tools that offer customizable migration. By creating custom .xml files, you can include migration capabilities for programs and settings not supported by Windows Easy Transfer. You can also specify files and settings to exclude from the migration.

Unlike Windows Easy Transfer, USMT does not work in an interactive fashion. While this reduces the burden on the end user whose user state is being migrated, it means more upfront work for the administrator. Perhaps more importantly, it means that all computers are migrated in the same way; aside from repeating the tasks of modifying the .xml files that control how USMT works, there's no provision for selectively customizing the process for individual computers.

The general procedure for using USMT involves three distinct stages:

1. **Plan your migration.**   Decide exactly what you want to migrate, where to store the data, and which of several methods you'll use for actually performing the migration on each system. Then use the command-line tool to set options and modify or create .xml files as needed to implement the plan.

2. **Collect files and settings from the old computer.**   Much as you do with Windows Easy Transfer, you back up the old computer and close all applications and then collect the user state into a migration file. You use the ScanState command-line tool, part of USMT, to perform this task.

3. **Restore files and settings on the new computer.**   After installing the operating system and all applications on the new computer (a task you can perform manually or in an automated fashion by using a setup created by the Windows Automated Installation Kit or Express Deployment Tool), you use the LoadState command to migrate the user state from the stored migration file.

You get USMT, along with its documentation, as part of the Windows Automated Installation Kit, which you can download from *w7io.com/22611*.

Working with Volume Licenses

You might assume, based on the name, that Microsoft's volume licensing (VL) program for Windows is exclusively for large organizations. That's only partially true. Yes, Fortune 500 corporations with tens of thousands of workers are the most obvious VL customers. But small businesses—even very small outfits with a literal handful of Windows PCs—can take advantage of VL upgrades as well, allowing them to lower overall costs or gain access to additional usage rights. Separate VL programs, often with significant discounts, are available for academic, charity, and government organizations.

Let's start by dispelling one common misconception. A volume license for Windows provides upgrade rights only. You cannot purchase a full license for Windows through a VL program. If you plan to deploy a new PC in your organization, you need to acquire a *qualifying operating system* for that computer before it is eligible for a volume license upgrade. The qualifying operating system can be a copy of Windows preinstalled on a PC by an OEM, or it can be a full packaged product purchased from a retail outlet.

> **Note**
>
> Although volume licensing agreements specify that the software is available as an upgrade only, that doesn't place any limits on how you install Windows. As long as you have a license for a qualifying operating system on the underlying hardware, you can perform a clean install or use a supported imaging tool. The choice is yours.

The rules for VL upgrades are complex, so much so that Microsoft regularly updates a lengthy product list document that spells out the rules in excruciating detail. (The latest version for your geographic region is available at *w7io.com/22690*.) The oversimplified version of these rules for business customers is that the qualifying operating system must be a business edition of Windows—Windows 7 Professional, Windows Vista Business, Windows XP Professional or Tablet PC edition—to qualify for Windows 7 volume licensing rights. (The rules are relaxed for charity and academic VL programs, in which consumer versions of Windows such as Windows Vista and Windows 7 Home Premium, Home Basic, and Starter editions qualify.)

Purchasing a volume license upgrade gives you the right to install the version of Windows that you think is most appropriate for your organization. For most businesses, the best choice is Windows 7 Enterprise edition, which offers (among other benefits) the right to run up to four additional copies of Windows in virtual machines on the licensed PC.

For an explanation of the differences between Windows 7 editions, see Appendix A, "Windows 7 Editions at a Glance."

Chapter 26

INSIDE OUT   Pay as you go for an Enterprise upgrade

The simplest way to purchase an upgrade to Windows 7 Enterprise edition is to do so as part of a Windows Intune subscription. This cloud-based suite of management services includes inventory monitoring, update management tools, and security software, all for a subscription fee of $10 per month. That price also includes an upgrade to Windows 7 Enterprise edition (or a newer version of Windows, when one is available). For more details about how Windows Intune works, see *w7io.com/22691*.

A VL upgrade completely replaces the qualifying operating system. Thus, if you purchased a PC in 2009 with Windows Vista Business, you can upgrade it to Windows 7 Enterprise by purchasing a VL upgrade.

Paradoxically, the list of benefits associated with a VL upgrade includes *downgrade rights*. Unlike a retail or OEM license, which describes a specific Windows version and edition, a VL upgrade allows you to install any supported version of Windows, including Windows Vista and Windows XP, to maintain compatibility with other PCs in your organization and then upgrade to Windows 7 when you are ready.

When you purchase a VL upgrade, you can also purchase a Software Assurance subscription, which provides additional support and training benefits. It also includes rights to use the Microsoft Desktop Optimization Pack, an assortment of superb and useful deployment and diagnostic tools.

Microsoft offers a comprehensive collection of details about volume licensing options at *microsoft.com/licensing*. For a full explanation of product use rights, visit *w7io.com/22693*.

Activating a Volume License

In Chapter 2, we covered activation options for retail and OEM copies of Windows 7. (See "Activating and Validating Windows 7" on page 59 for details.) VL upgrades to Windows 7 also require setup keys and activation, but the rules and infrastructure for the activation process are different.

For Windows 7, volume activation is required for systems that are covered under a VL agreement, regardless of how those VL upgrades were purchased. The technology was introduced with Windows Vista and is also used with Windows Server 2008 and Windows Server 2008 R2, as well as with Microsoft Office 2010 and related products.

You can use either of two models for volume activation of PCs running Windows 7:

- **Key Management Service (KMS)**   This option is most appropriate for large organizations that need to activate hundreds or thousands of systems within their own network. (The minimum number of Windows desktop systems to activate using this technology is 25.) The KMS host has its own product key, which is activated with a Microsoft server. Individual Windows 7 PCs must be set up using setup keys supplied by the Microsoft Volume Licensing Service Center. The KMS service can activate an unlimited number of computers using these keys.

- **Multiple Activation Key (MAK)**   If you have fewer than 25 VL systems, or if you don't want to install a KMS host locally, you can use this type of product key. When you activate a system that was set up using an MAK, it contacts Microsoft's activation servers to complete activation. Unlike retail and OEM keys, which are limited to a single activation, this type of key allows a predetermined number of activations, which is set by your VL agreement.

For more information on the differences between these activation technologies, see "Frequently Asked Questions About Volume License Keys" at *w7io.com/22692*.

Evaluation Programs

If you're not sure whether Windows 7 Enterprise is a good fit for your needs, you can download an evaluation copy and take it for a spin for up to 90 days. Details and download links are available at *w7io.com/22694*.

If you are a current volume license customer, you might already have the right to install and use an evaluation copy of Windows 7 Enterprise within your organization. Check your VL agreement for details.

In addition, Microsoft offers a variety of subscription-based programs aimed at customers who want the flexibility to evaluate and test Windows 7 and other products. These three are especially popular:

- TechNet subscriptions are available in Standard and Professional editions. Both offer access to full-version software, including multiple editions of Windows 7 and Microsoft Office, for testing and evaluation purposes. Windows 7 Enterprise is available as part of the Professional subscription only. For details, visit *technet.com/subscriptions*.

- Microsoft Developer Network (MSDN) offers a wide range of subscription options aimed primarily at software developers. All subscriptions include the option to download Windows 7 Enterprise for test and evaluation purposes. For details, visit *msdn.com/subscriptions*.

- Microsoft Action Pack Solution Provider is a program aimed at businesses that resell Microsoft software, either on new PCs or as part of other business services. A related program, Microsoft Action Pack Development and Design, serves software developers and web designers. In addition to evaluation software, an Action Pack subscription includes licensed copies of Windows and other software that can be used for production purposes. For details, visit *partner.microsoft.com/40016455*.

Automating Windows 7

IF you use your computer very often—and if you're reading this book you probably do—you likely find yourself performing certain ordinary tasks repeatedly. Such tasks might include routine maintenance activities, such as backing up your data or cleaning deadwood from your hard disk, or they might be jobs that require many steps. Computers excel at repetitive actions, and Windows 7 provides several ways to automate such tasks:

- **Task Scheduler** Probably the most important automation tool at your disposal is Task Scheduler, which lets you set up automated routines to be triggered by events or by a schedule and requires no programming expertise.

- **Batch programs** A carryover from the earliest days of MS-DOS, batch programming still offers an easy, reliable way to run sequences of tasks. Most Windows programs can be started from a command prompt, which means they can be started from a batch program.

- **Windows Script Host** This feature allows you to run scripts written in VBScript, JScript, and other languages. Although learning how to use Windows Script Host is more difficult than learning to create batch programs, scripts can interact with the operating system and with other programs in more powerful ways.

- **Windows PowerShell** Windows PowerShell is a .NET 2.0–based command-line shell and scripting language tailored to work with Windows 7. If you're serious about scripting Windows 7, you'll want to take a look at Windows PowerShell.

What's in Your Edition?

The options for automating Windows 7 are the same in all editions.

Using Task Scheduler

If you're accustomed to using Scheduled Tasks in Windows XP, you'll be pleased by the improvements that have been made in Windows Vista and Windows 7. To begin with, the user interface to the task scheduler is now a Microsoft Management Console (MMC) snap-in, which means you have access to more information about the properties, status, and run history of your tasks (and those that the operating system and your applications have established for you). Second, the Scheduled Tasks snap-in has been neatly integrated with the Event Viewer snap-in, making it easy for you to use events (an application crash or a disk-full error, for example) as triggers for tasks. Third and most important, the Task Scheduler now supports a much more extensive set of triggering and scheduling options. In addition to running programs or scripts at specified times, you can now launch actions when the computer has been idle for a specified time period, when particular users log on or off, and so on. You can use these (and other) triggers to send e-mail messages or display message windows, as well as to run programs or scripts.

For information about the Event Viewer snap-in, see "Digging Deeper with Event Viewer" on page 1023. For more general information about using Microsoft Management Console, see "Using Microsoft Management Console" on page 904.

To launch Task Scheduler, type **sched** in the Start menu search box. That should bring Task Scheduler to the top of the menu. Alternatively, press Windows logo key+R and type **taskschd.msc** on the Run line.

Figure 27-1 shows a sample of Task Scheduler in its default layout. As you can see, the window is divided vertically into three regions—a console tree on the left, an action pane on the right, and in between, various informative windows in the details pane. The console tree shows you which computer you're working with (the local machine or a network computer to which you have connected) and provides a folder tree of currently defined tasks. You can create your own folders here to organize the tasks that you create yourself, or you can add new tasks to existing folders.

The action pane provides a menu of things you can do. With rare (and probably unintended) exceptions, items here are also available on the menus at the top of the window, so if you're feeling cramped in the center, you might consider hiding the action pane. (Choose View, Customize, and then clear the check box for Action Pane.)

In the center part of the window, initially you'll see an overview message (this is a static bit of text; once you've read it, you can hide it by clicking the collapse arrow at the right), a status report of all tasks that have run (or were scheduled to run) during some period of time (by default, the most recent 24 hours), and a summary of all the currently enabled tasks. Entries in the Task Status list have outline controls; click an item's plus sign to see more details.

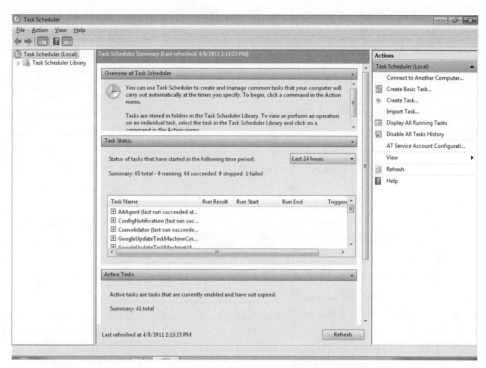

Figure 27-1 The Windows 7 Task Scheduler is implemented as an MMC snap-in.

The Task Status and Active Tasks displays are not updated automatically. To get the latest information, click Refresh at the bottom of the screen, in the action pane, or on the Action menu.

If this is your first visit to Task Scheduler, you might be surprised by the number of active tasks that Windows and your applications have already established. For example, if you use Backup And Restore to perform regular full and incremental backups, you'll find some backup-related items in the list. Unless you or someone else has disabled automatic disk defragmentation, there will be an item for it in the list. If you rely on a calendar program to remind you of appointments or task deadlines, chances are that functionality will be represented in the active tasks list. To see what tasks managed by Task Scheduler are currently running, click Display All Running Tasks in the action pane.

To satisfy your curiosity about what an active task does and how it has been set up, you'll need to locate it in the console tree. Expand the outline entries as needed and browse to an item of interest. The entries in the console tree are virtual folders, each of which can contain subfolders or one or more tasks. When you select a folder, the upper part of the details pane lists all tasks stored in the folder. The lower pane, meanwhile, shows a tabbed display of the properties of the selected task. Figure 27-2 shows the WindowsBackup folder selected in the console tree, the AutomaticBackup task selected in the upper pane, and the General tab of the AutomaticBackup properties displayed in the lower pane. (The action pane has been hidden in this figure.)

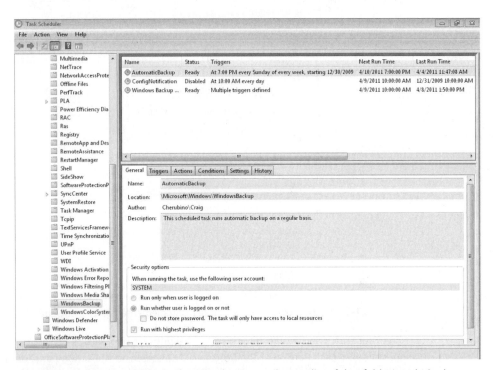

Figure 27-2 Selecting a folder in the console tree produces a list of that folder's tasks in the upper part of the details pane and a properties display in the lower part.

The properties display that appears is read-only. To edit the properties associated with a task, right-click the task name and choose Properties from the shortcut menu. (Or double-click the task's entry.) That will open a read/write dialog box in a separate window.

With the exception of the History tab, the properties dialog box is identical to the Create Task dialog box, one of the tools you can use to create a new task; we'll explore that dialog box in some detail in the following section, "Creating a Task." The History tab allows you to see exactly how, whether, and when a task has run. Figure 27-3 shows the History tab for AutomaticBackup.

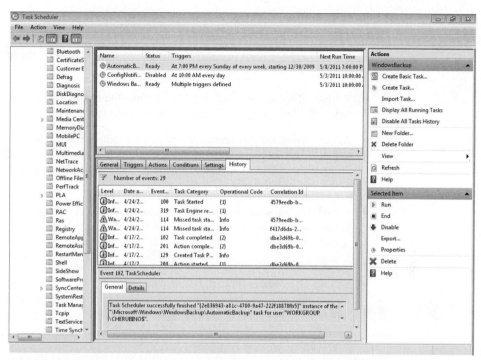

Figure 27-3 The History tab lets you confirm that a scheduled task is running as expected.

When you display the History tab, the relevant portion of the Event Viewer snap-in snaps in, showing you all the recent events related to the selected task. This is exactly what you would see if you ran Evntvwr.msc, navigated in the console tree to Applications And Services Logs\Microsoft\Windows\TaskScheduler\Operational, and filtered the resulting log to show events related to the selected task. (Obviously, if you want this information, it's quicker to find it in the Task Scheduler console than in the Event Viewer console.) If a task you've set up is not getting triggered when you expect it to or not running successfully when it should, you can double-click the appropriate event entry and read whatever details the event log has to offer.

INSIDE OUT   Use the History tab to troubleshoot tasks

Unlike the Scheduled Tasks folder in Windows XP (which recorded only the most recent error code generated by a failed task), the Windows 7 Task Scheduler maintains an ample history of the events generated by each task. If a task is failing regularly or intermittently, you can review all the causes by scrolling through the History tab of the task's properties display.

Task Scheduler Terminology

As you go through the steps to create or edit a task, you'll encounter the following terms:

- **Trigger**   The time at which a task is scheduled to run, or the event in response to which a task runs. A task can have multiple triggers.

- **Action**   What the task does. Possible actions include starting a program, sending an e-mail message, and displaying a message on the screen. A task can have multiple actions, in which case the actions occur sequentially in the order in which you assign them.

- **Condition**   An additional requirement that, along with the trigger, must be met for the task to run. For example, a condition might stipulate that the task run only if the computer has been idle for 10 minutes or only if it's running on AC power.

- **Setting**   A property that affects the behavior of a task. With settings, you can do such things as enable a task to run on demand or set retry parameters to be followed if a task fails to run when it's triggered.

Creating a Task

You can set up tasks on your own computer or any other computer to which you have access. If you're administering a remote computer, start by selecting the top item in the console tree—the one that says Task Scheduler (Local) if you haven't yet connected to a remote computer. Then choose Connect To Another Computer in the action pane or from the Action menu.

To begin creating a new task, select the folder in the console tree where you want the task to reside. If you need to create a new folder for this purpose, right-click the folder's parent in the console tree and choose New Folder from the shortcut menu.

You can create a new task in the Scheduled Tasks snap-in by using a wizard or by filling out the Create Task dialog box. The wizard, which you launch by choosing Create Basic Task (in the action pane or from the Action menu), is ideal for time-triggered tasks involving a single action. It's also fine for setting up a task to run when you log on or when Windows starts. For a more complex task definition, you'll need to work through the Create Task dialog box. Select the folder where you want the task to appear (in the console tree), and then choose Create Task in the action pane or from the Action menu. Figure 27-4 shows the General tab of the Create Task dialog box.

The one required entry on the General tab is a name for the task; everything else is optional. The task's author is you (you can't change that), and unless you specify otherwise, the task will run in your own security context. If you want it to run in the security context of a different user or group, click Change User Or Group and fill out the ensuing dialog box.

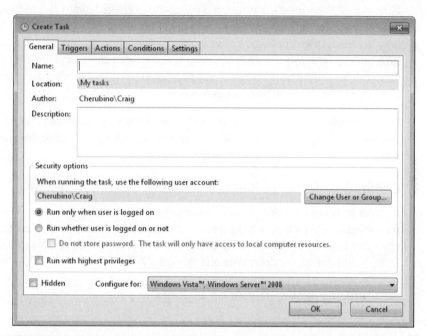

Figure 27-4 On the General tab, type a name for your new task and indicate the security context it should run in.

The circumstance under which you're most likely to need to change the security context is if you're setting up tasks to run on another computer. If you intend to run programs with which another user can interact, you should run those in the other user's security context. If you run them in your own, the tasks will run noninteractively (that is, the user will not see them).

Regardless of which user's security context the task is to run in, you have the option of allowing the task to run whether or not that user is logged on. If you select Run Whether User Is Logged On Or Not, you will be prompted for the user's password when you finish creating the task. If you don't happen to have that password, you can select Do Not Store Password. As the text beside this check box indicates, the task will have access to local resources only.

Creating a Task to Run with Elevated Privileges

If the task you're setting up is one that would generate a UAC prompt if run interactively, you'll want to select Run With Highest Privileges. If you're setting up a task to run with elevated privileges in the context of a user who does not have administrative credentials, you are asked to supply credentials when you complete the task-setup process.

Creating a Hidden Task

Windows XP Service Pack 2 introduced the ability to create hidden tasks—tasks that did not ordinarily appear in the Windows XP Scheduled Tasks folder. Such tasks could be created only by means of an application programming interface (API). In Windows 7, you can create such tasks without using the API by selecting the Hidden check box. Presumably the reason to do this is to make tasks that you set up for other users less visible (hence, less subject to alteration or deletion) on their target machines.

Note, however, that anyone with administrative credentials can make hidden tasks visible by choosing View, Show Hidden Tasks. And anyone running Task Scheduler can alter or delete tasks at will, regardless of who created them.

Configuring a Task to Run in a Different Operating System

If you're setting up a task on a remote computer that's running an operating system other than Windows 7, open the Configure For list and choose appropriately. Task Scheduler can configure tasks for Windows Server 2008, Windows Server 2003, Windows XP, or Windows 2000, in addition to Windows Vista and Windows 7.

Setting Up a Task's Trigger or Triggers

Tasks can be triggered in the following ways:

- On a schedule
- At logon
- At startup
- On idle
- On an event
- At task creation or modification
- On connection to a user session
- On disconnection from a user session
- On workstation lock
- On workstation unlock

You can establish zero, one, or several triggers for a task. If you don't set any triggers, you can still run the task on demand (unless you clear the Allow Task To Be Run On Demand check box on the Settings tab of the Create Task dialog box). This gives you a way to test a new task before committing it to a schedule, for example. If you set multiple triggers, the task runs when any one of the triggers occurs.

To set up a trigger, click the Triggers tab in the Create Task dialog box, and then click New. In the New Trigger dialog box that appears (shown in Figure 27-5), choose the type of trigger you want from the Begin The Task drop-down list.

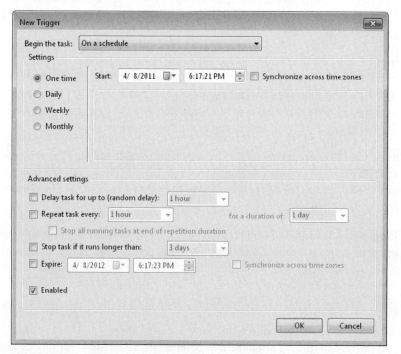

Figure 27-5 A task can have zero, one, or several triggers. Advanced Settings options let you set delay, repeat, and expiration parameters.

Note the Advanced Settings options at the bottom of the dialog box shown in Figure 27-5. These choices—which let you establish delay, repeat, and expiration parameters (among other things)—are not so easy to find when you're reviewing a task that you or someone has already created. They don't appear in the read-only version of a task's properties, and if you open the read/write version of the properties dialog box, you'll need to select a trigger (on the Triggers tab) and click Edit to see or change the advanced options.

Triggering a Task on Schedule   Time-triggered tasks can be set to run once or to recur at regular intervals. The choices are probably self-explanatory, with the possible exception of the Synchronize Across Time Zones check box. Time triggers are governed by the clock of the machine on which the task is to run, unless you select this check box—in which case, they are triggered by coordinated universal time (UTC). You might want to go with UTC if you're trying to coordinate time-triggered tasks on multiple machines in multiple time zones.

Triggering a Task at Logon   Logon tasks can be set for any user or a specific user or user group. If the user whose logon triggers the task is not the user in whose security context the task is running, the task will be noninteractive—in other words, essentially invisible. (The user can note the presence of the task—and terminate it—by running Windows Task Manager, going to the Processes tab, clicking Show Processes From All Users, and answering the UAC prompt.)

Triggering a Task at Startup   If you set a task to be triggered at startup, the trigger takes effect when you start your own computer (assuming you have Task Scheduler set to configure the local machine), but before you log on. Therefore, if you intend for the task to run on your own system, be sure to choose Run Whether User Is Logged On Or Not on the General tab of the Create Task dialog box. Otherwise, the task will never run.

If you use the Change User Or Group button on the General tab to specify another user on your domain, and you choose Run Only When User Is Logged On, the startup-triggered task will run on the remote system when you restart your own, provided the specified user actually is logged on.

Triggering a Task on Idle   If you set a task to be triggered when your computer is idle, you should also go to the Conditions tab of the Create Task dialog box to specify what you mean by "idle." For information about how Scheduled Tasks defines idleness, see "Starting and Running a Task Only If the Computer Is Idle" on page 976.

Note that you need to set an idle trigger on the Triggers tab only if idleness is the only trigger you want to use. If you're setting one or more other triggers but you want to ensure that the task starts only when the computer is idle, select Start The Task Only If The Computer Is Idle For on the Conditions tab.

Using an Event to Trigger a Task   Anything that generates an item in an event log can serve as a task trigger. The simplest way to use this feature is to launch Event Viewer (Eventvwr.msc), find the event that you want to use as a trigger, right-click it in Event Viewer, and choose Attach Task To This Event. This action launches the Create Basic Task wizard, with the trigger portion of the wizard already filled out. The new task appears in a folder called Event Viewer Tasks (newly created for you if it doesn't already exist), and you can modify it if needed by selecting it there and opening its properties dialog box.

For information about events and event logs, see "Digging Deeper with Event Viewer" on page 1023.

It's possible, of course, to create an event-driven task directly in Task Scheduler—by selecting On An Event in the New Trigger dialog box. If you set up the task in this fashion, however, you'll need to supply the Log, Source, and Event ID information yourself. It's more trouble to do it this way, and there's no need.

Triggering at Task Creation or Modification   The option to trigger a task at task creation or modification gives you an easy way to make a task run the moment you finish setting it up the first time or editing it subsequently. You can use this setting for testing purposes, or by combining it with other triggers, you can use it to make a task run immediately as well as subsequently.

Triggering a Task at User Connection or Disconnection   The options On Connection To A User Session and On Disconnect From A User Session give you some flexible ways to set tasks running in response to user activities. Option buttons associated with these choices let you specify whether the settings apply to any user or to a particular user or group. Additional options make the trigger apply to remote connections and disconnections or to local connections and disconnections. Setting a trigger to a particular user on the local computer, for example, would enable you to run a task in response to that user's connection via Remote Desktop Connection or the Switch User command.

Triggering a Task at Workstation Lock or Unlock   Like several other triggering choices, the On Workstation Lock and On Workstation Unlock options can be configured to apply to a particular user or group or to anyone who locks or unlocks the computer.

Setting Up a Task's Action or Actions

Besides its name (which you supply on the General tab of the Create Task dialog box), the only other task parameter you must provide is the action or actions the task is supposed to perform. This you do by clicking New on the Actions tab and filling out the rest of the dialog box. Three types of actions are possible:

- Start a program

- Send an e-mail

- Display a message

You can specify one or several actions. Multiple actions are carried out sequentially, with each new action beginning when the previous one is complete.

The Start A Program option can be applied to anything that Windows can execute—a Windows program, a batch program or script, a document associated with a program, or a shortcut. You can use the Browse button to simplify entry of long path specifications, add command-line parameters for your executable on the Add Arguments line, and specify a

Chapter 27

start-in folder for the executable. If your program needs elevated privileges to run successfully, be sure that you select Run With Highest Privileges on the General tab of the Create Task dialog box.

If you choose to send an e-mail, Task Scheduler will require the address of your outbound (SMTP) server. If you opt for a message, the dialog box will provide fields for the window title and message text. The Send An E-Mail and Display A Message options are not available for tasks set to run on Windows XP, Windows 2000, or Windows Server 2003.

Starting and Running a Task Only If the Computer Is Idle

On the Conditions tab of the Create Task dialog box (shown in Figure 27-6), you can require that the computer be idle for a specified period of time before a triggered task can begin. To do this, select Start The Task Only If The Computer Is Idle For, and specify the time period in the field to the right. Other check boxes in the Idle section of the Conditions tab let you specify what should happen if the task has begun during a required idle period but the computer subsequently becomes active again.

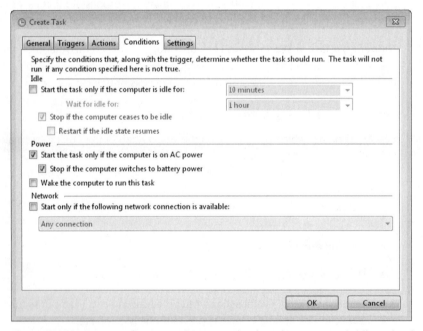

Figure 27-6 You can configure a task to run only when the computer is idle, only when it's running on AC power, or only when it's connected to a network.

Task Scheduler defines idleness as follows:

- If a screen saver is running, the computer is presumed to be idle.

- If a screen saver is not running, the system checks for idleness every 15 minutes, considering the machine to be idle if there has been no keyboard or mouse input during that interval and if the disk IO and CPU usage figures were at 0 percent for 90 percent of that time.

In addition to specifying a required period of idleness, you can tell Windows to wait some period of time after a task has been triggered before beginning to determine whether the computer is idle. Clearly, adjusting the idle parameters is a bit of an art; if you have precise requirements for some reason, you might need to experiment and test to get things just the way you want them.

Requiring AC Power

If you're setting up a task to run on a portable computer, consider whether you want the task to begin running while the computer is running on battery power. If you do not, select Start The Task Only If The Computer Is On AC Power in the Power section of the Conditions tab. A second check box below this one lets you decide whether the task, once begun, should cease if the computer switches to battery power.

Waking the Computer to Run a Task

If it's essential that your task run at some particular time, whether or not the computer is asleep, be sure to select Wake The Computer To Run This Task on the Conditions tab. Once aroused, the computer will then perform whatever duties you've assigned, returning to sleep on completion in accordance with whatever power plan is in effect.

If you do not want to disturb your computer's rest, you might want to stipulate that the task run as soon as possible after the machine awakes. You can do that by selecting Run Task As Soon As Possible After A Scheduled Start Is Missed on the Settings tab of the Create Task dialog box.

Requiring a Network Connection

If your task requires access to network resources, be sure to select Start Only If The Following Network Connection Is Available on the Conditions tab. Then use the drop-down list directly below this check box to specify which network connection is required. You might want to use this option in conjunction with Run Task As Soon As Possible After A Scheduled Start Is Missed, a check box on the Settings tab.

The option to require a network connection is not available for tasks set to run on Windows XP, Windows 2000, or Windows Server 2003.

Chapter 27

Running a Task on Demand

You can run a scheduled task on demand, as well as in response to various time or event triggers. You can turn this feature off for a task by clearing the Allow Task To Be Run On Demand check box on the Settings tab. But unless you're concerned that another user with access to your system might run a task against your wishes, it's hard to imagine why you would want to disallow on-demand execution.

To run a task on demand, assuming you have not disallowed it, locate the task's folder in the console tree, right-click the task in Task Scheduler's upper window, and choose Run from the shortcut menu.

Scheduling Tasks with the Schtasks Command

Task Scheduler provides a friendly and versatile method of creating and managing scheduled tasks. In some instances, however, you might find it easier to manage scheduled tasks from a command prompt. For these occasions. Windows 7 provides the Schtasks command, a replacement for the venerable At command that was included with earlier versions of the Windows NT platform. With Schtasks, you can create, modify, delete, end, view, and run scheduled tasks—and, of course, you can incorporate the command in batch programs and scripts.

Tasks created via Schtasks appear in the top-level folder (Task Scheduler Library) in the Task Scheduler console, and you can edit, run, or delete them from there as well as from the command prompt.

Schtasks is a rather complex command with lots of command-line switches and other parameters, but it has only six main variants:

- **Schtasks /Create**   This variant, which you use to create a new scheduled task, is the most complex because of all the available triggering options, conditions, and settings. For details, type **schtasks /create /?** at the command prompt.

- **Schtasks /Change**   This variant allows you to modify an existing task. Among other things, you can change the program that the task runs, the user account under which the task runs, or the password associated with that user account. For details, type **schtasks /change /?** at the command prompt.

- **Schtasks /Delete**   This variant deletes an existing task or, optionally, all tasks on a computer.

- **Schtasks /End**   This variant stops a program that was started by a scheduled task.

- **Schtasks /Query**   This variant displays, with optional verbosity, all scheduled tasks on the local or a remote computer. You can use arguments to restrict the display to particular tasks or tasks running in particular security contexts. For details, type **schtasks /query /?** at the command prompt.

- **Schtasks /Run**   This variant runs a specified task on demand.

A few examples should give you an idea of the power of the Schtasks command. Suppose, for example, that you want to take a break every four hours at 20 minutes past the hour to play a hand of Solitaire. The following command sets you up:

```
schtasks /create /tn "Solitaire break" /tr "%programfiles%\microsoft games\solitaire\
solitaire.exe" /sc hourly /mo 4 /st 00:20:00
```

In this example, the /Tn switch specifies the name of the task, /Tr specifies the path to the executable program, /Sc specifies the schedule type /Mo specifies the interval, and /St specifies the starting time.

The following example creates a task that runs a script on the last Friday of each calendar quarter. (The script isn't included with Windows; it's just an example.)

```
schtasks /create /tn "Quarterly wrap-up" /tr c:\apps\qtrwrap.vbs /sc monthly /mo last
/d fri /m mar,jun,sep,dec
```

By default, tasks scheduled via the Schtasks command run under the user account that's currently logged on. To make them run under a different account, use the /Ru switch followed by the account name you want to use; you'll also need to know the logon password for that account. To use the built-in System account, append /ru "System" to the command. No password is required for the System account, but because only administrators can use Schtasks, this doesn't present a problem.

Automating Command Sequences with Batch Programs

A *batch program* (also commonly called a *batch file*) is a text file that contains a sequence of commands to be executed. You execute the commands by entering the file name at a command prompt. Any action you can take by typing a command at a command prompt can be encapsulated in a batch program.

When you type the name of your batch program at the command prompt (or when you specify it as a task to be executed by Task Scheduler and the appropriate trigger occurs), the command interpreter opens the file and starts reading the statements. It reads the first line, executes the command, and then goes on to the next line. On the surface, this seems to operate just as if you were typing each line yourself at the command prompt. In fact, however, the batch program can be more complicated, because the language includes replaceable parameters, conditional and branching statements, the ability to call subroutines, and so on. Batch programs can also respond to values returned by programs and to the values of environment variables.

Batch programming is a venerable art, having been with us since the earliest days of MS-DOS (long before Windows was so much as a twinkle in Microsoft's eye). These days there are more powerful scripting tools at your disposal. Nevertheless, if you have already invested some time and energy in learning the language of batch programming, that investment can continue to serve you in Windows 7; your batch programs will run as well as they ever have, and you can execute them on or in response to events by means of Task Scheduler.

Automating Tasks with Windows Script Host

Microsoft Windows Script Host (WSH) provides a way to perform more sophisticated tasks than the simple jobs that batch programs are able to handle. You can control virtually any component of Windows and of many Windows-based programs with WSH scripts.

To run a script, you can type a script name at a command prompt or double-click the script's icon in Windows Explorer. WSH has two nearly equivalent programs—Wscript.exe and Cscript.exe—that, with the help of a language interpreter dynamic-link library such as Vbscript.dll, execute scripts written in VBScript or another scripting language. (Cscript.exe is a command-line program; Wscript.exe is its GUI counterpart.)

With WSH, the files can be written in several different languages, including VBScript (a scripting language similar to Microsoft Visual Basic) and JScript (a form of JavaScript). All the objects are available to any language, and in most situations, you can choose the language with which you are most comfortable. WSH doesn't care what language you use, provided the appropriate interpreter dynamic-link library (DLL) is available. VBScript and JScript interpreters come with Windows 7; interpreters for Perl, KiXtart (Kix), Python, Rexx, and other languages are available elsewhere.

Because WSH scripts can access ActiveX controls, they provide great flexibility. Several objects are provided with WSH that allow you basic control of Windows and your computer. By using ActiveX, you can control many of the programs on your computer. For example, you can create a script to display a chart in Microsoft Excel.

An Introduction to Windows PowerShell

Microsoft describes Windows PowerShell as a "task-based command-line shell and scripting language designed especially for system administrators." That means that you can use PowerShell for the same kinds of tasks you're accustomed to performing with Cmd.exe (the shell that has been included with all recent versions of Windows), and you can use its scripting power to automate routine work. If you're a Windows user who occasionally likes to take advantage of the power of text-based command-line tools such as Ipconfig or Netsh, you'll find that PowerShell lets you interact with the operating system in all the old familiar ways—and a good many new ones as well. If you're accustomed to using batch programs, VBScript, or Jscript to automate administrative tasks, you can retain your current scripting investment but take advantage of the additional capabilities afforded by PowerShell's object orientation and .NET Framework foundation as your scripting needs grow.

Among the advantages that PowerShell offers over previous shells and scripting platforms are the following:

- **Integration with the .NET Framework**   Like more traditional development languages, such as C#, PowerShell commands and scripts have access to the vast resources of the .NET Framework.

- **Object orientation and an object-based pipeline**   All PowerShell commands that generate output return .NET Framework objects rather than plain text, eliminating the need for text parsing when the output of one command provides input to a second (that is, when one command is "piped" to another).

- **A consistent, discoverable command model**   All of PowerShell's commands (or "cmdlets," as they are called) use a *verb-noun* syntax, with a hyphen separating the two components. All cmdlets that read information from the system begin with *Get*; all those that write information begin with *Set*. These and other similar consistencies make the language easy to learn and understand. Each cmdlet has a help topic that can be retrieved by typing **get-help *cmdletname*** (where *cmdletname* is the name of a cmdlet). A –Whatif parameter lets you test the effect of a cmdlet before you execute it.

- **Universal scripting capability**   A PowerShell script is a text file, with the extension .ps1, containing PowerShell commands. Any commands that can be used interactively can be incorporated into a script, and scripting structures, such as looping, branching, and variables, can also be used interactively—that is, outside the context of a script.

- **A focus on administrators**   PowerShell includes features of particular interest to system administrators, such as the ability to work with remote computers; access to system resources such as files, folders, registry keys, events, and logs; and the ability to start and stop services.

- **Extensibility**   Developers can extend the PowerShell language by importing modules—packages of PowerShell commands and other items.

The following pages provide an elementary introduction to PowerShell. Our discussion focuses primarily on the use of PowerShell as an interactive command shell because PowerShell scripting is itself a book-length subject. For sources of additional information, see "Finding Additional PowerShell Resources" on page 1004. For information about running

PowerShell scripts, including the scripts on this book's companion CD, see "Running Power-Shell Scripts" on page 999.

Starting PowerShell

PowerShell 2.0 is included with all versions of Windows 7. (PowerShell 2.0 was shipped in June 2010.) You'll find a Windows PowerShell folder in the Accessories folder of your Start menu. The Start Menu folder includes a command to launch the PowerShell Integrated Scripting Environment (Windows PowerShell ISE), as well as one to launch the shell itself. The ISE is a multitabbed graphical environment of particular use for developing and debugging scripts; for more information, see "Using the PowerShell ISE" on page 1002.

The 64-bit editions of Windows 7 include both the 32-bit and 64-bit versions of PowerShell. The 32-bit version is identified on the Start menu as Windows PowerShell (x86).

As a more direct route to PowerShell, type **power** in the Start menu search box and choose Windows PowerShell from the Programs section of the search results. To launch PowerShell from a command prompt, type **powershell**. For information about optional startup parameters for PowerShell, type **powershell /?** at a command prompt.

As Figure 27-7 shows, PowerShell's default appearance differs minimally from that of Cmd.exe. The caption *Windows PowerShell* and the letters *PS* at the beginning of the command prompt may be the only details you notice.

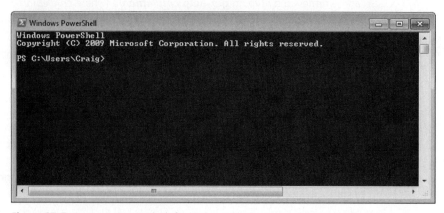

Figure 27-7 An uncustomized (default) PowerShell window looks a lot like Cmd.exe.

Personalizing PowerShell

You can customize the appearance of the PowerShell window by using many of the same techniques you would use to customize the appearance of Cmd.exe. (For details about those techniques, see "Customizing Command Prompt Windows" on page 1180.) Using the Control menu's Properties command, for example, you can change the display colors that PowerShell uses, alter the cursor size, change the font, toggle QuickEdit Mode and Insert Mode, and so on. Note, however, that PowerShell ignores the Defaults command on its Control menu. You can use your profile to tailor PowerShell's default characteristics. Your profile is a PowerShell script that is executed automatically when PowerShell is launched; for more information, see "Using Your Profile to Customize PowerShell" on page 1002.

Interacting with PowerShell

If you're an old hand at the command prompt but new to PowerShell, the first thing you might want to try is using some of Cmd.exe's familiar internal commands. You'll discover that such items—for example, *dir*, *cd*, *md*, *rd*, *pushd*, and *popd*—still work in PowerShell. Redirection symbols, such as > to send output to a file and >> to append output to a file, work as well, and you can pipe lengthy output to *more*, just as you are accustomed to doing in Cmd.exe. PowerShell uses *aliases* to map Cmd.exe commands to its own cmdlets. Thus, for example, *dir* is an alias for the PowerShell cmdlet *Get-Childitem*; *cd* is an alias for PowerShell's *Set-Location*. You can create your own aliases to simplify the typing of PowerShell commands that you use often; for details, see "Using and Creating Aliases" on page 991.

Like any other command prompt, PowerShell can be used to launch executables. Typing **regedit**, for example, launches Registry Editor; typing **taskschd** launches Task Scheduler. (Note that PowerShell also lets you work directly with the registry, without the use of Registry Editor; for details, see "Working with the Registry" on page 994.)

Using Cmdlets

The core of PowerShell 2.0's native vocabulary is a set of 236 cmdlets, each consisting of a verb, followed by a hyphen, followed by a noun—as, for example, *Start-Service*. (In this chapter, we generally follow the capitalization style used by PowerShell's help text and Microsoft's online support resources, but PowerShell itself doesn't care whether or how you use capital letters.) A cmdlet may be followed by one or more parameters; each parameter is preceded by a space and consists of a hyphen connected to the parameter's name followed by a space and the parameter's value. So, for example,

```
Get-Process -Name iexplore
```

Chapter 27

returns information about any currently running processes named iexplore:

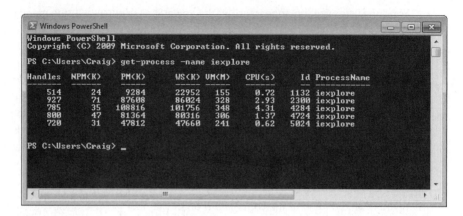

With parameters that accept multiple values, you can use a comma to separate the values. For example,

```
Get-Process -Name iexplore, winword, excel
```

would generate information about Word and Excel, as well as Internet Explorer.

Many cmdlets use positional parameters. For example, the –Name parameter for *Get-Process* is positional. PowerShell expects it to come first, so you may omit –Name and simply specify the names of the processes in which you're interested.

If you omit both the first positional parameter and its value, PowerShell typically assumes a value of *. So, for example,

```
Get-Process
```

returns information about all running processes, as shown in Figure 27-8.

In some cases, if you omit values for an initial positional parameter, PowerShell will prompt you to supply the parameter. For example, in response to

```
Get-Eventlog
```

PowerShell will do you the courtesy of prompting for the name of an event log. (Event logs are large; it wouldn't be reasonable to ask for all of them at once.)

For information about any particular cmdlet, type **get-help** followed by the cmdlet name.

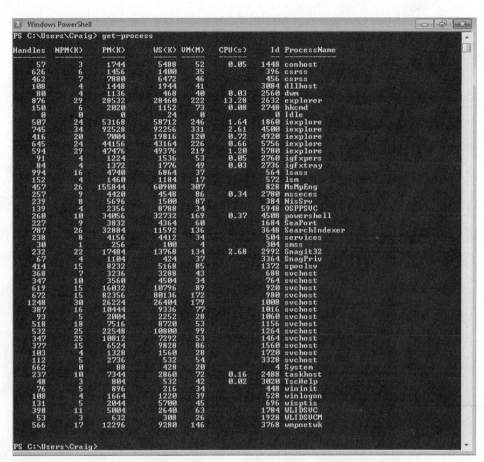

Figure 27-8 Typing *Get-Process* by itself, without parameters, produces information about all processes running on the local computer.

Using the Pipeline

The pipe operator (|) lets you supply the output of one cmdlet as input to another. You can connect as many cmdlets as you please in this manner, as long as each cmdlet to the right of a pipe operator understands the output of the cmdlet to its left. Because PowerShell cmdlets return full-fidelity .NET objects rather than text, a cmdlet to the right of a pipe operator can operate directly on properties or methods of the preceding cmdlet's output.

The following paragraphs provide examples of the use of piping to format, filter, and sort the output from various *Get-* cmdlets.

Chapter 27

Formatting Output as a List   The default output from many *Get-* cmdlets is a table that presents only some of the resultant object's properties (about as many as the width of your display is likely to accommodate). For example, the cmdlet

```
Get-Service
```

generates a three-column display that includes only the Status, Name, and DisplayName properties:

If you pipe the same output to *Format-List*,

```
Get-Service | Format-List
```

PowerShell, no longer constrained by display width, can display more of the object's properties (see Figure 27-9), including in this case such useful items as the dependencies of each service and whether the service can be paused or stopped.

```
Windows PowerShell
Copyright (C) 2009 Microsoft Corporation. All rights reserved.

PS C:\Users\Craig> get-service | format-list


Name                  : AeLookupSvc
DisplayName           : Application Experience
Status                : Stopped
DependentServices     : {}
ServicesDependedOn    : {}
CanPauseAndContinue   : False
CanShutdown           : False
CanStop               : False
ServiceType           : Win32ShareProcess

Name                  : ALG
DisplayName           : Application Layer Gateway Service
Status                : Stopped
DependentServices     : {}
ServicesDependedOn    : {}
CanPauseAndContinue   : False
CanShutdown           : False
CanStop               : False
ServiceType           : Win32OwnProcess

Name                  : AppIDSvc
DisplayName           : Application Identity
Status                : Stopped
DependentServices     : {}
ServicesDependedOn    : {AppID, CryptSvc, RpcSs}
CanPauseAndContinue   : False
CanShutdown           : False
CanStop               : False
ServiceType           : Win32ShareProcess

Name                  : Appinfo
DisplayName           : Application Information
Status                : Running
DependentServices     : {}
ServicesDependedOn    : {ProfSvc, RpcSs}
CanPauseAndContinue   : False
CanShutdown           : False
CanStop               : True
ServiceType           : Win32ShareProcess

Name                  : AppMgmt
DisplayName           : Application Management
Status                : Stopped
DependentServices     : {}
ServicesDependedOn    : {}
CanPauseAndContinue   : False
CanShutdown           : False
CanStop               : False
ServiceType           : Win32ShareProcess

Name                  : AudioEndpointBuilder
DisplayName           : Windows Audio Endpoint Builder
```

Figure 27-9 Piping a cmdlet to *Format-List* allows you to see more of a resultant object's properties.

In some cases, the *Format-List* cmdlet, with no parameters, is equivalent to *Format-List –Property* *. But this is by no means always the case. For example,

```
Get-Process | Format-List
```

returns four properties for each process: ID, Handles, CPU, and Name. Asking for all properties produces a wealth of additional information.

To generate a list of particular properties, add the –Property parameter to *Format-List* and supply a comma-separated list of the properties you want to see. To see what properties are available for the object returned by a cmdlet, pipe that cmdlet to *Get-Member*:

```
Get-Process | Get-Member -Itemtype property
```

(Omitting the –Itemtype parameter returns methods as well as properties.)

Creating a Multicolumn List with *Format-Wide*   By piping a cmdlet to *Format-Wide*, you can generate a multicolumn list displaying a single property, comparable to a List view in Windows Explorer. Use the –Column parameter to specify the number of columns you want. For example,

```
Get-Childitem hkcu:\appevents\eventlabels | Format-Wide -Column 2
```

generates a two-column list of the subkeys of HKCU:\Appevents\Eventlabels.

Formatting Output as a Table   Perhaps you want tabular output but with different properties than your cmdlet gives you by default. *Format-Table* does the trick. For example,

```
Get-Service | Format-Table -Property name, dependentservices, servicesdependedon
```

generates a table consisting of these three enumerated properties. Note that PowerShell's console output is constrained by your console width, no matter how many properties you ask to see. For results that are too wide to display, redirect output to a file (using the > operator) or try the *Out-Gridview* cmdlet, described next.

Generating an Interactive Graphical Table with *Out-Gridview*   Piping output to *Out-Gridview* generates a graphical tabular display that you can filter, sort, and copy easily into other programs, such as Excel, that accommodate tabular data. For example,

```
Get-Process | Select-Object * | Out-Gridview
```

produces output comparable to that shown in Figure 27-10. Note that in this example, *Get-Process* is piped first to *Select-Object* * because *Out-Gridview*, unlike *Format-Table*, does not include a –Property parameter. *Select-Object* * passes all properties of the object returned by *Get-Process* along the pipeline to *Out-Gridview*.

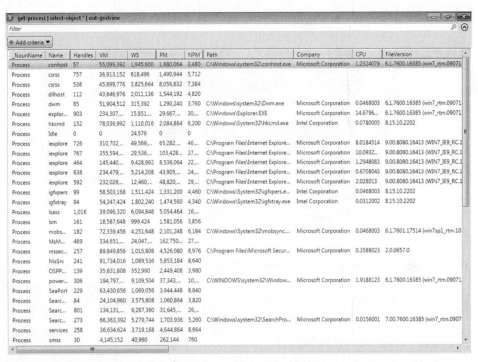

Figure 27-10 The *Out-Gridview* cmdlet produces a graphical tabular display that you can sort, filter, and copy into a spreadsheet.

You can manipulate the *Out-Gridview* display with techniques comparable to those used by many other programs:

- To sort the display, click a column heading; click a second time to reverse the sort.

- To change the position of a column, drag its heading. You can also rearrange columns by right-clicking any column head, choosing Select Columns, and then using the Move Down and Move Up buttons in the Select Columns dialog box.

- To remove columns from the display, right-click any column heading, choose Select Columns, and then use the << button in the Select Columns dialog box.

- To perform a quick filter, enter text in the line labeled *Filter*. For example, to limit the display in Figure 27-10 to processes with properties containing the word *Microsoft*, type **Microsoft** on the Filter line.

- To filter on one or more specific columns, click the Add Criteria button. In the drop-down list that appears, select check boxes for the columns on which you want to filter and then click Add. Filtering fields will appear in the area above the column headings:

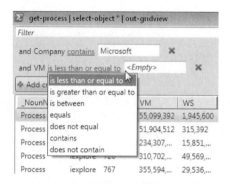

Filtering Output with *Where-Object* To filter output from a cmdlet, pipe it to the *Where-Object* cmdlet. With *Where-Object* you encapsulate filtering criteria in a script block, between curly braces. The following example filters output from *Get-Service* so that only services whose status is Stopped are displayed:

```
Get-Service | Where-Object {$_.Status -eq "Stopped"}
```

Where-Object in this example tests the value of the Status property of each object generated by *Get-Service* and returns only those whose Status property equals Stopped.

Sorting Output with *Sort-Object* The *Sort-Object* cmdlet lets you sort the output from a cmdlet, on one or more of the resultant object's properties, in a variety of useful ways. If you omit the –Property parameter, *Sort-Object* sorts on the default property. For example,

```
Get-Childitem | Sort-Object
```

sorts the contents of the current directory by Name, the default property in this case. To sort on multiple properties, follow –Property with a comma-separated list. *Sort-Object* sorts on the first named property first, sorting items with identical first properties by the second property, and so on. Sorts are ascending by default; to sort in descending order, add the parameter –Descending.

By piping *Sort-Object* to *Select-Object* you can do such things as returning the largest or smallest *n* items in a resultant object. For example,

```
Get-Process | Sort-Object -Property WS | Select-Object -Last 10
```

returns the processes with the 10 largest values of the working set (WS) property. Using –First 10 instead of –Last 10 would give you the items with the smallest values.

Piping Output to the Printer   To redirect output to the default printer, pipe it to *Out-Printer*. To use a nondefault printer, specify its name, in quotation marks, after *Out-Printer*. For example,

```
Get-Content G:\Users\Craig\Documents\Music\Sonata.sib | Out-Printer "Microsoft XPS
Document Writer"
```

sends the content of G:\Users\Craig\Documents\Music\Sonata.sib to the device named Microsoft XPS Document Writer.

Using PowerShell Features to Simplify Keyboard Entry

PowerShell is a wordy language and doesn't take kindly to misspelling. Fortunately, it includes many features to streamline and simplify the task of formulating acceptable commands.

Using and Creating Aliases   An alias is an alternative formulation for a cmdlet. As mentioned earlier, PowerShell uses aliases to translate Cmd.exe commands to its own native tongue—for example, *cd* to *Set-Location*. But it includes a great many more simply for your typing convenience; *gsv*, for example, is an alias for *Get-Service*. And you can create aliases of your own.

To see what aliases are currently available (including any that you have created yourself during the current session), type **get-alias**. To see if an alias is available for a particular cmdlet, pipe *Get-Alias* to *Where-Object*, like this:

```
Get-Alias | Where-Object { $_.definition -eq "Set-Variable" }
```

This particular command string inquires if an alias is available for the *Set-Variable* cmdlet. If you type this, you'll discover that PowerShell offers two—*sv* and *set*.

To create a new alias, type **set-alias *name value***, where *name* is the alias and *value* is a cmdlet, function, executable program, or script. If *name* already exists as an alias, *Set-Alias* redefines it. If *value* is not valid, PowerShell won't bother you with an error message—until you try to use the alias.

Aliases that you create are valid for the current session only. To make them available permanently, include them in your profile. See "Using Your Profile to Customize PowerShell" on page 1002.

Chapter 27

Abbreviating Parameter Names   Aliases are dandy for cmdlets, but they're no help for parameter names. Fortunately, PowerShell allows you to abbreviate such names. The commands *Get-Process -name iexplore* and *Get-Process -n iexplore* are equivalent. As soon as you've typed enough of a parameter name to let PowerShell recognize it unambiguously, you can give your fingers a rest. And, of course, you can combine aliases with parameter abbreviations to further lighten your load.

Using Tab Expansion   As a further convenience, PowerShell lets you complete the names of files, cmdlets, or parameters by pressing Tab. Type part of a name, press Tab, and Power-Shell presents the first potential completion. Continue pressing Tab to cycle through all the possibilities. Note, however, that Tab expansion works only with the noun portion of a cmdlet; type the verb and the hyphen, and then you can use Tab expansion for the noun.

Using Wildcards and Regular Expressions   Like all its Windows-shell predecessors, Power-Shell supports the * and ? wildcards, the former standing in for any combination of zero or more characters, the latter for any single character. PowerShell also provides a vast panoply of "regular expressions" for matching character strings. For details about regular expressions in PowerShell, type **Get-Help about_regular_expressions**.

Recalling Commands from the Command History   PowerShell maintains a history of your recent commands, which makes it easy to reuse (or edit and reuse) a command that you've already entered. To see the history, type **get-history**. Each item in the history is identified by an ID number. Type **invoke-history *ID*** to bring an item to the command line. On the command line, you can edit an item before executing it. With the exception of Alt+F7, the editing keys available in Cmd.exe work the same way in PowerShell. For a list of those editing keys, see Table B-1 on page 1173.

The number of history items retained in a PowerShell session is defined by the automatic variable $MaximumHistoryCount. By default, that variable is set to 64. If you find you need more, you can assign a larger number to the variable. For example, to double the default for the current session, type **$MaximumHistoryCount = 128**. To change the history size for all sessions, add a variable assignment to your profile. For more information, see "Using Your Profile to Customize PowerShell" on page 1002.

Using PowerShell Providers for Access to File System and Registry Data

PowerShell includes a set of built-in *providers* that give you access to various kinds of data stores. Providers are .NET Framework–based programs, and their data is exposed in the form of *drives*, comparable to familiar file-system drives. Thus, for example, you can access a key in the HKLM registry hive with a path structure similar to that of a file-system folder; for example, the path HKLM:\Hardware\ACPI specifies the ACPI key of the Hardware key of the HKLM hive. Or, to use a quite different example, you can use the command *Get-Childitem env:* to get a list of current environment variables and their values.

Table 27-1 lists PowerShell's built-in providers. For more information about providers, type **Get-Help about_Providers**.

Table 27-1 Built-in Providers

Provider	Drive	Data Store
Alias	Alias	Currently defined aliases
Certificate	Cert	X509 certificates for digital signatures
Environment	Env	Windows environment variables
FileSystem	(varies)	File-system drives, directories, and files
Function	Function	PowerShell functions
Registry	HKLM, HKCU	HKLM and HKCU registry hives
Variable	Variable	PowerShell variables
WSMan	WSMan	WS-Management configuration information

The following paragraphs provide some basic information about working with the file system and registry.

Working with the File System For very simple file-system operations, you might find that familiar Cmd.exe commands are adequate and easier to use than PowerShell cmdlets. The built-in aliases listed in Table 27-2 let you stick with time-honored methods. PowerShell supports the familiar single period (.) and double period (..) symbols for the current and parent directories, and it includes a built-in variable, $Home, that represents your home directory (equivalent to the HOMEPATH environment variable).

Table 27-2 File-System Aliases

Alias	PowerShell Cmdlet
cd	*Set-Location*
chdir	*Set-Location*
copy	*Copy-Item*
del	*Remove-Item*
dir	*Get-Childitem*
move	*Move-Item*
md, mkdir	*New-Item*
rd, rmdir	*Remove-Item*
type	*Get-Content*

Chapter 27

The PowerShell cmdlets, however, include valuable optional parameters:

- **–Confirm** and **–Whatif**   The –Confirm parameter, used with *Copy-Item, Move-Item, Remove-Item,* or *Clear-Content,* causes PowerShell to display a confirmation prompt before executing the command. (*Clear-Content* can be used to erase the contents of a file.) If you use the –Whatif parameter, PowerShell shows you the result of a command without executing it.

- **–Credential**   Use the –Credential parameter to supply security credentials for a command that requires them. Follow –Credential with the name of a user, within double quotation marks. PowerShell will prompt for a password.

- **–Exclude**   The –Exclude parameter allows you to make exceptions. For example, *Copy-Item directory1*.* directory2 –Exclude *.log* copies everything except *.log from Directory1 to Directory2.

- **–Recurse**   The –Recurse parameter causes a command to operate on subfolders of a specified path. For example, *Remove-Item x:\garbagefolder*.* –Recurse* deletes everything from X:\Garbagefolder, including files contained within that folder's subfolders.

- **–Include**   The –Include parameter, used in conjunction with –Recurse, allows you to restrict the scope of a command. For example, *Get-Childitem g:\users\craig\documents* –Recurse –Include *.xlsx* restricts a recursive listing of G:\Users\Craig\Documents to files with the extension .xlsx.

- **–Force**   The –Force parameter causes a command to operate on items that are not ordinarily accessible, such as hidden and system files.

For detailed information about using these parameters with *Set-Location, Get-Childitem, Move-Item, Copy-Item, Get-Content, New-Item, Remove-Item,* or *Get-Acl,* type **get-help cmdletname**.

Working with the Registry   The built-in registry provider provides drives for two registry hives, HKLM and HKCU. To change the working location to either of these, type **set-location hklm:** or **set-location hkcu:**. Use standard path notation to navigate to particular subkeys, but enclose paths that include spaces in quotation marks; for example, *set-location "hkcu:\control panel\accessibility"*.

To display the immediate subkeys of a registry key, use *Get-Childitem*. As Figure 27-11 shows, the object returned includes the Subkey Count (SKC) and Value Count (VC) properties. Undefined default values are not included in Value Count. In the example, the HKCU:\

control panel\powercfg key includes subkeys named GlobalPowerPolicy and PowerPolicies. The former has one value (Policies) and no subkeys; the latter has six subkeys.

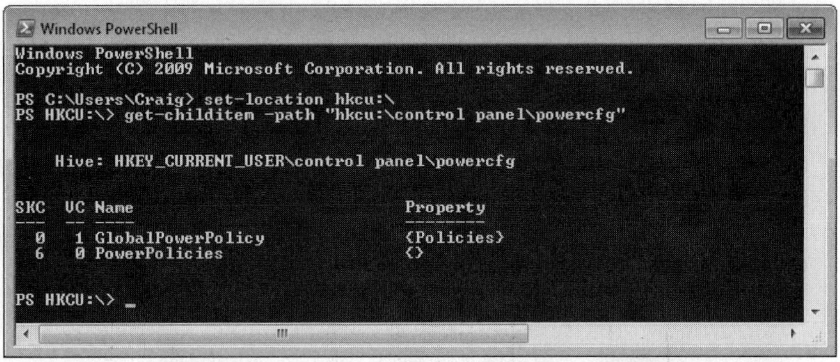

```
Windows PowerShell
Copyright (C) 2009 Microsoft Corporation. All rights reserved.

PS C:\Users\Craig> set-location hkcu:\
PS HKCU:\> get-childitem -path "hkcu:\control panel\powercfg"


    Hive: HKEY_CURRENT_USER\control panel\powercfg


SKC  VC Name                           Property
---  -- ----                           --------
  0   1 GlobalPowerPolicy              {Policies}
  6   0 PowerPolicies                  {}


PS HKCU:\> _
```

Figure 27-11 The registry object returned by *Get-Childitem* includes Subkey Count (SKC) and Value Count (VC) properties.

To display information about all subkeys of a key, use *Get-Childitem*. For example,

```
Get-Childitem -Path hkcu:\software\microsoft
```

returns information about all the subkeys of HKCU:\Software\Microsoft.

To add a key to the registry, use *New-Item*. For example,

```
New-Item -Path hkcu:\software\mynewkey
```

adds the key *mynewkey* to HKCU:\Software. To remove this key, type **remove-item –path hkcu:\software\mynewkey**.

To copy a key, use *Copy-Item* and specify the source and destination paths; like this, for example,

```
Copy-Item -Path hkcu:\software\mykey hkcu:\software\copyofmykey
```

To move a key, use *Move-Item*. The command

```
Move-Item -Path hkcu:\software\mykey -Destination hkcu:\software\myrelocatedkey
```

copies all properties and subkeys associated with HKCU:\Software\Mykey to HKCU:\Software\Myrelocatedkey and deletes HKCU:\Software\Mykey.

Chapter 27

To display the security descriptor associated with a key, use *Get-Acl*. To see all the properties of the security descriptor, pipe this to *Format-List –Property* *. For example,

```
Get-Acl -Path hkcu:\software\microsoft | Format-List -Property *
```

generates a display comparable to this:

For more information about working with the registry, type **get-help registry**.

Discovering PowerShell

PowerShell provides plenty of resources to help you learn as you go. You can display help information about any cmdlet by typing **get-help** *cmdletname*. For example, to read help about *Get-Help*, type **get-help get-help**. If you omit the first *get*, PowerShell helpfully pipes the help text to *more*. So, for example, if you type **help get-help**, PowerShell will pause the output after each screenful.

Among the useful parameters for *Get-Help* are the following:

- **–Examples**   To display only the name, synopsis, and examples associated with a particular help text, add the –Examples parameter.

- **–Parameter**   To get help for a particular parameter associated with a cmdlet, include –Parameter. Specify the parameter name in quotation marks.

- **–Detailed**   To get the description, syntax, and parameter details for a cmdlet, as well as a set of examples, use the –Detailed parameter. (Without this parameter, the examples are omitted; with –Examples, the syntax information is omitted.)

- **–Full**   For the works, including information about input and output object types and additional notes, specify –Full.

- **–Online**   For the latest information that Microsoft has, including additions or corrections to the native output of *Get-Help*, specify –Online. The relevant information, from the Microsoft TechNet Script Center, will appear in your browser.

PowerShell includes a compiled HTML (.chm) help file, which you can run from the Jump List that appears on the recent items or pinned items section of your Start menu (or on the taskbar if you pin PowerShell there). But the information made available via the –Online parameter is more current and more accurate than that provided in the .chm file. For direct access to the root of Microsoft TechNet's PowerShell information, point your browser to *w7io.com/22701*.

Getting Help on Conceptual Topics

The PowerShell help resources include a number of entries on conceptual topics, such as operators, parameters, variables, and pipelines. These topics all begin with *about*. You can generate a list by typing **get-help about*** or **get-help –category "helpfile"** (see Figure 27-12). To read information about aliases, for example, type **get-help about_aliases**. Note that the TechNet site described in the previous section also includes these conceptual topics.

Chapter 27

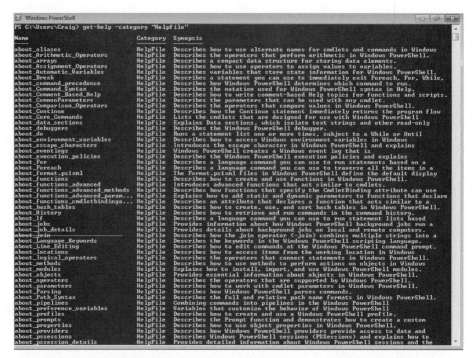

Figure 27-12 The PowerShell help system includes a sizable number of conceptual topics, all beginning with the word *about*.

Finding the Right Cmdlet to Use

The *Get-Command* cmdlet can help you figure out which cmdlet is the right one to use for a given task. Type **get-command** with no arguments to get the names and definitions of all available cmdlets, functions, and aliases. *Get-Command* can also give you information about non-PowerShell executables. If you type **get-command ***, for example, you'll get a huge list including all files in all folders included in your current Path environment variable.

Either global list (with or without the non-PowerShell executables) is likely to be less than useful when you just want to know which cmdlets are available for use with a particular object. To get such a focused list, add the –Noun parameter. For example, type **get-command –noun eventlog** to get a list of the cmdlets that use that noun; you'll be rewarded with the names and definitions of *Clear-Eventlog*, *Get-Eventlog*, *Limit-Eventlog*, *New-Eventlog*, *Remove-Eventlog*, *Show-Eventlog*, and *Write-Eventlog*. You can get a list focused similarly on a particular verb by using the –Verb parameter.

Scripting with PowerShell

A PowerShell script is a text file with the extension .ps1. You can create a script in any plain text editor (Notepad will do fine), or you can use the Interactive Scripting Environment (ISE) that comes with PowerShell 2.0. For details about the latter, see "Using the PowerShell ISE" on page 1002.

Anything that you do interactively with PowerShell you can also do in a script. The reverse is also true; you can take lines from a script, including those that involve looping or branching structures, and execute them individually outside the context of a script. For example, if you type

```
For ($i=1; $i -le 5; $i++}
{
    "Hello, World"
}
```

at the PowerShell command prompt, PowerShell will perform the familiar greeting five times.

Using PowerShell's history feature, you can easily transfer commands that you have used interactively into a script. That way you can easily test to see what works and how it works before committing text to a .ps1 file.

For example, the command

```
Get-History | Foreach-Object { $_.commandline } >> g:\scripts\mynewscript.ps1
```

appends the Commandline property from each item in your current history to the file G:\Scripts\Mynewscript.ps1. (If the path doesn't exist, the command returns an error.) Once you have transferred your history to Mynewscript.ps1 in this manner, you can edit it in Notepad by typing **notepad g:\scripts\mynewscript.ps1**.

Running PowerShell Scripts

Although files with the extension .ps1 are executable PowerShell scripts, running one is not quite as straightforward as double-clicking a .bat file. In the first place, if you double-click a .ps1 file in Windows Explorer, you'll get an Open File—Security Warning dialog box, from which the only forward step leads to Notepad. In effect, the default action for a PowerShell script in Windows Explorer is Edit.

Second, the first time you try to run a script by typing its name at the PowerShell command prompt, you might well see a distressing message like this:

When you see such a message, displayed in red letters and with possibly unwelcome detail, PowerShell has declined to run your script "because the execution of scripts is disabled on this system." You need to change PowerShell's "execution policy" (which has nothing to do with capital punishment); more about that in a moment.

Third, even after you've cleared the execution-policy hurdle, you might still be rebuffed if you try to run a script stored in the current directory. That's because PowerShell requires a full path specification—even when the item you're running is stored in the current directory. For example, to run Displayprocessor.ps1, which resides in the current directory, you must type **.\displayprocessor**.

Getting and Setting the Execution Policy   PowerShell's power can be used for evil ends. The majority of Windows users will never run PowerShell, but many will have .ps1 files lying about on their system or will download them inadvertently. To protect you from malice, PowerShell disables script execution until you explicitly enable it. Enabling execution requires a change to the execution policy.

Note that your profile script (if you have one) is subject to the same execution policy as any other script. (See "Using Your Profile to Customize PowerShell" on page 1002.) Therefore, it's pointless to set an execution policy by means of a profile script; that script itself will not run until you've enabled script execution elsewhere.

The following execution policies, listed here from least permissive to most, are available:

- **Restricted**   The default policy. No scripts are allowed to run.

- **AllSigned**   Any script signed by a trusted publisher is allowed to run. PowerShell presents a confirmation prompt before running a script signed by a publisher that you have not designated as "trusted."

- **RemoteSigned**   Scripts from local sources can run. Scripts downloaded from the Internet (including scripts that originated as e-mail or instant-messaging attachments) can run if signed by a trusted publisher.

- **Unrestricted**   All scripts can run, but PowerShell presents a confirmation prompt before running a script from a remote source.

- **Bypass**   All scripts are allowed to run.

Execution policies can be set separately for the following scopes:

- **Process**   Affects the current PowerShell session only. The execution policy is stored in memory and lost at the end of the session.

- **CurrentUser**   The execution policy is stored in a subkey of HKCU and applies to the current user only. The setting is retained between PowerShell sessions.

- **LocalMachine**   The execution policy is stored in a subkey of HKLM and applies to all users at this computer. The setting is retained between PowerShell sessions.

If policies are set at two or more of these scopes, the Process policy takes precedence over the CurrentUser policy, which takes precedence over the LocalMachine policy. Execution policy can also be set via Group Policy, however, and settings made in that manner trump any of the foregoing scopes. (Group Policy settings can be made in either the Computer Configuration or User Configuration node; a Computer Configuration setting trumps any other.)

To see the execution policies in effect at all scopes, type **get-executionpolicy –list**.

To set an execution policy, use *Set-ExecutionPolicy*. To set a policy at the LocalMachine scope, you need to be running PowerShell with administrative privileges. (On the Start menu, right-click Windows PowerShell and choose Run As Administrator.)

The default scope for *Set-ExecutionPolicy* is LocalMachine, so if you're planning to apply a policy to all users at your computer, you can omit the –Scope parameter. For example, if you're comfortable disabling all of PowerShell's script-execution security measures, including warning prompts, you can type **setexecutionpolicy bypass**. For a slightly more protective environment, type **setexecutionpolicy unrestricted**.

To set a policy at the CurrentUser or Process scope, add –Scope followed by CurrentUser or Process. Note that you can also set an execution policy at the Process scope by adding an –Executionpolicy argument to a command that launches PowerShell. For example, from a command prompt in Cmd.exe, in PowerShell, or on the Start menu, you could type **powershell –executionpolicy unrestricted** to launch PowerShell with an Unrestricted execution policy at the Process scope.

To remove an execution policy from a particular scope, set that scope's policy to Undefined. For example, if you have set a Process policy to, say, Bypass, and you would like PowerShell

Chapter 27

to revert to the policy at the next level of precedence (CurrentUser, if a policy is set there, or LocalMachine, if not), type **set-executionpolicy undefined –scope process**.

Using Your Profile to Customize PowerShell

Your profile is a script that PowerShell executes at the beginning of each session. You can use it to tailor your PowerShell environment to your preferences. Your profile must have the following path and file name:

$Home\Documents\WindowsPowerShell\Profile.ps1

where $Home is a system-generated PowerShell variable corresponding to the environment variable *UserProfile*. You can see where this is on your system by typing **$profile**, and you can edit an existing profile by typing **notepad $profile**. If you have not yet created a profile, you can type the following:

```
if (!(test-path $profile)){New-Item -Type file -Path $profile -Force}
```

PowerShell will create the file for you in the appropriate folder. Then you can type **notepad $profile** to edit the blank file.

You can use your profile to customize PowerShell in a variety of ways. Possibilities to consider include changing the default prompt and creating new aliases.

PowerShell's prompt is derived from a built-in function called Prompt. You can overwrite that function with your own. For example, the following function

```
Function prompt {"PS [$env:computername] $(Get-Date) > "}
```

replaces the built-in PowerShell prompt with the letters *PS*, followed by your computer name, followed by the current date and time. For more information about PowerShell prompts, type **get-help about_prompts**.

To add new aliases to the ones that PowerShell already offers, simply include *Set-Alias* statements in your profile. (See "Using and Creating Aliases" on page 991.)

Using the PowerShell ISE

A feature introduced with PowerShell 2.0 allows you to issue commands and work with scripts in a graphical environment. This Integrated Scripting Environment (ISE), shown in Figure 27-13, includes a command pane, a script pane, and an output pane. The output pane displays the results of any commands you issue in the command pane or any scripts that you run in the script pane.

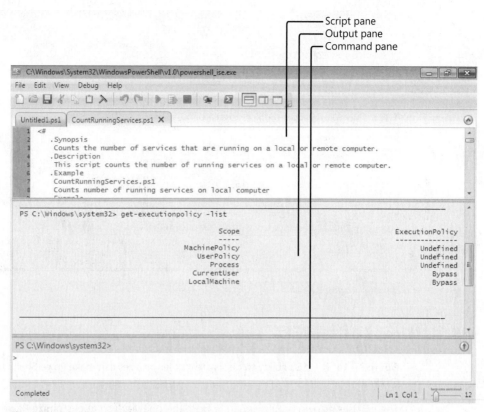

Figure 27-13 The ISE comes with separate panes for issuing commands and for running (or editing or debugging) scripts. Output from commands or scripts appears in the output pane.

The ISE supports multiple tabs, so you can open several scripts at once. Choose File, New to open a new blank tab (for example, to write a new script) or File, Open to open an existing script in a new tab. To run the current script, choose Run/Continue from the Debug menu, press F5, or click the green arrow in the middle of the toolbar. Other commands on the Debug menu allow you to set and remove breakpoints and step through execution.

The ISE offers all the usual amenities of a graphical environment. You can resize and rearrange the panes, for example. You can use the View menu's Zoom commands (or adjust the slider in the lower right corner of the window) to make the text display larger or smaller. (See Figure 27-14.) And you can easily select and copy text from one pane to another or from the ISE to another application.

Chapter 27

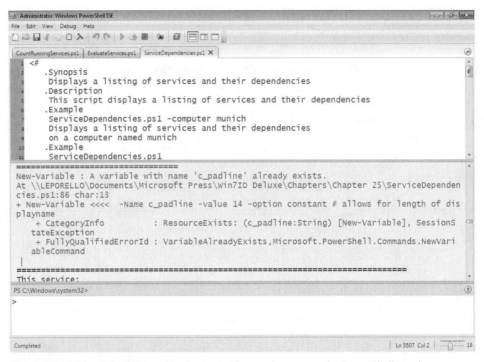

Figure 27-14 The ISE's ability to display text at larger sizes can make PowerShell's verbose error messages easier to read.

The ISE uses its own profile, separate from the one you use to customize PowerShell itself. The path and file name are as follows:

$Home\Documents\WindowsPowerShell\ProfileISE.ps1

and you create the file by typing:

```
if(!(Test-Path $profile)){New-Item -Type file -Path $profile -Force}
```

Finding Additional PowerShell Resources

This chapter's discussion of PowerShell has barely nicked the surface. For further exploration, we recommend the following:

- *Windows PowerShell 2.0 Best Practices*, by Ed Wilson with the Windows PowerShell Teams at Microsoft (Microsoft Press, 2010)

- *Windows PowerShell Cookbook*, Second Edition, by Lee Holmes (O'Reilly Media, 2010)

- "Scripting with Windows PowerShell" (part of the Microsoft TechNet Script Center) at *w7io.com/22702*

- The "Hey, Scripting Guy!" blog at *w7io.com/22703*

- "Windows PowerShell Getting Started Guide" (part of MSDN Library) at *w7io.com/22704*

Chapter 27

Troubleshooting Windows Errors and Crashes

T o paraphrase a popular bumper sticker from an earlier era, stuff happens. Although occurrences are far fewer with each new version of Windows, applications hang (stop responding) or crash (shut down unexpectedly). Once in a while, a feature of Windows walks off the job without warning. And on rare occasions, the grim BSOD (the "blue screen of death," more formally known as a Stop error or bugcheck) arrives, bringing your whole system to a halt.

In a fully debugged, perfect world, such occurrences would never darken your computer screen. But you don't live there, and neither do we. So the prudent course is to prepare for the unexpected—by making regular backups (including, if possible, a complete image backup of your system drive), letting the System Protection program create restore points regularly, keeping Windows Update enabled, and learning to use the other tools that Windows provides for error diagnosis and recovery. Those tools are the subject of this chapter.

For information about creating regular backups and image backups, see "Using the Windows Backup Program" on page 436. For information about System Protection, see "Configuring System Protection Options" on page 461.

What's in Your Edition?

The troubleshooting information in this chapter applies equally to all editions of Windows 7.

Reporting Problems and Finding Solutions

Often an early indication that something is amiss is an error message informing you that an application is "not responding"—as if you hadn't figured that out already. But this can be taken as a positive sign because it means that Windows Error Reporting is going into action. Windows Error Reporting (WER) is a feature that can report problem information to Microsoft. (In fact, although the service and programs that enable the feature are called Windows Error Reporting, the term you're more likely to see in Windows is *problem reporting*.) Microsoft makes this information available to the developers of the program that caused the error (whether it's from Microsoft or from another vendor), allowing them to see which errors occur most frequently and, ultimately, to develop fixes for the problems.

Windows Error Reporting has been streamlined and improved in the most recent versions of Windows. In Windows XP, the system was essentially manual; when an error occurred, you were invited to send a report to Microsoft. Following up an error report to see if a solution had become available was a cumbersome, discouraging process.

In Windows 7, you can automate this entire reporting and follow-up process. The salient features of Windows Error Reporting in Windows 7 are as follows:

- You now have the option of configuring Windows Error Reporting to transmit basic information to Microsoft automatically when an error occurs.

- You can configure Windows Error Reporting to transmit a more detailed problem report (but not personally identifiable information) automatically when the system requests it. Or you can provide this additional information on a case-by-case basis.

- You can configure Windows Error Reporting to notify you automatically when an error occurs for which a solution is available.

- Windows Error Reporting maintains a history of errors on your system. You can use this to review dates and events and to see what information has been sent to Microsoft. More importantly, you can use the history to check periodically for new solutions that might have been developed for problems that have occurred in the past.

In addition to the improvements in Windows Error Reporting, Windows offers application developers a set of application recovery and restart functions that allow them to respond more gracefully to hangs and crashes. An application written with these functions will probably respond to a crash by restarting and reopening the document you were working on. If you use Microsoft Office 2007 or later, you might already have seen these recovery and restart features in action. As time goes by, you can expect to see more and more programs that take advantage of these features.

Understanding Windows Error Reporting and Privacy

The information that Windows Error Reporting transmits to Microsoft is intended to help the company improve its product reliability. Microsoft engineers use this information for solving problems and making improvements, both to Windows and to Microsoft applications, such as Microsoft Office. In the past, a large number of the fixes that arrived in Windows service packs were the result of submitted error reports. In addition, Windows Error Reporting information involving a third-party application is available to that application's publisher so that its engineers can fix problems.

The basic report that Windows Error Reporting transmits typically includes information such as the application name and version, module name and version, exception (error) code, and offset. The likelihood that any of these items will convey personally identifiable information is essentially nil. The process does transmit your IP address to a Microsoft server, but Microsoft's privacy statement asserts that the IP address is used only to generate aggregate statistics, not to identify you.

If the Windows Error Reporting server requests additional information, that information will consist of one or more files, such as log files, temporary files, and memory dump files. Depending on the types of files and your problem reporting settings, Windows might display a dialog box that asks your permission to send the files; you can click View Details to see the names of the files. It is not impossible that one or more of these files might include some data that could be used to identify you. If you are concerned about that possibility, you can use a text editor, such as Notepad, to inspect the files before you make a decision about whether to send them. (You can't open the files from within the Windows Error Reporting dialog box, but you can navigate to them via Windows Explorer before responding to the dialog box.)

> **Note**
> Regardless of your settings for Windows Error Reporting, it never uploads data files that potentially contain personally identifiable data without your explicit consent.

If privacy is a major concern, you should, of course, read Microsoft's privacy statement. To find it, open Action Center (easiest way: click its flag icon in the notification area and click Open Action Center), click the arrow next to Maintenance to expand the category, and click the Privacy Policy link. Or simply type **privacy** in the Start menu search box and then click View The Microsoft Error Reporting Privacy Statement Online.

Understanding the Windows Error Reporting Process

Here is a blow-by-blow description of how Windows Error Reporting responds to a hang, crash, or Stop error:

1. Windows Error Reporting gathers the basic information (program name and version, module name and version, and so on) and either transmits this to Microsoft or requests your permission to do so, depending on how you have configured the system. You might see a dialog box similar to the one shown in Figure 28-1.

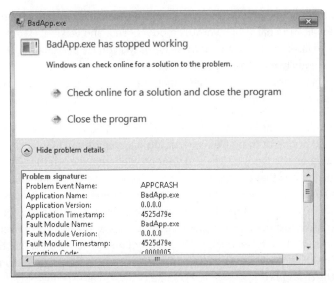

Figure 28-1 To display the information that will be sent (with your approval), click Show Problem Details.

2. If you click Check Online For A Solution And Close The Program (or if you have configured Windows Error Reporting to check online automatically), the Microsoft server checks to see if the error has resulted from a known problem. You might see something like this:

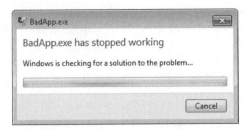

3. If the problem is known and a solution is available, the server sends this information to Windows Error Reporting, which displays it to you. If the problem is known but a

solution is still in development, the server reports that. It might also send a request for additional information.

4. If the server has requested more information, Windows Error Reporting gathers the information and requests your permission to transmit it.

5. The application that generated the error restarts if it can.

> **Note**
>
> BadApp.exe, which caused the error depicted in the preceding illustrations, is a harmless testing tool that you can download at no charge from *w7io.com/2301*.

For another approach to troubleshooting a program that reports it is "not responding," see "Troubleshooting Hangs and Other Problems with Resource Monitor" on page 1021.

Setting Windows Error Reporting Options

To configure the behavior of Windows Error Reporting, open Action Center. In Action Center's left pane, click Change Action Center Settings. Then click Problem Reporting Settings. (Alternatively, in the Start menu search box type **problem** and then click Choose How To Report Problems.) These steps take you to Problem Report Settings, shown in Figure 28-2.

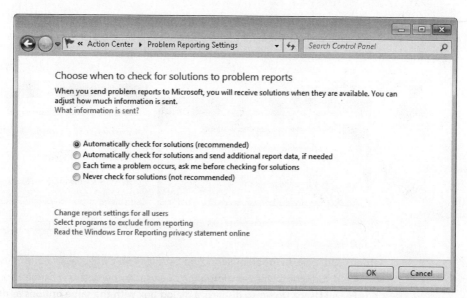

Figure 28-2 The initial setting depends on an option you choose during Windows setup and (if you didn't select the highest option at that time) the first time you open Action Center.

Select one of the four options:

- **Automatically Check For Solutions (Recommended)**   If you select this option, Windows Error Reporting sends basic information to Microsoft whenever a hang or crash occurs. If the server requests additional information, Windows Error Reporting displays a dialog box asking for permission to send the additional information. If you don't click Send Information in that dialog box, no additional data is sent.

- **Automatically Check For Solutions And Send Additional Report Data, If Needed**   With this option, Windows Error Reporting sends basic information to Microsoft whenever a hang or crash occurs. If the server requests additional information that does not contain any personally identifiable information (such as a mini dump), Windows Error Reporting sends that information automatically. If the request for additional information includes files that are more likely to contain personally identifiable information (such as a kernel memory dump), Windows Error Reporting displays a dialog box asking you for permission to send the additional information.

- **Each Time A Problem Occurs, Ask Me Before Checking For Solutions**   If a crash or hang occurs while this option is selected, Windows Error Reporting displays a dialog box similar to the one shown earlier in Figure 28-1. You must click Check Online For A Solution And Close The Program to send any information to Microsoft. If the server requests additional information, you'll be prompted again for your consent to send that information.

- **Never Check For Solutions (Not Recommended)**   This setting disables Windows Error Reporting. A crash or a hang produces a simple dialog box with few choices, similar to those shown here, and no information is sent to Microsoft.

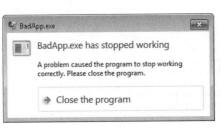
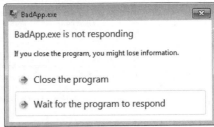

> **Note**
>
> Settings you make in Problem Reporting Settings apply only to the current user account. If your computer has more than one user account, click Change Report Settings For All Users. Doing so displays a dialog box with the same options as described above, allowing you to apply the same setting for all user accounts.

Although most people are understandably reluctant to send information to a faceless corporation, remember that this is a two-way street. You're sending information about a problem, and there's a good chance that, in return, you'll receive a solution to the problem, as explained in the next section. (Remember too that the engineers who analyze the problem information to develop solutions are not faceless!)

If you are developing an application yourself (or testing one in development), you probably don't want to deal with error-reporting prompts in any way when that application hangs or crashes. You can exclude particular programs from Windows Error Reporting's scrutiny. Click Select Programs To Exclude From Reporting, and in the ensuing dialog box specify the programs you don't want to report on.

Checking for Solutions to Problems

When Windows encounters an error such as a program crash or hang and you allow Windows Error Reporting to send a report, it also looks to see if a solution exists for the problem and reports its findings. If you miss that opportunity to investigate the solution, you'll have others. Action Center is on the lookout for reported problems, and when it finds one it displays a message that's visible by clicking Action Center's notification area icon. Open Action Center to see a complete list of maintenance-related problems, along with links to view more information (including, in some cases, a solution to the problem), as shown in Figure 28-3.

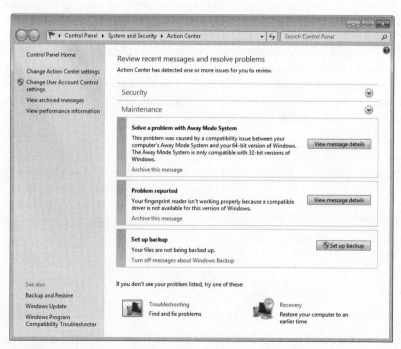

Figure 28-3 Problems are flagged with a yellow bar under the Maintenance heading.

The solution page, if one exists, typically provides information about how to implement the solution that Windows has found and includes a link to the provider of the misbehaving program or device where you can download a fix to the problem or learn more about it. A sample is shown here.

Compatibility issue between your fingerprint reader and Windows

Your fingerprint reader is not compatible with this version of Windows.
The model name of your fingerprint reader is Microsoft Fingerprint Reader.
➜ Click to go to the Microsoft Corporation website for more information and support options
▸ Which version of Windows am I using?

Don't assume because an item isn't marked *Solution Available* that it has no solution. To check for possible solutions to all the items in your problem history, open Action Center, and click the arrow to the right of Maintenance to expand the category. Then, under the heading Check For Solutions To Problem Reports, click Check For Solutions. After a moment or two, the new solutions appear in Action Center, or a dialog box appears to let you know that no new solutions are available.

Reviewing the Problem History

If you don't immediately act on this information, you can do so later. Windows Error Reporting maintains a history of the untoward events it has witnessed on your system. To review the log, in the Start menu search box or in Control Panel, type **history** and then click View All Problem Reports. Figure 28-4 shows a portion of the error history for a computer that has been heavily used in a production environment.

If the words *Solution Available* appear in the Status column for an item, right-click that item and choose View Solution from the shortcut menu. Note also that the right-click menu includes commands to group the entries in the list of problem reports by source (the default view, shown in Figure 28-4), summary, date, or status—or you can choose Ungroup to see the entire, uncategorized list. Grouped or not, you can sort by any field by clicking a column heading.

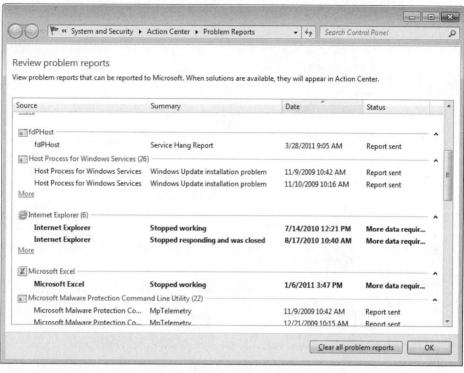

Figure 28-4 Problem Reports displays only the first two reports in each group; click More to see others.

You can see a more detailed report about any event in this log by double-clicking the event. The details might or might not be meaningful to you, but they could be helpful to a support technician. In the following report, for example, the problem description—"Windows Update installation problem"—probably tells you nothing that you didn't already know. On the other hand, the version and other details could be useful. And in many cases, the Description field is written clearly enough to provide news you can potentially use.

Chapter 28

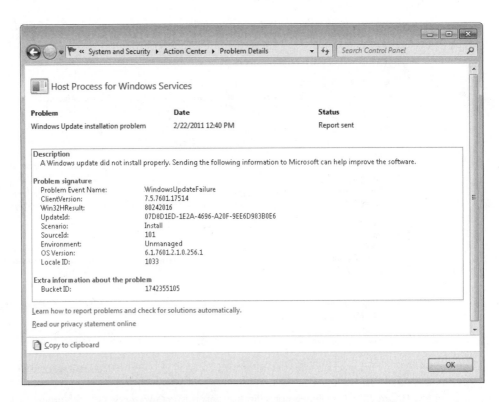

Curious about the item called Bucket ID? Microsoft sorts error reports received through Windows Error Reporting into virtual "buckets." A bucket is a unique identifier for all instances of a specific error associated with a particular version of a driver or application.

Using Troubleshooters to Solve Problems

Not all the problems you might encounter relate to calamitous events such as those that cause Windows Error Reporting to spring into action. To address a wide variety of other types of problems, big and small, Windows 7 includes a library of troubleshooting wizards. You can see a list of them by opening Action Center and clicking Troubleshooting, as shown in Figure 28-5.

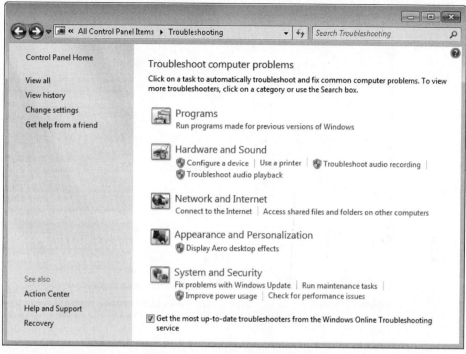

Figure 28-5 Each of the troubleshooters launches an interactive wizard that can identify and resolve common problems.

The troubleshooter system is designed to be extensible so that software developers, corporate help desks, and others can create additional troubleshooters. And, if you select the box at the bottom of the Troubleshooting window, Windows uses updated versions of the in-box troubleshooters when available. Other troubleshooters might be available online; click View All to see a complete list.

A troubleshooter might lead you through several steps and ask you to check various things before culminating in a troubleshooting report similar to the one shown in Figure 28-6.

You can explore the details of the troubleshooting report upon its completion or at any time later. In the Troubleshooting control panel (shown in Figure 28-5), click View History.

Figure 28-6 Each bit of light blue text in the troubleshooting report is a link to more detailed information. Black arrows (not shown here) expand the amount of information shown when clicked.

INSIDE OUT Microsoft Fix it provides another self-repair option

Using technology similar to the troubleshooting packs in Windows 7, Microsoft Fix it provides online configuration settings and solutions to a variety of problems. You can see a simple example in Microsoft Support article 299357 (*w7io.com/299357*), in which clicking the Microsoft Fix It button performs the steps necessary to reset your computer's TCP/IP connection. You can learn more about Microsoft Fix it in the team blog at *w7io.com/2302*.

Using Problem Steps Recorder to Get Help

Sometimes Windows Error Reporting doesn't find a solution for a problem you're having and the troubleshooter is unable to solve it. Although Windows provides many other tools—as explained in the rest of this chapter—you might decide instead to use your "phone a friend" lifeline. Windows 7 includes a new tool that lets you capture the steps that lead to a problem so that a support technician can review your actions and suggest a solution.

The tool is called Problem Steps Recorder, and you can start it by opening Action Center, clicking Troubleshooting, clicking Get Help From A Friend, and clicking Problem Steps Recorder. (If that journey is too long, in the Start menu search box or Control Panel, simply type **psr** and click Record Steps To Reproduce A Problem.) Problem Steps Recorder opens in a small window, as shown here.

When you're ready to reproduce the steps that demonstrate the problem, click Start Record, and then go through the problematic procedure. At any time, you can highlight a particular area of the screen and add an explanatory note by clicking Add Comment. When you're done, click Stop Record and save the file.

Before you send the file to your friend the computer whiz, double-click the saved file (a .zip archive saved, by default, on your desktop) and then double-click the file stored within the .zip archive. The file is a single-file HTML document that opens in your default web browser. You can now see exactly what the recipient will see: each step recorded as a screen capture with a highlight on the active area, along with a time stamp and a textual description. If that document accurately demonstrates the problem (and it doesn't show any onscreen information that you don't want the recipient to see), return to Problem Steps Recorder, click the arrow next to the help button, and choose Send To E-Mail Recipient. Problem Steps Recorder sends the most recently recorded steps as an e-mail attachment.

By default, Problem Steps Recorder saves its output files on your desktop. You can change the default location and also disable screen captures in the Problem Steps Recorder Settings dialog box, shown next. To open it, click the arrow next to the help button and choose Settings.

Chapter 28

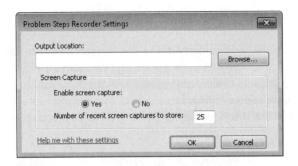

For details about another "phone a friend" option, see "Connecting to Another PC with Windows Remote Assistance" on page 90.

Reviewing Problem Reports with Reliability Monitor

Suppose you suddenly start experiencing errors in a program or a Windows feature that used to work flawlessly. To troubleshoot a problem like this, you might want to open Reliability Monitor, which is shown in Figure 28-7. To get there, open Action Center, click the arrow next to Maintenance to expand the category, and click View Reliability History.

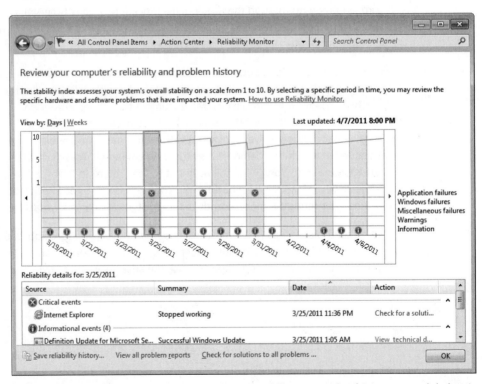

Figure 28-7 Reliability Monitor rates your system's stability on a scale of 1 (wear a crash helmet) through 10 (smooth sailing).

Chapter 28

Each column in the graphical display represents events of a particular day (or week, if you click that option in the upper left corner). Each red X along the first three lines below the graph (the various "Failures" lines) indicates a day on which problems occurred. The "Warnings" line describes minor problems unrelated to system reliability, such as a program whose installation process didn't complete properly. The last line below the graph—the line marked Information—identifies days on which an application or other software element (such as an ActiveX control) was installed or removed. You can see the details about the events of any day by clicking on the graph for that day. Reliability Monitor retains its system stability records for one year, giving you plenty of history to review.

Examine the critical events for a particular period, and see if they correspond with an informational item, such as a program installation. The alignment of these events could be mere coincidence, but it could also represent the first appearance of a long-term problem. Conjunctions of this sort are worth examining. If you think a new software application has destabilized your system, you can try uninstalling it.

Note also that you can click the link in the Action column to take additional steps, such as searching for a solution or viewing the technical details of a particular event.

Troubleshooting Hangs and Other Problems with Resource Monitor

Occasionally, you'll encounter a program that seems to be stuck. Sometimes "(Not Responding)" appears in the title bar, but the most obvious symptom is that nothing is happening and the program is apparently waiting for something—but what?

A Windows 7 enhancement to Resource Monitor can help to answer that question in some cases. To see why a program is hung, open Resource Monitor. (On the Performance tab in Task Manager, click Resource Monitor.)

On the Overview tab, under CPU, right-click the name of the executable file for the slow program (if Windows has recognized that the program is not responding, the name will be red) and choose Analyze Wait Chain. The dialog box that appears (see Figure 28-8) provides details about the holdup. If the program is running normally, Resource Monitor reports that fact in the Analyze Wait Chain dialog box. But if the program is waiting for another process, Analyze Wait Chain displays a tree-structured list of processes, organized by dependency. You can select and end any of these processes to remove the roadblock.

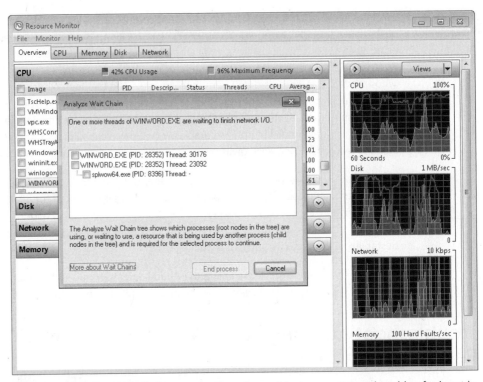

Figure 28-8 Analyze Wait Chain can sometimes be useful when a program is waiting for input in a dialog box that is hidden and inaccessible behind a window.

CAUTION

Note that ending a process can make things worse. When you do so, the process closes immediately, and you will lose any unsaved data. It might also lead to further system instability, for which the best cure is restarting your computer. Rather than using Resource Monitor to end a process, you're better off using the program's normal close procedure, if possible. Nonetheless, using Analyze Wait Chain in Resource Monitor can be an effective tool in identifying problems and—in some cases—bringing them to a quick end.

Note also that many programs depend on other processes and services as part of their normal operation, so the mere appearance of processes in the Analyze Wait Chain dialog box doesn't necessarily indicate a problem. If the process name on the Overview tab is not red, its status is Running, and everything is working normally, you shouldn't end a process or take any other action.

For more information about Resource Monitor, see "Using Resource Monitor" on page 847.

Digging Deeper with Event Viewer

You can also examine the history of errors on your system by creating a filtered view of the Application log in Event Viewer. In Windows, an *event* is any occurrence that is potentially noteworthy—to you, to other users, to the operating system, or to an application. Events are recorded by the Windows Event Log service, and their history is preserved in one of several log files, including Application, Security, Setup, System, and Forwarded Events. Event Viewer, a Microsoft Management Console (MMC) snap-in supplied with Windows, allows you to review and archive these event logs, as well as other logs created by the installation of certain applications and services.

Why would you want to do this? The most likely reasons are to troubleshoot problems that have occurred, to keep an eye on your system to forestall problems, and to watch out for security breaches. If a device has failed, a disk has filled close to capacity, a program has crashed repeatedly, or some other critical difficulty has arisen, the information recorded in the event logs can help you—or a technical support specialist—figure out what's wrong and what corrective steps are required.

To start Event Viewer, find it via the search box on the Start menu or in Control Panel. Figure 28-9 illustrates Event Viewer.

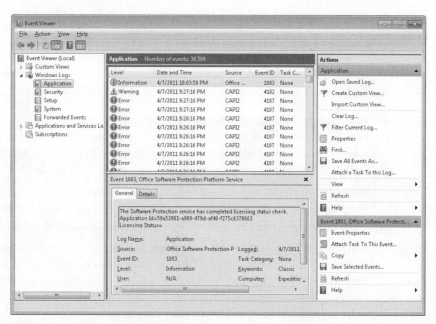

Figure 28-9 In Event Viewer, the action pane provides a menu of tasks relevant to the items highlighted in the console tree and details pane.

> **Note**
>
> Event Viewer requires administrator privileges for full functionality. If you start Event Viewer while logged on as a standard user, it starts without requesting elevation. However, the Security log is unavailable, along with some other features. To get access to all logs, right-click and choose Run As Administrator.

Types of Events

As a glance at the console tree confirms, events are recorded in one of several logs:

- **Application** Application events are generated by applications, including programs you install, programs that come with Windows 7, and operating system services. Program developers decide which events to record in the Application log and which to record in a program-specific log under Applications And Services Logs.

- **Security** Security events include logon attempts (successful and failed) and attempts to use secured resources, such as an attempt to create, modify, or delete a file.

- **Setup** Setup events are generated by application installations.

- **System** System events are generated by Windows itself and by installed features, such as device drivers. If a driver fails to load when you start a Windows session, for example, that event is recorded in the System log.

- **Forwarded Events** The Forwarded Events log contains events that have been gathered from other computers.

- **Applications And Services Logs** The Applications And Services Logs folder contains logs for individual applications and services. The other logs generally record events that are systemwide in nature, but each log in Applications And Services Logs records the events related only to a particular program or feature.

  Within the Applications And Services Logs folder resides a Microsoft\Windows folder, which contains a folder for each of many features that are part of Windows 7. Each of these folders contains one or more logs.

  Even more logs appear in Applications And Services Logs when you open the View menu and click Show Analytic And Debug Logs. These additional logs are generally needed only for a hard-core troubleshooting session, so they're hidden by default. Also note that these logs do not record events by default. To use either the Analytic or Debug log, right-click it and choose Enable Logging.

INSIDE OUT   Discover event sources

If you're curious about what elements of your system generate events and where those events are recorded, use Registry Editor to open the following registry key: HKLM\System\CurrentControlSet\Services\Eventlog. Then inspect the subkeys, such as Application, Security, and System. Each entity capable of generating an event has a subkey under one of those keys. (For details about using Registry Editor, see "Editing the Registry" on page 923.)

Accessing Event Logs with PowerShell Scripts

In the Scripts folder on the book's companion CD, we've included several scripts that you might find useful as building blocks for developing scripts to work with events and event logs:

- **Get-DiagnosticEventLogs.ps1**   This script lists the names of all the event logs on a computer.

- **CountErrors.ps1**   This script reports the number of error-level events in a particular log. You specify the log by appending its name (for example, **counterrors application** or **counterrors "windows powershell"**).

- **GetErrorsFromAllLogFiles.ps1**   This script lists any errors found among the 20 most recent entries in each of the three "classic" event logs (Application, Security, and System).

- **GetEventLogErrors.ps1**   This script lists recent error-level events in a particular log. By default, it looks at the last 200 entries in the local Application log, but you can append command-line parameters to look at a different computer, specify the event log, or change the number of events. For example, to look for errors among the last 300 System log events, type **geteventlogerrors –max 300 –log system**

- **FindUSBEvents.ps1**   This script lists each USB-related event in the Application log. The heart of the program uses the Get-EventLog cmdlet, which you can easily modify as needed:

```
Get-EventLog -LogName application -ComputerName $computer |
Where-Object { $_.source -like "*usb*" }
```

For information about using these scripts, see "Running PowerShell Scripts" on page 999.

Chapter 28

Events in most log files are classified as one of three levels: Error, Warning, or Information. Error events represent possible loss of data or functionality. Examples of errors include events related to a malfunctioning network adapter and loss of functionality caused by a device or service that doesn't load at startup. Warning events represent less significant or less immediate problems than error events. Examples of warning events include a nearly full disk, a timeout by the network redirector, and data errors on a backup tape. Other events that Windows logs are identified as information events.

The Security log file uses two different icons to classify events: a key icon identifies Audit Success events, and a lock icon identifies Audit Failure events. Both types of events are classified as Information-level events; "Audit Success" and "Audit Failure" are stored in the Keywords field of the Security log file.

Understanding the Event Logs Summary

When you select the top-level folder in Event Viewer's console tree, the details pane displays summary information, as shown in Figure 28-10. This view lets you see at a glance if any significant events that might require your attention have occurred in the past hour, day, or week. You can expand each category to see the sources of events of that event type. Seeing a count of events of various types in various time periods is interesting—but not particularly useful in and of itself. However, by right-clicking an event type or an event source under Summary Of Administrative Events and choosing View All Instances Of This Event, you can jump directly to those events, regardless of which logs they're in.

Viewing Individual Logs and Events

When you select in the console tree a log or a custom view, the details pane shows a single line for each event. By default, five columns of information—each known as an *event property*—are shown:

- **Level**   Each event is classified as one of three severity levels: Information, Warning, and Error.

- **Date And Time**   The Windows Event Log service records the date and time each event occurred in Coordinated Universal Time (UTC), and Event Viewer translates those time values into dates and times appropriate for your own time zone.

- **Source**   The Source column reports the application or Windows feature that generated an event.

- **Event ID**   Every event is identified by a numerical value. This number is associated with a text description that appears when you view an event's properties. No universal coding system is in use here—each event source's designer simply decides what numbers to use and records those numbers in a file—and there's no requirement that each event source use a unique set of numbers.

Chapter 28

- **Task Category**   Some event sources use categories to distinguish different types of events they might report. Many sources do not.

To view additional event properties, open the View menu and click Add/Remove Columns.

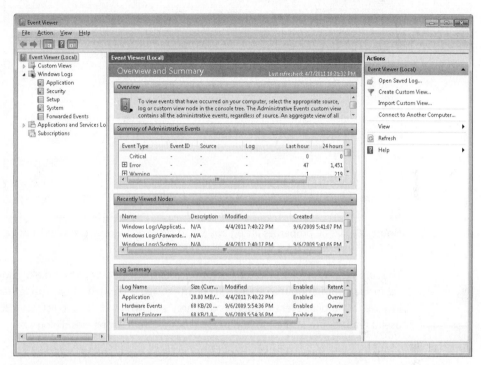

Figure 28-10 Under Summary Of Administrative Events, click a plus sign to expand a category of events of a certain type.

Viewing Event Details

When viewing events in a selected log or custom view, at the bottom of the details pane you'll see information about the currently selected event. Except on a monitor with very high resolution, this preview of the full details for a particular event doesn't impart much more information than the columnar display at the top of the details pane. (If you find the lower part of the details pane to be useless, you can banish it and use the window's full height for the events list. To do so, open the View menu and click Preview Pane.)

To learn more about an event than Event Viewer's details pane tells you, select the event you're interested in and click Event Properties in the action pane. Figure 28-11 shows the Event Properties dialog box for an event in the Application log.

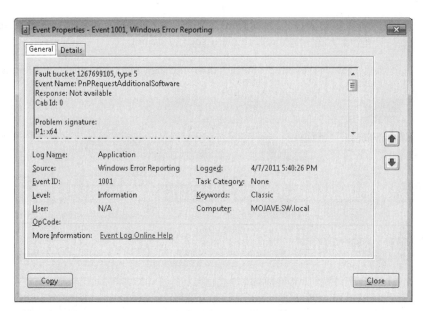

Figure 28-11 The properties dialog box for an event provides a textual description and data that are not shown in the main Event Viewer window.

The summary information in the bottom half of the Event Properties dialog box is identical to the information that appears in Event Viewer's columnar details pane—except that it includes additional event properties that aren't shown by default in list view. But the most useful features are at the top and bottom of the Event Properties dialog box.

At the top is a plain-language description of what has occurred. Near the bottom of the Event Properties dialog box is a Copy button. Clicking here sends the entire contents of the Event Properties dialog box to the Clipboard, allowing you, for example, to paste the information into an e-mail message and send it to a support technician. The copied information includes a plain-text rendition similar to the on-screen display, as well as the underlying data in XML format.

Also, near the bottom of the Event Properties dialog box is a link to more information online. Clicking this link opens a web page that provides more specific and detailed information about this particular combination of event source and event ID, including further action you might want to take in response to the event.

Sorting and Grouping Events

By default, events are sorted chronologically, with the most recent located at the top of the list. You can change the sort order by opening the View menu, clicking Sort By, and then clicking the name of the column you want to sort on. More simply, click a column heading. To revert to the default order, click View, Remove Sorting.

More powerful than sorting is the ability to group events. Grouping not only sorts the event list by the selected column, but it places them under group headings that can be collapsed or expanded, making it easier to find and focus on events of interest. Figure 28-12 shows an example.

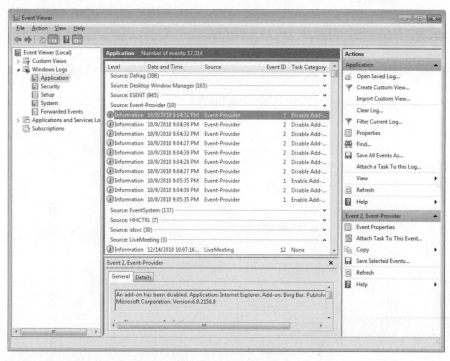

Figure 28-12 The Application log here is grouped by Source.

To group events in the currently displayed log or custom view, open the View menu, click Group By, and then click the name of the column you want to group by. (Note that Date And Time actually groups by date only.) To find your way more quickly to a group of interest, open the View menu and click Collapse All Groups. To revert to the standard, ungrouped event list, click View, Remove Grouping Of Events.

Filtering the Log Display

As you can see from a cursory look at your System log, events can pile up quickly, obscuring those generated by a particular source or those that occurred at a particular date and time. Sorting and grouping can help you to find that needle in a haystack, but to get the hay out of the way altogether, use filtering. With filtering, you can select events based on multiple criteria and, after a view is filtered, nonconforming events are hidden from view, making it much easier to focus on the items you currently care about.

To filter the currently displayed log or custom view, click Action, Filter Current Log. A dialog box like the one shown in Figure 28-13 appears. To fully appreciate the flexibility of filtering, click the arrow by each filter. You can, for example, filter events from the past hour, 12 hours, day, week, month, or any custom time period you specify. In the Event Sources, Task Category, and Keywords boxes, you can type text to filter on (separate multiple items with commas), but you'll probably find it easier to click the arrow and then click each of the items you want to include in your filtered view. In the Includes/Excludes Event IDs box, you can enter multiple ID numbers and number ranges, separated by commas; to exclude particular event IDs, precede their number with a minus sign.

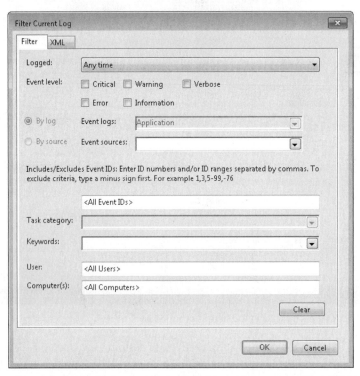

Figure 28-13 If you don't select any Event Level boxes, Event Viewer includes all levels in the filtered results. Similarly, any other field you leave blank includes all events without regard to the value of that property.

When you finish defining the broad strokes of your filter on the Filter tab, you might want to switch to the XML tab, where you can further refine your filter by editing the query. Click OK when you're finished.

To restore the unfiltered list, in the Event Viewer window click Action, Clear Filter.

> **Note**
>
> Event Viewer also includes an anemic search capability, which you access by clicking Action, Find. You can perform more precise searches by filtering.

Creating and Saving Custom Views

If you spend much time in Event Viewer or have a particularly troublesome program or device that sends you back to Event Viewer often, creating ad-hoc filtering, grouping, and sorting criteria becomes tiresome. Custom views to the rescue! To create a custom view, click Action, Create Custom View. You'll see a dialog box nearly identical to the Filter Current Log dialog box shown in Figure 28-13. One key difference: the Event Logs list is available, and you can specify any or all logs to include in your custom view.

After you create filter criteria and click OK, you need to specify a name and location for your custom view. You can store your custom view in the Custom Views folder or any of its subfolders. (To create a subfolder, click New Folder.) Select the All Users option if you want the view to be available to any user on your computer; clear it if you want the view to appear only when you log on.

You can now display your custom view by selecting its name in the console tree. You can apply sorting or grouping, and those changes are stored as part of the custom view. To modify the filter criteria, click Filter Current Log. To change the name or description for your custom view, click Action, Properties.

Exporting Event Data

You can save selected events, all events in the current view, or all events in a particular log to a file for archival purposes, for further analysis in a different program, or to share with a technical support specialist. (To select events for exporting, hold down the Ctrl key and click each event you want to include.) The command to do so is on the Action menu, and the command name varies depending on the current view and selection: Save Selected Events, Save Filtered Log File As, Save Events In Custom View As, or Save Events As.

Saving event data in Event Viewer's native (.evtx) format creates a file that you can view only in Event Viewer (or a third-party application capable of reading native event logs). However, Event Viewer can export log data to XML, tab-delimited, or comma-delimited text files, and you can easily import these into database, spreadsheet, or even word processing programs.

Creating a Task to Run When a Specific Event Occurs

Traditionally, troubleshooters delve into Event Viewer after a problem has occurred, poring through logs to find clues to the cause of the problem. To take a more proactive approach, you can configure a task to be performed automatically when a particular event happens.

You might want to be notified or have a program run if a particular event occurs. Task Scheduler monitors event logs so that an event can be a trigger to launch a task that runs a program, sends an e-mail message, or displays a message on the screen. To configure such a task from within Event Viewer, find an existing occurrence of the event, select it, and click Action, Attach Task To This Event. Doing so opens the Create Basic Task wizard, with the trigger and event information already completed. If you want to create a task based on an event that isn't currently in your log file, open Task Scheduler and click Action, Create Basic Task.

For more information about creating and configuring scheduled tasks, see "Using Task Scheduler" on page 966.

Understanding Stop Errors

If Windows has ever suddenly shut down, you've probably experienced that sinking feeling in the pit of your stomach. When Windows 7 encounters a serious problem that makes it impossible for the operating system to continue running, it shuts down immediately and displays an ominous text message whose technical details begin with the word *STOP* in capital letters. Because a Stop error typically appears in white letters on a blue background, this type of message is often referred to as a blue screen error or the Blue Screen of Death (BSOD). When a Stop error appears, it means that there is a serious problem that demands your immediate attention.

Windows 7 includes a variety of information sources and debugging tools that you can use to identify the cause of Stop errors. Many of the tools are intended for use by developers with professional debugging tools. These topics are covered in more detail in *Windows 7 Resource Kit* (Microsoft Press, 2009). If you know where to look, however, you can learn a lot from these error messages, and in many cases you can recover completely by using standard troubleshooting techniques.

Customizing How Windows Handles Stop Errors

When Windows encounters a serious error that forces it to stop running, it takes the following actions:

1. The system displays a Stop message.

2. Based on the preferences defined for the current Windows installation, the system writes debugging information to the page file. When the computer restarts, this information is saved as a crash dump file, which can be used to debug the specific cause of the error.

3. Again, based on the current preferences, the system either pauses with the Stop message on the screen or restarts when the crash dump information has been saved.

You can customize two crucial aspects of this process by defining the size of the crash dump files and specifying whether you want Windows to restart automatically after a Stop message appears. By default, Windows automatically restarts after a Stop message. That's the preferred strategy in response to a random, isolated Stop error. But if you're experiencing chronic Stop errors, you might have more troubleshooting success by reconfiguring Windows to halt at the Stop message and wait for you to manually restart the system. To make this change, follow these steps:

1. Open Control Panel, click System And Security, click System, and then click Advanced System Settings. (Or, in the Start menu search box, type the undocumented command **systempropertiesadvanced** and press Enter.)

2. On the Advanced tab of the System Properties dialog box, under Startup And Recovery, click Settings. The following dialog box appears:

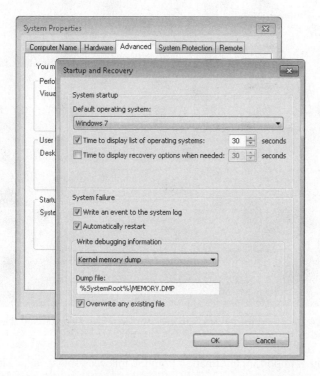

3. Clear the Automatically Restart check box and click OK.

From the same dialog box, you can also define the settings for crash dump files. By default, Windows saves a kernel memory dump. This option includes memory allocated to kernel-mode drivers and programs, which are most likely to cause Stop errors. Because this file does not include unallocated memory or memory allocated to user-mode programs, it will usually be smaller in size than the amount of RAM on your system. The exact size varies, but in general you can expect the file to be approximately one-third the size of installed physical RAM. The crash files are stored in %SystemRoot% using the file name Memory.dmp.

Chapter 28

If disk space is limited or you're planning to send the crash dump file to a support technician, you might want to consider setting the system to store a small memory dump (commonly called a mini dump). A small memory dump contains just a fraction of the information in a kernel memory dump, but it's often enough to determine the cause of a problem.

How to Read a Stop Error

The exact text of a Stop error varies according to what caused the error. But the format is predictable, as the example in Figure 28-14 shows.

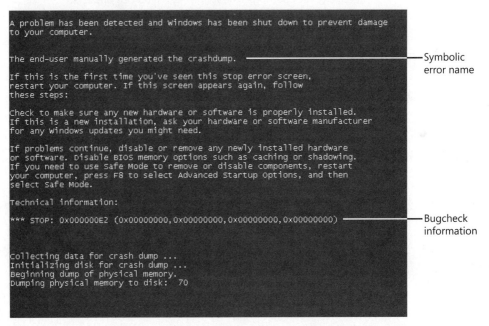

Figure 28-14 Decoding the information in a Stop error can help you find the underlying problem and fix it.

You can gather important information from the following message details:

- **Symbolic error name** This is the message that the error returned to the operating system. It corresponds to the Stop error number that appears at the bottom of the screen. The symbolic error name appears near the top of the screen, usually in all capital letters.

- **Troubleshooting recommendations** This generic text applies to all Stop errors of the specified type. Depending on the error number, you might be told to check available disk space, uninstall a piece of hardware, or remove or update recently installed drivers or software.

- **Error number and parameters** Developers call this section *bugcheck information*. The text following the word *STOP* includes the error number (in hexadecimal notation, as indicated by the 0x at the beginning of the code) and up to four parameters that are specific to the error type.

> **Note**
>
> Stop errors are a rare occurrence, especially at that precise time when you actually *want* to see one, such as when you're capturing example screens for a book. For that reason, we had to resort to a bug-generating trick built into Windows, which is why the symbolic error name correctly indicates that this is a manually generated error. If you'd like to try it for yourself, see Microsoft Support article 244139 (*w7io.com/244139*).

The blue screen offers tantalizingly incomplete bits of evidence—and it often disappears before you have an opportunity to examine it closely. After the fact, you can find these same details in Event Viewer. Windows 7 also displays the information in Reliability Monitor, under the heading Critical Events. Select the day on which the error occurred, and then click View Technical Details next to the event summary to display the bugcheck information, as shown in Figure 28-15. (For more information, see "Reviewing Problem Reports with Reliability Monitor" on page 1020.)

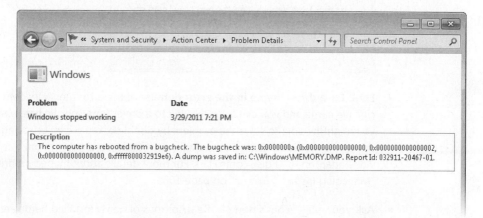

Figure 28-15 If the blue screen disappears before you can examine the details, you can find the same information in Reliability Monitor.

Dealing with Stop Errors

If you experience a Stop error, don't panic. Instead, run through the following troubleshooting checklist to isolate the problem and find a solution:

- **Don't rule out hardware problems** In many cases, software is the victim and not the cause of blue-screen errors. Common hardware failures such as a damaged hard disk, defective physical RAM, an overheated CPU chip, or even a bad cable can result in Stop errors. If the errors seem to happen at random and the message details vary each time, there is a very good chance that you are experiencing hardware problems.

- **Check your memory** Windows 7 includes a memory diagnostic tool that you can use if you suspect a faulty or failing memory chip. To run this diagnostic procedure, open Control Panel and type **memory** in the search box. Then, under Administrative Tools, click Diagnose Your Computer's Memory Problems. In the Windows Memory Diagnostic tool, shown here, click Restart Now And Check For Problems (Recommended) or Check For Problems The Next Time I Start My Computer.

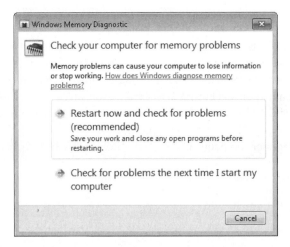

- **Look for a driver name in the error details** If the error message identifies a specific file name and you can trace that file to a driver for a specific hardware device, you might be able to solve the problem by disabling, removing, or rolling back that driver to an earlier version. The most likely offenders are network interface cards, video adapters, and disk controllers. For more details about managing driver files, see "Managing Installed Drivers" on page 1089.

- **Ask yourself, "What's new?"** Be suspicious of newly installed hardware and software. If you added a device recently, remove it temporarily and see whether the problem goes away. Take an especially close look at software in the categories that install services or file-system filter drivers—these hook into the core operating system files that manage the file system to perform tasks such as scanning for viruses. This category includes backup programs, multimedia applications, antivirus software, and CD-burning utilities. You might need to permanently uninstall or update the program to resolve the problem.

- **Search Microsoft Support**   Make a note of the error code and all parameters. Search Microsoft Support using both the full and short formats. For instance, if you're experiencing a KMODE_EXCEPTION_NOT_HANDLED error, use 0x1E and 0x0000001E as your search keywords.

- **Check your system BIOS carefully**   Is an update available from the manufacturer of the system or motherboard? Check the BIOS documentation carefully; resetting all BIOS options to their defaults can sometimes resolve an issue caused by overtweaking.

- **Are you low on system resources?**   Stop errors are sometimes the result of a critical shortage of RAM or disk space. If you can start in Safe Mode, check the amount of physical RAM installed and look at the system and boot drives to see how much free disk space is available.

- **Is a crucial system file damaged?**   To reinstall a driver, restart your computer, press F8, and start Windows in Safe Mode. In Safe Mode, only core drivers and services are activated. If your system starts in Safe Mode but not normally, you very likely have a problem driver. Try running Device Manager in Safe Mode and uninstalling the most likely suspect. Or run System Restore in Safe Mode. If restoring to a particular day cures the problem, use Reliability Monitor (shown earlier in Figure 28-7) to determine what changes occurred on or after that day.

> **Note**
> A good online resource for Stop errors can be found at *w7io.com/2303*.

Analyzing Crash Reports

In fact, the sparse information on the bugcheck screen is rarely enough to solve a problem. The real keys to troubleshooting are stored in dump files that are created after the system crashes and before it restarts. As noted earlier, when a Stop error occurs, a memory dump—essentially, the contents of RAM copied to a file on a storage device—is created. Depending on your selection in the Startup And Recovery dialog box, it can be a kernel memory dump or a mini dump. But what does one do with these files?

Chapter 28

Support technicians might request that you send a memory dump file either automatically via the Windows Error Reporting process or manually through e-mail or other means. The files can assist the technicians in determining what was going on when the error occurred.

INSIDE OUT   Create a troubleshooting CD

You can install the Crash Analyzer wizard locally and download the most recent version of the Debugging Tools for Windows and the symbols for the current version of Windows. That's a sensible strategy if you're doing long-term testing on your own development PC, but it's overkill if you're troubleshooting a recent crash on a client's PC. For that job, use the ERD Commander Boot Media wizard, another component of MDOP. You supply the installation media for the operating system you're debugging, and the wizard creates an ISO image that you can use to burn a recovery disk that includes an assortment of useful troubleshooting tools. (You'll need to create separate recovery media for x86 and x64 versions of Windows 7.)

When you boot from the recovery disk and choose the DaRT option, you see the complete set of tools shown here.

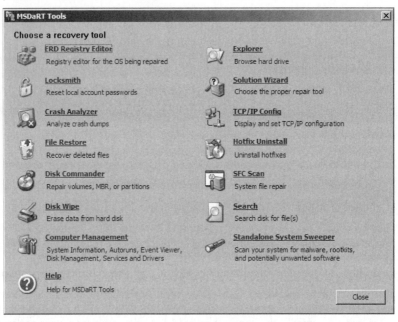

If you have the curiosity, the technical chops, and the right tools, you can dive into the files yourself. Microsoft customers with a Software Assurance subscription have access to the Microsoft Desktop Optimization Pack (MDOP); one of its components is the Microsoft Diagnostics and Recovery Toolset (DaRT), which includes a Crash Analyzer wizard. MDOP is also available for TechNet and MSDN subscribers, but subscribers should be sure to review their subscription terms of service, which limit how these tools can be used. For more information about MDOP, visit *w7io.com/2304*. Mitch Tulloch's series of articles beginning at *w7io.com/22803* provides a good introduction to using DaRT for troubleshooting.

The Crash Analyzer wizard uses two external components to work its magic:

- The Debugging Tools for Windows (*w7io.com/2305*) are typically used by developers during the course of creating drivers, applications, and services for Windows. They're available in 32-bit and 64-bit versions and are required to open crash dump files.

- Symbol packages (*w7io.com/22801*) contain information that the debugger needs to interpret variables and other details in the dump file. When debugging a Windows crash dump file, you must use the symbol package that matches the operating system that created the crash dump.

The Crash Analyzer wizard uses the PC's network connection to download the necessary components and symbols for the target operating system and then analyzes the most recent crash dump file stored on the target PC. When the wizard completes its analysis, it displays the results in a summary dialog box like the one shown in Figure 28-16.

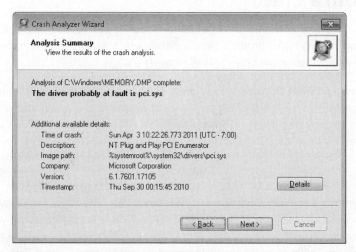

Figure 28-16 The Crash Analyzer wizard fingers the probable culprit (in this case, pci.sys) and shows details about the driver version.

You can examine more complete results by clicking the Details button, but in many cases the identification is enough to help you determine the root cause of the problem. A search for the name of the suspect driver along with the Stop code (which you can find by clicking Details and looking in the Crash Code box on the Crash Message tab) usually yields links to a Microsoft Support article or other solution. The Crash Analyzer wizard can't find the cause of every crash. Even when it does succeed in pinpointing a problem, you might be stymied if a replacement driver is unavailable or if uninstalling the offending application isn't an option. But at least you'll have information you can use to open a trouble ticket with Microsoft or the developer of the faulty code.

Other, less powerful, tools are available from Microsoft without a subscription. You can download Debugging Tools for Windows from *w7io.com/2305*. You'll need some of these tools to perform the analyses described in Microsoft Support article 315263, "How to read the small memory dump files that Windows creates for debugging" (*w7io.com/315263*).

Numerous other tools are available online, including a program called WhoCrashed (*w7io.com/2306*), which works with Debugging Tools for Windows to extract the crucial information into an easily understood form. Another tool for gleaning basic information from mini dump files is BlueScreenView (*w7io.com/22802*). Searching the web for "mini dump crash analyzer" turns up countless tools and tutorials on the subject. You're likely to discover that the mysterious and technical-looking BSOD is simply an obfuscation of information about crash causes that, in many cases, can be deciphered by mere mortals.

Recovering from a Crash

Windows 7 provides a full assortment of troubleshooting and repair options. The circumstances and severity of the problem usually dictate which tool is most appropriate. In this section, we cover two broad categories of recovery tools:

- **Advanced Boot Options**   If you press F8 while your system is starting up, Windows 7 displays a menu of diagnostic startup options. The most important of these is Safe Mode, which lets Windows start with only its most essential drivers and services. After you have started in Safe Mode, you can start and stop services, uninstall programs or drivers that might be causing problems, and run System Restore to return your system to an earlier, more stable, state.

- **Windows Recovery Environment (Windows RE)**   The Windows Recovery Environment provides a set of system recovery features in a small-footprint version of Windows. Even if you can't start your system in Safe Mode, you can use the Windows Recovery Environment to repair damaged system files, run System Restore, run memory diagnostics, restore a Complete PC Backup image, or perform diagnostic and recovery operations at a command prompt. The Windows Recovery Environment is a replacement for the Recovery Console in Windows XP.

Using Advanced Boot Options

Pressing F8 during the startup process takes you to the Advanced Boot Options menu, as shown in Figure 28-17.

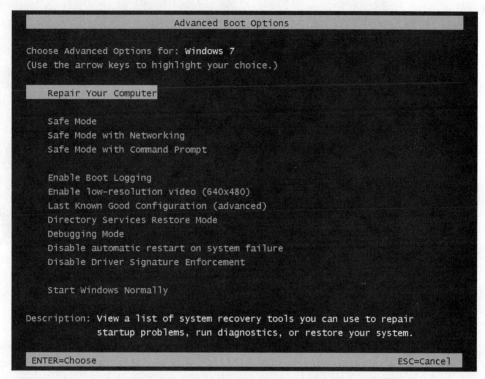

```
                    Advanced Boot Options

Choose Advanced Options for: Windows 7
(Use the arrow keys to highlight your choice.)

    Repair Your Computer

    Safe Mode
    Safe Mode with Networking
    Safe Mode with Command Prompt

    Enable Boot Logging
    Enable low-resolution video (640x480)
    Last Known Good Configuration (advanced)
    Directory Services Restore Mode
    Debugging Mode
    Disable automatic restart on system failure
    Disable Driver Signature Enforcement

    Start Windows Normally

Description: View a list of system recovery tools you can use to repair
            startup problems, run diagnostics, or restore your system.

ENTER=Choose                                            ESC=Cancel
```

Figure 28-17 A command that didn't appear in earlier Windows versions, Repair Your Computer, is at the top of the Advanced Boot Options menu in Windows 7.

For information about the first (and newest) item on the Advanced Boot Options menu, see "Making Repairs with the Windows Recovery Environment" on page 1046.

If Windows hangs at startup (that is, if you never get to the desktop or a logon prompt), use the power switch to restart your system. In that case, you might see the Windows Error Recovery menu (shown in Figure 28-18), which offers some of the same troubleshooting options as the Advanced Boot Options menu.

Chapter 28

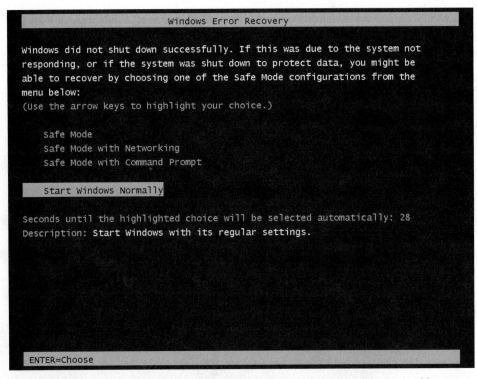

```
                    Windows Error Recovery

Windows did not shut down successfully. If this was due to the system not
responding, or if the system was shut down to protect data, you might be
able to recover by choosing one of the Safe Mode configurations from the
menu below:
(Use the arrow keys to highlight your choice.)


    Safe Mode
    Safe Mode with Networking
    Safe Mode with Command Prompt

    Start Windows Normally

Seconds until the highlighted choice will be selected automatically: 28
Description: Start Windows with its regular settings.








 ENTER=Choose
```

Figure 28-18 If power is lost unexpectedly or if you experience a Stop error, you see this menu when your computer restarts.

Using Safe Mode

As in previous versions, Windows 7 gives you the option to start your system in Safe Mode if you're unable to start reliably in the normal manner. In Safe Mode, Windows uses only services and drivers that are absolutely required to start your system. The operating system runs with a generic video driver at 800 by 600 resolution, with support for keyboard, mouse, monitor, local storage, and default system services. In Safe Mode, Windows does not install support for audio devices and nonessential peripherals. Your USB flash drives, hard disks, keyboard, and mouse will be supported, provided your system BIOS includes the option to recognize and enable these devices. All logon programs (programs in your Startup folder, for example) are bypassed.

INSIDE OUT Use an administrative account

To solve problems in Safe Mode, you need administrative credentials. With a standard account, you'll have read-only access to some diagnostic tools, but you won't be able to take any troubleshooting actions.

TROUBLESHOOTING

You can't display the Advanced Boot Options menu

Pressing F8 at precisely the right moment to cause the Advanced Boot Options menu to appear is sometimes difficult. If you're able to boot your computer normally at least once, you can use another method to start in Safe Mode or with other boot options.

To use the other method, while Windows is running type **msconfig** in the Start menu search box and press Enter to open System Configuration, shown here. Click the Boot tab, and then make selections under Boot Options. These options take effect the next time you restart your computer—without requiring you to first press F8. Select Safe Boot to invoke Safe Mode; the suboptions Minimal, Network, and Alternate Shell correlate to the three Safe Mode options on the Advanced Boot Options menu.

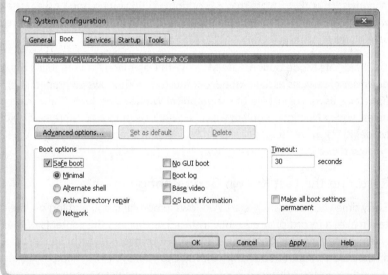

In Safe Mode, you can access certain essential configuration tools, including Device Manager, System Restore, and Registry Editor. All local Help And Support features are available; if you choose the Safe Mode With Networking option, you'll have access to online help as well.

One important troubleshooting tool that is not available in Safe Mode is Backup And Restore. To restore a system image backup, for example, you need to use the Windows Recovery Environment, not Safe Mode.

If Windows appears to work properly in Safe Mode, you can safely assume that there's no problem with the basic services. Use Device Manager, Driver Verifier Manager, and Event Viewer to try to figure out where the trouble lies. If you suspect that a newly installed device or program is the cause of the problem, you can remove the offending software while you're running in Safe Mode. Use Device Manager to uninstall or roll back a hardware driver; use Control Panel to remove a program. Then try restarting the system normally to see whether your changes have resolved the problem.

For information about using Device Manager, see "Managing Devices with Device Manager" on page 1070. For information about Driver Verifier Manager, see "Your computer experiences sporadic blue screens, lockups, or other strange behavior" on page 1091. For information about using Event Viewer, see "Digging Deeper with Event Viewer" on page 1023. For information about removing programs, see "Uninstalling Programs" on page 195.

If you need access to network connections, choose the Safe Mode With Networking option, which loads the base set of Safe Mode files and adds drivers and services required to start Windows networking. Note that this option will do you no good on a portable computer with a PC Card (PCMCIA) network adapter, because PC Card peripherals are disabled in Safe Mode.

The third Safe Mode option, Safe Mode With Command Prompt, loads the same stripped-down set of services as Safe Mode, but it uses the Windows command interpreter (Cmd.exe) as a shell instead of the graphical Windows Explorer. This option is unnecessary unless you're having a problem with the Windows graphical interface. The default Safe Mode also provides access to the command line. (Press Windows logo key+R, and then type **cmd.exe** in the Run dialog box.)

Restoring the Last Known Good Configuration

Every time you successfully start Windows in normal mode and log on, the operating system makes a record of all currently installed drivers and the contents of the registry key HKLM\System\CurrentControlSet. This record comes in handy if you install a driver or make a hardware configuration change that causes your system to hang at startup. When Windows displays the Advanced Boot Options menu, you can choose the Last Known Good Configuration (Advanced) option. This menu choice restores the previous, working registry key, effectively removing the changes that are causing the problem.

In general, System Restore is a more reliable method of restoring a prior working configuration than the Last Known Good Configuration option. That's because System Restore restores all Windows system files and the entire registry rather than just a single key. (For more information, see "Rolling Back to a Stable State with System Restore" on page 466.)

CAUTION❗

If you suspect that a driver change is causing system problems and you don't have a recent restore point to return to, don't log on in normal mode. As soon as you log on normally, Windows resets the Last Known Good Configuration information, effectively removing your safety net. Be especially careful if this computer is configured for dual boot and you have recently booted into an earlier version of Windows, such as Windows XP. Windows 7 restore points are erased when you boot into an operating system earlier than Windows Vista. If you suspect problems, start Windows in Safe Mode and perform basic troubleshooting. Logging on in Safe Mode does not update the Last Known Good Configuration information, so you can safely roll back to the Last Known Good Configuration if Safe Mode troubleshooting is unsuccessful.

Other Startup Options

Six additional choices on the Advanced Boot Options menu are of use in specialized circumstances:

- **Enable Boot Logging**   When you select this option, Windows starts up normally and creates a log file that lists the names and status of all drivers loaded into memory. To view the contents of this file, look for Ntbtlog.txt in the %SystemRoot% folder. If your system is hanging because of a faulty driver, the last entry in this log file might identify the culprit.

- **Enable Low-Resolution Video**   This option starts the computer in 640 by 480 resolution using the current video driver. Use this option to recover from video problems that are caused not by a faulty driver but by incorrect settings, such as an improper resolution or refresh rate.

- **Directory Services Restore Mode**   This option is used only with domain controllers running a server edition of Windows. Ignore it.

- **Debugging Mode**   This choice starts Windows in kernel debug mode. To take advantage of this capability, you must connect the system to another computer using a serial connection on COM2. The other computer must run a compatible debugger to perform troubleshooting and system analysis.

Chapter 28

- **Disable Automatic Restart On System Failure**   Use this option if you're getting a Stop error (a blue-screen crash) every time you start Windows and the operating system is configured to restart automatically after a crash. Under these circumstances your computer will continually reboot, crash, and reboot. To break the cycle, turn the machine off. Then press F8 during startup and choose Disable Automatic Restart On System Failure.

- **Disable Driver Signature Enforcement**   Use this option if Windows is refusing to start because of an unsigned driver. Windows will start normally, not in Safe Mode.

Advanced Boot Options also includes a Repair Your Computer command, which starts the Windows Recovery Environment. We discuss the Windows Recovery Environment next.

Making Repairs with the Windows Recovery Environment

If your system won't start even in Safe Mode, all is by no means lost. You can repair many serious problems with the Windows Recovery Environment (Windows RE). If the trouble stems from a corrupted system file, the Windows Recovery Environment might be able to get your system running again with almost no intervention or effort on your part.

Launching the Windows Recovery Environment

> **Note**
>
> Unlike in earlier versions of Windows, with Windows 7 the Windows Recovery Environment is installed by default, so it's not necessary to have a Windows DVD available to launch Windows RE. You *can*, however, open it from a Windows DVD, which can be useful on a system that is completely scrambled. To do so, boot from the Windows DVD. When you reach the Install Windows screen, make the appropriate selections for language, time, and keyboard, and then click Next. On the screen that follows, click Repair Your Computer.

To open the Windows Recovery Environment, follow these steps:

1. Press F8 while your computer is booting to display the Advanced Boot Options menu (shown earlier in Figure 28-17). Use the arrow keys to highlight Repair Your Computer, and press Enter.

After a few moments, a System Recovery Options dialog box appears, as shown here.

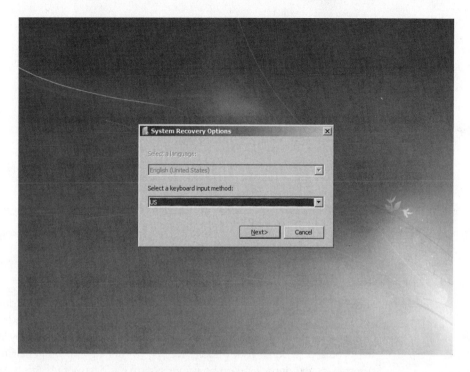

2. Select a keyboard input method and click Next. A logon dialog box appears.

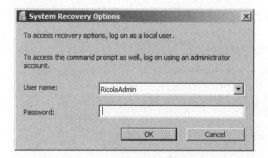

3. Select the name of a user account—preferably an administrator account—enter its password, and click OK. The System Recovery Options menu, shown in Figure 28-19, appears.

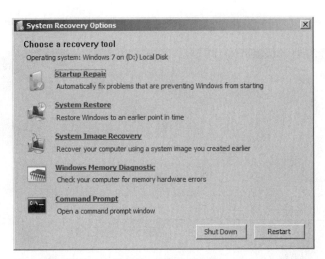

Figure 28-19 The main menu of the Windows Recovery Environment, titled System Recovery Options, offers a selection of five troubleshooting and repair commands.

Replacing Corrupted or Missing Files with Startup Repair

Startup Repair, the first item on the System Recovery Options menu, is designed to get you back up and running when Windows won't start because of damage to (or deletion of) one or more essential system files. Generally speaking, if you're not sure why Windows won't start, you should begin your troubleshooting by running Startup Repair. (Under some circumstances and depending on how your system has been set up, Startup Repair might run automatically when Windows fails to boot.)

Startup Repair begins by displaying the following:

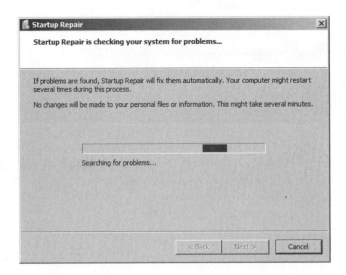

After a few moments, Startup Repair reports its results. This is not a promise that your system has been fixed—but it is encouraging. If you respond by clicking Finish, the system reboots. If no problems remain unsolved, you'll be heading straight back into Windows. If more repair is needed, Startup Repair runs again.

If you want more information about what Startup Repair has done, click the link at the bottom of the dialog box—View Diagnostic And Repair Details. Something akin to the following will appear, and you can use the scroll bar to read the full report.

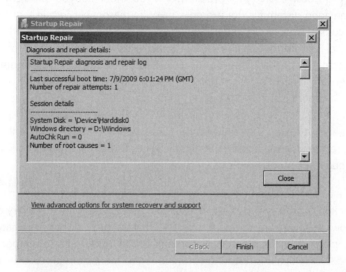

If Startup Repair is unable to solve your problem, you're likely to see a request that you consent to informing Microsoft about the problem. You might also see a message proposing an alternative troubleshooting approach—such as running System Restore.

INSIDE OUT   Check system files while Windows is running

If you receive an error message indicating a damaged system file while you are running Windows and you have an account with administrative privileges (or access to elevated credentials), try running the command-line utility Sfc (short for System File Checker). Open the Start menu, click All Programs, click Accessories, right-click Command Prompt, and choose Run As Administrator. Respond to the User Account Control prompt. Then, in the Command Prompt window, type **sfc /scannow**. The utility scans your system files and attempts to repair any damage that it finds. It might prompt you for Windows 7 distribution media to carry out its repairs. For more details about System File Checker, see Microsoft Support article 929833 (*w7io.com/929833*).

Another method for repairing startup problems—specifically, problems with the master boot record (MBR), the boot sector, or the Boot Configuration Data (BCD) store—is to use the Bootrec tool in a Command Prompt session. For more information about Command Prompt in Windows RE, see "Working at the Command Prompt" on page 1052. For details about Bootrec, see Microsoft Support article 927392 (*w7io.com/927392*).

Restoring Your Computer to Working Condition

If Startup Repair doesn't solve your problem, or if you know that your problem is not the result of a damaged system file (for example, if you're reasonably certain that a bad device driver is the culprit), you can try returning your system to a more stable state by means of System Restore. For information about using System Restore, see "Rolling Back to a Stable State with System Restore" on page 466, which describes the use of this tool from within Windows. The one difference between running it in Windows and running it in the Windows Recovery Environment is that in the latter case no new restore point is created at the time you perform the restore. Therefore, if you run System Restore from the Windows Recovery Environment and you're not pleased with the result, you won't have any simple method of undoing the restore. On the other hand, the fact that you're in the Windows Recovery Environment to begin with suggests that you have nothing to lose.

If, prior to the current emergency, you have used the Windows Backup program to create an image backup of your system disk, you can use the System Image Recovery command in the Windows Recovery Environment to restore that image. Restoring an image backup of a disk completely replaces the current contents of the disk. The restore program, in fact, formats the disk to which it is restoring before it begins the restore process—and it requires your acknowledgement and explicit consent before it begins. This might sound like a drastic step, but it can be a quick and effective way to get Windows running again in circumstances that Startup Repair is unable to address.

For complete details about Windows Backup, see "Creating a System Image Backup" on page 444 and "Restoring a System Image" on page 460.

INSIDE OUT   Using System Image Recovery with two or more unformatted hard disks

If you are using System Image Recovery to restore disk images to two or more "clean" hard disks—that is, disks with no disk signatures and no volumes—the program will fail with a cryptic error message. To work around the problem, go to the Windows Recovery Environment command prompt. Then use the DiskPart command to create and format volumes on the new disks. This workaround is required only when your computer has two or more fixed disks and all of the disks are clean.

CAUTION

If you keep your documents on the same volume as your system files, performing a system image recovery is likely to entail the loss of recent work—unless, of course, you have an up-to-date file backup or you have the good fortune to have made an image backup almost immediately before your current troubles began. The same is true if you save documents on a volume separate from your system files but you have included that data volume in your system image backup. If you have documents that have not been backed up, you can avoid losing recent work by copying them to a disk that will not be affected by the restore process—a USB flash drive, for example, or some other form of removable media. You can use the Command Prompt option in the Windows Recovery Environment to copy these documents. (For details about using the Command Prompt option, see "Working at the Command Prompt" on the next page.) If you do have a recent file backup, you will be able to restore files after you have used System Image Recovery to get your system running again.

Running the Windows Memory Diagnostic Tool

If Startup Repair is unable to get your system running again, and if neither System Restore nor System Image Recovery has returned your computer to a condition of reliable health, consider the possibility that your computer has failing memory. To test this hypothesis, click Windows Memory Diagnostic on the Startup Recovery Options menu. Windows Memory Diagnostic asks whether you want to restart immediately and check for problems (the recommended option) or check instead on your next startup. Because you're having trouble getting to that next startup, you presumably want the first option.

While the diagnostic program is running, you will see status messages on your screen. These will give you some idea how much longer the tests have to run and whether errors have been found. You can press F1 at any time to get to an options screen. Here you can choose between Basic, Standard, and Extended tests as well as select various other testing parameters. One of these parameters controls the number of test passes the tool will make. If you don't mind letting the tests run a long time—for example, overnight—select a number higher than the default 2. When you have configured the tests to your satisfaction, press F10 to continue.

Your system will restart—if it can—when the testing is complete. The results will be displayed when you log on.

Chapter 28

Working at the Command Prompt

To get to the command prompt, click Command Prompt on the System Recovery Options menu. (Note that this option is available only if you provided credentials for an administrator account when you started the Windows Recovery Environment.) Depending on whether you launch the Windows Recovery Environment from Advanced Boot Options or from a Windows DVD, you will land in the \Windows\System32 or \Sources subdirectory (folder) of a RAM disk identified by the drive letter X. From here, you have access to nearly a hundred command-line tools, including disk-management utilities such as Chkdsk, Format, and Disk-Part, as well as file-management items such as Copy, Rename, and Delete.

The Windows Recovery Environment command prompt is a vastly more versatile replacement for the Recovery Console that was introduced in Windows XP. Unlike Recovery Console, which imposed stringent restrictions on your command-line activities, the Windows Recovery Environment command prompt permits you to do just about anything you need to do. Among other things, you can copy, delete, rename, move, and type document files; partition and format hard disks (using DiskPart); and run diagnostic utilities.

INSIDE OUT   Access your network from the Windows Recovery Environment command prompt

Network functionality is not available by default at the Windows Recovery Environment command prompt. To enable it, type **wpeinit**.

Because the command prompt in the Windows Recovery Environment runs in the security context of the SYSTEM account, you have full read/write access there to every file on every accessible disk. This means, among other things, that you can generate backup copies of not only your own documents but those created under other accounts at your computer. It also means that you need to take care of the physical security of your computer, because anyone who knows how to get to the Windows Recovery Environment could wander your system at will, read your documents, take copies away on removable media, and otherwise wreak havoc upon your life.

If you're accustomed to answering UAC prompts for relatively risk-free operations in Windows (such as reading the event logs), or if you've had experience working in the restricted conditions of the Windows XP Recovery Console, the permissive nature of the Windows Recovery Environment command prompt might come as something of a surprise. In reality, though, the Windows Recovery Environment presents no security hazard that wasn't already there. Unless you prevent physical access to your computer by using Windows BitLocker Drive Encryption (or storing your computer in a locked closet), anyone with boot media and the appropriate file drivers could enjoy the same access to your resources that the Windows Recovery Environment command prompt affords.

I T's probably only a slight exaggeration to say that no two computers are alike. Motherboards, disks and controllers, video and network adapters, and peripherals of all shapes and sizes combine to create a nearly infinite number of possible computer configurations.

Windows 7 supports a long list of computer peripherals. For supported hardware upgrades, Windows detects the device automatically and installs the correct driver software so that you can use the device and its full array of features. As we note in this chapter, however, the compatibility bar has been raised for some classes of older devices, and for 64-bit versions of Windows 7 the list of compatible devices is even more exclusive.

If Windows has a problem with a device, you have your choice of troubleshooting tools. Device Manager, available as part of the Computer Management console and as a stand-alone snap-in for Microsoft Management Console (MMC), is the primary tool for gathering information about installed devices and drivers and adjusting their configuration details.

What's in Your Edition?

You'll encounter no differences in working with hardware devices when you switch between computers running different editions of Windows 7. The procedures for installing devices, working with device drivers, and troubleshooting hardware problems are the same in all editions.

Installing a New Plug and Play Device

Since its introduction in Windows 95, Plug and Play technology has evolved tremendously. Early incarnations of this technology were notoriously unreliable, leading some users to dismiss the feature as "plug and pray." In recent years, however, hardware and software standards have converged to make most device configuration tasks completely automatic. With true Plug and Play devices, Windows 7 handles virtually all the work of configuring computer hardware and attached devices. For Plug and Play to work properly, all the pieces of a computer system must be capable of working together to perform hardware configuration tasks. Specifically, they must have the following capabilities:

- The system BIOS must be capable of responding to Plug and Play and power management events. By definition, any system with an Advanced Configuration and Power Interface (ACPI) BIOS includes this capability. Non-ACPI computers with a Plug and Play BIOS are capable of performing a subset of Plug and Play functions but will not be as capable as ACPI computers.

- The operating system must be capable of responding to Plug and Play events. Windows 7 fully supports the Plug and Play standard.

- The device must be capable of identifying itself, listing its required resources (including drivers), and allowing software to configure it. Microsoft has created a single "Compatible with Windows 7" logo that identifies hardware that meets these requirements. (The same logo is used for software that has passed compatibility and reliability tests.)

- The device driver must be capable of interacting with the operating system and responding to device notification and power management events. A Plug and Play driver can load automatically when Windows detects that a device has been plugged in, and it can suspend and resume operation properly along with the system.

In Windows 7, Plug and Play support is optimized for USB, IEEE 1394 (FireWire), PCMCIA (PC Card), ExpressCard, PCI, and PCI Express (PCIe) devices. By definition, any USB, PCMCIA, or ExpressCard device is a Plug and Play device, as are virtually all PCI and PCIe devices. Devices that connect to a parallel or serial port might or might not be fully Plug and Play compatible. No legacy devices that use the ISA bus are capable of being managed by Plug and Play; for the most part, ISA devices are found only in computers manufactured before the year 2000, and it's unlikely that Windows 7 will run acceptably—if at all—on hardware of that vintage.

INSIDE OUT
Run setup software at the right time

In many cases, new hardware devices include a setup CD that contains driver files and utility software. The best time to run this CD is *before* plugging in the device. If the drivers are signed, the setup program copies the driver files and Setup Information (.inf) file to your driver store folder so that installation can proceed automatically when you plug in the device. Some newer advanced devices work in just the opposite fashion and will install drivers only if the device itself is physically installed. When in doubt, check the documentation.

When you install a Plug and Play device for the first time, Windows reads the Plug and Play identification tag in the hardware's BIOS or firmware. It then compares that ID tag with a master list of corresponding tags drawn from all the Setup Information files in the %SystemRoot%\Inf folder. If it finds a signed driver with a matching tag, it installs the correct driver file (or files) and makes other necessary system modifications with no intervention required from you. Windows 7 displays the progress of Plug and Play operations in pop-up messages in the notification area. You might see a series of these notifications, beginning with a taskbar balloon like this:

In a few moments, a success message appears, either as a balloon or (if you have been following the status of the installation) a Drive Software Installation dialog box like this:

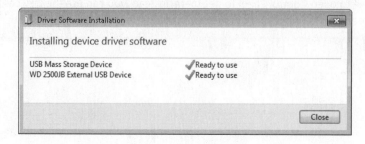

> **Note**
>
> Any user can install a new device if a driver for that device is included in the driver store. To add any signed or unsigned driver to the driver store when you are logged on as a member of the local Administrators group you must provide your consent in a User Account Control (UAC) dialog box. If you're logged on using an account without administrative permissions, you'll be prompted to supply an administrator's credentials to install a signed driver but will be unable to install any unsigned drivers.

If Windows detects a Plug and Play device (after you've plugged it into a USB port, for instance) but cannot locate a suitable signed device driver, it starts the Found New Hardware wizard. The purpose of this wizard is to assist you in the event that you know (or suspect) the location of a suitable driver. Start by clicking Locate And Install Driver Software (Recommended). Windows responds by searching all removable drives for a compatible driver. If the search is unsuccessful, you'll be prompted to insert the disc that came with your device. If your new device came with an installation CD containing drivers compatible with Windows 7, place that disc in your CD or DVD drive and allow installation to continue. If you've previously downloaded a Windows 7–compatible driver to your hard disk or to another form of removable media, click I Don't Have The Disk. Show Me Other Options. In the resulting dialog box, click Browse My Computer For Driver Software (Advanced). This option allows you to point the installer to a particular disk folder. Enter the full path of the folder that contains the downloaded driver and Setup Information file, or click Browse to point to this location. Click Next to search the specified location. Follow the prompts to complete the installation. Clear the Include Subfolders box if your downloaded driver package includes drivers for multiple Windows versions and you want to designate a specific version for installation.

Managing Devices with Devices And Printers

One of the significant usability improvements in Windows 7 is the Devices And Printers folder, shown in Figure 29-1. Devices And Printers resides within Control Panel, but you don't have to open Control Panel to get there. Instead, you can use the Devices And Printers command on the right side of the Start menu.

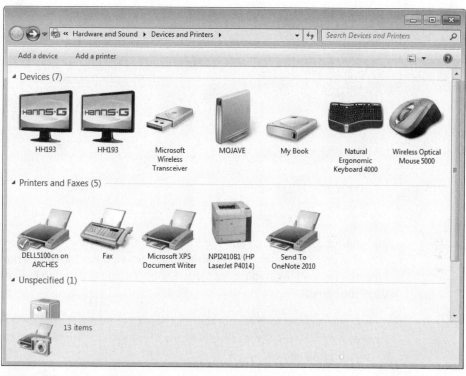

Figure 29-1 Devices And Printers gathers all your installed items in a single Control Panel folder, identifies them with friendly names and realistic icons, and provides appropriate action choices for each in a context-sensitive toolbar.

If you're a Windows veteran, you might be accustomed to digging through layers of Control Panel to do such things as change the pointer speed of your mouse or the repeat delay of your keyboard. You might also have made an occasional visit to Device Manager to see why a device isn't working as expected. You can still do all that in Windows 7, of course, but Devices And Printers might save you some of these trips.

Most essential configuration tasks for your printers and other hardware are now available via context menus in Devices And Printers. For some devices, such as monitors, keyboards, and mice, you'll find a settings command near the top of the menu. The settings command—such as the Keyboard Settings command shown next—opens the familiar properties dialog box similar to the ones in earlier versions of Windows.

Chapter 29

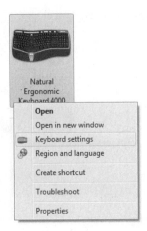

Some device context menus also sport Open and Open In New Window commands. Instead of opening traditional properties dialog boxes, these commands provide access to a modern alternative called Device Stage. For details, see "Managing Devices with Device Stage" on page 1067.

For complex devices, such as your computer itself, you'll find a rich assortment of options, some of which (Mouse Settings and Keyboard Settings, for example) duplicate commands found on individual peripherals:

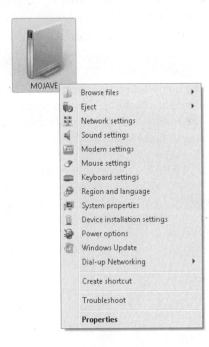

Three commands are common to all of these context menus: Create Shortcut, Troubleshoot, and Properties. Devices that aren't working properly are flagged with yellow exclamation points; the same familiar symbol highlights their Troubleshoot commands:

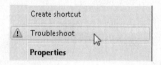

The Create Shortcut command plants a shortcut on your desktop, which makes the device's context menu accessible outside Devices And Printers. If you create a shortcut to the entry for your computer, for example, you can right-click that shortcut to go straight to such places as Sound Settings or Power Options.

The Properties command provides an alternative route to the dialog boxes that have traditionally been provided by Device Manager. We discuss those dialog boxes later in this chapter (see "Managing Devices with Device Manager" on page 1070).

INSIDE OUT   Get a free e-book on troubleshooting

Microsoft Press offers an e-book titled "What You Can Do Before You Call Tech Support" as a free download. Get it from *w7io.com/22901*.

Managing Printers and Print Queues

To configure a printer or work with a print queue, click the printer in Devices And Printers. Depending on the type of printer, you will see either a simple printer-queue dialog box or something more elaborate, like the one shown in Figure 29-2.

The top part of this display provides status information. In Figure 29-2, for example, we see that the Artisan 720 is set to print in portrait mode on letter-size paper and currently has nothing to do. The options below let you inspect and manipulate the print queue, change print settings (switch from portrait to landscape, for example), perform diagnostic tests and printer maintenance operations, scan documents and photos using the printer's built-in scanner, and obtain support information from the manufacturer.

Installing a Printer

To install a local printer that plugs into a USB port, you don't need to do anything in the Printers And Devices folder. Simply connect the device, and Plug and Play will do the rest. (See "Installing a New Plug and Play Device" on page 1056.) For information about installing a local printer that doesn't meet these standards, see the following section.

Chapter 29

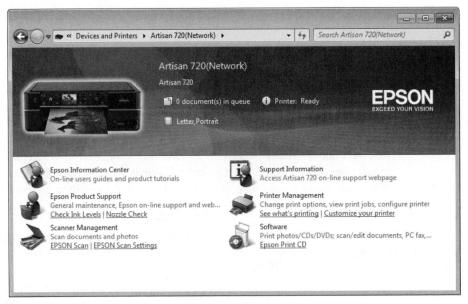

Figure 29-2 Clicking a printer in Devices And Printers might produce a dialog box similar to this, where you can see the status of the selected device, select print options, perform configuration tasks, and—in the case of a multifunction printer—scan documents and photos.

To make a networked printer available locally, click Add A Printer on the Devices And Printers toolbar. Then, in the Add Printer wizard, select the second option, Add A Network, Wireless Or Bluetooth Printer, and click Next. The wizard will scan the network for available printers:

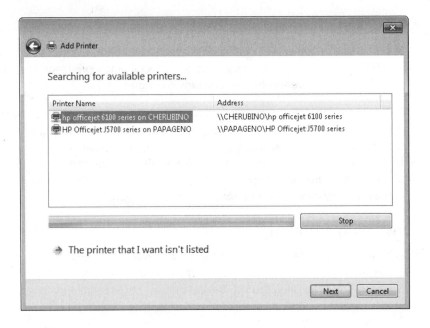

Select the printer you want to install, and click Next. If the network printer doesn't appear, click The Printer That I Want Isn't Listed, which brings up a dialog box (see Figure 29-3) that lets you use any of three methods to find the printer on the network:

- Select the first option to search Active Directory on a Windows Server–based network.

- Use the second option to enter the Uniform Naming Convention (UNC) path or Uniform Resource Locator (URL) for the network printer.

- Choose the third option to specify a printer using its TCP/IP address or host name. This method is typically used for network-attached printers that are not connected to a host computer and shared. If you use this method to identify a printer, you might want to give it a fixed IP address by using the printer's control panel (or its web-based settings page) or by configuring this on your network's DHCP server. If you use dynamic addressing and the address changes, you might not be able to print.

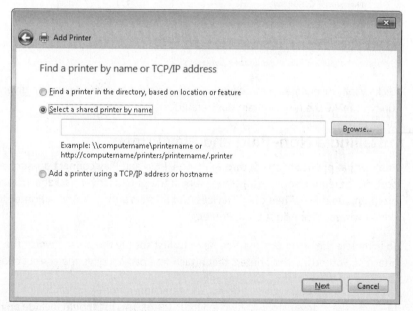

Figure 29-3 Depending on how your network is configured, you might have to search for the network printer.

INSIDE OUT Find a printer's TCP/IP address or host name

Often the easiest way to determine the TCP/IP address or host name for a printer is to use the printer's control panel to print a configuration page, which usually includes this information.

Because Windows requires a local copy of the network printer's driver, after you identify the network printer you want to use, you are likely to see a dialog box similar to the following:

Click Install Driver. In a moment, you'll receive a success message and be given the opportunity to make the new printer your default.

Installing a Non–Plug and Play Printer

Printers that physically attach through a non–Plug and Play connection, such as a parallel port, might require some extra setup work. If the printer driver package includes a setup program, run it first. Then open Devices And Printers and click Add A Printer. In the Add Printer wizard, click Add A Local Printer.

To complete the setup process, you need to first specify the port to which the printer is attached. For most older printers that attach to a parallel port, the correct choice is LPT1.

Click Next to select the correct driver. You can choose from a list of drivers available in the Windows 7 driver store (shown in Figure 29-4). This list should include any drivers you installed by running a setup program. If you have downloaded a printer driver that doesn't include a setup program, click Have Disk and browse to the correct location. If you don't have a driver, or if you suspect a more recent version might be available, click Windows Update to check Microsoft's collection of updated, signed drivers; after the update is complete, check the list again to see if your printer model is available.

The final step in the printer setup process is giving the printer a name. The default name typically includes the manufacturer's name and printer model; you can change this value to a more descriptive name now or later.

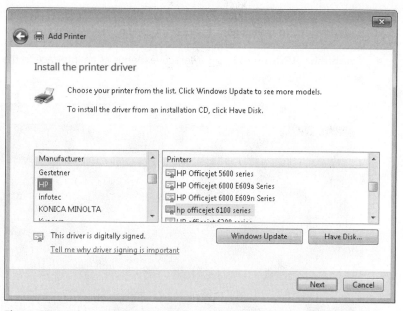

Figure 29-4 When installing a non–Plug and Play printer, use this dialog box to select the most up-to-date driver.

INSIDE OUT   Use a compatible driver

If you can't find a driver that's specifically designed for your printer, you might be able to get away with another driver. Check the hardware documentation to find out whether the printer emulates a more popular model, such as a Hewlett-Packard Laser-Jet. If so, choose that printer driver, and then print some test documents after completing setup. You might lose access to some advanced features available with your model of printer, but this strategy should allow you to perform basic printing tasks.

Using PowerShell Scripts to Manage Printers

Windows Management Instrumentation (WMI) provides methods for controlling all aspects of printers, including print queues and drivers. In the Scripts folder of this book's companion CD, you can find several sample scripts that you can use as is or incorporate into more full-featured scripts, including the following:

- **WorkWithPrinters.ps1** uses a command-line interface to perform a number of printer management tasks. For example, to list the printers on a computer, type **workwithprinters –computer** *computername* **–action list**. Other actions let you see which is the current default printer; set the default printer; print a test page; and pause, resume, or cancel jobs in the print queue.

- **TroubleshootPrinter.ps1** uses interactive menus as an interface to the built-in printer troubleshooters.

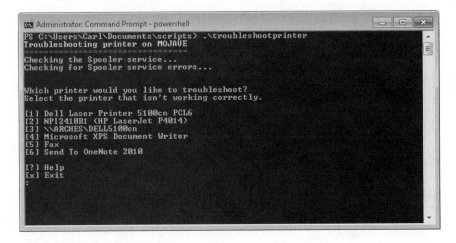

- **ListPrinters.ps1** displays a list of printers installed on a computer.

- **ListPrinterDrivers.ps1** displays details about each installed printer driver on a computer.

- **FindPrinterDrivers.ps1** displays a list of the printer setup installation files in the %SystemRoot%\Inf folder.

- **InstallPrinterDriver.ps1** installs a printer using a printer driver from the driver store. You must furnish the printer name as defined in the driver installation file.

- **InstallPrinterDriverFull.ps1** installs a printer using driver files stored in any location. You must furnish the printer name as well as the complete path to all files that make up the printer driver.

- **ListSharedPrintersAddPrintConnection.ps1** displays a list of shared printers on a remote computer and can create a connection to a remote shared computer.

- **Get-SharedPrinter.ps1** lists detailed information about each shared printer on a computer.

- **Get-PrinterPorts.ps1** displays a list of printer ports in use on a computer.

- **FindPrinterPorts.ps1** displays a list of printer ports in a range of IP addresses on a computer or network server.

- **Get-PrintQueueStatistics.ps1** displays statistics, such as the number of jobs and pages printed, about each installed printer.

For information about using these scripts, see "Running PowerShell Scripts" on page 999.

Managing Devices with Device Stage

Device Stage is a platform designed to provide a more pleasing assortment of status information and configuration options for peripheral devices. It's also intended to give device vendors a way of creating a more "branded" presentation for their end users. Device Stage is new in Windows 7, and you're likely to find support for Device Stage primarily on newer devices. (Although manufacturers can add Device Stage support to a driver fairly easily, the reality is that most manufacturers devote their development resources to new products instead of updating drivers for older products they no longer sell.) Figure 29-5 illustrates Device Stage, in this case for the Microsoft Natural Ergonomic Keyboard. As you can see in this example, Device Stage can include links to device vendors' websites (for support forums, driver downloads, opportunities to buy accessories, and more) and product documentation as well as access to settings.

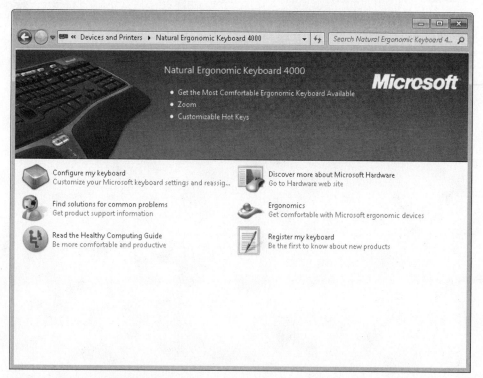

Figure 29-5 Device Stage provides a more pleasant, option-rich environment for using and configuring supported peripheral devices.

Chapter 29

Some devices that support Device Stage include an application that appears as a task-bar button when the device is connected. You can click such an icon to go straight to the device's Device Stage window, or you can hover your mouse over the icon to read status information. The taskbar button for a Sansa portable media player provides an example:

Right-clicking the taskbar button generates a context menu that typically includes the same commands that appear in the lower portion of the Device Stage window. By clicking Change General Settings on this menu, you can provide your own friendly name for the device. In the following example, we've renamed the Sansa m250 "My 2 GB Media Player."

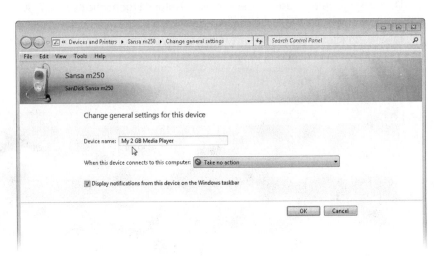

Using Windows Mobility Center

Windows Mobility Center is a special-purpose control panel (Mblctr.exe) that runs only on portable PCs running Windows 7 Home Premium or higher editions. (If you double-click the executable file on a desktop system, you'll get an error message.) You'll find Windows Mobility Center on the All Programs menu, in the Accessories folder. If you own a portable PC, however, we recommend that you memorize its keyboard shortcut, Windows logo key+X. Pressing that combination opens Windows Mobility Center.

On a clean installation of Windows 7, you'll see a collection of up to eight tiles, each of which controls a Windows setting. In addition, as the next example illustrates, PC manufacturers can include custom tiles and branding below the default configuration.

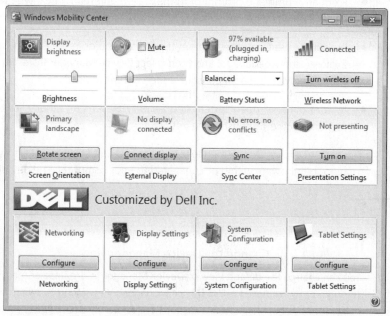

If some of the tiles shown here are missing on your portable PC, don't be alarmed. If your hardware doesn't support a particular setting (such as screen rotation), it won't appear here. Likewise, the Presentation Settings and Sync Center options are available only in the Professional or Ultimate editions.

Each of the tiles adheres to a common size, shape, and standard for interaction. Sliders allow you to quickly increase or decrease display brightness and speaker volume; buttons enable you to turn wireless adapters on or off. The hidden gem in each tile is the icon in the upper left corner, which is clickable and offers the most direct route to advanced settings. Clicking the Speaker icon, for example, opens the Sound Control Panel, and clicking the signal strength indicator in the Wireless Network tile opens the list of networks that are available for connection.

Chapter 29

Managing Devices with Device Manager

Knowing what hardware drivers are installed on your computer can make a huge difference when it comes to troubleshooting problems or configuring advanced features for a device. In every case, your starting point is Device Manager, a graphical utility that provides detailed information about all installed hardware, along with controls that you can use to configure devices, assign resources, and set advanced options. To open Device Manager, use any of the following techniques:

- In the Start menu search box, type **device**. Device Manager should appear near the top of the results list.

- From any command prompt or in the Start menu search box, type **devmgmt.msc** and press Enter.

- Right-click the Computer icon on the Start menu or in the Folders pane of Windows Explorer, choose Manage, and then select Device Manager from the left pane of the Computer Management console, under System Tools.

- In Control Panel, open System And Security, System, and then click the Device Manager link in the Tasks list in the left column.

As Figure 29-6 shows, Device Manager is organized as a hierarchical list that inventories every piece of hardware within or connected to your computer. The default view shows devices by type.

INSIDE OUT   Change the Device Manager view

You can change the default view of Device Manager to organize entries in the list by resource or by connection. Use Device Manager's View menu to switch between any of the four built-in views. Resource views are especially useful when you're trying to track down problems caused by interrupt request (IRQ) conflicts. Choosing either the Resources By Type view or the Resources By Connection view shows a list of all devices in which you can see how direct memory access (DMA), IO addresses, and IRQs are assigned. Another option on the View menu lets you show hidden devices.

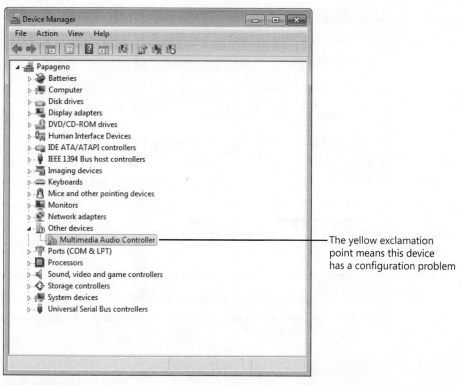

The yellow exclamation point means this device has a configuration problem

Figure 29-6 Click the plus sign to the left of each category in Device Manager to see individual devices within that category.

To view information about a specific device, double-click its entry in Device Manager's list of installed devices. Each device has its own multitabbed properties dialog box. At a minimum, each device includes two tabs, General and Driver. The General tab lists basic facts about the device, including the device name, the name of its manufacturer, and its current status, as shown in Figure 29-7.

The Driver tab, shown in Figure 29-8, lists version information about the currently installed driver for the selected device. Although the information shown here is sparse, it covers the essentials. You can tell at a glance who supplied the driver and whether it's digitally signed; you can also determine the date and version number of the driver, which is important when deciding whether you should download and install an available update.

Chapter 29

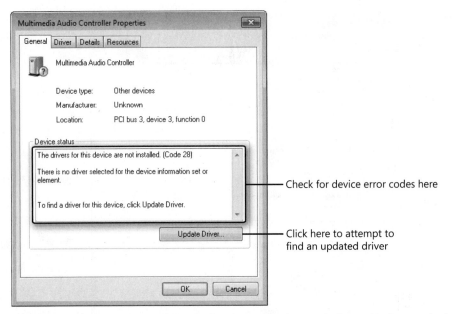

Check for device error codes here

Click here to attempt to find an updated driver

Figure 29-7 The General tab supplies basic information about a device and indicates whether it is currently functioning properly.

Figure 29-8 The Driver tab, which is available for every installed device, offers valuable information and tools for managing installed drivers.

To view additional information about an installed driver, click the Driver Details button on the Driver tab. As you can see from Figure 29-9, the Driver File Details dialog box provides far more comprehensive information, including the names and locations of all associated files. Selecting any file name from this list displays details for that file in the lower portion of the dialog box.

Figure 29-9 This detailed view of an installed driver provides important information about each file the device uses. In this example, the driver file is a Windows Hardware Quality Lab (WHQL)–certified driver, as shown by the Digital Signer field.

A separate Details tab provides, via a drop-down menu, a wealth of additional data points for the selected driver:

In addition to this basic information, the properties dialog box for a given device can include any number of custom tabs. The USB controller shown in Figure 29-10, for example, includes the basic information on the General and Driver tabs and adds a custom tab (Advanced) that allows you to view how much bandwidth is allotted to connected devices.

INSIDE OUT   Take inventory of installed drivers

If you want a more compact record of installed drivers in a format that you can review later, use the Driverquery command. Entering this command with no switches produces a simple list of installed devices and drivers. You can modify the output of the command with a variety of switches, and you can redirect the output of the command to a file so that you can load it in another program. For instance, you can use the /V switch to produce a detailed (verbose) listing, and add the /FO switch with the Csv parameter to generate the output in a format suitable for use in Microsoft Excel:

```
driverquery /v /fo csv > drvlist.csv
```

Open Drvlist.csv in Excel to see a neatly formatted and highly detailed list of all your hardware. (For a full list of the switches available for the Driverquery command, add the /? switch or search for Driverquery in Windows Help And Support.)

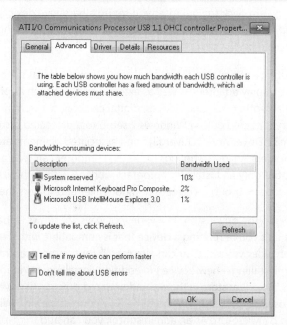

Figure 29-10 Some devices, including USB controllers and network adapters, allow you to view performance settings on an Advanced tab in the properties dialog box.

Chapter 29

By design, the information displayed in Device Manager is dynamic. When you add, remove, or reconfigure a device, the information stored here changes as well. In Windows XP, Device Manager included a Print command; this option is no longer available. To save a record of the settings for your system, including details about installed devices, you can generate a System Health report. To do this, open Performance Information And Tools in Control Panel, and then click Advanced Tools. Click the Generate A System Health Report option and wait about a minute until Windows finishes collecting data. The Devices section, under the Hardware Configuration category, includes all the information you normally find under Device Manager. You can save the resulting report as an HTML file (click Save As on the File menu), or click File, Print to send the full report to your default printer. The latter option, unfortunately, requires that you manually expand all the branches in the Devices category before printing.

A Crash Course in Device Drivers

Before Windows can work with any piece of hardware, it requires a compatible, properly configured device driver. *Drivers* are compact control programs that hook directly into Windows and handle the essential tasks of communicating your instructions to a hardware device and then relaying data back to you. After you set up a hardware device, its driver loads automatically and runs as part of the operating system, without requiring any further intervention on your part.

Windows 7 includes a library of drivers—for internal components such as sound cards, storage controllers, and display adapters as well as external add-ons such as printers, key-boards, scanners, mice and other pointing devices, digital cameras, and removable storage devices. This core library is copied during Windows 7 setup to a protected system folder, %SystemRoot%\System32\DriverStore. (Driver files and associated elements are stored in the FileRepository subfolder.) Anyone who logs on to the computer can read and execute files from this location, but only an installation program working with authorization from a member of the Administrators group can create or modify files and folders there.

You can add new drivers to the driver store in a variety of ways. Windows Update offers drivers when it detects that you're running a device that is compatible with that driver but is currently using an older version. (You can also search for the most recent driver via Windows Update when installing a new device.) In addition, installing a Windows service pack typically refreshes the driver store with new and updated drivers. All drivers that are copied here from Microsoft servers are certified to be fully compatible with Windows 7 and are digitally signed by Microsoft. As an administrator, you can add third-party drivers, signed or unsigned, to the driver store by specifically giving consent. All drivers added to the driver store in this fashion are saved in their own subfolder beneath the FileRepository folder, along with some supporting files created by Windows 7, which allows them to be reinstalled if necessary. Any driver that has been added to the store, signed or unsigned, is considered to be trusted and can be installed without prompts or administrator credentials.

In Windows 7, you do not have to be an administrator to install drivers; Windows checks the current driver installation policy to determine whether installation is permitted. When you install a new Plug and Play–compatible device, Windows checks the driver store first. If it finds a suitable driver, installation proceeds automatically. If no compatible driver is available, you're prompted to search for driver software.

By default, Windows 7 installs drivers from trusted publishers without prompts and never installs drivers from publishers that the user has chosen not to trust. When you attempt to install a signed third-party driver and have not previously designated the publisher as trusted or untrusted, you're presented with a consent dialog box. In addition to confirming the installation of the driver in question, this Windows Security dialog box gives you the opportunity to confer trust upon the driver's publisher. If you agree to trust the publisher, subsequent installations of drivers from that publisher will proceed without your explicit consent.

What if you're installing an unsigned driver? If you point the driver installer to an unsigned file while running a 32-bit version of Windows 7, you see a different Windows Security dialog box, one that warns you that Windows cannot verify the publisher of the driver you're trying to install. You can cancel the installation and look for a signed file (the default choice in this dialog box), or you can ignore the warning and continue.

To be properly installed in Windows 7, a hardware driver must have a Setup Information file (with the extension .inf). This is a text file that contains detailed information about the device to be installed, including the names of its driver files, the locations where they are to be installed, any required registry settings, and version information. All devices with drivers in the DriverStore folder include Setup Information files in the %SystemRoot%\Inf folder.

The basic structure of a Setup Information file is similar to an old-fashioned Windows 3.x–style .ini file. Each piece of setup information appears on its own line under a bracketed section heading. Windows will not allow the driver package to be copied into the driver store unless these sections are present and filled in correctly. In particular, an .inf file must contain valid [SourceDisksFiles] and [SourceDisksNames] sections. At the time the .inf file is copied into the driver store, Windows creates a folder for the driver files using the name of the .inf file with an eight-character hash appended to it. Inside that folder, Windows uses the data in the .inf file to create a Precompiled Setup Information file with the .pnf extension, which it uses for installation tasks.

Although the Setup Information file is a crucial part of the driver installation process, you don't work with it directly. Instead, this file supplies instructions that the operating system uses during Plug and Play detection or when you use the Add Hardware wizard or a setup program to install a device.

CAUTION !

> The syntax of Setup Information files is complex, and the intricacies of .inf files can trip up even experienced software developers. If you find that a driver setup routine isn't working properly, you might be tempted to try editing the Setup Information file to work around the hang-up. Trust us: that approach is almost certain to fail. In fact, by tinkering with .inf files, you run the risk of corrupting registry settings and crashing your system.

When Windows completes the installation of a driver package, it performs all the tasks specified by the Setup Information file and copies the driver files themselves to %SystemRoot%\System32\Drivers.

Is That Driver Signed?

As we noted earlier in this chapter, Windows 7 requires that all driver packages be trusted before they can be added to the driver store. Drivers pass an initial threshold of trust when they are digitally signed. But not all signatures are created equal. Here's a description of how Windows 7 handles different types of drivers:

- The highest level of trust is assigned to drivers that are signed by Microsoft's Windows Hardware Quality Lab (WHQL, often pronounced *wickle* by Microsoft insiders) through the Windows Logo Program. These so-called WHQL-signed drivers can be installed by any user, on any 32-bit or 64-bit version of Windows 7, without any warnings or requests for an administrator's consent. Any driver that is listed as Compatible with Windows 7 is also compatible with Windows Server 2008 R2, and vice versa.

- Drivers can also be signed by third parties by using Authenticode signatures, which use a certificate that is issued by a Certificate Authority whose certificate is stored in the Trusted Root Certification Authorities store. If an administrator has added the publisher's certificate to the Trusted Publishers store, the driver can be installed with no prompts by any user.

- If a driver is signed by a publisher whose certificate is not in the Trusted Publishers store, it can be installed by an administrator only. Installation will fail silently for users who are not members of the Administrators group. An administrator can also choose to add this type of signed driver to the driver store, after which it can be installed by any user with no prompts.

- Drivers that are unsigned, have a signature that is invalid or cannot be verified by a trusted Certificate Authority, or have a digital signature that has been altered can be installed by an administrator on 32-bit (x86) versions of Windows 7, but they cannot be installed on any 64-bit (x64) version of Windows 7.

To make the issue of driver signing even more confusing, there are two additional levels of digital signing to consider. For most driver packages, the only file that must be digitally signed is the *catalog file*, which uses a .cat extension. It lists the files included with the driver package and provides hashed digest numbers that uniquely identify each file and confirm that the file has not been tampered with. For drivers that start at boot-up on x64 versions of Windows 7, the driver file itself must contain an embedded signature. In addition, any device that is used to play back media that uses the Protected Media Path (PMP), such as Blu-ray discs and other formats that use the Advanced Access Content System (AACS) specification, must have a driver that is signed using a PMP-PE certificate. You can verify the contents of a Security Catalog file by double-clicking it in Windows Explorer.

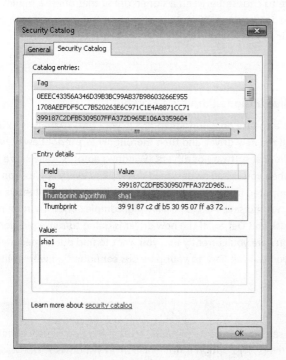

In general, you should prefer WHQL-signed drivers, which have undergone extensive compatibility testing using procedures established by Microsoft's hardware testing labs. These procedures provide strong assurance that the driver follows installation guidelines and

Chapter 29

that you can count on it not to cause your system to crash or become unstable. A digital signature from another trusted source doesn't confer the same assurance of reliability but does provide confidence that the driver hasn't been tampered with by other installation programs or by a virus or Trojan horse program.

Don't underestimate the negative consequences that can result from installing an unsigned driver that turns out to be faulty. Because hardware drivers access low-level functions in the operating system, a badly written driver is much more likely to cause Stop (blue screen) errors than a buggy program. Even a seemingly innocuous driver can result in sudden crashes that result in loss of data and prevent you from restarting your computer.

Sometimes you will have to make the difficult decision of whether to install an unsigned driver or give up the use of a piece of hardware. If the hardware device is essential and replacing it would be prohibitively expensive, and you're using a 32-bit version of Windows 7, you might decide that the risk is worth it. In other cases, the choice is more difficult, as when you have to choose between a signed driver that offers a minimal set of features and an unsigned alternative driver that allows you to take advantage of special features that are specific to your hardware.

INSIDE OUT Give unsigned drivers a workout

If you decide to take a chance on an unsigned driver, your best strategy is to back up your data first, install the new driver, and then thoroughly test it right away, without introducing any additional software or drivers. (Windows automatically sets a System Restore point when you install an unsigned driver.) Run every application that's installed on your computer. Try to run a few CPU-intensive and disk-intensive tasks at the same time. Open and save files, especially big, complex ones. Try running disk utilities such as Chkdsk and Defrag. If the new driver is going to cause problems with the hardware and software you currently use, you want to find out immediately after installing it so that you can roll back to your previous configuration with as little hassle as possible.

Windows XP allowed users to change the default settings and completely eliminate warnings about unsigned drivers. This option is not available in Windows 7 (nor was it in Windows Vista).

INSIDE OUT Dig deep for drivers

It's not always clear from the labeling on the outside of a CD or other installation media that the drivers it contains are for multiple Windows versions. Sometimes the structure of the disc itself can offer important clues. Look for a Windows 7 (or Windows Vista) subdirectory, for example, and point the Add Hardware wizard to that location when prompted. If a suitable .inf file is available, you might be able to complete the installation.

Configuring Legacy Devices

The Windows 7 driver store includes a small collection of drivers for legacy devices, mostly older printers, modems, scanners, infrared ports, PCMCIA controllers, and other oddball devices that don't use Plug and Play connections. As you might suspect, Windows will not automatically set up such devices, and you're rolling the dice if you find one of these old but still worthwhile devices and try to install an old driver. But what if the device in question is valuable to you and can't be easily replaced by a newer, supported one? Then by all means give it a try. Download the most recent hardware drivers you can find (ideally, for Windows XP or Windows Server 2003), and then use the Add Hardware wizard to complete the hardware setup process. Follow these steps:

1. If you've found a downloadable driver package or a CD that came with the device, look for a Setup program and run it. This option places the driver files on your hard disk and simplifies later installation steps.

2. Connect the new hardware to your computer. In the case of an internal device such as an add-in card, turn off the computer, add the device, and then restart.

3. Open Device Manager, select any item in the list of installed devices, and then click Add Legacy Hardware on the Action menu.

4. Click Next to skip past the Welcome screen. On the next wizard screen, choose how you want to select the device to be installed.

   - For printers, network cards, modems, and other devices that can be detected mechanically, choose Search For And Install The Hardware Automatically (Recommended). After you click Next, the wizard quickly runs a detection module that searches for anything on its list of non–Plug and Play devices. If it finds the new device, it installs the driver automatically, and your work is finished. If the wizard doesn't find any new hardware, you'll be prompted to click Next and look manually.

- If you have a driver on a disc, skip the detection process. Choose Install The Hardware That I Manually Select From A List (Advanced) and click Next.

5. From the Common Hardware Types list, select a hardware category (or the inclusive Show All Devices category) and click Next.

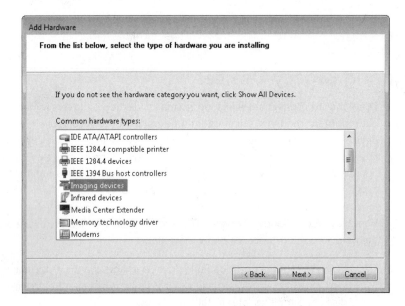

6. From the master list of available drivers, select the device manufacturer and the correct model. Click Next to continue. Follow the prompts to complete the wizard.

Changing Settings for an Installed Device

By default, Device Manager displays information about all currently installed and connected Plug and Play devices. To view devices that use non–Plug and Play drivers, as well as previously installed devices that are not currently connected, you need to tweak Device Manager slightly—for example:

- To view non–Plug and Play devices, open Device Manager and choose Show Hidden Devices from the View menu. In the default Devices By Type view, the formerly hidden devices appear under the Non–Plug And Play Drivers branch.

- To view devices that were once installed but are no longer attached to the computer, open a Command Prompt window using the Run As Administrator option and enter the command **set devmgr_show_nonpresent_devices=1**. Then, from the same command prompt, type **devmgmt.msc** to open Device Manager. Choose View, Show Hidden Devices. The new instance of Device Manager now shows "ghosted" entries for devices that were once present. This technique is especially useful for fixing problems caused by leftover drivers after replacing a network card or video card—just delete the ghosted device.

- To see advanced details about a device, open the properties dialog box for the device and look on the Details tab. The value shown under Device Instance Id is especially useful for tracking down devices that are detected incorrectly. The full details for a device ID shown here can be found in the registry, under HKLM\System\Current-ControlSet\Enum. Although we don't recommend idly deleting the found key, this information might be sufficient for figuring out why a device isn't being identified properly.

Setting the DEVMGR environment variable as described in this section affects only the instance of Device Manager launched from that Command Prompt window. If you want the change to be persistent, open Control Panel, open System, click Advanced System Settings, click Environment Variables on the Advanced tab, and define a new variable for this setting. If you add the variable to the User Variables section, the setting applies only to the current user; if you edit the System Variables section, the extra information is visible in Device Manager for all users of the current computer.

Adjusting Advanced Settings

Some devices include specialized tabs in the properties dialog box available from Device Manager. Controls on these additional tabs allow you to change advanced settings and properties for devices—for instance:

- Network cards and modems typically include a Power Management tab that allows you to control whether the device can force the computer to wake up from Sleep mode. This option is useful if you have fax capabilities enabled for a modem or if you use the Remote Desktop feature over the Internet on a machine that isn't always running at full power. On both portable and desktop computers, you can also use this option to allow Windows to turn off a device to save power.

- The Volumes tab for a disk drive contains no information when you first display the properties dialog box for that device. Click the Populate button to read the volume information for the selected disk. You can then choose any of the listed volumes, as shown in Figure 29-11, and click the Properties button to check the disk for errors, run the Defrag utility, or perform other maintenance tasks. Although you can perform these same tasks by right-clicking a drive icon in the Computer window, this option might be useful in situations where you have multiple hard disks installed and you suspect that one of those disks is having mechanical problems. Using this option allows you to quickly see which physical disk a given volume is stored on.

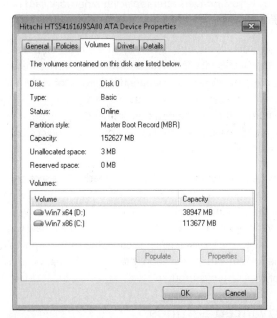

Figure 29-11 After you click the Populate button, the Volumes tab lists volumes on the selected drive and gives you full access to troubleshooting and maintenance tools.

- DVD drives offer an option to change the DVD region, which controls what discs can be played on that drive, as shown next.

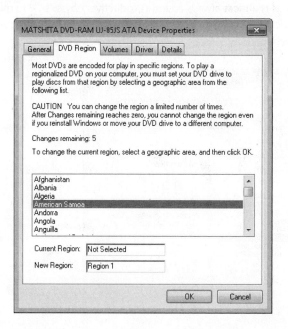

CAUTION

The DVD Region setting actually increments a counter on the physical drive itself, and that counter can be changed only a limited number of times. Be extremely careful with this setting, or you might end up losing the capability to play any regionally encoded DVDs in your collection.

- When working with network cards, you can often choose from a plethora of settings on an Advanced tab, as shown in the following example. Randomly tinkering with these settings is almost always counterproductive; however, you might be able to solve specific performance or connectivity problems by adjusting settings as directed by the device manufacturer or a Microsoft Support article.

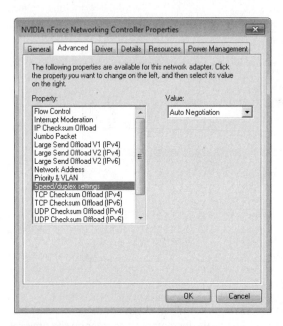

- Self-powered USB hubs (hubs that are connected to an AC power source) include a Power tab. Use the information on the Power tab to calculate the amount of power required by devices that draw power from the hub. If the total power requirement is more than the hub can supply, you might need a new hub.

Viewing and Changing Resource Assignments

If you're a PC veteran, you probably remember struggling with MS-DOS and early versions of Windows to resolve device conflicts, most often when two or more pieces of hardware lay claim to the same IRQ. On modern computers with an Advanced Configuration and Power Interface (ACPI) BIOS, those sorts of conflicts are practically extinct. In the original design of the IBM Personal Computer, IRQs were in short supply, with a total of 15 available, and many of those were reserved by system devices, such as communications ports, keyboards, and disk controllers. With older Windows versions, problems could occur when adding a new device such as a sound card or network adapter. If the new device was hard-wired to a specific IRQ that was already in use, or if there were no free IRQs, the device simply would not work.

On computers running Windows 2000, Windows XP, Windows Server 2003, Windows Server 2008, Windows Vista, or Windows 7 with a mix of PCI add-in cards, the operating system takes advantage of the ACPI features on the motherboard to share scarce IRQs among multiple devices. In Device Manager, you can check resource allocations at a glance by choosing Resources By Type or Resources By Connection from the View menu. In the example shown next, Windows 7 has assigned more than 130 IRQs; IRQs 19 and 20 are each being shared successfully by four PCI devices.

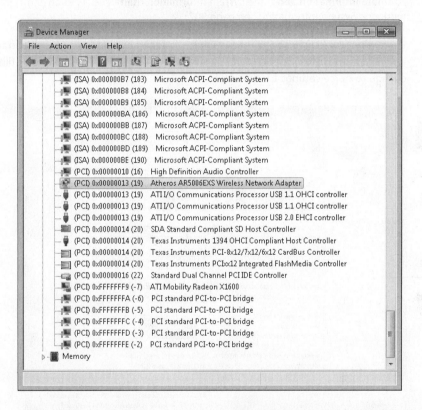

Under most circumstances, you cannot use Device Manager to change resource settings for a specific PCI or USB device. Resources are allocated automatically by the operating system at startup, and the controls to change resource settings are unavailable. Resource conflicts are most common with legacy devices that are not fully compatible with Plug and Play. In the rare event that you experience a resource conflict, you might be able to adjust resource settings manually from the Resources tab: clear the Use Automatic Settings check box, and cycle through different settings to see if any of the alternate configurations resolve the conflict.

If you suspect that a hardware problem is caused by a resource conflict, you can access an overview of resource usage by opening the System Information utility (Msinfo32.exe), which is found on the All Programs menu under Accessories, System Tools. Open Hardware Resources in the console pane, and pay special attention to the Conflicts/Sharing entry, shown in Figure 29-12, and the Forced Hardware item. Don't be alarmed if you see a number of devices sharing a single IRQ; that's perfectly normal.

For more information about the System Information utility, see "Finding and Decoding Information in System Information" on page 902.

For legacy devices whose resources can't be assigned by Windows, you'll need to adjust jumpers on the card or device or use a software-based setup/configuration utility to change resource settings for that device.

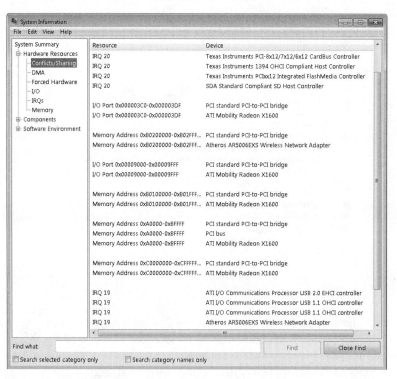

Figure 29-12 All the devices shown in this example are sharing resources properly. If two unrelated devices try to share a resource other than an IRQ, you might need to adjust device settings manually.

TROUBLESHOOTING

Resource conflicts prevent a device from working

If two devices are in conflict for a system resource, try any of these strategies to resolve the problem:

- With PCI and PCI Express devices, try swapping cards, two at a time, between slots. On some motherboards, IRQs and other resources are assigned on a per-slot basis, and moving a card can free up the proper resources. Check the motherboard documentation to see which IRQs are assigned to each slot, and experiment until you find an arrangement that works.

- If the conflict is caused by a legacy (ISA) device, replace it with a Plug and Play–compatible PCI device.

- Use jumpers or a software utility to change settings on a legacy device so that it reserves a different set of resources. You will need documentation from the manufacturer to accomplish this goal.

If you have problems with PCI devices, the device itself might not be to blame. When drivers and ACPI BIOS code interact improperly, conflicts can result. Check for an updated hardware driver (especially if the current driver is unsigned), and look for a motherboard BIOS update as well.

Managing Installed Drivers

If you're having a hardware problem that you suspect is caused by a device driver, your first stop should be Device Manager. Open the properties dialog box for the device, and use the following buttons on the Driver tab to perform maintenance tasks:

- **Update Driver** This choice starts the Hardware Update wizard.

- **Roll Back Driver** This option uninstalls the most recently updated driver and rolls back your system configuration to the previously installed driver. Unlike System Restore, this option affects only the selected device. If you have never updated the selected driver, this option is unavailable.

- **Uninstall** This button completely removes driver files and registry settings for the selected device. This option is available from Safe Mode if you need to remove a driver that is causing blue-screen (Stop) errors. You can also use this capability to remove a driver that you suspect was incorrectly installed and then reinstall the original driver or install an updated driver.

Chapter 29

INSIDE OUT Create a safety net before tinkering with drivers

When you install a new, unsigned hardware driver, Windows automatically attempts to create a new System Restore checkpoint. That doesn't mean it will be successful, especially if a problem with your System Restore settings has caused this utility to suspend operations temporarily. To make certain that you can roll back your changes if necessary, set a new System Restore checkpoint manually before making any kind of hardware configuration change. (For more details, see "Rolling Back to a Stable State with System Restore" on page 466.)

Updating a Device Driver

Microsoft and third-party device manufacturers frequently issue upgrades to device drivers. In some cases, the updates enable new features; in other cases, the newer version swats a bug that might or might not affect you. New WHQL-signed drivers are sometimes (but not always) delivered through Windows Update. Other drivers are available only by downloading them from the device manufacturer's website.

If the new driver includes a setup program, run it first so that the proper files are copied to your system. Then start the update process from Device Manager by selecting the entry for the device you want to upgrade and clicking the Update Driver button on the toolbar or the Update Driver option on the right-click shortcut menu. (You can also click Update Driver on the Driver tab of the properties dialog box for the device.) Click Search Automatically For Updated Driver Software if you want to look in local removable media and check Windows Update. Click Browse My Computer For Driver Software if you want to enter the location of a downloaded driver package or choose from a list of available drivers in the driver store.

INSIDE OUT Make sure that update is really an update

How do you know whether a downloaded version is newer than the currently installed driver on your system? A good Readme file should provide this information and is the preferred option for determining version information. In the absence of documentation, file dates offer some clues, but they are not always reliable. A better indicator is to inspect the properties of the driver files themselves. After unzipping the downloaded driver files to a folder on a local or network drive, right-click any file with a .dll or .sys extension and choose Properties. On the Version tab, you should be able to find details about the specific driver version, which you can compare to the driver details shown in Device Manager.

Rolling Back to a Previous Driver Version

Unfortunately, updated drivers can sometimes cause new problems that are worse than the woes they were intended to fix. This is especially true if you're experimenting with unsigned drivers or beta versions of new drivers. If your troubleshooting leads you to suspect that a newly installed driver is the cause of recent crashes or system instability, consider removing that driver and rolling your system configuration back to the previously installed driver.

To do this, open Device Manager and double-click the entry for the device you want to roll back. Then go to the Driver tab and click Roll Back Driver. The procedure that follows is straightforward and self-explanatory.

Uninstalling a Driver

There are at least three circumstances under which you might want to completely remove a device driver from your system:

- You're no longer using the device, and you want to prevent the previously installed drivers from loading or using any resources.

- You've determined that the drivers available for the device are not stable enough to use on your system.

- The currently installed driver is not working correctly, and you want to reinstall it from scratch.

To remove a driver permanently, open Device Manager and double-click the entry for the device in question. On the Driver tab, click Uninstall. Click OK when prompted to confirm that you want to remove the driver, and Windows removes the files and registry settings completely. If you installed the driver files from a downloaded file, the Confirm Device Uninstall dialog box includes a check box that allows you to remove the files from the driver store as well. This prevents a troublesome driver from being inadvertently reinstalled when you reinsert the device or restart the computer.

TROUBLESHOOTING

Your computer experiences sporadic blue screens, lockups, or other strange behavior

When your computer acts unpredictably, chances are good that a buggy device driver is at fault.

If you're experiencing unexplained computer problems, using a powerful trouble-shooting tool called Driver Verifier Manager (Verifier.exe) is a terrific way to identify flawed device drivers. Instead of your computer locking up at a most inopportune time with a misleading Blue Screen of Death (BSOD), Driver Verifier stops your computer

Chapter 29

predictably at startup with a BSOD that accurately explains the true problem. Although this doesn't sound like a huge improvement (your system still won't work, after all), Driver Verifier Manager performs a critical troubleshooting step: identifying the problem. You can then correct the problem by removing or replacing the offending driver. (If you're satisfied that the driver really is okay despite Driver Verifier Manager's warning, you can turn off Driver Verifier for all drivers or for a specific driver. Any driver that Driver Verifier chokes on should be regarded with suspicion, but some legitimate drivers bend the rules without causing problems.)

Driver Verifier works at startup to thoroughly exercise each driver. It performs many of the same tests that are run by WHQL as part of the certification and signing process, such as checking for the way the driver accesses memory.

Beware: If Driver Verifier Manager finds a nonconforming driver—even one that doesn't seem to be causing any problems—it will prevent your system from starting. Use Driver Verifier only if you're having problems. In other words, if it ain't broke...

To begin working with Driver Verifier Manager, type **verifier** at a command prompt. In the Driver Verifier Manager dialog box, shown here, select Create Standard Settings. In the next dialog box, select the type of drivers you want to verify. Unsigned drivers are a likely cause of problems, as are those created for an older version of Windows.

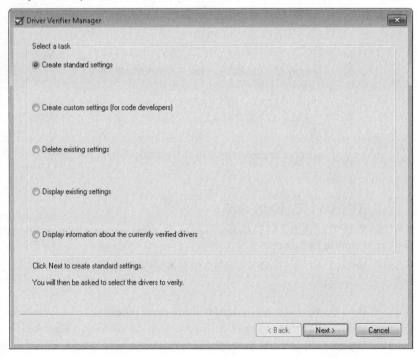

When you click Next, you get a list of all currently installed drivers that match the conditions you specified. Note that the list might contain a mix of hardware drivers and
some file-system filter drivers, such as those used by antivirus programs, CD-burning
software, and other low-level system utilities.

At this point, you have two choices:

- Go through the list and make a note of all drivers identified and then click Cancel. No changes are made to your system configuration; all you've done is gather
  a list of suspicious drivers, which you can then try to remove or disable manually.

- Click Finish to complete the wizard and restart your computer. Don't choose this
  option unless you're prepared to deal with the consequences, as explained in the
  remainder of this sidebar.

If your computer stops with a blue screen when you next log on, you've identified
a problem driver. The error message includes the name of the offending driver and
an error code. For information about the error codes, see Microsoft Support article
229903, "Partial List of Possible Error Codes with Driver Verifier," at *w7io.com/2401*.
(Although this article is specifically for Windows 2000, the information is valid for Windows XP, Windows Vista, and Windows 7.) To resolve the problem, boot into Safe Mode
(press F8 during startup) and disable or uninstall the problem driver. You'll then want to
check with the device vendor to get a working driver that you can install.

To disable Driver Verifier so that it no longer performs verification checks at startup,
run Driver Verifier Manager again and select Delete Existing Settings in the initial dialog box. Alternatively, at a command prompt, type **verifier /reset**. (If you haven't yet
solved the driver problem, of course, you'll be stopped at a BSOD, unable to disable
Driver Verifier. In that case, boot into Safe Mode and then disable Driver Verifier.)

You can configure Driver Verifier so that it checks only certain drivers. To do that, open
Driver Verifier Manager, select Create Standard Settings, click Next, and select the last
option, Select Driver Names From A List. This option lets you exempt a particular driver
from Driver Verifier's scrutiny—such as one that Driver Verifier flags but you are certain
is not the cause of your problem.

You can read more about Driver Verifier online in Microsoft Support article 244617,
"Using Driver Verifier to identify issues with Windows drivers for advanced users"
(*w7io.com/2402*).

INSIDE OUT Manage Plug and Play drivers

Removing and reinstalling the driver for a Plug and Play device requires a little extra effort. Because these drivers are loaded and unloaded dynamically, you can remove the driver only if the device in question is plugged in. Use the Uninstall button to remove the driver before unplugging the device. To reinstall the device driver without unplugging, open Device Manager and choose Action, Scan For Hardware Changes.

Enabling and Disabling Individual Devices

Installing and uninstalling device drivers can be a hassle. If all you want to do is enable or disable a specific device, you can do so from Device Manager. Select the device and click the Disable button on the Device Manager toolbar or right-click the device name and then click Disable on the shortcut menu. If a device is already disabled, both of these options toggle to Enable. The drivers for a disabled device remain available, but Windows does not load them.

You might choose to disable the driver for a device if all of the following conditions are true: you use it infrequently (or never), the device cannot be physically removed, and you want to avoid having it use resources or cause stability problems. This might be the case with an infrared receiver or Bluetooth adapter on a notebook, for example. Enable the device when you want to use it, and keep it disabled the rest of the time.

Note

In Windows XP, it was possible to define configurations called hardware profiles that could be chosen at startup. Each profile contained a list of installed devices that were enabled or disabled when that profile was selected. This feature was removed, beginning with Windows Vista. Will you miss it? Probably not. Hardware profiles are a relic of a bygone day, before Plug and Play, when portable computers were designed for use with docking stations containing add-in cards. Virtually all modern hardware devices, including docking stations, are capable of installing and uninstalling dynamically, making hardware profiles unnecessary.

Decoding Hardware Errors

When Windows encounters a problem with a device or its driver, it changes the icon in Device Manager and displays an error code on the General tab of the device's properties dialog box. Each code is identified by a number and a brief text description. Table 29-1 contains a partial list of error codes and suggested actions you should take to try to resolve them.

Table 29-1 **Common Device Manager Error Codes**

Error Code	Error Message	What to Do About It
1	This device is not configured correctly. (Code 1)	After downloading a compatible driver for the device, click the Update Driver button and follow the wizard's prompts to install the new driver.
3	The driver for this device might be corrupted, or your system might be running low on memory or other resources. (Code 3)	Check available memory and, if necessary, close some programs to free up RAM. If you have sufficient memory, try uninstalling and reinstalling the driver.
10	This device cannot start. (Code 10)	Click the Update Driver button to install updated drivers if any are available. The Troubleshoot button might provide useful information as well.
12	This device cannot find enough free resources that it can use. If you want to use this device, you need to disable one of the other devices on this system. (Code 12)	The device has been assigned one or more I/O ports, IRQs, or DMA channels used by another device. This error message can also appear if the BIOS is configured incorrectly (for example, if a USB controller doesn't get an IRQ from the BIOS). Check BIOS settings. Use the Resources tab to identify the conflicting device.
14	This device cannot work properly until you restart your computer. (Code 14)	The driver has probably been installed correctly, but it will not be started until you reboot the system.
16	Windows cannot identify all the resources this device uses. (Code 16)	A legacy device is improperly configured. Use the Resources tab to fill in the missing details.
18	Reinstall the drivers for this device. (Code 18)	Click the Update Driver button to start the Update Hardware wizard and reinstall the driver.
19	Your registry might be corrupted. (Code 19)	Incorrect or conflicting information is entered in the registry settings for this device. Try uninstalling and then reinstalling the driver. Try using System Restore to roll back the configuration to a point when the device worked properly.

Chapter 29

Error Code	Error Message	What to Do About It
21	Windows is removing this device. (Code 21)	Wait a few seconds, and then refresh the Device Manager view. If the device continues to display, restart the computer.
22	This device is disabled. (Code 22)	The device has been disabled using Device Manager. To enable it, click the Enable Device button.
24	This device is not present, is not working properly, or does not have all its drivers installed. (Code 24)	This is a catch-all error that can be caused by bad hardware or corrupt or incompatible drivers. This message also appears after you use the Remove Device option.
28	The drivers for this device are not installed. (Code 28)	After downloading a compatible driver for the device, click the Update Driver button and follow the wizard's prompts to install the new driver.
29	This device is disabled because the firmware of the device did not give it the required resources. (Code 29)	This is most commonly seen with SCSI adapters, third-party disk controllers, and other devices that supply their own BIOS. Check the documentation for the device to learn how to reenable it.
31	This device is not working properly because Windows cannot load the drivers required for this device. (Code 31)	Windows was unable to load the driver, probably because it is not compatible with Windows 7. After downloading a compatible driver for the device, click the Update Driver button and follow the wizard's prompts to install the new driver.
32	A driver service for this device was not required and has been disabled. (Code 32)	The driver has been disabled. The start type for this service is set to Disabled in the registry. If the driver really is required, change the start type in the BIOS by using the BIOS setup utility as defined in the documentation for the device. If the device previously worked properly, use System Restore to return to a working configuration.
33	Windows cannot determine which resources are required for this device. (Code 33)	This error typically indicates a misconfigured legacy device or a hardware failure. See the documentation for the device for more information.
34	Windows cannot determine the settings for this device. Consult the documentation that came with this device, and use the Resource tab to set the configuration. (Code 34)	This legacy device requires a forced configuration. Change the hardware settings (using jumpers or a software utility), and then use Device Manager's Resources tab to set the forced configuration.

Error Code	Error Message	What to Do About It
35	Your computer's system BIOS does not include enough information to properly configure and use this device. To use this device, contact your computer manufacturer to obtain a firmware or BIOS update. (Code 35)	This error is specific to multiprocessor systems. Check with the system manufacturer for a BIOS upgrade.
36	This device is requesting a PCI interrupt but is configured for an ISA interrupt (or vice versa). Please use the computer's system setup program to reconfigure the interrupt for this device. (Code 36)	IRQ translation failed. This error usually occurs on Advanced Power Management (APM) machines. Check BIOS settings to see if certain IRQs have been reserved incorrectly. Upgrade to an ACPI BIOS if possible.
37	Windows cannot initialize the device driver for this hardware. (Code 37)	After downloading a compatible driver for the device, click the Update Driver button and follow the wizard's prompts to install the new driver.
38	Windows cannot load the device driver for this hardware because a previous instance of the device driver is still in memory. (Code 38)	Restart the computer.
39	Windows cannot load the device driver for this hardware. The driver might be corrupted. (Code 39)	The driver is missing or corrupted, or it is in conflict with another driver. Look for an updated driver or reinstall the current driver. If the device worked previously, use System Restore to roll back to a working configuration.
40	Windows cannot access this hardware because its service key information in the registry is missing or recorded incorrectly. (Code 40)	Information in the registry's service key for the driver is invalid. Reinstall the driver.
41	Windows successfully loaded the device driver for this hardware but cannot find the hardware device. (Code 41)	This error occurs with legacy devices because Plug and Play cannot detect them. Use Device Manager to uninstall the driver and then use the Add Hardware wizard to reinstall it.
42	Windows cannot load the device driver for this hardware because there is a duplicate device already running in the system. (Code 42)	Restart the computer.

Error Code	Error Message	What to Do About It
43	Windows has stopped this device because it has reported problems. (Code 43)	A driver has reported a device failure. Uninstall and reinstall the device. If that doesn't work, contact the device manufacturer.
44	An application or service has shut down this hardware device. (Code 44)	The device has been halted by an application or a service. Restart the computer.
47	Windows cannot use this hardware device because it has been prepared for "safe removal," but it has not been removed from the computer. (Code 47)	The device has been prepared for ejection from a PCMCIA slot, USB port, or docking station. Unplug the device and plug it in again, or restart the computer.
48	The software for this device has been blocked from starting because it is known to have problems with Windows. Contact the hardware vendor for a new driver. (Code 48)	Contact the hardware vendor for a compatible driver.

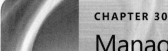

Managing Disks and Drives

W HEN you get right down to it, storage defines what you can and can't do with Windows. A big hard disk (or two or three) makes it possible for you to download and store an enormous amount of digital music, photos, and video; record and preserve television shows; manage large-scale, data-intensive projects; and keep your entire collection of digital resources safely backed up.

Using today's gigantic disks effectively, however, often entails partitioning them intelligently so that separate volumes can be assigned distinct purposes. For a variety of reasons, we recommend, for example, that you keep your operating system and personal data on separate volumes, that (if possible) you make a full image backup of the volume on which your Windows system files are stored, and that you make regular and frequent backups of your valuable data. All of this requires some planning and some familiarity both with disk-management concepts and with the management tools that Windows 7 provides.

For more information about file management, see Chapter 9, "Organizing Files and Information." For more information about backing up, see Chapter 12, "Backup, Restore, and Recovery."

In this chapter, we'll look at the disk-management tools provided by Windows 7 and survey some of the scenarios under which you might find these tools of use.

What's in Your Edition?

Disk management is the same in all editions of Windows 7.

The Windows 7 Disk-Management Toolkit

The principal disk-management tool in Windows 7 is the Disk Management console, Diskmgmt.msc. For those who need to incorporate disk-management tasks in scripts (as well as for those who simply prefer carrying out administrative tasks at the command prompt), Windows also provides a powerful command-prompt program called DiskPart. Everything that you can do with Disk Management you can also do using DiskPart; you just have to work harder and more carefully. Accessing Windows Management Instrumentation (WMI) through Windows PowerShell provides another method for managing disks. This method offers capabilities unavailable with the Disk Management console or DiskPart, and it has the additional advantage of custom programmability, which can be useful when you need to perform disk-management operations repeatedly on different computers.

If you've come to Windows 7 directly from Windows XP and have some familiarity with the disk-management tools in that earlier operating system, you'll find significant improvements in Windows 7. (These changes were introduced with Windows Vista.) Most notably, you can now shrink partitions as well as expand them from within the console. If you have a writable CD or DVD drive, you'll also appreciate the Windows 7 support for the Universal Disk Format (UDF). With UDF, you can write folders and files to CDs and DVDs as easily (if not as quickly) as you can write them to a hard disk. And if, like many others, you rely on portable computers or external hard disks (USB, IEEE 1394, or eSATA drives), you will be pleased to know that Windows now supports dynamic disks as well as basic disks on those devices.

Running Disk Management

To run Disk Management, do any of the following:

- At a command prompt, type **diskmgmt.msc**.

- Right-click Computer and choose Manage. The Computer Management console appears. In the console tree (the left pane), select Disk Management.

- In Control Panel, choose System And Security. Then, under the heading Administrative Tools, choose Create And Format Hard Disk Partitions.

> **Note**
> **Disk Management requires administrative credentials.**

Figure 30-1 illustrates the Disk Management console.

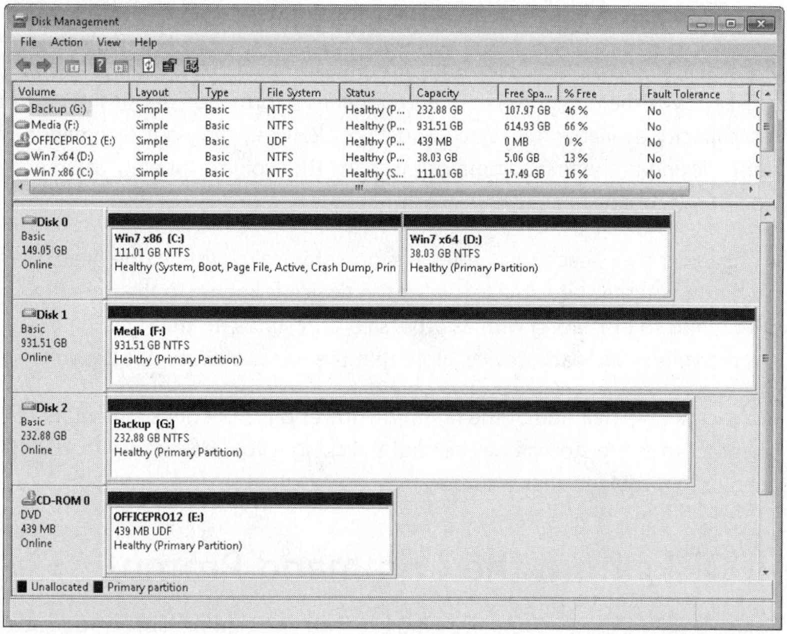

Figure 30-1 Use the Disk Management console to gather information about and manage hard disks and removable disks.

Disk Management provides a wealth of information about physical disks and the volumes, partitions, and logical drives in place on those disks. You can use this utility to perform the following disk-related tasks:

- Check the size, file system, status, and other properties of disks and volumes

- Create, format, and delete partitions, logical drives, and dynamic volumes

- Assign drive letters to hard disk volumes, removable disk drives, and optical drives

- Create mounted drives

- Convert basic disks to dynamic disks, and vice versa

- Create spanned and striped volumes

- Extend or shrink partitions

The Disk Management display is in two panes. In its default arrangement, the upper pane lists each volume on your system and provides information about the volume's type, status, capacity, available free space, and so on. You can carry out commands on a volume by right-clicking in the first column of this pane (the column labeled Volume) and choosing from the shortcut menu.

In the lower pane, each row represents one physical device. In the headings at the left of each row, you see the name by which the device is known to the operating system (Disk 0, Disk 1, and so on), along with its type, size, and status. To the right are rectangles representing the volumes of each device. Note that the rectangles are not drawn to scale.

Right-clicking a heading at the left in the lower pane provides a menu of commands pertinent to an entire storage device. Right-clicking a volume rectangle provides a menu of actions applicable to that volume.

Managing Disks from the Command Prompt

To use DiskPart, start by running Cmd.exe with elevated privileges. You can do that by opening the Start menu and choosing All Programs, Accessories. On the Accessories submenu, right-click Command Prompt, choose Run As Administrator, and then reply to the User Account Control (UAC) prompt.

For more information about the command prompt, see Appendix B, "Working with the Command Prompt."

When you run DiskPart, it opens a console window and dumps you at the DISKPART> prompt. If you type **help** and press Enter, you see a screen that lists all available commands, like the one shown next.

```
C:\Windows\system32\diskpart.exe

Microsoft DiskPart version 6.1.7601
Copyright (C) 1999-2008 Microsoft Corporation.
On computer: EXPLORER

DISKPART> help

Microsoft DiskPart version 6.1.7601

ACTIVE      - Mark the selected partition as active.
ADD         - Add a mirror to a simple volume.
ASSIGN      - Assign a drive letter or mount point to the selected volume.
ATTRIBUTES  - Manipulate volume or disk attributes.
ATTACH      - Attaches a virtual disk file.
AUTOMOUNT   - Enable and disable automatic mounting of basic volumes.
BREAK       - Break a mirror set.
CLEAN       - Clear the configuration information, or all information, off the
              disk.
COMPACT     - Attempts to reduce the physical size of the file.
CONVERT     - Convert between different disk formats.
CREATE      - Create a volume, partition or virtual disk.
DELETE      - Delete an object.
DETAIL      - Provide details about an object.
DETACH      - Detaches a virtual disk file.
EXIT        - Exit DiskPart.
EXTEND      - Extend a volume.
EXPAND      - Expands the maximum size available on a virtual disk.
FILESYSTEMS - Display current and supported file systems on the volume.
FORMAT      - Format the volume or partition.
GPT         - Assign attributes to the selected GPT partition.
HELP        - Display a list of commands.
IMPORT      - Import a disk group.
INACTIVE    - Mark the selected partition as inactive.
LIST        - Display a list of objects.
MERGE       - Merges a child disk with its parents.
ONLINE      - Online an object that is currently marked as offline.
OFFLINE     - Offline an object that is currently marked as online.
RECOVER     - Refreshes the state of all disks in the selected pack.
              Attempts recovery on disks in the invalid pack, and
              resynchronizes mirrored volumes and RAID5 volumes
              that have stale plex or parity data.
REM         - Does nothing. This is used to comment scripts.
REMOVE      - Remove a drive letter or mount point assignment.
REPAIR      - Repair a RAID-5 volume with a failed member.
RESCAN      - Rescan the computer looking for disks and volumes.
RETAIN      - Place a retained partition under a simple volume.
SAN         - Display or set the SAN policy for the currently booted OS.
SELECT      - Shift the focus to an object.
SETID       - Change the partition type.
SHRINK      - Reduce the size of the selected volume.
UNIQUEID    - Displays or sets the GUID partition table (GPT) identifier or
              master boot record (MBR) signature of a disk.

DISKPART> _
```

Even if you don't prefer the command prompt and don't intend to write disk-management scripts, you should know about DiskPart because if you ever find yourself needing to manage hard disks from the Windows Recovery Environment (Windows RE), you will have access to DiskPart but not to the Disk Management console. (Windows RE is a special environment that you can use for system-recovery purposes if a major hardware or software problem prevents you from starting Windows.)

For more information about Windows RE, see "Making Repairs with the Windows Recovery Environment" on page 1046.

Windows also includes a second command-line tool for file-system and disk management, called Fsutil. This utility allows you to find files by security identifier (SID), change the short name of a file, and perform other esoteric tasks.

CAUTION!

Fsutil and DiskPart are not for the faint of heart or casual experimentation. Both are intended primarily to be incorporated into scripts rather than for interactive use. DiskPart in particular is dense and cryptic, with a complex structure that requires you to list and select objects before you act on them. For more details about DiskPart, see Microsoft Support article 300415, "A Description of the DiskPart Command-Line Utility" (*w7io.com/2501*). Although this article dates from Windows XP days and some of the comparisons it makes between DiskPart and the Disk Management console are out of date, its tutorial information about the syntax and usage of DiskPart is still accurate.

PowerShell scripts that use WMI offer another command-line disk-management approach. As an example, a script called Get-VolumeInventory.ps1 on the companion CD displays information about the volumes on a specified computer, similar to this:

The heart of the script is this function, which relies on the Get-WmiObject cmdlet:

```
Function Get-VolumeInventory($computername)
{
 Get-WmiObject -Class Win32_Volume -filter "drivetype = 3" -ComputerName
    $computername
} # end get-DiskDriveInventory
```

You can find the complete script in the Scripts folder on the companion CD. Other disk-management scripts in that folder include the following:

- **Get-DiskPerformance.ps1** tests the disk performance on a computer and reports the percentage of time the disk is working.

- **Get-PageFile.ps1** displays the current page file settings. (For more information about the page file, see "Ensuring That You Have an Adequate Virtual-Memory Configuration" on page 856.)

- **Get-VolumeDirty.ps1** displays the status of the volume dirty bit, which determines whether the volume should be checked for errors the next time the computer is restarted.

- **Set-VolumeAutoCheck.ps1** sets the volume dirty bit, which causes the volume to be checked during the next restart. For this script to work properly, you must run it as an administrator; use the format **set-volumeautocheck –disk *d*:**, where *d* is the letter of the drive you want to mark for checking.

- **Get-VolumeLabel.ps1** displays the label for a specified volume. When prompted, enter the drive letter for the volume, followed by a colon.

- **Set-VolumeLabel.ps1** sets the label for a specified volume.

For information about using PowerShell scripts, see "An Introduction to Windows PowerShell" on page 980.

Understanding Disk-Management Terminology

The current version of Disk Management has simplified somewhat the arcane language of disk administration. Nevertheless, it's still important to have a bit of the vocabulary under your belt. The following terms and concepts are the most important:

- **Volume**   A *volume* is a disk or subdivision of a disk that is formatted and available for storage. If a volume is assigned a drive letter, it appears as a separate entity in Windows Explorer. A hard disk can have one or more volumes.

- **Mounted drive**   A *mounted drive* is a volume that is mapped to an empty folder on an NTFS-formatted disk. A mounted drive does not get a drive letter and does not appear separately in Windows Explorer. Instead, it behaves as though it were a subfolder on another volume.

- **Format**   To *format* a disk is to prepare it for storage using a particular file system (such as NTFS).

- **File system**   A *file system* is a method for organizing folders (directories) and files on a storage medium. Windows 7 supports the following file systems: FAT (File Allocation Table), NTFS (NT File System), CDFS (Compact Disc File System, also sometimes identified as ISO-9660), and UDF (Universal Disk Format).

- **Basic disk and dynamic disk**   The two principal types of hard-disk organization in Windows are called *basic* and *dynamic*:

  - A basic disk can be subdivided into as many as four partitions. (Disks that have been initialized using a GUID Partition Table can have more than four.) All volumes on a basic disk must be *simple* volumes. When you use Disk Management to create new simple volumes, the first three partitions it creates are *primary partitions*. The fourth is created as an *extended partition* using all remaining unallocated space on the disk. An extended partition can be organized into as many as two thousand *logical disks*. In use, a logical disk behaves exactly like a primary partition.

  - A dynamic disk offers organizational options not available on a basic disk. In addition to simple volumes, dynamic disks can contain *spanned* or *striped* volumes. These last two volume types combine space from multiple disks.

- **Simple volume**   A *simple volume* is a volume contained entirely within a single physical device. On a basic disk, a simple volume is also known as a *partition*.

- **Spanned volume**   A *spanned volume* is a volume that combines space from physically separate disks, making the combination appear and function as though it were a single storage medium.

- **Striped volume**   A *striped volume* is a volume in which data is stored in 64-KB strips across physically separate disks to improve performance.

- **MBR and GPT disks**   *MBR (master boot record)* and *GPT (GUID Partition Table)* are terms describing alternative methods for maintaining the information regarding a disk's subdivisions. GPT disks support larger volumes (up to 18 exabytes) and more partitions (as many as 128 on a basic disk). You can convert a disk from MBR to GPT (or vice versa) only before a disk has been partitioned for the first time (or after all partitions have been removed).

- **Active partition, boot partition, and system partition**   The *active partition* is the one from which an x86-based computer starts after you power it up. The first physical hard disk attached to the system (Disk 0) must include an active partition. The *boot partition* is the partition where the Windows system files are located. The *system partition* is the partition that contains the bootstrap files that Windows uses to start your system and display the boot menu.

Setting Up a New Hard Disk

Whether you're installing Windows on a brand new hard disk or simply adding a new disk to an existing system, it's a good idea to consider how you want to use the new storage space before you begin creating volumes. If your goal is to set up a large space for backup or media storage, for example, you might want to devote the entire disk to a single volume. On the other hand, if your plan is to establish two or more separate volumes—perhaps one for each family member on a shared home computer—decide how many gigabytes you want to assign to each partition. You can change your mind later (see "Managing Existing Disks and Volumes" on page 1114), but it's easiest to adjust the number of volumes on a disk and their relative sizes before you've put a lot of data on the platter.

Installing Windows on a New Disk

When you run the Windows 7 Setup program on a computer with a single, raw hard disk, Setup presents you with a screen identifying the disk and its size (see Figure 2-2 on page 35). If you want to create a single volume encompassing the entire disk, click Next to proceed. Otherwise click Drive Options (Advanced). On the screen that follows, you can use the Size control to specify how large a volume you want to create for your Windows installation:

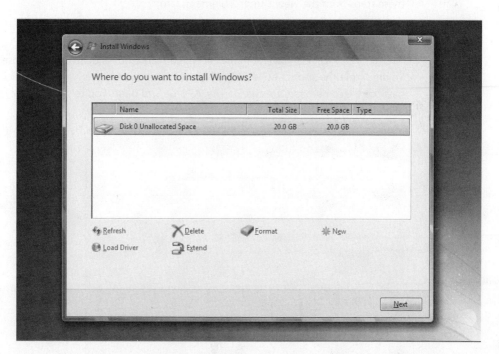

If you decide not to use the entire disk for Windows, you can create additional volumes from within the Setup program. But there's no particular need to do this. After you install

Windows, you can use Disk Management to create one or more additional volumes in the unallocated space remaining on the disk.

For more information about setting up Windows, see Chapter 2, "Installing and Configuring Windows 7."

Adding a New Disk to an Existing Windows Installation

In the graphical pane of Disk Management, a brand new hard disk, whether internal or external, appears like this:

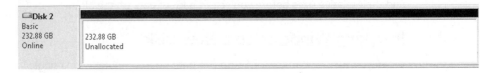

To make this disk available for storage, you need to create one or more volumes, assign drive letters, label the volumes (if you don't want them to be identified in Windows Explorer as simply "New Volume"), and format the new volumes. You can carry out all of these steps from the New Simple Volume wizard.

Specifying Volume Capacity

To begin, right-click anywhere in the rectangle marked Unallocated and choose New Simple Volume from the shortcut menu. The New Simple Volume wizard appears. Click Next to get past the welcome page. On the Specify Volume Size page, you're shown the maximum and minimum amounts of space you can devote to the new volume:

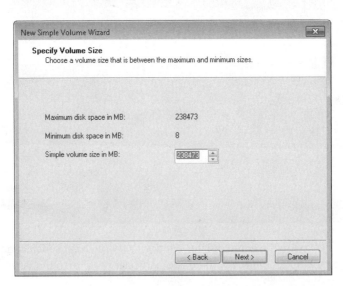

The wizard doesn't give you the option of designating volume space as a percentage of unallocated space, so if your goal is to create two or more volumes of equal size, you might want to do a bit of arithmetic before going on. Here, for example, if you wanted to split the disk into two equal partitions, you would enter 119236 in the Simple Volume Size In MB box.

Assigning a Drive Letter

After you have specified the volume size in megabytes and clicked Next, you are given the opportunity to assign a drive letter to the new volume. Note that the letters *A* and *B*, which used to be reserved for floppy disks, are no longer reserved:

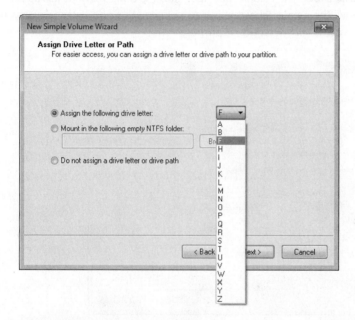

Formatting the New Volume

The Format Partition page, which follows the Assign Drive Letter Or Path page, gives you a chance to do just that, but it does not require that you do so. If you prefer to wait, you can always do the formatting later (right-click the volume's rectangle in the graphical pane of Disk Management and choose Format from the shortcut menu.) Figure 30-2 illustrates the Format Partition page.

Your choices are as follows:

- **File System**   For hard disk volumes larger than 4 GB (4,096 MB), your only options are NTFS (the default) and exFAT. If you are formatting removable media such as USB flash drives or a writable optical disc, other file systems are available. For more information, see "Choosing a File System" on page 1111.

- **Allocation Unit Size**   The allocation unit size (also known as the cluster size) is the smallest space that can be allocated to a file. The Default option, in which Windows 7 selects the appropriate cluster size based on volume size, is the best choice here.

- **Volume Label**   The volume label identifies the drive in Windows Explorer's Computer window. The default label text is New Volume. It's a good idea to give your new volume a name that describes its purpose.

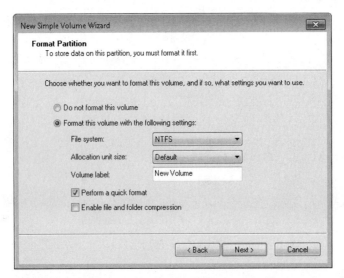

Figure 30-2 The Format Partition page lets you specify your new volume's file system, allocation unit size, and volume label.

Select Perform A Quick Format if you want Disk Management to skip the sometimes lengthy process of checking the disk media. Select Enable File And Folder Compression if you want all data on the new volume to use NTFS compression. (This option, which you can also apply later, is available only on NTFS volumes. For more information, see "Increase storage space with NTFS compression" on page 1115.)

The wizard's final page gives you one more chance to review your specifications. You should actually take a moment to read this display before you click Finish.

After Disk Management has done its work and disk formatting is complete, a dark blue bar appears over the new volume in the console's graphical pane:

If your disk still has unallocated space (as the disk in this example does), you can add another volume by right-clicking that part of the display and choosing New Simple Volume again.

Choosing a File System

Whether you're setting up a new disk or reformatting an existing one, the process of formatting entails choosing a file system. The choices available to you depend on the type of media you are formatting. With hard disks, the only options made available by Disk Management are NTFS and exFAT. If you want to format a hard disk in FAT or FAT32, you need to use the command-prompt Format command, with the /FS switch. (Type **format /?** at the command prompt for details.) The only good reason to do this, however, is for the sake of compatibility with systems running Windows 9x. (See "The Advantages of NTFS" on page 1112.) If you're dual-booting with Windows 9x and want the data on the volume you're formatting to be accessible to the Windows 9x partition, you should choose FAT32. Note that the 16-bit FAT, while still available, is a relic of much older days when disks were dramatically smaller.

If you're formatting a USB flash drive, on the other hand, FAT32 or exFAT is a reasonable choice. In the first place, a flash drive is likely to serve at times as a transfer medium, possibly with systems running earlier versions of Windows. Secondly, because NTFS is a journaling file system, reading and writing files on NTFS disks involves more disk input/output than similar operations on FAT32 and exFAT disks. Flash drives can perform a finite number of reads and writes before they need to be replaced—hence, they will likely have a longer life expectancy under FAT32 or exFAT than under NTFS. (For more information about exFAT, see "exFAT vs. FAT32" on page 1113.)

Choosing the Right UDF Version for Optical Media

If you're formatting a writable CD or DVD disc, your choices are various flavors of the Universal Disk Format (UDF). UDF, a successor to the CD-ROM file system (CDFS), is an evolving specification. Windows 7 can format discs using version 1.50, 2.00, 2.01, or 2.50. (Windows 7 can also use—but not format—discs using the latest version, which is 2.60.) Which to choose? It depends on whether you want the CDs or DVDs that you generate to be readable on systems running earlier versions of Windows or Windows Server 2003. The differences are as follows:

- **Version 1.50**   Can be read on systems running Windows 2000, Windows XP, Windows Vista, and Windows Server 2003.

- **Version 2.00 or 2.01**   Cannot be read on Windows 2000. Can be read on Windows XP Service Pack 3, Windows Vista, and Windows Server 2003. Note that version 2.01 is a minor revision of version 2.00. There is no reason to prefer version 2.00.

- **Version 2.50**   Can be read only on computers running Windows Vista, Windows 7, or Windows Server 2008 or later.

All of these variants are afforded read/write support by Windows 7, and none of them are supported in any form on Windows 9x platforms.

Choosing Between UDF and Mastered Optical Media

You do not have to format a CD or DVD (using one of the compatible UDF flavors) to store files on it. You can *burn* files to optical media in the manner introduced by Windows XP—by copying files to a temporary folder and transferring them *en masse* to the CD or DVD. Using UDF is somewhat more convenient because it allows you to read and write CD or DVD files as though they were stored on a USB flash drive or floppy disk. But the older method, sometimes called Mastered or ISO, offers greater compatibility with computers running other operating systems, and it's the only method that allows you to burn audio files and play them back on consumer audio devices.

Whatever choice you make, you have to make the same choice the next time you decide you want to transfer files to optical media. The default choice when you use Windows Explorer to burn files is UDF 2.01. To burn a mastered disk, you must explicitly change this option or use third-party software.

The Advantages of NTFS

As compensation for its incompatibility with Windows 9x, NTFS offers a number of important advantages over the earlier FAT and FAT32 file systems:

- **Security**   On an NTFS volume, you can restrict access to files and folders by using permissions. (For information about using NTFS permissions, see "What Are ACLs?" on page 644.) You can add an extra layer of protection by encrypting files if your edition of Windows 7 supports it. On a FAT or FAT32 drive, anyone with physical access to your computer can access any files stored on that drive.

- **Reliability**   Because NTFS is a journaling file system, an NTFS volume can recover from disk errors more readily than a FAT32 volume. NTFS uses log files to keep track of all disk activity. In the event of a system crash, Windows 7 can use this journal to repair file system errors automatically when the system is restarted. In addition, NTFS can dynamically remap clusters that contain bad sectors and mark those clusters as bad so that the operating system no longer uses them. FAT and FAT32 drives are more vulnerable to disk errors.

- **Expandability**   Using NTFS-formatted volumes, you can expand storage on existing volumes without having to back up, repartition, reformat, and restore.

- **Efficiency**   On partitions greater than 8 GB, NTFS volumes manage space more efficiently than FAT32. The maximum partition size for a FAT32 drive created by Windows 7 is 32 GB; by contrast, you can create a single NTFS volume of up to 16 terabytes (16,384 GB) using default settings, and by tweaking cluster sizes you can ratchet the maximum volume size up to 256 terabytes.

- **Optimized Storage of Small Files**   Files on the order of a hundred bytes or less can be stored entirely within the Master File Table (MFT) record, rather than requiring a minimum allocation unit outside the MFT. This results in greater storage efficiency for small files.

For more information about the NTFS, FAT, and UDF file systems, see the white paper at *w7io.com/2502*.

exFAT vs. FAT32

Microsoft introduced the Extended FAT (exFAT) file system first with Windows Embedded CE 6.0, an operating system designed for industrial controllers and consumer electronics devices. Subsequently, exFAT was made available in Windows Vista Service Pack 1 (SP1). Its principal advantage over FAT32 is scalability. The exFAT file system removes the 32-GB volume and 4-GB file-size limitations of FAT32. It also handles more than one thousand files per directory. Other benefits of exFAT are described at *w7io.com/23001*. Its principal disadvantage is limited backward compatibility. Systems running Windows XP, for example, require a hotfix to read exFAT32 devices, and non-PC consumer electronics devices, at this time, are more likely to be able to read earlier FAT systems than exFAT.

If you're formatting a high-capacity media player and expect to store large video files on it, exFAT might be a good file-system choice. If you're formatting a flash disk to use to transfer data from your Windows 7 system to other computers running Windows XP or Windows Vista, you're probably better off sticking with FAT32. And if you're planning to take that flash disk to a photo kiosk at your local convenience store, FAT32 is definitely the way to go.

INSIDE OUT Formatting does *not* remove a volume's data

Whatever formatting options you choose, you are warned that the action of formatting a volume makes that volume's data inaccessible. That's true. Whatever data is there when you format will no longer be available to you by normal means after you format. Unless you use the /P switch, the data remains in some form, however. If you're really concerned about covering tracks, either use the format /P:*x* (where *x* represents the number of passes) or wipe the disk after you format it by using the command-line program Cipher.exe, with the /W switch. (Type **cipher /?** at the command prompt for details. For information about other ways to clean a disk, see "Permanently Wiping All Data from a Disk" on page 1127.)

Managing Existing Disks and Volumes

No matter how well you plan, your approach to deploying storage resources is likely to change over time. Disk Management can help you adjust to changing requirements. You can expand volumes (assuming space is available), shrink volumes, reformat, relabel, assign new drive letters, and more. We'll consider these options next.

Extending a Volume

Disk Management will be happy to make an NTFS volume larger for you, provided unallocated space is available on the same or another hard disk. To accomplish the expansion, right-click the volume you want to expand and choose Extend Volume from the shortcut menu. Click Next to move past the Extend Volume wizard's welcome page. The Select Disks page, shown in Figure 30-3, appears.

The Selected list, on the right side of this dialog box, initially shows the disk whose volume you intend to extend. The Maximum Available Space In MB box shows you how much larger you can make the volume, assuming you want to confine your expansion to the current disk. The Select The Amount Of Space In MB box, initially set to equal the maximum available space, is where you declare the number of megabytes you want to add to the volume, and the Total Volume Size In Megabytes (MB) box shows you how big your volume is about to become. When you're ready to continue, click Next, review your orders on the ensuing page, and then click Finish. If your volume resided on a basic disk to begin with, it will remain basic after the expansion—provided the space into which you expanded was contiguous with the original volume. Note that no separate formatting step is required; the new territory acquires the same formatting as the original.

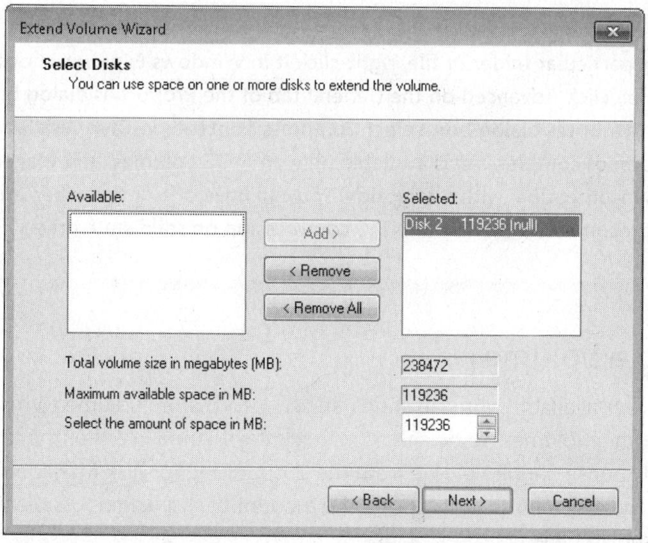

Figure 30-3 The Extend Volume wizard lets you extend a volume into unallocated space on the same or another hard disk with free space.

Volume extension is subject to the following limitations:

- Only NTFS-formatted volumes can be extended.

- A logical drive can be extended only within the extended partition that contains it.

- The system and boot partitions can be extended only into contiguous unallocated space.

- You cannot extend a striped volume.

INSIDE OUT   Increase storage space with NTFS compression

If you're thinking of expanding a partition because you're running short of space, consider compressing your files and folders instead. You can compress individual files, particular folders, or entire volumes. Items compressed in this manner are decompressed on the fly when you open them and recompressed when they are closed. You won't achieve huge savings in storage space this way—less than you would get by using compressed (zipped) folders—but the convenience of NTFS is high and the cost, in terms of performance, is virtually unnoticeable. To compress a volume, open Computer in Windows Explorer, right-click the volume, choose Properties, and then, on the General tab of the Properties dialog box, select Compress This Drive To Save Disk Space. To compress a particular folder or file, right-click it in Windows Explorer, choose Properties, and then click Advanced on the General tab of the Properties dialog box. In the Advanced Attributes dialog box, select Compress Contents To Save Disk Space. Note that this form of compression is available only on NTFS volumes, and that NTFS compression is incompatible with encryption. You can have one or the other, but not both. We do not recommend the use of NTFS compression on solid state drives (SSDs).

Shrinking a Volume

Provided space is available, you can shrink an NTFS-formatted volume to make more space available for other volumes. To do this, right-click the volume in either the tabular or graphical pane and choose Shrink Volume from the shortcut menu. Disk Management responds by analyzing the disk, and then it reports the amount of shrinkage possible in a dialog box like the one shown here.

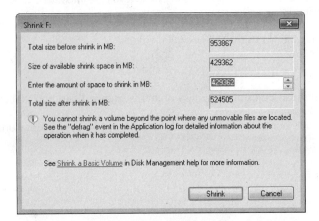

Enter the number of megabytes by which you want to reduce your volume, and then click Shrink. Disk Management defragments the disk, moving all its data to a contiguous block, and then performs the shrink.

Be aware that page files and volume shadow copy files cannot be moved during the defragmentation process. This means that you might not have as much room to shrink as you would like. Microsoft also advises that the amount by which you can shrink a volume is "transient" and depends on what is happening on the volume at the time. In other words, if you are trying to eliminate, say, 10 GB from the volume, and Disk Management can manage only 7, take the 7 and then try for more later.

INSIDE OUT   Force Windows to shrink a volume

The process of shrinking a volume in Windows 7 can be frustrating, especially after you've used that volume for any length of time. Even though Disk Management reports ample unused space on the disk, you might find yourself able to shrink the volume by only a small amount. In one recent example, we were working with a 366-GB disk that reportedly had 287 GB of free space. Disk Management, however, reported that it could shrink the volume by only 172 GB. So how do you make use of the extra space? Carefully. Try the following steps in order, checking after each one and stopping when you find that enough space is available:

1. Start by disabling System Restore on the volume. (Right-click Computer and choose Properties. Click System Protection, select the drive on which you want to disable System Restore, and then click Configure. In the System Protection dialog box, click Turn Off System Protection.) This action deletes all existing volume shadow copies on the volume and often frees up a significant amount of space.

2. Temporarily configure the volume to use no page file, using the procedure described in "Ensuring That You Have an Adequate Virtual-Memory Configuration" on page 856. Be sure to reset the page file after you complete the disk shrink operation.

3. Use a third-party defragmenter to reorganize data files, and choose the option to move the Master File Table (MFT) to the beginning of the volume. (You must use a third-party tool for this task; the Windows 7 Defrag tool doesn't offer this capability.) If the MFT is in the middle of the volume, you will be unable to take advantage of any shrink space between it and the end of the data area.

If none of these steps give you as much space as you were looking for, choose the most drastic option: make an image backup of the current volume (see "Creating a System Image Backup" on page 444). After verifying that the image is good, delete the volume and restore it from the image file. Immediately after completing the restore, attempt to shrink the volume again; you should find that virtually all free space is available for you to use.

Deleting a Volume

Deleting a volume is easy—and irreversible. All data is lost in the process, so be sure you have backed up or no longer need whatever the volume currently contains. Then right-click the volume and choose Delete Volume. The volume reverts to unallocated space, and if it happens to have been the last volume on a dynamic disk, the disk itself is converted to basic.

Chapter 30

Converting a FAT32 Disk to NTFS

To convert a FAT or FAT32 disk to NTFS, use the command-line Convert utility. The essential syntax is

```
convert d: /fs:ntfs
```

where *d* is the drive letter you want to convert. For information about optional parameters, type **convert /?** at the command prompt.

The Convert utility can do its work within Windows if the drive to be converted is not in use. However, if you want to convert the system volume or a volume that holds a page file, you might see an error message when you run Convert. In that case, you must schedule the conversion to occur the next time you start Windows. After you restart the computer, you'll see a prompt that warns you that the conversion is about to begin. You have 10 seconds to cancel the conversion. If you allow it to proceed, Windows will run the Chkdsk utility and perform the conversion automatically. During this process, your computer will restart twice.

> **CAUTION**
>
> Converting your system drive to NTFS makes it impossible to restore a previously installed operating system that requires FAT32, such as Windows 9x. The Convert utility warns you about this fact in no uncertain terms. If you have set up your system using a multiboot configuration so that you can continue to run Windows 9x, do not convert the system drive to NTFS; doing so will make it impossible to start your previous Windows version.

Assigning or Changing a Volume Label

In Windows 7, as in previous versions of Windows, you can assign a descriptive text label to any volume. Assigning a label is purely optional, but it's a good practice, especially if you have a multiboot system or if you've set up separate volumes to keep your data organized. You can use *Data* as the label for your data drive, *Music* for the drive that holds your collection of digital tunes, and so on. Volume labels appear in the Computer window alongside the drive letter for a volume, as in the example shown here:

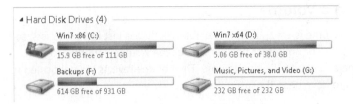

You can enter a volume label when you format a new volume, or you can do it at any time afterward by right-clicking a volume (in Disk Management or in Windows Explorer), choosing Properties, and entering text in the edit field near the top of the General tab.

 If you need to view or change the volume name programmatically, two scripts located in the Scripts folder on the companion CD, Get-VolumeLabel.ps1 and Set-VolumeLabel.ps1, provide a good starting point. (Note that when the scripts ask you to furnish a disk parameter, you must enter the drive letter followed by a colon.)

Assigning and Changing Drive Letters

You can assign one and only one letter to a volume. For all but the following volumes, you can change or remove the drive letter at any time:

- The boot volume

- The system volume

- Any volume on which the page (swap) file is stored

To change a drive-letter assignment, right-click the volume in Disk Management and choose Change Drive Letter And Paths. (You can do this in either the graphical or tabular pane.) To replace an existing drive letter, select it and click Change. To assign a drive letter to a volume that currently has none, click Add. Select an available drive letter from the Assign The Following Drive Letter list, and then click OK twice.

INSIDE OUT   Restore those missing card-reader drives

Windows 7, unlike Windows Vista, does not display empty drives by default. If your computer has a set of drives for memory cards, you're accustomed to seeing those drives listed in Windows Explorer whether the drives are empty or not. If you want to put things back the way they used to be, open Windows Explorer, choose Tools, Folder Options (start by pressing Alt if the menu bar isn't visible), click the View tab, and then clear Hide Empty Drives In The Computer Folder.

Mapping a Volume to an NTFS Folder

In addition to (or in place of) a drive letter, you can assign one or more paths to NTFS folders to a volume. Assigning a drive path creates a *mounted volume* (also known as a *mounted drive*, *mounted folder*, or *volume mount point*). A mounted volume appears as a folder within an NTFS-formatted volume that has a drive letter assigned to it. Besides allowing you to sidestep the limitation of 26 drive letters, mounted volumes offer these advantages:

- You can extend storage space on an existing volume that's running low on free space. For instance, if your digital music collection has outgrown your drive C, you can create a subfolder of your Music folder and call it, say, More Music. Then you can assign a drive path from a new volume to the More Music folder—in effect increasing the size of your original Music folder.

- You can make commonly used files available in multiple locations. Say you have an enormous collection of clip art that you store on drive X, and each user has a folder in his or her Documents folder where they store desktop publishing files. In each of those personal folders, you can create a subfolder called Clip Art and assign that folder's path to volume X. That way, the entire clip art collection is always available from any user's desktop publishing folder, and no one has to worry about creating shortcuts to X or changing drive letters while they work.

To create a mounted volume, follow these steps:

1. In Disk Management, right-click the volume you want to change. (You can do this in either the graphical pane or the tabular pane.) Choose Change Drive Letter And Paths from the shortcut menu.

2. Click Add to open the Add Drive Letter Or Path dialog box.

3. Select Mount In The Following Empty NTFS Folder. (This is the only option available if the volume already has an assigned drive letter.)

4. Click the Browse button. The Browse For Drive Path dialog box that appears shows only NTFS volumes, and the OK button is enabled only if you select an empty folder or click New Folder to create one.

5. Click OK to add the selected location in the Add Drive Letter Or Path dialog box, and then click OK to create the drive path.

You can manage files and subfolders in a mounted volume just as though it were a regular folder. In Windows Explorer, the folder icon will be marked by a shortcut arrow. If you right-click the folder icon and choose Properties, the General tab will reveal that the folder is actually a mounted volume, as shown next.

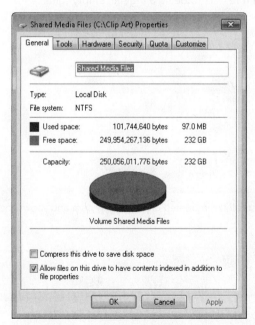

And, as Figure 30-4 shows, if you click the Properties button within that properties dialog box, you'll see more details about the drive to which the folder is mapped.

Figure 30-4 The properties dialog box for a mounted drive identifies the volume that actually holds its files.

If you use the Dir command in a Command Prompt window to display a folder directory, a mounted volume is identified as <JUNCTION> (for *junction point*, yet another name for mounted volume), whereas ordinary folders are identified as <DIR> (for *directory*, the MS-DOS term for a folder).

CAUTION

When creating mounted volumes, avoid establishing loops in the structure of a drive—for example, by creating a drive path from drive X that points to a folder on drive D and then creating a drive path on drive D that points to a folder on drive X. Windows allows you to do this, but it's invariably a bad idea, because an application that opens subfolders (such as a search) can go into an endless loop.

To see a list of all the mounted drives on your system, choose View, Drive Paths in Disk Management. A dialog box like the one shown in Figure 30-5 appears. Note that you can remove a drive path from this dialog box; if you do so, the folder remains in the same spot it was previously located, but it reverts to being a regular, empty folder.

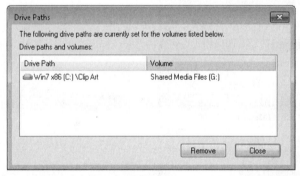

Figure 30-5 This dialog box lists all the mounted drives on a system and shows the volume label, if any, of each mounted drive.

INSIDE OUT Make a bootable flash disk

A bootable flash disk can be a great way to install Windows 7 on a netbook that lacks an external DVD drive. Putting the system files on a flash disk also makes the operating system a little easier to tote, if you happen to need the ultimate in portability. The trick is to make the flash disk's partition active, and Disk Management won't do that for you. Fortunately, DiskPart, the command-line disk-management utility, is willing and able. For a clearly written, well-illustrated set of step-by-step instructions, see "Windows 7: Setting Up a USB Bootable Device for Installs," by Microsoft blogger Jeff Alexander, at *w7io.com/2503*. For additional details, see "Expediting Multiple Windows Installations by Installing from a USB Flash Drive" on page 950.

INSIDE OUT Burn ISO images onto blank DVDs

Windows 7 makes it easy to transfer .ISO files to DVD. Simply right-click the .ISO file in Windows Explorer, choose Burn Disc Image from the context menu, and follow the prompts. No more scrambling for third-party disc-burning utilities. (You can also select the .ISO file and click Burn on the toolbar.)

Checking the Properties and Status of Disks and Volumes

As with previous Windows versions, you can check the properties of any drive—including the volume label, file system, and amount of free space available—by right-clicking the drive in Windows Explorer's Computer folder and choosing Properties from the shortcut menu. You can see the same details and more in Disk Management. Most of the crucial information is visible in the volume list, the tabular pane that appears by default at the top of the Disk Management window. Slightly less information is available in the graphical pane at the bottom of the window. Of particular interest is information about the status of a disk or volume. Figure 30-6 shows where to look for this information.

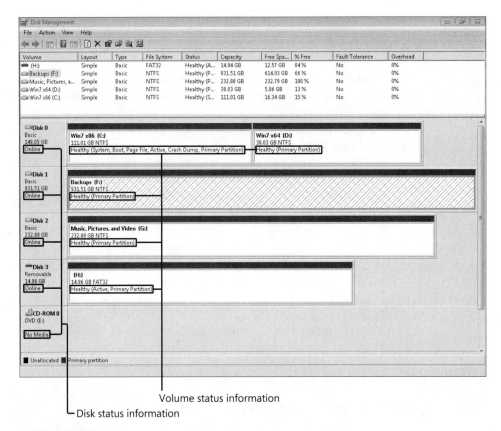

Volume status information

Disk status information

Figure 30-6 Disk Management displays information about the status of each disk and volume.

Under normal circumstances, the status information displayed here should report that each disk is online and each volume is healthy. Table 30-1 lists all possible disk status messages you might see on a system running Windows 7, along with suggested actions for resolving possible errors.

Table 30-1 **Disk Status Messages**

Status	Description	Action Required
Online	The disk is configured correctly and has no known problems.	None.
Online (Errors)	The operating system encountered errors when reading or writing data from a region of the disk. (This status message appears on dynamic disks only.)	Right-click the disk and choose Reactivate Disk to return its status to Online. If errors continue to occur, check for damage to the disk.
Offline	The disk was once available but is not currently accessible. The disk might be physically damaged, or it might be disconnected. (This status message appears on dynamic disks only.)	Check the physical connections between the disk and the power supply or disk controller. After repairing connections, right-click the disk and choose Reactivate Disk to return its status to Online. If the damage cannot be repaired, delete all volumes, right-click the disk, and choose Remove Disk.
Foreign	The disk was originally installed on another computer and has not yet been set up for use on your computer. (This status message appears on dynamic disks only.)	Right-click the disk and choose Import Foreign Disks.
Unreadable	All or part of the disk might be physically damaged, or (in the case of a dynamic disk) the dynamic disk database might be corrupted.	Restart the computer. If the problem persists, right-click the disk and choose Rescan Disks. If the status is still Unreadable, some data on the disk might be recoverable with third-party utilities.
Missing	The disk is corrupted, disconnected, or not powered on. (This status message appears on dynamic disks only.)	After you reconnect or power on the missing disk, right-click the disk and choose Reactivate Disk to return its status to Online.
Not Initialized	The disk does not contain a valid signature. It might have been prepared on a system running a non-Microsoft operating system, such as UNIX or Linux, or the drive might be brand new.	If the disk is used by another operating system, do nothing. To prepare a new disk for use with Windows 7, right-click the disk and choose Initialize Disk.
No Media	A disc is not inserted in the drive. (This status message appears only on removable media drives, such as CD and DVD drives.)	Insert a disc in the drive, and choose Action, Rescan Disks.

Chapter 30

Table 30-2 describes volume status messages you're likely to see.

Table 30-2 **Volume Status Messages**

Status	Description	Action Required
Healthy	The volume is properly formatted and has no known problems.	None.
Healthy (At Risk)	Windows encountered errors when reading from or writing to the underlying disk. Such errors are often caused by bad blocks on the disk. After encountering an error anywhere on the disk, Disk Management marks all volumes on that disk as Healthy (At Risk). (This status message appears on dynamic disks only.)	Right-click the disk and choose Reactivate Disk. Persistent errors often indicate a failing disk. Back up all data, and run a thorough diagnostic check using the hardware manufacturer's software; if necessary, replace the disk.
Healthy (Unknown Partition)	Windows does not recognize the partition; this occurs with some partitions created by another operating system or by a computer manufacturer that uses a partition to store system files. You cannot format or access data on an unknown partition.	If you're certain the partition is unnecessary, use Disk Management to delete it and create a new partition in the free space created.
Initializing	Disk Management cannot determine the disk status because the disk is initializing. (This status message appears on dynamic disks only.)	Wait. The drive status should appear in a few seconds.
Failed	The dynamic disk is damaged or the file system is corrupted.	To repair a failed dynamic volume, check to see whether the disk is online. (If not, right-click the disk and choose Reactivate Disk.) Then right-click the volume and choose Reactivate Volume. If the failed volume is on a basic disk, be sure that the disk is properly connected.
Unknown	The boot sector for the volume is corrupted, and you can no longer access data. This condition might be caused by a virus.	Use an up-to-date virus-scanning program to check for the presence of a boot-sector virus.

Permanently Wiping All Data from a Disk

Formatting a volume results in a root folder that appears to be empty. However, as we mentioned earlier in this chapter, someone with data-recovery tools might be able to restore deleted files even after you format the volume. If you're discarding or recycling an old computer or hard disk, you don't want to risk the possibility of it landing in the hands of someone who might search it for recoverable data that can be used for identity theft or other nefarious purposes.

If your old disk is headed for the dump, you can ensure the data can't be recovered by removing the disk drive from the computer and physically destroying the disk. Using tools as varied as a power saw, drill, torch, or sledge hammer, you can render the disk inoperable. Although this method is effective, it has several disadvantages: it takes time, considerable physical effort, and has all the usual risks associated with tools. (Be sure you're wearing safety goggles.) Perhaps most important, you're left with a disk that can't be sold or donated to someone who can use it.

As we mentioned earlier, the Format command (with the /P switch) and the Cipher command (with the /W switch) can be used to overwrite everything on a disk, but these tools are impractical for cleaning the system partition.

A better solution is to use a third-party disk-wiping tool. A free one that we like is Darik's Boot And Nuke (DBAN), which you can download from *dban.org*. DBAN is a bootable disk that securely wipes a computer's hard disks. If you're worried that DBAN or another purported disk-wiping utility might surreptitiously steal your data before destroying it, remove your concerns by disconnecting your computer from your network before using the program.

If your disk contains highly sensitive material and you want to be absolutely sure its data can't be recovered, search for a utility that conforms to the United States Department of Defense DoD 5220.22-M standard for clearing and sanitizing media. This standard requires each sector to be overwritten with different characters several times, thus defeating even the most sensitive data-recovery tools. Programs that meet the standard include Active@ KillDisk (*killdisk.com*) and BCWipe (*jetico.com*).

Working with Virtual Hard Disks

New in the Windows 7 version of Disk Management is the capability to create virtual hard disks in the .VHD format used by Microsoft Virtual PC and the Hyper-V feature of Windows Server 2008 R2. A .VHD file encapsulates all the characteristics of a simple disk volume in a single file. Once created, initialized, and formatted, it appears as a disk drive in Windows Explorer and Disk Management, but you can copy it, back it up, and do anything else with it that you might do with an ordinary file.

To create a virtual hard disk, open Disk Management and choose Action, Create VHD. Disk Management responds with the Create And Attach Virtual Hard Disk dialog box:

Specify a file name with a fully qualified path. It's easiest to do this with the help of the Browse button, but note that the file cannot be stored in your %SystemRoot% (usually C:\Windows) folder. If you want the disk to expand in size as you add files to it, choose Dynamically Expanding. Otherwise, choose Fixed Size (Recommended). Either way, you must also specify a size (that's an initial size if you choose Dynamically Expanding). The minimum size is 3 MB; the maximum is the amount of free space available on your (real) disk.

After you complete these steps, Disk Management adds the disk to its graphical display as an unknown, uninitialized disk with unallocated space:

Right-click the box at the left side of this display (the one with the disk number), and then choose Initialize Disk:

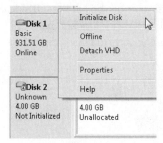

The Initialize Disk dialog box will give you the option of setting up a disk with a master boot record or a GUID Partition Table:

Choose MBR (Master Boot Record) unless you're working with a very large disk. On completion of these steps, you can follow the procedures described earlier in this chapter to create one or more volumes on the new disk. After you have created a volume, formatted it, and assigned it a drive letter, the disk appears like any other in Disk Management and Windows Explorer:

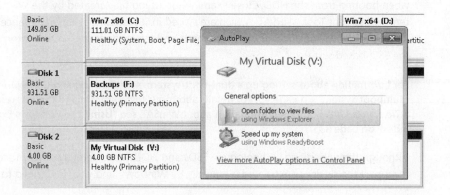

To remove a virtual hard disk, right-click the disk-number box at the left side of Disk Management's graphical display and choose Detach VHD. Disk Management will give you the option of deleting the disk file that encapsulated your virtual hard disk:

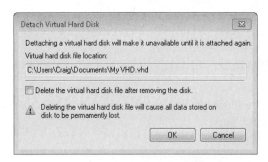

If you think you might need to use the virtual disk again, leave the check box clear. You can remount the disk subsequently by choosing Action, Attach VHD in Disk Management.

Working with Solid State Drives

Many newer computers are equipped with a solid state drive (SSD), which is a chunk of flash memory instead of a spinning magnetic disk. Such drives can provide improved performance, increased battery life, better durability, reduced likelihood of damage caused by drops and shocks, faster startup times, and reductions in noise, heat, and vibration. These benefits come at a price: SSDs typically cost more and have less storage capacity than current hard disk drive (HDD) models, although the gap is closing.

Conventional hard disk drives are typically the biggest performance bottleneck in any computing environment. If you can speed up disk activity, especially reads, the effects on system startup and application launch times can be breathtaking. On our test platform, which has a conventional hard disk and a solid state drive configured for dual booting, the total boot time when using the SSD is less than half the time (about 30 seconds) than when booting from the HDD. Close examination of log files created by the Windows System Assessment Tool (WinSAT), which are stored in %SystemRoot%\Performance\WinSAT\ DataStore, shows radically higher throughput and faster times in the DiskMetrics section of the SSD-based system.

For information about setting up a dual-boot system, see "Creating and Configuring a Multiboot System" on page 49. For details about our test platform and the test results, see w7io.com/23002. For more information about WinSAT, see "Using the Windows Experience Index" on page 835.

Although the underlying technology in SSDs and HDDs is completely different, for the most part the devices are treated identically by Windows, and you don't need to concern yourself with the differences. Behind the scenes, Windows does several things differently on SSDs, including:

- Defragmentation is disabled. Because SSDs can directly retrieve bits from random disk locations instead of waiting for a spinning disk to come into position, random access speeds are very fast, and defragmenting an SSD provides virtually no performance improvement. And because SSDs degrade with increased use, defragmenting can unnecessarily shorten the life of the SSD.

  For more information about defragmenting, see "Defragmenting Disks for Better Performance" on page 886.

- SuperFetch, ReadyBoost, ReadyBoot, and ReadyDrive, features designed to overcome hard disk bottlenecks, are also unnecessary and are disabled by default on most SSDs. (Windows analyzes disk performance and disables these features only on SSDs that are fast enough to make these features superfluous.)

- When creating a partition on an SSD, Windows properly aligns the partition for best performance.

- Windows 7 supports the TRIM command, which allows the system to properly erase blocks of data in the background. You can find more details in this white paper from MaximumPC: *w7io.com/23003*.

In general, there's little you need to do except enjoy the benefits. However, we do have some recommendations that ensure you get the best performance from your SSD:

- Be sure you're using the latest firmware for your SSD. Check with the computer manufacturer or SSD manufacturer to see if a firmware update is available. Particularly if your drive (and its firmware) came out before the release of Windows 7 in 2009, you might find that an update adds support for important performance features included in Windows 7 but not in earlier Windows versions.

CAUTION!

> In most cases, applying a firmware update wipes out all data on the drive. Therefore, you must first back up all your data and then update the firmware by following the manufacturer's instructions.

If you update the firmware (and, therefore, need to reinstall Windows), you should take the following additional steps:

1. In the system BIOS, set the Serial ATA (SATA) disk controller to Advanced Host Controller Interface (AHCI) mode. Using the legacy IDE or ATA mode prevents

you from installing the proper disk controller driver later and will result in reduced performance.

2. Boot from the Windows 7 media to begin the clean installation process. Use the Windows Setup utility to create the partition. If you have a partition created using any other tool, delete it and use the Windows 7 disk tools to create a new one. This ensures that the partition is properly aligned. For details about deleting and creating partitions during setup, see "Setup and Your Hard Disk" on page 42.

- Avoid using NTFS compression on SSDs—particularly for frequently used folders and small files. Because of the way Windows writes to disk, you're likely to notice a performance hit with this setup.

Using Pen, Touch, and Voice Input

I N this chapter, we discuss activities that by their very nature require hardware not found on a generic PC with the Windows operating system. In place of a keyboard and mouse, you can use your fingers, a digital pen, or your voice to manipulate objects on the screen, enter data, and control how Windows works.

The Tablet PC, which uses a special screen and a stylus to capture text and other input, has been a part of the Windows family since 2002. Those functions have been refined in Windows 7, including the ability to recognize even the most idiosyncratic (and in some cases downright sloppy) handwriting. Extensions to these features in Windows 7 allow you to perform many functions by tapping the screen with a fingertip and using simple gestures to read and navigate. If the screen is capable of recognizing multiple simultaneous touch points, the range of available gestures expands impressively; using a thumb and index finger together, for example, you can resize text and rotate images in a multitouch-aware program.

Voice recognition, the other unconventional input mode built into Windows 7, requires a microphone—typically, one that has more capabilities than the pinhole mikes that are standard on many notebooks. With a high-quality headset or an array microphone, you can turn dictation into text and control the Windows interface with the power of speech.

What's in Your Edition?

Speech recognition features are available in all editions of Windows 7. Pen and touch features require custom hardware and are supported in the Home Premium, Professional, Ultimate, and Enterprise editions.

Enabling and Customizing Pen and Touch Features

For years, touching a PC screen did nothing except leave a greasy smudge on the glass. That's still the case if you have a desktop or notebook PC with a conventional display—Windows 7 cannot magically turn your old LCD into a touch screen. But if your hardware includes a display that can recognize the touch of a pen or a finger, you can input text and manage windows, icons, and other on-screen objects directly.

For basic program management and web browsing, you can use a finger or the Tablet PC pen as a mouse and open programs, select menu options, move scroll bars, and click hyperlinks by pointing, dragging, and tapping. If your PC includes a pen, you can use it to enter handwritten notes directly on the screen, using pen-aware applications such as Windows Journal (included with Windows 7) or Microsoft OneNote. You can add handwritten annotations to Microsoft Word documents and Microsoft Excel spreadsheets and share the marked-up files—even if your coworker is using a conventional PC. You can send handwritten notes to other people via e-mail or Windows Live Messenger, or you can convert those scribbled notes to text and then insert the converted text into other documents.

The full range of features available to you depends on your hardware. At the time we wrote this chapter, widely available options included two basic categories of PC designs:

- **Touch-enabled PCs** These are typically all-in-one devices that integrate the motherboard, memory, and storage in the same housing as the display. You can use a keyboard or mouse for conventional computing tasks or hide those input devices and control media playback and other functions by using touch.

- **Tablet PCs** These are notebook computers that include the capability to let you enter and edit data by using a pen and a specially digitized screen. Tablet PC hardware typically uses one of two configurations. *Slate* designs do not include a built-in keyboard (although they can accept an external keyboard or mouse) and are intended for use primarily with a pen. *Convertible* designs resemble a conventional notebook, with a keyboard and pointing device; by rotating the screen on a hinge and folding it over the keyboard, you can switch the PC into a position that allows you to work with the pen in a more natural fashion. From a software point of view, there is no difference between the two designs.

The history of PC design suggests that these form factors will be joined in the future by new designs that take advantage of touch features for special-purpose applications. For example, it's easy to imagine a small touch-enabled device, powered by Windows 7, that is designed to sit on a living room table and control Windows Media Center functions on a big-screen TV.

INSIDE OUT   What makes a touch or tablet screen special?

The difference between a standard LCD display and one that is able to accept direct input from a pen or finger is an extra layer of technology called a *digitizer*. The specific implementations of this technology vary, depending on the intended application, and can typically be divided into two broad classes. An *active digitizer* responds only to a specific type of input device, such as a pen or stylus, which contains electronic components that transmit electromagnetic information to the sensor behind the LCD. This arrangement allows the digitizer to respond to input even if the point of the stylus is merely hovering over the screen; it also allows Windows to record different degrees of pressure with very high precision (to make thick and thin ink strokes, for example). A *passive digitizer*, which is typically used in dedicated devices such as ATMs and check-in kiosks at airports, is less precise and responds to any kind of pressure, including the press of a finger. Hybrid designs combine both types of digitizer technologies to allow handwriting input and simplified touch navigation.

If you have an older computer that supports pen or single-touch input only, you will not be able to enable the multitouch features in Windows 7. In fact, even some PC designs that bill themselves as multitouch might not provide you access to the new touch features in Windows 7. If in doubt, look for the logo indicating that the computer has passed Microsoft's stringent compatibility tests for touch support. Finally, if your computer has a touchpad that is capable of accepting multitouch input, prepare to be at least a little disappointed. These features are supplied by device manufacturers only and are not supported by the Windows Touch subsystem in Windows 7.

If you purchase a new PC with Windows 7, any drivers and utilities required to enable touch and pen input will already be installed by the PC maker. If you upgrade to Windows 7 or perform a clean install, you might need to visit the hardware manufacturer's website to download and install required drivers. To check the status of pen and touch support, open Control Panel, click System (under the System And Security heading), and look at the last line under the System heading. The system whose properties are shown here includes support for the full range of pen and multitouch features.

System	
Rating:	**3.5** Windows Experience Index
Processor:	Intel(R) Core(TM)2 Duo CPU U7700 @ 1.33GHz 1.33 GHz
Installed memory (RAM):	3.00 GB (2.75 GB usable)
System type:	32-bit Operating System
Pen and Touch:	Pen and Touch Input Available with 4 Touch Points

To see the full range of hardware settings, you need to familiarize yourself with the options under the Pen And Touch heading in Control Panel.

For a touch-enabled PC, the most important options are available on the Touch tab of the Pen And Touch dialog box, which is shown in Figure 31-1.

Figure 31-1 Use the settings in this dialog box to enable or disable touch input and to customize its behavior.

The check boxes at the top of this dialog box allow you to enable or disable touch and multitouch input. The Touch Actions section in the center includes options for customizing the touch behaviors that correspond to common mouse actions. Select either entry from the list, and then click or tap Settings to change the way it works. These options are especially useful if you need to increase or decrease the sensitivity of the response to a double-tap action.

The check box in the Touch Pointer section at the bottom is normally not selected. When this option is enabled, touching the screen displays a large, transparent pointer in the shape of a mouse. Click either of the virtual buttons on this virtual mouse to simulate a click or right-click.

INSIDE OUT   Right-click with one or two fingers

On a PC with limited touch support, you can simulate a right-click by pressing the screen and holding your finger until you see a large circle. When you remove your finger from the screen, the shortcut menu appears just as if you had clicked the right mouse button. On a PC that supports multitouch features, you have an additional choice to simulate a right-click: touch the screen with your index finger, and then tap with the middle finger.

The Pen Options tab of the Pen And Touch dialog box, shown in Figure 31-2, offers a similar set of options for Tablet PCs.

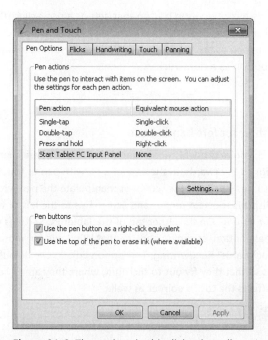

Figure 31-2 The options in this dialog box allow you to fine-tune the behavior of the pen when it's used as a pointing device.

Table 31-1 lists the four pen actions and the possible adjustments you can make by selecting the pen action and then clicking Settings.

Table 31-1 **Settings for Pen Actions**

Pen Action	Settings
Single-tap (click)	Settings cannot be adjusted.
Double-tap (double-click)	Use the Speed control to define the maximum pause that can occur between the two taps that make up a double-tap; use the Spatial Tolerance slider to define the distance that can separate the two taps that make up a double-tap.
Press and hold (right-click)	Use the Speed and Duration sliders to define the amount of time you need to press and hold the pen against the screen to emulate a right-click.
Start Input Panel gesture	By default, this setting is disabled; select the check box to enable and then define the extent of the side-to-side movement you need to make with the pen to open the Input Panel.

Some pens with buttons have a combination button that acts as a right-click if pushed one way and as an eraser if pressed differently. The Pen Options tab includes a setting for whether to use the top of the pen as an eraser. You can select this setting independently of the setting to use the pen button as a right-click equivalent.

INSIDE OUT   Adjusting for left-handed use

Are you left-handed? If so, you're probably accustomed to a world where everything seems to have been designed backwards. In the case of a PC with pen or touch support, the operating system assumes you'll tap the screen or manipulate the pen with your right hand, and thus it displays shortcut menus and ScreenTips to the left of wherever you're tapping, sliding, or writing. On the Other tab of the Tablet PC Settings dialog box, adjust the Handedness option, as shown here, so that Windows can more accurately recognize your "backwards" handwriting. This option adjusts the default position of menus and ScreenTips so that they fly out to the right, where they aren't covered by your hand. This option affects the touch pointer as well.

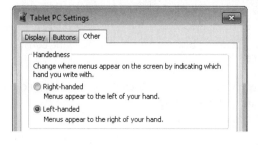

Calibrating the Screen

Many PCs that support pen and touch input require you to go through a calibration step on first use; you can repeat the calibration process any time if you notice that your taps aren't working as expected.

When you use an active digitizer, accurately mapping the relationship between pen and screen is essential. The precision with which you can control the pointer's location with the pen depends in part on how you hold the pen and your posture in relation to your tablet. If the digitizer is off by even a few pixels, tapping the screen to click a button or select a menu option might not produce the expected result. Calibrating a touch screen is less crucial, because most touch operations don't involve precision activities, but it's still a good practice.

You'll find the calibration options in the Tablet PC Settings dialog box. On the Display tab, tap Calibrate. If your PC supports both pen and touch input, you'll need to calibrate each input mode separately.

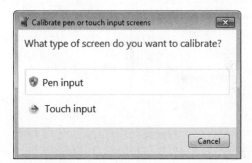

The calibration process displays a series of between 4 and 16 on-screen targets in the form of crosshairs; tap the center of each target in turn, and then save the calibration data when prompted. Calibration has to be performed separately for both landscape and portrait orientations, and if you use the screen upside-down in either orientation (denoted as Secondary Portrait and Secondary Landscape), you have to run through the calibration procedure for those orientations as well.

Changing Orientation

Tablet PCs are designed so that you can change the screen orientation from landscape to portrait (and back to landscape) without rebooting. This versatility is especially important in convertible Tablet PCs, where you might work in landscape orientation for part of your day, using the keyboard and built-in pointing device to create and edit a spreadsheet, and then switch into portrait mode to take handwritten notes at a meeting. Most convertible PCs change screen orientation automatically when you pivot the screen on its hinge; to change orientation manually, right-click the desktop and select Screen Resolution from the shortcut menu, make a selection from the drop-down Orientation list, and then click or tap Apply or OK.

This change in orientation happens almost instantaneously.

If opening this dialog box seems like a cumbersome way to change orientation, you're right. It's much easier to use the Screen Orientation options in Windows Mobility Center (Windows logo key+X). To change the predetermined sequence of orientations, click the Display tab of the Tablet PC Settings dialog box, and then tap or click Go To Orientation. This option allows you to enter up to four orientations in the numbered boxes, as shown in Figure 31-3. (If you want to cycle between two orientations, set options 3 and 4 to None). Windows switches to the next item in this sequence each time you tap the Rotate Screen button in Windows Mobility Center. If you have a hardware button that is dedicated to this function, it respects your settings here as well.

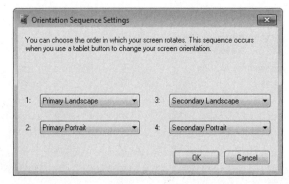

Figure 31-3 The order you assign in this dialog box determines how the screen responds when you tap the Rotate Screen button.

Redefining Tablet PC Buttons

Tablet buttons allow access to some common functions when a keyboard is unavailable. Typically, these buttons are built into the computer's case, in the bezel alongside the display, within easy reach of your hands when using the computer as a tablet. It's common to find a Security button, for example, which has the same effect when pressed as does the Ctrl+Alt+Delete combination on a conventional keyboard.

Each Tablet PC design is different, but many hardware designers include buttons that you can customize to perform any of a long list of actions, including standard keyboard commands (Down Arrow, Up Arrow, and Enter, for example) or running an application. To customize them, open the Tablet PC Settings dialog box from Control Panel and tap the Buttons tab. Figure 31-4 shows the available settings for a Dell Latitude XT Tablet PC with six customizable buttons.

Figure 31-4 If your Tablet PC includes support for customizable hardware buttons, this tab will be visible. The images shown here are specific to this model.

By default, the tablet buttons perform the same actions for all screen orientations; however, you can assign different actions to the buttons for different orientations. Using the buttons for actions associated with the keyboard is most helpful when you're using the tablet with pen input only. When browsing the web, for instance, you might find it helpful to redefine the Up Arrow and Down Arrow buttons so that they emulate the Mouse Wheel Up and Mouse Wheel Down actions instead. Having quick access to these actions is not nearly as helpful on a convertible Tablet PC when the full keyboard is available, nor is it necessary if touch input is available. For that configuration, consider defining the tablet buttons to launch applications you use frequently.

Reading, Writing, and Editing with Pen and Touch Tools

On a PC that accepts pen or touch input, you can use taps and double-taps wherever you would normally click or double-click a mouse; you can press and hold to emulate a right-click and press and drag to emulate the familiar click-and-drag mouse action. But those simple mouse alternatives barely scratch the surface when it comes to making yourself more productive.

In this section, we show you how to use gestures to enhance the experience of reading web pages and long documents. You'll learn how to scroll smoothly through long documents with a flick of the finger and how to use a two-finger tap to zoom in for a closer view of text and images.

We also explain how to use pen or touch input in lieu of a regular keyboard by using the writing pad and touch keyboard in the Tablet PC Input Panel.

Using Gestures in Windows 7

There's more to touch (and pen) support than just replacing a mouse. Once you learn the full range of gestures that Windows 7 supports, you'll realize that touch input enables some capabilities you can't use with a mouse alone. (Some of the basic touch capabilities we describe in this section are available with older computers that support only pen or single-touch input, but the full set of gestures requires a modern PC with multitouch support.)

INSIDE OUT   Resize the Windows interface for better response

A touch interface is most effective when menus and buttons are large enough to serve as convenient touch targets. Trying to control applications with touch can be frustrating if you keep hitting the wrong menu option or missing a small button. If you use touch features extensively, consider bumping up the size of the Windows interface to 125 percent of normal size. To access this option, open Control Panel and click or tap Display, under the Appearance And Personalization heading. Choose Medium – 125%, and then click or tap Apply. Note that you must log off and then log back on to change the size of the display. If you prefer the display at its normal size but occasionally want the ability to zoom in on a part of the screen to make it easier to touch a button or menu, pin the Magnifier utility to the taskbar or Start menu and use it as needed. With applications that support the Zoom gesture, such as Internet Explorer, you can zoom in to a portion of a page to click a link and then zoom back out to resume reading.

With touch-enabled hardware and the proper drivers, you can use a basic set of gestures with any program, regardless of whether its programmers explicitly enabled touch features. Gestures in this group include all basic mouse alternatives: tap and double-tap (tolerances are set to be larger than the equivalent mouse actions); drag (moving objects and selecting text, for example); and the two right-click replacements—press and hold or press and tap with a second finger.

Three specific gestures are available in many applications without explicit support for touch input. They are as follows:

- **Scroll**   Use one or two fingers to drag the content within a window and scroll up or down. This gesture typically works in any window that has scroll bars. It takes a bit of unlearning to master this technique; unlike a scroll bar, where you drag down to move the contents up and vice versa, the scrolling gesture moves the page in the direction that you drag. (If it helps, imagine the contents of the window as a piece of paper and use your finger to push the paper up or down.)

The more energy you put into a drag motion, the more the contents scroll. Move your finger (or fingers) slowly to read a web page, a Word document, or a lengthy e-mail message closely. "Toss" the page with a sweeping up or down gesture to move several screens at a time. The tossing action includes inertia, which causes the scrolling to go quickly at first and then slow as it finishes. If the Aero theme is enabled, you'll notice a small bounce in the entire program window when you reach the top or bottom of the contents you're scrolling through.

INSIDE OUT   Scroll and pan with two fingers

Although you can scroll up and down and pan left and right with a single finger, executing this gesture with two fingers offers a tangible advantage. With a single finger, you might end up accidentally selecting text or an object at the point where you began the scroll or pan. By using two fingers, you effectively tell Windows that making a selection is not an option.

- **Flick**   Drag your finger quickly left or right to execute this gesture. Flicks typically work in any program that has Back and Forward buttons, including Internet Explorer, Windows Explorer, and Windows Photo Viewer. In Internet Explorer, a flick to the right loads the previous page (the same as if you had clicked the Back button) and a flick to the left goes to the next page (as if you had clicked or tapped Forward). In either case, you'll notice a transition effect as the current page slides out and the new page appears.

- **Zoom**   Pinch two fingers together or move them apart to zoom in or out, respectively, on the contents of the current window, as shown in the following diagram. This gesture works in programs that support zooming with the mouse wheel, including Internet Explorer, Windows Photo Viewer, Windows Live Photo Gallery, and programs in the Microsoft Office family such as Word and Excel. The zoom gesture is especially useful when you are looking at photos or reading documents on a small portable computer.

The final two members of the multitouch gesture set in Windows 7 must be specifically enabled by program developers before they can be used. They are as follows:

- **Two-finger tap**   Tap with two fingers simultaneously to change the zoom factor on a point between the two fingers. This gesture is enabled by default in Internet Explorer, where you can use a two-finger tap to zoom in to a hyperlink (making it easier to double-click) and then repeat the gesture to return to the normal zoom level.

- **Rotate**   Touch two spots on a digital photo and twist to rotate it just like a real photo. You can move both fingers simultaneously or allow one finger to remain stationary while you move the other, as shown in the following diagram. Windows Photo Viewer and Windows Live Photo Gallery both support this capability.

Several parts of the Windows 7 shell change behavior slightly when used on a multitouch-enabled PC. When you use touch to drag a window to the edge of the screen to snap it into position (Aero Snap), the tolerances are more forgiving and the snap occurs when you get close to the edge instead of hitting it precisely. The Show Desktop button at the right of the taskbar is twice as wide on a touch-enabled PC as it is on a conventional display. You can open Jump Lists with a quick flick of a taskbar button as well; when you do, the spacing between items on the Jump List is increased in comparison to the Jump List you see if you right-click.

Some programs and utilities included with Windows 7 behave differently on a touch-enabled PC as well. In Paint, you can choose a brush and then finger-paint with as many fingers as your display supports. Windows Media Center allows direct panning in all directions in most scrollable views and menus, and Windows Media Player offers larger active areas for play and navigation controls. In the Games category, both Hearts and Solitaire have been optimized for touch, which means that you can legitimately claim that you're polishing your PC skills instead of wasting time if you use either game on a touch-enabled PC. In that same vein, look for a group of optional games and screen savers called the Touch Pack, which are specifically designed to show off the features of a multitouch PC.

Internet Explorer offers the richest assortment of touch support of any application in Windows 7, including zoom, panning in all directions, and flicks. Try dragging the address bar menu down to see a list of recent sites, with increased spacing to make it easier to hit a target from the list. Likewise, using the Favorites menu with multitouch gestures adds extra spacing between items compared to the same menu displayed in response to a mouse click. One especially useful shortcut is this simple gesture: to open any link in a new tab, drag the link a short distance in any direction.

Using the Writing Pad and Touch Keyboard

When you use a PC without a keyboard, how do you enter text into dialog boxes, web forms, your browser's address bar, or a document? For those tasks, use the Tablet PC Input Panel. (Don't be fooled by the name, which is a carryover from its roots in older Windows versions; this feature works on touch-enabled PCs as well as Tablet PCs.) The Input Panel is a relatively small box that appears on demand. Using small buttons in the upper left corner of the Input Panel, you can switch between its two views. Use the *writing pad* to edit existing text or to enter handwritten characters that are converted on the fly and inserted as if you had typed them; use the *touch keyboard* (shown in Figure 31-5) to enter text and keyboard commands directly.

Figure 31-5 The touch keyboard is larger by default on a touch-enabled PC than on a Tablet PC. In either case, it allows you to enter text and commands as you would with an actual keyboard.

Normally, the Input Panel is completely hidden. If you tap the display with a finger or a pen, a few pixels of the Input Panel's right edge become visible on the left side of the screen. To open the Input Panel, tap this small edge to expose a larger portion of the Input Panel and then tap to open the Input Panel in the center of the screen.

The Input Panel also offers to appear when it's needed for specific text-entry tasks. Tap to position the insertion point in the Start menu search box, a dialog box, a form, a document, or any place where you would normally use the keyboard to enter text. Tap with a finger or allow the pen point to hover for a second until the Input Panel icon appears. Then tap the icon to open a floating Input Panel.

> **Note**
>
> If you used a Tablet PC with Windows XP Tablet PC Edition, you might remember the Input Panel gesture. This gesture (a side-to-side slashing motion akin to the mark of Zorro) is disabled by default in Windows 7, as it was in Windows Vista. To reenable it, open the Pen And Touch dialog box, choose Start Tablet PC Input Panel from the Pen Actions list on the Pen Options tab, and click Settings. Select Enable Start Input Panel Gesture, and click or tap OK to save the new setting. You'll find a slew of other ways to customize the behavior of the Input Panel in the Options dialog box, available from the Tools menu at the top of the Input Panel.

Under some circumstances, you might prefer to dock the Input Panel. This option is useful when you expect to enter a few characters at a time in several locations within a document you're editing and you don't want to continually make the Input Panel visible. To switch between floating and docked modes, tap the Tools menu above the Input Panel and then choose Dock At Top Of Screen or Dock At Bottom Of Screen.

The two buttons in the top left corner of the Input Panel allow you to switch between the touch keyboard and the writing pad. The writing pad offers a blank surface for editing existing text or entering free-form text. The example in Figure 31-6 shows the writing pad after selecting a misspelled word from a Microsoft Word document.

Figure 31-6 Use the writing pad to show a selection of text from the current document and correct misspellings like the one shown here.

When you enter handwritten text in the writing pad, it is converted to text on the fly but remains in the entry window. To erase text you've entered here, use the scratch-out gesture, a quick left-and-right slashing motion. Make sure that your pen stays on the screen as you make the gesture—directly on the text you want to erase—and keep the lines horizontal; if you're unsuccessful, you might need to draw more or longer lines. The text does not appear at the insertion point until you tap Insert.

INSIDE OUT Using ink and handwriting

When you use a Tablet PC pen to scribble a handwritten note or sketch a figure within a pen-aware application, you create a type of data called *ink*. Although it superficially resembles a simple bitmap, ink-based data contains a wealth of information in addition to the simple shape. Windows records the direction, pressure, speed, and location of the tablet pen as it moves and stores the resulting marks as a compressed graphic. If you enlarge a piece of data that was stored as ink, Windows uses this stored data to ensure that it keeps its proper shape.

By recognizing the combinations of strokes that represent handwritten letters, the operating system can convert even bad handwriting into text, and with surprising accuracy. You don't have to convert ink into text to get the benefits of handwriting recognition, either. The handwriting recognizer automatically converts handwriting to text in the background, storing the resulting text along with the ink and adding the recognized words and phrases to the Windows Search index.

Applications that fully support ink as a data type are relatively rare, but you can perform some remarkable feats with those that do exist. Using Microsoft Office Word 2007 or later, for instance, you can insert handwritten comments and annotations into a document. Another member of the Office family, OneNote, goes even further, building an index of your handwritten notes and allowing you to search through an entire collection for a word or phrase.

Although you need a stylus to create ink on a Tablet PC, anyone who uses any edition of Windows 7, Windows Vista, Windows XP, Windows Server 2003, or Windows Server 2008 can view ink-based data.

To edit a selection of text using a pen or touch input, open the writing pad and tap the selection. This action breaks the selected text into individual slots for each letter or number, as shown in Figure 31-7.

Figure 31-7 You can use the Input Panel to edit text, even in programs that don't support ink. Select a word or phrase with the pen, and tap the text to open this editing panel.

In this editing mode, the writing pad supports four editing gestures: correcting, deleting, splitting, and joining. The button in the upper right corner of the writing pad (to the left of the Close button) allows you to show or hide a strip of help buttons, each of which displays a small animation that illustrates the selected gesture.

INSIDE OUT   Make logons more secure

The touch keyboard is available on the Welcome screen, allowing you to log on to your account by entering your password. To toggle its display, click the icon in the lower left corner of the Welcome screen. Using the touch keyboard presents some potential security issues: you don't want a casual bystander or a deliberate snoop to look over your shoulder and watch each character of your password flash as you enter it. To adjust the behavior of the touch keyboard for logons, open the Options dialog box, click the Advanced tab, and use the slider to choose a higher or lower degree of security. The available help text does a concise job of explaining what each option does.

Using Speech Recognition and Voice Commands

The crew of the starship *Enterprise* thought nothing of talking to the computer that ran the ship and its systems. Windows Speech Recognition, a feature introduced in Windows Vista and available in all editions of Windows 7, comes closest to fulfilling that futuristic vision of computing. You won't be able to blast Klingon warships into space dust with voice commands, but if you set slightly more realistic expectations, we predict you'll be extremely impressed with Windows Speech Recognition.

Before you can get started, you need to have the right gear. The most important piece of equipment, naturally, is a high-quality microphone. Microsoft recommends a USB headset model for best performance. The headset ensures a consistent distance between your mouth and the microphone, and a USB connection has an all-digital signal path, unlike direct connections to an onboard sound card. Both factors increase your chances of success in accurate speech recognition.

Tuning and Tweaking Windows Speech Recognition

After installing your hardware and any required drivers, you're ready to begin using Windows Speech Recognition. You need to run through a quick setup routine, which in turn strongly encourages you to complete the Windows Speech Recognition tutorial. Even if you normally prefer to dive right in to a new feature, we recommend that you make an exception for this tutorial. In small part, that's because the tutorial does an excellent job of introducing the Speech Recognition feature. Much more important, though, is the fact that the speech recognition engine uses your responses during the tutorial to train itself to recognize your voice and phrasing. (And it's really not that long, honest.)

With the tutorial out of the way, you can start Windows Speech Recognition by using its shortcut on the Start menu. If you need to adjust any setup options, you can do so from Speech Recognition in Control Panel.

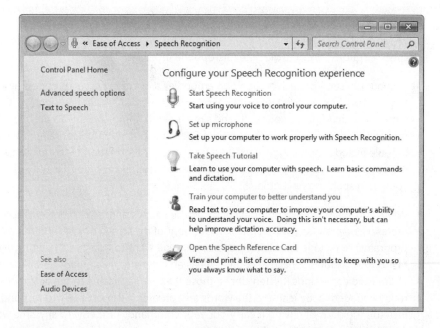

When Speech Recognition is running, you see the capsule-shaped microphone interface pinned to the top of the screen. When the microphone icon is blue and the word *Listening* appears, the speech recognition engine is hanging on your every word—or for that matter, on stray sounds, which it will try to convert into text or commands. If you're not actively dictating, click the microphone button (or say "Stop listening"). The microphone icon turns gray. If you chose manual activation in the initial setup, you'll need to click the microphone icon again (or press Ctrl+Windows logo key) to resume; if you chose voice activation mode, the word *Sleeping* appears to indicate that it is listening only for the magic phrase "Start listening" to begin again.

INSIDE OUT   Hide or move the speech recognition interface

If you find that the speech recognition interface covers up important information when docked at the top of the screen, you have several choices. You can move it so that it floats on the screen, or you can hide it by speaking the command "Hide speech recognition." To make the interface visible once again, just say "Show speech recognition."

To see a list of all options that you can adjust for Windows Speech Recognition, say "Show speech options" or right-click the microphone interface.

Without question, speech recognition embodies a learning curve. A modest amount of time and effort expended up front pays substantial dividends in the long run. One technique that can improve your skills and simultaneously improve the accuracy of the speech recognition engine is to run through the Speech Recognition Voice Training sessions. Each module includes tips, suggestions, and background information that you read out loud. The more modules you complete, the more information the computer has to work with when you begin speaking next time.

When you speak to the computer, it parses the sounds and tries to determine whether they represent commands (which control movement of on-screen objects and the behavior of programs) or dictation (which represents text you want to insert in an editing window or a text box). Windows Speech Recognition has an extensive vocabulary, and it's smart enough to limit the commands it listens for to those that are applicable to the activity you're currently engaged in. By learning the words and phrases it is most likely to respond to, you increase the odds of having it carry out your commands properly. At any time, you can say "What can I say?" This all-purpose command opens the Windows Speech Recognition Quick Reference Card, a Help And Support dialog box that breaks most commands down into related groups.

Controlling a PC with Voice Commands

The guiding principle for working with windows, dialog boxes, menus, and other on-screen objects is simple: "Say what you see." So, for example, you can say "Start," and Windows Speech Recognition will display the Start menu. You can then say "All Programs" to open that menu and continue working your way to the program you want by saying the names of objects and menu items you see on the screen. If you know the name of the program you want to open, you can skip that navigation and just say "Open *program.*"

You can also "click what you see" (or double-click or right-click). If a window has menus available, you can speak the names of those menus ("File," "Open") just as if you were clicking them.

If you can't figure out what to say to get Windows Speech Recognition to click an object on the screen, make a note of where the object you want to see is located, and then say "Show numbers." This command enumerates every clickable object on the screen and overlays a number on each one, as shown in Figure 31-8, which depicts what happens to Control Panel when you choose this option.

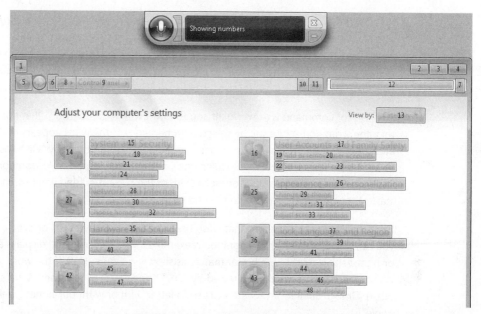

Figure 31-8 When you say "Show numbers," Windows Speech Recognition tags every clickable object with a number. Say "click" or "double-click" followed by the number to accomplish your goal.

Show Numbers works equally well with web pages, identifying clickable regions and objects on the page. It also works with the Start menu and the taskbar, offering an easy way to open and switch programs. If you prefer, you can use the "Switch to *program*" command, substituting the text in the title bar for the program you want to switch to. To work with individual windows, you can use the "Minimize," "Maximize," and "Close" commands, followed by the name of the program. For the currently selected window, use the shortcut "that," as in "Minimize that." To minimize all open windows, say "Show desktop."

To scroll through text in a window, say "Scroll up" or "Scroll down." For more control over scrolling, add a number from 1 through 20 after the command (the larger the number, the greater the scrolling).

Using Speech to Enter and Edit Data

If it can't interpret what you say as a command, Windows Speech Recognition assumes that you're trying to dictate. It then inserts its best guess at what you meant to say at the current insertion point. The accuracy of speech recognition is reasonably good after a short period of training, and it gets much better after time and practice. But it's not perfect, nor are you likely to dictate smooth sentences with perfect syntax. As a result, you'll want to master the basics of text editing by using the voice commands in this section.

To delete the most recent word or phrase you dictated, say "Undo" or "Undo that."

If you want to change a word, phrase, or sentence, start by saying "Select *word*" or, for a phrase, "Select *word* through *word*," substituting the actual text for the italicized entries here. "Select next [or previous] sentence" works, as does "Select previous five words" or "Select next two sentences." After you make a selection, you can delete it or copy it to the Clipboard ("Copy that").

The "Go to" command is powerful. If you follow it with a unique word that appears in the text, the word you spoke will be selected immediately. If the word appears multiple times, each one is highlighted with a number. Say the number and then say "OK." You can say "Go to before" or "Go to after" a particular word, and Windows Speech Recognition will obey your commands. To go to the top or bottom of the current editing window, say "Go to the start of the document" or "Go to the end of the document."

If you need to correct a word that wasn't recognized correctly, say "Correct *word*." When you do, Windows Speech Recognition reexamines what you said and displays a list of words or phrases that might be a better match, as shown in Figure 31-9. If the word you spoke is on the list, say its number, followed by "OK." If the word isn't on the list, try saying it again. Or say "Spell it" and then recite each letter, with or without phonetic helpers ("A as in apple").

Punctuation is easy: to insert a period, comma, colon, semicolon, or apostrophe, just say the word. Literally. The Quick Reference Card has a long list of punctuation marks the speech recognition engine will translate.

To enter a carriage return, say "New paragraph" or "New line."

You can simulate the action of pressing any key by saying "Press *key*," substituting the name of the key for the italicized word. To repeat a key, say "Press *key nn* times," substituting a number for *nn*. A handful of special keys are recognized without the magic introductory word "press": Home, End, Space, Tab, Enter, and Backspace all fall into this category.

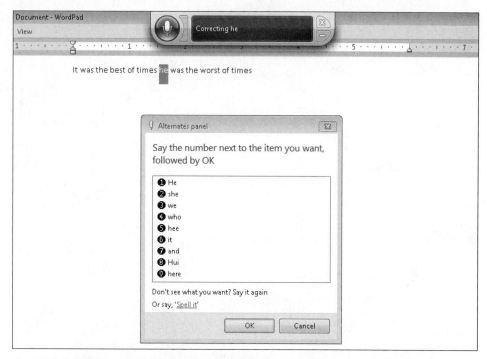

Figure 31-9 Windows Speech Recognition takes these corrections to heart, adjusting its recognition database to ensure it doesn't make the same mistake twice.

Appendixes

Windows 7 Editions at a Glance

WITH Windows 7, Microsoft has sliced and diced operating system features into five distinct editions intended to meet different user needs and price points. In this appendix, we list the features you can expect to find in each edition. We start with a lengthy list of features that are common to all editions. Then we look at features that are added as you upgrade to the next higher edition in the Windows 7 family.

You can use this information to make intelligent purchase decisions when shopping for a new home or office PC. You can also use the data in these tables to help decide whether it makes economic and technological sense to purchase a Windows Anytime Upgrade package to move up to a more feature-rich edition.

We start with a brief discussion of hardware configurations. Table A-1 lists technical limits related to CPU and memory support that might affect your purchase or upgrade decision.

Table A-1 Supported Hardware Configurations in Windows 7

Hardware Component	Supported Configurations
Number of CPUs/cores	Starter, Home Basic: One physical processor, unlimited cores Home Premium and higher editions: One or two physical processors, unlimited cores
64-bit CPU support	64-bit versions available for all editions except Starter
Addressable memory (RAM), 32-bit editions	All editions: 4 GB maximum (because of 32-bit memory architecture, usable memory is typically 3.5 GB or less)
Addressable memory (RAM), 64-bit editions	Starter, Home Basic: 8 GB maximum Home Premium: 16 GB maximum Professional and higher editions: 192 GB maximum

Features Available in All Windows 7 Editions

With some minor exceptions, which are noted here, the Windows 7 features listed in Table A-2 are available in all retail editions of Windows 7 sold worldwide.

Table A-2 Features Available in All Windows 7 Editions

Feature	Description
Core Windows Features	
Windows Search	Indexed search of local files, programs, and Control Panel items.
Windows shell enhancements	Window arrangement with mouse gestures (Aero Snap), Jump Lists, and Windows Flip (Alt+Tab).
Desktop Gadgets	Choose from default gadgets in Desktop Gadget Gallery; download and install additional third-party gadgets.
Power management	Edit default power schemes; create custom schemes.
Windows ReadyBoost	Support for multiple flash drives used as supplemental memory to improve performance.
Device Stage	Simplified interface for managing and configuring user-installed devices such as cameras, phones, and printers.
Sync Center	Manages synchronization with mobile devices.
Windows Easy Transfer	Transfer files and settings from an old computer (or previous Windows installation) to a new one.
Windows Speech Recognition	Enter and edit text and issue voice commands using a microphone.
Ease of Access features	High-contrast themes, Ease of Access Center, Magnifier, Narrator, and On-Screen Keyboard.
Virtual hard drive (VHD) support	Create a new VHD; attach (mount) an existing VHD.
Included Applications	
Internet Explorer 8	Default web browser for Windows 7.
Games Explorer with basic games	FreeCell, Hearts, Minesweeper, Purble Place, Solitaire, and Spider Solitaire.
Basic productivity applications	Calculator, Paint, Notepad, and WordPad.
Windows Fax and Scan	Scan documents, send and receive faxes. Requires properly configured scanner, fax modem, or both.
Windows PowerShell and Integrated Scripting Environment	Command-line shell and graphical host application for scripting administrative tasks.
XPS Document Writer and Viewer	Provides the capability to create and view documents using the XML Paper Specification.

Feature	Description
Security and Reliability	
Windows Update	Automatic and manual updates for Windows; option to download and install updates for other Microsoft products.
User Account Control	Also includes Protected Mode in Internet Explorer 8.
Action Center	Messages and updates about security and maintenance issues.
Windows Defender	Antispyware protection.
Windows Firewall	Blocks unsolicited inbound network connections; includes Advanced Security interface to manage inbound and outbound connections.
System Repair Disc/Windows Recovery Environment	Provides the ability to access a troubleshooting/repair environment at startup without requiring original installation media.
Windows Backup	Perform manual or scheduled backups by file type or location; includes the ability to create a system image.
Previous Versions	Provides the ability to recover changed or deleted files from automatic or manual restore points and backups.
Parental Controls	Set time limits on computer usage, and block access to specific games and programs.
Windows Remote Assistance	Allows direct network connections between two Windows PCs for troubleshooting and repair.
Digital Media	
Windows Media Player 12	Play back all supported music and video formats, including unprotected MPEG-4 audio and QuickTime Movie files.
DVD playback capability	Requires MPEG-2 decoder, which is included in premium editions but must be installed separately in the Starter and Home Basic editions.
Windows Photo Viewer	Import photos from digital cameras; rotate photos, send them via e-mail, burn them to CD/DVD, or print them.
Photo slide shows	Basic features only; no transitions or other special effects.
Sound Recorder	Basic sound-recording capabilities.
Networking	
Remote Desktop client	Connect via a network to a Remote Desktop host.
SMB network connections	Maximum of 20 simultaneous connections. Because each PC or device requires two Server Message Block (SMB) connections, 10 PCs or devices can be connected at once.
Ability to join a homegroup	Share local resources and access shared resources on other Windows 7 machines that are part of the same homegroup.

Appendix A

Windows 7 Starter and Home Basic

The two entry-level editions of Windows 7 deserve special discussion.

Windows 7 Starter is available worldwide, but it is not sold in boxed editions or on desktop PCs. Microsoft authorizes its sale only when preinstalled by PC makers on new portable computers that meet certain hardware standards. Its primary purpose is to power small, light, inexpensive PCs popularly known as *netbooks*.

Windows 7 Starter offers the Windows Basic interface only and lacks support for most effects in the Aero user experience, including glass effects on window borders and live thumbnails on the Windows taskbar. It also offers a sparse menu of personalization features. Despite the fact that it is available only on portable computers, it does not include the Windows Mobility Center, a convenient utility for managing notebook features. If you are willing to accept those limitations, you'll find that Windows 7 Starter is fully capable of running virtually all Windows programs.

The other unconventional member of the Windows 7 family is Home Basic. This edition is available for sale only in so-called emerging markets. It cannot legally be sold in the United States, Western Europe, Japan, Australia, and the rest of the developed world.

Windows 7 Home Basic offers the Windows Standard interface, which includes a subset of Aero features: it lacks glass effects, for example, but provides live taskbar previews. It is distinctly more feature rich than the Starter edition, offering Windows Mobility Center and some personalization features. However, it lacks many of the signature features of Windows 7 Home Premium, such as support for multitouch and Tablet PC features. It also lacks the MPEG-2 decoder required to play DVDs in Windows Media Player (you'll need to supply that component separately) and does not offer Windows Media Center.

Windows 7 Home Premium

Windows 7 Home Premium includes all the common Windows 7 features as well as those listed in Table A-3.

Table A-3 **Features Available Only in Windows 7 Home Premium or Higher Editions**

Feature	Description
Core Windows Features	
Aero graphics and user experience	Full support for Aero features, including themes, glass, taskbar previews, Aero Peek, Flip 3D, Aero Shake, and desktop slide shows.
Personalization features	Control Panel for changing desktop backgrounds, window colors, and sound schemes; also allows saving settings as a theme or theme pack.

Feature	Description
Fast User Switching	Log on to multiple user accounts simultaneously.
Multimonitor support	With properly configured hardware, extend the main display to include a second (or third, fourth, and so on) monitor.
Windows Mobility Center	Central location for managing power, display, network, and other settings on a notebook PC.
Windows SideShow	Support for auxiliary display devices.
Touchscreen/Tablet PC support	With appropriate hardware and drivers, adds support for touch, multitouch, and pen input.
Included Applications	
Snipping Tool	Capture all or part of a screen and save it to the Clipboard or as a file.
Sticky Notes	Save free-form notes.
Premium games	Chess Titans, Hearts, Internet Backgammon, Internet Checkers, Internet Spades, and Mahjong Titans.
Tablet PC utilities	Windows Journal and Math Input Panel.
Digital Media	
Windows Media Center	Simplified media playback interface optimized for use with a remote control; includes support for up to four TV tuners of each type.
Remote Media Streaming	Allows streaming of music, videos, and recorded TV from your home computer to a remote computer or Digital Living Network Alliance (DLNA)–compatible device.
MPEG-2 decoding	Enables DVD playback with Dolby Digital audio in Windows Media Player and Media Center.
Windows DVD Maker	Create and edit video DVDs.
Networking	
Create and manage a homegroup	Set up a homegroup for sharing resources among Windows 7 machines; view and change the homegroup password.
Internet Information Services	Lightweight web and FTP server (disabled by default).
Internet Connection Sharing	Provide Internet access to other computers on a local area network.

Appendix A

Windows 7 Professional

Windows 7 Professional includes all features in Windows 7 Home Premium plus those listed in Table A-4.

Table A-4 **Features Available Only in Windows 7 Professional, Ultimate, or Enterprise Editions**

Feature	Description
Core Windows Features	
Presentation Mode	Disables a screen saver, taskbar alerts, and other potential distractions during a PC-based presentation.
Encrypting File System	Enables strong encryption of files on an NTFS-formatted volume.
Windows XP Mode	Downloadable option enables Windows Virtual PC with a licensed copy of Windows XP Professional.
Networking	
Connect to network projector	Mirror your computer's display on a projector connected to a wired or wireless network.
Backup to network	Adds an option to back up files and system images to network locations.
Offline Files	Synchronize, cache, and index network files locally so that they are available when the computer is disconnected from the network.
Domain support	Allows a client to join a Windows domain on an enterprise network.
Remote Desktop host	Allows authorized users to log on to a computer using Remote Desktop Protocol over a network connection.

Windows 7 Ultimate/Enterprise

Windows 7 Ultimate is sold in retail channels; Windows 7 Enterprise is available to enterprise customers who purchase volume licenses. These editions are functionally identical and include all features in Windows 7 Professional as well as those listed in Table A-5.

Table A-5 Features Available Only in Windows 7 Ultimate or Enterprise Editions

Feature	Description
Core Windows Features	
Boot from virtual hard drive (VHD)	Configure a VHD as a boot device.
Language packs	Change the Windows 7 interface to display menus, dialog boxes, and other elements in a user-selected language.
Subsystem for UNIX-based Applications	Compatibility subsystem for compiling and running custom UNIX-based applications.
Networking	
BranchCache	Increases network responsiveness of applications on Windows Server 2008 R2.
DirectAccess	Provides secure connections (without a virtual private network, or VPN) between a client PC running Windows 7 and Windows Server 2008 R2.
Location-aware printing	Helps domain-joined computers find the correct printer when a user moves between office and home networks.
Security and Reliability	
AppLocker	Enables administrators of enterprise networks to create an authorized list of programs that users can install and run.
BitLocker	Allows an entire drive to be encrypted, protecting its contents from unauthorized access if the computer is lost or stolen.
BitLocker To Go	Encrypts data on removable media such as USB flash drives.

Appendix A

Working with the Command Prompt

P RESERVING a tradition that goes back decades, with Windows 7 you can enter commands, run batch programs, and run applications by typing commands in a Command Prompt window. If you're accustomed to performing administrative tasks at the command line, you don't need to change your ways in Windows 7. (Note, however, that Windows 7 also includes a far more powerful tool for performing administrative tasks at the command line. This newer, more versatile shell, called Windows PowerShell, is described in Chapter 27, "Automating Windows 7.")

> ## What's in Your Edition?
> The command prompt works identically in all editions of Windows 7.

Starting and Ending a Command Prompt Session

To get to the command prompt, run Cmd.exe, which you can do in any of the following ways:

- Type **cmd** in the Start menu search box, and click the Cmd shortcut when it appears, under Programs, at the top of the menu.

- Press Windows logo key+R, and type **cmd** in the Open box.

- Choose Start, All Programs, Accessories, Command Prompt.

- Double-click the Cmd icon in your %SystemRoot%\System32 folder.

- Double-click any shortcut for Cmd.exe.

You can open as many Command Prompt windows as you like. With each additional window, you start another Command Prompt session. For example, you might want to open two Command Prompt windows to see two directories in side-by-side windows. To open another Command Prompt window, repeat any of the preceding methods or type **start** or **start cmd** at the command prompt. (These commands produce the same result. If you don't type a program name after typing **start**, Windows assumes that you want to start Cmd.exe.)

> **Note**
>
> Your activities in a Command Prompt session are subject to the same User Account Control (UAC) restrictions as anything else you do in Windows 7. At times, you might find it convenient to start a Command Prompt session with an administrator token; such a session is sometimes called an *elevated command prompt*. To do this, right-click any shortcut for Cmd.exe and choose Run As Administrator from the shortcut menu. If you do this as a standard user, you will be prompted to supply administrative credentials.

INSIDE OUT   Easy ways to invoke administrator Command Prompt sessions

A quick way to open a Command Prompt session as an administrator is to press the Windows logo key (to open the Start menu), type **cmd** in the Start menu search box, and press Ctrl+Shift+Enter.

If you often need a Command Prompt session with administrator privileges, create a shortcut to Cmd.exe, open the shortcut's properties dialog box, click the Shortcut tab, click Advanced, and select Run As Administrator.

It's a good idea to visually differentiate this high-powered Command Prompt session from others so that you'll know at a glance that you're using a more powerful session—power that comes with the potential to cause damage. Windows inserts the word *Administrator* in the title bar of each Command Prompt window that has administrator privileges. You can also make the window visually distinctive by applying different fonts and colors; for details, see "Customizing Command Prompt Windows" on page 1180.

When the Command Prompt window is active, you can end a Command Prompt session in any of the following ways:

- Type **exit** at the command prompt.

- Click the Close button.

- Click the Control menu icon, and choose Close.

- Double-click the Control menu icon.

If you are running a character-based program in the Command Prompt window, you should use the program's normal exit command to quit the program before attempting to close the window and end the Command Prompt session. Otherwise, it's possible that you'll lose unsaved data. However, if you are sure that the program doesn't have any unsaved information, you can safely and quickly close it by using one of the last three methods in the preceding list. If a program is running, a dialog box appears asking whether you really want to terminate the program.

Starting Command Prompt at a Particular Folder

If you run Cmd.exe from a shortcut or from %SystemRoot%\System32, the session begins with that folder as the current directory. (*Directory* is the MS-DOS–era term for *folder*, and you'll encounter it frequently in command names, help files, and so on.) If you run Cmd from the Start menu, it begins in your %UserProfile% folder. To run a Command Prompt session at a different folder, hold down the Shift key while you right-click the folder in Windows Explorer. On the shortcut menu, choose Open Command Window Here.

INSIDE OUT   Cmd.exe vs. Command.com

Cmd.exe is the Windows command processor. Command.com—the 16-bit command processor from the MS-DOS days—is still supported in 32-bit Windows 7 editions but is unavailable on PCs running 64-bit Windows 7 editions. Unless you have a legacy application that requires Command.com, you should use Cmd.exe. You can run external MS-DOS commands, batch programs, and other executables with either processor, but Cmd includes several internal commands and options not available in Command.com, which hasn't been significantly updated in many years. Cmd offers full support for long file and folder names; Command.com can display long names but accepts only MS-DOS–style short equivalents as input.

Starting Command Prompt and Running a Command

The /C and /K command-line arguments allow you to start a Command Prompt session and immediately run a command or program. The difference between the two is that Cmd /C *commandstring* terminates the Command Prompt session as soon as *commandstring* has finished, whereas Cmd /K *commandstring* keeps the Command Prompt session open after *commandstring* has finished. Note the following:

- You must include either /C or /K if you want to specify a command string as an argument to Cmd. If you type **cmd *commandstring***, the command processor simply ignores *commandstring*.

- While *commandstring* is executing, you can't interact with the command processor. To run a command or program and keep the Command Prompt window interface, use the Start command. For example, to run Mybatch.bat and continue issuing commands while the batch program is running, type

  ```
  cmd /k start mybatch.bat
  ```

- If you include other command-line arguments along with /C or /K, /C or /K must be the last argument before *commandstring*.

For more information about using Command Prompt's command-line syntax, see "Using Cmd's Command-Line Syntax" on page 1169.

Using AutoRun to Execute Commands When Command Prompt Starts

By default, Command Prompt executes on startup whatever it finds in the following two registry values:

- The AutoRun value in HKLM\Software\Microsoft\Command Processor

- The AutoRun value in HKCU\Software\Microsoft\Command Processor

The AutoRun value in HKLM affects all user accounts on the current machine. The AutoRun value in HKCU affects only the current user account. If both values are present, both are executed—HKLM before HKCU.

Both AutoRun values are of data type REG_SZ, which means they can contain a single string. (You can enter a multistring value, but Windows ignores all but the first string.) To execute a sequence of separate Command Prompt statements, therefore, you must use command symbols or store the sequence as a batch program and then use AutoRun to call the batch program.

To specify an AutoRun value, open a registry editor and navigate to the Command Processor key in either HKLM or HKCU. Create a new string value there, and name it AutoRun. Then specify your command string as the data for AutoRun, exactly as you would type it at the command prompt.

To disable AutoRun commands for a particular Command Prompt session, start Cmd with /D. For more about Command Prompt's command-line syntax, see the next section.

Using Cmd's Command-Line Syntax

The complete command-line syntax for Cmd.exe is

```
cmd [/a | /u] [/q] [/d] [/e:on | /e:off] [/f:on | /f:off] [/v:on | /v:off]
    [[/s] [/c | /k] commandstring]
```

All arguments are optional. The available arguments are as follows:

- **/A | /U**   This argument lets you specify the encoding system used for text that's piped to a file or other device. Use /A for ANSI or /U for Unicode. (The default is ANSI.)

- **/Q**   The /Q argument starts Command Prompt with echo off. (With echo off, you don't need to include an @Echo Off line to suppress screen output in a batch program. To turn echo back on after starting Command Prompt with /Q, type **echo on** at the command prompt.)

- **/D**   The /D argument disables execution of any AutoRun commands specified in the registry. (For more information, see the preceding section.)

- **/E:on | /E:off**   The /E argument allows you to override the current registry settings that affect command extensions, which are enhancements to several internal commands; some extensions might be incompatible with last-century programs or work habits. Command extensions are enabled by default. To disable extensions by default, set the DWORD value EnableExtensions in HKLM\Software\Microsoft\Command Processor to 0.

- **/F:on | /F:off**   The /F argument allows you to override the current registry settings regarding file-name and folder-name completion. (See "Using File-Name and Folder-Name Completion" on page 1171.)

- **/V:on | /V:off**   The /V argument lets you enable or disable delayed variable expansion. With /V:on, for example, the variable !var! is expanded only when executed. The default is /V:off. To turn on delayed variable expansion as a default, add the DWORD value DelayedExpansion to HKLM\Software\Microsoft\Command Processor (for all users at the current machine) or HKCU\Software\Microsoft\Command Processor (for the current user account only) and set DelayedExpansion to 1. (Delayed variable expansion is useful in conditional statements and loop constructs in batch programs. For more information, type **help set** at the command prompt.)

- **/S [/C | /K] *commandstring*** The alternative /C and /K arguments allow you to run a command when Command Prompt starts—with /C terminating the session at the command's completion and /K keeping it open. (For more information, see "Starting Command Prompt and Running a Command" on page 1167.) Including /S before /C or /K affects the processing of quotation marks in *commandstring*.

  If you do not include /S, *and* there are exactly two quotation marks in *commandstring*, *and* there are no "special" characters (&, <, >, (,), @, ^, or |) in *commandstring*, *and* there are one or more white-space characters (spaces, tabs, or linefeeds, for example) between the two quotation marks, *and commandstring* is the name of an executable file, then Command Prompt preserves the two quotation characters.

  If the foregoing conditions are not met and if the first character in *commandstring* is a quotation mark, Command Prompt strips the first and last quotation marks from *commandstring*.

Appendix B

Using Commands

In most respects, entering commands or running programs at the Windows command prompt is the same as using the command prompt of any other operating system that offers a command-line interface, such as MS-DOS, Macintosh OS X, or Linux. Every operating system has a command to delete files, another to display lists of files, another to copy files, and so on. The names and details might differ, but it's the same cast of characters.

INSIDE OUT   Type /? for help

You can get help on any Command Prompt command by typing its name followed by **/?**. For example, to see a list and explanation of the command-line switches for the Dir command, type **dir /?**. Alternatively, type the word **help** followed by the command name—for example, **help dir**. For help with network-related commands, precede your help request with **net**. For example, type **net view /?** or **net help view** for information about the Net View command. (With the Net commands, **net help *command*** provides more detailed help than **net *command* /?**.) You can also type **help** with no arguments to get a list of the internal commands and system utilities provided with Windows.

Starting Programs

You can start all kinds of programs at the command prompt—programs for Windows 7, earlier versions of Windows, or MS-DOS—so you don't need to know a program's origin or type to run it. If it's on your disk, simply type its name (and path, if needed) followed by any parameters. It should run with no problem.

If you're starting a character-based program, it runs in the Command Prompt window. When you terminate the application, the command prompt returns. If you start a Windows-based program, it appears in its own window, and you can continue to work in the Command Prompt window.

For additional control over the programs you start from a command prompt, you can use the Start command. For instance, for Windows-based programs, you can use /Min or /Max to open a program in a minimized or maximized window. For character-based programs, you can enter (in quotation marks) the title that you want to appear in the program window. Place any parameters or switches that you use with the Start command *before* the name of the program or command you want to start—for example, **start /max myprog.exe**. Anything after the program name is passed to the program as a command-line parameter and is ignored by Start. For more information about the Start command, type **start /?** at the command prompt.

Appendix B

INSIDE OUT   Open Windows Explorer at the current Command Prompt folder

If you type **start.** (with a period) at a command prompt, a Windows Explorer window opens on the current folder. This amounts to the opposite of Shift+right-clicking a folder in Windows Explorer to open a Command Prompt session at the selected folder.

Using File-Name and Folder-Name Completion

Command Prompt offers an invaluable file-name and folder-name completion feature that can save you the trouble of typing long paths or file names. If you start typing a command string and then press Tab (the default *completion character*), Command Prompt proposes the next file or folder name that's consistent with what you've typed so far. For example, to switch to a folder that starts with the letter *Q*, you can type **cd q** and press the folder-name completion character as many times as necessary until the folder you want appears.

INSIDE OUT   Use a different completion character

By default, the completion character for both file names and folder names is the Tab key. You can select a different completion character by modifying the CompletionChar and PathCompletionChar values in the HKCU\Software\Microsoft\Command Processor registry key. These DWORD values specify the file and folder completion characters, respectively, for the current user. (To change the settings for all users, modify the same values in HKLM\Software\Microsoft\Command Processor.) If you decide to experiment with these registry settings, keep in mind the following: If CompletionChar is defined and PathCompletionChar is either absent or set to the hexadecimal value 0x40, the CompletionChar setting works for both file completion and folder completion. In all cases, the completion characters should be specified as hexadecimal values—for example, 0x9 for Tab, 0x4 for Ctrl+D, 0x6 for Ctrl+F, 0xC for Ctrl+L, and so on.

You can also override the registry settings for an individual Command Prompt session by starting the session with Cmd /F:on or Cmd /F:off. Cmd /F:on starts a Command Prompt session with Ctrl+D as the path-completion character and Ctrl+F as the file-completion character, disabling the completion characters set in the registry. Cmd /F:off starts a Command Prompt session with no completion characters, regardless of your registry settings. Cmd /F:on and Cmd /F:off both disable the Tab key as a completion character.

Using Wildcards

Wildcards offer an alternative shortcut to entering file and path specifications in a Command Prompt session. Windows, like MS-DOS, recognizes two wildcard characters: ? and *. The question mark represents any single character in a file name. The asterisk matches any number of characters. Typing **cd pro***, for example, might take you to your Program Files folder (depending, of course, on where you are when you type it.) Because you can include multiple wildcards in a string, you can even create formulations such as cd pro*\com*\mic* to get to Program Files\Common Files\Microsoft Shared.

Editing the Command Line

When working at a command prompt, you often enter the same command several times, or enter several similar commands. If you make a mistake when typing a command line, you don't want to retype the whole thing—you just need to fix the part that was wrong. Windows includes a feature that recalls previous commands and allows you to edit them on the current command line. Table B-1 lists these editing keys and what they do.

Table B-1 **Command-Line Editing Keys**

Key	Function
Up Arrow	Recalls the previous command in the command history
Down Arrow	Recalls the next command in the command history
Page Up	Recalls the earliest command used in the session
Page Down	Recalls the most recent command used
Left Arrow	Moves left one character
Right Arrow	Moves right one character
Ctrl+Left Arrow	Moves left one word
Ctrl+Right Arrow	Moves right one word
Home	Moves to the beginning of the line
End	Moves to the end of the line
Esc	Clears the current command
F7	Displays the command history in a scrollable pop-up box
F8	Displays commands that start with characters currently on the command line
Alt+F7	Clears the command history

The command-line recall feature maintains a history of the commands entered during the Command Prompt session. To display this history, press F7, which opens a window that shows your recently entered commands. Scroll through the history with the arrow keys, and then press Enter to reuse the selected command, or press the Left Arrow key to place the selected text on the command line without executing the command. (This allows you to edit the command before executing it.)

It's not necessary to display the pop-up window to use the command history. You can scroll through the history within the Command Prompt window with the Up Arrow and Down Arrow keys.

The F8 key provides a useful alternative to the Up Arrow key. The Up Arrow key moves you through the command history to the top of the command buffer and then stops. F8 does the same, except that when you get to the top of the buffer, it cycles back to the bottom. Furthermore, F8 displays only commands in the buffer that begin with whatever you typed before you pressed F8. Type **d** at the command prompt (don't press Enter), and then press F8 a few times. You'll cycle through recently entered commands that start with *d*, such as Dir and Del. Now type **e** (after the *d*), and press F8 a few more times. You'll cycle through Del commands along with any others that start with *de*. You can save a lot of keystrokes using F8 if you know the first letters of the command you're looking for.

Using Command Symbols

Old-fashioned programs that take all of their input from a command line and then run unaided can be useful in a multitasking system. You can turn them loose to perform complicated processing in the background while you continue to work with other programs in the foreground.

To work better with other programs, many command-line programs follow a set of conventions that control their interaction:

- By default, programs take all of their input as lines of text typed at the keyboard. But input in the same format also can be redirected from a file or any device capable of sending lines of text.

- By default, programs send all of their output to the screen as lines of text. But output in the same format also can be redirected to a file or another line-oriented device, such as a printer.

- Programs set a number called a *return value* when they terminate, to indicate the results of the program.

When programs are written according to these rules, you can use the symbols in Table B-2 to control a program's input and output and to connect or chain programs together.

Table B-2 **Command Symbols**

Symbol	Function
<	Redirects input
>	Redirects output
>>	Appends redirected output to existing data
|	Pipes output
&	Separates multiple commands in a command line
&&	Runs the command after && only if the command before && is successful
||	Runs the command after || only if the command before || fails
^	Treats the next symbol as a character
(and)	Groups commands

The Redirection Symbols

As in MS-DOS and UNIX, Command Prompt sessions in Windows allow you to override the default source for input (the keyboard) or the default destination for output (the screen).

Redirecting Output   To redirect output to a file, type the command followed by a greater than sign (>) and the name of the file. For example, to send the output of the Dir command to a file instead of the screen, type the following:

```
dir /b *.bat > batch.lst
```

This command line creates a file called Batch.lst that contains the names of all the .bat files in the current folder.

Using two greater than signs (>>) redirects output and appends it to an existing file. For example:

```
dir /b *.cmd >> batch.lst
```

This command line appends a list of .cmd files to the previously created file containing .bat files. (If you use >> to append to a file that doesn't exist, Windows creates the file.)

Redirecting Input   To redirect input from a file, type the command followed by a less than sign (<) and the name of the file. The Sort and More commands are examples of commands that can accept input from a file. The following example uses Sort to filter the file created with the Dir command just shown:

```
sort < batch.lst
```

The input file, Batch.lst, contains a list of .bat files followed by a list of .cmd files (assuming you have some of each in the current folder). The output to the screen is the same list of files sorted alphabetically by file name.

Redirecting Input and Output   You can redirect both input and output in a command line. For example, to use Batch.lst as input to the Sort command and send its output to a file named Sorted.lst, type the following:

```
sort < batch.lst > sorted.lst
```

Standard Output and Standard Error   Programs can be written to send their output either to the standard output device or to the standard error device. Sometimes programs are written to send different types of output to each device. You can't always tell which is which because, by default, both devices are the screen.

The Type command illustrates the difference. When used with wildcards, the Type command sends the name of each matching file to the standard error device and sends the contents of the file to the standard output device. Because they both go to the screen, you see a nice display with each file name followed by its contents.

However, if you try to redirect output to a file like this:

```
type *.bat > std.out
```

the file names still appear on your screen because standard error is still directed to the screen. Only the file contents are redirected to Std.out.

Windows allows you to qualify the redirection symbol by preceding it with a number. Use 1> (or simply >) for standard output and 2> for standard error. For example:

```
type *.bat 2> err.out
```

This time the file contents go to the screen and the names are redirected to Err.out. You can redirect both to separate files with this command line:

```
type *.bat 2> err.out 1> std.out
```

The Pipe Symbol

The pipe symbol (|) is used to send or *pipe* the output of one program to a second program as the second program's input. Piping is commonly used with the More utility, which displays multiple screenfuls of output one screenful at a time. For example:

```
help dir | more
```

This command line uses the output of Help as the input for More. The More command filters out the first screenful of Help output, sends it to the screen as its own output, and then waits for a keypress before sending more filtered output.

The Command Combination Symbols

Windows allows you to enter multiple commands on a single command line. Furthermore, you can make later commands depend on the results of earlier commands. This feature can be particularly useful in batch programs and Doskey macros, but you might also find it convenient at the command prompt.

To simply combine commands without regard to their results, use the ampersand (&) symbol:

```
copy f:file.dat & edit file.dat
```

If the first command fails (because there is no File.dat on drive F, for example), the second command is unlikely to work as you expect. Windows provides two command symbols for better control over situations like this:

- The && symbol causes the second command to run only if the first command succeeds.

- The || symbol causes the second command to run only if the first command fails.

Consider this modified version of the earlier example:

```
copy f:file.dat && edit file.dat
```

With this command line, if the Copy command fails, the Edit command is ignored.

Sometimes you want the opposite effect—execute the second command only if the first fails:

```
copy f:file.dat || copy g:file.dat
```

This command line tries to copy the file from drive F. If that doesn't work, it tries to copy the file from drive G.

Pausing or Canceling Commands

You can pause or cancel a command that you enter at the command prompt as the command is running. (Keep this in mind if you accidentally request a directory of all the files—or worse, enter a command to delete all the files—on a huge network server drive!)

To pause the output of a command, press Ctrl+S or the Pause key. To resume output, press any key.

If you have enabled QuickEdit mode for your Command Prompt window (see "Setting Other Options" on page 1183), simply click in the window to pause command output. To resume output, right-click in the window.

To cancel a command, press Ctrl+C or Ctrl+Break. With either key, your command is canceled, and the command prompt returns. Be aware, though, that any action (such as deleting files) that occurs before you cancel the command is done—and cannot be undone.

Simplifying Command Entry with Doskey Macros

The Doskey utility lets you encapsulate command strings as easy-to-enter macros. For example, by typing the following at the command prompt:

```
doskey 50=mode con:lines=50
```

you create a macro named 50 that executes the command string *mode con:lines=50*. To run a macro, you simply enter its name (in this example, 50) at a command prompt. You can create as many macros as you like with Doskey, but your macros are effective only for the current Command Prompt session. To create a reusable set of Doskey macros, save them in a plain-text file by using an editor such as Notepad. Then load them from the command prompt by using Doskey's /Macrofile switch. For example, if your macros are stored in your profile folder in a file named MyMacros.txt, typing

```
doskey /macrofile=%userprofile%\mymacros.txt
```

Appendix B

makes those macros available for the current Command Prompt session. If you regularly use the same macro file, consider using the AutoRun feature to load your macros. See "Using AutoRun to Execute Commands When Command Prompt Starts" on page 1168. For more information about using Doskey, type **doskey /?** at the command prompt.

Using Environment Variables

Operating systems traditionally use environment variables as a means for programs to share information and read global settings. (Windows—and applications written for Windows—also use the registry for this purpose.) To use an environment variable in a command, program, or address, enclose it between percent signs, like this: %UserName%. Capitalization is ignored.

Viewing Environment Variables

The Set command allows you to examine as well as set environment variables. To examine the current environment variables, open a Command Prompt window and type **set** (without any arguments). Windows displays a list of all the current environment variables and their values.

Modifying Environment Variables

Command Prompt gets its environment variables from three sources:

- Any variables set in your Autoexec.bat file

- System variables, as recorded in HKLM\System\CurrentControlSet\Control\Session Manager\Environment

- User variables, as recorded in HKCU\Environment

When you log on, Windows scans the Autoexec.bat file in the root folder of your boot drive for environment variables initialized with Set statements. Both system and user variables are stored in the registry, but you don't need to launch a registry editor to change them. Open System in Control Panel instead. Click Advanced System Settings to get to the System Properties dialog box. Click the Advanced tab and then Environment Variables.

Changes to environment variables made via Control Panel affect your next and subsequent Command Prompt sessions (but not current ones). Changes made via Autoexec.bat are not effective until the next time you log on. In case of conflicting assignments, user variables take precedence over system variables, which take precedence over variables declared in

Autoexec.bat. The Path variable, however, is cumulative. That is, changes made in any venue are appended to any changes made elsewhere.

Within a given Command Prompt session, you can change environment variables by means of Set statements. Such statements affect only the current session and any applications (including additional Command Prompt sessions) spawned from the current session.

Predefined Environment Variables

Many of the environment variables you see when you use the Set command are ones that Windows automatically sets with information about your system. You can use these values in batch programs, Doskey macros, and command lines—and if you're a programmer, in the programs you write. The system-defined environment variables include the following:

- **Information about your place in the network**   COMPUTERNAME contains the name of your computer, USERDOMAIN contains the name of the domain you logged on to, and USERNAME contains your logon name.

- **Information about your computer**   PROCESSOR_ARCHITECTURE contains the type of processor (such as "x86"), and PROCESSOR_IDENTIFIER, PROCES-SOR_LEVEL, and PROCESSOR_REVISION provide specific information about the processor version.

- **Information about Windows**   SystemRoot contains the drive and folder in which Windows is installed; SystemDrive contains only the drive letter.

- **Information about your programs**   When you type a program name (to start the program) without typing its path, Windows looks first in the current folder. If the program isn't located in the current folder, Windows looks in each folder listed in the Path variable.

- **Information about your file locations**   The APPDATA, LOCALAPPDATA, PUBLIC, and USERPROFILE variables each contain a pointer to a folder that many applications use as a default storage location for documents and other data files.

- **Information about the command prompt**   PROMPT contains codes that define the appearance of the command prompt itself. (For details, type **prompt /?** at the prompt.)

Appendix B

Customizing Command Prompt Windows

You can customize the appearance of a Command Prompt window in several ways. You can change its size, select a font, and even use eye-pleasing colors. And you can save these settings independently for each shortcut that launches a Command Prompt session so that you can make appropriate settings for different tasks.

To customize a Command Prompt window, you make settings in a properties dialog box that you can reach in any of three ways:

- Right-click a shortcut that opens a Command Prompt window and choose Properties from the shortcut menu. Changes you make here affect all future Command Prompt sessions launched from this shortcut.

- Click the Control menu icon in a Command Prompt window, and then choose Properties from the Control menu. (If Command Prompt is running in full-screen mode, press Alt+Enter to switch to window display.) Changes you make here affect the current session. When you leave the properties dialog box, you'll be given the option of propagating your changes to the shortcut from which this session was launched. If you accept, all future sessions launched from that shortcut will have the new properties.

- Click the Control menu icon in a Command Prompt window, and then choose Defaults from the Control menu. Changes here do not affect the current session. Instead, they affect all future sessions, except those launched from a shortcut whose properties you have modified. They also affect future sessions in character-mode, MS-DOS-based applications that do not have a program information file (PIF) and do not store their own settings.

Setting the Window Size and Position

To change the screen position where a newly launched Command Prompt window appears, open the window's properties dialog box and click the Layout tab. (See Figure B-1.)

The dialog box maintains two different sizes—the screen buffer size and the window size. The width for both sizes is specified in columns (characters); the height is specified in rows (text lines).

The screen buffer settings control the size of the "virtual screen," which is the maximum extent of the screen. Standard screen sizes are 80 by 25, 80 by 43, or 80 by 50, but you can set your Command Prompt session to any size you want. (Some programs that you launch from a Command Prompt session, however, might work correctly only with standard screen sizes. In such cases, Windows automatically adjusts the screen buffer size to the closest size that the program understands.)

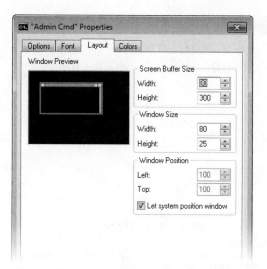

Figure B-1 Settings on the Layout tab control the number of lines and characters per line that a Command Prompt window can display.

The window size settings control the size of the Command Prompt window on your screen. In most cases, you'll want it to be the same size as the screen buffer. But if your screen is crowded, you can reduce the window size. If you do, scroll bars are added so that you can scroll to different parts of the virtual screen. The window size settings cannot be larger than the screen buffer size settings.

Because you size a window by specifying how many rows and columns of characters it should have, the size of those characters also affects the amount of space the window occupies on your display. For information about changing the character size, see "Selecting a Font" below.

Setting the Window Size and Position Visually

Rather than guess at the settings for window size and position, you can drag the borders of a Command Prompt window to adjust its size and drag its title bar to adjust its position. To retain the settings for future sessions, click the Control menu icon, choose Properties, and click the Layout tab. You'll see the settings that reflect the window's current condition. Click OK to apply these settings.

Selecting a Font

Unlike most Windows-based applications, applications in a Command Prompt can display only one font at a time. Your choice is relatively limited, as you'll see if you click the Font tab in the Command Prompt window's properties dialog box, shown in Figure B-2.

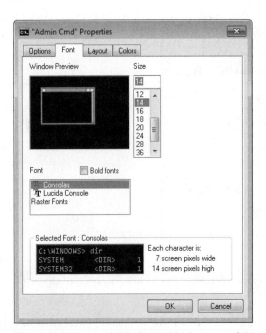

Figure B-2 The small window at the bottom of this dialog box shows an actual-size sample of the selected font; the window at the top shows the relative size and shape of the Command Prompt window if you use the selected font.

Make a selection in the Font list first because your choice here determines the contents of the Size list. If you select the Consolas or Lucida Console font, you'll find point sizes to choose from in the Size list. If you select Raster Fonts, you'll find character widths and height in pixels.

Setting Colors

You can set the color of the text and the background of the Command Prompt window. You can also set the color of the text and the background of pop-up windows that originate from the command prompt, such as the command history.

To set colors, click the Colors tab in the Command Prompt window's properties dialog box. Here you can set separate foreground and background colors for the Command Prompt window and pop-up windows, such as the command history window that appears when you press F7.

Setting Other Options

The Options tab in the Command Prompt window's properties dialog box, shown in Figure B-3, offers a variety of options that affect how your Command Prompt window operates:

- **Cursor Size** These options control the size of the blinking cursor in a Command Prompt window.

- **Command History** These options control the buffer used by Doskey. Buffer Size specifies the number of commands to save in each command history. Number Of Buffers specifies the number of command history buffers to use. (Certain character-based programs other than Cmd.exe use Doskey's command history. Doskey maintains a separate history for each such program that you start.) Discard Old Duplicates, if selected, uses the history buffers more efficiently by not saving duplicate commands.

- **QuickEdit Mode** This option provides a fast, easy way to copy text from (and paste text into) Command Prompt windows with a mouse. If you don't select QuickEdit Mode, you can use commands on the Control menu to copy and paste text.

- **Insert Mode** This option (on by default) allows you to insert text at the cursor position. To overstrike characters instead, clear the Insert Mode check box.

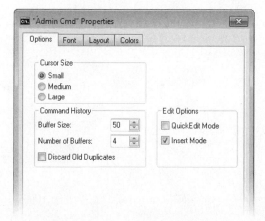

Appendix B

Figure B-3 You can set cursor size, set the size of your command history buffer, and control editing features on the Options tab.

Fixes Included in Windows 7 Service Pack 1

M ICROSOFT released Windows 7 Service Pack 1 on February 22, 2011. This update is available as a standalone installer for x86 and x64 systems, or as a much smaller download via Windows Update. The service pack incorporates many hotfixes and updates delivered after the original release of Windows 7.

This appendix lists all the previously issued updates that are included in SP1, arranged by category using a taxonomy developed by the Windows 7 Inside Out author team. Each entry in the following list includes the number and title of the Knowledge Base (KB) article that corresponds to that fix. To look up a specific KB article, make a note of its number and then enter it in the address bar of your web browser using the following syntax: *http://support.microsoft.com/kb/nnnnn* (or *w7io.com/nnnnn*), replacing *nnnnn* with the KB article number you're interested in.

Note that some of the fixes in SP1 pertain only to the server editions of Windows. Those we have omitted from the list.

Application Compatibility

974332	Windows 7 and Windows Server 2008 R2 Application Compatibility Update
974333	Updates Windows 7 and Windows Server 2008 R2 to fix common application compatibility issues by using Dynamic Update functionality
976264	Application Compatibility Update for Windows Vista, Windows Server 2008, Windows 7, and Windows Server 2008 R2: February 2010
976419	You cannot connect to an instance of SQL Server Analysis Services from an application in Windows 7 or in Windows Server 2008 R2 after you install Office Live Add-in 1.4 or Windows Live ID Sign-in Assistant 6.5
977225	Incorrect lines are printed when a Word document is printed on a computer that is running Windows XP, Windows Server 2003, or Windows Vista
977627	You cannot open a remote application or a remote desktop by using Forefront UAG
978884	A "Request For Permission to Use a Key" dialog box appears every time that you send an e-mail message in Outlook 2007
979643	The Right-to-Left alignment does not work correctly for a Visual Basic application that runs in Windows 7 or in Windows Server 2008 R2
980681	Mail merge in Microsoft Word does not work on a computer that is running Windows 7 or Windows Server 2008 R2
980846	Description of an update to the backward compatibility feature in Windows 7 and in Windows Server 2008 R2
982323	Visual Studio 2010 does not render correctly when Desktop Window Manager is enabled
982519	Application Compatibility Update for Windows Vista, Windows Server 2008, Windows 7, and Windows Server 2008 R2: June 2010
982520	Windows Vista, Windows Server 2008, Windows 7 and Windows Server 2008 R2 Application Compatibility Update through Dynamic Update: June 2010
983315	Description of the 2007 Office system hotfix package (Oart-x-none.msp, Oart-conv-x-none.msp): June 29, 2010
2069802	You cannot safely remove a device that has an embedded USB host controller from a computer that is running Windows 7 if the computer has Windows Virtual PC and Windows XP mode installed

2254157 Error message when you use Outlook to try to forward an email message that contains a TIFF image on a computer that is running Windows 7 or Windows Server 2008 R2: "Cannot send this item"

2255746 You cannot publish IRM-protected content in Microsoft Office 2010 on a computer that is running Windows Server 2008 R2

2272691 Application Compatibility Update for Windows 7 and Windows Server 2008 R2: August 2010

2300535 Windows Ribbon is not displayed correctly in an application that uses the /largeaddressaware option on a computer that is running Windows 7, Windows Server 2008 R2, Windows Vista or Windows Server 2008

2315936 Colors are printed incorrectly when you print an image in 2007 Microsoft Office system or in Microsoft Office 2010 on a computer that is running a 32-bit version of Windows

Computer Management, Administration, and Tools

968930 Windows Management Framework Core package (Windows PowerShell 2.0 and WinRM 2.0)

969867 FIX: You cannot import or paste some group policies across domains by using the "Group Policy Management" MMC snap-in

971163 The STDIN, the STDOUT, and the STDERR redirections do not work in a WOW64 child process if the CreateProcessWithTokenW function creates the child process

975778 The Chkdsk.exe program does not start correctly on a Windows 7-based computer

976329 Error message when you run the ChkDsk.exe utility in read-only mode on a Windows-based computer: "The Volume Bitmap is incorrect" or "Error detected in index $I30 for file 5"

976398 LDAP filters in the Group Policy preference settings do not take effect on a computer that is running Windows Server 2008 R2 or Windows 7

976399 FIX: You cannot apply Group Policy settings on a computer that is running Windows 7 or Windows Server 2008 R2 when security group filters are used in Group Policy preference settings

977096   You are unable to diagnose whether a snapshot creation failure is caused by issues in VSS hardware providers running in Windows 7 and in Windows Server 2008 R2

977542   A hotfix is available to block standard users from logging on to a Window 7-based or Windows Server 2008 R2-based computer in safe mode

977620   You may receive an error message when you run the Msinfo32.exe tool in Windows 7 or Windows Server 2008 R2

978387   FIX: The connectivity test that is run by the Dcdiag.exe tool fails together with error code 0x621

978838   Error message when you run the "Set-GPPermission" cmdlet or the "Get-GPPermission" cmdlet: ""_ploc" is not a valid security group"

979645   You cannot use a script to join a computer automatically into a specified OU in a Windows 2000 domain when the computer is running Windows 7 or Windows Server 2008 R2

979731   Some Group Policy preferences are not applied successfully on computers that are running Windows Vista, Windows Server 2008, Windows 7 or Windows Server 2008 R2

980628   The "Load a specific theme" Group Policy setting is not applied correctly on a computer that is running Windows 7 or Windows Server 2008 R2

981577   The "Invoke-WmiMethod" cmdlet dispatches incorrect results on a computer that is running Windows 7 or Windows Server 2008 R2

982502   You cannot back up a file in Windows Server 2008 R2 or in Windows 7 if the path length is longer than 260 characters

983402   The debug symbol file that corresponds to Dsadmin.dll is missing in Active Directory Lightweight Directory Services (AD LDS) for Windows 7

983426   Some noncritical volumes are included in the system state backup image when you use the "-allCritical" switch in Windows Server 2008 R2 or in Windows 7

983440   An ASP.NET 2.0 hotfix rollup package is available for Windows 7 and for Windows Server 2008 R2

983544   The "Modified time" file attribute of a registry hive file is updated when an application loads and then unloads the registry hive file without making any changes on a computer that is running Windows Server 2008 R2 or Windows 7

983618 Some Group Policy settings are not displayed in the Group Policy Results report in Windows Server 2008, in Windows Vista, in Windows Server 2008 R2, or in Windows 7

983633 You cannot bring a volume online when the Snapshot Protection mode is enabled in Windows Server 2008 R2 or in Windows 7

2028962 The "Active Directory Users and Computers" MMC snap-in does not list all the accounts that have passwords cached on the RODC in Windows

2029006 You cannot restore Windows Vista or Windows Server 2008 in a Windows PE 3.0 environment

2157973 The Security event that has Event ID 4625 does not contain the user account name on a computer that is running Windows Vista, Windows Server 2008, Windows 7, or Windows Server 2008 R2

2209360 "c0000225" error occurs when you try to start a Windows PE RAM disk image on a UEFI-enabled computer that is running Windows 7 or Windows Server 2008 R2

2258620 You cannot find the "Find Now," "Stop," and "Clear All" buttons in the GPMC snap-in on a computer that is running Windows 7 or Windows Server 2008 R2

2261826 You cannot find a network drive in the "Browse For Folder" dialog box in the GPMC MMC snap-in on a computer that is running Windows Server 2008, Windows Vista, Windows Server 2008 R2, or Windows 7

2268318 Duplicated data may be in the Performance log when you use the Performance Logs and Alerts service to collect performance data in Windows Server 2008, in Windows Vista, in Windows 7, or in Windows Server 2008 R2

2277998 You cannot run the BCDBoot.exe tool to repair the BCD store of a Windows 7-based or Windows Server 2008 R2-based system partition by using a computer that is running Windows XP

2280699 All remote PowerShell operations fail together with the "E_ACCESSDENIED" error message when you use the CredSSP in a remote PowerShell session in Windows 7 or in Windows Server 2008 R2

2283445 The backup process requires significantly more time when you use the Windows Backup utility in Windows 7 if the size of the backup files increases

2284538   "Apply once and do not reapply" Group Policy setting is never applied after the first GPO deployment fails on a client computer that is running Windows 7 or Windows Server 2008 R2

2288055   The backup data is corrupted when you use the Windows Backup utility to back up some SQL Server databases or the AD LDS instance data in Windows 7

2379592   "Object reference not set to an instance of an object" error message when you view the GPO backup settings in the Group Policy Management Console

2382370   You cannot apply a Wi-Fi Protected Access 2 (WPA2) pre-authentication Group Policy setting to some client computers that are running Windows 7

2385838   Item-level targeting object picker dialog box shows only the domain in which the Gpmc.msc is started in Windows Server 2008 R2, in Windows 7, in Windows Vista or in Windows Server 2008

2387778   You find a very large increase in the DFS Replication backlogs

2397463   A hotfix is available that updates localized Windows PowerShell Help files for Windows Server AppFabric

2462856   You may receive an error message when you try to access a multilevel entry in an MMC by using the Taskpad view on a computer that is running Windows Server 2008 R2 or Windows 7

Desktop and Shell

955547   You cannot create or rename files as expected when you try to use similar file names that differ only in capitalization in an NFS shared directory that was exported from a Windows Server 2003 R2-based or Windows Server 2008 R2-based NFS Server

971257   Formatted content that is copied and then pasted from an RTF document is not displayed correctly on a computer that is running a 64-bit version of Windows

975214   An End-User Defined Character (EUDC) font that was created in Windows XP cannot be deployed to a computer that is running Windows 7 or Windows Server 2008 R2

975741   Some function keys or keyboard shortcuts do not work correctly on a computer that is running Windows 7

976090 The On-Screen Keyboard displays the numeric keypad incorrectly after you set the default input language to Chinese (Simplified, PRC) in Windows 7 and in Windows Server 2008 R2

976525 Incorrectly displayed Arabic characters in Windows 7 or in Windows Server 2008 R2

976883 A program icon in the notification area may be lost after the corresponding program is updated in Windows 7 or in Windows Server 2008 R2

977346 The Welcome screen may be displayed for 30 seconds during the logon process after you set a solid color as the desktop background in Windows 7 or in Windows Server 2008 R2

977380 The "Search programs and files" box does not display search results correctly in Windows 7 and in Windows 2008 R2

977944 The "Desktop Wallpaper" Group Policy setting is not applied in Windows 7 or in Windows Server 2008 R2

978909 The wrong fonts appear in Web pages, in printed Word documents, or in printed PowerPoint presentations after you install security update 961371

979140 The Gabriola font incorrectly displays fractions when you enable a feature that combines the fraction into one symbol in Windows 7 or Windows Server 2008 R2

979155 FIX: The Taskbar is reset to the default settings when you use the "Automatically Log On" feature in Windows 7 and in Windows Server 2008 R2

979158 Files do not go into the Recycle Bin when you delete more than 1000 files at the same time in Windows 7 or in Windows Server 2008 R2

979164 Gadgets intermittently do not start in Windows 7

979560 The position of the windows is not restored correctly after you turn on the "Restore previous folder windows at logon" feature on a Windows 7 or Windows Server 2008 R2-based computer

980120 A file in the Public Desktop folder disappears from the desktop immediately after you rename the file on a computer that is running Windows 7 or Windows Server 2008 R2

Appendix C

980369   The caption buttons of all the windows disappear when you load a mirror drive on a computer that is running Windows 7 or Windows Server 2008 R2

980409   You cannot log on to a Swedish or to a German edition of Windows 7 when you enter "Benutzer" or "Gäste" as a user name

980994   A namespace extension under the Start Menu is not displayed correctly on a computer that is running Windows 7 or Windows Server 2008 R2

981177   You can still unpin a program from the taskbar unexpectedly when you enable the "Do not allow pinning programs to the Taskbar" Group Policy on a computer that is running Windows 7 or Windows Server 2008 R2

981187   The "Close" button on the title bar is clickable, but the button appears to be unavailable on a computer that is running Windows 7 or Windows Server 2008 R2

981306   An EUDC character does not load when you switch between the Phonetic IME and the ChangJie IME on a computer that is running Windows 7 or Windows Server 2008 R2

981813   You cannot save private characters by using eudcedit.exe on a computer that is running Windows 7 or Windows Server 2008 R2

981890   The user profile is not updated when you configure a client computer that is running Windows 7 or Windows Server 2008 R2 to use roaming user profiles

982405   "Unspecified error" error message when you click Personalization on the shortcut menu on a computer that is running Windows 7 or Windows Server 2008 R2

982709   Only the first search term is searched for when you configure the "Pin Internet search sites to the 'Search again' links and the Start menu" Group Policy setting in Windows 7 or Windows Server 2008 R2

2259539   An update is available that enables the thumbnail controls of certain applications to be displayed correctly on the taskbar in Windows 7 or in Windows Server 2008 R2

2353143   The taskbar is three times wider than expected after you change the orientation and the position of multiple monitors in the Display settings of a computer that is running Windows 7 or Windows Server 2008 R2

Development Tools, Including .NET Framework and Data Components

959162	FIX: You receive error MSB4018 when you run MSBuild.exe at a Visual Studio 2008 SP1 command prompt to build a large solution
971601	FIX: The performance counters that monitor an application stop responding when the application exits and restarts and you receive the System.InvalidOperationException exception on a computer that is running .NET Framework 2.0
971988	FIX: The CPU usage increases significantly when you run a .NET Framework 2.0-based Multi-AppDomain application that uses objects whose finalizers start ThreadPool methods
972848	FIX: A minidump file generation is slow and the size of the file is larger than expected when the information that the file collects is not of the MiniDumpWithFullMemory type in the .NET Framework 2.0
973685	Description of an update for Microsoft XML Core Services 4.0 Service Pack 3
973688	Description of an update for Microsoft XML Core Services 4.0 Service Pack 2
973746	FIX: A System.Runtime.InteropServices.COMException exception occurs when you use COM components in the .NET Framework 2.0 to access form data or querystring data that contains a TAB character
973975	FIX: The WCF security stack does not support the SHA-256 hashing algorithm in the .NET Framework 3.5
974065	A hotfix is available that resolves the System.InsufficientMemoryException exception and enhances the heap balancing on a computer that has over 8 processors for the .NET Framework 2.0 Service Pack 2
974168	FIX: An access violation occurs when you pass structs as parameters through remoting or reflection in 64-bit applications in the .NET Framework 3.5 SP1 or the .NET Framework 2.0 SP2
974286	FIX: A WPF application that is based on the .NET Framework 3.5 SP1 crashes and a System.ExecutionEngineException exception is thrown when you select and drag text in a text box control that is in the application
974372	FIX: The top of the call stack shows the mscorwks!WKS::gc_heap::mark_object_simple function after an exception occurs in a .NET Framework 2.0-based application

974477   FIX: A System.InvalidCastException exception occurs when you run a .NET Framework 3.5-based Windows Presentation Foundation (WPF) application

974842   A hotfix is available that lets you use the Security Token Reference-Transform mechanism to reference issued tokens in a .NET Framework 3.5-based WCF application

974893   FIX: An unexpected Failure Audit event is logged for the local credential when you run a .NET Framework 2.0-based application that tries to connect to a remote computer

975525   The WCF service that uses the .NET Framework 3.5 does not support the Windows Azure feature that rewrites the SERVER_PORT variable

975849   Memory usage increases for a .NET Framework 2.0-based application when you use the ImageList.ImageCollection.Item property to obtain an image or when you call the ImageList.ImageCollection.GetEnumerator method

975974   FIX: When you run a .NET Framework 2.0-based application, a System.AccessViolationException exception occurs, or a dead-lock occurs on two threads in an application domain

976117   FIX: A System.OutOfMemoryException exception occurs or the IDE responds slowly after you build a solution that contains many WPF projects several times by using the .NET Framework 3.5 SP1

976127   An update is available that provides additional features and improvements for ADO.NET Data Services in the .NET Framework 3.5 SP1 on a computer that is running Windows 7 or Windows Server 2008 R2

976462   A hotfix for the .NET Framework 3.5 Service Pack 1 is available for Windows 7 and for Windows Server 2008 R2 as a prerequisite for Microsoft Office SharePoint Server 2010

976566   A hotfix is available that automatically streamlines the RequireSSL and SSLRequireCert IIS settings with corresponding WCF settings in the .NET Framework 3.5 SP1

976816   Web requests take a long time to be completed when you call the System.Net.HttpWebRequest class to create the requests in a .NET Framework 2.0-based application

976898   FIX: After you use the ThreadPool.SetMinThreads method in the Microsoft .NET Framework 3.5, threads maintained by the thread pool do not work as expected

977020   FIX: An application that is based on the Microsoft .NET Framework 2.0 Service Pack 2 and that invokes a Web service call asynchronously throws an exception on a computer that is running Windows 7

977069   FIX: You receive a System.InvalidOperationException exception when you start a .NET Framework-based application that runs Extensible Object Markup Language workflows on a computer that has the FIPS algorithm enabled

977182   FIX: A .NET Framework 3.5-based WPF application behaves unpredictably or crashes when a HwndHost control or a WindowsFormsHost control is removed from the visual tree and tries to make a call on a message window

977420   A hotfix rollup is available to fix problems in Windows Communication Foundation in the .NET Framework 3.5 SP1 for Windows 7 and for Windows Server 2008 R2

977866   FIX: You cannot run .NET Framework 3.5-based Entity Framework applications in a partial trust environment on a computer that is running Windows 7 Client or Windows Server 2008 R2

978249   FIX: You receive a FatalExecutionEngineError exception when a domain neutral assembly is unloaded and a debugger that uses Just My Code detaches from a .NET Framework 2.0-based process

978254   FIX: The CLR cannot start the Dr. Watson tool to report errors or to generate dump files when a .NET Framework 2.0-based application process runs in an impersonated user context

979533   Description of a hotfix that adds the SuppressPreamble property into the HttpResponseMessageProperty class in the .NET Framework 3.5 SP1

979562   A NullReferenceException exception occurs when a TextBox control in a WPF-based application receives the focus in the .NET Framework 3.5

979744   A .NET Framework 2.0-based Multi-AppDomain application stops responding when you run the application

979900   An update is available for the .NET Framework 3.5 Service Pack 1 in Windows 7 and in Windows Server 2008 R2

980138   FIX: A .NET Framework 3.5 SP1-based WPF application throws a System.ArgumentException exception on a computer that uses a multi-touch screen

980251   FIX: A memory leak occurs in a .NET Framework 3.5 SP1-based Windows Presentation Foundation (WPF) application that uses the ResourceDictionary class and the MergedDictionaries property to manage resources

Appendix C

980817   FIX: A .NET Framework 3.5-based application becomes unresponsive when a time-out issue occurs on a request to a service that uses the SSL protocol

980951   FIX: A workflow takes a long time to open when you use the workflow designer in a .NET Framework 3.5 SP1-based solution

981002   A hotfix rollup is available for Windows Communication Foundation in the .NET Framework 3.5 SP1 for Windows 7 and Windows Server 2008 R2

981107   A hotfix is available that resolves some memory leak issues for WPF in the .NET Framework 3.0 SP2

981119   FIX: You cannot run an ASP.NET 3.5-based application that uses a ScriptManager control

981145   Workflows gradually take longer to load in a workflow designer that is re-hosted in the .NET Framework 2.0

981266   Referenced assemblies of a .NET Framework 2.0-based 32-bit application are loaded multiple times

981429   Some XPS file text is printed incorrectly by a .NET Framework 3.0-based WPF application

981574   The splash screen stays open longer than usual when you try to start Excel on a computer that has the .NET Framework 3.5 SP1 installed

981575   A memory leak occurs in a .NET Framework 2.0-based application that uses the AesCryptoServiceProvider class

981619   A hotfix is available that improves the performance of CLR when a .NET Framework 3.5 SP1-based application runs in a virtualized environment

981667   An exception occurs when a WCF client sends a request to a .NET Framework 3.5-based WCF service that uses an IPv6 address for the binding

981773   East Asian text is displayed incorrectly when you run a Windows Form application in the .NET Framework 2.0

981878   FIX: A dump file is not generated for a .NET Framework 2.0-based application after the application closes

982307   Description of the update for ADO.NET Data Services Update for .NET Framework 3.5 SP1 for Windows 7 and Windows Server 2008 R2: May 7, 2010

982671   The .NET Framework 4 is available on Windows Update

982967   WCF services that are hosted by computers together with a NLB fail in .NET Framework 3.5 SP1

983590   MS10-060 Description of the security update for the Microsoft .NET Framework 3.5 in Windows 7 and in Windows Server 2008 R2: August 10, 2010

2077754   A .NET Framework 2.0-based application that targets to the x64 platform crashes for an uncaught ThreadAbortException exception

2254512   FIX: The TextFieldParser.EndOfData method returns True when the TextFieldParser object does not reach the end of text data in a Microsoft .NET Framework 2.0-based application or a Microsoft .NET Framework 3.5 SP1-based application

2276255   FIX: An application that is based on the .NET Framework 2.0 stops responding on a computer that has more than 32 processors, and the .NET Framework 2.0 Service Pack 2 or the .NET Framework 3.5 Service Pack 1 is installed

2282372   "Loading this assembly would produce a different grant set from other instances" error message when you run a .NET Framework 2.0-based application on a computer that is running a 64-bit version of Windows

2289553   FIX: Inline data-binding expressions in a templated web user control disappear after you generate a local resource for an ASP.NET 2.0 web application

Hardware and Drivers

975891   HP Multifunction Printers and HP Full Feature Software or HP Basic Driver solutions do not work as expected after a computer upgrades from Windows Vista to Windows 7

976759   WFP drivers may cause a failure to disconnect the RDP connection to a multi-processor computer that is running Windows Vista, Windows Server 2008, Windows 7 or Windows Server 2008 R2

978044   A USB composite device that supports consumer infrared does not work correctly on a computer that is running Windows 7

978462   A computer that is running Windows 7 or Windows Server 2008 R2 stops responding when you disable or remove a CD-ROM or DVD-ROM device in Device Manager

978977   An exclamation mark (!) may be displayed next to the smartcard reader in Device Manager after you start Windows 7 or Windows Server 2008 R2

979681   FIX: A legacy HP printer driver may crash when you run a 32-bit application on a computer that is running a 64-bit version of Windows 7 or of Windows Server 2008 R2

981214   There is high CPU usage when using a USB audio device connected to a USB 2.0 EHCI host controller

981377   An SDIO wireless device is not detected on a computer that is running Windows 7

2182039   Some USB 2.0 audio devices that have an MIDI out port do not work correctly in Windows Vista, Windows Server 2008, Windows 7, or Windows Server 2008 R2

2281456   Windows Explorer does not correctly recognize the DVD drive and the DVD disc after you use Windows DVD Maker to create a DVD disc in Windows 7 or in Windows Server 2008 R2

International/Localization

976782   Text in the General tab of the Windows Backup task in the Task Scheduler Library is not displayed in the localized language in Windows 7 or Windows Server 2008 R2

979745   The legacy Vista-style green progress bar shows when you start or restart Chinese Traditional HK version of Windows 7

982115   The decimal point and the thousands separator do not change to match native "Hindi" formats when you use Microsoft Office applications to process financial data in Windows 7 or in Windows Server 2008 R2

2030901   The DateTimePicker control displays short dates in the "yyyy/MM/dd" format unexpectedly when "Hebrew (Israel)" is specified as date and time format in Windows 7 and Windows Server 2008 R2

2446496   An update is available that changes the currency symbol of Estonia to the euro (€) in Windows

Internet Explorer

888092 You may receive an error message in module Mshtml.dll and Internet Explorer quits when you run a custom Web program in Internet Explorer 6

925681 When you try to download a file from the Internet by using Internet Explorer, the download stops responding

925683 In Internet Explorer 6 or in Internet Explorer 8, the OnChange event in a field does not occur when you change the "ß" character to "ss" characters, or when you change "ss" characters to the "ß" character

951422 The WTSQuerySessionInformation function returns ambiguous IPv6 address data on a computer that is running Windows Vista, Windows 7, Windows Server 2008 or Windows Server 2008 R2

970840 Some settings in Group Policy Preferences for Internet Explorer do not deploy correctly to computers that are running Windows Server 2008, Windows Vista, Windows 7 or Windows Server 2008 R2

971447 The SetCursorPos function does not move the pointer to the link that receives keyboard focus in Internet Explorer 8 on Windows Vista and on Windows Server 2008

972260 MS09-034 Cumulative security update for Internet Explorer

972774 The Platform for Privacy Preferences privacy policy of a Web site is lost when the Encoding option of Internet Explorer is set to "Auto-Select"

973528 The "window.focus" and "window.blur" methods do not set the focus on a new window in Internet Explorer 8 if the window was created by another Iexplorer.exe process

973533 Text takes a long time to appear on the screen when you type inside a TEXTAREA element in a Web page in Internet Explorer 8 Standards mode

973534 Internet Explorer 8 crashes when you click an element that uses expressions in cascading style sheets

973535 A Web page is not displayed correctly in Internet Explorer 8 on a computer that is running Windows Vista

973536 Internet Explorer 8 is slow to load a Web page that contains the BASE tag

973538 You cannot print a page and you receive an error message in an application that hosts a WebOC that uses a custom print template in Internet Explorer 8

974043 CPU usage reaches almost 100 percent when you reply to or forward an e-mail message in Outlook 2003 on a computer that has Internet Explorer 7 or Internet Explorer 8 installed

974322 "Operation aborted" error message when you open a Web page that uses the appendChild method in Internet Explorer 8 or in Internet Explorer 7

974455 MS09-054 Cumulative security update for Internet Explorer

974537 Part of a pop-up window appears off-screen in Internet Explorer 8

975169 The application that hosts a WebBrowser control crashes when you use a custom MIME filter on a computer that has Internet Explorer installed

975624 User's data in local storage is occasionally lost in Internet Explorer 8

976002 What is the Browser Choice update?

976425 A file name extension is displayed as .soi instead of .xsl in Microsoft Office Excel 2003 on a computer that has Internet Explorer 8 installed

976662 An update is available for the native JSON feature in Internet Explorer 8

977416 Some table cells are not displayed when you use Internet Explorer 8 to browse a HTML webpage

977417 You are prompted to provide authentication again when you open a new tab or a new window in a SSL Web site in Internet Explorer 8

978019 Cascading pop-up windows overlap incorrectly in Internet Explorer 8

978207 MS10-002 Cumulative security update for Internet Explorer

978896 Table column width shrinks when you use the table-layout:fixed attribute in Internet Explorer 8

979898 A text block moves together with the mouse pointer when you click the LEFT ARROW key or the RIGHT ARROW key in a Microsoft SharePoint Web application in Internet Explorer 8

979926 The history.length value is calculated incorrectly in Internet Explorer 8 when the Automatic Crash Recovery feature is enabled

979942 The option to select an alternative file source does not display when you use Internet Explorer 8 to view a PDF document that contains an embedded media

979954   The Window.focus method does not work in Internet Explorer 8

980073   Focus is lost when the Print Picture option is selected in Internet Explorer 8

980182   MS10-018 Cumulative security update for Internet Explorer

981286   A webpage that uses the "table-layout:fixed" attribute is displayed unexpectedly in Compatibility View in Internet Explorer 8

981991   Internet Explorer 8 crashes when you try to print a webpage that contains a frameset inside an IFRAME element

982070   Internet Explorer 8 crashes when you select a search item from the dynamic candidate list in www.google.co.jp on a Tablet PC that is running Windows 7

982085   An ActiveX control that is used to hide or to reset the browser chrome does not work correctly in Internet Explorer 8

982086   The title of a custom toolbar is not displayed in Internet Explorer 8

982087   Internet Explorer 8 may crash intermittently if you enable SmartScreen Filter

982094   A memory leak occurs if the content in a frame on a webpage is reloaded repeatedly in Internet Explorer 8

982367   InfoPath.exe stops working when you press an arrow key on a computer that has Internet Explorer 8 installed

982368   You cannot save a webpage as the complete Web page format or as the single file web archive format in Internet Explorer 8

982370   You receive a "Work Offline" dialog box in Internet Explorer 8 after the computer resumes from sleep or from hibernation

982372   The "Load time" fields of some BHOs are blank in Internet Explorer 8

982375   The IDM_SHOWZEROBORDERATDESIGNTIME command ID does not work in Internet Explorer 8

982381   MS10-035 Cumulative security update for Internet Explorer

2029558   The keys that you type and any mouse movement do not work on the VM when you access the VM in Internet Explorer 8 by using the Terminal Services ActiveX control in Windows 7 or in Windows Server 2008 R2

2078942   The CertEnroll control does not work in Internet Explorer 8 on a computer that is running Windows 7 or Windows Server 2008 R2

Appendix C

2175840   Internet Explorer 7 and Internet Explorer 8 stop responding intermittently

2183461   MS10-053 Cumulative Security update for Internet Explorer

2221763   You cannot open a web folder by using the httpFolder behavior from a webpage in Internet Explorer 8 on a computer that is running Windows 7 or Windows Server 2008 R2

2310259   A hyperlink that is specified to open in a 32-bit instance of Internet Explorer 8 opens in a 64-bit instance of Internet Explorer 8

2386759   Group Policy preference settings for the settings on the Advanced tab in Internet Explorer 8 do not work as expected on a client computer that is running Windows 7 or Windows Server 2008 R2

2416400   MS10-090 Cumulative security update for Internet Explorer

2447568   A Compatibility View list update is available for Windows Internet Explorer 8: November 23, 2010

Multimedia

975499   A black rectangle appears on the secondary screen when you play some media from the Start menu on a Windows 7-based computer

978206   FIX: MPEG-2 Program Stream content does not play on a computer that is running Windows 7 or Windows Server 2008 R2

979532   Windows Media Photo encoder generates a lossless compressed image instead of a lossy compressed image as expected

979567   An update is available that addresses some issues with the Microsoft Media Foundation source reader and sink writer in Windows 7

980393   Two users accounts that are logged on to the same computer cannot use Windows Photo Viewer at the same time in Windows 7 and in Windows Server 2008 R2

981013   A memory leak issue occurs in the Audiodg.exe process when you play audio on a computer that is running Windows 7, Windows Server 2008 R2, Windows Vista or Windows Server 2008

981621   Streaming issues that are related to Microsoft Media Foundation in Windows 7

981679   An application that captures and plays audio stops responding in Windows 7 or in Windows Server 2008 R2

981738   Hardware-accelerated video playback stops responding for more than 10 seconds in Windows Server 2008 R2 or in Windows 7

2120976   Streaming issues that are related to Microsoft Media Foundation in Windows 7

Networking

954664   MIB interface information that is collected by the IP Helper API is blank or incomplete on a computer that is running a non-English version of Windows Server 2008 or Windows Vista

971277   You cannot access an administrative share on a computer after you set the SrvsvcDefaultShareInfo registry entry to configure the default share permissions for a network share

974636   AD RMS may stop working when it queries Active Directory global catalogs on a computer that is running Windows Server 2008 R2

978622   The setsockopt function does not bind a PGM packet to a network interface that has more than two IP addresses on a computer that is running Windows 7 or Windows Server 2008 R2

978738   You cannot use DirectAccess to connect to a corporate network from a computer that is running Windows 7 or Windows Server 2008 R2

978836   You cannot create or delete managed service accounts in a perimeter network in Windows 7 or in Windows Server 2008 R2

978869   Error message when you try to open a network-shared application on a client computer that is running Windows 7 or Windows Server 2008 R2: 0xc000000f

979101   The command "netsh interface ipv4 dump" does not export the subnet mask setting in Windows 7, in Windows Server 2008 R2, in Windows Server 2008, and in Windows Vista

979346   The DNS server entry for a WAN miniport adapter is removed on a computer that is running Windows Server 2008 R2 or Windows 7

979373   The DirectAccess connection is lost on a computer that is running Windows 7 or Windows Server 2008 R2 that has an IPv6 address

979548   You cannot enter an agreement number of a volume license that contains more than seven digits in Remote Desktop Licensing Manager or in TS Licensing Manager

Appendix C

979751   A domain user account that has a blank password cannot be used to authenticate against Microsoft SharePoint Server 2010 or against Windows Live SkyDrive

981054   The Group Policy preference settings for the "Terminal Session" item-level targeting item are not applied in Windows 7 or in Windows Server 2008 R2

981152   A shared printer does not appear in Windows 7 or Windows Server 2008 R2

981197   DNS query of multi-label SRV records cause the KMS auto-detection feature not to work

981382   You may be unable to connect to a network by using a 3G modem after you remove the 3G modem in Windows 7 or in Windows Server 2008 R2

981636   SharePoint document libraries are displayed in WebDav style instead of SharePoint HTML style in the Open dialog box and in the Save As dialog box on a computer that is running Windows 7 or Windows Server 2008 R2

983620   You cannot access a DFS share through a mapped network drive on a computer that is running Windows 7 or Windows Server 2008 R2

2028749   A "Set Network Location" dialog box appears when you first log on to a domain-joined Windows 7-based client computer

2028827   The applications that use the TDI driver for network traffic may stop responding in Windows Server 2008 R2 or in Windows 7

2028965   Data corruption when multiple users perform read and write operations to a shared file in the SMB2 environment

2157332   You are denied access when you try to open the properties dialog of a network interface on a 64-bit version of Windows Server 2008 R2 or Windows 7 even if you use the correct credentials

2175609   You may encounter unexpected behavior when you use multiple IPv4 addresses on a computer that is running Windows 7 or Windows Server 2008 R2

2182005   You receive an incorrect error message when you experience name collision in a shared network folder in Windows 7

2194664   You cannot access a remote server that shares files and printers by using the SMB protocol from a computer that is running Windows Server 2008 R2 or Windows 7

2257487   You cannot mount shares from an NFS file server on a client computer that is running Windows 7 or Windows Server 2008 R2 when you use NFS version 2 on the file server

2265741 IPSec communication fails between a computer that is running Windows Server 2008 R2 or Windows 7 and a computer that is running Windows XP

2275950 An error occurs when you try to establish SSL connections to the nodes by using the alias name from an LDAPS client computer that is running Windows 7 or Windows Server 2008 R2

2291175 The shared type icons do not appear when you use Windows Explorer to view the sharing status of some shared folders in Windows 7 or in Windows Server 2008 R2

2309371 "HTTP 401" error message when you try to access web resources that require Kerberos authentication on a computer that is running Windows 7 or Windows Server 2008 R2

2344959 The DHCP traffic is blocked after you enable the "Do not allow exception" and "Prohibit unicast response to multicast or broadcast requests" Windows Firewall settings in Windows 7 or in Windows Server 2008 R2

2383827 FIX: You receive an error message when no file is found on an FTP 7.5 server: "550-The system cannot find the file specified"

2385405 An application that uses the WLAN API displays an incorrect location for the current user after you resume a Windows 7-based computer from a new access point on a wireless network

2386184 IP addresses are still registered on the DNS servers even if the IP addresses are not used for outgoing traffic on a computer that is running Windows 7 or Windows Server 2008 R2

2393659 A DHCP client computer that has multiple network adapters and that is running Windows 7 or Windows Server 2008 R2 cannot renew a DHCP lease when the computer wakes

2409615 The WinHTTP API cannot obtain content from a website that contains special characters in Windows 7 or in Windows Server 2008 R2

Networking: IIS and WebDAV Issues

907286 FIX: "System.NotSupportedException" exception occurs after you configure a "Negotiable 2-based" authentication provider on an IIS virtual directory that hosts a .NET Framework 3.5 SP1-based WCF service

972251 FIX: A System.NotSupportedException exception is thrown when you run an IIS hosted WCF service that uses a client certificate for SSL authentication

Appendix C

975443   FIX: Windows Process Activation Service (WAS) does not start when you use the IISRESET /RESTART command to restart IIS 7.0 or IIS 7.5

977787   Calls to CreateActCtx fail when the calls try to set a process-wide manifest inside an IIS 7.5 application

979543   You cannot open some IIS 7.5-hosted PDF documents by using a Web browser that has the Adobe PDF Reader plug-in enabled

979917   Two issues occur when you deploy an ASP.NET 2.0-based application on a server that is running IIS 7.0 or IIS 7.5 in Integrated mode

980368   A update is available that enables certain IIS 7.0 or IIS 7.5 handlers to handle requests whose URLs do not end with a period

980423   FIX: You experience several issues when you use Powershell cmdlets or AppFabric features in IIS 7.0 or IIS 7.5

981124   FIX: The MIME mapping list cannot be parsed by using the earlier version of the ADSI provider in IIS 7.0

981898   A file does not download from an IIS 7.5 server that is running Windows 7 or Windows Server 2008 R2

982386   FIX: IISCertObj methods fail on a computer that is running Internet Information Services (IIS) 7.5

983484   Some services are preloaded unexpectedly when you start a website that contains multiple applications in IIS 7.5

2078804   A "200" HTTP status code is incorrectly logged in the IIS log when a partial content client request succeeds in IIS 7.5 in Windows 7 or in Windows Server 2008 R2

2277918   FIX: A PHP application that depends on the REQUEST_URI server variable may fail when a request whose URL contains UTF-8 characters is sent to IIS 7.5

2278855   FIX: It takes a long time to add a new website in a shared hosting environment on a web server that is running IIS 7.0 or IIS 7.5

2288297   You are unexpectedly prompted to enter your credentials when you try to access a WebDAV resource in a corporate network by using a DirectAccess connection in Windows 7 or in Windows Server 2008 R2

2386854   Files remain encrypted after you copy the files from an encrypted folder to a WebDAV share if the files are copied by using a computer that is running Windows 7 or Windows Server 2008 R2

2414971 FIX: Requests for URLs are not traced after you enable the UseUrlFilter flag in IIS 7.0 or in IIS 7.5

2465204 In Office 2003, you cannot open a file that is on a WebDAV share when Office is running on a Windows 7-based computer

Networking: Remote Access, VPN

973062 The audio redirection feature does not work when you use Remote Desktop Connection Client for Mac 2.0 to make a terminal server session to a computer that is running Windows Server 2008 x64 Edition or Windows Vista x64 Edition

975488 A Cisco VPN server does not provide differential services if you connect to the VPN server through a VPN connection that is based on the IKEv2 protocol from a computer that is running Windows 7 or Windows Server 2008 R2

979425 A combo box item in a RemoteApp application is updated incorrectly when you connect by using Remote Desktop Connection (RDC) 7.0

979443 You do not receive a warning message when a remote desktop connection fails from a Windows 7 or Windows Server 2008 R2-based computer

979734 Description of an update for Remote Desktop Services BPA

980399 "0x0000009F" Stop error when you use L2TP over IPsec tunnel to initialize a VPN connection to a corporate network from a client computer that is running Windows 7 or Windows Server 2008 R2 and later you try to use hibernate mode.

981637 An application cannot receive multicast data from a private enterprise server through a VPN connection on a client computer that is running Windows 7, Windows Server 2008, Windows Vista, or Windows Server 2008 R2

2096902 Virtual machines in a VDI environment are not rolled back as expected if the disconnected Remote Desktop connections on the virtual machines are stopped by Group Policy

2273487 Error message when you shadow a remote desktop service session in Windows Server 2008 R2 or in Windows 7: "Because of a protocol error, this session will be disconnected. Please try connecting to the remote computer again."

2301288 A Remote Desktop Services session is disconnected automatically if you apply the "Interactive logon: smart card removal behavior" Group Policy setting in Windows Server 2008 R2 or in Windows 7

2388381 You cannot start a RemoteAPP program that is hosted on a Windows XP SP3 virtual machine through Terminal Services Web Access or Remote Desktop Web Access in Windows Server 2008 R2, in Windows 7 or in Windows Vista

Appendix C

Offline Files

977229   You are unable to update the target location of offline file shares in the Offline File client side cache without administrative permission in Windows Server 2008 R2 or in Windows 7

977397   The icon of an offline file that you changed in offline mode always indicates that synchronization is successful even when the synchronization fails on a client computer that is running Windows 7

2028960 The Offline Files Disk Usage Limits settings do not reflect the settings that are defined in the GPO in Windows 7

Performance and Reliability

951418   Stop error in Windows Vista, Windows 7, Windows Server 2008, or Windows Server 2008 R2: "0x00000050 PAGE_FAULT_IN_NONPAGED_AREA"

970360   You experience high CPU utilization when an application uses the IPMI driver to communicate with the baseboard management controller on a computer that is running Windows Vista or Windows Server 2008

970924   FIX: The performance of applications that use the CreateType method decrease as you add more type objects to a dynamic assembly module in the .NET Framework 2.0 SP2

973510   Downloaded files do not inherit the permissions from the parent folder when you use the Ftp.exe program to download files in Windows Vista, in Windows Server 2008, in Windows 7 or in Windows Server 2008 R2

974431   The October 2009 stability and reliability update for Windows 7 and Windows Server 2008 R2 is available.

974639   SceCli 1202 events are logged every time Computer Group Policy settings are refreshed on a computer that is running Windows Server 2008 R2 or Windows 7

974813   FIX: You cannot send or receive messages by using Message Queuing 4.0 or Message Queuing 5.0 after you configure the BindInterfaceIP registry entry.

974930   An application or service that queries information about a failover cluster by using the WMI provider may experience low performance or a time-out exception

975243 The DirectX Diagnostics Tool incorrectly reports DirectX 11 devices as DirectX 10.1 devices on a computer that is running Windows 7 or Windows Server 2008 R2

975332 Users and applications cannot access authorization rules that are stored in Authorization Manager

975363 A time-out error occurs when many NTLM authentication requests are sent from a computer that is running Windows Server 2008 R2, Windows 7, Windows Server 2008, or Windows Vista in a high latency network

975415 Error message when you pass a variant between a COM client and a COM server in Windows: "0x800706F7 (The stub received bad data)"

975688 A snapshot may become corrupted when the Volume Shadow Copy Service (VSS) snapshot providers take more than 10 seconds to create it on a computer that is running Windows 7 or Windows Server 2008 R2

975858 An application or service that calls the InitializeSecurityContext function together with the ISC_REQ_EXTENDED_ERROR flag may encounter a TLS/SSL negotiation failure on a computer that is running Windows Server 2008 R2 or Windows 7

975921 You may be unable to perform certain disk-related operations after an exception when a hardware provider tries to create a snapshot in Windows Server 2008 R2 or in Windows 7

975992 After you enable large pages for a process in Windows 7 or in Windows Server 2008 R2, the process stops responding intermittently

976038 Exceptions that are thrown from an application that runs in a 64-bit version of Windows are ignored

976099 VSS snapshot creation may fail after a LUN resynchronization on a computer that is running Windows 7 or Windows Server 2008 R2

976417 High CPU usage in the Explorer.exe process when you open a folder that contains corrupted .wav files in Windows 7 or in Windows Server 2008 R2

976418 After you change the SATA mode of disk devices to use the AHCI specification, the computer or certain applications randomly stop responding for 60 seconds or for longer in Windows 7 and in Windows Server 2008 R2

976424 Error code when the kpasswd protocol fails after you perform an authoritative restore: "KDC_ERROR_S_PRINCIPAL_UNKNOWN"

Appendix C

976427   Computers that are running Windows 7 or Windows Server 2008 R2 stop responding at a black screen if a screen saver is enabled

976443   Stop error message when you retrieve WMI connection statistics for iSCSI after you change the iSCSI configurations on a computer that is running Windows Server 2008 R2 or Windows 7: "0x00000019 BAD_POOL_HEADER"

976494   Error 1789 when you use the LookupAccountName function on a computer that is running Windows 7 or Windows Server 2008 R2

976538   File corruption may occur if you run a program that uses a file system filter driver in Windows 7, Windows Server 2008 R2, Windows Vista, or Windows Server 2008

976586   Error in Windows 7 or Windows Server 2008 R2 when unlocking a computer or switching users

976658   The memory of the nonpaged pool may leak when you enable IPsec on a computer that is running Windows Server 2008 R2 or Windows 7

976700   An application stops responding, experiences low performance, or experiences high privileged CPU usage if many large I/O operations are performed in Windows 7 or Windows Server 2008 R2

976746   Error message when a Windows Server 2008 R2-based or a Windows 7-based computer enters hibernation: "STOP: 0x0000000A"

977067   You receive a stop error after you enable the RequireinClearout mode on an IPv6 network on Windows Server 2008 R2 or in Windows 7

977074   The January 2010 stability and reliability update for Windows 7 and Windows Server 2008 R2 is available.

977158   DNS updates may be incorrectly reported as failed when you use a third-party DNS server application for DNS registration on a computer that is running Windows Server 2008 R2 or Windows 7

977206   Error message about hardware-assisted virtualization for Windows XP Mode in Windows Virtual PC on a computer that is running Windows 7

977353   A Group Policy Immediate Task preference item does not run on a client computer that is running Windows 7 or Windows Server 2008 R2

977357   A memory leak issue occurs in the Windows Management Instrumentation service on a computer that is running Windows Server 2008 R2 or Windows 7

977579   Error message when you try to open a 3DES encrypted file that is migrated from Windows XP to Windows 7 or to Windows Server 2008 R2: "Access Denied"

977589   An application or a service that uses the Wmiaprpl.dll module crashes when the application or the service enumerates the returned performance objects under the HKEY_PERFORMANCE_DATA registry key

977643   The Presentationhost.exe process that is associated with an XBAP application incorrectly remains in memory

977648   An application that calls the ReadConsoleOutputCharacter function closes unexpectedly or data becomes corrupted when the application runs in Windows 7 or in Windows Server 2008 R2

977695   The SceCli 1202 events are logged when some Group Policy settings are refreshed in Windows Server 2008 R2 and in Windows 7

977911   The system language is changed or you receive a Stop error after you restart a computer that is running a preinstalled version of Windows 7: "0x00000021a"

978042   FIX: A memory leak may occur when you use the Microsoft ActiveX Data Objects Library in Windows Vista, in Windows 7, in Windows Server 2008, or in Windows Server 2008 R2

978048   The SUA application stops responding when you run a mixed-mode SUA application that calls the fork function on a computer that is running Windows 7 or Windows Server 2008 R2

978116   In an MIT realm, user authentication fails after invalid credentials are received on a computer that is running Windows 7 or Windows Server 2008 R2

978155   A memory leak occurs when an ADO Recordset object calls the UpdateBatch method

978265   FIX: The memory allocation and processor usage for the Ocspsvc.exe process keeps increasing if a large CRL is loaded

978277   Error message when you try to change a password on a computer that is running Windows 7 or Windows Server 2008 R2: "The specified account does not exist"

978330   FIX: The message-signaled interrupts (MSIs) feature is not enabled on VIA processors on a computer that is running Windows 7 or Windows Server 2008 R2

978347   Many connections have a CLOSE_WAIT status after you map some network drives on a Windows 7 or Windows Server 2008 R2-based client computer and access them several times on an NFS server

Appendix C

978433   Windows Explorer crashes and then restarts when you access a third-party Control Panel item on a computer that is running Windows 7 or Windows Server 2008 R2

978489   Logoff process stops responding after you create a logoff Group Policy script on a client computer that is running Windows Vista or Windows Server 2008

978491   FIX: A server that is running Server Message Block Version 2 does not respond to certain FSCTL_SRV_NOTIFY_TRANSACTION requests from clients that are running Windows Vista or Windows Server 2008

978516   You experience significant delays when you read the same set of files several times on a read-only volume in Windows 7 or in Windows Server 2008 R2

978526   FIX: Windows Explorer may stop responding when you insert a recordable BD-R into the Blu-Ray drive on a computer that is running Windows 7 or Windows Server 2008 R2

978535   Stop error on a blue screen when you remove an SD card from a Windows 7-based or Windows Server 2008 R2-based computer: "0x000000D1"

978637   An application runs in a Windows Vista context instead of in a Windows 7 context on a computer that is running an x64 edition of Windows 7 or of Windows Server 2008 R2

978714   Error message in Windows 7 or in Windows Server 2008 R2: 0x8007007E

978837   The Group Policy Management Editor window crashes when you apply some changes for NRPT policy settings

978898   You cannot access a volume in Windows 7 or in Windows 2008 R2 when the volume is encrypted by a third-party encryption driver

979149   A computer that is running Windows 7 or Windows Server 2008 R2 becomes unresponsive when you run a large application

979223   A nonpaged pool memory leak occurs when you use a WFP callout driver in Windows Vista, Windows 7, Windows Server 2008, or in Windows Server 2008 R2

979241   No event is added to the System log or to an operational channel when a print job is canceled or deleted

979275   You cannot start a second application from an application by using the CreateProcess function in Windows 7 or in Windows Server 2008 R2

979278   Using two Windows Filtering Platform (WFP) drivers causes a computer to crash when the computer is running Windows Vista, Windows 7, or Windows Server 2008

979294   The Dcdiag.exe tool takes a long time to run in Windows Server 2008 R2 and in Windows 7

979366   The burning operation fails with a time-out error when you try to burn files to a DVD-R Dual Layer disc in Windows 7 or in Windows Server 2008 R2

979383   After you apply a WMI filter, the GPO does not take effect on a client computer that is running Windows 7 or Windows Server 2008 R2

979444   Error message on a blue screen on a computer that is running Windows 7 or Windows Server 2008 R2: "STOP: 0x0000000A"

979491   Computer that has an nVidia MCP7A-GeForce 9300 rev B1 motherboard together with an LSI Logic FW533 or an FW643 1394 Host controller crashes after you install Windows 7 or Windows Server 2008 R2

979619   Tracing is inefficient when you diagnose issues that are related to iSCSI Initiator in Windows Server 2008 R2 or in Windows 7

979711   Stop error message on a computer that is running Windows 7 or Windows Server 2008 R2 and that has iSCSI storage: "0x0000000A"

979791   A computer that is running Windows Server 2008 R2 or Windows 7 cannot come out of quarantine if you install the System Center Configuration Manager System health agent on the computer

979940   A VDS application cannot enumerate FC HBA ports in the presence of SAS HBA ports in Windows Server 2008 R2 and in Windows 7

980082   Stop error in Win7 and in Win2008 R2 when you run a backup application: "0x0000007E SYSTEM_THREAD_EXCEPTION_NOT_HANDLED"

980226   "STOP: 0X000000D5" error message on a computer that is running Windows Vista, Windows 7, Windows Server 2008, or Windows Server 2008 R2

980254   The "dsget user -memberof -expand" command returns incorrect results in Windows Server 2008 R2 and in Windows 7

980259   The SNMP service does not respond to any SNMP requests after a Group Policy refresh in Windows Vista, in Windows Server 2008, in Windows 7 or in Windows Server 2008 R2

Appendix C

980295 No response to 802.1X authentication requests after authentication fails on a computer that is running Windows 7 or Windows Server 2008 R2

980358 Stop error when you startup Windows Preinstallation Environment on a computer that has the Pentium 233 MHz MMX process installed: "STOP 0x00000078"

980382 The computer stops responding when you rename a folder in Windows Server 2008, in Windows Vista, in Windows 7 and in Windows Server 2008 R2

980385 The disconnected sessions are not deleted on a computer that is running Windows Server 2008 R2 or Windows 7 after a time-out if the users log on by using the Fast User Switching feature

980663 Stop error in Windows 7 and in Windows Server 2008 R2 if a heavy load situation exists or if connectivity issues exist: "STOP: 0x000000B8"

980731 A computer that is running Windows 7 or Windows Server 2008 R2 stops responding when you run DirectX applications

980794 System state backup error in Windows Server 2008, in Windows Vista, in Windows 7 and in Windows Server 2008 R2: "Enumeration of the files failed"

980922 Some stability issues occur when you run an application that uses the DirectWrite API

980932 "STOP 0x0000003B" Stop error on a computer that is running Windows 7 or Windows Server 2008 R2 when you use some IEEE 1394 devices

981109 "0x00000027" Stop error when you try to log on a client computer that is running Windows 7 or Windows Server 2008 R2

981118 The CryptDecrypt function fails when you try to decrypt encrypted content on a computer that is running Windows 7 or Windows Server 2008 R2

981180 Stop error message when you run an application that transfers data by using the UDP protocol in Windows Server 2008 R2 or in Windows 7: "STOP 0x0000007F"

981194 The input or output stream is redirected incorrectly in a Korn shell

981208 Poor performance when you transfer many small files on a computer that is running Windows 7 or Windows Server 2008 R2

981314 The "Win32_Service" WMI class leaks memory in Windows Server 2008 R2 and in Windows 7

981344 An application may receive the "10054" error when the application receives data from a connection on a computer that is running Windows 7 or Windows Server 2008 R2 if a TDI filter driver is installed

981357 The handle count of the system process keeps increasing in Windows Server 2008, in Windows Vista, in Windows 7 or in Windows Server 2008 R2

981394 A computer restarts when multiple Kerberos authentication requests are made at the same time in Windows 7 or in Windows Server 2008 R2

981466 An event log may not be saved when you "Save and Clear" an event log in Windows 7 or Windows Server 2008 R2

981506 "SSL Certificate add failed, Error: 1312" error message when you try to add a CTL in Windows Server 2008 R2 or in Windows 7

981542 A Windows 7 or a Windows Server 2008 R2 image deployment process stops when you try to deploy the image on another computer

981603 "The destination folder path is invalid" Error message when you extract a compressed file on a computer that is running Windows 7 or Windows Server 2008 R2

981613 Transferred data is corrupted or the data transfer stops between an IEEE 1394 device and a computer that is running Windows 7 or Windows Server 2008 R2

981709 You experience a long delay when the IVssBackupComponents::AddComponent is used to add thousands of components in Windows Server 2008 R2 or in Windows 7

981710 An application that invokes the configuration page for a scheduled task crashes after you change some task settings in Windows 7 or Windows Server 2008 R2

981711 "0x000000D5" Stop error when you run an application or transfer some data from a shared DVD disc on a server in Windows 7 or Windows Server 2008 R2

981721 A portable computer display does not switch back to the internal monitor after you play a DVD on an external monitor and disconnect the HDMI cable in Windows 7

981730 You cannot create an event in an event log in Windows 7 or in Windows Server 2008 R2 if the source field contains a single quotation mark

981750 Error message occurs when you use GPMC to view a software restriction Group Policy setting in Windows 7 and in Windows Server 2008 R2: "An error has occurred while collecting data for Software Restriction Policies"

981765 The network performance is not as fast as expected on a computer that has NUMA-based processors and that is running Windows Server 2008 R2 or Windows 7

981830   Slow logon for roaming profile users on client computers that are running Windows 7 or Windows Server 2008 R2

981845   The Windows Remote Management service stops responding in Windows 7 or in Windows Server 2008 R2

981851   The backup operation fails and the Wbengine.exe service stops in Windows Server 2008 R2 or in Windows 7 if one of the volumes in the operation does not exists any longer

981872   Access to a redirected folder or a home drive disconnects regularly on a computer that is running Windows Server 2008 R2 and Windows 7

981884   FIX: "The length of the string exceeds the value set on the maxJsonLength property" error message when you access an ASP.NET 3.5 web form

981892   Syntax error message when you run the unmask command in Windows Server 2008 R2 or Windows 7 and when VDS hardware provider is "VDS_HWT_HYBRID" type

982110   The QueryPathOfRegTypeLib function does not return the correct path for a 32-bit version of an application in a 64-bit edition of Windows 7 or in Windows Server 2008 R2

982199   The "CreateProcess" function fails in a 64-bit version of Windows 7 for Embedded Systems or of Windows Server 2008 R2 for Embedded Systems if the file system redirection feature is disabled

982293   The Svchost.exe process that has the WMI service crashes in Windows Server 2008 R2 or in Windows 7

982300   A computer stops responding when you install or run Windows 7 or Windows Server 2008 R2 if the 1394 bus host controller is enabled

982383   You encounter a decrease in I/O performance under a heavy disk I/O load on a Windows Server 2008 R2-based or Windows 7-based computer

982606   The value of the "State" registry item is changed after a Group Policy preferences setting is applied in Windows Server 2008, in Windows Vista or in Windows Server 2008 R2

982613   The "GetTempFileName" function fails together with an access denied error in Windows 7 or in Windows Server 2008 R2

982643   "Windows cannot connect to the printer" error message when you try to add a printer that uses IPP to a client computer that is running Windows Vista, Windows Server 2008, Windows 7, or Windows Server 2008 R2

982669   The nonpaged pool memory is low after an isochronous data transfer between an IEEE 1394 device and a Windows 7 or Windows Server 2008 R2-based computer

982674   "Stop 0x000000D1" error after you enable an iSCSI Initiator data digest setting that uses CRC or that uses checksum in Windows Server 2008 R2 or in Windows 7

982822   Some providers may receive an incorrect password value from the OLEDB32 component if the password in the connection string is blank in Windows 7 or in Windows Server 2008 R2

982847   "Error(s) occurred while invoke of Open on object xmlDOM" error message when you load an XML file that uses ISO-10646-UCS-2 encoding by using Microsoft XML Core Services 6.0

982927   You receive an error message that states the file system is broken in Windows 7 or in Windows Server 2008 R2

983224   The GetLastError function returns an incorrect value when the StartDoc function fails in a computer that is running a 64-bit version operating system

983246   "Type Mismatch" error message when you run a VBA macro in a 64-bit version of an Office 2010 application

983289   The "ZwAllocateVirtualMemory" function fails together with a STATUS_INSUFFICIENT_RESOURCES error randomly when you have sufficient memory in Windows 7 or in Windows Server 2008 R2

983396   A 32-bit OLE object may be displayed as an icon instead of the actual object when you insert it into a 64-bit process on a 64-bit version of Windows 7 or Windows Server 2008 R2

983401   A long delay occurs when you print a large file on a Windows 7 or Windows Server 2008 R2-based computer

983466   "A fatal error has occurred." error message when you use Windows Update on a Windows 7 or Windows Server 2008 R2-based computer that has a third-party filter driver installed

983478   You experience low performance when you call the TreeView_SetItem macro of a tree-view control on a Windows 7 or Windows Server 2008 R2-based computer

Appendix C

983528   The TCP receive window autotuning feature does not work correctly in Windows Server 2008 R2 or in Windows 7

983531   You experience a significant delay when you try to log on to an Active Directory site from a computer that is running Windows 7 or Windows Server 2008 R2

983533   The pop-up windows are hidden and the TS RemoteApp application stops responding in Windows Vista, in Windows 7, in Windows Server 2008, and in Windows Server 2008 R2

983543   "STOP 0x000000D1" error message when you try to access a device that is not a PCI device in Windows 7 or in Windows Server 2008 R2

983545   Stop error when you add RAM by using the Hot Add Memory feature in a virtual machine that is running Windows 7

983550   You cannot use Imjpuexc.exe to change a custom dictionary back to the default IME dictionary in Windows 7 or in Windows Server 2008 R2

983551   Windows 7 or Windows Server 2008 R2 stops responding at the "Please wait" screen before you are requested to press Ctrl+ALT+DEL

2028560   An update is available for Windows 7 and for Windows Server 2008 R2 which provides new functionality and performance improvements for the graphics platform

2028566   A copy-on-write snapshot may become corrupted in Windows Server 2008 R2 or in Windows 7 if some snapshots that are stored on the same volume are deleted

2028605   You receive a "registry.pol" corruption error in Windows Server 2008 R2 and in Windows 7 if you enable the "Certificate Services Client – Certificate Enrollment Policy" policy

2028610   The Image.Save method in GDI+ does not save JPEG images correctly on a computer that is running Windows 7 or Windows Server 2008 R2

2028687   You cannot specify a NUMA node when you create a process by using the "start" command in Windows Server 2008 R2 or in Windows 7

2028815   "0x00000050" Stop error message occurs when you use multiple volume managers in Windows Server 2008 or in Windows Server 2008 R2

2028997   FIX: Message Queuing may become unresponsive in Windows 7 or in Windows Server 2008 R2

2029054   An application which calls the ReadFile function on a named pipe server may stop responding when you run the application on a computer that is running Windows Vista, Windows Server 2008, Windows 7 or Windows Server 2008 R2

2064460   The "BackupRead" function randomly fails together with error code 58 in Windows Server 2008 R2 or in Windows 7

2102850   The image is not drawn correctly when you run an application that calls the LineTo function together with the BS-PATTERN style to display an image in Windows 7 or in Windows Server 2008 R2

2154088   The "HBA_SendCTPassThruV2" function fails in Windows Server 2008 R2 or in Windows 7

2159238   Error message when you set the screen saver to a 3D screen saver in Windows 7 or in Windows Server 2008 R2: "The screen saver can't run because it requires a newer video card or one that's compatible with Direct3D"

2171571   You incorrectly receive an error message when you join a computer that is running Windows 7 or Windows Server 2008 R2 to a Samba 3-based domain

2173749   The download or update process fails when you try to download firmware to an IEEE 1394 Firewire device or to update the firmware on an IEEE 1394 Firewire device on a computer that is running Windows 7 or Windows Server 2008 R2

2182466   "2155347997 (0x8078001D)" error code when you perform a system state backup operation in Windows 7 or in Windows Server 2008 R2

2203302   An RDP connection that uses SSL authentication and CredSSP protocol fails in Windows 7, in Windows Server 2008 R2, in Windows Vista and in Windows Server 2008

2203330   "STOP: 0x00000001" error occurs in Windows Server 2008 R2 or in Windows 7

2217044   The "FaxEnumJobs" function does not enumerate all fax jobs in Windows Server 2008 R2 or in Windows 7

2248145   IPsec connection in the IKEv1 tunnel mode fails from a computer that is running Windows 7 or Windows Server 2008 R2

2249715   You cannot copy a large file and paste the file to a multi-core computer that is running Windows 7 when the computer contains a network adapter that does not support the RSS feature

Appendix C

2253063 The direction flag is set incorrectly after an APC during an alterable wait of an exception handler when you run a 32-bit application on a computer that is running a 64-bit version of Windows 7 or of Windows Server 2008 R2

2253693 A VSS writer cannot create a snapshot on a computer that is running Windows 7 or Windows Server 2008 R2 if the snapshot set of the VSS writer has no disk volumes

2254251 A Bluetooth Personal Area Network device may stop responding after a surprise removal of the device from a computer that is running Windows 7

2254754 You experience a GPO report-generation issue in the GPMC window when you try to generate the report in a localized version of Windows 7 or of Windows Server 2008 R2

2260182 "0x0000003B" Stop error may occur when you run an App-V application on a computer that has App-V RDS client installed and that is running Windows 7 or Windows Server 2008 R2

2261116 IEEE 1394 asynchronous requests are completed, but they have incorrect data or status under high transfer rates in Windows 7 or in Windows Server 2008 R2

2265716 A computer that is running Windows Server 2008 R2 or Windows 7 stops responding randomly

2266686 The TunnelMTU registry entry does not work in Windows 7 and in Windows Server 2008 R2

2268596 The "Search programs and files" box on the Start menu does not search files on network locations that are not indexed in Windows 7 or in Windows Server 2008 R2

2275315 You cannot read the GPO in the SYSVOL directory in Windows 7 or in Windows Server 2008 R2 if you enable the "Deny write" permission of the GPO

2276597 "LDAP_AUTH_UNKNOWN (0x56)" error code occurs when you call the "ldap_set_option" function in Windows 7 or in Windows Server 2008 R2 if you use the "LDAP_OPT_SASL_METHOD" session option

2277956 You see a black desktop background after the computer switches between graphics adapters in Windows 7 or in Windows Server 2008 R2

2280515 A user is added to the wrong group on a client computer that is running Windows 7 or Windows Server 2008 R2

2287812   The "DwmEnableBlurBehindWindow" function does not work correctly for a non-rectangular window in Windows 7 and in Windows Server 2008 R2

2288487   Data corruption occurs when you write data to a partition on a disk through an IDE port or a SATA port that uses IDE emulation on a Windows Server 2008 R2-based or a Windows 7-based computer

2294419   A Message Queuing trigger on Windows 7 or on Windows 2008 R2 stops processing messages after the Message Queuing service is restarted on the computer that hosts the message queue

2295825   Poor printing performance in Windows 7 or in Windows Server 2008 R2 compared to the performance in Windows Vista or in Windows Server 2008

2299380   "0x0000007E" Stop error when you back up a Windows Server 2008 R2-based or Windows 7-based computer that is running virtual machines

2300639   The desktop stops responding for some time after you resume the display on a computer that is running Windows 7

2302026   You cannot dial another number if there is no answer when you dial out by using a modem on a Windows 7-based computer

2302077   You experience poor performance when you call the "CryptAcquireContext" function in Windows Server 2008 R2 or in Windows 7

2304914   All "LINE_CALLSTATE" messages do not arrive at an x64-based version of Windows 7 or of Windows Server 2008 R2

2316513   The Lanmanserver service cannot start after you restart a computer that is running Windows 7 or Windows Server 2008 R2 if a volume that is referenced in the PATH variable is inaccessible

2320550   Stop error on a Windows Server 2008 R2-based or Windows 7-based computer when the operating system uses a virtual storport miniport driver to save a dump file or a hibernation file: "0x000000D1"

2344941   "0x0000007B" Stop error when you replace an iSCSI network adapter or a motherboard with an identical device on a Windows Server 2008 R2-based or Windows 7-based computer

2354868   A handle leak occurs when an .exe file is called by the CreateProcess function after a file system filter driver denies the execution of the .exe file in Windows 7 or in Windows Server 2008 R2

Appendix C

2359223   "0x0000003B" Stop error occurs in Windows Server 2008 R2 and in Windows 7 when an application or a service performs a GUI-related operation

2384602   The pop-up windows of a RemoteApp program may be hidden in Windows Server 2008 R2 and in Windows 7

2386730   An item-level targeting security group filter in Group Policy preferences settings does not work on a computer that is running Windows Server 2008 R2 or Windows 7 in a disjoint namespace

2386792   Windows crashes when you run applications that use the D3D and GDI Interop surfaces on a computer that has multiple monitors attached and that is running Windows 7 or Windows Server 2008 R2

2386802   The user cannot log back on to a client computer that is running Windows 7 or Windows Server 2008 R2 after you reset the password and then lock the computer

2388028   IShareEngine fails in a Windows Home Server-based computer when you publish a share

2389167   The "User Notice" value of the policy extension is displayed incorrectly in Windows Server 2008 R2 or in Windows 7 if the "UTF8String" data type is used

2390986   Folder redirection fails in Windows 7 and in Windows Server 2008 R2 when you use a large Fdeploy1.ini file to configure the Folder Redirection policy

2391536   An application or service that receives event log information by using a WMI interface stops responding in Windows Server 2008 or in Windows Vista

2394120   "0xC00E5201" error code occurs when you try to create an .msp file in Windows 7

2403142   A WIA application crashes when you try to adjust the brightness or contrast of a picture that is scanned in Windows 7, in Windows Server 2008 R2, in Windows Vista or in Windows Server 2008

2408903   An MS-DOS-based program that uses the MS-DOS protected mode interface crashes on a computer that is running Windows 7

2409336   "Unable to cast object of type 'System.String' to type 'Microsoft.Group.Policy.Reporting.Extensions.Registry.RegistryValue'." error message when you try to generate a report for a GPO in Windows Server 2008 R2 or in Windows 7

2409711   A 30-second delay occurs when you log on to a computer after you configure the "Hide all icons on Desktop" Group Policy and the "Normal Wallpaper" Group Policy in Windows 7 or in Windows Server 2008

2410263   A 32-bit iSCSI provider cannot retrieve an instance of MSiSCSIInitiator_Persistent-Device in 64-bit versions of Windows 7 or of Windows Server 2008 R2

2434932   Temporary files do not synchronize correctly to a non-DFS share on a server from a client computer that is running Windows 7 or Windows Server 2008 R2

2454826   A performance and functionality update is available for Windows 7 and for Windows Server 2008 R2

Printing and Scanning Technologies

959554   Only the header and footer information in an XPS document are printed when you print the document on a computer that is running Windows XP, Windows Vista SP1, or Windows Server 2008

978917   A PostScript printer prints an error message instead of the expected document

979163   Many pages are printed when you try to print an Excel worksheet by using a redirected printer if the Terminal Services Easy Print feature is used

981070   "Windows can't open Add Printer" error in a 64-bit version of Win7 or of Windows Server 2008 R2

981076   A print job fails on a print device that uses a 64-bit printer driver when you use a 32-bit application to print the job in Windows 7 or Windows Server 2008 R2

981431   A PostScript printer does not print a document that contains multiple paper sizes correctly on a computer that is running Windows 7, Windows Server 2008 R2, Windows Vista or Windows Server 2008

981559   No print jobs are displayed in the IPP print queue on a computer that is running Windows 7 or Windows Server 2008 R2

981620   You cannot print a Web page by using an IPP printer in Windows 7 or in Windows Server 2008 R2

982728   "Windows cannot connect to printer" error message when you try to create a Point and Print connection to a remote printer from a Windows 7 or Windows Server 2008 R2-based client computer

Appendix C

983476   Poor performance occurs when you try to view print jobs in a queue on a computer that is running Windows Server 2008 R2 or Windows 7 if the print queue has many print jobs

2028551   An update is available that contains improvements to XPS in Windows 7 or in Windows Server 2008 R2

2121850   A booklet layout setting does not work when you print a multiple-page document in Windows 7 or in Windows Server 2008 R2 if you use a printer driver that uses Unidrv.dll

2249684   A Web Services for Devices (WSD)-based scanner does not work after the device is restarted on a computer that is running in Windows 7 or Windows Server 2008 R2

2280758   The print job fails when you try to print to a non-Windows-based IPP server on a client computer that is running Windows 7 or Windows Server 2008 R2

2344949   The printing operation stops responding when you print a document for a 64-bit Office application to a PostScript printer in Windows 7 or in Windows Server 2008 R2

2388142   A computer that is running Windows 7 or Windows Server 2008 R2 intermittently cannot use a shared network printer to print

2388144   Some print jobs fail and raise Event 6161 when the Print to File option is used on a multiprocessor computer that is running Windows 7 or Windows Server 2008 R2 and is under heavy stress

2406635   You cannot open a scanned TIFF file by using a standard third-party imaging application in Windows 7 or in Windows Server 2008 R2

2413679   You cannot install a printer that uses a DOT4 port on a computer that is running Windows 7 or Windows Server 2008 R2

Security

971468   MS10-012 Vulnerabilities in SMB Server could allow remote code execution

972270   MS10-001 Vulnerability in the Embedded OpenType Font Engine could allow remote code execution

973525   MS09-055 Cumulative Security Update of ActiveX Kill Bits

974571 MS09-056 Vulnerabilities in CryptoAPI could allow spoofing

975467 MS09-059 Vulnerability in the Local Security Authority Subsystem Service could allow denial of service

975561 MS10-016 Vulnerability in Windows Movie Maker could allow remote code execution

976323 MS10-024 Description of the security update for Windows SMTP Service: April 13, 2010 and July 13, 2010

977222 No private key is associated with a certificate after you successfully install the certificate on a computer that is running Windows 7 or Windows Server 2008 R2

977377 Microsoft Security Advisory: Vulnerability in TLS/SSL could allow spoofing

978262 MS10-008 Cumulative Security Update of ActiveX Kill Bits

978601 MS10-019 Description of the security update for Windows Authenticode Signature Verification: April 13, 2010

978886 MS10-058 Vulnerabilities in TCP/IP could allow elevation of privilege

979309 MS10-019 Description of the security update for Windows Cabinet File Viewer Shell Extension: April 13, 2010

979495 A secure channel is broken after you change the computer password on a Windows 7 or Windows Server 2008 R2-based client computer

979559 MS10-032 Vulnerabilities in Windows Kernel-Mode drivers could allow remote code execution

979688 MS10-083 Description of the security update for Windows Shell: October 12, 2010

979808 "Robocopy /B" does not copy the security information such as ACL in Windows 7 and in Windows Server 2008 R2

980232 MS10-020 Vulnerabilities in SMB client could allow remote code execution

980436 MS10-049 Vulnerabilities in SChannel could allow remote code execution

981957 MS10-073 Vulnerabilities in Windows kernel-mode drivers could allow elevation of privilege

982132	MS10-076 Vulnerability in the Embedded OpenType Font Engine could allow remote code execution
982214	MS10-054 Vulnerabilities in SMB Server could allow remote code execution
983458	You cannot save documents to a folder or change the permission settings of folders on a SMB 1.0-based remote server from a Windows-based computer that has security update 980232 (MS10-020) installed
2032276	MS10-043 Vulnerability in canonical display driver could allow remote code execution
2079403	MS10-051 Vulnerability in Microsoft XML Core Services could allow remote code execution
2207559	MS10-101 Vulnerability in Windows NetLogon Service could allow denial of service
2281679	MS10-075 Vulnerability in Media Player Network Sharing service could allow remote code execution
2286198	MS10-046 Vulnerability in Windows Shell could allow remote code execution
2296011	MS10-081 Vulnerability in the Windows common control library could allow remote code execution
2309344	A publisher name incorrectly has double ampersands (&&) in the "File Download - Security Warning" dialog box in Windows 7 or in Windows Server 2008 R2 if the publisher name has one ampersand (&)
2347290	MS10-061 Vulnerability in Print Spooler Service could allow remote code execution
2385678	MS10-095 Vulnerability in Microsoft Windows could allow remote code execution
2387149	MS10-074 Vulnerability in Microsoft Foundation Classes could allow remote code execution
2393802	MS11-011 Vulnerabilities in Windows Kernel could allow elevation of privilege
2436673	MS10-098 Vulnerabilities in Windows Kernel could allow elevation of privilege
2442962	MS10-100 Vulnerability in Consent User Interface could allow elevation of privilege

Setup, Deployment, Backup, and Activation

971033 Description of the update for Windows Activation Technologies

972831 The IEEE 802.1X authentication protocol is not supported in Windows Preinstall Environment (PE) 3.0

974624 Integrated device drivers do not work after you log on to a system that was prepared by using the Sysprep.exe utility in Windows 7 or in Windows Server 2008 R2

974674 Description of the Windows NT Backup Restore Utility for Windows 7 and for Windows Server 2008 R2

977015 You are repeatedly prompted to insert a new disk when you use the Backup and Restore tool in Windows 7 or the Windows Server Backup tool in Windows Server 2008 R2 to back up your files or to create a system image on a recordable Blu-ray disc (BD-R)

980711 An ACPI APIC UP HAL operating system image cannot be deployed if a Windows 7 boot image is used in the deployment process

2276755 Driver load times are much longer in Windows PE 3.0 than in Windows PE 2.1 on a computer that is running Windows 7 or Windows Server 2008 R2

Sleep/Hibernation and Power Management

958685 A Windows-based portable computer does not resume correctly if you close the lid while the computer is asleep

974259 A Windows 7-based computer that is equipped with a hybrid television tuner does not enter sleep mode

974410 "STOP 0x000000FE" error in Windows 7 or in Windows Server 2008 R2 when the computer enters or resumes from sleep (S3) or from hibernation (S4)

974476 The computer stops responding when an USB device resumes from the USB Selective Suspend state in Windows 7 or in Windows Server 2008 R2

975599 Stop error when you put a computer that is running Windows 7 or Windows Server 2008 R2 to sleep or into hibernation, or when you restart the computer: "0x9F"

Appendix C

975851   When you resume a computer that is running Windows 7, WWAN devices do not automatically connect to the target 3G network

976240   PCI devices are unexpectedly enabled after you resume a Windows Vista or Windows 7 system from hibernation

976373   A computer that is connected to an IEEE 802.1X authenticated network through a VOIP phone does not connect to the correct network after you resume it from Hibernate mode or Sleep mode

976755   A new user cannot use touch capacity to log on to a computer that is running Windows 7 or Windows Server 2008 R2 after it resumes from sleep or hibernation

976781   A computer may enter sleep or hibernation before the CD or DVD burning process is complete in Windows 7 or Windows Server 2008 R2

977186   Error message when you try to resume a Windows 7-based or a Windows Server 2008 R2-based computer from hibernation: "Stop 0x0000009F"

977307   You cannot make a computer that is running Windows 7 shut down or sleep

978258   USB devices that are connected to a computer may not work after the computer is idle for more than one hour Windows 7 or in Windows Server 2008 R2

978571   Stop error when you try to put the computer into hibernation (S4) in Windows 7 or in Windows Server 2008 R2: "STOP: 0x0000000A IRQL_NOT_LESS_OR_EQUAL"

978982   Stop error when you resume a computer that is running Windows 7 or Windows Server 2008 R2 from sleep or from hibernation: "STOP: 0x000000D1"

980078   The USB selective suspend feature may be disabled when you use DC/AC on a computer that is running Windows 7 or Windows Server 2008 R2

980985   Windows 7 or Windows Server 2008 R2 enters sleep mode automatically when you use a scanner to scan a document

980992   A computer that is running Windows 7 or Windows Server 2008 R2 shuts down shortly after you resume the computer from hibernation

981112   Computer cannot enter sleep or hibernation when you do not share media files

981761   An optical drive that supports DIPM does not enter a low power state when it is installed on a computer that is running Windows 7 or Windows Server 2008 R2

981848   "0x0000009F" Stop error message when a computer enters and resumes from hibernation in Windows 7 or Windows Server 2008 R2

982046   A Bluetooth device stops working, and you receive error code 43 together with event 17 after you resume a computer that is running Windows 7 from sleep

982479   Old data is displayed for an SD card that you reinsert into a Windows 7, Windows Server 2008 R2, Windows Server 2008 or Windows Vista-based computer that is in standby or in hibernation

982635   The computer screen dims after you log on to resume a computer from hibernation in Windows 7

2122063   The audio applications stop responding in Windows 7 or in Windows Server 2008 R2 after you resume the computer from the S3 sleep mode

2293330   You may incorrectly receive a "Consider replacing your battery" warning message on some older HP notebook computers that are running Windows 7

2315295   "0x0000009F" Stop error when you resume a computer that is running Windows Server 2008 R2 or Windows 7 from sleep

2345131   The logon screen appears two times when you resume a Windows 7-based or Windows Server 2008 R2-based computer from Sleep (S3) or from Hibernation (S4)

Startup/Shutdown

969851   Instead of the specified startup program, the whole desktop is started on a remote desktop connection when you change the "Terminal Services Profile" setting for the user account

974719   A computer that is running Windows 7 does not start after you force the computer to shut down

975538   Audio devices are missing or are displayed as "Not plugged in" after you restart a the computer that is running Windows 7 or Windows Server 2008 R2

975777   There is a delay when you shut down, restart, or log off a computer that is running Windows 7 or Windows Server 2008 R2

977419   Unexpectedly slow startup in Windows 7 or in Windows Server 2008 R2

981275   A UEFI-enabled computer may "hang" at a black screen in the startup process for Windows 7 or Windows 2008 R2

982929   "Boot failed" error when you start a UEFI-enabled computer from a 64-bit version of Windows 7 or Windows Server 2008 R2 installation DVD (Package 1)

983460   Startup takes a long time on a Windows 7 or Windows Server 2008 R2-based computer that has an Intel Nehalem-EX CPU installed

2223832   "Boot failed" error message when you start a UEFI-enabled computer from the installation DVD of a 64-bit version of Windows 7 or Windows Server 2008 R2 (Package 2)

2292867   You experience a long startup time on a Windows 7-based computer that has an unused external SATA port

Storage

975617   An update is available for the UDF file system driver (Udfs.sys) for Windows 7 and Windows Server 2008 R2

975680   Virtual Disk Service (VDS) crashes when you try to extend a dynamic volume in an NTFS file system on a computer that is running Windows Vista, Windows Server 2008, Windows Server 2008 R2, or Windows 7

976092   An update is available to fix a data corruption issue for Secure Digital (SD) cards in Windows 7

976187   FIX: The DVD drive is not recognized after you install Windows 7 or Windows Server 2008 R2

976422   The capacity of a Secure Digital (SD) card that is larger than 32 GB is reported incorrectly in Windows 7 and in Windows Server 2008 R2

979344   An attached eSATA drive is considered as a fixed data drive on a computer that is running Windows 7 or Windows Server 2008 R2

982018   An update that improves the compatibility of Windows 7 and Windows Server 2008 R2 with Advanced Format Disks is available

982667   Windows intermittently does not detect the optical disk drive when you start a computer that is running Windows 7 or Windows Server 2008 R2

2223201   Event ID 82 may be logged in the System log after you extend the protected dynamic volume on a Windows 7-based or Windows Server 2008 R2-based computer

2360987   FIX: The wrong volume is formatted when a raw volume is mounted on an NTFS folder on a computer that is running Windows Server 2008 R2 or Windows 7

Time Zone/Daylight Saving Time

970413 The Win32_Process class returns incorrect CreationDate property during the first week after daylight saving time begins or ends

974176 Daylight saving time (DST) 2009 hotfix for the "(GMT+02:00) Cairo" and "(GMT+08:00) Perth" time zones for Windows XP, Windows Server 2003, Windows Vista, Windows 7, Windows Server 2008, and Windows Server 2008 R2

976098 December 2009 cumulative time zone update for Microsoft Windows operating systems

977615 A hotfix is available for Windows Services for UNIX and for Subsystem for UNIX-based Applications to incorporate a cumulative DST update for December 2009

977748 A hotfix is available to update the Daylight Saving Time for the Fiji Standard Time time zone for the year 2009 for Windows XP, Windows Server 2003, Windows Vista, Windows Server 2008, Windows 7 and Windows Server 2008 R2-based computers

981128 A hotfix is available to update the Daylight Saving Time for the "(UTC-04:00) Asuncion", "(UTC+12:00) Fiji" and "(UTC-04:00) Santiago" time zone for Windows Operating Systems

981793 May 2010 cumulative time zone update for Windows operating systems

982615 A hotfix is available to update the Daylight Saving Time for the "(UTC) Casablanca" time zone for Windows Operating Systems

2158563 September 2010 cumulative time zone update for Windows operating systems

2443685 December 2010 cumulative time zone update for Windows operating systems

Windows Media Center

976627 You cannot use Windows Media Center to play a Microsoft Recorded TV Show file (.dvr-ms) if you set the system locale to Arabic (Saudi Arabia) in Windows 7

977071 When you configure Windows Media Center for Windows 7 to display a visualization when you play music, the memory usage continually increases

977716 An update is available for third-party extensibility applications that start DVD playback in Windows Media Center for Windows 7

977863   February 2010 Windows Media Center Cumulative Update for Windows 7

978632   Extensibility applications that provide TV playback stop responding in Windows Media Center of Windows 7

981129   An update to the TV tuner functionality in Windows Media Center is available for Windows 7

981130   Windows Media Center may display Low Bit Rate overlay messages on a computer that is running Windows 7

981770   You frequently experience a music library issue when you access the music library in Windows Media Center or in Windows Media Center Extender

2266287   "Copying Prohibited" error when you use Windows Media Center to watch live TV shows or recorded TV shows on a computer that is running Windows 7

2277775   "Tuner conflict" message when you try to change the channel in Windows Media Center on a computer that is running Windows 7

2284742   October 2010 Cumulative Update for Windows Media Center in Windows 7

Windows Media Player and Related Technologies

974324   Black and white pixels unexpectedly appear on the right side of the screen when you run Windows Media Center in full-screen mode in Windows 7 or in Windows Vista

974912   Windows Media Center crashes in windowed mode on a computer that is running Windows 7 when you start certain Web applications while you are playing an ISDB-T TV program

975053   Description of the Windows Media Center update for Windows 7 that addresses some output issues with ISDB broadcasts

975762   Black screen or error message when you watch ISDB-T television programs in Windows Media Center on a Windows 7-based computer

975806   The video image flickers when you configure Windows Media Player 12 to display the subtitles of a DVD in Windows 7 or in Windows Server 2008 R2

976483   When you use Windows Media Player 12 to play a DVD in full screen mode and display subtitles, the shortcut menu disappears when a new line of subtitles is displayed in Windows 7 or in Windows Server 2008 R2

977314   Windows Media Player 12 does not play all the media files in an ASX playlist on a computer that is running Windows 7

977609   Windows Media Player 12 stops responding after you resume the computer from sleep and you try to play a DVD: "Windows Media Player is not responding"

978205   FIX: MPEG-2 transport streams or certain variable bit rate WMV files may not play in Windows Media Player on a computer that is running Windows 7 or Windows Server 2008 R2

978529   Windows Media Player 12 cannot transcode some music files

979224   A video protected by Digital Rights Management may not play correctly when you install multiple third-party digital signal processor plug-ins for Windows Media Player

2385296   Windows Media Player stops responding in Windows 7 when you play an AVI video or a playlist that consists of AVI videos

2408734   The aspect ratio of an ASF file is lost when you try to select a different audio stream for the file in Windows Media Player in Windows 7 or in Windows Vista

Windows Portable Devices

2257924   The stylus or the touchscreen does not work after you close and then open the lid on a Tablet PC that is running Windows 7

2385146   A hotfix is available for Windows 7 to resolve some Tablet PC issues

Windows 7 Certifications

M ICROSOFT provides certifications to information technology professionals that validate their skills and proficiency with various Microsoft products and technologies. These certifications, which are based on standardized training and examinations and widely recognized by IT organizations, can help you hone and demonstrate your technical competence, prove your worth in the marketplace, and move ahead in your career. The Microsoft Certification Program also provides you with access to a member website and to contact with a global network of other certified professionals.

Microsoft provides two levels of certification for professionals with Windows 7 expertise: Microsoft Certified Technology Specialist (MCTS) and Microsoft Certified IT Professional (MCITP). The MCITP certification is the more advanced of the two and requires an MCTS certification as a prerequisite. Generally speaking, the MCTS certifications are for IT professionals with at least a year's experience. The MCITP certifications are intended for professionals with at least two years of experience who already have earned one or more MCTS certifications.

More information about the certification program, as it relates to Windows 7, is available at *w7io.com/23501*.

The available certifications and the examinations you are required to pass to achieve them are listed in Table D-1.

Table D-1 **Windows 7 Certifications**

Certification Level	Certification	Exam Number	Exam Title
MCTS	MCTS Windows 7 Configuration	70-680	Windows 7, Configuring
MCTS	MCTS Windows 7 and Office 2010 Desktop Deployment	70-681	Windows 7 and Office 2010, Deploying
MCITP	MCITP Windows 7 Enterprise Desktop Support Technician	70-680, 70-685	Windows 7, Enterprise Desktop Support Technician
MCITP	MCITP Windows 7 Enterprise Desktop Administrator	70-680, 70-686	Windows 7, Enterprise Desktop Administrator

The content areas covered by exams 70-680, 70-681, 70-685, and 70-686 are listed in Table D-2.

Table D-2 **Skills Measured**

Exam	Skills
70-680	Installing, upgrading, and migrating to Windows 7 (14 percent) Deploying Windows 7 (13 percent) Configuring hardware and applications (14 percent) Configuring network connectivity (14 percent) Configuring access to resources (13 percent) Configuring mobile computing (10 percent) Monitoring and maintaining systems that run Windows 7 (11 percent) Configuring backup and recovery options (11 percent)
70-681	Configuring a deployment infrastructure (24 percent) Creating and configuring images (25 percent) Deploying Windows 7 (27 percent) Configuring and deploying Office 2010 (24 percent)
70-685	Identifying cause of and resolving desktop application issues (20 percent) Identifying cause of and resolving networking issues (23 percent) Managing and maintaining systems that run Windows 7 client (21 percent) Supporting mobile users (18 percent) Identifying cause of and resolving security issues (18 percent)
70-686	Planning and managing a client life cycle strategy Designing a standard image Designing client configurations Designing a Windows 7 client deployment Designing application packages for deployment Identifying and resolving deployment and client configuration issues

Preparing for Certification Exams

Microsoft Learning offers classroom training, e-learning packages, and distance-learning courses to assist you in preparation for certification exams. Classroom training options are available through Microsoft partners in major cities throughout the world. E-learning courses are self-paced; many include a virtual lab component to simulate hands-on experience. Distance-learning courses combine online classroom training, live discussion, and self-directed study using real-world examples.

To explore the training options available to you, begin at the Microsoft Learning Windows 7 and Windows Vista Training Portal, *w7io.com/23502*.

Microsoft Press also offers three excellent self-paced training kits to help the motivated student prepare for exams 70-680, 70-685, and 70-686. The books, entitled *Configuring Windows 7* (70-680), *Windows 7 Enterprise Desktop Support Technician* (70-685), and *Windows 7 Enterprise Desktop Administrator* (70-686), include chapters devoted to each major exam topic, along with review questions for each topic. Each book also includes a DVD with lesson reviews and practice tests. The tests present randomized questions designed to simulate the certification exams. You can take these tests again and again, as needed, until you're ready to test for certification. Figure D-1 shows a sample of a practice test from the book for Exam 70-680.

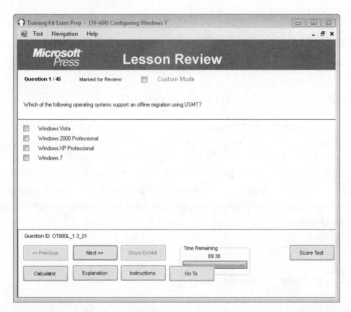

Figure D-1 Timed practice tests included with the Microsoft Press training kits let you hone your skills in preparation for an actual certification exam.

Here are a few questions chosen at random from the training kits:

Exam 70-680, Configuring Windows 7

Which of the following installation sources can you use to perform an upgrade of a computer running Windows Vista to the Windows 7 operating system? (Each correct answer presents a complete solution. Choose three.)

❏ A DVD-ROM.

❏ A network share.

❏ Windows Deployment Services (WDS).

❏ A USB storage device.

Which of the following components must be installed on the computer running Windows Server 2008 that you install the Microsoft Deployment Toolkit (MDT) 2010 on if you want to support light touch deployment to clients with Preboot Execution Environment (PXE)–compatible network adapters? (Each correct answer presents part of the solution. Choose two.)

❏   Windows Deployment Services (WDS).

❏   Windows Server Update Services (WSUS).

❏   System Center Data Protection Manager 2007.

❏   Windows Automated Installation Kit (Windows AIK).

❏   System Center Operations Manager 2007.

As a security measure, you want to block users in your organization from writing data to removable disks, portable media players, and cellular phones that they might connect to their computers running Windows 7 Enterprise. Which of the following Group Policy items could you configure to accomplish this goal? (Each correct answer presents part of the solution. Choose two.)

❏   Windows Devices: Deny Execute Access.

❏   Floppy Drives: Deny Execute Access.

❏   Removable Disks: Deny Write Access.

❏   Removable Disks: Deny Execute Access.

❏   Floppy Drives: Deny Write Access.

❏   WPD Devices: Deny Write Access.

Your organization wants to implement BranchCache at each branch office. All computers in your organization are members of the same Active Directory Domain Services domain. There is a server running Windows Server 2008 R2 at each branch office. BranchCache is needed to speed up access to files located on head-office file servers. You are configuring the clients running Windows 7 and the server running Windows Server 2008 R2 named Branch-FS1 from the command line. Which of the following commands should you use to accomplish this goal? (Each correct answer presents part of the solution. Choose two.)

❏   Execute the command **netsh branchcache set service distributed** on each client running Windows 7.

❏   Execute the command **netsh branchcache set service hostedclient location=Branch-FS1** on Branch-FS1.

❑ Execute the command **netsh branchcache set service distributed** on Branch-FS1.

❑ Execute the command **netsh branchcache set service hostedserver clientauthentication=domain** on each client running Windows 7.

❑ Execute the command **netsh branchcache set service hostedserver clientauthentication=domain** on Branch-FS1.

❑ Execute the command **netsh branchcache set service hostedclient location=Branch-FS1** on each client running Windows 7.

You have created a reference installation of Windows 7 Enterprise (x64) and Windows 7 Professional (x86). Which of the following Windows PE images and ImageX utilities do you need to use to capture these installations as WIM files?

❑ Windows PE (x86), ImageX (x86).

❑ Windows PE (x64), ImageX (x64).

❑ Windows PE (x64), ImageX (x86).

❑ Windows PE (x86), ImageX (x64).

Exam 70-685, Windows 7 Enterprise Desktop Support Technician

You are a systems administrator for an enterprise network. To meet your organization's security requirements, you must configure event forwarding to use a Secure Sockets Layer (SSL) certificate for encryption. Which of the following must you do to enable event forwarding for Normal event subscriptions using Hypertext Transfer Protocol Secure (HTTPS)? (Each correct answer presents part of the solution. Choose two.)

❑ Configure the collecting computer with a computer certificate.

❑ Put the **winrm quickconfig –transport:https** command on the computer collecting the forwarded events.

❑ Create a Windows Firewall exception for TCP port 443 on the forwarding computer.

❑ Configure the forwarding computer with a computer certificate.

You are a help desk operator in a support center. A user's computer refuses to start Windows 7. However, startup is failing at different times. Occasionally, it fails immediately. Sometimes, it reaches the logon screen before failing. Often, the computer shows a Stop error with the message Physical Memory Error. You would like to test the computer's memory without starting the operating system. How can you do this? (Each correct answer presents a complete solution. Choose two.)

❐   Install the Windows 7 Setup DVD.

❐   When the computer starts to boot, press F8. Then select Safe Mode With Command Prompt.

❐   When the computer starts to boot, press F8. Then select Debugging Mode.

❐   Select Launch Startup Repair from the Windows Error Recovery menu.

You are a systems administrator managing Windows 7 images that are used when deploying new computers. Microsoft has released a critical update that you need automatically deployed to new computers. Which tool would you use to add a new software update to an existing image?

❐   Windows System Image Manager.

❐   Application Compatibility Toolkit (ACT).

❐   Use State Migration Tool (USMT).

❐   ImageX.

You are a systems administrator for an enterprise network. You are planning to upgrade computers from Windows XP with Microsoft Internet Explorer 6 to Windows 7 with Windows Internet Explorer 8. Currently, users access an internal web application that relies on an ActiveX object. You want to ensure that users can install the ActiveX object, which was developed for Internet Explorer 6 and has not been updated. Users do not currently have administrative privileges. Which of the following allows you to accomplish this? (Each correct answer presents a complete solution. Choose two.)

❐   Add the website to the list of Trusted Sites.

❐   Disable Protected Mode for the zone containing the website.

❐   Have the developers create a non-admin installation package.

❐   Enable Internet Explorer 8 Accelerators.

❐   Grant the users administrative privileges.

Exam 70-686, Windows 7 Enterprise Desktop Administrator

Your organization uses Multiple Activation Key (MAK) activation with several hundred Windows 7 Enterprise edition clients. You are planning procedures for regular licensing compliance audits. Which of the following tools can you use to audit MAK key usage at your organization? (Each correct answer presents a complete solution. Choose three.)

❐   Volume Activation Management Tool (VAMT).

❐   System Center Operations Manager 2007.

❐   Active Directory Users and Computers.

❐   System Center Configuration Manager 2007.

❐   Slmgr.vbs.

You are planning to deploy 50 computers running Windows 7 at a remote mining outpost in the Australian outback. The network you will be deploying these computers on is not connected to the Internet, so you want to perform the Microsoft Windows Activation by using a telephone rather than the Internet. You want to minimize the number of telephone calls you need to make and you do not want to make any additional calls if you introduce new Windows 7 clients to the network. Which of the following volume activation methods should you use?

❐   Multiple Activation Keys (MAK) Independent Activation.

❐   Multiple Activation Keys (MAK) Proxy Activation.

❐   Retail product keys.

❐   Key Management Services (KMS) keys.

Automatic updates are set to install each day at 3 A.M. You want to ensure that computers that are hibernating wake for update installation. You also want to ensure that computers that are not hibernating but are switched off at night install updates 10 minutes after they next boot. Which of the following policies should you configure to accomplish this goal? (Each correct answer presents part of the solution. Choose two.)

❐   Pre-Prompt For Restart With Scheduled Installations.

❐   Reschedule Automatic Update Scheduled Installations.

❐   Enabling Windows Update Power Management To Automatically Wake Up The System To Install Scheduled Updates.

❐   Allow Automatic Updates Immediate Installation.

You are visiting a branch office and need to deploy Windows 7 to 20 new computers. The branch office has a single Windows Server 2008 Server Core server that is configured as a read-only domain controller (RODC). None of the 20 new computers have optical media drives. All of these computers have PXE-compliant network adapters. Which of the following steps should you take to deploy Windows 7 to the computers at this branch office? (Each correct answer presents part of the solution. Choose three.)

❏ Boot the computers from a USB device with Windows PE.

❏ Install Windows Deployment Services (WDS) on the Windows Server 2008 RODC.

❏ Copy the Windows 7 Installation files to the shared folder.

❏ Configure a shared folder on the Windows Server 2008 RODC.

❏ Add the Windows 7 installation image to the Windows Deployment Services (WDS) server.

❏ Boot the computers from a USB device that has a Windows Deployment Services (WDS) discover image.

Some Useful Accessory Programs

W INDOWS 7 comes with dozens of useful accessory tools (some are GUI applications, and others are text-based). Most of them are mentioned in one place or another in the pages of this book. But some are not. In this appendix, we provide short descriptions of interesting items that are not discussed elsewhere.

Our Favorite Five

The following five are Windows programs we use every week, if not every day. Some of them, like Calculator and Paint, have been around forever but keep appearing in new and improved versions. Snipping Tool, in contrast, is a new and welcome addition to the Windows toolkit.

Calculator

It's not Microsoft Excel, but at what it does it now excels more than ever. The humble Calculator remained unchanged from Windows 3.0 (1990) through Windows Vista, but it got a serious makeover in Windows 7. New options at the bottom of the View menu cause Calculator to sprout special-purpose calculators to the right of the familiar keypad. These options execute all types of unit conversions, calculate monthly mortgage payments, perform automobile lease calculations, and let you measure fuel economy. Want to know the number of days elapsed between two dates? Calculator will do that, too.

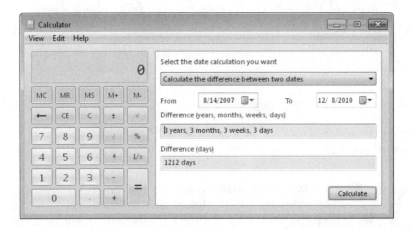

Calculator offers standard, scientific, programmer, and statistics modes and maintains a history window that you can copy to your favorite text editor or spreadsheet. If you haven't looked at Calculator in a while, type **calc** in the Start menu search box and check it out. It won't sing or dance, but it does load more quickly than Excel.

Paint

The free bitmap editor included with Windows is useful for all sorts of graphic manipulations, including adding lines and shapes to pictures and performing text annotations. Need to add callouts to an illustration? Paint might be the quickest way to get it done. Paint is also handy for converting images from one format to another. Using Paint's Save As command, for example, you can easily and quickly convert a large BMP file to a space-saving JPEG. (Other supported formats include PNG, GIF, TIFF, and monochrome BMP.) Cropping, resizing, and rotating tools, all accessible in the Image group of Paint's new ribbon interface, let you carry out other common manipulations. The Resize and Skew dialog box lets you maintain aspect ratio or not, as you choose; skewing options let you turn boring images into fun-house amusements:

The quickest way to run Paint is to type **Paint** in the Start menu search box.

Snipping Tool

Every version of Windows, from Windows 1.0 on down, has let you copy an image of the current window or current screen to the Clipboard (by pressing Alt+PrintScreen or Print-Screen). But when it comes to serious screen capturing—for presentations, book pages, or whatever—Windows 7 offers a snappier way to snip. Snipping Tool includes the window and full-screen capture modes of yore, but it adds rectangular region captures and irregularly shaped (lasso) captures to boot:

As soon as you've snipped, a capture appears in Snipping Tool's rudimentary editor, where you can add pen and highlighter annotations (no text tools, unfortunately), and save, copy, or send the finished shot. The program saves JPEGs by default, but you can also save in PNG, GIF, or MHT (single-file HTML) formats.

To run Snipping Tool, type **snip** in the Start menu search box.

Character Map and Private Character Editor

When your text-oriented program lacks the special character you need (or just makes it too hard to find), call on Character Map. This venerable Windows accessory offers your system's complete repertoire of accents, symbols, ligatures, and foreign alphabets. You can explore the characters available in any typeface—including those of symbol-oriented fonts such as Webdings and Wingdings—by choosing from the Font menu. When you select a character in the grid that occupies the main part of the window, Character Map magnifies it to help you confirm that it's the one you want. Then you can click Select to put it in the Characters To Copy box and then Copy to put it on the Clipboard. If you're having trouble locating a character you need, select the Advanced View check box, and then type all or part of the character's name in the Search For box. For example, if you're looking for a capital *A* with a grave accent (À), you can search for "grave," and Character Map will present all the grave-accented characters in the current font. The Group By drop-down list, which also appears after you select Advanced View, provides another way to gather groups of related characters:

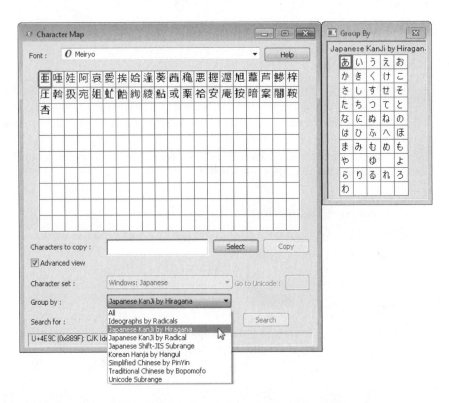

Appendix E

If Character Map doesn't have the character you need, you can create it yourself using a related accessory, Private Character Editor. When you first run Private Character Editor, a Select Code grid will appear, in which you can specify a Unicode value for the character you're about to create. Once you've done that and clicked OK, you'll see a pixel-level editor, in which you can draw a character or paste one in from another application (Character Map, for example) and edit it:

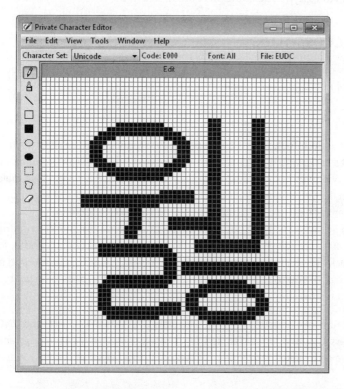

After you've drawn or edited the character to your satisfaction, press Ctrl+S to save it. Your character will then be available in Character Map. To use it, choose All Fonts (Private Characters) in Character Map's Fonts drop-down list.

To run either Character Map or Private Character Editor, type **char** in the Start menu search box. The applications will appear in the Programs section of the search results.

Sticky Notes

If you're the sort of person who likes to plaster sticky-note reminders on your monitor, Windows can show you a better way. The reminders you post with the Sticky Notes accessory won't fall off your screen (and if you haven't deleted them, they'll still be there the next time you start Windows). Right-click a note to choose a background color (the default is yellow). Press Ctrl+Shift+L to get a bullet list (press it again to switch to a numbered list). To tick an item off your list (strike it through), select it and press Ctrl+T. Use Ctrl+B, Ctrl+I, and Ctrl+U for bold, italic, and underlined text. Press Ctrl+Shift+> to make text larger, or Ctrl+Shift+< to make it smaller. Click the X in the upper-right corner to peel a note off and throw it away.

To run Sticky Notes, type **stic** in the Start menu search box.

Other Handy Accessories

We don't rely on the following five programs as much as the previous five, but these are still worthy of notice and mention.

Windows Fax And Scan

Your scanner undoubtedly has its own options for scanning pictures and documents, but sometimes it's easier and quicker to use the Windows Fax And Scan program. Click New Scan on the Windows Fax And Scan toolbar, and then fill out the New Scan dialog box. Options there let you choose a scanning device, specify the source of your document (Flatbed or Feeder, for example), indicate the color format you're looking for (Color, Grayscale, or Black And White), specify an output file type, and choose resolution, brightness, and contrast. If you're scanning something smaller than a full page (a 4 x 5 photo, for example), be sure to click Preview rather than Scan. In the Preview window you can drag handles to indicate the size of your document. That way you won't get a lot of extra white space in your scanned image.

A scanned image can be saved in various formats (JPEG, BMP, GIF, TIFF, and PNG), attached to e-mail messages, and forwarded as a fax. The fax component of the program assumes that you have an installed fax modem or can point to a fax server on your network.

XPS Viewer

The Open XML Paper Specification (XPS) is Microsoft's solution to the need for full-fidelity portable documents. Comparable in many respects to Adobe Systems's PDF (Portable Document Format), XPS provides a way for you to transfer formatted documents from one system to another with the assurance that they maintain the same appearance wherever they are viewed and printed.

If you have received or downloaded an XPS file, you can view and print it using the XPS Viewer application. To create an XPS document, simply print to the Microsoft XPS Document Writer device.

XPS Viewer also lets you digitally sign a document (ensuring that the document will not subsequently be changed without your awareness) and to attach permissions (provided you have a digital rights management account on your system).

Sound Recorder

It's absolutely a one-trick pony, but Sound Recorder is invaluable if you need to record sound annotations for a document or a vocal attachment for an e-mail message. Simply make sure your microphone is plugged in and working, and then click Start Recording. When you click Stop Recording, a Save As dialog box lets you save your sound bite as a WMA file.

WordPad

As its name suggests, WordPad occupies an immediate plateau between the speedy plain-text Notepad and a full-featured graphical word processor. Because virtually everyone has one of the latter these days, WordPad is less indispensable than it might once have been. Nevertheless, there are still times when you might find it handier (and quicker) to open, say, a Rich Text Format (RTF) document in WordPad than in Microsoft Word. And WordPad does have a few talents. It can read documents in Word's native DOCX format, as well as plain text, RTF, and ODT (OpenDocument) formats. And it can save documents as RTF, Open XML, ODT, or plain text. If you want to make it behave more like a plain-text editor, you can turn word wrap off.

Windows Journal

Windows Journal lets users of tablet PCs create handwritten notes with their styluses. With its array of built-in templates, the program creates electronic paper for such things as calendars, to-do lists, graphs, and music staves. You can choose from a variety of pen styles, highlighter colors, and eraser sizes.

System Management Tools

The following are useful system management tools.

Winver

Run Winver (Windows Version) to get information about your Windows version and build number. In the window that appears, you can also click a link to read the terms of your Microsoft Software License in fine lawyerly detail.

Boot Configuration Data Editor (BCDEdit)

If you have installed multiple operating systems on your computer, you can use the System section of Control Panel to specify the default operating system and the length of time the boot routine will display the boot menu before launching the default. (To do this, choose Advanced System Settings, then click Settings in the Startup And Recovery section of the Advanced tab of the System Properties dialog box.) But if you want to make other changes to the multiboot routine (such as the names that appear on the boot menu), you need the Boot Configuration Data Editor (BCDEdit). Launch BCDEdit from an elevated command prompt.

Use this tool with caution, and don't use it at all if you aren't sure you know what you're doing. For a detailed treatise on the architecture of boot configuration data in Windows Vista and Windows 7, and a "cookbook" of things you can do with BCDEdit, see the white paper "Boot Configuration Data in Windows Vista" at *w7io.com/23601*.

Color Management

Color Management is a corner of Control Panel of importance primarily to graphics professionals. It allows you to attach profiles to output devices or adjust those already in place, ensuring that colors are displayed with consistency across devices.

DirectX Diagnostic Tool (DXDiag)

If you're having trouble getting a game or movie to play properly, a good place to begin troubleshooting is the DirectX Diagnostic Tool (DXDiag). Run DXDiag from any command prompt, and Windows will immediately begin testing each DirectX device on your system, reporting any problems that it finds. You can click Save All Information to preserve its finding in a text file.

DOSKey

The DOSKey utility lets you encapsulate command strings as easy-to-enter macros. For example, by typing the following at a Cmd prompt:

```
Doskey 50=mode con:lines=50
```

you create a macro named 50 that executes the command string *mode con:lines=50*. To run a macro, you simply enter its name (in this example, 50) at a command prompt. You can create as many macros as you like with DOSKey, but your macros are effective only for the current session. To create a reusable set of macros, save them in a plain-text file, then load them from the command prompt using DOSKey's /Macrofile switch.

Historical Curiosities

If your kids are curious about the bad-old early days of personal computing, show them these three museum pieces. In the 32-bit editions of Windows, they're all still there.

Edlin

Tim Paterson, then of Seattle Computer Products, wrote QDOS (Quick and Dirty Operating System), which, when bought and renamed MS-DOS by Microsoft, became the first operating system to run on the IBM Personal Computer. Along with an operating system, Paterson supplied Microsoft with a primitive line-oriented text editor. You can still run it by typing **edlin <*filename*>** at a command prompt.

Edlin uses terse commands that address text lines by number. To delete line 9 from your file, for example, type **9d**. As this illustration shows, you can get a complete list of Edlin's command repertoire by typing **?** at the prompt.

Edit

For a full-screen character-mode editor, type **edit** at a command prompt. Like pre-Windows versions of Microsoft Word, the editor that appears supports the mouse but does not do graphics. Still, it's a mighty step up from Edlin.

Debug

Like Edlin, Debug was written by Tim Paterson for QDOS. Much loved and much used by programmers in the early 1980s, Debug included a mini assembler and could access specific disk sectors and memory addresses (within the first 640 KB of memory). For an interesting summary of Debug's history and capabilities, see Daniel B. Sedory's "A Guide to DEBUG" at *w7io.com/23602*.

Index to Troubleshooting Topics

Index

Symbols and Numbers

* (asterisk)
  PowerShell values and, 984
  PowerShell wildcards, 992
  searching, 383
  wildcard searches, 392–393
  wildcards in Command Prompt, 1172
. or .. (periods) in PowerShell, 993
| (pipe operator), 985–991
? (question mark)
  PowerShell wildcards, 992
  wildcard searches, 393
  wildcards in Command Prompt, 1172
~ (tilde) in wildcard searches, 393
1:1 pixel mapping, 586
3G support, 685
3GPP/3GPP2 support, 477
10Base-T standard, 691
16-bit programs, 184
32-bit browsers, 212
32-bit programs
  determining if 32- or 64-bit, 185
  running in 64-bit Windows, 184–185
32-bit versions of PowerShell, 982
32-bit versions of Windows 7
  compared to 64-bit, 28–29
  editions available in, 7
  hardware minimum requirements, 27
  installing from 64-bit editions prohibited, 31
  memory issues, 853–854
64-bit browsers, 212
64-bit programs, 185
64-bit versions of PowerShell, 982
64-bit versions of Windows 7
  16-bit programs not installable, 184
  32-bit programs running in, 184–185
  compared to 32-bit, 28–29
  device driver signing requirement, 1079
  driver availability, 28
  hardware minimum requirements, 27
  increasing prevalence of, 7

installing from 32-bit editions prohibited, 31
installing programs in, 184–185
memory requirements and limitations, 852
security features of, 600
100Base-T standard, 691
802.1_ standards. *See* wireless networking

A

AAC (Advanced Audio Coding) format, 477, 480, 520
AACS (Advanced Access Content System), 1079
abnormal shutdowns, 854
about:blank pages, 218
about:Tabs pages, 218
academic volume licensing, 961
accelerators, Internet Explorer 9, 234–235, 239–240
accent marks, 1246–1247
AcceptPause.ps1 script, 922
access control
  Advanced Sharing settings, 746
  children. *See* Parental Controls
  discretionary approach to, 642
  effective permissions, 746–747
  entries. *See* ACEs (access control entries)
  Full Control access, 645
  integrity levels, 646
  List Folder Contents permissions, 645
  lists. *See* ACLs (access control lists)
  Modify access, 645
  NTFS permissions. *See* ACLs (access control lists)
  permissions. *See* permissions
  Read & Execute permission, 645
  Read permission, 645
  rights, 646
  security access tokens for, 642–643
  Sharing wizard, 644
  SIDs, 642–643
  Special Permissions, 645
  UAC interactions with, 645
  user accounts. *See* user accounts
  Write permission, 645

About the Authors

Ed Bott is an award-winning author and technology journalist who has been researching and writing about Windows and PC technology, in print and on the Internet, for nearly two decades, with no intention of stopping anytime soon. He has written more than 25 books, all on Microsoft Windows and Office, which in turn have been translated into dozens of different languages and read worldwide. You can catch up with Ed's latest opinions and get hands-on advice at Ed Bott's Microsoft Report on ZDNet (*blogs.zdnet.com/bott*) and Ed Bott's Windows Expertise (*edbott.com/weblog*). Ed and his wife, Judy, live in northern New Mexico with a house full of very lucky pets—Katy the cat, who was plucked from a shelter in the Puget Sound area in 1997, and Mackie and Lucy, who were adopted with the help of English Springer Rescue America (*springerrescue.org*). All three make cameo appearances in this book.

Carl Siechert began his writing career at age eight as editor of the *Mesita Road News*, a neighborhood newsletter that reached a peak worldwide circulation of 43 during its eight-year run. Following several years as an estimator and production manager in a commercial printing business, Carl returned to writing with the formation of Siechert & Wood Professional Documentation, a Pasadena, California, firm that specializes in writing and producing product documentation for the personal computer industry. Carl is a coauthor of more than 20 books, covering operating systems from MS-DOS 3.0 to Windows 7 and productivity applications from Microsoft Works 3 to Office 2010. In a convergence of new and old technology, Carl's company now operates a popular website for hobby machinists, *littlemachineshop.com*. Carl hiked the Pacific Crest Trail from Mexico to Canada in 1977 and would rather be hiking right now. He and his wife, Jan, live in Southern California.

Craig Stinson, an industry journalist since 1981, was editor of *Softalk for the IBM Personal Computer*, one of the earliest IBM-PC magazines. He is the author or coauthor of numerous books about Microsoft Windows and Microsoft Excel. Craig is an amateur musician and reformed music critic, having reviewed classical music for various newspapers and trade publications, including *Billboard, The Boston Globe, The Christian Science Monitor,* and *Musical America*. He lives in Bloomington, Indiana.

The authors have set up a website for readers of this book. At the site, you can find updates, corrections, links to other resources, and more useful tips. In addition, you can discuss Windows 7 with the authors and with other readers. We hope you'll join us at *w7io.com*.

What do you think of this book?

We want to hear from you!
To participate in a brief online survey, please visit:

microsoft.com/learning/booksurvey

Tell us how well this book meets your needs—what works effectively, and what we can do better. Your feedback will help us continually improve our books and learning resources for you.

Thank you in advance for your input!